Praise for Danny Goodman's *JavaScript™ Bible*

"JavaScript™ Bible *is the definitive resource in JavaScript programming. I am never more than three feet from my copy.*"
— **Steve Reich, CEO, PageCoders**

"*This book is a must-have for any web developer or programmer.*"
— **Thoma Lile, President, Kanis Technologies, Inc.**

"*Outstanding book. I would recommend this book to anyone interested in learning to develop advanced Web sites. Mr. Goodman did an excellent job of organizing this book and writing it so that even a beginning programmer can understand it.*"
— **Jason Hensley, Director of Internet Services, NetVoice, Inc.**

"*Goodman is always great at delivering clear and concise technical books!*"
— **Dwayne King, Chief Technology Officer, White Horse**

"JavaScript™ Bible *is well worth the money spent!*"
— **Yen C.Y. Leong, IT Director, Moo Mooltimedia, a member of SmartTransact Group**

"*A must-have book for any internet developer.*"
— **Uri Fremder, Senior Consultant, TopTier Software**

"*I love this book! I use it all the time, and it always delivers. It's the only JavaScript book I use!*"
— **Jason Badger, Web Developer**

"*Whether you are a professional or a beginner, this is a great book to get.*"
— **Brant Mutch, Web Application Developer, Wells Fargo Card Services, Inc.**

"*I never thought I'd ever teach programming before reading your book [*JavaScript™ Bible*]. It's so simple to use—the Programming Fundamentals section brought it all back! Thank you for such a wonderful book, and for breaking through my programming block!*"
— **Susan Sann Mahon, Certified Lotus Instructor, TechNet Training**

"*I continue to get so much benefit from* JavaScript™ Bible. *What an amazing book! Danny Goodman is the greatest!*"
— **Patrick Moss**

"*Danny Goodman is very good at leading the reader into the subject.* JavaScript™ Bible *has everything we could possibly need.*"
— **Philip Gurdon**

"An excellent book that builds solidly from whatever level the reader is at. A book that is both witty and educational."
— **Dave Vane**

"I continue to use the book on a daily basis and would be lost without it."
— **Mike Warner, Founder, Oak Place Productions**

"JavaScript™ Bible *is by **far** the best JavaScript resource I've ever seen (and I've seen quite a few)."*
— **Robert J. Mirro, Independent Consultant, RJM Consulting**

"First, I want to thank you for writing THE definitive book on JavaScript. I spent many hours in the computer aisles of bookstores, looking for a text to use for my class, and yours is hands-down the best I've seen. It's now a required text for the course."
— **Tom Travers, Instructor, University of New England**

JavaScript™ Bible

4th Edition

Danny Goodman
With a foreword by Brendan Eich, JavaScript's creator

Hungry Minds™

Hungry Minds, Inc.

New York, NY ✦ Cleveland, OH ✦ Indianapolis, IN

JavaScript™ Bible, 4th Edition

Published by
Hungry Minds, Inc.
909 Third Avenue
New York, NY 10022
www.hungryminds.com

Library of Congress Control Number: 200101676

ISBN: 0-7645-3342-8

Printed in the United States of America

10 9 8 7 6 5 4 3 2 1

4B/SR/QT/QR/IN

Distributed in the United States by Hungry Minds, Inc.

Distributed by CDG Books Canada Inc. for Canada; by Transworld Publishers Limited in the United Kingdom; by IDG Norge Books for Norway; by IDG Sweden Books for Sweden; by IDG Books Australia Publishing Corporation Pty. Ltd. for Australia and New Zealand; by TransQuest Publishers Pte Ltd. for Singapore, Malaysia, Thailand, Indonesia, and Hong Kong; by Gotop Information Inc. for Taiwan; by ICG Muse, Inc. for Japan; by Intersoft for South Africa; by Eyrolles for France; by International Thomson Publishing for Germany, Austria, and Switzerland; by Distribuidora Cuspide for Argentina; by LR International for Brazil; by Galileo Libros for Chile; by Ediciones ZETA S.C.R. Ltda. for Peru; by WS Computer Publishing Corporation, Inc., for the Philippines; by Contemporanea de Ediciones for Venezuela; by Express Computer Distributors for the Caribbean and West Indies; by Micronesia Media Distributor, Inc. for Micronesia; by Chips Computadoras S.A. de C.V. for Mexico; by Editorial Norma de Panama S.A. for Panama; by American Bookshops for Finland.

For general information on Hungry Minds' products and services please contact our Customer Care department within the U.S. at 800-762-2974, outside the U.S. at 317-572-3993 or fax 317-572-4002.

For sales inquiries and reseller information, including discounts, premium and bulk quantity sales, and foreign-language translations, please contact our Customer Care department at 800-434-3422, fax 317-572-4002 or write to Hungry Minds, Inc., Attn: Customer Care Department, 10475 Crosspoint Boulevard, Indianapolis, IN 46256.

For information on licensing foreign or domestic rights, please contact our Sub-Rights Customer Care department at 212-884-5000.

For information on using Hungry Minds' products and services in the classroom or for ordering examination copies, please contact our Educational Sales department at 800-434-2086 or fax 317-572-4005.

For press review copies, author interviews, or other publicity information, please contact our Public Relations department at 317-572-6168 or fax 317-572-4168.

For authorization to photocopy items for corporate, personal, or educational use, please contact Copyright Clearance Center, 222 Rosewood Drive, Danvers, MA 01923, or fax 978-750-4470.

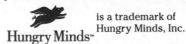

is a trademark of
Hungry Minds, Inc.

About the Author

Danny Goodman is the author of numerous critically acclaimed and best-selling books, including *The Complete HyperCard Handbook, Danny Goodman's AppleScript Handbook*, and *Dynamic HTML: The Definitive Reference*. He is a renowned authority and expert teacher of computer scripting languages and is widely known for his "JavaScript Apostle" articles at Netscape's *ViewSource* online developer newsletter. His writing style and pedagogy continue to earn praise from readers and teachers around the world. To help keep his finger on the pulse of real-world programming challenges, Goodman frequently lends his touch as consulting programmer and designer to leading-edge World Wide Web and intranet sites from his home base in the San Francisco area.

Credits

Acquisitions Editor
Debra Williams Cauley

Project Editor
Neil Romanosky

Technical Editor
David Wall

Copy Editors
Jerelind Charles
Victoria Lee O'Malley

Proof Editor
Cordelia Heaney

Project Coordinator
Regina Snyder

Graphics and Production Specialists
Sean Decker
LeAndra Johnson
Stephanie Jumper
Barry Offringa
Kristin Pickett
Jill Piscitelli
Jeremey Unger
Erin Zeltner

Quality Control Technicians
Laura Albert
Valery Bourke
Joel Draper
Dwight Ramsey

Permissions Editor
Laura Moss

Media Development Specialist
Greg Stephens

Media Development Coordinator
Marisa Pearman

Book Designer
Kurt Krames

Proofreading
York Production Services

Indexer
Johnna VanHoose Dinse

Cover Illustrator
Kate Shaw

Foreword

As JavaScript's creator, I would like to say a few words about where JavaScript has been, where it is going, and how the book you're holding will help you to make the most of the language.

JavaScript was born out of a desire to let HTML authors write scripts directly in their documents. This may seem obvious now, but in the spring of 1995 it was novel and more than a little at odds with both the conventional wisdom (that HTML should describe static document structure only) and the Next Big Thing (Java applets, which were hyped as the one true way to enliven and extend Web pages). Once I got past these contentions, JavaScript quickly shaped up along the following lines:

✦ "Java-lite" syntax. Although the "natural language" syntax of HyperTalk was fresh in my mind after a friend lent me *The Complete HyperCard Handbook* by some fellow named Goodman, the Next Big Thing weighed heavier, especially in light of another goal: scripting Java applets. If the scripting language resembled Java, then those programmers who made the jump from JavaScript to Java would welcome similarities in syntax. But insisting on Java's class and type declarations, or on a semicolon after each statement when a line ending would do, were out of the question — scripting for most people is about writing short snippets of code, quickly and without fuss.

✦ Events for HTML elements. Buttons should have onClick event handlers. Documents load and unload from windows, so windows should have onLoad and onUnload handlers. Users and scripts submit forms: thus the onSubmit handler. Although not initially as flexible as HyperCard's messages (whose handlers inspired the onEvent naming convention), JavaScript events let HTML authors take control of user interaction from remote servers and respond quickly to user gestures and browser actions. With the adoption of the W3C DOM Level 2 event handling recommendations, JavaScript in modern browsers has fully flexible control over events.

✦ Objects without classes. The Self programming language proved the notion of prototype-based inheritance. For JavaScript, I wanted a single prototype per object (for simplicity and efficiency), based by default on the function called using the new operator (for consonance with Java). To avoid distinguishing constructors from methods from functions, all functions receive the object naming them as the property that was called, in the this parameter. Although prototypes didn't appear until Navigator 3, they were prefigured in Version 2 by quoted text being treated as an object (the String object prototype, to which users could attach methods).

✦ Generated HTML. Embedding JavaScript in HTML gave rise to a thought: Let the script speak HTML, as if the emitted text and markup were loaded in place of the script itself. The possibilities went beyond automating current or last-modified dates, to computing whole trees of tables where all the repeated structure was rolled up in a scripted loop, while the varying contents to be tabulated came in minimal fashion from JavaScript objects forming a catalog or mini-database.

At first, I thought JavaScript would most often find use in validating input to HTML forms. But before long, I was surprised to see how many Web designers devised compelling applications by way of script-generated HTML and JavaScript objects. It became clear from user demonstration and feedback that Web designers sought to build significant applications quickly and effectively with just a few images, HTML, and JavaScript. Eventually they demanded that the browser support what is now known as "Dynamic HTML" (one fun link: `http://www.javascript-games.org/`).

As legions of Web authors embraced the authoring power of JavaScript, they, in turn, demonstrated the crucial advantages of a scripting environment over old-school application development. Not only were the HTML and JavaScript languages comparatively easy to use, but development did not require the programming expertise needed to light all pixels and handle all events as in a big, traditional application.

The primacy of JavaScript on the Web today vindicates our early belief in the value of a scripting language for HTML authors. By keeping the "pixel-lighting" bar low, HTML with images has made Web designers out of millions of people. By keeping the "event-handling" bar low, JavaScript has helped many thousands of those designers become programmers. Perhaps the ultimate example of web development's convergence with application development is the Mozilla browser, wherein all of the user-interface and even some custom widgets and modular components are implemented entirely using JavaScript, Cascading Style Sheets (CSS), custom XML-based markup languages, and images.

JavaScript is also a general language, useful apart from HTML and XML. It has been embedded in servers, authoring tools, browser plug-ins, and other kinds of browsers (for such things as 3D graphical worlds). Its international standard, ECMA-262 (ISO 16262), has advanced to a Third Edition. But compared to languages such as Perl and even Java, it is still relatively young. Work toward a Fourth Edition of the language, supporting optional types, classes, and versioning facilities, progresses within the ECMA technical committee (see the "JS2" proposal to the ECMA technical committee documented at `http://www.mozilla.org/js/language/js20/`).

It is clear to me that JavaScript would not have survived without a creative, loyal, and patient community of developers; I owe them each a huge debt of thanks. Those developers who took up the beta releases of Navigator 2, and disseminated vital workarounds and feature requests by e-mail and net-news, are the language's godparents. Developer support and feedback continue to make JavaScript the eclectic, rambunctious success it is.

The book in your hands compiles thousands of those "developer miles" with the insight of an expert guide and teacher. Danny didn't know at the time how much inspiration I found in his HyperCard book, but it was on my desk throughout the development of JavaScript in 1995. His energy, compassion, and clear prose helped me keep the goal of "a language for all" in mind. It is enormously gratifying to write the foreword to the fourth edition of this book, which has earned so many "satisfied reader miles."

I highly recommend Danny Goodman's *JavaScript Bible* to anyone who wants to learn JavaScript, and especially to those HTML authors who've so far written only a few scripts or programs — you're in for a lifetime of fun on the "scripting road" with a trusty guide at your side.

— *Brendan Eich*
The Mozilla Organization (http://www.mozilla.org)

Preface

For nearly 20 years, I have written the books I wished had already been written to help me learn or use a new technology. Whenever possible, I like to get in at the very beginning of a new authoring or programming environment, feel the growing pains, and share with readers the solutions to my struggles. This fourth edition of the *JavaScript Bible* represents knowledge and experience accumulated over five years of daily work in JavaScript and a constant monitoring of newsgroups for questions, problems, and challenges facing scripters at all levels. My goal is to help you avoid the same frustration and head scratching I and others have experienced through multiple generations of scriptable browsers.

While previous editions of this book focused on the then predominant Netscape Navigator browser, the swing of the browser market share pendulum currently favors Microsoft Internet Explorer. At the same time, Netscape has accomplished the admirable task of reinventing its own browser in light of rapidly advancing industry standards. As a result of both of these trends, this massively revised and expanded fourth edition treats both brands of browsers as equals as far as scripters are concerned. You hear my praise and dismay at various scripting features of both browser families. But empowering you to design and write good scripts is my passion, regardless of browser. Therefore, the book contains details about proprietary and standard implementations to equip you to choose the development path that best fits your content's audience. If you detect any bias of mine throughout this book, it is a desire, where possible, to write scripts that work on as many browsers as possible.

Organization and Features of This Edition

Because of the greatly expanded range of vocabularies that scripts may use in the latest browser versions, the biggest change to the structure of the book is in the reference portion. In this edition, you find a greater distinction between the document object model and core JavaScript language reference sections. This new division should help those readers who are primarily interested in only the JavaScript language (for use in other applications) find what they need more quickly. Here are some details about the book's structure.

Part I

Part I of the book begins with a chapter that shows how JavaScript compares with Java and discusses its role within the rest of the World Wide Web. The Web browser and scripting world have undergone significant changes since JavaScript first arrived on the scene. That's why Chapter 2 is devoted to addressing challenges facing scripters who must develop applications for both single- and cross-platform browser audiences amid rapidly changing standards efforts. Chapter 3 provides the first foray into JavaScript, where you get to write your first practical script.

Part II

All of Part II is handed over to a tutorial for newcomers to JavaScript. Nine lessons provide you with a gradual path through browser internals, basic programming skills, and genuine JavaScript scripting. With only a couple of clearly labeled items, the lessons cover scripting topics that apply to all scriptable browsers. Exercises follow at the end of each lesson to help reinforce what you just learned and challenge you to use your new knowledge (you'll find answers to the exercises in Appendix C). The goal of the tutorial is to equip you with sufficient experience to start scripting simple pages right away while making it easier for you to understand the in-depth discussions and examples in the rest of the book. By the end of the final lesson, you'll know how to script multiple frame environments and even create the mouse-rollover image swapping effect that is popular in a lot of Web pages these days.

Part III

Part III, the largest section of the book, provides in-depth coverage of the document object models as implemented in browsers from the earliest days to today. In all reference chapters, a compatibility chart indicates the browser version that supports each object and object feature. One chapter in particular, Chapter 15, contains reference material that is shared by most of the remaining chapters of Part III. To help you refer back to Chapter 15 from other chapters, a dark tab along the outside edge of the page shows you at a glance where the chapter is located. Additional navigation aids include guide words at the bottoms of most pages to indicate which object and object feature is covered on the page.

Part IV

Reference information for the core JavaScript language fills Part IV. As with reference chapters of Part III, the JavaScript chapters display browser compatibility charts for every JavaScript language term. Guide words at the bottoms of pages help you find a particular term quickly.

Part V

In Part V, I get down to the business of deploying JavaScript. Here are the practical aspects of JavaScript, such as Chapter 43's coverage of client-side form data validation and Chapter 44's coverage of blending Java applets and plug-ins into pages. Debugging scripts is the focus of Chapter 45, with tips on understanding error messages, building your own debugging tools, and using Netscape's debugger. Chapter 46 goes into great detail about security issues for JavaScript-enabled applications.

Dynamic HTML in a cross-browser environment is the subject of Chapter 47, while Chapter 48 introduces you to Microsoft's behaviors mechanism for Windows.

The remaining nine chapters consist of full-fledged applications of JavaScript. These applications are designed not necessarily as plug-and-play modules you can put into your pages right away. Instead, their goal is to demonstrate many of the concepts described earlier in the book by way of real-world examples. New for this edition are some examples based on XML data islands in Internet Explorer for Windows.

 On the CD-ROM   You can find all of the Part V chapters on the CD-ROM that accompanies this book.

Part VI

Finally, several appendixes at the end of the book provide helpful reference information. These resources include a JavaScript and Browser Objects Quick Reference in Appendix A, a list of JavaScript reserved words in Appendix B, answers to Part II's tutorial exercises in Appendix C, and Internet resources in Appendix D. In Appendix E, you also find information on using the CD-ROM that comes with this book.

CD-ROM

The accompanying CD-ROM contains over 300 ready-to-run HTML documents that serve as examples of most of the document object model and JavaScript vocabulary words in Parts III and IV. You can run these examples with your JavaScript-enabled browser, but be sure to use the `index.html` page in the listings folder as a gateway to running the listings. This page shows you the browsers that are compatible with each example listing. I could have provided you with humorous little sample code fragments out of context, but I think that seeing full-fledged HTML documents (simple though they may be) for employing these concepts is important. I intentionally omitted the script listings from the tutorial part (Part II) of this book to encourage you to type the scripts. I believe you learn a lot, even by aping listings from the book, as you get used to the rhythms of typing scripts in documents. You also find listings from Parts I and V on the CD-ROM.

The CD-ROM holds another valuable resource: dozens and dozens of Example sections for Parts III and IV. Many of these sections reveal detailed descriptions of HTML listings that illustrate a particular object model or language feature. Even more Example sections invite you to try out an object model or language feature with the help of an interactive workbench, called The Evaluator — a *JavaScript Bible* exclusive! You see instant results and quickly learn how the feature works.

The Quick Reference from Appendix A is in .pdf format on the CD-ROM for you to print out and assemble as a handy reference, if desired. Adobe Acrobat Reader is also included on the CD-ROM so that you can read this .pdf file. Finally, the text of the book is in a .pdf file format on the CD-ROM for easy searching.

Prerequisites to Learning JavaScript

Although this book doesn't demand that you have a great deal of programming experience behind you, the more Web pages you've created with HTML, the easier you will find it to understand how JavaScript interacts with the familiar elements you normally place in your pages. Occasionally, you will need to modify HTML tags to take advantage of scripting. If you are familiar with those tags already, the JavaScript enhancements will be simple to digest.

Forms and their elements (text fields, buttons, and selection lists) play an especially important role in much of typical JavaScript work. You should be familiar with these elements and their HTML attributes. Fortunately, you won't need to know about server scripting or passing information from a form to a server. The focus here is on client-side scripting, which operates independently of the server after the JavaScript-enhanced HTML page is fully loaded into the browser.

The basic vocabulary of the current HTML standard should be part of your working knowledge. When we get to using frames, for instance, the focus is on how to script these elements, not on designing pages with them. Microsoft, Netscape, and other online sources provide more detailed explanations of frames.

If you've never programmed before

To someone who learned HTML from a slim guidebook a few years ago, the size of this book must be daunting. JavaScript may not be the easiest language in the world to learn, but believe me, it's a far cry from having to learn a full programming language, such as Java or C. Unlike developing a full-fledged monolithic application (such as the productivity programs you buy in the stores), JavaScript lets you experiment by writing small snippets of program code to accomplish big things. The JavaScript interpreter built into every scriptable browser does a great deal of the technical work for you.

Programming, at its most basic level, consists of nothing more than writing a series of instructions for the computer to follow. We humans follow instructions all the time, even if we don't realize it. Traveling to a friend's house is a sequence of small instructions: Go three blocks that way; turn left here; turn right there. Amid these instructions are some decisions that we have to make: If the stoplight is red, then stop; if the light is green, then go; if the light is yellow, then floor it. Occasionally, we must repeat some operations several times (kind of like having to go around the block until a parking space opens up). A computer program not only contains the main sequence of steps, but it also anticipates what decisions or repetitions may be needed to accomplish the program's goal (such as how to handle the various states of a stoplight or what to do if someone just stole the parking spot you were aiming for).

The initial hurdle of learning to program is becoming comfortable with the way a programming language wants its words and numbers organized in these instructions. Such rules are called syntax, the same as in a living language. Because computers generally are dumb electronic hulks, they aren't very forgiving if you don't communicate with them in the specific language they understand. When speaking to another human, you can flub a sentence's syntax and still have a good chance of the other person's understanding you fully. Not so with computer programming languages. If the syntax isn't perfect (or at least within the language's range of knowledge that it can correct), the computer has the brazenness to tell you that you have made a syntax error.

The best thing you can do is to just chalk up the syntax errors you receive as learning experiences. Even experienced programmers get them. Every syntax error you get — and every resolution of that error made by rewriting the wayward statement — adds to your knowledge of the language.

If you've done a little programming before

Programming experience in a procedural language, such as BASIC or Pascal, may almost be a hindrance rather than a help to learning JavaScript. Although you may have an appreciation for precision in syntax, the overall concept of how a program fits into the world is probably radically different from JavaScript. Part of this has to do with the typical tasks a script performs (carrying out a very specific task in response to user action within a Web page), but a large part also has to do with the nature of object-oriented programming.

In a typical procedural program, the programmer is responsible for everything that appears on the screen and everything that happens under the hood. When the program first runs, a great deal of code is dedicated to setting up the visual environment. Perhaps the screen contains several text entry fields or clickable buttons. To determine which button a user clicks, the program examines the coordinates of the click and compares those coordinates against a list of all button coordinates on the screen. Program execution then branches out to perform the instructions reserved for clicking in that space.

Object-oriented programming is almost the inverse of that process. A button is considered an object — something tangible. An object has properties, such as its label, size, alignment, and so on. An object may also contain a script. At the same time, the system software and browser, working together, can send a message to an object — depending on what the user does — to trigger the script. For example, if a user clicks in a text entry field, the system/browser tells the field that somebody has clicked there (that is, has set the focus to that field), giving the field the task of deciding what to do about it. That's where the script comes in. The script is connected to the field, and it contains the instructions that the field carries out after the user activates it. Another set of instructions may control what happens when the user types an entry and tabs or clicks out of the field, thereby changing the content of the field.

Some of the scripts you write may seem to be procedural in construction: They contain a simple list of instructions that are carried out in order. But when dealing with data from form elements, these instructions work with the object-based nature of JavaScript. The form is an object; each radio button or text field is an object as well. The script then acts on the properties of those objects to get some work done.

Making the transition from procedural to object-oriented programming may be the most difficult challenge for you. When I was first introduced to object-oriented programming a number of years ago, I didn't get it at first. But when the concept clicked — a long, pensive walk helped — so many light bulbs went on inside my head that I thought I might glow in the dark. From then on, object orientation seemed to be the only sensible way to program.

If you've programmed in C before

By borrowing syntax from Java (which, in turn, is derived from C and C++), JavaScript shares many syntactical characteristics with C. Programmers familiar with C will feel right at home. Operator symbols, conditional structures, and repeat loops follow very much in the C tradition. You will be less concerned about data types in JavaScript than you are in C. In JavaScript, a variable is not restricted to any particular data type.

With so much of JavaScript's syntax familiar to you, you will be able to concentrate on document object model concepts, which may be entirely new to you. You will still need a good grounding in HTML (especially form elements) to put your expertise to work in JavaScript.

If you've programmed in Java before

Despite the similarity in their names, the two languages share only surface aspects: loop and conditional constructions, C-like "dot" object references, curly braces for grouping statements, several keywords, and a few other attributes. Variable declarations, however, are quite different, because JavaScript is a loosely typed language. A variable can contain an integer value in one statement and a string in the next (though I'm not saying that this is good style). What Java refers to as methods, JavaScript calls methods (when associated with a predefined object) or functions (for scripter-defined actions). JavaScript methods and functions may return values of any type without having to state the data type ahead of time.

Perhaps the most important aspects of Java to suppress when writing JavaScript are the object-oriented notions of classes, inheritance, instantiation, and message passing. These aspects are simply non-issues when scripting. At the same time, however, JavaScript's designers knew that you'd have some hard-to-break habits. For example, although JavaScript does not require a semicolon at the end of each statement line, if you type one in your JavaScript source code, the JavaScript interpreter won't balk.

If you've written scripts (or macros) before

Experience with writing scripts in other authoring tools or macros in productivity programs is helpful for grasping a number of JavaScript's concepts. Perhaps the most important concept is the idea of combining a handful of statements to perform a specific task on some data. For example, you can write a macro in Microsoft Excel that performs a data transformation on daily figures that come in from a corporate financial report on another computer. The macro is built into the Macro menu, and you run it by choosing that menu item whenever a new set of figures arrives.

More sophisticated scripting, such as that found in Toolbook or HyperCard, prepares you for the object orientation of JavaScript. In those environments, screen objects contain scripts that are executed when a user interacts with those objects. A great deal of the scripting you will do in JavaScript matches that pattern exactly. In fact, those environments resemble the scriptable browser environment in another way: They provide a finite set of predefined objects that have fixed sets of properties and behaviors. This predictability makes learning the entire environment and planning an application easier to accomplish.

Formatting and Naming Conventions

The script listings and words in this book are presented in a `monospace font` to set them apart from the rest of the text. Because of restrictions in page width, lines of script listings may, from time to time, break unnaturally. In such cases, the remainder of the script appears in the following line, flush with the left margin of the listing, just as they would appear in a text editor with word wrapping turned on. If these line breaks cause you problems when you type a script listing into a document yourself, I encourage you to access the corresponding listing on the CD-ROM to see how it should look when you type it.

As soon as you reach Part III of this book, you won't likely go for more than a page before reading about an object model or language feature that requires a specific minimum version of one browser or another. To make it easier to spot in the text when a particular browser and browser version is required, most browser references consist of a two-letter abbreviation and a version number. For example, IE5 means Internet Explorer 5 for any operating system; NN6 means Netscape Navigator 6 for any operating system. If a feature is introduced with a particular version of browser and is supported in subsequent versions, a plus symbol (+) follows the number. For example, a feature marked IE4+ indicates that Internet Explorer 4 is required at a minimum, but the feature is also available in IE5, IE5.5, and so on. Occasionally, a feature or some highlighted behavior applies to only one operating system. For example, a feature marked IE4+/Windows means that it works only on Windows versions of Internet Explorer 4 or later. As points of reference, the first scriptable browsers were NN2, IE3/Windows, and IE3.01/Macintosh. Moreover, IE3 for Windows can be equipped with one of two versions of the JScript .dll file. A reference to the earlier version is cited as IE3/J1, while the later version is cited as IE3/J2. You will see this notation primarily in the compatibility charts throughout the reference chapters.

   Note, Tip, and Caution icons occasionally appear in the book to flag important points.

 On the CD-ROM icons point you to useful examples and code listings found on this book's companion CD-ROM.

Acknowledgments

Before closing, I would like to acknowledge the contributions of many folks who helped make this edition possible: Eric Krock, Tom Pixley, Vidur Apparao, and especially the ever-patient, all-knowing Brendan Eich (Mozilla); Martin Honnen (Netscape DevEdge Champion); Tantek Celik (Microsoft's Macintosh development group); Brenda McLaughlin, Walt Bruce, Michael Roney, Debra Williams Cauley, Neil Romanosky, Eric Newman, Jerelind Charles, and Victoria Lee O'Malley (Hungry Minds, Inc.); technical reviewer David Wall; "cookie man" Bill Dortch (hIdaho Design); Red and his friends (Mars, Incorporated); and fellow scripters and newsgroup kibitzers, who unwittingly advised me as to where scripters were having trouble with the language. Above all, I want to thank the many readers of the first three editions of this book (with both titles, *Danny Goodman's JavaScript Handbook* and *JavaScript™ Bible*) for investing in this ongoing effort. I wish I had the space here to acknowledge by name so many who have sent e-mail notes and suggestions: Your input has been most welcome and greatly appreciated. Now it's time to get down to the fun of learning JavaScript. Enjoy!

A Word from the Publisher

The expanded content of this edition far exceeds the number of pages we can bind into a softcover volume. In our goal to deliver to you the author's comprehensive expertise within these physical limits, we have moved selected chapters of more advanced subjects to the CD-ROM in searchable Acrobat format. We trust that the added value of these unabridged electronic chapters outweighs the associated inconvenience.

Contents at a Glance

Contents

Chapter 23: The Form and Related Objects **625**

Chapter 24: Button Objects **651**

Part IV: JavaScript Core Language Reference   891

Getting Started with JavaScript

JavaScript's Role in the World Wide Web and Beyond

Many of the technologies that make the World Wide Web possible have far exceeded their original visions. Envisioned at the outset as a medium for publishing static text and image content across a network, the Web is forever being probed, pushed, and pulled by content authors. By taking for granted so much of the "dirty work" of establishing the connection and conveying the bits between server and client computers, content developers and programmers dream of using that connection to generate new user experiences and operating system-independent applications. A developer community essentially taking ownership of a technology and molding it to do new and exciting things is not new. It's the enormous popularity of the Web and the accessibility of the technologies to everyday folks who have intriguing ideas that has led to an unprecedented explosion in turning the World Wide Web from a bland publishing medium into a highly interactive, operating system-agnostic authoring platform.

The JavaScript language is a Web-enhancing technology. When employed on the client computer, the language can help turn a static page of content into an engaging, interactive, and intelligent experience. Applications can be as subtle as welcoming a site's visitor with the greeting "Good morning!" when it is morning in the client computer's time zone — even though it is dinnertime where the server is located. Or applications can be much more obvious, such as delivering the content of a slide show in one-page download while JavaScript controls the sequence of hiding, showing, and "flying slide" transitions while navigating through the presentation.

Of course, JavaScript is not the only technology that can give life to drab Web content. Therefore, it is important to understand where JavaScript fits within the array of standards, tools, and other technologies at your disposal. The alternative technologies described in this chapter are HTML, server programs, plug-ins, and Java applets. In most cases, JavaScript can work side by side with these other technologies, even though the hype around some make them sound like one-stop shopping places for all your interactive needs. That's rarely the case. Finally, you learn about the origins of JavaScript and what role it plays in today's advanced Web browsers.

Competition on the Web

Web page publishers revel in logging as many visits to their sites as possible. Regardless of the questionable accuracy of Web page *hit* counts, a site consistently logging 10,000 dubious hits per week is clearly far more popular than one with 1,000 dubious hits per week. Even if the precise number is unknown, relative popularity is a valuable measure.

Encouraging people to visit a site frequently is the Holy Grail of Web publishing. Competition for viewers is enormous. Not only is the Web like a ten million-channel television, but the Web competes for viewers' attention with all kinds of computer-generated information. That includes anything that appears onscreen as interactive multimedia.

Users of entertainment programs, multimedia encyclopedias, and other colorful, engaging, and mouse finger-numbing actions are accustomed to high-quality presentations. Frequently, these programs sport first-rate graphics, animation, live-action video, and synchronized sound. In contrast, the lowest common denominator Web page has little in the way of razzle-dazzle. Even with the help of recent advances in Dynamic HTML and style sheets, the layout of pictures and text is highly constrained compared with the kinds of desktop publishing documents you see all the time. Regardless of the quality of its content, a vanilla HTML document is flat. At best, interaction is limited to whatever navigation the author offers in the way of hypertext links or forms whose filled-in content magically disappears into the Web site's server.

With so many ways to spice up Web sites and pages, you can count on competitors for your site's visitors to do their darndest to make their sites more engaging than yours. Unless you are the sole purveyor of information that is in high demand, you continually must devise ways to keep your visitors coming back and entice new ones. If you design an intranet, your competition is the drive for improved productivity by the colleagues who use the internal Web sites for getting their jobs done.

These are all excellent reasons why you should care about using one or more Web technologies to raise your pages above the noise. Let's look at the major technologies you should know about.

Hypertext Markup Language (HTML)

As an outgrowth of *SGML (Standard Generalized Markup Language)*, *HTML* is generally viewed as nothing more than a document formatting, or *tagging*, language. The tags (inside <> delimiter characters) instruct a viewer program (the *browser* or, more generically, the *client*) how to display chunks of text or images.

Relegating HTML to the category of a tagging language does disservice not only to the effort that goes into fashioning a first-rate Web page, but also to the way users interact with the pages. To my way of thinking, any collection of commands and other syntax that directs the way users interact with digital information is *programming*. With HTML, a Web page author controls the user experience with the content just as the engineers who program Microsoft Excel craft the way users interact with spreadsheet content and functions.

Recent enhancements to the published standards for HTML (HTML 4.0 and later) endeavor to define more narrowly the purpose of HTML to assign context to content, leaving the appearance to a separate standard for style sheets. In other words, it's not HTML's role to signify that some text is italic, but rather to signify *why* it is italic. (For example, you tag a chunk of text that conveys emphasis regardless of how the style sheet or browser sets the appearance of that emphasized text.)

The most interactivity that HTML lets authors play with is associated with fill-in-the-blank forms. Browsers display text boxes, radio buttons, checkboxes, and select lists in response to HTML tags for those types of form controls. But that's as far as HTML goes. Any processing of the choices or information entered into the form by the user is the job of other technologies, such as programs on the server or client-side scripts.

CGI Scripting

One way to enhance the interaction between user and content is to have the page communicate with the Web server that houses the Web pages. Popular Web search sites, such as Yahoo!, Google, and Lycos, enable users to type search criteria and click a button or two to specify the way the search engine should treat the query. E-commerce sites enable you to gather products in a virtual shopping cart and then click a button to submit an order for processing. When you click the Submit or Search buttons, your browser sends your entries from a form to the server. On the server, a program known as a *CGI (Common Gateway Interface)* script formats the data you enter and sends this information to a database or other program running on the server. The CGI script then sends the results to your browser, sometimes in the form of a new page or as information occupying other fields in the form.

Writing customized CGI scripts typically requires considerable programming skill. Most CGI scripts are written in languages such as Perl, Java, and C or C++. Very few servers are equipped to run server scripts written in JavaScript.

Whatever language you use, the job definitely requires the Web page author to be in control of the server, including whatever *back-end* programs (such as databases) are needed to supply results or massage the information coming from the user. Even with the new, server-based Web site design tools available, CGI scripting often is not a task that a content-oriented HTML author can do without handing it off to a more experienced programmer.

As interesting and useful as CGI scripting is, it burdens the server with the job of processing queries. A busy server may process hundreds of CGI scripts at a time, while the client computers — the personal computers running the browsers — sit idle as the browser's logo icon dances its little animation. This wastes desktop processing horsepower, especially if the process running on the server doesn't need to access big databases or other external computers. That's why some people regard browsing a basic Web page as little more than using a dumb terminal to access some server content.

Of Helpers and Plug-ins

In the early days of the World Wide Web, a browser needed to present only a few kinds of data before a user's eyes. The power to render text (tagged with HTML) and images (in popular formats such as GIF and JPEG) was built into browsers intended for desktop operating systems. Not to be limited by those data types, developers worked hard to extend browsers so that data in other formats could be rendered on the client computer. It was unlikely, however, that a browser would ever be built that could download and render, say, any of several sound file formats.

One way to solve the problem was to allow the browser, upon recognizing an incoming file of a particular type, to launch a separate application on the client machine to render the content. As long as this helper application was installed on the client computer (and the association with the helper program set in the browser's preferences), the browser would launch the program and send the incoming file to that program. Thus, you might have one helper application for a MIDI sound file and another for a WAV sound file.

Beginning with Netscape Navigator 2, software *plug-ins* for browsers enabled developers to extend the capabilities of the browser without having to modify the browser. Unlike a helper application, a plug-in can enable external content to blend into the document seamlessly.

The most common plug-ins are those that facilitate the playback of audio and video from the server. Audio may include music tracks that play in the background while visiting a page or live (streaming) audio, similar to a radio station. Video and animation can operate in a space on the page when played through a plug-in that knows how to process such data.

Today's browsers tend to ship with plug-ins that decode the most common sound file types. Developers of plug-ins for Internet Explorer for the Windows operating system commonly implement plug-ins as ActiveX controls — a distinction that is important to the underpinnings of the operating system, but not to the user.

Plug-ins and helpers are valuable for more than just audio and video playback. A popular helper application is the *Adobe Acrobat Reader*, which displays Acrobat files that are formatted just as if they were being printed. But for interactivity, developers today frequently rely on Macromedia Corporation's *Flash* plug-in. Created using the Macromedia Flash authoring environment, a Flash document can have active clickable areas and draggable elements. Some authors even simulate artistic video games and animated stories in Flash. A browser equipped with the Flash plug-in displays the content in a rectangular area embedded within the browser page.

One potential downside for authoring interactive content in Flash or similar environments is that if the user does not have the plug-in installed, it can take some time to download the plug-in (if the user even wants to bother). Moreover, once the plug-in is installed, highly graphic and interactive content can take longer to download to the client (especially on a dial-up connection) than some users are willing to wait. This is one of those situations in which you must balance your creative palette with the user's desire for your interactive content.

Java Applets

When the interaction between user and Web page exceeds the capabilities of HTML, experienced programmers may prefer to "roll their own" programs to handle the special needs not available in existing plug-ins. The Java programming language fills this need. Developed by Sun Microsystems, this language enables programmers to write small applications *(applets)* that download to the browser as separate files. An applet runs as the user needs it and then is automatically discarded from memory when the user moves elsewhere in the Web.

Animation, including animated text whose content can change over time, is a popular application of the Java applet in an HTML page. Because applets can also communicate with the Internet as they run (it is a very network-centric programming language), they are also used for real-time, data-streaming applications that display up-to-the-minute news, stock market, and sports data as this information comes across the wires. Standard HTML content can surround all of this activity as the Web page designer sees fit.

To play a Java applet, a browser company must license the technology from Sun and build it into its browser (or link up with a Java engine that is part of the operating system). Netscape was the first third-party browser supplier to license and produce a browser capable of running Java applets (Navigator 2 under Windows 95 and UNIX). Today, both Netscape Navigator and Microsoft Internet Explorer (IE) can load and run Java applets on almost every operating system platform supported by the browser.

Despite a flash of popularity in the early Java days, Java is used less and less for browser applets. It is quite popular, however, on the server, where it is used frequently to create small server application modules called *servlets*. On the client, Java applets suffer the same problem as some plug-ins: the delay required to download the file. Also, not every browser is equipped with the desired Java component, causing potential compatibility conflicts.

JavaScript: A Language for All

The Java language is derived from C and C++, but it is a distinct language. Its main audience is the experienced programmer. That leaves out many Web page authors. I was dismayed at this situation when I first read about Java's specifications. I would have preferred a language that casual programmers and scripters who were comfortable with authoring tools such as Apple's once-formidable HyperCard and Microsoft's Visual Basic could adopt quickly. As these accessible development platforms have shown, nonprofessional authors can dream up many creative applications, often for very specific tasks that no professional programmer would have the inclination to work on. Personal needs often drive development in the classroom, office, den, or garage. But Java was not going to be that kind of inclusive language.

My spirits lifted several months later, in November 1995, when I heard of a scripting language project brewing at Netscape. Initially born under the name LiveScript, this language was developed in parallel with Netscape's Web server software. The language was to serve two purposes with the same syntax. One purpose was as a scripting language that Web server administrators could use to manage the server and connect its pages to other services, such as back-end databases and search engines for users looking up information. Extending the "Live" brand name further, Netscape assigned the name LiveWire to the database connectivity usage of JavaScript on the server.

On the client side — in HTML documents — authors could employ scripts written in this new language to enhance Web pages in a number of ways. For example, an author could use LiveScript to make sure that the information a user enters into a form is of the proper type. Instead of forcing the server or database to do the data validation (requiring data exchanges between the client browser and the server), the user's computer handles all the calculation work — putting some of that otherwise wasted horsepower to work. In essence, LiveScript could provide HTML-level interaction for the user.

As the intensity of industry interest in Java grew, Netscape saw another opportunity for LiveScript: as a way for HTML documents (and their users) to communicate with Java applets. For example, a user might make some preference selections from checkboxes and pop-up selection lists located at the top of a Web page. Scrolling down to the next screenful, the user sees text in the Java applet scrolling banner on the page that is customized to the settings made above. In this case, the LiveScript script sends the text that is to appear in the scrolling banner to the applet (and perhaps a new color to use for the banner's background and text). While this is happening, the server doesn't have to worry a bit about it, and the user hasn't had to wait for communication between the browser and the server. As great an idea as this was initially, this connectivity feature didn't make it into Navigator 2 when JavaScript first became available.

LiveScript becomes JavaScript

In early December 1995, just prior to the formal release of Navigator 2, Netscape and Sun jointly announced that the scripting language thereafter would be known as JavaScript. Though Netscape had several good marketing reasons for adopting this name, the changeover may have contributed more confusion to both the Java and HTML scripting worlds than anyone expected.

Before the announcement, the language was already related to Java in some ways. Many of the basic syntax elements of the scripting language were reminiscent of the C and C++ style of Java. For client-side scripting, the language was intended for very different purposes than Java — essentially to function as a programming language integrated into HTML documents rather than as a language for writing applets that occupy a fixed rectangular area on the page (and that are oblivious to anything else on the page). Instead of Java's full-blown programming language vocabulary (and conceptually more difficult to learn object-oriented approach), JavaScript had a small vocabulary and a more easily digestible programming model.

The true difficulty, it turned out, was making the distinction between Java and JavaScript clear to the world. Many computer journalists made major blunders when they said or implied that JavaScript provided a simpler way of building Java applets. To this day, many programmers believe JavaScript is synonymous with the Java language: They post Java queries to JavaScript-specific Internet newsgroups and mailing lists.

The fact remains today that Java and JavaScript are more different than they are similar. The two languages employ entirely different interpreter engines to execute their lines of code. Whereas JavaScript support shipped in every platform-specific version of Navigator 2 in February 1996, Java was not available for Windows 3.1 users until late in the life of Navigator 3. (Many squirrelly technical issues make it difficult for this modern language to work in an "ancient" MS-DOS operating system.)

The Microsoft world

Although the JavaScript language originated at Netscape, Microsoft acknowledged the potential power and popularity of the language by implementing it (under the JScript name) in Internet Explorer 3. Even if Microsoft would rather that the world use the VBScript (Visual Basic Script) language that it provides in the Windows versions of IE, the fact that JavaScript is available on more browsers and operating systems makes it the client-side scripter's choice for anyone who must design for a broad range of users.

In keeping with the competitive nature of the Web browser market, Netscape and Microsoft continue to attract developers to their camps with different philosophies. As this book is written, Netscape is waving the banner of support for published Web standards; Microsoft, on the other hand, provides only partial standards support but many proprietary extensions that are useful, especially when the clients are running Win32 operating systems exclusively. If you develop pages for an audience that uses both browser brands and multiple operating systems, this creates challenges. I address these issues in the next chapter and in several technical sections in Parts III and IV.

JavaScript: The Right Tool for the Right Job

Knowing how to match an authoring tool to a solution-building task is an important part of being a well-rounded Web page author. A Web page designer who ignores JavaScript is akin to a plumber who bruises his knuckles by using pliers instead of the wrench at the bottom of the toolbox.

By the same token, JavaScript won't fulfill every dream. The more you understand about JavaScript's intentions and limitations, the more likely you will be to turn to it immediately when it is the proper tool. In particular, look to JavaScript for the following kinds of solutions:

✦ Getting your Web page to respond or react directly to user interaction with form elements (input fields, text areas, buttons, radio buttons, checkboxes, selection lists) and hypertext links — a class of application I call the *serverless CGI*

✦ Distributing small collections of database-like information and providing a friendly interface to that data

✦ Controlling multiple-frame navigation, plug-ins, or Java applets based on user choices in the HTML document

✦ Preprocessing data on the client before submission to a server

✦ Changing content and styles in modern browsers dynamically and instantly in response to user interaction

At the same time, understanding what JavaScript is *not* capable of doing is vital. Scripters waste many hours looking for ways of carrying out tasks for which JavaScript was not designed. Most of the limitations are designed to protect visitors from invasions of privacy or unauthorized access to their desktop computers. Therefore, unless a visitor uses a modern browser and explicitly gives you permission to access protected parts of his or her computer, JavaScript cannot surreptitiously perform any of the following actions:

✦ Setting or retrieving the browser's preferences settings, main window appearance features, action buttons, and printing

✦ Launching an application on the client computer

✦ Reading or writing files or directories on the client or server computer

✦ Capturing live data streams from the server for retransmission

✦ Sending secret e-mails from Web site visitors to you

Web site authors are constantly seeking tools that will make their sites engaging (if not "cool") with the least amount of effort. This is particularly true when the task is in the hands of people more comfortable with writing, graphic design, and page layout than with hard-core programming. Not every Webmaster has legions of experienced programmers on hand to whip up some special, custom enhancement for the site. Nor does every Web author have control over the Web server that physically houses the collection of HTML and graphics files. JavaScript brings programming power within reach of anyone familiar with HTML, even when the server is a black box at the other end of a telephone line.

✦   ✦   ✦

Authoring Challenges Amid the Browser Wars

If you are starting to learn JavaScript at this point in the brief history of scriptable browsers, you have both a distinct advantage and disadvantage. The advantage is that you have the wonderful capabilities of the latest browser offerings from Netscape and Microsoft at your bidding. The disadvantage is that you have not experienced the painful history of authoring for older browser versions that were buggy and at times incompatible with one another due to a lack of standards. You have yet to learn the anguish of carefully devising a scripted application for the browser version you use only to have site visitors sending you voluminous e-mail messages about how the page triggers all kinds of script errors when run on a different browser brand, generation, or operating system platform.

Welcome to the real world of scripting Web pages in JavaScript. Several dynamics are at work to help make an author's life difficult if the audience for the application uses more than a single type of browser. This chapter introduces you to these challenges before you type your first word of JavaScript code. My fear is that the subjects I raise may dissuade you from progressing further into JavaScript and its powers. But as a developer myself—and as someone who has been using JavaScript since the earliest days of its public pre-release availability—I dare not sugarcoat the issues facing scripters today. Instead, I want to make sure you have an appreciation of what lies ahead to assist you in learning the language. I believe if you understand the big picture of the browser-scripting world as it stands in the year 2001, you will find it easier to target JavaScript usage in your Web application development.

Leapfrog

Browser compatibility has been an issue for authors since the earliest days of rushing to the Web — long before JavaScript. Despite the fact that browser developers and other interested parties voiced their opinions during formative stages of standards development, HTML authors could not produce a document that appeared the same pixel by pixel on all client machines. It may have been one thing to establish a set of standard tags for defining heading levels and line breaks, but it was rare for the actual rendering of content inside those tags to look identical on different brands of browsers.

Then, as the competitive world heated up — and Web browser development transformed itself from a volunteer undertaking into profit-seeking businesses — creative people defined new features and new tags that helped authors develop more flexible and interesting looking pages. As happens a lot in any computer-related industry, the pace of commercial development easily outpaced the studied processing of standards. A browser maker would build a new HTML feature into a browser and only then propose that feature to the relevant standards body. Web authors were using these features (sometimes for prerelease browser versions) before the proposals were published for review.

When the deployment of content depends almost entirely on an interpretive engine on the client computer receiving the data — the HTML engine in a browser, for example — authors face an immediate problem. Unlike a standalone computer program that can extend and even invent functionality across a wide range and have it run on everyone's computer (at least for a given operating system), Web content providers must rely on the functionality built into the browser. This led to questions such as, "If not all browsers coming to my site support a particular HTML feature, then should I apply newfangled HTML features for visitors only at the bleeding edge?" and "If I do deploy the new features, what do I do for those with older browsers?"

Authors who developed pages in the earliest days of the Web wrestled with these questions for many HTML features that we today take for granted. Tables and frames come to mind. Eventually, the standards caught up with the proposed HTML extensions — but not without a lot of author anguish along the way.

The same game continues today. But the field of players has shrunk to two primary players: Netscape and Microsoft. The independent Opera browser runs a distant third in the browser race. For all of these companies, the stakes are higher than ever before — market share, investor return on investment, and so on. Pick a business buzzword, and you'll find a reason behind the competition. What had begun years ago as a friendly game of leapfrog (long before Microsoft even acknowledged the Web) has become an out-and-out war.

Duck and Cover

Sometimes it is difficult to tell from week to week where the battles are being fought. Marketing messages from the combatants turn on a dime. You can't tell if the message is proactive to stress a genuinely new corporate strategy or reactive to match the opponent's latest salvo. The combatants keep touting to each other: "Anything you can do, we can do better!" Or, in a more recent salvo: "We support Web standards!" and "We integrate seamlessly with the operating system!"

If it were a case of Netscape and Microsoft pitching their server and browser software to customers for the creation of monolithic intranets, I could understand and appreciate such efforts. The battle lines would be clearly drawn, and potential customers would base their decisions on unemotional criteria — how well the solution fits the customer's information distribution and connectivity goals. In fact, if you develop for an organization-wide intranet, whose browser choice is dictated by management, you are in luck because authoring for a single browser brand and version is a piece of cake. But you are not in the majority.

As happens in war, civilian casualties mount when the big guns start shooting. The battle lines have shifted dramatically in only a few years. The huge market share territory once under Netscape's command now lies in Microsoft hands (no doubt aided by the millions of America Online users who receive IE as part of the AOL software). While a fair amount of authoring common ground exists between the latest versions of the two browsers, the newest features cause the biggest problems for authors wishing to deploy on both browsers. Trying to determine where the common denominator is may be the toughest part of the authoring job.

Compatibility Issues Today

Allow me to describe the current status of compatibility between Netscape Navigator and Internet Explorer. The discussion in the next few sections intentionally does not get into specific scripting technology very deeply — some of you may know very little about programming. In many chapters throughout Parts III and IV, I offer scripting suggestions to accommodate both browsers.

Separating language from objects

Although early JavaScript authors initially treated client-side scripting as one environment that permitted the programming of page elements, the scene has changed as the browsers have matured. Today, a clear distinction exists between specifications for the core JavaScript language and for the elements you script in a document (for example, buttons and fields in a form).

On one level, this separation is a good thing. It means that one specification exists for basic programming concepts and syntax that enables you to apply the same language to environments that may not even exist today. You can think of the core language as basic wiring. Once you know how electric wires work, you can connect them to all kinds of electrical devices, including some that may not be invented yet. Similarly, JavaScript today is used to wire together page elements in an HTML document. Tomorrow, operating systems could use the core language to enable users to wire together desktop applications that need to exchange information automatically.

At the ends of today's JavaScript wires are the elements on the page. In programming jargon, these items are known as *document objects*. By keeping the specifications for document objects separate from the wires that connect them, you can use other kinds of wires (other languages) to connect them. It's like designing telephones that can work with any kind of wire, including a type of wire that hasn't been invented yet. Today the devices can work with copper wire or fiber optic cable. You get a good picture of this separation in Internet Explorer, whose set of document objects can be scripted with JavaScript or VBScript. They're the same objects, just different wiring.

The separation of core language from document objects enables each concept to have its own standards effort and development pace. But even with recommended standards for each factor, each browser maker is free to extend the standards. Furthermore, authors may have to expend more effort to devise one version of a page or script that plays on both browsers unless the script adheres to a common denominator (or uses some other branching techniques to let each browser run its own way).

Core language standard

Keeping track of JavaScript language versions requires study of history and politics. History covers the three versions developed by Netscape; politics covers Microsoft's versions and the joint standards effort. The first version of JavaScript (in Navigator 2) was Version 1.0, although that numbering was not part of the language usage. JavaScript was JavaScript. Version numbering became an issue when Navigator 3 was released. The version of JavaScript associated with that Navigator version was JavaScript 1.1. As you will learn later in this book, the version number is sometimes necessary in an attribute of the HTML tags that surround a script. The Navigator 4.x generation increased the language version one more notch with JavaScript 1.2.

Microsoft's scripting effort contributes confusion for scripting newcomers. The first version of Internet Explorer to include scripting was Internet Explorer 3. The timing of Internet Explorer 3 was roughly coincidental to Navigator 3. But as scripters soon discovered, Microsoft's scripting effort was one generation behind. Microsoft did not license the JavaScript name. As a result, the company called its language

JScript. Even so, the HTML tag attribute that requires naming the language of the script inside the tags could be either JScript or JavaScript for Internet Explorer. Internet Explorer 3 could understand a JavaScript script written for Navigator 2.

During this period of dominance by Navigator 3 and Internet Explorer 3, scripting newcomers were often confused because they expected the scripting languages to be the same. Unfortunately for the scripters, there were language features in JavaScript 1.1 that were not available in the older JavaScript version in Internet Explorer 3. Microsoft improved JavaScript in IE3 with an upgrade to the .dll file that gives IE its JavaScript syntax. However, it's hard to know which .dll is installed in any given visitor's IE3. The situation smoothed out for Internet Explorer 4. Its core language was essentially up to the level of JavaScript 1.2 in Navigator 4. Microsoft still officially called the language JScript. Almost all language features that were new in Navigator 4 (including the script tag attribute identifying JavaScript 1.2) were understood when you loaded the scripts into Internet Explorer 4.

While all of this jockeying for JavaScript versions was happening, Netscape, Microsoft, and other concerned parties met to establish a core language standard. The standards body is a Switzerland-based organization originally called the European Computer Manufacturer's Association and now known simply as ECMA (commonly pronounced ECK-ma). In mid-1997, the first formal language specification was agreed on and published (ECMA-262). Due to licensing issues with the JavaScript name, the body created a new name for the language: ECMAScript.

With only minor and esoteric differences, this first version of ECMAScript was essentially the same as JavaScript 1.1 found in Navigator 3. Both Navigator 4 and Internet Explorer 4 supported the ECMAScript standard. Moreover, as happens so often when commerce meets standards bodies, both browsers went beyond the ECMAScript standard. Fortunately, the common denominator of this extended core language is broad, lessening authoring headaches on this front.

IE5 advances to JavaScript Version 1.3, while NN6 has the luxury of implementing JavaScript 1.5. In the meantime, the ECMA standard has evolved to a new release that incorporates features found in JavaScript 1.3 and 1.5.

While the core language tends to exhibit the most compatibility between IE and NN, authors must pay attention to which language features are available in the browsers visiting scripted pages. Older browser versions are not equipped to handle newer JavaScript features. But you can sometimes script around these incompatibilities (as described throughout the language reference in Part IV).

Document object model

If NN and IE are close in core JavaScript language compatibility, nothing could be further from the truth when it comes to the document objects. Internet Explorer 3 based its document object model (DOM) on that of Netscape Navigator 2, the same browser level it used as a model for the core language. When Netscape added a couple of new objects to the model in Navigator 3, the addition caused further headaches for neophyte scripters who expected those objects to appear in Internet Explorer 3. Probably the most commonly missed object in Internet Explorer 3 was the image object, which lets scripts swap the image when a user rolls the cursor atop a graphic — *mouse rollovers,* they're commonly called.

In the Level 4 browsers, however, Internet Explorer's document object model jumped way ahead of the object model \Netscape implemented in Navigator 4. The two most revolutionary aspects of IE4 were the ability to script virtually every element in an HTML document and the instant reflow of a page when the content changed. This opened the way for HTML content to be genuinely dynamic without requiring the browser to fetch a rearranged page from the server. NN4 implemented only a small portion of this dynamism, without exposing all elements to scripts or reflowing the page. Inline content could not change as it could in IE4. Suffice it to say IE4 was an enviable implementation.

At the same time, a DOM standard was being negotiated under the auspices of the World Wide Web Consortium (W3C). The hope among scripters was that once a standard was in place, it would be easier to develop dynamic content for all browsers that supported the standard.

Netscape took this wish to heart and designed an almost entirely new browser: Navigator 6. It incorporates all of the W3C DOM Level 1 and a good chunk of Level 2. Even though Microsoft participated in the W3C DOM standards development, IE5 implements only some of the W3C DOM standard — in some cases, just enough to allow cross-browser scripting that adheres to the standard. Of course, the standard is not perfect either, and it brings to the DOM several brand-new concepts for scripters. When you take these issues into account, and add to the mix the number of older browsers still in use, scripting HTML objects is touchy business. It requires a good knowledge of compatibility, as described in the object discussions throughout this book.

Cascading Style Sheets

Navigator 4 and Internet Explorer 4 were the first browsers to claim compatibility with a W3C recommendation called *Cascading Style Sheets Level 1 (CSS1)*. This specification customized content in an organized fashion throughout a document (and thus minimized the HTML in each tag); it was also an effort to extend the Web's tradition of publishing static content. As implementations go, NN4 had a lot of rough edges, especially when trying to mix style sheets and tables. But IE4 was no angel, either, especially when comparing the results of style sheet assignments as rendered in the Windows and Macintosh versions of the browser.

CSS Level 2 adds more style functionality to the standard, and both IE5 and NN6 support a good deal of Level 2. Rendering of styled content is more harmonious between both browsers, largely thanks to more stringent guidelines about how styles should render.

JavaScript plays a role in style sheets in IE4+ and NN6 because those browsers' object models permit dynamic modification to styles associated with any content on the page. Style sheet information is part of the object model and is therefore accessible and modifiable from JavaScript.

Dynamic HTML

Perhaps the biggest improvements to the inner workings of the Level 4 browsers from both Netscape and Microsoft revolve around a concept called *Dynamic HTML (DHTML)*. The ultimate goal of DHTML is to enable scripts in documents to control the content, content position, and content appearance in response to user actions. To that end, the W3C organization developed another standard for the precise positioning of HTML elements on a page as an extension of the CSS standards effort. The CSS-Positioning recommendation was later blended into the CSS standard, and both are now part of CSS Level 2. With positioning, you can define an exact location on the page where an element should appear, whether the item should be visible, and what stacking order it should take among all the items that might overlap it.

IE4+ adheres to the positioning standard syntax and makes positionable items subject to script control. Navigator 4 followed the standard from a conceptual point of view, but it implemented an alternative methodology involving an entirely new, and eventually unsanctioned, tag for layers. Such positionable items were scriptable in Navigator 4 as well, although a lot of the script syntax differed from that used in Internet Explorer 4. Fortunately for DHTML authors, NN6, by its adherence to the CSS standard, is more syntactically in line with DHTML style properties employed in IE4+. Cross-browser scripting can be challenging, yet it is certainly possible if you understand the limitations imposed by following a common denominator.

Developing a Scripting Strategy

Browsers representing the latest generation contain a hodgepodge of standards and proprietary extensions. Even if you try to script to a common denominator among today's browsers, your code probably won't take into account the earlier versions of both the JavaScript core language and the browser document object models.

The true challenge for authors these days is determining the audience for which scripted pages are intended. You will learn techniques in Chapter 13 that enable you to redirect users to different paths in your Web site based on their browser capabilities. In Chapter 14, you will discover the alternatives you can take depending on the object model version(s) and specific features you need to support. Each new browser generation not only brings with it new and exciting features you are probably eager to employ in your pages, it also adds to the fragmentation of the audience visiting a publicly accessible page. With each new browser upgrade, fewer existing users are willing to download megabytes of browser merely to have the latest and greatest browser version. For many pioneers — and certainly for most non-techie users — there is an increasingly smaller imperative to upgrade browsers, unless that browser comes via a new computer or operating system upgrade.

As you work your way through this book, know that the common denominator you choose depends on where you draw the line for browser support. Even if you wish to adhere to the absolutely lowest common denominator of scripting, I've got you covered: The Part II tutorial focuses on language and object aspects that are compatible with every version of JavaScript and every document object model.

At the same time, I think it is important for you to understand that the cool application you see running on your latest, greatest browser may not translate to Internet Explorer 3 or Navigator 2. Therefore, when you see a technique that you'd like to emulate, be realistic in your expectations of adapting that trick for your widest audience. Only a good working knowledge of each language term's compatibility and an examination of the cool source code will reveal how well it will work for your visitors.

✦   ✦   ✦

Your First JavaScript Script

In this chapter, you set up a productive script-writing and previewing environment on your computer, and then you write a simple script whose results you can see in your JavaScript-compatible browser.

Because of differences in the way various personal computing operating systems behave, I present details of environments for two popular variants: Win32 operating systems (Windows 95/98/NT/2000/ME) and the MacOS. For the most part, your JavaScript authoring experience is the same regardless of the operating system platform you use — including Linux or UNIX. Although there may be slight differences in font designs depending on your browser and operating system, the information remains the same. Most illustrations of browser output in this book are made from the Win32 version of Internet Explorer 5.*x*. If you run another browser or version, don't fret if every pixel doesn't match with the illustrations in this book.

The Software Tools

The best way to learn JavaScript is to type the HTML and scripting code into documents in a text editor. Your choice of editor is up to you, although I provide you with some guidelines for choosing a text editor in the next section.

Choosing a text editor

For the purposes of learning JavaScript in this book, avoid WYSIWYG (What You See Is What You Get) Web page authoring tools, such as FrontPage and DreamWeaver, for now. These tools certainly will come in handy afterward when you can productively use those facilities for molding the bulk of your content and layout. But the examples in this book focus more on script content (which you must type in anyway), so there isn't much HTML that you have to type. Files for all complete Web page listings (except for the tutorial chapters) also appear on the companion CD-ROM.

An important factor to consider in your choice of editor is how easy it is to save standard text files with an .html filename extension. In the case of Windows, any program that not only saves the file as text by default but also enables you to set the extension to .htm or .html prevents a great deal of problems. If you use Microsoft Word, for example, the program tries to save files as binary Word files — something that no Web browser can load. To save the file initially as a text or .html extension file requires mucking around in the Save As dialog box. This requirement is truly a nuisance.

Nothing's wrong with using bare-essentials text editors. In Windows, that includes the WordPad program or a more fully featured product such as the shareware editor called TextPad. For the MacOS, SimpleText is also fine — although the lack of a search-and-replace function may get in the way when you start managing your Web site pages. A favorite among Mac HTML authors and scripters is BBEdit (Bare Bones Software), which includes a number of useful aids for scripters, such as optional line numbers (which help in debugging JavaScript).

Choosing a browser

The other component that is required for learning JavaScript is the browser. You don't have to be connected to the Internet to test your scripts in the browser. You can perform all testing offline. This means you can learn JavaScript and create cool, scripted Web pages with a laptop computer — even on a boat in the middle of an ocean.

The browser brand and version you use is up to you. Until you reach Chapter 12, virtually everything you script will run in every scriptable browser. For page development, however, you want a more modern browser, such as IE5.x or NN6. And to derive the most benefit from the examples scattered throughout this book, you should have the latest versions of IE and NN available for your primary operating system.

Note   Many example listings in this book demonstrate language or document object model (DOM) features that work on only specific browsers and versions. Check the compatibility listing for that language or DOM feature to make sure you use the right browser to load the page.

Setting up Your Authoring Environment

To make the job of testing your scripts easier, make sure that you have enough free memory in your computer to let both your text editor and browser run simultaneously. You need to be able to switch quickly between editor and browser as you experiment and repair any errors that may creep into your code. The typical work-flow entails the following steps:

1. Enter HTML and script code into the source document in the text editor.
2. Save the latest version to disk.
3. Switch to the browser.
4. Do one of the following: If this is a new document, open the file via the browser's Open menu. If the document is already loaded, reload the file into the browser.

Steps 2 through 4 are the key ones you will follow frequently. I call this three-step sequence the save-switch-reload sequence. You will perform this sequence so often as you script that the physical act quickly will become second nature to you. How you arrange your application windows and effect the save-switch-reload sequence varies according to your operating system.

Windows

You don't have to have either the editor or browser window maximized (at full screen) to take advantage of them. In fact, you may find them easier to work with if you adjust the size and location of each window so both windows are as large as possible while still enabling you to click a sliver of the other's window. Or, you can leave the taskbar visible so you can click the desired program's button to switch to its window (Figure 3-1). A monitor that displays more than 640 × 480 pixels certainly helps in offering more screen real estate for the windows and the taskbar.

In practice, however, the Windows Alt+Tab task-switching keyboard shortcut makes the job of the save-switch-reload steps outlined earlier a snap. If you run Windows and also use a Windows-compatible text editor (which more than likely has a Ctrl+S file-saving keyboard shortcut), you can effect the save-switch-reload sequence from the keyboard all with the left hand: Ctrl+S (save the source file); Alt+Tab (switch to the browser); Ctrl+R (reload the saved source file).

As long as you keep switching between the browser and text editor via Alt+Tab task switching, either program is always just an Alt+Tab away.

MacOS

If you expand the windows of your text editor and browser to full screen, you have to use the rather inconvenient Application menu (right-hand icon of the menu bar) to switch between the programs. A better method is to adjust the size and location of the windows of both programs so they overlap, while allowing a portion of the inactive window to remain visible (Figure 3-2). That way, all you have to do is click anywhere on the inactive window to bring its program to the front.

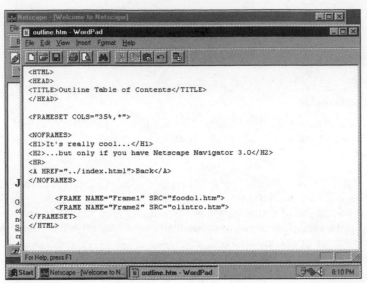

Figure 3-1: Editor and browser window arrangement in Windows 98

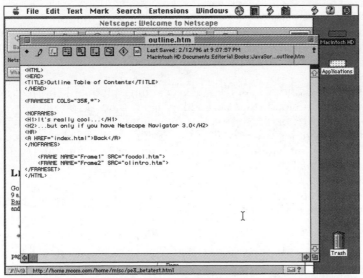

Figure 3-2: Editor and browser window arrangement on the Macintosh screen

With this arrangement, the save-switch-reload sequence is a two-handed affair:

1. Press Ô-S (save the source file).
2. Click in the browser window.
3. Press Ô-R (reload the saved source file).

To return to editing the source file, click any exposed part of the text editor's window.

A useful utility called *Program Switcher* (`http://www.kamprath.net/claireware`) puts the Alt+Tab program switching functionality on the Mac keyboard. It is more convenient than using the Application menu.

Reloading issues

For the most part, a simple page reload is enough to let you test a revised version of a script right away. But sometimes the browser's cache (with its default settings) can preserve parts of the previous page's attributes when you reload, even though you have changed the source code. To perform a more thorough reload, hold down the Shift key while clicking the browser's Reload/Refresh button. Alternatively, you can turn off the browser's cache in the preferences area, but that setting may negatively affect the overall performance of the browser during your regular Web surfing.

What Your First Script Will Do

For the sake of simplicity, the kind of script you look at in the next section is the kind that runs automatically when the browser loads the HTML page. Although all scripting and browsing work done here is offline, the behavior of the page is identical if you place the source file on a server and someone accesses it via the Web.

Figure 3-3 shows the page as it appears in the browser after you're finished. (The exact wording differs slightly if you run your browser on an operating system platform other than Win32 or if you use a browser other than Internet Explorer.) The part of the page that is defined in regular HTML contains nothing more than an <H1>-level header with a horizontal rule under it. If someone does not use a JavaScript-equipped browser, all he or she sees is the header and horizontal rule (unless that person has a truly outmoded browser, in which case some of the script words appear in the page).

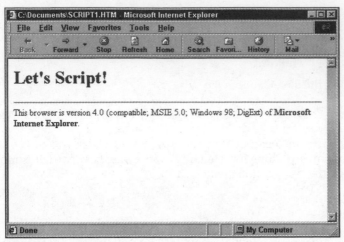

Figure 3-3: The finished page of your first JavaScript script

Below the rule, the script displays plain body text that combines static text with information about the browser you use to load the document. The script writes a stream of HTML information to the browser, including a tag to render a portion of the information in boldface. Even though two lines of code are writing information to the page, the result is rendered as one line — just as it is when all the text is hard-coded in HTML.

Entering Your First Script

It's time to start creating your first JavaScript script. Launch your text editor and browser. If your browser offers to dial your Internet service provider (ISP) or begins dialing automatically, cancel or quit the dialing operation. If the browser's Stop button is active, click it to halt any network searching it may try to do. You may receive a dialog box message indicating that the URL for your browser's home page (usually the home page of the browser's publisher — unless you've changed the settings) is unavailable. That's fine. You want the browser open, but you shouldn't be connected to your ISP. If you're automatically connected via a local area network in your office or school, that's also fine. However, you don't need the network connection for now. Next, follow these steps to enter and preview your first JavaScript script:

1. Activate your text editor and create a new, blank document.

2. Type the script into the window exactly as shown in Listing 3-1.

Listing 3-1: **Source Code for script1.htm**

```
<HTML>
<HEAD>
<TITLE>My First Script</TITLE>
</HEAD>

<BODY>
<H1>Let's Script...</H1>
<HR>
<SCRIPT LANGUAGE="JavaScript">
<!-- hide from old browsers
document.write("This browser is version " + navigator.appVersion)
document.write(" of <B>" + navigator.appName + "</B>.")
// end script hiding -->
</SCRIPT>
</BODY>
</HTML>
```

3. Save the document with the name `script1.htm`. (This is the lowest common denominator filenaming convention for Windows 3.1 — feel free to use an .html extension if your operating system allows it.)

4. Switch to your browser.

5. Choose Open (or Open File on some browsers) from the File menu and select `script1.htm`. (On some browsers, you have to click a Browse button to reach the File dialog box.)

If you typed all lines as directed, the document in the browser window should look like the one in Figure 3-3 (with minor differences for your computer's operating system and browser version). If the browser indicates that a mistake exists somewhere as the document loads, don't do anything about it for now. (Click the OK button if you see a script error dialog box.) Let's first examine the details of the entire document so you understand some of the finer points of what the script is doing.

Examining the Script

You do not need to memorize any of the commands or syntax discussed in this section. Instead, relax and watch how the lines of the script become what you see in the browser. In Listing 3-1, all of the lines up to the `<SCRIPT>` tag are very standard HTML. Your JavaScript-enhanced HTML documents should contain the same style of opening tags you normally use.

The <SCRIPT> tag

Any time you include JavaScript verbiage in an HTML document, you must enclose those lines inside a <SCRIPT>...</SCRIPT> tag pair. These tags alert the browser program to begin interpreting all the text between these tags as a script. Because other scripting languages (such as Microsoft's VBScript) can take advantage of these script tags, you must specify the precise name of the language in which the enclosed code is written. Therefore, when the browser receives this signal that your script uses the JavaScript language, it employs its built-in JavaScript interpreter to handle the code. You can find parallels to this setup in real life: If you have a French interpreter at your side, you need to know that the person with whom you're conversing also knows French. If you encounter someone from Russia, the French interpreter can't help you. Similarly, if your browser has only a JavaScript interpreter inside, it can't understand code written in VBScript.

Now is a good time to instill an aspect of JavaScript that will be important to you throughout all your scripting ventures: JavaScript is case-sensitive. Therefore, you must enter any item in your script that uses a JavaScript word with the correct uppercase and lowercase letters. Your HTML tags (including the <SCRIPT> tag) can be in the case of your choice, but everything in JavaScript is case-sensitive. When a line of JavaScript doesn't work, look for the wrong case first. Always compare your typed code against the listings printed in this book and against the various vocabulary entries discussed throughout it.

A script for all browsers

The next line after the <SCRIPT> tag in Listing 3-1 appears to be the beginning of an HTML comment tag. It is, but the JavaScript interpreter treats comment tags in a special way. Although JavaScript dutifully ignores a line that begins with an HTML comment start tag, it treats the next line as a full-fledged script line. In other words, the browser begins interpreting the next line after a comment start tag. If you want to put a comment inside JavaScript code, the comment must start with a double slash (//). Such a comment may go near the end of a line (such as after a JavaScript statement that is to be interpreted by the browser) or on its own line. In fact, the latter case appears near the end of the script. The comment line starts with two slashes.

Step back for a moment and notice that the entire script (including comments) is contained inside a standard HTML comment tag (<!--comment-->). The value of this containment is not clear until you see what happens to your scripted HTML document in a non-JavaScript-compatible browser. Such a browser blows past the <SCRIPT> tag as being an advanced tag it doesn't understand. But it treats a line of script as regular text to be displayed in the page. If you enclose script lines between HTML comment tags, most older browsers don't display the script lines. Still, some old browsers can get tripped up and present some ugliness because they interpret any > symbol (not the whole --> symbol) as an end-of-comment character. Figure 3-4 shows the results of your first script when viewed in a now obsolete version of the America Online Web browser (Version 2.5 for Windows).

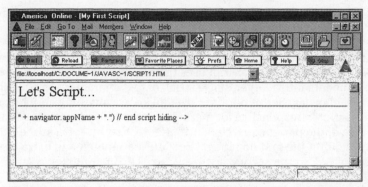

Figure 3-4: If you enclose script lines between HTML comments, the entire script is ignored by most, but not all, non-JavaScript browsers. Here, an old America Online browser shows part of the script anyway.

Remember, too, that some users don't have access to modern browsers or graphical browsers. (They use the Lynx text-oriented UNIX Web reader software or Lynx-like browsers in handheld computers.) By embracing your script lines within these comments, your Web pages don't look completely broken in relatively modern, non-JavaScript browsers.

Note   Notice that the comment lines that shield older browsers from your scripts go inside the `<SCRIPT>...</SCRIPT>` tags. Do not put these comment lines above the `<SCRIPT>` tag or below the `</SCRIPT>` tag and expect them to work.

One more issue about the script-hiding comment lines in this book. To save space on the page, most examples do not have comment lines inserted in them. But as you can see in the full-fledged application examples from Chapters 49 through 57 on the CD-ROM, the comment lines are where they should be. For any pages you produce for public consumption, always encase your script lines inside these comments.

Displaying some text

Both script lines in Listing 3-1 use one of the possible actions a script can ask a document to perform (`document.write()`, meaning display text in the current document). You learn more about the `document` object in Chapter 18.

Whenever you ask an object (a document in this case) to perform a task for you, the name of the task is always followed by a set of parentheses. In some cases — the `write()` task, for example — JavaScript needs to know what information it should act on. That information (called a *parameter*) goes inside parentheses after the name of the task. Thus, if you want to write the name of the first U.S. president to a document, the command to do so is

```
document.write("George Washington")
```

The line of text that the script writes starts with some static text (`"This browser is version"`) and adds some evaluated text (the version of the browser) to it. The writing continues with more static text that includes an HTML tag (`"of <B>"`), more evaluated text (the name of the browser application), and an HTML closing tag and the sentence's period (`"</B>."`). JavaScript uses the plus symbol (+) to join *(concatenate)* text components into a larger, single string of text characters to be written by the document. Neither JavaScript nor the + symbol knows anything about words and spaces, so the script is responsible for making sure that the proper spaces are passed along as part of the parameters. Notice, therefore, that an extra space exists after the word "version" in the first `document.write()` parameter, and extra spaces exist on both sides of "of" in the second `document.write()` parameter.

To fetch the information about the browser version and name for your parameters, you call upon JavaScript to extract the corresponding properties from the `navigator` object. You extract a property by appending the property name to the object name (`navigator` in this case) and separating the two names with a period. If you're searching for some English to mentally assign to this scheme as you read it, start from the right side and call the right item a property "of" the left side: the `appVersion` property of the `navigator` object. This dot syntax looks a great deal like the `document.write()` task, but a property name does not have parentheses after it. In any case, the reference to the property in the script tells JavaScript to insert the value of that property in the spot where the call is made. For your first attempt at the script, JavaScript substitutes the internal information about the browser as part of the text string that gets written to the document.

Have Some Fun

If you encounter an error in your first attempt at loading this document into your browser, go back to the text editor and check the lines of the script section against Listing 3-1, looking carefully at each line in light of the explanations. There may be a single character out of place, a lowercase letter where an uppercase one belongs, or a quote or parenthesis missing. Make necessary repairs, switch to your browser, and click Reload.

To see how dynamic the script in `script1.htm` is, go back into the text editor and replace the word "browser" with "client software." Save, switch, and reload to see how the script changes the text in the document. Feel free to substitute other text for the quoted text in the `document.write()` statement. Or, add more text with additional `document.write()` statements. The parameters to `document.write()` are HTML text, so you can even write `"<BR>"` to make a line break. Always be sure to save, switch, and reload to see the results of your handiwork.

✦   ✦   ✦

JavaScript Tutorial

Browser and Document Objects

This chapter marks the first of nine tutorial chapters
(which compose Part II) tailored to Web authors who
have at least basic grounding in HTML concepts. In this chapter, you see several practical applications of JavaScript and
begin to see how a JavaScript-enabled browser turns familiar
HTML elements into objects that your scripts control. Most of
what you learn throughout the tutorial can be applied to all
scriptable browsers (back to Navigator 2 and Internet
Explorer 3). I clearly label a handful of fancy features that
require recent browser versions.

Scripts Run the Show

If you have authored Web pages with HTML, you are familiar
with how HTML tags influence the way content is rendered on
a page when viewed in the browser. As the page loads, the
browser recognizes angle-bracketed tags as formatting
instructions. Instructions are read from the top of the document downward, and elements defined in the HTML document
appear onscreen in the same order in which they appear in
the document's source code. As an author, you do a little work
one time and up front — adding the tags to text content — and
the browser does a lot more work every time a visitor loads
the page into a browser.

Assume for a moment that one of the elements on the page is
a text input field inside a form. The user is supposed to enter
some text in the text field and then click the Submit button to
send that information back to the Web server. If that information must be an Internet e-mail address, how do you ensure
the user includes the "@" symbol in the address?

One way is to have a Common Gateway Interface (CGI) program on the server inspect the submitted form data after the user clicks the Submit button and the form information is transferred to the server. If the user omits or forgets the "@" symbol, the CGI program serves the page back to the browser—but this time with an instruction to include the symbol in the address. Nothing is wrong with this exchange, but it means a significant delay for the user to find out that the address does not contain the crucial symbol. Moreover, the Web server has to expend some of its resources to perform the validation and communicate back to the visitor. If the Web site is a busy one, the server may try to perform hundreds of these validations at any given moment, probably slowing the response time to the user even more.

Now imagine that the document containing that text input field has some intelligence built into it that makes sure the text field entry contains the "@" symbol before ever submitting one bit (literally!) of data to the server. That kind of intelligence would have to be embedded in the document in some fashion—downloaded with the page's content so it can stand ready to jump into action when called upon. The browser must know how to run that embedded program. Some user action must start the program, perhaps when the user clicks the Submit button. If the program runs inside the browser and detects a lack of the "@" symbol, an alert message should appear to bring the problem to the user's attention. The same program also should be capable of deciding if the actual submission can proceed or if it should wait until a valid e-mail address is entered into the field.

This kind of pre-submission data entry validation is but one of the practical ways JavaScript adds intelligence to an HTML document. Looking at this example, you might recognize that a script must know how to look into what is typed in a text field; a script must also know how to let a submission continue or how to abort the submission. A browser capable of running JavaScript programs conveniently treats elements such as the text field as *objects*. A JavaScript script controls the action and behavior of objects—most of which you see on the screen in the browser window.

JavaScript in Action

By adding lines of JavaScript code to your HTML documents, you control onscreen objects in whatever way your applications require. To give you an idea of the scope of applications you can create with JavaScript, I show you several applications on the CD-ROM (in the folders for Chapters 49 through 57). I strongly suggest you open the applications and play with them in your browser as they are described in the next several pages.

Interactive user interfaces

HTML hyperlinks do a fine job, but they're not necessarily the most engaging way to present a table of contents for a large site or document. With a bit of JavaScript, you can create an interactive, expandable table of contents listing that displays the hierarchy of a large body of material (see Figure 4-1). Just like the text listings (or *tree views*) in operating system file management windows, the expandable table of contents lets the user see as much or as little as possible while displaying the big picture of the entire data collection.

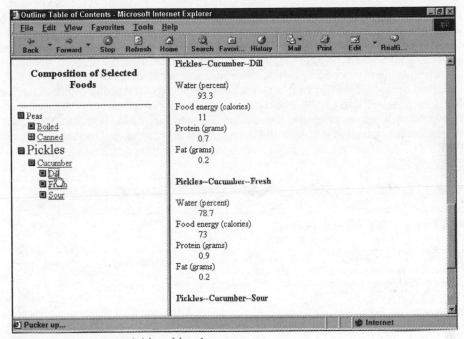

Figure 4-1: An expandable table of contents

Click a gray widget icon to expand the items underneath. An endpoint item has an orange and black widget icon. Items in the outline can be links to other pages or descriptive information. You also maintain the same kind of font control over each entry, as expected from HTML. While such outlines have been created with server CGIs in the past, the response time between clicks is terribly slow. By placing all of the smarts behind the outline inside the page, it downloads once and runs quickly after each click.

As demonstrated in the detailed description of this outline in the application Outline-Style Table of Contents (Chapter 52 on the CD-ROM), you can implement the scriptable workings within straight HTML for Navigator 2 and 3 — although limitations in page rendering require rewriting the page after each click. Internet Explorer 4+ and Navigator 6+ automatically reflow the page in response to changes of content, turning this outliner into a truly dynamic HTML application. Either way you do it, the quick response and action on the screen makes for a more engaging experience for Web surfers who are in a hurry to scout your site.

Small data lookup

A common application on the Web is having a CGI program present a page that visitors use to access large databases on the server. Large data collections are best left on the server where search engines and other technologies are the best fit. But if your page acts as a *front end* to a small data collection lookup, you can consider embedding that data collection in the document (out of view) and letting JavaScript act as the intermediary between user and data.

I do just that in a Social Security prefix lookup system shown in Figure 4-2. I convert a printed table of about 55 entries into a JavaScript list that occupies only a few hundred bytes. When the visitor types the three-character prefix of his or her Social Security number into the field and clicks the Search button, a script behind the scenes compares that number against the 55 or so ranges in the table. When the script finds a match, it displays the corresponding state of registration in a second field.

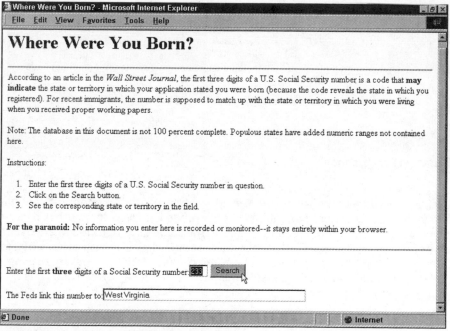

Figure 4-2: Looking up data in a small table

If the application were stored on the server and the data stored in a server database, each click of the Search button would mean a delay of many seconds as the server processed the request, got the data from the database, and reformulated the page with the result for the user. Built instead as a JavaScript application, once the page downloads the first time, scripts perform all lookups instantaneously.

Forms validation

I've already used data entry form validation as an example of when JavaScript is a good fit. In fact, the data entry field in the Social Security lookup page (see Figure 4-2) includes scripting to check the validity of the entered number. Just as a CGI program for this task has to verify that the entry is a three-digit number, so, too, must the JavaScript program verify the entered value. If a mistake appears in the entry—perhaps a finger slips and hits a letter key—the visitor is advised of the problem and directed to try another entry. The validation script even preselects the text in the entry field for the visitor so that typing a new value replaces the old one.

Interactive data

JavaScript opens opportunities for turning static information into interactive information. Figure 4-3 shows a graphical calculator for determining the value of an electrical component (called a *resistor*) whose only markings are colored bars.

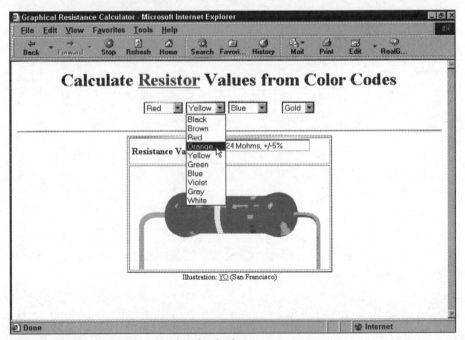

Figure 4-3: An interactive graphical calculator

The image in the bottom half of the page is composed of seven images in vertical slices all bunched up against each other. Four slices display the colored bands, while the remaining three slices contain the ends of the resistor and the spacer between groups of bands. As the visitor selects a color from a pop-up list near the top, the associated image slice changes to the selected color and the resistance value is calculated and displayed.

Again, once the page is loaded, response time is instantaneous. Conversely, a server-based version of this calculator would take many seconds between color changes. Moreover, JavaScript provides the power to preload all possible images into the browser cache while the main page loads. Therefore, with only a slight extra delay to download all images with the page, no further delay occurs when a visitor chooses a new color. Not only is the application practical (for its intended audience), but it's just plain fun to play with.

Multiple frames

While frames are the domain of HTML, they suddenly become more powerful with some JavaScript behind them. The Decision Helper application shown in Figure 4-4 takes this notion to the extreme.

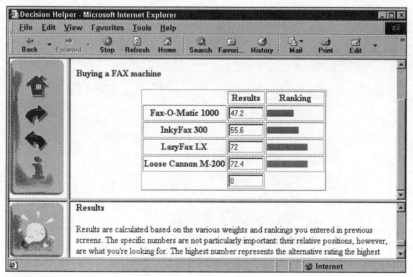

Figure 4-4: The Decision Helper

The Decision Helper is a full-fledged application that includes four input screens and one screen that displays the results of some fairly complex calculations based on the input screens. Results are shown both in numbers and in a bar graph form, as displayed in Figure 4-4.

Interaction among the three frames requires JavaScript. For example, suppose the user clicks one of the directional arrows in the top-left frame. Not only does the top-right frame change to another document, but the instructions document in the bottom frame also shifts to the anchor point that parallels the content of the input screen. Scripting behind the top-right frame documents uses various techniques to preserve entry information as the user navigates through the sequence of input pages. These are the same techniques you might use to build an online product catalog and shopping cart — accumulating the customer's selections from various catalog pages and then bringing them together in the checkout order form.

Certainly you could fashion this application out of a CGI program on the server. But the high level of interaction and calculation required would turn this now speedy application into a glacially slow exchange of information between user and server.

Dynamic HTML

Starting with the version 4 browsers from both Netscape and Microsoft, you can modify more and more content on the page with the help of client-side scripts. In Figure 4-5, for example, scripts in the page control the dragging of map pieces in the puzzle. Highlighted colors change as you click the state maps, instruction panels fly in from the edge of the screen, and another item appears when you place all the states in their proper positions.

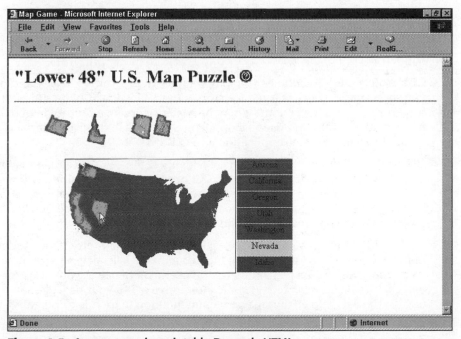

Figure 4-5: A map game in scriptable Dynamic HTML

The browser feature that makes this level of script control possible is *Dynamic HTML (DHTML)*. JavaScript becomes the vital connection between the user and dynamically respositionable elements on the screen. Not even a program on the server could help this application because you need immediate programmatic control in the page to respond to user mouse motion and instantaneous changes to screen elements.

When to use JavaScript

The preceding examples demonstrate a wide range of applications for JavaScript, but by no means do they come close to exhausting JavaScript's possibilities. When faced with a Web application task, I look to client-side JavaScript for help with the following requirements:

✦ **Data entry validation:** If form fields need to be filled out for processing on the server, I let client-side scripts prequalify the data entered by the user.

✦ **Serverless CGIs:** I use this term to describe processes that, were it not for JavaScript, would be programmed as CGIs on the server, yielding slow performance because of the interactivity required between the program and user. This includes tasks such as small data collection lookup, modification of images, and generation of HTML in other frames and windows based on user input.

✦ **Dynamic HTML interactivity:** It's one thing to use DHTML's capabilities to precisely position elements on the page — you don't need scripting for that. But if you intend to make the content dance on the page, scripting makes that happen.

✦ **CGI prototyping:** Sometimes you may want a CGI program to be at the root of your application because it reduces the potential incompatibilities among browser brands and versions. It may be easier to create a prototype of the CGI in client-side JavaScript. Use this opportunity to polish the user interface before implementing the application as a CGI.

✦ **Offloading a busy server:** If you have a highly trafficked Web site, it may be beneficial to convert frequently used CGI processes to client-side JavaScript scripts. Once a page is downloaded, the server is free to serve other visitors. Not only does this lighten server load, but users also experience quicker response to the application embedded in the page.

✦ **Adding life to otherwise dead pages:** HTML by itself is pretty "flat." Adding a blinking chunk of text doesn't help much; animated GIF images more often distract from, rather than contribute to, the user experience at your site. But if you can dream up ways to add some interactive zip to your page, it may engage the user and encourage a recommendation to friends or repeat visits.

✦ **Creating "Web pages that think":** If you let your imagination soar, you may develop new, intriguing ways to make your pages appear "smart." For example, in the application Intelligent "Updated" Flags (Chapter 54), you see how (without a server CGI or database) an HTML page can "remember" when a visitor last came to the page. Then any items that have been updated since the last visit—regardless of the number of updates you've done to the page—are flagged for that visitor. That's the kind of subtle, thinking Web page that best displays JavaScript's powers.

The Document Object Model

Before you can truly start scripting, you should have a good feel for the kinds of objects you will be scripting. A scriptable browser does a lot of the work of creating software objects that generally represent the visible objects you see in an HTML page in the browser window. Obvious objects include form controls (text boxes and buttons) and (in recent browsers) images. However, there may be other objects that aren't so obvious by looking at a page, but which make perfect sense when you consider the HTML tags used to generate a page's content—frames of a frameset, for example.

To help scripts control these objects—and to help authors see some method to the madness of potentially dozens of objects on a page—the browser makers define a *document object model (DOM)*. A model is like a prototype or plan for the organization of objects on a page.

Object models implemented in browsers have grown rapidly with each generation of browser. Moreover, Microsoft and Netscape have added their own touches from time to time in a competitive features race. The lack of compatibility among browser versions and brands can drive scripters to distraction, especially if (at the outset) they learn the object model only of the latest version of only one brand—unaware of limits in earlier browsers or those from other makers.

Proprietary and Standard Object Models

Object model features that are proprietary to one browser version and/or brand are perfectly usable provided you know that your audience uses that brand or version exclusively (for example, in a corporate environment where a browser version might be mandated for all employees). If you develop in this kind of controlled environment, then be assured that browser-specific features are covered in the reference portions of this book.

An industry standards effort (by the W3C) has begun specifying a common set of object model features and syntax that provide more flexibility than the original implementations. The biggest improvement is that every HTML element becomes an object that scripts can manipulate (a feature also found in IE4's object model). This DOM, built upon the original object model you learn in this tutorial, is implemented in varying degrees of completion in IE5+ and NN6+ (the latter offering a much more complete W3C DOM implementation). The scripter's dream is that one day W3C DOM-compatible browsers will be the majority of the installed base, and creating cross-browser, highly dynamic pages will be easier than today. In the meantime, you have lots of fundamentals to learn—knowledge that you'll use for many years to come.

All is not lost, however. This tutorial focuses on the document object model that you can find in every scriptable browser. Figure 4-6 shows a map of the lowest common denominator object model, which is safe to use on all browsers. At this stage of the learning process, it is not important to memorize the model but rather to get a general feel for what's going on.

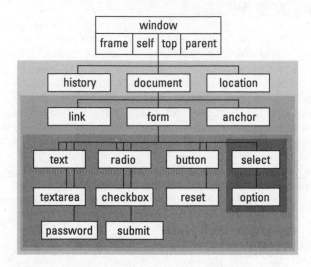

Figure 4-6: Lowest common denominator document object model for all scriptable browsers

One misconception you must avoid at the outset is that the model shown in Figure 4-6 is the model for every document that loads into the browser. On the contrary — it represents an idealized version of a document that includes one of every possible type of object that the browser knows. In a moment, I will show you how the document object model stored in the browser at any given instant reflects the HTML in the document. But for now, I want to impress an important aspect of the structure of the idealized model: its hierarchy.

Containment hierarchy

Notice in Figure 4-6 that objects are grouped together in various levels designated by the density of the gray background. Objects are organized in a *hierarchy*, not unlike the hierarchy of a company's organization chart of job positions. At the top is the president. Reporting to the president are several vice presidents. One of the vice presidents manages a sales force that is divided into geographical regions. Each region has a manager who reports to the vice president of sales; each region then has several salespeople. If the president wants to communicate to a salesperson who handles a big account, the protocol dictates that the president should route the message through the hierarchy—to the vice president of sales; to the sales manager; to the salesperson. The hierarchy clearly defines each unit's role and relationship to the other units.

This hierarchical structure applies to the organization of objects in a document. Allow me to highlight the key objects in Figure 4-6 and explain their relationships to others.

✦ **Window object:** At the top of the hierarchy is the window. This object represents the content area of the browser window where HTML documents appear. In a multiple-frame environment, each frame is also a window (but don't concern yourself with this just yet). Because all document action takes place inside the window, it is the outermost element of the object hierarchy. Its physical borders contain the document.

✦ **Document object:** Each HTML document that gets loaded into a window becomes a `document` object. Its position in the object hierarchy is an important one, as you can see in Figure 4-6. The `document` object contains most of the other kinds of objects in the model. This makes perfect sense when you think about it: The document contains the content that you are likely to script.

✦ **Form object:** Users don't see the beginning and ending of forms on a page, only their elements. But a form is a distinct grouping of content inside an HTML document. Everything that is inside the `<FORM>...</FORM>` tag set is part of the form object. A document might have more than one pair of `<FORM>` tags if dictated by the page design. If so, the map of the objects for that particular document has two form objects instead of the one that appears in Figure 4-6.

✦ **Form control elements:** Just as your HTML defines form elements within the confines of the `<FORM>...</FORM>` tag pair, so does a form object contain all the elements defined for that object. Each one of those form elements—text fields, buttons, radio buttons, checkboxes, and the like—is a separate object. Unlike the one-of-everything model shown in Figure 4-6, the precise model for any document depends on the HTML tags in the document.

When a Document Loads

Programming languages, such as JavaScript, are convenient intermediaries between your mental image of how a program works and the true inner workings of the computer. Inside the machine, every word of a program code listing influences the storage and movement of bits (the legendary 1s and 0s of the computer's binary universe) from one RAM storage slot to another. Languages and object models are inside the computer (or, in the case of JavaScript, inside the browser's area of the computer) to make it easier for programmers to visualize how a program works and what its results will be. The relationship reminds me a lot of knowing how to drive an automobile from point A to point B without knowing exactly how an internal combustion engine, steering linkages, and all that other internal "stuff" works. By controlling high-level objects such as the ignition key, gearshift, gas pedal, brake, and steering wheel, I can get the results I need.

Of course, programming is not exactly like driving a car with an automatic transmission. Even scripting requires the equivalent of opening the hood and perhaps knowing how to check the transmission fluid or change the oil. Therefore, now it's time to open the hood and watch what happens to the document object model as a page loads into the browser.

A simple document

Figure 4-7 shows the HTML and corresponding object model for a very simple document. When this page loads, the browser maintains in its memory a map of the objects generated by the HTML tags in the document. The window object is always there for every document. Every window object also contains an object called the location object (it stores information about the URL of the document being loaded). I'll skip that object for now, but acknowledge its presence (as a dimmed box in the diagram) because it is part of the model in the browser memory. Finally, because a document has been loaded, the browser generates a document object in its current map.

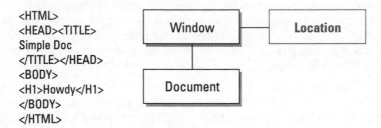

```
<HTML>
<HEAD><TITLE>
Simple Doc
</TITLE></HEAD>
<BODY>
<H1>Howdy</H1>
</BODY>
</HTML>
```

Figure 4-7: A simple document and object map

Note   In IE4+ and the W3C DOM, every HTML element (such as the H1 element of Figure 4-7) becomes an object contained by the document. But this tutorial observes the original model, which turns only a handful (albeit an important handful) of HTML elements into scriptable objects.

Add a form

Now, I modify the HTML file to include a blank <FORM> tag set and reload the document. Figure 4-8 shows what happens to both the HTML (changes in boldface) and the object map as constructed by the browser. Even though no content appears in the form, the <FORM> tags are enough to tell the browser to create that form object.

Also note that the `form` object is contained by the document in the hierarchy of objects in the current map. This mirrors the structure of the idealized map shown in Figure 4-6.

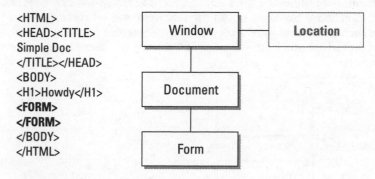

```
<HTML>
<HEAD><TITLE>
Simple Doc
</TITLE></HEAD>
<BODY>
<H1>Howdy</H1>
<FORM>
</FORM>
</BODY>
</HTML>
```

Figure 4-8: Adding a form

Add a text input element

I modify and reload the HTML file again, this time including an `<INPUT>` tag that defines the text field form element shown in Figure 4-9. As mentioned earlier, the containment structure of the HTML (the `<INPUT>` tag goes inside a `<FORM>` tag set) is reflected in the object map for the revised document. Therefore, the window contains a document; the document contains a form; and the form contains a text input element.

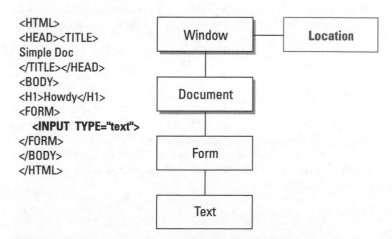

```
<HTML>
<HEAD><TITLE>
Simple Doc
</TITLE></HEAD>
<BODY>
<H1>Howdy</H1>
<FORM>
   <INPUT TYPE="text">
</FORM>
</BODY>
</HTML>
```

Figure 4-9: Adding a text input element to the form

Add a button element

The last modification I make to the file is to add a button input element to the same form as the one that holds the text input element (see Figure 4-10). Notice that the HTML for the button is contained by the same <FORM> tag set as the text field. As a result, the object map hierarchy shows both the text field and button contained by the same form object. If the map were a corporate organization chart, the employees represented by the Text and Button boxes would be at the same level reporting to the same boss.

```
<HTML>
<HEAD><TITLE>
Simple Doc
</TITLE></HEAD>
<BODY>
<H1>Howdy</H1>
<FORM>
   <INPUT TYPE="text">
   <INPUT TYPE="button">
</FORM>
</BODY>
</HTML>
```

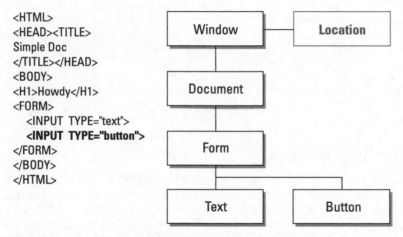

Figure 4-10: Adding a button element to the same form

Now that you see how objects are created in memory in response to HTML tags, the next step is to figure out how scripts can communicate with these objects. After all, scripting is mostly about controlling these objects.

Object References

After a document is loaded into the browser, all of its objects are safely stored in memory in the containment hierarchy structure specified by the browser's document object model. For a script to control one of those objects, there must be a way to communicate with an object and find out something about it such as, "Hey, Mr. Text Field, what did the user type?"

The JavaScript language uses the containment hierarchy structure to let scripts get in touch with any object in a document. For a moment, pretend you are the browser with a document loaded into your memory. You have this road map of objects handy. If a script needs you to locate one of those objects, it would be a big help if the script showed you what route to follow in the map to reach that object. That is precisely what an *object reference* in a script does for the browser.

Object naming

The biggest aid in creating script references to objects is assigning names to every scriptable object in your HTML. Scriptable browsers, such as modern versions of Navigator and Internet Explorer, acknowledge an optional tag attribute called NAME. This attribute enables you to assign a unique name to each object. Here are some examples of NAME attributes added to typical tags:

```
<FORM NAME="dataEntry" METHOD=GET>

<INPUT TYPE="text" NAME="entry">

<FRAME SRC="info.html" NAME="main">
```

The only rules about object names (also called *identifiers*) are that they

- ✦ May not contain spaces
- ✦ Should not contain punctuation except for the underscore character
- ✦ Must be inside quotes when assigned to the NAME attribute
- ✦ Must not start with a numeric character

Think of assigning names the same as sticking nametags on everyone attending a conference meeting. The name of the object, however, is only one part of the actual reference that the browser needs to locate the object. For each object, the reference must include the steps along the object hierarchy from the top down to the object — no matter how many levels of containment are involved. In other words, the browser cannot pick out an object by name only. A reference includes the names of each object along the path from the window to the object. In the JavaScript language, each successive object name along the route is separated from another by a period.

To demonstrate what real references look like within the context of an object model you've already seen, I retrace the same model steps shown earlier but this time I show the reference to each object as the document acquires more objects.

NAME versus ID Attributes

The HTML 4.0 specification introduces a new way to assign an identifier to HTML elements: the ID attribute. The ID attribute is helpful for some aspects of Cascading Style Sheets (CSS) and Dynamic HTML. Even so, the NAME attribute is still required for common denominator elements covered in this tutorial — FRAME, FORM, and INPUT elements, for example. The newest browsers can access an element by name or ID, but authors typically use the ID attribute for HTML element objects not shown in Figure 4-6. You can read more about the ID attribute (and id property) in Chapter 15 after you finish the tutorial.

A simple document

I start with the model whose only objects are the window (and its location object) and document from the simple HTML file. Figure 4-11 shows the object map and references for the two main objects. Every document resides in a window, so to reference the window object you start with window. Also fixed in this reference is the document because there can be only one document per window (or frame). Therefore, a reference to the document object is window.document.

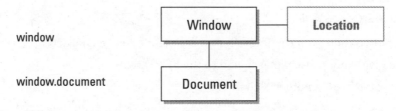

Figure 4-11: References to the window and document

Add a form

Modifying the document to include the empty <FORM> tag generates the form object in the map. If I do the job right, the <FORM> tag also includes a NAME attribute. The reference to the form object, as shown in Figure 4-12, starts with the window, wends through the document, and reaches the form, which I call by name: window.document.*formName* (the italics meaning that in a real script, I would substitute the form's name for *formName*).

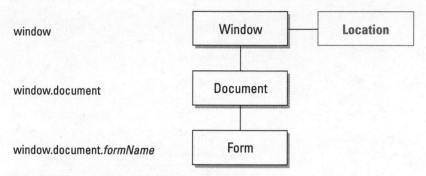

Figure 4-12: Reference to the form object

Add a text input element

As the hierarchy gets deeper, the object reference gets longer. In Figure 4-13, I add a text input object to the form. The reference to this deeply nested object still starts at the window level and works its way down to the name I assigned to the object in its <INPUT> tag: window.document.*formName*.*textName*.

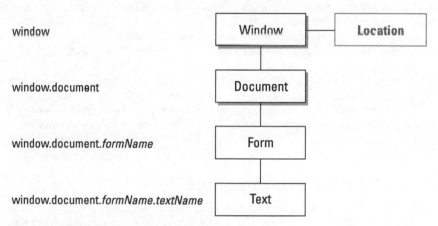

Figure 4-13: Reference to the text field object

Add a button element

When I add a button to the same form as the text object, the reference stays the same length (see Figure 4-14). All that changes is the last part of the reference where the button name goes in place of the text field name: window.document.*formName*.*buttonName*.

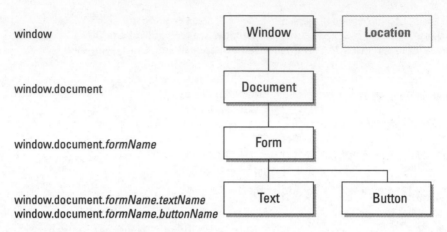

Figure 4-14: Reference to the button object

About the Dot Syntax

JavaScript uses the period to separate components of a hierarchical reference. This convention is adopted from Java, which, in turn, based this formatting on the C language. Every reference typically starts with the most global scope—the window for client-side JavaScript—and narrows focus with each "dot" (.) delimiter.

If you have not programmed before, don't be put off by the dot syntax. You are probably already using it, such as when you access Usenet newsgroups. The methodology for organizing the thousands of newsgroups is to group them in a hierarchy that makes it relatively easy to both find a newsgroup and visualize where the newsgroup you're currently reading is located in the scheme of things.

Newsgroup organization model

Let me briefly dissect a typical newsgroup address to help you understand dot syntax: `rec.sport.skating.inline`. The first entry (at the left edge) defines the basic group—recreation—among all the newsgroup categories. Other group categories, such as `comp` and `alt`, have their own sections and do not overlap with what goes on in the `rec` section. Within the `rec` section are dozens of subsections, one of which is `sport`. That name distinguishes all the sport-related groups from, say, the automobile or music groups within recreational newsgroups.

Like most broad newsgroup categories, rec.sport has many subcategories, with each one devoted to a particular sport. In this case, it is skating. Other sport news-groups include rec.sport.rugby and rec.sport.snowboarding. Even within the rec.sport.skating category, a further subdivision exists to help narrow the sub-ject matter for participants. Therefore, a separate newsgroup just for inline skaters exists, just as a group for roller-skating exists (rec.sport.skating.roller). As a narrower definition is needed for a category, a new level is formed by adding a dot and a word to differentiate that subgroup from the thousands of newsgroups on the Net. When you ask your newsgroup software to view messages in the rec.sport.skating.inline group, you're giving it a map to follow in the news-group hierarchy to go directly to a single newsgroup.

Another benefit of this syntactical method is that names for subcategories can be reused within other categories, if necessary. For example, with this naming scheme, it is possible to have two similarly named subcategories in two separate newsgroup classifications (such as rec.radio.scanners and alt.radio.scanners). When you ask to visit one, the hierarchical address, starting with the rec or alt classifi-cation, ensures you get to the desired place. Neither collection of messages is auto-matically connected with the other (although subscribers frequently cross-post to both newsgroups).

For complete newbies to the Net, this dot syntax can be intimidating. Because the system was designed to run on UNIX servers (the UNIX operating system is written in C), the application of a C-like syntax for newsgroup addressing is hardly surprising.

What Defines an Object?

When an HTML tag defines an object in the source code, the browser creates a slot for that object in memory as the page loads. But an object is far more complex internally than, say, a mere number stored in memory. The purpose of an object is to represent some "thing." Because in JavaScript you deal with items that appear in a browser window, an object may be an input text field, a button, or the whole HTML document. Outside of the pared-down world of a JavaScript browser, an object can also represent abstract entities, such as a calendar program's appoint-ment entry or a layer of graphical shapes in a drawing program.

Every object is unique in some way, even if two or more objects look identical to you in the browser. Three very important facets of an object define what it is, what it looks like, how it behaves, and how scripts control it. Those three facets are prop-erties, methods, and event handlers. They play such key roles in your future JavaScript efforts that the Quick Reference in Appendix A summarizes the proper-ties, methods, and event handlers for each object in the object models imple-mented in various browser generations. You might want to take a quick peek at that road map of the original object model if for no other reason than to gain an appreci-ation for the size of the scripting vocabulary that this tutorial covers.

Properties

Any physical object you hold in your hand has a collection of characteristics that defines it. A coin, for example, has shape, diameter, thickness, color, weight, embossed images on each side, and any number of other attributes that distinguish it from, say, a feather. Each of those features is called a *property*. Each property has a value of some kind attached to it (even if the value is empty or null). For example, the shape property of a coin might be "circle" — in this case, a text value. In contrast, the denomination property is most likely a numeric value.

You may not have known it, but if you've written HTML for use in a scriptable browser, you have set object properties without writing one iota of JavaScript. Tag attributes are the most common way to set an HTML object's initial properties. The presence of JavaScript often adds optional attributes whose initial values you can set when the document loads. For example, the following HTML tag defines a `button` object that assigns two property values:

```
<INPUT TYPE="button" NAME="clicker" VALUE="Hit Me...">
```

In JavaScript parlance, then, the `name` property holds the word "clicker," while the `value` property is the text that appears on the button label, "Hit Me. . . ." In truth, a button has more properties than just these, but you don't have to set every property for every object. Most properties have default values that are automatically assigned if nothing special is set in the HTML or later from a script.

The contents of some properties can change while a document is loaded and the user interacts with the page. Consider the following text input tag:

```
<INPUT TYPE="text" NAME="entry" VALUE="User Name?">
```

The `name` property of this object is the word "entry." When the page loads, the text of the `VALUE` attribute setting is placed in the text field — the automatic behavior of an HTML text field when the `VALUE` attribute is specified. But if a user enters some other text into the text field, the `value` property changes — not in the HTML, but in the memory copy of the object model that the browser maintains. Therefore, if a script queries the text field about the content of the `value` property, the browser yields the current setting of the property — which isn't the one specified by the HTML if a user changes the text.

To gain access to an object's property, you use the same kind of dot syntax, hierarchical addressing scheme you saw earlier for objects. A property is contained by its object, so the reference to it consists of the reference to the object plus one more extension naming the property. Therefore, for the button and text object tags just shown, references to various properties are

```
document.formName.clicker.name
document.formName.clicker.value
document.formName.entry.value
```

You may wonder what happened to the `window` part of the reference. It turns out that there can be only one document contained in a window, so references to objects inside the document can omit the `window` portion and start the reference with `document`. You cannot omit the `document` object, however, from the reference. In IE4+, you can reference an element object by simply referring to the element's `ID` attribute if one is assigned. Even so, I strongly recommend spelling out references so that your code is easier to read and understand long after you've written it. Notice, too, that the button and text fields both have a property named `value`. These properties represent very different attributes for each object. For the button, the property determines the button label; for the text field, the property reflects the current text in the field. You now see how the (sometimes lengthy) hierarchical referencing scheme helps the browser locate exactly the object and property your script needs. No two items in a document can have identical references even though parts of these references may have the same component names.

Methods

If a property is like a descriptive adjective for an object, then a method is a verb. A *method* is all about action related to the object. A method either does something to the object or with the object that affects other parts of a script or document. They are commands of a sort, but whose behaviors are tied to a particular object.

An object can have any number of methods associated with it (including none at all). To set a method into motion (usually called *invoking a method*), a JavaScript statement must include a reference to it — via its object with a pair of parentheses after the method name — as in the following examples:

```
document.orderForm.submit()
document.orderForm.entry.select()
```

The first is a scripted way of clicking a Submit button to send a form (named `orderForm`) to a server. The second selects the text inside a text field named `entry` (which is contained by a form named `orderForm`).

Sometimes a method requires that you send additional information with it so that it can do its job. Each chunk of information passed with the method is called a *parameter* or *argument* (you can use the terms interchangeably). You saw examples of passing a parameter in your first script in Chapter 3. Two script statements invoked the `write()` method of the `document` object:

```
document.write("This browser is version " + navigator.appVersion)
document.write(" of <B>" + navigator.appName + "</B>.")
```

As the page loaded into the browser, each `document.write()` method sent whatever text was inside the parentheses to the current document. In both cases, the content being sent as a parameter consisted of straight text (inside quotes) and the values of two object properties: the `appVersion` and `appName` properties of the `navigator` object. (The `navigator` object does not appear in the object hierarchy diagram of Figure 4-6 because in early browsers this object exists outside of the document object model.)

Some methods require more than one parameter. If so, the multiple parameters are separated by commas. For example, version 4 and later browsers support a `window` object method that moves the window to a particular coordinate point on the screen. A coordinate point is defined by two numbers that indicate the number of pixels from the left and top edges of the screen where the top-left corner of the window should be. To move the browser window to a spot 50 pixels from the left and 100 pixels from the top, the method is

```
window.moveTo(50,100)
```

As you learn more about the details of JavaScript and the document objects you can script, pay close attention to the range of methods defined for each object. They reveal a lot about what an object is capable of doing under script control.

Event handlers

One last characteristic of a JavaScript object is the *event handler*. *Events* are actions that take place in a document, usually as the result of user activity. Common examples of user actions that trigger events include clicking a button or typing a character into a text field. Some events, such as the act of loading a document into the browser window or experiencing a network error while an image loads, are not so obvious.

Almost every JavaScript object in a document receives events of one kind or another — summarized for your convenience in the Quick Reference of Appendix A. What determines whether the object does anything in response to the event is an extra attribute you enter into the object's HTML definition. The attribute consists of the event name, an equal sign (just like any HTML attribute), followed by instructions about what to do when the particular event fires. Listing 4-1 shows a very simple document that displays a single button with one event handler defined for it.

Listing 4-1: **A Simple Button with an Event Handler**

```
<HTML>
<BODY>
<FORM>
<INPUT TYPE="button" VALUE="Click Me" onClick="window.alert ('Ouch!')">
</FORM>
</BODY>
</HTML>
```

The form definition contains what, for the most part, looks like a standard input item. But notice the last attribute, `onClick="window.alert('Ouch!')"`. Button objects, as you see in their complete descriptions in Chapter 24, react to mouse clicks. When a user clicks the button, the browser sends a click event to the button. In this button's definition, the attribute says that whenever the button receives that message, it should invoke one of the `window` object's methods, `alert()`. The `alert()` method displays a simple alert dialog box whose content is whatever text is passed as a parameter to the method. Like most arguments to HTML attributes, the attribute setting to the right of the equal sign goes inside quotes. If additional quotes are necessary, as in the case of the text to be passed along with the event handler, those inner quotes can be single quotes. In actuality, JavaScript doesn't distinguish between single or double quotes but does require that each set be of the same type. Therefore, you can write the attribute this way:

```
onClick='alert("Ouch!")'
```

Exercises

1. Which of the following applications are well suited to client-side JavaScript? Why or why not?

   a. Music jukebox

   b. Web-site visit counter

   c. Chat room

   d. Graphical Fahrenheit-to-Celsius temperature calculator

   e. All of the above

   f. None of the above

2. General Motors has separate divisions for its automobile brands: Chevrolet, Pontiac, Buick, and Cadillac. Each brand has several models of automobile. Following this hierarchy model, write the dot-syntax equivalent reference to the following three vehicle models:

   a. Chevrolet Malibu

   b. Pontiac Firebird

   c. Pontiac GrandAm

3. Which of the following object names are valid in JavaScript? For each one that is invalid, explain why.

   a. `lastName`

   b. `company_name`

   c. `1stLineAddress`

   d. `zip code`

   e. `today's_date`

4. An HTML document contains tags for one link and one form. The form contains tags for three text boxes, one checkbox, a Submit button, and a Reset button. Using the object hierarchy diagram from Figure 4-6 for reference, draw a diagram of the object model that the browser would create in its memory for these objects. Give names to the link, form, text fields, and checkbox, and write the references to each of those objects.

5. Write the HTML tag for a button input element named "Hi," whose visible label reads "Howdy" and whose onClick event handler displays an alert dialog box that says "Hello to you, too!"

✦   ✦   ✦

Scripts and HTML Documents

In this chapter's tutorial, you begin to see how scripts are embedded within HTML documents and what comprises a script statement. You also see how script statements can run when the document loads or in response to user action. Finally, you find out where script error information is hiding.

Where Scripts Go in Documents

Chapter 4 did not thoroughly cover what scripts look like or how you add them to an HTML document. That's where this lesson picks up the story.

The <SCRIPT> tag

To assist the browser in recognizing lines of code in an HTML document as belonging to a script, you surround lines of script code with a `<SCRIPT>...</SCRIPT>` tag set. This is common usage in HTML where start and end tags encapsulate content controlled by that tag, whether the tag set is for a form or a paragraph.

Depending on the browser, the `<SCRIPT>` tag has a variety of attributes you can set that govern the script. One attribute shared by scriptable browsers is the `LANGUAGE` attribute. This attribute is essential because each browser brand and version accepts a different set of scripting languages. One setting that all scriptable browsers accept is the JavaScript language, as in

```
<SCRIPT LANGUAGE="JavaScript">
```

A Future Attribute

The HTML 4.0 specification does not endorse the popular LANGUAGE attribute for script tags. Instead, it suggests the TYPE attribute, which requires a value in the form of a *MIME (Multipurpose Internet Mail Extensions)* type descriptor:

```
TYPE="text/javascript"
```

Only browsers with W3C DOM capabilities (such as IE5+ and NN6+) support the TYPE attribute, but the LANGUAGE attribute continues to be supported and should be for some time to come. All examples in this book use the compatible LANGUAGE attribute.

Other possibilities include later versions of JavaScript (version numbers are part of the language name), Microsoft's JScript variant, and the separate VBScript language. You don't need to specify any of these other languages unless your script intends to take specific advantage of a particular language version to the exclusion of all others. Until you learn the differences among the language versions, you can safely specify plain JavaScript on all scriptable browsers.

Be sure to include the ending tag for the script. Lines of JavaScript code go between the two tags:

```
<SCRIPT LANGUAGE="JavaScript">
  one or more lines of JavaScript code here
</SCRIPT>
```

If you forget the closing script tag, the script may not run properly and the HTML elsewhere in the page may look strange.

Although you don't work with it in this tutorial, another attribute works with more recent browsers to blend the contents of an external script file into the current document. An SRC attribute (similar to the SRC attribute of an <IMG> tag) points to the file containing the script code. Such files must end with a .js extension. The tag set looks like the following:

```
<SCRIPT LANGUAGE="JavaScript" SRC="myscript.js"></SCRIPT>
```

All script lines are in the external file, so no script lines are included between the start and end script tags in the document.

Tag positions

Where do these tags go within a document? The answer is, anywhere they're needed in the document. Sometimes it makes sense to include the tags nested within the <HEAD>...</HEAD> tag set; other times it is essential that you drop the script into a very specific location in the <BODY>...</BODY> section.

In the following four listings, I demonstrate — with the help of a skeletal HTML document — some of the possibilities of <SCRIPT> tag placement. Later in this lesson, you see why scripts may need to go in different places within a page depending on the scripting requirements.

Listing 5-1 shows the outline of what may be the most common position of a <SCRIPT> tag set in a document: in the <HEAD> tag section. Typically, the *Head* is a place for tags that influence noncontent settings for the page — so-called HTML "directive" elements, such as <META> tags and the document title. It turns out that this is also a convenient place to plant scripts that are called on in response to user action.

Listing 5-1: **Scripts in the Head**

```
<HTML>
<HEAD>
<TITLE>A Document</TITLE>
<SCRIPT LANGUAGE="JavaScript">
    //script statement(s) here
    ...
</SCRIPT>
</HEAD>
<BODY>
</BODY>
</HTML>
```

On the other hand, if you need a script to run as the page loads so that the script generates content in the page, the script goes in the <BODY> portion of the document, as shown in Listing 5-2. If you check the code listing for your first script in Chapter 3, you see that the script tags are in the Body because the script needs to fetch information about the browser and write the results to the page as the page loads.

Listing 5-2: **A Script in the Body**

```
<HTML>
<HEAD>
<TITLE>A Document</TITLE>
</HEAD>
<BODY>
<SCRIPT LANGUAGE="JavaScript">
    //script statement(s) here
    ...
</SCRIPT>
</BODY>
</HTML>
```

It's also good to know that you can place an unlimited number of <SCRIPT> tag sets in a document. For example, Listing 5-3 shows a script in both the Head and Body portions of a document. Perhaps this document needs the Body script to create some dynamic content as the page loads, but the document also contains a button that needs a script to run later. That script is stored in the Head portion.

Listing 5-3: **Scripts in the Head and Body**

```
<HTML>
<HEAD>
<TITLE>A Document</TITLE>
<SCRIPT LANGUAGE="JavaScript">
    //script statement(s) here
    ...
</SCRIPT>
</HEAD>
<BODY>
<SCRIPT LANGUAGE="JavaScript">
    //script statement(s) here
    ...
</SCRIPT>
</BODY>
</HTML>
```

You also are not limited to one <SCRIPT> tag set in either the Head or Body. You can include as many <SCRIPT> tag sets in a document as are needed to complete your application. In Listing 5-4, for example, two <SCRIPT> tag sets are located in the Body portion, with some other HTML between them.

Listing 5-4: **Two Scripts in the Body**

```
<HTML>
<HEAD>
<TITLE>A Document</TITLE>
</HEAD>
<BODY>
<SCRIPT LANGUAGE="JavaScript">
    //script statement(s) here
    ...
</SCRIPT>
<MORE HTML>
<SCRIPT LANGUAGE="JavaScript">
    //script statement(s) here
    ...
</SCRIPT>
</BODY>
</HTML>
```

Handling older browsers

Only browsers that include JavaScript in them know to interpret the lines of code between the `<SCRIPT>`...`</SCRIPT>` tag pair as script statements and not HTML text for display in the browser. This means that a pre-JavaScript browser not only ignores the tags, but it also treats the JavaScript code as page content. As you saw at the end of Chapter 3 in an illustration of your first script running on an old browser, the results can be disastrous to a page.

You can reduce the risk of old browsers displaying the script lines by playing a trick. The trick is to enclose the script lines between HTML comment symbols, as shown in Listing 5-5. Most nonscriptable browsers completely ignore the content between the `<!--` and `-->` comment tags, whereas scriptable browsers ignore those comment symbols when they appear inside a `<SCRIPT>` tag set.

Listing 5-5: **Hiding Scripts from Most Old Browsers**

```
<SCRIPT LANGUAGE="JavaScript">
<!--
    //script statement(s) here
    ...
// -->
</SCRIPT>
```

The odd construction right before the ending script tag needs a brief explanation. The two forward slashes are a JavaScript comment symbol. This symbol is necessary because JavaScript otherwise tries to interpret the components of the ending HTML symbol (-->). Therefore, the forward slashes tell JavaScript to skip the line entirely; a nonscriptable browser simply treats those slash characters as part of the entire HTML comment to be ignored.

Despite the fact that this technique is often called *hiding scripts,* it does not disguise the scripts entirely. All client-side JavaScript scripts are part of the HTML document and download to the browser just like all other HTML. Furthermore, you can view them as part of the document's source code. Do not be fooled into thinking that you can hide your scripts entirely from prying eyes.

JavaScript Statements

Virtually every line of code that sits between a <SCRIPT>...</SCRIPT> tag pair is a JavaScript statement. To be compatible with habits of experienced programmers, JavaScript accepts a semicolon at the end of every statement. Fortunately for newcomers, this semicolon is optional. The carriage return at the end of a statement suffices for JavaScript to know the statement has ended.

A statement must be in the script for a purpose. Therefore, every statement does "something" relevant to the script. The kinds of things that statements do are

✦ Define or initialize a variable

✦ Assign a value to a property or variable

✦ Change the value of a property or variable

✦ Invoke an object's method

✦ Invoke a function routine

✦ Make a decision

If you don't yet know what all of these mean, don't worry — you will by the end of this tutorial. The point I want to stress is that each statement contributes to the scripts you write. The only statement that doesn't perform any explicit action is the *comment.* A pair of forward slashes (no space between them) is the most common way to include a comment in a script. You add comments to a script for your benefit. They usually explain in plain language what a statement or group of statements does. The purpose of including comments is to remind you six months from now how your script works.

When Script Statements Execute

Now that you know where scripts go in a document, it's time to look at when they run. Depending on what you need a script to do, you have four choices for determining when a script runs:

✦ While a document loads

✦ Immediately after a document loads

✦ In response to user action

✦ When called upon by other script statements

The determining factor is how the script statements are positioned in a document.

While a document loads – immediate execution

Your first script in Chapter 3 (reproduced in Listing 5-6) runs while the document loads into the browser. For this application, it is essential that a script inspects some properties of the navigator object and includes those property values in the content being rendered for the page as it loads. It makes sense, therefore, to include the <SCRIPT> tags and statements in the Body portion of the document. I call the kind of statements that run as the page loads *immediate statements*.

Listing 5-6: **HTML Page with Immediate Script Statements**

```
<HTML>
<HEAD>
<TITLE>My First Script</TITLE>
</HEAD>

<BODY>
<H1>Let's Script...</H1>
<HR>
<SCRIPT LANGUAGE="JavaScript">
<!-- hide from old browsers
document.write("This browser is version " + navigator.appVersion)
document.write(" of <B>" + navigator.appName + "</B>.")
// end script hiding -->
</SCRIPT>
</BODY>
</HTML>
```

Deferred scripts

The other three ways that script statements run are grouped together as what I called *deferred scripts*. To demonstrate these deferred script situations, I must introduce you briefly to a concept covered in more depth in Chapter 7: the function. A *function* defines a block of script statements summoned to run some time after those statements load into the browser. Functions are clearly visible inside a <SCRIPT> tag because each function definition begins with the word function followed by the function name (and parentheses). Once a function is loaded into the browser (commonly in the Head portion so it loads early), it stands ready to run whenever called upon.

One of the times a function is called upon to run is immediately after a page loads. The Window object has an event handler called onLoad. Unlike most event handlers, which are triggered in response to user action (for example, clicking a button), the onLoad event handler fires the instant that all of the page's components (including images, Java applets, and embedded multimedia) are loaded into the browser. The onLoad event handler goes in the <BODY> tag, as shown in Listing 5-7. Recall from Chapter 4 (Listing 4-1) that an event handler can run a script statement directly. But if the event handler must run several script statements, it is usually more convenient to put those statements in a function definition and then have the event handler *invoke* that function. That's what happens in Listing 5-7: When the page completes loading, the onLoad event handler triggers the done() function. That function (simplified for this example) displays an alert dialog box.

Listing 5-7: **Running a Script from the onLoad Event Handler**

```
<HTML>
<HEAD>
<TITLE>An onLoad script</TITLE>
<SCRIPT LANGUAGE="JavaScript">
<!--
function done() {
    alert("The page has finished loading.")
}
// -->
</SCRIPT>
</HEAD>
<BODY onLoad="done()">
Here is some body text.
</BODY>
</HTML>
```

Don't worry about the curly braces or other oddities in Listing 5-7 that cause you concern at this point. Focus instead on the structure of the document and the flow. The entire page loads without running any script statements, although the page loads the done() function in memory so that it is ready to run at a moment's notice. After the document loads, the browser fires the onLoad event handler, which causes the done() function to run. Then the user sees the alert dialog box.

Getting a script to execute in response to a user action is very similar to the preceding example for running a deferred script right after the document loads. Commonly, a script function is defined in the Head portion, and an event handler in, say, a form element calls upon that function to run. Listing 5-8 includes a script that runs when a user clicks a button.

Listing 5-8: **Running a Script from User Action**

```
<HTML>
<HEAD>
<TITLE>An onClick script</TITLE>
<SCRIPT LANGUAGE="JavaScript">
<!--
function alertUser() {
    alert("Ouch!")
}
// -->
</SCRIPT>
</HEAD>
<BODY>
Here is some body text.
<FORM>
    <INPUT TYPE="text" NAME="entry">
    <INPUT TYPE="button" NAME="oneButton" VALUE="Press Me!"
onClick="alertUser()">
</FORM>
</BODY>
</HTML>
```

Not every object must have an event handler defined for it in the HTML, as shown in Listing 5-8 — only the ones for which scripting is needed. No script statements execute in Listing 5-8 until the user clicks the button. The alertUser() function is defined as the page loads, and it waits to run as long as the page remains loaded in the browser. If it is never called upon to run, there's no harm done.

The last scenario for when script statements run also involves functions. In this case, a function is called upon to run by another script statement. Before you see how that works, it helps to read through the next lesson (Chapter 6). Therefore, I will hold off on this example until later in the tutorial.

Viewing Script Errors

In the early days of JavaScript in browsers, script errors displayed themselves in very obvious dialog boxes. These boxes were certainly helpful for scripters who wanted to debug their scripts. However, if a bug got through to a page served up to a non-technical user, the error alert dialog boxes were not only disruptive, but also scary. To prevent such dialog boxes from disturbing unsuspecting users, the browser makers tried to diminish the visual impact of errors in the browser window. Unfortunately for scripters, it is often easy to overlook the fact that your script contains an error because the error is not so obvious. Recent versions of IE and NN have different ways of letting scripters see the errors.

In IE5+, you can set its preferences so that scripts do not generate error dialog boxes (got to Tools ➪ Internet Options ➪ Advanced ➪ Browsing and find the checkbox entry that says "Display a notification about every script error"). Even with error dialog boxes turned off, error indications are displayed subtly at the left edge of the browser window's status bar. An alert icon and message ("Error on page.") appear in the status bar. If you double-click the icon, the error dialog box appears (see Figure 5-1). Be sure to expand the dialog box by clicking the Show Details button. Unless you turn on script error dialog boxes and keep them coming, you have to train yourself to monitor the status bar when a page loads and after each script runs.

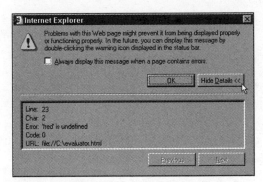

Figure 5-1: The expanded IE error dialog box

For NN 4.07 and later, the status bar is also your first indication of a script error. A message appears in the status bar that instructs you to go to the location `javascript:` to see the error details. Viewing the details of the error requires different steps, depending on the Navigator version. For NN 4.07 and all subsequent 4.*x* versions, choose File ➪ Open and enter

```
javascript:
```

For NN6, choose Tasks ➪ Tools ➪ JavaScript Console. The JavaScript console window (a separate window from the Java console) opens to reveal the error message details (see Figure 5-2). You can keep this window open all the time if you like. Unless you clear the window, subsequent error messages are appended to the bottom of the window.

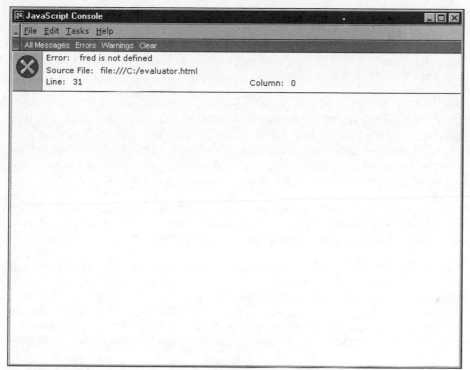

Figure 5-2: The NN6 JavaScript Console window

Understanding error messages and doing something about them is a very large subject, reserved for advanced discussion in Chapter 45. During this tutorial, however, you can use the error messages to see if you have perhaps mistyped a script from a listing in the book.

Scripting versus Programming

You may get the impression that scripting is easier than programming. "Scripting" simply sounds easier or more friendly than "programming." In many respects, this is true. One of my favorite analogies is the difference between a hobbyist who builds model airplanes from scratch and a hobbyist who builds model airplanes from commercial kits. The "from scratch" hobbyist carefully cuts and shapes each piece of wood and metal according to very detailed plans before the model starts to take shape. The commercial kit builder starts with many prefabricated parts and assembles them into the finished product. When both builders are finished, you may not be able to tell which airplane was built from scratch and which one came out of a box of components. In the end, both builders used many of the same techniques to complete the assembly, and each can take pride in the result.

As you've seen with the document object model, the browser gives scripters many prefabricated components with which to work. Without the browser, you'd have to be a pretty good programmer to develop from scratch your own application that served up content and offered user interaction. In the end, both authors have working applications that look equally professional.

Beyond the document object model, however, "real programming" nibbles its way into the scripting world. That's because scripts (and programs) work with more than just objects. When I said earlier in this lesson that each statement of a JavaScript script does something, that "something" involves *data* of some kind. Data is the information associated with objects or other pieces of information that a script pushes around from place to place with each statement.

Data takes many forms. In JavaScript, the common incarnations of data are numbers; text (called *strings*); objects (both from the object model and others you can create with scripts); and true and false (called *Boolean values*).

Each programming or scripting language determines numerous structures and limits for each kind of data. Fortunately for newcomers to JavaScript, the universe of knowledge necessary for working with data is smaller than in a language such as Java. At the same time, what you learn about data in JavaScript is immediately applicable to future learning you may undertake in any other programming language — don't believe for an instant that your efforts in learning scripting will be wasted.

Because deep down scripting is programming, you need to have a basic knowledge of fundamental programming concepts to consider yourself a good JavaScript scripter. In the next two lessons, I set aside most discussion about the document object model and focus on the programming principles that will serve you well in JavaScript and future programming endeavors.

Exercises

1. Write the complete script tag set for a script whose lone statement is

   ```
   document.write("Hello, world.")
   ```

2. Build an HTML document and include the answer to the previous question such that the page executes the script as it loads. Open the document in your browser.

3. Add a comment to the script in the previous answer that explains what the script does.

4. Create an HTML document that displays an alert dialog box immediately after the page loads and displays a different alert dialog box when the user clicks a form button.

5. Carefully study the document in Listing 5-9. Without entering and loading the document, predict

   a. What the page looks like

   b. How users interact with the page

   c. What the script does

Then type the listing into a text editor as shown (observe all capitalization and punctuation). **Do not type a carriage return after the "=" sign in the upperMe function statement; let the line word-wrap as it does in the following listing.** It's okay to use a carriage return between attribute name/value pairs, as shown in the first `<INPUT>` tag. Save the document as an HTML file, and load the file into your browser to see how well you did.

Listing 5-9: **How Does This Page Work?**

```
<HTML>
<HEAD>
<TITLE>Text Object Value</TITLE>
<SCRIPT LANGUAGE="JavaScript">
<!--
function upperMe() {
    document.converter.output.value =
document.converter.input.value.toUpperCase()
}
// -->
</SCRIPT>
</HEAD>

<BODY>
Enter lowercase letters for conversion to uppercase:<BR>
<FORM NAME="converter">
    <INPUT TYPE="text" NAME="input" VALUE="sample"
        onChange="upperMe()"><BR>
    <INPUT TYPE="text" NAME="output" VALUE="">
</FORM>
</BODY>
</HTML>
```

✦ ✦ ✦

Programming Fundamentals, Part I

The tutorial breaks away from HTML and documents for a while as you begin to learn programming fundamentals that apply to practically every scripting and programming language you will encounter. Here, you start learning about variables, expressions, data types, and operators — things that might sound scary if you haven't programmed before. Don't worry. With a little practice, you will become quite comfortable with these terms and concepts.

What Language Is This?

The language you're studying is called JavaScript. But the language has some other names that you may have heard. JScript is Microsoft's name for the language. By leaving out the "ava," the company doesn't have to license the "Java" name from its trademark owner: Sun Microsystems.

A standards body called ECMA (pronounced ECK-ma) now governs the specifications for the language (no matter what you call it). The document that provides all of the details about the language is known as *ECMA-262* (it's the 262nd standard published by ECMA). Both JavaScript and JScript are ECMA-262 compatible. Some earlier browser versions exhibit very slight deviations from ECMA-262 (which came later than the earliest browsers). The most serious discrepancies are noted in the core language reference in Part IV of this book.

Working with Information

With rare exception, every JavaScript statement you write does something with a hunk of information — *data*. Data may be text information displayed on the screen by a JavaScript statement or the on/off setting of a radio button in a form. Each single piece of information in programming is also called a *value*. Outside of programming, the term *value* usually connotes a number of some kind; in the programming world, however, the term is not as restrictive. A string of letters is a value. A number is a value. The setting of a check box (whether it is checked or not) is a value.

In JavaScript, a value can be one of several types. Table 6-1 lists JavaScript's formal data types, with examples of the values you will see displayed from time to time.

Table 6-1
JavaScript Value (Data) Types

Type	Example	Description
String	"Howdy"	A series of characters inside quote marks
Number	4.5	Any number not inside quote marks
Boolean	true	A logical true or false
Null	null	Completely devoid of any value
Object		A software "thing" that is defined by its properties and methods (arrays are also objects)
Function		A function definition

A language that contains these few data types simplifies programming tasks, especially those involving what other languages consider to be incompatible types of numbers (integers versus real or floating-point values). In some definitions of syntax and parts of objects later in this book, I make specific reference to the type of value accepted in placeholders. When a string is required, any text inside a set of quotes suffices.

You will encounter situations, however, in which the value type may get in the way of a smooth script step. For example, if a user enters a number into a form's text input field, the browser stores that number as a string value type. If the script is to perform some arithmetic on that number, you must convert the string to a number before you can apply the value to any math operations. You see examples of this later in this lesson.

Variables

Cooking up a dish according to a recipe in the kitchen has one advantage over cooking up some data in a program. In the kitchen, you follow recipe steps and work with real things: carrots, milk, or a salmon fillet. A computer, on the other hand, follows a list of instructions to work with data. Even if the data represents something that looks real, such as the text entered into a form's input field, once the value gets into the program, you can no longer reach out and touch it.

In truth, the data that a program works with is merely a collection of bits (on and off states) in your computer's memory. More specifically, data in a JavaScript-enhanced Web page occupies parts of the computer's memory set aside for exclusive use by the browser software. In the olden days, programmers had to know the numeric address in memory (RAM) where a value was stored to retrieve a copy of it for, say, some addition. Although the innards of a program have that level of complexity, programming languages such as JavaScript shield you from it.

The most convenient way to work with data in a script is to first assign the data to a *variable*. It's usually easier to think of a variable as a basket that holds information. How long the variable holds the information depends on a number of factors. But the instant a Web page clears the window (or frame), any variables it knows about are immediately discarded.

Creating a variable

You have a couple of ways to create a variable in JavaScript, but one covers you properly in all cases. Use the `var` keyword, followed by the name you want to give that variable. Therefore, to *declare* a new variable called `myAge`, the JavaScript statement is

```
var myAge
```

That statement lets the browser know that you can use that variable later to hold information or to modify any of the data in that variable.

To assign a value to a variable, use one of the *assignment operators*. The most common one by far is the equal sign. If I want to assign a value to the `myAge` variable at the same time I declare it (a combined process known as *initializing the variable*), I use that operator in the same statement as the `var` keyword:

```
var myAge = 45
```

On the other hand, if I declare a variable in one statement and later want to assign a value to it, the sequence of statements is

```
var myAge
myAge = 45
```

Use the var keyword **only for declaration or initialization** — once for the life of any variable name in a document.

A JavaScript variable can hold any value type. Unlike many other languages, you don't have to tell JavaScript during variable declaration what type of value the variable will hold. In fact, the value type of a variable can change during the execution of a program. (This flexibility drives experienced programmers crazy because they're accustomed to assigning both a data type and a value to a variable.)

Variable names

Choose the names you assign to variables with care. You'll often find scripts that use vague variable names, such as single letters. Other than a few specific times where using letters is a common practice (for example, using i as a counting variable in repeat loops in Chapter 7), I recommend using names that truly describe a variable's contents. This practice can help you follow the state of your data through a long series of statements or jumps, especially for complex scripts.

A number of restrictions help instill good practice in assigning names. First, you cannot use any reserved keyword as a variable name. That includes all keywords currently used by the language and all others held in reserve for future versions of JavaScript. The designers of JavaScript, however, cannot foresee every keyword that the language may need in the future. By using the kind of single words that currently appear in the list of reserved keywords (see Appendix B), you always run a risk of a future conflict.

To complicate matters, a variable name cannot contain space characters. Therefore, one-word variable names are fine. Should your description really benefit from more than one word, you can use one of two conventions to join multiple words as one. One convention is to place an underscore character between the words; the other is to start the combination word with a lowercase letter and capitalize the first letter of each subsequent word within the name — I refer to this as the *interCap format*. Both of the following examples are valid variable names:

```
my_age
myAge
```

My preference is for the second version. I find it easier to type as I write JavaScript code and easier to read later. In fact, because of the potential conflict with future keywords, using multiword combinations for variable names is a good idea. Multiword combinations are less likely to appear in the reserved word list.

Variable names have a couple of other important restrictions. Avoid all punctuation symbols except for the underscore character. Also, the first character of a variable name cannot be a numeral. If these restrictions sound familiar, it's because they're identical to those for HTML element identifiers described in Chapter 5.

Expressions and Evaluation

Another concept closely related to the value and variable is *expression evaluation*—perhaps the most important concept of learning how to program a computer.

We use expressions in our everyday language. Remember the theme song of *The Beverly Hillbillies*?

> *Then one day he was shootin' at some food*
>
> *And up through the ground came a-bubblin' crude*
>
> *Oil that is. Black gold. Texas tea.*

At the end of the song, you find four quite different references ("crude," "oil," "black gold," and "Texas tea"). They all mean oil. They're all *expressions* for oil. Say any one of them and other people know what you mean. In our minds, we *evaluate* those expressions to mean one thing: oil.

In programming, a variable always evaluates to its contents, or value. For example, after assigning a value to a variable, such as

```
var myAge = 45
```

anytime the variable is used in a statement, its value (45) is automatically applied to whatever operation that statement calls. Therefore, if you're 15 years my junior, I can assign a value to a variable representing your age based on the evaluated value of myAge:

```
var yourAge = myAge - 15
```

The variable, yourAge, evaluates to 30 the next time the script uses it. If the myAge value changes later in the script, the change has no link to the yourAge variable because myAge evaluated to 45 when it was used to assign a value to yourAge.

Expressions in script1.htm

You probably didn't recognize it at the time, but you saw how expression evaluation came in handy in your first script of Chapter 3. Recall the second document.write() statement:

```
document.write(" of " + navigator.appName + ".")
```

Testing Evaluation in Navigator

You can begin experimenting with the way JavaScript evaluates expressions with the help of The Evaluator Jr. (seen in the following figure), an HTML page you can find on the companion CD-ROM. (I introduce the Senior version in Chapter 13.) Enter any JavaScript expression into the top text box, and either press Enter/Return or click the Evaluate button.

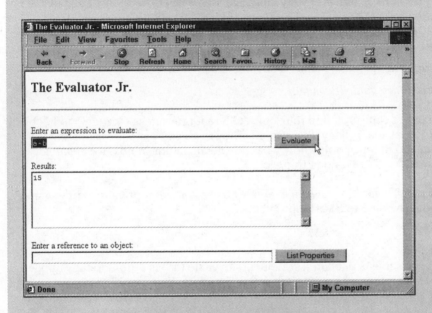

The Evaluator Jr. for testing expression evaluation

The Evaluator Jr. has 26 variables (lowercase a through z) predefined for you. Therefore, you can assign values to variables, test comparison operators, and even do math here. Using the age variable examples from earlier in this chapter, type each of the following statements into the upper text box and observe how each expression evaluates in the Results field. Be sure to observe case-sensitivity in your entries.

```
a = 45
a
b = a - 15
b
a - b
a > b
```

To start over, click the Refresh/Reload button.

The `document.write()` method (remember, JavaScript uses the term *method* to mean *command*) requires a parameter in parentheses: the text string to be displayed on the Web page. The parameter here consists of one expression that joins three distinct strings:

```
" of "
navigator.appName
"."
```

The plus symbol is one of JavaScript's ways of joining strings. Before JavaScript can display this line, it must perform some quick evaluations. The first evaluation is the value of the `navigator.appName` property. This property evaluates to a string of the name of your browser. With that expression safely evaluated to a string, JavaScript can finish the job of joining the three strings in the final evaluation. That evaluated string expression is what ultimately appears on the Web page.

Expressions and variables

As one more demonstration of the flexibility that expression evaluation offers, this section shows you a slightly different route to the `document.write()` statement. Rather than join those strings as the direct parameter to the `document.write()` method, I can gather the strings in a variable and then apply the variable to the `document.write()` method. Here's how that method looks, as I simultaneously declare a new variable and assign it a value:

```
var textToWrite = " of " + navigator.appName + "."
document.write(textToWrite)
```

This method works because the variable, `textToWrite`, evaluates to the combined string. The `document.write()` method accepts that string value and does its display job. As you read a script or try to work through a bug, pay special attention to how each expression (variable, statement, object property) evaluates. I guarantee that as you learn JavaScript (or any language), you will end up scratching your head from time to time because you haven't stopped to examine how expressions evaluate when a particular kind of value is required in a script.

Data Type Conversions

I mentioned earlier that the type of data in an expression can trip up some script operations if the expected components of the operation are not of the right type. JavaScript tries its best to perform internal conversions to head off such problems, but JavaScript cannot read your mind. If your intentions differ from the way JavaScript treats the values, you won't get the results you expect.

A case in point is adding numbers that may be in the form of text strings. In a simple arithmetic statement that adds two numbers together, you get the expected result:

```
3 + 3          // result = 6
```

But if one of those numbers is a string, JavaScript leans toward converting the other value to a string — thus turning the plus sign's action from arithmetic addition to joining strings. Therefore, in the statement

```
3 + "3"        // result = "33"
```

the "string-ness" of the second value prevails over the entire operation. The first value is automatically converted to a string, and the result joins the two strings. Try this yourself in The Evaluator Jr.

If I take this progression one step further, look what happens when another number is added to the statement:

```
3 + 3 + "3"    // result = "63"
```

This might seem totally illogical, but there is logic behind this result. The expression is evaluated from left to right. The first plus operation works on two numbers, yielding a value of 6. But as the 6 is about to be added to the "3," JavaScript lets the "string-ness" of the "3" rule. The 6 is converted to a string, and two string values are joined to yield "63."

Most of your concern about data types will focus on performing math operations like the ones here. However, some object methods also require one or more parameters of particular data types. While JavaScript provides numerous ways to convert data from one type to another, it is appropriate at this stage of the tutorial to introduce you to the two most common data conversions: string to number and number to string.

Converting strings to numbers

As you saw in the last section, if a numeric value is stored as a string — as it is when entered into a form text field — your scripts will have difficulty applying that value to a math operation. The JavaScript language provides two built-in functions to convert string representations of numbers to true numbers: parseInt() and parseFloat().

There is a difference between integers and floating-point numbers in JavaScript. *Integers* are always whole numbers, with no decimal point or numbers to the right of a decimal. *Floating-point numbers,* on the other hand, can have fractional values to the right of the decimal. By and large, JavaScript math operations don't differentiate between integers and floating-point numbers: A number is a number. The only time you need to be cognizant of the difference is when a method parameter requires an integer because it can't handle fractional values. For example, parameters to the `scroll()` method of a window require integer values of the number of pixels vertically and horizontally you want to scroll the window. That's because you can't scroll a window a fraction of a pixel on the screen.

To use either of these conversion functions, insert the string value you wish to convert as a parameter to the function. For example, look at the results of two different string values when passed through the `parseInt()` function:

```
parseInt("42")       // result = 42
parseInt("42.33")    // result = 42
```

Even though the second expression passes the string version of a floating-point number to the function, the value returned by the function is an integer. No rounding of the value occurs here (although other math functions can help with that if necessary). The decimal and everything to its right are simply stripped off.

The `parseFloat()` function returns an integer if it can; otherwise, it returns a floating-point number as follows:

```
parseFloat("42")     // result = 42
parseFloat("42.33")  // result = 42.33
```

Because these two conversion functions evaluate to their results, you simply insert the entire function wherever you need a string value converted to a number. Therefore, modifying an earlier example in which one of three values was a string, the complete expression can evaluate to the desired result:

```
3 + 3 + parseInt("3")  // result = 9
```

Converting numbers to strings

You'll have less need for converting a number to its string equivalent than the other way around. As you saw in the previous section, JavaScript gravitates toward strings when faced with an expression containing mixed data types. Even so, it is good practice to perform data type conversions explicitly in your code to prevent any potential ambiguity. The simplest way to convert a number to a string is to take advantage of JavaScript's string tendencies in addition operations. By adding an empty string to a number, you convert the number to its string equivalent:

```
("" + 2500)          // result = "2500"
("" + 2500).length   // result = 4
```

In the second example, you can see the power of expression evaluation at work. The parentheses force the conversion of the number to a string. A *string* is a JavaScript object that has properties associated with it. One of those properties is the `length` property, which evaluates to the number of characters in the string. Therefore, the length of the string "2500" is 4. Note that the length value is a number, not a string.

Operators

You will use lots of *operators* in expressions. Earlier, you used the equal sign (=) as an assignment operator to assign a value to a variable. In the preceding examples with strings, you used the plus symbol (+) to join two strings. An operator generally performs some kind of calculation (operation) or comparison with two values (the value on each side of an operator is called an *operand*) to reach a third value. In this lesson, I briefly describe two categories of operators — arithmetic and comparison. Chapter 40 covers many more operators, but once you understand the basics here, the others are easier to grasp.

Arithmetic operators

It may seem odd to talk about text strings in the context of "arithmetic" operators, but you have already seen the special case of the plus (+) operator when one or more of the operands is a string. The plus operator instructs JavaScript to *concatenate* (pronounced kon-KAT-en-eight), or join, two strings together precisely where you place the operator. The string concatenation operator doesn't know about words and spaces, so the programmer must make sure that any two strings to be joined have the proper word spacing as part of the strings — even if that means adding a space:

```
firstName = "John"
lastName = "Doe"
fullName = firstName + " " + lastName
```

JavaScript uses the same plus operator for arithmetic addition. When both operands are numbers, JavaScript knows to treat the expression as an arithmetic addition rather than a string concatenation. The standard math operators for addition, subtraction, multiplication, and division (+, -, *, /) are built into JavaScript.

Comparison operators

Another category of operator helps you compare values in scripts — whether two values are the same, for example. These kinds of comparisons return a value of the Boolean type — `true` or `false`. Table 6-2 lists the comparison operators. The operator that tests whether two items are equal consists of a pair of equal signs to distinguish it from the single equal sign assignment operator.

Symbol	Description
==	Equals
!=	Does not equal
>	Is greater than
>=	Is greater than or equal to
<	Is less than
<=	Is less than or equal to

Table 6-2
JavaScript Comparison Operators

Where comparison operators come into greatest play is in the construction of scripts that make decisions as they run. A cook does this in the kitchen all the time: If the sauce is too watery, add a bit of flour. You see comparison operators in action in the next chapter.

Exercises

1. Which of the following are valid variable declarations or initializations? Explain why each one is or is not valid. If an item is invalid, how do you fix it so that it is?

   a. `my_name = "Cindy"`

   b. `var how many = 25`

   c. `var zipCode = document.form1.zip.value`

   d. `var 1address = document.nameForm.address1.value`

2. For each of the statements in the following sequence, write down how the `someVal` expression evaluates after the statement executes in JavaScript.

   ```
   var someVal = 2
   someVal = someVal + 2
   someVal = someVal * 10
   someVal = someVal + "20"
   someVal = "Robert"
   ```

3. Name the two JavaScript functions that convert strings to numbers. How do you give the function a string value to convert to a number?

4. Type and load the HTML page and script shown in Listing 6-1. Enter a three-digit number into the top two fields and click the Add button. Examine the code and explain what is wrong with the script. How do you fix the script so the proper sum is displayed in the output field?

Listing 6-1: **What's Wrong with This Page?**

```
<HTML>
<HEAD>
<TITLE>Sum Maker</TITLE>
<SCRIPT LANGUAGE="JavaScript">
<!--
function addIt() {
    var value1 = document.adder.inputA.value
    var value2 = document.adder.inputB.value
    document.adder.output.value = value1 + value2
}
// -->
</SCRIPT>
</HEAD>

<BODY>
<FORM NAME="adder">
<INPUT TYPE="text" NAME="inputA" VALUE="0" SIZE=4><BR>
<INPUT TYPE="text" NAME="inputB" VALUE="0" SIZE=4>
<INPUT TYPE="button" VALUE="Add" onClick="addIt()">
<P>_____</P>
<INPUT TYPE="text" NAME="output" SIZE=6> <BR>
</FORM>
</BODY>
</HTML>
```

5. What does the term *concatenate* mean in the context of JavaScript programming?

✦   ✦   ✦

Programming Fundamentals, Part II

Y our tour of programming fundamentals continues in this
chapter with subjects that have more intriguing possibilities. For example, I show you how programs make decisions and why a program must sometimes repeat statements
over and over. Before you're finished here, you will learn how
to use one of the most powerful information holders in the
JavaScript language: the array.

Decisions and Loops

Every waking hour of every day you make decisions of some
kind—most of the time you probably don't even realize it.
Don't think so? Well, look at the number of decisions you
make at the grocery store, from the moment you enter the
store to the moment you clear the checkout aisle.

No sooner do you enter the store than you are faced with a
decision. Based on the number and size of items you intend to
buy, do you pick up a hand-carried basket or attempt to extri-
cate a shopping cart from the metallic conga line near the
front of the store? That key decision may have impact later
when you see a special offer on an item that is too heavy to
put into the hand basket.

Next, you head for the food aisles. Before entering an aisle,
you compare the range of goods stocked in that aisle against
items on your shopping list. If an item you need is likely to be
found in this aisle, you turn into the aisle and start looking for
the item; otherwise, you skip the aisle and move to the head
of the next aisle.

Later, you reach the produce section in search of a juicy tomato. Standing in front of the bin of tomatoes, you begin inspecting them one by one—picking one up, feeling its firmness, checking the color, looking for blemishes or signs of pests. You discard one, pick up another, and continue this process until one matches the criteria you set in your mind for an acceptable morsel. Your last stop in the store is the checkout aisle. "Paper or plastic?" the clerk asks. One more decision to make. What you choose impacts how you get the groceries from the car to the kitchen as well as your recycling habits.

In your trip to the store, you go through the same kinds of decisions and repetitions that your JavaScript programs also encounter. If you understand these frameworks in real life, you can now look into the JavaScript equivalents and the syntax required to make them work.

Control Structures

In the vernacular of programming, the kinds of statements that make decisions and loop around to repeat themselves are called *control structures*. A control structure directs the execution flow through a sequence of script statements based on simple decisions and other factors.

An important part of a control structure is the condition. Just as you may travel different routes to work depending on certain conditions (for example, nice weather, nighttime, attending a soccer game), so, too, does a program sometimes have to branch to an execution route if a certain condition exists. Each condition is an expression that evaluates to `true` or `false`—one of those Boolean data types mentioned in Chapter 6. The kinds of expressions commonly used for conditions are expressions that include a comparison operator. You do the same in real life: If it is true that the outdoor temperature is less than freezing, then you put on a coat before going outside. In programming, however, the comparisons are strictly comparisons of number or string values.

JavaScript provides several kinds of control structures for different programming situations. Three of the most common control structures you'll use are `if` constructions, `if...else` constructions, and `for` loops.

Chapter 39 covers in great detail other common control structures you should know, some of which were introduced only in Navigator 4 and Internet Explorer 4. For this tutorial, however, you need to learn about the three common ones just mentioned.

if constructions

The simplest program decision is to follow a special branch or path of the program if a certain condition is true. Formal syntax for this construction follows. Items in italics get replaced in a real script with expressions and statements that fit the situation.

```
if (condition) {
    statement[s] if true
}
```

Don't worry about the curly braces yet. Instead, get a feel for the basic structure. The keyword, if, is a must. In the parentheses goes an expression that evaluates to a Boolean value. This is the condition being tested as the program runs past this point. If the condition evaluates to true, then one or more statements inside the curly braces execute before continuing on with the next statement after the closing brace. If the condition evaluates to false, then the statements inside the curly brace are ignored and processing continues with the next statement after the closing brace.

The following example assumes that a variable, myAge, has had its value set earlier in the script (exactly how is not important for this example). The condition expression compares the value myAge against a numeric value of 18.

```
if (myAge < 18) {
    alert("Sorry, you cannot vote.")
}
```

The data type of the value inside myAge must be a number so that the proper comparison (via the < comparison operator) does the right thing. For all instances of myAge less than 18, the nested statement inside the curly braces runs and displays the alert to the user. After the user closes the alert dialog box, the script continues with whatever statement follows the entire if construction.

if . . . else constructions

Not all program decisions are as simple as the one shown for the if construction. Rather than specifying one detour for a given condition, you might want the program to follow either of two branches depending on that condition. It is a fine, but important, distinction. In the plain if construction, no special processing is performed when the condition evaluates to false. But if processing must follow one of two special paths, you need the if...else construction. The formal syntax definition for an if...else construction is as follows:

```
if (condition) {
    statement[s] if true
} else {
    statement[s] if false
}
```

Everything you know about the condition for an `if` construction applies here. The only difference is the `else` keyword, which provides an alternate path for execution to follow if the condition evaluates to `false`.

As an example, the following `if...else` construction determines how many days are in February for a given year. To simplify the demo, the condition simply tests whether the year divides equally by 4. (True testing for this value includes special treatment of end-of-century dates, but I'm ignoring that for now.) The % operator symbol is called the *modulus operator* (covered in more detail in Chapter 40). The result of an operation with this operator yields the remainder of division of the two values. If the remainder is zero, then the first value divides evenly by the second.

```
var febDays
var theYear = 1993
if (theYear % 4 == 0) {
    febDays = 29
} else {
    febDays = 28
}
```

The important point to see from this example is that by the end of the `if...else` construction, the `febDays` variable is set to either 28 or 29. No other value is possible. For years evenly divisible by 4, the first nested statement runs. For all other cases, the second statement runs. Processing then picks up with the next statement after the `if...else` construction.

About Repeat Loops

Repeat loops in real life generally mean the repetition of a series of steps until some condition is met, thus enabling you to break out of that loop. Such was the case earlier in this chapter when you looked through a bushel of tomatoes for the one that came closest to your ideal tomato. The same can be said for driving around the block in a crowded neighborhood until a parking space opens up.

A *repeat loop* lets a script cycle through a sequence of statements until some condition is met. For example, a JavaScript data validation routine might inspect every character that you enter into a form text field to make sure that each one is a number. Or if you have a collection of data stored in a list, the loop can check whether an entered value is in that list. Once that condition is met, the script can then break out of the loop and continue with the next statement after the loop construction.

The most common repeat loop construction used in JavaScript is called the `for` loop. It gets its name from the keyword that begins the construction. A `for` loop is a powerful device because you can set it up to keep track of the number of times the loop repeats itself. The formal syntax of the for loop is as follows:

```
for ([initial expression]; [condition]; [update expression]) {
    statement[s] inside loop
}
```

The square brackets mean that the item is optional. However, until you get to know the for loop better, I recommend designing your loops to utilize all three items inside the parentheses. The *initial expression* portion usually sets the starting value of a counter. The *condition*—the same kind of condition you saw for if construc- tions—defines the condition that forces the loop to stop going around and around. Finally, the *update expression* is a statement that executes each time all of the state- ments nested inside the construction complete running.

A common implementation initializes a counting variable, i, increments the value of i by one each time through the loop, and repeats the loop until the value of i exceeds some maximum value, as in the following:

```
for (var i = startValue; i <= maxValue; i++) {
    statement[s] inside loop
}
```

Placeholders startValue and maxValue represent any numeric values, including explicit numbers or variables holding numbers. In the update expression is an oper- ator you have not seen yet. The ++ operator adds 1 to the value of i each time the update expression runs at the end of the loop. If startValue is 1, the value of i is 1 the first time through the loop, 2 the second time through, and so on. Therefore, if maxValue is 10, the loop repeats itself 10 times (in other words, as long as i is less than or equal to 10). Generally speaking, the statements inside the loop use the value of the counting variable in their execution. Later in this lesson, I show how the variable can play a key role in the statements inside a loop. At the same time, you see how to break out of a loop prematurely and why you may need to do this in a script.

Functions

In Chapter 5, you saw a preview of the JavaScript function. A *function* is a definition of a set of deferred actions. Functions are invoked by event handlers or by state- ments elsewhere in the script. Whenever possible, good functions are designed for reuse in other documents. They can become building blocks you use over and over again.

If you have programmed before, you can see parallels between JavaScript functions and other languages' subroutines. But unlike some languages that distinguish between procedures (which carry out actions) and functions (which carry out actions and return values), only one classification of routine exists for JavaScript. A function is capable of returning a value to the statement that invoked it, but this is not a requirement. However, when a function does return a value, the calling statement treats the function call like any expression — plugging in the returned value right where the function call is made. I will show some examples in a moment.

Formal syntax for a function is as follows:

```
function functionName ( [parameter1]...[,parameterN] ) {
    statement[s]
}
```

Names you assign to functions have the same restrictions as names you assign HTML elements and variables. You should devise a name that succinctly describes what the function does. I tend to use multiword names with the interCap (internally capitalized) format that start with a verb because functions are action items, even if they do nothing more than get or set a value.

Another practice to keep in mind as you start to create functions is to keep the focus of each function as narrow as possible. It is possible to generate functions that are literally hundreds of lines long. Such functions are usually difficult to maintain and debug. Chances are that you can divide the long function into smaller, more tightly focused segments.

Function parameters

In Chapter 5, you saw how an event handler invokes a function by calling the function by name. Any call to a function, including one that comes from another JavaScript statement, works the same way: a set of parentheses follows the function name.

You also can define functions so they receive parameter values from the calling statement. Listing 7-1 shows a simple document that has a button whose onClick event handler calls a function while passing text data to the function. The text string in the event handler call is in a *nested string* — a set of single quotes inside the double quotes required for the entire event handler attribute.

Listing 7-1: **Calling a Function from an Event Handler**

```
<HTML>
<HEAD>
<SCRIPT LANGUAGE="JavaScript">
function showMsg(msg) {
    alert("The button sent: " + msg)
}
</SCRIPT>
</HEAD>
<BODY>
<FORM>
    <INPUT TYPE="button" VALUE="Click Me"
    onClick="showMsg ('The button has been clicked!')">
</FORM>
</BODY>
</HTML>
```

Parameters (also known as *arguments*) provide a mechanism for "handing off" a value from one statement to another by way of a function call. If no parameters occur in the function definition, both the function definition and call to the function have only empty sets of parentheses (as shown in Chapter 5, Listing 5-8).

When a function receives parameters, it assigns the incoming values to the variable names specified in the function definition's parentheses. Consider the following script segment:

```
function sayHiToFirst(a, b, c) {
    alert("Say hello, " + a)
}
sayHiToFirst("Gracie", "George", "Harry")
sayHiToFirst("Larry", "Moe", "Curly")
```

After the function is defined in the script, the next statement calls that very function, passing three strings as parameters. The function definition automatically assigns the strings to variables a, b, and c. Therefore, before the alert() statement inside the function ever runs, a evaluates to "Gracie," b evaluates to "George," and c evaluates to "Harry." In the alert() statement, only the a value is used and the alert reads

```
Say hello, Gracie
```

When the user closes the first alert, the next call to the function occurs. This time through, different values are passed to the function and assigned to a, b, and c. The alert dialog box reads

```
Say hello, Larry
```

Unlike other variables that you define in your script, function parameters do not use the var keyword to initialize them. They are automatically initialized whenever the function is called.

Variable scope

Speaking of variables, it's time to distinguish between variables that are defined outside and those defined inside of functions. Variables defined outside of functions are called *global variables*; those defined inside functions are called *local variables*.

A global variable has a slightly different connotation in JavaScript than it has in most other languages. For a JavaScript script, the "globe" of a global variable is the current document loaded in a browser window or frame. Therefore, when you initialize a variable as a global variable, it means that all script statements in the page (including those inside functions) have direct access to that variable value. Statements can retrieve and modify global variables from anywhere in the page. In programming terminology, this kind of variable is said to have *global scope* because everything on the page can "see" it.

It is important to remember that the instant a page unloads itself, all global variables defined in that page are erased from memory. If you need a value to persist from one page to another, you must use other techniques to store that value (for example, as a global variable in a framesetting document, as described in Chapter 16; or in a cookie, as described in Chapter 18). While the var keyword is usually optional for initializing global variables, I strongly recommend you use it for all variable initializations to guard against future changes to the JavaScript language.

In contrast to the global variable, a local variable is defined inside a function. You already saw how parameter variables are defined inside functions (without var keyword initializations). But you can also define other variables with the var keyword (absolutely required for local variables). The scope of a local variable is only within the statements of the function. No other functions or statements outside of functions have access to a local variable.

Local scope allows for the reuse of variable names within a document. For most variables, I strongly discourage this practice because it leads to confusion and bugs that are difficult to track down. At the same time, it is convenient to reuse certain kinds of variable names, such as for loop counters. These are safe because they are always reinitialized with a starting value whenever a for loop starts. You cannot, however, nest a for loop inside another without specifying a different loop counting variable.

To demonstrate the structure and behavior of global and local variables — and show you why you shouldn't reuse most variable names inside a document — Listing 7-2 defines two global and two local variables. I intentionally use bad form by initializing a local variable that has the same name as a global variable.

Listing 7-2: **Global and Local Variable Scope Demonstration**

```
<HTML>
<HEAD>
<SCRIPT LANGUAGE="JavaScript">
var aBoy = "Charlie Brown"    // global
var hisDog = "Snoopy"         // global
function demo() {
    // using improper design to demonstrate a point
    var hisDog = "Gromit"     // local version of hisDog
    var output = hisDog + " does not belong to " + aBoy + ".<BR>"
    document.write(output)
}
</SCRIPT>
</HEAD>
<BODY>
<SCRIPT LANGUAGE="JavaScript">
demo()          // runs as document loads
document.write(hisDog + " belongs to " + aBoy + ".")
</SCRIPT>
</BODY>
</HTML>
```

When the page loads, the script in the Head portion initializes the two global variables (aBoy and hisDog) and defines the demo() function in memory. In the Body, another script begins by invoking the function. Inside the function, a local variable is initialized with the same name as one of the global variables — hisDog. In JavaScript, such a local initialization overrides the global variable for all statements inside the function. (But note that if the var keyword is left off of the local initialization, the statement reassigns the value of the global version to "Gromit.")

Another local variable, output, is merely a repository for accumulating the text that is to be written to the screen. The accumulation begins by evaluating the local version of the hisDog variable. Then it concatenates some hard-wired text (note the extra spaces at the edges of the string segment). Next comes the evaluated value of the aBoy global variable — any global not overridden by a local is available for use inside the function. The expression is accumulating HTML to be written to the page, so it ends with a period and a <BR> tag. The final statement of the function writes the content to the page.

After the function completes its task, the next statement in the Body script writes another string to the page. Because this script statement is executing in global space (that is, not inside any function), it accesses only global variables — including those defined in another <SCRIPT> tag set in the document. By the time the complete page finishes loading, it contains the following text lines:

```
Gromit does not belong to Charlie Brown.
Snoopy belongs to Charlie Brown.
```

About Curly Braces

Despite the fact that you probably rarely — if ever — use curly braces ({ }) in your writing, there is no mystery to their usage in JavaScript (and many other languages). Curly braces enclose blocks of statements that belong together. While they do assist humans who are reading scripts in knowing what's going on, curly braces also help the browser to know which statements belong together. You always must use curly braces in matched pairs.

You use curly braces most commonly in function definitions and control structures. In the function definition in Listing 7-2, curly braces enclose four statements that make up the function definition (including the comment line). The closing brace lets the browser know that whatever statement comes next is a statement outside of the function definition.

Physical placement of curly braces is not critical (nor is the indentation style you see in the code I provide). The following function definitions are treated identically by scriptable browsers:

```
function sayHiToFirst(a, b, c) {
    alert("Say hello, " + a)
}

function sayHiToFirst(a, b, c)
{
    alert("Say hello, " + a)
}

function sayHiToFirst(a, b, c) {alert("Say hello, " + a)}
```

Throughout this book, I use the style shown in the first example because I find that it makes lengthy and complex scripts easier to read — especially scripts that have many levels of nested control structures.

Arrays

The JavaScript array is one of the most useful data constructions you have available to you. You can visualize the structure of a basic array as if it were a single-column spreadsheet. Each row of the column holds a distinct piece of data, and each row is numbered. Numbers assigned to rows are in strict numerical sequence, starting with zero as the first row (programmers always start counting with zero). This row number is called an *index*. To access an item in an array, you need to know the name of the array and the index for the row. Because index values start with zero, the total number of items of the array (as determined by the array's length property) is always one more than the highest index value of the array. More advanced array concepts enable you to create the equivalent of an array with multiple columns (described in Chapter 37). For this tutorial, I stay with the single-column basic array.

Data elements inside JavaScript arrays can be any data type, including objects. And, unlike a lot of other programming languages, different rows of the same JavaScript array can contain different data types.

Creating an array

An array is stored in a variable, so when you create an array you assign the new array object to the variable. (Yes, arrays are JavaScript objects, but they belong to the core JavaScript language rather than the document object model.) A special keyword — new — preceding a call to the JavaScript function that generates arrays creates space in memory for the array. An optional parameter to the Array() function enables you to specify at the time of creation how many elements (rows) of data eventually will occupy the array. JavaScript is very forgiving about this because you can change the size of an array at any time. Therefore, if you omit a parameter when generating a new array, your script incurs no penalty.

To demonstrate the array creation process, I create an array that holds the names of the 50 states plus the District of Columbia (a total of 51). The first task is to create that array and assign it to a variable of any name that helps me remember what this collection of data is about:

```
var USStates = new Array(51)
```

At this point, the USStates array is sitting in memory like a 51-row table with no data in it. To fill the rows, I must assign data to each row. Addressing each row of an array requires a special way of indicating the index value of the row: square brackets after the name of the array. The first row of the USStates array is addressed as

```
USStates[0]
```

To assign the string name of the first state of the alphabet to that row, I use a simple assignment operator:

```
USStates[0] = "Alabama"
```

To fill in the rest of the rows, I include a statement for each row:

```
USStates[1] = "Alaska"
USStates[2] = "Arizona"
USStates[3] = "Arkansas"
...
USStates[50] = "Wyoming"
```

Therefore, if you want to include a table of information in a document from which a script can look up information without accessing the server, you include the data in the document in the form of an array creation sequence. When the statements run as the document loads, by the time the document finishes loading into the browser, the data collection array is built and ready to go. Despite what appears to be the potential for a lot of statements in a document for such a data collection, the amount of data that must download for typical array collections is small enough not to severely impact page loading — even for dial-up users at 28.8 Kbps.

Accessing array data

The array index is the key to accessing an array element. The name of the array and an index in square brackets evaluates to the content of that array location. For example, after the USStates array is built, a script can display an alert with Alaska's name in it with the following statement:

```
alert("The largest state is " + USStates[1] + ".")
```

Just as you can retrieve data from an indexed array element, so can you change the element by reassigning a new value to any indexed element in the array.

Although I don't dwell on it in this tutorial, you can also use string names as index values instead of numbers. In essence, this enables you to create an array that has named labels for each row of the array — a definite convenience for certain circumstances. But whichever way you use to assign data to an array element, the first time dictates the way you must access that element thereafter in the page's scripts.

Parallel arrays

Now I show you why the numeric index methodology works well in JavaScript. To help with the demonstration, I generate another array that is parallel with the

USStates array. This new array is also 51 elements long, and it contains the year in which the state in the corresponding row of USStates entered the Union. That array construction looks like the following:

```
var stateEntered = new Array(51)
stateEntered [0] = 1819
stateEntered [1] = 1959
stateEntered [2] = 1912
stateEntered [3] = 1836
...
stateEntered [50] = 1890
```

In the browser's memory, then, are two tables that you can visualize as looking like the model in Figure 7-1. I can build more arrays that are parallel to these for items such as the postal abbreviation and capital city. The important point is that the zeroth element in each of these tables applies to Alabama, the first state in the USStates array.

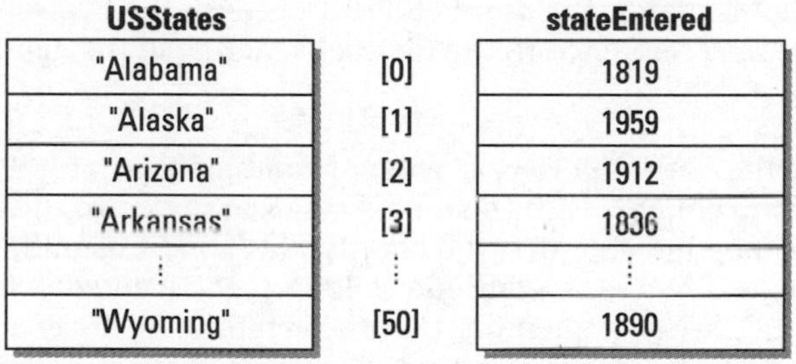

USStates		stateEntered
"Alabama"	[0]	1819
"Alaska"	[1]	1959
"Arizona"	[2]	1912
"Arkansas"	[3]	1836
⋮	⋮	⋮
"Wyoming"	[50]	1890

Figure 7-1: Visualization of two related parallel tables

If a Web page included these tables and a way for a user to look up the entry date for a given state, the page would need a way to look through all of the USStates entries to find the index value of the one that matches the user's entry. Then, that index value could be applied to the stateEntered array to find the matching year.

For this demo, the page includes a text entry field in which the user types the name of the state to look up. In a real application, this methodology is fraught with peril unless the script performs some error checking in case the user makes a mistake.

But for now, I assume that the user always types a valid state name. (Don't ever make this assumption in your Web site's pages.) An event handler from either the text field or a clickable button calls a function that looks up the state name, fetches the corresponding entry year, and displays an alert message with the information. The function is as follows.

```
function getStateDate() {
    var selectedState = document.entryForm.entry.value
    for ( var i = 0; i < USStates.length; i++) {
        if (USStates[i] == selectedState) {
            break
        }
    }
    alert("That state entered the Union in " + stateEntered[i] + ".")
}
```

In the first statement of the function, I grab the value of the text box and assign the value to a variable, selectedState. This is mostly for convenience because I can use the shorter variable name later in the script. In fact, the usage of that value is inside a for loop, so the script is marginally more efficient because the browser doesn't have to evaluate that long reference to the text field each time through the loop.

The key to this function is in the for loop. Here is where I combine the natural behavior of incrementing a loop counter with the index values assigned to the two arrays. Specifications for the loop indicate that the counter variable, i, is initialized with a value of zero. The loop is directed to continue as long as the value of i is less than the length of the USStates array. Remember that the length of an array is always one more than the index value of the last item. Therefore, the last time the loop runs is when i is 50, which is both less than the length of 51 and equal to the index value of the last element. Each time after the loop runs, the counter increments by one.

Nested inside the for loop is an if construction. The condition it tests is the value of an element of the array against the value typed in by the user. Each time through the loop, the condition tests a different row of the array starting with row zero. In other words, this if construction can be performed dozens of times before a match is found, but each time the value of i is one larger than the previous try.

The equality comparison operator (==) is very strict when it comes to comparing string values. Such comparisons respect the case of each letter. In our example, the user must type the state name exactly as it is stored in the USStates array for the match to be found. In Chapter 10, you learn about some helper methods that eliminate case and sensitivity in string comparisons.

When a match is found, the statement nested inside the if construction runs. The break statement is designed to help control structures bail out if the program needs it. For this application, it is imperative that the `for` loop stop running when a match for the state name is found. When the `for` loop breaks, the value of the `i` counter is fixed at the row of the `USStates` array containing the entered state. I need that index value to find the corresponding entry in the other array. Even though the counting variable, `i`, is initialized in the `for` loop, it is still "alive" and in the scope of the function for all statements after the initialization. That's why I can use it to extract the value of the row of the `stateEntered` array in the final statement that displays the results in an alert message.

This application of a `for` loop and array indexes is a common one in JavaScript. Study the code carefully and be sure you understand how it works. This way of cycling through arrays plays a role not only in the kinds of arrays you create in your code, but also with the arrays that browsers generate for the document object model.

Document objects in arrays

If you look at the `document` object portions of the Quick Reference in Appendix A, you can see that the properties of some objects are listed with square brackets after them. These are, indeed, the same kind of square brackets you just saw for array indexes. That's because when a document loads, the browser creates arrays of like objects in the document. For example, if your page includes two `<FORM>` tag sets, then two forms appear in the document. The browser maintains an array of form objects for that document. References to those forms are

```
document.forms[0]
document.forms[1]
```

Index values for document objects are assigned according to the loading order of the objects. In the case of form objects, the order is dictated by the order of the `<FORM>` tags in the document. This indexed array syntax is another way to reference forms in an object reference. You can still use a form's name if you prefer — and I heartily recommend using object names wherever possible because even if you change the physical order of the objects in your HTML, references that use names still work without modification. But if your page contains only one form, you can use the reference types interchangeably, as in the following examples of equivalent references to a text field's `value` property in a form:

```
document.entryForm.entry.value
document.forms[0].entry.value
```

In examples throughout this book, you can see that I often use the array type of reference to simple forms in simple documents. But in my production pages, I almost always use named references.

Exercises

1. With your newly acquired knowledge of functions, event handlers, and control structures, use the script fragments from this chapter to complete the page that has the lookup table for all of the states and the years they entered into the Union. If you do not have a reference book for the dates, then use different year numbers starting with 1800 for each entry. In the page, create a text entry field for the state and a button that triggers the lookup in the arrays.

2. Examine the following function definition. Can you spot any problems with the definition? If so, how can you fix the problems?

```
function format(ohmage) {
    var result
    if ohmage >= 1e6 {
        ohmage = ohmage / 1e5
        result = ohmage + " Mohms"
    } else {
        if (ohmage >= 1e3)
            ohmage = ohmage / 1e2
            result = ohmage + " Kohms"
        else
            result = ohmage + " ohms"
    }
    alert(result)
```

3. Devise your own syntax for the scenario of looking for a ripe tomato at the grocery store, and write a `for` loop using that object and property syntax.

4. Modify Listing 7-2 so it does not reuse the `hisDog` variable inside the function.

5. Given the following table of data about several planets of our solar system, create a Web page that enables users to enter a planet name and, at the click of a button, have the distance and diameter appear either in an alert box or (as extra credit) in separate fields of the page.

Planet	Distance from the Sun	Diameter
Mercury	36 million miles	3,100 miles
Venus	67 million miles	7,700 miles
Earth	93 million miles	7,920 miles
Mars	141 million miles	4,200 miles

✦   ✦   ✦

Window and Document Objects

Now that you have exposure to programming fundamentals, it is easier to demonstrate how to script objects in documents. Starting with this lesson, the tutorial turns back to the document object model, diving more deeply into each of the objects you will place in many of your documents.

Document Objects

As a refresher, study the lowest common denominator document object hierarchy in Figure 8-1. This chapter focuses on objects at or near the top of the hierarchy: window, location, history, and document. The goal is not only to equip you with the basics so you can script simple tasks, but also to prepare you for in-depth examinations of each object and its properties, methods, and event handlers in Part III of this book. I introduce only the basic properties, methods, and event handlers for objects in this tutorial — you can find far more in Part III. Examples in that part of the book assume you know the programming fundamentals covered in previous chapters.

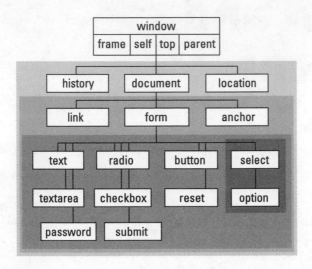

Figure 8-1: The lowest common denominator document object model for all scriptable browsers

The Window Object

At the very top of the document object hierarchy is the window object. This object gains that exalted spot in the object food chain because it is the master container for all content you view in the Web browser. As long as a browser window is open— even if no document is loaded in the window—the window object is defined in the current model in memory.

In addition to the content part of the window where documents go, a window's sphere of influence includes the dimensions of the window and all of the "stuff" that surrounds the content area. The area where scrollbars, toolbars, the status bar, and (non-Macintosh) menu bar live is known as a window's *chrome*. Not every browser has full scripted control over the chrome of the main browser window, but you can easily script the creation of additional windows sized the way you want and have only the chrome elements you wish to display in that subwindow.

Although the discussion about frames comes in Chapter 11, I can safely say now that each frame is also considered a window object. If you think about it, that makes sense because each frame can hold a different document. When a script runs in one of those documents, it regards the frame that holds the document as the window object in its view of the object hierarchy.

As you learn in this chapter, the `window` object is a convenient place for the document object model to attach methods that display modal dialog boxes and adjust the text that displays in the status bar at the bottom of the browser window. A `window` object method enables you to create a separate window that appears on the screen. When you look at all of the properties, methods, and event handlers defined for the `window` object (see Chapter 16), it should be clear why they are attached to window objects — visualize their scope and the scope of a browser window.

Accessing window properties and methods

You can word script references to properties and methods of the `window` object in several ways, depending more on whim and style than on specific syntactical requirements. The most logical and common way to compose such references includes the `window` object in the reference:

```
window.propertyName
window.methodName([parameters])
```

A `window` object also has a synonym when the script doing the referencing points to the window that houses the document. The synonym is `self`. Reference syntax then becomes

```
self.propertyName
self.methodName([parameters])
```

You can use these initial reference object names interchangeably, but I tend to reserve the use of `self` for more complex scripts that involve multiple frames and windows. The `self` moniker more clearly denotes the current window holding the script's document. It makes the script more readable — by me and by others.

Back in Chapter 4, I indicated that because the `window` object is always "there" when a script runs, you could omit it from references to any objects inside that window. Therefore, the following syntax models assume properties and methods of the current window:

```
propertyName
methodName([parameters])
```

In fact, as you will see in a few moments, some methods may be more understandable if you omit the `window` object reference. The methods run just fine either way.

Creating a window

A script does not create the main browser window. A user does that by virtue of launching the browser or by opening a URL or file from the browser's menus (if the window is not already open). But a script can generate any number of subwindows once the main window is open (and that window contains a document whose script needs to open subwindows).

The method that generates a new window is `window.open()`. This method contains up to three parameters that define window characteristics, such as the URL of the document to load, its name for `TARGET` attribute reference purposes in HTML tags, and physical appearance (size and chrome contingent). I don't go into the details of the parameters here (they're covered in great depth in Chapter 16), but I do want to expose you to an important concept involved with the `window.open()` method.

Consider the following statement that opens a new window to a specific size and with an HTML document from the same server directory that holds the current page:

```
var subWindow = window.open("define.html","def","HEIGHT=200,WIDTH=300")
```

The important thing to note about this statement is that it is an assignment statement. Something gets assigned to that variable `subWindow`. What is it? It turns out that when the `window.open()` method runs, it not only opens up that new window according to specifications set as parameters, but it also evaluates to a reference to that new window. In programming parlance, the method is said to *return a value*—in this case, a genuine object reference. The value returned by the method is assigned to the variable.

Your script can now use that variable as a valid reference to the second window. If you need to access one of its properties or methods, you must use that reference as part of the complete reference. For example, to close the subwindow from a script in the main window, use this reference to the `close()` method for that subwindow:

```
subWindow.close()
```

If you issue `window.close()`, `self.close()`, or just `close()` in the main window's script, the method closes the main window and not the subwindow. To address another window, then, you must include a reference to that window as part of the complete reference. This has an impact on your code because you probably want the variable holding the reference to the subwindow to be valid as long as the main document is loaded into the browser. For that to happen, the variable has to be initialized as a global variable, rather than inside a function (although you can set its value inside a function). That way, one function can open the window while another function closes it.

Listing 8-1 is a page that has a button for opening a blank, new window and closing that window from the main window. To view this demonstration, shrink your main browser window to less than full screen. Then when the new window is generated, reposition the windows so you can see the smaller, new window when the main window is in front. (If you "lose" a window behind another, use the browser's

Window menu to choose the hidden window.) The key point of Listing 8-1 is that the newWindow variable is defined as a global variable so that both the makeNewWindow() and closeNewWindow() functions have access to it. When a variable is declared with no value assignment, its value is null. A null value is interpreted to be the same as false in a condition, while the presence of any non-zero value is the same as true in a condition. Therefore, in the closeNewWindow() function, the condition tests whether the window has been created before issuing the subwindow's close() method. Then, to clean up, the function sets the newWindow variable to null so that another click of the Close button doesn't try to close a nonexistent window.

Listing 8-1: **References to Window Objects**

```
<HTML>
<HEAD>
<TITLE>Window Opener and Closer</TITLE>
<SCRIPT LANGUAGE="JavaScript">
var newWindow
function makeNewWindow() {
    newWindow = window.open("","","HEIGHT=300,WIDTH=300")
}
function closeNewWindow() {
    if (newWindow) {
        newWindow.close()
        newWindow = null
    }
}
</SCRIPT>
</HEAD>

<BODY>
<FORM>
<INPUT TYPE="button" VALUE="Create New Window" onClick="makeNewWindow()">
<INPUT TYPE="button" VALUE="Close New Window" onClick="closeNewWindow()">
</FORM>
</BODY>
</HTML>
```

Window Properties and Methods

The one property and three methods for the window object described in this section have an immediate impact on user interaction. They work with all scriptable browsers. You can find extensive code examples in Part III for each property and method. You can also experiment with the one-statement script examples by entering them in the top text box of The Evaluator Jr. (from Chapter 16).

window.status property

The status bar at the bottom of the browser window normally displays the URL of a link when you roll the mouse pointer atop it. Other messages also appear in that space during document loading, Java applet initialization, and the like. However, you can use JavaScript to display your own messages in the status bar at times that may be beneficial to your users. For example, rather than display the URL of a link, you can display a friendlier, plain-language description of the page at the other end of the link (or a combination of both to accommodate both newbies and geeks).

You can assign the `window.status` property some other text at any time. To change the status bar text of a link as the cursor hovers atop the link, you trigger the action with an `onMouseOver` event handler of a link object. A peculiarity of the `onMouseOver` event handler for setting the status bar is that an additional statement — `return true` — must be part of the event handler. This is very rare in JavaScript, but it is required here for your script to successfully override the status bar.

Due to the simplicity of setting the `window.status` property, it is most common for the script statements to run as inline scripts in the event handler definition. This is handy for short scripts because you don't have to specify a separate function or add `<SCRIPT>` tags to your page. You simply add the script statements to the `<A>` tag:

```
<A HREF="http://home.netscape.com" onMouseOver=
"window.status='Visit the Netscape Home page (home.netscape.com)'; return true">
Netscape</A>
```

Look closely at the script statements assigned to the `onMouseOver` event handler. The two statements are

```
window.status='Visit the Netscape Home page (home.netscape.com)'
return true
```

When you run these as inline scripts, you must separate the two statements with a semicolon. (The space after the semicolon is optional, but often improves readability.) Equally important, the entire set of statements is surrounded by double quotes ("..."). To nest the string being assigned to the `window.status` property inside the double-quoted script, you surround the string with single quotes ('...'). You get a big payoff for a little bit of script when you set the status bar. The downside is that scripting this property is how those awful status bar scrolling banners are created. Yech!

window.alert() method

I have already used the `alert()` method many times so far in this tutorial. This window method generates a dialog box that displays whatever text you pass as a parameter (see Figure 8-2). A single OK button (whose label you cannot change) enables the user to dismiss the alert.

Figure 8-2: A JavaScript alert dialog box (old style)

The appearance of this and two other JavaScript dialog boxes (described next) has changed since the first scriptable browsers. In older browser versions (as shown in Figure 8-2), the browser inserted words clearly indicating that the dialog box was a "JavaScript Alert." Different browsers display different title bars whose content cannot be altered by script. You can change only the other message content.

All three dialog box methods are good cases for using a `window` object's methods without the reference to the window. Even though the `alert()` method is technically a `window` object method, no special relationship exists between the dialog box and the window that generates it. In production scripts, I usually use the shortcut reference:

```
alert("This is a JavaScript alert dialog.")
```

window.confirm() method

The second style of dialog box presents two buttons (Cancel and OK in most versions on most platforms) and is called a confirm dialog box (see Figure 8-3). More importantly, this is one of those methods that returns a value: `true` if the user clicks OK, `false` if the user clicks Cancel. You can use this dialog box and its returned value as a way to have a user make a decision about how a script progresses.

Figure 8-3: A JavaScript confirm dialog box (IE5/Win32 style)

Because the method always returns a Boolean value, you can use the evaluated value of the entire method as a condition statement in an `if` or `if...else` construction. For example, in the following code fragment, the user is asked about starting the application over. Doing so causes the default page of the site to load into the browser.

```
if (confirm("Are you sure you want to start over?")) {
    location.href = "index.html"
}
```

window.prompt() method

The final dialog box of the `window` object, the prompt dialog box (see Figure 8-4), displays a message that you set and provides a text field for the user to enter a response. Two buttons, Cancel and OK, enable the user to dismiss the dialog box with two opposite expectations: canceling the entire operation or accepting the input typed into the dialog box.

Figure 8-4: A JavaScript prompt dialog box (IE5/Win32 style)

The `window.prompt()` method has two parameters. The first is the message that acts as a prompt to the user. You can suggest a default answer in the text field by including a string as the second parameter. If you don't want any default answer to appear, then include an empty string (two double quotes without any space between them).

This method returns one value when the user clicks either button. A click of the Cancel button returns a value of `null`, regardless of what the user types into the field. A click of the OK button returns a string value of the typed entry. Your scripts can use this information in conditions for `if` and `if...else` constructions. A value of `null` is treated as `false` in a condition. It turns out that an empty string is also treated as `false`. Therefore, a condition can easily test for the presence of real characters typed into the field to simplify a condition test, as shown in the following fragment:

```
var answer = prompt("What is your name?","")
if (answer) {
    alert("Hello, " + answer + "!")
}
```

The only time the `alert()` method is called is when the user enters something into the prompt dialog box and clicks the OK button.

onLoad event handler

The `window` object reacts to several system and user events, but the one you will probably use most often is the event that fires as soon as everything in a page finishes loading. This event waits for images, Java applets, and data files for plug-ins to download fully to the browser. It can be dangerous to script access to elements of a document object while the page loads because if the object has not loaded yet (perhaps due to a slow network connection or server), a script error results. The advantage of using the onLoad event to invoke functions is that you are assured that all document objects are in the browser's document object model. All window event handlers are placed inside the <BODY> tag. Even though you will come to associate the <BODY> tag's attributes with the document object's properties, it is the window object's event handlers that go inside the tag.

The Location Object

Sometimes an object in the hierarchy represents something that doesn't seem to have the kind of physical presence that a window or a button does. That's the case with the location object. This object represents the URL loaded into the window. This differs from the document object (discussed later in this lesson) because the document is the real content; the location is simply the URL.

Unless you are truly Web-savvy, you may not realize a URL consists of many components that define the address and method of data transfer for a file. Pieces of a URL include the protocol (such as http:) and the hostname (such as www.giantco.com). You can access all of these items as properties of the location object. For the most part, though, your scripts will be interested in only one property: the href property, which defines the complete URL.

Setting the location.href property is the primary way your scripts navigate to other pages:

```
location.href = "http://www.dannyg.com"
```

You can generally navigate to a page in your own Web site by specifying a relative URL (that is, relative to the currently loaded page) rather than the complete URL with protocol and host information. For pages outside of the domain of the current page, you need to specify the complete URL.

If the page to be loaded is in another window or frame, the window reference must be part of the statement. For example, if your script opens a new window and assigns its reference to a variable named newWindow, the statement that loads a page into the subwindow is

```
newWindow.location.href = "http://www.dannyg.com"
```

The History Object

Another object that doesn't have a physical presence on the page is the history object. Each window maintains a list of recent pages that the browser has visited. While the history object's list contains the URLs of recently visited pages, those

URLs are not generally accessible by script due to privacy and security limits imposed by browsers. But methods of the `history` object allow for navigating backward and forward through the history relative to the currently loaded page. You can find details in Chapter 17.

The Document Object

The `document` object holds the real content of the page. Properties and methods of the `document` object generally affect the look and content of the document that occupies the window. Only more recent browsers (IE4+ and NN6+) allow script access to the text contents of a page once the document has loaded. However, as you saw in your first script of Chapter 3, the `document.write()` method lets a script dynamically create content as the page loads. A great many of the `document` object's properties are established by attributes of the `<BODY>` tag. Many other properties are arrays of other objects in the document.

Accessing a `document` object's properties and methods is straightforward, as shown in the following syntax examples:

```
[window.]document.propertyName
[window.]document.methodName([parameters])
```

The `window` reference is optional when the script is accessing the `document` object that contains the script. If you want a preview of the `document` object properties of the browser you're using, enter `document` into the bottom text box of The Evaluator Jr. and press Enter/Return. The object's properties and current values appear in the Results box.

document.forms[] property

One of the object types contained by a document is the FORM element object. Because conceivably there can be more than one form in a document, forms are stored as arrays in the `document.forms[]` property. As you recall from the discussion of arrays in Chapter 7, an index number inside the square brackets points to one of the elements in the array. To find out how many FORM objects are in the current document, use

```
document.forms.length
```

To access the first form in a document, for example, the reference is

```
document.forms[0]
```

In general, however, I recommend that you access a form by way of a name you assign to the form in its NAME attribute, as in

```
document.formName
```

Either methodology reaches the same object. When a script needs to reference elements inside a form, the complete address to that object must include document and form references.

document.title property

Not every property of a document object is set in a <BODY> tag attribute. If you assign a title to the page in the <TITLE> tag set within the Head portion, that title text is reflected by the document.title property. A document's title is mostly a cosmetic setting that gives a plain-language name of the page appearing in the browser's title bar, as well as the user's history listing and bookmark of your page.

document.write() method

The document.write() method operates in both immediate scripts to create content in a page as it loads and in deferred scripts that create new content in the same or different window. The method requires one string parameter, which is the HTML content to write to the window or frame. Such string parameters can be variables or any other expressions that evaluate to a string. Very often, the written content includes HTML tags.

Bear in mind that after a page loads, the browser's *output stream* is automatically closed. After that, any document.write() method issued to the current page opens a new stream that immediately erases the current page (along with any variables or other values in the original document). Therefore, if you wish to replace the current page with script-generated HTML, you need to accumulate that HTML in a variable and perform the writing with just one document.write() method. You don't have to explicitly clear a document and open a new data stream; one document.write() call does it all.

One last piece of housekeeping advice about the document.write() method involves its companion method, document.close(). Your script must close the output stream when it finishes writing its content to the window (either the same window or another). After the last document.write() method in a deferred script, be sure to include a document.close() method. Failure to do this may cause images and forms not to appear. Also, any document.write() method invoked later will only append to the page, rather than clear the existing content to write anew. To demonstrate the document.write() method, I show two versions of the same application. One writes to the same document that contains the script; the other writes to a separate window. Type in each document in a new text editor document, save it with an .html file name extension, and open it in your browser.

Listing 8-2 creates a button that assembles new HTML content for a document, including HTML tags for a new document title and color attribute for the <BODY> tag. An operator in the listing that may be unfamiliar to you is +=. It appends a string on its right side to whatever string is stored in the variable on its left side.

This operator is a convenient way to accumulate a long string across several separate statements. With the content gathered in the `newContent` variable, one `document.write()` statement blasts the entire new content to the same document, obliterating all vestiges of the content of Listing 8-2. The `document.close()` statement, however, is required to close the output stream properly. When you load this document and click the button, notice that the document title in the browser's title bar changes accordingly. As you click back to the original and try the button again, notice that the dynamically written second page loads much faster than even a reload of the original document.

Listing 8-2: **Using document.write() on the Current Window**

```
<HTML>
<HEAD>
<TITLE>Writing to Same Doc</TITLE>
<SCRIPT LANGUAGE="JavaScript">
function reWrite() {
    // assemble content for new window
    var newContent = "<HTML><HEAD><TITLE>A New Doc</TITLE></HEAD>"
    newContent += "<BODY BGCOLOR='aqua'><H1>This document is brand new.</H1>"
    newContent += "Click the Back button to see original document."
    newContent += "</BODY></HTML>"
    // write HTML to new window document
    document.write(newContent)
    document.close() // close layout stream
}
</SCRIPT>
</HEAD>
<BODY>
<FORM>
<INPUT TYPE="button" VALUE="Replace Content" onClick="reWrite()">
</FORM>
</BODY>
</HTML>
```

In Listing 8-3, the situation is a bit more complex because the script generates a subwindow to which is written an entirely script-generated document. To keep the reference to the new window alive across both functions, the `newWindow` variable is declared as a global variable. As soon as the page loads, the `onLoad` event handler invokes the `makeNewWindow()` function. This function generates a blank subwindow. I added a property to the third parameter of the `window.open()` method that instructs the status bar of the subwindow to appear.

A button in the page invokes the `subWrite()` method. The first task it performs is to check the `closed` property of the subwindow. This property (which exists only in newer browser versions) returns `true` if the referenced window is closed. If that's the case (if the user manually closed the window), the function invokes the `makeNewWindow()` function again to reopen that window.

With the window open, new content is assembled as a string variable. As with Listing 8-2, the content is written in one blast (although that isn't necessary for a separate window), followed by a `close()` method. But notice an important difference: both the `write()` and `close()` methods explicitly specify the subwindow.

Listing 8-3: **Using document.write() on Another Window**

```
<HTML>
<HEAD>
<TITLE>Writing to Subwindow</TITLE>
<SCRIPT LANGUAGE="JavaScript">
var newWindow
function makeNewWindow() {
    newWindow = window.open("","","status,height=200,width=300")
}

function subWrite() {
    // make new window if someone has closed it
    if (newWindow.closed) {
        makeNewWindow()
    }
    // bring subwindow to front
    newWindow.focus()
    // assemble content for new window
    var newContent = "<HTML><HEAD><TITLE>A New Doc</TITLE></HEAD>"
    newContent += "<BODY BGCOLOR='coral'><H1>This document is brand new.</H1>"
    newContent += "</BODY></HTML>"
    // write HTML to new window document
    newWindow.document.write(newContent)
    newWindow.document.close() // close layout stream
}
</SCRIPT>
</HEAD>
<BODY onLoad="makeNewWindow()">
<FORM>
<INPUT TYPE="button" VALUE="Write to Subwindow" onClick="subWrite()">
</FORM>
</BODY>
</HTML>
```

The Link Object

Belonging to the `document` object in the hierarchy is the link object. A link object is the object model equivalent of an `<A>` tag when the tag includes an `HREF` attribute. A document can have any number of links, so references to links (if necessary) are usually made via the array index method:

```
document.links[n].propertyName
```

More commonly, though, links are not scripted. However, there is an important JavaScript component to these objects. When you want to click a link to execute a script rather than navigate directly to another URL, you can redirect the `HREF` attribute to call a script function. The technique involves a pseudo-URL called the `javascript:` URL. If you place the name of a function after the `javascript:` URL, then a scriptable browser runs that function. So as not to mess with the minds of users, the function should probably perform some navigation in the end. However, the script can do other things as well, such as simultaneously changing the content of two frames within a frameset.

The syntax for this construction in a link is as follows:

```
<A HREF="javascript:void functionName([parameter1]...[parameterN])">...</A>
```

The `void` keyword prevents the link from trying to display any value that the function may return. Remember this `javascript:` URL technique for all tags that include `HREF` and `SRC` attributes: If an attribute accepts a URL, it can accept this `javascript:` URL as well. This can come in handy as a way to script actions for client-side image maps that don't necessarily navigate anywhere, but which cause something to happen on the page just the same.

The next logical step past the document level in the object hierarchy is the form. That's where you will spend the next lesson.

Exercises

1. Which of the following references are valid and which are not? Explain what is wrong with the invalid references.

   a. `window.document.form[0]`

   b. `self.entryForm.entryField.value`

   c. `document.forms[2].name`

   d. `entryForm.entryField.value`

   e. `newWindow.document.write("Howdy")`

2. Write the JavaScript statement that displays a message in the status bar welcoming visitors to your Web page.

3. Write the JavaScript statement that displays the same message to the document as an <H1>-level headline on the page.

4. Create a page that prompts the user for his or her name as the page loads (via a dialog box) and then welcomes the user by name in the body of the page.

5. Create a page with any content you like, but one that automatically displays a dialog box after the page loads to show the user the URL of the current page.

✦   ✦   ✦

Forms and Form Elements

Most interactivity between a Web page and the user takes place inside a form. That's where a lot of the interactive HTML stuff lives for every browser: text fields, buttons, checkboxes, option lists, and so on. As you can tell from the (by now) familiar basic object hierarchy diagram (refer back to Figure 8-1), a form is always contained by a document. Even so, the document object must be part of the reference to the form and its elements.

The FORM Object

A FORM object can be referenced either by its position in the array of forms contained by a document or by name (if you assign an identifier to the NAME attribute inside the <FORM> tag). If only one form appears in the document, it is still a member of an array (a one-element array) and is referenced as follows:

```
document.forms[0]
```

Notice that the array reference uses the plural version of the word, followed by a set of square brackets containing the index number of the element (zero is always first). But if you assign a name to the form, simply plug the form's name into the reference:

```
document.formName
```

Form as object and container

In the simplified, compatible object model of this tutorial, a form has a relatively small set of properties, methods, and event handlers. Almost all of the properties are the same as the attributes for forms. All scriptable versions of Navigator, and most versions of Internet Explorer, allow scripts to change these properties under script control, which gives your scripts potentially significant power to direct the behavior of a form submission in response to user selections on the page.

A form is contained by a document, and the form in turn contains any number of elements (sometimes called *form controls*). All of those interactive elements that enable users to enter information or make selections belong to the form object. This relationship mirrors the HTML tag organization in which items such as <INPUT> tags are nested between the <FORM> and </FORM> tag "bookends."

Accessing form properties

Forms are created entirely from standard HTML tags in the page. You can set attributes for NAME, TARGET, ACTION, METHOD, and ENCTYPE. Each of these is a property of a FORM object, accessed by all lowercase versions of those words, as in

```
document.forms[0].action
document.formName.action
```

To change any of these properties, simply assign new values to them:

```
document.forms[0].action = "http://www.giantco.com/cgi/login.pl"
```

form.elements[ ] property

In addition to keeping track of each type of element inside a form, the browser also maintains a list of all control elements within a form. This list is another array, with items listed according to the order in which their HTML tags appear in the source code. It is generally more efficient to create references to elements directly, using their names. However, sometimes a script needs to look through all of the elements in a form. This is especially true if the content of a form changes with each loading of the page because the number of text fields changes based on the user's browser type. (For example, a script on the page uses document.write() to add an extra text box for information required only from Windows users.)

The following code fragment shows the form.elements[] property at work in a for repeat loop that looks at every element in a form to set the contents of text fields to an empty string. The script cannot simply barge through the form and set every element's content to an empty string because some elements may be buttons, which don't have a value property that you can set to an empty string.

```
var form = window.document.forms[0]
for (var i = 0; i < form.elements.length; i++) {
    if (form.elements[i].type == "text") {
        form.elements[i].value = ""
    }
}
```

In the first statement, I create a variable—form—that holds a reference to the first form of the document. I do this so that when I make many references to form elements later in the script, the typical length of each reference is much shorter (and marginally faster). I can use the form variable as a shortcut to building references to items more deeply nested in the form.

Next, I start looping through the items in the elements array for the form. Each form element has a type property, which reveals what kind of form element it is: text, button, radio, checkbox, and so on. I'm interested in finding elements whose type is text. For each of those, I set the value property to an empty string.

I return to forms later in this chapter to show you how to submit a form without a Submit button and how client-side form validation works.

Form Controls as Objects

Three kinds of HTML elements nested inside a <FORM> tag become scriptable objects in all browser document object models. Most of the objects owe their existence to the <INPUT> tag in the page's source code. Only the value assigned to the TYPE attribute of an <INPUT> tag determines whether the element is a text box, password entry field, hidden field, button, checkbox, or radio button. The other two kinds of form controls, TEXTAREA and SELECT, have their own tags.

While form controls have several properties in common, some properties are unique to a particular control type or related types. For example, only a SELECT object offers a property that reveals which item in its list is currently selected. But checkbox and radio buttons both have a property that indicates whether the control is currently set to "on." Similarly, all text-oriented controls operate the same way for reading and modifying their content.

Having a good grasp of the scriptable features of form control objects is important to your success with JavaScript. In the next sections, you meet the most important form control objects and see how scripts interact with them.

Text-related objects

Each of the four text-related HTML form elements—text, password, hidden, and TEXTAREA—is an element in the document object hierarchy. All but the hidden object display themselves in the page, enabling users to enter information. These objects also display text information that changes in the course of using a page (although Dynamic HTML in IE4+ and NN6+ also allows the scripted change of body text in a document).

Text Object Behavior

Many scripters look to JavaScript to solve what are perceived as shortcomings or behavioral anomalies with text-related objects in forms. I want to single these out early in your scripting experience so that they do not confuse you later.

First, only the most recent browsers let scripts reliably alter the font, font size, font style, and text alignment of a text object's content. You can access changes through the element's style-related properties (Chapter 30).

Second, most browser forms practice a behavior that was recommended long ago as an informal standard by Web pioneers. When a form contains only one text INPUT object, a press of the Enter/Return key while the text object has focus automatically submits the form. For two or more fields in browsers other than IE5/Mac, you need another way to submit the form (for example, a Submit button). This one-field submission scheme works well in many cases, such as the search page of most Web search sites. But if you are experimenting with simple forms containing only one field, you can submit the form with a press of the Enter/Return key. Submitting a form that has no other action or target specified means the page performs an unconditional reload — wiping out any information entered into the form. You can, however, cancel the submission through an onSubmit event handler in the form, as shown later in this chapter. Also, starting with version 4 browsers, you can script the press of the Enter/Return key in any text field to submit a form (see Chapter 29).

To make these objects scriptable in a page, you do nothing special to their normal HTML tags — with the possible exception of assigning a NAME attribute. I strongly recommend assigning unique names to every form control element if your scripts will be getting or setting properties or invoking their methods. Besides, if the form is actually submitted to a server program, the NAME attributes must be assigned in order for the server to process the element's data.

For the visible objects in this category, event handlers are triggered from many user actions, such as giving a field focus (getting the text insertion pointer in the field) and changing text (entering new text and leaving the field). Most of your text field actions are triggered by the change of text (the onChange event handler). In IE and NN version 4 browsers and later, event handlers fire in response to individual keystrokes as well.

Without a doubt, the single most used property of a text-related element is the value property. This property represents the current contents of the text element. A script can retrieve and set its content at any time. Content of the value property is always a string. This may require conversion to numbers (see Chapter 6) if text fields are used to enter values for some math operations.

To demonstrate how a text field's value property can be read and written, Listing 9-1 provides a complete HTML page with a single-entry field. Its onChange event handler invokes the upperMe() function, which converts the text to uppercase. In the upperMe() function, the first statement assigns the text object reference to a more convenient variable: `field`. A lot goes on in the second statement of the function. The right side of the assignment statement performs a couple of key tasks. The reference to the `value` property of the object (`field.value`) evaluates to whatever content is in the text field at that instant. That string is then handed over to one of JavaScript's string functions, `toUpperCase()`, which converts the value to uppercase. The evaluated result of the right side statement is then assigned to the second variable: `upperCaseVersion`. Nothing has changed yet in the text box. That comes in the third statement where the `value` property of the text box is assigned whatever the `upperCaseVersion` variable holds. The need for the second statement is more for learning purposes, so you can see the process more slowly. In practice, you can combine the actions of steps two and three into one power-packed statement:

```
field.value = field.value.toUpperCase()
```

Listing 9-1: **Getting and Setting a Text Object's value Property**

```
<HTML>
<HEAD>
<TITLE>Text Object value Property</TITLE>
<SCRIPT LANGUAGE="JavaScript">
function upperMe() {
    var field = document.forms[0].converter
    var upperCaseVersion = field.value.toUpperCase()
    field.value = upperCaseVersion
}
</SCRIPT>
</HEAD>
<BODY>
<FORM onSubmit="return false">
<INPUT TYPE="text" NAME="converter" VALUE="sample" onChange="upperMe()">
</FORM>
</BODY>
</HTML>
```

Later in this chapter, I show you how to reduce even further the need for explicit references in functions such as `upperMe()` in Listing 9-1. In the meantime, notice for a moment the `onSubmit` event handler in the `<FORM>` tag. I delve more deeply into this event handler later in this chapter, but I want to point out the construction that prevents a single-field form from being submitted when you press the Enter key.

The Button Object

I have used the button INPUT element in many examples up to this point in the tutorial. The button is one of the simplest objects to script. In the simplified object model of this tutorial, the button object has only a few properties that are rarely accessed or modified in day-to-day scripts. Like the text object, the visual aspects of the button are governed not by HTML or scripts, but by the operating system and browser that the page visitor uses. By far, the most useful event handler of the button object is the onClick event handler. It fires whenever the user clicks the button. Simple enough. No magic here.

The Checkbox Object

A checkbox is also a simple element of the FORM object, but some of the properties may not be intuitive entirely. Unlike the value property of a plain button object (the text of the button label), the value property of a checkbox is any other text you want associated with the object. This text does not appear on the page in any fashion, but the property (initially set via the VALUE tag attribute) might be important to a script that wants to know more about the purpose of the checkbox within the form.

The key property of a checkbox object is whether or not the box is checked. The checked property is a Boolean value: true if the box is checked, false if not. When you see that a property is a Boolean value, it's a clue that the value might be usable in an if or if...else condition expression. In Listing 9-2, the value of the checked property determines which alert box the user sees.

Listing 9-2: **The Checkbox Object's checked Property**

```
<HTML>
<HEAD>
<TITLE>Checkbox Inspector</TITLE>
<SCRIPT LANGUAGE="JavaScript">
function inspectBox() {
    if (document.forms[0].checkThis.checked) {
        alert("The box is checked.")
    } else {
        alert("The box is not checked at the moment.")
    }
}
</SCRIPT>
</HEAD>
<BODY>
<FORM>
<INPUT TYPE="checkbox" NAME="checkThis">Check here<BR>
<INPUT TYPE="button" VALUE="Inspect Box" onClick="inspectBox()">
</FORM>
</BODY>
</HTML>
```

Checkboxes are generally used as preferences setters, rather than as action inducers. While a checkbox object has an `onClick` event handler, a click of a checkbox should never do anything drastic, such as navigate to another page.

The Radio Object

Setting up a group of radio objects for scripting requires a bit more work. To let the browser manage the highlighting and unhighlighting of a related group of buttons, you must assign the same name to each of the buttons in the group. You can have multiple groups within a form, but each member of the same group must have the same name.

Assigning the same name to a form element forces the browser to manage the elements differently than if they each had a unique name. Instead, the browser maintains an array list of objects with the same name. The name assigned to the group becomes the name of the array. Some properties apply to the group as a whole; other properties apply to individual buttons within the group and must be addressed via array index references. For example, you can find out how many buttons are in a group by reading the `length` property of the group:

```
document.forms[0].groupName.length
```

If you want to find out if a particular button is currently highlighted — via the same checked property used for the checkbox — you must access the button element individually:

```
document.forms[0].groupName[0].checked
```

Listing 9-3 demonstrates several aspects of the radio button object, including how to look through a group of buttons to find out which one is checked and how to use the `VALUE` attribute and corresponding property for meaningful work.

The page includes three radio buttons and a plain button. Each radio button's `VALUE` attribute contains the full name of one of the Three Stooges. When the user clicks the button, the `onClick` event handler invokes the `fullName()` function. In that function, the first statement creates a shortcut reference to the form. Next, a `for` repeat loop looks through all of the buttons in the `stooges` radio button group. An `if` construction looks at the checked property of each button. When a button is highlighted, the `break` statement bails out of the `for` loop, leaving the value of the `i` loop counter at the number where the loop broke ranks. The alert dialog box then uses a reference to the value property of the `i`th button so that the full name can be displayed in the alert.

Listing 9-3: **Scripting a Group of Radio Objects**

```
<HTML>
<HEAD>
<TITLE>Extracting Highlighted Radio Button</TITLE>
<SCRIPT LANGUAGE="JavaScript">
function fullName() {
    var form = document.forms[0]
    for (var i = 0; i < form.stooges.length; i++) {
        if (form.stooges[i].checked) {
            break
        }
    }
    alert("You chose " + form.stooges[i].value + ".")
}
</SCRIPT>
</HEAD>

<BODY>
<FORM>
<B>Select your favorite Stooge:</B>
<INPUT TYPE="radio" NAME="stooges" VALUE="Moe Howard" CHECKED>Moe
<INPUT TYPE="radio" NAME="stooges" VALUE="Larry Fine" >Larry
<INPUT TYPE="radio" NAME="stooges" VALUE="Curly Howard" >Curly<BR>
<INPUT TYPE="button" NAME="Viewer" VALUE="View Full Name..."
onClick="fullName()">
</FORM>
</BODY>
</HTML>
```

As you learn about form elements in later chapters of this book, the browser's tendency to create arrays out of identically named objects of the same type (except for Internet Explorer 3) can be a benefit to scripts that work with, say, columns of fields in an HTML order form.

The SELECT Object

The most complex form element to script is the SELECT element object. As you can see from the lowest common denominator object hierarchy diagram (Figures 4-6 or 8-1), the SELECT object is really a compound object: an object that contains an array of OPTION objects. Moreover, you can establish this object in HTML to display itself as either a pop-up list or a scrolling list — the latter configurable to accept multiple selections by users. For the sake of simplicity at this stage, this lesson focuses on deployment as a pop-up list that allows only single selections.

Some properties belong to the entire SELECT object; others belong to individual options inside the SELECT object. If your goal is to determine which item the user selects, you must use properties of both the SELECT and OPTION objects.

The most important property of the SELECT object itself is the `selectedIndex` property, accessed as follows:

```
document.form[0].selectName.selectedIndex
```

This value is the index number of the currently selected item. As with most index counting schemes in JavaScript, the first item (the one at the top of the list) has an index of zero. The `selectedIndex` value is critical for enabling you to access properties of the selected option. Two important properties of an option item are `text` and `value`, accessed as follows:

```
document.forms[0].selectName.options[n].text
document.forms[0].selectName.options[n].value
```

The `text` property is the string that appears onscreen in the SELECT object. It is unusual for this information to be exposed as a FORM object property because in the HTML that generates a SELECT object, the text is defined outside of the `<OPTION>` tag. But inside the `<OPTION>` tag, you can set a `VALUE` attribute, which, like the radio buttons shown earlier, enables you to associate some hidden string information with each visible entry in the list.

To read the `value` or `text` property of a selected option most efficiently, you can use the SELECT object's `selectedIndex` property as an index value to the option. References for this kind of operation get pretty long, so take the time to understand what's happening here. In the following function, the first statement creates a short-cut reference to the SELECT object. The `selectedIndex` property of the SELECT object is then substituted for the `index` value of the `options` array of that same object:

```
function inspect() {
    var list = document.forms[0].choices
    var chosenItemText = list.options[list.selectedIndex].text
}
```

To bring a SELECT object to life, use the `onChange` event handler. As soon as a user makes a new selection in the list, this event handler runs the script associated with that event handler (except for Windows versions of Navigator 2, whose `onChange` event handler doesn't work for SELECT objects). Listing 9-4 shows a common application for a SELECT object. Its text entries describe places to go in and out of a Web site, while the `VALUE` attributes hold the URLs for those locations. When a user makes a selection in the list, the `onChange` event handler triggers a script that extracts the `value` property of the selected option and assigns that value to the `location` object to effect the navigation. Under JavaScript control, this kind of navigation doesn't need a separate Go button on the page.

Listing 9-4: **Navigating with a SELECT Object**

```
<HTML>
<HEAD>
<TITLE>Select Navigation</TITLE>
<SCRIPT LANGUAGE="JavaScript">
function goThere() {
    var list = document.forms[0].urlList
    location = list.options[list.selectedIndex].value
}
</SCRIPT>
</HEAD>

<BODY>
<FORM>
Choose a place to go:
<SELECT NAME="urlList" onChange="goThere()">
    <OPTION SELECTED VALUE="index.html">Home Page
    <OPTION VALUE="store.html">Shop Our Store
    <OPTION VALUE="policies.html">Shipping Policies
    <OPTION VALUE="http://www.yahoo.com">Search the Web
</SELECT>
</FORM>
</BODY>
</HTML>
```

Note   Internet Explorer and NN6 expose the `value` property of the selected option item as the `value` property of the SELECT object. While this is certainly a logical and convenient shortcut, for compatibility reasons you should use the long way shown in Listing 9-4.

There is much more to the SELECT object, including the ability to change the contents of a list in newer browsers. Chapter 26 covers the object in depth.

Passing Form Data and Elements to Functions

In all of the examples so far in this lesson, when an event handler invokes a function that works with form elements, the form or form element is explicitly referenced in the function. But valuable shortcuts do exist for transferring information about the form or form control directly to the function without dealing with those typically long references that start with the `window` or `document` object level.

JavaScript features a keyword — this — that always refers to whatever object contains the script in which the keyword is used. Thus, in an onChange event handler for a text field, you can pass a reference to the text object to the function by inserting the this keyword as a parameter to the function:

```
<INPUT TYPE="text" NAME="entry" onChange="upperMe(this)">
```

At the receiving end, the function defines a parameter variable that turns that reference into a variable that the rest of the function can use:

```
function upperMe(field) {
    statement[s]
}
```

The name you assign to the function's parameter variable is purely arbitrary, but it is helpful to give it a name that expresses what the reference is. Importantly, this reference is a "live" connection back to the object. Therefore, statements in the script can get and set property values of the object at will.

For other functions, you may wish to receive a reference to the entire form, rather than just the object calling the function. This is certainly true if the function needs to access other elements of the same form. To pass the entire form, you reference the form property of the INPUT object, still using the this keyword:

```
<INPUT TYPE="button" VALUE="Click Here" onClick="inspect(this.form)">
```

The function definition should then have a parameter variable ready to be assigned to the form object reference. Again, you decide the name of the variable. I tend to use the variable name form as a way to remind me exactly what kind of object is referenced.

```
function inspect(form) {
    statement[s]
}
```

Listing 9-5 demonstrates passing both an individual form element and the entire form in the performance of two separate acts. This page makes believe it is connected to a database of Beatles songs. When you click the Process Data button, it passes the form object, which the processData() function uses to access the group of radio buttons inside a for loop. Additional references using the passed form object extract the value properties of the selected radio button and the text field.

The text field has its own event handler, which passes just the text field to the verifySong() function. Notice how short the reference is to reach the value property of the song field inside the function.

Listing 9-5: Passing a Form Object and Form Element to Functions

```
<HTML>
<HEAD>
<TITLE>Beatle Picker</TITLE>
<SCRIPT LANGUAGE="JavaScript">
function processData(form) {
    for (var i = 0; i < form.Beatles.length; i++) {
        if (form.Beatles[i].checked) {
            break
        }
    }
    // assign values to variables for convenience
    var beatle = form.Beatles[i].value
    var song = form.song.value
    alert("Checking whether " + song + " features " + beatle + "...")
}

function verifySong(entry) {
    var song = entry.value
    alert("Checking whether " + song + " is a Beatles tune...")
}
</SCRIPT>
</HEAD>

<BODY>
<FORM onSubmit="return false">
Choose your favorite Beatle:
<INPUT TYPE="radio" NAME="Beatles" VALUE="John Lennon" CHECKED>John
<INPUT TYPE="radio" NAME="Beatles" VALUE="Paul McCartney">Paul
<INPUT TYPE="radio" NAME="Beatles" VALUE="George Harrison">George
<INPUT TYPE="radio" NAME="Beatles" VALUE="Ringo Starr">Ringo<P>

Enter the name of your favorite Beatles song:<BR>
<INPUT TYPE="text" NAME="song" VALUE = "Eleanor Rigby"
onChange="verifySong(this)"><P>
<INPUT TYPE="button" NAME="process" VALUE="Process Request..."
onClick="processData(this.form)">
</FORM>
</BODY>
</HTML>
```

Get to know the usage of the `this` keyword in passing `form` and `form element` objects to functions. The technique not only saves you typing in your code, but it also ensures accuracy in references to those objects.

Submitting and Prevalidating Forms

If you have worked with Web pages and forms before, you are familiar with how simple it is to add a Submit-style button that sends the form to your server. However, design goals for your page may rule out the use of ugly system-generated buttons. If you'd rather display a pretty image, the link tag surrounding that image should use the `javascript:` URL technique to invoke a script that submits the form (the image type of `INPUT` element is not recognized prior to IE4 and NN6).

The scripted equivalent of submitting a form is the FORM object's `submit()` method. All you need in the statement is a reference to the form and this method:

```
document.forms[0].submit()
```

One limitation might inhibit your plans to secretly have a script send you an e-mail message from every visitor who comes to your Web site. If the form's `ACTION` attribute is set to a `mailTo:` URL, JavaScript does not pass along the `submit()` method to the form. See Chapter 23 for cautions about using the `mailTo:` URL as a form's action.

Before a form is submitted, you may wish to perform some last-second validation of data in the form or in other scripting (for example, changing the form's `action` property based on user choices). You can do this in a function invoked by the form's `onSubmit` event handler. Specific validation routines are beyond the scope of this tutorial (but are explained in substantial detail in Chapter 43), but I want to show you how the `onSubmit` event handler works.

In all but the first generation of scriptable browsers from Microsoft (IE3) and Netscape (NN2), you can let the results of a validation function cancel a submission if the validation shows some incorrect data or empty fields. To control submission, the `onSubmit` event handler must evaluate to `return true` (to allow submission to continue) or `returnfalse` (to cancel submission). This is a bit tricky at first because it involves more than just having the function called by the event handler return `true` or `false`. The `return` keyword must be part of the final evaluation.

Listing 9-6 shows a page with a simple validation routine that ensures all fields have something in them before allowing submission to continue. (The form has no `ACTION` attribute, so this sample form doesn't get sent to the server.) Notice how the `onSubmit` event handler (which passes a reference to the FORM object as a parameter — in this case the `this` keyword points to the FORM object because its tag holds the event handler) includes the `return` keyword before the function name. When the function returns its `true` or `false` value, the event handler evaluates to the requisite `return true` or `return false`.

Listing 9-6: Last-Minute Checking Before Form Submission

```
<HTML>
<HEAD>
<TITLE>Validator</TITLE>
<SCRIPT LANGUAGE="JavaScript">
function checkForm(form) {
    for (var i = 0; i < form.elements.length; i++) {
        if (form.elements[i].value == "") {
        alert("Fill out ALL fields.")
        return false
        }
        }
    return true
}
</SCRIPT>
</HEAD>

<BODY>
<FORM onSubmit="return checkForm(this)">
Please enter all requested information:<BR>
First Name:<INPUT TYPE="text" NAME="firstName"><BR>
Last Name:<INPUT TYPE="text" NAME="lastName"><BR>
Rank:<INPUT TYPE="text" NAME="rank"><BR>
Serial Number:<INPUT TYPE="text" NAME="serialNumber"><BR>

<INPUT TYPE="submit">
</FORM>
</BODY>
</HTML>
```

One quirky bit of behavior involving the submit() method and onSubmit event handler needs explanation. While you might think (and logically so, in my opinion) that the submit() method would be the exact scripted equivalent of a click of a real Submit button, it's not. In Navigator, the submit() method does not cause the form's onSubmit event handler to fire at all. If you want to perform validation on a form submitted via the submit() method, invoke the validation in the script function that ultimately calls the submit() method.

So much for the basics of forms and form elements. In the next chapter, you step away from HTML for a moment to look at more advanced JavaScript core language items: strings, math, and dates.

Exercises

1. Rework Listings 9-1, 9-2, 9-3, and 9-4 so that the script functions all receive the most efficient form or form element references from the invoking event handler.

2. Modify Listing 9-6 so that instead of the Submit button making the submission, the submission is performed from a hyperlink. Be sure to include the form validation in the process.

3. In the following HTML tag, what kind of information do you think is being passed with the event handler? Write a function that displays in an alert dialog box the information being passed.

   ```
   <INPUT TYPE="text"NAME="phone" onChange="format(this.value)">
   ```

4. A document contains two forms named `specifications` and `accessories`. In the `accessories` form is a field named `acc1`. Write two different statements that set the contents of that field to `Leather Carrying Case`.

5. Create a page that includes a SELECT object to change the background color of the current page. The property that you need to set is `document.bgColor`, and the three values you should offer as options are `red`, `yellow`, and `green`. In the SELECT object, the colors should display as `Stop`, `Caution`, and `Go`. Note: If you use a Macintosh or UNIX version of Navigator, you must employ version 4 or later for this exercise.

✦   ✦   ✦

Strings, Math, and Dates

For most of the lessons in the tutorial so far, the objects at the center of attention belong to the document object model. But as indicated in Chapter 2, a clear dividing line exists between the document object model and the JavaScript language. The language has some of its own objects that are independent of the document object model. These objects are defined such that if a vendor wished to implement JavaScript as the programming language for an entirely different kind of product, the language would still use these core facilities for handling text, advanced math (beyond simple arithmetic), and dates. You can find formal specifications of these objects in the ECMA-262 recommendation.

Core Language Objects

It is often difficult for newcomers to programming — or even experienced programmers who have not worked in object-oriented worlds before — to think about objects, especially when attributed to "things" that don't seem to have a physical presence. For example, it doesn't require lengthy study to grasp the notion that a button on a page is an object. It has several physical properties that make perfect sense. But what about a string of characters? As you learn in this chapter, in an object-based environment such as JavaScript, everything that moves is treated as an object — each piece of data from a Boolean value to a date. Each such object probably has one or more properties that help define the content; such an object may also have methods associated with it to define what the object can do or what you can do to the object.

I call all objects that are not part of the document object model *core language objects*. You can see the full complement of them in the Quick Reference in Appendix A. In this chapter, I focus on the String, Math, and Date objects.

String Objects

You have already used `String` objects many times in earlier lessons. A *string* is any text inside a quote pair. A quote pair consists of either double quotes or single quotes. This allows one string to nest inside another, as often happens in event handlers. In the following example, the `alert()` method requires a quoted string as a parameter, but the entire method call also must be inside quotes.

```
onClick="alert('Hello, all')"
```

JavaScript imposes no practical limit on the number of characters that a string can hold. However, most older browsers have a limit of 255 characters in length for a script statement. This limit is sometimes exceeded when a script includes a lengthy string that is to become scripted content in a page. You need to divide such lines into smaller chunks using techniques described in a moment.

You have two ways to assign a string value to a variable. The simplest is a basic assignment statement:

```
var myString = "Howdy"
```

This works perfectly well except in some exceedingly rare instances. Beginning with Navigator 3 and Internet Explorer 4, you can also create a string object using the more formal syntax that involves the `new` keyword and a constructor function (that is, it "constructs" a new object):

```
var myString = new String("Howdy")
```

Whichever way you use to initialize a variable with a string, the variable receiving the assignment can respond to all `String` object methods.

Joining strings

Bringing two strings together as a single string is called *concatenating* strings, a term you learned in Chapter 6. String concatenation requires one of two JavaScript operators. Even in your first script in Chapter 3, you saw how the addition operator (+) linked multiple strings together to produce the text dynamically written to the loading Web page:

```
document.write(" of <B>" + navigator.appName + "</B>.")
```

As valuable as that operator is, another operator can be even more scripter friendly. This operator is helpful when you are assembling large strings in a single variable. The strings may be so long or cumbersome that you need to divide the building process into multiple statements. The pieces may be combinations of *string literals* (strings inside quotes) or variable values. The clumsy way to do it (perfectly doable in JavaScript) is to use the addition operator to append more text to the existing chunk:

```
var msg = "Four score"
msg = msg + " and seven"
msg = msg + " years ago,"
```

But another operator, called the *add-by-value operator*, offers a handy shortcut. The symbol for the operator is a plus and equal sign together (+=). This operator means "append the stuff on the right of me to the end of the stuff on the left of me." Therefore, the preceding sequence is shortened as follows:

```
var msg = "Four score"
msg += " and seven"
msg += " years ago,"
```

You can also combine the operators if the need arises:

```
var msg = "Four score"
msg += " and seven" + " years ago"
```

I use the add-by-value operator a lot when accumulating HTML text to be written to the current document or another window.

String methods

Of all the core JavaScript objects, the `String` object has the most diverse collection of methods associated with it. Many methods are designed to help scripts extract segments of a string. Another group, rarely used in my experience, wraps a string with one of several style-oriented tags (a scripted equivalent of tags for font size, style, and the like).

To use a string method, the string being acted upon becomes part of the reference followed by the method name. All methods return a value of some kind. Most of the time, the returned value is a converted version of the string object referred to in the method call — but the original string is still intact. To capture the modified version, you need to assign the results of the method to a variable:

```
var result = string.methodName()
```

The following sections introduce you to several important string methods available to all browser brands and versions.

Changing string case

Two methods convert a string to all uppercase or lowercase letters:

```
var result = string.toUpperCase()
var result = string.toLowerCase()
```

Not surprisingly, you must observe the case of each letter of the method names if you want them to work. These methods come in handy when your scripts need to compare strings that may not have the same case (for example, a string in a lookup table compared with a string typed by a user). Because the methods don't change the original strings attached to the expressions, you can simply compare the evaluated results of the methods:

```
var foundMatch = false
if (stringA.toUpperCase() == stringB.toUpperCase()) {
    foundMatch = true
}
```

String searches

You can use the *string*.indexOf() method to determine if one string is contained by another. Even within JavaScript's own object data, this can be useful information. For example, another property of the navigator object in Chapter 3 (navigator.userAgent) reveals a lot about the browser that loads the page. A script can investigate the value of that property for the existence of, say, "Win" to determine that the user has a Windows operating system. That short string might be buried somewhere inside a long string, and all the script needs to know is whether the short string is present in the longer one — wherever it might be.

The *string*.indexOf() method returns a number indicating the index value (zero based) of the character in the larger string where the smaller string begins. The key point about this method is that if no match occurs, the returned value is -1. To find out whether the smaller string is inside, all you need to test is whether the returned value is something other than -1.

Two strings are involved with this method: the shorter one and the longer one. The longer string is the one that appears in the reference to the left of the method name; the shorter string is inserted as a parameter to the indexOf() method. To demonstrate the method in action, the following fragment looks to see if the user is running Windows:

```
var isWindows = false
if (navigator.userAgent.indexOf("Win") != -1) {
    isWindows = true
}
```

The operator in the if construction's condition (!=) is the inequality operator. You can read it as meaning "is not equal to."

Extracting copies of characters and substrings

To extract a single character at a known position within a string, use the charAt() method. The parameter of the method is an index number (zero based) of the character to extract. When I say *extract*, I don't mean delete, but rather grab a snapshot of the character. The original string is not modified in any way.

For example, consider a script in a main window that is capable of inspecting a variable, `stringA`, in another window that displays map images of different corporate buildings. When the window has a map of Building C in it, the `stringA` variable contains "Building C." The building letter is always at the tenth character position of the string (or number 9 in a zero-based counting world), so the script can examine that one character to identify the map currently in that other window:

```
var stringA = "Building C"
var bldgLetter = stringA.charAt(9)
    // result: bldgLetter = "C"
```

Another method — *string*.`substring()` — enables you to extract a contiguous sequence of characters, provided you know the starting and ending positions of the substring of which you want to grab a copy. Importantly, the character at the ending position value is not part of the extraction: All applicable characters, up to but not including that character, are part of the extraction. The string from which the extraction is made appears to the left of the method name in the reference. Two parameters specify the starting and ending index values (zero based) for the start and end positions:

```
var stringA = "banana daiquiri"
var excerpt = stringA.substring(2,6)
    // result: excerpt = "nana"
```

String manipulation in JavaScript is fairly cumbersome compared to some other scripting languages. Higher-level notions of words, sentences, or paragraphs are completely absent. Therefore, sometimes it takes a bit of scripting with string methods to accomplish what seems like a simple goal. And yet you can put your knowledge of expression evaluation to the test as you assemble expressions that utilize heavily nested constructions. For example, the following fragment needs to create a new string that consists of everything from the larger string except the first word. Assuming the first word of other strings can be of any length, the second statement utilizes the *string*.`indexOf()` method to look for the first space character and adds 1 to that value to serve as the starting index value for an outer *string*.`substring()` method. For the second parameter, the `length` property of the string provides a basis for the ending character's index value (one more than the actual character needed).

```
var stringA = "The United States of America"
var excerpt = stringA.substring(stringA.indexOf(" ") + 1, stringA.length)
    // result: excerpt = "United States of America"
```

Creating statements like this one is not something you are likely to enjoy over and over again, so in Chapter 34 I show you how to create your own library of string functions you can reuse in all of your scripts that need their string-handling facilities. More powerful string matching facilities are built into NN4+ and IE4+ by way of regular expressions (see Chapters 34 and 38).

The Math Object

JavaScript provides ample facilities for math—far more than most scripters who don't have a background in computer science and math will use in a lifetime. But every genuine programming language needs these powers to accommodate clever programmers who can make windows fly in circles on the screen.

The `Math` object contains all of these powers. This object is unlike most of the other objects in JavaScript in that you don't generate copies of the object to use. Instead your scripts summon a single `Math` object's properties and methods. (One `Math` object actually occurs per window or frame, but this has no impact whatsoever on your scripts.) Programmers call this kind of fixed object a *static object*. That `Math` object (with an uppercase M) is part of the reference to the property or method. Properties of the `Math` object are constant values, such as pi and the square root of two:

```
var piValue = Math.PI
var rootOfTwo = Math.SQRT2
```

`Math` object methods cover a wide range of trigonometric functions and other math functions that work on numeric values already defined in your script. For example, you can find which of two numbers is the larger:

```
var larger = Math.max(value1, value2)
```

Or you can raise one number to a power of ten:

```
var result = Math.pow(value1, 10)
```

More common, perhaps, is the method that rounds a value to the nearest integer value:

```
var result = Math.round(value1)
```

Another common request of the `Math` object is a random number. Although the feature was broken on Windows and Macintosh versions of Navigator 2, it works in all other versions and brands since. The `Math.random()` method returns a floating-point number between 0 and 1. If you design a script to act like a card game, you need random integers between 1 and 52; for dice, the range is 1 to 6 per die. To generate a random integer between zero and any top value, use the following formula:

```
Math.floor(Math.random() * (n + 1))
```

where n is the top number. (`Math.floor()` returns the integer part of any floating-point number.) To generate random numbers between one and any higher number, use this formula:

```
Math.floor(Math.random() * n) + 1
```

where n equals the top number of the range. For the dice game, the formula for each die is

```
newDieValue = Math.floor(Math.random() * 6) + 1
```

To see this, enter the right-hand part of the preceding statement in the top text box of The Evaluator Jr. and repeatedly press the Evaluate button.

One bit of help JavaScript doesn't offer except in IE5.5 and NN6 is a way to specify a number-formatting scheme. Floating-point math can display more than a dozen numbers to the right of the decimal. Moreover, results can be influenced by each operating system's platform-specific floating-point errors, especially in earlier versions of scriptable browsers. For browsers prior to IE5.5 and NN6 you must perform any number formatting — for dollars and cents, for example — through your own scripts. Chapter 35 provides an example.

The Date Object

Working with dates beyond simple tasks can be difficult business in JavaScript. A lot of the difficulty comes with the fact that dates and times are calculated internally according to *Greenwich Mean Time (GMT)* — provided the visitor's own internal PC clock and control panel are set accurately. As a result of this complexity, better left for Chapter 36, this section of the tutorial touches on only the basics of the JavaScript Date object.

A scriptable browser contains one global Date object (in truth, one Date object per window) that is always present, ready to be called upon at any moment. The Date object is another one of those static objects. When you wish to work with a date, such as displaying today's date, you need to invoke the Date object constructor to obtain an instance of a Date object tied to a specific time and date. For example, when you invoke the constructor without any parameters, as in

```
var today = new Date()
```

the Date object takes a snapshot of the PC's internal clock and returns a date object for that instant. Notice the distinction between the static Date object and a date object instance, which contains an actual date value. The variable, today, contains not a ticking clock, but a value that you can examine, tear apart, and reassemble as needed for your script.

Internally, the value of a date object instance is the time, in milliseconds, from zero o'clock on January 1, 1970, in the Greenwich Mean Time zone — the world standard reference point for all time conversions. That's how a date object contains both date and time information.

You can also grab a snapshot of the `Date` object for a particular date and time in the past or future by specifying that information as parameters to the `Date` object constructor function:

```
var someDate = new Date("Month dd, yyyy hh:mm:ss")
var someDate = new Date("Month dd, yyyy")
var someDate = new Date(yy,mm,dd,hh,mm,ss)
var someDate = new Date(yy,mm,dd)
var someDate = new Date(GMT milliseconds from 1/1/1970)
```

If you attempt to view the contents of a raw date object, JavaScript converts the value to the local time zone string as indicated by your PC's control panel setting. To see this in action, use The Evaluator Jr.'s top text box to enter the following:

```
new Date()
```

Your PC's clock supplies the current date and time as the clock calculates them (even though JavaScript still stores the date object's millisecond count in the GMT zone). You can, however, extract components of the date object via a series of methods that you apply to a date object instance. Table 10-1 shows an abbreviated listing of these properties and information about their values.

Table 10-1   Some Date Object Methods

Method	Value Range	Description
dateObj.getTime()	0-...	Milliseconds since 1/1/70 00:00:00 GMT
dateObj.getYear()	70-...	Specified year minus 1900; four-digit year for 2000+
dateObj.getFullYear()	1970-...	Four-digit year (Y2K-compliant); version 4+ browsers
dateObj.getMonth()	0-11	Month within the year (January = 0)
dateObj.getDate()	1-31	Date within the month
dateObj.getDay()	0-6	Day of week (Sunday = 0)
dateObj.getHours()	0-23	Hour of the day in 24-hour time
dateObj.getMinutes()	0-59	Minute of the specified hour
dateObj.getSeconds()	0-59	Second within the specified minute
dateObj.setTime(val)	0-...	Milliseconds since 1/1/70 00:00:00 GMT
dateObj.setYear(val)	70-...	Specified year minus 1900; four-digit year for 2000+
dateObj.setMonth(val)	0-11	Month within the year (January = 0)
dateObj.setDate(val)	1-31	Date within the month

Method	Value Range	Description
dateObj.setDay(val)	0-6	Day of week (Sunday = 0)
dateObj.setHours(val)	0-23	Hour of the day in 24-hour time
dateObj.setMinutes(val)	0-59	Minute of the specified hour
dateObj.setSeconds(val)	0-59	Second within the specified minute

Caution Be careful about values whose ranges start with zero, especially the months. The getMonth() and setMonth() method values are zero based, so the numbers are one less than the month numbers you are accustomed to working with (for example, January is 0, December is 11).

You may notice one difference about the methods that set values of a date object. Rather than returning some new value, these methods actually modify the value of the date object referenced in the call to the method.

Date Calculations

Performing calculations with dates requires working with the millisecond values of the date objects. This is the surest way to add, subtract, or compare date values. To demonstrate a few date object machinations, Listing 10-1 displays the current date and time as the page loads. Another script calculates the date and time seven days from the current date and time value.

Listing 10-1: **Date Object Calculations**

```
<HTML>
<HEAD>
<TITLE>Date Calculation</TITLE>
<SCRIPT LANGUAGE="JavaScript">
function nextWeek() {
    var todayInMS = today.getTime()
    var nextWeekInMS = todayInMS + (60 * 60 * 24 * 7 * 1000)
    return new Date(nextWeekInMS)
}
</SCRIPT>
</HEAD>

<BODY>
Today is:
<SCRIPT LANGUAGE="JavaScript">
var today = new Date()
```

Continued

Listing 10-1 *(continued)*

```
document.write(today)
</SCRIPT>
<BR>
Next week will be:
<SCRIPT LANGUAGE="JavaScript">
document.write(nextWeek())
</SCRIPT>
</BODY>
</HTML>
```

In the Body portion, the first script runs as the page loads, setting a global variable (today) to the current date and time. The string equivalent is written to the page. In the second Body script, the document.write() method invokes the nextWeek() function to get a value to display. That function utilizes the today global variable, copying its millisecond value to a new variable: todayInMS. To get a date seven days from now, the next statement adds the number of milliseconds in seven days (60 seconds times 60 minutes times 24 hours times seven days times 1000 milliseconds) to today's millisecond value. The script now needs a new date object calculated from the total milliseconds. This requires invoking the Date object constructor with the milliseconds as a parameter. The returned value is a date object, which is automatically converted to a string version for writing to the page. Letting JavaScript create the new date with the accumulated number of milliseconds is more accurate than trying to add 7 to the value returned by the date object's getDate() method. JavaScript automatically takes care of figuring out how many days there are in a month as well as in leap years.

Many other quirks and complicated behavior await you if you script dates in your page. As later chapters demonstrate, however, the results may be worth the effort.

Exercises

1. Create a Web page that has one form field for entry of the user's e-mail address and a Submit button. Include a pre-submission validation routine that verifies that the text field has the @ symbol found in all e-mail addresses before you allow submission of the form.

2. Given the string "Netscape Navigator," fill in the blanks of the myString.substring() method parameters here that yield the results shown to the right of each method call:

```
var myString = "Netscape Navigator"
myString.substring(___,___) // result = "Net"
myString.substring(___,___) // result = "gator"
myString.substring(___,___) // result = "cape Nav"
```

3. Fill in the rest of the function in the listing that follows so that it looks through every character of the entry field and counts how many times the letter "e" appears in the field. (Hint: All that is missing is a `for` repeat loop.)

```
<HTML>
<HEAD>
<TITLE>Wheel o' Fortuna</TITLE>
<SCRIPT LANGUAGE="JavaScript">
function countE(form) {
    var count = 0
    var inputString = form.mainstring.value.toUpperCase()
    missing code
    alert("The string has " + count + " instances of the letter e.")
}
</SCRIPT>
</HEAD>

<BODY>
<FORM>
Enter any string: <INPUT TYPE="text" NAME="mainstring" SIZE=30><BR>
<INPUT TYPE="button" VALUE="Count the Es"
onClick="countE(this.form)">
</FORM>
</BODY>
</HTML>
```

4. Create a page that has two fields and one button. The button should trigger a function that generates two random numbers between 1 and 6, placing each number in one of the fields. (Think of using this page as a substitute for rolling a pair of dice in a board game.)

5. Create a page that displays the number of days between today and next Christmas.

✦   ✦   ✦

Scripting Frames and Multiple Windows

◆   ◆   ◆   ◆

In This Chapter

Relationships among frames in the browser window

How to access objects and values in other frames

How to control navigation of multiple frames

Communication skills between separate windows

◆   ◆   ◆   ◆

One of the cool aspects of JavaScript on the client is that it allows user actions in one frame or window to influence what happens in other frames and windows. In this section of the tutorial, you extend your existing knowledge of object references to the realm of multiple frames and windows.

Frames: Parents and Children

You probably noticed that at the top of the simplified document object hierarchy diagram (refer to Figure 8-1) the window object has some other object references associated with it. In Chapter 8, you learned that self is synonymous with window when the reference applies to the same window that contains the script's document. In this lesson, you learn the roles of the other three object references — frame, top, and parent.

Loading an ordinary HTML document into the browser creates a model in the browser that starts out with one window object and the document it contains. (The document likely contains other elements, but I'm not concerned with that stuff yet.) The top rungs of the hierarchy model are as simple as can be, as shown in Figure 11-1. This is where references begin with window or self (or with document because the current window is assumed).

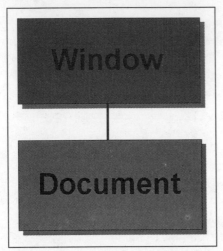

Figure 11-1: Single-frame window and document hierarchy

The instant a framesetting document loads into a browser, the browser starts building a slightly different hierarchy model. The precise structure of that model depends entirely on the structure of the frameset defined in that framesetting document. Consider the following skeletal frameset definition:

```
<HTML>
<FRAMESET COLS="50%,50%">
    <FRAME NAME="leftFrame" SRC="somedoc1.html">
    <FRAME NAME="rightFrame" SRC="somedoc2.html">
</FRAMESET>
</HTML>
```

This HTML splits the browser window into two frames side by side, with a different document loaded into each frame. The model is concerned only with structure — it doesn't care about the relative sizes of the frames or whether they're set up in columns or rows.

Framesets establish relationships among the frames in the collection. Borrowing terminology from the object-oriented programming world, the framesetting document loads into a *parent window*. Each of the frames defined in that parent window document is a *child frame*. Figure 11-2 shows the hierarchical model of a two-frame environment. This illustration reveals a lot of subtleties about the relationships among framesets and their frames.

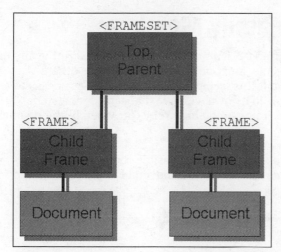

Figure 11-2: Two-frame window and document hierarchy

It is often difficult at first to visualize the frameset as a window object in the hierarchy. After all, with the exception of the URL showing in the Location/Address field, you don't see anything about the frameset in the browser. But that window object exists in the object model. Notice, too, that in the diagram the framesetting parent window has no document object showing. This may also seem odd because the window obviously requires an HTML file containing the specifications for the frameset. In truth, the parent window has a document object associated with it, but it is omitted from the diagram to better portray the relationships among parent and child windows. A frameset parent's document cannot contain most of the typical HTML objects such as forms and controls, so references to the parent's document are rarely, if ever, used.

If you add a script to the framesetting document that needs to access a property or method of that window object, references are like any single-frame situation. Think about the point of view of a script located in that window. Its immediate universe is the very same window.

Things get more interesting when you start looking at the child frames. Each of these frames contains a document object whose content you see in the browser window. And the structure is such that each document is entirely independent of the other. It is as if each document lived in its own browser window. Indeed, that's why each child frame is also a window type of object. A frame has the same kinds of properties and methods of the window object that occupies the entire browser.

From the point of view of either child window in Figure 11-2, its immediate container is the parent window. When a parent window is at the very top of the hierarchical model loaded in the browser, that window is also referred to as the top object.

References among Family Members

Given the frame structure of Figure 11-2, it's time to look at how a script in any one of those windows can access objects, functions, or variables in the others. An important point to remember about this facility is that if a script has access to an object, function, or global variable in its own window, that same item can be reached by a script from another frame in the hierarchy (provided both documents come from the same Web server).

A script reference may need to take one of three possible routes in the two-generation hierarchy described so far: parent to child; child to parent; or child to child.

Each of the paths between these windows requires a different reference style.

Parent-to-child references

Probably the least common direction taken by references is when a script in the parent document needs to access some element of one of its frames. The parent contains two or more frames, which means the parent maintains an array of the child frame objects. You can address a frame by array syntax or by the name you assign to it with the NAME attribute inside the <FRAME> tag. In the following examples of reference syntax, I substitute a placeholder named *ObjFuncVarName* for whatever object, function, or global variable you intend to access in the distant window or frame. Remember that each visible frame contains a document object, which is generally the container of elements you script — be sure references to the element include document. With that in mind, a reference from a parent to one of its child frames follows either of these models:

```
[window.]frames[n].ObjFuncVarName
[window.]frameName.ObjFuncVarName
```

Index values for frames are based on the order in which their <FRAME> tags appear in the framesetting document. You will make your life easier, however, if you assign recognizable names to each frame and use the frame's name in the reference. Note that some problems existed in early scriptable browsers when references to other frames started with window. I recommend omitting window from all such references.

Child-to-parent references

It is not uncommon to place scripts in the parent (in the Head portion) that multiple child frames or multiple documents in a frame use as a kind of script library. By loading in the frameset, these scripts load only once while the frameset is visible. If other documents load into the frames over time, they can take advantage of the parent's scripts without having to load their own copies into the browser.

From the child's point of view, the next level up the hierarchy is called the `parent`. Therefore, a reference from a child frame to items at the parent level is simply

```
parent.ObjFuncVarName
```

If the item accessed in the parent is a function that returns a value, the returned value transcends the parent/child borders down to the child without hesitation.

When the parent window is also at the very top of the object hierarchy currently loaded into the browser, you can optionally refer to it as the *top window*, as in

```
top.ObjFuncVarName
```

Using the `top` reference can be hazardous if for some reason your Web page gets displayed in some other Web site's frameset. What is your top window is not the master frameset's top window. Therefore, I recommend using the `parent` reference whenever possible (unless you want to blow away an unwanted framer of your Web site).

Child-to-child references

The browser needs a bit more assistance when it comes to getting one child window to communicate with one of its siblings. One of the properties of any window or frame is its `parent` (whose value is `null` for a single window). A reference must use the `parent` property to work its way out of the current frame to a point that both child frames have in common — the parent in this case. Once the reference is at the parent level, the rest of the reference can carry on as if starting at the parent. Thus, from one child to one of its siblings, you can use either of the following reference formats:

```
parent.frames[n].ObjFuncVarName
parent.frameName.ObjFuncVarName
```

A reference from the other sibling back to the first looks the same, but the `frames[]` array index or `frameName` part of the reference differs. Of course, much more complex frame hierarchies exist in HTML. Even so, the document object model and referencing scheme provide a solution for the most deeply nested and gnarled frame arrangement you can think of — following the same precepts you just learned.

Frame Scripting Tips

One of the first mistakes that frame scripting newcomers make is writing immediate script statements that call upon other frames while the pages load. The problem here is that you cannot rely on the document loading sequence to follow the frameset source code order. All you know for sure is that the parent document *begins* loading first. Regardless of the order of <FRAME> tags, child frames can begin loading at any time. Moreover, a frame's loading time depends on other elements in the document, such as images or Java applets.

Fortunately, you can use a certain technique to initiate a script once all of the documents in the frameset are completely loaded. Just as the onLoad event handler for a document fires when that document is fully loaded, a parent's onLoad event handler fires after the onLoad event handler in its child frames is fired. Therefore, you can specify an onLoad event handler in the <FRAMESET> tag. That handler might invoke a function in the framesetting document that then has the freedom to tap the objects, functions, or variables of all frames throughout the object hierarchy.

Controlling Multiple Frames — Navigation Bars

If you are enamored of frames as a way to help organize a complex Web page, you may find yourself wanting to control the navigation of one or more frames from a static navigation panel. Here, I demonstrate scripting concepts for such control using an application called Decision Helper (which you can find in Chapter 54 on the CD-ROM). The application consists of three frames (see Figure 11-3). The top-left frame is one image that has four graphical buttons in it. The goal is to turn that image into a client-side image map and script it so the pages change in the right-hand and bottom frames. In the upper-right frame, the script loads an entirely different document along the sequence of five different documents that go in there. In the bottom frame, the script navigates to one of five anchors to display the segment of instructions that applies to the document loaded in the upper-right frame.

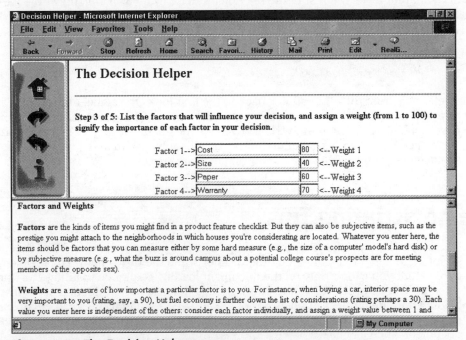

Figure 11-3: The Decision Helper screen

Listing 11-1 shows a slightly modified version of the actual file for the Decision Helper application's navigation frame. The listing contains a couple of new objects and concepts not yet covered in this tutorial. But as you will see, they are extensions to what you already know about JavaScript and objects. To help simplify the discussion here, I remove the scripting and HTML for the top and bottom button of the area map. In addition, I cover only the two navigation arrows.

Listing 11-1: **A Graphical Navigation Bar**

```
<HTML>
<HEAD>
<TITLE>Navigation Bar</TITLE>
<SCRIPT LANGUAGE="JavaScript">
<!-- start
function goNext() {
    var currOffset = parseInt(parent.currTitle)
    if (currOffset < 5) {
        currOffset += 1
        parent.entryForms.location.href = "dh" + currOffset + ".htm"
        parent.instructions.location.hash = "help" + currOffset
    } else {
        alert("This is the last form.")
    }
}
function goPrev() {
    var currOffset = parseInt(parent.currTitle)
    if (currOffset > 1) {
        currOffset -= 1
        parent.entryForms.location.href = "dh" + currOffset + ".htm"
        parent.instructions.location.hash = "help" + currOffset
    } else {
        alert("This is the first form.")
    }
}
// end -->
</SCRIPT>
</HEAD>
<BODY bgColor="white">
<MAP NAME="navigation">
<AREA SHAPE="RECT" COORDS="25,80,66,116" HREF="javascript:goNext()">
<AREA SHAPE="RECT" COORDS="24,125,67,161" HREF="javascript:goPrev()">
</MAP>
<IMG SRC="dhNav.gif" HEIGHT=240 WIDTH=96 BORDER=0 USEMAP="#navigation">
</BODY>
</HTML>
```

Look first at the HTML section for the Body portion. Almost everything there is standard stuff for defining client-side image maps. The coordinates define rectangles around each of the arrows in the larger image. The HREF attributes for the two areas point to JavaScript functions defined in the Head portion of the document.

In the frameset that defines the Decision Helper application, names are assigned to each frame. The upper-right frame is called entryForms; the bottom frame is called instructions.

Knowing that navigation from page to page in the upper-right frame requires knowledge of which page is currently loaded there, I build some other scripting into both the parent document and each of the documents that loads into that frame. A global variable called currTitle is defined in the parent document. Its value is an integer indicating which page of the sequence (1 through 5) is currently loaded. An onLoad event handler in each of the five documents (named dh1.htm, dh2.htm, dh3.htm, dh4.htm, and dh5.htm) assigns its page number to that parent global variable. This arrangement allows all frames in the frameset to share that value easily.

When a user clicks the right-facing arrow to move to the next page, the goNext() function is called. The first statement gets the currTitle value from the parent window and assigns it to a local variable: currOffset. An if...else construction tests whether the current page number is less than five. If so, the add-by-value operator adds one to the local variable so I can use that value in the next two statements.

In those next two statements, I adjust the content of the two right frames. Using the parent reference to gain access to both frames, I set the location.href property of the top-right frame to the name of the file next in line (by concatenating the number with the surrounding parts of the filename). The second statement sets the location.hash property (which controls the anchor being navigated to) to the corresponding anchor in the instructions frame (anchor names help1, help2, help3, help4, and help5).

A click of the left-facing arrow reverses the process, subtracting 1 from the current page number (using the subtract-by-value operator) and changing the same frames accordingly.

The example shown in Listing 11-1 is one of many ways to script a navigation frame in JavaScript. Whatever methodology you use, much interaction occurs among the frames in the frameset.

More about Window References

In Chapter 8, you saw how to create a new window and communicate with it by way of the window object reference returned from the window.open() method. In this section, I show you how one of those subwindows can communicate with objects, functions, and variables in the window or frame that creates the subwindow.

In scriptable browsers (except for Navigator 2), every window has a property called `opener`. This property contains a reference to the window or frame that held the script whose `window.open()` statement generated the subwindow. For the main browser window and frames therein, this value is `null`. Because the `opener` property is a valid window reference, you can use it to begin the reference to items in the original window — just like a script in a child frame uses `parent` to access items in the parent document. The parent-child terminology doesn't apply to subwindows, however.

Listings 11-2 and 11-3 contain documents that work together in separate windows. Listing 11-2 displays a button that opens a smaller window and loads Listing 11-3 into it. The main window document also contains a text field that gets filled in when you enter text into a corresponding field in the subwindow.

In the main window document, the `newWindow()` function generates the new window. Because no other statements in the document require the reference to the new window just opened, the statement does not assign its returned value to any variable. This is an acceptable practice in JavaScript if you don't need the returned value of a function or method.

Listing 11-2: **A Main Window Document**

```
<HTML>
<HEAD>
<TITLE>Main Document</TITLE>
<SCRIPT LANGUAGE="JavaScript">
function newWindow() {
    window.open("subwind.htm","sub","HEIGHT=200,WIDTH=200")
}
</SCRIPT>
</HEAD>

<BODY>
<FORM>
<INPUT TYPE="button" VALUE="New Window" onClick="newWindow()">
<BR>
Text incoming from subwindow:
<INPUT TYPE="Text" NAME="entry">
</FORM>
</BODY>
</HTML>
```

All of the action in the subwindow document comes in the `onChange` event handler of the text field. It assigns the subwindow field's own value to the value of the field in the opener window's document. Remember that the contents of each window and frame belong to a document. So even after your reference targets a specific window or frame, the reference must continue helping the browser find the ultimate destination, which is generally some element of the document.

Listing 11-3: **A Subwindow Document**

```
<HTML>
<HEAD>
<TITLE>A SubDocument</TITLE>
</HEAD>
<BODY>
<FORM onSubmit="return false">
Enter text to be copied to the main window:
<INPUT TYPE="text"
onChange="opener.document.forms[0].entry.value = this.value">
</FORM>
</BODY>
</HTML>
```

Just one more lesson to go before I let you explore all the details elsewhere in the book. I use the final tutorial chapter to show you some fun things you can do with your Web pages, such as changing images when the user rolls the mouse atop a picture.

Exercises

Before answering the first three questions, study the structure of the following frameset for a Web site that lists college courses:

```
<FRAMESET ROWS="85%,15%">
    <FRAMESET COLS="20%,80%">
        <FRAME NAME="mechanics" SRC="history101M.html">
        <FRAME NAME="description" SRC="history101D.html">
    </FRAMESET>
    <FRAMESET COLS="100%">
        <FRAME NAME="navigation" SRC="navigator.html">
    </FRAMESET>
</FRAMESET>
</HTML>
```

1. Whenever a document loads into the description frame, it has an onLoad event handler that stores a course identifier in the framesetting document's global variable called currCourse. Write the onLoad event handler that sets this value to "history101".

2. Draw a block diagram that describes the hierarchy of the windows and frames represented in the frameset definition.

3. Write the JavaScript statements located in the navigation frame that loads the file `"french201M.html"` into the mechanics frame and the file `"french201D.html"` into the description frame.

4. While a frameset is still loading, a JavaScript error message suddenly appears saying that "window.document.navigation.form.selector is undefined." What do you think is happening in the application's scripts, and how can you solve the problem?

5. A script in a child frame of the main window uses `window.open()` to generate a second window. How can a script in the second window access the location object (URL) of the parent window in the main browser window?

Images and Dynamic HTML

◆   ◆   ◆   ◆

In This Chapter

How to precache
images

How to swap images
for mouse rollovers

What you can do
with Dynamic HTML
and scripting

◆   ◆   ◆   ◆

The previous eight lessons have been intensive, covering a lot of ground for both programming concepts and JavaScript. Now it's time to apply those fundamentals to the learning of more advanced techniques. I cover two areas here. First, I show you how to implement the ever-popular *mouse rollover* in which images swap when the user rolls the cursor around the screen. Then I introduce you to concepts surrounding scripted control of Dynamic HTML in the version 4 and later browsers.

The Image Object

One of the objects contained by the document is the image object. Unfortunately, this object is not available in all scriptable browsers. The earliest browsers that you can use this technique with are NN3 and IE4. Therefore, everything you learn here about the image object doesn't apply to NN2 (all versions) or IE3 (for Windows). Even so, I show you how to insert rollover code in pages so that it doesn't cause errors in earlier browsers.

Because a document can have more than one image, image object references for a document are stored in the object model as an array belonging to the document object. You can therefore reference an image by array index or image name. Moreover, the array index can be a string version of the image's name. Thus, all of the following are valid references to an image object:

```
document.images[n]
document.images["imageName"]
document.imageName
```

Each of the <IMG> tag's attributes is accessible to JavaScript as a property of the image object. No mouse-related event handlers are affiliated with the image object (until you get to IE4+ and NN6+). If you want to make an image a clickable item in older browsers, surround it with a link (and set the image's border to zero) or attach a client-side image map to it. The combination of a link and image is how you make a clickable image button (the image type of form input element is not a scriptable object until IE4+ and NN6+).

Interchangeable images

The advantage of having a scriptable image object is that a script can change the image occupying the rectangular space already occupied by an image. In IE4+ and NN6+, the images can even change size, with surrounding content reflowing accordingly.

The script behind this kind of image change is simple enough. All it entails is assigning a new URL to the image object's src property. The size of the image on the page is governed by the HEIGHT and WIDTH attributes set in the <IMG> tag as the page loads. The most common image rollovers use the same size image for each of the rollover states. In NN3 and NN4, the image can't change size on the page, which causes a differently sized replacement image to scale to fit the original dimensions.

Precaching images

Images often take several extra seconds to download from a Web server. If you design your page so an image changes in response to user action, you usually want the same fast response that users are accustomed to in multimedia programs. Making the user wait many seconds for an image to change can severely detract from enjoyment of the page.

JavaScript comes to the rescue by enabling scripts to load images into the browser's memory cache without displaying the image, a technique called *precaching images*. The tactic that works best is to preload the image into the browser's image cache when the page initially loads. Users are less impatient for those few extra seconds as the main page loads than waiting for an image to download in response to some mouse action.

Precaching an image requires constructing an image object in memory. An image object created in memory differs in some respects from the document image object that you create with the <IMG> tag. Memory-only objects are created by script, and you don't see them on the page at all. But their presence in the document code forces the browser to load the images as the page loads. The object model provides an Image object constructor function to create the memory type of image object as follows:

```
var myImage = new Image(width, height)
```

Parameters to the constructor function are the pixel width and height of the image. These dimensions should match the <IMG> tag's WIDTH and HEIGHT attributes. Once the image object exists in memory, you can then assign a filename or URL to the src property of that image object:

```
myImage.src = "someArt.gif"
```

When the browser encounters a statement assigning a URL to an image object's src property, the browser goes out and loads that image into the image cache. All the user sees is some extra loading information in the status bar, as if another image were in the page. By the time the entire page loads, all images generated in this way are tucked away in the image cache. You can then assign your cached image's src property or the actual image URL to the src property of the document image created with the <IMG> tag:

```
document.images[0].src = myImage.src
```

The change to the image in the document is instantaneous.

Listing 12-1 is a simple listing for a page that has one <IMG> tag and a select list that enables you to replace the image in the document with any of four precached images (including the original image specified for the tag). If you type this listing — as I strongly recommend — you can obtain copies of the four image files from the companion CD-ROM in the Chapter 12 directory of listings (you must still type the HTML and code, however).

Listing 12-1: **Precaching Images**

```
<HTML>
<HEAD>
<TITLE>Image Object</TITLE>
<SCRIPT LANGUAGE="JavaScript1.1">
// pre-cache four images
image1 = new Image(120,90)
image1.src = "desk1.gif"
image2 = new Image(120,90)
image2.src = "desk2.gif"
image3 = new Image(120,90)
image3.src = "desk3.gif"
image4 = new Image(120,90)
image4.src = "desk4.gif"

// load an image chosen from select list
function loadCached(list) {
    var img = list.options[list.selectedIndex].value
    document.thumbnail.src = eval(img + ".src")
}
```

Continued

Listing 12-1 *(continued)*

```
</SCRIPT>
</HEAD>

<BODY >
<H2>Image Object</H2>
<IMG SRC="desk1.gif" NAME="thumbnail" HEIGHT=90 WIDTH=120>
<FORM>
<SELECT NAME="cached" onChange="loadCached(this)">
<OPTION VALUE="image1">Bands
<OPTION VALUE="image2">Clips
<OPTION VALUE="image3">Lamp
<OPTION VALUE="image4">Erasers
</SELECT>
</FORM>
</BODY>
</HTML>
```

As the page loads, it executes several statements immediately. These statements create four new memory image objects and assign filenames to the objects' src properties. These images are loaded into the image cache as the page loads. Down in the Body portion of the document, an <IMG> tag stakes its turf on the page and loads one of the images as a starting image.

A SELECT element lists user-friendly names for the pictures while housing the names of image objects already precached in memory. When the user makes a selection from the list, the loadCached() function extracts the selected item's value — which is a string version of the image object name. To convert a string name to a reference to the object of that same name, use the eval() function (part of the core JavaScript language). You need the src property of that object, so the eval() function is applied to a string version of the reference to an image object's src property. The src property of the chosen image object is assigned to the src property of the visible image object on the page, and the precached image appears instantaneously.

Creating image rollovers

A favorite technique to add some pseudo-excitement to a page is to swap button images as the user rolls the cursor atop them. The degree of change to the image is largely a matter of taste. The effect can be subtle — a slight highlight or glow around the edge of the original image — or drastic — a radical change of color. Whatever your approach, the scripting is the same.

When several of these graphical buttons occur in a group, I tend to organize the memory image objects as arrays and create naming and numbering schemes that facilitate working with the arrays. Listing 12-2 shows such an arrangement for four buttons that control a jukebox. The code in the listing is confined to the image-swapping portion of the application. This is the most complex and lengthiest listing of the tutorial, so it requires a bit of explanation as it goes along.

Listing 12-2: **Image Rollovers**

```
<HTML>
<HEAD>
<TITLE>Jukebox/Image Rollovers</TITLE>
<SCRIPT LANGUAGE="JavaScript">
```

Only browsers capable of handling image objects should execute statements that precache images. Therefore, the entire sequence is nested inside an `if` construction that tests for the presence of the `document.images` array. In older browsers, the condition evaluates to "undefined," which an `if` condition treats as `false`.

```
if (document.images) {
```

Image precaching starts by building two arrays of image objects. One array stores information about the images depicting the graphical button's "off" position; the other is for images depicting their "on" position. These arrays use strings (instead of integers) as index values. The string names correspond to the names given to the visible image objects whose tags come later in the source code. The code is clearer to read (for example, you know that the `offImgArray["play"]` entry has to do with the Play button image). Also, as you see later in this listing, rollover images don't conflict with other visible images on the page (a possibility if you rely exclusively on numeric index values when referring to the visible images for the swapping).

After creating the array and assigning new blank image objects to the first four elements of the array, I go through the array again, this time assigning file pathnames to the `src` property of each object stored in the array. These lines of code execute as the page loads, so the images load into the image cache along the way.

```
// precache all 'off' button images
var offImgArray = new Array()
offImgArray["play"] = new Image(75,33)
offImgArray["stop"] = new Image(75,33)
offImgArray["pause"] = new Image(75,33)
offImgArray["rewind"] = new Image(86,33)

// off image array -- set 'off' image path for each button
offImgArray["play"].src = "images/playoff.jpg"
offImgArray["stop"].src = "images/stopoff.jpg"
offImgArray["pause"].src = "images/pauseoff.jpg"
offImgArray["rewind"].src = "images/rewindoff.jpg"
```

```
    // precache all 'on' button images
    var onImgArray = new Array()
    onImgArray["play"] = new Image(75,33)
    onImgArray["stop"] = new Image(75,33)
    onImgArray["pause"] = new Image(75,33)
    onImgArray["rewind"] = new Image(86,33)

    // on image array -- set 'on' image path for each button
    onImgArray["play"].src = "images/playon.jpg"
    onImgArray["stop"].src = "images/stopon.jpg"
    onImgArray["pause"].src = "images/pauseon.jpg"
    onImgArray["rewind"].src = "images/rewindon.jpg"
}
```

As you can see in the following HTML, when the user rolls the mouse atop any of the visible document image objects, the onMouseOver event handler (from the link object surrounding the image in the document) invokes the imageOn() function, passing the name of the particular image. The imageOn() function uses that name to synchronize the document.images array entry (the visible image) with the entry of the in-memory array of "on" images from the onImgArray array. The src property of the array entry is assigned to the corresponding document image src property.

```
// functions that swap images & status bar
function imageOn(imgName) {
    if (document.images) {
        document.images[imgName].src = onImgArray[imgName].src
    }
}
```

The same goes for the onMouseOut event handler, which needs to turn the image off by invoking the imageOff() function with the same index value.

```
function imageOff(imgName) {
    if (document.images) {
        document.images[imgName].src = offImgArray[imgName].src
    }
}
```

Both the onMouseOver and onMouseOut event handlers set the status bar to prevent the ugly javascript: URL from appearing there as the user rolls the mouse atop the image. The onMouseOut event handler sets the status bar message to an empty string.

```
function setMsg(msg) {
    window.status = msg
    return true
}
```

For this demonstration, I disable the functions that control the jukebox. But I leave the empty function definitions here so they catch the calls made by the clicks of the links associated with the images.

```
// controller functions (disabled)
function playIt() {
}
function stopIt() {
}
function pauseIt(){
}
function rewindIt() {
}
</SCRIPT>
</HEAD>

<BODY>
<CENTER>
<FORM>
Jukebox Controls<BR>
```

I surround each image in the document with a link because the link object has the event handlers needed to respond to the mouse rolling over the area for compatibility back to NN3. Each link's onMouseOver event handler calls the imageOn() function, passing the name of the image object to be swapped. Because both the onMouseOver and onMouseOut event handlers require a return true statement to work, I combine the second function call (to setMsg()) with the return true requirement. The setMsg() function always returns true and is combined with the return keyword before the call to the setMsg() function. It's just a trick to reduce the amount of code in these event handlers.

Note   If you are typing this listing to try it out, be sure to keep each entire <A> tag and its attributes in one unbroken line; or insert a carriage return *before* any event handler name.

```
<A HREF="javascript:playIt()"
   onMouseOver="imageOn('play'); return setMsg('Play the selected tune')"
   onMouseOut="imageOff('play'); return setMsg('')">
<IMG SRC="images/playoff.jpg" NAME="play" HEIGHT=33 WIDTH=75 BORDER=0>
</A>
<A HREF="javascript:stopIt()"
   onMouseOver="imageOn('stop'); return setMsg('Stop the playing tune')"
   onMouseOut="imageOff('stop'); return setMsg('')">
<IMG SRC="images/stopoff.jpg" NAME="stop" HEIGHT=33 WIDTH=75 BORDER=0>
</A>
<A HREF="javascript:pauseIt()"
   onMouseOver="imageOn('pause'); return setMsg('Pause the playing tune')"
   onMouseOut="imageOff('pause'); return setMsg('')">
<IMG SRC="images/pauseoff.jpg" NAME="pause" HEIGHT=33 WIDTH=75 BORDER=0>
</A>
<A HREF="javascript:rewindIt()"
   onMouseOver="imageOn('rewind'); return setMsg('Rewind tune')"
   onMouseOut="imageOff('rewind'); return setMsg('')">
```

```
<IMG SRC="images/rewindoff.jpg" NAME="rewind" HEIGHT=33 WIDTH=86 BORDER=0>
</A>
</FORM>
</CENTER>
</BODY>
</HTML>
```

You can see the results of this lengthy script in Figure 12-1. As the user rolls the mouse atop one of the images, it changes from a light to dark color by swapping the entire image. You can access the image files on the CD-ROM, and I encourage you to enter this lengthy listing and see the magic for yourself.

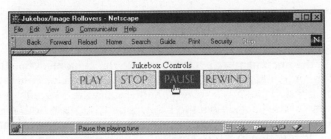

Figure 12-1: Typical mouse rollover image swapping

More Dynamism in HTML

The image object swapping technique is but a preview of what the newest developments in Dynamic HTML are all about. In IE4+ and NN6+, you can script changes to HTML element styles and content. Content can literally "dance" on the page.

Due to different approaches to document object models that Microsoft and Netscape have taken over the years, it is only with adoption of the W3C DOM in the IE5 and NN6 browsers that a lot of the same DHTML script code can run interchangeably on both IE and NN. (But even then, IE5 and IE5.5 do not support the W3C DOM as fully as NN6 does.) If your audience uses IE exclusively, you also have the option of using Microsoft's proprietary object model for compatibility back to IE4 (although with occasional compatibility problems accruing to the Macintosh version of IE4).

In Chapter 14, I provide some suggestions on how to approach the diversity of object models when developing content. Until W3C DOM-compatible browsers represent the majority of browsers accessing your pages, you may have to weigh a delicate balance between the gain to your Web site's prestige with very cool DHTML features and the pain in making those features work on a range of incompatible browsers. But even if you sit on the DHTML sidelines for a while, there is plenty to do with fully compatible scripting techniques demonstrated throughout this tutorial.

And so ends the final lesson of the *JavaScript Bible, Fourth Edition* tutorial. If you have gone through every lesson and tried your hand at the exercises, you are now ready to dive into the rest of the book to learn the fine details and many more features of both the document object model and the JavaScript language. You can work sequentially through the chapters of Parts III and IV, but before too long, you should also take a peek at Chapter 45 to learn some debugging techniques that help the learning process.

Exercises

1. Explain the difference between a document image object and the memory type of image object.

2. Write the JavaScript statements needed to precache an image named
   jane.jpg that later will be used to replace the document image defined by
   the following HTML:

   ```
   <IMG NAME="people" SRC="john.jpg" HEIGHT=120 WIDTH=100>
   ```

3. With the help of the code you wrote for Question 2, write the JavaScript statement that replaces the document image with the memory image.

4. Backward-compatible document image objects do not have event handlers for mouse events. How do you trigger scripts needed to swap images for mouse rollovers?

✦   ✦   ✦

Document Objects Reference

JavaScript Essentials

Whenever JavaScript is discussed in the context of the Web browser environment, it is sometimes difficult to distinguish between JavaScript the scripting language and the objects that you use the language to control. Even so, it's important to separate the language from the object model just enough to help you make important design decisions when considering JavaScript-enhanced pages. You may come to appreciate the separation in the future if you use JavaScript for other object models, such as server-side programming. All the basics of the language are identical. Only the objects differ.

This chapter elaborates on many of the fundamental subjects about the core JavaScript language raised throughout the tutorial (Part II), particularly as they relate to deploying scripts in a world in which visitors to your pages may use a wide variety of browsers. Along the way, you receive additional insights into the language itself. You can find details about the JavaScript core language syntax in Part IV.

JavaScript Versions

The JavaScript language has its own numbering system, which is completely independent of the version numbers assigned to browsers. The language's creator, Netscape, by and large controls the numbering system.

The first version, logically enough, was JavaScript 1.0. This was the version implemented in Navigator 2 and the first release of Internet Explorer 3. As the language evolved with succeeding browser versions, the JavaScript version number incremented in small steps. Internet Explorer 5, for example, uses JavaScript 1.3, whereas Navigator 6 uses JavaScript 1.5.

Each successive generation employs additional language features. For example, in JavaScript 1.0, arrays were not developed fully, causing scripted arrays to not track the number of items in the array. JavaScript 1.1 filled that hole by providing a constructor function for generating arrays and an inherent `length` property for any generated array. Later in this chapter, you see how to direct a browser to use a specific version of JavaScript for script execution if that makes sense to your application.

In practice, however, the JavaScript version implemented in a browser is not always a good predictor of core language features available for that browser. For example, while JavaScript 1.2 (as implemented by Netscape in NN4) includes broad support for regular expressions, not all of those features appear in Microsoft's JavaScript 1.2 implementation in IE4. By the same token, Microsoft implemented `try-catch` error handling in its version of JavaScript 1.3 in IE5, but Netscape didn't include that feature until its NN6 implementation of JavaScript 1.5. Therefore, the language version number is far less important than the browser version in determining which language features to use.

Core Language Standard — ECMAScript

Although Netscape first developed the JavaScript language, Microsoft incorporated the language in Internet Explorer 3. Because Microsoft did not want to license the "Java" name from its trademark owner (Sun Microsystems), the language became known in the IE environment as JScript. Except for some very esoteric exceptions and the pace of newly introduced features, the two languages are essentially identical. The levels of compatibility between browser brands for a comparable generation are remarkably high for the core language (unlike the vast disparities in object model implementations discussed in Chapter 14).

As mentioned in Chapter 2, standards efforts have been under way to create industry-wide recommendations for browser makers to follow (to make developers' lives easier). The core language was among the first components to achieve standard status. Through the European standards body called ECMA, a formal standard for the language has been agreed to and published. The first specification for the language, dubbed ECMAScript by the standards group, was roughly the same as JavaScript 1.1 in Netscape Navigator 3. The standard defines how various data types are treated, how operators work, what a particular data-specific syntax looks like, and other language characteristics. A newer version (called version 3) adds many enhancements to the core language (version 2 was version 1 with errata fixed). You can view the current version of the ECMA-262 specification at `http://www.ecma.ch`. If you are a student of programming languages, you will find the document fascinating; if you simply want to script your pages, you will probably find the minutia mind-boggling.

Both Netscape and Microsoft have pledged to make their browsers compliant with the ECMA standard. The vast majority of the ECMAScript standard has appeared in Navigator since version 3 and Internet Explorer since version 4. And, as new features are added to the ECMA standard, they tend to find their way into newer browsers as well.

Embedding Scripts in HTML Documents

Scriptable browsers offer several ways to include scripts or scripted elements in your HTML documents. Not all approaches are available in all versions of every browser, but you have sufficient flexibility starting with Navigator 3 and some versions of Internet Explorer 3.

<SCRIPT> tags

The simplest and most compatible way to include script statements in an HTML document is inside a `<SCRIPT>. . .</SCRIPT>` tag set that specifies the scripting language via the `LANGUAGE` attribute. You can have any number of such tag sets in your document. For example, you can define some functions in the Head section to be called by event handlers in HTML tags within the Body section. Another tag set can reside within the Body to write part of the content of the page as the page loads. Place only script statements and comments between the start and end tags of the tag set. Do not place any HTML tags inside unless they are part of a string parameter to a `document.write()` statement that creates content for the page.

Every opening `<SCRIPT>` tag should specify the `LANGUAGE` attribute. Because the `<SCRIPT>` tag is a generic tag indicating that the contained statements are to be interpreted as executable script and not renderable HTML, the tag is designed to accommodate any scripting language the browser knows.

Specifying the language version

All scriptable browsers (from Navigator 2 onward and Internet Explorer 3 onward) recognize the `LANGUAGE="JavaScript"` attribute setting. However, more recent browsers typically acknowledge additional versions of JavaScript or, in the case of Internet Explorer, other languages such as VBScript. For example, the JavaScript interpreter built into Navigator 3 knows the JavaScript 1.1 version of the language; Navigator 4 and Internet Explorer 4 include the JavaScript 1.2 version. For versions beyond the original JavaScript, you specify the language version by appending the version number after the language name without any spaces, as in

```
<SCRIPT LANGUAGE="JavaScript1.1">...</SCRIPT>

<SCRIPT LANGUAGE="JavaScript1.2">...</SCRIPT>
```

How you use these later-version attributes depends on the content of the scripts and your intended audience. For example, while Navigator 6 is JavaScript 1.5-compatible, it works with all previous versions of the JavaScript LANGUAGE attribute as well. Features of the language that are new in JavaScript 1.5 are executed if the LANGUAGE attribute is set to only "JavaScript". On rare occasions (detailed where necessary in Part IV), the behavior of the language changes in a browser if you specify a later language version (usually to force the script to adhere to the ECMA specification when it varies from earlier implementations).

Writing scripts for a variety of browser versions requires a bit of care, especially when the scripts may contain language features available only in newer browsers. As demonstrated in an extensive discussion about browser detection later in this chapter, there may be a need to include multiple versions of a script function, each in its own <SCRIPT> tag with a different LANGUAGE attribute value.

Note   The HTML 4.0 specification defines the <SCRIPT> tag, but does not endorse the LANGUAGE attribute. In its place, HTML 4 recommends the TYPE attribute as a way of specifying a MIME type for the tag's content. Only IE5+ and NN6+ browsers recognize this attribute. Assign the attribute as TYPE="text/javascript" (IE5+ also accepts text/ecmascript). JavaScript versions, however, are not taken into account with this methodology. To be both backward compatible and forward looking, you can specify both the LANGUAGE and TYPE attributes in your <SCRIPT> tags because older browsers ignore the TYPE attribute.

<SCRIPT FOR> tags

Internet Explorer 4 (and later) offers a variation on the <SCRIPT> tag that binds a <SCRIPT> tag's statements to a specific object and event generated by that object. In addition to the language specification, the tag's attributes must include FOR and EVENT attributes (not part of the HTML 4.0 specification). The value assigned to the FOR attribute is a reference to the desired object. Most often, this is simply the identifier assigned to the object's ID attribute (IE4+ enables you to reference an object by either *document.all.objectID* or just *objectID*). The EVENT attribute is the event handler name that you wish the script to respond to. For example, if you design a script to perform some action upon a mouseDown event in a paragraph whose ID is myParagraph, the script statements are enclosed in the following tag set:

```
<SCRIPT FOR="myParagraph" EVENT="onmousedown" LANGUAGE="JavaScript"
TYPE="text/javascript">
...
</SCRIPT>
```

Statements inside the tag set execute only upon the firing of the event. No function definitions are required.

This way of binding an object's event to a script means that there is no event handler defined in the element's tag. Therefore, it guarantees that only IE4 or later can carry out the script when the event occurs. But the tag and attributes contain a lot of source code overhead for each object's script, so this is not a technique that you should use for script statements that need to be called by multiple objects.

Also be aware that you cannot use this tag variation if non-IE or pre-IE4 browsers load the page. In such browsers, script statements execute as the page loads, which certainly causes script errors.

JavaScript versus JScript and VBScript

As previously explained, Internet Explorer's version of JavaScript is called JScript. As a result, Internet Explorer's default script language is JScript. While Internet Explorer acknowledges the LANGUAGE="JavaScript" attribute, Netscape Navigator ignores the LANGUAGE="JScript" attribute. Therefore, if you write scripts that must work in all scriptable browsers, you can specify one language ("JavaScript") and count on all browsers interpreting the code correctly (assuming you take into account other browser compatibility issues).

An entirely different issue is Internet Explorer's other scripting language, VBScript. This language, a derivative of Visual Basic, works only in Win32 versions of IE. You can mix scripts from both languages in the same document, but their tag sets must be separate with the LANGUAGE attributes clearly specifying the language for each <SCRIPT> tag.

Hiding script statements from older browsers

As more versions of scriptable browsers spread among the user community, the installed base of older, nonscriptable browsers diminishes. However, public Web sites can still attract a variety of browsers that date back to the World Wide Web Stone Age (before A.D.1996). But even new devices, such as palm-sized computers, typically employ compact browsers that don't have built-in JavaScript interpreters.

Nonscriptable browsers do not know about the <SCRIPT> tag. Normally, browsers ignore tags they don't understand. That's fine when a tag is just one line of HTML, but a <SCRIPT> tag sets off any number of script statement lines in a document. Old browsers don't know to expect a closing </SCRIPT> tag. Therefore, their natural inclination is to render any lines they encounter after the opening <SCRIPT> tag. Unfortunately, this places script statements squarely in the document — surely to confuse anyone who sees such gibberish on the page.

You can, however, exercise a technique that tricks most older browsers into ignoring the script statements: surround the script statements — inside the <SCRIPT> tag set — with HTML comment markers. An HTML comment begins with the sequence <!-- and ends with -->. Therefore, you should embed these comment sequences in your scripts according to the following format:

```
<SCRIPT LANGUAGE="JavaScript">
<!--
script statements here
//-->
</SCRIPT>
```

JavaScript interpreters also know to ignore a line that begins with the HTML beginning comment sequence, but the interpreter needs a little help with the ending
sequence. The close of the HTML comment starts with a JavaScript comment
sequence (//). This tells JavaScript to ignore the line; but a nonscriptable browser
sees the ending HTML symbols and begins rendering the page with the next HTML
tag or other text in the document. An older browser doesn't know what the
</SCRIPT> tag is, so the tag is ignored and rendering begins after that.

Even with this subterfuge, not all browsers handle HTML comment tags gracefully.
Some older America Online browsers display the script statements no matter what
you do. Fortunately, these browsers are disappearing.

If you design your pages for public access, include these HTML comment lines in all
your <SCRIPT> tag sets. Make sure they go inside the tags, not outside. Also note
that most of the script examples in this book do not include these comments for
the sake of saving space in the listings.

Hiding scripts entirely?

It may be misleading to say that this HTML comment technique "hides" scripts from
older browsers. In truth, the comments hide the scripts from being rendered by the
browsers. The tags and script statements, however, are still downloaded to the
browser and appear in the source code when viewed by the user.

A common wish among authors is to truly hide scripts from visitors to a page.
Client-side JavaScript must be downloaded with the page and is, therefore, visible
in the source view of pages. There are, of course, some tricks you can implement
that may disguise client-side scripts from prying eyes. The most easily implemented technique is to let the downloaded page contain no visible elements, only
scripts that assemble the page that the visitor sees. Source code for such a page is
simply the HTML for the page. But that page is not interactive because no scripting
is attached unless it is written as part of the page—defeating the goal of hiding
scripts. Any scripted solution for disguising scripts is immediately defeatable by
the user turning off scripting temporarily before downloading the page. All of your
code is ready for source view.

If you are worried about other scripters "stealing" your scripts, your best protection is to include a copyright notification in your page's source code. Not only are
your scripts visible to the world, but so, too, are a thief's scripts. This way you can
easily see when someone lifts your scripts verbatim.

Script libraries (.js files)

If you do a lot of scripting or script a lot of pages for a complex Web application, you will certainly develop some functions and techniques that you can use for several pages. Rather than duplicate the code in all of those pages (and go through the nightmare of making changes to all copies for new features or bug fixes), you can create reusable script library files and link them to your pages.

Such an external script file contains nothing but JavaScript code — no <SCRIPT> tags, no HTML. The script file you create must be a text-only file, but its filename must end with the two-character extension .js. To instruct the browser to load the external file at a particular point in your regular HTML file, you add an SRC attribute to the <SCRIPT> tag as follows:

```
<SCRIPT LANGUAGE="JavaScript" SRC="hotscript.js"></SCRIPT>
```

This kind of tag should go at the top of the document so it loads before any other in-document <SCRIPT> tags load. If you load more than one external library, include a series of these tag sets at the top of the document.

Note For complex pages and pages that link multiple external .js files, Navigator 3 and 4 sometimes do not execute immediate statements in the .js file as it loads. If you encounter this problem, surround the statements in a function, and invoke the function from a script statement in the main document.

Take notice of two features about this external script tag construction. First, the <SCRIPT> . . . </SCRIPT> tag pair is required, even though nothing appears between them. You can mix <SCRIPT> tag sets that specify external libraries with in-document scripts in the same document. Second, avoid putting other script statements between the start and end tags when the start tag contains an SRC attribute.

How you reference the source file in the SRC attribute depends on its physical location and your HTML coding style. In the preceding example, the .js file is assumed to reside in the same directory as the HTML file containing the tag. But if you want to refer to an absolute URL, the protocol for the file is http:// (just like with an HTML file):

```
<SCRIPT LANGUAGE="JavaScript" SRC="http://www.cool.com/hotscript.js">
</SCRIPT>
```

A very important prerequisite for using script libraries with your documents is that your Web server software must know how to map files with the .js extension to a MIME type of application/x-javascript. If you plan to deploy JavaScript in this manner, be sure to test a sample on your Web server beforehand and arrange for any necessary server adjustments.

When a user views the source of a page that links in an external script library, code from the `.js` file does not appear in the window even though the browser treats the loaded script as part of the current document. However, the name or URL of the `.js` file is plainly visible (displayed exactly as it appears in your source code). Anyone can then turn off JavaScript in the browser and open that file (using the `http://` protocol) to view the `.js` file's source code. In other words, an external JavaScript source file is no more hidden from view than JavaScript embedded directly in an HTML file.

Tip   NN3 exhibits a bug if you specify an external `.js` library file in a tag that specifies JavaScript 1.2 as the language. Unfortunately, NN3 ignores the language version and loads the external file no matter what language you specify in that tag. Therefore, if you don't want those scripts to run in NN3, surround the scripts in the external file in a version-checking `if` clause:

```
if (parseInt(navigator.appVersion) > 3) {
    statements to run here
}
```

Library compatibility issues

On the Netscape Navigator side, the external library capability was introduced with NN3. Therefore, the SRC attribute is ignored in NN2, and none of the external scripts become part of the document.

The situation is more clouded on the Internet Explorer side. When IE3 shipped for Windows, the external script library feature was not available. By most accounts, IE version 3.02 included support for external libraries, but I heard reports that this was not the case. I know that the version 3.02 installed on my Windows 95 computers loads external libraries from `.js` files. It may be a wise tactic to specify a complete URL for the `.js` file because this is known to assist IE3 in locating the script library file associated with an HTML file.

Navigator 3&4 JavaScript entities

A feature valid only for Navigator 3 and 4 is the JavaScript entity. The idea behind this technique is to provide a way for the browser to use script expressions to fill in the value for any HTML tag attribute. *Entities* are strings that allow special characters or symbols to be embedded in HTML. They begin with an ampersand symbol (&) and end with a semicolon (;). For example, the `&copy;` entity is rendered in browsers as a copyright symbol (©).

To assign a JavaScript expression to an entity, the entity still begins and ends like all entities, but curly braces surround the expression. For example, consider a document containing a function that returns the current day of the week:

```
function today() {
    var days = new Array("Sunday","Monday","Tuesday","Wednesday","Thursday",
    "Friday","Saturday")
    var today = new Date()
    return days[today.getDay()]
}
```

You can assign this function to a JavaScript entity such that the label of a button is created with the returned value of the function:

```
<INPUT TYPE="button" VALUE="&{today()};" onClick="handleToday()">
```

You can use expressions to fulfill only attribute assignments, not other parts related to a tag, such as the text for a document title or link. Those items can be generated dynamically via `document.write()` statements as the document loads.

The dynamic content capabilities of NN6 (and IE4+) provide ample substitutes for JavaScript entities. At load time, a script can modify any element's attribute after the HTML creates the element, including those that impact its size or layout. The only difference is that with the dynamic version, the user sees both the "before" and "after" versions while the page loads.

Browser Version Detection

Without question, the biggest challenge facing many client-side scripters is how to program an application that accommodates a wide variety of browser versions and brands, each one of which can bring its own quirks and bugs. Happy is the intranet developer who knows for a fact that the company has standardized its computers with a particular brand and version of browser. But that is a rarity, especially in light of the concept of the *extranet* — private corporate networks and applications that open up for access to the company's suppliers and customers.

Having dealt with this problem since the original scripted browser (NN2) had to work alongside a hoard of nonscriptable browsers, I have identified several paths that an application developer can follow. Unless you decide to be autocratic about browser requirements for using your site, you must make compromises in desired functionality or provide multiple paths in your Web site for two or more classes of browsers. In this section, I give you several ideas about how to approach development in an increasingly fragmented browser world.

Is JavaScript on?

Very often, the first decision an application must make is whether the client accessing the site is JavaScript-enabled. Non-JavaScript-enabled browsers fall into two categories: a) JavaScript-capable browsers that have JavaScript turned off in the preferences; and b) browsers that have no built-in JavaScript interpreter.

Using the <NOSCRIPT> tag

Except for some of the earliest releases of NN2, all JavaScript-capable browsers have a preferences setting to turn off JavaScript (and a separate one for Java). You should know that even though JavaScript is turned on by default in most browsers, many institutional deployments turn it off when the browser is installed on client machines. The reasons behind this MIS deployment decision vary from scares about Java security violations incorrectly associated with JavaScript, valid JavaScript security concerns on some browser versions, and the fact that some firewalls try to filter JavaScript lines from incoming HTML streams.

All JavaScript-capable browsers include a set of <NOSCRIPT>. . .</NOSCRIPT> tags to balance the <SCRIPT>. . .</SCRIPT> tag set. If one of these browsers has JavaScript turned off, the <SCRIPT> tag is ignored but the <NOSCRIPT> tag is observed. As with the <NOFRAMES> tag, you can use the body of a <NOSCRIPT> tag set to display HTML that lets users know JavaScript is turned off, and therefore the full benefit of the page isn't available unless they turn on JavaScript. Listing 13-1 shows a skeletal HTML page that uses these tags.

Listing 13-1: **Employing the <NOSCRIPT> Tag**

```
<HTML>
<HEAD>
<TITLE>Some Document</TITLE>
<SCRIPT LANGUAGE="JavaScript">
    // script statements
</SCRIPT>
<NOSCRIPT>
<B>Your browser has JavaScript turned off.</B><BR>
You will experience a more enjoyable time at this Web site if you turn
JavaScript on.
<HR>
</NOSCRIPT>
</HEAD>
<BODY>
<H2>The body of your document.</H2>
</BODY>
</HTML>
```

You can display any standard HTML within the `<NOSCRIPT>` tag set. An icon image is a colorful way to draw the user's attention to the special advice at the top of the page. If your document is designed to create content dynamically in one or more places in the document, you may have to include a `<NOSCRIPT>` tag set after more than one `<SCRIPT>` tag set to let users know what they're missing. Do not include the HTML comment tags that you use in hiding JavaScript statements from older browsers. Their presence inside the `<NOSCRIPT>` tags prevents the HTML from rendering.

Other nonscriptable browsers

At this juncture, I must point out that newcomers to scripting frequently want to know what script to write to detect whether JavaScript is turned on. Because scripters are so ready to write a script to work around all situations, it takes some thought to realize that a non-JavaScript browser cannot execute such a script: If no JavaScript interpreter exists in the browser (or it is turned off), the script is ignored. I suppose that the existence of a JavaScript-accessible method for Java detection — the `navigator.javaEnabled()` method — promises a parallel method for JavaScript. But logic fails to deliver on that unspoken promise.

Another desire is to have JavaScript substitute document content when the browser is JavaScript-enabled. Only in IE4+ and NN6+ can a script replace regular HTML with scripted content. If you develop content that must be backward compatible with older browsers, remember that all HTML in a document appears in the browser window, while scripted content can be additive only.

You can use this additive scripting to create unusual effects when displaying different links and (with a caveat) body text for scriptable and nonscriptable browsers. Listing 13-2 shows a short document that uses HTML comment symbols to trick nonscriptable browsers into displaying a link to Netscape's Web site and two lines of text. A scriptable browser takes advantage of a behavior that allows only the nearest `<A>` tag to be associated with a closing `</A>` tag. Therefore, the Netscape link isn't rendered at all, but the link to my Web site is. For the body text, the script assigns the same text color to a segment of HTML body text as the document's background. While the colored text is camouflaged in a scriptable browser (and some other text written to the document), the "hidden" text remains invisible in the document. HTML fans frown upon this kind of element spoofing, which will likely run afoul of HTML validators. However, it can be fun to play with.

Listing 13-2: Rendering Different Content for Scriptable and Nonscriptable Browsers

```
<HTML>
<BODY BGCOLOR="#FFFFFF">
<A HREF="http://home.netscape.com">
<SCRIPT LANGUAGE="JavaScript">
<!--
document.writeln("<A HREF='http://www.dannyg.com'>")
//-->
</SCRIPT>
Where?</A>
<HR>
<SCRIPT LANGUAGE="JavaScript">
<!--
document.write("Howdy from the script!<FONT COLOR='#FFFFFF'>")
//-->
</SCRIPT>
If you can read this, JavaScript is not available.
<SCRIPT LANGUAGE="JavaScript">
<!--
document.write("</FONT>")
//-->
</SCRIPT>
<BR>
Here's some stuff afterward.
</BODY>
</HTML>
```

Scripting for different browsers

The number of solutions for accommodating different client browsers is large because the specific compatibility need might be as simple as letting a link navigate to a scripted page for script-enabled browsers, as involved as setting up distinct areas of your application for different browser classes, or any degree in between. The first step in planning for compatibility is determining what your goals are for various visitor classes.

Establishing goals

Once you map out your application, you must then look at the implementation details to see which browser is required for the most advanced aspect of the application. For example, if the design calls for image swapping on mouse rollovers, that feature requires NN3+ and IE4+. In implementing Dynamic HTML features, you have potentially three different ways to implement tricks (such as movable elements or changeable content) because the document object models require different scripting (and sometimes HTML) for NN4, IE4+, and the W3C DOM implemented in NN6 and IE5+.

In an ideal scenario, you have an appreciation for the kinds of browsers that your visitors use. For example, if you want to implement some DHTML features, but NN4 usage is only a small and decreasing percentage of hits, then you can probably get by with designing for the IE4+ and NN6 document object models. Or you may wish to forget the past and design your DHTML exclusively for W3C DOM-compatible browsers. If your Web hosting service maintains a log of visitor activity to your site, you can study the browsers listed among the hits to see which browsers your visitors use.

After you determine the lowest common denominator for the optimum experience, you then must decide how gracefully you want to degrade the application for visitors whose browsers do not meet the common denominator. For example, if you plan a page or site that requires a W3C DOM-compatible browser for all the bells and whistles, you can provide an escape path with content in a simple format that every browser from Lynx to IE4 and NN4 can view. Or perhaps you can provide for users of older scriptable browsers a third offering with limited scriptability that works on all scriptable browsers.

Creating an application or site that has multiple paths for viewing the same content may sound good at the outset, but don't forget that maintenance chores lie ahead as the site evolves. Will you have the time, budget, and inclination to keep all paths up to date? Despite whatever good intentions a designer of a new Web site may have, in my experience the likelihood that a site will be maintained properly diminishes rapidly with the complexity of the maintenance task.

Implementing a branching index page

If you decide to offer two or more paths into your application or content, one place you can start visitors down their individual paths is at the default page for your site. Numerous techniques are available that can redirect visitors to the appropriate perceived starting point of the site.

One design to avoid is placing the decision about the navigation path in the hands of the visitor. Offering buttons or links that describe the browser requirements may work for users who are HTML and browser geeks, but average consumers surfing the Web these days likely don't have a clue about what level of HTML their browsers support or whether they are JavaScript-enabled. It is incumbent upon the index page designer to automate the navigation task as much as possible.

A *branching index page* has almost no content. It is not the "home page" per se of the site, rather a gateway to the entire Web site. Its job is to redirect users to what appears to be the home page for the site. Listing 13-3 shows what such a branching index page looks like.

Listing 13-3: **A Branching Index Page**

```
<HTML>
<HEAD>
  <TITLE>GiantCo On The Web</TITLE>
  <SCRIPT LANGUAGE="JavaScript">
  <!--
      window.location.href = "home1.html"
  //-->
  </SCRIPT>
  <META HTTP-EQUIV="REFRESH"
  CONTENT="0; URL=http://www.giantco.com/home2.html">
</HEAD>

<BODY>
<CENTER>
   <A HREF="home2.html"><IMG SRC="images/giantcoLogo.gif" HEIGHT=60 WIDTH=120
BORDER=0 ALT="Go To GiantCo Home Page"></A>
</CENTER>
</BODY>
</HTML>
```

Notice that the only visible content is an image surrounded by a standard link. The <BODY> tag contains no background color or art. A single script statement is located in the Head. A <META> tag is also in the Head to automate navigation for some users. To see how a variety of browsers respond to this page, here are what three different classes of browser do with Listing 13-3:

A JavaScript-enabled browser. Although the entire page may load momentarily (at most, flashing the company logo for a brief moment), the browser executes the script statement that loads home1.html into the window. In the meantime, the image is preloaded into the browser's memory cache. This image should be reused in home1.html so the download time isn't wasted on a one-time image. If your pages require a specific browser brand or minimum version number, this is the place to filter out browsers that don't meet the criteria (which may include the installation of a particular plug-in). Use the properties of the navigator object (Chapter 28) to write a *browser sniffer script* that allows only those browsers meeting your design minimum to navigate to the scripted home page. All other browsers fall through to the next execution possibility.

A modern browser with JavaScript turned off or missing. Several modern browsers recognize the special format of the <META> tag as one that loads a URL into the current window after a stated number of seconds. In Listing 13-3, that interval is zero seconds. The <META> tag is executed only if the browser ignores the <SCRIPT> tag. Therefore, any scriptable browser that has JavaScript turned off or any browser that knows <META> tags but no scripting follows the refresh command for the <META> tag. If you utilize this tag, be very careful to observe the tricky formatting of the CONTENT attribute value. A semicolon and the subattribute URL follow the number of seconds. A complete URL for your nonscriptable home page version is required for this subattribute. Importantly, the entire CONTENT attribute value is inside one set of quotes.

Older graphical browsers, PDA browsers, and Lynx. The last category includes graphical browsers some call "brain-dead," as well as intentionally stripped down browsers. Lynx is designed to work in a text-only VT-100 terminal screen; personal digital assistants (PDAs) such as the Palm handheld computer have browsers optimized for usage through slow modems and viewing on small screens. If such browsers do not understand the <META> tag for refreshing content, they land at this page with no further automatic processing. But by creating an image that acts as a link, the user will likely click (or tap) on it to continue. The link then leads to the nonscriptable home page. Also note that the ALT attribute for the image is supplied. This takes care of Lynx and PDA browsers (with image loading off) because these browsers show the ALT attribute text in lieu of the image. Users click or tap on the text to navigate to the URL referenced in the link tag.

I have a good reason to keep the background of the branching index page plain. For those whose browsers automatically lead them to a content-filled home page, the browser window flashes from a set background color to the browser's default background color before the new home page and its background color appear. By keeping the initial content to only the company logo, less screen flashing and obvious navigation are visible to the user.

One link — alternate destinations

Another filtering technique is available directly from links. With the exceptions of NN2 and IE3, a link can navigate to one destination via a link's onClick event handler and to another via the HREF attribute if the browser is not scriptable.

The trick is to include an extra return false statement in the onClick event handler. This statement cancels the link action of the HREF attribute. For example, if a nonscriptable browser should go to one version of a page at the click of a link and the scriptable browser should go to another, the link tag is as follows:

```
<A HREF="nonJSCatalog.html" onClick="location.href='JSCatalog.html';return
false">Product Catalog</A>
```

Only nonscriptable browsers, NN2, and IE3 go to the nonJSCatalog.html page; all others go to the JSCatalog.html page.

Multiple-level scripts

Each new JavaScript level brings more functionality to the language. You can use the LANGUAGE attribute of the <SCRIPT> tag to provide road maps for the execution of functions according to the power available in the browser. For example, consider a button whose event handler invokes a function. You can write that function in such a way that users of each JavaScript version get special treatment with regard to unique features of that version. To make sure all scriptable browsers handle the event handler gracefully, you can create multiple versions of the function, each wrapped inside its own <SCRIPT> tag and specifying a particular language version.

Listing 13-4 shows the outline of a page that presents different versions of the same event handler. For this technique to work properly, you must lay out the <SCRIPT> tags in ascending order of JavaScript version. In other words, the last function that the browser knows how to read (according to the LANGUAGE version) is the one that gets executed. In Listing 13-4, for instance, NN3 (whose JavaScript version is 1.1) gets only as far as the middle version and executes only that one.

Listing 13-4: **Multiple Script Versions**

```
<HTML>
<HEAD>
    <SCRIPT LANGUAGE="JavaScript">
    <!--
    function doIt() {
        // statements for JavaScript 1.0 browsers
    }
    //-->
    </SCRIPT>

    <SCRIPT LANGUAGE="JavaScript1.1">
    <!--
    function doIt() {
        // statements for JavaScript 1.1 browsers
    }
    //-->
    </SCRIPT>

    <SCRIPT LANGUAGE="JavaScript1.2">
    <!--
    function doIt() {
        // statements for JavaScript 1.2 browsers
    }
    //-->
    </SCRIPT>
</HEAD>
<BODY>
<FORM>
    <INPUT TYPE=button VALUE="Click Me" onClick="doIt()">
</FORM>
</BODY>
</HTML>
```

If you use this technique, you must define an event handler for the lowest common version to catch the oldest browsers. For example, failure to include a version for JavaScript 1.0 in Listing 13-4 results in a script error for users of NN2 and IE3. If you don't want an older browser to execute a function (because the browser doesn't support the functionality required for the action), include a *dummy function* (a function definition with no nested script statements) in the lower-version `<SCRIPT>` tag to catch the event handlers of less-capable browsers.

Scripting event handlers as object properties

Along the same lines of Listing 13-4, you can define event handlers for objects within separate language versions. This works for NN3+ and IE4+ because in those browsers you can assign event handlers as properties of an object instead of by way of tag attribute event handlers. For example, in Listing 13-5, a button is assigned an event handler within the context of a JavaScript 1.1-level script. NN2 and IE3 users don't have their button's event handler set because the HTML tag doesn't have an event handler. Even though the `doIt()` function is not restricted to any JavaScript version, it is invoked only in browsers capable of JavaScript version 1.1 or later.

Listing 13-5: **Event Handler Assignments**

```
<<HTML>
<HEAD>
    <SCRIPT LANGUAGE="JavaScript">
    <!--
    function doIt() {
        // statements
    }
    //-->
    </SCRIPT>
</HEAD>
<BODY>
<FORM>
    <INPUT TYPE=button NAME=janeButton VALUE="Click Me">
    <SCRIPT LANGUAGE="JavaScript1.1">
    <!--
        document.forms[0].janeButton.onclick=doIt
    //-->
    </SCRIPT>
</FORM>
</BODY>
</HTML>
```

Object detection

The final methodology for implementing browser version branching is known as *object detection*. The principle is simple: If an object type exists in the browser's object model, then it is safe to execute script statements that work with that object.

Perhaps the best example of object detection is the way scripts can swap images on a page in newer browsers without tripping up on older browsers that don't implement images as objects. In a typical image swap, onMouseOver and onMouseOut event handlers (assigned to a link surrounding an image, to be backward compatible) invoke functions that change the src property of the desired image. Each of those functions is invoked for all scriptable browsers, but you want them to run their statements only when images can be treated as objects.

Object models that implement images always include an array of image objects belonging to the document object. The document.images array always exists, even with a length of zero when no images are on the page. Therefore, if you wrap the image swapping statements inside an if construction that lets browsers pass only if the document.images array exists, older browsers simply skip over the statements:

```
function imageSwap(imgName, url) {
    if (document.images) {
        document.images[imgName].src = url
    }
}
```

Object detection works best when you know for sure how all browsers implement the object. In the case of document.images, the implementation across browsers is identical, so it is a very safe branching condition. That's not always the case, and you should use this feature cautiously. For example, IE4 introduced a document object array called document.all, which is used very frequently in building references to HTML element objects. NN4, however, did not implement that array, but instead had a document-level array object called layers, which was not implemented in IE4. Unfortunately, many scripters used the existence of these array objects as determinants for browser version. They set global variables signifying a minimum version of IE4 and NN4 based on the existence of these array objects. This is most dangerous because there is no way of knowing if a future version of a browser may adopt the object of the other browser brand. What happens, for instance, if the W3C DOM in a future version should adopt the document.all array? If a future version of Navigator implements that array, the browser sniffing code from the old page will treat Navigator as if it were Internet Explorer, and scripts will likely break left and right.

This is why I recommend object detection not for browser version sniffing but for object availability branching, as shown previously for images. Moreover, it is safest to implement object detection only when all major browser brands (and the W3C DOM recommendation) have adopted the object so that behavior is predictable wherever your page loads in the future.

Techniques for object detection include testing for the availability of an object's method. A reference to an object's method returns a value, so such a reference can be used in a conditional statement. For example, the following code fragment demonstrates how a function can receive an argument containing the string ID of an element and convert the string to a valid object reference for three different document object models:

```
function myFunc(elemID) {
    var obj
    if (document.all) {
        obj = document.all(elemID)
    } else if (document.getElementById) {
        obj = document.getElementById(elemID)
    } else if (document.layers) {
        obj = document.layers[elemID]
    }
    if (obj) {
        // statements that work on the object
    }
}
```

It no longer matters which browser brand, operating system, and version supports a particular way of changing an element ID to an object reference. Whichever of the three document object properties or method is supported by the browser (or the first one, if the browser supports more than one), that is the property or method used to accomplish the conversion. If the browser supports none of them, then no further statements execute.

If your script wants to check for the existence of an object's property or method, you may also have to check for the existence of the object beforehand if that object is not part of all browers' object models. An attempt to reference a property of a non-existent object in a conditional expression generates a script error. To avoid the error, you can cascade the conditional tests with the help of the && operator. The following fragment tests for the existence of both the document.body object and the document.body.style property:

```
if (document.body && document.body.style) {
    // statements that work on the body's style property
}
```

If the test for document.body fails, JavaScript bypasses the second test.

One potential "gotcha" to using conditional expressions to test for the existence of an object's property is that even if the property exists but its value is zero or an empty string, the conditional test reports that the property does not exist. To workaround this potential problem, the conditional expression can examine the data type of the value to ensure that the property genuinely exists. A non-existent property for an object reports a data type of undefined. Use the typeof operator (Chapter 40) to test for a valid property:

```
if (document.body && typeof document.body.scroll != "undefined") {
    // statements that work on the body's scroll property
}
```

Object detection is the wave of the future, and I wholeheartedly recommend designing your scripts to take advantage of it in lieu of branching on particular browser name strings and version numbers. Scriptable features are gradually finding their way into browsers embedded in a wide range of non-traditional computing devices. These browsers may not go by the same names and numbering systems that we know today, yet such browsers may be able to interpret your scripts. By testing for browser functionality, your scripts will likely require less maintenance in the future. You can see more object detection at work in Chapters 47 and 56.

Designing for Compatibility

Each new major release of a browser brings compatibility problems for page authors. It's not so much that old scripts break in the new versions (well-written scripts rarely break in new versions with the rare exception of the jump from NN4 to NN6). No, the problems center on the new features that attract designers when the designers forget to accommodate visitors who have not advanced to the latest and greatest browser version yet or who don't share your browser brand preference.

Adding to these problems are numerous bugs, particularly in first-generation browsers from both Netscape and Microsoft. Worse still, some of these bugs affect only one operating system platform among the many supported by the browser. Even if you have access to all the browsers for testing, the process of finding the errors, tracking down the bugs, and implementing workarounds that won't break later browsers can be quite frustrating—even when you've scripted pages from the earliest days and have a long memory for ancient bug reports.

Catering only to the lowest common denominator can more than double your development time due to the expanded testing matrix necessary to ensure a good working page in all operating systems and on all versions. Decide how important the scripted functionality you employ in a page is for every user. If you want some functionality that works only in a later browser, then you may have to be a bit autocratic in defining the minimum browser for scripted access to your page—any lesser browser gets shunted to a simpler presentation of your site's data.

Another possibility is to make a portion of the site accessible to most, if not all, browsers, and restrict the scripting to only the occasional enhancement that non-scriptable browser users won't miss. Once the application reaches a certain point in the navigation flow, then the user needs a more capable browser to get to the really good stuff. This kind of design is a carefully planned strategy that lets the site welcome all users up to a point, but then enables the application to shine for users of, say, W3C DOM-compatible browsers.

The ideal page is one that displays useful content on any browser, but whose scripting enhances the experience of the page visitor — perhaps by offering more efficient site navigation or interactivity with the page's content. That is certainly a worthy goal to aspire to. But even if you can achieve this ideal on only some pages, you will reduce the need for defining entirely separate, difficult-to-maintain paths for browsers of varying capabilities.

Dealing with beta browsers

If you have crafted a skillfully scripted Web page or site, you may be concerned when a prerelease (or *beta*) version of a browser available to the public causes script errors or other compatibility problems to appear on your page. Do yourself a favor — don't overreact to bugs and errors that occur in prerelease browser versions. If your code is well written, it should work with any new generation of browser. If the code doesn't work correctly, consider the browser to be buggy. Report the bug (preferably with a simplified test case script sample) to the browser maker.

The exception to the "it's a beta bug" rule arose in the transition from NN4 to NN6. As you learn in Chapter 14, a conscious effort to eliminate a proprietary NN4 feature (the <LAYER> tag and corresponding scriptable object) caused many NN4 scripts to break on NN6 betas (and final release). Had scripters gone to report the problem to the new browsers' developer (Mozilla), they would have learned of the policy change, and planned for the new implementation. It is extremely rare for a browser to eliminate a popular feature so quickly, but it can happen.

It is often difficult to prevent yourself from getting caught up in browser makers' enthusiasm for a new release. But remember that a prerelease version is not a shipping version. Users who visit your page with prerelease browsers should know that there may be bugs in the browser. That your code does not work with a prerelease version is not a sin, nor is it worth losing sleep over. Just be sure to connect with the browser's maker either to find out if the problem will continue in the final release or to report the bug so the problem doesn't make it into the release version.

IE Browser Version Headaches

As described more fully in the discussion of the `navigator` object in Chapter 28, your scripts can easily determine which browser is the one running the script. However, the properties that reveal the version don't always tell the whole story about Internet Explorer. For one thing, the Windows and Macintosh versions of the same major browser version (3.0x) implement slightly different object models. The Mac version includes the ever-popular `image` object for mouse rollover image swapping; the Windows version does not, and any attempt to use such code in the Windows version results in script errors.

Next, the first release of Internet Explorer 3 for the Macintosh was not scriptable at all — the JavaScript interpreter was left out. Macintosh version 3.01 was the first scriptable Mac version. Even among minor generation releases of Internet Explorer 3 for Windows, Microsoft implemented some new features here and there.

Probably the most troublesome problem is that an improved JavaScript interpreter (in the `JScript.dll` file) underwent substantial improvements between version 1 and version 2 for Windows. Many copies of browser version 3.02 for Windows shipped with version 1 of the `.dll`. Some users updated their browsers if they knew to download the new `.dll` from Microsoft. Unfortunately, the interpreter version is not reflected in any `navigator` object property. A nasty Catch-22 in this regard is that version 2 of the interpreter includes a new property that enables you to examine the interpreter version, but testing for that property in a browser that has version 1 of the interpreter installed results in an error message.

Due to the insecurity of knowing exactly what will and won't work in a browser that identifies itself as Internet Explorer 3.0x, you might decide to redirect all users of Internet Explorer 3 to pages in your application that include no scripting. But before you think I'm bashing Internet Explorer 3, you should also consider doing the same redirection for Navigator 2 users due to the number of platform-specific bugs that littered that first round of JavaScript. Object model and core language implementations in NN3+ and IE4+ are much more stable and reliable platforms on which to build scriptable applications (and you get genuine array objects!). If you have an opportunity to study the access logs of your Web site, analyze the proportion of different browser versions over several days before deciding where you set your lowest common denominator for scripted access.

Even with IE5, browser detection remains a challenge. As you can see in detail in Chapter 28, the `navigator.appVersion` property for IE5 for Windows reports version 4 (the same as IE4). You can still "sniff" for version 5 (you can find the designation `MSIE 5` in the `navigator.userAgent` property), but the process is not as straightforward as it could be — especially if you need to look for any version greater than or equal to 5. The best advice is to be vigilant when new browsers come on the scene or adopt object detection techniques in your scripts.

The Evaluator Sr.

In Chapter 6, you were introduced to a slimmed-down version of The Evaluator Jr., which provides an interactive workbench to experiment with expression evaluation and object inspection. At this point, you should meet The Evaluator Sr., a tool you will use in many succeeding chapters to help you learn both core JavaScript and DOM terminology.

Figure 13-1 shows the top part of the page. Two important features differentiate this full version from the Jr. version in Chapter 6.

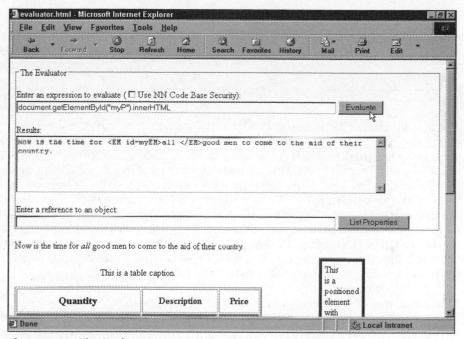

Figure 13-1: The Evaluator Sr.

First, you can try some Netscape secure features if you have Code Base Principles turned on for your browser (Chapter 46) and you check the Use Code Base Security checkbox (NN4+ only). Second, the page has several HTML elements preinstalled, which you can use to explore DOM properties and methods. As with the smaller version, a set of 26 one-letter global variables (a through z) are initialized and ready for you to assign values for extended evaluation sequences.

You should copy the file `evaluator.html` from the companion CD-ROM to a local hard disk and set a bookmark for it in all of your test browsers. Feel free to add your own elements to the bottom of the page to explore other objects. I describe a version of The Evaluator for embedding in your projects as a debugging tool in Chapter 45.

Compatibility ratings in reference chapters

With the proliferation of scriptable browser versions since Navigator 2, it is important to know up front whether a particular language or object model object, property, method, or event handler is supported in the lowest common denominator for which you are designing. Therefore, beginning with Chapter 15 of this reference part of the book, I include frequent compatibility charts, such as the following example:

	NN2	NN3	NN4	NN6	IE3/J1	IE3/J2	IE4	IE5	IE5.5
Compatibility	✓	✓	✓	✓	(✓)	✓	✓	✓	✓

The first four columns represent Navigator versions 2, 3, 4, and 6, respectively (there was no release numbered 5). For Internet Explorer, two columns appear for version 3. One, marked IE3/J1, represents the combination of Internet Explorer 3 and JScript.dll version 1; IE3/J2 represents Internet Explorer 3 and JScript.dll version 2. Internet Explorer 4 and later come with their own JScript.dll versions, so there is no sub-version listed. A checkmark means the feature is compatible with the designated browser. You will also occasionally see one or more of the checkmarks surrounded in parentheses. This means some bug or partial implementation for that browser is explained in the body text. Look to the feature's text if there are version issues related to operating system, especially for items that are new with IE4 or later, where many features operate only in Windows.

I also recommend that you print the JavaScript and Browser Objects Quick Reference file shown in Appendix A. The file is on the companion CD-ROM in Adobe Acrobat format. This quick reference clearly shows each object's properties, methods, and event handlers, along with keys to the browser version in which each language item is supported. You should find the printout to be valuable as a day-to-day resource.

Language Essentials for Experienced Programmers

In this section, experienced programmers can read the highlights about the core JavaScript language in terms that may not make complete sense to those with limited or no scripting experience. This section is especially for you if you found the tutorial of Part II rudimentary. Here, then, is the quick tour of the essential issues surrounding the core JavaScript language.

JavaScript is a scripting language. The language is intended for use in an existing *host environment* (for example, a Web browser) that exposes objects whose properties and behaviors are controllable via statements written in the language. Scripts execute within the context of the host environment. The host environment controls what, if any, external environmental objects may be addressed by language statements running in the host environment. For security and privacy reasons, Web browsers generally afford little or no direct access via JavaScript to browser preferences, the operating system, or other programs beyond the scope of the browser. The exception to this rule is that modern browsers allow deeper client access (with the user's permission) through trust mechanisms such as signed scripts (Netscape) or trusted ActiveX controls (Microsoft).

JavaScript is object-based. Although JavaScript exhibits many syntactic parallels with the Java language, JavaScript is not as pervasively object-oriented as Java. The core language includes several built-in static objects from which working objects are generated. Objects are created via a call to a constructor function for any of the built-in objects plus the new operator. For example, the following expression generates a String object and returns a reference to that object:

```
new String("Hello")
```

Table 13-1 lists the built-in objects with which scripters come in contact.

Table 13-1 **JavaScript Built-in Objects**			
Array[1]	Boolean	Date	Error[2]
EvalError[2]	Function[1]	Math	Number[1]
Object[1]	RangeError[2]	ReferenceError[2]	RegExp[3]
String[1]	SyntaxError[2]	TypeError[2]	URIError[2]

[1]Although defined in ECMA Level 1, was first available in NN3 and IE3/J2

[2]Defined in ECMA Level 3; implemented in NN6

[3]Defined in ECMA Level 3; implemented fully in NN4, partially in IE4

JavaScript is loosely typed. Variables, arrays, and function return values are not defined to be of any particular data type. In fact, an initialized variable can hold different data type values in subsequent script statements (obviously not good practice, but possible nonetheless). Similarly, an array may contain values of multiple types. The range of built-in data types is intentionally limited:

Boolean (true or false)

Null

Number (double-precision 64-bit format IEEE 734 value)

Object (encompassing the `Array` object)

String

Undefined

The host environment defines global scope. Web browsers traditionally define a browser window or frame to be the global context for script statements. When a document unloads, all global variables defined by that document are destroyed.

JavaScript variables have either global or local scope. A global variable in a Web browser is typically initialized in `var` statements that execute as the document loads. All statements in that document can read or write that global variable. A local variable is initialized inside a function (also with the `var` operator). Only statements inside that function may access that local variable.

Scripts sometimes access JavaScript static object properties and methods. Some static objects encourage direct access to their properties or methods. For example, all properties of the `Math` object act as constant values (for example, `Math.PI`).

You can add properties or methods to working objects at will. To add a property to an object, simply assign a value of any type to it. For example, to add an `author` property to a string object named `myText`, use:

```
myText.author = "Jane"
```

Assign a function reference to an object property to give that object a new method:

```
// function definition
function doSpecial(arg1) {
    // statements
}
// assign function reference to method name
myObj.handleSpecial = doSpecial
...
// invoke method
myObj.handleSpecial(argValue)
```

Inside the function definition, the `this` keyword refers to the object that owns the method.

JavaScript objects employ prototype-based inheritance. All object constructors create working objects whose properties and methods inherit the properties and methods defined for the *prototype* of that object. Starting with NN3 and IE3/J2, scripts can add and delete custom properties and/or methods associated with the static object's prototype so that new working objects inherit the current state of the prototype. Scripts can freely override prototype property values or assign different functions to prototype methods in a working object if desired without affecting the static object prototype. But if inherited properties or methods are not modified in the current working object, any changes to the static object's prototype are reflected in the working object. (The mechanism is that a reference to an object's property works its way up the prototype inheritance chain to find a match to the property name.)

JavaScript includes a large set of operators. You can find most operators that you are accustomed to working with in other languages.

JavaScript provides typical control structures. All versions of JavaScript offer `if`, `if-else`, `for`, and `while` constructions. JavaScript 1.3 (NN4+ and IE4+) also add `do-while` and `switch` constructions. Iteration constructions provide `break` and `continue` statements to modify control structure execution.

JavaScript functions may or may not return a value. There is only one kind of JavaScript function. A value is returned only if the function includes a `return` keyword followed by the value to be returned. Return values can be of any data type.

JavaScript functions cannot be overloaded. A JavaScript function accepts zero or more arguments, regardless of the number of parameter variables defined for the function. All arguments are automatically assigned to the `arguments` array, which is a property of a function object. Parameter variable data types are not predefined.

Values are passed "by reference" and "by value." An object passed to a function is actually a reference to that object, offering full read/write access to properties and methods of that object. But other types of values (including object properties) are passed by value, with no reference chain to the original object. Thus, the following nonsense fragment empties the text box when the `onChange` event fires:

```
function emptyMe(arg1) {
    arg1.value = ""
}
...
<INPUT TYPE="text" VALUE="Howdy" onChange="emptyMe(this)">
```

But in the following version, nothing happens to the text box:

```
function emptyMe(arg1) {
    arg1 = ""
}
...
<INPUT TYPE="text" VALUE="Howdy" onChange="emptyMe(this.value)">
```

The local variable (`arg1`) simply changes from `"Howdy"` to an empty string.

Error trapping techniques depend on JavaScript version. There is no error trapping in NN2 or IE3. Error trapping in NN3, NN4, and IE4 is event-driven in the Web browser object model. JavaScript, as implemented in IE5 and NN6, supports `try-catch` and `throw` statements, as well as built-in error objects that are not dependent on the host environment.

Memory management is not under script control. The host environment manages memory allocation, including garbage collection. Different browsers may handle memory in different ways.

White space (other than a line terminator) is insignificant. Space and tab characters may separate lexical units (for example, keywords, identifiers, and so on).

A line terminator is usually treated as a statement delimiter. Except in very rare constructions, JavaScript parsers automatically insert the semicolon statement delimiter whenever they encounter one or more line terminators (for example, carriage returns or line feeds). A semicolon delimiter is required between two statements on the same physical line of source code. Moreover, string literals may not have carriage returns in their source code (but an escaped newline character (\n) may be a part of the string).

Onward to Object Models

The core language is only a small part of what you work with while scripting Web pages. The bulk of your job entails understanding the ins and outs of document object models as implemented in several generations of browsers. That's where the next chapter picks up the "essentials" story.

✦   ✦   ✦

Document Object Model Essentials

◆ ◆ ◆ ◆

In This Chapter

Object models versus
browser versions

Proprietary model
extensions

Structure of the W3C
DOM

Mixing object models
in a single document

◆ ◆ ◆ ◆

Without question, the biggest challenge facing client-side Web scripters is the sometimes-baffling array of document object models that have competed for our attention throughout the short history of scriptable browsers. Netscape got the ball rolling in Navigator 2 with the first object model. By the time the version 4 browsers came around, the original object model had gained not only some useful cross-browser features, but also a host of features that were unique to only Navigator or Internet Explorer. The object models were diverging, causing no end of headaches for page authors whose scripts had to run on as many browsers as possible. A ray of hope emerged from the standards process of the World Wide Web Consortium (W3C) in the form of a document object model (DOM) recommendation. The new DOM brings forward much of the original object model, plus new ways of addressing every object in a document. The goal of this chapter is to put each of the object models into perspective and help you select the model(s) you intend to support in your Web applications. But before we get to those specifics, let's examine the role of the object model in designing scripted applications.

The Object Model Hierarchy

In the tutorial chapters of Part II, you were introduced to the fundamental ideas behind a document object hierarchy in scriptable browsers. In other object-oriented environments, object hierarchy plays a much greater role than it does in JavaScript-able browsers. (In JavaScript, you don't have to worry about related terms, such as classes, inheritance, and instances.) Even so, you cannot ignore the hierarchy concept because much of your code relies on your ability to write references to objects that depend on their positions within the hierarchy.

Calling these objects "JavaScript objects" is not entirely correct. These are really browser document objects: you just happen to use the JavaScript language to bring them to life. Some scripters of Microsoft Internet Explorer use the VBScript language to script the very same document objects. Technically speaking, JavaScript objects apply to data types and other core language objects separate from the document. The more you can keep document and core language objects separate in your head, the more quickly you can deal with browser brand compatibility issues.

Hierarchy as road map

For the programmer, the primary role of the document object hierarchy is to provide scripts with a way to reference a particular object among all the objects that a browser window can contain. The hierarchy acts as a road map the script can use to know precisely which object to address.

Consider, for a moment, a scene in which you and your friend Tony are in a high school classroom. It's getting hot and stuffy as the afternoon sun pours in through the wall of windows on the west side of the room. You say to Tony, "Would you please open a window?" and motion your head toward a particular window in the room. In programming terms, you've issued a command to an object (whether or not Tony appreciates the comparison). This human interaction has many advantages over anything you can do in programming. First, by making eye contact with Tony before you speak, he knows that he is the intended recipient of the command. Second, your body language passes along some parameters with that command, pointing ever so subtly to a particular window on a particular wall.

If, instead, you are in the principal's office using the public address system, and you broadcast the same command, "Would you please open a window?," no one knows what you mean. Issuing a command without directing it to an object is a waste of time because every object thinks, "That can't be meant for me." To accomplish the same goal as your one-on-one command, the broadcast command has to be something like, "Would Tony Jeffries in Room 312 please open the middle window on the west wall?"

Let's convert this last command to JavaScript *dot syntax* form (see Chapter 4). Recall from the tutorial that a reference to an object starts with the most global point of view and narrows to the most specific point of view. From the point of view of the principal's office, the location hierarchy of the target object is

```
room312.Jeffries.Tony
```

You can also say that Tony's knowledge about how to open a window is one of Tony's methods. The complete reference to Tony and his method then becomes

```
room312.Jeffries.Tony.openWindow()
```

Your job isn't complete yet. The method requires a parameter detailing which window to open. In this case, the window you want is the middle window of the west wall of Room 312. Or, from the hierarchical point of view of the principal's office, it becomes

```
room312.westWall.middleWindow
```

This object road map is the parameter for Tony's openWindow() method. Therefore, the entire command that comes over the PA system is

```
room312.Jeffries.Tony.openWindow(room312.westWall.middleWindow)
```

If, instead of barking out orders while sitting in the principal's office, you attempt the same task via radio from an orbiting space shuttle to all the inhabitants on Earth, imagine how laborious your object hierarchy is. The complete reference to Tony's openWindow() method and the window that you want opened has to be mighty long to distinguish the desired objects from the billions of objects within the space shuttle's view.

The point is that the smaller the scope of the object-oriented world you're programming, the more you can assume about the location of objects. For client-side JavaScript, the scope is no wider than the browser itself. In other words, every object that a JavaScript script can work with resides within the browser application. With few exceptions, a script does not access anything about your computer hardware, operating system, other applications, desktop, or any other stuff beyond the browser program.

The browser document object road map

Figure 14-1 shows the lowest common denominator document object hierarchy that is implemented in all scriptable browsers. Notice that the window object is the topmost object in the entire scheme. Everything you script in JavaScript is in the browser's window.

Pay attention to the shading of the concentric rectangles. Every object in the same shaded area is at the same level relative to the window object. When a line from an object extends to the next darker shaded rectangle, that object contains all the objects in darker areas. There exists, at most, one of these lines between levels. The window object contains the document object; the document object contains a form object; a form object contains many different kinds of form elements.

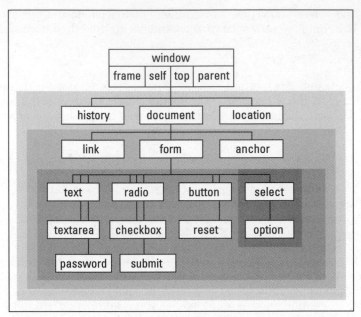

Figure 14-1: The lowest common denominator browser document object hierarchy

Study Figure 14-1 to establish a mental model for the basic scriptable elements of a Web page. Models of more recent browsers have more objects in their hierarchies, but the fundamental organization remains. After you script these objects several times, the object hierarchy will become second nature to you — even if you don't necessarily remember every detail (property, method, and event handler) of every object. At least you know where to look for information.

How Document Objects Are Born

Most of the objects that a browser creates for you are established when an HTML document loads into the browser. The same kind of HTML code you use to create links, anchors, and input elements tells a JavaScript-enhanced browser to create those objects in memory. The objects are there whether or not your scripts call them into action.

The only visible differences to the HTML code for defining those objects are the one or more optional attributes specifically dedicated to JavaScript. By and large, these attributes specify the event you want the user interface element to react to and what JavaScript should do when the user takes that action. By relying on the document's HTML code to perform the object generation, you can spend more time figuring out how to do things with those objects or have them do things for you.

Bear in mind that objects are created in their load order. And if you create a multiframe environment, a script in one frame cannot communicate with another frame's objects until both frames load. This trips up a lot of scripters who create multiframe and multiwindow sites (more in Chapter 16).

Object Properties

A property generally defines a particular current setting of an object. The setting may reflect a visible attribute of an object, such as the state of a checkbox (checked or not); it may also contain information that is not so obvious, such as the action and method of a submitted form.

Document objects have most of their initial properties assigned by the attribute settings of the HTML tags that generate the objects. Thus, a property may be a word (for example, a name) or a number (for example, a size). A property can also be an array, such as an array of images contained by a document. If the HTML does not include all attributes, the browser usually fills in a default value for both the attribute and the corresponding JavaScript property.

A Note to Experienced Object-Oriented Programmers

Although the basic object model hierarchy appears to have a class/subclass relationship, many of the traditional aspects of a true, object-oriented environment don't apply to the model. The original JavaScript document object hierarchy is a *containment hierarchy*, not an *inheritance hierarchy*. No object inherits properties or methods of an object higher up the chain. Nor is there any automatic message passing from object to object in any direction. Therefore, you cannot invoke a window's method by sending a message to it via the document or a form object. All object references must be explicit.

Predefined document objects are generated only when the HTML code containing their definitions loads into the browser. You cannot modify many properties, methods, and event handlers in early object models once you load the document into the browser. In Chapter 41, you learn how to create your own objects, but those objects do not present new visual elements on the page that go beyond what HTML, Java applets, and plug-ins can portray.

Inheritance *does* play a role, as you will see later in this chapter, in the object model defined by the W3C. The new hierarchy is of a more general nature to accommodate requirements of XML as well as HTML. But the containment hierarchy for HTML objects, as described in this section, is still valid in W3C DOM-compatible browsers.

When used in script statements, property names are case-sensitive. Therefore, if you see a property name listed as `bgColor`, you must use it in a script statement with that exact combination of lowercase and uppercase letters. But when you set an initial value of a property by way of an HTML attribute, the attribute name (like all of HTML) is not case-sensitive. Thus, `<BODY BGCOLOR="white">` and `<body bgcolor="white">` both set the same `bgColor` property value.

Each property determines its own read/write status. Some properties are read-only, whereas you can change others on the fly by assigning a new value to them. For example, to put some new text into a text box object, you assign a string to the object's `value` property:

```
document.forms[0].phone.value = "555-1212"
```

Once an object contained by the document exists (that is, its HTML is loaded into the document), you can also add one or more custom properties to that object. This can be helpful if you wish to associate some additional data with an object for later retrieval. To add such a property, simply specify it in the same statement that assigns a value to it:

```
document.forms[0].phone.delimiter = "-"
```

Any property you set survives as long as the document remains loaded in the window and scripts do not overwrite the object. Be aware, however, that reloading the page usually destroys custom properties.

Object Methods

An object's method is a command that a script can give to that object. Some methods return values, but that is not a prerequisite for a method. Also, not every object has methods defined for it. In a majority of cases, invoking a method from a script causes some action to take place. The resulting action may be obvious (such as resizing a window) or something more subtle (such as sorting an array in memory).

All methods have parentheses after them, and they always appear at the end of an object's reference. When a method accepts or requires parameters, the parameter values go inside the parentheses (with multiple parameters separated by commas).

While an object has its methods predefined by the object model, you can also assign one or more additional methods to an object that already exists (that is, after its HTML is loaded into the document). To do this, a script in the document (or in another window or frame accessible by the document) must define a JavaScript function and then assign that function to a new property name of the object. In the following example written to take advantage of version 4 or later browser features, the `fullScreen()` function invokes one `window` object method and adjusts two `window` object properties. By assigning the function reference to the new `window.maximize` property, I define a `maximize()` method for the `window` object. Thus, a button's event handler can call that method directly.

```
// define the function
function fullScreen() {
    this.moveTo(0,0)
    this.outerWidth = screen.availWidth
    this.outerHeight = screen.availHeight
}
// assign the function to a custom property
window.maximize = fullScreen
...
<!-- invoke the custom method -->
<INPUT TYPE="button" VALUE="Maximize Window" onClick="window.maximize()">
```

Object Event Handlers

An *event handler* specifies how an object reacts to an event that is triggered by a user action (for example, a button click) or a browser action (for example, the completion of a document load). Going back to the earliest JavaScript-enabled browser, event handlers were defined inside HTML tags as extra attributes. They included the name of the attribute, followed by an equal sign (working as an assignment operator) and a string containing the script statement(s) or function(s) to execute when the event occurs (see Chapter 5). Event handlers also have other forms. In NN3+ and IE4+, event handlers have corresponding methods for their objects and every event handler is a property of its object.

Event handlers as methods

Consider a button object whose sole event handler is `onClick`. This means whenever the button receives a click event, the button triggers the JavaScript expression or function call assigned to that event handler in the button's HTML definition:

```
<INPUT TYPE="button" NAME="clicker" VALUE="Click Me" onClick="doIt()">
```

Normally, that click event is the result of a user physically clicking the button in the page. In NN3+ and IE4+, you can also trigger the event handler with a script by calling the event handler as if it were a method of the object:

```
document.formName.clicker.onclick()
```

Notice that when summoning an event handler as a method, the method name is all lowercase regardless of the case used in the event handler attribute within the original HTML tag. This lowercase reference is a requirement.

Invoking an event handler this way is different from using a method to simulate the physical action denoted by the event. For example, imagine a page containing three simple text fields. One of those fields has an onFocus event handler defined for it. Physically tabbing to or clicking in that field brings focus to the field and thereby triggers its onFocus event handler. If the field does not have focus, a button can invoke that field's onFocus event handler by referencing it as a method:

```
document.formName.fieldName.onfocus()
```

This scripted action does not bring physical focus to the field. The field's own focus() method, however, does that under script control.

A byproduct of an event handler's capability to act like a method is that you can define the action of an event handler by defining a function with the event handler's name. For example, instead of specifying an onLoad event handler in a document's <BODY> tag, you can define a function like this:

```
function onload() {
    statements
}
```

This capability is particularly helpful if you want event handler actions confined to a script running in NN3, IE4, or later. Your scripts don't require special traps for Navigator 2 or Internet Explorer 3.

Event handlers as properties

Although event handlers are commonly defined in an object's HTML tag, you also have the power in NN3+ and IE4+ to assign or change an event handler just like you assign or change the property of an object. The value of an event handler property looks like a function definition. For example, given this HTML definition:

```
<INPUT TYPE="text" NAME="entry" onFocus="doIt()">
```

the value of the object's onfocus (all lowercase) property is

```
function onfocus() {
    doIt()
}
```

You can, however, assign an entirely different function to an event handler by assigning a function reference to the property. Such references don't include the parentheses that are part of the function's definition. (You see this again much later in Chapter 41 when you assign functions to object properties.)

Using the same text field definition you just looked at, you can assign a different function to the event handler because based on user input elsewhere in the document you want the field to behave differently when it receives the focus. If you define a function like this

```
function doSomethingElse() {
    statements
}
```

you can then assign the function to the field with this assignment statement:

```
document.formName.entry.onfocus = doSomethingElse
```

Because the new function reference is written in JavaScript, you must observe case for the function name. Although NN4 accepts interCap versions of the event handler names, you are best served across all browsers by sticking with all lowercase event handler names as properties.

Caution

Be aware, however, that as with several settable object properties that don't manifest themselves visually, any change you make to an event handler property disappears with a document reload. Therefore, I advise you not to make such changes except as part of a script that also invokes the event handler like a method: Any gap in time leaves room for users to reload the page accidentally or intentionally.

Because every event handler operates as both property and method, I don't list these properties and methods as part of each object's definition in the next chapters. You can be assured this feature works for every JavaScript object that has an event handler starting with Navigator 3 and Internet Explorer 4.

Object Model Smorgasbord

A survey of the entire evolution of scriptable browsers from NN2 and IE3 through IE5.5 and NN6 reveals six (yes, six!) distinct document object model families. Even if your job entails developing content for just one current browser version, you may be surprised that family members from more than one document object model inhabit your authoring space.

Studying the evolution of the object model is extremely valuable for newcomers to scripting. It is too easy to learn the latest object model gadgets in your current browser, only to discover that your heroic scripting efforts are lost on earlier browsers accessing your pages. Therefore, take a look at the six major object model types and how they came into being. Table 14-1 lists the object model families (in chronological order of their release) and the browser versions that support them. Later in this chapter are some guidelines you can follow to help you choose the object model(s) that best suit your users' "appetites."

Table 14-1 **Object Model Families**	
Model	**Browser Support**
Basic Object Model	NN2, NN3, IE3/J1, IE3/J2, NN4, IE4, IE5, NN6, IE5.5
Basic Plus Images	NN3, IE3.01 (Mac only), NN4, IE4, IE5, NN6, IE5.5
NN4 Extensions	NN4
IE4 Extensions	IE4, IE5, IE5.5 (some features in all versions require Win32 OS)
IE5 Extension	IE5, IE5.5 (some features in all versions require Win32 OS)
W3C DOM (I and II)	IE5 (partial), IE5.5 (partial), NN6 (most)

Basic Object Model

The first scriptable browser, Netscape Navigator 2, implemented a very basic document object model. Figure 14-1 provides a visual guide to the objects that were exposed to scripting. The hierarchical structure starts with the window and drills inward toward the document, forms, and form elements. A document is a largely immutable page on the screen. Only elements that are by nature interactive — links and form elements such as text fields, buttons, and so on — are treated as objects with properties, methods, and event handlers.

The heavy emphasis on form elements opened up numerous possibilities that were radical ideas at the time. Because a script could inspect the values of form elements, forms could be pre-validated on the client. If the page included a script that performed some calculations, data entry and calculated results were displayed via editable text fields.

Additional objects that exist outside of the document — window, history, and location objects — provide scriptable access to simple yet practical properties of the browser that loads the page. The most global view of the environment is the navigator object, which includes properties about the browser brand and version.

When Internet Explorer 3 arrived on the scene, the short life of Navigator 2 was nearing its end. Even though NN3 was already widely available in prerelease form, IE3 implemented the basic object model from NN2 (plus one window object property from NN3). Therefore, despite the browser version number discrepancy, NN2 and IE3 are essentially the same with respect to their document object models. For a brief moment in Internet Time, there was nearly complete harmony between Microsoft and Netscape document object models — albeit at a very simple level.

Basic Object Model Plus Images

A very short time after IE3 was released, Netscape released Navigator 3 with an object model that built upon the original version. A handful of existing objects — especially the `window` object — gained new properties, methods, and/or event handlers. Scripts could also communicate with Java applets as objects. But the biggest new object on the scene was the `Image` object and the array of image objects exposed to the `document` object.

Most of the properties for an NN3 image object gave read-only access to values typically assigned to attributes in the `<IMG>` tag. But you could modify one property — the `src` property — after the page loaded. Scripts could swap out images within the fixed image rectangle. Although these new image objects didn't have mouse-related event handlers, nesting an image inside a link (which had `onMouseOver` and new `onMouseOut` event handlers) let scripts implement "image rollovers" to liven up a page.

As more new scripters investigated the possibilities of adding JavaScript to their pages, frustration ensued when the image swapping they implemented for NN3 failed to work in IE3. Although you could easily script around the lack of an image object to prevent script errors in IE3 (see Chapter 12), the lack of this "cool" page feature disappointed many. Had they also taken into account the installed base of NN2 in the world, they would have been disappointed there, too. To confuse matters even more, the Macintosh version of IE 3.01 (the second release of the IE3/Mac browser) implemented scriptable image objects.

Despite these rumblings of compatibility problems to come, the object model implemented in Navigator 3 eventually became the baseline reference for future document object models. With few exceptions, code written for this object model runs on all browsers from NN3 and IE4 through the latest versions of both brands. Exceptions primarily involve Java applet object support in non-Windows versions of IE4+.

Navigator 4-Only Extensions

The next browser released to the world was Netscape Navigator 4. Numerous additions to the existing objects put more power into the hands of scripters. You could move and resize browser windows within the context of script-detectable `screen` object properties (for example, how big the user's monitor screen was). Two concepts that represented new thinking about the object model were an enhanced event model and the layer object.

Event Capture Model

Navigator 4 added many new events to the repertoire. Keyboard events and more mouse events (onMouseDown and onMouseUp) allowed scripts to react to more user actions on form elements and links. All of these events worked as they did in previous object models in which event handlers were typically assigned as attributes to an element's tag (although you could also assign event handlers as properties in script statements). To facilitate some of the Dynamic HTML potential in the rest of the Navigator 4 object model, the event model was substantially enhanced.

At the root of the system is the idea that when a user performs some physical action on an event-aware object (for example, clicking a form button), the event reaches that button from top down through the document object hierarchy. If you have multiple objects that share the same event handler, it may be more convenient to capture that event in just one place — the window or document object level — rather than assigning the same event handler to all the elements. The default behavior of Navigator 4 allowed the event to reach the target object, just as it had in earlier browsers. But you could also turn on *event capture* in the window, document, or layer object. Once captured, the event could be handled at the upper level, preprocessed before being passed onto its original target, or redirected to another object altogether.

To engage event capture in NN4, scripts must invoke the captureEvents() method of the window, document, or layer object and pass as parameters constant values that denote the specific events to be captured (constants of the Event object). If you no longer need to capture an event, you can turn off event capture via the releaseEvents() method.

Whether or not you capture events, the Navigator 4 event model produces an event object (lowercase "e" to distinguish from the static Event object) for each event. That object contains properties that reveal more information about the specific event, such as the keyboard character pressed for a keyboard event or the position of a click event on the page. Any event handler can inspect event object properties to learn more about the event and process the event accordingly.

Layers

Perhaps the most radical addition to the NN4 object model was a new object that reflected an entirely new HTML element, the LAYER element. A *layer* is a container that is capable of holding its own HTML document, yet it exists in a plane in front of the main document. You can move, size, and hide a layer under script control. This new element allowed, for the first time, overlapping elements in an HTML page.

To accommodate the layer object in the document object hierarchy, Netscape defined a nesting hierarchy such that a layer was contained by a document. As the result, the document object acquired a property (document.layers) that was an array of layer objects in the document. This array exposed only the first level of layer(s) in the current `document` object. References to a layer in the main document started with any one of the following:

```
document.layerName
document.layers[n]
document.layers[layerName]
```

Each layer had its own `document` object because each layer could load an external HTML document if desired. Thus, if a script needed access to, say, a form element inside a layer, the reference would begin:

```
document.layerName.document.forms[0]....
```

If a layer contained yet another layer, the reference grew even longer:

```
document.outerLayerName.document.innerLayerName.document.forms[0]...
```

As a positionable element, a layer object had numerous properties and methods that allowed scripts to move, hide, show, and change its stacking order.

Unfortunately for Netscape, the W3C did not agree to make the `<LAYER>` tag a part of the HTML 4.0 specification. As such, it is an orphan element that exists only in Navigator 4 (not implemented in NN6 or later). The same goes for the scripting of the layer object and its nested references. Navigator 4 does, however, implement a little bit of the HTML 4.0 and CSS specifications for positionable elements because you can assign CSS style sheets (with the position and related attributes) to `DIV` and `SPAN` elements in NN4. Navigator treats positioned `DIV` or `SPAN` elements as near equivalents of layer objects for scripting purposes. This means, however, that even if you can get the HTML to work the same across browsers (not always guaranteed due to occasionally different rendering characteristics of positioned `DIV` elements in NN4 and IE4), the scripting for NN4 must adhere to the layer syntax, which differs from the IE4 CSS syntax.

Internet Explorer 4+ Extensions

Microsoft broke important new ground with the release of IE4, which came several months after the release of NN4. The main improvements were in the exposure of all HTML elements, scripted support of CSS, and a new event model. Some other additions were available only on Windows 32-bit operating system platforms.

HTML element objects

The biggest change to the object model world was that every HTML element became a scriptable object, while still supporting the original object model.

Microsoft invented the document.all array (also called a *collection*). This array contains references to every element in the document, regardless of element nesting. If you assign an identifier (name) to the ID attribute of an element, you can reference the element by the following syntax:

document.all.*elementID*

In most cases, you can also drop the document.all. part of the reference and begin with only the element ID.

Every element object has an entirely new set of properties and methods that give scripters a level of control over document content unlike anything seen before. Table 14-2 shows the properties and methods that all HTML element objects have in common in IE4 (properties followed by brackets are arrays).

Table 14-2 **IE4 HTML Element Features in Common**

Properties	Methods
all[]	click()
children[]	contains()
className	getAttribute()
document	insertAdjacentHTML()
filters[]	insertAdjacentText()
id	removeAttribute()
innerHTML	scrollIntoView()
innerText	setAttribute()
isTextEdit	
lang	
language	
offsetHeight	
offsetLeft	
offsetParent	
offsetTop	
offsetWidth	
outerHTML	
outerText	
parentElement	
parentTextEdit	

Properties	Methods
sourceIndex	
style	
tagName	
title	

You can find details for all of the items from Table 4-1 in Chapter 15. But several groups of properties deserve special mention here.

Four properties (innerHTML, innerText, outerHTML, and outerText) provide read/write access to the actual content within the body of a document. This means that you no longer must use text boxes to display calculated output from scripts. You can modify content inside paragraphs, table cells, or anywhere on the fly. The browser's rendering engine immediately reflows a document when the dimensions of an element's content change. That feature puts the "Dynamic" in "Dynamic HTML." To those of us who scripted the static pages of earlier browsers, this feature—now taken for granted—was nothing short of a revelation.

The series of "offset" properties are related to the position of an element on the page. These properties are distinct from the kind of positioning performed by CSS. Therefore, you can get the dimensions and location of any element on the page, making it easier to move positionable content atop elements that are part of the document and may appear in various locations due to the browser window's current size.

Finally, the style property is the gateway to CSS specifications defined for the element. Importantly, the script can modify the numerous properties of the style object. Therefore, you can modify font specifications, colors, borders, and the positioning properties after the page loads. The dynamic reflow of the page takes care of any layout changes that the alteration requires (for example, adjusting to a bigger font size).

Element containment hierarchy

While IE4 still recognizes the element hierarchy of the original object model (Figure 14-1), the document object model for IE4 does not extend this kind of hierarchy fully into other elements. If it did, it would mean that TD elements inside a table might have to be addressed via its next outer TR or TABLE element (just as a form control element must be addressed via its containing FORM element). See in Figure 14-2 how all HTML elements are grouped together under the document object. The document.all array flattens the containment hierarchy as far as referencing object goes. A reference to the most deeply nested TD element is still document.all.cellID. The highlighted pathway from the window object is the predominant reference path used when working with the IE4 document object hierarchy.

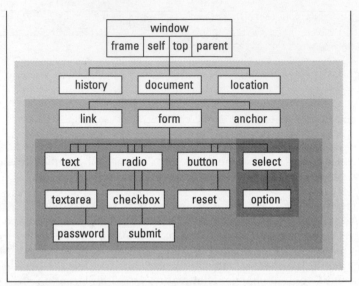

Figure 14-2: The IE4 document object hierarchy

Element containment in IE4, however, is important for other reasons. Because an element can inherit some style sheet attributes from an element that contains it, you should devise a document's HTML by embedding every piece of content inside a container. Paragraph elements are text containers (with start and end tags), not tall line breaks between text chunks. IE4 introduces the notion of a parent-child relationship between a container and elements nested within it. Also, the position of an element may be calculated relative to the position of its next outermost positioning context.

The bottom line here is that element containment doesn't have anything to do with object references (like the original object model). It has everything to do with the *context* of an element relative to the rest of the page's content.

Cascading Style Sheets

By arriving a bit later to market with its version 4 browser than Netscape, Microsoft benefited from having the CSS Level 1 specification more fully developed before the browser's release. Therefore, the implementation is far more complete than that of NN4 (but it is not 100% compatible with the standard).

I should point out that the scriptability of style sheet properties is a bit at odds with the first-generation CSS specification, which seemed to ignore the potential of scripting styles with JavaScript. Many CSS attribute names are hyphenated words (for example, text-align, z-index). But hyphens are not allowed in identifier names in JavaScript. This necessitated conversion of the multiword CSS attribute names to interCap JavaScript property names. Therefore, `text-align` becomes `textAlign` and `z-index` becomes `zIndex`. You can access all of these properties through an element's `style` property:

`document.all.elementID.style.stylePropertyName`

One byproduct of the scriptability of style sheets in IE4 and later is what some might call the *phantom page syndrome*. This occurs when the layout of a page is handled after the primary HTML for the page has downloaded to the browser. As the page loads, not all content may be visible, or it may be in a visual jumble. An `onLoad` event handler in the page then triggers scripts to set styles and/or content for the page. Elements jump around to get to their final resting places. This may be disconcerting to some users who at first see a link to click; but by the time the cursor reaches the click location, the page has reflowed, thereby moving the link to somewhere else on the page.

Event bubbling

Just as Netscape invented an event model for NN4, so, too, did Microsoft invent one for IE4. Unfortunately for cross-browser scripters, the two event models are quite different. Instead of events trickling down the hierarchy to the target element, an IE event starts at the target element and, unless instructed otherwise, "bubbles up" through the element containment hierarchy to eventually reach the `window` object. At any object along the way, an event handler can perform additional processing on that event if desired. Therefore, if you want a single event handler to process all click events for the page, assign the event handler to the `body` or `window` object so the events reach those objects (provided the event bubbling isn't cancelled by some other object along the containment hierarchy).

IE also has an `event` object (a property of the `window` object) that contains details about the event, such as the keyboard key pressed for a keyboard event and the location of a mouse event. Names for these properties are entirely different from the event object properties of NN4.

Despite what seems like incompatible, if not completely opposite, event models in NN4 and IE4, you can make a single set of scripts handle events in both browsers (see Chapters 29 and 56 for examples). In fact, the two event models are made to work together in the W3C DOM Level 2 specification, described later in this chapter.

Event binding of scripts

IE4 introduced an additional way of binding events to objects via a `<SCRIPT>` tag that has two additional, non-W3C attributes: `FOR` and `EVENT` (see a syntax example in Chapter 13). The value assigned to the `FOR` attribute is the ID of an element object for which the script is intended; the value of the `EVENT` attribute is the name of the event handler (for example, `onclick`) by which the script statements within the tag are to be triggered.

Inside the tags are straight script statements, but when the browser sees the special attributes, execution is deferred until the event fires for the designated object. The instant the event fires for the object, the script statements inside the tag execute. This special form of script tag takes the place of a function definition assigned to the event handler by other means. This technique appears to have been a "dry run" for what eventually became DHTML behaviors in IE5/Windows (see the following section).

You can use this binding method only if you run the page inside IE4+. All other browsers, including IE3, ignore the special attributes and treat the statements inside the tags as statements to execute as the page loads.

Win32 features

For Internet Explorer users with 32-bit Windows operating systems, IE4 includes some extra features in the object model that can enhance presentations. *Filters* are style sheet additives that offer a variety of visual effects on body text. For example, you can add a drop shadow or a glowing effect to text by simply applying filter styles to the text. Although filters follow the CSS syntax, they are not a part of the W3C specification.

Two special filters provide animation for transitions between hidden and visible content. For example, you can create the equivalent of a slide presentation by placing the content of each slide in a positioned DIV element. As you hide one DIV and show the other (under script control), the transition filter can perform a transition such as a wipe or an expanding circle — very much like the transitions you specify in PowerPoint or other presentation programs.

Internet Explorer 5+ Extensions

With the release of IE5, Microsoft built more onto the proprietary object model it launched in IE4. Although the range of objects remained pretty much the same, the number of properties, methods, and event handlers for the objects increased dramatically. Some of those additions were added to meet some of the specifications of the W3C DOM (discussed in the next section), occasionally causing a bit of incompatibility with IE4. But Microsoft also pushed ahead with efforts for Windows users only that may not necessarily become industry standards: DHTML behaviors and HTML applications.

A *DHTML behavior* is a chunk of script — saved as an external file — that defines some action (usually a change of one or more style properties) that you can apply to any kind of element. The goal is to create a reusable component that you can load into any document whose elements require that behavior. The behavior file is known as an *HTML component*, and the file has an .htc extension. Components are

XML documents whose XML tags specify events and event-handling routines for whatever element is assigned that behavior. Script statements in .htc documents are written inside <SCRIPT> tag sets just as in regular, scriptable HTML documents. As an example of a DHTML behavior, you can define a behavior that turns an element's text to red whenever the cursor rolls atop it and reverts to black when the cursor rolls out. When you assign the behavior to an element in the document (via CSS-like rule syntax), the element picks up that behavior and responds to the user accordingly. You can apply that same behavior to any element(s) you like in the document. (Microsoft has submitted behaviors to the W3C for possible inclusion into CSS Level 3.) You can see an example of a DHTML behavior in Chapter 15's description of the addBehavior() method and read an extended discussion in Chapter 47.

HTML applications (*HTAs* in Microsoft parlance) are HTML files that include an XML element known as the HTA:APPLICATION element. You can download an HTA to IE5 from the server as if it were a Web page (although its file extension is .hta rather than .htm or .html). A user can also install an HTA on a client machine so it behaves very much like an application with a Desktop icon and significant control over the look of the window. HTAs are granted greater security privileges on the client so that this "application" can behave more like a regular program. In fact, you can elect to turn off the system menu bar and use DHTML techniques to build your own menu bar for the application. Implementation details of HTAs are beyond the scope of this book, but you should be aware of their existence. More information is available at http://msdn.microsoft.com.

The W3C DOM

Conflicting browser object models from Netscape and Microsoft made life difficult for developers. Scripters craved a standard that would serve as a common denominator much like HTML and CSS standards did for content and styles. The W3C took up the challenge of creating a document object model standard, the W3C DOM.

The charter of the W3C DOM working group was to create a document object model that could be applied to both HTML and XML documents. Because an XML document can have tags of virtually any name (as defined by the Document Type Definition), it has no intrinsic structure or fixed vocabulary of elements like an HTML document does. As a result, the DOM specification had to accommodate the known structure of HTML (as defined in the HTML 4.0 specification) as well as the unknown structure of an XML document.

To make this work effectively, the working group divided the DOM specification into two sections. The first, called the *Core DOM*, defines specifications for the basic document structure that both HTML and XML documents share. This includes notions of a document containing elements that have tag names and attributes; an element is capable of containing zero or more other elements. The second part of the DOM specification addresses the elements and other characteristics that apply only to HTML. The HTML portion "inherits" all the features of the Core DOM, while providing a measure of backward compatibility to object models already implemented in legacy browsers and providing a framework for new features.

It is important for veteran scripters to recognize that the W3C DOM does not specify all features from existing browser object models. Many features of the Internet Explorer 4 (and later) object model are not part of the W3C DOM specification. This means that if you are comfortable in the IE environment and wish to shift your focus to writing for the W3C DOM spec, you have to change some practices as highlighted in this chapter. Navigator 4 page authors lose the <LAYER> tag (which is not part of HTML 4.0 and likely will never see the light of day in a standard) as well as the layer object. In many respects, especially with regard to Dynamic HTML applications, the W3C DOM is an entirely new DOM with new concepts that you must grasp before you can successfully script in the environment.

By the same token, you should be aware that whereas NN6 goes to great lengths to implement all of DOM Level 1 and most of Level 2, Microsoft (for whatever reason) features only a partial implementation of the W3C DOM through IE5.5. This is true even though Microsoft participated in the W3C DOM working group and had more than ample time to put more of the W3C DOM into IE version 5.5.

DOM levels

Like most W3C specifications, one version is rarely enough. The job of the DOM working group was too large to be swallowed whole in one sitting. Therefore, the DOM is a continually evolving specification. The timeline of specification releases rarely coincides with browser releases. Therefore, it is very common for any given browser release to include only some of the most recent W3C version.

The first formal specification, DOM Level 1, was released well after NN4 and IE4 shipped. The HTML portion of Level 1 includes DOM Level 0. This is essentially the object model as implemented in Navigator 3 (and for the most part in Internet Explorer 3 plug image objects). Perhaps the most significant omission from Level 1 is an event model (it ignores even the simple event model implemented in NN2 and IE3).

DOM Level 2 builds on the work of Level 1. In addition to several enhancements of both the Core and HTML portions of Level 1, Level 2 adds significant new sections on the event model, ways of inspecting a document's hierarchy, XML namespaces, text ranges, style sheets, and style properties.

What stays the same

By adopting DOM Level 0 as the starting point of the HTML portion of the DOM, the W3C provided a way for a lot of existing script code to work even in a W3C DOM-compatible browser. Every object you see in the original object model starting with the document object (Figure 14-1) plus the image object are in DOM Level 0. Almost all of the same object properties and methods are also available.

More importantly, when you consider the changes to referencing other elements in the W3C DOM (discussed in the next section), we're lucky that the old ways of referencing objects such as forms, form elements, and images still work. Had the working group been planning from a clean slate, it is unlikely that the document object would have been given properties consisting of arrays of forms, links, and images.

The only potential problems you could encounter with your existing code have to do with a handful of properties that used to belong to the document object. In the new DOM, four style-related properties of the document object (alinkColor, bgColor, linkColor, and vlinkColor) become properties of the body object (referenced as document.body). In addition, the three link color properties pick up new names in the process (aLink, link, vLink). It appears, however, that for now, IE5.x and NN6 maintain backward compatibility with the older document object color properties.

Also, note that the DOM specification concerns itself only with the document and its content. Objects such as window, navigator, and screen are not part of the DOM specification through Level 2. Scripters are still at the mercy of browser makers for compatibility in these areas, but the window object likely will be added to the W3C DOM in the future.

What isn't available

As mentioned earlier, the W3C DOM is not simply a restatement of existing browser specifications. Many convenience features of the IE and NN object models do not appear in the W3C DOM. If you develop Dynamic HTML content in IE4+ or NN4, you have to learn how to get along without some of these conveniences.

Navigator 4's experiment with the <LAYER> tag was not successful in the W3C process. As a result, both the tag and the scripting conventions surrounding it do not exist in the W3C DOM. To some scripters' relief, the document.layerName referencing scenario (even more complex with nested layers) disappears from the object model entirely. A positioned element is treated as just another element that has some special style sheet attributes that enable you to move it anywhere on the page, stack it amid other positioned elements, and hide it from view.

Among popular IE4+ features missing from the W3C DOM are the document.all collection of HTML elements and four element properties that facilitate dynamic content: innerHTML, innerText, outerHTML, and outerText. A new W3C way provides for acquiring an array of all elements in a document, but generating HTML content to replace existing content or be inserted in a document requires a tedious sequence of statements (see the section "New DOM concepts" later in this chapter). Netscape, however, has implemented the innerHTML property for HTML element objects in NN6. If you have a lot of legacy IE4 code that uses the other missing properties that you want to use for NN6, see the section "Simulating IE4 Syntax in NN6" later in this chapter.

"New" HTML practices

Exploitation of Dynamic HTML possibilities in both IE4+ and the W3C DOM relies on some HTML practices that may be new to long-time HTML authors. At the core of these practices (espoused by the HTML 4.0 specification) is making sure that all content is within an HTML container of some kind. Therefore, instead of using the <P> tag as a separator between blocks of running text, surround each paragraph of the running text with a <P>...</P> tag set. If you don't do it, the browser treats each <P> tag as the beginning of a paragraph and ends the paragraph element just before the next <P> tag or other block-level element.

While recent browsers continue to accept the omission of certain end tags (for TD, TR, and LI elements, for instance), it is best to get in the habit of supplying these end tags. If for no other reason, they help you visualize where an element's sphere of influence truly begins and ends.

Any element that you intend to script — whether to change its content or its style — should have an identifier assigned to the element's ID attribute. Form control elements still require NAME attributes if you submit the form content to a server. But you can freely assign a different identifier to a control's ID attribute. Scripts can use either the ID or the document.*formReference*.*elementName* reference to reach a control object. Identifiers are essentially the same as the values you assign to the NAME attributes of form and form input elements. Following the same rules for the NAME attribute value, an ID identifier must be a single word (no white space), it cannot begin with a numeral (to avoid conflicts in JavaScript), and it should avoid punctuation symbols except for the underscore. While an element can be accessed by numeric index within the context of some surrounding element (such as the BODY), this is a risky practice when content is under construction. Unique identifiers make it much easier for scripts to reference objects and are not affected by changes in content order.

New DOM concepts

With the W3C DOM come several concepts that may be entirely new to you unless you have worked extensively with the terminology of tree hierarchies. Concepts that have the most impact on your scripting are new ways of referencing elements and nodes.

Element referencing

Script references to objects in the DOM Level 0 are observed in the W3C DOM for backward compatibility. Therefore, a form input element whose NAME attribute is assigned the value userName is addressed just like it always is:

```
document.forms[0].userName
```

or

```
document.formName.userName
```

But because all elements of a document are exposed to the `document` object, you can use the new `document` object method to access any element whose ID is assigned. The method is `document.getElementById()`, and the sole parameter is a string version of the identifier of the object whose reference you wish to get. To help put this in context with what you may have used with the IE4 object model, consider the following HTML paragraph tag:

```
<P ID="myParagraph">...</P>
```

In IE4+, you can reference this element with

```
var elem = document.all.myParagraph
```

IE4+ also enables you to omit the `document.all.` portion of the reference — although for the sake of script readability (especially by others who want to study the script), I recommend that you use the `document.all.` prefix.

Although the `document.all` collection is not implemented in the W3C DOM, use the new `document` object method (available in IE5+ and NN6+) that enables you to access any element by its ID:

```
var elem = document.getElementById("myParagraph")
```

Unfortunately for scripters, this method is difficult to type (it is case-sensitive — watch out for that ending lowercase "d"). But the W3C DOM includes another `document` object method that enables you to simulate the `document.all` convenience collection. See the section, "Simulating IE4 Syntax in NN6" later in this chapter.

A hierarchy of nodes

The issue surrounding containers (described earlier) comes into play for the underlying architecture of the W3C DOM. Every element or freestanding chunk of text in an HTML (or XML) document is an object that is contained by its next outermost container. Let's look at a simple HTML document to see how this system works. Listing 14-1 is formatted to show the containment hierarchy of elements and string chunks.

Listing 14-1: A Simple HTML Document

```
<HTML>
    <HEAD>
        <TITLE>
            A Simple Page
        </TITLE>
    </HEAD>
    <BODY>
        <P ID="paragraph1">
            This is the
            <EM ID="emphasis1">
                one and only
            </EM>
            paragraph on the page.
        </P>
    </BODY>
</HTML>
```

What you don't see in the listing is a representation of the document object. The document object exists automatically when this page loads into a browser. Importantly, the document object encompasses everything you see in Listing 14-1. Therefore, the document object has a single nested element: the HTML element. The HTML element, in turn, has two nested elements: HEAD and BODY. The HEAD element contains the TITLE element, while the TITLE element contains a chunk of text. Down in the BODY element, the P element contains three pieces: a string chunk, the EM element, and another string chunk.

According to W3C DOM terminology, each container, standalone element (such as a BR element), or text chunk is known as a *node* — a fundamental building block of the W3C DOM. Nodes have parent-child relationships when one container holds another. As in real life, parent-child relationships extend only between adjacent generations, so a node can have zero or more children. However, the number of third-generation nodes further nested within the family tree does not influence the number of children associated with a parent. Therefore, in Listing 14-1, the HTML node has two child nodes, HEAD and BODY, which are *siblings* that share the same parent. The BODY element has one child (P) even though that child contains three children (two text nodes and an EM element node).

If you draw a hierarchical tree diagram of the document in Listing 14-1, it should look like the illustration in Figure 14-3.

Note   If the document's source code contains a Document Type Definition (DTD) above the `<HTML>` tag, the browser treats that DTD node as a sibling of the HTML element node. In that case, the root document node contains two child nodes.

```
document
+--<HTML>
   +--<HEAD>
   |   +--<TITLE>
   |      +--"A Simple Page"
   +--<BODY>
      +--<P ID="paragraph1">
         +--"This is the  "
         +--<EM ID="emphasis1">
         |   +--"one and only"
         +--" paragraph on the page."
```

Figure 14-3: Tree diagram of nodes for the document in Listing 14-1

The W3C DOM (through Level 2) defines 12 different types of nodes, seven of which have direct application in HTML documents. These seven types of nodes appear in Table 14-3 (the rest apply to XML). Of the 12 types, the three most common are the document, element, and text fragment types. The latter two are implemented in both IE5+ and NN6 (all are implemented in NN6).

Table 14-3   W3C DOM HTML-Related Node Types

Type	Number	nodeName	nodeValue	Description	IE5+	NN6
Element	1	tag name	null	Any HTML or XML tagged element	Yes	Yes
Attribute	2	attribute name	attribute value	A name-value attribute pair in an element	No	Yes
Text	3	#text	text content	A text fragment contained by an element	Yes	Yes
Comment	8	#comment	comment text	HTML comment	No	Yes
Document	9	#document	null	Root document object	No	Yes
DocumentType	10	DOCTYPE	null	DTD specification	No	Yes
Fragment	11	#document-fragment	null	Series of one or more nodes outside of the document	No	Yes

Applying the node types of Table 14-3 to the node diagram in Figure 14-3, you can see that the simple page consists of one document node, six element nodes, and four text nodes.

Node properties

A node has many properties, most of which are references to other nodes related to the current node. Table 14-4 lists all properties shared by all node types in DOM Level 2.

Table 14-4	**Node Object Properties (W3C DOM Level 2)**				
Property	**Value**	**Description**	**IE5/Win**	**IE5/Mac**	**NN6**
nodeName	String	Varies with node type (see Table 14-3)	Yes	Yes	Yes
nodeValue	String	Varies with node type (see Table 14-3)	Yes	Yes	Yes
nodeType	Integer	Constant representing each type	Some	Yes	Yes
parentNode	Object	Reference to next outermost container	Yes	Yes	Yes
childNodes	Array	All child nodes in source order	Yes	Yes	Yes
firstChild	Object	Reference to first child node	Yes	Yes	Yes
lastChild	Object	Reference to last child node	Yes	Yes	Yes
previousSibling	Object	Reference to sibling node up in source order	Yes	Yes	Yes
nextSibling	Object	Reference to sibling node next in source order	Yes	Yes	Yes
attributes	NodeMap	Array of attribute nodes	No	Yes	Yes
ownerDocument	Object	Containing document object	No	Yes	Yes
namespaceURI	String	URI to namespace definition (element and attribute nodes only)	No	No	Yes
prefix	String	Namespace prefix (element and attribute nodes only)	No	No	Yes
localName	String	Applicable to namespace-affected nodes	No	No	Yes

Note You can find all of the properties shown in Table 14-4 that also show themselves to be implemented in IE5 or NN6 in Chapter 15's listing of properties that all HTML element objects have in common. That's because an HTML element, as a type of node, inherits all of the properties of the prototypical node.

To help you see the meanings of the key node properties, Table 14-5 shows the property values of several nodes in the simple page shown in Listing 14-1. For each node column, find the node in Figure 14-3 and then follow the list of property values for that node, comparing the values against the actual node structure in Figure 14-3.

Table 14-5	**Properties of Selected Nodes for a Simple HTML Document**			
Properties	**Nodes**			
	document	HTML	P	"one and only"
nodeType	9	1	1	3
nodeName	#document	HTML	P	#text
nodeValue	null	null	null	"one and only"
parentNode	null	document	BODY	EM
previousSibling	null	null	null	null
nextSibling	null	null	null	null
childNodes	HTML	HEAD BODY	"This is the " EM " paragraph on the page."	(none)
firstChild	HTML	HEAD	"This is the "	null
lastChild	HTML	BODY	" paragraph on the page."	null

The nodeType property is an integer that is helpful in scripts that iterate through an unknown collection of nodes. Most content in an HTML document is of type 1 (HTML element) or 3 (text fragment), with the outermost container, the document, of type 9. A node's nodeName property is either the name of the node's tag (for an HTML element) or a constant value (preceded by a # [hash mark] as shown in Table 14-3). And, what may surprise some, the nodeValue property is null except for the text fragment node type, in which case the value is the actual string of text of the node. In other words, for HTML elements, the W3C DOM does not expose a container's HTML as a string.

The Object-Oriented W3C DOM

If you are familiar with concepts of object-oriented (OO) programming, you will appreciate the OO tendencies in the way the W3C defines the DOM. The Node object includes sets of properties (Table 14-4) and methods (Table 14-6) that are inherited by every object based on the Node. Most of the objects that inherit the Node's behavior have their own properties and/or methods that define their specific behaviors. The following figure shows (in W3C DOM terminology) the inheritance tree from the Node root object. Most items are defined in the Core DOM, while items shown in boldface are from the HTML DOM portion.

```
Node
+--Document
|   +--HTMLDocument
+--CharacterData
|   +--Text
|   |   +--CDATASection
|   +--Comment
+--Attr
+--Element
|   +--HTMLElement
|       +-- (Each specific HTML element)
+--DocumentType
+--DocumentFragment
+--Notation
+--Entity
+--Entity Reference
+--ProcessingInstruction
```

You can see from the preceding figure that individual HTML elements inherit properties and methods from the generic HTML element, which inherits from the Core Element object, which, in turn, inherits from the basic Node.

It isn't important to know the Node object inheritance to script the DOM. But it does help explain the ECMA Script Language Binding appendix of the W3C DOM recommendation, as well as explain how a simple element object winds up with so many properties and methods associated with it.

It is doubtful that you will use all of the relationship-oriented properties of a node, primarily because there is some overlap in how you can reach a particular node from any other. The parentNode property is important because it is a reference to the current node's immediate container. While the firstChild and lastChild properties point directly to the first and last children inside a container, most scripts generally use the childNodes property with array notation inside a for loop to iterate through child nodes. If there are no child nodes, then the childNodes array has a length of zero.

Note The IE5/Windows incomplete implementation of the W3C DOM does not treat the `document` object as a node in the true sense. It has no `nodeType` property defined for it, nor does the document node appear as the parent node of the HTML node of a page. Even so, the `document` object remains the root of all references in a page's scripts.

Node methods

Actions that modify the HTML content of a node in the W3C DOM world primarily involve the methods defined for the prototype `Node`. Table 14-6 shows the methods and their support in the W3C DOM-capable browsers.

Table 14-6	**Node Object Methods (W3C DOM Level 2)**		
Method	**Description**	**IE5**	**NN6**
`appendChild(newChild)`	Adds child node to end of current node	Yes	Yes
`cloneNode(deep)`	Grabs a copy of the current node (optionally with children)	Yes	Yes
`hasChildNodes()`	Determines whether current node has children (Boolean)	Yes	Yes
`insertBefore(new, ref)`	Inserts new child in front of another child	Yes	Yes
`removeChild(old)`	Deletes one child	Yes	Yes
`replaceChild(new, old)`	Replaces an old child with a new one	Yes	Yes
`supports(feature, version)`	Determines whether the node supports a particular feature	No	Yes

The important methods for modifying content are `appendChild()`, `insertBefore()`, `removeChild()`, and `replaceChild()`. Notice, however, that all of these methods assume that the point of view for the action is from the parent of the nodes being affected by the methods. For example, to delete an element (using `removeChild()`), you don't invoke that method on the element being removed, but rather on its parent element. This leaves open the possibility for creating a library of utility functions that obviate having to know too much about the precise containment hierarchy of an element. A simple function that lets a script appear to delete an element actually does so from its parent:

```
function removeElement(elemID) {
    var elem = document.getElementById(elemID)
    elem.parentNode.removeChild(elem)
}
```

If this seems like a long way to go to accomplish the same result as setting the `outerHTML` property of an IE4+ object to empty, you are right. While some of this convolution makes sense for XML, unfortunately the W3C working group doesn't seem to have HTML scripters' best interests in mind. All is not lost, however, as you see later in this chapter.

Generating new node content

The final point about the node structure of the W3C DOM focuses on the similarly gnarled way scripters must go about generating content they want to add or replace on a page. For text-only changes (for example, the text inside a table cell), there is both an easy and hard way to perform the task. For HTML changes, there is only the hard way (plus a couple of handy workarounds discussed later). Let's look at the hard way first and then pick up the easy way for text changes.

To generate a new node in the DOM, you look to the variety of methods that are defined for the Core DOM's `document` object (and are therefore inherited by the HTML `document` object). A node creation method is defined for nearly every node type in the DOM. The two important ones for HTML documents are `createElement()` and `createTextNode()`. The first generates an element with whatever tag name (string) you pass as a parameter; the second generates a text node with whatever text you pass.

When you first create a new element, it exists only in the browser's memory and not as part of the document containment hierarchy. Moreover, the result of the `createElement()` method is a reference to an empty element except for the name of the tag. For example, to create a new P element, use

```
var newElem = document.createElement("P")
```

The new element has no ID, attributes, or any content. To assign some attributes to that element, you can use the `setAttribute()` method (a method of every element object) or assign a value to the object's corresponding property. For example, to assign an identifier to the new element, use either

```
newElem.setAttribute("id", "newP")
```

or

```
newElem.id = "newP"
```

Both ways are perfectly legal. Even though the element has an ID at this point, it is not yet part of the document so you cannot retrieve it via the `document.getElementById()` method.

To add some content to the paragraph, you next generate a text node as a separate object:

```
var newText = document.createTextNode("This is the second paragraph.")
```

Again, this node is just sitting around in memory waiting for you to apply it as a child of some other node. To make this text the content of the new paragraph, you can append the node as a child of the paragraph element that is still in memory:

```
newElem.appendChild(newText)
```

If you were able to inspect the HTML that represents the new paragraph element, it would look like the following:

```
<P ID="newP">This is the second paragraph.</P>
```

The new paragraph element is ready for insertion into a document. Using the document shown in Listing 14-1, you can append it as a child of the BODY element:

```
document.body.appendChild(newElem)
```

At last, the new element is part of the document containment hierarchy. You can now reference it just like any other element in the document.

Replacing node content

The addition of the paragraph shown in the last section requires a change to a portion of the text in the original paragraph (the first paragraph is no longer the "one and only" paragraph on the page). As mentioned earlier, you can perform text changes either via the `replaceChild()` method or by assigning new text to a text node's `nodeValue` property. Let's see how each approach works to change the text of the first paragraph's EM element from "one and only" to "first."

To use `replaceChild()`, a script must first generate a valid text node with the new text:

```
var newText = document.createTextNode("first ")
```

Because strings are dumb (in other words, they don't know about words and spaces), the new text node includes a space to accommodate the existing space layout of the original text. The next step is to use the `replaceChild()` method. But recall that the point of view for this method is the parent of the child being replaced. The child here is the text node inside the EM element, so you must invoke the `replaceChild()` method on the EM element. Also, the `replaceChild()` method requires two parameters: the first is the new node; the second is a reference to the node to be replaced. Because the script statements get pretty long with the getElementById() method, an intermediate step grabs a reference to the text node inside the EM element:

```
var oldChild = document.getElementById("emphasis1").childNodes[0]
```

Now the script is ready to invoke the replaceChild() method on the EM element, swapping the old text node with the new:

```
document.getElementById("emphasis1").replaceChild(newText, oldChild)
```

If you want to capture the old node before it disappears entirely, be aware that the replaceChild() method returns a reference to the replaced node (which is only in memory at this point, and not part of the document node hierarchy). You can assign the method statement to a variable and use that old node somewhere else, if needed.

This may seem like a long way to go; it is, especially if the HTML you are generating is complex. Fortunately, you can take a simpler approach for replacing text nodes. All it requires is a reference to the text node being replaced. You can assign that node's nodeValue property its new string value:

```
document.getElementById("emphasis1").childNodes[0].nodeValue = "first "
```

When an element's content is entirely text (for example, a table cell that already has a text node in it), this is the most streamlined way to swap text on the fly using W3C DOM syntax. This doesn't work for the creation of the second paragraph text earlier in this chapter because the text node did not exist yet. The createTextNode() method had to explicitly create it.

Also remember that a text node does not have any inherent style associated with it. The style of the containing HTML element governs the style of the text. If you want to change not only the text node's text but also how it looks, you have to modify the style property of the text node's parent element. Browsers that perform these kinds of content swaps and style changes automatically reflow the page to accommodate changes in the size of the content.

To summarize, Listing 14-2 is a live version of the modifications made to the original document shown in Listing 14-1. The new version includes a button and script that makes the changes described throughout this discussion of nodes. Reload the page to start over.

Listing 14-2: **Adding/Replacing DOM Content**

```
<HTML>
<HEAD>
<TITLE>A Simple Page</TITLE>
<SCRIPT LANGUAGE="JavaScript">
```

```
function modify() {
    var newElem = document.createElement("P")
    newElem.id = "newP"
    var newText = document.createTextNode("This is the second paragraph.")
    newElem.appendChild(newText)
    document.body.appendChild(newElem)
    document.getElementById("emphasis1").childNodes[0].nodeValue = "first "
}
</SCRIPT>
</HEAD>
<BODY>
<BUTTON onClick="modify()">Add/Replace Text</BUTTON>
<P ID="paragraph1">This is the <EM ID="emphasis1">one and only </EM>paragraph on
the page.</P>
</BODY>
</HTML>
```

Chapter 15 details node properties and methods that are inherited by all HTML elements. Most are implemented in both IE5 and NN6. Also look to the reference material for the document object in Chapter 18 for other valuable W3C DOM methods.

Although not part of the W3C DOM, the innerHTML property (originally devised by Microsoft for IE4) is available in NN6 for the sake of convenience. To speed the conversion of legacy IE4 dynamic content code that uses other popular IE conveniences to run in NN6, see the section "Simulating IE4 Syntax in NN6" later in this chapter.

Static W3C DOM HTML objects

The NN6 DOM (but unfortunately not IE5.x) adheres to the core JavaScript notion of prototype inheritance with respect to the object model. When a page loads into NN6, the browser creates HTML objects based on the prototypes of each object defined by the W3C DOM. For example, if you use The Evaluator (Chapter 13) to see what kind of object the myP paragraph object is (enter document. getElementById("myP") into the top text box and click the Evaluate button), it reports that the object is based on the HTMLParagraphElement object of the DOM. Every "instance" of a P element object in the page inherits its default properties and methods from HTMLParagraphElement (which, in turn, inherits from HTMLElement, Element, and Node objects — all detailed in the JavaScript binding appendix of the W3C DOM specification).

You can use scripting to add properties to the prototypes of some of these static objects. To do so, you must use new features added to NN6. Two new methods — __defineGetter__() and __defineSetter__() — enable you to assign functions to a custom property of an object.

Note   These methods are Netscape-specific. To prevent their possible collision with standardized implementations of these features in future implementations of
ECMAScript, the underscore characters on either side of the method name are
pairs of underscore characters.

The functions execute whenever the property is read (the function assigned via the
__defineGetter__() method) or modified (the function assigned via the
__defineSetter__() method). The common way to define these functions is in
the form of an anonymous function (Chapter 41). The formats for the two statements that assign these behaviors to an object prototype are as follows:

```
object.prototype.__defineGetter__("propName", function([param1[,...[,paramN]]])
{
    // statements
    return returnValue
})
object.prototype.__defineSetter__("propName", function([param1[,...[,paramN]]])
{
    // statements
    return returnValue
})
```

The example in Listing 14-3 demonstrates how to add a read-only property to
every HTML element object in the current document. The property, called
childNodeDetail, returns an object; the object has two properties, one for the
number of element child nodes and one for the number of text child nodes. Note
that the script is wrapped inside a script tag that specifies JavaScript 1.5. Also note
that the this keyword in the function definition is a reference to the object for
which the property is calculated. And because the function runs each time a script
statement reads the property, any scripted changes to the content after the page
loads are reflected in the returned property value.

Listing 14-3: **Adding a Read-Only Prototype Property to All HTML Element Objects**

```
<SCRIPT LANGUAGE="JavaScript1.5">
if (HTMLElement) {
    HTMLElement.prototype.__defineGetter__("childNodeDetail", function() {
        var result = {elementNodes:0, textNodes:0}
        for (var i = 0; i < this.childNodes.length; i++) {
            switch (this.childNodes[i].nodeType) {
                case 1:
                    result.elementNodes++
                    break
                case 3:
                    result.textNodes++
                    break
```

```
        }
      }
      return result
   })
}
</SCRIPT>
```

To access the property, use it like any other property of the object. For example:

```
var BodyNodeDetail = document.body.childNodeDetail
```

The returned value in this example is an object, so you use regular JavaScript syntax to access one of the property values:

```
var BodyElemNodesCount = document.body.childNodeDetail.elementNodes
```

Bidirectional event model

Despite the seemingly conflicting event models of NN4 (trickle down) and IE4 (bubble up), the W3C DOM event model (defined in Level 2) manages to employ both models. This gives the scripter the choice of where along an event's propagation path the event gets processed. To prevent conflicts with existing event model terminology, the W3C model invents many new terms for properties and methods for events. Some coding probably requires W3C DOM-specific handling in a page aimed at multiple object models.

The W3C event model also introduces a new concept called the *event listener*. An event listener is essentially a mechanism that instructs an object to respond to a particular kind of event — very much like the way the event handler attributes of HTML tags respond to events. But the DOM recommendation points out that it prefers use of a more script-oriented way of assigning event listeners: the addEventListener() method available for every node in the document hierarchy. Through this method, you advise the browser whether to force an event to bubble up the hierarchy (the default behavior that is also in effect if you use the HTML attribute type of event handler) or to be captured at a higher level.

Functions invoked by the event listener receive a single parameter consisting of the event object whose properties contain contextual details about the event (details such as the position of a mouse click, character code of a keyboard key, or a reference to the target object). For example, if a form includes a button whose job is to invoke a calculation function, the W3C DOM prefers the following way of assigning the event handler:

```
document.getElementById("calcButton").addEventListener("click", doCalc, false)
```

The addEventListener() method takes three parameters. The first parameter is a string of the event to listen for; the second is a reference to the function to be invoked when that event fires; and the third parameter is a Boolean value. When you set this Boolean value to true, it turns on event capture whenever this event is directed to this target. The function then takes its cue from the event object passed as the parameter:

```
function doCalc(evt) {
    // get shortcut reference to input button's form
    var form = evt.target.form
    var results = 0
    // other statements to do the calculation //
    form.result.value = results
}
```

To modify an event listener, you use the removeEventListener() method to get rid of the old listener and then employ addEventListener() with different parameters to assign the new one.

Preventing an event from performing its default action is also a different procedure in the W3C event model than in IE. In IE4 (as well as NN3 and NN4), you can cancel the default action by allowing the event handler to evaluate to return false. While this still works in IE5, Microsoft includes another property of the window.event object, called returnValue. Setting that property to false anywhere in the function invoked by the event handler also kills the event before it does its normal job. But the W3C event model uses a method of the event object, preventDefault(), to keep the event from its normal task. You can invoke this method anywhere in the function that executes when the event fires.

Unfortunately, IE5.x does not implement the W3C DOM event syntax, so using the event listener terminology requires code branching for a cross-browser page. But part of the burden is lifted because the HTML 4.0 way of binding events to elements by way of attributes as well as assignment of events as object properties continues to be supported in IE5.x and NN6. NN6 treats "old fashioned" event handler syntax the same as adding an event listener.

Mixing Object Models

The more browsers that your audience uses, the more likely you will want to make your pages work on as many browsers as possible. You've seen in this chapter that scripts written for older browsers, such as Navigator 2 and Internet Explorer 3, tend to work in even the latest browsers without modification. But aiming at that compatibility target doesn't let you take advantage of more advanced features, in particular Dynamic HTML. You must balance the effort required to support as many as four classifications of browsers (non-DHTML, NN4, IE4/5, and W3C DOM common denominator in IE5 and NN6) against the requirements of your audience. Moreover, those requirements can easily change over time. For example, the share of the audience using non-DHTML and NN4 browsers will diminish over time, while the installed base of browsers capable of using the Microsoft IE DOM (for IE4+) and the W3C DOM (IE5+ and NN6+) will increase. If the percentage of visitors using NN4 is not significant at this point, you may well decide to not worry about implementing DHTML features for that browser and lump NN4 together with the rest of the non-DHTML browsers.

For any given application or Web site, it is important to develop a strategy to apply to the deployment of scripted features. But be aware that one strategy simply cannot fit all situations. The primary considerations are the breadth of browser versions reaching your site (many for public sites; perhaps only one for a tightly controlled intranet) and the amount of DHTML you intend to implement.

In the rest of this section, you see three scenarios and strategies employed to meet the developer's requirements. Although they are labeled as three different levels of aggressiveness, it is likely that you can apply individual techniques from each of the levels in establishing a strategy of your own.

The conservative approach

In the first scenario, the content requires a modest level of data entry interaction with a user via a form as well as image rollovers. Supported browsers encompass the entire range of nonscriptable and scriptable browsers, with one version of each page to serve all visitors.

If the form gathers information from the user for submission to a server CGI that stores the data in a database or performs a search based on user-supplied criteria, the obvious mode of entry is through traditional form elements. Scriptable browsers can perform pre-submission validations to hasten the correction of any improperly formatted fields. Event handlers attached to the text fields (onChange event handlers) and an onSubmit event handler for the form itself can do the validation on the client. Nonscriptable browsers ignore the event handlers, and the form is submitted as usual, relying on server-side validation of input data (and the slow back-and-forth processing that this entails when there is an error or missing field data).

For image rollovers, links surround the image elements. The onMouseOver and onMouseOut event handlers for the links trigger functions that swap images. By wrapping the statements in the event handler functions in if constructions that test for the presence of the document.images array, first-generation scriptable browsers that don't implement images as objects perform no action:

```
function imageOn(imgName) {
    if (document.images) {
        document.images[imgName].src = onImages[imgName].src
    }
}
```

The same goes for script statements in the Head that precache the swappable images as the page loads:

```
if (document.images) {
    var onImages = new Array()
    onImages["home"] = new Image(50,30)
    onImages["home"].src = "images/homeOn.gif"
    ...
}
```

This scenario can also provide added content on the page for scriptable browser users by embedding scripts within the body that use `document.write()` to generate content as the page loads. For example, the page can begin with a time-sensitive greeting ("Good Morning," "Good Afternoon," and so on), while nonscriptable browser users see a standard greeting inside the `<NOSCRIPT>` tag pair.

Middle ground

The second scenario includes pages that employ style sheets. The goal again is to support all browser users with the same HTML pages, but also provide users of modern browsers with an enhanced experience. Where supported by the browser, styles of objects change in response to user action (for example, links highlight with a special font color and background during rollover). One of the design elements on the page is a form within a table. As users enter values into some text boxes, calculated results appear at the bottom of the table, preferably as regular content within a table cell (otherwise in another text box).

This scenario requires browser version branching in several places to allow for variations in browser treatment of the features and to avoid problems with older scriptable browsers and nonscriptable browsers alike. You can (and should) perform some (if not all) of the branching via object detection, as you will see in a moment. Table 14-7 highlights the major feature requirements for this scenario and describes the browser support for each.

Table 14-7	**Features and Support for a Typical "Middle Ground" Scenario**
Feature	*Support and Approach*
Dynamic Styles	IE4+ and NN6+ through the `style` property of any HTML element object
Form Calculations	Unless requiring Y2K date compliance or regular expression parsing of input, should work with all scriptable browsers without any branching required

Feature	Support and Approach
Dynamic Content	IE4+ and NN6+ support Dynamic HTML content within a cell, but MS and W3C object models require different ways of changing a table cell's content. (Or you can use the nonstandard, but convenient, `innerHTML` property of the cell.) For older scriptable browsers, the cell should contain a text box to display the results; for nonscriptable browsers, the cell should contain a button that submits the form to a server CGI to process the calculation and return a new page with the results.

Dynamic styles

For dynamic styles, both the IE4+ and W3C object models provide access to style sheet settings via the `style` property of any HTML element. This simplifies matters because you can wrap modifications to `style` properties inside `if` clauses that check for the existence of the `style` property for the specified object:

```
function hilite(elem) {
    if (elem.style) {
        elem.style.fontWeight = "bold"
    }
}
```

If the event handler that triggers the change can be localized to the affected element (for example, an `onMouseOver` event handler for a SPAN element surrounding some text), then the event doesn't fire in browsers that don't also support the `style` property. (By good fortune, browsers that implement the `style` property also expose all elements to the object model.) To compensate for the differences in object references between the IE4+ and W3C models, you can pass the object as a parameter to event handler functions:

```
<SPAN onMouseOver="hilite(this)" onMouseOut="revert(this)"
onClick="go('...')>...</SPAN>
```

This technique obviates the need to use browser version detection because the functions invoked by the event handlers do not have to build DOM-specific references to the objects to adjust the style.

Branching variables

If, for now, you continue to be more comfortable with browser version detection than object detection, you can apply version detection for this "middle ground" scenario by establishing branches for the IE4+ and W3C object models. Global variables that act as flags elsewhere in your page's scripts are still the primary mechanism. For this scenario, you can initialize two global variables as follows:

```
function getIEVersion() {
    var ua = navigator.userAgent
    var IEoffset = ua.indexOf("MSIE ")
    return parseFloat(ua.substring(IEoffset+5, ua.indexOf(";", Ieoffset)))
}
var isIE4 = ((navigator.appName.indexOf("Microsoft") == 0 &&
    parseInt(getIEVersion()) >= 4))
var isW3C = (document.documentElement) ? true : false
```

Notice how the `getIEVersion()` function digs out the precise IE version from deep within the `navigator.userAgent` property. Both global variables are Boolean values. While each variable conveys valuable information on its own, the combination of the two reveals even more about the browser environment if necessary. Figure 14-4 shows the truth table for using the AND (&&) operator in a conditional clause with both values. For example, if you need a branch that works only in IE4, the `if` clause is

```
if (isIE4 && !isW3C) {...}
```

isIE4	isW3C	isIE4 && isW3C
true	true	IE5+
true	false	IE4 Only
false	true	NN6+
false	false	Older browser

Figure 14-4: Truth table for two browser version variables with the AND operator

The overlap between MS and the W3C object models in IE5 means that you need to determine for each branch which model to use when the script is running. This governs the order of nested `if` conditions when they arise. If you trap for the W3C version first, IE5 runs the branch containing the W3C DOM syntax.

Dynamic content

Once you have the branching variables in place, your scripts can use them for executing functions invoked by event handlers as well as for scripts that run while the page loads. The importance of the second type comes when you want a page to display one kind of HTML for one class of browsers and other HTML for other classes (or all of the rest). The design for the current scenario calls for a table cell to display the results of a form's calculation in HTML where capable. In lesser scriptable browsers, the results should appear in a text box in the table. Nonscriptable browsers should display a button to submit the form.

In the Body of the page, a script should take over and use `document.write()` for the TD element that is to show the results. Buggy behavior in early versions of Navigator require that at least the entire TD element be written dynamically, instead of just the cell's content. (In fact, I usually recommend writing the entire table dynamically if a lot of users have older Navigators.) The structure of such a form and table is as follows:

```
...
<FORM NAME="calculator" ACTION="http://xxx/cgi-bin/calculate.pl"
onSubmit="return false">
<TABLE>
...
<TR>
    <TD>...</TD>
    <SCRIPT LANGUAGE="JavaScript">
    if (isIE4 || isW3C) {
        document.write("<TD ID='result'>0</TD>")
    } else {
        document.write("<TD>"
        document.write("<INPUT TYPE='text' NAME='result' SIZE='10' VALUE='0'>")
        document.write("</TD>")
    }
    </SCRIPT>
    <NOSCRIPT>
        <TD>Click 'Submit' for Results</TD>
    </NOSCRIPT>
</TR>
</TABLE>
<NOSCRIPT>
    <INPUT TYPE="submit">
</NOSCRIPT>
</FORM>
...
```

The preceding code assumes that other table cells contain text boxes whose `onChange` event handlers trigger a calculation script. That calculation script must also branch for the two classes of scriptable browser so that results are displayed to fit the browser's object model:

```
function calculate(form) {
    var results
    ...
    // statements here that perform math and stuff answer into 'results'
variable //
    ...
    if (isIE4) {
        document.all.result.innerText = results
    } else if (isW3C) {
        document.getElementById("result").childNodes[0].nodeValue = results
    } else {
        document.calculator.result.value = results
    }
}
```

Adding dynamic content for NN4 requires a little more planning. The technique usually involves nesting an absolute-positioned DIV inside a relative-positioned SPAN. Scripts can then use `document.write()` to create new content for the deeply nested DIV element. Pulling this off successfully entails pretty complex references through multiple layers and their documents, as described in Chapter 31. But no matter what lengths you go to in an effort to employ dynamic content in NN4, the new content does not automatically resize the table or cell to accommodate larger or smaller chunks of text. Without automatic reflow of the page, as is found in IE4+ and NN6+, writing to an NN4 positioned layer does not force other page content to move.

A radical approach

By "radical," I mean that the page content is designed to employ extensive DHTML features, including positioned (if not flying) elements on the page. Perhaps some clicking and dragging of elements can add some fun to the page while you're at it.

Employing these kinds of features requires some extensive forethought about your audience and the browsers they use. While some aspects of DHTML, such as CSS, degrade gracefully in older browsers (the content is still presented, although not in optimum font display perhaps), positioned elements do not degrade well at all. The problem is that older browsers ignore the CSS attributes that control positioning, stacking order, and visibility. Therefore, when the page loads in a pre-version 4 browser, all content is rendered in source code order. Elements that are supposed to be positioned, hidden, or overlapped are drawn on the page in "old fashioned" rendering.

To use element positioning for the greatest effect, your Web site should preexamine the browser at some earlier page in the navigation sequence to reach the DHTML-equipped page. Only browsers capable of your fancy features should be allowed to pass onto the "cool" pages. All other browsers get diverted to another page or pathway through your application so they can at least get the information they came for, if not in the most lavish presentation. Techniques detailed in Chapter 13 demonstrate how to make a branching index page.

By filtering out non-DHTML-capable browsers, some of your job is easier — but not all. On the plus side, you can ignore a lot of weirdness that accrues to scripting bugs in earlier browsers. But you must still decide which of the three element positioning models to follow: IE4+, NN4, or W3C. Chances are that you will want to support at least two of the three unless you are in the luxurious position of designing for a single browser platform (or have taken a stand that you will support only one DOM).

Of the three models, NN4's DOM is the trickiest one to deal with at the HTML level. While it may be possible that your content design will look the same using positioned DIV and SPAN elements in all DHTML-capable browsers, often the appearance in NN4 is unacceptable. At that point, you will probably have to use scripts in your Body to dynamically generate HTML, specifying the `<LAYER>` tag for NN4 and positioned `<DIV>` elements for the rest.

Note   Although IE4 and IE5.*x* can use the same basic Microsoft object model, not all DHTML code renders the same on both generations of browsers. Microsoft made some changes here and there to the way some style attributes are rendered so that IE5.*x* comes into better compliance with the CSS recommendation.

Using script libraries

As long as you plan to use scripts to dynamically generate HTML for the page, you might consider creating separate, external .js libraries for each of the object models you want to support for the page. Scripts in each library contain code for both the HTML accumulation (for use with document.write() in the main page) and for processing user interaction. Assuming that only DHTML-capable browsers reach the page, branching is required only at the beginning of the document where an object model-specific library is loaded:

```
var isIE4 = ((navigator.appName.indexOf("Microsoft") == 0 &&
    parseInt(navigator.appVersion) == 4))
var isW3C = (document.documentElement) ? true : false
if (isW3C) {
    // give priority to W3C model for IE5.x
    document.write("<SCRIPT LANGUAGE='JavaScript' SRC='page3_W3C.js'><" +
        "\/SCRIPT>")
} else if (isIE4) {
    document.write("<SCRIPT LANGUAGE='JavaScript' SRC='page3_IE4.js'><" +
        "\/SCRIPT>")
} else {
    document.write("<SCRIPT LANGUAGE='JavaScript' SRC='page3_generic.js'><" +
        "\/SCRIPT>")
}
```

Each of the statements that writes the <SCRIPT> tag includes a workaround that is required on some browsers (NN4 especially) to facilitate using document.write() to write script tags to the page.

Once these libraries are specified for the page, script statements anywhere later in the page can invoke functions defined in each library to generate a particular element or set of elements in the object model HTML optimized for the current browser. Of course, it's not necessary to have one library devoted to each object model. You might find it more convenient for authoring and maintenance to keep all the code in one library that has numerous internal branchings for browser versions. Branches in a library can use the version sniffing global variables defined in the main HTML page's scripts. Better still, a library can be entirely self-contained by using object detection. You can see an example of such a DHTML library in Chapter 48.

Handling events

Thanks to the W3C DOM's event model implementing a similar event bubbling scheme as IE4+, you can apply that event propagation model to IE4+ and W3C DOM browsers. There are differences in the details, however. IE's approach does not pass the event object as a parameter to a function invoked by an event handler. Instead, the IE `event` object is a property of the `window` object. Therefore, your functions have to look for the passed parameter and substitute the `window.event` object in its place for IE:

```
function calculate(evt) {
    evt = (evt) ? evt : window.event
    // more statements to handle the event //
}
```

Additional branching is necessary to inspect many details of the event. For example, IE calls the object receiving the event the `srcElement`, while the W3C DOM calls it the `target`. Canceling the default behavior of the event (for example, preventing a form's submission if it fails client-side validation) is also different for the models (although the "old-fashioned" way of letting HTML-type event handlers evaluate to `return false` still works). You can find more event object details in Chapter 29.

Simulating IE4+ Syntax in NN6

With so much IE4+ DHTML-related JavaScript code already in use, scripters are certainly eager to leverage as much of their old code as possible in W3C DOM browsers such as NN6. While NN6 helps a bit by implementing the IE `innerHTML` property for HTML elements, this section shows you how a simple `.js` library can provide NN6 with a few more common convenience properties of the IE4+ object model. By linking this library into your pages, you can give NN6 the valuable HTML element properties shown in Table 14-8.

Table 14-8   IE4+ HTML Element Property Simulation for NN6

Property	Read	Write	Replaces in W3C DOM
all	yes	no	getElementsByTagName("*")
innerText	yes	yes	nodeValue property for text nodes; creating a text fragment node and inserting it into existing node structure
outerHTML	no	yes	(No equivalent)

Scripts that make these simulations possible use the prototype inheritance behavior of static objects described earlier in this chapter. Because they require NN6-specific features in that browser's implementation of JavaScript 1.5, link the `.js` library with the following tag:

```
<SCRIPT LANGUAGE="JavaScript1.5" TYPE="text/javascript"
SRC="IE4Simulator.js"></SCRIPT>
```

All scripts that follow belong in the .js library. They're divided into two groups to allow for detailed discussion.

The all property simulator

Nearly every HTML element can be a container of other elements (with the exception of a handful of leaf nodes, such as <BR>). The all property in IE returns a collection of references to all element objects nested inside the current object, no matter how deeply nested the containment hierarchy is. That's why the document.all reference is such a convenient way to access any element in the entire document that has an ID attribute.

As illustrated earlier in the sidebar figure, the Node static object is the object from which all elements are derived. That object's prototype is enhanced here because you have to make sure that all nodes, especially the document node, can acquire the all property. Listing 14-4a shows the segment of the library that defines the all property for the Node object prototype.

Listing 14-4a: **Simulator for the all Property**

```
if (!document.all) {
    Node.prototype.__defineGetter__("all", function() {
        if (document.getElementsByTagName("*").length) {
            switch (this.nodeType) {
                case 9:
                    return document.getElementsByTagName("*")
                    break
                case 1:
                    return this.getElementsByTagName("*")
                    break
            }
        }
        return ""
    })
    Node.prototype.__defineSetter__("all", function() {})
}
```

This portion of the library exhibits a rare instance in which using object detection for document.all does the right thing now and in the future. The prototype should not execute if the browser loading the page already has a document.all property.

The anonymous function first establishes a branch in the code only for the object model if it supports the wildcard parameter for the document. getElementsByTagName() method. The function then performs slightly different extractions depending on whether the node is the document (type 9) or an element (type 1). If the all property should be queried for any other kind of node, the returned value is an empty string. Each time the all property is accessed, the anonymous function executes to pick up all elements nested inside the current node. Therefore, the collection returned by the all property is always up to date, even if the node structure of the current object changes after the document loads.

While this simulator code provides NN6 scripts with IE4-like syntax for referencing elements, the collection returned by the native document.all in IE and calculated document.all in NN6 may not always have an identical length — the collections are derived slightly differently. The important thing to know, however, is that by employing this prototype modifier in NN6, you have the ability to reference elements by their IDs in the form document.all.*elementID*.

The content properties simulators

The remaining code of this library lets NN6 use the same innerText and outerHTML properties as IE4 for modifying all element objects. Listing 14-4b contains the NN6 JavaScript code that prepares the browser to set an element object's outerHTML property, as well as get and set the innerText properties. The code again uses anonymous functions assigned to getter and setter behaviors of prototype properties. Because the properties here apply only to HTML elements, the static object whose prototype is being modified is HTMLElement. All specific HTML element objects inherit properties and methods from the HTMLElement object. All four prototype adjustment blocks are nested inside a condition that makes sure the static HTMLElement object is exposed in the browser's object model (which it is in NN6+).

All functions in Listing 14-4b use the W3C DOM Range object (Chapter 19). Two of them use a Netscape-proprietary method of the Range object as a shortcut to converting a string into a node hierarchy.

Listing 14-4b: Simulator for the innerText and outerHTML Properties

```
if (HTMLElement) {
    HTMLElement.prototype.__defineSetter__("innerText", function (txt) {
        var rng = document.createRange()
        rng.selectNodeContents(this)
        rng.deleteContents()
        var newText = document.createTextNode(txt)
        this.appendChild(newText)
        return txt
    })
    HTMLElement.prototype.__defineGetter__("innerText", function () {
```

```
        var rng = document.createRange()
        rng.selectNode(this)
        return rng.toString()
    })
    HTMLElement.prototype.__defineSetter__("outerHTML", function (html) {
        var rng = document.createRange()
        rng.selectNode(this)
        var newHTML = rng.createContextualFragment(html)
        this.parentNode.replaceChild(newHTML,this)
        return html
    })
    HTMLElement.prototype.__defineGetter__("outerHTML", function() {return ''})
}
```

The getter function for the innerText property creates a range whose boundaries encompass the current object. Because a range includes only the text part of a document, the adjustment of the range boundaries to the current node encompasses all text, including text nodes of nested elements. Returning the string version of the range provides a copy of all text inside the current element.

For the setter action, the anonymous function defines one parameter variable, which is the text to replace the text inside an element. With the help, again, of the Range object, the range is cinched up to encompass the contents of the current node. Those contents are deleted, and new text node is created out of the value assigned to the property (in other words, passed as a parameter to the anonymous function). With the current object no longer containing any nodes after the deletion, the appendChild() method inserts the new text node as a child to the current object.

Setting the outerHTML property starts out the same as setting the innerText, but the new content — which arrives as a string assigned to the parameter variable — is converted into a fully formed set of nested nodes via the createContextualFragment() method. This method is invoked on any range object, but it does not affect the range to which it is attached. The value returned from the method is what's important, containing a node whose content is already set up as genuine DOM nodes. That's why the returned value can be passed to the replaceChild() method to replace the new content as HTML rather than plain text. But because the outerHTML property applies to the entire current element, it must use the roundabout way of replacing itself as a child of its parent. This prevents the accidental modification of any siblings in the process.

Where to Go from Here

These past two chapters provided an overview of the core language and object model issues that anyone designing pages that use JavaScript must confront. The goal here is to stimulate your own thinking about how to embrace or discard levels of compatibility with your pages as you balance your desire to generate "cool" pages and serve your audience. From here on, the difficult choices are up to you.

To help you choose the objects, properties, methods, and event handlers that best suit your requirements, the rest of the chapters in Part III and all of Part IV provide in-depth references to the document object model and core JavaScript language features. Observe the compatibility ratings for each language term very carefully to help you determine which features best suit your audience's browsers. Most example listings are complete HTML pages that you can load in various browsers to see how they work. Many others invite you to explore how things work via The Evaluator (Chapter 13). Play around with the files, making modifications to build your own applications or expanding your working knowledge of JavaScript in the browser environment.

The language and object models have grown in the handful of years they have been in existence. The amount of language vocabulary has increased astronomically. It takes time to drink it all in and feel comfortable that you are aware of the powers available to you. Don't worry about memorizing the vocabulary. It's more important to acquaint yourself with the features, and then come back later when you need the implementation details.

Be patient. Be persistent. The reward will come.

✦   ✦   ✦

Generic HTML Element Objects

The object model specifications implemented in Internet
Explorer 4+ and Netscape Navigator 6 both feature a
large set of scriptable objects that represent what we often
call "generic" HTML elements. Generic elements can be
divided into two groups. One group, such as the B and STRIKE
elements, define font styles to be applied to enclosed
sequences of text. The need for these elements (and the
objects that represent them) is receding as more browsers
accommodate style sheets. The second group of elements
assigns context to content within their start and end tags.
Examples of contextual elements include H1, BLOCKQUOTE,
and the ubiquitous P element. While browsers sometimes
have consistent visual ways of rendering contextual elements
by default (for example, the large, bold font of an <H1> tag),
the specific rendering is not the intended purpose of the tags.
No formal standard dictates that text within an EM element
must be italicized: the style simply has become the custom
since the very early days of browsers.

All of these generic elements share a large number of scriptable properties, methods, and event handlers. The sharing
extends not only among generic elements, but also among virtually every renderable element — even if it has additional,
element-specific properties, methods, and/or event handlers
that I cover in depth in other chapters of this reference.
Rather than repeat the details of these shared properties,
methods, and event handlers for each object throughout this
reference, I describe them in detail only in this chapter
(unless there is a special behavior, bug, or trick associated
with the item in some object described elsewhere). In succeeding reference chapters, each object description includes
a list of the object's properties, methods, and event handlers,
but I do not list shared items over and over (making it hard to
find items that are unique to a particular element). Instead,
you see a pointer back to this chapter for the items in

common with generic HTML element objects. A dark tab at the bottom of this chapter's pages should make it easy to find this chapter in a hurry.

Generic Objects

Table 15-1 lists all of the objects that I treat in this reference as "generic" objects. All of these objects share the properties, methods, and event handlers described in succeeding sections and have no special items that require additional coverage elsewhere in this book.

Table 15-1	Generic HTML Element Objects
Formatting Objects	*Contextual Objects*
B	ACRONYM
BIG	ADDRESS
CENTER	CITE
I	CODE
NOBR	DFN
RT	DEL
RUBY	DIV
S	EM
SMALL	INS
STRIKE	KBD
SUB	LISTING
SUP	P
TT	PLAINTEXT
U	PRE
WBR	SAMP
	SPAN
	STRONG
	VAR
	XMP

Properties	Methods	Event Handlers
accessKey	addBehavior()	onActivate
all	addEventListener()	onBeforeCopy
attributes	appendChild()	onBeforeCut
behaviorUrns	applyElement()	onBeforeDeactivate
canHaveChildren	attachEvent()	onBeforeEditFocus
canHaveHTML	blur()	onBeforePaste
childNodes	clearAttributes()	onBlur
children	click()	onClick
className	cloneNode()	onContextMenu
clientHeight	componentFromPoint()	onControlSelect
clientLeft	contains()	onCopy
clientTop	detachEvent()	onCut
clientWidth	dispatchEvent()	onDblClick
contentEditable	fireEvent()	onDeactivate
currentStyle	focus()	onDrag
dataFld	getAdjacentText()	onDragEnd
dataFormatAs	getAttribute()	onDragEnter
dataSrc	getAttributeNode()	onDragLeave
dir	getBoundingClientRect()	onDragOver
disabled	getClientRects()	onDragStart
document	getElementsByTagName()	onDrop
filters	getExpression()	onFilterChange
firstChild	hasChildNodes()	onFocus
height	insertAdjacentElement()	onHelp
hideFocus	insertAdjacentHTML()	onKeyDown
id	insertAdjacentText()	onKeyPress
innerHTML	insertBefore()	onKeyUp
innerText	item()	onLoseCapture
isContentEditable	mergeAttributes()	onMouseDown
isDisabled	normalize()	onMouseEnter

Continued

elementObject

	Table 15-1 *(continued)*	
Properties	*Methods*	*Event Handlers*
isMultiLine	releaseCapture()	onMouseLeave
isTextEdit	removeAttribute()	onMouseMove
lang	removeAttributeNode()	onMouseOut
language	removeBehavior()	onMouseOver
lastChild	removeChild()	onMouseUp
length	removeEventListener()	onPaste
localName	removeExpression()	onPropertyChange
namespaceURI	removeNode()	onReadyStateChange
nextSibling	replaceAdjacentText()	onResize
nodeName	replaceChild()	onResizeEnd
nodeType	replaceNode()	onResizeStart
nodeValue	scrollIntoView()	onSelectStart
offsetHeight	setActive()	
offsetLeft	setAttribute()	
offsetParent	setAttributeNode()	
offsetTop	setCapture()	
offsetWidth	setExpression()	
outerHTML	supports()	
outerText	swapNode()	
ownerDocument	tags()	
parentElement	urns()	
parentNode		
parentTextEdit		
prefix		
previousSibling		
readyState		
recordNumber		
runtimeStyle		
scopeName		
scrollHeight		

Properties	Methods	Event Handlers
scrollLeft		
scrollTop		
scrollWidth		
sourceIndex		
style		
tabIndex		
tagName		
tagUrn		
title		
uniqueID		

Syntax

To access element properties or methods, use this:

```
(IE4+)      [document.all.]objectID.property | method([parameters])
(IE5+/NN6)   document.getElementById(objectID).property | method([parameters])
```

About these objects

All objects listed in Table 15-1 are DOM representations of HTML elements that influence either the font style or the context of some HTML content. The large set of properties, methods, and event handlers associated with these objects also applies to virtually every other DOM object that represents an HTML element. Discussions about object details in this chapter apply to dozens of other objects described in succeeding chapters of this reference section.

Properties

accessKey

Value: One-Character String   Read/Write

	NN2	NN3	NN4	NN6	IE3/J1	IE3/J2	IE4	IE5	IE5.5
Compatibility							✓	✓	✓

For many elements, you can specify a keyboard character (letter, numeral, or punctuation symbol) that, when typed as an Alt+key combination (on the Win32 OS platform) or Ctrl+key combination (on the MacOS), brings focus to that element. An element that has focus is the one that is set to respond to keyboard activity. If the newly focused element is out of view in the document's current scroll position, the document is scrolled to bring that focused element into view (also see the scrollIntoView() method). The character you specify can be an uppercase or lowercase value, but these values are not case-sensitive. If you assign the same letter to more than one element, the user can cycle through all elements associated with that accessKey value.

For IE4, not all elements can receive focus in a meaningful way. For that browser version, you should limit this property to elements that can actually receive focus, such as form elements and links. One way to see what elements on a page can receive focus is to repeatedly press the Tab key while the document is visible. In the Windows platforms, either a dotted line around the element or a text insertion pointer flashing inside a text entry element indicates the focus. Not all operating system platforms provide focus to the same set of elements. IE4 for the Macintosh, for example, does not give focus to button elements. For IE5.5, however, any element can receive focus — even if no visible outline explicitly indicates this state.

Internet Explorer gives some added powers to the accessKey property in some cases. For example, if you assign an accessKey value to a LABEL element object, the focus is handed to the form element associated with that label. Also, when elements such as buttons have focus, pressing the spacebar acts the same as clicking the element with a mouse.

Exercise some judgement in selecting characters for accessKey values. If you assign a letter that is normally used to access one of the Windows version browser's built-in menus (for example, Alt+F for the File menu), that accessKey setting overrides the browser's normal behavior. To users who rely on keyboard access to menus, your control over that key combination can be disconcerting.

On the CD-ROM   Example (with Listing 15-1) on the CD-ROM

Related Item: scrollIntoView() method.

all

Value: Array of nested element objects.   Read-Only

	NN2	NN3	NN4	NN6	IE3/J1	IE3/J2	IE4	IE5	IE5.5
COMPATIBILITY							✓	✓	✓

The `all` property is a collection (array) of every HTML element and (in IE5+) XML tag within the scope of the current object. Items in this array appear in source-code order, and the array is oblivious to element containment among the items. For HTML element containers, the source-code order is dependent on the position of the start tag for the element — end tags are not counted. But for XML tags, end tags appear as separate entries in the array.

Every `document.all` collection contains objects for the HTML, HEAD, TITLE, and BODY element objects even if the actual HTML source code omits the tags. The object model creates these objects for every document that is loaded into a window or frame. While the `document.all` reference may be the most common usage, the `all` property is available for any container element. For example, `document.forms[0].all` exposes all elements defined within the first form of a page.

You can access any element that has an identifier assigned to its `ID` attribute by that identifier in string form (as well as by index integer). Rather than use the performance-costly `eval()` function to convert a string to an object reference, use the string value of the name as an array index value:

```
var paragraph = document.all["myP"]
```

Internet Explorer enables you to use either square brackets or parentheses for single collection index values. Thus, the following two examples evaluate identically:

```
var paragraph = document.all["myP"]
var paragraph = document.all("myP")
```

In the rare case that more than one element within the `all` collection has the same ID, the syntax for the string index value returns a collection of just those identically named elements. But you can use a second argument (in parentheses) to signify the integer of the initial collection and thus single out a specific instance of that named element:

```
var secondRadio = document.all("group0",1)
```

As a more readable alternative, you can use the `item()` method (described later in this chapter) to access the same kinds of items within a collection:

```
var secondRadio = document.all.item("group0",1)
```

Also see the `tags()` method (later in this chapter) as a way to extract a set of elements from an `all` collection that matches a specific tag name.

You can simulate the behavior of IE's `all` property in NN6. See Chapter 14 for the code you need to add to make that happen.

On the
CD-ROM   Example on the CD-ROM

Related Items: item(), tags() methods.

attributes

Value: Array of attribute object references.   Read-Only

	NN2	NN3	NN4	NN6	IE3/J1	IE3/J2	IE4	IE5	IE5.5
Compatibility				✓				✓	✓

The attributes property consists of an array of attributes specified for an element. In IE5, the attributes array contains an entry for every possible property that the browser has defined for its elements — even if the attribute is not set explicitly in the HTML tag. Also, any attributes that you add later via script facilities such as the setAttribute() method are not reflected in the attributes array. In other words, the IE5 attributes array is fixed, using default values for all properties except those that you explicitly set as attributes in the HTML tag.

NN6's attributes property returns an array that is a named node map (in W3C DOM terminology). NN6 does not implement all W3C DOM Level 2 methods for a named node map, but you can use the getNamedItem(attrName) and item(index) methods on the array returned from the attributes property to access individual attribute objects via W3C DOM syntax.

IE5 and NN6 have different ideas about what an attribute object should be. Table 15-2 shows the variety of properties of an attribute object as defined by the two object models. The larger set of properties in NN6 reveals its dependence on the W3C DOM node inheritance model discussed in Chapter 14.

Table 15-2 **Attribute Object Properties**

Property	IE5.x	NN6	Description
attributes	No	Yes	Array of nested attribute objects (null)
childNodes	No	Yes	Child node array
firstChild	No	Yes	First child node
lastChild	No	Yes	Last child node

Property	IE5.x	NN6	Description
localName	No	Yes	Name within current namespace
name	No	Yes	Attribute name
nameSpaceURI	No	Yes	XML namespace URI
nextSibling	No	Yes	Next sibling node
nodeName	Yes	Yes	Attribute name
nodeType	No	Yes	Node type (2)
nodeValue	Yes	Yes	Value assigned to attribute
ownerDocument	No	Yes	document object reference
ownerElement	No	Yes	Element node reference
parentNode	No	Yes	Parent node reference
prefix	No	Yes	XML namespace prefix
previousSibling	No	Yes	Previous sibling node
specified	Yes	Yes	Whether attribute is explicitly specified (Boolean)
value	No	Yes	Value assigned to attribute

The most helpful property of an attribute object is the Boolean specified property. In IE, this lets you know whether the attribute is explicitly specified in the element's tag. Because NN6 returns only explicitly specified attributes in the attributes array, the value in NN6 is always true.

On the CD-ROM

Example on the CD-ROM

Related Items: mergeAttributes(), removeAttribute(), setAttribute() methods.

behaviorUrns

Value: Array of behavior URN strings   Read-Only

	NN2	NN3	NN4	NN6	IE3/J1	IE3/J2	IE4	IE5	IE5.5
Compatibility								✓	✓

The `behaviorUrns` property is designed to provide a list of addresses, in the form of *URNs (Uniform Resource Names),* of all behaviors assigned to the current object. If there are no behaviors, the array has a length of zero. In practice, however, IE5 always returns an array of empty strings. Perhaps the potential exposure of URNs by script was deemed to be a privacy risk.

Example on the CD-ROM

Related Item: `urns()` method.

canHaveChildren

Value: Boolean   Read-Only

	NN2	NN3	NN4	NN6	IE3/J1	IE3/J2	IE4	IE5	IE5.5
Compatibility								✓	✓

Useful in some dynamic content situations, the `canHaveChildren` property (not implemented in IE5/Mac) reveals whether a particular element is capable of containing a child (nested) element. Most elements that have start and end tags (particularly the generic elements covered in this chapter) can contain nested elements. In modern object models, a nested element is referred to as a child of its parent container.

Example (with Listing 15-2) on the CD-ROM

Related Items: `childNodes`, `firstChild`, `lastChild`, `parentElement`, `parentNode` properties; `appendChild()`, `hasChildNodes()`, `removeChild()` methods.

canHaveHTML

Value: Boolean   Read-Only

	NN2	NN3	NN4	NN6	IE3/J1	IE3/J2	IE4	IE5	IE5.5
Compatibility									✓

While most HTML elements are containers of HTML content, not all are. The canHaveHTML property lets scripts find out whether a particular object can accept HTML content, such as for insertion or replacement by object methods. The value for a P element, for example, is true. The value for a BR element is false.

On the CD-ROM   Example on the CD-ROM

Related Items: appendChild(), insertAdjacentHTML(), insertBefore() methods.

childNodes

Value: Array of node objects.   Read-Only

	NN2	NN3	NN4	NN6	IE3/J1	IE3/J2	IE4	IE5	IE5.5
Compatibility				✓			✓	✓	

The childNodes property consists of an array of node objects contained by the current object. Note that child nodes consist of both element objects and text nodes. Therefore, depending on the content of the current object, the number of childNodes and children collections may differ.

Caution   If you use the childNodes array in a for loop that iterates through a sequence of HTML (or XML) elements, watch out for the possibility that the browser treats source code whitespace (blank lines between elements and even simple carriage returns between elements) as text nodes. This potential problem affects IE5/Mac and NN6 (although later versions may repair the problem). If present, these extra text nodes occur primarily surrounding block elements.

Most looping activity through the childNodes array aims to examine, count, or modify element nodes within the collection. If that is your script's goal, then test each node returned by the childNodes array, and verify that the nodeType property is 1 (element) before processing that node. Otherwise, skip over the node. The skeletal structure of such a loop follows:

```
for (var i = 0; i < myElem.childNodes.length; i++) {
    if (myElem.childNodes[i].nodeType == 1) {
        statements to work on element node i
    }
}
```

The presence of these "phantom" text nodes also impacts the nodes referenced by the firstChild and lastChild properties, described later in this chapter.

Example (with Listing 15-3) on the CD-ROM

Related Items: nodeName, nodeType, nodeValue, parentNode properties; cloneNode(), hasChildNodes(), removeNode(), replaceNode(), swapNode() methods.

children

Value: Array of element objects   Read-Only

	NN2	NN3	NN4	NN6	IE3/J1	IE3/J2	IE4	IE5	IE5.5
Compatibility							✓	✓	✓

The children property consists of an array of element objects contained by the current object. Unlike the childNodes property, children does not take into account text nodes but rather focuses strictly on the HTML (and XML) element containment hierarchy from the point of view of the current object. Children exposed to the current object are immediate children only. If you want to get all element objects nested within the current object (regardless of how deeply nested they are), use the all collection instead.

Example (with Listing 15-4) on the CD-ROM

Related Items: canHaveChildren, firstChild, lastChild, parentElement properties; appendChild(), removeChild(), replaceChild() methods.

className

Value: String   Read/Write

	NN2	NN3	NN4	NN6	IE3/J1	IE3/J2	IE4	IE5	IE5.5
Compatibility				✓			✓	✓	✓

A *class name* is an identifier that is assigned to the CLASS attribute of an element. To associate a CSS rule with several elements in a document, assign the same identifier to the CLASS attributes of those elements, and use that identifier (preceded by a period) as the CSS rule's selector. An element's className property enables the application of different CSS rules to that element under script control.

On the CD-ROM Example (with Listing 15-5) on the CD-ROM

Related Items: rule, stylesheet objects (Chapter 30); id property.

clientHeight
clientWidth

Value: Integer   Read-Only

	NN2	NN3	NN4	NN6	IE3/J1	IE3/J2	IE4	IE5	IE5.5
Compatibility							✓	✓	✓

These two properties by and large reveal the pixel height and width of the content with an element whose style sheet rule includes height and width settings. In theory, these measures do not take into account any margins, borders, or padding that you add to an element by way of style sheets. In practice, however, different combinations of borders, margins, and padding influence these values in unexpected ways. One of the more reliable applications of the clientHeight property enables you to discover, for example, where the text of an overflowing element ends.

For the document.body object, the clientHeight and clientWidth properties return the inside height and width of the window or frame (plus or minus a couple of pixels). These take the place of desirable, but nonexistent, window properties in IE.

Internet Explorer 5 expands the number of objects that employ these properties to include virtually all objects that represent HTML elements. For IE4, these properties apply only to the following objects: BODY, BUTTON, CAPTION, DIV, EMBED, FIELDSET, LEGEND, MARQUEE, TABLE, TD, TEXTAREA, TH, and TR.

On the CD-ROM Example (with Listing 15-6) on the CD-ROM

Related Items: offsetHeight, offsetWidth properties.

clientLeft
clientTop

Value: Integer   Read-Only

	NN2	NN3	NN4	NN6	IE3/J1	IE3/J2	IE4	IE5	IE5.5
Compatibility							✓	✓	✓

The purpose and names of the `clientLeft` and `clientTop` properties are confusing at best. Unlike the `clientHeight` and `clientWidth` properties, which apply to the content of an element, the `clientLeft` and `clientTop` properties return essentially no more information than the thickness of a border around an element — provided the element is positioned. If you do not specify a border or do not position the element, the values are zero (although the `document.body` object can show a couple of pixels in each direction without explicit settings). If you are trying to read the left and top coordinate positions of an element, the `offsetLeft` and `offsetTop` properties are more valuable in IE/Windows; as shown in Listing 15-6, however, the `clientTop` property returns a suitable value in IE/Mac. Virtually all elements have the `clientLeft` and `clientTop` properties in IE5+; in IE4, the properties apply only to the BODY, BUTTON, CAPTION, EMBED, FIELDSET, LEGEND, MARQUEE, and TEXTAREA objects.

Related Items: `offsetLeft`, `offsetTop` properties.

contentEditable

Value: Boolean   Read/Write

	NN2	NN3	NN4	NN6	IE3/J1	IE3/J2	IE4	IE5	IE5.5
Compatibility									✓

IE5.5 introduces the concept of editable HTML content on a page. Element tags can include a `CONTENTEDITABLE` attribute, whose value is echoed via the `contentEditable` property of the element. The default value for this property is `inherit`, which means that the property inherits whatever setting this property

has in the hierarchy of HTML containers outward to the body. If you set the `contentEditable` property to `true`, then that element and all nested elements set to inherit the value become editable; conversely, a setting of `false` turns off the option to edit the content.

Example (with Listing 15-7) on the CD-ROM

Related Item: `isContentEditable` property.

currentStyle

Value: `style` object   Read-Only

	NN2	NN3	NN4	NN6	IE3/J1	IE3/J2	IE4	IE5	IE5.5
Compatibility								✓	✓

Every element has style attributes applied to it, even if those attributes are the browser's default settings. Because an element's `style` object reflects only those properties whose corresponding attributes are explicitly set via CSS statements, you cannot use the `style` property of an `element` object to view default style settings applied to an element. That's where the `currentStyle` property comes in.

This property returns a read-only `style` object that contains values for every possible `style` property applicable to the element. If a `style` property is explicitly set via CSS statement or script adjustment, the current reading for that property is also available here. Thus, a script can inquire about any property to determine if it should change to meet some scripted design goal. For example, if you surround some text with an `<EM>` tag, the browser by default turns that text into an italic font style. This setting is not reflected in the element's `style` object (`fontStyle` property) because the italic setting was not set via CSS; in contrast, the `element` object's `currentStyle.fontStyle` property reveals the true, current `fontStyle` property of the element as italic.

To change a `style` property setting, access it via the element's `style` object.

Example on the CD-ROM

Related Items: `runtimeStyle`, `style` objects (Chapter 30).

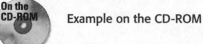

dataFld
dataFormatAs
dataSrc

Value: String   Read/Write

	NN2	NN3	NN4	NN6	IE3/J1	IE3/J2	IE4	IE5	IE5.5
Compatibility							✓	✓	✓

The dataFld, dataFormatAs, and dataSrc properties (along with more element-specific properties such as dataPageSize and recordNumber) are part of the Internet Explorer data-binding facilities based on ActiveX controls. The Win32 versions of IE4 and later have several ActiveX objects built into the browsers that facilitate the direct communication between a Web page and a data source. Data sources include text files, XML data, HTML data, and external databases. Data binding is a very large topic, much of which extends more to discussions about Microsoft Data Source Objects (DSOs), ODBC, and JDBC — subjects well beyond the scope of this book. But data binding is a powerful tool and can be of use even if you are not a database guru. Therefore, this discussion of the three primary properties — dataFld, dataFormatAs, and dataSrc — briefly covers data binding through Microsoft's *Tabular Data Control DSO*. This allows any page to access, sort, display, and filter (but not update) data downloaded into a Web page from an external text file (commonly comma- or tab-delimited data).

You can load data from an external text file into a document with the help of the Tabular Data Control (TDC). You retrieve the data by specifying the TDC object within an <OBJECT> tag set and specifying additional parameters such as the URL of the text file and field delimiter characters. The OBJECT element can go anywhere within the BODY of your document. (I tend to put it at the bottom of the code so that all normal page rendering happens before the control loads.) Retrieving the data simply brings it into the browser and does not, on its own, render the data on the page.

If you haven't worked with embedded objects in IE, the CLASSID attribute value might seem a bit strange. The most perplexing part to some is the long value of numeric data signifying the Globally Unique Identifier (GUID) for the object. You must enter this value exactly as shown in the following example for the proper ActiveX TDC to run. The HTML syntax for this object is as follows:

```
<OBJECT ID="objName" CLASSID="clsid:333C7BC4-460F-11D0-BC04-0080C7055A83">
    <PARAM NAME="DataURL" VALUE="URL">
    [additional optional parameters]
</OBJECT>
```

Table 15-3 lists the parameters available for the TDC. Only the `DataURL` parameter is required; others — such as `FieldDelim`, `UseHeader`, `RowDelim`, and `EscapeChar` — may be helpful depending on the nature of the data source.

Table 15-3	**Tabular Data Control Parameters**
Parameter	**Description**
CharSet	Character set of the data source file. Default is `latin1`.
DataURL	URL of data source file (relative or absolute).
EscapeChar	Character used to "escape" delimiter characters that are part of the data. Default is empty. A common value is `"\"`.
FieldDelim	Delimiter character between fields within a record. Default is comma (`,`). For a Tab character, use a value of `&#09;`.
Language	ISO language code of source data. Default is `en-us`.
TextQualifier	Optional character surrounding a field's data. Default is empty.
RowDelim	Delimiter character between records. Default is newline (`NL`).
UseHeader	Set to `true` if the first row of data in the file contains field names. Default is `false`.

The value you assign to the OBJECT element's `ID` attribute is the identifier that your scripts use to communicate with the data after the page and data completely load. You can therefore have as many uniquely named TDCs loaded in your page as there are data source files you want to access at once.

The initial binding of the data to HTML elements usually comes when you assign values to the `DATASRC` and `DATAFLD` attributes of the elements. The `DATASRC` attribute points to the `DSO` identifier (matching the `ID` attribute of the OBJECT element, preceded with a hash symbol), while the `DATAFLD` attribute points to the name of the field whose data should be extracted. When you use data binding with an interactive element such as a table, multiple records are displayed in consecutive rows of the table (more about this in a moment).

Adjust the `dataSrc` and `dataFld` properties if you want the same HTML element (other than a table) to change the data that it displays. These properties apply to a subset of HTML elements that can be associated with external data: A, APPLET, BODY, BUTTON, DIV, FRAME, IFRAME, IMG, INPUT (most types), LABEL, MARQUEE, OBJECT, PARAM, SELECT, SPAN, and TEXTAREA objects.

In some cases, your data source may store chunks of HTML-formatted text for rendering inside an element. Unless directed otherwise, the browser renders a data source field as plain text — even if the content contains HTML formatting tags. But if you want the HTML to be observed during rendering, you can set the dataFormatAs property (or, more likely, the DATAFORMATAS attribute of the tag) to HTML. The default value is text.

Example (with Listings 15-8 and 15-9) on the CD-ROM

Related Items: recordNumber, TABLE.dataPageSize properties.

dir

Value: "ltr" | "rtl"   Read/Write

	NN2	NN3	NN4	NN6	IE3/J1	IE3/J2	IE4	IE5	IE5.5
Compatibility				✓				✓	✓

The dir property (based on the DIR attribute of virtually every text-oriented HTML element) controls whether an element's text is rendered left-to-right (the default) or right-to-left. Depending on the default language and character set of the IE5 browser running a page, selecting a value other than the default may require the user to install Microsoft's Uniscribe add-in component. By and large, this property (and HTML attribute) is necessary only when you need to override the default direction-ality of a language's character set as defined by the Unicode standard.

Example on the CD-ROM

Related Item: lang property.

disabled

Value: Boolean   Read/Write

	NN2	NN3	NN4	NN6	IE3/J1	IE3/J2	IE4	IE5	IE5.5
Compatibility				(✓)			✓	✓	✓

While some elements have a disabled property in IE4, IE5, and NN6 this property is associated with every HTML element in IE5.5. Disabling an HTML element (like form elements) usually gives the element a "dimmed" look, indicating that it is not active.

A disabled element does not receive any events. It also cannot receive focus, either manually or by script (although disabled text fields in IE4/Mac errantly manage to receive focus). But a user can still select and copy a disabled body text element.

Note

If you disable a form control element, the element's data is not submitted to the server with the rest of the form elements. If you need to keep a form control "locked down," but still submit it to the server, use the FORM element's `onSubmit` event handler to enable the form control right before the form is submitted.

On the CD-ROM Example on the CD-ROM

Related Item: `isDisabled` property.

document

Value: `document` object   Read-Only

	NN2	NN3	NN4	NN6	IE3/J1	IE3/J2	IE4	IE5	IE5.5
Compatibility							✓	✓	✓

In the context of HTML element objects as exposed in IE4+, the `document` property is a reference to the document that contains the object. While it is unlikely that you will need to use this property, `document` may come in handy for complex scripts and script libraries that handle objects in a generic fashion and do not know the reference path to the document containing a particular object. You might need a reference to the document to inspect it for related objects. The W3C version of this property (implemented in IE5/Mac but not in IE5.5/Windows) is `ownerDocument`.

On the CD-ROM Example on the CD-ROM

Related Item: `ownerDocument` property.

filters

Value: Array   Read-Only

	NN2	NN3	NN4	NN6	IE3/J1	IE3/J2	IE4	IE5	IE5.5
Compatibility							✓	✓	✓

Filters are IE-specific style sheet add-ons that offer a greater variety of font rendering (such as drop shadows) and transitions between hidden and visible elements. Each filter specification is a `filter` object. The `filters` property contains an array of `filter` objects defined for the current element. You can apply filters to the following set of elements: BODY, BUTTON, IMG, INPUT, LI, MARQUEE, OL, TABLE, TD, TEXTAREA, TH, UL, and positioned DIV and SPAN elements. See Chapter 30 for details about style sheet filters.

Related Item: `filter` object.

firstChild
lastChild

Value: Node object reference   Read-Only

	NN2	NN3	NN4	NN6	IE3/J1	IE3/J2	IE4	IE5	IE5.5
Compatibility				✓				✓	✓

W3C DOM-based document object models are built around an architecture known as a *node map*. Each object defined by HTML is a node in the map. A node has relationships with other nodes in the document — relationships described in family terms of parents, siblings, and children.

A *child node* is an element that is contained by another element. The container is the parent of such a child. Just as an HTML element can contain any number of child elements, so can a parent object have zero or more children. A list of those children (returned as an array) can be read from an object by way of its `childNodes` property:

```
var nodeArray = document.getElementById("elementID").childNodes
```

While you can use this array (and its `length` property) to get a reference to the first or last child node, the `firstChild` and `lastChild` properties offer shortcuts to those positions. These are helpful when you wish to insert a new child before or after all of the others and you need a reference point for the IE `insertAdjacentElement()` method or other method that adds elements to the document's node list.

Caution   See the discussion of the `childNodes` property earlier in this chapter about the presence of "phantom" nodes in some browser versions. The problem may influence your use of the `firstChild` and `lastChild` properties.

Example (with Listing 15-10) on the CD-ROM

Related Items: nextSibling, parentElement, parentNode, previousSibling properties; appendChild(), hasChildNodes(), removeChild(), removeNode(), replaceChild(), replaceNode() methods.

height
width

Value: Integer or Percentage String   Read/Write and Read-Only

	NN2	NN3	NN4	NN6	IE3/J1	IE3/J2	IE4	IE5	IE5.5
Compatibility			✓	✓			✓	✓	✓

The height and width properties described here are not the identically named properties that belong to an element's style. Rather, these properties reflect the values normally assigned to HEIGHT and WIDTH attributes of elements such as IMG, APPLET, and TABLE, and so on. As such, these properties are accessed directly from the object (for example, document.all.myTable.width in IE4+) rather than through the style object (for example, document.all.myDIV.style.width). Only elements for which the HTML 4.x standard provides HEIGHT and WIDTH attributes have the corresponding properties.

Values for these properties are either integer pixel values (numbers or strings) or percentage values (strings only). If you need to perform some math on an existing percentage value, use the parseInt() function to extract the numeric value for use with math calculations. If an element's HEIGHT and WIDTH attributes are set as percentage values, you can use the clientHeight and clientWidth properties in IE4+ to get the rendered pixel dimensions.

Property values are read/write for the image object in most recent browser versions because you can resize an image object in IE4+ and NN6 after the page loads. Properties are read/write for some other objects (such as the TABLE object) — but not necessarily all others that support these properties.

Support for these properties in NN4 is limited to the IMAGE object. In that browser, both properties are read-only.

In general, you cannot set the value of these properties to something less than is required to render the element. This is particularly true of a table. If you attempt to set the `height` value to less than the amount of pixels required to display the table as defined by its style settings, your changes have no effect (even though the property value retains its artificially low value). For other objects, however, you can set the size to anything you like and the browser scales the content accordingly (images, for example). If you want to see only a segment of an element (in other words, to crop the element), use a style sheet to set the element's clipping region.

Example on the CD-ROM

Related Items: `clientHeight`, `clientWidth` properties; `style.height`, `style.width` properties.

hideFocus

Value: Boolean   Read/Write

	NN2	NN3	NN4	NN6	IE3/J1	IE3/J2	IE4	IE5	IE5.5
Compatibility									✓

In IE for Windows, button types of form controls and links display a dotted rectangle around some part of the element whenever that element has focus. If you set the `TABINDEX` attribute or `tabIndex` property of any other kinds of elements in IE5+, they, too, display that dotted line when given focus. You can still let an element receive focus, but hide that dotted line, by setting the `hideFocus` property of the element object to `true` (default value is `false`).

Hiding focus does not disable the element. In fact, if the element about to receive focus is scrolled out of view, the page scrolls to bring the element into view. Form controls that respond to keyboard action (for example, pressing the spacebar to check or uncheck a checkbox control) also continue to work as normal. For some designers, the focus rectangle harms the design goals of the page. The `hideFocus` property gives them more control over the appearance while maintaining consistency of operation with other pages. There is no corresponding HTML attribute for a tag, so you can use an `onLoad` event handler in the page to set the `hideFocus` property of desired objects after the page loads.

Example on the CD-ROM

Related Items: `tabIndex` property; `srcollIntoView()` method.

id

Value: String (See text)

	NN2	NN3	NN4	NN6	IE3/J1	IE3/J2	IE4	IE5	IE5.5
Compatibility				✓			✓	✓	✓

The id property returns the identifier assigned to an element's ID attribute in the HTML code. A script cannot modify the ID of an existing element nor assign an ID to an element that lacks one. But if a script creates a new element object, an identifier may be assigned to it by way of the id property.

On the CD-ROM

Example on the CD-ROM

Related Item: className property.

innerHTML
innerText

Value: String Read/Write

	NN2	NN3	NN4	NN6	IE3/J1	IE3/J2	IE4	IE5	IE5.5
Compatibility				(✓)			✓	✓	✓

One way that Internet Explorer exposes the contents of an element is through the innerHTML and innerText properties. (Navigator 6 offers only the innerHTML property.) All content defined by these "inner" properties consists of document data that is contained by an element's start and end tags, but not including the tags themselves (see outerText and outerHTML properties). Setting these inner properties is a common way to modify a portion of a page's content after the page loads.

The innerHTML property contains not only the text content for an element as seen on the page, but also every bit of HTML tagging that is associated with that content. (If there are no tags in the content, the text is rendered as is.) For example, consider the following bit of HTML source code:

```
<P ID="paragraph1">"How <EM>are</EM> you?" he asked.</P>
```

The value of the paragraph object's `innerHTML` property (`document.all.`
`paragraph1.innerHTML`) is:

```
"How <EM>are</EM> you?" he asked.
```

The browser interprets any HTML tags that you include in a string you assign to an
element's `innerHTML` property as tags. This also means that you can introduce
entirely new nested elements (or child nodes in the modern terminology) by assigning a slew of HTML content to an element's `innerHTML` property. The document's
object model adjusts itself to the newly inserted content.

In contrast, the `innerText` property knows only about the text content of an element container. In the example you just saw, the value of the paragraph's
`innerText` property (`document.all.paragraph1.innerText`) is:

```
"How are you?" he asked.
```

It's important to remember that if you assign a string to the `innerText` property of
an element and that string contains HTML tags, the tags and their angle brackets
appear in the rendered page and are not interpreted as live tags.

Do not modify the `innerHTML` property to adjust the HTML for `FRAMESET`, `HTML`,
`HEAD`, `TITLE`, or table-related objects. You should modify table constructions
through the various table-related methods that create or delete rows, columns, and
cells (see Chapter 27). It is safe, however, to modify the contents of a cell by setting
its `innerHTML` or `innerText` properties.

When the HTML you insert includes a `<SCRIPT>` tag, be sure to include the `DEFER`
attribute to the opening tag. This even goes for scripts that contain function definitions, which you might consider to be deferred automatically.

If your audience includes Internet Explorer 4 for the Macintosh, know that several
elements do not support these properties. Be sure to test your page thoroughly
on this platform combination. Also, if you want to have the convenience of the
`innerText` property in Navigator 6, see Chapter 14 for instructions on how to
add that property to all elements. Alternatively, you can use the NN6-compatible
`innerHTML` property to assign new text content to an element, even though the
content contains no HTML tags.

**On the
CD-ROM**   Example (with Listing 15-11) on the CD-ROM

Related Items: `outerHTML`, `outerText` properties; `replaceNode()` method.

isContentEditable

Value: Boolean   Read-Only

	NN2	NN3	NN4	NN6	IE3/J1	IE3/J2	IE4	IE5	IE5.5
Compatibility									✓

The isContentEditable property returns a Boolean value indicating whether a particular element object is set to be editable (see the preceding discussion of the contentEditable property). This property is helpful because if a parent element's contentEditable property is set to true, a nested element's contentEditable property likely is set to its default value inherit. But because its parent is editable, the isContentEditable property of the nested element returns true.

Example on the CD-ROM

Related Item: contentEditable property.

isDisabled

Value: Boolean   Read-Only

	NN2	NN3	NN4	NN6	IE3/J1	IE3/J2	IE4	IE5	IE5.5
Compatibility									✓

The isDisabled property returns a Boolean value that indicates whether a particular element object is set to be disabled (see the preceding discussion of the disabled property). This property is helpful; if a parent element's disabled property is set to true, then a nested element's disabled property likely is set to its default value of false. But because its parent is disabled, the isDisabled property of the nested element returns true. In other words, the isDisabled property returns the actual disabled status of an element regardless of its disabled property.

Example on the CD-ROM

Related Item: disabled property.

isMultiLine

Value: Boolean   Read-Only

	NN2	NN3	NN4	NN6	IE3/J1	IE3/J2	IE4	IE5	IE5.5
Compatibility									✓

The isMultiLine property returns a Boolean value that reveals whether the element object is capable of occupying or displaying more than one line of text. Importantly, this value does not reveal whether the element actually occupies multiple lines; rather, it indicates the potential of doing so. For example, a text INPUT element cannot wrap to multiple lines, so its isMultiLine property is false. However, a BUTTON element can display multiple lines of text for its label, so it reports true for the isMultiLine property.

Example on the CD-ROM

isTextEdit

Value: Boolean   Read-Only

	NN2	NN3	NN4	NN6	IE3/J1	IE3/J2	IE4	IE5	IE5.5
Compatibility							✓	✓	✓

The isTextEdit property reveals whether an object can have an IE/Windows TextRange object created with its content. (See the TextRange object in Chapter 19.) You can create TextRange objects only from a limited selection of objects in IE4+ for Windows: BODY, BUTTON, certain form elements (text, password, hidden, button, reset, and submit types), and TEXTAREA. This property always returns false in IE5/Mac.

Example on the CD-ROM

Related Items: createRange() method; TextRange object (Chapter 19).

lang

Value: ISO language code string   Read/Write

	NN2	NN3	NN4	NN6	IE3/J1	IE3/J2	IE4	IE5	IE5.5
Compatibility				✓			✓	✓	✓

The lang property governs the written language system used to render an element's text content when overriding the default browser's language system. The default value for this property is an empty string unless the corresponding LANG attribute is assigned a value in the element's tag. Modifying the property value by script control does not appear to have any effect in the current browser implementations.

On the
CD-ROM   Example on the CD-ROM

language

Value: String   Read/Write

	NN2	NN3	NN4	NN6	IE3/J1	IE3/J2	IE4	IE5	IE5.5
Compatibility							✓	✓	✓

IE4+'s architecture allows for multiple scripting engines to work with the browser. Two engines are included with the basic Windows version browser: JScript (compatible with JavaScript) and Visual Basic Scripting Edition (VBScript). The default scripting engine is JScript. But if you wish to use VBScript or some other scripting language in statements that are embedded within event handler attributes of a tag, you can specifically direct the browser to apply the desired scripting engine to those script statements by way of the LANGUAGE attribute of the tag. The language property provides scripted access to that property. Unless you intend to modify the event handler HTML code and replace it with a statement in VBScript (or any other non-JScript-compatible language installed with your browser), you do not need to modify this property (or read it, for that matter).

Valid values include JScript, javascript, vbscript, and vbs. Third-party scripting engines have their own identifier for use with this value. Because the LANGUAGE attribute is also used in the <SCRIPT> tag, Internet Explorer 5 observes LANGUAGE="XML" as well.

Example on the CD-ROM

Related Item: SCRIPT element object.

lastChild
(See firstchild)

length

Value: Integer   Read-Only and Read/Write

	NN2	NN3	NN4	NN6	IE3/J1	IE3/J2	IE4	IE5	IE5.5
Compatibility	✓	✓	✓	✓	✓	✓	✓	✓	✓

The length property returns the number of items in an array or collection of objects. Its most common application is as a boundary condition in a for loop. While arrays and collections commonly use integer values as index values (always starting with zero), the length value is the actual number of items in the group. Therefore, to iterate through all items of the group, the condition expression should include a less-than (<) symbol rather than a less-than-or-equal (<=) symbol, as in the following:

```
for (var i = 0; i < someArray.length; i++) {...}
```

For decrementing through an array (in other words, starting from the last item in the array and working toward the first), the initial expression must initialize the counting variable as the length minus one:

```
for (var i = someArray.length - 1; i >= 0; i--) {...}
```

For most arrays and collections, the length property is read-only and governed solely by the number of items in the group. But in more recent versions of the browsers, you can assign values to some object arrays (areas, options, and the SELECT object) to create placeholders for data assignments. See discussions of the AREA, SELECT, and OPTION element objects for details. A plain JavaScript array can also have its length property value modified by script to either trim items from the end of the array or reserve space for additional assignments. See Chapter 37 for more about the Array object.

Example on the CD-ROM

Related Items: AREA, SELECT, OPTION, and `Array` objects.

localName
namespaceURI
prefix

Value: String   Read-Only

	NN2	NN3	NN4	NN6	IE3/J1	IE3/J2	IE4	IE5	IE5.5
Compatibility				✓					

The three properties, `localName`, `namespaceURI`, and `prefix`, apply to any node in an XML document that associates a Namespace URI with an XML tag. Although NN6 exposes all three properties for all element (and node) objects, the properties do not return the desired values. Future versions of NN6 should remedy the situation. In the meantime, this description provides a preview of what values these three properties will represent.

Consider the following XML content:

```
<x xmlns:bk='http://bigbooks.org/schema'>
    <bk:title>To Kill a Mockingbird</bk:title>
</x>
```

The element whose tag is `<bk:title>` is associated with the Namespace URI defined for the block, and the element's `namespaceURI` property would return the string `http://bigbooks.org/schema`. The tag name consists of a prefix (before the colon) and the local name (after the colon). In the above example, the `prefix` property for the element defined by the `<bk:title>` tag would be `bk`, while the `localName` property would return `title`. The `localName` property of any node returns the same value as its `nodeName` property value, such as `#text` for a text node.

For more information about XML Namespaces, visit `http://www.w3.org/TR/REC-xml-names`.

Related Items: `scopeName`, `tagUrn` properties.

nextSibling
previousSibling

Value: Object reference   Read-Only

	NN2	NN3	NN4	NN6	IE3/J1	IE3/J2	IE4	IE5	IE5.5
Compatibility				✓				✓	✓

A *sibling element* is one that is at the same nested level as another element. For example, the following P element has two child nodes (the EM and SPAN elements). Those two child nodes are siblings of each other.

```
<P>MegaCorp is <EM>the</EM> source of the <SPAN CLASS="hot">hottest</SPAN>
gizmos.</P>
```

Sibling order is determined solely by the source code order of the elements. Therefore, in the previous example, the EM element has no previousSibling property. Meanwhile, the SPAN element has no nextSibling property (meaning that these properties return null). These properties provide another way to iterate through all elements at the same level.

On the CD-ROM   Example on the CD-ROM

Related Items: firstChild, lastChild, childNodes properties; hasChildNodes(), insertAdjacentElement() methods.

nodeName

Value: String   Read-Only

	NN2	NN3	NN4	NN6	IE3/J1	IE3/J2	IE4	IE5	IE5.5
Compatibility				✓				✓	✓

For HTML and XML elements, the name of a node is the same as the tag name. The nodeName property is provided for the sake of consistency with the node architecture specified by the formal W3C DOM standard. The value, just like the tagName property, is an all-uppercase string of the tag name (even if the HTML source code is written with lowercase tags).

Some nodes, such as the text content of an element, do not have a tag. The nodeName property for such a node is a special value: #text. Another kind of node is an attribute of an element. For an attribute, the nodeName is the name of the attribute. See Chapter 14 for more about Node object properties.

Example on the CD-ROM

Related Item: tagName property.

nodeType

Value: Integer   Read-Only

	NN2	NN3	NN4	NN6	IE3/J1	IE3/J2	IE4	IE5	IE5.5
Compatibility				✓				✓	✓

The W3C DOM specification identifies a series of constant values that denote categories of nodes. Not all of these values are implemented in the W3C DOM-capable browsers, although NN6 includes more than the two supplied by IE5. Table 15-4 lists the nodeType values implemented in recent browsers.

Table 15-4   nodeType Property Values

Value	Description	IE5/5.5	Nav6 & IE5/Mac
1	Element node	✓	✓
2	Attribute node		✓
3	Text (#text) node	✓	✓
8	Comment node		✓
9	Document node		✓

The nodeType value is automatically assigned to an element, whether the element exists in the document's HTML source code or it is generated on the fly via a script.

For example, if you create a new element through any of the ways available by script (for example, by assigning a string encased in HTML tags to the `innerHTML` property or by explicitly invoking the `document.createElement()` method), the new element assumes a `nodeType` of 1.

NN6 goes one step further in supporting the W3C DOM specification by implementing a set of `Node` object property constants for each of the `nodeType` values. Table 15-5 lists the entire set as defined in the DOM Level 2 specification (not all of which are implemented in NN6). Substituting these constants for `nodeType` integers can improve readability of a script. For example, instead of

```
if (myElem.nodeType == 1) {...}
```

it is much easier to see what's going on with

```
if (myElem.nodeType == Node.ELEMENT_NODE) {...}
```

Table 15-5 **W3C DOM nodeType Constants**

Reference	nodeType Value
Node.ELEMENT_NODE	1
Node.ATTRIBUTE_NODE	2
Node.TEXT_NODE	3
Node.CDATA_SECTION_NODE	4
Node.ENTITY_REFERENCE_NODE	5
Node.ENTITY_NODE	6
Node.PROCESSING_INSTRUCTION_NODE	7
Node.COMMENT_NODE	8
Node.DOCUMENT_NODE	9
Node.DOCUMENT_TYPE_NODE	10
Node.DOCUMENT_FRAGMENT_NODE	11
Node.NOTATION_NODE	12

On the CD-ROM Example on the CD-ROM

Related Item: `nodeName` property.

nodeValue

Value: Number, string, or null   Read/Write

	NN2	NN3	NN4	NN6	IE3/J1	IE3/J2	IE4	IE5	IE5.5
Compatibility				✓				✓	✓

Of the node types implemented in the W3C DOM-capable browsers, only the text and attribute types have readable values. An element's node value returns a `null` value.

For a text node, the `nodeValue` property consists of the actual text for that node. Such a node cannot contain any further nested elements, so the `nodeValue` property offers another way of reading and modifying what Internet Explorer implements as an element's `innerText` property.

For an attribute node, the `nodeValue` property consists of the value assigned to that attribute. According to the W3C DOM standard, attribute values should be reflected as strings. IE5/Windows, however, returns values of type `Number` when the value is all numeric characters. Even if you assign a string version of a number to such a `nodeValue` property, it is converted to a `Number` type internally. NN6 and IE5/Mac return `nodeValue` values as strings in all cases (and convert numeric assignments to strings).

On the CD-ROM

Example on the CD-ROM

Related Items: `attributes`, `innerText`, `nodeType` properties.

offsetHeight
offsetWidth

Value: Integer   Read-Only

	NN2	NN3	NN4	NN6	IE3/J1	IE3/J2	IE4	IE5	IE5.5
Compatibility				✓			✓	✓	✓

It is nearly impossible to reconcile the actual behavior of these properties with the descriptions provided by Microsoft for Internet Explorer. The genuine complexity comes when an element has one or more of the following style features attached: borders, margins, and padding. The property values, especially offsetWidth, are heavily influenced by the height and width attributes assigned to an element's style sheet rule. The permutations of elements and their styles plus the vastly roving range of resulting values make it difficult to recommend the offsetHeight and offsetWidth properties unless you manage to find the magic combination that works for your page layout. Differences abound in these properties' treatment across operating system versions of IE.

One advantage that offsetHeight and offsetWidth have over clientHeight and clientWidth is that the offset properties have values even when you do not set dimensions for the element in the HTML tag attributes. That's because these values are set in relation to the element's parent element—most often the BODY element.

Be aware that for a normal element whose height and width are not specified, the offsetHeight is determined by the actual height of the content after all text flows. But the offsetWidth always extends the full width (plus or minus borders, margins, and padding) of the containing element. Therefore, the offsetWidth property does not reveal the rendered width of text content that is narrower than the full parent element width. (Through IE5, no property reveals this information.) To find out the actual width of text within a full-width, block-level element, wrap the text within an inline element (such as a SPAN) and inspect the offsetWidth property of the SPAN.

Although the offsetHeight and offsetWidth properties are not part of the W3C DOM specification, Netscape has implemented these properties in NN6 because they are convenient for some scriptable Dynamic HTML tasks. Through these two properties, a script can read the height and width of any block-level or inline element. As with IE, the NN6 offsetWidth of a text-oriented block-level element is the width of the element's container. For example, a P element consisting of only a few words may report an offsetWidth of many hundreds of pixels because the paragraph's block extends the full width of the BODY element that represents the containing parent of the P element.

On the CD-ROM   Example on the CD-ROM

Related Items: clientHeight, clientWidth properties.

offsetLeft
offsetTop

Value: Integer   Read-Only

	NN2	NN3	NN4	NN6	IE3/J1	IE3/J2	IE4	IE5	IE5.5
Compatibility				✓			✓	✓	✓

The offsetLeft and offsetTop properties can suffer from the same version vagaries that afflict offsetHeight and offsetWidth properties when borders, margins, and padding are associated with an element. However, the offsetLeft and offsetTop properties are valuable in providing pixel coordinates of an element within the positioning context of the parent element — even when the elements are not positioned explicitly.

Note The offsetLeft and offsetTop properties for positioned elements in IE/Macintosh do not return the same values as the style.left and style.top properties of the same element. See Listing 31-17 for an example of how to correct these discrepancies without having to hard-wire the precise pixel differences in your code.

The element used as a coordinate context for these properties is whatever element the offsetParent property returns. This means that to determine the precise position of any element, you may have to add some code that iterates through the offsetParent hierarchy until that property returns null.

Although the offsetLeft and offsetTop properties are not part of the W3C DOM specification, Netscape has implemented these properties in NN6 because they are convenient for some scriptable Dynamic HTML tasks. Through these two properties, a script can read the pixel coordinates of any block-level or inline element. Measurements are made relative to the BODY element, but this may change in the future. See the discussion later in this chapter about the offsetParent property.

On the CD-ROM Example on the CD-ROM

Related Items: clientLeft, clientTop, offsetParent properties.

offsetParent

Value: Object reference   Read-Only

	NN2	NN3	NN4	NN6	IE3/J1	IE3/J2	IE4	IE5	IE5.5
Compatibility				✓			✓	✓	✓

The offsetParent property returns a reference to the object that acts as a positioning context for the current element. Values for the offsetLeft and offsetTop properties are measured relative to the top-left corner of the offsetParent object.

The returned object is usually, but not always, the next outermost block-level container. For most document elements, the offsetParent object is the document. body object (with exceptions for some elements in some browsers).

Table cells, for example, have different offsetParent elements in different browsers:

Browser	*TD offsetParent*
IE4/Windows	TR
IE5+/Windows	TABLE
IE/Mac	TABLE
NN6	BODY

Positioned elements also have different results among browsers. In IE, a first-level positioned element's offsetParent element is the BODY; the offsetParent of a nested positioned element (for example, one absolute-positioned DIV inside another) is the next outer container (in other words, the positioning context of the inner element).

The situation for NN6, however, is not as straightforward as it could be. The offsetParent for any unpositioned element on the page is the BODY element. But the offsetParent property for a positioned element (or any element nested inside a positioned element) returns null. Even so, the offsetLeft and offsetTop properties of a positioned element (and its contents) treat the BODY element as the positioning context. This approach complicates the calculation of the position of an element inside a positioned element relative to its container. Future versions of NN6 will likely bring the behavior of the `offsetParent` property in line with the IE behavior. See Chapter 31 for more details on browser-specific treatment of positionable elements.

Example (with Listing 15-12) on the CD-ROM

Related Items: `offsetLeft`, `offsetTop`, `offsetHeight`, `offsetWidth` properties.

outerHTML
outerText

Value: String   Read/Write

	NN2	NN3	NN4	NN6	IE3/J1	IE3/J2	IE4	IE5	IE5.5
Compatibility							✓	✓	✓

One way that Internet Explorer exposes an entire element to scripting is by way of the `outerHTML` and `outerText` properties. The primary distinction between these two properties is that `outerHTML` includes the element's start and end tags whereas `outerText` includes only rendered text that belongs to the element (including text from any nested elements).

The `outerHTML` property contains not only the text content for an element as seen on the page, but also every bit of HTML tagging associated with that content. For example, consider the following bit of HTML source code:

```
<P ID="paragraph1">"How <EM>are</EM> you?" he asked.</P>
```

The value of the P object's `outerHTML` property (`document.all.paragraph1.outerHTML`) is exactly the same as that of the source code.

The browser interprets any HTML tags in a string that you assign to an element's `outerHTML` property. This means that you can delete (set the property to an empty string) or replace an entire tag with this property. The document's object model adjusts itself to whatever adjustments you make to the HTML in this manner.

In contrast, the `outerText` property knows only about the text content of an element container. In the preceding example, the value of the paragraph's `outerText` property (`document.all.paragraph1.innerText`) is:

```
"How are you?" he asked.
```

If this looks familiar, it's because in most cases the `innerText` and `outerText` properties of an existing element return the exact same strings.

If your audience includes Internet Explorer 4 for the Macintosh, be aware that several elements do not support these properties. In addition, IE5/Mac is downright buggy when you try to assign new content to either property. Be sure to test your page thoroughly on these platform combinations. Also see Chapter 14 for some code to add to a page that simulates the `outerHTML` property for writing in NN6.

Example (with Listing 15-13) on the CD-ROM

Related Items: `innerHTML`, `innerText` properties; `replaceNode()` method.

ownerDocument

Value: `document` object reference   Read-Only

	NN2	NN3	NN4	NN6	IE3/J1	IE3/J2	IE4	IE5	IE5.5
Compatibility				✓					

The `ownerDocument` property belongs to any element or node in the W3C and NN6 DOM. The property's value is a reference to the document node that ultimately contains the element or node. If a script encounters a reference to an element or node (perhaps it has been passed as a parameter to a function), the object's `ownerDocument` property provides a way to build references to other objects in the same document or to access properties and methods of the document objects. IE's version of this property is simply `document`.

Example on the CD-ROM

Related Item: `document` object.

parentElement

Value: Element object reference or `null`   Read-Only

	NN2	NN3	NN4	NN6	IE3/J1	IE3/J2	IE4	IE5	IE5.5
Compatibility							✓	✓	✓

The `parentElement` property returns a reference to the next outermost HTML element from the current element. This parent–child relationship of elements is often, but not always, the same as a parent–child node relationship (see `parentNode` property later in this chapter). The difference is that the `parentElement` property deals only with HTML elements as reflected as document objects, whereas a node is not necessarily an HTML element (for example, an attribute or text chunk).

There is also a distinction between `parentElement` and `offsetParent` properties. The latter returns an element that may be many generations removed from a given element but is the immediate parent with regard to positioning context. For example, a TD element's `parentElement` property is most likely its enclosing TR element, but (in IE5 at least) a TD element's `offsetParent` property is its TABLE element.

A script can "walk" the element hierarchy outward from an element with the help of the `parentElement` property. The top of the parent chain is the HTML element. Its `parentElement` property returns `null`.

Example on the CD-ROM

Related Items: `offsetParent`, `parentNode` properties.

parentNode

Value: Node object reference or `null`   Read-Only

	NN2	NN3	NN4	NN6	IE3/J1	IE3/J2	IE4	IE5	IE5.5
Compatibility				✓				✓	✓

The `parentNode` property returns a reference to the next outermost node that is reflected as an object belonging to the document. For a standard element object, the `parentNode` property is the same as IE's `parentElement` because both objects happen to have a direct parent–child node relationship as well as a parent–child element relationship.

Other kinds of content, however, can be nodes. This includes text fragments within an element. A text fragment's `parentNode` property is the next outermost node or element that encompasses that fragment. A text node object in IE does not have a `parentElement` property.

Example on the CD-ROM

Related Items: childNodes, nodeName, nodeType, nodeValue, parentElement properties.

parentTextEdit

Value: Element object reference or null   Read-Only

	NN2	NN3	NN4	NN6	IE3/J1	IE3/J2	IE4	IE5	IE5.5
Compatibility							✓	✓	✓

Only a handful of objects in IE's object model are capable of creating text ranges (see the TextRange object in Chapter 19). To find an object's next outermost container capable of generating a text range, use the parentTextEdit property. If an element is in the hierarchy, that element's object reference is returned. Otherwise (for example, document.body.parentTextEdit), the value is null. IE5/Mac through version 5 does not implement text ranges or associated properties and methods.

On the CD-ROM   Example (with Listing 15-14) on the CD-ROM

Related Items: isTextEdit property; TextRange object (Chapter 19).

previousSibling

(See nextSibling)

readyState

Value: String (integer for OBJECT object)   Read-Only

	NN2	NN3	NN4	NN6	IE3/J1	IE3/J2	IE4	IE5	IE5.5
Compatibility							✓	✓	✓

A script can query an element to find out if it has loaded all ancillary data (for example, external image files or other media files) before other statements act on that object or its data. The readyState property lets you know the loading status of an element.

Table 15-6 lists the possible values and their meanings.

	Table 15-6	**readyState Property Values**
HTML Value	**OBJECT Value**	**Description**
complete	4	Element and data fully loaded
interactive	3	Data may not be loaded fully, but user can interact with element
loaded	2	Data is loaded, but object may be starting up
loading	1	Data is loading
uninitialized	0	Object has not started loading data yet

For most HTML elements, this property always returns complete. Most of the other states are used by elements such as IMG, EMBED, and OBJECT, which load external data and even start other processes (such as ActiveX controls) to work.

In IE4, the readyState property was limited to the following objects: document, EMBED, IMG, LINK, OBJECT, SCRIPT, and STYLE. For IE5+, this property is available to essentially every element.

One word of caution: Do not expect the readyState property to reveal if an object exists yet in the document (for example, uninitialized). If the object does not exist, it cannot have a readyState property—the result is a script error for an undefined object. If you want to run a script only after every element and its data are fully loaded, trigger the function by way of the onLoad event handler for the BODY element or the onReadyStateChange event handler for the object (and check that the readyState property is complete).

On the CD-ROM   Example on the CD-ROM

Related Items: onReadyStateChange event handler.

recordNumber

Value: Integer or null   Read-Only

	NN2	NN3	NN4	NN6	IE3/J1	IE3/J2	IE4	IE5	IE5.5
Compatibility							✓	✓	✓

Virtually every object has a `recordNumber` property, but it applies only to elements used in Internet Explorer (for Windows) data binding to represent repeated data. For example, if you display 30 records from an external data store in a table, the TR element in the table is represented only once in the HTML. However, the browser repeats the table row (and its component cells) to accommodate all 30 rows of data. If you click a row, you can use the `recordNumber` property of the TR object to see which record was clicked. A common application of this facility is in data binding situations that allow for updating records. For example, script a table so that clicking on an uneditable row of data displays that record's data in editable text boxes elsewhere on the page. If an object is not bound to a data source, or it is a non-repeating object bound to a data source, the `recordNumber` property is `null`.

Example (with Listing 15-15) on the CD-ROM

Related Items: `dataFld`, `dataSrc` properties; TABLE, TR objects (Chapter 27).

runtimeStyle

Value: `style` object   Read-Only

	NN2	NN3	NN4	NN6	IE3/J1	IE3/J2	IE4	IE5	IE5.5
Compatibility								✓	✓

You can determine the browser default settings for style sheet attributes with the help of the `runtimeStyle` property. The `style` object that this property returns contains all style attributes and the default settings at the time the page loads. This property does not reflect values assigned to elements by style sheets in the document or by scripts. The default values returned by this property differ from the values returned by the `currentStyle` property. The latter includes data about values that are not assigned explicitly by style sheets, yet are influenced by the default behavior of the browser's rendering engine. In contrast, the `runtimeStyle` property shows unassigned style values as empty or zero.

To change a style property setting, access it via the element's `style` object.

Example on the CD-ROM

Related Items: `currentStyle` property; `style` object (Chapter 30).

scopeName

Value: String   Read-Only

	NN2	NN3	NN4	NN6	IE3/J1	IE3/J2	IE4	IE5	IE5.5
Compatibility								✓	✓

The `scopeName` property is associated primarily with XML that is embedded within a document. When you include XML, you can specify one or more XML Namespaces that define the "owner" of a custom tag name, thus aiming toward preventing conflicts of identical custom tags from different sources in a document. (See Chapter 33 for more about XML objects.)

The XML Namespace is assigned (in IE5+) as an attribute of the `<HTML>` tag that surrounds the entire document:

```
<HTML XMLNS:Fred='http://www.someURL.com'>
```

After that, the Namespace value precedes all custom tags linked to that Namespace:

```
<Fred:FIRST Name ID="fredFirstName"/>
```

To find out the Namespace "owner" of an element, you can read the `scopeName` property of that element. For the preceding example, the `scopeName` returns `Fred`. For regular HTML elements, the returned value is always `HTML`. The `scopeName` property is available only in Win32 and UNIX flavors of IE5. The comparable property in the W3C DOM is `localName`.

On the CD-ROM   Example on the CD-ROM

Related Item: `tagUrn` property.

scrollHeight
scrollWidth

Value: Integer   Read-Only

	NN2	NN3	NN4	NN6	IE3/J1	IE3/J2	IE4	IE5	IE5.5
Compatibility							✓	✓	✓

The scrollHeight and scrollWidth properties contain the pixel measures of an object, regardless of how much of the object is visible on the page. Therefore, if the browser window displays a vertical scrollbar, and the body extends below the bottom of the viewable space in the window, the scrollHeight takes into account the entire height of the body as if you were to scroll downward and see the entire element. For most elements that don't have their own scrollbars, the scrollHeight and scrollWidth properties have the same values as the clientHeight and clientWidth properties.

A few compatibility cautions are necessary, however. While these properties are available for virtually every element in IE5+, they are available for only the BODY, BUTTON, CAPTION, DIV, FIELDSET, LEGEND, MARQUEE, and TEXTAREA objects in IE4 for Windows. Moreover, IE for the Macintosh yields the viewable height and width of the BODY element, rather than its true scrolling height and width. The values are accurate, however, for other content elements.

Example on the CD-ROM

Related Items: clientHeight, clientWidth **properties;** window.scroll() method.

scrollLeft
scrollTop

Value: Integer   Read-Only

	NN2	NN3	NN4	NN6	IE3/J1	IE3/J2	IE4	IE5	IE5.5
Compatibility							✓	✓	✓

If an element is scrollable (in other words, it has its own scrollbars), you can find out how far the element is scrolled in the horizontal and vertical direction via the scrollLeft and scrollTop properties. These values are pixels. For non-scrollable elements, these values are always zero — even if they are contained by elements that are scrollable. For example, if you scroll a browser window (or frame in a multi-frame environment) vertically, the scrollTop property of the body object is whatever the pixel distance is between the top of the object (now out of view) and the first visible row of pixels of the element. But the scrollTop value of a table that is in the document remains at zero.

These properties are available only to the BODY, BUTTON, CAPTION, DIV, FIELDSET, LEGEND, MARQUEE, SPAN, and TEXTAREA objects in IE4. For IE5+, the properties are available to virtually every element.

NN treats scrolling of a BODY element from the point of view of the window. If you want to find out the scrolled offset of the current page in NN4+, use `window.scrollX` and `window.scrollY`.

Example on the CD-ROM

Related Items: `clientLeft`, `clientTop` properties; `window.scroll()` method.

sourceIndex

Value: Integer   Read-Only

	NN2	NN3	NN4	NN6	IE3/J1	IE3/J2	IE4	IE5	IE5.5
Compatibility							✓	✓	✓

The `sourceIndex` property returns the numeric index (zero-based) of the object within the `document.all` collection. This property is useful if a script needs to access an adjacent object on a page. For example, the following function receives an object reference as a parameter and returns a reference to the object that is next in the source code object order:

```
function getNextObject(obj) {
    return document.all[(obj.sourceIndex + 1)]
}
```

Or if you know only the ID of an object and want to retrieve a reference to the next object in source code order, you can use the following version:

```
function getNextObject(objName) {
    var index = document.all[objName].sourceIndex
    return document.all[(index + 1)]
}
```

Example on the CD-ROM

Related Item: `item()` method.

style

Value: style object reference   Read/Write

	NN2	NN3	NN4	NN6	IE3/J1	IE3/J2	IE4	IE5	IE5.5
Compatibility				✓			✓	✓	✓

The style property is the gateway to an element's style sheet settings. The property's value is a style object whose properties enable you to read and write the style sheet settings for the element. While scripts do not usually manipulate the style object as a whole, it is quite common in a Dynamic HTML page for scripts to get or set multiple properties of the style object to effect animation, visibility, and all appearance parameters of the element.

Changing properties of the style object may affect the layout of the page. For example, setting the font size of an element to a larger value forces the paragraph to reflow to accommodate the enlarged text. This page reflow is available in IE4+ and NN6. Because NN4 cannot reflow content, severe limitations are placed on changing content after the page loads.

You can find significant differences in the breadth of properties of the style object in IE compared with NN. See Chapter 30 for more details on the style object.

Example on the CD-ROM

Related Items: currentStyle, runtimeStyle properties; style object (Chapter 30).

tabIndex

Value: Integer   Read/Write

	NN2	NN3	NN4	NN6	IE3/J1	IE3/J2	IE4	IE5	IE5.5
Compatibility				✓			✓	✓	✓

The tabIndex property controls where in the tabbing sequence the current object receives focus. This property obviously applies only to elements that can receive focus. IE5+ permits giving focus to more elements than IE4 or NN6; but for all browsers compatible with this property, the primary elements for which you may want to control focus (namely form input elements) are covered. IE4/Mac does not give focus to elements other than those that accept text input.

The default value of the `tabIndex` property is 0 (although it is -1 in NN6). A value of 0 (or -1 in NN6) means that elements receive focus in the normal tabbing order on the page, following source code order from the first focusable element. In general, the browsers treat form elements as focusable elements by default. Nonform elements usually don't receive focus unless you specifically set their `tabIndex` properties (or `TABINDEX` tag attributes). If you set the `tabIndex` property of one form element to 1, then that element is first in the tabbing order. Meanwhile, the rest fall into source code tabbing order on successive presses of the Tab key. If you set two elements to, say, 1, then the tabbing proceeds in source code order for those two elements and then onto the rest of the elements in source code order starting with the top of the page.

In Internet Explorer, you can remove an element from tabbing order entirely by setting its `tabIndex` property to 1. Users can still click those elements to make changes to form element settings, but tabbing bypasses the element.

 On the CD-ROM   Example (with Listing 15-16) on the CD-ROM

Related Items: `blur()`, `focus()` methods.

tagName

Value: String   Read-Only

	NN2	NN3	NN4	NN6	IE3/J1	IE3/J2	IE4	IE5	IE5.5
Compatibility				✓			✓	✓	✓

The `tagName` property returns a string of the HTML or (in IE5+ and NN6) XML tag name belonging to the object. All `tagName` values are returned in all uppercase characters, even if the source code is written in all lowercase or a mixture. This consistency makes it easier to perform string comparisons. For example, you can create a generic function that contains a `switch` statement to execute actions for some tags and not others. The skeleton of such a function looks like the following:

```
function processObj(objRef) {
    switch (objRef.tagName) {
        case "TR":
            [statements to deal with table row object]
            break
        case "TD":
            [statements to deal with table cell object]
            break
        case "COLGROUP":
            [statements to deal with column group object]
            break
        default:
            [statements to deal with all other object types]
    }
}
```

Example on the CD-ROM

Related Items: nodeName property; getElementsByTagName() method.

tagUrn

Value: String   Read-Only

	NN2	NN3	NN4	NN6	IE3/J1	IE3/J2	IE4	IE5	IE5.5
Compatibility								✓	✓

The tagUrn property is associated primarily with XML that is embedded within a document. When you include XML, you can specify one or more XML Namespaces that define the "owner" of a custom tag name—thus preventing conflicts of identical custom tags from different sources in a document. (See Chapter 33 for more about XML objects.) A Namespace definition can include a Uniform Resource Name (URN) that lets a page link to a destination on the network that further defines such Namespace aspects as a behavior associated with a custom XML element.

The XML Namespace is assigned (in IE5+) as an attribute of the <HTML> tag that surrounds the entire document.

```
<HTML XMLNS:Fred="http://www.giantco.com/xmllib/">
```

After that, the namespace value precedes all custom tags linked to that Namespace:

```
<Fred:FIRST_Name ID="fredFirstName"/>
```

To find out the URN of the namespace "owner" of an element, you can read the tagUrn property of that element. For the preceding example, the tagURN property returns www.giantco.com/xmllib. For regular HTML elements, the returned value is always null. The corresponding property in the W3C DOM and NN6 is namespaceURI.

 Example on the CD-ROM

Related Item: scopeName property.

title

Value: String   Read/Write

	NN2	NN3	NN4	NN6	IE3/J1	IE3/J2	IE4	IE5	IE5.5
Compatibility				✓			✓	✓	✓

The W3C standard states that you should use the title property (and TITLE attribute) in an "advisory" role. The main browsers interpret that role as text assigned to tooltips that pop up momentarily while the cursor rests atop an element. The advantage of having this property available for writing is that your scripts can modify an element's tooltip text in response to other user interaction on the page.

A tooltip can provide brief help about the behavior of icons or links on the page. It can also convey a summary of key facts from the destination of a link, thus enabling a visitor to see vital information without having to navigate to the other page. For example, Microsoft's Web authoring documentation online (http://msdn.microsoft.com) uses the tooltips in listings of scriptable properties to display a list of elements for which the property is available. While this information also appears on the destination of the link for each property, you can see at a glance, for instance, which instance of the two listings for the same property name apply to the object in which you're interested. The browser governs tooltip font and color characteristics, which are not changeable via scripting.

As with setting the status bar, I don't recommend using tooltips for conveying mission-critical information to the user. Not all users are patient enough to let the pointer pause for the tooltip to appear. On the other hand, a user may be more likely to notice a tooltip once it appears rather than a status bar message (even though the latter appears instantaneously).

Example (with Listing 15-17) on the CD-ROM

Related Item: `window.status` property.

uniqueID

Value: String   Read-Only

	NN2	NN3	NN4	NN6	IE3/J1	IE3/J2	IE4	IE5	IE5.5
Compatibility								✓	✓

You can let the IE5+/Windows browser generate an identifier (`id` property) for a dynamically generated element on the page with the aid of the `uniqueID` property. You should use this feature with care because the ID it generates at any given time may differ from the ID generated the next time the element is created in the page. Therefore, you should use the `uniqueID` property when your scripts require an unknown element to have an `id` property but the algorithms are not expecting any specific identifier.

To guarantee that an element gets only one ID assigned to it while the object exists in memory, assign the value via the `uniqueID` property of that same object—not some other object. Once you retrieve the `uniqueID` property of an object, the property's value stays the same no matter how often you access the property again. In general, you assign the value returned by the `uniqueID` property to the object's `id` property for other kinds of processing. (For example, the parameter of a `getElementById()` method requires the value assigned to the `id` property of an object.)

Example (with Listing 15-18) on the CD-ROM

Related Items: `id` property; `getElementById()` method.

Methods

addBehavior("*URL*")

Returns: Integer ID.

	NN2	NN3	NN4	NN6	IE3/J1	IE3/J2	IE4	IE5	IE5.5
Compatibility								✓	✓

The addBehavior() method imports an external Internet Explorer behavior and attaches it to the current object, thereby extending the properties and/or methods of that object. See Chapter 48 for details on IE behaviors (new in IE5 for Windows).

The sole parameter of the addBehavior() method is a URL pointer to the behavior component's code. This component may be in an external file (with an .htc extension), in which case the parameter can be a relative or absolute URL. IE also includes a library of built-in (default) behaviors, whose URLs are in the following format:

#default#behaviorName

Here, *behaviorName* is one of the default behaviors (see Chapter 48). If the behavior is imported into the document via the OBJECT tag, the addBehavior() method parameter is the ID of that element in the following format:

#objectID

When you add a behavior, the loading of the external code occurs asynchronously. This means that even though the method returns a value instantly, the behavior is not necessarily ready to work. Only when the behavior is fully loaded can it respond to events or allow access to its properties and methods. Behaviors loaded from external files observe domain security rules. The behavior component and the HTML page that loads it must come from the same server and domain; they also must load via the same protocol (for example, http://, https://, and file:// are mutually exclusive, mismatched protocols).

On the CD-ROM   Example (with Listings 15-19a and 15-19b) on the CD-ROM

Related Items: readyState property; removeBehavior() method; behaviors (Chapter 48).

addEventListener("*eventType*", *listenerFunc*, *useCapture*)
removeEventListener("*eventType*", *listenerFunc*, *useCapture*)

Returns: Nothing.

	NN2	NN3	NN4	NN6	IE3/J1	IE3/J2	IE4	IE5	IE5.5
Compatibility				✓					

The W3C DOM's event mechanism accommodates both event bubbling and trick-ling (see Chapter 29). While the new mechanism supports the long-standing notion of binding an event to an element by way of HTML attributes (for example, the old `onClick` event handler), it encourages binding events by registering an event lis-tener with an element. (In browsers that support the W3C event model, other ways of binding events — such as event handler attributes — are internally converted to registered events.)

To tell the DOM that an element should "listen" for a particular kind of event, use the `addEventListener()` method on the element object. The method requires three parameters. The first is a string version of the event type for which the ele-ment should listen. Event type strings do not include the well-used "on" prefix of event handlers. Instead, the names consist only of the event and are usually in all lowercase (except for some special system-wide events preceded by DOM). Table 15-7 shows all the events recognized by the W3C DOM specification (although NN6 may not implement them all).

Table 15-7   W3C DOM Event Listener Types

`abort`	`error`
`blur`	`focus`
`change`	`load`
`click`	`mousedown`
`DOMActivate`	`mousemove`
`DOMAttrModified`	`mouseout`
`DOMCharacterDataModified`	`mouseover`
`DOMFocusIn`	`mouseup`
`DOMFocusOut`	`reset`
`DOMNodeInserted`	`resize`
`DOMNodeInsertedIntoDocument`	`scroll`
`DOMNodeRemoved`	`select`
`DOMNodeRemovedFromDocument`	`submit`
`DOMSubtreeModified`	`unload`

elementObject.addEventListener()

Note that the event types specified in the DOM Level 2 are more limited than the wide range of events defined in IE4+. Also, the W3C temporarily tabled the issue of keyboard events until DOM Level 3. Fortunately, Netscape implements keyboard events in a fashion that likely will appear as part of the W3C DOM.

The second parameter of the addEventListener() method is a reference to the JavaScript function to be invoked. This is the same form used to assign a function to an event property of an object (for example, *objReference*.onclick = *someFunction*), and it should *not* be a quoted string. This approach also means that you cannot specify parameters in the function call. Therefore, functions that need to reference forms or form control elements must build their own references (with the help of the event object's property that says which object is the event's target).

By default, the W3C DOM event model has events bubble upward through the element container hierarchy starting with the target object of the event (for example, the button being clicked). However, if you specify true for the third parameter of the addEventListener() method, event capture is enabled for this particular event type whenever the current object is the event target. This means that any other event type targeted at the current object bubbles upward unless it, too, has an event listener associated with the object and the third parameter is set to true.

 Caution NN6 does not always set event capture for an element, even when you specify true as the third parameter of addEventListener(). For the most part, you can make do with event bubbling by adding an event listener to a container higher up the element hierarchy. Because event capture is a part of the W3C DOM event model, this feature will likely be implemented in a future version of NN.

Using the addEventListener() method requires that the object to which it is attached already exist. Therefore, you most likely will use the method inside an initialization function triggered by the onLoad event handler for the page. (The document object can use addEventListener() for the load event immediately because the document object exists early in the loading process.)

A script can also eliminate an event listener that was previously added by script. The removeEventListener() method takes the same parameters as addEventListener(), which means that you can turn off one listener without disturbing others. In fact, because you can add two listeners for the same event and listener function (one set to capture and one not — a rare occurrence, indeed), the three parameters of the removeEventListener() enable you to specify precisely which listener to remove from an object.

Unlike the event capture mechanism of NN4, the W3C DOM event model does not have a "global" capture mechanism for an event type regardless of target. And with respect to IE5, the addEventListener() method is closely analogous to the IE5 attachEvent() method. Also, event capture in IE5 is enabled via the setCapture() method. Both the W3C and IE5 event models use their separate syntaxes to bind objects to event handling functions, so the actual functions may be capable of serving both models with browser version branching required only for event binding. See Chapter 29 for more about event handling with these two event models.

On the CD-ROM   Example (with Listing 15-20) on the CD-ROM

Related Items: attachEvent(), detachEvent(), dispatchEvent(), fireEvent(), removeEventListener() methods.

appendChild(*nodeObject*)

Returns: Node object reference.

	NN2	NN3	NN4	NN6	IE3/J1	IE3/J2	IE4	IE5	IE5.5
Compatibility				✓				✓	✓

Using the W3C DOM parent, node, and child terminology, you can create cross-browser code (for IE5+ and NN6) that modifies HTML content on the page. The appendChild() method inserts an element or text node (defined by other code that comes before it) as the new, last child of the current element.

Aside from the more obvious application of adding a new child element to the end of a sequence of child nodes, the appendChild() method is also practical for building element objects and their content before appending, replacing, or inserting the element into an existing document. The document.createElement() method generates a reference to an element of whatever tag name you assign as that method's parameter. But this does nothing to populate the element's attributes or its content. While IE4+ offers nonstandard innerText and innerHTML shortcut properties to assign content to an element (and NN6 provides innerHTML), the DOM standard recommends adding child nodes to the new element (for more details, see Chapter 14). For example, if you wish to create a B element and its content, you first create the element and then append a text node, as in the following sequence:

```
var newB = document.createElement("B")
newB.appendChild(document.createTextNode("Important!"))
```

At this point, you can append or insert the newB element. It appears with its content ready to go. The appendChild() method returns a reference to the appended node object. This reference differs from the object that is passed as the method's parameter because the returned value represents the object as part of the document rather than as a freestanding object in memory.

On the CD-ROM   Example (with Listing 15-21) on the CD-ROM

Related Items: removeChild(), replaceChild() methods; nodes and children (Chapter 14).

applyElement(*elementObject*[, *type*])

Returns: Nothing.

	NN2	NN3	NN4	NN6	IE3/J1	IE3/J2	IE4	IE5	IE5.5
Compatibility								✓	✓

The applyElement() method (not implemented in IE5/Mac) enables you to insert a new element as the parent or child of the current object. An important feature of this method is that the new object is wrapped around the current object (if the new element is to become the parent) or the current object's content (if the new element is to become a child). When the new element becomes a child, all previous children are nested further by one generation to become immediate children of the new element. You can imagine how the resulting action of this method affects the containment hierarchy of the current element, so you must be careful in how you use the applyElement() method.

One parameter, a reference to the object to be applied, is required. This object may be generated from constructions such as document.createElement() or from one of the child or node methods that returns an object. The second parameter is optional, and it must be one of the following values:

Parameter Value	Description
outside	New element becomes the parent of the current object
inside	New element becomes the immediate child of the current object

If you omit the second parameter, the default value (outside) is assumed.

On the CD-ROM   Example (with Listing 15-22) on the CD-ROM

Related Items: insertBefore(), appendChild(), insertAdjacentElement() methods.

attachEvent("*eventName*", *functionRef*)
detachEvent("*eventName*", *functionRef*)

Returns: Boolean.

	NN2	NN3	NN4	NN6	IE3/J1	IE3/J2	IE4	IE5	IE5.5
Compatibility								✓	✓

The attachEvent() method is used primarily within code that specifies IE behaviors (see Chapter 48). But you can also use it in regular scripting as yet another way to bind an event handler to an object. The following example characterizes the more typical approach to assigning an event handler:

```
myObject.onmousedown = setHilite
```

The version with attachEvent() is as follows:

```
myObject.attachEvent("onmousedown", setHilite)
```

Both parameters are required. The first parameter is a string version (case-insensitive) of the event name. The second is a reference to the function to be invoked when the event fires for this object. A *function reference* is an unquoted, case-sensitive identifier for the function without any parentheses (which also means that you cannot pass parameters in this function call).

There is a subtle benefit to using attachEvent() over the event property binding approach. When you use attachEvent(), the method returns a Boolean value of true if the event binding succeeds. IE triggers a script error if the function reference fails, so don't rely on a returned value of false to catch these kinds of errors. Also, there is no validation that the object recognizes the event name.

If you have used attachEvent() to bind an event handler to an object's event, you can disconnect that binding with the detachEvent() method. The parameters are the same as for attachEvent(). The detachEvent() method cannot unbind events whose associations are established via tag attributes or event property settings.

The W3C DOM event model provides functionality similar to these IE-only methods: addEventListener() and removeEventListener().

 On the CD-ROM   **Example on the CD-ROM**

Related Items: `addEventListener()`, `detachEvent()`, `dispatchEvent()`, `fireEvent()`, `removeEventListener()` methods; Event binding (Chapter 14).

blur()
focus()

Returns: Nothing.

	NN2	NN3	NN4	NN6	IE3/J1	IE3/J2	IE4	IE5	IE5.5
Compatibility	✓	✓	✓	✓	✓	✓	✓	✓	✓

The `blur()` method removes focus from an element, while the `focus()` method gives focus to an element. Even though the `blur()` and `focus()` methods have been around since the earliest scriptable browsers, not every focusable object has enjoyed these methods since the beginning. Browsers prior to IE4 and NN6 limited these methods primarily to the `window` object and form control elements.

Windows

For window objects, the `blur()` method (NN3+, IE4+) pushes the referenced window to the back of all other open windows. If other browser suite windows (such as e-mail or news reader windows) are open, the window receiving the `blur()` method is placed behind these windows as well.

Caution

The `window.blur()` method does not adjust the stacking order of the current window in NN6. But a script in a window can invoke the `focus()` method of another window to bring that other window to the front (provided a scriptable linkage, such as the `window.opener` property, exists between the two windows).

The minute you create another window for a user in your Web site environment, you must pay attention to window layer management. With browser windows so easily activated by the slightest mouse click, a user can lose a smaller window behind a larger one in a snap. Most inexperienced users don't think to check the Windows taskbar or browser menu bar (if the browser is so equipped) to see if a smaller window is still open and then activate it. If that subwindow is important to your site design, then you should present a button or other device in each window that enables users to safely switch among windows. The `window.focus()` method brings the referenced window to the front of all the windows.

Rather than supply a separate button on your page to bring a hidden window forward, you should build your window-opening functions in such a way that if the window is already open, the function automatically brings that window forward (as shown in Listing 15-23). This removes the burden of window management from your visitors.

The key to success with this method is making sure that your references to the desired windows are correct. Therefore, be prepared to use the `window.opener` property to refer to the main window if a subwindow needs to bring the main window back into focus.

Form elements

The `blur()` and `focus()` methods apply primarily to text-oriented form controls: text input, SELECT, and TEXTAREA elements.

Just as a camera lens blurs when it goes out of focus, a text object "blurs" when it loses focus — when someone clicks or tabs out of the field. Under script control, `blur()` deselects whatever may be selected in the field, and the text insertion pointer leaves the field. The pointer does not proceed to the next field in tabbing order, as it does if you perform a blur by tabbing out of the field manually.

For a text object, having focus means that the text insertion pointer is flashing in that text object's field. Giving a field focus is like opening it up for human editing.

Setting the focus of a text field or TEXTAREA does not, by itself, enable you to place the cursor at any specified location in the field. The cursor usually appears at the beginning of the text. To prepare a field for entry to remove the existing text, use both the `focus()` and `select()` methods in series. Be aware, however, that the `focus()` method does not work reliably in Navigator 3 for UNIX clients: While the `select()` method selects the text in the designated field, focus is not handed to the field.

One other caveat about using `focus()` and `select()` together to preselect the content of a text field for immediate editing: Many versions of Internet Explorer fail to achieve the desired results due to an internal timing problem. You can work around this problem (and remain compatible with Navigator) by initiating the focus and selection actions through a `setTimeout()` method. See Chapter 43 on data validation for an example.

A common design requirement is to position the insertion pointer at the end of a text field or TEXTAREA so that a user can begin appending text to existing content immediately. This is possible in IE4+ with the help of the `TextRange` object. The following script fragment moves the text insertion pointer to the end of a TEXTAREA element whose ID is `myTextarea`:

```
var range = document.all.myTextarea.createTextRange()
range.move("textedit")
range.select()
```

You should be very careful in combining `blur()` or `focus()` methods with `onBlur` and `onFocus` event handlers — especially if the event handlers display alert boxes. Many combinations of these events and methods can cause an infinite loop in which it is impossible to dismiss the alert dialog box completely. On the other hand, there is a useful combination for older browsers that don't offer a `disabled` property for text boxes. The following text field event handler can prevent users from entering text in a text field:

```
onFocus = "this.blur()"
```

Some operating systems and browsers enable you to give focus to elements such as buttons (including radio and checkbox buttons) and hypertext links (encompassing both A and AREA elements). Typically, once such an element has focus, you can accomplish the equivalent of a mouse click on the element by pressing the space-bar on the keyboard. This is helpful for accessibility to those who have difficulty using a mouse.

An unfortunate side effect of button focus in Win32 environments is that the focus highlight (a dotted rectangle) remains around the button after a user clicks it and until another object gets focus. You can eliminate this artifact for browsers and objects that implement the onMouseUp event handler by including the following event handler in your buttons:

```
onMouseUp = "this.blur()"
```

IE5.5 recognizes the often undesirable effect of that dotted rectangle and lets scripts set the hideFocus property of an element to true to keep that rectangle hidden while still giving the element focus. It is a tradeoff for the user, however, because there is no visual feedback about which element has focus.

Other elements

For other kinds of elements that support the focus() method, you can bring an element into view in lieu of the scrollIntoView() method. Link (A) and AREA elements in Windows versions of IE display the dotted rectangle around them after a user brings focus to them. To eliminate that artifact, use the same

```
onMouseUp = "this.blur()"
```

event handler as (or IE5.5 hideFocus property) just described for form controls. Microsoft increased the breadth of objects that support the blur() and focus() methods in IE5.

On the CD-ROM   Example (with Listing 15-23) on the CD-ROM

Related Items: window.open(), document.*formObject*.*textObject*.select() methods.

clearAttributes()

Returns: Nothing.

	NN2	NN3	NN4	NN6	IE3/J1	IE3/J2	IE4	IE5	IE5.5
Compatibility								✓	✓

The `clearAttributes()` method removes all attributes from an element except the NAME and ID values. Thus, styles and event handlers are removed, as are custom attributes assigned in either the HTML source code or later by script. You should know that the `clearAttributes()` method does not alter the length of the element's `attributes` collection because the collection always contains all possible attributes for an element. (See the `attributes` property for elements earlier in this chapter.)

This method is handy if you wish to construct an entirely new set of attributes for an element and prefer to start out with a blank slate. Be aware, however, that unless your scripts immediately assign new attributes to the element, the appearance of the element reverts to its completely unadorned form until you assign new attributes. This means that even positioned elements find their way back to their source code order until you assign a new positioning style. If you simply want to change the value of one or more attributes of an element, it is faster to use the `setAttribute()` method or adjust the corresponding property.

To accomplish a result in NN6 that simulates that of IE5's `clearAttributes()`, you must iterate through all attributes of an element and remove those attributes (via the `removeAttribute()` method) whose names are other than ID and NAME.

 Example on the CD-ROM

Related Items: `attributes` property; `getAttribute()`, `setAttribute()`, `removeAttribute()`, `mergeAttributes()`, and `setAttributeNode()` methods.

click()

Returns: Nothing.

	NN2	NN3	NN4	NN6	IE3/J1	IE3/J2	IE4	IE5	IE5.5
Compatibility	✓	✓	✓	✓	✓	✓	✓	✓	✓

The `click()` method lets a script perform nearly the same action as clicking an element. While this method was available in one form or another since the beginning of scripting, it was available only on INPUT elements that act as buttons (input type button, reset, submit, radio, and checkbox). Most element objects received the method in IE4 and NN6.

The behavior of the `click()` method has also changed over time. Prior to NN4 and IE4, the `click()` method invoked on a button did not trigger the `onClick` event handler for the object. This has significant impact if you expect the `onClick` event handler of a button to function even if a script performs the "click." For earlier browser versions, you have to invoke the event handler statements directly. Also, just because a script is "clicking" a button, not all buttons in all platforms change their appearance in response. For example, NN4 on the Mac does not change the state of a checkbox when clicked remotely. (Win32 versions of version 4 browsers do change state.)

If you want to script the action of "clicking" a button, you can safely invoke the resulting event handler function directly. And if the element is a radio button or checkbox, handle the change of state directly (for example, set the `checked` property of a checkbox) rather than expect the browser to take care of it for you.

On the CD-ROM

Example on the CD-ROM

Related Item: `onClick` event handler.

cloneNode(*deepBoolean*)

Returns: Node object reference.

	NN2	NN3	NN4	NN6	IE3/J1	IE3/J2	IE4	IE5	IE5.5
Compatibility				✓				✓	✓

The `cloneNode()` method makes an exact copy of the current node object. This copy does not have a parent node or other relationship with any element once the copy exists (of course, the original node remains in place). The clone also does not become part of the document's object model unless you explicitly insert or append the node somewhere on the page. The copy includes all element attributes, including the `ID` attribute. Because the value returned by the `cloneNode()` method is a genuine `Node` object, you can operate on it with any `Node` object methods while it is still in the non-document object state.

The Boolean parameter of the `cloneNode()` method controls whether the copy of the node includes all child nodes (`true`) or just the node itself (`false`). For example, if you clone a paragraph element by itself, the clone consists only of the raw element (equivalent of the tag pair, including attributes in the start tag) and none of its content. But including child nodes makes sure that all content within that paragraph element is part of the copy. This parameter is optional in IE5 (defaulting to `false`), but it is required in NN6 and the W3C DOM.

On the CD-ROM   Example on the CD-ROM

Related Items: `Node` object (Chapter 14); `appendChild()`, `removeChild()`, `removeNode()`, `replaceChild()`, and `replaceNode()` methods.

componentFromPoint(*x*,*y*)

Returns: String.

	NN2	NN3	NN4	NN6	IE3/J1	IE3/J2	IE4	IE5	IE5.5
Compatibility								✓	✓

The `componentFromPoint()` method assists in some event-related tasks. You can use it for a kind of collision detection (in other words, to determine whether an event occurs inside or outside of a particular element). If the element has scrollbars, the method can provide additional information about the event such as precisely which component of the scrollbar the user activates. The method is not implemented in IE5/Mac.

A key aspect of this method is that you invoke it on any element that you want to use as the point of reference. For example, if you want to find out if a `mouseup` event occurs in an element whose ID is `myTable`, invoke the method as follows:

```
var result = document.all.myTable.componentFromPoint(event.clientX,
event.clientY)
```

Parameters passed to the method are x and y coordinates. These coordinates do not have to come from an event, but the most likely scenario links this method with an event of some kind. Mouse events (other than `click`) work best.

The value returned by the method is a string that provides details about where the coordinate point is with respect to the current element. If the coordinate point is inside the element's rectangle, the returned value is an empty string. Conversely, if the point is completely outside of the element, the returned value is the string `"outside"`. For scrollbar pieces, the list of possible returned values is quite lengthy (as shown in Table 15-8). Microsoft defines additional values representing pieces of element resizing handles when the browser is set to what the company calls DHTML authoring mode in Windows. This mode involves a special ActiveX control that is outside the scope of this book. Table 15-8 lists these extra values just the same.

Table 15-8   Returned Values for componentFromPoint()

Returned String	Element Component at Coordinate Point
scrollbarDown	Scrollbar down arrow
scrollbarHThumb	Scrollbar thumb on horizontal bar
scrollbarLeft	Scrollbar left arrow
scrollbarPageDown	Scrollbar page-down region
scrollbarPageLeft	Scrollbar page-left region
scrollbarPageRight	Scrollbar page-right region
scrollbarPageUp	Scrollbar page-up region
scrollbarRight	Scrollbar right arrow
scrollbarUp	Scrollbar up arrow
scrollbarVThumb	Scrollbar thumb on vertical bar
handleBottom	Resize handle at bottom
handleBottomLeft	Resize handle at bottom left
handleBottomRight	Resize handle at bottom right
handleLeft	Resize handle at left
handleRight	Resize handle at right
handleTop	Resize handle at top
handleTopLeft	Resize handle at top left
handleTopRight	Resize handle at top right

You do not have to use this method for most collision or event detection, however. The event object's srcElement property returns a reference to whatever object receives the event.

On the CD-ROM

Example (with Listing 15-24) on the CD-ROM

Related Item: event object.

contains(*elementObjectReference*)

Returns: Boolean.

	NN2	NN3	NN4	NN6	IE3/J1	IE3/J2	IE4	IE5	IE5.5
Compatibility							✓	✓	✓

The contains() method reports whether the current object contains another known object within its HTML containment hierarchy. Note that this is not geographical collision detection of overlapping elements, but rather the determination of whether one element is nested somewhere within another.

The scope of the contains() method extends as deeply within the current object's hierarchy as is necessary to locate the object. In essence, the contains() method examines all of the elements that are part of an element's all array. Therefore, you can use this method as a shortcut replacement for a for loop that examines each nested element of a container for the existence of a specific element.

The parameter to the contains() method is a reference to an object. If you have only the element's ID as a string to go by, you can use the document.all.item() method to generate a valid reference to the nested element. If the parameter is a reference to an element that has the same ID as another within the scope of the method, a script error results because a reference to such an element returns an array of elements rather than a valid object reference.

Note   An element always contains itself.

On the CD-ROM   Example on the CD-ROM

Related Items: item(), document.getElementById() methods.

detachEvent()

See attachEvent().

dispatchEvent(*eventObject*)

Returns: Boolean.

	NN2	NN3	NN4	NN6	IE3/J1	IE3/J2	IE4	IE5	IE5.5
Compatibility				✓					

The dispatchEvent() method allows a script to fire an event aimed at any object capable of supporting that event. This is the W3C event model way of generalizing mechanisms that earlier browsers sometimes mimic with object methods such as click() and focus().

The process of generating one of these events is similar to the way a script generates a new node and inserts that node somewhere in the document object model. For events, however, the object that is created is an Event object, which is generated via the document.createEvent() method. An event generated in this manner is simply a specification about an event. Use properties of an event object to supply specifics about the event, such as its coordinates or mouse button. Then dispatch the event to a target object by invoking that target object's dispatchEvent() method and passing the newly created Event object as the sole parameter.

Interpreting the meaning of the Boolean value that the dispatchEvent() method returns is not straightforward. The browser follows the dispatched event through whatever event propagation is in effect for that object and event type (either bubbling or capture). If any of the event listener functions that are triggered by this dispatched event invoke the preventDefault() method, the dispatchEvent() method returns false to indicate that the event did not trigger the native action of the object; otherwise, the method returns true. Notice that this returned value indicates nothing about propagation type or how many event listeners run as a result of dispatching this event.

Caution

While the dispatchEvent() method is implemented in NN6, the browser does not yet provide a way to generate new events from scratch. And if you attempt to redirect an existing event to another object via the dispatchEvent() method, the browser is prone to crashing.

On the CD-ROM

Example (with Listing 15-25) on the CD-ROM

Related Item: fireEvent() method.

fireEvent("*eventType*"[, *eventObjectRef*])

Returns: Boolean.

	NN2	NN3	NN4	NN6	IE3/J1	IE3/J2	IE4	IE5	IE5.5
Compatibility									✓

While some objects have methods that emulate physical events (for example, the `click()` and `focus()` methods), IE5.5 generalizes the mechanism by letting a script direct any valid event to any object. The `fireEvent()` method is the vehicle.

One required parameter is the event type, formatted as a string. IE event types are coded just like the property names for event handlers (for example, `onclick`, `onmouseover`, and so on).

A second, optional parameter is a reference to an existing `event` object. This object can be an event that some user or system action triggers (meaning that the `fireEvent()` method is in a function invoked by an event handler). The existing event can also be an object created by the IE5.5 `document.createEventObject()` method. In either case, the purpose of providing an existing `event` object is to set the properties of the `event` object that the `fireEvent()` method creates. The event type is defined by the method's first parameter, but if you have other properties to set (for example, coordinates or a keyboard key code), then those properties are picked up from the existing object. Here is an example of a sequence that creates a new `mousedown` event, stuffs some values into its properties, and then fires the event at an element on the page:

```
var newEvent = document.createEventObject()
newEvent.clientX = 100
newEvent.clientY = 30
newEvent.cancelBubble = false
newEvent.button = 1
document.all.myElement.fireEvent("onmousedown", newEvent)
```

Events generated by the `fireEvent()` method are just like regular IE `window.event` objects, and they have several important `event` object properties that the browser presets. Importantly, `cancelBubble` is set to `false` and `returnValue` is set to `true`—just like a regular user- or system-induced event. This means that if you want to prevent event bubbling and/or prevent the default action of the event's source element, then the event handler functions must set these `event` object properties just like normal event handling in IE.

The `fireEvent()` method returns a Boolean value that the `returnValue` property of the event determines. If the `returnValue` property is set to `false` during event handling, then the `fireEvent()` method returns `false`. Under normal processing, the method returns `true`.

Although the W3C DOM Level 2 event model includes the dispatchEvent() method to accommodate script-generated events (and Event object methods to create event objects), Microsoft has so far elected to ignore the standard recommendation. While there is some similarity between the basic operations of fireEvent() and dispatchEvent(), the two methods diverge significantly in advanced applications (for example, the way events can propagate and the W3C notion of an Event object).

On the CD-ROM   Example (with Listing 15-26) on the CD-ROM

Related Item: dispatchEvent() method.

focus()

See blur().

getAdjacentText("*position*")

Returns: String.

	NN2	NN3	NN4	NN6	IE3/J1	IE3/J2	IE4	IE5	IE5.5
Compatibility								✓	✓

The getAdjacentText() method enables you to extract plain text components of an element object (in other words, without any HTML tag information). This method is not implemented in IE5/Mac. The sole parameter is one of four case-insensitive string constant values that indicate from where, in relation to the current object, the text should be extracted. The values are:

Parameter Value	Description
beforeBegin	Text immediately in front of the element's tag, back to the preceding tag
afterBegin	Text that begins inside the element tag, up to the next tag (whether it be a nested element or the element's end tag)
beforeEnd	Text immediately in front of the element's end tag, back to the preceding tag (whether it be a nested element or the element's start tag)
afterEnd	Text immediately following the element's end tag, forward until the next tag

If the current object has no nested elements, then the afterBegin and beforeEnd versions both return the same as the object's innerText property. When the current object is encased immediately within another element (for example, a TD element inside a TR element), there is no text before the element's beginning or after the element's end so these values are returned as empty strings.

The strings returned from this method are roughly equivalent to values of text fragment nodes in the W3C DOM, but IE5 treats these data pieces only as string data types rather than as text node types. Cross-browser DOM equivalents for the four versions are:

```
document.getElementById("objName").previousSibling.nodeValue
document.getElementById("objName").firstChild.nodeValue
document.getElementById("objName").lastChild.nodeValue
document.getElementById("objName").nextSibling.nodeValue
```

 Example on the CD-ROM

Related Items: childNodes, data, firstChild, lastChild, nextSibling, nodeValue, and previousSibling properties.

getAttribute("*attributeName*"[, *caseSensitivity*])

Returns: See text.

	NN2	NN3	NN4	NN6	IE3/J1	IE3/J2	IE4	IE5	IE5.5
Compatibility				✓			✓	✓	✓

The getAttribute() method returns the value assigned to a specific attribute of the current object. You can use this method as an alternative to retrieving properties of an object, particularly when your script presents you with the attribute name as a string (in contrast to a fully formed reference to an object and its property). Thus, the following example statements yield the same data:

```
var mult = document.all.mySelect.multiple
var mult = document.all.mySelect.getAttribute("multiple")
```

Returned value types from getAttribute() are either strings (including attribute values assigned as unquoted numeric values) or Booleans (for example, the multiple property of a SELECT element object).

Note

The W3C DOM Level 2 standard recommends getAttribute() and setAttribute() for reading and writing element object attribute values, rather than reading and writing those values by way of their corresponding properties. While using these methods is certainly advisable for XML elements, the same DOM standard sends conflicting signals by defining all kinds of properties for HTML element objects. Browsers, of course, will support access via properties well into the future, so don't feel obligated to change your ways.

All browsers that support the getAttribute() method require one parameter, which is a string of the attribute name. By default, this parameter is not case-sensitive. Note that this has impact on custom attributes that you might assign to HTML or XML elements in your documents. Attribute names are automatically converted to lowercase when they are turned into properties of the object. Therefore, you must avoid reusing attribute names, even if you use different case letters in the source code assignments.

IE includes an optional extension to the method in the form of a second parameter that enables you to be more specific about the case-sensitivity of the first parameter. The default value of the second parameter is false, which means that the first parameter is not case-sensitive. A value of true makes the first parameter case-sensitive. This matters only if you use setAttribute() to add a parameter to an existing object and in the IE version of that method insists on case-sensitivity. The default behavior of setAttribute() respects the case of the attribute name. See also the discussion of the setAttribute() method later in this chapter with regard to setAttribute()'s influence over the IE attributes property.

On the CD-ROM

Example on the CD-ROM

Related Items: attributes property; document.createAttribute(), setAttribute() methods.

getAttributeNode("*attributeName*")

Returns: Attribute node object.

	NN2	NN3	NN4	NN6	IE3/J1	IE3/J2	IE4	IE5	IE5.5
Compatibility				✓					

In the W3C DOM, an attribute is an object that inherits all the properties of a Node object (see Chapter 14). As its name implies, an attribute object represents a name–value pair of an attribute that is explicitly defined inside an element's tag. The ability to treat attributes as node objects is far more important when working with XML than HTML, but it is helpful to understand attribute nodes within the context of the W3C DOM object-oriented view of a document. Importantly, attribute nodes specifically are not recognized as nodes of a document hierarchy. Therefore, an attribute node is not a child node of the element that defines the attribute.

But the "nodeness" of attributes comes into play when comparing the contents of an object's `attributes` property in the IE and W3C DOM worlds. In IE5+, the `attributes` property returns an array of all attributes for an element (whether or not the attributes are explicitly included in the tag). But the W3C `attributes` property builds on the DOM's formal structure by returning an object known (internally) as a *named node map*. Like an array, the named node map has a `length` property (facilitating `for` loop interation through the map), plus several methods that allow for inserting, removing, reading, or writing attribute name–value pairs within the node map. To a script, the value of the `attributes` property can behave the same in both IE5 and the W3C DOM provided that scripts don't have to dig too deeply into the nature of each object model's idea of what an attribute object is.

In IE5, an attribute object is a relatively simple object consisting of `nodeName`, `nodeValue`, and `specified` properties. In the W3C DOM, an attribute object is something more substantial, primarily because it inherits all the properties of the `Node` object. Table 5-9 compares the properties of an attribute object in NN6 and IE5.

Table 5-9   Attribute Object Properties in NN6 and IE5

NN6	IE5
attributes	
childNodes	
firstChild	
lastChild	
name	
nextSibling	
nodeName	nodeName
nodeType	
nodeValue	nodeValue
ownerDocument	
parentNode	
previousSibling	
specified	specified
value	

Admittedly, the three properties implemented in IE5 are the most important, but the shortcut approach negates the object-oriented system of the W3C DOM.

All of this is a long way to explain the W3C DOM `getAttributeNode()` method, which returns a W3C DOM attribute object. The sole parameter of the method is a case-insensitive string version of the attribute's name. You can then use any of the properties shown in Table 15-9 to get or set attribute values. Of course, HTML attributes are generally exposed as properties of HTML elements, so it is usually easier to read or write the object's properties directly.

Example on the CD-ROM

Related Items: `attributes` property; `getAttribute()`, `removeAttributeNode()`, `setAttributeNode()` methods.

getBoundingClientRect()

Returns: `TextRectangle` object.

	NN2	NN3	NN4	NN6	IE3/J1	IE3/J2	IE4	IE5	IE5.5
Compatibility								✓	✓

IE5+ assigns to every content-holding element a rectangle that describes the space that the element occupies on the page. This rectangle is called a *bounding rectangle*, and it is expressed in the IE5/Windows object model as a `TextRectangle` object (even when the content is an image or some other kind of object). A `TextRectangle` object has four properties (`top`, `left`, `bottom`, and `right`) that are the pixel coordinates that define the rectangle. The `getBoundingClientRect()` method returns a `TextRectangle` object that describes the bounding rectangle of the current object. You can access an individual measure of an object's bounding rectangle, as in the following example:

```
var parTop = document.all.myP.getBoundingClientRect().top
```

For elements that consist of text, such as paragraphs, the dimensions of individual `TextRectangle`s for each line of text in the element influence the dimensions of the bounding rectangle. For example, if a paragraph contains two lines, and the second line extends only halfway across the width of the first line, the width of the second line's `TextRectangle` object is only as wide as the actual text in the second line. But because the first line extends close to the right margin, the width of the encompassing bounding rectangle is governed by that wider, first line `TextRectangle`. Therefore, an element's bounding rectangle is as wide as its widest line and as tall as the sum of the height of all `TextRectangle` objects in the paragraph.

Another method, getClientRects(), enables you to obtain a collection of line-by-line TextRectangle objects for an element. Neither method is implemented in IE5/Mac.

On the CD-ROM   Example (with Listing 15-27) on the CD-ROM

Related Items: getClientRects() method; TextRectangle object (Chapter 19).

getClientRects()

Returns: Array of TextRectangle objects.

	NN2	NN3	NN4	NN6	IE3/J1	IE3/J2	IE4	IE5	IE5.5
Compatibility								✓	✓

The getClientRects() method returns an array of all TextRectangle objects that fall within the current object the moment the method is invoked. Each TextRectangle object has its own top, left, bottom, and right coordinate properties. You can then, for example, loop through all objects in this array to calculate the pixel width of each line. If you want to find out the aggregate height and/or maximum width of the entire collection, you can use the getBoundingClientRect() method as a shortcut. This method is not implemented in IE5/Mac.

On the CD-ROM   Example on the CD-ROM

Related Items: getBoundingClientRect() method; TextRectangle object (Chapter 19).

getElementsByTagName("*tagName*")

Returns: Array of element objects.

	NN2	NN3	NN4	NN6	IE3/J1	IE3/J2	IE4	IE5	IE5.5
Compatibility				✓				✓	✓

The getElementsByTagName() method returns an array of all elements of the current object whose tags match the tag name supplied as the sole parameter to the method.

The tag name parameter must be in the form of a string and is case-insensitive. The group of elements returned in the array includes only those elements that are within the containment scope of the current object. Therefore, if you have two table objects in a document and you invoke the getElementsByTagName("td") method on one of them, the list of returned table cell elements is confined to those cells within the current table object. The current element is not included in the returned array.

The W3C DOM (but not implemented in IE5.x/Windows) accepts a wildcard character ("*") as a parameter to the getElementsByTagName() method. The resulting array of elements is similar to what IE4+ returns via the document.all collection. See Chapter 14 for ideas on simulating document.all in NN6 using this technique.

Internet Explorer provides additional alternate syntax for this method: the tags() method of the all collection. This alternate syntax also works in IE4 (see the all property earlier in this chapter).

Example on the CD-ROM

Related Items: getElementById(), tags() methods.

getExpression("*attributeName*")

Returns: String.

	NN2	NN3	NN4	NN6	IE3/J1	IE3/J2	IE4	IE5	IE5.5
Compatibility								✓	✓

The getExpression() method (not implemented in IE5/Mac) returns the text of the expression that was assigned to an element's attribute via the setExpression() method. The returned value is not the value of the expression, but rather the expression itself. If you want to find out the current value of the expression (assuming that the variables used are within the scope of your script), you can use the eval() function on the call to getExpression(). This action converts the string to a JavaScript expression and returns the evaluated result.

One parameter, a string version of the attribute name, is required.

Example on the CD-ROM

Related Items: document.recalc(), removeExpression(), setExpression() methods.

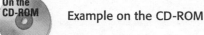

hasChildNodes()

Returns: Boolean.

	NN2	NN3	NN4	NN6	IE3/J1	IE3/J2	IE4	IE5	IE5.5
Compatibility				✓				✓	✓

The `hasChildNodes()` method returns `true` if the current object has child nodes nested within; it returns `false` otherwise. A child node is not necessarily the same as a child element, so the following two expressions return `true` when the current object has at least one child node:

```
document.getElementById("myObject").hasChildNodes()
document.getElementById("myObject").childNodes.length > 0
```

You cannot use the second expression interchangeably with the following statement (which uses the IE-only `children` property):

```
document.getElementById("myObject").children.length > 0
```

You generally use the `hasChildNodes()` method in a conditional expression to make sure such nodes exist before performing operations on them:

```
if (document.getElementById("myObject").hasChildNodes() {
    statements that apply to child nodes
}
```

 Example on the CD-ROM

Related Items: `childNodes` property; `appendChild()`, `removeChild()`, `replaceChild()` methods.

insertAdjacentElement("*location*", *elementObject*)

Returns: Object.

	NN2	NN3	NN4	NN6	IE3/J1	IE3/J2	IE4	IE5	IE5.5
Compatibility								✓	✓

The `insertAdjacentElement()` method (not implemented in IE5/Mac) inserts an element object (coming from a variety of sources) in a specific position relative to the current object. Both parameters are required. The first must be one of four possible case-insensitive locations for the insertion, shown in the following table:

Location	Description
beforeBegin	Before the current element's start tag
afterBegin	After the start tag, but before any nested content
beforeEnd	Before the end tag, but after all other nested content
afterEnd	After the end tag

These locations are relative to the current object. The element type of the current object (a block-level or inline element) has great bearing on how the inserted element is rendered. For example, suppose you create a B element (using `document.createElement()`) and assign some inner text to it. You then use `insertAdjacentElement()` in an effort to insert this B element before some text in a P element. Because a P element is a block-level element, the location `beforeBegin` places the new B element before the start tag of the P element. This means, however, that the bold text appears in a text line above the start of the P element because a `<P>` tag begins a new block at the left margin of its container (unless instructed otherwise by style sheets). The resulting HTML looks like the following:

```
<B>The new element.</B><P>The original paragraph element.</P>
```

To make the new B element a part of the P element — but in front of the existing P element's content — use the `afterBegin` location. The resulting HTML looks like the following:

```
<P><B>The new element.</B>The original paragraph element.</P>
```

To complete the demonstration of the four location types, the following is the result of the `beforeEnd` location:

```
<P>The original paragraph element. <B>The new element.</B></P>
```

and this is the result of the `afterEnd` location:

```
<P>The original paragraph element.</P><B>The new element.</B>
```

The object to be inserted is a reference to an element object. The object reference can come from any expression that evaluates to an element object or, more likely, from the result of the `document.createElement()` method. Bear in mind that the object generated by `document.createElement()` initially has no content, and all attribute values are set to default values. Moreover, the object is passed to `insertAdjacentElement()` by reference, which means that there is only one instance of that object. If you attempt to insert that object in two places with two statements, the object is moved from the first location to the second. If you need to copy an existing object so that the original is not moved or otherwise disturbed by this method, use the `cloneNode()` method to specify the `true` parameter to capture all nested content of the node.

Do not use this method to insert new table elements into a table. Instead, use the many table-specific insertion methods that better treat rows, columns, and cells of a table (see Chapter 27). And if you wish to insert an element that surrounds the current element or wraps all of the content of the current element, use the `applyElement()` method.

Example on the CD-ROM

Related Items: `document.createElement()`, `applyElement()` methods.

insertAdjacentHTML("*location*", "*HTMLtext*") insertAdjacentText("*location*", "*text*")

Returns: Nothing.

	NN2	NN3	NN4	NN6	IE3/J1	IE3/J2	IE4	IE5	IE5.5
Compatibility							✓	✓	✓

These two methods insert HTML or straight text at a location relative to the current element. They are intended for use after a page loads, rather than inserting content while the page loads (in which case you can use `document.write()` wherever you need evaluated content to appear on the page).

The first parameter must be one of four possible case-insensitive locations for the insertion, shown in the following table:

Location	*Description*
`beforeBegin`	Before the current element's start tag
`afterBegin`	After the start tag, but before any nested content
`beforeEnd`	Before the end tag, but after all other nested content
`afterEnd`	After the end tag

These locations yield the same results as described in the insertAdjacentElement() function discussed earlier.

Whether you use insertAdjacentHTML() or insertAdjacentText() depends on the nature of your content and what you want the browser to do with it. If the content contains HTML tags that you want the browser to interpret and render as if it were part of the page source code, then use the insertAdjacentHTML() method. All tags become objects in the document's object model. But if you want only to display some text (including HTML tags in their "raw" form), use insertAdjacentText(). The rendering engine does not interpret any tags included in the string passed as the second parameter. Instead, these tags are displayed as characters on the page. This distinction is identical to the one between the innerHTML and innerText properties.

The difference between insertAdjacentHTML() and insertAdjacentElement() is the nature of the content that you insert. The former enables you to accumulate the HTML as a string, while the latter requires the creation of an element object. Also, the two methods in this section work with IE4+ (including Mac versions), whereas insertAdjacentElement() requires the newer object model of IE5 and later.

If the HTML you pass as the second parameter of insertAdjacentHTML() contains <SCRIPT> tags, you must set the DEFER attribute in the opening tag. This prevents script statements from executing as you insert them.

For inserting new elements into an existing table, use the variety of table object methods for managing rows, columns, and cells (see Chapter 27).

Example on the CD-ROM

Related Items: innerText, innerHTML, outerText, outerHTML properties; insertAdjacentElement(), replaceAdjacentText() methods.

insertBefore(*newChildNodeObject*[, *referenceChildNode*])

Returns: Node object.

	NN2	NN3	NN4	NN6	IE3/J1	IE3/J2	IE4	IE5	IE5.5
Compatibility				✓				✓	✓

The insertBefore() method is the W3C DOM syntax for inserting a new child node into an existing element. Node references for both parameters must be valid Node objects (including those that document.createElement() generates).

The behavior of this method might seem counter-intuitive at times. If you include the second parameter (a reference to an existing child node of the current element), the new child node is inserted before that existing one. But if you omit the second parameter (or its value is null), the new child node is inserted as the last child of the current element — in which case, the method acts the same as the appendChild() method. The true power of this method is summoned when you specify that second parameter; from the point of view of a parent element, you can drop a new child into any spot among its existing children.

Bear in mind that the insertBefore() method works from a parent element. Internet Explorer provides additional methods, such as insertAdjacentElement(), to operate from the perspective of what will become a child element.

On the CD-ROM   Example (with Listing 15-28) on the CD-ROM

Related Items: appendChild(), replaceChild(), removeChild(), insertAdjacentElement() methods.

item(*index* | "*index*" [, *subIndex*])

Returns: Object.

	NN2	NN3	NN4	NN6	IE3/J1	IE3/J2	IE4	IE5	IE5.5
Compatibility				✓			✓	✓	✓

The item() method works with most objects that are themselves collections of other objects. In the W3C DOM framework, these kinds of objects are known as *named node lists* (for objects such as nodes and attributes) or *HTML collections* (for objects such as elements of a form). While the W3C DOM defines the item() method, it does so with a single numeric parameter that is the index value of the desired object within the collection. NN6 implements this version. If you know the index number of the item, you can use JavaScript array syntax instead. The following two statements return the same object reference:

```
document.getElementById("myTable").childNodes.item(2)
document.getElementById("myTable").childNodes[2]
```

And for IE's `all` object, the index value for a given element is the same as the element's `sourceIndex` property.

IE4+ extends the possibilities by also allowing a string of the ID of an object within the collection. (Integer values are required for the `attributes`, `rules`, and `TextRectangle` objects, however.) Additionally, if the collection has more than one object with the same ID (never a good idea except when necessary), a second numeric parameter enables you to select which identically named group you want (using zero-based index values within that subgroup). This obviously does not apply to collections, such as attributes and rules, which have no ID associated with them.

The method returns a reference to the object specified by the parameters.

On the CD-ROM   Example on the CD-ROM

Related Items: All object element properties that return collections (arrays) of other objects.

mergeAttributes("*sourceObject*")

Returns: Nothing.

	NN2	NN3	NN4	NN6	IE3/J1	IE3/J2	IE4	IE5	IE5.5
Compatibility								✓	✓

The `mergeAttributes()` method (not implemented in IE5/Mac) is a convenient way to propagate attributes in newly created elements without painstakingly adding attributes one at a time. Once you have an object whose attributes can function as a prototype for other elements, those attributes (except for the `ID` attribute) can be applied to a newly created element instantaneously.

On the CD-ROM   Example (with Listing 15-29) on the CD-ROM

Related Items: `clearAttributes()`, `cloneNode()`, `removeAttributes()` methods.

normalize()

Returns: Nothing.

	NN2	NN3	NN4	NN6	IE3/J1	IE3/J2	IE4	IE5	IE5.5
Compatibility				✓					

In the course of appending, inserting, removing, and replacing child nodes of an element, it is conceivable that two text nodes can end up adjacent to each other. While this typically has no effect on the rendering of the content, some XML-centric applications that rely heavily on the document node hierarchy to interpret content properly may not like having two text nodes sitting next to each other. The "proper" form of a node hierarchy is for a single text node to be bounded by other node types. The `normalize()` method sweeps through the child nodes of the current node object and combines adjacent text nodes into a single text node. The effect obviously impacts the number of child nodes of an element, but it also cleanses the nested node hierarchy.

On the CD-ROM   Example on the CD-ROM

Related Items: `document.createTextNode()`, `appendChild()`, `insertBefore()`, `removeChild()`, `replaceChild()` methods.

releaseCapture()
setCapture(*containerBoolean*)

Returns: Nothing.

	NN2	NN3	NN4	NN6	IE3/J1	IE3/J2	IE4	IE5	IE5.5
Compatibility								✓	✓

You can instruct a single object on an IE5+/Windows page to capture all mouse events (`onmousedown`, `onmouseup`, `onmousemove`, `onmouseout`, `onmouseover`, `onclick`, and `ondblclick`) via the IE-specific `setCapture()` method. This type of event capture is somewhat similar to event capture mechanisms of NN4 and NN6 (which are quite different in and of themselves). However, the syntax is entirely different, as is the overall approach to the code that handles events (see Chapter 29 on the `Event` object).

A primary scenario for IE mouse event capture is when some content appears on the page that you wish to leave as the center of user focus — items such as pull-down menus, context menus, or simulated modal window areas. When such items appear on the screen, you want the effect of blocking all mouse events except those that apply to the menu or currently visible pseudowindow. When the region disappears, mouse events can be released so that individual elements (such as buttons and links elsewhere on the page) respond to mouse events.

Event capture does not block the events. Instead, the events are redirected to the object set to capture all mouse events. Events bubble up from that point unless explicitly cancelled (see Chapter 29). For example, consider a document that has a `<BODY>` tag containing an `onClick` event handler that governs the entire document at all times. If you turn on event capture for a DIV somewhere in the document, the click event first goes to the DIV. That DIV might have an `onClick` event handler that looks to process click events when they occur in some of its child elements. If the event handler for the DIV does not also cancel the bubbling of that click event, the BODY element's `onClick` event handler eventually receives and processes the event, even though the DIV initially captured the event.

Deciding which object should capture events is an important design issue to confront. With event capture engaged, all mouse events (no matter where they occur) get funneled to the object set to capture the events. Therefore, if you design an application whose entire interface consists of clicking and dragging positionable elements, you can set one of those elements (or even the `document` object) to perform the capturing. For pop-up regions, however, it is generally more logical and convenient for your coding to assign the capture mechanism to the primary container of the pop-up content (usually a positioned DIV).

The `setCapture()` method has one optional Boolean parameter. The parameter controls whether mouse events on child elements within the capturing object are under control of the event capture mechanism. The default value (`true`) means that all mouse events targeted at elements within the current object go to the current object rather than to the original target—the most likely way you will use `setCapture()` for things such as pop-up and context menus. But if you specify `false` as the parameter, then mouse events occurring in child elements of the capturing container receive their events directly. From there, regular event bubbling upward from the target ensues (see Chapter 29).

You may encounter odd behavior when the region you set up to capture mouse events contains form elements such as text input fields and SELECT lists. Because these elements require mouse events to gain focus for interaction, the event capture mechanism inhibits access to these items. To work around this behavior, you can examine the click event's `srcElement` property to see if the click was on one of these elements and script the focus of that element (or instruct the user to press the Tab key until the element gets focus manually).

Once an object is set to capture events, your other code must define which events actually do something; and decide whether events should bubble up beyond the capturing element. You need to worry about bubbling only if your design includes mouse event handlers in elements higher up the element containment hierarchy.

elementObject.**releaseCapture()**

You may not wish for those event handlers to fire while event capture is on; in this case, you need to cancel the bubbling of those events in the capturing object.

If your application design requires that the pop-up area be hidden and event handling be returned to normal (such as after the user makes a pop-up menu selection), use the `releaseCapture()` method in conjunction with hiding the container. Because event capture can be engaged for only one element at a time, you can release capture by invoking the `releaseCapture()` method from the container or from the `document` object.

Event capture is automatically disengaged when the user performs any of the following actions:

- ✦ Gives focus to any other window
- ✦ Displays any system modal dialog window (for example, alert window)
- ✦ Scrolls the page
- ✦ Opens a browser context menu (by right-clicking)
- ✦ Tabs to give focus to the Address field in the browser window

Therefore, you may want to set the `document` object's `onLoseCapture` event handler to hide any container that your script displays in concert with event capture.

Also be aware that even though mouse events may be captured to prevent mouse access to the rest of the page, keyboard events are not captured. Thus, using the event capture mechanism to simulate modal windows is not foolproof: a user can tab to any form element or link in the page and press the spacebar or Enter key to activate that element.

Event capture, as defined in the W3C DOM, operates differently from IE event capture. In the W3C DOM, you can instruct the browser to substitute event capture of any kind of event for the normal event bubbling behavior. For example, you can attach an event listener to the BODY element in such a way that it sees all click events aimed at elements contained by the BODY element before the events reach their target elements. (See Chapters 14 and 29 for more on the W3C DOM event model and how to integrate it into cross-browser applications.)

On the
CD-ROM   Example (with Listing 15-30) on the CD-ROM

Related Items: `addEventListener()`, `dispatchEvent()`, `fireEvent()`, `removeEventListener()` **methods;** `onlosecapture` **event;** Event **object** (Chapter 29).

removeAttribute("*attributeName*"[, *caseSensitivity*])

Returns: Boolean (IE); Nothing (NN).

	NN2	NN3	NN4	NN6	IE3/J1	IE3/J2	IE4	IE5	IE5.5
Compatibility				✓			✓	✓	✓

If you create an attribute with the setAttribute() method, you can eliminate that attribute from the element object via the removeAttribute() method. The required parameter is the name of the attribute. IE4+ permits you to set and remove attributes such that the attribute names are case-sensitive. The default behavior of removeAttribute() in IE (the second parameter is a Boolean value) is false. Therefore, if you supply a value of true for the case-sensitivity parameter in setAttribute(), you should set the parameter to true in removeAttribute() to ensure a proper balance between created and removed attributes.

The NN6 (and W3C) version of the removeAttribute() method has a single parameter (a case-insensitive attribute name) and returns no value. The returned value in IE is true if the removal succeeds and false if it doesn't succeed (or the attribute is one that you set in some other manner).

On the CD-ROM   Example on the CD-ROM

Related Items: attributes property; document.createAttribute(), getAttribute(), and setAttribute() methods.

removeAttributeNode(*attributeNode*)
setAttributeNode(*attributeNode*)

Returns: Attribute object.

	NN2	NN3	NN4	NN6	IE3/J1	IE3/J2	IE4	IE5	IE5.5
Compatibility				✓					

As discussed in the coverage of the getAttributeNode() method earlier in this chapter, the W3C DOM treats a name–value attribute pair as an attribute object.

As discussed in the coverage of the `getAttributeNode()` method earlier in this chapter, the W3C DOM treats a name–value attribute pair as an attribute object. An attribute object is a distinct node within a named node map — a collection of attribute objects belonging to an element. Understanding named node maps and attribute objects is more useful in an XML environment where attributes cannot only contain valuable data, but are not exposed to the document object model as properties you can access via script. Instead of accessing an object's properties, you work with the actual attributes.

If you want to insert an attribute in the formal W3C methodology, you can use `document.createAttribute()` to generate a new attribute object. Subsequent script statements assign values to the `nodeName` and `nodeValue` properties to give the attribute its traditional name–value pair. You can then insert that new attribute object into the attribute list of an object via the `setAttributeNode()` method. The sole parameter is an attribute object, and the return value is a reference to the newly inserted attribute object.

To remove an attribute node from an element using this syntax, employ the `removeAttributeNode()` method. Again, the sole parameter is an attribute object. If your script knows only the attribute's name, you can use `getAttributeNode()` to obtain a valid reference to the attribute object. The `removeAttributeNode()` method returns a reference to the removed attribute object. That object remains in the browser's memory, but it is not part of the document hierarchy. By capturing this removed attribute object in a variable, you have the flexibility to modify and assign it to another object elsewhere in the document.

Caution   A bug in NN6 prevents the `setAttributeNode()` method from returning a reference to an attribute when the attribute being set is not specified in the element's tag. The new attribute succeeds in becoming part of the element, but your script does not automatically receive a reference to it. This behavior may disrupt a design plan to create an attribute node via `document.createAttribute()`, insert the new attribute temporarily via `setAttributeNode()`, and use the reference returned by `setAttributeNode()` as the parameter to `removeAttributeNode()` later.

In practice, you may rarely, if ever, need to address attributes as nodes. Other methods — notably `getAttribute()`, `removeAttribute()`, and `setAttribute()` — do the job when your scripts have only the name (as a string) of an attribute belonging to an element.

On the CD-ROM   Example on the CD-ROM

Related Items: `attributes` property; `document.createAttribute()`, `getAttribute()`, `getAttributeNode()`, `setAttribute()` methods.

removeBehavior(*ID*)

Returns: Boolean.

	NN2	NN3	NN4	NN6	IE3/J1	IE3/J2	IE4	IE5	IE5.5
Compatibility								✓	✓

The removeBehavior() method detaches a behavior from an object. It assumes that the behavior was added to the object via the addBehavior() method. The return value of the addBehavior() method is a unique identifier for that particular behavior. This identifier is the required parameter for the removeBehavior() method. Thus, you can add two behaviors to an object and remove just one of them if so desired. If the removal succeeds, the removeBehavior() method returns true; otherwise, it returns false.

 Example on the CD-ROM

Related Item: addBehavior() method.

removeChild(*nodeObject*)

Returns: Node object reference.

	NN2	NN3	NN4	NN6	IE3/J1	IE3/J2	IE4	IE5	IE5.5
Compatibility				✓				✓	✓

The removeChild() method erases a child element from the current element. Content associated with the child element is no longer visible on the page, and the object is no longer part of the document object hierarchy.

As destructive as that sounds, the specifications for the deleted object are not lost to the ether necessarily. The removeChild() method returns a reference to the removed node. By assigning this value to a variable, you can hold onto that object specification for insertion later in the session. You are free to use this value as a parameter to such methods as appendChild(), replaceChild(), swapNode(), and insertBefore().

Remember that removeChild() is invoked from the point of view of a parent element. If you simply want to remove an element, you can do so more directly (in IE5+) with the removeNode() method.

Example on the CD-ROM

Related Items: appendChild(), replaceChild(), removeNode() methods.

removeEventListener()

See addEventListener().

removeExpression("*propertyName*")

Returns: Boolean.

	NN2	NN3	NN4	NN6	IE3/J1	IE3/J2	IE4	IE5	IE5.5
Compatibility								✓	✓

If you assign an expression to an object property (including an object's style object) via the setExpression() method, you can remove it under script control with the removeExpression() method. The sole parameter is the name of the property in string form. Property names are case-sensitive.

The method returns true if the removal succeeds; otherwise, false is returned. Be aware that removing an expression does not alter the value that is currently assigned to the property. In other words, you can use setExpression() to set a property's value and then remove the expression so that no further changes are made when the document recalculates expressions. If this is your goal, however, you are probably better served by simply setting the property directly via scripting.

Example on the CD-ROM

Related Items: document.recalc(), getExpression(), setExpression() methods.

removeNode(*removeChildrenFlag*)

Returns: Node object reference.

	NN2	NN3	NN4	NN6	IE3/J1	IE3/J2	IE4	IE5	IE5.5
Compatibility								✓	✓

You can use the removeNode() method to delete the current node from an element hierarchy in IE5+. The sole parameter is a Boolean value that directs the method to remove only itself (without its child nodes) or the node and all of its children (value of true). Exercise care with this method when you use a default parameter value of false: If the node has child nodes (for example, you attempt to remove a TABLE but not its child nodes), IE5 can crash on you. However, you can safely remove the node and all of its children.

The method returns a reference to the node object removed. This removed object is no longer accessible to the document object model. But the returned value contains all properties of the object as it existed before you removed it (including properties such as outerHTML and explicitly set style sheet rules). Thus, you can use this value as a parameter to insert the node elsewhere in the document.

While the W3C and Navigator 6 DOM do not have a removeNode() method, the cross-browser method whose behavior most closely resembles removeNode() is the removeChild() method. The scope of the removeChild() method is one level up the object hierarchy from the object you use for the removeNode() method.

 On the CD-ROM   Example on the CD-ROM

Related Items: Node object; appendChild(), cloneChild(), removeChild(), replaceChild(), replaceNode() methods.

replaceAdjacentText("*location*", "*text*")

Returns: String.

	NN2	NN3	NN4	NN6	IE3/J1	IE3/J2	IE4	IE5	IE5.5
Compatibility								✓	✓

The replaceAdjacentText() method (not implemented in IE5/Mac) enables you to replace one chunk of document text with another in a specific position relative to the current object. Be aware that this method works only for plain text and not HTML tags. The returned value is the string of the text that you replace.

Both parameters are required. The first must be one of four possible case-insensitive locations for the insertion, shown in the following table:

Location	Description
beforeBegin	Before the current element's start tag
afterBegin	After the start tag, but before any nested content
beforeEnd	Before the end tag, but after all other nested content
afterEnd	After the end tag

This method is best used with inline (rather than block) elements when specifying the beforeBegin and afterEnd parameters. For example, if you attempt to use replaceAdjacentText() with beforeBegin on the second of two consecutive paragraph elements, the replacement text is inserted into the end of the first paragraph. You can think of the replaceAdjacentText() method in terms of text fragment nodes (even though IE5 does not fully support this W3C DOM feature). The method replaces the text fragment node (given any one of the four position parameters) with new text. Replacing the text of a simple element with either the afterBegin or beforeEnd locations is the same as assigning that text to the object's innerText property.

Example on the CD-ROM

Related Items: innerText, outerText properties; getAdjacentText(), insertAdjacentHTML(), insertAdjacentText() methods.

replaceChild(*newNodeObject, oldNodeObject*)

Returns: Node object reference.

	NN2	NN3	NN4	NN6	IE3/J1	IE3/J2	IE4	IE5	IE5.5
Compatibility				✓				✓	✓

The replaceChild() method enables you to swap an existing child node object for a new node object. Parameters for the replaceChild() method are node object references, and they must be in the order of the new object followed by the object you want to replace. The old object must be an immediate child node of the parent used to invoke the method, and the new object must also be a "legal" child element within the document containment hierarchy.

The method returns a reference to the child object that you replaced with the new object. This reference can be used as a parameter to any of the node-oriented insertion or replacement methods.

Remember that replaceChild() is invoked from the point of view of a parent element. If you simply want to change an element, you can do so more directly with the swapNode() method (or, in IE5, the replaceNode() method).

Example on the CD-ROM

Related Items: appendChild(), removeChild(), replaceNode(), swapNode() methods.

replaceNode(*newNodeObject*)

Returns: Node object reference.

	NN2	NN3	NN4	NN6	IE3/J1	IE3/J2	IE4	IE5	IE5.5
Compatibility								✓	✓

The replaceNode() method (not implemented in IE5/Mac) is related to the replaceChild() method, but you invoke this method on the actual node you want to replace (instead of the object's parent). The sole parameter is a reference to a valid node object, which you can generate via the document.createElement() method or copy from an existing node. The value returned from the method is a reference to the object that you replace. Thus, you can preserve a copy of the replaced node by storing the results in a variable for use later.

If the node you replace contains other nodes, the replaceNode() method removes all contained nodes of the original from the document. Therefore, if you want to change a wrapper node but want to maintain the original children, your script must capture the children and put them back into the new node as shown in the following example.

Example (with Listing 15-31) on the CD-ROM

Related Items: removeChild(), removeNode(), replaceChild(), swapNode() methods.

scrollIntoView(*topAlignFlag*)

Returns: Nothing.

	NN2	NN3	NN4	NN6	IE3/J1	IE3/J2	IE4	IE5	IE5.5
Compatibility							✓	✓	✓

The scrollIntoView() method scrolls the page (vertically and/or horizontally as needed) such that the current object is visible within the window or frame that contains it. A single parameter, a Boolean value, controls the location of the element within the viewable space. A value of true (the default) causes the element to be displayed so that its top is aligned with the top of the window or frame (provided the document beneath it is long enough to allow this amount of scrolling). But a value of false causes the bottom of the element to align with the bottom of the viewable area. In most cases, you want the former so that the beginning of a page section is at the top of the viewable area. But if you don't want a user to see content below a certain element when you jump to the new view, then use the false parameter.

For form elements, you must use the typical form element reference (document. *formName*.*elementName*.scrollIntoView()) unless you also specify an ID attribute for the element (document.all.*elementID*.scrollIntoView()).

Example on the CD-ROM

Related Items: window.scroll(), window.scrollBy(), window.scrollTo() methods.

setActive()

Returns: Nothing.

	NN2	NN3	NN4	NN6	IE3/J1	IE3/J2	IE4	IE5	IE5.5
Compatibility									✓

The setActive() method lets a script designate an element object as the active element. However, unlike the focus() method, the window does not scroll the active element into view. Any onFocus event handler defined for the element fires when setActive() is invoked, without the browser giving the element focus.

Example on the CD-ROM

Related Item: focus() method.

setAttribute("*attributeName*", *value*[, *caseSensitivity*])

Returns: Nothing.

	NN2	NN3	NN4	NN6	IE3/J1	IE3/J2	IE4	IE5	IE5.5
Compatibility				✓			✓	✓	✓

The setAttribute() method assigns a new value to an existing attribute of the current object or inserts an entirely new attribute name–value pair among the attributes of the current object. This method represents an alternative syntax to setting a property of the object directly.

Note

The W3C DOM Level 2 standard recommends getAttribute() and setAttribute() for reading and writing element object attribute values, rather than reading and writing those values by way of their corresponding properties. While using these methods is certainly advisable for XML elements, the same DOM standard sends conflicting signals by defining all kinds of properties for HTML element objects. Browsers, of course, will support access via properties well into the future, so don't feel obligated to change your ways.

The first two parameters of setAttribute() are required. The first is the name of the attribute. The default behavior of this method respects the case of the attribute name. Therefore, if you use setAttribute() to adjust the value of an existing attribute in default mode, the first parameter must match the case of the attribute as known by the object model for the current document. Remember that all names of all attributes assigned as inline source code attributes are automatically converted to lowercase letters.

A value you assign to the attribute is the second parameter. For cross-browser compatibility, the value should be either a string or Boolean data type.

IE provides an optional third parameter to control the case-sensitivity issue for the attribute name. The default value (`true`) has a different impact on your object depending on whether you use `setAttribute()` to assign a new attribute or reassign an existing one. In the former case, the third parameter as `true` means that the attribute name assigned to the object observes the case of the first parameter. In the latter case, the third parameter as `true` means that the attribute isn't reassigned unless the first parameter matches the case of the attribute currently associated with the object. Instead, a new attribute with a different case sequence is created.

Attempting to manage the case-sensitivity of newly created attributes is fraught with peril, especially if you try to reuse names but with different case sequences. I strongly recommend using default case-sensitivity controls for `setAttribute()` and `getAttribute()`.

IE4+ imposes some limitations on the action resulting from the `setAttribute()` method. Any attribute you add via `setAttribute()` does not become part of the `attributes` collection associated with the element. While you can extract the value of such a newly added attribute via `getAttribute()`, you cannot access the new attribute from the `attributes` collection. Thus, after creating a new attribute as follows:

```
document.all.myTable.setAttribute("currYear", (new Date()).getFullYear())
```

you can access that attribute value through either of the following two statements:

```
var tableYear = document.all.myTable.getAttribute("curryear")
var tableYear = document.all.myTable.currYear
```

However, you cannot access the attribute value with the following statement:

```
var tableYear = document.all.myTable.attributes["currYear"]
```

See also the W3C DOM facilities for treating attributes as node objects in the discussions of the `getAttributeNode()` and `removeAttributeNode()` methods earlier in this chapter.

On the CD-ROM   Example on the CD-ROM

Related Items: `attributes` property; `document.createAttribute()`, `getAttribute()`, `getAttributeNode()`, `removeAttribute()`, `removeAttributeNode()`, `setAttributeNode()` methods.

setAttributeNode()

See `removeAttributeNode()`.

setCapture(*containerBoolean*)

See releaseCapture().

setExpression("*propertyName*", "*expression*","*language*")

Returns: Nothing.

	NN2	NN3	NN4	NN6	IE3/J1	IE3/J2	IE4	IE5	IE5.5
Compatibility								✓	✓

Use the setExpression() method (not implemented in IE5/Mac) to assign the result of an executable expression to the value of an element object property. This method can assign values to both HTML element objects and style objects that belong to them.

The setExpression() method is a scripted way of assigning expressions to attributes. But you can also assign expressions directly to style sheet definitions in the HTML tag of an element using the expression() syntax, as in the following example:

```
<P STYLE="width:expression(document.body.style.width * 0.75)">
```

The setExpression() method requires three parameters. The first parameter is the name of the property (in string form) to which you assign the expression. Property names are case-sensitive. The second parameter is a string form of the expression to be evaluated to supply a value for the property. Expressions can refer to global variables or properties of other objects in the same document (provided the property is anything other than an array). An expression may also contain math operators.

Pay close attention to the data type of the evaluated value of the expression. The value must be a valid data type for the property. For example, the URL of the body background image must be a string. But for numeric values, you can generally use number and string types interchangeably because the values are converted to the proper type for the property. Even for expressions that evaluate to numbers, encase the expression inside quotes. It may not be necessary in all cases, but if you get into the habit of using quotes, you'll have fewer problems for strings or complex expressions that require them.

You are not limited to using JavaScript as the language for the expression because you also specify the scripting language of the expression in the third parameter. Acceptable parameter values for the language are

```
JScript
VBScript
JavaScript
```

For all intents and purposes, JScript and JavaScript are the same. Both languages are ECMA-262 compatible.

One reason to use `setExpression()` for dynamic properties is to let the property always respond to the current conditions on the page. For example, if you set a property that is dependent on the current width of the body, then you want a recalculation that is applied to the property if the user resizes the window. The browser automatically responds to many events and updates any dynamic properties. In essence, the browser recalculates the expressions and applies the new values to the property. Keyboard events, in particular, trigger this kind of automatic recalculation for you. But if your scripts perform actions on their own (in other words, not triggered by events), then your scripts need to force the recalculation of the expressions. The `document.recalc()` method takes care of this, but you must invoke it to force the recalculation of dynamic properties in these cases.

Example (with Figure 15-1 and Listing 15-32) on the CD-ROM

Related Items: `document.recalc()`, `removeExpression()`, `setExpression()` methods.

swapNode(*otherNodeObject*)

Returns: Node object reference.

	NN2	NN3	NN4	NN6	IE3/J1	IE3/J2	IE4	IE5	IE5.5
Compatibility								✓	✓

The `swapNode()` method (not implemented in IE5/Mac) exchanges the positions of two nodes within an element hierarchy. Contents of both nodes are preserved in their entirety during the exchange. The single parameter must be a valid node object (perhaps created with `document.createElement()` or copied from an existing node). A return value is a reference to the object whose `swapNode()` method was invoked.

Example on the CD-ROM

Related Items: `removeChild()`, `removeNode()`, `replaceChild()`, `replaceNode()` methods.

tags("*tagName*")

Returns: Array of element objects.

	NN2	NN3	NN4	NN6	IE3/J1	IE3/J2	IE4	IE5	IE5.5
Compatibility							✓	✓	✓

The `tags()` method does not belong to every element, but it is a method of every collection of objects (such as `all`, `forms`, and `elements`). The method is best thought of as a kind of filter for the elements that belong to the current collection. For example, to get an array of all P elements inside a document, use this expression:

```
document.all.tags("P")
```

You must pass a parameter string consisting of the tag name you wish to extract from the collection. The tag name is case-insensitive.

The return value is an array of references to the objects within the current collection whose tags match the parameter. If there are no matches, the returned array has a length of zero. If you need cross-browser compatibility, use the `getElementsByTagName()` method described earlier in this chapter.

Example on the CD-ROM

Related Item: `getElementsByTagName()` method.

urns("*behaviorURN*")

Returns: Array of element objects.

	NN2	NN3	NN4	NN6	IE3/J1	IE3/J2	IE4	IE5	IE5.5
Compatibility								✓	✓

The urns() method does not belong to every element, but it is a method of every collection of objects. You must pass a parameter string consisting of the URN (Uniform Resource Name) of a behavior resource (most typically .htc for IE5) assigned to one or more elements of the collection. The parameter does not include the extension of the filename. If there is no matching behavior URN for the specified parameter, the urns() method returns an array of zero length. This method is related to the behaviorUrns property, which contains an array of behavior URNs assigned to a single element object.

Note   Neither the behaviorUrns property nor the urns() method appear to be working as described by Microsoft. Perhaps the potential exposure of URNs by script was deemed a privacy risk. As proven thus far with IE5 for Win32, the urns() method always returns an array of zero length.

On the CD-ROM   Example on the CD-ROM

Related Item: behaviorUrns property.

Event handlers
onActivate
onBeforeDeactivate
onDeactivate

	NN2	NN3	NN4	NN6	IE3/J1	IE3/J2	IE4	IE5	IE5.5
Compatibility									✓

The onActivate and onDeactivate event handlers are new with IE5.5. But in some circumstances, they are very similar to the onFocus and onBlur event handlers, respectively. If an element receives focus, the onActivate event fires for that element just before the onFocus event fires; conversely, just prior to the element losing focus, events fire in the sequence: onBeforeDeactivate, onDeactivate, onBlur. Only elements that, by their nature, can accept focus (for example, links and form input controls) or that have a TABINDEX attribute set can become the active element (and therefore fire these events).

IE5.5 maintains the original onFocus and onBlur event handlers. But because the behaviors are so close to those of the onActivate and onDeactivate events, I don't recommend mixing the old and new event handler names in your coding style. If you script exclusively for IE5.5+, then you can use the new terminology throughout.

Example on the CD-ROM

Related Items: onBlur, onFocus event handlers.

onBeforeCopy

	NN2	NN3	NN4	NN6	IE3/J1	IE3/J2	IE4	IE5	IE5.5
Compatibility								✓	✓

The onBeforeCopy event handler (not implemented in IE5/Mac) fires before the actual copy action takes place whenever the user initiates a content copy action via the Edit menu (including the Ctrl+C keyboard shortcut) or the right-click context menu. If the user accesses the Copy command via the Edit or context menu, the onBeforeCopy event fires before either menu displays. In practice, the event may fire twice even though you expect it only once. Just because the onBeforeCopy event fires, it does not guarantee that a user will complete the copy operation (for example, the context menu may close before the user makes a selection).

Unlike paste-related events, the onBeforeCopy event handler does not work with form input elements. Just about any other HTML element is fair game, however.

Example (with Listing 15-33) on the CD-ROM

Related Items: onBeforeCut, onCopy event handlers.

onBeforeCut

	NN2	NN3	NN4	NN6	IE3/J1	IE3/J2	IE4	IE5	IE5.5
Compatibility								✓	✓

The onBeforeCut event handler fires before the actual cut action takes place whenever the user initiates a content cut via the Edit menu (including the Ctrl+X keyboard shortcut) or the right-click context menu. If the user accesses the Cut command via the Edit or context menu, the onBeforeCut event fires before either menu displays. In practice, the event may fire twice even though you expect it only once. Just because the onBeforeCut event fires, it does not guarantee that a user will complete the cut operation (for example, the context menu may close before the user makes a selection). If you add the onBeforeCut event handler to an HTML element, the context menu usually disables the Cut menu item. But assigning a JavaScript call to this event handler brings the Cut menu item to life.

Example on the CD-ROM

Related Items: onBeforeCopy, onCut event handlers.

onBeforeDeactivate

See: onActivate event handler.

onBeforeEditFocus

	NN2	NN3	NN4	NN6	IE3/J1	IE3/J2	IE4	IE5	IE5.5
Compatibility								✓	✓

The onBeforeEditFocus event handler (not implemented in IE5/Mac) is triggered whenever you edit an element on a page in an environment such as Microsoft's DHTML Editing ActiveX control or with the editable page content feature of IE5.5. This discussion focuses on the latter scenario because it is entirely within the scope of client-side JavaScript. The onBeforeEditFocus event fires just before the element receives its focus. (There may be no onscreen feedback that editing is turned on unless you script it yourself.) The event fires each time a user clicks the element, even if the element just received edit focus elsewhere in the same element.

Example on the CD-ROM

Related Items: document.designMode, contentEditable, isContentEditable properties.

onBeforePaste

	NN2	NN3	NN4	NN6	IE3/J1	IE3/J2	IE4	IE5	IE5.5
Compatibility								✓	✓

Like onBeforeCopy and onBeforeCut, the onBeforePaste event (not implemented in IE5/Mac) occurs just prior to the display of either the context or menu bar Edit menu when the current object is selected (or has a selection within it). The primary value of this event comes when you use scripts to control the copy and paste process of a complex object. Such an object may have multiple kinds of data associated with it, but your script captures only one of the data types. Or, you may want to put some related data about the copied item (for example, the id property of the element) into the clipboard. By using the onBeforePaste event handler to set the event.returnValue property to false, you guarantee that the pasted item is enabled in the context or Edit menu (provided the clipboard is holding some content). A handler invoked by onPaste should then apply the specific data subset from the clipboard to the currently selected item.

Example on the CD-ROM

Related Items: onCopy, onCut, onPaste event handlers.

onBlur

	NN2	NN3	NN4	NN6	IE3/J1	IE3/J2	IE4	IE5	IE5.5
Compatibility	✓	✓	✓	✓	✓	✓	✓	✓	✓

The onBlur event fires when an element that has focus is about to lose focus because some other element is about to receive focus. For example, a text input element fires the onBlur event when a user tabs from that element to the next one inside a form. The onBlur event of the first element fires before the onFocus event of the next element.

The availability of the onBlur event has expanded with succeeding generations of script-capable browsers. In the earlier versions, blur and focus were largely confined to text-oriented input elements (including the SELECT element). These are safe to use with all scriptable browser versions. The window object received the onBlur event handler starting with NN3 and IE4. IE4 also extended the event handler to more form elements, predominantly on the Windows operating system because that OS has a user interface clue (the dotted rectangle) when items such as buttons and links receive focus (so that you may act upon them by pressing the keyboard's spacebar). For IE5, the onBlur event handler is available to virtually every HTML element. For most of those elements, however, blur and focus are not possible unless you assign a value to the TABINDEX attribute of the element's tag. For example, if you assign TABINDEX=1 inside a <P> tag, the user can bring focus to that paragraph (highlighted with the dotted rectangle in Windows) by clicking the paragraph or pressing the Tab key until that item receives focus in sequence.

If you plan to use the onBlur event handler on window or text-oriented input elements, be aware that there might be some unexpected and undesirable consequences of scripting for the event. For example, in IE, a window object that has focus loses focus (and triggers the onBlur event) if the user brings focus to any element on the page (or even clicks a blank area on the page). Similarly, the interaction between onBlur, onFocus, and the alert() dialog box can be problematic with text input elements. This is why I generally recommend using the onChange event handler to trigger form validation routines. If you should employ both the onBlur and onChange event handler for the same element, the onChange event fires before onBlur. For more details about using this event handler for data validation, see Chapter 43.

IE5.5 adds the onDeactivate event handler, which fires immediately before the onBlur event handler. Both the onBlur and onDeactivate events can be blocked if the onBeforeDeactivate event handler function sets event.returnValue to false.

Example (with Listing 15-34) on the CD-ROM

Related Items: blur(), focus() methods; onDeactivate, onBeforeDeactivate, onFocus, onActivate event handlers.

onClick

	NN2	NN3	NN4	NN6	IE3/J1	IE3/J2	IE4	IE5	IE5.5
Compatibility	✓	✓	✓	✓	✓	✓	✓	✓	✓

The onClick event fires when a user presses down (with the primary mouse button) and releases the button with the pointer atop the element (both the down and up strokes must be within the rectangle of the same element). The event also fires with non-mouse click equivalents in operating systems such as Windows 95 and later. For example, you can use the keyboard to give focus to a clickable object and then press the spacebar or Enter key to perform the same action as clicking the element. In IE, if the element object supports the click() method, the onClick event fires with the invocation of that method (notice that this does not apply to Navigator).

The availability of the onClick event has expanded with succeeding generations of script-capable browsers. In the earlier versions, the event was limited primarily to button style input elements (including checkbox and radio input elements) and links (A elements with HREF attributes assigned to them). You can safely use this event handler for elements that date back to the earliest scriptable browsers.

In Navigator 4, the AREA element gained the onClick event (and window, document, and layer objects could capture onClick events, as described in Chapter 29). In IE4+, virtually every element that you can see on a page can have an onClick event handler defined for it and thereby respond to user clicks.

Beginning with version 4 browsers, scripters could access more mouse-related events. It is important to know the sequence of these incremental events as a user clicks or double-clicks an element. The other related events are onMouseDown, onMouseUp, and onDoubleClick. The onMouseDown event fires when the user makes contact with the mouse switch on the downstroke of a click action. Next comes the onMouseUp event (when the contact breaks). Only then does the onClick event fire—provided that the onMouseDown and onMouseUp events have fired in the same object. See the discussions on the onMouseDown and onMouseUp events later in this chapter for examples of their usage.

Interaction with the onDblClick event is simple: the onClick event fires first (after the first click), followed by the onDblClick event (after the second click). See the discussion of the onDblClick event handler later in this chapter for more about the interaction of these two event handlers.

When used with objects that have intrinsic actions when users click them (namely links and areas), the onClick event handler can perform all of the action—including navigating to the destination normally assigned to the HREF attribute of the element. For example, to be compatible with all scriptable browsers, you can make an image clickable if you surround its tag with an <A> link tag. This lets the onClick event of that tag substitute for the missing onClick event handler of earlier <IMG> tags. If you assign an onClick event handler without special protection, the event handler will execute and the intrinsic action of the element will be carried out. Therefore, you need to block the intrinsic action. To accomplish this, the event handler must evaluate to the statement return false. You can do this in two ways. The first is to append a return false statement to the script statement assigned to the event handler:

```
<A HREF="#" onClick="yourFunction(); return false"><IMG...></A>
```

As an alternative, you can let the function invoked by the event handler supply the false part of the return false statement, as shown in the following sequence:

```
function yourFunction() {
    [statements that do something here]
    return false
}
...
<A HREF="#" onClick="return yourFunction()"><IMG...></A>
```

Either methdology is acceptable. A third option is to not use the onClick event handler at all, but assign a javascript: pseudo-URL to the HREF attribute (see the link object in Chapter 21).

The event model in IE5+ provides one more way to prevent the intrinsic action of an object from firing when a user clicks it. If the onClick event handler function sets the returnValue property of the event object to false, the intrinsic action is cancelled. Simply include the following statement in the function invoked by the event handler:

```
event.returnValue = false
```

The event model of the W3C DOM has a different approach to cancelling the default action. In the event handler function for an event, invoke the eventObj.cancelDefault() method.

A common mistake made by scripting beginners is to use a submit type input button as a button intended to perform some script action rather than submitting a form. The typical scenario is an INPUT element of type submit assigned an onClick event handler to perform some local action. The submit input button has an intrinsic behavior, just like links and areas. While you can block the intrinsic behavior, as just described, you should use an INPUT element of type button.

If you are experiencing difficulty with an implementation of the onClick event handler (such as trying to find out which mouse button was used for the click), it may be that the operating system or default browser behavior is getting in the way of your scripting. But you can usually get what you need via the onMouseDown event handler. (The onMouseUp event may not fire when you use the secondary mouse button to click an object.) Use the onClick event handler whenever possible to capture user clicks because this event behaves most like users are accustomed to in their daily computing work. But fall back on onMouseDown in an emergency.

Example (with Listing 15-35) on the CD-ROM

Related Items: click() method; onContextMenu, onDblClick, onMouseDown, onMouseUp event handlers.

onContextMenu

	NN2	NN3	NN4	NN6	IE3/J1	IE3/J2	IE4	IE5	IE5.5
Compatibility								✓	✓

The onContextMenu event (not implemented in IE5/Mac) fires when the user clicks an object with the secondary (usually the right-hand) mouse button. The only click-related events that fire with the secondary button are onMouseDown and onContextMenu.

To block the intrinsic application menu display of the onContextMenu event, use any of the three event cancellation methodologies available in IE5+ (as just described in the onClick event handler description: two variations of evaluating the event handler to return false; assigning false to the event.returnValue property). It is not uncommon to wish to block the context menu from appearing so that users are somewhat inhibited from downloading copies of images or viewing the source code of a frame. Be aware, however, that if a user turns Active Scripting off in IE5+, the event handler cannot prevent the context menu from appearing.

Another possibility for this event is to trigger the display of a custom context menu constructed with other DHTML facilities. In this case, you must also disable the intrinsic context menu so that both menus do not display at the same time.

On the CD-ROM

Example on the CD-ROM

Related Items: releaseCapture(), setCapture() methods.

onControlSelect

	NN2	NN3	NN4	NN6	IE3/J1	IE3/J2	IE4	IE5	IE5.5
Compatibility									✓

The onControlSelect event should fire just before a user makes a selection on what Microsoft calls a *control selection*. Microsoft is less than clear in explaining what a control selection is, but it appears to have something to do with a user edit mode. I have not been able to have this event fire naturally in IE5.5. If I receive further details, they will appear at the *JavaScript(tm) Bible, 4th Edition* Support Center (http://www.dannyg.com).

Related Items: onResizeEnd, onResizeStart event handlers.

onCopy
onCut

	NN2	NN3	NN4	NN6	IE3/J1	IE3/J2	IE4	IE5	IE5.5
Compatibility								✓	✓

The onCopy and onCut events (not implemented in IE5/Mac) fire immediately after the user or script initiates a copy or cut edit action on the current object. Each event is preceded by its associated "before" event, which fires before any Edit or context menu appears (or before the copy or cut action, if initiated by keyboard shortcut).

Use these event handlers to provide edit functionality to elements that don't normally allow copying or cutting. In such circumstances, you need to enable the Copy or Cut menu items in the context or Edit menu by setting the event.returnValue for the onBeforeCopy or onBeforeCut event handlers to false. Then your onCopy or onCut event handlers must manually stuff a value into the clipboard by way of the setData() method of the clipboardData object. If you use the setData() method in your onCopy or onCut event handler, you must also set the event.returnValue property to false in the handler function to avoid the default copy or cut action from wiping out your clipboard contents.

Because you are in charge of what data is stored in the clipboard, you are not limited to a direct copy of the data. For example, you might wish to store the value of the src property of an image object so that the user can paste it elsewhere on the page.

In the case of the onCut event handler, your script is also responsible for cutting the element or selected content from the page. To eliminate all of the content of an element, you can set the element's innerHTML or innerText property to an empty string. For a selection, use the selection.createRange() method to generate a TextRange object whose contents you can manipulate through the TextRange object's methods.

Example (with Listing 15-36) on the CD-ROM

Related Items: onBeforeCopy, onBeforeCut, onBeforePaste, and onPaste event handlers.

onDblClick

	NN2	NN3	NN4	NN6	IE3/J1	IE3/J2	IE4	IE5	IE5.5
Compatibility			✓	✓			✓	✓	✓

The onDblClick event fires after the second click of a double-click sequence. The timing between clicks depends on the client's mouse control panel settings. The onClick event also fires, but only after the first of the two clicks.

NN4 implements the onDblClick event handler only for link objects (but not at all on the Macintosh version of NN4). IE4 introduced the event to virtually every HTML element.

In general, it is rarely a good design to have an element perform one task when the mouse is single-clicked and a different task if double-clicked. With the event sequence employed in modern browsers, this isn't practical anyway (the onClick event always fires, even when the user double-clicks). But it is not uncommon to have the mouse down action perform some helper action. You see this in most icon-based file systems: if you click a file icon, it is highlighted at mouse down to select the item; you can double-click the item to launch it. In either case, one event's action does not impede the other nor confuse the user.

Example on the CD-ROM

Related Items: onClick, onMouseDown, onMouseUp event handlers.

onDrag

	NN2	NN3	NN4	NN6	IE3/J1	IE3/J2	IE4	IE5	IE5.5
Compatibility								✓	✓

The onDrag event fires after the onDragStart event and continues firing repeatedly while the user drags a selection or object on the screen. Unlike the onMouseMove event, which fires only as the cursor moves on the screen, the onDrag event continues to fire even when the cursor is stationary. In the IE5+ environment, users can drag objects to other browser windows or other applications. The event fires while the dragging extends beyond the browser window.

Because the event fires regardless of what is underneath the dragged object, you can use it in a game or training environment in which the user has only a fixed amount of time to complete a dragging operation (for example, matching similar pairs of objects). If future versions of the browser accommodate downloadable cursors, the onDrag event could cycle the cursor through a series of cursor versions to resemble an animated cursor.

Understanding the sequence of drag-related events during a user drag operation can be helpful if your scripts need to micromanage the actions (usually not necessary for basic drag-and-drop operations). Consider the drag-and-drop operation shown in Figure 15-2.

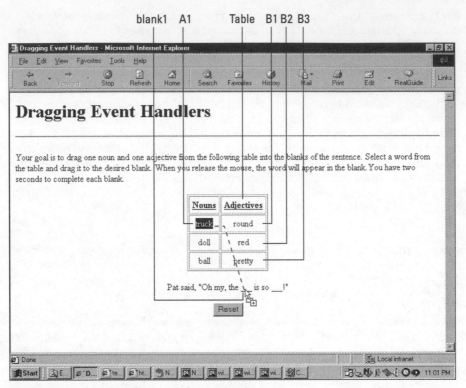

Figure 15-2: A typical drag-and-drop operation

It helps to imagine that the cells of the table with draggable content are named like spreadsheet cells: "truck" is cell A1; "round" is B1; "doll" is A2; and so on. During the drag operation, many objects are the targets of a variety of drag-related events. Table 15-10 lists the event sequence and the event targets.

Table 15-10   Events and Their Targets During a Typical Drag-and-Drop Operation

Event	Target	Discussion
onDragStart	cell A1	The very first event that fires during a drag-and-drop operation.
onDrag	cell A1	Fires continually on this target throughout the entire operation. Other events get interspersed, however.
onDragEnter	cell A1	Even though the cursor hasn't moved from cell A1 yet, the onDragEnter event fires upon first movement within the source element.

Event	Target	Discussion
onDragOver	cell A1	Fires continually on whatever element the cursor rests on at that instant. If the user simply holds the mouse button down and does not move the cursor during a drag, the onDrag and onDragOver events fire continually, alternating between the two.
(repetition)	cell A1	onDrag and onDragOver events fire alternately while the cursor remains atop cell A1.
onDragEnter	TABLE	The TABLE element, represented by the border and/or cell padding, receives the onDragEnter event when the cursor touches its space.
onDragLeave	cell A1	Notice that the onDragLeave event fires after the onDragEnter event fires on another element.
onDrag	cell A1	Still firing away.
onDragOver	TABLE	The source element for this event shifts to the TABLE because that's what the cursor is "over" at this instant. If the cursor doesn't move from this spot, the onDrag (cell A1) and onDragOver (TABLE) events continue to fire in turn.
onDragEnter	cell B1	The drag is progressing from the TABLE border space to cell B1.
onDragLeave	TABLE	
onDrag	cell A1	The onDrag event continues to fire on the cell A1 object.
onDragOver	cell B1	The cursor is atop cell B1 now, so the onDragOver event fires for that object. Fires multiple times (depending on the speed of the computer and the user's drag action), alternating with the previous onDrag event.

[More of the same as the cursor progresses from cell B1 through the TABLE border again to cell B2, the TABLE again, cell B3, and the outermost edge of the TABLE.]

Event	Target	Discussion
onDragEnter	BODY	Dragging is free of the TABLE and is floating free on the bare BODY element.
onDragLeave	TABLE	Yes, you just left the TABLE.
onDrag	cell A1	Still alive and receiving this event.
onDragOver	BODY	That's where the cursor is now. Fires multiple times (depending on the speed of the computer and the user's drag action), alternating with the previous onDrag event.
onDragEnter	blank1	The cursor reaches the SPAN element whose ID is blank1, where the empty underline is.
onDragLeave	BODY	Just left the BODY for the blank.
onDrag	cell A1	Still kicking.

Table 15-10 *(continued)*

Event	Target	Discussion
onDragOver	blank1	That's where the cursor is now. Fires multiple times (depending on the speed of the computer and the user's drag action), alternating with the previous onDrag event.
onDrop	blank1	The SPAN element gets the notification of a recent drop.
onDragEnd	cell A1	The original source element gets the final word that dragging is complete. This event fires even if the drag does not succeed because the drag does not end on a drop target.

In practice, some of the events shown in Table 15-10 may not fire. Much has to do with how many event handlers you trap that need to execute scripts along the way. The other major factor is the physical speed at which the user performs the drag-and-drop operation (which interacts with the CPU processing speed). The kinds of events that are most likely to be skipped are the onDragEnter and onDragLeave events, and perhaps some onDragOver events if the user flies over an object before its onDragOver event has a chance to fire.

Despite this uncertainty about drag-related event reliability, you can count on several important ones to fire all the time. The onDragStart, onDrop (if over a drop target), and onDragEnd events — as well some interstitial onDrag events — will definitely fire in the course of dragging on the screen. All but onDrop direct their events to the source element, while onDrop fires on the target.

On the CD-ROM   Example (with Listing 15-37) on the CD-ROM

Related Items: event.dataTransfer object; onDragEnd, onDragEnter, onDragLeave, onDragOver, onDragStart, onDrop event handlers.

onDragEnter
onDragLeave

	NN2	NN3	NN4	NN6	IE3/J1	IE3/J2	IE4	IE5	IE5.5
Compatibility								✓	✓

These events (not implemented in IE5/Mac) fire during a drag operation. When the cursor enters the rectangular space of an element on the page, the onDragEnter event fires on that element. Immediately thereafter, the onDragLeave event fires on the element from which the cursor came. While this may seem to occur out of sequence from the physical action, the events always fire in this order. Depending on the speed of the client computer's CPU and the speed of the user's dragging action, one or the other of these events may not fire—especially if the physical action outstrips the computer's capability to fire the events in time. See the discussion of the onDrag event handler earlier in this chapter for more details on the sequence of drag-related events.

Example (with Listing 15-38) on the CD-ROM

Related Items: onDrag, onDragEnd, onDragOver, onDragStart, onDrop event handlers.

onDragOver

	NN2	NN3	NN4	NN6	IE3/J1	IE3/J2	IE4	IE5	IE5.5
Compatibility								✓	✓

The onDragOver event (not implemented in IE5/Mac) fires continually while a dragged cursor is atop an element. In the course of dragging from one point on the page to another, the onDragOver event target changes with the element beneath the cursor. If no other drag-related events are firing (the mouse button is still down in the drag operation, but the cursor is not moving), the onDrag and onDragOver events fire continually, alternating between the two.

You should have the onDragOver event handler of a drop target element set the event.returnValue property to false. See the discussion of the onDrag event handler earlier in this chapter for more details on the sequence of drag-related events.

Example on the CD-ROM

Related Items: event.dataTransfer object; onDrag, onDragEnd, onDragEnter, onDragLeave, onDragStart, onDrop event handlers.

onDragStart

	NN2	NN3	NN4	NN6	IE3/J1	IE3/J2	IE4	IE5	IE5.5
Compatibility							✓	✓	✓

The onDragStart event handler is the first event to fire in the long sequence of events that occur in a typical drag-and-drop operation by the user. This event handler is associated with the element that is the source element of the drag operation. Typically, the onDragStart event handler sets the dataTransfer.effectAllowed property in IE5 for Windows, packages the data being passed along with the drag (via the dataTransfer.setData() method), and overrides default behavior by setting the event.returnValue property to false. See the discussion of the onDrag event handler earlier in this chapter for more details on the sequence of drag-related events.

Example on the CD-ROM

Related Items: event.dataTransfer object; onDrag, onDragEnd, onDragEnter, onDragLeave, onDragOver, onDrop event handlers.

onDrop

	NN2	NN3	NN4	NN6	IE3/J1	IE3/J2	IE4	IE5	IE5.5
Compatibility								✓	✓

The onDrop event (not implemented in IE5/Mac) fires on the drop target element as soon as the user releases the mouse button at the end of a drag-and-drop operation. Microsoft recommends that you denote a drop target by applying the onDragEnter, onDragOver, and onDrop event handlers to the target element. In each of those event handlers, you should set the dataTransfer.dropEffect to the transfer effect you wish to portray in the drag-and-drop operation (signified by a different cursor for each type). These settings should match the dataTransfer.effectAllowed property that is usually set in the onDragStart event handler. Each of the three drop-related handlers should also override the default event behavior by setting the event.returnValue property to false. See the discussion of the onDrag event handler earlier in this chapter for more details on the sequence of drag-related events.

Example on the CD-ROM

Related Items: event.dataTransfer object; onDrag, onDragEnd, onDragEnter, onDragLeave, onDragOver, onDragStart event handlers.

onFilterChange

	NN2	NN3	NN4	NN6	IE3/J1	IE3/J2	IE4	IE5	IE5.5
Compatibility							✓	✓	✓

The onFilterChange event (not implemented in IE5/Mac) fires whenever an object's visual filter switches to a new state or a transition completes (a transition may be extended over time). Only objects that accommodate filters and transitions in IE (primarily block elements and form controls) receive the event.

A common usage of the onFilterChange event is to trigger the next transition within a sequence of transition activities. This may include an infinite loop transition, for which the object receiving the event toggles between two transition states. If you don't want to get into a loop of that kind, place the different sets of content into their own positionable elements and use the onFilterChange event handler in one to trigger the transition in the other.

Example (with Listing 15-39) on the CD-ROM

Related Item: filter object.

onFocus

	NN2	NN3	NN4	NN6	IE3/J1	IE3/J2	IE4	IE5	IE5.5
Compatibility	✓	✓	✓	✓	✓	✓	✓	✓	✓

The onFocus event fires when an element receives focus, usually following some other object losing focus. (The element losing focus receives the onBlur event before the current object receives the onFocus event.) For example, a text input element fires the onFocus event when a user tabs to that element while navigating through a form via the keyboard. Clicking an element also gives that element focus, as does making the browser the frontmost application on the client desktop.

The availability of the onFocus event has expanded with succeeding generations of script-capable browsers. In earlier versions, blur and focus were largely confined to text-oriented input elements (including the SELECT element). The window object received the onFocus event handler starting with NN3 and IE4. IE4 also extended the event handler to more form elements, predominantly on the Windows operating system because that OS has a user interface clue (the dotted rectangle) when items such as buttons and links receive focus (so that users may act upon them by pressing the keyboard's spacebar). For IE5, the onFocus event handler is available to virtually every HTML element. For most of those elements, however, you cannot use blur and focus unless you assign a value to the TABINDEX attribute of the element's tag. For example, if you assign TABINDEX=1 inside a <P> tag, the user can bring focus to that paragraph (highlighted with the dotted rectangle in Windows) by clicking the paragraph or pressing the Tab key until that item receives focus in sequence.

If you plan to use the onFocus event handler on window or text-oriented input elements, be aware that there might be some unexpected and undesirable consequences of scripting for the event. For example, in IE5 (but not IE4), some object almost always has focus. In most cases, the window has focus but loses it when the user clicks an element wired to receive focus. Clicking anywhere on an unwired element brings focus back to the window object. Similarly, the interaction between onBlur, onFocus, and the alert dialog box can be problematic with text input elements.

IE5.5 adds the onActivate event handler, which fires immediately before the onFocus event handler. You can use one or the other, but there is little need to include both event handlers for the same object unless you temporarily wish to block an item from receiving focus. To prevent an object from receiving focus in IE5.5, include an event.returnValue=false statement in the onActivate event handler for the same object. In older browsers, you can usually get away with assigning onFocus="this.blur()" as an event handler for elements such as form controls. However, this is not a foolproof way to prevent a user from changing a control's setting. Unfortunately, there are few reliable alternatives.

On the CD-ROM   Example on the CD-ROM

Related Items: onActivate, onBlur, onDeactivate event handlers.

onHelp

	NN2	NN3	NN4	NN6	IE3/J1	IE3/J2	IE4	IE5	IE5.5
Compatibility							✓	✓	✓

The onHelp event handler fires in Windows whenever an element of the document has focus and the user presses the F1 function key on a Windows PC. As of IE5/Mac, the event fires only on the window (in other words, event handler specified in the <BODY> tag) and does so via the dedicated Help key on a Mac keyboard. Browser Help menu choices do not activate this event. To prevent the browser's Help window from appearing, the event handler must evaluate to return false (for IE4+) or set the `event.returnValue` property to `false` (IE5+). Because the event handler can be associated with individual elements of a document in the Windows version, you can create a context-sensitive help system. However, if the focus is in the Address field of the browser window, you cannot intercept the event. Instead, the browser's Help window appears.

Example (with Listing 15-40) on the CD-ROM

Related Items: `window.showHelp()`, `window.showModalDialog()` methods.

onKeyDown
onKeyPress
onKeyUp

	NN2	NN3	NN4	NN6	IE3/J1	IE3/J2	IE4	IE5	IE5.5
Compatibility			✓	✓			✓	✓	✓

When someone presses and releases a keyboard key, a sequence of three events fires in quick succession. The `onKeyDown` event fires when the key makes its first contact. This is followed immediately by the `onKeyPress` event. When contact is broken by the key release, the `onKeyUp` event fires. If you hold a character key down until it begins auto-repeating, the `onKeyDown` and `onKeyPress` events fire with each repetition of the character.

The sequence of events can be crucial in some keyboard event handling. Consider the scenario that wants the focus of a series of text fields to advance automatically after the user enters a fixed number of characters (for example, date, month, and two-digit year). By the time the `onKeyUp` event fires, the character associated with the key press action is already added to the field and you can accurately determine the length of text in the field, as shown in this simple example:

```
<HTML>
<HEAD>
<SCRIPT Language="JavaScript">
function jumpNext(fromFld, toFld) {
    if (fromFld.value.length == 2) {
        document.forms[0].elements[toFld].focus()
        document.forms[0].elements[toFld].select()
    }
}
</SCRIPT>
</HEAD>
```

```
<BODY>
<FORM>
Month: <INPUT Name="month" Type="text" Size="3" VALUE=""
    onKeyUp="jumpNext(this, day)"  maxLength="2">
Day: <INPUT Name="day" Type="text" Size="3" VALUE=""
    onKeyUp ="jumpNext(this, year)"  maxLength="2">
Year: <INPUT Name="year" Type="text" Size="3" VALUE=""
    onKeyUp ="jumpNext(this, month)"  maxLength="2">
</FORM>
</BODY>
</HTML>
```

These three events do not fire for all keys of the typical PC keyboard on all browser versions that support keyboard events. The only keys that you can rely on supporting the events in all browsers shown in the preceding compatibility chart are the alphanumeric keys represented by ASCII values. This includes keys such as the spacebar and Enter (Return on the Mac), but it excludes all function keys, arrow keys, and other navigation keys. Modifier keys, such as Shift, Ctrl (PC), Alt (PC), Command (Mac), and Option (Mac), generate some events on their own (depending on browser and version). However, functions invoked by other key events can always inspect the pressed states of these modifier keys.

Scripting keyboard events almost always entails examining which key is pressed so that some processing or validation can be performed on that key press. This is where the situation gets very complex if you are writing for cross-browser implementation. In some cases, even writing just for Internet Explorer gets tricky because non-alphanumeric keys generate only the onKeyDown and onKeyUp events.

In fact, to fully comprehend keyboard events, you need to make a distinction between *key codes* and *character codes*. Every PC keyboard key has a key code associated with it. This key code is always the same regardless of what other keys you press at the same time. Only the alphanumeric keys (letters, numbers, spacebar, and so on), however, generate character codes. The code represents the typed character produced by that key. The value might change if you press a modifier key. For example, if you type the "A" key by itself, it generates a lowercase "a" character (character code 97); if you also hold down the Shift key, that same key produces an uppercase "A" character (character code 65). The key code for that key (65 for Western language keyboards) remains the same no matter what.

That brings us, then, to where these different codes are made available to scripts. In all cases, the code information is conveyed as one or two properties of the browser's event object. IE's event object has only one such property — keyCode. It contains key codes for onKeyDown and onKeyUp events, but character codes for onKeyPress events. The NN6 event object, on the other hand, contains two separate properties: charCode and keyCode. You can find more details and examples about these event object properties in Chapter 29.

The bottom-line script consideration is to use either `onKeyDown` or `onKeyUp` event handlers when you want to look for non-alphanumeric key events (for example, function keys, arrow and page navigation keys, and so on). To process characters as they appear in text boxes, use the `onKeyPress` event handler. You can experiment with these events and codes in Listing 15-41 as well as in examples from Chapter 29.

Common keyboard event tasks

IE4+ (but not NN) enables you to modify the character that a user who is editing a text box enters. The `onKeyPress` event handler can modify the `event.keyCode` property and allow the event to continue (in other words, don't evaluate to `return false` or set the `event.returnValue` property to `false`). The following IE function (invoked by an `onKeyPress` event handler) makes sure text entered into a text field is all uppercase, even if you type it as lowercase:

```
function assureUpper() {
    if (event.charCode >= 97 && event.charCode <= 122) {
        event.charCode = event.charCode - 32
    }
}
```

Doing this might confuse (or frustrate) users, so think carefully before implementing such a plan.

To prevent a keyboard key press from becoming a typed character in a text field, the `onKeyPress` event handler prevents the default action of the event. For example, the following (NN4+, IE4+) HTML page shows how to inspect a text field's entry for numbers only:

```
<HTML>
<HEAD>
<TITLE>Keyboard Capture</TITLE>
<SCRIPT LANGUAGE="JavaScript">
function checkIt(evt) {
    var charCode = (evt.which) ? evt.which : event.keyCode
    if (charCode > 31 && (charCode < 48 || charCode > 57)) {
        alert("Please make sure entries are numbers only.")
        return false
    }
    return true
}
</SCRIPT>
</HEAD>

<BODY>
<FORM>
```

```
Enter any positive integer: <INPUT TYPE="text" NAME="numeric"
    onKeyPress="return checkIt(event)">
</FORM>
</BODY>
</HTML>
```

Whenever a user enters a non-number, the user receives a warning and the character is not appended to the text box's text.

Keyboard events also enable you to script the submission of a form when a user presses the Enter (Return on the Mac) key within a text box. The ASCII value of the Enter/Return key is 13. Therefore, you can examine each key press in a text box and submit the form whenever value 13 arrives, as shown in the following function, which works in IE4+ and NN4+:

```
function checkForEnter(evt) {
    evt = (evt) ? evt : event
    var charCode = (evt.which) ? evt.which : evt.keyCode
    if (charCode == 13) {
        document.forms[0].submit()
        return false
    }
    return true
}
```

By assigning the `checkForEnter()` function to each field's `onKeyPress` event handler, you suddenly add some extra power to a typical HTML form.

You can intercept Ctrl+keyboard combinations (letters only) in HTML pages most effectively in Internet Explorer, but only if the browser itself does not use the combination. In other words, you cannot redirect Ctrl+key combinations that the browser uses for its own control. The `onKeyPress` `keyCode` value for Ctrl+ combinations ranges from 1 through 26 for letters A through Z (except for those used by the browser, in which case no keyboard event fires).

On the CD-ROM

Example (with Listing 15-41) on the CD-ROM

Related Item: `String.fromCharCode()` method.

onLoseCapture

	NN2	NN3	NN4	NN6	IE3/J1	IE3/J2	IE4	IE5	IE5.5
Compatibility								✓	✓

The onLoseCapture event handler fires whenever an object that has event capture turned on no longer has that capture. Event capture is automatically disengaged when the user performs any of the following actions:

✦ Gives focus to any other window

✦ Displays any system modal dialog box (for example, alert window)

✦ Scrolls the page

✦ Opens a browser context menu (right-clicking)

✦ Tabs to give focus to the Address field in the browser window

A function associated with the onLoseCapture event handler should perform any cleanup of the environment due to an object no longer capturing mouse events.

Example on the CD-ROM

Related Items: releaseCapture(), setCapture() methods.

onMouseDown
onMouseUp

	NN2	NN3	NN4	NN6	IE3/J1	IE3/J2	IE4	IE5	IE5.5
Compatibility			✓	✓			✓	✓	✓

The onMouseDown event handler fires when the user presses any button of a mouse. The onMouseUp event handler fires when the user releases the mouse button, provided the object receiving the event also received an onMouseDown event. When a user performs a typical click of the mouse button atop an object, mouse events occur in the following sequence: onMouseDown, onMouseUp, onClick. But if the user presses the mouse atop an object and then slides the cursor away from the object, only the onMouseDown event fires. In NN4, these two mouse events were limited to button, radio button, checkbox, link, and area objects.

These events enable authors and designers to add more application-like behavior to images that act as action or icon buttons. If you notice the way most buttons work, the appearance of the button changes while you press the mouse button and reverts to its original style when you release the mouse button (or you drag the cursor out of the button). These events enable you to emulate that behavior.

The event object created with every mouse button action has a property that reveals which mouse button the user pressed. NN4's event model calls that property the `which` property. IE4+ and NN6 call it the `button` property (but with different values for the buttons). It is most reliable to test for the mouse button number on either the `onMouseDown` or `onMouseUp` event, rather than on `onClick`. The `onClick` event object does not always contain the button information.

On the CD-ROM

Example (with Listing 15-42) on the CD-ROM

Related Item: `onClick` event handler.

onMouseEnter
onMouseLeave

	NN2	NN3	NN4	NN6	IE3/J1	IE3/J2	IE4	IE5	IE5.5
Compatibility									✓

Two event handlers that are new with IE5.5 are `onMouseEnter` and `onMouseLeave`. Both event handlers operate just like the `onMouseOver` and `onMouseOut` event handlers, respectively. Microsoft simply offers an alternate terminology. The old and new events continue to fire in IE5.5. The old ones fire just before the new ones for each act of moving the cursor atop, and exiting from atop, the object. If you are scripting exclusively for IE5.5+, then you should use the new terminology; otherwise, stay with the older versions.

On the CD-ROM

Example on the CD-ROM

Related Items: `onMouseOver`, `onMouseOut` event handlers.

onMouseMove

	NN2	NN3	NN4	NN6	IE3/J1	IE3/J2	IE4	IE5	IE5.5
Compatibility			(✓)	✓			✓	✓	✓

The `onMouseMove` event handler fires whenever the cursor is atop the current object and the mouse is moved, even by a single pixel. You do not have to press the mouse button for the event to fire, although the event is most commonly used in element dragging — especially in NN, where no onDrag event handler is available.

Even though the granularity of this event can be at the pixel level, you should not use the number of event firings as a measurement device. Depending on the speed of cursor motion and the performance of the client computer, the event may not fire at every pixel location.

In NN4, you cannot assign the onMouseMove event handler to any object by way of tag attributes. But you can use the NN4 event capturing mechanism to instruct (via scripting) a window, document, or layer object to capture mouseMove events. This allows for NN4 scripts to produce positioned element (layer) dragging. In IE4+ and NN6+, however, you can assign the onMouseMove event handler to any element (although you can drag only with positioned elements). When designing a page that encourages users to drag multiple items on a page, it is most common to assign the onMouseMove event handler to the document object and let all such events bubble up to the document for processing.

 On the CD-ROM Example (with Listing 15-43) on the CD-ROM

Related Items: onDrag, onMouseDown, onMouseUp event handlers.

onMouseOut
onMouseOver

	NN2	NN3	NN4	NN6	IE3/J1	IE3/J2	IE4	IE5	IE5.5
Compatibility	✓	✓	✓	✓	✓	✓	✓	✓	✓

The onMouseOver event fires for an object whenever the cursor rolls into the rectangular space of the object on the screen (one event per entry into the object — except for a bug in NN4/Windows, which causes the onMouseOver event to fire with mouse movement). The onMouseOut event handler fires when you move the cursor outside the object's rectangle. These events most commonly display explanatory text about an object in the window's status bar and effect image swapping (so-called mouse rollovers). Use the onMouseOver event handler to change the state to a highlighted version; use the onMouseOut event handler to restore the image or status bar to its normal setting.

While these two events have been in object models of scriptable browsers since the beginning, they were not available to most objects in earlier browsers. The onMouseOver event was available only to the link object until the version 4 browsers. Even then, NN4 still restricted this event to link, area, and layer objects. The `onMouseOut` event handler first surfaced for link and area objects in Navigator 3. IE4+ and NN6+ provide support for these events on every element that occupies space on the screen. IE5.5 includes an additional pair of event handlers — `onMouseEnter` and `onMouseLeave` — that duplicate the `onMouseOver` and `onMouseOut` events but with different terminology. The old event handlers fire just before the new versions.

> **Note**   The `onMouseOut` event handler commonly fails to fire if the event is associated with an element that is near a frame or window edge and the user moves the cursor quickly outside of the current frame.

On the CD-ROM

Example (with Listing 15-44) on the CD-ROM

Related Items: `onMouseEnter`, `onMouseLeave`, `onMouseMove` event handlers.

onPaste

	NN2	NN3	NN4	NN6	IE3/J1	IE3/J2	IE4	IE5	IE5.5
Compatibility								✓	✓

The `onPaste` event (not implemented in IE5/Mac) fires immediately after the user or script initiates a paste edit action on the current object. The event is preceded by the `onBeforePaste` event, which fires prior to any edit or context menu that appears (or before the paste action if initiated by keyboard shortcut).

Use this event handler to provide edit functionality to elements that don't normally allow pasting. In such circumstances, you need to enable the Paste menu item in the context or Edit menu by setting the `event.returnValue` for the `onBeforePaste` event handler to `false`. Then your `onPaste` event handler must manually retrieve data from the clipboard (by way of the `getData()` method of the `clipboardData` object) and handle the insertion into the current object.

Because you are in charge of what data is stored in the clipboard, you are not limited to a direct copy of the data. For example, you might wish to store the value of the `src` property of an image object so that you can paste it elsewhere on the page.

On the CD-ROM

Example (with Listing 15-45) on the CD-ROM

Related Items: `onCopy`, `onCut`, `onBeforePaste` event handlers.

onPropertyChange

	NN2	NN3	NN4	NN6	IE3/J1	IE3/J2	IE4	IE5	IE5.5
Compatibility								✓	✓

The `onPropertyChange` event fires in Windows versions of IE5+ whenever a script modifies an object's property. This includes changes to the properties of an object's style. Changing properties by way of the `setAttribute()` method also triggers this event.

A script can inspect the nature of the property change because the `event.propertyName` property contains the name (as a string) of the property that was just changed. In the case of a change to an object's `style` object, the `event.propertyName` value begins with `"style."` as in `style.backgroundcolor`.

You can use this event handler to localize any object-specific post-processing of changes to an object's properties. Rather than include the post-processing statements inside the function that makes the changes, you can make that function generalized (perhaps to modify properties of multiple objects).

On the CD-ROM Example (with Listing 15-46) on the CD-ROM

Related Items: `style` property; `setAttribute()` method.

onReadyStateChange

	NN2	NN3	NN4	NN6	IE3/J1	IE3/J2	IE4	IE5	IE5.5
Compatibility							✓	✓	✓

The `onReadyStateChange` event handler fires whenever the ready state of an object changes. See details about these states in the discussion of the `readyState` property earlier in this chapter (and notice the limits for IE4). The change of state does not guarantee that an object is, in fact, ready for script statements to access its properties. Always check the `readyState` property of the object in any script that the `onReadyStateChange` event handler invokes.

This event fires for objects that are capable of loading data: APPLET, document, FRAME, FRAMESET, IFRAME, IMG, LINK, OBJECT, SCRIPT, and XML objects. The event doesn't fire for other types of objects unless a Microsoft DHTML behavior is associated with the object. The onReadyStateChange event does not bubble, nor can you cancel it.

Example on the CD-ROM

Related Item: readyState property.

onResize

	NN2	NN3	NN4	NN6	IE3/J1	IE3/J2	IE4	IE5	IE5.5
Compatibility			✓	✓			✓	✓	✓

The onResize event handler fires whenever an object is resized in response to a variety of user or scripted actions. In NN4+, the onResize event handler is available only for the window object; IE4 includes this event handler for the APPLET, AREA, BUTTON, DIV, FIELDSET, FRAMESET, IMG, MARQUEE, SELECT, TABLE, TD, TH, and window objects. Virtually every content-containing element in IE5+ has this event handler, provided the object has dimensional style attributes (for example, height, width, or position) assigned to it.

Window resizing presents potentially serious problems in NN4, especially when the page contains positioned elements. Unlike IE4+ and NN6, the NN4 rendering engine typically fails to redraw a resized page properly. A reload of the page usually fixes the problems. You can use the onResize event handler in NN4 to repair the damage:

```
window.onresize = restorePage
function restorePage() {
    history.go(0)
}
```

But there is one additional complication in NN4 for Windows when the content of a window or frame requires scrollbars. The application of the scrollbars forces another resize event. In concert with the preceding code, the page gets in an infinite loop of reloading the page. To guard against this, your script must compare the innerWidth and innerHeight of the window before and after the resize event:

```
var Nav4 = ((navigator.appName == "Netscape") &&
(parseInt(navigator.appVersion) == 4))
window.onresize = restorePage
if (Nav4) {
    var startWidth = window.innerWidth
    var startHeight = window.innerHeight
}
function restorePage() {
    if (Nav4) {
        if (startWidth != window.innerWidth ||
startHeight != window.innerHeight) {
            history.go(0)
        }
    }
}
```

In IE4+ and NN6, the onResize event does not bubble. Resizing the browser window or frame does not cause the window's onLoad event handler to fire.

Example on the CD-ROM

Related Item: window.resize() method.

onResizeEnd
onResizeStart

	NN2	NN3	NN4	NN6	IE3/J1	IE3/J2	IE4	IE5	IE5.5
Compatibility									✓

The onResizeEnd and onResizeStart event handlers fire only on a resizable object in Windows edit mode. As mentioned in the discussion of the onControlSelect event handler, an authoritative description or example is not available yet.

Related Item: onControlSelect event handler.

onSelectStart

	NN2	NN3	NN4	NN6	IE3/J1	IE3/J2	IE4	IE5	IE5.5
Compatibility							✓	✓	✓

The onSelectStart event handler fires when a user begins to select content on the page. Selected content can be inline text, images, or text within an editable text field. If the user selects more than one object, the event fires in the first object affected by the selection.

On the CD-ROM Example (with Listing 15-47) on the CD-ROM

Related Item: onSelect event handler for a variety of objects

✦   ✦   ✦

Window and Frame Objects

✦ ✦ ✦ ✦

In This Chapter

Scripting
communication
among multiple
frames

Creating and
managing new
windows

Controlling the size,
position, and
appearance of the
browser window

Details of Window,
FRAME, FRAMESET,
and IFRAME objects

✦ ✦ ✦ ✦

A quick look at the basic document object model diagram
in Chapter 14 (Figure 14-1) reveals that the window
object is the outermost, most global container of all docu-
ment-related objects that you script with JavaScript. All HTML
and JavaScript activity takes place inside a window. That window may be a standard Windows, Mac, or Xwindows application-style window, complete with scrollbars, toolbars, and
other "chrome;" you can also generate windows that have
only some of a typical window's chrome. A frame is also a window, even though a frame doesn't have many accoutrements
beyond scrollbars. The window object is where everything
begins in JavaScript references to object. IE4+ and NN6 treat
the frameset as a special kind of window object, so that it is
also covered in this chapter.

Of all the objects associated with browser scripting, the window and window-related objects have by far the most object-
specific terminology associated with them. This necessitates
a rather long chapter to keep the discussion in one place. Use
the running footers as a navigational aid through this substantial collection of information.

Window Terminology

The window object is often a source of confusion when you
first learn about the document object model. A number of syn-
onyms for window objects muck up the works: top, self,
parent, and frame. Aggravating the situation is that these
terms are also properties of a window object. Under some conditions, a window is its own parent, but if you define a frameset with two frames, you have only one parent among a total
of three window objects. It doesn't take long before the whole
subject can make your head hurt.

If you do not use frames in your Web applications, all of these headaches never appear. But if frames are part of your design plan, you should get to know how frames affect the object model.

Frames

The application of frames has become a religious issue among Web designers: some swear by them, while others swear at them. I believe there can be compelling reasons to use frames at times. For example, if you have a document that requires considerable scrolling to get through, you may want to maintain a static set of navigation controls visible at all times. By placing those controls — be they links or image maps — in a separate frame, you have made the controls available for immediate access, regardless of the scrolled condition of the main document.

Creating frames

The task of defining frames in a document remains the same whether or not you're using JavaScript. The simplest framesetting document consists of tags that are devoted to setting up the frameset, as follows:

```
<HTML>
<HEAD>
<TITLE>My Frameset</TITLE>
</HEAD>
<FRAMESET>
    <FRAME NAME="Frame1" SRC="document1.html">
    <FRAME NAME="Frame2" SRC="document2.html">
</FRAMESET>
</HTML>
```

The preceding HTML document, which the user never sees, defines the frameset for the entire browser window. Each frame must have a URL reference (specified by the SRC attribute) for a document to load into that frame. For scripting purposes, assigning a name to each frame with the NAME attribute greatly simplifies scripting frame content.

The frame object model

Perhaps the key to successful frame scripting is understanding that the object model in the browser's memory at any given instant is determined by the HTML tags in the currently loaded documents. All canned object model graphics, such as Figure 16-1 in this book, do not reflect the precise object model for your document or document set.

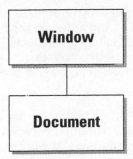

Figure 16-1: The simplest window–document relationship

For a single, frameless document, the object model starts with just one window object, which contains one document, as shown in Figure 16-1. In this simple structure, the window object is the starting point for all references to any loaded object. Because the window is always there—it must be there for a document to load into—a reference to any object in the document can omit a reference to the current window.

In a simple two-framed frameset model (Figure 16-2), the browser treats the container of the initial, framesetting document as the parent window. The only visible evidence that the document exists is that the framesetting document's title appears in the browser window title bar.

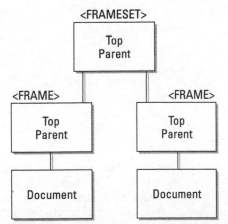

Figure 16-2: The parent and frames are part of the object model.

Each <FRAME> tag inside the <FRAMESET> tag set creates another window object into which a document is loaded. Each of those frames, then, has a document object associated with it. From the point of view of a given document, it has a single window container, just as in the model shown in Figure 16-1. And although the par-ent object is not visible to the user, it remains in the object model in memory. The presence of the parent often makes it a convenient repository for variable data that need to be shared by multiple child frames or must persist between loading of different documents inside a child frame.

In even more complex arrangements, as shown in Figure 16-3, a child frame itself may load a framesetting document. In this situation, the differentiation between the parent and top objects starts to come into focus. The top window is the only one in common with all frames in Figure 16-3. As you see in a moment, when frames need to communicate with other frames (and their documents), you must fashion references to the distant object via the window object that they all have in common.

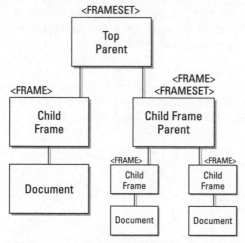

Figure 16-3: Three generations of window objects

Referencing frames

The purpose of an object reference is to help JavaScript locate the desired object in the object model currently held in memory. A reference is a road map for the browser to follow, so that it can track down, say, the value of a particular text field in a particular document. Therefore, when you construct a reference, think about where the script appears in the object model and how the reference can help the browser determine where it should go to find the distant object. In a two-generation scenario, such as the one shown in Figure 16-2, three intergenerational references are possible:

✦ Parent-to-child

✦ Child-to-parent

✦ Child-to-child

Assuming that you need to access an object, function, or variable in the relative's frame, the following are the corresponding reference structures:

✦ `frameName.objFuncVarName`

✦ `parent.objFuncVarName`

✦ `parent.frameName.objFuncVarName`

The rule is this: Whenever a reference must point to another frame, begin the reference with the `window` object that the two destinations have in common. To demonstrate that rule on the complex model in Figure 16-3, if the left-hand child frame's document needs to reference the document at the bottom right of the map, the reference structure is

`top.frameName.frameName.document. ...`

Follow the map from the top `window` object down through two frames to the final document. JavaScript has to take this route, so your reference must help it along.

Top versus parent

After seeing the previous object maps and reference examples, you may be wondering, Why not use `top` as the leading object in all trans-frame references? From an object model point of view, you'll have no problem doing that: A parent in a two-generation scenario is also the top window. What you can't count on, however, is your framesetting document always being the `top` window object in someone's browser. Take the instance where a Web site loads other Web sites into one of its frames. At that instant, the `top` window object belongs to someone else. If you always specify `top` in references intended just for your parent window, your references won't work and will probably lead to script errors for the user. My advice, then, is to use `parent` in references whenever you mean one generation above the current document.

Preventing framing

You can use your knowledge of `top` and `parent` references to prevent your pages from being displayed inside another Web site's frameset. Your top-level document must check whether it is loaded into its own top or parent window. When a document is in its own top window, a reference to the `top` property of the current window is equal to a reference to the current window (the `window` synonym `self` seems most grammatically fitting here). If the two values are not equal, you can script your document to reload itself as a top-level document. When it is critical that your document be a top-level document, include the script in Listing 16-1 in the head portion of your document:

Listing 16-1: **Prevention from Getting "Framed"**

```
<SCRIPT LANGUAGE="JavaScript">
if (top != self) {
    top.location = location
}
</SCRIPT>
```

Your document may appear momentarily inside the other site's frameset, but then the slate is wiped clean, and your top-level document rules the browser window.

Ensuring framing

When you design a Web application around a frameset, you may want to make sure that a page always loads the complete frameset. Consider the possibility that a visitor adds only one of your frames to a bookmarks list. On the next visit, only the bookmarked page appears in the browser, without your frameset, which may contain valuable navigation aids to the site.

A script can make sure that a page always loads into its frameset by comparing the URLs of the top and self windows. If the URLs are the same, it means that the page needs to load the frameset. Listing 16-2 shows the simplest version of this technique, which loads a fixed frameset. The listing includes a workaround for an NN4-specific behavior that prevents printing a frame. (NN4 for Windows and Unix reloads a page into a separate hidden window for printing and runs any immediate scripts in the process.) For a more complete implementation that passes a parameter to the frameset so that it opens a specific page in one of the frames, see the location.search property in Chapter 17.

Listing 16-2: **Forcing a Frameset to Load**

```
<SCRIPT LANGUAGE="JavaScript">
var isNav4 = (navigator.appName == "Netscape" &&
parseInt(navigator.appVersion) == 4)
if (top.location.href == window.location.href) {
    if (isNav4) {
        if (window.innerWidth != 0) {
            top.location.href = "myFrameset.html"
        }
    } else {
        top.location.href = " myFrameset.html"
```

```
    }
  }
</SCRIPT>
```

Switching from frames to frameless

Some sites load themselves in a frameset by default and offer users the option of getting rid of the frames. Only IE4+ and NN6+ let you modify a frameset's `cols` or `rows` properties on the fly to simulate adding or removing frames from the current view (see the FRAMESET element object later in this chapter). In other browsers, you cannot dynamically change the makeup of a frameset after it has loaded, but you can load the content page of the frameset into the main window. Simply include a button or link whose action loads that document into the `top` window object:

```
top.location.href = "mainBody.html"
```

A switch back to the frame version entails nothing more complicated than loading the framesetting document.

Inheritance versus containment

Scripters who have experience in object-oriented programming environments probably expect frames to inherit properties, methods, functions, and variables defined in a parent object. That's not the case with scriptable browsers. You can, however, still access those parent items when you make a call to the item with a complete reference to the parent. For example, if you want to define a deferred function in the framesetting parent document that all frames can share, the scripts in the frames refer to that function with this reference:

```
parent.myFunc()
```

You can pass arguments to such functions and expect returned values.

Navigator 2 Bug: Parent Variables

Some bugs in Navigator 2 cause problems when accessing variables in a parent window from one of its children. If a document in one of the child frames unloads, a parent variable value that depends on that frame may get scrambled or disappear. Using a temporary `document.cookie` for global variable values may be a better solution. For Navigator 3, you should declare parent variables that are updated from child frames as first-class string objects (with the `new String()` constructor) as described in Chapter 34.

Frame synchronization

A pesky problem for some scripters' plans is that including immediate scripts in the framesetting document is dangerous — if not crash-prone in Navigator 2. Such scripts tend to rely on the presence of documents in the frames being created by this framesetting document. But if the frames have not yet been created and their documents have not yet loaded, the immediate scripts will likely crash and burn.

One way to guard against this problem is to trigger all such scripts from the frameset's onLoad event handler. In theory, this handler won't trigger until all documents have successfully loaded into the child frames defined by the frameset. Unfortunately, IE4+ for Windows has a nasty bug that fires the onLoad event handler in the frameset even if the loading has been interrupted by the browser's Stop button or pressing the Esc key. At the same time, be careful with onLoad event handlers in the documents going into a frameset's frames. If one of those scripts relies on the presence of a document in another frame (one of its brothers or sisters), you're doomed to eventual failure. Anything coming from a slow network or server to a slow modem can get in the way of other documents loading into frames in the ideal order.

One way to work around these problems is to create a Boolean variable in the parent document to act as a flag for the successful loading of subsidiary frames. When a document loads into a frame, its onLoad event handler can set that flag to true to indicate that the document has loaded. Any script that relies on a page being loaded should use an if construction to test the value of that flag before proceeding.

Despite the horrible IE4+/Windows bug described above, it is best to construct the code so that the parent's onLoad event handler triggers all the scripts that you want to run after loading. Depending on other frames is a tricky business, but the farther the installed base of Web browsers gets from Navigator 2, the less the associated risk. For example, beginning with Navigator 3, if a user resizes a window, the document does not reload itself, as it used to in Navigator 2. Even so, you still should test your pages thoroughly for any residual effects that may accrue if someone resizes a window or clicks Reload.

Blank frames

Often, you may find it desirable to create a frame in a frameset but not put any document in it until the user has interacted with various controls or other user interface elements in other frames. Navigator and recent IE versions have a somewhat empty document in one of its internal URLs (about:blank). But with Navigator 2 and 3 on the Macintosh, an Easter egg–style message appears in that window when it displays. This URL is also not guaranteed to be available on all browsers. If you need a blank frame, let your framesetting document write a generic HTML document to the frame directly from the SRC attribute for the frame, as shown in the skeletal code in Listing 16-3. Loading an "empty" HTML document requires no additional transactions.

> **Listing 16-3: Creating a Blank Frame**

```
<HTML>
<HEAD>
<SCRIPT LANGUAGE="JavaScript">
<!--
function blank() {
    return "<HTML></HTML>"
}
//-->
</SCRIPT>
</HEAD>
<FRAMESET>
    <FRAME NAME="Frame1" SRC="someURL.html">
    <FRAME NAME="Frame2" SRC="javascript:parent.blank()">
</FRAMESET>
</HTML>
```

Viewing frame source code

Studying other scripters' work is a major learning tool for JavaScript (or any programming language). With most scriptable browsers you can easily view the source code for any frame, including those frames whose content is generated entirely or in part by JavaScript. Click the desired frame to activate it (a subtle border may appear just inside the frame on some browser versions, but don't be alarmed if the border doesn't appear). Then select Frame Source (or equivalent) from the View menu (or right-click submenu). You can also print or save a selected frame.

Frames versus FRAME element objects

With the expansion of object models that expose every HTML element to scripting (IE4+, NN6), a terminology conflict comes into play. Everything that you have read about frames thus far in the chapter refers to the original object model, where a frame is just another kind of window, with a slightly different referencing approach. That still holds true, even in the latest browsers.

But when the object model also exposes HTML elements, then the notion of the FRAME element object is somewhat distinct from the frame object of the original model. The FRAME element object represents an object whose properties are dominated by the attributes you set inside the <FRAME> tag. This provides access to settings, such as the frame border and scrollability—the kinds of properties that are not exposed to the original frame object.

References to the frame and FRAME element objects are also different. You've seen plenty of examples of how to reference an old-fashioned frame earlier in this chapter. But access to a FRAME element object is either via the element's ID attribute or through the child node relationship of the enclosing FRAMESET element (you cannot use the parentNode property to back your way out of the current document to the FRAME element that encloses the document). The way I prefer is to assign an ID attribute to <FRAME> tags and access the FRAME element object by way of the document object that lives in the parent (or top) of the frameset hierarchy. Therefore, to access the frameBorder property of a FRAME element object from a script living in any frame of a frameset, the syntax is

```
parent.document.all.frameID.frameBorder
```

or, for IE5+ and NN6+

```
parent.document.getElementById("frameID").frameBorder
```

There is no access to the document contained by a frame when the reference goes through the FRAME element object.

Window Object

Properties	Methods	Event Handlers
appCore	alert()	onAbort††
clientInformation	attachEvent()†	onAfterPrint
clipboardData	back()	onBeforePrint
closed	blur()†	onBeforeUnload
Components	captureEvents()	onBlur†
controllers	clearInterval()	onChange††
crypto	clearTimeout()	onClick††
defaultStatus	close()	onClose††
dialogArguments	confirm()	onDragDrop
dialogHeight	createPopup()	onError
dialogLeft	detachEvent()†	onFocus†
dialogTop	disableExternalCapture()	onHelp
dialogWidth	enableExternalCapture()	onKeyDown††

Properties	Methods	Event Handlers
directories	execScript()	onKeyPress††
document	find()	onKeyUp††
event	fireEvent()†	onLoad
external	focus()†	onMouseDown††
frameElement	forward()	onMouseMove††
frames	GetAttention()	onMouseOut††
history	handleEvent()	onMouseOver††
innerHeight	home()	onMouseUp††
innerWidth	moveBy()	onMove
length	moveTo()	onReset††
loading	navigate()	onResize
location	open()	onScroll
locationbar	print()	onSelect††
menubar	prompt()	onSubmit††
name	releaseEvents()	onUnload
navigator	resizeBy()	
offscreenBuffering	resizeTo()	
opener	routeEvent()	
outerHeight	scroll()	
outerWidth	scrollBy()	
pageXOffset	scrollTo()	
pageYOffset	setActive()†	
parent	setCursor()	
personalbar	setInterval()	
pkcs11	setTimeout()	
prompter	showHelp()	
returnValue	showModalDialog()	
screen	showModelessDialog()	
screenLeft	sizeToContent()	

Continued

Properties	Methods	Event Handlers
screenTop	stop()	
screenX		
screenY		
scrollbars		
scrollX		
scrollY		
self		
sidebar		
status		
statusbar		
toolbar		
top		
window		

†See Chapter 15.
††To handle captured or bubbled events of other objects in IE4+ and NN6

Syntax

Creating a window:

```
var windowObject = window.open([parameters])
```

Accessing window properties or methods:

```
window.property | method([parameters])

self.property | method([parameters])

windowObject.property | method([parameters])
```

About this object

The window object has the unique position of being at the top of the object hierarchy, encompassing even the almighty document object. This exalted position gives the window object a number of properties and behaviors unlike those of any other object.

Chief among its unique characteristics is that because everything takes place in a window, you can usually omit the `window` object from object references. You've seen this behavior in previous chapters when I invoked document methods, such as `document.write()`. The complete reference is `window.document.write()`. But because the activity was taking place in the window that held the document running the script, that window was assumed to be part of the reference. For single-frame windows, this concept is simple enough to grasp.

As previously stated, among the list of properties for the `window` object is one called `self`. This property is synonymous with the `window` object itself (which is why it shows up in hierarchy diagrams as an object). Having a property of an object that is the same name as the object may sound confusing, but this situation is not that uncommon in object-oriented environments. I discuss the reasons why you may want to use the `self` property as the window's object reference in the `self` property description that follows.

As indicated earlier in the syntax definition, you don't always have to specifically create a `window` object in JavaScript code. After you start your browser, it usually opens a window. That window is a valid `window` object, even if the window is blank. Therefore, after a user loads your page into the browser, the `window` object part of that document is automatically created for your script to access as it pleases.

One conceptual trap to avoid is believing that a `window` object's event handler or custom property assignments outlive the document whose scripts make the assignments. Except for some obvious physical properties of a window, each new document that loads into the window starts with a clean slate of window properties and event handlers.

Your script's control over an existing (already open) window's user interface elements varies widely with the browser and browser version for which your application is intended. Before the version 4 browsers, the only change you can make to an open window is to the status line at the bottom of the browser window. With IE4+ and NN4+, however, you can control such properties as the size, location, and (with signed scripts in Navigator) the presence of "chrome" elements (toolbars and scrollbars, for example) on the fly. Many of these properties can be changed beyond specific safe limits only if you cryptographically sign the scripts (see Chapter 46) and/or the user grants permission for your scripts to make those modifications.

Window properties are far more flexible on all browsers when your scripts generate a new window (with the `window.open()` method): You can influence the size, toolbar, or other view options of a window. Recent browser versions provide even more options for new windows, including the position of the window and whether the window should even display a title bar. Again, if an option can conceivably be used to deceive a user (for example, silently hiding one window that monitors activity in another window), signed scripts and/or user permission are necessary.

The `window` object is also the level at which a script asks the browser to display any of three styles of dialog boxes (a plain alert dialog box, an OK/Cancel confirmation dialog box, or a prompt for user text entry). Although dialog boxes are extremely helpful for cobbling together debugging tools for your own use (Chapter 45), they can be very disruptive to visitors who navigate through Web sites. Because most JavaScript dialog boxes are modal (that is, you cannot do anything else in the browser — or anything at all on a Macintosh — until you dismiss the dialog box), use them sparingly, if at all. Remember that some users may create macros on their computers to visit sites unattended. Should such an automated access of your site encounter a modal dialog box, it is trapped on your page until a human intervenes.

All dialog boxes generated by JavaScript identify themselves as being generated by JavaScript (less egregiously so in version 4 browsers and later). This is primarily a security feature to prevent deceitful scripts from creating system- or application-style dialog boxes that convince visitors to enter private information. It should also discourage dialog box usage in Web page design. And that's good, because dialog boxes tend to annoy users.

With the exception of the IE-specific modal and modeless dialog boxes (see the `window.showModalDialog()` and `window.showModeless()` methods), JavaScript dialog boxes are not particularly flexible in letting you fill them with text or graphic elements beyond the basics. In fact, you can't even change the text of the dialog box buttons or add a button. With DHTML-capable browsers, you can use positioned DIV or IFRAME elements to simulate dialog box behavior in a cross-browser way.

Properties

```
appCore
Components
controllers
prompter
sidebar
```

Values: See Text   Read-Only

	NN2	NN3	NN4	NN6	IE3/J1	IE3/J2	IE4	IE5	IE5.5
Compatibility				✓					

Navigator 6 provides scriptable access to numerous services that are part of the xpconnect package ("xp" stands for "cross-platform"). These services allow scripts to work with COM objects and the mozilla.org XUL (XML-based User Interface Language) facilities — lengthy subjects that extend well beyond the scope of this book. You can begin to explore this subject within the context of Navigator 6 and scripting at `http://www.mozilla.org/scriptable/`.

clientInformation

Value: `navigator` object   Read-only

	NN2	NN3	NN4	NN6	IE3/J1	IE3/J2	IE4	IE5	IE5.5
Compatibility							✓	✓	✓

In an effort to provide scriptable access to browser-level properties while avoiding reference to the Navigator browser brand, Microsoft provides the `clientInformation` property. Its value is identical to that of the `navigator` object — an object name that is also available in IE. Use the `navigator` object for cross-browser applications. (See Chapter 28.)

Related Items: `navigator` object.

clipboardData

Value: Object   Read/Write

	NN2	NN3	NN4	NN6	IE3/J1	IE3/J2	IE4	IE5	IE5.5
Compatibility								✓	✓

Use the `clipboardData` object (not implemented in IE5/Mac) to transfer data for such actions as cutting, copying, and pasting under script control. The object contains data of one or more data types associated with a transfer operation. Use this property only when editing processes via the Edit menu (or keyboard equivalents) or context menu controlled by script — typically in concert with edit-related event handlers.

Working with the `clipboardData` object requires knowing about its three methods shown in Table 16-1. Familiarity with the edit-related event handlers ("before" and "after" versions of cut, copy, and paste) is also helpful (see Chapter 15).

Table 16-1	**window.clipboardData Object Methods**	
Method	*Returns*	*Description*
clearData([*format*])	Nothing	Removes data from the clipboard. If no format parameter is supplied, all data is cleared. Data formats can be one or more of the following strings: Text, URL, File, HTML, Image.
getData(*format*)	String	Retrieves data of the specified format from the clipboard. The format is one of the following strings: Text, URL, File, HTML, Image. The clipboard is not emptied when you get the data, so that the data can be retrieved in several sequential operations.
setData(*format*, *data*)	Boolean	Stores string data in the clipboard. The format is one of the following strings: Text, URL, File, HTML, Image. For non-text data formats, the data must be a string that specifies the path or URL to the content. Returns true if the transfer to the clipboard is successful.

You cannot use the clipboardData object to transfer data between pages that originate from different domains or arrive via different protocols (http versus https).

On the CD-ROM   Example on the CD-ROM

Related Items: event.dataTransfer property; onBeforeCopy, onBeforeCut, onBeforePaste, onCopy, onCut, onPaste event handlers.

closed

Value: Boolean   Read-Only

	NN2	NN3	NN4	NN6	IE3/J1	IE3/J2	IE4	IE5	IE5.5
Compatibility		✓	✓	✓			✓	✓	✓

When you create a subwindow with the `window.open()` method, you may need to access object properties from that subwindow, such as setting the value of a text field. Access to the subwindow is via the `window` object reference that is returned by the `window.open()` method, as in the following code fragment:

```
var newWind = window.open("someURL.html","subWind")
...
newWind.document.entryForm.ZIP.value = "00000"
```

In this example, the `newWind` variable is not linked "live" to the window, but is only a reference to that window. If the user should close the window, the `newWind` variable still contains the reference to the now missing window. Thus, any script reference to an object in that missing window will likely cause a script error. What you need to know before accessing items in a subwindow is whether the window is still open.

The `closed` property returns `true` if the `window` object has been closed either by script or by the user. Any time you have a script statement that can be triggered after the user has an opportunity to close the window, test for the `closed` property before executing that statement.

As a workaround for Navigator 2, any property of a closed window reference returns a `null` value. Thus, you can test whether, say, the `parent` property of the new window is `null`: If so, the window has already closed. Internet Explorer 3, on the other hand, triggers a scripting error if you attempt to access a property of a closed window — you have no error-free way to detect whether a window is open or closed in Internet Explorer 3.

 On the CD-ROM   Example (with Listing 16-4) on the CD-ROM

Related Items: `window.open()`, `window.close()` methods.

Components
See `appCore`.

controllers
See `appCore`.

crypto
pkcs11

Values: Object References   Read-Only

	NN2	NN3	NN4	NN6	IE3/J1	IE3/J2	IE4	IE5	IE5.5
Compatibility				✓					

The crypto and pkcs11 properties return references to browser objects that are
relevant to internal public-key cryptography mechanisms. These subjects are
beyond the scope of this book, but you can read more about Netscape's efforts on
this front at http://www.mozilla.org/projects/security/.

defaultStatus

Value: String   Read/Write

	NN2	NN3	NN4	NN6	IE3/J1	IE3/J2	IE4	IE5	IE5.5
Compatibility	✓	✓	✓	✓	✓	✓	✓	✓	✓

After a document is loaded into a window or frame, the statusbar's message field
can display a string that is visible any time the mouse pointer is not atop an object
that takes precedence over the statusbar (such as a link object or an image map).
The window.defaultStatus property is normally an empty string, but you can set
this property at any time. Any setting of this property will be temporarily overridden when a user moves the mouse pointer atop a link object (see window.status
property for information about customizing this temporary statusbar message).

Probably the most common time to set the window.defaultStatus property is
when a document loads into a window. You can do this as an immediate script
statement that executes from the Head or Body portion of the document or as part
of a document's onLoad event handler.

Tip   The defaultStatus property does not work well in Navigator 2 or Internet
Explorer 3, and experiences problems in Navigator 3, especially on the Macintosh
(where the property doesn't change even after loading a different document into
the window). Many users simply don't notice the statusbar change during Web
surfing, so don't put mission-critical information in the statusbar.

Example (with Listing 16-5) on the CD-ROM

Related Items: `window.status` property.

dialogArguments

Value: Varies   Read-only

	NN2	NN3	NN4	NN6	IE3/J1	IE3/J2	IE4	IE5	IE5.5
Compatibility							✓	✓	✓

The `dialogArguments` property is available only in a window that is generated by the IE-specific `showModalDialog()` or `showModelessDialog()` methods. Those methods allow a parameter to be passed to the dialog box window, and the `dialogArguments` property lets scripts inside the dialog box window's scripts to access that parameter value. The value can be in the form of a string, number, or JavaScript array (convenient for passing multiple values).

Example on the CD-ROM

Related Items: `window.showModalDialog()`, `window.showModelessDialog()` methods.

dialogHeight
dialogWidth

Value: String   Read/Write

	NN2	NN3	NN4	NN6	IE3/J1	IE3/J2	IE4	IE5	IE5.5
Compatibility							✓	✓	✓

Scripts in a document located inside an IE-specific modal or modeless dialog box (generated by showModalDialog() or showModelessDialog()) can read or modify the height and width of the dialog box window via the dialogHeight and dialogWidth properties. Scripts can access these properties from the main window only for modeless dialog boxes, which remain visible while the user can control the main window contents.

Values for these properties are strings and include the unit of measure, the pixel (px).

Example on the CD-ROM

Related Items: window.dialogLeft, window.dialogTop properties.

dialogLeft
dialogTop

Value: String   Read/Write

	NN2	NN3	NN4	NN6	IE3/J1	IE3/J2	IE4	IE5	IE5.5
Compatibility							✓	✓	✓

Scripts in a document located inside an IE-specific modal or modeless dialog box (generated by showModalDialog() or showModelessDialog()) can read or modify the left and top coordinates of the dialog box window via the dialogLeft and dialogTop properties. Scripts can access these properties from the main window only for modeless dialog boxes, which remain visible while the user can control the main window contents.

Values for these properties are strings and include the unit of measure, the pixel (px). If you attempt to change these values so that any part of the dialog box window would be outside the video monitor, the browser overrides the settings to keep the entire window visible.

Example on the CD-ROM

Related Items: window.dialogHeight, window.dialogTopWidth properties.

```
directories
locationbar
menubar
personalbar
scrollbars
statusbar
toolbar
```

Value: Object   Read/Write (with signed scripts)

	NN2	NN3	NN4	NN6	IE3/J1	IE3/J2	IE4	IE5	IE5.5
Compatibility			✓	✓					

Beyond the rectangle of the content region of a window (where your documents appear), the Netscape browser window displays an amalgam of bars and other features known collectively as *chrome*. All browsers can elect to remove these chrome items when creating a new window (as part of the third parameter of the `window.open()` method), but until signed scripts were available in Navigator 4, these items could not be turned on and off in the main browser window or any existing window.

Navigator 4 promotes these elements to first-class objects contained by the `window` object. Navigator 6 adds one more feature, called the directories bar — a frame-like device that can be opened or hidden from the left edge of the browser window. At the same time, however, NN6 no longer permits hiding and showing the browser window's scrollbars. Figure 16-4 points out where each of the six bars appears in a fully chromed Navigator 4 window. The only element that is not part of this scheme is the window's title bar. You can create a new window without a title bar (with a signed script), but you cannot hide and show the title bar on an existing window.

Chrome objects have but one property: `visible`. Reading this Boolean value (possible without signed scripts) lets you inspect the visitor's browser window for the elements currently engaged. There is no intermediate setting or property for the expanded/collapsed state of the toolbar, locationbar, and personalbar in NN4.

Menubar

Toolbar Locationbar   Personalbar   Statusbar   Scrollbar

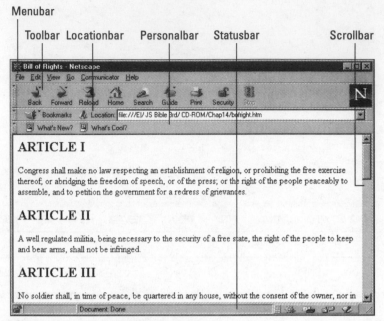

Figure 16-4: Window chrome items

Changing the visibility of these items on the fly alters the relationship between the inner and outer dimensions of the browser window. If you must carefully size a window to display content, you should adjust the chrome elements before sizing the window. Before you start changing chrome visibility before the eyes of your page visitors, weigh the decision carefully. Experienced users have fine-tuned the look of their browser windows to just the way they like them. If you mess with that look, you may anger your visitors. Fortunately, changes you make to a chrome element's visibility are not stored to the user's preferences. However, the changes you make survive an unloading of the page. If you change the settings, be sure you first save the initial settings and restore them with an onUnload event handler.

Tip   The Macintosh menu bar is not part of the browser's window chrome. Therefore, its visibility cannot be adjusted from a script.

On the CD-ROM   Example (with Listing 16-6) on the CD-ROM

Related Items: window.open() method.

document

Value: Object

Read-only

	NN2	NN3	NN4	NN6	IE3/J1	IE3/J2	IE4	IE5	IE5.5
Compatibility	✓	✓	✓	✓	✓	✓	✓	✓	✓

I list the `document` property here primarily for completeness. Each `window` object contains a single `document` object (although in Navigator 4, a window may also contain layers, each of which has a `document` object, as described in Chapter 31). The value of the `document` property is the `document` object, which is not a displayable value. Instead, you use the `document` property as you build references to properties and methods of the document and to other objects contained by the document, such as a form and its elements. To load a different document into a window, use the `location` object (see Chapter 17). The `document` object is described in detail in Chapter 18.

Related Items: `document` object.

event

Value: Object

Read/Write

	NN2	NN3	NN4	NN6	IE3/J1	IE3/J2	IE4	IE5	IE5.5
Compatibility							✓	✓	✓

Only IE4+ treats the `event` object as a property of the `window` object. Navigator 4+ and the W3C DOM pass an instance of the `Event` object as an argument to event handler functions. The connection with the `window` object in IE is relatively inconsequential, because all action involving the `event` object occurs in event handler functions. The only difference is that the object can be treated as a more global object when one event handler function invokes another. Instead of having to pass the `event` object parameter to the next function, IE functions can access the `event` object directly (with or without the `window.` prefix in the reference).

For complete details about the `event` object in all browsers, see Chapter 29.

Related Items: `event` object.

external

Value: Object   Read-only

	NN2	NN3	NN4	NN6	IE3/J1	IE3/J2	IE4	IE5	IE5.5
Compatibility							✓	✓	✓

The external property (not implemented in IE5/Mac) is useful only when the browser window is a component in another application. The property provides a gateway between the current browser window and the application that acts as a host to the browser window component.

With IE4+ acting as a component to the host operating system, the external property can be used to access several methods that influence behaviors outside of the browser. Perhaps the three most useful methods to regular Web page scripters are AddDesktopComponent(), AddFavorite(), and NavigateAndFind(). The first two methods display the same kind of alert dialog box that users get after making these choices from the browser or desktop menus, so that you won't be able to sneak your Web site onto desktops or Favorites listings without the visitor's approval. Table 16-2 describes the parameters for these three methods.

Table 16-2   Popular window.external Object Methods

Method	Description
AddDesktopComponent ("URL", "type"[, left, top, width, height])	Adds a Web site or image to the Active Desktop (if turned on in the user's copy of Windows). The type parameter value is either website or image. Dimensional parameters (optional) are all integer values.
AddFavorite("URL"[, "title"])	Adds the specified URL to the user's Favorites list. The optional title string parameter is how the URL should be listed in the menu (if missing, the URL appears in the list).
NavigateAndFind("URL", "findString", "target")	Navigates to the URL in the first parameter and opens the page in the target frame (an empty string opens in the current frame). The findString is text to be searched for on that page and highlighted when the page loads.

To learn more about the `external` object and how to extend the MS object model, visit `http://msdn.microsoft.com.workshop/browser/overview/Overview.asp#Extending_the_Dynami`.

 On the CD-ROM Example on the CD-ROM

frameElement

Values: FRAME or IFRAME Object Reference   Read-Only

	NN2	NN3	NN4	NN6	IE3/J1	IE3/J2	IE4	IE5	IE5.5
Compatibility									✓

If the current window exists as a result of a `<FRAME>` or `<IFRAME>` tag, the window's `frameElement` property returns a reference to the hosting element. As is made clear in the discussion later in this chapter about the FRAME element object, a reference to a FRAME or IFRAME element object provides access to the properties that echo the attributes of the HTML element object. For a window that is not part of a frameset, the frameElement property returns `null`.

The convenience of this property becomes apparent when a single document is loaded into multiple framesets. A script in the document can still refer to the containing FRAME element, even when the ID of the element changes from one frameset to another. The FRAMESET element is also accessible via the `parentElement` property of the `frameElement` property:

```
var frameSetObj = self.frameElement.parentElement
```

A reference to the FRAMESET element opens possibilities of adjusting frame sizes.

Related Items: FRAME, IFRAME objects.

frames

Value: Array   Read-only

	NN2	NN3	NN4	NN6	IE3/J1	IE3/J2	IE4	IE5	IE5.5
Compatibility	✓	✓	✓	✓	✓	✓	✓	✓	✓

In a multiframe window, the top or parent window contains any number of separate frames, each of which acts as a full-fledged `window` object. The `frames` property (note the plural use of the word as a property name) plays a role when a statement must reference an object located in a different frame. For example, if a button in one frame is scripted to load a document in another frame, the button's event handler must be able to tell JavaScript precisely where to display the new HTML document. The `frames` property assists in that task.

To use the `frames` property to communicate from one frame to another, it should be part of a reference that begins with the `parent` or `top` property. This lets JavaScript make the proper journey through the hierarchy of all currently loaded objects to reach the desired object. To find out how many frames are currently active in a window, use this expression:

```
parent.frames.length
```

This expression returns a number indicating how many frames the parent window defines. This value does not, however, count further nested frames, should a third generation of frame be defined in the environment. In other words, no single property exists that you can use to determine the total number of frames in the browser window if multiple generations of frames are present.

The browser stores information about all visible frames in a numbered (indexed) array, with the first frame (that is, the topmost <FRAME> tag defined in the framesetting document) as number 0:

```
parent.frames[0]
```

Therefore, if the window shows three frames (whose indexes are `frames[0]`, `frames[1]`, and `frames[2]`, respectively), the reference for retrieving the `title` property of the document in the second frame is

```
parent.frames[1].document.title
```

This reference is a road map that starts at the parent window and extends to the second frame's document and its `title` property. Other than the number of frames defined in a parent window and each frame's name (`top.frames[i].name`), no other values from the frame definitions are directly available from the frame object via scripting until you get to IE4 and NN6 (see the FRAME element object later in this chapter). In these browsers, individual FRAME element objects have several properties that reveal <FRAME> tag attributes.

Using index values for frame references is not always the safest tactic, however, because your frameset design may change over time, in which case the index values will also change. Instead, you should take advantage of the NAME attribute of the <FRAME> tag, and assign a unique, descriptive name to each frame. A value you assign to the NAME attribute is also the name that you use for TARGET attributes of links to force a linked page to load in a frame other than the one containing the link. You can use a frame's name as an alternative to the indexed reference. For example, in Listing 16-7, two frames are assigned distinctive names. To access the title of a document in the JustAKid2 frame, the complete object reference is

```
parent.JustAKid2.document.title
```

with the frame name (case-sensitive) substituting for the frames[1] array reference. Or, in keeping with JavaScript flexibility, you can use the object name in the array index position:

```
parent.frames["JustAKid2"].document.title
```

The supreme advantage to using frame names in references is that no matter how the frameset structure may change over time, a reference to a named frame will always find that frame, although its index value (that is, position in the frameset) may change.

On the CD-ROM

Example (with Figure 16-5 and Listings 16-7 and 16-8) on the CD-ROM

Related Items: frame, frameset objects; window.parent, window.top properties.

history

Value: Object   Read-only

	NN2	NN3	NN4	NN6	IE3/J1	IE3/J2	IE4	IE5	IE5.5
Compatibility	✓	✓	✓	✓	✓	✓	✓	✓	✓

See the discussion of the history object in Chapter 17.

```
innerHeight
innerWidth
outerHeight
outerWidth
```

Value: Integer   Read/Write

	NN2	NN3	NN4	NN6	IE3/J1	IE3/J2	IE4	IE5	IE5.5
Compatibility			✓	✓					

Navigator 4+ lets scripts adjust the height and width of any window, including the main browser window by setting properties (NN4+ and IE4+ have methods that also resize the browser window). This adjustment can be helpful when your page shows itself best with the browser window sized to a particular height and width. Rather than relying on the user to size the browser window for optimum viewing of your page, you can dictate the size of the window (although the user can always manually resize the main window). And because you can examine the operating system of the visitor via the navigator object (see Chapter 28), you can size a window to adjust for the differences in font and form element rendering on different platforms.

Netscape provides two different points of reference for measuring the height and width of a window: inner and outer. Both are measured in pixels. The inner measurements are that of the active document area of a window (sometimes known as a window's content region). If the optimum display of your document depends on the document display area being a certain number of pixels high and/or wide, the innerHeight and innerWidth properties are the ones to set.

In contrast, the outer measurements are of the outside boundary of the entire window, including whatever chrome is showing in the window: scrollbars, statusbar, and so on. Setting the outerHeight and outerWidth is generally done in concert with a reading of screen object properties (Chapter 28). Perhaps the most common usage of the outer properties is to set the browser window to fill the available screen area of the visitor's monitor.

A more efficient way of modifying both outer dimensions of a window is with the window.resizeTo() method, which is also available in IE4+. The method takes pixel width and height (as integer values) as parameters, thus accomplishing a window resizing in one statement. Be aware that resizing a window does not adjust the location of a window. Therefore, just because you set the outer dimensions of a window to the available space returned by the screen object doesn't mean that the window will suddenly fill the available space on the monitor. Application of the window.moveTo() method is necessary to ensure the top-left corner of the window is at screen coordinates 0,0.

Despite the freedom that these properties afford the page author, Netscape has built in a minimum size limitation for scripts that are not cryptographically signed. You cannot set these properties such that the outer height and width of the window is smaller than 100 pixels on a side. This limitation is to prevent an unsigned script from setting up a small or nearly invisible window that monitors activity in other windows. With signed scripts, however, windows can be made smaller than 100×100 pixels with the user's permission. IE4+ maintains a smaller minimum size to prevent resizing a window to zero size.

On the CD-ROM Example (with Listing 16-9) on the CD-ROM

Related Items: window.resizeTo(), window.moveTo() methods; screen object; navigator object.

loading

Value: Boolean   Read-only

	NN2	NN3	NN4	NN6	IE3/J1	IE3/J2	IE4	IE5	IE5.5
Compatibility			✓						

This NN4-specific property allows you to query whether the window is still loading content. The property returns true if the page is still loading and false if the page has completed loading all of its content.

location

Value: Object   Read/Write

	NN2	NN3	NN4	NN6	IE3/J1	IE3/J2	IE4	IE5	IE5.5
Compatibility	✓	✓	✓	✓	✓	✓	✓	✓	✓

See the discussion of the location object in Chapter 17.

locationbar

See `directories`.

name

Value: String   Read/Write

	NN2	NN3	NN4	NN6	IE3/J1	IE3/J2	IE4	IE5	IE5.5
Compatibility	✓	✓	✓	✓	✓	✓	✓	✓	✓

All `window` objects can have names assigned to them. Names are particularly useful for working with frames, because a good naming scheme for a multiframe environment can help you determine precisely which frame you're working with in references coming from other frames.

The main browser window, however, has no name attached to it by default. Its value is an empty string. There aren't many reasons to assign a name to the window, because JavaScript and HTML provide plenty of other ways to refer to the `window` object (the `top` property, the `_top` constant for `TARGET` attributes, and the `opener` property from subwindows).

If you want to attach a name to the main window, you can do so by setting the `window.name` property at any time. But be aware that because this is one window property whose life extends beyond the loading and unloading of any given document, chances are that your scripts would use the reference in only one document or frameset. Unless you restore the default empty string, your programmed window name will be present for any other document that loads later. My suggestion in this regard is to assign a name in a window's or frameset's `onLoad` event handler, and then reset it to empty in a corresponding `onUnload` event handler:

```
<BODY onLoad="self.name = 'Main'"  onUnload="self.name = ''">
```

You can see an example of this application in Listing 16-16, where setting a parent window name is helpful for learning the relationships among parent and child windows.

Related Items: `top` property; `window.open()`, `window.sizeToContent()` methods.

navigator

Value: Object   Read-only

	NN2	NN3	NN4	NN6	IE3/J1	IE3/J2	IE4	IE5	IE5.5
Compatibility				✓			✓	✓	✓

Although the navigator object appears as a property of the window object only in the most recent browsers, the navigator object has been around since the very beginning (see Chapter 28). In previous browsers, the navigator object was referenced as a standalone object. And because you can omit any reference to the window object for a window object's properties, you can use the same window-less reference syntax for compatibility across all scriptable browsers (at least for the navigator object properties that exist across all browsers). That's the way I recommend referring to the navigator object.

Example on the CD-ROM

Related Items: navigator object.

offscreenBuffering

Value: Boolean or String   Read/Write

	NN2	NN3	NN4	NN6	IE3/J1	IE3/J2	IE4	IE5	IE5.5
Compatibility							✓	✓	✓

Internet Explorer 4+ (for Win32 platforms) by default initially renders a page in a buffer (a chunk of memory) before it is blasted to the video screen. You can control this behavior explicitly by modifying the window.offscreenBuffering property.

The default value of the property is the string auto. You can also assign Boolean true or false to the property to override IE's normal automatic handling of this behavior.

Example on the CD-ROM

onerror

Value: Function   Read/Write

	NN2	NN3	NN4	NN6	IE3/J1	IE3/J2	IE4	IE5	IE5.5
Compatibility		✓	✓	✓			✓	✓	✓

The `onerror` property is an exception to the rule of this book to not describe event handlers as properties within object reference sections. The reason is that the `onError` event brings along some special properties that are useful to control by setting the event handler property in scripts.

Recent browsers (IE5+ and NN4+) are designed to prevent script errors from being intrusive if a user encounters a script error while loading or interacting with a page. Even so, even the subtle hints about problems (messages or icons in the statusbar) can be confusing for users who have no idea what JavaScript is. JavaScript lets you turn off the display of script error windows or messages as someone executes a script on your page. The question is: When should you turn off these messages?

Script errors generally mean that something is wrong with your script. The error may be the result of a coding mistake or, conceivably, a bug in JavaScript (perhaps on a platform version of the browser that you haven't been able to test). If such errors occur, often the script won't continue to do what you intended. Hiding the script error from yourself during development would be foolhardy, because you'd never know whether unseen errors are lurking in your code. It can be equally dangerous to turn off error dialog boxes for users who may believe that the page is operating normally, when, in fact, it's not. Some data values may not be calculated or displayed correctly.

That said, I can see some limited instances of when you may want to keep such dialog box windows from appearing. For example, if you know for a fact that a platform-specific bug trips the error message without harming the execution of the script, you may want to prevent that error alert dialog box from appearing in the files posted to your Web site. You should do this only after extensive testing to ensure that the script ultimately behaves correctly, even with the bug or error.

Note   IE fires the `onError` event handler only for runtime errors. This means that if you have a syntactical error in your script that trips the browser as the page loads, the `onError` event doesn't fire, and you cannot trap that error message. Moreover, if the user has the IE script debugger installed, any code you use to prevent browser error messages from appearing will not work.

When the browser starts, the `window.onerror` property is `<undefined>`. In this state, all errors are reported via the normal JavaScript error window or message. To turn off error alerts, set the `window.onerror` property to invoke a function that does absolutely nothing:

```
function doNothing() {return true}
window.onerror = doNothing
```

To restore the error messages, reload the page.

You can, however, also assign a custom function to the `window.onerror` property. This function then handles errors in a more friendly way under your script control. Whenever error messages are turned on (the default behavior), a script error (or Java applet or class exception) invokes the function assigned to the `onerror` property, passing three parameters:

✦ Error message

✦ URL of document causing the error

✦ Line number of the error

You can essentially trap for all errors and handle them with your own interface (or no user notification at all). The last statement of this function must be `return true` if you do not want the JavaScript script error message to appear.

Note
NN6 does not pass error-related parameters to a function invoked by `onError`. This may be an attempt to lure scripters to the more modern `try-catch` error trapping mechanism (see Chapter 39). But it means that NN6 cannot take complete advantage of older error reporting code, including that shown in Listing 16-10.

If you are using LiveConnect to communicate with a Java applet or (in NN3+) to call up Java class methods directly from your scripts, you can use the same scheme to handle any exception that Java may throw. A Java exception is not necessarily a mistake kind of error: Some methods assume that the Java code will trap for exceptions to handle special cases (for example, reacting to a user's denial of access when prompted by a signed script dialog box). See Chapter 44 for an example of trapping for a specific Java exception. Also, see Chapter 39 for JavaScript exception handling introduced for W3C DOM-compatible browsers.

On the CD-ROM
Example (with Figure 16-6 and Listing 16-10) on the CD-ROM

Related Items: `location.reload()` method; JavaScript exception handling (Chapter 39); debugging scripts (Chapter 45).

opener

Value: Window object reference   Read/Write

	NN2	NN3	NN4	NN6	IE3/J1	IE3/J2	IE4	IE5	IE5.5
Compatibility		✓	✓	✓	✓	✓	✓	✓	✓

Many scripters make the mistake of thinking that a new browser window created with the window.open() method has a child–parent relationship similar to the one that frames have with their parents. That's not the case at all. New browser windows, once created, have a very slim link to the window from whence they came: via the opener property. The purpose of the opener property is to provide scripts in the new window with valid references back to the original window. For example, the original window may contain some variable values or general-purpose functions that a new window at this Web site wants to use. The original window may also have form elements whose settings are either of value to the new window or get set by user interaction in the new window.

Because the value of the opener property is a reference to a genuine window object, you can begin references with the property name. Or, you may use the more complete window.opener or self.opener reference. But the reference must then include some object or property of that original window, such as a window method or a reference to something contained by that window's document.

Although this property was new for Navigator 3 (and was one of the rare Navigator 3 features to be included in Internet Explorer 3), you can make your scripts backward compatible to Navigator 2. For every new window you create, make sure it has an opener property as follows:

```
var newWind = window.open()
if (newWind.opener == null) {
    newWind.opener = self
}
```

For Navigator 2, this step adds the opener property to the window object reference. Then, no matter which version of JavaScript-enabled Navigator the user has, the opener property in the new window's scripts points to the desired original window.

If a subwindow opens yet another subwindow, the chain is still valid, albeit one step longer. The third window can reach the main window with a reference that begins:

```
opener.opener....
```

It's a good idea for the third window to store in a global variable the value of `opener.opener` while the page loads. Thus, if the user closes the second window, the variable can be used to start a reference to the main window.

When a script that generates a new window is within a frame, the `opener` property of the subwindow points to that frame. Therefore, if the subwindow needs to communicate with the main window's parent or another frame in the main window, you have to very carefully build a reference to that distant object. For example, if the subwindow needs to get the `checked` property of a checkbox in a sister frame of the one that created the subwindow, the reference is

`opener.parent.`*`sisterFrameName`*`.document.`*`formName`*`.`*`checkboxName`*`.checked`

It is a long way to go, indeed, but building such a reference is always a case of mapping out the path from where the script is to where the destination is, step-by-step.

On the CD-ROM   Example (with Figure 16-7 and Listings 16-11 and 16-12) on the CD-ROM

Related Items: `window.open()`, `window.focus()` methods.

outerHeight
outerWidth

See `innerHeight` and `innerWidth`, earlier.

pageXOffset
pageYOffset

Value: Integer   Read-only

	NN2	NN3	NN4	NN6	IE3/J1	IE3/J2	IE4	IE5	IE5.5
Compatibility			✓	✓					

The top-left corner of the content (inner) region of the browser window is an important geographical point for scrolling documents. When a document is scrolled all the way to the top and flush left in the window (or when a document is small enough to fill the browser window without displaying scrollbars), the document's location is said to be 0,0, meaning zero pixels from the top and zero pixels from the left. If you were to scroll the document, some other coordinate point of the document would be under that top-left corner. That measure is called the page offset, and the `pageXOffset` and `pageYOffset` properties let you read the pixel value of the document at the inner window's top-left corner: `pageXOffset` is the horizontal offset, and `pageYOffset` is the vertical offset.

The value of these measures becomes clear if you design navigation buttons in your pages to carefully control paging of content being displayed in the window. For example, you might have a two-frame page in which one of the frames features navigation controls, while the other displays the primary content. The navigation controls take the place of scrollbars, which, for aesthetic reasons, are turned off in the display frame. Scripts connected to the simulated scrolling buttons can determine the `pageYOffset` value of the document, and then use the `window.scrollTo()` method to position the document precisely to the next logical division in the document for viewing.

IE4+ has corresponding values as `body` object properties: `body.scrollLeft` and `body.scrollTop` (see Chapter 18).

 On the CD-ROM   Example (with Listing 16-13) on the CD-ROM

Related Items: `window.innerHeight`, `window.innerWidth`, `body.scrollLeft`, `body.scrollTop` properties; `window.scrollBy()`, `window.scrollTo()` methods.

parent

Value: Window object reference   Read-only

	NN2	NN3	NN4	NN6	IE3/J1	IE3/J2	IE4	IE5	IE5.5
Compatibility	✓	✓	✓	✓	✓	✓	✓	✓	✓

The `parent` property (and the `top` property that follows later in this section) comes into play primarily when a document is to be displayed as part of a multiframe window. The HTML documents that users see in the frames of a multiframe browser window are distinct from the document that specifies the frameset for the entire window. That document, though still in the browser's memory (and appearing as the URL in the location field of the browser), is not otherwise visible to the user (except in the Source View).

If scripts in your visible documents need to reference objects or properties of the frameset window, you can reference those frameset window items with the `parent` property (do not, however, expand the reference by preceding it with the `window` object, as in `window.parent.`*`propertyName`*, as this causes problems in early browsers). In a way, the `parent` property seems to violate the object hierarchy because, from a single frame's document, the property points to a level seemingly higher in precedence. If you didn't specify the `parent` property or instead specified the `self` property from one of these framed documents, the object reference is to the frame only, rather than to the outermost framesetting `window` object.

A nontraditional but perfectly legal way to use the `parent` object is as a means of storing temporary variables. Thus, you could set up a holding area for individual variable values or even an array of data. These values can then be shared among all documents loaded into the frames, including when documents change inside the frames. You have to be careful, however, when storing data in the parent on the fly (that is in response to user action in the frames). Variables can revert to their default values (that is, the values set by the parent's own script) if the user resizes the window in early browsers.

A child window can also call a function defined in the parent window. The reference for such a function is

```
parent.functionName([parameters])
```

At first glance, it may seem as though the `parent` and `top` properties point to the same framesetting `window` object. In an environment consisting of one frameset window and its immediate children, that's true. But if one of the child windows was, itself, another framesetting window, then you wind up with three generations of windows. From the point of view of the "youngest" child (for example, a window defined by the second frameset), the `parent` property points to its immediate parent, whereas the `top` property points to the first framesetting window in this chain.

On the other hand, a new window created via the `window.open()` method has no parent–child relationship to the original window. The new window's `top` and `parent` point to that new window. You can read more about these relationships in the "Frames" section earlier in this chapter.

 Example (with Figure 16-8 and Listings 16-14 and 16-15) on the CD-ROM

Related Items: `window.frames`, `window.self`, `window.top` properties.

`personalbar`

See `directories`.

returnValue

Value: Any data type   Read/Write

	NN2	NN3	NN4	NN6	IE3/J1	IE3/J2	IE4	IE5	IE5.5
Compatibility							✓	✓	✓

Scripts use the returnValue property in a document that loads into the IE-specific modal dialog box. A modal dialog box is generated via the showModalDialog() method, which returns whatever data has been assigned to the returnValue property of the dialog box window before it closes. This is possible because script processing in the main window freezes while the modal dialog box is visible. As the dialog box closes, a value can be returned to the main window's script right where the modal dialog box was invoked, and the main window's script resumes executing statements.

On the CD-ROM   Example on the CD-ROM

Related Items: showModalDialog() method.

screen

Value: screen Object   Read-only

	NN2	NN3	NN4	NN6	IE3/J1	IE3/J2	IE4	IE5	IE5.5
Compatibility				✓			✓	✓	✓

Although the screen object appears as a property of the window object only in the most recent browsers, the screen object is also available in NN4 (see Chapter 28), but as a standalone object. Because you can omit any reference to the window object for a window object's properties, the same window-less reference syntax can be used for compatibility across all browsers that support the screen object. That's the way I recommend referring to the screen object.

Example

See Chapter 28 for examples of using the screen object to determine the video monitor characteristics of the computer running the browser.

Related Items: screen object.

screenLeft
screenTop

Value: Integer   Read-only

	NN2	NN3	NN4	NN6	IE3/J1	IE3/J2	IE4	IE5	IE5.5
Compatibility								✓	✓

IE5+ (but not IE5/Mac) provides the screenLeft and screenTop properties of the window object to let you read the pixel position (relative to the top-left 0,0 coordinate of the video monitor) of what Microsoft calls the *client area* of the browser window. The client area excludes most window chrome, such as the title bar, address bar, and the window sizing bar. Therefore, when the IE5 browser window is maximized (meaning that no sizing bars are exposed), the screenLeft property of the window is 0, while the screenTop property varies depending on the combination of toolbars the user has elected to display. For non-maximized windows, if the window has been positioned so that the top and/or left part of the client area are out of view, their property values will be negative integers.

These two properties are read-only. You can position the browser window via the window.moveTo() and window.moveBy() methods, but these methods position the top-left corner of the entire browser window, not the client area. IE browsers, through Version 5.5, do not provide properties for the position of the entire browser window.

Example on the CD-ROM

Related Items: window.moveTo(), window.moveBy() methods.

screenX
screenY

Value: Integer   Read/Write

	NN2	NN3	NN4	NN6	IE3/J1	IE3/J2	IE4	IE5	IE5.5
Compatibility				✓					

NN6 provides the `screenX` and `screenY` properties to read the position of the outer boundary of the browser window relative to the top-left coordinates (0,0) of the video monitor. The browser window includes the four-pixel wide window sizing bars that surround Win32 windows. Therefore, when the NN6/Win32 browser window is maximized, the values for both `screenX` and `screenY` are `-4`. Netscape does not provide the equivalent measures of the browser window client area as found in the `screenLeft` and `screenTop` properties of IE5. You can, however, find out if various toolbars are visible in the browser window (see `window.directories`).

Both properties can be changed by script to alter the location of the window, but the `window.moveTo()` and `window.moveBy()` methods are more convenient, because only one statement is needed to handle both coordinates.

Example on the CD-ROM

Related Items: `window.moveTo()`, `window.moveBy()` methods.

scrollbars

See `directories`.

scrollX
scrollY

Value: Integer   Read-Only

	NN2	NN3	NN4	NN6	IE3/J1	IE3/J2	IE4	IE5	IE5.5
Compatibility				✓					

The NN6 `scrollX` and `scrollY` properties let you determine the horizontal and vertical scrolling of a window. Scrolling is possible only if the window displays scrollbars along the desired axis. Values are pixel integers.

While the IE DOM does not provide similar properties for the window, the same information can be derived from the `body.scrollLeft` and `body.scrollTop` properties.

Example on the CD-ROM

Related Items: `body.scrollLeft`, `body.scrollTop` properties.

self

Value: Window object reference   Read-only

	NN2	NN3	NN4	NN6	IE3/J1	IE3/J2	IE4	IE5	IE5.5
Compatibility	✓	✓	✓	✓	✓	✓	✓	✓	✓

Just as the `window` object reference is optional, so too is the `self` property when the object reference points to the same window as the one containing the reference. In what may seem to be an unusual construction, the `self` property represents the same object as the `window`. For instance, to obtain the title of the document in a single-frame window, you can use any of the following three constructions:

```
window.document.title
self.document.title
document.title
```

Although `self` is a property of a window, you should not combine the references within a single-frame window script (for example, don't begin a reference with `window.self`, which has been known to cause numerous scripting problems). Specifying the `self` property, though optional for single-frame windows, can help make an object reference crystal clear to someone reading your code (and to you, for that matter). Multiple-frame windows are where you need to pay particular attention to this property.

JavaScript is pretty smart about references to a statement's own window. Therefore, you can generally omit the `self` part of a reference to a same-window document element. But when you intend to display a document in a multiframe window, complete references (including the `self` prefix) to an object make it much easier on anyone who reads or debugs your code to track who is doing what to whom. You are free to retrieve the `self` property of any window. The value that comes back is a `window` object reference.

 On the CD-ROM Example (with Listing 16-16) on the CD-ROM

Related Items: `window.frames`, `window.parent`, `window.top` properties.

sidebar

See `appCore`.

status

Value: String   Read/Write

	NN2	NN3	NN4	NN6	IE3/J1	IE3/J2	IE4	IE5	IE5.5
Compatibility	✓	✓	✓	✓	✓	✓	✓	✓	✓

At the bottom of the browser window is a statusbar. Part of that bar includes an area that normally discloses the document loading progress or the URL of a link that the mouse is pointing to at any given instant. You can control the temporary content of that field by assigning a text string to the window object's status property (Figure 16-9). You should adjust the status property only in response to events that have a temporary effect, such as a link or image map area object's onMouseOver event handler. When the status property is set in this situation, it overrides any other setting in the statusbar. If the user then moves the mouse pointer away from the object that changes the statusbar, the bar returns to its default setting (which may be empty on some pages).

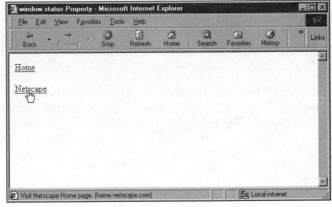

Figure 16-9: The statusbar can be set to display a custom message when the pointer rolls over a link.

Use this window property as a friendlier alternative to displaying the URL of a link as a user rolls the mouse around the page. For example, if you'd rather use the statusbar to explain the nature of the destination of a link, put that text into the statusbar in response to the onMouseOver event handler. But be aware that experienced Web surfers like to see URLs down there. Therefore, consider creating a hybrid message for the statusbar that includes both a friendly description followed by the URL in parentheses. In multiframe environments, you can set the `window.status` property without having to worry about referencing the individual frame.

On the CD-ROM Example (with Listings 16-17, 16-18, and 16-19) on the CD-ROM

Related Items: `window.defaultStatus` property; `onMouseOver`, `onMouseOut` event handlers; `link` object.

statusbar
toolbar

See `locationbar`.

top

Value: Window object refererence   Read-only

	NN2	NN3	NN4	NN6	IE3/J1	IE3/J2	IE4	IE5	IE5.5
Compatibility	✓	✓	✓	✓	✓	✓	✓	✓	✓

The `window` object's `top` property refers to the topmost window in the document object hierarchy. For a single-frame window, the reference is to the same object as the window itself (including the `self` and `parent` properties), so do not include `window` as part of the reference. In a multiframe window, the top window is the one that defines the first frameset (in case of nested framesets). Users don't ever really see the top window in a multiframe environment, but the browser stores it as an object in its memory. The reason is that the top window has the road map to the other frames (if one frame should need to reference an object in a different frame), and its children frames can call upon it. Such a reference looks like

```
top.functionName([parameters])
```

For more about the distinction between the `top` and `parent` properties, see the in-depth discussion about scripting frames at the beginning of this chapter. See also the example of the `parent` property for listings that demonstrate the values of the `top` property.

Related Items: `window.frames`, `window.self`, `window.parent` properties.

window

Value: Window object   Read-only

	NN2	NN3	NN4	NN6	IE3/J1	IE3/J2	IE4	IE5	IE5.5
Compatibility	✓	✓	✓	✓	✓	✓	✓	✓	✓

Listing the `window` property as a separate property may be more confusing than helpful. The `window` property is the same object as the `window` object. You do not need to use a reference that begins with `window.window`. Although the `window` object is assumed for many references, you can use `window` as part of a reference to items in the same window or frame as the script statement that makes that reference. You should not, however, use `window` as a part of a reference involving items higher up in the hierarchy (`top` or `parent`).

Methods

alert("*message*")

Returns: Nothing.

	NN2	NN3	NN4	NN6	IE3/J1	IE3/J2	IE4	IE5	IE5.5
Compatibility	✓	✓	✓	✓	✓	✓	✓	✓	✓

An alert dialog box is a modal window that presents a message to the user with a single OK button to dismiss the dialog box. As long as the alert dialog box is showing, no other application or window can be made active. The user must dismiss the dialog box before proceeding with any more work in the browser.

The single parameter to the `alert()` method can be a value of any data type, including representations of some unusual data types whose values you don't normally work with in JavaScript (such as complete objects). This makes the alert dialog box a handy tool for debugging JavaScript scripts. Anytime you want to monitor the value of an expression, use that expression as the parameter to a temporary `alert()` method in your code. The script proceeds to that point and then stops to show you the value. (See Chapter 45 for more tips on debugging scripts.)

What is often disturbing to application designers is that all JavaScript-created modal dialog boxes (via the `alert()`, `confirm()`, and `prompt()` methods) identify themselves as being generated by JavaScript or the browser. The look is particularly annoying in browsers before NN4 and IE4, because the wording appears directly in the dialog box's content area, rather than in the title bar of the dialog box. The purpose of this identification is to act as a security precaution against unscrupulous scripters who might try to spoof system or browser alert dialog boxes, inviting a user to reveal passwords or other private information. These identifying words cannot be overwritten or eliminated by your scripts. You can simulate a modal dialog box window in a cross-browser fashion (see an article at `http://developer.netscape.com/viewsource/goodman_modal/goodman_modal.html`), but it is not as robust as a genuine modal window, which you can create in IE4+ via the `window.showModalDialog()` method.

Because the `alert()` method is of a global nature (that is, no particular frame in a multiframe environment derives any benefit from laying claim to the alert dialog box), a common practice is to omit all `window` object references from the statement that calls the method. Restrict the use of alert dialog boxes in your HTML documents and site designs. The modality of the windows is disruptive to the flow of a user's navigation around your pages. Communicate with users via forms or by writing to separate document window frames.

Example (with Figure 16-10 and Listing 16-20) on the CD-ROM

Related Items: `window.confirm()`, `window.prompt()` methods.

back()
forward()

Returns: Nothing.

	NN2	NN3	NN4	NN6	IE3/J1	IE3/J2	IE4	IE5	IE5.5
Compatibility			✓	✓					

The purpose of the `window.back()` and `window.forward()` methods in NN4 is to offer a scripted version of the global back and forward navigation buttons, while allowing the `history` object to control navigation strictly within a particular window or frame—as it should. These window methods did not catch on in IE (and the `window` object is out of the scope of the W3C DOM Level 2), so you are better off staying with the history object's methods for navigating through browser history. For more information about version compatibility and the back and forward navigation, see the history object in Chapter 17.

On the CD-ROM   Example on the CD-ROM

Related Items: history.back(), history.forward(), history.go() methods.

captureEvents(*eventTypeList*)

Returns: Nothing.

	NN2	NN3	NN4	NN6	IE3/J1	IE3/J2	IE4	IE5	IE5.5
Compatibility			✓						

In Navigator 4, an event filters down from the window object and eventually reaches its intended target. For example, if you click a button, the click event first reaches the window object; then it goes to the document object; and eventually (in a split second) it reaches the button, where an onClick event handler is ready to act on that click.

The NN4 "trickle-down" event propagation mechanism allows window, document, and layer objects to intercept events and process them prior to reaching their intended targets (or preventing them from reaching their destinations entirely). But for one of these outer containers to grab an event, your script must instruct it to capture the type of event your application is interested in preprocessing. If you want the window object to intercept all events of a particular type, use the window.captureEvents() method to turn that facility on.

Note   NN6 (and future browsers that implement the W3C DOM event model) has both a trickle-down and bubble-up event model combination. The syntax for using event capture in NN6 is quite different from that in NN4. The discussions of the captureEvents(), releaseEvents(), handleEvent(), and routeEvent() methods of the window, document, and layer objects apply only to Navigator 4. If your DHTML page design does not need to support NN4, you can skip these discussions.

The window.captureEvents() method takes one or more event types as parameters. An event type is a constant value built inside the Navigator 4 Event object. One event type exists for every kind of event handler you see in all of the

Navigator 4 document objects. The syntax is the event object name (`Event`) and the event name in all uppercase letters. For example, if you want the window to intercept all click events, the statement is

```
window.captureEvents(Event.CLICK)
```

For multiple events, add them as parameters, separated by the pipe (|) character:

```
window.captureEvents(Event.MOUSEDOWN | Event.KEYPRESS)
```

After an event type is captured by the `window` object, a function must be ready to deal with the event. For example, perhaps the function looks through all `Event.MOUSEDOWN` events and looks to see if the right mouse button was the one that triggered the event and what form element (if any) is the intended target. The goal is to perhaps display a pop-up menu (as a separate layer) for a right-click. If the click comes from the left mouse button, the event is routed to its intended target.

To associate a function with a particular event type captured by a `window` object, assign a function to the event. For example, to assign a custom `doClickEvent()` function to `click` events captured by the `window` object, use the following statement:

```
window.onclick=doClickEvent
```

Note that the function name is assigned only as a reference name (no quotes or parentheses), not like an event handler within a tag. The function itself is like any function, but it has the added benefit of automatically receiving an instance of the `Event` object as a parameter. To turn off event capture for one or more event types, use the `window.releaseEvent()` method.

Note   Capturing events at the `window`, `document`, or layer level in NN4 does not always work the way you might like. This is especially true if your page contains tables. For example, capturing mouse events has no effect in the Windows version of NN4 unless the cursor is atop a cell border. Event capture works most reliably when a scriptable object has an event handler defined for it (even if it is an empty string) and the element is the target of the event (for example, you are about to type into a text field). For all other elements, events may simply not be captured at the document or window level.

On the CD-ROM   Example (with Listing 16-21) on the CD-ROM

Related Items: `window.disableExternalCapture()`, `window.enableExternalCapture()`, `window.handleEvent()`, `window.releaseEvents()`, `window.routeEvent()` methods.

clearInterval(*intervalIDnumber*)

Returns: Nothing.

	NN2	NN3	NN4	NN6	IE3/J1	IE3/J2	IE4	IE5	IE5.5
Compatibility			✓	✓			✓	✓	✓

Use the `window.clearInterval()` method to turn off an interval loop action started with the `window.setInterval()` method. The parameter is the ID number returned by the `setInterval()` method. A common application for the JavaScript interval mechanism is animation of an object on a page. If you have multiple intervals running, each has its own ID value in memory. You can turn off any interval by its ID value. As soon as an interval loop stops, your script cannot resume that interval: It must start a new one, which generates a new ID value.

On the CD-ROM Example on the CD-ROM

Related Items: `window.setInterval()`, `window.setTimeout()`, `window.clearTimeout()` methods.

clearTimeout(*timeoutIDnumber*)

Returns: Nothing.

	NN2	NN3	NN4	NN6	IE3/J1	IE3/J2	IE4	IE5	IE5.5
Compatibility	✓	✓	✓	✓	✓	✓	✓	✓	✓

Use the `window.clearTimeout()` method in concert with the `window.setTimeout()` method, as described later in this chapter, when you want your script to cancel a timer that is waiting to run its expression. The parameter for this method is the ID number that the `window.setTimeout()` method returns when the timer starts ticking. The `clearTimeout()` method cancels the specified timeout. A good practice is to check your code for instances where user action may negate the need for a running timer — and to stop that timer before it goes off.

Example (with Figure 16-11 and Listing 16-22) on the CD-ROM

Related Items: `window.setTimeout()` method.

close()

Returns: Nothing.

	NN2	NN3	NN4	NN6	IE3/J1	IE3/J2	IE4	IE5	IE5.5
Compatibility	✓	✓	✓	✓	✓	✓	✓	✓	✓

The `window.close()` method closes the browser window referenced by the `window` object. Most likely, you will use this method to close subwindows created from a main document window. If the call to close the window comes from a window other than the new subwindow, the original `window` object must maintain a record of the subwindow object. You accomplish this by storing the value returned from the `window.open()` method in a global variable that will be available to other objects later (for example, a variable not initialized inside a function). If, on the other hand, an object inside the new subwindow calls the `window.close()` method, the `window` or `self` reference is sufficient.

Be sure to include a window as part of the reference to this method. Failure to do so may cause JavaScript to regard the statement as a `document.close()` method, which has different behavior (see Chapter 18). Only the `window.close()` method can close the window via a script. Closing a window, of course, forces the window to trigger an `onUnload` event handler before the window disappears from view; but after you've initiated the `window.close()` method, you cannot stop it from completing its task. Moreover, `onUnload` event handlers that attempt to execute time-consuming processes (such as submitting a form in the closing window) may not complete because the window can easily close before the process completes — a behavior that has no workaround (with the exception of the `onBeforeUnload` event handler in IE4+).

While I'm on the subject of closing windows, a special case exists when a subwindow tries to close the main window (via a statement such as `self.opener.close()`) when the main window has more than one entry in its session history. As a safety precaution against scripts closing windows they did not create, NN3+ and IE4+ ask the user whether he or she wants the main window to close (via a browser-generated dialog box). This security precaution cannot be overridden except in NN4+ via a signed script when the user grants permission to control the browser (Chapter 46).

Example on the CD-ROM

Related Items: `window.open()`, `document.close()` methods.

confirm("*message*")

Returns: Boolean.

	NN2	NN3	NN4	NN6	IE3/J1	IE3/J2	IE4	IE5	IE5.5
Compatibility	✓	✓	✓	✓	✓	✓	✓	✓	✓

A confirm dialog box presents a message in a modal dialog box along with OK and Cancel buttons. Such a dialog box can be used to ask a question of the user, usually prior to a script performing actions that will not be undoable. Querying a user about proceeding with typical Web navigation in response to user interaction on a form element is generally a disruptive waste of the user's time and attention. But for operations that may reveal a user's identity or send form data to a server, a JavaScript confirm dialog box may make a great deal of sense. Users can also accidentally click buttons, so you should provide avenues for backing out of an operation before it executes.

Because this dialog box returns a Boolean value (OK = `true`; Cancel = `false`), you can use this method as a comparison expression or as an assignment expression. In a comparison expression, you nest the method within any other statement where a Boolean value is required. For example:

```
if (confirm("Are you sure?")) {
    alert("OK")
} else {
    alert("Not OK")
}
```

Here, the returned value of the confirm dialog box provides the desired Boolean value type for the `if...else` construction (Chapter 39).

This method can also appear on the right side of an assignment expression, as in

```
var adult = confirm("You certify that you are over 18 years old?")
if (adult) {
    //statements for adults
} else {
    //statements for children
}
```

You cannot specify other alert icons or labels for the two buttons in JavaScript confirm dialog box windows.

Tip

Be careful how you word the question in the confirm dialog box. In Navigator 2 and 3, the buttons are labeled OK and Cancel in Windows browsers; the Mac versions, however, label the buttons Yes and No. If your visitors may be using older Mac Navigators, be sure your questions are logically answered with both sets of button labels.

On the CD-ROM

Example (with Figure 16-12 and Listing 16-23) on the CD-ROM

Related Items: `window.alert()`, `window.prompt()`, `form.submit()` methods.

createPopup()

Returns: Popup Object reference.

	NN2	NN3	NN4	NN6	IE3/J1	IE3/J2	IE4	IE5	IE5.5
Compatibility									✓

An IE pop-up window is a chrome-less rectangular space that overlaps the current window. Unlike the dialog boxes generated by the `showModalDialog()` and `showModelessDialog()` methods, the pop-up window's entire content must be explicitly controlled by script. That also goes for the size and location of the window. Generating the window via the `createPopup()` method simply creates the object in memory without displaying it. You can then use the reference to the pop-up window that is returned by the method to position the window, populate its content, and make it visible. See details in the description of the `popup` object later in this chapter.

On the CD-ROM

Example on the CD-ROM

Related Items: `popup` object.

disableExternalCapture()
enableExternalCapture()

Returns: Nothing.

	NN2	NN3	NN4	NN6	IE3/J1	IE3/J2	IE4	IE5	IE5.5
Compatibility			✓						

NN4 security restrictions prevent one frame from monitoring events in another frame (when a different domain is in that second frame) unless the user has granted permission to a signed script. Controlling this cross-frame access requires two special `window` object methods: `enableExternalCapture()` and `disableExternalCapture()`.

Putting these methods to work is a little trickier than manipulating the regular `window.captureEvents()` method. You have to turn on external capture in the frame doing the capture, but then set `captureEvents()` and the event handler in the frame whose events you want to capture. Moreover, when a new document loads into the second frame, you must set the `captureEvents()` and event handler for that frame again. See Chapter 46 for details about signed scripts.

On the
CD-ROM   Example on the CD-ROM

Related Items: `window.captureEvents()` method; `event` object; signed scripts (Chapter 46).

execScript("*exprList*"[, *language*])

Returns: Nothing.

	NN2	NN3	NN4	NN6	IE3/J1	IE3/J2	IE4	IE5	IE5.5
Compatibility							✓	✓	✓

The IE-specific `window.execScript()` method executes one or more script statements that are passed as string expressions. The first parameter is a string version of one or more script statements (multiple statements must be separated by semicolons). The second, optional parameter is the language interpreter the browser should use to execute the script statement. Acceptable values for the language are `JavaScript`, `JScript`, `VBS`, and `VBScript`. The default value is `JScript`, so you can omit the second parameter when supplying expressions in JavaScript.

Unlike the JavaScript core language `eval()` function (which also executes string versions of JavaScript statements), the `execScript()` method returns no values.

Even so, the method operates within the global variable space of the window holding the current document. For example, if a document's script declares a global variable as follows

```
var myVar
```

the execScript() method can read or write to that variable:

```
window.execScript("myVar = 10; myVar += 5")
```

After the above statement runs, the global variable myVar has a value of 15.

Example on the CD-ROM

Related Items: eval() function.

find(["*searchString*" [, *matchCaseBoolean*, *searchUpBoolean*]])

Returns: Boolean value for nondialog searches.

	NN2	NN3	NN4	NN6	IE3/J1	IE3/J2	IE4	IE5	IE5.5
Compatibility			✓						

The NN4-specific window.find() method mimics the powers of the browser's Find dialog box, accessible from the Find button in the toolbar.

If you specify no parameters, the browser's Find dialog box appears, just as if the user had clicked the Find button in the toolbar. With no parameters, this function does not return a value.

You can specify a search string as a parameter to the function. The search is based on simple string matching and is not in any way connected with the regular expression kind of search (see Chapter 38). If the search finds a match, the browser scrolls to that matching word and highlights the word, just as if using the browser's own Find dialog box. The function also returns a Boolean true after a match is found. If no match is found in the document or no more matches occur in the current search direction (the default direction is from top to bottom), the function returns false.

Two optional Boolean parameters to the scripted find action let you specify whether the search should be case-sensitive and whether the search direction should be upward from the bottom of the document. These choices are identical to the ones that appear in the NN4's Find dialog box. Default behavior is case-insensitive and searches from top to bottom. If you specify any one of these two optional parameters, you must specify both of them.

IE4+ also has a text search facility, but it is implemented in an entirely different way (using the `TextRange` object described in Chapter 19). The visual behavior also differs in that it does not highlight and scroll to a matching string in the text.

Example on the CD-ROM

Related Items: `TextRange`, `Range` objects (Chapter 19).

forward()

See `window.blur()`.

GetAttention()

Returns: Nothing.

	NN2	NN3	NN4	NN6	IE3/J1	IE3/J2	IE4	IE5	IE5.5
Compatibility				✓					

While the `window.GetAttention()` method is intended for use more by programmers of NN6 user interface themes than by scripters, the object model nevertheless exposes the method to scripters. The purpose of the method is to alert the user that the browser needs attention when the browser is not the frontmost application on the desktop. Each operating system has a different way of signalling this attention to users. Windows flashes the Taskbar rectangle for the browser window needing attention; the MacOS beeps and places a bullet next to the application's name in the Application menu. If the browser window is already the frontmost window on the desktop, then no signals flash or beep.

It is highly unlikely that you would design a script that runs long enough for the user to need to switch to another application. But you might have some scripted mechanism (using the `setTimeout()` method described later in this chapter) that signals the user if the page has no activity for a set number of minutes.

Example on the CD-ROM

handleEvent(*event*)

Returns: Nothing.

	NN2	NN3	NN4	NN6	IE3/J1	IE3/J2	IE4	IE5	IE5.5
Compatibility			✓						

When you explicitly capture events in the NN4 window, document, or layer object (by invoking the captureEvents() method for that object), you can control where the events go after their initial capture. To let an event continue to its original target (for example, a button that was clicked by a user), you use the routeEvent() method. But if you want to redirect an event (or class of events) to a particular event handler elsewhere in the document, use the handleEvent() method.

Every NN4 object that has event handlers associated with it also has a handleEvent() method. Thus, if you are capturing click events in a window, you can redirect the events to, say, a particular button or link on the page because both of those objects know what to do with click events. Consider the following code excerpt:

```
<SCRIPT LANGUAGE="JavaScript">
// function to run when window captures a click event
function doClicks(evt) {
    // send all clicks to the first link in the document
    document.links[0].handleEvent(evt)
}
// set window to capture click events
window.captureEvents(Event.CLICK)
// assign doClick() function to click events captured by window
window.onclick = doClicks
</SCRIPT>
```

The window is set up to capture all click events and invoke the doClicks() function each time the user clicks a clickable item in the window. In the doClicks() function is a single statement that instructs the first link in the document to handle the click event being passed as a parameter. The link must have an onClick event handler defined for this to be meaningful. Because an event object is passed along automatically, the link's event handler can examine event properties (for example, location of the click) and perhaps alter some of the link's properties before letting it perform its linking task. The preceding example is really showing how to use handleEvent() with a link object, rather than a window object. There is little opportunity for other objects to capture events that normally go to the window, but this method is part of every event-aware object in NN4.

The corresponding method in the W3C event model's capture mechanism is dispatchEvent(), and the IE5+ equivalent is fireEvent().

Example

See Chapter 29 for details and in-depth examples of working with event objects.

Related Items: window.captureEvents(), window.releaseEvents(), window.routeEvent() methods; event object.

home()

Returns: Nothing.

	NN2	NN3	NN4	NN6	IE3/J1	IE3/J2	IE4	IE5	IE5.5
Compatibility			✓	✓					

Like many of the window methods new to Navigator 4, the window.home() method provides an NN-specific scripted way of replicating the action of a toolbar button: the Home button. The action navigates the browser to whatever URL is set in the browser preferences for home page location. You cannot control the default home page of a visitor's browser.

Related Items: window.back(), window.forward() methods; window.toolbar property.

moveBy(*deltaX,deltaY*)
moveTo(*x,y*)

Returns: Nothing.

	NN2	NN3	NN4	NN6	IE3/J1	IE3/J2	IE4	IE5	IE5.5
Compatibility			✓	✓			✓	✓	✓

In IE4+ and NN4+, JavaScript can adjust the location of a browser window on the screen. This applies to the main window or any subwindow generated by script. Netscape regards the possibility of a window moved out of screen view as a potential security hole, so signed scripts are needed in NN4+ to move a window off screen.

You can move a window to an absolute position on the screen or adjust it along the horizontal and/or vertical axis by any number of pixels, irrespective of the absolute pixel position. The coordinate space for the x (horizontal) and y (vertical) position is the entire screen, with the top-left corner representing 0,0. The point of the window you set with the `moveBy()` and `moveTo()` methods is the very top-left corner of the outer edge of the browser window. Therefore, when you move the window to point 0,0, that sets the window flush with the top-left corner of the screen. This may not be the equivalent of a truly maximized window for all browsers and operating systems, however, because a maximized window's coordinates may be negative by a handful of pixels.

If you try to adjust the position of the window in NN4 such that any edge falls beyond the screen area, the window remains at the edge of the screen — unless you are using a signed script and have the user's permission to adjust the window partially or completely off screen. Moving the only visible browser window entirely off screen is dangerous because the user has no way to get it back into view without quitting and relaunching the browser.

The difference between the `moveTo()` and `moveBy()` methods is that one is an absolute move, while the other is relative with respect to the current window position. Parameters you specify for `moveTo()` are the precise horizontal and vertical pixel counts on the screen where you want the upper-left corner of the window to appear. In contrast, the parameters for `moveBy()` indicate how far to adjust the window location in either direction. If you want to move the window 25 pixels to the right, you must still include both parameters, but the y value will be zero:

```
window.moveBy(25,0)
```

To move to the left, the first parameter must be a negative number.

Example (with Listing 16-24) on the CD-ROM

Related Items: `window.outerHeight`, `window.outerWidth` properties; `window.resizeBy()`, `window.resizeTo()` methods.

navigate("*URL*")

Returns: Nothing.

	NN2	NN3	NN4	NN6	IE3/J1	IE3/J2	IE4	IE5	IE5.5
Compatibility					✓	✓	✓	✓	✓

The `window.navigate()` method is an IE-specific method that lets you load a new document into a window or frame. This method's action is the same as assigning a URL to the `location.href` property—a property that is available on all scriptable NN and IE browsers. If your audience is entirely IE-based, then this method is safe. Otherwise, I recommend the `location.href` property as the best navigation approach.

 On the CD-ROM   Example on the CD-ROM

Related Items: `location` object.

open("*URL*", "*windowName*" [, "*windowFeatures*"][,*replaceFlag*])

Returns: A window object representing the newly created window; `null` if method fails.

	NN2	NN3	NN4	NN6	IE3/J1	IE3/J2	IE4	IE5	IE5.5
Compatibility	✓	✓	✓	✓	✓	✓	✓	✓	✓

With the `window.open()` method, a script provides a Web site designer with an immense range of options for the way a second or third Web browser window looks on the user's computer screen. Moreover, most of this control can work with all JavaScript-enabled browsers without the need for signed scripts. Because the interface elements of a new window are easier to envision, I cover those aspects of the `window.open()` method parameters first.

Setting new window features

The optional *windowFeatures* parameter is one string, consisting of a comma-separated list of assignment expressions (behaving something like HTML tag attributes). **Important:** For the best browser compatibility, do not put spaces after the commas. If you omit the third parameter, JavaScript creates the same type of new window you get from the New Web Browser menu choice in the File menu. But you can control which window elements appear in the new window with the third parameter. Remember this important rule: If you specify even one of the method's original set of third parameter values, all other features are turned off unless the parameters specify the features to be switched on. Table 16-3 lists the attributes that you can control for a newly created window in all browsers. Except where noted, all Boolean values default to `yes` if you do not specify the third parameter.

Table 16-3: window.open() Method Attributes Controllable via Script

Attribute	Browsers	Description
alwaysLowered[3]	NN4+	(Boolean) Always behind other browser windows
alwaysRaised[3]	NN4+	(Boolean) Always in front of other browser windows
channelmode	IE4+	(Boolean) Theater mode with channel band (default is no)
copyhistory	NN2+, IE3+	(Boolean) Duplicates Go menu history for new window
dependent	NN4+	(Boolean) Subwindow closes if the opener window closes
directories	NN2+, IE3+	(Boolean) "What's New" and other buttons in the row
fullscreen	IE4+	(Boolean) No title bar or menus (default is no)
height	NN2+, IE3+	(Integer) Content region height in pixels
hotkeys	NN4+	(Boolean) If true, disables menu shortcuts (except Quit and Security Info) when menubar is turned off
innerHeight[4]	NN4+	(Integer) Content region height; same as old height property
innerWidth[4]	NN4+	(Integer) Content region width; same as old width property
left	IE4+	(Integer) Horizontal position of top-left corner on screen
location	NN2+, IE3+	(Boolean) Field displaying the current URL
menubar[1]	NN2+, IE3+	(Boolean) Menubar at top of window
outerHeight[4]	NN4+	(Integer) Visible window height
outerWidth[4]	NN4+	(Integer) Visible window width
resizable[2]	NN2+, IE3+	(Boolean) Interface elements that allow resizing by dragging
screenX[4]	NN4+	(Integer) Horizontal position of top-left corner on screen
screenY[4]	NN4+	(Integer) Vertical position of top-left corner on screen

	Table 16-3: *(continued)*	
Attribute	**Browsers**	**Description**
scrollbars	NN2+, IE3+	(Boolean) Displays scrollbars if document is larger than window
status	NN2+, IE3+	(Boolean) Statusbar at bottom of window
titlebar[3]	NN4+	(Boolean) Title bar and all other border elements
title	IE5	(Boolean) Title bar
toolbar	NN2+, IE3+	(Boolean) "Back," "Forward," and other buttons in the row
top	IE4+	(Integer) Horizontal position of top-left corner on screen
width	NN2+, IE3+	(Integer) Content region width in pixels
z-lock[3]	NN4+	(Boolean) Window layer is fixed below browser windows

1. Not on Macintosh because the menubar is not in the browser window; when off in NN4/Mac, displays an abbreviated Mac menubar.

2. Macintosh windows are always resizable.

3. Requires a signed script.

4. Requires a signed script to size or position a window beyond safe threshold.

Boolean values are handled a bit differently than you might expect. The value for true can be either yes, 1, or just the feature name by itself; for false, use a value of no or 0. If you omit any Boolean attributes, they are rendered as false. Therefore, if you want to create a new window that shows only the toolbar and statusbar and is resizable, the method looks like this:

```
window.open("newURL","NewWindow", "toolbar,status,resizable")
```

A new window that does not specify the height and width is set to the default size of the browser window that the browser creates from a File menu's New Web Browser command. In other words, a new window does not automatically inherit the size of the window making the window.open() method call. A new window created via a script is positioned somewhat arbitrarily, unless you use the window positioning attributes available in NN4+ and IE4+. Notice that the position attributes are different for each browser (screenX and screenY for NN; left and top for IE). You can include both sets of attributes in a single parameter string because the browser ignores attributes it doesn't recognize.

Netscape-only signed scripts

Many NN-specific attributes are deemed to be security risks and thus require signed scripts and the user's permission before they are recognized. If the user fails to grant permission, the secure parameter is ignored.

A couple of these attributes have different behaviors on different operating system platforms, due to the way the systems manage their application windows. For example, the alwaysLowered, alwaysRaised, and z-locked styles can exist in layers that range behind Navigator's own windows in the Windows platform; on the Mac, however, such windows are confined to the levels occupied by Navigator. The difference is that Windows allows windows from multiple applications to interleave each other, while the Mac keeps each application's windows in contiguous layers.

To apply signed scripts to opening a new window with the secure window features, you must enable UniversalBrowserWrite privileges as you do for other signed scripts (see Chapter 46). A code fragment that generates an alwaysRaised style window follows:

```
<SCRIPT LANGUAGE="JavaScript" ARCHIVE="myJar.jar" ID="1">
function newRaisedWindow() {
    netscape.security.PrivilegeManager.enablePrivilege("UniversalBrowserWrite")
    var newWindow = window.open("","","HEIGHT=100,WIDTH=300,alwaysRaised")
    netscape.security.PrivilegeManager.disablePrivilege("UniversalBrowserWrite")
    var newContent = "<HTML><BODY><B> "On top of spaghetti!"</B>"
    newContent += "<FORM><CENTER><INPUT TYPE='button' VALUE='OK'"
    newContent += "onClick='self.close()'></CENTER></FORM></BODY></HTML>"
    newWindow.document.write(newContent)
    newWindow.document.close()
}
</SCRIPT>
```

You can experiment with the look and behavior of new windows with any combination of attributes with the help of the script in Listing 16-25. This page presents a table of all NN-specific new window Boolean attributes and creates a new 300×300 pixel window based on your choices. This page assumes that if you are using NN4, you have codebase principals turned on for signed scripts (see Chapter 46).

Be careful with turning off the title bar and hotkeys. With the title bar off, the content appears to float in space, because absolutely no borders are displayed. With hotkeys still turned on, you can use Ctrl+W to close this borderless window (except on the Mac, for which the hotkeys are always disabled with the title bar off). This is how you can turn a computer into a kiosk by sizing a window to the screen's dimensions and setting the window options to

```
"titlebar=no,hotkeys=no,alwaysRaised=yes"
```

Listing 16-25: **New Window Laboratory**

```
<HTML>
<HEAD>
<TITLE>window.open() Options</TITLE>
<SCRIPT LANGUAGE="JavaScript">
var isNav4 = (navigator.appName == "Netscape" &&
navigator.appVersion.charAt(0) >= 4) ? true : false

function makeNewWind(form) {
    if (isNav4) {netscape.security.PrivilegeManager.enablePrivilege↵
("UniversalBrowserWrite")
    }
    var attr = "HEIGHT=300,WIDTH=300"
    for (var i = 0; i < form.elements.length; i++) {
        if (form.elements[i].type == "checkbox") {
            attr += "," + form.elements[i].name + "="
            attr += (form.elements[i].checked) ? "yes" : "no"
        }
    }
    var newWind = window.open("bofright.htm","subwindow",attr)
    if (isNav4) {netscape.security.PrivilegeManager.revertPrivilege↵
("UniversalBrowserWrite")
    }
}
</SCRIPT>
</HEAD>
<BODY>
<FORM>
<B>Select new window options:</B>
<TABLE BORDER=2>
<TR>
    <TD COLSPAN=2 BGCOLOR="yellow" ALIGN="middle">All Browsers Features:</TD>
</TR>
<TR>
    <TD><INPUT TYPE="checkbox" NAME="toolbar">toolbar</TD>
    <TD><INPUT TYPE="checkbox" NAME="location">location</TD>
</TR>
<TR>
    <TD><INPUT TYPE="checkbox" NAME="directories">directories</TD>
    <TD><INPUT TYPE="checkbox" NAME="status">status</TD>
</TR>
<TR>
    <TD><INPUT TYPE="checkbox" NAME="menubar">menubar</TD>
    <TD><INPUT TYPE="checkbox" NAME="scrollbars">scrollbars</TD>
</TR>
<TR>
    <TD><INPUT TYPE="checkbox" NAME="resizable">resizable</TD>
    <TD><INPUT TYPE="checkbox" NAME="copyhistory">copyhistory</TD>
```

```
</TR>
<TR>
    <TD COLSPAN=2 BGCOLOR="yellow" ALIGN="middle">Communicator Features:</TD>
</TR>
<TR>
    <TD><INPUT TYPE="checkbox" NAME="alwaysLowered">alwaysLowered</TD>
    <TD><INPUT TYPE="checkbox" NAME="alwaysRaised">alwaysRaised</TD>
</TR>
<TR>
    <TD><INPUT TYPE="checkbox" NAME="dependent">dependent</TD>
    <TD><INPUT TYPE="checkbox" NAME="hotkeys" CHECKED>hotkeys</TD>
</TR>
<TR>
    <TD><INPUT TYPE="checkbox" NAME="titlebar" CHECKED>titlebar</TD>
    <TD><INPUT TYPE="checkbox" NAME="z-lock">z-lock</TD>
</TR>
<TR>
    <TD COLSPAN=2 ALIGN="middle"><INPUT TYPE="button" NAME="forAll"
    VALUE="Make New Window" onClick="makeNewWind(this.form)"></TD>
</TR>
</TABLE>
<BR>
</FORM>
</BODY>
</HTML>
```

Specifying a window name

Getting back to the other parameters of `window.open()`, the second parameter is the name for the new window. Don't confuse this parameter with the document's title, which would normally be set by whatever HTML text determines the content of the window. A window name must be the same style of one-word identifier that you use for other object names and variables. This name is also an entirely different entity than the `window` object that the `open()` method returns. You don't use the name in your scripts. At most, the name can be used for `TARGET` attributes of links and forms.

Loading content into a new window

A script generally populates a window with one of two kinds of information:

   ✦ An existing HTML document whose URL is known beforehand

   ✦ An HTML page created on the fly

To create a new window that displays an existing HTML document, supply the URL as the first parameter of the `window.open()` method. If your page is having difficulty loading a URL into a new page (except as noted in the sidebar "A Navigator 2 Bug Workaround"), try specifying the complete URL of the target document (instead of just the filename).

Leaving the first parameter as an empty string forces the window to open with a blank document, ready to have HTML written to it by your script (or loaded separately by another statement that sets that window's location to a specific URL). If you plan to write the content of the window on the fly, assemble your HTML content as one long string value and then use the `document.write()` method to post that content to the new window. If you plan to append no further writing to the page, also include a `document.close()` method at the end to tell the browser that you're finished with the layout (so that the `Layout:Complete` or `Done` message appears in the statusbar, if your new window has one).

A call to the `window.open()` method returns a reference to the new window's object if the window opens successfully. This value is vitally important if your script needs to address elements of that new window (such as when writing to its document).

To allow other functions in your script to reference the subwindow, you should assign the result of a `window.open()` method to a global variable. Before writing to the new window the first time, test the variable to make sure that it is not a `null` value—the window may have failed to open because of low memory, for instance. If everything is okay, you can use that variable as the beginning of a reference to any property or object within the new window. For example:

```
var newWindow
...
function createNewWindow() {
    newWindow = window.open("","")
    if (newWindow != null) {
        newWindow.document.write("<HTML><HEAD><TITLE>Hi!</TITLE></HEAD>")
    }
}
```

That global variable reference continues to be available for another function that perhaps closes the subwindow (via the `close()` method).

A Navigator 2 Bug Workaround

If you're concerned about backward compatibility with Navigator 2, you should be aware of a bug in the Macintosh and UNIX flavors of the browser. In those versions, if you include a URL as a parameter to `window.open()`, Navigator opens the window but does not load the URL. A second call to the `window.open()` method is required. Moreover, the second parameter must be an empty string if you add any third-parameter settings. Here is a sample listing you can adapt for your own usage:

```
<HTML>
<HEAD>
<TITLE>New Window</TITLE>
<SCRIPT LANGUAGE="JavaScript">
// workaround for window.open() bug on X and Mac platforms
function makeNewWindow() {
    var newWindow =
    window.open("http://www.dannyg.com","","status,height=200,width=300")
    if (parseInt(navigator.appVersion) == 2 && navigator.appName == "Netscape") {
        newWindow =
          window.open("http://www.dannyg.com","","status,height=200,width=300")
    }
}
</SCRIPT>
</HEAD>
<BODY>
<FORM>
<INPUT TYPE="button" NAME="newOne" VALUE="Create New Window"
onClick="makeNewWindow()">
</FORM>
</BODY>
</HTML>
```

This workaround can also be used without penalty in Windows versions of Navigator.

When scripts in the subwindow need to communicate with objects and scripts in the originating window, you must make sure that the subwindow has an `opener` property if the level of JavaScript in the visitor's browser doesn't automatically supply one. See the discussion about the `window.opener` property earlier in this chapter.

Invoking multiple `window.open()` methods with the same window name parameter (the second parameter) does not create additional copies of that window in Netscape browsers (although it does in Internet Explorer). JavaScript prevents you from creating two windows with the same name. Also be aware that a `window.open()` method does not bring an existing window of that name to the front of the window layers: Use `window.focus()` for that.

Internet Explorer idiosyncracies

Creating subwindows in IE can be complicated at times by undesirable behavior by the browser. One of the most common problems occurs when you attempt to use `document.write()` to put content into a newly created window. IE, including some of the latest versions, fails to complete the window opening job before the script statement that uses `document.write()` executes. This causes a script error because the reference to the subwindow is not yet valid. To work around this, you should put the HTML assembly and `document.write()` statements in a separate function that gets invoked via a `setTimeout()` method after the window is created. You can see an example of this in Listing 16-26.

Another problem that affects IE is the occasional security violation ("access denied") warning when a script attempts to access a subwindow. This problem goes away when the page that includes the script for opening and accessing the subwindow is served from an http server, rather than accessed from a local hard disk.

Finally, an all-too common bug in Windows 95/98 allows the Registry to become mildly corrupted in some key areas that IE needs for opening and referencing new windows. The most common symptom of the problem is a script error on the statement that invokes `window.open()`, but other indications include error messages that the `document.write()` method is not supported in the subwindow or that the "RPC server" is not available. The problem cannot be fixed by JavaScript but requires human intervention on the affected PC. Here are the steps to repair the problem:

1. Click Start and then click Run.

2. In the Open box, type the following line: `regsvr32 actxprxy.dll`

3. Click OK and then click OK again after you receive the following message:

    `DllRegisterServer in actxprxy.dll succeeded.`

4. Click Start and then click Run.

5. In the Open box, type the following line: `regsvr32 shdocvw.dll`

6. Click OK and then click OK again after you receive the following message:

    `DllRegisterServer in shdocvw.dll succeeded.`

7. Shut down and restart your computer.

The corruption is reported to be caused by application installers and uninstallers that don't clean up after themselves the way they should. The fact that this problem is rather common in IE4 under both Windows 95 and 98 might make you gunshy about utilizing multiple windows in your application.

 On the CD-ROM

Example (with Listing 16-26) on the CD-ROM

Related Items: window.close(), window.blur(), window.focus() methods; window.closed property.

print()

Returns: Nothing.

	NN2	NN3	NN4	NN6	IE3/J1	IE3/J2	IE4	IE5	IE5.5
Compatibility			✓	✓				✓	✓

The print() method provides a scripted way of sending the window or a frame from a frameset to the printer. In all cases, the Print dialog box appears for the user to make the typical printer choices when printing manually. This prevents a rogue print() command from tying up a printer without the user's permission.

The precise behavior of the print() method varies a bit with the different ways NN and IE (not to mention operating systems) handle printing. In NN4+ (except for the Windows OS), you can print all frames of a frameset in one print() command when it is invoked for the framesetting (parent) document. NN4 for Windows, however, does not print the entire frameset at once. You can write a script that iterates through all frames and prints them with delays to let the content be sent to the print spooler:

```
function printFrames(n) {
    parent.frames[n++].print()
    if (n < parent.frames.length) {
        setTimeout("printFrames(" + n + ")",5000)
    }
}
```

Invoke this function as printFrames(0), and the function does the rest.

In IE5, the print dialog box gives the user the choice of printing just one frame or all of the frames. Make sure that the print() method is invoked for the desired frame when you want only that frame to print. The browser defaults to printing just that frame.

IE5 introduces some print-specific event handlers that are triggered by scripted printing as well as manual printing. The events begin to fire after the user has accepted the Print dialog box. An onBeforePrint event handler can be used to show content that might be hidden from view but should appear in the printout. After the content has been sent to the print spooler, the onAfterPrint event can restore the page.

Example (with Listings 16-27 and 16-28) on the CD-ROM

NN4 printing anomalies

The Windows and Unix versions of NN4 handle printing in a way that can cause the page to not print what the user sees because before the page prints, it is loaded into a hidden window. Any immediate scripts in the page run again, but any user-induced, scripted content modifications will most likely not be a part of the page.

While there is no known workaround for resurrecting modified content, your script can at least know if the page is being loaded into one of these hidden windows: The NN-specific `window.outerHeight` and `window.outerWidth` properties are zero. If you don't want an immediate script statement to run before being printed, use an `if` construction to let the nested statement(s) run only if either of those dimension properties is greater than zero.

Printing in IE4

While the `window.print()` method is not available in IE4, it is possible to script printing in the Win32 OS platforms via the built-in browser object. To use this ActiveX object, you must first include the following HTML somewhere in your document (at the end of the BODY is fine):

```
<OBJECT ID="IEControl" WIDTH=0 HEIGHT=0
CLASSID="clsid:8856F961-340A-11D0-A96B-00C04FD705A2">
</OBJECT>
```

The long `CLASSID` attribute must be copied exactly. This HTML adds an object to the document object model that can be scripted. The object has several commands available, one of which provides printing services. The commands are numbered, and the one for printing is the following:

```
IEControl.ExecWB(6, 1)
```

If the user cancels the Print dialog box, a script error may appear, so be sure to trap for errors (see the `window.onerror` property earlier in this chapter). If you change the second parameter to 2, the Print dialog box does not appear, but that isn't a very user-friendly way to treat printing.

Related Items: `window.back()`, `window.forward()`, `window.home()`, `window.find()` methods.

prompt("*message*", "*defaultReply*")

Returns: String of text entered by user or `null`.

	NN2	NN3	NN4	NN6	IE3/J1	IE3/J2	IE4	IE5	IE5.5
Compatibility	✓	✓	✓	✓	✓	✓	✓	✓	✓

The third kind of dialog box that JavaScript can display includes a message from the script author, a field for user entry, and two buttons (OK and Cancel, or Yes and No on Mac versions of Navigator 2 and 3). The script writer can supply a prewritten answer so that a user confronted with a prompt dialog box can click OK (or press Enter) to accept that answer without further typing. Supplying both parameters to the window.prompt() method is important. Even if you don't want to supply a default answer, enter an empty string as the second parameter:

```
prompt("What is your postal code?","")
```

If you omit the second parameter, JavaScript inserts the string undefined into the dialog box's field. This string is disconcerting to most Web page visitors.

The value returned by this method is a string in the dialog box's field when the user clicks the OK button. If you're asking the user to enter a number, remember that the value returned by this method is a string. You may need to perform data-type conversion with the parseInt() or parseFloat() functions (see Chapter 42) to use the returned values in math calculations.

When the user clicks the prompt dialog box's OK button without entering any text into a blank field, the returned value is an empty string (""). Clicking on the Cancel button, however, makes the method return a null value. Therefore, the scripter must test for the type of returned value to make sure that the user entered some data that can be processed later in the script, as in

```
var entry = prompt("Enter a number between 1 and 10:","")
if (entry != null) {
    //statements to execute with the value
}
```

This script excerpt assigns the results of the prompt dialog box to a variable and executes the nested statements if the returned value of the dialog box is not null (if the user clicked the OK button). The rest of the statements then include data validation to make sure that the entry is a number within the desired range (see Chapter 43).

It may be tempting to use the prompt dialog box as a handy user input device. But, as with the other JavaScript dialog boxes, the modality of the prompt dialog box is disruptive to the user's flow through a document and can also trap automated macros that some users activate to capture Web sites. In forms, HTML fields are better user interface elements for attracting user text entry. Perhaps the safest way to use a prompt dialog box is to have it appear when a user clicks a button element on a page—and then only if the information you require of the user can be provided in a single prompt dialog box. Presenting a sequence of prompt dialog boxes is downright annoying to users.

On the CD-ROM

Example (with Figure 16-13 and Listing 16-29) on the CD-ROM

Related Items: `window.alert()`, `window.confirm()` method.

releaseEvents(*eventTypeList*)

Returns: Nothing.

	NN2	NN3	NN4	NN6	IE3/J1	IE3/J2	IE4	IE5	IE5.5
Compatibility			✓						

If your scripts have enabled NN4-specific event capture for the `window` object (or `document` or `layer`, for that matter), you can turn off that capture with the `releaseEvents()` method. This method does not inhibit events from reaching their intended target. In fact, by releasing capture from a higher object, released events don't bother stopping at those higher objects anymore. Parameters for the `releaseEvents()` method are one or more event types. Each event type is its own entity, so if your window captures three event types at one point, you can release some or all of those event types as the visitor interacts with your page. For example, if the page loads and captures three types of events, as in

```
window.captureEvents(Event.CLICK | Event.KEYPRESS | Event.CHANGE)
```

you can later turn off window event capture for all but the `click` event:

```
window.releaseEvents(Event.KEYPRESS | Event.CHANGE)
```

The window still captures and processes `click` events, but `keyPress` and `change` events go directly to their target objects.

A new mechanism (removing an event listener) is implemented in NN6 based on the W3C event model. See Chapters 14 and 29 for more information.

Related Items: `window.captureEvents()`, `window.routeEvent()` methods.

resizeBy(*deltaX,deltaY*)
resizeTo(*outerwidth,outerheight*)

Returns: Nothing.

	NN2	NN3	NN4	NN6	IE3/J1	IE3/J2	IE4	IE5	IE5.5
Compatibility			✓	✓			✓	✓	✓

Starting with NN4 and IE4, scripts can control the size of the current browser window on the fly. While you can set the individual inner and (in NN) outer width and height properties of a window, the resizeBy() and resizeTo() methods let you adjust both axis measurements in one statement. In both instances, all adjustments affect the lower-right corner of the window: To move the top-left corner, use the window.moveBy() or window.moveTo() methods.

Each resize method requires a different kind of parameter. The resizeBy() method adjusts the window by a certain number of pixels along one or both axes. Therefore, it is not concerned with the specific size of the window beforehand — only by how much each axis is to change. For example, to increase the current window size by 100 pixels horizontally and 50 pixels vertically, the statement is

```
window.resizeBy(100, 50)
```

Both parameters are required, but if you only want to adjust the size in one direction, set the other to zero. You may also shrink the window by using negative values for either or both parameters.

You find a greater need for the resizeTo() method, especially when you know that on a particular platform the window needs adjustment to a specific width and height to best accommodate that platform's display of form elements. Parameters for the resizeTo() method are the actual pixel width and height of the outer dimension of the window — the same as NN's window.outerWidth and window.outerHeight properties.

To resize the window such that it occupies all screen real estate (except for the Windows Taskbar and Macintosh menubar), use the screen object properties that calculate the available screen space:

```
window.resizeBy(screen.availWidth, screen.availHeight)
```

This action, however, is not precisely the same in Windows as maximizing the window. To achieve that same effect, you must move the window to coordinates -4, -4 and add eight to the two parameters of resizeBy():

```
window.moveTo(-4,-4)
window.resizeTo(screen.availWidth + 8, screen.availHeight + 8)
```

This hides the window's own four-pixel wide border, as occurs during OS-induced window maximizing. See also the screen object discussion (Chapter 28) for more OS-specific details.

In practice, NN4 does not give reliable results setting a window's size via the resizeTo() method. On some platforms, the dimensions are applied to the inner width and height, rather than outer. If a specific outer size is necessary, use the NN-specific window.outerHeight and window.outerWidth properties instead.

Navigator imposes some security restrictions for maximum and minimum size for a window. For both methods, you are limited to the viewable area of the screen and visible minimums unless the page uses signed scripts (see Chapter 46). With signed scripts and the user's permission, for example, you can adjust windows beyond the available screen borders.

On the CD-ROM   Example (with Listing 16-30) on the CD-ROM

Related Items: window.outerHeight, window.outerWidth properties; window.moveTo(), window.sizeToContent() methods.

routeEvent(*event*)

Returns: Nothing.

	NN2	NN3	NN4	NN6	IE3/J1	IE3/J2	IE4	IE5	IE5.5
Compatibility			✓						

If you turn on NN4-specific event capturing in the window, document, or layer object (via their respective captureEvents() methods), the handlers you assign to those events really capture those events, preventing them from ever reaching their intended targets. For some page designs, this is intentional, as it allows the higher-level object to handle all events of a particular type. But if your goal is to perform some preprocessing of events before they reach their destination, you need a way to pass that event along its regular path. That's what the routeEvent() method is for.

Perhaps a more common reason for capturing events at the window (or similar) level is to look for special cases, such as when someone Ctrl+clicks on an element. In this case, even though the window event handler receives all click events, it performs further processing only when the event.modifiers property indicates the Ctrl key is also pressed and the *eventObj*.target property reveals the item being clicked is a link rather than a button. All other instances of the click event are routed on their way to their destinations. The event object knows where it's going, so that your routeEvent() method doesn't have to worry about that.

The parameter for the routeEvent() method is the event object that is passed to the function that processes the high-level event, as shown here:

```
function flashRed(evt) {
    [statements that filter specific events to flash background color red]
    routeEvent(evt)
}
```

The event object, evt, comes into the function while passing unmodified to the object that was clicked.

In the W3C DOM event model (as implemented in NN6), a captured event continues onward to the target after event handlers higher up the containment chain finish their work.

 Example on the CD-ROM

Related Items: window.captureEvents(), window.releaseEvents(), window.handleEvent() methods; event object (Chapter 29).

scroll(*horizontalCoord, verticalCoord*)

Returns: Nothing.

	NN2	NN3	NN4	NN6	IE3/J1	IE3/J2	IE4	IE5	IE5.5
Compatibility	✓	✓	✓				✓	✓	✓

The window.scroll() method was introduced in NN3 and has been implemented in all scriptable browsers since then. But in the meantime, the method has been replaced by the window.scrollTo() method, which is in more syntactic alliance with many other window methods. Use the window.scroll() method only if your audience is still using NN3; for an audience of NN4+ and IE4+, use the window.scrollTo() method instead.

The `window.scroll()` method takes two parameters, the horizontal (x) and vertical (y) coordinates of the document that is to be positioned at the top-left corner of the window or frame. You must realize that the window and document have two similar, but independent, coordinate schemes. From the window's point of view, the top-left pixel (of the content area) is point 0,0. All documents also have a 0,0 point: the very top-left of the document. The window's 0,0 point doesn't move, but the document's 0,0 point can move — via manual or scripted scrolling. Although `scroll()` is a window method, it seems to behave more like a document method, as the document appears to reposition itself within the window. Conversely, you can also think of the window moving to bring its 0,0 point to the designated coordinate of the document.

Although you can set values beyond the maximum size of the document or to negative values, the results vary from platform to platform. For the moment, the best usage of the `window.scroll()` method is as a means of adjusting the scroll to the very top of a document (`window.scroll(0,0)`) when you want the user to be at a base location in the document. For vertical scrolling within a text-heavy document, an HTML anchor may be a better alternative for now (though it doesn't readjust horizontal scrolling).

 Example (with Listings 16-31, 16-32, and 16-33) on the CD-ROM

Related Items: `window.scrollBy()`, `window.scrollTo()` methods.

scrollBy(*deltaX,deltaY*)
scrollTo(*x,y*)

Returns: Nothing.

	NN2	NN3	NN4	NN6	IE3/J1	IE3/J2	IE4	IE5	IE5.5
Compatibility			✓	✓			✓	✓	✓

NN4+ and IE4+ provide a related pair of window scrolling methods. The `window.scrollTo()` method is the new version of the `window.scroll()` method. The two work identically to position a specific coordinate point of a document at the top-left corner of the inner window region.

Unwanted User Scrolling

Many Windows-compatible personal computers ship with a mouse that includes a scroll wheel that is activated by pressing down on the wheel and spinning the wheel. Be aware that even if your page design loads into frames or new windows that intentionally lack scrollbars, the page will be scrollable via this wheel if the document or its background image are larger than the window or frame. Users may not even be aware that they have scrolled the page (because there are no scrollbar visual clues). If this affects your design, you may need to build in a routine (via `setTimeout()`) that periodically sets the scroll of the window to 0,0.

In contrast, the `window.scrollBy()` method allows for relative positioning of the document. Parameter values indicate by how many pixels the document should scroll in the window (horizontally and vertically). Negative numbers are allowed if you want to scroll to the left and/or upward. The `scrollBy()` method comes in handy if you elect to hide the scrollbars of a window or frame and offer other types of scrolling controls for your users. For example, to scroll down one entire screen of a long document, you can use the `window.innerHeight` (in NN) or `document.body.clientHeight` (in IE) properties to determine what the offset from the current position would be:

```
// assign IE body clientHeight to window.innerHeight
if (document.body && document.body.clientHeight) {
    window.innerHeight = document.body.clientHeight
}
window.scrollBy(0, window.innerHeight)
```

To scroll upward, use a negative value for the second parameter:

```
window.scrollBy(0, -window.innerHeight)
```

Scrolling the document in the Macintosh exhibits some buggy behavior. At times it appears as though you are allowed to scroll well beyond the document edges. In truth, the document has stopped at the border, but the window or frame may not have refreshed properly.

The window scroll methods are not the ones to use to produce the scrolling effect of a positioned element. That kind of animation is accomplished by adjusting `style` position properties (see Chapter 31).

On the CD-ROM Example (with Listings 16-34 and 16-35) on the CD-ROM

Related Items: `window.pageXOffset`, `window.pageYOffset` properties; `window.scroll()` method.

setCursor("*cursorType*")

Returns: Nothing.

	NN2	NN3	NN4	NN6	IE3/J1	IE3/J2	IE4	IE5	IE5.5
Compatibility				✓					

The NN6 window.setCursor() method is an alternative to the cursor style sheet attribute. In the meantime, NN6 user interface theme authors have been using it, and you can experiment with it, too.

The method requires one parameter, a string name of one of the accepted cursor types. Recognized cursor types are as follows:

alias	auto	cell
context-menu	copy	count-down
count-up	count-up-down	crosshair
default	e-resize	grab
grabbing	help	move
n-resize	ne-resize	nw-resize
pointer	s-resize	se-resize
spinning	sw-resize	text
w-resize	wait	

Each operating system provides its own suite of cursor designs, but not all operating systems provide a unique cursor design for each type. Also be aware that setting the cursor via this method does not lock the cursor. If the user rolls the cursor atop form controls (especially text boxes), the cursor reverts to its "auto" setting.

On the CD-ROM   Example on the CD-ROM

Related Item: style.cursor property (Chapter 30).

```
setInterval("expr", msecDelay [, language])
setInterval(funcRef, msecDelay [, funcarg1,
..., funcargn])
```

Returns: Interval ID integer.

	NN2	NN3	NN4	NN6	IE3/J1	IE3/J2	IE4	IE5	IE5.5
Compatibility			✓	✓			✓	✓	✓

It is important to understand the distinction between the setInterval() and setTimeout() methods. Before the setInterval() method was part of JavaScript, authors replicated the behavior with setTimeout(), but the task often required reworking scripts a bit.

Use setInterval() when your script needs to call a function or execute some expression repeatedly with a fixed time delay between calls to that function or expression. The delay is not at all like a wait state in some languages: Other processing does not halt while the delay is in effect. Typical applications include animation by moving an object around the page under controlled speed (instead of letting the JavaScript interpreter whiz the object through its path at CPU-dependent speeds). In a kiosk application, you can use setInterval() to advance "slides" that appear in other frames or as layers, perhaps changing the view every ten seconds. Clock displays and countdown timers would also be suitable usage of this method (even though you see examples in this book that use the old-fashioned setTimeout() way to perform timer and clock functions).

In contrast, setTimeout() is best suited for those times when you need to carry out a function or expression one time in the future — even if that future is only a second or two away. See the discussion of the setTimeout() method later in this chapter for details on this application.

While the primary functionality of the setInterval() method is the same in both NN and IE, each browser offers some extra possibilities depending on the way you use parameters to the method. For simple invocations of this method, the same parameters work in all browsers that support the method. First, I address the parameters that all browsers have in common.

The first parameter of the setInterval() method is the name of the function or expression to run after the interval elapses. This item must be a quoted string. If the parameter is a function, no function arguments are allowed inside the function's parentheses unless the arguments are literal strings (but see the section "Passing Function Parameters").

The second parameter of this method is the number of milliseconds (1,000 per second) that JavaScript should use as the interval between invocations of the function or expression. Even though the measure is in extremely small units, don't rely on 100 percent accuracy of the intervals. Various other internal processing delays may throw off the timing just a bit.

Just as with setTimeout(), setInterval() returns an integer value that is the ID for the interval process. That ID value lets you turn off the process with the clearInterval() method. That method takes the ID value as its sole parameter. This mechanism allows for the setting of multiple interval processes running, while giving your scripts the power to stop individual processes at any time without interrupting the others.

IE4+ uses the optional third parameter to specify the scripting language of the statement or function being invoked in the first parameter. As long as you are scripting exclusively in JavaScript (the same as JScript), there is no need to include this parameter.

Passing function parameters

NN4+ provides a mechanism for easily passing evaluated parameters to a function invoked by setInterval(). To use this mechanism, the first parameter of setInterval() must not be a string, but rather a reference to the function (no trailing parentheses). The second parameter remains the amount of delay. But beginning with the third parameter, you can include evaluated function arguments as a comma-delimited list:

```
intervalID = setInterval(cycleAnimation, 500, "figure1")
```

The function definition receives those parameters in the same form as any function.

```
function cycleAnimation(elemID) {...}
```

For use with a wider range of browsers, you can also cobble together the ability to pass parameters to a function invoked by setInterval(). Because the call to the other function is a string expression, you can use computed values as part of the strings via string concatenation. For example, if a function uses event handling to find the element that a user clicked (to initiate some animation sequence), that element's ID, referenced by a variable, can be passed to the function invoked by setInterval():

```
function findAndCycle() {
    var elemID
    // statements here that examine the event info
    // and extract the ID of the clicked element,
    // assigning that ID to the elemID variable
    intervalID = setInterval("cycleAnimation(" + elemID + ")", 500)
}
```

If you need to pass ever-changing parameters with each invocation of the function from `setInterval()`, look instead to using `setTimeout()` at the end of a function to invoke that very same function again.

On the CD-ROM   Example (with Listings 16-36 and 16-37) on the CD-ROM

Related Items: `window.clearInterval()`, `window.setTimeout()` methods.

setTimeout("*expr*", *msecDelay* [, *language*]) setTimeout(*functionRef*, *msecDelay* [, *funcarg1*, ..., *funcargn*])

Returns: ID value for use with `window.clearTimeout()` method.

	NN2	NN3	NN4	NN6	IE3/J1	IE3/J2	IE4	IE5	IE5.5
Compatibility	✓	✓	✓	✓	✓	✓	✓	✓	✓

The name of this method may be misleading, especially if you have done other kinds of programming involving timeouts. In JavaScript, a *timeout* is an amount of time (in milliseconds) before a stated expression evaluates. A timeout is not a wait or script delay, but rather a way to tell JavaScript to hold off executing a statement or function for a desired amount of time. Other statements following the one containing `setTimeout()` execute immediately.

Say that you have a Web page designed to enable users to interact with a variety of buttons or fields within a time limit (this is a Web page running at a free-standing kiosk). You can turn on the timeout of the window so that if no interaction occurs with specific buttons or fields lower in the document after, say, two minutes (120,000 milliseconds), the window reverts to the top of the document or to a help screen. To tell the window to switch off the timeout after a user does navigate within the allotted time, you need to have any button that the user interacts with call the other side of a `setTimeout()` method—the `clearTimeout()` method—to cancel the current timer. (The `clearTimeout()` method is explained earlier in this chapter.) Multiple timers can run concurrently and are completely independent of each other.

While the primary functionality of the `setTimeout()` method is the same in both NN and IE, each browser offers some extra possibilities depending on the way you use parameters to the method. For simple invocations of this method, the same parameters work in all browsers that support the method. I first address the parameters that all browsers have in common.

The expression that comprises the first parameter of the method `window.setTimeout()` is a quoted string that can contain either a call to any function or method or a standalone JavaScript statement. The expression evaluates after the time limit expires.

Understanding that this timeout does not halt script execution is very important. In fact, if you use a `setTimeout()` method in the middle of a script, the succeeding statements in the script execute immediately; after the delay time, the expression in the `setTimeout()` method executes. Therefore, I've found that the best way to design a timeout in a script is to plug it in as the last statement of a function: Let all other statements execute and then let the `setTimeout()` method appear to halt further execution until the timer goes off. In truth, however, although the timeout is "holding," the user is not prevented from performing other tasks. And after a time-out timer is ticking, you cannot adjust its time. Instead, clear the timeout and start a new one.

If you need to use `setTimeout()` as a delay inside a function, break the function into two parts, using the `setTimeout()` method as a bridge between the two functions. You can see an example of this in Listing 16-26, where IE needs a little delay to finish opening a new window before content can be written for it. If it weren't for the required delay, the HTML assembly and writing would have been accomplished in the same function that opens the new window.

It is not uncommon for a `setTimeout()` method to invoke the very function in which it lives. For example, if you have written a Java applet to perform some extra work for your page and you need to connect to it via LiveConnect, your scripts must wait for the applet to load and carry out its initializations. While an `onLoad` event handler in the document ensures that the applet object is visible to scripts, it doesn't know whether the applet has finished its initializations. A JavaScript function that inspects the applet for a clue might need to poll the applet every 500 milliseconds until the applet sets some internal value indicating all is ready, as shown here:

```
var t
function autoReport() {
    if (!document.myApplet.done) {
        t = setTimeout("autoReport()",500)
    } else {
        clearTimeout(t)
        // more statements using applet data //
    }
}
```

JavaScript provides no built-in equivalent for a `wait` command. The worst alternative is to devise a looping function of your own to trap script execution for a fixed amount of time. In NN3+, you can also use LiveConnect (see Chapter 44) to invoke a

Java method that freezes the browser's thread for a fixed amount of time. Unfortunately, both of these practices prevent other processes from being carried out, so you should consider reworking your code to rely on a `setTimeout()` method instead.

NN4+ provides a mechanism for passing parameters to functions invoked by `setTimeout()`. See the section "Passing Parameters" in the discussion of `window.setInterval()` for details on this and passing parameters in other browser versions.

As a note to experienced programmers, neither `setInterval()` nor `setTimeout()` spawn new threads in which to run their invoked scripts. When the timer expires and invokes a function, the process gets at the end of the queue of any pending script processing in the JavaScript execution thread.

 Example (with Listing 16-38) on the CD-ROM

Related Items: `window.clearTimeout()`, `window.setInterval()`, `window.clearInterval()` methods.

showHelp("*URL*",["*contextID*"])

Returns: Nothing

	NN2	NN3	NN4	NN6	IE3/J1	IE3/J2	IE4	IE5	IE5.5
Compatibility							✓	✓	✓

The IE-specific `showHelp()` method (not implemented in IE5/Mac) lets a script open a Winhelp window with a particular `.hlp` file. This method is specific to the Win32 operating systems.

If your Winhelp file has context identifiers specified in various places, you can pass the ID as an optional second parameter. This lets the call to `showHelp()` navigate to a particular area of the `.hlp` file that applies to a specific element on the page.

Example
See the Microsoft Visual Studio authoring environment for details on building Winhelp files.

```
showModalDialog("URL"[, arguments][,
features])
showModelessDialog("URL"[, arguments][,
features])
```

Returns: `returnValue` (modal) or `window` object (modeless).

	NN2	NN3	NN4	NN6	IE3/J1	IE3/J2	IE4	IE5	IE5.5
Compatibility							(✓)	✓	✓

IE4+ provides methods for opening a modal dialog box window, which always stays in front of the main browser window while making the main window inaccessible to the user. In IE5 (but not IE5/Mac), Microsoft added the modeless type of dialog box, which also stays in front, but allows user access to whatever can be seen in the main window. You can load any HTML page or image that you like into the dialog box window, by providing a URL as the first parameter. Optional parameters let you pass data to a dialog box and give you considerable control over the look of the window. Unfortunately, these types of dialog box windows are not available in Navigator. At best, you can simulate modal and modeless dialog box windows, but the job is not for beginners (see `http://developer.netscape.com/viewsource/goodman_modal/goodman_modal.html` for one example).

The windows generated by both methods are (almost) full-fledged `window` objects with some extra properties that are useful for what these windows are intended to do. Perhaps the most important property is the `window.dialogArgument` property. This property lets a script read the data that is passed to the window via the second parameter of both `showModalDialog()` and `showModelessDialog()`. Passed data can be in any valid JavaScript data type, including objects and arrays.

Displaying a modal dialog box has some ramifications for scripts. In particular, script execution in the main window halts at the statement that invokes the `showModalDialog()` method as long as the modal dialog box remains visible. Scripts are free to run in the dialog box window during this time. The instant the user closes the dialog box, execution resumes in the main window. A call to show a modeless dialog box, on the other hand, does not halt processing because scripts in the main page or dialog box window are allowed to communicate "live" with the other window.

Retrieving dialog data

To send data back to the main window's script from a modal dialog box window, a script in the dialog box window can set the `window.returnValue` property to any

JavaScript value. It is this value that gets assigned to the variable receiving the returned value from the `setModelDialog()` method, as shown in the following example:

```
var specifications = window.showModalDialog("preferences.html")
```

The makeup and content of the returned data is in the hands of your scripts. No data is automatically returned for you.

Because a modeless dialog box coexists with your live main page window, returning data is not as straightforward as for a modal dialog box. The second parameter of the `showModelessDialog()` method takes on a special task that isn't exactly the same as passing parameters to the dialog box. Instead, if you define a global variable or a function in the main window's script, pass a reference to that variable or function as the second parameter to display the modeless dialog box. A script in the modeless dialog box can then point to that reference as the way to send data back to the main window before the dialog box closes (or when a user clicks something, such as an Apply button). This mechanism even allows for passing data back to a function in the main window. For example, say that the main window has a function defined as the following:

```
function receivePrefsDialogData(a, b, c) {
    // statements to process incoming values //
}
```

Then pass a reference to this function when opening the window:

```
dlog = showModelessDialog("prefs.html", receivePrefsDialogData)
```

A script statement in the dialog box window's document can pick up that reference so that other statements can use it, such as a function for an Apply button's `onClick` event handler:

```
var returnFunc = window.dialogArguments
...
function apply(form) {
    returnFunc(form.color.value, form.style.value, form.size.value)
}
```

While this approach seems to block ways of getting parameters to the dialog box when it opens, you can always reference the dialog box in the main window's script and set form or variable values directly:

```
dlog = showModelessDialog("prefs.html", receivePrefsDialogData)
dlog.document.forms[0].userName.value = GetCookie("userName")
```

Be aware that a dialog box window opened with either of these methods does not maintain a connection to the originating window via the `opener` property. The `opener` property for both dialog box types is undefined.

Dialog window features

Both methods provide an optional third property that lets you specify visible features of the dialog box window. Omitting the property sets all features to their default values. All parameters are to be contained by a single string, and each parameter's name-value pair is in the form of CSS `attribute:value` syntax. Table 16-4 lists all of the window features available for the two window styles. If you are designing for compatibility with IE4, you are restricted to the modal dialog box and a subset of features, as noted in the table. All values listed as Boolean take only the following four values: `yes`, `no`, `1`, `0`.

Table 16-4   IE Dialog Box Window Features

Feature	Type	Default	Description
center	Boolean	yes	Whether to center dialog box (overridden by `dialogLeft` and/or `dialogTop`).
dialogHeight	Length	varies	Outer height of the dialog box window. IE4 default length unit is `em`; IE5 is pixel (`px`).
dialogLeft	Integer	varies	Pixel offset of dialog box from left edge of screen.
dialogTop	Integer	varies	Pixel offset of dialog box from top edge of screen.
dialogWidth	Length	varies	Outer width of the dialog box window. IE4 default length unit is `em`; IE5 is pixel (`px`).
help	Boolean	yes	Display Help icon in title bar.
resizable	Boolean	no	Dialog box is resizable (IE5+ only).
status	Boolean	varies	Display statusbar at window bottom (IE5+ only). Default is `yes` for untrusted dialog box; `no` for trusted dialog box.

The CSS-type of syntax for these features lets you string multiple features together by separating each pair with a semicolon within the string. For example:

```
var dlogData = showModalDialog("prefs.html", defaultData,
"dialogHeight:300px; dialogWidth:460px; help:no")
```

Although not explicitly listed as one of the window features, scroll bars are normally displayed in the window if the content exceeds the size assigned or available to the dialog box. If you don't want scroll bars to appear, have your dialog box document's script set the `document.body.scroll` property to `false` as the page opens.

Dialog cautions

A potential user problem to watch for is that typically a dialog box window does not open until the HTML file for the dialog box has loaded. Therefore, if there is substantial delay before a complex document loads, the user does not see any action indicating that something is happening. You may want to experiment with setting the `cursor` style sheet property and restoring it when the dialog box's document loads.

One of the reasons I call a dialog box window an (almost) `window` object is that some normal behavior is not available in IE4. For example, if you load a frameset into the dialog box window, scripts in documents within the frames cannot refer back to the parent document to access variables or parent window methods. Thus, a button in a frame of an IE4 modal dialog box cannot issue `parent.close()` to close the dialog box. This anomaly is repaired in IE5.

Example (with Listings 16-39 through 16-42) on the CD-ROM

Related Items: `window.open()` method.

sizeToContent()

Returns: Nothing.

	NN2	NN3	NN4	NN6	IE3/J1	IE3/J2	IE4	IE5	IE5.5
Compatibility				✓					

The NN6 `window.sizeToContent()` method can be a valuable aid in making sure that a window (especially a subwindow) is sized for the optimum display of the window's content. But you must also be cautious with this method, or it will do more harm than good.

Invoking the `sizeToContent()` method resizes the window so that all content is visible. Concerns about variations in OS-specific rendering become a thing of the past. Naturally, you should perform this action only on a window whose content at the most occupies a space smaller than the smallest video monitor running your code (typically 640 × 480 pixels, but conceivably much smaller for future versions of the browser used on handheld computers).

You can get the user in trouble, however, if you invoke the method twice on the same window that contains the resizing script. This action can cause the window to expand to a size that may exceed the pixel size of the user's video monitor. Successive invocations fail to cinch up the window's size to its content again. Multiple invocations are safe, however, on subwindows when the resizing script statement is in the main window.

On the CD-ROM   Example on the CD-ROM

Related Item: `window.resizeTo()` method.

stop()

Returns: Nothing.

	NN2	NN3	NN4	NN6	IE3/J1	IE3/J2	IE4	IE5	IE5.5
Compatibility			✓	✓					

The Navigator-specific `stop()` method offers a scripted equivalent of clicking the Stop button in the toolbar. Availability of this method allows you to create your own toolbar on your page and hide the toolbar (in the main window with signed scripts or in a subwindow). For example, if you have an image representing the Stop button in your page, you can surround it with a link whose action stops loading, as in the following:

```
<A HREF="javascript: void stop()"><IMG SRC="myStop.gif" BORDER=0></A>
```

A script cannot stop its own document from loading, but it can stop loading of another frame or window. Similarly, if the current document dynamically loads a new image or a multimedia MIME type file as a separate action, the `stop()` method can halt that process. Even though the `stop()` method is a window method, it is not tied to any specific window or frame: Stop means stop.

Related Items: `window.back()`, `window.find()`, `window.forward()`, `window.home()`, `window.print()` methods.

Event handlers

onAfterPrint
onBeforePrint

	NN2	NN3	NN4	NN6	IE3/J1	IE3/J2	IE4	IE5	IE5.5
Compatibility								✓	✓

Each of these event handlers (not implemented in IE5/Mac) fires after the user has clicked the OK button in IE's Print dialog box. This goes for printing that is invoked manually (via menus and browser shortcut buttons) and the `window.print()` method.

Although printing is usually WYSIWYG, it is conceivable that you may want the printed version of a document to display more or less of the document than is showing at that instant. For example, you may have a special copyright notice that you want printed at the end of a page whenever it goes to the printer. In that case, the element with that content can have its `display` style sheet property set to `none` when the page loads. Before the document is sent to the printer, a script needs to adjust that style property to display the element as a block item; after printing, have your script revert the setting to `none`.

Immediately after the user clicks the OK button in the Print dialog box, the `onBeforePrint` event handler fires. As soon as the page(s) is sent to the printer or spooler, the `onAfterPrint` event handler fires.

On the CD-ROM   Example on the CD-ROM

onBeforeUnload

	NN2	NN3	NN4	NN6	IE3/J1	IE3/J2	IE4	IE5	IE5.5
Compatibility							✓	✓	✓

Any user or scripted action that normally forces the current page to be unloaded or replaced causes the onBeforeUnload event handler to fire (not implemented in IE5/Mac). Unlike the onUnload event handler, however, onBeforeUnload is a bit better behaved when it comes to allowing complex scripts to finish before the actual unloading takes place. Moreover, you can assign a string value to the event.returnValue property in the event handler function. That string becomes part of a message in an alert window that gives the user a chance to stay on the page. If the user agrees to stay, the page does not unload, and any action that caused the potential replacement is cancelled.

Example (with Listing 16-43) on the CD-ROM

Related Items: onUnload event handler.

onDragDrop

	NN2	NN3	NN4	NN6	IE3/J1	IE3/J2	IE4	IE5	IE5.5
Compatibility			✓						

With closer integration between the computer desktop and browsers these days, it is increasingly possible that shortcuts (or aliases) to Web URLs can be represented on our desktops and other kinds of documents. With NN4, you can script awareness of dragging and dropping of such items onto the browser window. The window's dragDrop event fires whenever a user drops a file or other URL-filled object onto the window.

You can add an onDragDrop event handler to the <BODY> tag of your document and pass along the event object that has some juicy tidbits about the drop: the object on which the item was dropped and the URL of the item. The function called by the event handler receives the event object information and can process it from there. Because this event is a window event, you don't have to turn on window.captureEvents() to get the window to feel the effect of the event.

The juiciest tidbit of the event, the URL of the dropped item, can be retrieved only with a signed script and the user's permission (see Chapter 46). Listing 16-44 shows a simple document that reveals the URL and screen location, as derived from the event object passed with the dragDrop event. You must have codebase principals turned on to get the full advantage of this listing, and it works best with Windows.

Listing 16-44: Analyzing a dragDrop Event

```
<HTML>
<HEAD>
<TITLE>DragDrop Event</TITLE>
<SCRIPT LANGUAGE="JavaScript">
function reportDrag(e) {
    var msg = "You dropped the file:\n"
    netscape.security.PrivilegeManager.enablePrivilege("UniversalBrowserRead")
    msg += e.data
    netscape.security.PrivilegeManager.disablePrivilege("UniversalBrowserRead")
    msg += "\nonto the window object at screen location ("
    msg += e.screenX + "," + e.screenY + ")."
    alert(msg)
    return false
}
</SCRIPT>
</HEAD>
<BODY onDragDrop="return reportDrag(event)">
<B>Drag and Drop a file onto this window</B>
</BODY>
</HTML>
```

The dragDrop event is the only one that uses the data property of the NN4 event object. That property contains the URL. The target property reveals only the window object, but you can access the event object's screenX and screenY properties to get the location of the mouse release.

Related Items: event object (Chapter 29).

onError

	NN2	NN3	NN4	NN6	IE3/J1	IE3/J2	IE4	IE5	IE5.5
Compatibility		✓	✓	✓			✓	✓	✓

See the discussion of the window.onerror property earlier in this chapter.

onHelp

	NN2	NN3	NN4	NN6	IE3/J1	IE3/J2	IE4	IE5	IE5.5
Compatibility							✓	✓	✓

The generic onHelp event handler is discussed in Chapter 15, but it also fires when the user activates the context-sensitive help within a modal or modeless dialog box. In the latter case, a user can click the Help icon in the dialog box's title bar, at which time the cursor changes to a question mark. The user can then click on any element in the window. At that second click, the onHelp event handler fires, and the event object contains information about the element clicked (the event.srcElement is a reference to the specific element), allowing a script to supply help about that element.

To prevent the brower's built-in help window from appearing, the event handler must evaluate to return false (IE4+) or set the event.returnValue property to false (IE5).

Example

The following script fragment can be embedded in the IE5-only modeless dialog box code in Listing 16-44 to provide context-sensitive help within the dialog box. Help messages for only two of the form elements are shown here, but in a real application you add messages for the rest.

```
function showHelp() {
    switch (event.srcElement.name) {
        case "bgColor" :
            alert("Choose a color for the main window\'s background.")
            break
        case "name" :
            alert("Enter your first name for a friendly greeting.")
            break
        default :
            alert("Make preference settings for the main page styles.")
    }
    event.returnValue = false
}
window.onhelp = showHelp
```

Because this page's help focuses on form elements, the switch construction cases are based on the name properties of the form elements. For other kinds of pages, the id properties may be more appropriate.

Related Items: event object (Chapter 29); switch construction (Chapter 39).

onLoad

	NN2	NN3	NN4	NN6	IE3/J1	IE3/J2	IE4	IE5	IE5.5
Compatibility	✓	✓	✓	✓	✓	✓	✓	✓	✓

The onLoad event handler fires in the current window at the end of the document loading process (after all text and image elements have been transferred from the source file server to the browser, and after all plug-ins and Java applets have loaded and started running). At that point, the browser's memory contains all the objects and script components in the document that the browser can possibly know about.

The onLoad handler is an attribute of a <BODY> tag for a single-frame document or of the <FRAMESET> tag for the top window of a multiple-frame document. When the handler is an attribute of a <FRAMESET> tag, the event triggers only after all frames defined by that frameset have completely loaded.

Use either of the following scenarios to insert an onLoad handler into a document:

```
<HTML>
<HEAD>
</HEAD>
<BODY [other attributes] onLoad="statementOrFunction">
[body content]
</BODY>
</HTML>


<HTML>
<HEAD>
</HEAD>
<FRAMESET [other attributes] onLoad="statementOrFunction">
    <FRAME>frame specifications</FRAME>
</FRAMESET>
</HTML>
```

This handler has a special capability when part of a frameset definition: The handler won't fire until the onLoad event handlers of all child frames in the frameset have fired. Therefore, if some initialization scripts depend on components existing in other frames, trigger them from the frameset's onLoad event handler. This brings up a good general rule of thumb for writing JavaScript: Scripts that execute during a document's loading should contribute to the process of generating the document and its objects. To act immediately on those objects, design additional functions that are called by the onLoad event handler for that window.

onLoad Bugs and Anomalies

The onLoad event has changed its behavior over the life of JavaScript in Navigator. In Navigator 2, the onLoad event handler fired whenever the user resized the window. Many developers considered this a bug because the running of such scripts destroyed data that were carefully gathered since the document originally loaded. From Navigator 3 onward (and including IE3+), a window resize does not trigger a load event.

Two onLoad bugs haunt Navigator 3 when used in conjunction with framesets. The first bug affects only Windows versions. The problem is that the frameset's onLoad event handler is not necessarily the last one to fire among all the frames. It is possible that one frame's onLoad event may still not have processed before the frameset's onLoad event handler goes. This can cause serious problems if your frameset's onLoad event handler relies on that final frame being fully loaded.

The second bug affects all versions of NN3, but at least a workaround exists. If a frame contains a Java applet, the frameset's onLoad event handler will fire before the applet has fully loaded and started. But if you place an onLoad event handler in the applet's document (even a dummy onLoad="" in the <BODY> tag), the frameset's onLoad event handler behaves properly.

The type of operations suited for an onLoad event handler are those that can run quickly and without user intervention. Users shouldn't be penalized by having to wait for considerable post-loading activity to finish before they can interact with your pages. At no time should you present a modal dialog box as part of an onLoad handler. Users who design macros on their machines to visit sites unattended may get hung up on a page that automatically displays an alert, confirm, or prompt dialog box. On the other hand, an operation such as setting the window.defaultStatus property is a perfect candidate for an onLoad event handler, as are initializing event handlers as properties of element objects in the page.

Related Items: onUnload event handler; window.defaultStatus property.

onMove

	NN2	NN3	NN4	NN6	IE3/J1	IE3/J2	IE4	IE5	IE5.5
Compatibility			✓						

If a user drags an NN4 window around the screen, the action triggers a move event for the window object. When you assign a function to the event (for example, window.onmove = handleMoves), the function receives an event object whose screenX and screenY properties reveal the coordinate point (relative to the entire screen) of the top-left corner of the window after the move.

Related Items: event object (Chapter 29).

onResize

	NN2	NN3	NN4	NN6	IE3/J1	IE3/J2	IE4	IE5	IE5.5
Compatibility			✓	✓			✓	✓	✓

If a user resizes a window, the action causes the onResize event handler to fire for the window object. When you assign a function to the event (for example, window.onresize = handleResizes), the NN event object conveys width and height properties that reveal the outer width and height of the entire window. A window resize should not reload the document such that an onLoad event handler fires (although some early Navigator versions did fire the extra event).

Note: Resizing the Navigator 4 browser window, especially if that window contains positioned elements (as DIV or LAYER elements) causes serious problems not only for the content, but also for scripts in the page. Content can get jumbled, and scripts may disappear. Your only hope is to use an onResize event handler to reload the page and get back to a known point. For some ideas on handling this problem, see the article at http://developer.netscape.com/viewsource/goodman_resize/goodman_resize.html. One point not covered in the article is that the Windows version of NN4 issues a resize event when scroll bars appear in a window. This resize event can make any reload-on-resize strategy turn into an infinite loop. To guard against this, you have to inspect the window.innerWidth and window.innerHeight properties to see if the window has really changed (the property values don't change when the scrollbars appear). Here is an example of script statements that go in the Head script of a page that has to worry about this problem in NN4:

```
var Nav4 = (navigator.appName == "Netscape" &&
parseInt(navigator.appVersion) == 4)
if (Nav4) {
    var loadWidth = window.innerWidth
    var loadHeight = window.innerHeight
}

function restore() {
    if (loadWidth != window.innerWidth || loadHeight != window.innerHeight) {
        history.go(0)
    }
}
if (Nav4) window.onresize = restore
```

Related Items: event object (Chapter 29).

onUnload

	NN2	NN3	NN4	NN6	IE3/J1	IE3/J2	IE4	IE5	IE5.5
Compatibility	✓	✓	✓	✓	✓	✓	✓	✓	✓

An unload event reaches the current window just before a document is cleared from view. The most common ways windows are cleared are when new HTML documents are loaded into them or when a script begins writing new HTML on the fly for the window or frame.

Limit the extent of the onUnload event handler to quick operations that do not inhibit the transition from one document to another. Do not invoke any methods that display dialog boxes. You specify onUnload event handlers in the same places in an HTML document as the onLoad handlers: as a <BODY> tag attribute for a single-frame window or as a <FRAMESET> tag attribute for a multiframe window. Both onLoad and onUnload event handlers can appear in the same <BODY> or <FRAME-SET> tag without causing problems. The onUnload event handler merely stays safely tucked away in the browser's memory, waiting for the unload event to arrive for processing as the document gets ready to clear the window.

Let me pass along one caution about the onUnload event handler. Even though the event fires before the document goes away, don't burden the event handler with time-consuming tasks, such as generating new objects or submitting a form. The document will probably go away before the function completes, leaving the function looking for objects and values that no longer exist. The best defense is to keep your onUnload event handler processing to a minimum.

Related Items: onLoad event handler.

FRAME Element Object

For HTML element properties, methods, and event handlers, see Chapter 15.

Properties	Methods	Event Handlers
borderColor		
contentDocument		
Document		

Properties	Methods	Event Handlers
frameBorder		
height		
longDesc		
marginHeight		
marginWidth		
noResize		
scrolling		
src		
width		

Syntax

Accessing properties or methods of a FRAME element object from a FRAMESET:

```
(IE4+)    document.all.frameID. property | method([parameters])
(IE5+/NN6) document.getElementById("frameID"). property | method([parameters])
```

Accessing properties of methods of a FRAME element from a frame document:

```
(IE4+)    parent.document.all.frameID. property | method([parameters])
(IE5+/NN6) parent.document.getElementById("frameID"). property |
          method([parameters])
```

About this object

As noted in the opening section of this chapter, a FRAME element object is distinct from the frame object that acts as a window object in a document hierarchy. The FRAME element object is available to scripts only when all HTML elements are exposed in the object model, as in IE4+ and NN6.

Because the FRAME element object is an HTML element, it shares the properties, methods, and event handlers of all HTML elements, as described in Chapter 15. By and large, you access the FRAME element object to set or modify an attribute value in the <FRAME> tag. If so, you simplify matters if you assign an identifier to the ID attribute of the tag. Your tag still needs a NAME attribute if your scripts refer to frames through the original object model (a parent.frameName reference). While there is no law against using the same identifier for both NAME and ID attributes, using different names to prevent potential conflict with references in browsers that recognize both attributes is best.

To modify the dimensions of a frame, you must go the FRAMESET element object that defines the COLS and ROWS attributes for the frameset. These properties can be modified on the fly in IE4+ and NN6.

Properties

borderColor

Value: Hexadecimal triplet or color name string   Read/Write

	NN2	NN3	NN4	NN6	IE3/J1	IE3/J2	IE4	IE5	IE5.5
Compatibility							✓	✓	✓

If a frame displays a border (as determined by the FRAMEBORDER attribute of the FRAME element or BORDER attribute of the FRAMESET element), it can have a color set separately from the rest of the frames. The initial color (if different from the rest of the frameset) is usually set by the BORDERCOLOR attribute of the <FRAME> tag. After that, scripts can modify settings as needed.

Modifying a single frame's border can be risky at times, depending on your color combinations. In practice, different browers appear to follow different rules when it comes to negotiating conflicts or defining just how far a single frame's border extends into the border space. Moreover, IE5/Windows exhibits some strange coloration behavior when applying a border color to a single frame. Color changes to individual frame borders do not always render. Verify your designs on as many browsers and operating system variations as you can to test your combinations.

Example on the CD-ROM

Related Items: FRAME.frameBorder, FRAMESET.frameBorder properties.

contentDocument

Value: document object reference   Read-Only

	NN2	NN3	NN4	NN6	IE3/J1	IE3/J2	IE4	IE5	IE5.5
Compatibility				✓					

The contentDocument property of a FRAME element object is nothing more than a reference to the document contained by that frame. This property bridges the gap between the FRAME element object and the frame object. Both of these objects contain the same document object, but from a scripting point of view, references most typically use the frame object to reach the document inside a frame, while the FRAME element is used to access properties equated with the FRAME tag's attributes. But if your script finds that it has a reference to the FRAME element object, you can use the contentDocument property to get a valid reference to the document, and therefore any other content of the frame.

 Example on the CD-ROM

Related Items: document object.

Document

Value: document object   Read-Only

	NN2	NN3	NN4	NN6	IE3/J1	IE3/J2	IE4	IE5	IE5.5
Compatibility							✓	✓	✓

Because IE4 for Windows implements frames as what are known as ActiveX Web Browser objects, there are times when the properties of the Web Brower object can fill in when the regular object model has a gap. Such is the case when trying to gain access to the document object contained by a FRAME element object. Recall (from Chapter 15) that the document property of an HTML element refers to the document that contains the current object. In the case of a FRAME element, that would be the framesetting document. But to jump across the normal element node hierarchy from the FRAME element to the document it contains, you can use the Document (uppercase "D") property.Even though IE5 no longer uses the Web Browser object for frames, the Document property continues to be available.

 Example on the CD-ROM

Related Items: window.document property.

frameBorder

Value: yes | no | 1 | 0 as strings   Read/Write

	NN2	NN3	NN4	NN6	IE3/J1	IE3/J2	IE4	IE5	IE5.5
Compatibility				✓			✓	✓	✓

The frameBorder property offers scripted access to a FRAME element object's FRAMEBORDER attribute setting. IE4+ does not respond well to modifying this property after the page has loaded.

Values for the frameBorder property are strings that substitute for Boolean values. Values yes or 1 mean that the border is (supposed to be) turned on; no or 0 turn off the border.

On the CD-ROM   Example on the CD-ROM

Related Items: FRAMESET.frameBorder properties.

height
width

Value: Integer   Read-Only

	NN2	NN3	NN4	NN6	IE3/J1	IE3/J2	IE4	IE5	IE5.5
Compatibility							✓	✓	✓

IE4+ lets you retrieve the height and width of a FRAME element object. These values are not necessarily the same as the document.body.clientHeight and document.body.clientWidth, because the frame dimensions include chrome associated with the frame, such as scrollbars. These values are read-only. If you need to modify the dimensions of a frame, do so via the FRAMESET element object's rows and/or cols properties. Reading integer values for a frame's height and width properties is much easier than trying to parse the rows and cols string properties.

Example on the CD-ROM

Related Items: FRAMESET object.

longDesc

Value: URL String   Read/Write

	NN2	NN3	NN4	NN6	IE3/J1	IE3/J2	IE4	IE5	IE5.5
Compatibility				✓					

The longDesc property is the scripted equivalent of the LONGDESC attribute of the
<FRAME> tag. This HTML 4.0 attribute is intended to provide browsers with a URL to a
document that contains a long description of the element. Future browsers can use
this feature to provide information about the frame for visually impaired site visitors.

marginHeight
marginWidth

Value: Integer   Read/Write

	NN2	NN3	NN4	NN6	IE3/J1	IE3/J2	IE4	IE5	IE5.5
Compatibility				✓			✓	✓	✓

Browsers tend to automatically insert content within a frame by adding a margin
between the content and the edge of the frame. These values are represented by
the marginHeight (top and bottom edges) and marginWidth (left and right edges)
properties. Although the properties are not read-only, changing the values after the
frameset has loaded does not alter the appearance of the document in the frame. If
you need to alter the margin(s) of a document inside a frame, adjust the document.
body.style margin properties.

Also be aware that although the default values of these properties are empty (meaning when no MARGINHEIGHT or MARGINWIDTH attributes are set for the <FRAME> tag), margins are built into the page. The precise pixel count of those margins varies with operating system.

Related Items: style object (Chapter 30).

noResize

Value: Boolean   Read/Write

	NN2	NN3	NN4	NN6	IE3/J1	IE3/J2	IE4	IE5	IE5.5
Compatibility				✓			✓	✓	✓

Web designers commonly fix their framesets so that users cannot resize the frames (by dragging any divider border between frames). The noResize property lets you read and adjust that behavior of a frame after the page has loaded. For example, during some part of the interaction with a user on a page, you may allow the user to modify the frame size manually while in a certain mode. Or you may grant the user one chance to resize the frame. When the onResize event handler fires, a script sets the noResize property of the FRAME element to false. If you turn off resizing for a frame, all edges of the frame become non-resizable, regardless of the noResize value setting of adjacent frames. Turning off resizability has no effect on the ability of scripts to alter the sizes of frames via the FRAMESET element object's cols or rows properties.

On the CD-ROM   Example on the CD-ROM

Related Items: FRAMESET.cols, FRAMESET.rows properties.

scrolling

Value: yes | no | 1 | 0 as strings   Read/Write

	NN2	NN3	NN4	NN6	IE3/J1	IE3/J2	IE4	IE5	IE5.5
Compatibility				✓			✓	✓	✓

The scrolling property lets scripts turn scrollbars on and off inside a single frame of a frameset. By default, scrolling is turned on unless overridden by the SCROLL attribute of the <FRAME> tag.

Values for the scrolling property are strings that substitute for Boolean values. Values yes or 1 mean that scrollbars are visible (provided there is more content than can be viewed without scrolling); no or 0 hide scrollbars in the frame. IE4+ also recognizes (and sets as default) the auto value.

Note   This property is partially broken in IE5.5/Windows. While the object records changes to the property, the frame's appearance does not change. NN6 has the same problem, plus some others, such as the property not returning a value unless the SCROLLING attribute is specified in the FRAME element's tag.

On the CD-ROM   Example (with Listing 16-45) on the CD-ROM

src

Value: URL String   Read/Write

	NN2	NN3	NN4	NN6	IE3/J1	IE3/J2	IE4	IE5	IE5.5
Compatibility				✓			✓	✓	✓

The src property of a FRAME element object offers an additional way of navigating to a different page within a frame (meaning other than assigning a new URL to the location.href property of the frame object). For backward compatibility with older browsers, however, continue using location.href for scripted navigation. Remember that the src property belongs to the FRAME element object, not the window object it represents. Therefore, references to the src property must be via the element's ID and/or node hierarchy.

On the CD-ROM   Example on the CD-ROM

Related Items: location.href property.

FRAMESET Element Object

For HTML element properties, methods, and event handlers, see Chapter 15.

Properties	Methods	Event Handlers
border		
borderColor		
cols		
frameBorder		
frameSpacing		
rows		

Syntax

Accessing properties or methods of a FRAMESET element object from a FRAMESET:

```
(IE4+)     document.all.framesetID. property | method([parameters])
(IE5+/NN6) document.getElementById("framesetID"). property |
           method([parameters])
```

Accessing properties of methods of a FRAMESET element from a frame document:

```
(IE4+)     parent.document.all.framesetID. property | method([parameters])
(IE5+/NN6) parent.document.getElementById("framesetID"). property |
           method([parameters])
```

About this object

The FRAMESET element object is the script-accessible equivalent of the element generated via the `<FRAMESET>` tag. This element is different from the parent (window-type) object from the original object model. A FRAMESET element object has properties and methods that impact the HTML element; in contrast, the `window` object referenced from documents inside frames via the `parent` or `top` window references contains a document and all the content that goes along with it.

When framesets are nested in one another, a node parent–child relationship exists between containing and contained framesets. For example, consider the following skeletal nested frameset structure:

```
<FRAMESET ID="outerFrameset" COLS="30%, 70%">
    <FRAME ID="frame1">
    <FRAMESET ID="innerFrameset" ROWS="50%,50%">
        <FRAME ID="frame2">
        <FRAME ID="frame3">
    </FRAMESET>
</FRAMESET>
```

When writing scripts for documents that go inside any of the frames of this structure, references to the framesetting window and frames are a flatter hierarchy than the HTML signifies. A script in any frame references the framesetting window via the `parent` reference; a script in any frame references another frame via the `parent.frameName` reference. In other words, the `window` objects of the frameset defined in a document are all siblings and share the same parent.

Such is not the case when viewing the above structure from the perspective of W3C node terminology. Parent–child relationships are governed by the nesting of HTML elements, irrespective of whatever windows get generated by the browser. Therefore, frame `frame2` has only one sibling, `frame3`. Both of those share one parent, `innerFrameset`. Both `innerFrameset` and `frame1` are children of `outerFrameset`. If your script were sitting on a reference to `frame2`, and you wanted to change the `cols` property of `outerFrameset`, you would have to traverse two generations of nodes:

```
frame2Ref.parentNode.parentNode.cols = "40%,60%"
```

What might confuse matters ever more in practice is that a script belonging to one of the frames must use window object terminology to jump out of the current `window` object to the frameset that generated the frame window for the document. In other words, there is no immediate way to jump directly from a document to the FRAME element object that defines the frame in which the document resides. The document's script accesses the node hierarchy of its frameset via the `parent.document` reference. But this reference is to the `document` object that contains the entire frameset structure. Fortunately, the W3C DOM provides the `getElementById()` method to extract a reference to any node nested within the document. Thus, a document inside one of the frames can access the FRAME element object just as if it were any element in a typical document (which it is):

```
parent.document.getElementById("frame2")
```

No reference to the containing FRAMESET element object is necessary. Or, to make that column width change from a script inside one of the frame windows, the statement would be:

```
parent.document.getElementById("outerFrame").cols = "40%,60%"
```

The inner frameset is equally accessible by the same syntax.

Properties

border

Value: Integer   Read/Write

	NN2	NN3	NN4	NN6	IE3/J1	IE3/J2	IE4	IE5	IE5.5
Compatibility							✓	✓	✓

The border property of a FRAMESET element object lets you read the thickness (in pixels) of the borders between frames of a frameset. If you do not specify a BORDER attribute in the frameset's tag, the property is empty, rather than reflecting the actual border thickness applied by default.

On the CD-ROM   Example on the CD-ROM

Related Items: FRAMESET.frameBorder property.

borderColor

Value: Hexadecimal triplet or color name string   Read/Write

	NN2	NN3	NN4	NN6	IE3/J1	IE3/J2	IE4	IE5	IE5.5
Compatibility							✓	✓	✓

The borderColor property lets you read the value of the color assigned to the BORDERCOLOR attribute of the frameset's tag. Although the property is read/write, changing the color by script does not alter the border colors rendered in the browser window. Attribute values set as color names are returned as hexadecimal triplets when you read the property value.

On the CD-ROM   Example on the CD-ROM

Related Items: FRAME.borderColor, FRAMESET.frameBorder properties.

cols
rows

Value: String   Read/Write

	NN2	NN3	NN4	NN6	IE3/J1	IE3/J2	IE4	IE5	IE5.5
Compatibility				✓			✓	✓	✓

The cols and rows properties of a FRAMESET element object let you read and modify the sizes of frames after the frameset has loaded. These two properties are
defined in the W3C DOM. Values for both properties are strings, which may include
percent symbols or asterisks. Therefore if you are trying to increase or decrease
the size of a frame column or row gradually, you must parse the string for the necessary original values before performing any math on them (or, in IE4+, use the
FRAME element object's height and width properties to gauge the current frame
size in pixels).

IE4+ lets you completely modify the frameset by adjusting these properties. This
includes adding or removing columns or rows to the frameset grid. Because a
change in the frameset structure could impact scripts by changing the size of the
frames array associated with the parent window or unloading documents that contain needed data, be sure to test your scripts with both states of your frameset. If
you want to remove a frame from a frameset view, you might be safer to specify the
size of zero for that particular row or column in the frameset. Of course a size of
zero still leaves a one-pixel frame, but it is essentially invisible if borders are not
turned on and the one-pixel frame shares the same background color as the other
frames. Another positive by-product of this technique is that you can restore the
other frame with its document state identical from when it was hidden.

When you have nested framesets defined in a single document, be sure to reference
the desired FRAMESET element object. One object may be specifying the columns,
while another (nested) one specifies the rows for the grid. Assign a unique ID to
each FRAMESET element so that references can be reliably directed to the proper
object.

Example (with Listings 16-46, 16-47, and 16-48) on the CD-ROM

Related Items: FRAME object.

frameBorder

Value: yes | no | 1 | 0 as strings   Read/Write

	NN2	NN3	NN4	NN6	IE3/J1	IE3/J2	IE4	IE5	IE5.5
Compatibility							✓	✓	✓

The frameBorder property offers scripted access to a FRAMESET element object's FRAMEBORDER attribute setting. IE4+ does not respond well to modifying this property after the page has loaded.

Values for the frameBorder property are strings that substitute for Boolean values. Values yes or 1 mean that the border is (supposed to be) turned on; no or 0 turn off the border.

Example on the CD-ROM

Related Items: FRAME.frameBorder properties.

frameSpacing

Value: Integer   Read/Write

	NN2	NN3	NN4	NN6	IE3/J1	IE3/J2	IE4	IE5	IE5.5
Compatibility							✓	✓	✓

The frameSpacing property of a FRAMESET element object lets you read the spacing (in pixels) between frames of a frameset. If you do not specify a FRAMESPACING attribute in the frameset's tag, the property is empty, rather than reflecting the actual border thickness applied by default (usually 2).

Example on the CD-ROM

Related Items: FRAMESET.border property.

IFRAME Element Object

For HTML element properties, methods, and event handlers, see Chapter 15.

Properties	Methods	Event Handlers
align		
contentDocument		
Document		
frameBorder		
frameSpacing		
hspace		
longDesc		
marginHeight		
marginWidth		
scrolling		
src		
vspace		

Syntax

Accessing properties or methods of an IFRAME element object from a containing document:

```
(IE4+)     document.all.iframeID. property | method([parameters])
(IE4+/NN6) window.frames["iframeName"]. property | method([parameters])
(IE5+/NN6) document.getElementById("iframeID"). property | method([parameters])
```

Accessing properties of methods of an IFRAME element from a document inside the IFRAME element:

```
(IE4+)     parent.document.all.iframeID. property | method([parameters])
(IE5+/NN6) parent.document.getElementById("iframeID"). property |
method([parameters])
```

About this object

An IFRAME element (IE4+ and NN6) allows HTML content from a separate source to be loaded within the body of another document. In some respects, the NN4 LAYER element was a precursor to the IFRAME concept, but unlike the LAYER, an IFRAME element is not inherently positionable. It is positionable, the same way as any other HTML element, by assigning positioning attributes to a style sheet associated with the IFRAME. Without explicit positioning, an IFRAME element appears in the body of a document in normal source code order of elements. Unlike a frame of a frameset, you can place an IFRAME arbitrarily in the middle of any document. If the FRAME changes size under script control, the surrounding content moves out of the way or cinches up.

What truly separates the IFRAME apart from other HTML elements is its ability to load and display external HTML files and, with the help of scripts, have different pages loaded into the IFRAME without disturbing the rest of the content of the main document. Pages loaded into the IFRAME can also have scripts and any other features that you may like to put into an HTML document (including XML).

The IFRAME element has a rich set of attributes that let the HTML author control the look, size (`HEIGHT` and `WIDTH`), and, to some degree, behavior of the frame. Most of those are accessible to scripts as properties of an IFRAME element object.

It is important to bear in mind that an IFRAME element is in many respects like a FRAME element, especially when it comes to window kinds of relationships. If you plant an IFRAME element in a document of the main window, that element shows up in the main window's object model as a frame, accessible via common frames terminology:

```
window.frames[i]
window.frames[frameName]
```

Within that IFRAME frame object is a document and all its contents. All references to the document objects inside the IFRAME must flow through the "portal" of the IFRAME frame.

Conversely, scripts in the document living inside an IFRAME can communicate with the main document via the `parent` reference. Of course, you cannot replace the content of the main window with another HTML document (using `location.href`, for instance) without destroying the IFRAME that was in the original document.

Properties

`align`

Value: String   Read/Write

	NN2	NN3	NN4	NN6	IE3/J1	IE3/J2	IE4	IE5	IE5.5
Compatibility				✓			✓	✓	✓

The `align` property governs how an IFRAME element aligns itself with respect to surrounding content on the page. Two of the possible values (`left` and `right`) position the IFRAME along the left and right edge (respectively) of the IFRAME's containing element (usually the BODY). Just as with an image, when an IFRAME is floated along the left and right edges of a container, other content wraps around the element. Table 16-5 shows all possible values and their meanings.

Table 16-5:   **Values of the align Property**

Value	Description
absbottom	Aligns the bottom of the IFRAME with the imaginary line that extends along character descenders of surrounding text.
absmiddle	Aligns the middle of the IFRAME with the center point between the surrounding text's `top` and `absbottom`.
baseline	Aligns the bottom of the IFRAME with the baseline of surrounding text.
bottom	Same as `baseline` in IE.
left	Aligns the IFRAME flush with left edge of the containing element.
middle	Aligns the imaginary vertical centerline of surrounding text with the same for the IFRAME element.
right	Aligns the IFRAME flush with the right edge of the containing element.
texttop	Aligns the top of the IFRAME element with the imaginary line that extends along the tallest ascender of surrounding text.
top	Aligns the top of the IFRAME element with the surrounding element's top.

As your script changes the value of the `align` property, the page automatically reflows the content to suit the new alignment.

Example on the CD-ROM

Related Items: `IFRAME.hspace`, `IFRAME.vspace` properties.

contentDocument

Value: document object reference   Read-Only

	NN2	NN3	NN4	NN6	IE3/J1	IE3/J2	IE4	IE5	IE5.5
Compatibility				✓					

The `contentDocument` property of an IFRAME element object is nothing more than a reference to the document contained by that frame. If your script finds that it has a reference to an IFRAME element object, you can use the `contentDocument` property to get a valid reference to the document, and therefore any other content of the frame.

Example on the CD-ROM

Related Items: document object.

Document

Value: document object   Read-Only

	NN2	NN3	NN4	NN6	IE3/J1	IE3/J2	IE4	IE5	IE5.5
Compatibility							✓	✓	✓

See the `FRAME.Document` property for details on this property of the ActiveX Web Browser object. You find less need for this property with an IFRAME element, because you can use the `window` object behavior of IFRAMEs to transcend the document object hierarchies of the main window and the IFRAME window.

Related Items: `FRAME.Document` property.

frameBorder

Value: `yes | no | 1 | 0` as strings   Read/Write

	NN2	NN3	NN4	NN6	IE3/J1	IE3/J2	IE4	IE5	IE5.5
Compatibility				✓			✓	✓	✓

The `frameBorder` property offers scripted access to an IFRAME element object's `FRAMEBORDER` attribute setting. IE4+ does not respond well to modifying this property after the page has loaded.

Values for the `frameBorder` property are strings that substitute for Boolean values. Values `yes` or `1` mean that the border is (supposed to be) turned on; `no` or `0` turn off the border.

 Example on the CD-ROM

Related Items: `FRAME.frameBorder` properties.

frameSpacing

Value: Integer   Read/Write

	NN2	NN3	NN4	NN6	IE3/J1	IE3/J2	IE4	IE5	IE5.5
Compatibility							✓	✓	✓

The `frameSpacing` property is included in IE5 for backward compatibility to IE4's erroneous inclusion of this property for an IFRAME element. Do not use it.

hspace
vspace

Value: Integer   Read/Write

	NN2	NN3	NN4	NN6	IE3/J1	IE3/J2	IE4	IE5	IE5.5
Compatibility							✓	✓	✓

These IE-specific properties allow for margins to be set around an IFRAME element. In general, hspace and vspace properties (and their HTML attributes) have been replaced by CSS margins and padding. These properties and their attributes are not recognized by any W3C standard (including HTML 4.0).

Values for these properties are integers representing the number of pixels of padding between the element and surrounding content. The hspace value assigns the same number of pixels to the left and right sides of the element; the vspace value is applied to both the top and bottom edges. Scripted changes to these values have no effect in IE5/Windows.

On the CD-ROM   Example on the CD-ROM

Related Items: style.padding property.

longDesc

Value: URL String   Read/Write

	NN2	NN3	NN4	NN6	IE3/J1	IE3/J2	IE4	IE5	IE5.5
Compatibility				✓					

The longDesc property is the scripted equivalent of the LONGDESC attribute of the <IFRAME> tag. This HTML 4.0 attribute is intended to provide browsers with a URL to a document that contains a long description of the element. Future browsers can use this feature to provide information about the frame for visually impaired site visitors.

`marginHeight`
`marginWidth`

Value: Integer   Read/Write

	NN2	NN3	NN4	NN6	IE3/J1	IE3/J2	IE4	IE5	IE5.5
Compatibility				✓			✓	✓	✓

Browsers tend to automatically insert content within a frame by adding a margin between the content and the edge of the frame. These values are represented by the `marginHeight` (top and bottom edges) and `marginWidth` (left and right edges) properties. Although the properties are not read-only, changing the values after the frameset has loaded does not alter the appearance of the document in the frame. If you need to alter the margin(s) of a document inside a frame, adjust the `document. body.style` margin properties.

Also be aware that although the default values of these properties are empty (that is, when no `MARGINHEIGHT` or `MARGINWIDTH` attributes are set for the `<IFRAME>` tag), margins are built into the page. The precise pixel count of those margins varies with different operating systems.

Related Items: `style` object (Chapter 30).

`scrolling`

Value: yes | no | 1 | 0 as strings   Read/Write

	NN2	NN3	NN4	NN6	IE3/J1	IE3/J2	IE4	IE5	IE5.5
Compatibility				✓			✓	✓	✓

The `scrolling` property lets scripts turn scrollbars on and off inside an IFRAME element. By default, scrolling is turned on unless overridden by the `SCROLL` attribute of the `<IFRAME>` tag.

Values for the `scrolling` property are strings that substitute for Boolean values. Values `yes` or `1` mean that scrollbars are visible (provided there is more content than can be viewed without scrolling); `no` or `0` hide scrollbars in the frame. IE4+ also recognizes (and sets as default) the `auto` value.

Example on the CD-ROM

Related Items: FRAME.scrolling property.

src

Value: URL String   Read/Write

	NN2	NN3	NN4	NN6	IE3/J1	IE3/J2	IE4	IE5	IE5.5
Compatibility				✓			✓	✓	✓

The src property of an IFRAME element object offers an additional way of navigating to a different page within an inline frame (that is, other than assigning a new URL to the location.href property of the frame object). Remember that the src property belongs to the IFRAME element object, not the window object it represents. Therefore, references to the src property must be via the element's ID and/or node hierarchy.

Example on the CD-ROM

Related Items: location.href property.

popup Object

Properties	*Methods*	*Event Handlers*
document	hide()	
isOpen	show()	

Syntax

Creating a popup object:

```
var popupObj = window.createPopup()
```

Accessing properties or methods of a popup object from a document in the window that created the pop-up:

```
popupObj.property | method([parameters])
```

	NN2	NN3	NN4	NN6	IE3/J1	IE3/J2	IE4	IE5	IE5.5
Compatibility									✓

About this object

A popup object is a chrome-less window space, which overlaps the window whose document generates the pop-up. A pop-up also appears in front of any dialog boxes. Unlike the dialog box windows generated via IE's showModalDialog() and showModelessDialog() methods, your scripts must not only create the window, but also put content into it, and then define where on the screen and how big it will be.

Because the pop-up window has no chrome (that is, title bar, resize handles, and so forth), you should populate its content with a border and/or background color so that it stands out from the main window's content. The following statements reflect a typical sequence of creating, populating, and showing a popup object:

```
var popup = window.createPopup()
var popupBody = popup.document.body
popupBody.style.border = "solid 2px black"
popupBody.style.padding = "5px"
popupBody.innerHTML = "<P>Here is some text in a popup window</P>"
popup.show(200,100, 200, 50, document.body)
```

The pop-up window that IE creates is, in fact, a window, but only from the point of view of the document that it contains. In other words, while the number of properties and methods for the popup object is small, the parentWindow property of the document inside the pop-up points to a genuine window property. Even so, be aware that this pop-up does not appear as a distinct window among windows listed in the Windows Taskbar. If a user clicks outside of the pop-up or switches to another application, the pop-up disappears, and you must reinvoke the show() method by script (complete with dimension and position parameters) to force the pop-up to reappear.

When you assign content to a pop-up, you are also responsible for making sure that the content fits the size of the pop-up you specify. If the content runs past the rectangular space (body text word wraps within the pop-up's rectangle), no scrollbars appear.

Properties

document

Value: document object reference   Read-Only

	NN2	NN3	NN4	NN6	IE3/J1	IE3/J2	IE4	IE5	IE5.5
Compatibility									✓

Use the document property as a gateway to the content of a pop-up window. This property is the only access point available from the script that creates the pop-up to the pop-up itself. The most common application of this property is to set document properties governing the content of the pop-up window. For example, to give the pop-up a border (because the pop-up itself has no window chrome), the script that creates the window can assign values to the style property of the document in the pop-up window, as follows:

```
myPopup.document.body.style.border = "solid 3px gray"
```

Beware that the document object of a pop-up window may not implement the full flexibility you know about primary window document objects. For example, you are not allowed to assign a URL to the document.URL property in a pop-up window.

On the CD-ROM   Example on the CD-ROM

Related Items: document object.

isOpen

Value: Boolean   Read-Only

	NN2	NN3	NN4	NN6	IE3/J1	IE3/J2	IE4	IE5	IE5.5
Compatibility									✓

While a pop-up window is visible, its isOpen property returns true; otherwise the property returns false. Because any user action in the browser causes the pop-up to hide itself, the property is useful only for script statements that are running on their own after the pop-up is made visible.

Example on the CD-ROM

Related Items: popup.show() method.

Methods

```
hide()
show(left, top, width, height[,
positioningElementRef])
```

FTR:

Returns: Nothing.

	NN2	NN3	NN4	NN6	IE3/J1	IE3/J2	IE4	IE5	IE5.5
Compatibility									✓

After you have created a popup object with the window.createPopup() method and populated it with content, you must explicitly show the window via the show() method. If the window is hidden because a user clicked the main browser window somewhere, the show() method (and all its parameters) must be invoked again. To have a script hide the window, invoke the hide() method for the popup object.

The first four parameters of the show() method are required and define the pixel location and size of the pop-up window. By default, the coordinate space for the left and top parameters is the video display. Thus, a left and top setting of zero places the pop-up in the upper-left corner of the video screen. But you can also define a different coordinate space by adding an optional fifth parameter. This parameter must be a reference to an element on the page. To confine the coordinate space to the content region of the browser window, specify the document. body object as the positioning element reference.

Example (with Listing 16-49) on the CD-ROM

Related Items: popup.isOpen property, window.createPopup() method.

✦   ✦   ✦

Location and History Objects

Not all objects in the document object model are
"things" you can see in the content area of the browser
window. Each browser window or frame maintains a bunch of
other information about the page you are currently visiting
and where you have been. The URL of the page you see in the
window is called the *location*, and browsers store this information in the `location` object. As you surf the Web, the
browser stores the URLs of your past pages in the `history`
object. You can manually view what that object contains by
looking in the browser menu that enables you to jump back to
a previously visited page. This chapter is all about these two
nearly invisible, but important, objects.

Not only are these objects valuable to your browser, but they
are also valuable to snoopers who might want to write scripts
to see what URLs you're viewing in another frame or the URLs
of other sites you've visited in the last dozen mouse clicks. As
a result, security restrictions built into browsers limit access
to some of these objects' properties (unless you use signed
scripts in NN4+). For older browsers, these properties simply
are not available from a script.

Location Object

Properties	Methods	Event Handlers
hash	assign()	None
host	reload()	
hostname	replace()	
href		
pathname		
port		
protocol		
search		

Syntax

Loading a new document into the current window:

```
[window.]location.href = "URL"
```

Accessing location object properties or methods:

```
[window.]location.property | method([parameters])
```

About this object

In its place one level below window-style objects in the document object hierarchy, the location object represents information about the URL of any currently open window or of a specific frame. A multiple-frame window displays the parent window's URL in the Location (or Address) field of the browser. Each frame also has a location associated with it, although you may not see any overt reference to the frame's URL in the browser. To get URL information about a document located in another frame, the reference to the location object must include the window frame reference. For example, if you have a window consisting of two frames, Table 17-1 shows the possible references to the location objects for all frames comprising the Web presentation.

Note

Scripts cannot alter the URL displayed in the browser's Location/Address box. For security and privacy reasons, that text box cannot display anything other than the URL of a current page or URL in transit.

Table 17-1	**Location Object References in a Two-Frame Browser Window**
Reference	**Description**
`location` (or `window.location`)	URL of frame displaying the document that runs the script statement containing this reference
`parent.location`	URL information for parent window that defines the `<FRAMESET>`
`parent.frames[0].location`	URL information for first visible frame
`parent.frames[1].location`	URL information for second visible frame
`parent.otherFrameName.location`	URL information for another named frame in the same frameset

Most properties of a `location` object deal with network-oriented information. This information involves various data about the physical location of the document on the network including the host server, the protocol being used, and other components of the URL. Given a complete URL for a typical WWW page, the `window.location` object assigns property names to various segments of the URL, as shown here:

```
http://www.giantco.com:80/promos/newproducts.html#giantGizmo
```

Property	**Value**
`protocol`	`"http:"`
`hostname`	`"www.giantco.com"`
`port`	`"80"`
`host`	`"www.giantco.com:80"`
`pathname`	`"/promos/newproducts.html"`
`hash`	`"#giantGizmo"`
`href`	`"http://www.giantco.com:80/promos newproducts.html#giantGizmo"`

The `window.location` object is handy when a script needs to extract information about the URL, perhaps to obtain a base reference on which to build URLs for other documents to be fetched as the result of user action. This object can eliminate a nuisance for Web authors who develop sites on one machine and then upload them to a server (perhaps at an Internet service provider) with an entirely different directory structure. By building scripts to construct base references from the directory location of the current document, you can construct the complete URLs for loading documents. You don't have to manually change the base reference data in your documents as you shift the files from computer to computer or from directory to directory. To extract the segment of the URL and place it into the enclosing directory, use the following:

```
var baseRef = location.href.substring(0,location.href.lastIndexOf("/") + 1)
```

Caution

Security alert: To allay fears of Internet security breaches and privacy invasions, scriptable browsers prevent your script in one frame from retrieving `location` object properties from other frames whose domain and server are not your own (unless you use signed scripts in NN4+ or you set the IE browser to trust the site). This restriction puts a damper on many scripters' well-meaning designs and aids for Web watchers and visitors. If you attempt such property accesses, however, you receive an "access denied" (or similar) security warning dialog box.

Setting the value of some `location` properties is the preferred way to control which document gets loaded into a window or frame. Though you may expect to find a method somewhere in JavaScript that contains a plain language "Go" or "Open" word (to simulate what you see in the browser menu bar), you "point your browser" to another URL by setting the `window.location.href` property to that URL, as in

```
window.location.href = "http://www.dannyg.com/"
```

The equals assignment operator (=) in this kind of statement is a powerful weapon. In fact, setting the `location.href` object to a URL of a different MIME type, such as one of the variety of sound and video formats, causes the browser to load those files into the plug-in or helper application designated in your browser's settings. The `location.assign()` method was originally intended for internal use by the browser, but it is available for scripters (although I don't recommend using it for navigation). Internet Explorer's object model includes a `window.navigate()` method that also loads a document into a window, but you can't use it for cross-browser applications.

Two other methods complement the `location` object's capability to control navigation. One method is the script equivalent of clicking Reload; the other method enables you to replace the current document's entry in the history with that of the next URL of your script's choice.

Properties

hash

Value: String   Read/Write

	NN2	NN3	NN4	NN6	IE3/J1	IE3/J2	IE4	IE5	IE5.5
Compatibility	✓	✓	✓	✓	✓	✓	✓	✓	✓

The *hash mark* (#) is a URL convention that directs the browser to an anchor located in the document. Any name you assign to an anchor (with the `<A NAME="...">` ...`</A>` tag pair) becomes part of the URL after the hash mark. A `location` object's `hash` property is the name of the anchor part of the current URL (which consists of the hash mark and the name).

If you have written HTML documents with anchors and directed links to navigate to those anchors, you have probably noticed that although the destination location shows the anchor as part of the URL (for example, in the Location field), the window's anchor value does not change as the user manually scrolls to positions in the document where other anchors are defined. An anchor appears in the URL only when the window has navigated there as part of a link or in response to a script that adjusts the URL.

Just as you can navigate to any URL by setting the `window.location.href` property, you can navigate to another hash in the same document by adjusting only the `hash` property of the location without the hash mark (as shown in the following example). Such navigation, even within a document, sometimes causes IE to reload the document. No reload occurs in NN3+.

On the CD-ROM   Example (with Listing 17-1) on the CD-ROM

Related Item: `location.href` property.

host

Value: String   Read/Write

	NN2	NN3	NN4	NN6	IE3/J1	IE3/J2	IE4	IE5	IE5.5
Compatibility	✓	✓	✓	✓	✓	✓	✓	✓	✓

The `location.host` property describes both the hostname and port of a URL. The port is included in the value only when the port is an explicit part of the URL. If you navigate to a URL that does not display the port number in the Location field of the browser, the `location.host` property returns the same value as the `location.hostname` property.

Use the `location.host` property to extract the `hostname:port` part of the URL of any document loaded in the browser. This capability may be helpful for building a URL to a specific document that you want your script to access on the fly.

On the CD-ROM   Example (with Listings 17-2, 17-3, and 17-4) on the CD-ROM

Related Items: `location.port`, `location.hostname` properties.

hostname

Value: String   Read/Write

	NN2	NN3	NN4	NN6	IE3/J1	IE3/J2	IE4	IE5	IE5.5
Compatibility	✓	✓	✓	✓	✓	✓	✓	✓	✓

The hostname of a typical URL is the name of the server on the network that stores the document you view in the browser. For most Web sites, the server name includes not only the domain name, but also the `www.` prefix. The hostname does not, however, include the port number if the URL specifies such a number.

On the CD-ROM   Example on the CD-ROM

Related Items: `location.host`, `location.port` properties.

href

Value: String

Read/Write

	NN2	NN3	NN4	NN6	IE3/J1	IE3/J2	IE4	IE5	IE5.5
Compatibility	✓	✓	✓	✓	✓	✓	✓	✓	✓

Of all the `location` object properties, `href` (hypertext reference) is probably the one most often called upon in scripting. The `location.href` property supplies a string of the entire URL of the specified `window` object.

Using this property on the left side of an assignment statement is the JavaScript way of opening a URL for display in a window. Any of the following statements can load my Web site's index page into a single-frame browser window:

```
window.location="http://www.dannyg.com"
window.location.href="http://www.dannyg.com"
```

At times, you may encounter difficulty by omitting a reference to a window. JavaScript may get confused and reference the `document.location` property. To prevent this confusion, the `document.location` property was deprecated (put on the no-no list) and replaced by the `document.URL` property. In the meantime, you can't go wrong by always specifying a window in the reference.

Note   You should be able to omit the `href` property name when assigning a new URL to the `location` object (for example, `location = "http://www.dannyg.com"`). While this works in most browsers most of the time, some early browsers (especially IE3) behave more reliably if you assign a URL explicitly to the `location.href` property. I recommend using `location.href` at all times.

Sometimes you must extract the name of the current directory in a script so another statement can append a known document to the URL before loading it into the window. Although the other `location` object properties yield an assortment of a URL's segments, none of them provides the full URL to the current URL's directory. But you can use JavaScript string manipulation techniques to accomplish this task. Listing 17-5 shows such a possibility.

Depending on your browser, the values for the `location.href` property may be encoded with ASCII equivalents of non-alphanumeric characters. Such an ASCII value includes the % symbol and the ASCII numeric value. The most common encoded character in a URL is the space: %20. If you need to extract a URL and display that value as a string in your documents, you can safely pass all such potentially encoded strings through the JavaScript unescape() function. For example, if a URL to one of Giantco's pages is http://www.giantco.com/product%20list, you can convert it by passing it through the unescape() function, as in the following example.

```
var plainURL = unescape(window.location.href)
    // result = "http://www.giantco.com/product list"
```

The inverse function, escape(), is available for sending encoded strings to CGI programs on servers. See Chapter 42 for more details on these functions.

Example (with Listing 17-5) on the CD-ROM

Related Items: location.pathname, document.location **properties;** String **object (Chapter 34).**

pathname

Value: String   Read/Write

	NN2	NN3	NN4	NN6	IE3/J1	IE3/J2	IE4	IE5	IE5.5
Compatibility	✓	✓	✓	✓	✓	✓	✓	✓	✓

The pathname component of a URL consists of the directory structure relative to the server's root volume. In other words, the root (the server name in an http: connection) is not part of the pathname. If the URL's path is to a file in the root directory, then the location.pathname property is a single slash (/) character. Any other pathname starts with a slash character, indicating a directory nested within the root. The value of the location.pathname property also includes the document name.

Example on the CD-ROM

Related Item: location.href **property.**

port

Value: String   Read/Write

	NN2	NN3	NN4	NN6	IE3/J1	IE3/J2	IE4	IE5	IE5.5
Compatibility	✓	✓	✓	✓	✓	✓	✓	✓	✓

These days, few consumer-friendly Web sites need to include the port number as part of their URLs. You see port numbers mostly in the less-popular protocols, in URLs to sites used for private development purposes, or in URLs to sites that have no assigned domain names. You can retrieve the value with the `location.port` property. If you extract the value from one URL and intend to build another URL with that component, be sure to include the colon delimiter between the server's IP address and port number.

On the CD-ROM   Example on the CD-ROM

Related Item: `location.host` property.

protocol

Value: String   Read/Write

	NN2	NN3	NN4	NN6	IE3/J1	IE3/J2	IE4	IE5	IE5.5
Compatibility	✓	✓	✓	✓	✓	✓	✓	✓	✓

The first component of any URL is the protocol used for the particular type of communication. For World Wide Web pages, the Hypertext Transfer Protocol (`http`) is the standard. Other common protocols you may see in your browser include HTTP-Secure (`https`), File Transfer Protocol (`ftp`), File (`file`), and Mail (`mailto`). Values for the `location.protocol` property include not only the name of the protocol, but also the trailing colon delimiter. Thus, for a typical Web page URL, the `location.protocol` property is

```
http:
```

Notice that the usual slashes after the protocol in the URL are not part of the
`location.protocol` value. Of all the `location` object properties, only the full
URL (`location.href`) reveals the slash delimiters between the protocol and other
components.

On the
CD-ROM   **Example on the CD-ROM**

Related Item: `location.href` property.

search

Value: String   Read/Write

	NN2	NN3	NN4	NN6	IE3/J1	IE3/J2	IE4	IE5	IE5.5
Compatibility	✓	✓	✓	✓	✓	✓	✓	✓	✓

Perhaps you've noticed the long, cryptic URL that appears in the Location/Address
field of your browser whenever you ask one of the WWW search services to look up
matches for items you enter into the keyword field. The URL starts the regular
way — with protocol, host, and pathname values. But following the more traditional
URL are search commands that are submitted to the search engine (a CGI program
running on the server). You can retrieve or set that trailing search query by using
the `location.search` property.

Each search engine has its own formula for query submissions based on the
designs of the HTML forms that obtain details from users. These search queries
come in an encoded format that appears in anything but plain language. If you plan
to script a search query, be sure you fully understand the search engine's format
before you start assembling a string to assign to the `location.search` property of
a window.

The most common format for search data is a series of name/value pairs. An equal
symbol (=) separates a name and its value. Multiple name/value pairs have amper-
sands (&) between them. You should use the `escape()` function to convert the data
into URL-friendly format, especially when the content includes spaces.

The `location.search` property also applies to any part of a URL after the filename, including parameters being sent to CGI programs on the server.

Passing data among pages via URLs

It is not uncommon to want to preserve some pieces of data that exist in one page so that a script in another page can pick up where the script processing left off in the first page. You can achieve persistence across page loads through one of three techniques: the `document.cookie` (Chapter 18), variables in framesetting documents, and the search string of a URL. That's really what happens when you visit search and e-commerce sites that return information to your browser. Rather than store, say, your search criteria on the server, they spit the criteria back to the browser as part of the URL. The next time you activate that URL, the values are sent to the server for processing (for example, to send you the next page of search results for a particular query).

Passing data among pages is not limited to client/server communication. You can use the search string strictly on the client side to pass data from one page to another. Unless some CGI process on the server is programmed to do something with the search string, a Web server regurgitates the search string as part of the location data that comes back with a page. A script in the newly loaded page can inspect the search string (via the `location.search` property) and tear it apart to gather the data and put it into script variables. The example on the CD-ROM demonstrates a powerful application of this technique.

On the CD-ROM Example (with Listings 17-6, 17-7, and 17-8) on the CD-ROM

Related Item: `location.href` property.

Methods

`assign("URL")`

Returns: Nothing.

	NN2	NN3	NN4	NN6	IE3/J1	IE3/J2	IE4	IE5	IE5.5
Compatibility	✓	✓	✓	✓	✓	✓	✓	✓	✓

In earlier discussions about the `location` object, I said that you navigate to another page by assigning a new URL to the `location` object or `location.href` property. The `location.assign()` method does the same thing. In fact, when you set the location object to a URL, JavaScript silently applies the assign() method. No particular penalty or benefit comes from using the assign() method, except perhaps to make your code more understandable to others. I don't recall the last time I used this method in a production document, but you are free to use it if you like.

Related Item: location.href property.

reload(*unconditionalGETBoolean*)

Returns: Nothing.

	NN2	NN3	NN4	NN6	IE3/J1	IE3/J2	IE4	IE5	IE5.5
Compatibility	✓	✓	✓				✓	✓	✓

The location.reload() method may be named inappropriately because it makes you think of the Reload/Refresh button in the browser toolbar. The reload() method is actually more powerful than the Reload/Refresh button.

Many form elements retain their screen states when you click Reload/Refresh (except in IE3). Text and TEXTAREA objects maintain whatever text is inside them; radio buttons and checkboxes maintain their checked status; SELECT objects remember which item is selected. About the only items the Reload/Refresh button destroys are global variable values and any settable, but not visible, property (for example, the value of a hidden INPUT object). I call this kind of reload a *soft reload*.

Browsers are frustratingly irregular about the ways they reload a document in the memory cache. In theory, an application of the location.reload() method should retrieve the page from the cache if the page is still available there (while the history.go(0) method should be even gentler, preserving form element settings). Adding a true parameter to the method is supposed to force an *unconditional GET* to the server, ignoring the cached version of the page. Yet when it is crucial for your application to get a page from the cache (for speed) or from the server (to guarantee a fresh copy), the browser behaves in just the opposite way you want it to behave. Meta tags supposedly designed to prevent caching of a page rarely, if ever, work. Some scripters have had success in reloading the page from the server by setting location.href to the URL of the page, plus a slightly different search string (for example, based on a string representation of the Date object) so that there is no match for the URL in the cache.

The bottom line is to be prepared to try different schemes to achieve the effect you want. And also be prepared to not get the results you need.

Example (with Listing 17-9) on the CD-ROM

Related Item: `history.go()` method.

replace("*URL*")

Returns: Nothing.

	NN2	NN3	NN4	NN6	IE3/J1	IE3/J2	IE4	IE5	IE5.5
Compatibility		✓	✓	✓			✓	✓	✓

In a complex Web site, you may have pages that you do not want to appear in the user's history list. For example, a registration sequence may lead the user to one or more intermediate HTML documents that won't make much sense to the user later. You especially don't want users to see these pages again if they use the Back button to return to a previous URL. The `location.replace()` method navigates to another page, but it does not let the current page stay in the queue of pages accessible via the Back button.

Although you cannot prevent a document from appearing in the history list while the user views that page, you can instruct the browser to load another document into the window and replace the current history entry with the entry for the new document. This trick does not empty the history list but instead removes the current item from the list before the next URL is loaded. Removing the item from the history list prevents users from seeing the page again by clicking the Back button later.

Example (with Listing 17-10) on the CD-ROM

Related Item: `history` object.

History Object

Property	Method	Event Handler
current	back()	(None)
length	forward()	
next	go()	
previous		

Syntax

Accessing history object properties or methods:

[window.]history.*property* | *method*([*parameters*])

About this object

As a user surfs the Web, the browser maintains a list of URLs for the most recent stops. This list is represented in the scriptable object model by the history object. A script cannot surreptitiously extract actual URLs maintained in that list unless you use signed scripts (in NN4+ — see Chapter 46) and the user grants permission. Under unsigned conditions, a script can methodically navigate to each URL in the history (by relative number or by stepping back one URL at a time), in which case the user sees the browser navigating on its own as if possessed by a spirit. Good Netiquette dictates that you do not navigate a user outside of your Web site without the user's explicit permission.

One application for the history object and its back() or go() methods is to provide the equivalent of a Back button in your HTML documents. That button triggers a script that checks for any items in the history list and then goes back one page. Your document doesn't have to know anything about the URL from which the user lands at your page.

The behavior of the Back and Forward buttons in Netscape Navigator underwent a significant change between versions 2 and 3. If you script these actions and need to support the older Navigator versions, you should understand how these browsers handle backward and forward navigation.

In Navigator 2, one history list applies to the entire browser window. You can load a frameset into the window and navigate the contents of each frame individually with wild abandon. But if you then click the Back button, Navigator unloads the frameset and takes you back to the page in history prior to that frameset.

In Navigator 3, each frame (`window` object) maintains its own history list. Thus, if you navigate within a frame, a click of the Back button steps you back out frame by frame. Only after the initial frameset documents appear in the window does the next Back button click unload the frameset. That behavior persists today in all other scriptable browsers.

JavaScript's reaction to the change of behavior over the generations is a bit murky. In Navigator 2, the `history.back()` and `history.forward()` methods act like the toolbar buttons because there is only one kind of history being tracked. In Navigator 3, however, there is a disconnect between JavaScript behavior and what the browser does internally with history: JavaScript fails to connect history entries to a particular frame. Therefore, a reference to `history.back()` built with a given frame name does not prevent the method from exceeding the history of that frame. Instead, the behavior is more like a global back operation, rather than being frame-specific.

For NN4, there is one more sea change in the relationship between JavaScript and these `history` object methods. The behavior of the Back and Forward buttons is also available through a pair of window methods: `window.back()` and `window.forward()`. The `history` object methods are not specific to a frame that is part of the reference. When the `parent.frameName.history.back()` method reaches the end of history for that frame, further invocations of that method are ignored.

IE's history mechanism is not localized to a particular frame of a frameset. Instead, the `history.back()` and `history.forward()` methods mimic the physical act of clicking the toolbar buttons. If you want to ensure cross-browser, if not cross-generational, behavior in a frameset, address references to the `history.back()` and `history.forward()` methods to the parent window.

So much for the history of the `history` object. As the tale of history object method evolution indicates, you must use the `history` object and its methods with extreme care. Your design must be smart enough to "watch" what the user is doing with your pages (for example, by checking the current URL before navigating with these methods). Otherwise, you run the risk of confusing your user by navigating to unexpected places. Your script can also get into trouble because it cannot detect where the current document is in the Back–Forward sequence in history.

Properties

```
current
next
previous
```

Value: String   Read-Only

	NN2	NN3	NN4	NN6	IE3/J1	IE3/J2	IE4	IE5	IE5.5
Compatibility		(✓)	✓	✓					

To know where to go when you click the Back and Forward buttons, the browser maintains a list of URLs visited. To someone trying to invade your privacy and see what sites and pages you frequent, this information is valuable. That's why the three NN-specific properties that expose the actual URLs in the history list are restricted to pages with signed scripts and whose visitors have given permission to read sensitive browser data (see Chapter 46).

With signed scripts and permission, you can look through the entire array of history entries in any frame or window. Because the list is an array, you can extract individual items by index value. For example, if the array has 10 entries, you can see the fifth item by using normal array indexing methods:

```
var fifthEntry = window.history[4]
```

No property or method exists that directly reveals the index value of the currently loaded URL, but you can script an educated guess by comparing the values of the current, next, and previous properties of the history object against the entire list.

I personally don't like some unknown entity watching over my shoulder while I'm on the Net, so I respect that same feeling in others and therefore discourage the use of these powers unless the user is given adequate warning. The signed script permission dialog box does not offer enough detail about the consequences of revealing this level of information.

Notice that in the above compatibility chart these properties were available in some form in NN3. Access to them required a short-lived security scheme called *data tainting*. That mechanism was never implemented fully and was replaced by signed scripts.

Related Item: history.length property.

length

Value: Number   Read-Only

	NN2	NN3	NN4	NN6	IE3/J1	IE3/J2	IE4	IE5	IE5.5
Compatibility	✓	✓	✓	✓	✓	✓	✓	✓	✓

Use the `history.length` property to count the items in the history list. Unfortunately, this nugget of information is not particularly helpful in scripting navigation relative to the current location because your script cannot extract anything from the place in the history queue where the current document is located. If the current document is at the top of the list (the most recently loaded), you can calculate relative to that location. But users can use the Go/View menu to jump around the history list as they like. The position of a listing in the history list does not change by virtue of navigating back to that document. A `history.length` of 1, however, indicates that the current document is the first one the user loaded since starting the browser software.

 On the CD-ROM   Example (with Listing 17-11) on the CD-ROM

Related Items: None.

Methods

back()

Returns: Nothing.

	NN2	NN3	NN4	NN6	IE3/J1	IE3/J2	IE4	IE5	IE5.5
Compatibility	✓	✓	✓	✓	✓	✓	✓	✓	✓

The behavior of the `history.back()` method has changed in Netscape's browsers between versions 3 and 4. Prior to Navigator 4, the method acted identically to clicking the Back button. (Even this unscripted behavior changed between Navigator 2 and 3 to better accommodate frame navigation.) IE3+ follows this behavior. In Navigator 4, however, the `history.back()` method is window/frame-specific. Therefore, if you direct successive `back()` methods to a frame within a frameset, the method is ignored once it reaches the first document to be loaded into that frame. The Back button (and the new `window.back()` method) unload the frameset and continue taking you back through the browser's global history.

If you deliberately lead a user to a dead end in your Web site, you should make sure that the HTML document provides a way to navigate back to a recognizable spot. Because you can easily create a new window that has no toolbar or menu bar (non-Macintosh browsers), you may end up stranding your users because they have no way of navigating out of a cul-de-sac in such a window. A button in your document should give the user a way back to the last location.

Unless you need to perform some additional processing prior to navigating to the previous location, you can simply place this method as the parameter to the event handler attribute of a button definition. To guarantee compatibility across all browsers, direct this method at the parent document when used from within a frameset.

On the CD-ROM Example (with Listings 17-12 and 17-13) on the CD-ROM

Related Items: `history.forward()`, `history.go()` methods.

forward()

Returns: Nothing.

	NN2	NN3	NN4	NN6	IE3/J1	IE3/J2	IE4	IE5	IE5.5
Compatibility	✓	✓	✓	✓	✓	✓	✓	✓	✓

Less likely to be scripted than the `history.back()` action is the method that performs the opposite action: navigating forward one step in the browser's history list. The only time you can confidently use the `history.forward()` method is to balance the use of the `history.back()` method in the same script — where your script closely keeps track of how many steps the script heads in either direction. Use the `history.forward()` method with extreme caution, and only after performing extensive user testing on your Web pages to make sure that you've covered all user possibilities. The same cautions about differences introduced in NN4 for `history.back()` apply equally to `history.forward()`: Forward progress extends only through the history listing for a given window or frame, not the entire browser history list. See Listings 17-12 and 17-13 for a demonstration.

Related Items: `history.back()`, `history.go()` methods.

go(*relativeNumber* | *"URLOrTitleSubstring"*)

Returns: Nothing.

	NN2	NN3	NN4	NN6	IE3/J1	IE3/J2	IE4	IE5	IE5.5
Compatibility	✓	✓	✓	✓	✓	✓	✓	✓	✓

Use the `history.go()` method to script navigation within the history list currently stored in the browser. If you elect to use a URL as a parameter, however, that precise URL must already exist in the history listing. Therefore, do not regard this method as an alternate to setting the `window.location` object to a brand-new URL.

For navigating n steps in either direction along the history list, use the *relativeNumber* parameter of the `history.go()` method. This number is an integer value that indicates which item in the list to use, relative to the current location. For example, if the current URL is at the top of the list (that is, the Forward button in the toolbar is dimmed), then you need to use the following method to jump to the URL two items backward in the list:

```
history.go(-2)
```

In other words, the current URL is the equivalent of `history.go(0)` (a method that reloads the window). A positive integer indicates a jump that many items forward in the history list. Thus, `history.go(-1)` is the same as `history.back()`, whereas `history.go(1)` is the same as `history.forward()`.

Alternatively, you can specify one of the URLs or document titles stored in the browser's history list (titles appear in the Go/View menu). The method is a bit lenient with the string you specify as a parameter. It compares the string against all listings. The first item in the history list to contain the parameter string is regarded as the match. But, again, no navigation takes place if the item you specify does not appear in the history.

Like most other history methods, your script finds it difficult to manage the history list or the current URL's spot in the queue. That fact makes it even more difficult for your script to intelligently determine how far to navigate in either direction or to which specific URL or title matches it should jump. Use this method only for situations in which your Web pages are in strict control of the user's activity (or for designing scripts for yourself that automatically crawl around sites according to a fixed regimen). Once you give the user control over navigation, you have no guarantee that the history list will be what you expect, and any scripts you write that depend on a `history` object will likely break.

In practice, this method mostly performs a soft reload of the current window using the 0 parameter.

Tip   If you are developing a page for all scriptable browsers, be aware that Internet Explorer's `go()` method behaves a little differently than Netscape's. First, a bug in Internet Explorer 3 causes all invocations of `history.go()` with a non-zero value to behave as if the parameter were `-1`. Second, the string version does not work at all in IE3 (it generates an error alert); for IE4+, the matching string must be part of the URL and not part of the document title, as in Navigator. Finally, the reloading of a page with `history.go(0)` often returns to the server to reload the page rather than reloading from the cache.

On the CD-ROM   Example (with Listing 17-14) on the CD-ROM

Related Items: `history.back()`, `history.forward()`, `location.reload()` methods.

✦   ✦   ✦

The Document and Body Objects

◆   ◆   ◆   ◆

In This Chapter

Accessing arrays of
objects contained by
the document object

Writing new docu-
ment content to a
window or frame

Using the BODY ele-
ment for IE window
measurements

◆   ◆   ◆   ◆

User interaction is a vital aspect of client-side JavaScript scripting, and most of the communication between script and user takes place by way of the document object and its components. Understanding the scope of the document object within each of the object models you support is key to implementing successful cross-browser applications.

Review the document object's place within the original object hierarchy. Figure 18-1 clearly shows that the document object is a pivotal point for a large percentage of JavaScript objects.

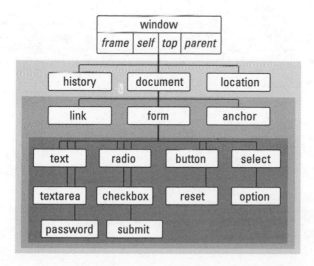

Figure 18-1: The basic document object model hierarchy

In fact, the document object and all that it contains is so big that I have divided its discussion into many chapters, each focusing on related object groups. This chapter looks at the document object and body object (which have conceptual relationships), while each of the succeeding chapters in this part of the book details objects contained by the document object.

I must stress at the outset that many newcomers to JavaScript have the expectation that they can, on the fly, modify sections of a loaded page's content with ease: replace some text here, change a table cell there. However, understanding that these capabilities — an important part of what is called Dynamic HTML — are available only in more recent browsers, specifically IE4+ and NN6+, is very important. Not only do these browsers expose every HTML element to script languages, but they also automatically reflow the page when the size of content changes under script control. Pages on all previous browsers are limited to a small set of modifiable objects, such as images and form elements. (NN4 also has a layer object that is useful for DHTML, but that object is unique to NN4 only.)

If your application requires compatibility with all scriptable browsers, you will be limited to changing only a handful of other invisible properties after the page loads. If these compatible pages need to modify their contents based on user input or timed updates, consider designing your pages so that scripts write the contents; then let the scripts rewrite the entire page with your new settings.

Document Object

Properties	Methods	Event Handlers
activeElement	attachEvent()†	onActivate†
alinkColor	captureEvents()	onBeforeCut†
all†	clear()	onBeforeDeactivate†
anchors	clearAttributes()†	onBeforeEditFocus†
applets	close()	onBeforePaste†
attributes†	createAttribute()	onClick†
bgColor	createElement()	onContextMenu†
body	createEventObject()	onControlSelect†
charset	createStyleSheet()	onCut†

Properties	Methods	Event Handlers
characterSet	createTextNode()	onDblClick†
childNodes†	detachEvent()†	onDrag†
cookie	elementFromPoint()	onDragEnd†
defaultCharset	execCommand()	onDragEnter†
designMode	focus()†	onDragLeave†
doctype	getElementById()	onDragOver†
documentElement	getElementsByName()	onDragStart†
domain	getElementsByTagName()†	onDrop†
embeds	getSelection()	onHelp†
expando	handleEvent()	onKeyDown†
fgColor	hasFocus()†	onKeyPress†
fileCreatedDate	mergeAttributes()†	onKeyUp†
fileModifiedDate	open()	onMouseDown†
fileSize	queryCommandEnabled()	onMouseMove†
firstChild†	queryCommandIndterm()	onMouseOut†
forms	queryCommandState()	onMouseOver†
frames	queryCommandSupported()	onMouseUp†
height	queryCommandText()	onPaste†
ids	queryCommandValue()	onPropertyChange†
images	recalc()	onReadyStateChange†
implementation	releaseCapture()†	onResizeEnd†
lastChild†	releaseEvents()	onResizeStart†
lastModified	†routeEvent()	onSelectionChange
layers	setActive()†	onStop
linkColor	write()	
links	writeln()	
location		

Continued

document

Properties	Methods	Event Handlers
media		
mimeType		
namespaces		
namespaceURI		
nextSibling†		
nodeName†		
nodeType†		
ownerDocument†		
parentNode†		
parentWindow		
plugins		
previousSibling†		
protocol		
readyState†		
referrer		
scripts		
security		
selection		
styleSheets		
tags		
title		
uniqueID†		
URL		
URLUnencoded		
VlinkColor		
width		

†See Chapter 15.

Syntax

Accessing document object properties or methods:

```
[window.]document.property | method([parameters])
```

About this object

A document object encompasses the totality of what exists inside the content region of a browser window or window frame (excluding toolbars, status lines, and so on). The document is a combination of the content and interface elements that make the Web page worth visiting. In more recent browsers, which treat HTML elements as nodes of a hierarchical tree, the document object is the root node—that from which all other nodes grow.

Because the document object isn't explicitly represented in an HTML document by tags or any other notation, the original designers of JavaScript and object models decided to make the document object the portal to many settings that were represented in HTML as belonging to the BODY element. That element's tag contains attributes for document-wide attributes, such as background color (BGCOLOR) and link colors in various states (ALINK, LINK, and VLINK). The BODY element also served as an HTML container for forms, links, and anchors. The document object, therefore, assumed a majority of the role of the BODY element. But even then, the document object became the most convenient place to bind some properties that extend beyond the BODY element, such as the TITLE element and the URL of the link that referred the user to the page. When viewed within the context of the HTML source code, the original document object is somewhat schizophrenic. Even so, the document object has worked well as the basis for references to original object model objects, such as forms, images, and applets.

This, of course, was before every HTML element, including the BODY element, was exposed as an object via modern object models. Amazingly, even with the IE4+ object model and W3C DOM—both of which treat the BODY element as an object separate from the document object—script compatibility with the original object model is quite easily accomplished. The document object has assumed a new schizophrenia, splitting its personality between the original object model and the one that places the document object at the root of the hierarchy, quite separate from the BODY element object it contains. The object knows which "face" to put on based on the rest of the script syntax that follows it. This means that quite often there are multiple ways to achieve the same reference. For example, you can use the following statement in all scriptable browsers to get the number of form objects in a document:

```
document.forms.length
```

In IE4+, you can also use

```
document.tags["FORM"].length
```

And in the W3C DOM as implemented in IE5+ and NN6, you can use

```
document.getElementsByTagName("FORM").length
```

The more modern versions provide generic ways of accessing elements (the `tags` array in IE4+ and the `getElementsByTagName()` method in the W3C DOM) to meet the requirements of object models that expose every HTML (and XML) element as an object.

Promoting the BODY element to the ranks of exposed objects presented its own challenges to the new object model designers. The BODY element is the true "owner" of some properties that the original `document` object had to take on by default. Most properties that had belonged to the original `document` object were renamed in their transfer to the BODY element. For example, the original `document.alinkColor` property is the `body.aLink` property in the new model. But the `bgColor` property has not been renamed. For the sake of code compatibility, the current versions of browsers recognize both properties, even though the W3C DOM (in an effort to push the development world ahead) has removed the old versions as properties of what it conceives as the `document` object.

As confusing as all of this may sound on the surface, understanding when to refer to the original `document` object and when to use the new syntax doesn't take long. It all depends on what you hang off the right edge of the reference. Original properties and methods are recognized as using the original `document` object; new properties and methods summon the powers of the new `document` object. It's all quite automatic. Thankfully.

Properties

activeElement

Value: Object Reference   Read-Only

	NN2	NN3	NN4	NN6	IE3/J1	IE3/J2	IE4	IE5	IE5.5
Compatibility							✓	✓	✓

In IE4+, a script can examine the document.activeElement property to see which element currently has focus. The value returned is an element object reference. You can use any of the properties and methods listed in Chapter 15 to find out more about the object. Be aware that not all elements in all operating systems receive focus. For example, buttons in IE4 for the Macintosh do not receive focus.

Although the element used to generate a mouse or keyboard event will most likely have focus (except for IE4/Mac buttons), don't rely on the activeElement property to find out which element generated an event. The IE event.srcElement property is far more reliable.

On the CD-ROM

Example on the CD

Related Items: event.srcElement property.

alinkColor
bgColor
fgColor
linkColor
vlinkColor

Value: Hexadecimal triplet or color name string　　　　　　　　Mostly Read/Write

	NN2	NN3	NN4	NN6	IE3/J1	IE3/J2	IE4	IE5	IE5.5
Compatibility	✓	✓	✓	✓	✓	✓	✓	✓	✓

These five properties are the script equivalent of the <BODY> tag attributes of the same name (although the property names are case-sensitive). All five settings can be read via scripting, but the ability to change some or all of these properties varies widely with browser and client platform. Table 18-1 shows a summary of which browsers and platforms can set which of the color properties.

Table 18-1	**Setting Document Colors on the Fly (Browser Versions)**					
	Navigator			*Internet Explorer*		
Color Property	*Windows*	*Mac*	*UNIX*	*Windows*	*Mac*	*UNIX*
bgColor	All	4+	4+	All	All	4+
All others	6	6	6	All	All	4+

If you experiment with setting `document.bgColor` on Mac or UNIX versions of Navigator 2 and 3, you may be fooled into thinking that the property is being set correctly. While the property value may stick, these platforms do not refresh their windows properly: If you change the color after all content is rendered, the swath of new color obscures the content until a reload of the window. The safest, backward-compatible scripted way of setting document color properties is to compose the content of a frame or window by script and set the `<BODY>` tag color attributes dynamically when `document.write()` puts the content into the window.

Values for all color properties can be either the common HTML hexadecimal triplet value (for example, `"#00FF00"`) or any of the Netscape color names. Internet Explorer recognizes these plain language color names, as well. But also be aware that some colors work only when the user has the monitor set to 16- or 24-bit color settings.

If you are scripting exclusively for IE4+ and NN6, you should use the `document.body` object to access these properties.

On the CD-ROM   Example on the CD with Listing 18-1

Related Items: `body.aLink`, `body.bgColor`, `body.link`, `body.text`, `body.vLink` properties.

anchors

Value: Array of anchor objects   Read-Only

	NN2	NN3	NN4	NN6	IE3/J1	IE3/J2	IE4	IE5	IE5.5
Compatibility	✓	✓	✓	✓	✓	✓	✓	✓	✓

Anchor objects (described in Chapter 21) are points in an HTML document marked with `<A NAME="">` tags. Anchor objects are referenced in URLs by a hash value between the page URL and anchor name. Like other object properties that contain a list of nested objects, the `document.anchors` property (notice the plural) delivers an indexed array of anchors in a document. Use the array references to pinpoint a specific anchor for retrieving any anchor property.

Anchor arrays begin their index counts with 0: The first anchor in a document, then, has the reference `document.anchors[0]`. And, as is true with any built-in array object, you can find out how many entries the array has by checking the length property. For example

```
var anchorCount = document.anchors.length
```

The `document.anchors` property is read-only. To script navigation to a particular anchor, assign a value to the `window.location` or `window.location.hash` object, as described in Chapter 17's `location` object discussion.

On the CD-ROM

Example on the CD with Listing 18-2

Related Items: anchor, `location` objects; `document.links` property.

applets

Value: Array of applet objects   Read-Only

	NN2	NN3	NN4	NN6	IE3/J1	IE3/J2	IE4	IE5	IE5.5
Compatibility		✓	✓	✓			✓	✓	✓

The `applets` property refers to Java applets defined in a document by the `<APPLET>` tag. An applet is not officially an object in the document until the applet loads completely.

Most of the work you do with Java applets from JavaScript takes place via the methods and variables defined inside the applet. Although you can reference an applet according to its indexed array position within the `applets` array, you will more likely use the applet object's name in the reference to avoid any confusion. Note that applets are not accessible to JavaScript in IE/Mac. For more details, see the discussion of the applet object in Chapter 32 and the LiveConnect discussion in Chapter 44.

Example on the CD

Related Items: applet object.

bgColor

See alinkColor

body

Value: BODY Element Object   Read/Write

	NN2	NN3	NN4	NN6	IE3/J1	IE3/J2	IE4	IE5	IE5.5
Compatibility				✓			✓	✓	✓

The document.body property is a shortcut reference to the BODY element object in modern object models. As you can see in the discussion of the BODY element object later in this chapter, that object has many key properties that govern the look of the entire page. Because the document object is the root of all references within any window or frame, the document.body property is easier to use to get to the BODY properties, rather than longer references normally used to access HTML element objects in both the IE4+ and W3C object models.

Example on the CD

Related Items: BODY element object.

charset

Value: String   Read/Write

	NN2	NN3	NN4	NN6	IE3/J1	IE3/J2	IE4	IE5	IE5.5
Compatibility							✓	✓	✓

The charset property reveals the character set used by the browser to render the current document (the NN6 version of this property is called characterSet). You can find possible values for this property at `ftp://ftp.isi.edu/in-notes/iana/assignments/character-sets`

Each browser and operating system has its own default character set. Values may also be set via a `<META>` tag.

Example on the CD

Related Items: `characterSet`, `defaultCharset` properties.

characterSet

Value: String   Read/Write

	NN2	NN3	NN4	NN6	IE3/J1	IE3/J2	IE4	IE5	IE5.5
Compatibility				✓					

The `characterSet` property reveals the character set used by the browser to render the current document (the IE4+ version of this property is called `charset`). You can find possible values for this property at

`ftp://ftp.isi.edu/in-notes/iana/assignments/character-sets`

Each browser and operating system has its own default character set. Values may also be set via a `<META>` tag.

Example on the CD

Related Items: `charset` property.

cookie

Value: String   Read/Write

	NN2	NN3	NN4	NN6	IE3/J1	IE3/J2	IE4	IE5	IE5.5
Compatibility	✓	✓	✓	✓	✓	✓	✓	✓	✓

The cookie mechanism in a Web browser lets you store small pieces of information on the client computer in a reasonably secure manner. In other words, when you need some tidbit of information to persist at the client level while either loading diverse HTML documents or moving from one session to another, the cookie mechanism saves the day. You can find Netscape's technical documentation (much of which is written from the perspective of a server writing to a cookie) on the Web at `http://www.netscape.com/newsref/std/cookie_spec.html`.

The cookie is commonly used as a means to store the username and password you enter into a password-protected Web site. The first time you enter this information into a CGI-governed form, the CGI program has Navigator write the information back to a cookie on your hard disk (usually after encrypting the password). Rather than bothering you to enter the username and password the next time you access the site, the server searches the cookie data stored for that particular server and extracts the username and password for automatic validation processing behind the scenes.

Other applications of the cookie include storing user preferences and information about the user's previous visit to the site. Preferences may include font styles or sizes and whether the user prefers viewing content inside a frameset or not. As shown in Chapter 54, a time stamp of the previous visit can allow a coded HTML page to display highlighted images next to content that has changed since the user's last visit, even if you have updated the page several times in the interim. Rather than hard-wiring "New" flags for *your* last visit, the scripts highlight what's new for the visitor.

> **Note**   I cover the technical differences between Navigator and Internet Explorer cookies later in this section. But for IE3, be aware that the browser neither reads nor writes cookies when the document accessing the cookie is on the local hard disk. IE4+ works with cookies generated by local files.

The cookie file

Allowing some foreign CGI program to read from and write to your hard disk may give you pause, but browser cookie mechanisms don't just open up your drive's directory for the world to see (or corrupt). Instead, the cookie mechanism provides access to just one special text file (Navigator) or type of text file (Internet Explorer) located in a platform-specific spot on your drive.

In Windows versions of Navigator 4, for example, the cookie file is named `cookies.txt` and is located in a directory reserved for a user's Navigator preferences; Mac users can find the `MagicCookie` file inside the Netscape folder, which is located within the System Folder:Preferences folder. Internet Explorer for Windows uses a different filing system: all cookies for each domain saved in a domain-specific file inside a `Cookies` directory within system directories. File names include the user name and domain of the server that wrote the cookie.

A cookie file is a text file (but because NN's Macintosh MagicCookie file's type is not TEXT, Mac users can open it only via applications capable of opening any kind of file). If curiosity drives you to open a cookie file, I recommend you do so only with a copy saved in another directory or folder. Any alteration to the existing file can mess up whatever valuable cookies are stored there for sites you regularly visit. The data format for NN and IE differs, in line with the different methodologies used for filing cookies. Inside the Netscape file (after a few comment lines warning you not to manually alter the file) are lines of tab-delimited text. Each return-delimited line contains one cookie's information. The cookie file is just like a text listing of a database. In each of the IE cookie files, the same data points are stored for a cookie as for Navigator, but the items are in a return-delimited list. The structure of these files is of no importance to scripting cookies, because both browsers utilize the same syntax for reading and writing cookies through the `document.cookie` property.

Note

As you experiment with browser's cookies, you will be tempted to look into the cookie file after a script writes some data to the cookie. The cookie file will not contain the newly written data, because cookies are transferred to disk only when the user quits the browser; conversely, the cookie file is read into the browser's memory when it is launched. While you read, write, and delete cookies during a browser session, all activity is performed in memory (to speed up the process) to be saved later.

A cookie record

Among the "fields" of each cookie record are the following (not necessarily in this order):

✦ Domain of the server that created the cookie

✦ Information on whether you need a secure HTTP connection to access the cookie

✦ Pathname of URL(s) capable of accessing the cookie

✦ Expiration date of the cookie

✦ Name of the cookie entry

✦ String data associated with the cookie entry

Notice that cookies are domain-specific. In other words, if one domain creates a cookie, another domain cannot access it through the browser's cookie mechanism behind your back. That reason is why it's generally safe to store what I call *throw-away passwords* (the username/password pairs required to access some free registration-required sites) in cookies. Moreover, sites that store passwords in a cookie usually do so as encrypted strings, making it more difficult for someone to hijack the cookie file from your unattended PC and figure out what your personal password scheme may be.

Cookies also have expiration dates. Because some browsers may allow no more than a fixed number of cookies (300 in NN), the cookie file can get pretty full over the years. Therefore, if a cookie needs to persist past the current browser session, it should have an expiration date established by the cookie writer. Browsers automatically clean out any expired cookies.

Not all cookies have to last beyond the current session, however. In fact, a scenario in which you use cookies temporarily while working your way through a Web site is quite typical. Many shopping sites employ one or more temporary cookie records to behave as the shopping cart for recording items you intend to purchase. These items are copied to the order form at checkout time. But after you submit the order form to the server, that client-side data has no particular value. As it turns out, if your script does not specify an expiration date, the browser keeps the cookie fresh in memory without writing it to the cookie file. When you quit the browser, that cookie data disappears as expected.

JavaScript access

Scripted access of cookies from JavaScript is limited to setting the cookie (with a number of optional parameters) and getting the cookie data (but with none of the parameters).

The original object model defines cookies as properties of documents, but this description is somewhat misleading. If you use the default path to set a cookie (that is, the current directory of the document whose script sets the cookie in the first place), then all documents in that same server directory have read and write access to the cookie. A benefit of this arrangement is that if you have a scripted application that contains multiple documents, all documents served from the same directory can share the cookie data. NN and IE, however, impose a limit of 20 named cookie entries for any domain; IE3 imposes an even more restrictive limit of one cookie (that is, one name/value pair) per domain. If your cookie requirements are extensive, then you need to fashion ways of concatenating cookie data (I do this in the Decision Helper application in Chapter 55).

Saving cookies

To write cookie data to the cookie file, you use a simple JavaScript assignment operator with the `document.cookie` property. But the formatting of the data is crucial to achieving success. Here is the syntax for assigning a value to a cookie (optional items are in brackets):

```
document.cookie = "cookieName=cookieData
          [; expires=timeInGMTString]
          [; path=pathName]
          [; domain=domainName]
          [; secure]"
```

Examine each of the properties individually.

Name/Data

Each cookie must have a name and a string value (even if that value is an empty string). Such name/value pairs are fairly common in HTML, but they look odd in an assignment statement. For example, if you want to save the string "Fred" to a cookie named "userName," the JavaScript statement is

```
document.cookie = "userName=Fred"
```

If the browser sees no existing cookie in the current domain with this name, it automatically creates the cookie entry for you; if the named cookie already exists, the browser replaces the old data with the new data. Retrieving `document.cookie` at this point yields the following string:

```
userName=Fred
```

You can omit all the other cookie-setting properties, in which case the browser uses default values, as explained in a following section. For temporary cookies (those that don't have to persist beyond the current browser session), the name/value pair is usually all you need.

The entire name/value pair must be a single string with no semicolons, commas, or character spaces. To take care of spaces between words, preprocess the value with the JavaScript `escape()` function, which URL-encodes the spaces as %20 (and then be sure to `unescape()` the value to restore the human-readable spaces when you retrieve the cookie later).

You cannot save a JavaScript array or object to a cookie. But with the help of the `Array.join()` method, you can convert an array to a string; use `String.split()` to re-create the array after reading the cookie at a later time. These two methods are available in NN3+ and IE4+.

Expires

Expiration dates, when supplied, must be passed as Greenwich Mean Time (GMT) strings (see Chapter 36 about time data). To calculate an expiration date based on today's date, use the JavaScript `Date` object as follows:

```
var exp = new Date()
var oneYearFromNow = exp.getTime() + (365 * 24 * 60 * 60 * 1000)
exp.setTime(oneYearFromNow)
```

Then convert the date to the accepted GMT string format:

```
document.cookie = "userName=Fred; expires=" + exp.toGMTString()
```

In the cookie file, the expiration date and time is stored as a numeric value (seconds) but, to set it, you need to supply the time in GMT format. You can delete a cookie before it expires by setting the named cookie's expiration date to a time and date earlier than the current time and date. The safest expiration parameter is

```
expires=Thu, 01-Jan-70 00:00:01 GMT
```

Omitting the expiration date signals the browser that this cookie is temporary. The browser never writes it to the cookie file and forgets it the next time you quit the browser.

Path

For client-side cookies, the default path setting (the current directory) is usually the best choice. You can, of course, create a duplicate copy of a cookie with a separate path (and domain) so that the same data is available to a document located in another area of your site (or the Web).

Domain

To help synchronize cookie data with a particular document (or group of documents), the browser matches the domain of the current document with the domain values of cookie entries in the cookie file. Therefore, if you were to display a list of all cookie data contained in a `document.cookie` property, you would get back all the name/value cookie pairs from the cookie file whose domain parameter matches that of the current document.

Unless you expect the document to be replicated in another server within your domain, you can usually omit the `domain` parameter when saving a cookie. Default behavior automatically supplies the domain of the current document to the cookie file entry. Be aware that a domain setting must have at least two periods, such as

```
.mcom.com
.hotwired.com
```

Or, you can write an entire URL to the domain, including the `http://` protocol.

SECURE

If you omit the `SECURE` parameter when saving a cookie, you imply that the cookie data is accessible to any document or CGI program from your site that meets the other domain- and path-matching properties. For client-side scripting of cookies, you should omit this parameter when saving a cookie.

Retrieving cookie data

Cookie data retrieved via JavaScript is contained in one string, including the whole name-data pair. Even though the cookie file stores other parameters for each cookie, you can retrieve only the name-data pairs via JavaScript. Moreover, when two or more (up to a maximum of 20) cookies meet the current domain criteria, these cookies are also lumped into that string, delimited by a semicolon and space. For example, a document.cookie string may look like this:

```
userName=Fred; password=NikL2sPacU
```

In other words, you cannot treat named cookies as objects. Instead, you must parse the entire cookie string, extracting the data from the desired name-data pair.

When you know that you're dealing with only one cookie (and that no more will ever be added to the domain), you can customize the extraction based on known data, such as the cookie name. For example, with a cookie name that is seven characters long, you can extract the data with a statement such as this:

```
var data = unescape(document.cookie.substring(7,document.cookie.length))
```

The first parameter of the substring() method includes the equals sign to separate the name from the data.

A better approach is to create a general-purpose function that can work with single- or multiple-entry cookies. Here is one I use in some of my pages:

```
function getCookieData(labelName) {
    var labelLen = labelName.length
    // read cookie property only once for speed
    var cookieData = document.cookie
    var cLen = cookieData.length
    var i = 0
    var cEnd
    while (i < cLen) {
        var j = i + labelLen
        if (cookieData.substring(i,j) == labelName) {
            cEnd = cookieData.indexOf(";",j)
            if (cEnd == -1) {
                cEnd = cookieData.length
            }
            return unescape(cookieData.substring(j+1, cEnd))
        }
        i++
    }
    return ""
}
```

Calls to this function pass the label name of the desired cookie as a parameter. The function parses the entire cookie string, chipping away any mismatched entries (through the semicolons) until it finds the cookie name.

If all of this cookie code still makes your head hurt, you can turn to a set of functions devised by experienced JavaScripter and Web site designer Bill Dortch of hIdaho Design. His cookie functions provide generic access to cookies that you can use in all of your cookie-related pages. Listing 18-3 shows Bill's cookie functions, which include a variety of safety nets for date calculation bugs that appeared in some versions of Netscape Navigator 2. Don't be put off by the length of the listing: Most of the lines are comments. Updates to Bill's functions can be found at `http://www.hidaho.com/cookies/cookie.txt`.

Listing 18-3: **Bill Dortch's Cookie Functions**

```
<html>
<head>
<title>Cookie Functions</title>
</head>
<body>
<script language="javascript">
<!-- begin script
//
//  Cookie Functions -- "Night of the Living Cookie" Version (25-Jul-96)
//
//  Written by:  Bill Dortch, hIdaho Design <bdortch@hidaho.com>
//  The following functions are released to the public domain.
//
//  This version takes a more aggressive approach to deleting
//  cookies.  Previous versions set the expiration date to one
//  millisecond prior to the current time; however, this method
//  did not work in Netscape 2.02 (though it does in earlier and
//  later versions), resulting in "zombie" cookies that would not
//  die.  DeleteCookie now sets the expiration date to the earliest
//  usable date (one second into 1970), and sets the cookie's value
//  to null for good measure.
//
//  Also, this version adds optional path and domain parameters to
//  the DeleteCookie function.  If you specify a path and/or domain
//  when creating (setting) a cookie**, you must specify the same
//  path/domain when deleting it, or deletion will not occur.
//
//  The FixCookieDate function must now be called explicitly to
//  correct for the 2.x Mac date bug.  This function should be
//  called *once* after a Date object is created and before it
//  is passed (as an expiration date) to SetCookie.  Because the
//  Mac date bug affects all dates, not just those passed to
```

```
//   SetCookie, you might want to make it a habit to call
//   FixCookieDate any time you create a new Date object:
//
//     var theDate = new Date();
//     FixCookieDate (theDate);
//
//   Calling FixCookieDate has no effect on platforms other than
//   the Mac, so there is no need to determine the user's platform
//   prior to calling it.
//
//   This version also incorporates several minor coding improvements.
//
//   **Note that it is possible to set multiple cookies with the same
//   name but different (nested) paths.  For example:
//
//     SetCookie ("color","red",null,"/outer");
//     SetCookie ("color","blue",null,"/outer/inner");
//
//   However, GetCookie cannot distinguish between these and will return
//   the first cookie that matches a given name.  It is therefore
//   recommended that you *not* use the same name for cookies with
//   different paths.  (Bear in mind that there is *always* a path
//   associated with a cookie; if you don't explicitly specify one,
//   the path of the setting document is used.)
//
//   Revision History:
//
//     "Toss Your Cookies" Version (22-Mar-96)
//       - Added FixCookieDate() function to correct for Mac date bug
//
//     "Second Helping" Version (21-Jan-96)
//       - Added path, domain and secure parameters to SetCookie
//       - Replaced home-rolled encode/decode functions with Netscape's
//         new (then) escape and unescape functions
//
//     "Free Cookies" Version (December 95)
//
//
//   For information on the significance of cookie parameters,
//   and on cookies in general, please refer to the official cookie
//   spec, at:
//
//       http://www.netscape.com/newsref/std/cookie_spec.html
//
//********************************************************************
//
// "Internal" function to return the decoded value of a cookie
//
function getCookieVal (offset) {
  var endstr = document.cookie.indexOf (";", offset);
```

Continued

Listing 18-3 *(continued)*

```
    if (endstr == -1)
      endstr = document.cookie.length;
    return unescape(document.cookie.substring(offset, endstr));
}
//
//  Function to correct for 2.x Mac date bug.  Call this function to
//  fix a date object prior to passing it to SetCookie.
//  IMPORTANT:  This function should only be called *once* for
//  any given date object!  See example at the end of this document.
//
function FixCookieDate (date) {
  var base = new Date(0);
  var skew = base.getTime(); // dawn of (Unix) time - should be 0
  if (skew > 0)  // Except on the Mac - ahead of its time
    date.setTime (date.getTime() - skew);
}
//
//  Function to return the value of the cookie specified by "name".
//    name - String object containing the cookie name.
//    returns - String object containing the cookie value, or null if
//      the cookie does not exist.
//
function GetCookie (name) {
  var arg = name + "=";
  var alen = arg.length;
  var clen = document.cookie.length;
  var i = 0;
  while (i < clen) {
    var j = i + alen;
    if (document.cookie.substring(i, j) == arg)
      return getCookieVal (j);
    i = document.cookie.indexOf(" ", i) + 1;
    if (i == 0) break;
  }
  return null;
}
//
//  Function to create or update a cookie.
//    name - String object containing the cookie name.
//    value - String object containing the cookie value.  May contain
//      any valid string characters.
//    [expires] - Date object containing the expiration data of the cookie.  If
//      omitted or null, expires the cookie at the end of the current session.
//    [path] - String object indicating the path for which the cookie is valid.
//      If omitted or null, uses the path of the calling document.
//    [domain] - String object indicating the domain for which the cookie is
//      valid. If omitted or null, uses the domain of the calling document.
```

```
//     [secure] - Boolean (true/false) value indicating whether cookie transmis-
sion
//       requires a secure channel (HTTPS).
//
// The first two parameters are required.  The others, if supplied, must
// be passed in the order listed above.  To omit an unused optional field,
// use null as a place holder.  For example, to call SetCookie using name,
// value and path, you would code:
//
//       SetCookie ("myCookieName", "myCookieValue", null, "/");
//
// Note that trailing omitted parameters do not require a placeholder.
//
// To set a secure cookie for path "/myPath", that expires after the
// current session, you might code:
//
//       SetCookie (myCookieVar, cookieValueVar, null, "/myPath", null, true);
//
function SetCookie (name,value,expires,path,domain,secure) {
  document.cookie = name + "=" + escape (value) +
    ((expires) ? "; expires=" + expires.toGMTString() : "") +
    ((path) ? "; path=" + path : "") +
    ((domain) ? "; domain=" + domain : "") +
    ((secure) ? "; secure" : "");
}


// Function to delete a cookie. (Sets expiration date to start of epoch)
//   name -   String object containing the cookie name
//   path -   String object containing the path of the cookie to delete.  This
MUST
//           be the same as the path used to create the cookie, or null/omit-
ted if
//           no path was specified when creating the cookie.
//   domain - String object containing the domain of the cookie to delete.
This MUST
//           be the same as the domain used to create the cookie, or
null/omitted if
//           no domain was specified when creating the cookie.
//
function DeleteCookie (name,path,domain) {
  if (GetCookie(name)) {
    document.cookie = name + "=" +
      ((path) ? "; path=" + path : "") +
      ((domain) ? "; domain=" + domain : "") +
      "; expires=Thu, 01-Jan-70 00:00:01 GMT";
  }
}


//
// Examples
```

Continued

Listing 18-3 *(continued)*

```
//
var expdate = new Date ();
FixCookieDate (expdate); // Correct for Mac date bug - call only once for given
Date object!
expdate.setTime (expdate.getTime() + (24 * 60 * 60 * 1000)); // 24 hrs from now
SetCookie ("ccpath", "http://www.hidaho.com/colorcenter/", expdate);
SetCookie ("ccname", "hIdaho Design ColorCenter", expdate);
SetCookie ("tempvar", "This is a temporary cookie.");
SetCookie ("ubiquitous", "This cookie will work anywhere in this
domain",null,"/");
SetCookie ("paranoid", "This cookie requires secure communications",exp-
date,"/",null,true);
SetCookie ("goner", "This cookie must die!");
document.write (document.cookie + "<br>");
DeleteCookie ("goner");
document.write (document.cookie + "<br>");
document.write ("ccpath = " + GetCookie("ccpath") + "<br>");
document.write ("ccname = " + GetCookie("ccname") + "<br>");
document.write ("tempvar = " + GetCookie("tempvar") + "<br>");
// end script -->
</script>
</body>
</html>
```

Extra batches

You may design a site that needs more than 20 cookies for a given domain. For example, in a shopping site, you never know how many items a customer may load into the shopping cart cookie.

Because each named cookie stores plain text, you can create your own text-based data structures to accommodate multiple pieces of information per cookie. (But also watch out for a practical limit of 2,000 characters per name/value pair within the 4,000 character maximum for any domain's combined cookies.) The trick is determining a delimiter character that won't be used by any of the data in the cookie. In Decision Helper (in Chapter 55), for example, I use a period to separate multiple integers stored in a cookie.

With the delimiter character established, you must then write functions that con-catenate these "subcookies" into single cookie strings and extract them on the other side. It's a bit more work, but well worth the effort to have the power of per-sistent data on the client.

Example on the CD

Related Items: String object methods (Chapter 34).

defaultCharset

Value: String   Read/Write

	NN2	NN3	NN4	NN6	IE3/J1	IE3/J2	IE4	IE5	IE5.5
Compatibility							✓	✓	✓

The `defaultCharset` property reveals the character set used by the browser to render the current document. You can find possible values for this property at

```
ftp://ftp.isi.edu/in-notes/iana/assignments/character-sets
```

Each browser and operating system has its own default character set. Values may also be set via a `<META>` tag. The difference between the `defaultCharset` and `charset` properties is not clear, especially because both are read/write (although modifying the `defaultCharset` property has no visual effect on the page). However, if your scripts temporarily modify the `charset` property, you can use the `defaultCharset` property to return to the original character set:

```
document.charset = document.defaultCharset
```

Example on the CD

Related Items: `charset`, `characterSet` properties.

designMode

Value: String   Read/Write

	NN2	NN3	NN4	NN6	IE3/J1	IE3/J2	IE4	IE5	IE5.5
Compatibility								✓	✓

The designMode property is applicable only when IE5 technology is being used as a component in another application. More information can be found at http://msdn.microsoft.com/workshop/browser/default.asp. The property controls whether the browser module is being used for HTML editing. Modifying the property from within a typical HTML page in the IE5 browser has no effect.

doctype

Value: DocumentType object reference   Read-Only

	NN2	NN3	NN4	NN6	IE3/J1	IE3/J2	IE4	IE5	IE5.5
Compatibility				✓					

The doctype property comes from the W3C Core DOM and returns a DocumentType object — a representation of the DTD information for the document. In IE5.5 and NN6, the DocumentType object (even if one is not explicitly defined in the source code) is the first child node of the root document node (and is thus a sibling to the HTML element).

As of NN6, only a couple of properties of this still-evolving W3C DOM specification are implemented. Table 18-2 shows the typical DocumentType object property list and values for a generic HTML page. Future DOM specifications will allow these properties to be read/write.

Table 18-2   DocumentType Object in NN6

Property	Value
entities	null
internalSubset	(empty)
name	HTML
notations	null
publicId	-//W3C//DTD HTML 3.2 Final//EN
systemId	(empty)

Related Items: Node object (Chapter 14).

documentElement

Value: HTML or XML element object reference   Read-Only

	NN2	NN3	NN4	NN6	IE3/J1	IE3/J2	IE4	IE5	IE5.5
Compatibility				✓				✓	✓

The documentElement property returns a reference to the HTML (or XML) element object that contains all of the content of the current document. The naming of this property is a bit misleading, because the root document node is not an element, but its only child node is the HTML (or XML) element for the page. At best, you can think of this property as providing scripts with an "element face" to the document object and document node associated with the page currently loaded in the browser.

On the CD-ROM   Example on the CD

Related Items: ownerDocument property (Chapter 15).

domain

Value: String   Read/Write

	NN2	NN3	NN4	NN6	IE3/J1	IE3/J2	IE4	IE5	IE5.5
Compatibility		✓	✓	✓			✓	✓	✓

Security restrictions can get in the way of sites that have more than one server at their domain. Because some objects, especially the location object, prevent access to properties of other servers displayed in other frames, legitimate access to those properties are blocked. For example, it's not uncommon for popular sites to have their usual public access site on a server named something such as www.popular.com. If a page on that server includes a front end to a site search engine located at search.popular.com, visitors who use browsers with these security restrictions are denied access.

To guard against that eventuality, a script in documents from both servers can instruct the browser to think both servers are the same. In the preceding example, you would set the document.domain property in both documents to popular.com.

Without specifically setting the property, the default value includes the server name as well, thus causing a mismatch between host names.

Before you start thinking that you can spoof your way into other servers, be aware that you can set the `document.domain` property only to servers with the same domain (following the "two-dot" rule) as the document doing the setting. Therefore, documents originating only from `xxx.popular.com` can set their `document.domain` properties to `popular.com` server.

Related Items: `window.open()` method; `window.location` object; security (Chapter 46).

embeds

Value: Array of EMBED element objects   Read-Only

	NN2	NN3	NN4	NN6	IE3/J1	IE3/J2	IE4	IE5	IE5.5
Compatibility		✓	✓	✓			✓	✓	✓

Whenever you want to load data that requires a plug-in application to play or display, you use the `<EMBED>` tag. The `document.embeds` property is merely one way to determine the number of such tags defined in the document:

```
var count = document.embeds.length
```

For controlling those plug-ins in Navigator, you can use the LiveConnect technology, described in Chapter 44.

Related Items: EMBED element object (Chapter 32).

expando

Value: Boolean   Read/Write

	NN2	NN3	NN4	NN6	IE3/J1	IE3/J2	IE4	IE5	IE5.5
Compatibility							✓	✓	✓

Microsoft calls any custom property that is not a native property of the `document` object an *expando* property. By default, most objects in recent generations of browsers allow scripts to add new properties of objects as a way to temporarily store data without explicitly defining global variables. For example, if you want to maintain an independent counter of how often a function is invoked, you can create a custom property of the document object and use it as the storage facility:

```
document.counter = 0
```

IE4+ lets you control whether the document object is capable of accepting expando properties. The default value of the document.expando property is true, thus allowing custom properties. But the potential downside to this permissiveness, especially during the page construction phase, is that a misspelled native property name is gladly accepted by the document object. You may not be aware of why the title bar of the browser window doesn't change when you assign a new string to the document.Title property (which, in the case-sensitive world of JavaScript, is distinct from the native document.title property).

On the CD-ROM Example on the CD

Related Items: prototype property of custom objects (Chapter 41).

fgColor

See alinkColor.

fileCreatedDate
fileModifiedDate
fileSize

Value: String, Integer (fileSize)   Read-Only

	NN2	NN3	NN4	NN6	IE3/J1	IE3/J2	IE4	IE5	IE5.5
Compatibility							✓	✓	✓

These three IE-specific properties return information about the file that holds the current document. Two of the properties (not implemented in IE5/Mac) reveal the dates on which the current document's file was created and modified. For an unmodified file, its creation and modified dates are the same. The fileSize property reveals the number of bytes of the file.

Date values returned for the first two properties are formatted differently between IE4 and IE5. The former provides a full readout of the day and date; the latter in a format similar to mm/dd/yyyy. Note, however, that the values contain only the date and not the time. In any case, you can use the values as the parameter to a `new Date()` constructor function. You can then use date calculations for such information as the number of days between the current day and the most recent modification.

Not all servers may provide the proper date or size information about a file or in a format that IE can interpret. Test your implementation on the deployment server to ensure compatibility.

Also, be aware that these properties can be read only for a file that is loaded in the browser. JavaScript by itself cannot get this information about files that are on the server but not loaded in the browser.

IE5.5 exposes a property called `fileUpdatedDate`, but the property does not return any data. This property may be a phantom property left over from a prerelease version.

On the CD-ROM

Example on the CD with Listing 18-4

Related Items: `lastModified` property.

forms

Value: Array   Read-Only

	NN2	NN3	NN4	NN6	IE3/J1	IE3/J2	IE4	IE5	IE5.5
Compatibility	✓	✓	✓	✓	✓	✓	✓	✓	✓

As I show in Chapter 23, which is dedicated to the form object, an HTML form (anything defined inside a `<FORM>`...`</FORM>` tag pair) is a JavaScript object unto itself. You can create a valid reference to a form according to its name (assigned via a form's `NAME` attribute). For example, if a document contains the following form definition

```
<FORM NAME="phoneData">
    input item definitions
</FORM>
```

your scripts can refer to the form object by name:

```
document.phoneData
```

However, a document object also tracks its forms in another way: as an array of Form objects. The first item of a document.forms array is the form that loaded first (it was first from the top of the HTML code). If your document defines one form, the forms property is an array one entry in length; with three separate forms in the document, the array is three entries long.

Use standard array notation to reference a particular form from the document.forms array. For example, the first form in a document (the "zeroth" entry of the document.forms array) is referenced as

```
document.forms[0]
```

Any of the form object's properties or methods are available by appending the desired property or method name to the reference. For example, to retrieve the value of an input text field named homePhone from the second form of a document, the reference you use is

```
document.forms[1].homePhone.value
```

One advantage to using the document.forms property for addressing a form object or element instead of the actual form name is that you may be able to generate a library of generalizable scripts that know how to cycle through all available forms in a document and hunt for a form that has some special element and property. The following script fragment (part of a *repeat loop* described more fully in Chapter 39) uses a loop-counting variable (i) to help the script check all forms in a document:

```
for (var i = 0; i < document.forms.length; i++) {
    if (document.forms[i]. ... ) {
        statements
    }
}
```

One more variation on forms array references lets you substitute the name of a form (as a string) for the forms array index. For example, the form named phoneData can be referenced as

```
document.forms["phoneData"]
```

If you use a lot of care in assigning names to objects, you will likely prefer the document.*formName* style of referencing forms. In this book, you see both indexed array and form name style references. The advantage of using name references is that even if you redesign the page and change the order of forms in the document, references to the named forms will still be valid, whereas the index numbers of the forms will have changed. See also the discussion in Chapter 23 of the form object and how to pass a form's data to a function.

Example on the CD with Listing 18-5

Related Items: form object (Chapter 23).

frames

Value: Array   Read-Only

	NN2	NN3	NN4	NN6	IE3/J1	IE3/J2	IE4	IE5	IE5.5
Compatibility							✓	✓	✓

The document.frames property is similar to the window.frames property, but its association with the document object may seem a bit illogical at times. The objects contained by the array returned from the property are window objects, which means they are the window objects of any FRAME elements (from a framesetting document) or IFRAME elements (from a plain HTML document) defined for the document. Distinguishing the window objects from the element objects is important. Window objects have different properties and methods than the FRAME and IFRAME element objects. The latter's properties typically represent the attributes for those element's tags. If a document contains no IFRAME elements, the frames array length is zero.

While you can access an individual frame object via the typical array syntax (for example, document.frames[0]), you can also use alternate syntax that Microsoft provides for collections of objects. The index number can also be placed inside parentheses, as in

```
document.frames(0)
```

Moreover, if the frames have values assigned to their NAME attributes, you can use the name (in string form) as a parameter:

```
document.frames("contents")
```

And if the collection of frames has more than one frame with the same name, you must take special care. Using the duplicated name as a parameter forces the reference to return a collection of frame objects that share that name. Or, you can limit the returned value to a single instance of the duplicate-named frames by specifying an optional second parameter indicating the index. For example, if a document has two IFRAME elements with the name contents, a script could reference the second window object as

```
document.frames("contents", 1)
```

Chapter 18 ✦ **The Document and Body Objects** 535

For the sake of cross-browser compatibility, my preference for referencing frame window objects is via the `window.frames` property.

Example on the CD

Related Items: `window.frames` property.

height
width

Value: Integer   Read-Only

	NN2	NN3	NN4	NN6	IE3/J1	IE3/J2	IE4	IE5	IE5.5
Compatibility			✓	✓					

The `height` and `width` properties of the NN4+ `document` object provide the pixel dimensions of the content within the current window (or frame). If the document's content is smaller than the size of the browser's content region, the dimensions returned by these properties include the blank space to the right and/or bottom edges of the content area of the window. But if the content extends beyond the viewable edges of the content region, the dimensions include the unseen content as well. The corresponding measures in IE4+ are the `document.body.scrollHeight` and `document.body.scrollWidth` properties.

Example on the CD

Related Items: `document.body.scrollHeight`, `document.body.scrollWidth` properties.

ids

Value: Array   Read-Only

	NN2	NN3	NN4	NN6	IE3/J1	IE3/J2	IE4	IE5	IE5.5
Compatibility			✓						

The NN4-specific `ids` property is used in the browser's alternative, JavaScript-based style sheet syntax. Deployment of JavaScript style sheets is exceedingly rare. In some ways, the `document.ids` property behaves similarly to the IE4+ `document.all` property, but `document.ids` cannot be used in regular scripts to access element objects.

Related Items: `tags` property.

images

Value: Array   Read-Only

	NN2	NN3	NN4	NN6	IE3/J1	IE3/J2	IE4	IE5	IE5.5
Compatibility		✓	✓	✓	(✓)		✓	✓	✓

With images treated as first-class objects beginning with NN3 and IE4 (and IE Version 3.01 on the Mac), it's only natural for a document to maintain an array of all the image tags defined on the page (just as it does for links and anchors). The prime importance of having images as objects is that you can modify their content (the source file associated with the rectangular space of the image) on the fly. You can find details about the image object in Chapter 22.

Use image array references to pinpoint a specific image for retrieval of any image property or for assigning a new image file to its `src` property. Image arrays begin their index counts with 0: The first image in a document has the reference `document.images[0]`. And, as with any array object, you can find out how many images the array contains by checking the length property. For example:

```
var imageCount = document.images.length
```

Images can also have names, so if you prefer, you can refer to the image object by its name, as in

```
var imageLoaded = document.imageName.complete
```

or

```
var imageLoaded = document.images[imageName].complete
```

The `document.images` array is a useful guide to knowing whether a browser supports swappable images. Any browser that treats an IMG element as an object always forms a `document.images` array in the page. If no images are defined in the page, the array is still there, but its length is zero. The array's existence, however, is the clue about image object compatibility. Because the document.images array evaluates to an array object when present, the expression can be used as a condition expression for branching to statements that involve image swapping:

```
if (document.images) {
    // image swapping or precaching here
}
```

Earlier browsers that don't have this property evaluate document.images as undefined and thus the condition is treated as a false value.

Example on the CD

Related Items: Image object (Chapter 22).

implementation

Value: Object   Read-Only

	NN2	NN3	NN4	NN6	IE3/J1	IE3/J2	IE4	IE5	IE5.5
Compatibility				✓					

The Core W3C DOM defines the document.implementation property as an avenue to let scripts find out what DOM features (that is, modules of the DOM standard) are implemented for the current environment. While the object returned by the property (a DOMImplementation object) has no properties, it has a method, hasFeature(), which lets scripts find out, for example, whether the environment supports HTML or just XML. The first parameter of the hasFeature() method is the feature in the form of a string. The second parameter is a string form of the version number. The method returns a Boolean value.

A section of the W3C DOM specification, called "Conformance," governs the module names (the standard also allows browser-specific features to be tested via the hasFeature() method). Module names include strings such as HTML, XML, MouseEvents, and so on.

Version numbering for W3C DOM modules corresponds to the W3C DOM level. Thus, the version for the XML DOM module in DOM Level 2 is known as 2.0. Note that versions refer to DOM modules and not, for instance, the separate HTML standard.

NN6 reports that it conforms to many modules defined in the W3C DOM Level 2, as shown in Table 18-3. But the indicated support may be misleading. According to the

W3C standard, conformance for a module and version should indicate support for "all the interfaces for that module and the associated semantics." In some cases, however, NN6 has merely reserved placeholders for objects, properties, and methods that are not yet implemented. As a result, it is risky to use the hasFeature() method as a substitute for object detection in scripts. For now, you can trust the reported conformance only as a coarse indication of feature support.

Table 18-3 NN6 document.implementation.hasFeature() Support	
Feature	**Versions**
XML	1.0, 2.0
HTML	1.0, 2.0
Views	2.0
StyleSheets	2.0
CSS	2.0
Events	2.0
MouseEvents	2.0
HTMLEvents	2.0
Range	2.0

Example on the CD

lastModified

Value: Date String   Read-Only

	NN2	NN3	NN4	NN6	IE3/J1	IE3/J2	IE4	IE5	IE5.5
Compatibility	✓	✓	✓	✓	✓	✓	✓	✓	✓

Every disk file maintains a modified timestamp, and most (but not all) servers are configured to expose this information to a browser accessing a file. This information is available by reading the document.lastModified property. If your server supplies this information to the client, you can use the value of this property to present this information for readers of your Web page. The script automatically updates the value for you, rather than requiring you to hand-code the HTML line every time you modify the home page.

If the value returned to you displays itself as a date in 1969, it means that you are positioned somewhere west of GMT, or Greenwich Mean Time (some number of time zones west of GMT at 1 January 1970), and the server is not providing the proper data when it serves the file. Sometimes server configuration can fix the problem, but not always.

The returned value is not a date object (Chapter 36) but rather a straight string consisting of time and date, as recorded by the document's file system. The format of the string varies from browser to browser and version to version. You can, however, usually convert the date string to a JavaScript date object and use the date object's methods to extract selected elements for recompilation into readable form. Listing 18-6 shows an example.

Note Some browser versions running in Windows 95 may return a two-digit year, which will lead to Y2K problems when generating a date object.

Even local file systems don't necessarily provide the correct data for every browser to interpret. For example, in Navigator of all generations for the Macintosh, dates from files stored on local disks come back as something from the 1920s (although Internet Explorer manages to reflect the correct date). But put that same file on a UNIX or NT Web server, and the date appears correctly when accessed via the Net.

On the CD-ROM Example on the CD with Listing 18-6

Related Items: Date object (Chapter 36).

layers

Value: Array   Read-Only

	NN2	NN3	NN4	NN6	IE3/J1	IE3/J2	IE4	IE5	IE5.5
Compatibility			✓						

The layer object (Chapter 31) is the NN4 way of exposing positioned elements to the object model. Thus, the document.layers property is an array of positioned elements in the document. But due to the nonstandard way that NN4 implements positioned elements, not every positioned element is represented in the document.layers array. More deeply nested positioned elements must be referenced through a hierarchy of layers.

Note   The layer object and `document.layers` property are orphaned in NN4, and their importance diminishes as the installed base of NN4 shrinks. The remaining discussion is included only for those Web authors who must support positioned elements in NN4. In NN6, the layer is represented by any HTML element whose style sheet definition includes a `position` attribute. References to such elements can be made through the `document.getElementById()` method or shortcuts described in Chapter 14.

A Netscape layer is a container for content that can be precisely positioned on the page. Layers can be defined with the NN4-specific `<LAYER>` tag or with W3C standard style sheet positioning syntax, as explained in Chapter 31. Each layer contains a `document` object—the true holder of the content displayed in that layer. Layers can be nested within each other, but a reference to `document.layers` reveals only the first level of layers defined in the document. Consider the following HTML skeleton.

```
<HTML>
<BODY>
<LAYER NAME="Europe">
    <LAYER NAME="Germany"></LAYER>
    <LAYER NAME="Netherlands"></LAYER>
</LAYER>
</BODY>
</HTML>
```

From the point of view of the primary document, there is one layer (Europe). Therefore, the length of the `document.layers` array is 1. But the Europe layer has a document, in which two more layers are nested. A reference to the array of those nested layers is

```
document.layers[1].document.layers
```

or

```
document.Europe.document.layers
```

The length of this nested array is two: The Germany and Netherlands layers. No property exists that reveals the entire set of nested arrays in a document, but you can create a `for` loop to crawl through all nested layers (shown in Listing 18-7).

On the CD-ROM   Example on the CD with Listing 18-7

Related Items: layer object (Chapter 31).

linkColor

See `alinkColor`.

links

Value: Array   Read-Only

	NN2	NN3	NN4	NN6	IE3/J1	IE3/J2	IE4	IE5	IE5.5
Compatibility	✓	✓	✓	✓	✓	✓	✓	✓	✓

The `document.links` property is similar to the `document.anchors` property, except that the objects maintained by the array are link objects — items created with `<A HREF="">` tags. Use the array references to pinpoint a specific link for retrieving any link property, such as the target window specified in the link's HTML definition.

Link arrays begin their index counts with 0: The first link in a document has the reference `document.links[0]`. And, as with any array object, you can find out how many entries the array has by checking the `length` property. For example:

```
var linkCount = document.links.length
```

Entries in the `document.links` property are full-fledged `location` objects.

On the CD-ROM

Example on the CD

Related Items: link object; `document.anchors` property.

location
URL

Value: String   Read/Write and Read-Only (see text)

	NN2	NN3	NN4	NN6	IE3/J1	IE3/J2	IE4	IE5	IE5.5
Compatibility	(✓)	✓	✓	✓	(✓)	(✓)	✓	✓	✓

The fact that JavaScript frequently reuses the same terms in different contexts may be confusing to the language's newcomers. Such is the case with the `document.location` property. You may wonder how this property differs from the `location` object (Chapter 17). In practice, many scripts also get the two confused when references don't include the `window` object. As a result, a new property name, document.URL, was introduced in NN3 and IE4 to take the place of document.location. You can still use document.location, but the term may eventually disappear from the object model vocabulary. To help you get into the future mindset, the rest of this discussion refers to this property as document.URL.

The remaining question is how the window.location object and document.URL property differ. The answer lies in their respective data types.

A location object, you may recall from Chapter 17, consists of a number of properties about the document currently loaded in a window or frame. Assigning a new URL to the location object (or location.href property) tells the browser to load the page from that URL into the frame. The document.URL property, on the other hand, is simply a string (read-only in Navigator) that reveals the URL of the current document. The value may be important to your script, but the property does not have the "object power" of the window.location object. You cannot change (assign another value to) this property value because a document has only one URL: its location on the Net (or your hard disk) where the file exists, and what protocol is required to get it.

This may seem like a fine distinction, and it is. The reference you use (window.location object or document.URL property) depends on what you are trying to accomplish specifically with the script. If the script is changing the content of a window by loading a new URL, you have no choice but to assign a value to the window.location object. Similarly, if the script is concerned with the component parts of a URL, the properties of the location object provide the simplest avenue to that information. To retrieve the URL of a document in string form (whether it is in the current window or in another frame), you can use either the document.URL property or the window.location.href property.

On the CD-ROM   Example on the CD with Listings 18-8, 18-9, and 18-10

Related Items: location object; location.href, URLUnencoded properties.

media

Value: String   Read/Write

	NN2	NN3	NN4	NN6	IE3/J1	IE3/J2	IE4	IE5	IE5.5
Compatibility									✓

At its introduction in IE5.5, the document.media property is limited to one value besides the default value of empty: print. Details of this property are sketchy, but the intention appears to be to provide a way to use scripting to set the equivalent of the CSS2 @media rule (one of the so-called "at" rules because of the at symbol). This style sheet rule allows browsers to assign separate styles for each type of output device on which the page is rendered (for example, perhaps a different font for a printer versus the screen). In practice, however, this property is not modifiable in IE5.5.

Related Items: None.

mimeType

Value: String   Read-Only

	NN2	NN3	NN4	NN6	IE3/J1	IE3/J2	IE4	IE5	IE5.5
Compatibility								✓	✓

Although this property is readable in IE5+, its value is not strictly speaking a MIME type, or at least not in traditional MIME format. Moreover, the results are inconsistent between IE5 and IE5.5. Perhaps this property will be of more use in an XML, rather than HTML, document environment. In any case, this property in no way exposes supported MIME types in the current browser.

namespaces

Value: Array of namespace objects   Read-Only

	NN2	NN3	NN4	NN6	IE3/J1	IE3/J2	IE4	IE5	IE5.5
Compatibility									✓

A namespace object (new in IE5.5) can dynamically import an XML-based IE Element Behavior. The namespaces property returns an array of all namespace objects defined in the current document. For more details on how to utilize Element Behaviors and ViewLinks (custom controls devised out of HTML and scripting) in IE5.5, visit http://msdn.microsoft.com/workshop/author/behaviors/overview/identityb_ovw.asp.

Related Items: None.

parentWindow

Value: window object reference   Read-Only

	NN2	NN3	NN4	NN6	IE3/J1	IE3/J2	IE4	IE5	IE5.5
Compatibility							✓	✓	✓

The document.parentWindow property returns a reference to the window object containing the current document. The value is the same as any reference to the current window.

On the CD-ROM

Example on the CD

Related Items: window object.

plugins

Value: Array   Read-Only

	NN2	NN3	NN4	NN6	IE3/J1	IE3/J2	IE4	IE5	IE5.5
Compatibility			✓	✓			✓	✓	✓

The document.plugins property returns the same array of EMBED element objects that you get from the document.embeds property. This property appears to have been deprecated in favor of document.embeds.

Related Items: document.embeds property.

protocol

Value: String   Read/Write

	NN2	NN3	NN4	NN6	IE3/J1	IE3/J2	IE4	IE5	IE5.5
Compatibility							✓	✓	✓

The IE-specific `document.protocol` property returns the plain-language version of the protocol that was used to access the current document. For example, if the file is accessed from a Web server, the property returns `Hypertext Transfer Protocol`. This property differs from the `location.protocol` property, which returns the portion of the URL that includes the often more cryptic protocol abbreviation (for example, `http:`). As a general rule, you want to hide all of this stuff from a Web application user.

Example on the CD

Related Items: `location.protocol` property.

referrer

Value: String   Read-Only

	NN2	NN3	NN4	NN6	IE3/J1	IE3/J2	IE4	IE5	IE5.5
Compatibility	✓	✓	✓	✓	✓	✓	✓	✓	✓

When a link from one document leads to another, the second document can, under JavaScript control, reveal the URL of the document containing the link. The `document.referrer` property contains a string of that URL. This feature can be a useful tool for customizing the content of pages based on the previous location the user was visiting within your site. A referrer contains a value only when the user reaches the current page via a link. Any other method of navigation (such as through the history, bookmarks, or by manually entering a URL) sets this property to an empty string.

The `document.referrer` property is broken in Windows versions of IE3 and IE4. In the Windows version, the current document's URL is given as the referrer; the proper value is returned in the Macintosh versions. For IE5+, the property returns empty when the referrer document is accessed via the `file:` protocol.

Example on the CD with Listings 18-11 and 18-12

Related Items: link object.

scripts

Value: Array   Read-Only

	NN2	NN3	NN4	NN6	IE3/J1	IE3/J2	IE4	IE5	IE5.5
Compatibility							✓	✓	✓

The IE-specific `document.scripts` property returns an array of all SCRIPT element objects in the current document. You can reference an individual SCRIPT element object to read not only the properties it shares with all HTML element objects (Chapter 15) but also script-specific properties, such as `defer`, `src`, and `htmlFor`. The actual scripting is accessible either through the `innerText` or `text` properties for any SCRIPT element object.

While the `document.scripts` array is read-only, many properties of individual SCRIPT element objects are modifiable. Adding or removing SCRIPT elements impacts the length of the `document.scripts` array. Don't forget, too, that if your scripts need to access a specific SCRIPT element object, you can assign an `ID` attribute to it and reference the element directly.

This property is an IE-specific convenience property that is the same as the IE4+ and NN6 expression `document.getElementsByTagName("SCRIPT")`, which returns an array of the same objects.

 Example on the CD

Related Items: SCRIPT element object (Chapter 20).

security

Value: String   Read-Only

	NN2	NN3	NN4	NN6	IE3/J1	IE3/J2	IE4	IE5	IE5.5
Compatibility									✓

The `security` property reveals information about a security certificate, if one is associated with the current document. As of this writing, the property is not formally documented by Microsoft, so its range of possibilities is not clear for now. For a standard document, the value of the property is `This type of document does not have a security certificate`.

selection

Value: Object   Read-Only

	NN2	NN3	NN4	NN6	IE3/J1	IE3/J2	IE4	IE5	IE5.5
Compatibility							✓	✓	✓

The `document.selection` property returns a `selection` object whose content is represented in the browser window as a body text selection. That selection can be explicitly performed by the user (by clicking and dragging across some text) or created under script contol via the IE/Windows `TextRange` object (see Chapter 19). Because script action on a selection (for example, finding the next instance of selected text) is performed via the `TextRange` object, converting a selection to a `TextRange` object using the `document.selection.createRange()` method is common practice. See the `selection` object in Chapter 19 for more details.

Be aware that you cannot script interaction with text selections through user interface elements, such as buttons. Clicking a button gives focus to the button and deselects the selection. Use other events, such as `document.onmouseup` to trigger actions on a selection.

 Example on the CD

Related Items: `selection`, `TextRange` objects.

styleSheets

Value: Array   Read-Only

	NN2	NN3	NN4	NN6	IE3/J1	IE3/J2	IE4	IE5	IE5.5
Compatibility				✓			✓	✓	✓

The `document.styleSheets` array consists of references to all STYLE element objects in the document. Not included in this array are style sheets that are assigned to elements by way of the STYLE attribute inside a tag or linked in via LINK elements. See Chapter 30 for details about the `styleSheet` object.

Related Items: `styleSheet` object (Chapter 30).

tags

Value: Array   Read-Only

	NN2	NN3	NN4	NN6	IE3/J1	IE3/J2	IE4	IE5	IE5.5
Compatibility			✓						

The NN4-specific `tags` property is used in the browser's alternate, JavaScript-based style sheet syntax. Deployment of JavaScript style sheets is exceedingly rare. In some ways, the `document.tags` property behaves like the IE4+ and NN5 `document.getElementsByTagName()` method, but `document.tags` cannot be used in regular scripts to access element objects.

Related Items: `ids` property.

title

Value: String   Read-Only and Read/Write

	NN2	NN3	NN4	NN6	IE3/J1	IE3/J2	IE4	IE5	IE5.5
Compatibility	✓	✓	✓	✓	✓	✓	✓	✓	✓

A document's title is the text that appears between the `<TITLE>...</TITLE>` tag pair in an HTML document's Head portion. The title usually appears in the title bar of the browser window in a single-frame presentation. Only the title of the topmost framesetting document appears as the title of a multiframe window. Even so, the `title` property for an individual document within a frame is available via scripting. For example, if two frames are available (`UpperFrame` and `LowerFrame`), a script in the document occupying the `LowerFrame` frame can reference the `title` property of the other frame's document, such as this:

```
parent.UpperFrame.document.title
```

This property is read-only in browsers prior to IE4 and NN6.

The `document.title` property is a holdover from the original document object model. HTML elements in recent browsers have an entirely different application of the `title` property (see Chapter 15). In IE4+ and NN6, you should address the document's title by way of the TITLE element object directly.

UNIX versions of Navigator 2 fail to return the document.title property value. Also, in Navigator 4 for the Macintosh, if a script creates the content of another frame, the document.title property for that dynamically written frame returns the filename of the script that wrote the HTML, even when it writes a valid <TITLE> tag set.

Related Items: history object.

URL

See location.

URLUnencoded

Value: String   Read-Only

	NN2	NN3	NN4	NN6	IE3/J1	IE3/J2	IE4	IE5	IE5.5
Compatibility									✓

The document.URL property returns a URL-encoded string, meaning that non-alphanumeric characters in the URL are converted to URL-friendly characters (for example, a space becomes %20). You can always use the unescape() function on the value returned by the document.URL property, but the URLUnencoded property does that for you. If there are no URL-encoded characters in the URL, then both properties return identical strings.

Related Items: document.URL property.

vlinkColor

See alinkColor.

width

See height.

Methods

captureEvents(*eventTypeList*)

Returns: Nothing.

	NN2	NN3	NN4	NN6	IE3/J1	IE3/J2	IE4	IE5	IE5.5
Compatibility			✓						

In Navigator 4 only, the natural propagation of an event is downward from the window object, through the document object, and eventually reaching its target. For example, if you click a button, the click event first reaches the window object; then it goes to the document object; if the button is defined within a layer, the event also filters through that layer; eventually (in a split second) the event reaches the button, where an onClick event handler is ready to act on that click.

The NN4 mechanism allows window, document, and layer objects to intercept events and process them prior to reaching their intended targets (or preventing them from reaching their destinations entirely). But for an outer container to grab an event, your script must instruct it to capture the type of event your application is interested in preprocessing. If you want the document object to intercept all events of a particular type, use the document.captureEvents() method to turn that facility on.

Note Event capture with different syntax has been standardized in the W3C DOM and is implemented in NN6. See the addEventListener() method in Chapter 15 for the W3C counterpart to the NN4 captureEvents() method. Also, see Chapter 29 for more details on the combination of event capture and event bubbling in the W3C DOM.

The document.captureEvents() method takes one or more event types as parameters. An event type is a constant value built inside the NN4 Event object. One event type exists for every kind of event handler that you see in all of the document objects of NN4. The syntax consists of a reference to the Event object and the event name in all uppercase letters. For example, if you want the document to intercept all click events, the statement is

```
document.captureEvents(Event.CLICK)
```

For multiple events, add them as parameters, separated by the pipe (|) character:

```
document.captureEvents(Event.MOUSEDOWN | Event.KEYPRESS)
```

After the `document` object is set to capture an event type, it must have a function ready to deal with the event. For example, perhaps the function looks through all `Event.MOUSEDOWN` events and looks to see if the right mouse button is the one that triggers the event and what form element (if any) is the intended target. The goal is perhaps to display a pop-up menu (as a separate layer) for a right-click. If the click comes from the left mouse button, then the event is routed to its intended target.

To associate a function with a particular event type captured by a `document` object, assign a function to the event. For example, to assign a custom `doClickEvent()` function to click events captured by the `wdocument` object, use the following statement:

```
document.onclick=doClickEvent
```

Notice that the function name is assigned only as a reference name, unlike an event handler within a tag. The function, itself, is like any function, but it has the added benefit of automatically receiving the event object as a parameter. To turn off event capture for one or more event types, use the `document.releaseEvent()` method. See Chapter 29 for details of working with NN4 events.

Note   Capturing events at the `window`, `document`, or layer level in NN4 does not always work the way you may want, which is especially true if your page contains tables. For example, capturing mouse events has no effect in the Windows version of NN4 unless the cursor is atop a cell border. Event capture works most reliably when a scriptable object has an event handler defined for it (even if the handler is an empty string), and the element is the target of the event (for example, you are about to type into a text field). For all other elements, event capture may simply not be captured at the `document` or `window` level.

On the CD-ROM   Example on the CD

Related Items: `document.handleEvent()`, `document.releaseEvents()`, `document.routeEvent()` methods; parallel `window` object event methods.

clear()

Returns: Nothing.

	NN2	NN3	NN4	NN6	IE3/J1	IE3/J2	IE4	IE5	IE5.5
Compatibility	✓	✓	✓	✓	✓	✓	✓	✓	✓

Ever since NN2, the `document.clear()` method was intended to clear the current document from the browser window. This method is quite impractical, because you typically need some further scripts to execute after you clear the document, but if the scripts are gone, nothing else happens.

In practice, the document.clear() method never did what it was supposed to do (and in earlier browsers easily caused browser crashes). I recommend against using document.clear(), including in preparation for generating a new page's content with document.write(). The document.write() method clears the original document from the window before adding new content. If you truly want to empty a window or frame, then use document.write() to write a blank HTML document or to load an empty HTML document from the server.

Related Items: document.close(), document.write(), document.writeln() methods.

close()

Returns: Nothing.

	NN2	NN3	NN4	NN6	IE3/J1	IE3/J2	IE4	IE5	IE5.5
Compatibility	✓	✓	✓	✓	✓	✓	✓	✓	✓

Whenever a layout stream is opened to a window via the document.open() method or either of the document writing methods (which also open the layout stream), you must close the stream after the document is written. This causes the Layout:Complete and Done messages to appear in the status line (although you may experience some bugs in the status message on some platforms). The document closing step is very important to prepare the window for the next potential round of replenishment with new script-assembled HTML. If you don't close the document, subsequent writing is appended to the bottom of the document.

Some or all of the data specified for the window won't display properly until you invoke the document.close() method, especially when images are being drawn as part of the document stream. A common symptom is the momentary appearance and then disappearance of the document parts. If you see such behavior, look for a missing document.close() method after the last document.write() method.

Fixing the Sticky Wait Cursor

IE4+ frequently fails to restore the cursor to normal after document.write() and document.close() (and some other content-modifying scripts). The cursor stubbornly remains in the wait mode when, in truth, all processing has been completed. One, albeit ugly, workaround that I have found effective is to force an extra `document.close()` via a `javascript:` pseudo-URL (just adding another `document.close()` to your script doesn't do the trick). For use within a frameset, the `javascript:` URL must be directed to the top of the frameset hierarchy, while the `document.close()` is aimed at the frame that had its content changed. For example, if the change is made to a frame named `content`, create a function, such as the following:

```
function recloseDoc() {
    if (isIE) {
        top.location.href="javascript:void (parent.content.
        document.close())"
    }
}
```

This assumes, of course, that you have browser-sniffing working in the script that sets the `isIE` global variable to `true` when the browser is running in IE. If you place this function in the framesetting document, scripts that modify the content frame can invoke this script after any operation that prevents the normal cursor from appearing.

On the CD-ROM   Example on the CD

Related Items: `document.open()`, `document.clear()`, `document.write()`, `document.writeln()` methods.

createAttribute("*attributeName*")

Returns: Attribute object reference

	NN2	NN3	NN4	NN6	IE3/J1	IE3/J2	IE4	IE5	IE5.5
Compatibility				✓					

The `document.createAttribute()` method generates an attribute node object (formally known as an `Attr` object in W3C DOM terminology) and returns a reference to the newly created object. Invoking the method assigns only the name of the attribute, so it is up to your script to assign a value to the object's `nodeValue` property and then plug the new attribute into an existing element via that element's `setAttributeNode()` method (described in Chapter 15). The following sequence generates an attribute that becomes an attribute of a TABLE element:

```
var newAttr = document.createAttribute("width")
newAttr.nodeValue = "80%"
document.getElementById("myTable").setAttributeNode(newAttr)
```

Attributes do not always have to be attributes known to the HTML standard, because the method also works for XML elements, which have custom attributes.

On the CD-ROM

Example on the CD

Related Items: setAttributeNode() method (Chapter 15).

createElement("*tagName*")

Returns: Element object reference

	NN2	NN3	NN4	NN6	IE3/J1	IE3/J2	IE4	IE5	IE5.5
Compatibility				✓			✓	✓	✓

The document.createElement() method generates an element object for whatever HTML (or XML) tag name you pass as the parameter. This object is not officially part of the current document object model because it has not yet been placed into the document. But this method is the way you begin assembling an element object that eventually gets inserted into the document.

The returned value is a reference to the object. Properties of that object include all properties (set to default values) that the browser's object model defines for that element object. Your scripts can then address the object via this reference to set the object's properties. Typically you do this before the object is inserted into the document, especially because otherwise read-only properties can be modified before the element is inserted into the document.

After the object is inserted into the document, the original reference (for example, a global variable used to store the value returned from the createElement() method) still points to the object, even while it is in the document and being displayed for the user. To demonstrate this effect, consider the following statements that create a simple paragraph element containing a text node:

```
var newText = document.createTextNode("Four score and seven years ago...")
var newElem = document.createElement("P")
newElem.id = "newestP"
newElem.appendChild(newText)
document.body.appendChild(newElem)
```

At this point, the new paragraph is visible in the document. But you can now modify, for example, the style of the paragraph by addressing either the element in the document object model or the variable that holds the reference to the object you created:

```
newElem.style.fontSize = "20pt"
```

or

```
document.getElementById("newestP").style.fontSize = "20pt"
```

The two references are inextricably connected and always point to the exact same object. Therefore, if you want to use a script to generate a series of similar elements (for example, a bunch of LI elements), then you can use `createElement()` to make the first one and set all properties that the items have in common. Then use `cloneNode()` to make a new copy, which you can then treat as a separate element (and probably assign unique IDs to each one).

Scripting in the W3C DOM environment (to the extent that it is supported in both IE5 and NN6), you may rely on `document.createElement()` frequently to generate new content for a page or portion thereof (unless you prefer to use the convenience `innerHTML` property to add content in the form of strings of HTML). In a strict W3C DOM environment, creating new elements is not a matter of assembling HTML strings, but rather creating genuine element (and text node) objects.

 Example on the CD

Related Items: `document.createTextNode()` method.

createEventObject([*eventObject*])

Returns: event Object.

	NN2	NN3	NN4	NN6	IE3/J1	IE3/J2	IE4	IE5	IE5.5
Compatibility									✓

The IE-specific `createEventObject()` method creates an `event` object, which can then be passed as a parameter to the `fireEvent()` method of any element object. The `event` object created by this event is just like an `event` object created by a user or system action.

An optional parameter lets you base the new event on an existing `event` object. In other words, the properties of the newly created `event` object pick up all the properties of the `event` object passed as a parameter, which lets you then modify properties of your choice. If you provide no parameter to the method, then you must fill the essential properties manually. For more about the properties of an event object, see Chapter 29.

Example on the CD

Related Items: fireEvent() method (Chapter 15); event object (Chapter 29).

createStyleSheet(["*URL*"[, *index*]])

Returns: styleSheet object reference.

	NN2	NN3	NN4	NN6	IE3/J1	IE3/J2	IE4	IE5	IE5.5
Compatibility							✓	✓	✓

The IE-specific createStyleSheet() method creates a styleSheet object, a type of object that includes STYLE element objects as well as style sheets that are imported into a document via the LINK element. Thus you can dynamically load an external style sheet even after a page has loaded. Note that this method does not work in IE4 for the Macintosh.

Unlike the other "create" methods entering W3C DOM usage, the createStyleSheet() method not only creates the style sheet, but it inserts the object into the document object model immediately. Thus, any style sheet rules that belong (or are assigned to) that object take effect on the page right away. If you'd rather create a style sheet and delay its deployment, you should use the createElement() method and element object assembly techniques.

If you don't specify any parameters to the method, an empty styleSheet object is created. It is assumed that you will then use styleSheet object methods, such as addRule() (not implemented in IE5/Mac) to add the details to the style sheet. To link in an external style sheet file, assign the file's URL to the first parameter of the method. The newly imported style sheet is appended to the end of the document. styleSheets array of styleSheet objects. An optional second parameter lets you specify precisely where in the sequence of style sheet elements the newly linked style sheet should be inserted. A style sheet rule for any given selector is overridden by a style sheet for the same selector that appears later in the sequence of style sheets in a document.

Example on the CD with Listing 18-13

Related Items: styleSheet object (Chapter 30).

createTextNode("*text*")

Returns: Text node object.

	NN2	NN3	NN4	NN6	IE3/J1	IE3/J2	IE4	IE5	IE5.5
Compatibility				✓				✓	✓

A text node is a W3C DOM object that contains body text without any HTML (or XML) tags, but is usually contained by (meaning, is a child of) an HTML (or XML) element. Without the IE innerText convenience property for modifying the text of an element, the W3C DOM relies on the node hierarchy of a document (NN6 exceeds the W3C DOM by providing an innerHTML property, which you can use to replace text in an element). To insert or replace text inside an HTML element in the W3C DOM way, you create the text node and then use methods of the parent element (for example, appendChild(), insertBefore(), and replaceChild(), all described in Chapter 15) to modify the document's content. To generate a fresh text node, use document.createTextNode().

The sole parameter of the createTextNode() method is a string whose text becomes the nodeValue of the text node object returned by the method. You can also create an empty text node (passing an empty string) and assign a string to the nodeValue of the object later. As soon as the text node is present in the document object model, scripts can simply change the nodeValue property to modify text of an existing element. For more details on the role of text nodes in the W3C DOM, see Chapter 14.

Example on the CD

Related Items: document.createElement() method.

elementFromPoint(*x, y*)

Returns: Element Text node object reference.

	NN2	NN3	NN4	NN6	IE3/J1	IE3/J2	IE4	IE5	IE5.5
Compatibility							✓	✓	✓

The IE-specific `elementFromPoint()` method returns a reference to whatever element object occupies the point whose integer coordinates are supplied as parameters to the method. The coordinate plane is that of the document, whose top-left corner is at point 0,0. This coordinate plane can be very helpful in interactive designs that need to calculate collision detection between positioned objects or mouse events.

When more than one object occupies the same point (for example, one element is positioned atop another), the element with the highest z-index value is returned. A positioned element always wins when placed atop a normal body-level element. And if multiple overlapping positioned elements have the same z-index value (or none by default), the element that comes last in the source code order is returned for the coordinate that they share in common.

On the CD-ROM   Example on the CD with Listing 18-14

Related Items: `event.clientX`, `event.clientY` properties; positioned objects (Chapter 31).

execCommand("*commandName*"[, *UIFlag*] [, *param*])

Returns: Boolean.

	NN2	NN3	NN4	NN6	IE3/J1	IE3/J2	IE4	IE5	IE5.5
Compatibility							✓	✓	✓

IE4+ includes a large set of commands that are outside of the methods defined for objects in the object model. These commands are also accessible to programmers who build an Internet Explorer ActiveX control into their applications. The `execCommand()` method (not implemented in IE5/Mac) is the JavaScript gateway to those commands. A series of related methods (`queryCommandEnable()` and others) also facilitate management of these commands.

The syntax for the `execCommand()` method requires at least one parameter, a string version of the command name. Command names are not case-sensitive. An optional second parameter is a Boolean flag to instruct the command to display any user interface artifacts that may be associated with the command. The default is `false`. For the third parameter, some commands require that an attribute value be passed for the command to work. For example, to set the font size of a text range, the syntax is

```
myRange.execCommand("FontSize", true, 5)
```

The execCommand() method returns Boolean true if the command is successful; false if not successful; undefined in IE5/Mac. Some commands can return values (for example, finding out the font name of a selection), but those are accessed through the queryCommandValue() method.

Most of these commands operate on body text selections that are TextRange objects. As described in Chapter 19, a TextRange object must be created under script control. But a TextRange object can be done in response to a user selecting some text in the document. Because a TextRange object is independent of the element hierarchy (indeed, a TextRange can spread across multiple nodes), it cannot respond to style sheet specifications. Thus, many of the commands that can operate on a TextRange object have to do with formatting or modifying the text. For a list of commands that work exclusively on TextRange objects, see the TextRange.execCommand() method in Chapter 19.

While many of the commands intended for the TextRange also work when invoked from the document object, in this section the focus is on those commands that have scope over the entire document. Table 18-4 lists those few commands that work with the document. Also listed are many commands that work exclusively on text selections in the document, whether the selections are made manually by the user or with the help of the TextRange object (see Chapter 19).

Table 18-4 document.execCommand() Commands

Command	Parameter	Description
Refresh	None	Reloads the page.
SelectAll	None	Selects entire page content.
Unselect	None	Unselects any page selection.
BackColor	Color String	Encloses the current selection with a FONT element whose STYLE attribute sets the background-color style to the parameter value.
CreateBookmark	Anchor String	Encloses the current selection (or text range) with an anchor element whose NAME attribute is set to the parameter value.
CreateLink	URL String	Encloses the current selection with an A element whose HREF attribute is set to the parameter value.
FontName	Font Face(s)	Encloses the current selection with a FONT element whose FACE attribute is set to the parameter value.
FontSize	Size String	Encloses the current selection with a FONT element whose SIZE attribute is set to the parameter value.

Continued

Table 18-4 *(continued)*

Command	Parameter	Description
FontColor	Color String	Encloses the current selection with a FONT element whose COLOR attribute is set to the parameter value.
Indent	None	Indents the current selection.
JustifyCenter	None	Centers the current selection.
JustifyFull	None	Full-justifies the current selection.
JustifyLeft	None	Left-justifies the current selection.
JustifyRight	None	Right-justifies the current selection.
Outdent	None	Outdents the current selection.
RemoveFormat	None	Removes formatting for the current selection.
SelectAll	None	Selects all text of the document.
UnBookmark	None	Removes anchor tags that surround the current selection.
Unlink	None	Removes link tags that surround the current selection.
Unselect	None	Deselects the current selection anywhere in the document.

On the
CD-ROM   Example on the CD

Related Items: queryCommandEnabled(), queryCommandIndterm(), queryCommandState(), queryCommandSupported(), queryCommandText(), queryCommandValue() methods.

getElementById("*elementID*")

Returns: Element object reference.

	NN2	NN3	NN4	NN6	IE3/J1	IE3/J2	IE4	IE5	IE5.5
Compatibility				✓				✓	✓

The document.getElementById() method is the W3C DOM syntax for retrieving a reference to any element in a document that has a unique identifier assigned to its ID attribute. If the document contains more than one instance of an ID, the method returns a reference to the first element in source code order with that ID. Because this method is such an important avenue to writing references to objects that are to be modified under script control, you can see how important it is to assign unique IDs to elements.

This method's name is quite a finger twister for scripters, especially compared to the IE4+ convention of letting a reference to any element begin simply with the object's ID. But unless you utilize the document.all normalization trick for NN6 as described in Chapter 15, the getElementById() method is the cross-browser way of gaining an element's reference for IE5+ and NN6+. When you type this method, be sure to use a lowercase "d" as the last character of the method name.

Unlike some other element-oriented methods (for example, getElementsByTagName()), which can be invoked on any element in a document, the getElementById() method works exclusively with the document object.

Example on the CD

Related Items: getElementsByTagName() method (Chapter 15).

getElementsByName("*elementName*")

Returns: Array.

	NN2	NN3	NN4	NN6	IE3/J1	IE3/J2	IE4	IE5	IE5.5
Compatibility				✓				✓	✓

The document.getElementsByName() method returns an array of references to objects whose NAME attribute is assigned the element name passed as the method's attribute. Although NN6 recognizes NAME attributes even for elements that don't have them by default, IE5+ does not. Therefore, for maximum cross-browser compatibility, use this method only to locate elements that have NAME attributes defined for them by default, such as form control elements. If the element does not exist in the document, the method returns an array of zero length.

For the most part, you are best served by using IDs on elements and the getElementById() method to unearth references to individual objects. But some elements, especially the INPUT element of type radio, use the NAME attribute to group elements together. In that case, a call to getElementsByName() returns an array of all elements that share the name—facilitating perhaps a for loop that inspects the checked property of a radio button group. Thus, instead of using the old-fashioned (although entirely backward compatible) approach by way of the containing form object

```
var buttonGroup = document.forms[0].radioGroupName
```

you can go more directly:

```
var buttonGroup = document.getElementsByName(radioGroupName)
```

In the latter case, you operate independently of the containing form object's index number or name. This assumes, of course, that a group name is not shared elsewhere on the page.

 Example on the CD

Related Items: document.getElementsById(), getElementsByTagName() methods.

getSelection()

Returns: String.

	NN2	NN3	NN4	NN6	IE3/J1	IE3/J2	IE4	IE5	IE5.5
Compatibility			✓	✓					

Many Web browser users aren't aware that they can select and copy body text in a document for pasting into other application documents. Even so, NN4+ offers a scripted way of capturing the text selected by a user in a page. The document.getSelection() method returns the string of text selected by the user. If nothing is selected, an empty string is the result. Returned values consist only of the visible text on the page and not the underlying HTML or style of the text.

The IE4+ equivalent involves the document.selection property, which returns an IE selection object (not implemented in IE5/Mac). To derive the text from this object, you must create a TextRange object from it and then inspect the text property:

```
var selectedText = document.selection.createRange().text
```

 Example on the CD with Listing 18-15

Related Items: document.selection property.

handleEvent(*event*)

Returns: Nothing.

	NN2	NN3	NN4	NN6	IE3/J1	IE3/J2	IE4	IE5	IE5.5
Compatibility			✓						

When you explicitly capture NN4 events in the window, document, or layer object (by invoking the captureEvents() method for that object), you can control where the events go after their initial capture. To let an event continue to its original target (for example, a button that is clicked by a user), you use the routeEvent() method. But if you want to redirect an event (or class of events) to a particular event handler elsewhere in the document, use the handleEvent() method.

See the discussion of the handleEvent() method for the window object in Chapter 16. The behavior of the handleEvent() method for all objects is the same.

Related Items: document.captureEvents(), document.releaseEvents(), document.routeEvent() methods; event object (Chapter 29).

open(["*mimeType*"] [, *replace*])

Returns: Nothing.

	NN2	NN3	NN4	NN6	IE3/J1	IE3/J2	IE4	IE5	IE5.5
Compatibility	✓	✓	✓	✓	✓	✓	✓	✓	✓

Opening a document is different from opening a window. In the case of a window, you're creating a new object, both on the screen and in the browser's memory. Opening a document, on the other hand, tells the browser to get ready to accept some data for display in the window named or implied in the reference to the document.open() method. (For example, parent.frames[1].document.open() may refer to a different frame in a frameset, whereas document.open() implies the current window or frame.) Therefore, the method name may mislead newcomers because the document.open() method has nothing to do with loading documents from the Web server or hard disk. Rather, this method is a prelude to sending data to a window via the document.write() or document.writeln() methods. In a sense, the document.open() method merely opens the valve of a pipe; the other methods send the data down the pipe like a stream, and the `document.close()` method closes that valve as soon as the page's data has been sent in full.

The `document.open()` method is optional because a `document.write()` method that attempts to write to a closed document automatically clears the old document and opens the stream for a new one. Whether or not you use the `document.open()` method, be sure to use the `document.close()` method after all the writing has taken place.

An optional parameter to the `document.open()` method lets you specify the nature of the data being sent to the window. A MIME (Multipurpose Internet Mail Extension) type is a specification for transferring and representing multimedia data on the Internet (originally for mail transmission, but now applicable to all Internet data exchanges). You've seen MIME depictions in the list of helper applications in your browser's preferences settings. A pair of data type names separated by a slash represent a MIME type (such as `text/html` and `image/gif`). When you specify a MIME type as a parameter to the `document.open()` method, you're instructing the browser about the kind of data it is about to receive, so that it knows how to render the data. Common values that most browsers accept are

```
text/html
text/plain
image/gif
image/jpeg
image/xbm
```

If you omit the parameter, JavaScript assumes the most popular type, `text/html` — the kind of data you typically assemble in a script prior to writing to the window. The `text/html` type includes any images that the HTML references. Specifying any of the image types means that you have the raw binary representation of the image that you want to appear in the new document — possible, but unlikely.

Another possibility is to direct the output of a `write()` method to a plug-in. For the `mimeType` parameter, specify the plug-in's MIME type (for example, `application/x-director` for Shockwave). Again, the data you write to a plug-in must be in a form that it knows how to handle. The same mechanism also works for writing data directly to a helper application.

 Note   IE3 does not accept any parameters for the `document.open()` method. IE4 accepts only the `text/html` MIME type parameter.

NN4+ and IE5+ include a second, optional parameter to the method: `replace`. This parameter does for the `document.open()` method what the `replace()` method does for the `location` object. For `document.open()`, it means that the new document you are about to write replaces the previous document in the window or frame from being recorded to that window or frame's history.

Tip   Avoid `document.open()` entirely for NN2 in the same window or frame as the one containing the script that invokes the `document.open()` method. Attempting to reopen the script's own document with this method in Navigator 2 usually leads to a crash of the browser.

On the CD-ROM   Example on the CD

Related Items: `document.close()`, `document.clear()`, `document.write()`, `document.writeln()` methods.

`queryCommandEnabled("commandName")`
`queryCommandIndterm("commandName")`
`queryCommandCommandState("commandName")`
`queryCommandSupported("commandName")`
`queryCommandText("commandName")`
`queryCommandValue("commandName")`

Returns: Various values.

	NN2	NN3	NN4	NN6	IE3/J1	IE3/J2	IE4	IE5	IE5.5
Compatibility							✓	✓	✓

These six methods (not implemented in IE5/Mac) lend further support to the `execCommand()` method for `document` and `TextRange` objects. If you choose to use the `execCommand()` method to achieve some stylistic change on a text selection, you can use some of these query methods to make sure the browser supports the desired command and to retrieve any returned values. Table 18-5 summarizes the purpose and returned values for each of the methods.

Table 18-5 IE Query Commands

queryCommand	*Returns*	*Description*
`Enabled`	**Boolean**	Reveals whether the `document` or `TextRange` object is in a suitable state to be invoked.
`Indterm`	**Boolean**	Reveals whether the command is in an indeterminate state.

Continued

Table 18-5 (continued)		

queryCommand	Returns	Description
CommandState	Boolean | null	Reveals whether the command has been completed (true), is still working (false), or is in an indeterminate state (null).
Supported	Boolean	Reveals whether the command is supported in the current browser.
Text	String	Returns any text that may be returned by a command.
Value	Varies	Returns whatever value (if any) is returned by a command.

Because the execCommand() method cannot be invoked on a page while it is still loading, any such invocations that may collide with the loading of a page should check with queryCommandEnabled() prior to invoking the command. Validating that the browser version running the script supports the desired command (especially for commands that have been introduced after IE4) is also a good idea. Therefore, you may want to wrap any command call with the following conditional structure:

```
if (queryCommandEnabled(commandName) && queryCommandSupported(commandName)) {...}
```

When using a command to read information about a selection, use the queryCommandText() or queryCommandValue() methods to catch that information (recall that the execCommand() method itself returns a Boolean value regardless of the specific command invoked).

On the CD-ROM   Example on the CD

Related Items: TextRange object (Chapter 19); execCommand() method.

recalc([allFlag])

Returns: Nothing.

	NN2	NN3	NN4	NN6	IE3/J1	IE3/J2	IE4	IE5	IE5.5
Compatibility								✓	✓

IE5 introduced the concept of dynamic properties. With the help of the setExpression() method of all elements and the expression() style sheet value, you can establish dependencies between object properties and potentially dynamic properties, such as a window's size or a draggable element's location. After those dependencies are established, the document.recalc() method causes those dependencies to be recalculated — usually in response to some user action, such as resizing a window or dragging an element.

The optional parameter is a Boolean value. The default value, false, means that the recalculations are performed only on expressions for which the browser has detected any change since the last recalculation. If you specify true, however, all expressions are recalculated whether they have changed or not.

On the CD-ROM

Example on the CD

Related Items: getExpression(), removeExpression(), setExpression() methods (Chapter 15).

releaseEvents(*eventTypeList*)

Returns: Nothing.

	NN2	NN3	NN4	NN6	IE3/J1	IE3/J2	IE4	IE5	IE5.5
Compatibility			✓						

If your NN4 scripts have enabled event capture for the document object (or window or layer, for that matter), you can turn off that capture with the releaseEvents() method. This method does not inhibit events from reaching their intended target. In fact, by releasing capture from a higher object, released events don't bother stopping at those higher objects anymore.

See the discussion of the releaseEvents() method for the window object in Chapter 16. The behavior of the releaseEvents() method for all objects is the same.

Related Items: document.captureEvents(), document.routeEvent() methods.

routeEvent(*event*)

Returns: Nothing.

	NN2	NN3	NN4	NN6	IE3/J1	IE3/J2	IE4	IE5	IE5.5
Compatibility			✓						

If you turn on NN4 event capturing in the `window`, `document`, or layer object (via their respective `captureEvents()` methods), the event handler you assign to those events really captures those events, preventing them from ever reaching their intended targets. For some page designs, this capturing is intentional, for it allows the higher-level object to handle all events of a particular type. But if your goal is to perform some preprocessing of events before they reach their destination, you need a way to pass that event along its regular path, which is what the `routeEvent()` method is for.

See the discussion of the `routeEvent()` method for the `window` object in Chapter 16. The behavior of the `routeEvent()` method for all objects is the same.

Related Items: document.captureEvents(), document.releaseEvents() methods.

write("string1" [,"string2" ... [, "stringn"]])
writeln("*string1*" [,"*string2*" ... [, "*stringn*"]])

Returns: Boolean `true` if successful.

	NN2	NN3	NN4	NN6	IE3/J1	IE3/J2	IE4	IE5	IE5.5
Compatibility	✓	✓	✓	✓	✓	✓	✓	✓	✓

Both of these methods send text to a document for display in its window. The only difference between the two methods is that `document.writeln()` appends a carriage return to the end of the string it sends to the document. This carriage return is helpful for formatting source code when viewed through the browser's source view window. For new lines in rendered HTML that is generated by these methods, you must still write a `<BR>` to insert a line break.

Note Not all browsers and versions display the source code that is dynamically generated by a client-side script when you attempt to view the source. In NN3 and NN4, the browser frequently shows the source code of such a page to have a `wysiwyg:` protocol, meaning that the document exists only in memory. Don't fool yourself into believing that this is a way to hide scripts from nosey visitors. Other browsers or versions (perhaps on a different operating system) are able to view the rendered source without any problem. Plus, a browser with scripting turned off is able to view the page that dynamically generated the code in the first place. See the section "Hiding scripts entirely?" in Chapter 13.

A common, incorrect conclusion that many JavaScript newcomers make is that these methods enable a script to modify the contents of an existing document, which is not true. As soon as a document has loaded into a window (or frame), the only fully backward compatible text that you can modify without reloading or rewriting the entire page is the content of text and TEXTAREA objects. In IE4+, you can modify HTML and text via the `innerHTML`, `innerText`, `outerHTML`, and `outerText` properties of any element. For NN6 and IE5+, you can modify an element's text by setting its `nodeValue` or `innerHTML` properties; strict adherence to the W3C DOM requires creating and inserting or replacing new elements, as described in Chapter 15.

The two safest ways to use the `document.write()` and `document.writeln()` methods are to

✦ Write some or all of the page's content by way of scripts embedded in the document

✦ Send HTML code either to a new window or to a separate frame in a multiframe window

For the first case, you essentially interlace script segments within your HTML. The scripts run as the document loads, writing whatever scripted HTML content you like. This task is exactly what you did in `script1.htm` in Chapter 3. This task is also how you can have one page generate browser-specific HTML when a particular class of browser requires unique syntax.

In the latter case, a script can gather input from the user in one frame and then algorithmically determine the layout and content destined for another frame. The script assembles the HTML code for the other frame as a string variable (including all necessary HTML tags). Before the script can write anything to the frame, it can optionally open the layout stream (to close the current document in that frame) with the `parent.frameName.document.open()` method. In the next step, a `parent.frameName.document.write()` method pours the entire string into the other frame. Finally, a `parent.frameName.document.close()` method ensures that the total data stream is written to the window. Such a frame looks just the same as if it were created by a source document on the server rather than on the fly in memory.

The document object of that window or frame is a full citizen as a standard document object. You can, therefore, even include scripts as part of the HTML specification for one of these temporary HTML pages.

NN2 has some nasty bugs when you use document.write() to write to the current window, but in NN3+ and IE3+, you can write to the current window without problems. Even so, you should be prepared for the consequences. After an HTML document (containing the script that is going to do the writing) loads completely, the page's incoming stream closes automatically. If you then attempt to apply a series of document.write() statements, the first document.write() method completely removes all vestiges of the original document. That includes all of its objects and scripted variable values. Therefore, if you try to assemble a new page with a series of document.write() statements, the script and variables from the original page will be gone before the second document.write() statement executes. To get around this potential problem, assemble the content for the new screen of content as one string variable and then pass that variable as the parameter to a single document.write() statement. Also be sure to include a document.close() statement in the next line of script.

Assembling HTML in a script to be written via the document.write() method often requires skill in concatenating string values and nesting strings. A number of JavaScript String object shortcuts facilitate the formatting of text with HTML tags (see Chapter 34 for details).

If you are writing to a different frame or window, you are free to use multiple document.write() statements if you like. Whether your script sends lots of small strings via multiple document.write() methods or assembles a larger string to be sent via one document.write() method depends partly on the situation and partly on your own scripting style. From a performance standpoint, a fairly standard procedure is to do more preliminary work in memory and place as few I/O (input/output) calls as possible. On the other hand, making a difficult-to-track mistake is easier in string concatenation when you assemble longer strings. My personal preference is to assemble longer strings, but you should use the system that's most comfortable for you.

You may see another little-known way of passing parameters to these methods. Instead of concatenating string values with the plus (+) operator, you can also bring string values together by separating them with commas. For example, the following two statements produce the same results:

```
document.write("Today is " + new Date())
document.write("Today is ",new Date())
```

Neither form is better than the other, so use the one that feels more comfortable to your existing programming style.

Note

Dynamically generating scripts requires an extra trick, especially in NN. The root of the problem is that if you try code, such as `document.write` (`"<SCRIPT></SCRIPT>"`), the browser interprets the end script tag as the end of the script that is doing the writing. You have to trick the browser by separating the end tag into a couple of components. Escaping the forward slash also helps. For example, if you want to load a different `.js` file for each class of browser, the code looks similar to the following:

```
// variable 'browserVer' is a browser-specific string and
// 'page' is the HTML your script is accumulating for document.write()
page += "<SCRIPT LANGUAGE='JavaScript' SRC='" + browseVer + ".js'><" +
"\/SCRIPT>"
```

Using the `document.open()`, `document.write()`, and `document.close()` methods to display images in a document requires some small extra steps. First, any URL assignments that you write via `document.write()` must be complete (not relative) URL references (especially for users of Navigator 2). Alternatively, you can write the `<BASE>` tag for the dynamically generated page so that its `HREF` attribute value matches that of the file that is writing the page.

The other image trick is to be sure to specify `HEIGHT` and `WIDTH` attributes for every image, scripted or otherwise. Navigator 2 requires these attributes (as does the HTML 4.0 specification), and document-rendering performance is improved on all platforms, because the values help the browser lay out elements even before their details are loaded.

In addition to the `document.write()` example that follows (see Listings 18-16 through 18-18), you can find fuller implementations that use this method to assemble images and bar charts in many of the applications in Chapters 48 through 57. Because you can assemble any valid HTML as a string to be written to a window or frame, a customized, on-the-fly document can be as elaborate as the most complex HTML document that you can imagine.

On the CD-ROM

Example on the CD with Figure 18-2 and Listings 18-16, 18-17, and 18-18

Related Items: `document.open()`; `document.close()`; `document.clear()` methods.

Event handlers

onSelectionChange

	NN2	NN3	NN4	NN6	IE3/J1	IE3/J2	IE4	IE5	IE5.5
Compatibility									✓

The onSelectionChange event can be triggered by numerous user actions, although all of those actions occur on elements that are under the influence of the IE5.5/Windows edit mode.

Related Items: onControlSelect event handler.

onStop

	NN2	NN3	NN4	NN6	IE3/J1	IE3/J2	IE4	IE5	IE5.5
Compatibility								✓	✓

The onStop event fires in IE5 when the user clicks the browser's Stop button. Use this event handler to stop potentially runaway script execution on a page, because the Stop button does not otherwise control scripts after a page has loaded. If you are having a problem with a runaway repeat loop during development, you can temporarily use this event handler to let you stop the script for debugging.

On the CD-ROM   Example on the CD with Listing 18-19

Related Items: Repeat loops (Chapter 39).

BODY Element Object

For HTML element properties, methods, and event handlers, see Chapter 15.

Properties	Methods	Event Handlers
alink	createControlRange()	onAfterPrint
background	createTextRange()	onBeforePrint
bgColor	doScroll()	onScroll
bgProperties		
bottomMargin		
leftMargin		
link		
noWrap		
rightMargin		
scroll		
scrollLeft		
scrollTop		
text		
topMargin		
vLink		

Syntax

Accessing BODY element object properties or methods:

[window.] document.body.*property* | *method*([*parameters*])

	NN2	NN3	NN4	NN6	IE3/J1	IE3/J2	IE4	IE5	IE5.5
Compatibility				✓			✓	✓	✓

About this object

In object models that reveal HTML element objects, the BODY element object is the primary container of the content that visitors see on the page. The BODY contains all rendered HTML. This special place in the node hierarchy gives the BODY object some special powers, especially in the IE object model.

As if to signify the special relationship, both the IE and W3C object models provide the same shortcut reference to the BODY element: `document.body`. As a first-class HTML element object (as evidenced by the long lists of properties, methods, and event handlers covered in Chapter 15), you are also free to use other syntaxes to reach the BODY element.

You are certainly familiar with several BODY element attributes that govern body-wide content appearance, such as link colors (in three states) and background (color or image). But IE and NN (and the W3C so far) have some very different ideas about the BODY element's role in scripting documents. Many methods and properties that NN considers to be the domain of the window (for example, scrolling, inside window dimensions, and so forth), IE puts into the hands of the BODY element object. Therefore, while NN scrolls the window (and whatever it may contain), IE scrolls the body (inside whatever window it lives). And because the BODY element fills the entire viewable area of a browser window or frame, that viewable rectangle is determined in IE by the body's `scrollHeight` and `scrollWidth` properties, whereas NN4+ features `window.innerHeight` and `window.innerWidth` properties. This distinction is important to point out because when you are scripting window- or document-wide appearance factors, you may have to look for properties and methods for the `window` or BODY element object, depending on your target browser(s).

Note   Use caution when referencing the `document.body` object while the page is loading. The object may not officially exist until the page has completely loaded. If you need to set some initial properties via scripting, do so in response to the `onLoad` event handler located in the `<BODY>` tag. Attempts at setting BODY element object properties in immediate scripts inside the HEAD element may result in error messages about the object not being found.

Properties

```
aLink
bgColor
link
text
vLink
```

Value: Hexadecimal triplet or color name string   Read/Write

	NN2	NN3	NN4	NN6	IE3/J1	IE3/J2	IE4	IE5	IE5.5
Compatibility				✓			✓	✓	✓

The aLink, link, and vLink properties are the new versions of the document properties alinkColor, linkColor, and vlinkColor. The bgColor is the same as the old document.bgColor property, while the text property is the new version of the document.fgColor property. These new properties are the scripted equivalents of the HTML attributes for the BODY element — the property names more closely align themselves with the HTML attributes than the old property names.

Link colors that are set via pseudo-class selectors in style sheets (as STYLE attributes of the BODY element) must be accessed via the style property for the BODY object. Over time, these properties will likely fall into disuse as style sheets become more common.

Example on the CD

Related Items: document.alinkColor, document.bgColor, document.fgColor, document.linkColor, document.vlinkColor **properties.**

background

Value: URL String   Read/Write

	NN2	NN3	NN4	NN6	IE3/J1	IE3/J2	IE4	IE5	IE5.5
Compatibility				✓			✓	✓	✓

The background property lets you set or get the URL for the background image (if any) assigned to the BODY element. A BODY element's background image overlays the background color in case both attributes or properties are set. To remove an image from the document's background, set the document.body.background property to an empty string.

Example on the CD

Related Items: body.bgColor, body.bgProperties **properties.**

bgColor

See aLink

bgProperties

Value: String constant   Read/Write

	NN2	NN3	NN4	NN6	IE3/J1	IE3/J2	IE4	IE5	IE5.5
Compatibility							✓	✓	✓

The IE-specific bgProperties property is an alternative way of adjusting whether the background image should remain fixed when the user scrolls the document or if it should scroll with the document. Initial settings for this behavior should be done via the background-attachment CSS attribute and modified under script control by way of the BODY element's style.backgroundAttachment property.

No matter which way you reference this property, the only allowable values are string constants scroll (the default) or fixed.

Example on the CD

Related Items: body.background property.

bottomMargin
leftMargin
rightMargin
topMargin

Value: Integer   Read/Write

	NN2	NN3	NN4	NN6	IE3/J1	IE3/J2	IE4	IE5	IE5.5
Compatibility							✓	✓	✓

The four IE-specific margin properties are alternatives to setting the corresponding four margin style sheet attributes for the BODY element (body.style.marginBottom, and so on). Style sheet margins represent blank space between the edge of an element's content and its next outermost container. In the case of the BODY element, that container is an invisible document container.

Of the four properties, only the one for the bottom margin may be confusing if the content does not fill the vertical space of a window or frame. The margin value is not automatically increased to accommodate the extra blank space.

Different versions and operating system implementations of IE4+ offer a variety of default integer values for these properties. But be aware that their values are not necessarily returned by these properties unless they are explicitly set in the IE-proprietary BODY element attributes of the same name. Therefore, even though a default BODY has a visible margin, the property does not return that default value.

 Example on the CD

Related Items: style object.

leftMargin

See bottomMargin.

link

See aLink.

noWrap

Value: Boolean   Read/Write

	NN2	NN3	NN4	NN6	IE3/J1	IE3/J2	IE4	IE5	IE5.5
Compatibility							✓	✓	✓

The noWrap property lets you modify the BODY element behavior normally set via the NOWRAP attribute. Because the property name is a negative, the Boolean logic needed to control it can get confusing.

The default behavior for a BODY element is for text to wrap within the width of the window or frame. This behavior occurs when the value of noWrap is its default value of false. By turning noWrap to true, a line of text continues to render past the right edge of the window or frame until the HTML contains a line break (or end of paragraph). If the text continues on past the right edge of the window, the window (or frame) gains a horizontal scrollbar (of course, not if a frame is set to not scroll).

By and large, users don't like to scroll in any direction if they don't have to. Unless you have a special need to keep single lines intact, let the default behavior rule the day.

On the CD-ROM Example on the CD

Related Items: None.

rightMargin

See bottomMargin.

scroll

Value: Constant String   Read/Write

	NN2	NN3	NN4	NN6	IE3/J1	IE3/J2	IE4	IE5	IE5.5
Compatibility							✓	✓	✓

The IE-specific scroll property provides scripted access to the IE-specific SCROLL attribute of a BODY element. By default, an IE BODY element displays a vertical scrollbar even if the height of the content does not warrant it; a horizontal scrollbar appears only when the content is forced to be wider than the window or frame. You can make sure that both scrollbars are hidden by setting the SCROLL attribute to "no" or changing it via script. Possible values for this property are the constant strings yes and no.

Other than frame attributes and NN4+ signed scripts, other browsers do not provide facilities for turning off scrollbars under script control. You can generate a new window (via the window.open() method) and specify that its scrollbars be hidden.

On the CD-ROM Example on the CD

Related Items: window.scrollbars property; window.open() method.

scrollLeft
scrollTop

Value: Integer   Read/Write

	NN2	NN3	NN4	NN6	IE3/J1	IE3/J2	IE4	IE5	IE5.5
Compatibility							✓	✓	✓

Even though the `scrollLeft` and `scrollTop` properties of the BODY object are the same as those for generic HTML element objects, they play an important roll in determining the position of positioned elements (described more fully in Chapter 31). Because the mouse event and element position properties tend to be relative to the visible content region of the browser window, you must take the scrolling values of the `document.body` object into account when assigning an absolute position. Values for both of these properties are integers representing pixels.

Example on the CD with Listing 18-20

Related Items: `window.pageXOffset`, `window.pageYOffset` properties.

text

See `aLink`.

topMargin

See `bottomMargin`.

vLink

See `aLink`.

Methods

createControlRange()

Returns: Array.

	NN2	NN3	NN4	NN6	IE3/J1	IE3/J2	IE4	IE5	IE5.5
Compatibility								✓	✓

This method is listed here for the sake of completeness. Microsoft has so far provided few clues as to when or how to use a controlRange object, except that it has something to do with a document in edit mode. In regular document view mode, the createControlRange() method (not implemented in IE5/Mac) returns an empty array.

createTextRange()

Returns: TextRange Object.

	NN2	NN3	NN4	NN6	IE3/J1	IE3/J2	IE4	IE5	IE5.5
Compatibility							✓	✓	✓

The BODY element object is the most common object to use to generate a TextRange object in IE4+, especially when the text you are about to manipulate is part of the document's body text. The initial TextRange object returned from the createTextRange() method (not implemented in IE5/Mac) encompasses the entire BODY element's HTML and body text. Further action on the returned object is required to set the start and end point of the range. See Chapter 19's discussion of the TextRange object for more details.

Example on the CD

Related Items: TextRange object (Chapter 19).

doScroll(["*scrollAction*"])

Returns: Nothing.

	NN2	NN3	NN4	NN6	IE3/J1	IE3/J2	IE4	IE5	IE5.5
Compatibility								✓	✓

Use the doScroll() method (not implemented in IE5/Mac) to simulate user action on the scrollbars inside a window or frame that holds the current document. This method comes in handy if you are creating your own scrollbars in place of the standard system scrollbars. Scrolling is instantaneous, however, rather than with animation even if the Display control panel is set for animated scrolling. The parameter for this method is one of the string constant values shown in Table 18-6. In practice, occasionally the longer scroll action names more closely simulate an actual click on the scrollbar component, whereas the shortcut versions may scroll at a slightly different increment.

Table 18-6	**document.body.doScroll() Parameters**	
Long Parameter	*Short Parameter*	*Scroll Action Simulates*
scrollbarDown	down	Clicking the down arrow.
scrollbarHThumb	n/a	Clicking the horizontal scrollbar thumb (no scrolling action).
scrollbarLeft	left	Clicking the left arrow.
scrollbarPageDown	pageDown	Clicking the page down area or pressing PgDn (default).
scrollbarPageLeft	pageLeft	Clicking the page left area.
scrollbarPageRight	pageRight	Clicking the page right area.
scrollbarPageUp	pageUp	Clicking the page up area or pressing PgUp.
scrollbarVThumb	n/a	Clicking the vertical scrollbar thumb (no scrolling action).

Unlike scrolling to a specific pixel location (by setting the BODY element's scrollTop and scrollLeft properties), the doScroll() method depends entirely on the spatial relationship between the body content and the window or frame size. Also, the doScroll() method triggers the onScoll event handler for the BODY element object.

Be aware that scripted modifications to body content can alter these spatial relationships. IE is prone to being sluggish in updating all of its internal dimensions after content has been altered. Should you attempt to invoke the doScroll() method after such a layout modification, the scroll may not be performed as expected. You may find the common trick of using setTimeout() to delay the invocation of the doScroll() method by a fraction of a second.

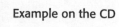

Example on the CD

Related Items: body.scroll, body.scrollTop, body.scrollLeft properties; window.scroll(), window.scrollBy(), window.scrollTo() methods.

Event handlers

onAfterPrint
onBeforePrint

See the onAfterPrint event handler for the window object, Chapter 16.

onScroll

	NN2	NN3	NN4	NN6	IE3/J1	IE3/J2	IE4	IE5	IE5.5
Compatibility							✓	✓	✓

The onScroll event handler fires for the BODY element object as the result of manual scrolling of the document (via scrollbars or navigation keyboard keys) and scripted scrolling via the doScroll() method, scrollIntoView() method, or adjusting the scrollTop and/or scrollLeft properties of the BODY element object. For manual scrolling and scrolling by doScroll(), the event seems to fire twice in succession. Moreover, the event.srcElement property is null, even when the BODY element is handling the onScroll event handler.

On the CD-ROM   Example on the CD with Listing 18-21

Related Items: body.scrollTop, body.scrollLeft properties; srcollIntoView(), body.doScroll() methods.

✦   ✦   ✦

Body Text Objects— Summary

On the CD-ROM

The full version of Chapter 19 is on the CD-ROM.

A large number of HTML elements fall into a catchall category of elements whose purposes are slightly more targeted than contextual elements covered in Chapter 15. In this group are some very widely used elements, such as the H1 through H6 header elements, plus several elements that are not yet widely used because their full support may be lacking in even some of the most modern browsers. In this chapter, you find all sorts of text-related objects, excluding those objects that act as form controls (text boxes and such, which are covered in Chapter 25). Consult the full chapter on the CD-ROM for details about the following elements covered in this category:

BLOCKQUOTE	BR
FONT	H1
H2	H3
H4	H5
H6	HR
LABEL	MARQUEE
Q	

For the most part, properties, methods, and event handlers of these objects are the generic ones covered in Chapter 15. Only those items that are unique to each object are covered in this chapter.

✦ ✦ ✦ ✦

In This Chapter

Objects that display running body text in documents

Using the NN Range and IE TextRange objects

Scripting search and replace actions

✦ ✦ ✦ ✦

Beyond the HTML element objects covered in this chapter, you also meet the `TextRange` object, first introduced in IE4, and the corresponding `Range` object from the W3C DOM implemented in NN6. This object is a very powerful one for scripters because it allows scripts to work very closely with body content—not in terms of, for example, the `innerText` or `nodeValue` properties of elements, but rather in terms of the text as it appears on the page in what users see as paragraphs, lists, and the like. The `TextRange` and `Range` objects essentially give your scripts cursor control over running body text for functions, such as cutting, copying, pasting, and applications that extend from those basic operations—search and replace, for instance. Bear in mind that everything you read in this chapter requires in the least the dynamic object models of IE4+ and NN6+; some items require IE5+. Unfortunately, the IE `TextRange` object is not implemented in IE5/Mac.

A few more related objects round out the chapter. These include the `selection`, `TextRectangle`, and `TextNode` objects for IE/Windows, and the `Text` object for NN6. From among these objects, the `selection` object is the most practical, especially when used with text ranges. You learn how to convert a user selection to an object whose content can be easily manipulated.

✦   ✦   ✦

HTML Directive Objects— Summary

On the CD-ROM

The full version of Chapter 20 is on the CD-ROM.

Thanks to the modern browser's desire to expose all HTML elements to the document object model, we can now (in IE4 and NN6) access a variety of objects that represent many HTML elements that are normally invisible to the human viewer of a page. These elements are called *directive elements* because they predominantly contain instructions for the browser — instructions that direct the browser to locate associated content on the page, link in external specifications, treat content as executable script statements, and more.

As you browse through the objects of this chapter, you may wonder why they have so many properties that normally indicate that the elements occupy space on the rendered page. After all, how can a META element have dimension or position on the page when it has no renderable content? The reason is that modern browsers internally employ some form of object-oriented behavior that lets all HTML elements — rendered or not — inherit the same set of properties, methods, and event handlers that any generic element has (see Chapter 15). The logical flaw is that unrendered elements can have properties and methods that don't genuinely apply to them. In such cases, their property values may be zero, an empty string, or an empty array. Yet the properties and methods exist in the objects just the same. Therefore, despite the large number of objects covered in this chapter, there are relatively few properties and methods that are not shared already with all HTML elements (as covered in Chapter 15).

Elements included in this category are the HTML, HEAD, LINK, TITLE, META, BASE, and SCRIPT elements. Most of these elements have a few properties that apply only to them, such as the `content` property of the META object.

It is highly unlikely that your scripts ever need to access the properties of directive elements. Moreover, the presence of these elements and the values of their attributes by and large impact the page only while the page loads into the browser. Modifying most properties has no effect. One exception is the `href` property of the LINK element objects: In IE5+/Windows, you can swap linked style sheets by assigning a new URL to the `href` property.

✦   ✦   ✦

Link and Anchor Objects

◆   ◆   ◆   ◆

In This Chapter

Differences between
link, anchor, and A
element objects

Scripting a link to
invoke a script
function

Scripting a link to
swap an image on
mouse rollovers

◆   ◆   ◆   ◆

The Web is based on the notion that the world's information can be strung together by way of the *hyperlink* — the
clickable hunk of text or image that enables an inquisitive
reader to navigate to a further explanation or related material.
Of all the document objects you work with in JavaScript, the
link is the one that makes that connection. Anchors also
provide guideposts to specific locations within documents.

As scriptable objects going back to the first scriptable
browsers, links and anchors are comparatively simple
devices. But this simplicity belies their significance in the
entire scheme of the Web. Under script control, links can be
far more powerful than mere tethers to locations on the Web.

In modern browsers (IE4+ and NN6), the notion of separating
links and anchors as similar yet distinctly different object
begins to fade. The association of the word "link" with objects
is potentially confused by the newer browsers' recognition of
the LINK element (see Chapter 20), which has an entirely
different purpose, as a scriptable object. Taking the place of
the anchor and link objects is an HTML element object
representing the element created by the <A> tag. As an
element object, the A element assumes all of the properties,
methods, and event handlers that accrue to all HTML element
objects in modern object models. To begin making that
transition, this chapter treats all three types of objects at
once. If you develop pages that must be compatible with early
scriptable browsers, pay special attention to the comments
about properties and event handler compatibility.

Anchor, Link, and A Element Objects

For HTML element properties, methods, and event handlers, see Chapter 15.

Properties	Methods	Event Handlers
charset		
coords		
hash		
host		
hostname		
href		
hreflang		
Methods		
mimeType		
name		
nameProp		
pathname		
port		
protocol		
protocolLong		
rel		
rev		
search		
shape		
target		
text		
type		
urn		
x		
y		

Syntax

Accessing link object properties:

```
(all)      [window.]document.links[index].property
```

Accessing A element object properties:

```
(IE4+)     [window.]document.all.elemID.property | method([parameters])
(IE5+/NN6) [window.]document.getElementById("elemID").property |
           method([parameters])
```

About this object

A little scripting history can help you to understand where the link and anchor objects came from and how the A element object evolved from them.

Using the terminology of the original object model, the anchor and link objects are both created in the object model from the <A> tag. What distinguishes a link from an anchor is the presence of the HREF attribute in the tag. Without an HREF attribute, the element is an anchor object, which (prior to version 4 browsers) has no properties, events, or event handlers associated with it. And even in NN4, the anchor object gains only four properties, all but one of which (name) disappear in NN6. Table 21-1 shows the implementation schedule for backward-compatible (and NN4-specific) properties associated with an anchor object.

Table 21-1 anchor Object Backward-Compatible Properties

Property	NN	IE
name	4	4
text	4	n/a
x	4	n/a
y	4	n/a

A link, on the other hand, is much more alive as an object — all just because of the inclusion of an HREF attribute, which usually points to a URL to load into a window or frame. In fact, the majority of early object model properties for the link object are the same as those of the early location object — properties that reveal information about the URL assigned to the HREF attribute. The other vital part of the original link object — especially as distinct from an anchor object — is that a link can respond to events. Initially, event handlers were limited to just onClick and onMouseOver. By NN4, additional mouse events and an onDblClick event joined the repertoire. Table 21-2 shows the properties and event handlers (there were no methods) for backward compatibility prior to the existence of the A element object.

Table 21-2	link Object Backward-Compatible Properties and Event Handlers	
Property	**NN**	**IE**
hash	2	3
host	2	3
hostname	2	3
href	2	3
pathname	2	3
prot	2	3
protocol	2	3
search	2	3
target	2	3
text	4	n/a
x	4	n/a
y	4	n/a
Event Handler	**NN**	**IE**
onClick	2	3
onDblClick	4[1]	4
onMouseDown	4	4
onMouseOut	3	4
onMouseOver	2	3
onMouseUp	4	4

[1]Not in NN4/Mac

When object models treat HTML elements as objects (IE4+ and NN6), both the anchor and link objects are subsumed by the A element object. Even so, one important characteristic from the original object still holds true: all A element objects that behave as link objects (by virtue of the presence of an HREF attribute) are members of the document.links property array. Therefore, if your scripts need to inspect or modify properties of all link objects on a page, they can do so by way of a for loop through the array of link objects. This is true even if you script solely for modern browsers and want to, say, change a style attribute of all links (for example, changing their style.textDecoration property from none to underline). The fact that the same element can have different behaviors depending on the existence of one attribute makes me think of the A element object as potentially two different animals. Thus, you see references to link and anchor objects throughout this book when the distinction between the two is important.

Scripting newcomers are often confused about the purpose of the TARGET attribute of an A element when they want a scripted link to act on a different frame or window. Under plain HTML, the TARGET attribute points to the frame or window into which the new document (the one assigned to the HREF attribute) is to load, leaving the current window or frame intact. But if you intend to use event handlers to navigate (by setting the location.href property), the TARGET attribute does not apply to the scripted action. Instead, assign the new URL to the location.href property of the desired frame or window. For example, if one frame contains a table of contents consisting entirely of links, the onClick event handlers of those links can load other pages into the main frame by assigning the URL to the parent.main.location.href property. You must also cancel the default behavior of any link, as described in the discussion of the generic onClick event handler in Chapter 15.

When you want a click of the link (whether the link consists of text or an image) to initiate an action without actually navigating to another URL, you can use a special technique—the javascript: pseudo-URL—to direct the URL to a JavaScript function. The URL javascript:*functionName*() is a valid parameter for the HREF attribute (and not just in the link object). Browsers that don't have JavaScript enabled do not respond to clicks on such a link.

If you don't want the link to do anything other than change the statusbar in the onMouseOver event handler, define an empty function and set the URL to that empty JavaScript function (such as HREF="javascript:doNothing()"). Starting with NN3 and IE4, you can also add a special void operator that guarantees that the called function does not trigger any true linking action (HREF="javascript: void someFunction()"). Specifying an empty string for the HREF attribute yields an FTP-like file listing for the client computer—an undesirable artifact. Don't forget, too, that if the URL leads to a type of file that initiates a browser helper application (for example, to play a RealAudio sound file), then the helper app or plug-in loads and plays without changing the page in the browser window.

A single link can change the content of more than one frame at once with the help of JavaScript. If you want only JavaScript-enabled browsers to act on such links, use a javascript: pseudo-URL to invoke a function that changes the location.href properties of multiple frames. For example, consider the following function, which changes the content of two frames:

```
function navFrames(url1, url2) {
    parent.product.location.href = url1
    parent.accessories.location.href = url2
}
```

You can then have a `javascript:` pseudo-URL invoke this multipurpose function and pass the specifics for the link as parameters:

```
<A HREF="javascript: void navFrames('products/gizmo344.html',
'access/access344.html')">Deluxe Super Gizmo</A>
```

Or if you want one link to do something for everyone, but something extra for JavaScript-enabled browsers, you can combine the standard link behavior with an `onClick` event handler to take care of both situations:

```
function setAccessFrame(url) {
    parent.accessories.location.href = url
}
...
<A HREF="products/gizmo344.html" TARGET="product"
onClick="setAccessFrame('access/access344.html')">Deluxe Super Gizmo</A>
```

Notice here that the `TARGET` attribute is necessary for the standard link behavior, while the script assigns a URL to a frame's `location.href` property.

One additional technique allows a single link tag to operate for both scriptable and nonscriptable browsers (NN3+ and IE4+). For nonscriptable browsers, establish a genuine URL to navigate from the link. Then make sure that the link's `onClick` event handler evaluates to `return false`. At click time, a scriptable browser executes the event handler and ignores the `HREF` attribute; a nonscriptable browser ignores the event handler and follows the link. See the discussion of the generic `onClick` event handler in Chapter 15 for more details.

As you design your links, consider building `onMouseOver` and `onMouseOut` event handlers into your link definitions. The most common applications for these event handlers are as a means of adjusting the `window.status` property or swapping images. (Early IMG element objects do not have event handlers of their own, so you must wrap them inside A elements to gain the event handler effect.) Thus, as a user rolls the mouse pointer atop a link, a descriptive label (perhaps more detailed or friendly than what the link text or image may indicate) appears in the status line at the bottom of the window. Whether a user notices the change down there is another issue, so don't rely on the status line as a medium for mission-critical communication. Image swaps, however, are more dramatic and enable a user to receive visual feedback that the mouse pointer is atop a particular button image. Thanks to the `onMouseDown` event handler in NN4 and IE4, you can even swap the image when the user presses down with the mouse button atop the link.

Properties

charset

Value: String
Read/Write

	NN2	NN3	NN4	NN6	IE3/J1	IE3/J2	IE4	IE5	IE5.5
Compatibility				✓					

The `charset` property represents the HTML 4.0 `CHARSET` attribute of an A element. It advises the browser of the character set used by the document to which the `HREF` attribute points. The value is a string of one of the character set codes from the registry found at `ftp://ftp.isi.edu/in-notes/iana/assignments/character-sets`.

coords
shape

Value: Strings
Read/Write

	NN2	NN3	NN4	NN6	IE3/J1	IE3/J2	IE4	IE5	IE5.5
Compatibility				✓					

HTML 4.0 provides specifications for A elements that accommodate different shapes (rect, circle, and poly) and coordinates when the link surrounds an image. Although the `coords` and `shape` properties are present for A element objects in NN6 (as directed by the W3C DOM), active support for the feature is not present in NN6.

hash
host
hostname
pathname
port
protocol
search

Value: Strings
Read/Write

	NN2	NN3	NN4	NN6	IE3/J1	IE3/J2	IE4	IE5	IE5.5
Compatibility	✓	✓	✓	✓	✓	✓	✓	✓	✓

This large set of properties is identical to the same-named properties of the location object (see Chapter 17). All properties are components of the URL that is assigned to the link object's HREF attribute. Although none of these properties appear in the W3C DOM specification for the A element object, they survive in modern browsers for backward compatibility. If you want to script the change of the destination for a link, try modifying the value of the object's href property rather than individual components of the URL.

Related Item: location object.

href

Value: String   Read/Write

	NN2	NN3	NN4	NN6	IE3/J1	IE3/J2	IE4	IE5	IE5.5
Compatibility	✓	✓	✓	✓	✓	✓	✓	✓	✓

The href property (included in the W3C DOM) is the URL of the destination of an A element equipped to act as a link. URLs can be relative or absolute.

In IE4+ and NN6, you can turn an anchor object into a link object by assigning a value to the href property even if the A element has no HREF attribute in the HTML that loads from the server. Naturally, this conversion is temporary, and it lasts only as long as the page is loaded in the browser. When you assign a value to the href property of an A element that surrounds text, the text assumes the appearance of a link (either the default appearance or whatever style you assign to links).

Related Item: location object.

hrefLang

Value: String   Read/Write

	NN2	NN3	NN4	NN6	IE3/J1	IE3/J2	IE4	IE5	IE5.5
Compatibility				✓					

The `hrefLang` property advises the browser (if the browser takes advantage of it) about the written language used for the content to which the A element's `HREF` attribute points. Values for this property must be in the form of the standard language codes (for example, `en-us` for U.S. English).

Methods

Value: String   Read/Write

	NN2	NN3	NN4	NN6	IE3/J1	IE3/J2	IE4	IE5	IE5.5
Compatibility							✓	✓	✓

The `Methods` property (note the uppercase "M") represents the HTML 4.0 `METHODS` attribute for an A element. Values for this attribute and property serve as advisory instructions to the browser about which HTTP method(s) to use for accessing the destination document. This is a rare case in which an HTML 4.0 attribute is not echoed in the W3C DOM. In any case, while IE4+ supports the property, the IE browsers do nothing special with the information.

mimeType

Value: String   Read-Only

	NN2	NN3	NN4	NN6	IE3/J1	IE3/J2	IE4	IE5	IE5.5
Compatibility							✓	✓	✓

Introduced in IE4 (but not IE4/Mac), the `mimeType` property is still present in IE5 but apparently is no longer supported. The HTML 4.0 and W3C DOM specifications define a `TYPE` attribute and `type` property instead. Perhaps this property was intended as an advisory to allow the browser to "know" ahead of time the MIME type of the destination document. In such a scenario, different MIME types can trigger scripts to use different cursors while hovering atop the link. The property has no actual control over the MIME type of the destination document.

name

Value: String   Read/Write

	NN2	NN3	NN4	NN6	IE3/J1	IE3/J2	IE4	IE5	IE5.5
Compatibility			✓	✓			✓	✓	✓

While a NAME attribute is optional for an A element serving solely as a link object, it is required for an anchor object. This value is exposed to scripting via the name property. While it is unlikely you will need to change the value by scripting, you can use this property as a way to identify a link object from among the document.links arrays in a repeat loop. For example:

```
for (var i = 0; i < document.links.length; i++) {
    if (document.links[i].name == "bottom" {
        // statements dealing with the link named "bottom"
    }
}
```

nameProp

Value: String   Read-Only

	NN2	NN3	NN4	NN6	IE3/J1	IE3/J2	IE4	IE5	IE5.5
Compatibility							✓	✓	✓

The IE-specific nameProp property is a convenience property that retrieves the segment of the HREF to the right of the rightmost forward slash character of the URL. Most typically, this value is the name of the file from a URL. But if the URL also includes a port number, that number is returned as part of the nameProp value.

protocolLong

Value: String   Read-Only

	NN2	NN3	NN4	NN6	IE3/J1	IE3/J2	IE4	IE5	IE5.5
Compatibility							✓	✓	✓

The IE-specific `protocolLong` property returns a verbose rendition of the `protocol` property as indicated in the A element's `HREF` attribute. For example, if the `HREF` attribute points to an `http:` protocol, the `protocolLong` property returns `HyperText Transfer Protocol`. Introduced in IE4 (but not IE4/Mac), the `protocolLong` property is still present in IE5 but apparently is no longer supported.

rel
rev

Value: String   Read/Write

	NN2	NN3	NN4	NN6	IE3/J1	IE3/J2	IE4	IE5	IE5.5
Compatibility				✓			✓	✓	✓

The `rel` and `rev` properties define relationships in the forward and back directions with respect to the destination document of the A element. Browsers have yet to exploit most of the potential of these attributes and properties.

A long list of values are predefined for these properties, based on the corresponding attribute values specified in HTML 4.0. If the browser does nothing with a particular value, the value is ignored. You can string together multiple values in a space-delimited list inside a single string. Accepted values are as follows:

`alternate`	`contents`	`index`	`start`
`appendix`	`copyright`	`next`	`stylesheet`
`bookmark`	`glossary`	`prev`	`subsection`
`chapter`	`help`	`section`	

target

Value: String   Read/Write

	NN2	NN3	NN4	NN6	IE3/J1	IE3/J2	IE4	IE5	IE5.5
Compatibility	✓	✓	✓	✓	✓	✓	✓	✓	✓

An important property of the link object is the `target`. This value reflects the window name supplied to the `TARGET` attribute in the A element.

You can temporarily change the target for a link. But, as with most transient object properties, the setting does not survive soft reloads. Rather than altering the target this way, you can safely force the target change by letting the `HREF` attribute call a `javascript:functionName()` psuedo-URL in which the function assigns a document to the desired `window.location`. If you have done extensive HTML authoring before, you will find it hard to break the habit of relying on the `TARGET` attribute.

Related Item: `document.links` property.

text

Value: String   Read-Only

	NN2	NN3	NN4	NN6	IE3/J1	IE3/J2	IE4	IE5	IE5.5
Compatibility			✓						

Between the start and end tags of a link goes the text (or image) that is highlighted in the distinguishing link color of the document. Navigator 4 enables you to read that text with the `link.text` property. This property is read-only. For later browsers, use the IE4+ and/or W3C DOM syntax for reading the text node (`innerText`, `innerHTML`, or `nodeValue`) property of the A element.

Note   This property was not implemented in releases of Navigator 4 prior to version 4.02.

type

Value: String   Read/Write

	NN2	NN3	NN4	NN6	IE3/J1	IE3/J2	IE4	IE5	IE5.5
Compatibility				✓					

The `type` property represents the HTML 4.0 `TYPE` attribute, which specifies the MIME type for the content of the destination document to which the element's `HREF` attribute points. This is primarily an advisory property for browsers that wish to, say, display different cursor styles based on the anticipated type of content at the other end of the link. Thus far, browsers do not take advantage of this feature. However, you can assign MIME type values to the attribute (for example, `video/mpeg`) and let scripts read those values for making style changes to the link text after the page loads. IE4+ implements this property as the `mimeType` property.

Related Item: `A.mimeType` property.

urn

Value: String   Read/Write

	NN2	NN3	NN4	NN6	IE3/J1	IE3/J2	IE4	IE5	IE5.5
Compatibility							✓	✓	✓

The `urn` property represents the IE-specific `URN` attribute, which enables authors to use a URN (Uniform Resource Name) for the destination of the A element. (See `http://www.ietf.org/rfc/rfc2141.txt` for information about URNs.) This property is not in common use.

x
y

Value: Integer   Read-Only

	Nav2	Nav3	Nav4	Nav6	IE3/J1	IE3/J2	IE4/J3	IE5
Compatibility			✓					

Your Navigator 4 script can retrieve the x and y coordinates of a link object (the top-left corner of the rectangular space occupied by the linked text or image) via the `link.x` and `link.y` properties. With IE4+ and NN6, you can get the coordinates of a typical link via the A element's `offsetLeft` and `offsetTop` properties.

✦   ✦   ✦

Image, Area, and Map Objects

✦ ✦ ✦ ✦

In This Chapter

How to precache images

Swapping images after a document loads

Creating interactive, client-side image maps

✦ ✦ ✦ ✦

For NN3+ and IE4+ browsers, images and areas — those items created by the ⟨IMG⟩ and ⟨AREA⟩ tags — are first-class objects that you can script for enhanced interactivity. You can swap the image displayed in an ⟨IMG⟩ tag with other images (restricted to images of the same size in NN3 and NN4), perhaps to show the highlighting of an icon button when the cursor rolls atop it. And with scriptable client-side area maps, pages can be smarter about how they respond to users' clicks on image regions.

One further benefit afforded scripters is that they can preload images into the browser's image cache as the page loads. With cached images, the user experiences no delay when the first swap occurs.

Image and IMG Element Objects

For HTML element properties, methods, and event handlers, see Chapter 15.

Properties	Methods	Event Handlers
align		onAbort
alt		onError
border		onLoad
complete		
dynsrc		
fileCreatedDate		
fileModifiedDate		
fileSize		

Continued

Properties (continued)	Methods	Event Handlers
fileUpdatedDate		
height		
href		
hspace		
isMap		
longDesc		
loop		
lowsrc		
name		
nameProp		
protocol		
src		
start		
useMap		
vspace		
width		
x		
y		

Syntax

Creating an image object:

```
imageName = new Image([pixelWidth, pixelHeight])
```

Accessing IMG element and image object properties or methods:

```
(NN3+/IE4+)    [window.]document.imageName. property | method([parameters])
(NN3+/IE4+)    [window.]document.images[index]. property | method([parameters])
(NN3+/IE4+)    [window.]document.images["imageName"]. property |
               method([parameters])
(IE4+)         [window.]document.all.elemID.property | method([parameters])
(IE5+/NN6+)    [window.]document.getElementById("elemID").property |
               method([parameters])
```

	NN2	NN3	NN4	NN6	IE3/J1	IE3/J2	IE4	IE5	IE5.5
Compatibility		✓	✓	✓	(✓)		✓	✓	✓

About this object

Before getting into detail about images as objects, it's important to understand the distinction between instances of the static Image object and IMG element objects. The former exist only in the browser's memory without showing anything to the user; the latter are the elements on the page generated via the <IMG> (or nonsanctioned, but accepted, <IMAGE>) tag. Scripts use Image objects to precache images for a page, but Image objects obviously have fewer applicable properties, methods, and event handlers because they are neither visible on the page nor influenced by tag attributes.

IMG elements have been in the HTML vocabulary since the earliest days, but Netscape Navigator 3 was the first to treat them like first-class objects along with the companion Image object for precaching images. Internet Explorer 3.01 for the Macintosh includes a partial implementation of both objects (to allow image precaching and swapping), and all flavors of IE4+ treat IMG elements as true document objects. The primary advantage of treating IMG elements as objects is that scripts can change the image that occupies the IMG object's space on the page, even after the document has loaded and displayed an initial image. The key to this scriptability is the src property of an image.

In a typical scenario, a page loads with an initial image. That image's tags specify any of the extra attributes, such as HEIGHT and WIDTH (which help speed the rendering of the page), and specify whether the image uses a client-side image map to make it interactive. (See the AREA object later in this chapter.) As the user spends time on the page, the image can then change (perhaps in response to user action or some timed event in the script), replacing the original image with a new one in the same space. In browsers prior to IE4 and NN6 that support the IMG element object, the height and width of the initial image that loads into the element establishes a fixed-sized rectangular space for the image. Attempts to fit an image of another size into that space forces the image to scale (up or down, as the case may be) to fit the rectangle. But in IE4+ and NN6+, a change in the image's size is reflected by an automatic reflow of the page content around the different size.

The benefit of the separate Image object is that a script can create a virtual image to hold a preloaded image. (The image is loaded into the image cache but the browser does not display the image.) The hope is that one or more unseen images will load into memory while the user is busy reading the page or waiting for the page to download. Then, in response to user action on the page, an image can change instantaneously rather than forcing the user to wait for the image to load on demand.

To preload an image, begin by assigning a new, empty image object to a global variable. The new image is created via the constructor function available to the `Image` object:

```
var imageVariable = new Image(width, height)
```

You help the browser allocate memory for the image if you provide the pixel height and width of the precached image as parameters to the constructor function. All that this statement does is create an object in memory whose properties are all empty. To force the browser to load the image into the cache, assign an image file URL to the object's `src` property:

```
var oneImage = new Image(55,68)
oneImage.src = "neatImage.gif"
```

As this image loads, you see the progress in the statusbar just like any image. Later, assign the `src` property of this stored image to the `src` property of the IMG element object that appears on the page:

```
document.images["someImage"].src = oneImage.src
```

Depending on the type and size of image, you will be amazed at the speedy response of this kind of loading. With small-palette graphics, the image displays instantaneously.

A popular user-interface technique is to change the appearance of an image that represents a clickable button when the user rolls the mouse pointer atop that art. This action assumes that a mouse event fires on an element associated with the object. Prior to IE4 and NN6, IMG element objects did not respond to mouse events on their own. The required technique was to encase the IMG element inside an A element. This allowed the events associated with rollovers (`onMouseOver` and `onMouseOut`) and a user click on the image to effect some change (usually to navigate to another page). While IE4+ and NN6+ provide these events directly for IMG element objects, you can guarantee your pages to be backward-compatible if you continue to surround your images with A elements. You can see examples of these kinds of actions in Chapters 12 and 22.

Image rollovers are most commonly accomplished in two different image states: normal and highlighted. But you may want to increase the number of states to more closely simulate the way clickable buttons work in application programs. In some instances, a third state signifies that the button is switched on. For example, if you use rollovers in a frame for navigational purposes and the user clicks a button to navigate to the Products area, that button stays selected but in a different style than the rollover highlights. Some designers go one step further by providing a fourth state that appears briefly when the user mouses down an image. Each one of these states requires the download of yet another image, so you have to gauge the effect of the results against the delay in loading the page.

The speed with which image swapping takes place may lead you to consider using this method for animation. Though this method may be practical for brief bursts of animation, the many other ways of introducing animation to your Web page (such as via GIF89a-standard images, Java applets, and a variety of plug-ins) produce animation that offers better speed control. In fact, swapping preloaded JavaScript image objects for some cartoon-like animations may be too fast. You can build a delay mechanism around the `setInterval()` method, but the precise timing between frames varies with client processor performance.

All browsers that implement the IMG element object also implement the `document.images` array. You can (and should) use the availability of this array as a conditional switch before any script statements that work with the IMG element or `Image` object. The construction to use is as follows:

```
if (document.images) {
    // statements working with images as objects
}
```

Earlier browsers treat the absence of this array as the equivalent of `false` in the `if` clause's conditional statement.

Tip

If you place an image inside a table cell, Navigator 3 sometimes generates two copies of the image object in its object model. This can disturb the content of the `document.images` array for your scripts. Specifying `HEIGHT` and `WIDTH` attributes for the image sometimes cures the problem. Otherwise, you have to craft scripts so they don't rely on the `document.images` array.

Most of the properties discussed here mirror attributes of the IMG HTML element. For more details on the meanings and implications of attribute values on the rendered content, consult the HTML 4.0 specification (`http://www.w3.org/TR/REC-html40`) and Microsoft's extensions for IE (`http://msdn.microsoft.com/workshop/author/dhtml/reference/objects/img.asp`).

Properties

`align`

Value: String   Read/Write

	NN2	NN3	NN4	NN6	IE3/J1	IE3/J2	IE4	IE5	IE5.5
Compatibility				✓			✓	✓	✓

The align property defines how the image is oriented in relation to surrounding text content. It is a double-duty property because you can use it to control the vertical or horizontal alignment depending on the value (and whether the image is influenced by a float style attribute). Values are string constants, as follows:

```
absbottom     middle
absmiddle     right
baseline      texttop
bottom        top
left
```

The default alignment for an image is bottom. Increasingly, element alignment is handed over to style sheet control.

Example (with Listing 22-1) on the CD-ROM

Related Items: text-align, float style sheet attributes.

alt

Value: String   Read/Write

	NN2	NN3	NN4	NN6	IE3/J1	IE3/J2	IE4	IE5	IE5.5
Compatibility				✓			✓	✓	✓

The alt property enables you to set or modify the text that the browser displays in the image's rectangular space (if height and width are specified in the tag) before the image downloads to the client. Also, if a browser has images turned off (or is incapable of displaying images), the alt text helps users identify what is normally displayed in that space. You can modify this alt text even after the page loads.

Example on the CD-ROM

Related Item: title property.

border

Value: Integer   Read/Write

	NN2	NN3	NN4	NN6	IE3/J1	IE3/J2	IE4	IE5	IE5.5
Compatibility		✓	✓	✓			✓	✓	✓

The `border` property defines the thickness in pixels of a border around an image. Remember that if you wrap an image inside an A element to make use of the mouse events (for rollovers and such), be sure to set the `BORDER=0` attribute of the `<IMG>` tag to prevent the browser from generating the usual link kind of border around the image. Even though the default value of the attribute is zero, surrounding the image with an A element or attaching the image to a client-side image map puts a border around the image.

On the CD-ROM

Example on the CD-ROM

Related Items: `isMap`, `useMap` properties.

complete

Value: Boolean   Read-Only

	NN2	NN3	NN4	NN6	IE3/J1	IE3/J2	IE4	IE5	IE5.5
Compatibility		✓	✓	✓			✓	✓	✓

Sometimes you may want to make sure that an image is not still in the process of loading before allowing another process to take place. This situation is different from waiting for an image to load before triggering some other process (which you can do via the image object's `onLoad` event handler). To verify that the IMG object displays a completed image, check for the Boolean value of the `complete` property. To verify that a particular image file has loaded, first find out whether the `complete` property is `true`; then compare the `src` property against the desired filename.

An image's `complete` property switches to `true` even if only the specified `LOWSRC` image has finished loading. Do not rely on this property alone for determining whether the `SRC` image has loaded if both `SRC` and `LOWSRC` attributes are specified in the `<IMG>` tag.

One of the best ways to use this property is in an `if` construction's conditional statement:

```
if (document.myImage.complete) {
    // statements that work with document.myImage
}
```

Note The `complete` property is not reliable in Navigator 4 and some versions of Internet Explorer 4. For those browsers, the value returns `true` in all instances.

Example (with Listing 22-2) on the CD-ROM

Related Items: `IMG.src`, `IMG.lowsrc`, `IMG.readyState` properties; onLoad event handler.

dynsrc

Value: URL String   Read/Write

	NN2	NN3	NN4	NN6	IE3/J1	IE3/J2	IE4	IE5	IE5.5
Compatibility							✓	✓	✓

The `dynsrc` property is a URL to a video source file, which (in IE) you can play through an IMG element. You can turn a space devoted to a static image into a video viewer by assigning a URL of a valid video source (for example, an `.avi` or `.mpg` file) to the `dynsrc` property of the image element object. Unlike the `src` property of image objects, assigning a URL to the `dynsrc` property does not precache the video.

You may experience buggy behavior in various IE versions when you assign a value to an image's `dynsrc` property after the IMG element renders a `.gif` or `.jpg` image. In IE5/Windows, the status bar indicates that the video file is still downloading, even though the download is complete. Clicking the Stop button has no effect. IE5.5/Windows may not even load the video file, leaving a blank space on the page. IE5/Macintosh changes between static and motion images with no problems, but playing the video file multiple times causes the IMG element to display black space beyond the element's rectangle. You can experience all this behavior in the example provided in Listing 22-3. None of these bugs is fatal, but they should discourage you from using the IMG element as a vehicle for video content.

Example (with Listing 22-3) on the CD-ROM

Related Items: `IMG.loop`, `IMG.start` properties.

fileCreatedDate
fileModifiedDate
fileSize

Value: String, Integer (fileSize)   Read-Only

	NN2	NN3	NN4	NN6	IE3/J1	IE3/J2	IE4	IE5	IE5.5
Compatibility							✓	✓	✓

These three IE-specific properties return information about the file displayed in the IMG element (whether still or motion image). Two of the properties reveal the dates on which the current image's file was created and modified. For an unmodified file, its creation and modified dates are the same. The fileSize property reveals the number of bytes of the file.

Date values returned for the first two properties are formatted differently between IE4 and IE5. The former provides a full readout of the day and date; the latter returns a format similar to mm/dd/yyyy. Note, however, that the values contain only the date and not the time. In any case, you can use the values as the parameter to a new Date() constructor function. This enables you to then use date calculations for such information as the number of days between the current day and the most recent modification.

Not all servers provide the proper date or size information about a file or in a format that IE can interpret. Test your implementation on the deployment server to ensure compatibility.

Also, be aware that these properties can be read-only for a file that is loaded in the browser. JavaScript by itself cannot get this information about files on the server that are not loaded in the browser.

Note

All of these file-related properties are present in the Mac version of IE, but the values are empty.

On the CD-ROM

Example on the CD-ROM

Related Items: None.

height
width

Value: Integer   Read/Write (see text)

	NN2	NN3	NN4	NN6	IE3/J1	IE3/J2	IE4	IE5	IE5.5
Compatibility		✓	✓	✓			✓	✓	✓

The height and width properties return and (in later browsers) control the pixel height and width of an image object. The property is read-only in NN3 and NN4, but it is read/write in all others that support the IMG element object.

If you adjust the height property of an image, the browser automatically scales the image within the same proportions as the original. But adjusting the width property has no effect on the height property in most browser versions. Scaling of an image may cause unwanted pixelation in the image, so modify an image's size with extreme care.

 Example on the CD-ROM

Related Items: hspace, vspace properties.

href

See src property.

hspace
vspace

Value: Integer   Read/Write

	NN2	NN3	NN4	NN6	IE3/J1	IE3/J2	IE4	IE5	IE5.5
Compatibility		✓	✓	✓			✓	✓	✓

The hspace and vspace properties control the pixel width of a transparent margin surrounding an image. Specifically, hspace controls the margins at the top and bottom of the image; vspace controls the left and right side margins. Images, by default, have margins of zero pixels.

Example on the CD-ROM

Related Items: height, width properties.

isMap

Value: Boolean   Read/Write

	NN2	NN3	NN4	NN6	IE3/J1	IE3/J2	IE4	IE5	IE5.5
Compatibility				✓			✓	✓	✓

The isMap property enables you to set whether the image should act as a server-side image map. When set as a server-side image map, pixel coordinates of the click are passed as parameters to whatever link HREF surrounds the image. For client-side image maps, see the useMap property later in this chapter.

longDesc

Value: URL String   Read/Write

	NN2	NN3	NN4	NN6	IE3/J1	IE3/J2	IE4	IE5	IE5.5
Compatibility				✓					

The longDesc property is a URL of a file that is intended to provide a detailed description of the image associated with the IMG element. While NN6 recognizes this property, the browser does not appear to do anything special with this information—whether specified by script or the LONGDESC attribute.

Related Item: alt property.

Example on the CD-ROM

Related Item: IMG.useMap property.

loop

Value: Integer   Read/Write

	NN2	NN3	NN4	NN6	IE3/J1	IE3/J2	IE4	IE5	IE5.5
Compatibility							✓	✓	✓

The loop property represents the number of times a video clip playing through the IMG element object should run. After the video plays that number of times, only the first frame of the video appears in the image area. The default value is 1; but if you set the value to -1, the video plays continuously. Unfortunately, setting the property to 0 prior to assigning a URL to the dynsrc property does not prevent the movie from playing at least once (except on the Mac, as noted in the dynsrc property discussion earlier in this chapter).

On the CD-ROM   Example on the CD-ROM

Related Item: dynsrc property.

lowsrc
lowSrc

Value: URL String   Read/Write

	NN2	NN3	NN4	NN6	IE3/J1	IE3/J2	IE4	IE5	IE5.5
Compatibility		✓	✓	✓			✓	✓	✓

For image files that take several seconds to load, recent browsers enable you to specify a lower-resolution image or some other quick-loading placeholder to stand in while the big image crawls to the browser. You assign this alternate image via the LOWSRC attribute in the <IMG> tag. The attribute is reflected in the lowsrc property of an image object.

All compatible browsers recognize the all-lowercase version of this property. But the W3C DOM specification calls for the interCap "S". NN6 recognizes this version as well.

Be aware that if you assign a URL to the LOWSRC attribute, the complete property switches to true and the onLoad event handler fires when the alternate file finishes loading: The browser does not wait for the main SRC file to load.

Example on the CD-ROM

Related Items: IMG.src, IMG.complete properties.

name

Value: Identifier String   Read/Write

	NN2	NN3	NN4	NN6	IE3/J1	IE3/J2	IE4	IE5	IE5.5
Compatibility	✓	✓	✓	✓	(✓)		✓	✓	✓

The name property returns the value assigned to the NAME attribute of an IMG element. Starting with IE4 and NN6, you can use the ID of the element to reference the IMG element object via document.all and document.getElementById(). But references in the form of document.imageName and document.images [imageName] must use only the value assigned to the NAME attribute.

In some designs, it may be convenient to assign numerically sequenced names to IMG elements, such as img1, img2, and so on. As with any scriptable identifier, the name cannot begin with a numeric character. Rarely, if ever, will you need to change the name of an IMG element object.

Example on the CD-ROM

Related Item: id property.

nameProp

Value: Filename String   Read-Only

	NN2	NN3	NN4	NN6	IE3/J1	IE3/J2	IE4	IE5	IE5.5
Compatibility								✓	✓

Unlike the src property, which returns a complete URL in IE, the IE nameProp property (not implemented in IE5/Mac) returns only the filename exclusive of and path. If your image swapping script needs to read the name of the file currently assigned to the image (to determine which image to show next), the nameProp property makes it easier to get the actual filename without having to perform extensive parsing of the URL.

Example on the CD-ROM

Related Item: IMG.src property.

protocol

Value: String   Read-Only

	NN2	NN3	NN4	NN6	IE3/J1	IE3/J2	IE4	IE5	IE5.5
Compatibility							✓	✓	✓

The IE protocol property returns only the protocol portion of the complete URL returned by the src property. This allows your script, for example, to see if the image is sourced from a local hard drive or a Web server. Values returned are not the actual protocol strings; rather, they are descriptions thereof: HyperText Transfer Protocol or File Protocol.

Example on the CD-ROM

Related Items: IMG.src, IMG.nameProp properties.

src

Value: URL String   Read/Write

	NN2	NN3	NN4	NN6	IE3/J1	IE3/J2	IE4	IE5	IE5.5
Compatibility		✓	✓	✓	(✓)		✓	✓	✓

The src property is the gateway to precaching images (in instances of the Image object that are stored in memory) and performing image swapping (in IMG element objects). Assigning a URL to the src property of an image object in memory causes the browser to load the image into the browser's cache (provided the user has the cache turned on). Assigning a URL to the src property of an IMG element object causes the element to display the new image. To take advantage of this powerful combination, you preload alternate versions of swappable images into image objects in memory and then assign the src property of the image object to the src property of the desired IMG element object. These powers are available in IE3 only in the Macintosh version (specifically, Version 3.01, which was the first scriptable version of IE3 for the Mac).

In NN3 and NN4 (all OS platforms) and IE3 for the Mac, the size of the image defined by the IMG element's attributes (or, if not specified, then calculated by the browser from the size of the incoming image) governs the rectangular space devoted to that image. An attempt to assign an image of a different size to that IMG element object causes the image to rescale to fit the rectangle (usually resulting in a distorted image). In all later browsers, however, the IMG element object resizes itself to accommodate the image, and the page content reflows around the new size.

Note that when you read the src property, it returns a fully formed URL of the image file including protocol and path. This often makes it inconvenient to let the name of the file guide your script to swap images with another image in a sequence of your choice. Some other mechanism (such as storing the current filename in a global variable) may be easier to work with (and see the IE5+/Windows nameProp property).

IE4+ replicates the src property as the href property for an image object. This may be deprecated in IE, so stick with the src property when dealing with the URL of a still image.

Example (with Figure 22-1 and Listing 22-4) on the CD-ROM

Related Items: IMG.lowsrc, IMG.nameProp properties.

start

Value: String   Read/Write

	NN2	NN3	NN4	NN6	IE3/J1	IE3/J2	IE4	IE5	IE5.5
Compatibility							✓	✓	✓

The start property works in conjunction with video clips viewed through the IMG element in IE4+. By default, a clip starts playing (except on the Macintosh) when the image file opens. This follows the default setting of the start property:

"fileopen". Another recognized value is "mouseover", which prevents the clip from running until the user rolls the mouse pointer atop the image.

Example on the CD-ROM

Related Items: IMG.dynsrc, IMG.loop properties.

useMap

Value: Identifier String   Read/Write

	NN2	NN3	NN4	NN6	IE3/J1	IE3/J2	IE4	IE5	IE5.5
Compatibility				✓			✓	✓	✓

The useMap property represents the USEMAP attribute of an IMG element, pointing to the name assigned to the AREA element in the page (see Listing 22-7 on the CD-ROM). This AREA element contains the details about the client-side image map (described later in this chapter). The value for the useMap property must include the hash mark that defines an internal HTML reference on the page. If you need to switch among two or more image maps for the same IMG element (for example, you swap images or the user is in a different mode), you can define multiple MAP elements each with a different name. Then change the value of the useMap property for the IMG element object to associate a different map with the image.

Related Item: isMap property.

vspace

See hspace.

width

See height.

x
y

Value: Integer   Read-Only

	NN2	NN3	NN4	NN6	IE3/J1	IE3/J2	IE4	IE5	IE5.5
Compatibility			✓						

An NN4 script can retrieve the x and y coordinates of an IMG element (the top-left corner of the rectangular space occupied by the image) via the x and y properties. These properties are read-only. They were supplanted in NN6 via the offsetLeft and offsetTop properties of any element.

Even without Dynamic HTML, you can use the information from these properties to help scroll a NN4 document to a precise position (with the window.scrollTo() method) as a navigational aid in your page. Due to the different ways each operating system platform renders pages and the different sizes of browser windows, you can dynamically locate the position of an image (in other words, scroll the document) given the current client conditions.

On the CD-ROM   **Example on the CD-ROM**

Related Items: IMG.offsetLeft, IMG.offsetTop properties; IMG.scrollIntoView(), window.scrollTo() methods.

Event handlers
onAbort
onError

	NN2	NN3	NN4	NN6	IE3/J1	IE3/J2	IE4	IE5	IE5.5
Compatibility		✓	✓	✓			✓	✓	✓

Your scripts may need to be proactive when a user clicks the Stop button while an image loads or when a network or server problem causes the image transfer to fail. Use the onAbort event handler to activate a function in the event of a user clicking the Stop button; use the onError event handler for the unexpected transfer snafu.

In practice, these event handlers don't supply all the information you may like to have in a script, such as the filename of the image loading at the time. If such information is critical to your scripts, then the scripts need to store the name of a currently loading image to a variable before they set the image's `src` property. You also don't know the nature of the error that triggers an error event. You can treat such problems by forcing a scripted page to reload or by navigating to an entirely different spot in your Web site.

Example on the CD-ROM

onLoad

	NN2	NN3	NN4	NN6	IE3/J1	IE3/J2	IE4	IE5	IE5.5
Compatibility		✓	✓	✓			✓	✓	✓

An IMG object's `onLoad` event handler fires when one of three actions occurs: an image's LOWSRC image finishes loading; in the absence of a LOWSRC image specification, the SRC image finishes loading; or when each frame of an animated GIF (GIF89a format) appears.

It's important to understand that if you define a LOWSRC file inside an `<IMG>` tag, the IMG object receives no further word about the SRC image having completed its loading. If this information is critical to your script, verify the current image file by checking the `src` property of the image object.

Be aware, too, that an IMG element's `onLoad` event handler may fire before the other elements on the page have completed loading. If the event handler function refers to other elements on the page, the function should verify the existence of other elements prior to addressing them.

The `onLoad` event handler for images appears to be broken in Navigator 4.

Example (with Listing 22-5) on the CD-ROM

Related Items: `IMG.src`, `IMG.lowsrc` properties.

AREA Element Object

For HTML element properties, methods, and event handlers, see Chapter 15.

Properties	Methods	Event Handlers
alt		
coords		
hash		
host		
hostname		
href		
noHref		
pathname		
port		
protocol		
search		
shape		
target		

Syntax

Accessing AREA element object properties:

```
(NN3+/IE4+)    [window.]document.links[index].property
(IE4+)         [window.]document.all.elemID.property | method([parameters])
(IE4+)         [window.]document.all.MAPElemID.areas[index].property |
               method([parameters])
(IE5+/NN6+)    [window.]document.getElementById("MAPElemID).areas[index].
               property | method([parameters])
(IE5+/NN6+)    [window.]document.getElementById("elemID").property |
               method([parameters])
```

	NN2	NN3	NN4	NN6	IE3/J1	IE3/J2	IE4	IE5	IE5.5
Compatibility		✓	✓	✓			✓	✓	✓

About this object

Document object models treat an image map area object as one of the link (A element) objects in a document (see the anchor object in Chapter 21). When you think about it, such treatment is not illogical at all because clicking a map area generally leads the user to another document or anchor location in the same document—a hyperlinked reference.

Although the HTML definitions of links and map areas differ greatly, the earliest scriptable implementations of both kinds of objects had nearly the same properties and event handlers. Therefore, to read about the details for these items, refer to the discussion about the link object in Chapter 21. The one difference is that in NN3 and NN4, a map area object does not have the same full array of mouse event handlers—you can count upon having only the onClick (NN4+), onMouseOver, and onMouseOut event handlers for those browsers.

Starting with IE4 and NN6, all AREA element attributes are accessible as scriptable properties. Moreover, you can change the makeup of client-side image map areas by way of the MAP element object. The MAP element object contains an array of AREA element objects nested inside. You can remove, modify, or add to the AREA elements inside the MAP element.

Client-side image maps are fun to work with, and they have been well documented in HTML references since Netscape Navigator 2 introduced the feature. Essentially, you define any number of areas within the image based on shape and coordinates. Many graphics tools can help you capture the coordinates of images that you need to enter into the COORDS attribute of the <AREA> tag.

Tip   If one gotcha exists that trips up most HTML authors, it's the tricky link between the <IMG> and <MAP> tags. You must assign a name to the <MAP>; in the <IMG> tag, the USEMAP attribute requires a hash symbol (#) and the map name. If you forget the hash symbol, you can't create a connection between the image and its map.

Tip   The onClick event handler appears in Netscape's area object beginning with Navigator 4. To be backward compatible with Navigator 3, use a javascript: URL for the HREF attribute if you want to navigate to another page with a click of the region.

On the CD-ROM   Example (with Listing 22-6) on the CD-ROM

Properties

alt

Value: String   Read/Write

	NN2	NN3	NN4	NN6	IE3/J1	IE3/J2	IE4	IE5	IE5.5
Compatibility				✓			✓	✓	✓

The `alt` property represents the ALT attribute of an AREA. Future browsers may implement this attribute to provide additional information about the link associated with the AREA element.

Related Item: `title` property.

coords
shape

Value: String   Read/Write

	NN2	NN3	NN4	NN6	IE3/J1	IE3/J2	IE4	IE5	IE5.5
Compatibility				✓			✓	✓	✓

The `coords` and `shape` properties control the location, size, and shape of the image hot spot governed by the AREA element. Shape values that you can use for this property control the format of the `coords` property values, as follows:

Shape	Coordinates	Example
`circ`	center-x, center-y, radius	`"30, 30, 20"`
`circle`	center-x, center-y, radius	`"30, 30, 20"`
`poly`	x1, y1, x2, y2,...	`"0, 0, 0, 30, 15, 30, 0, 0"`
`polygon`	x1, y1, x2, y2,...	`"0, 0, 0, 30, 15, 30, 0, 0"`
`rect`	left, top, right, bottom	`"10, 20, 60, 40"`
`rectangle`	left, top, right, bottom	`"10, 20, 60, 40"`

The default shape for an AREA is a `rectangle`.

On the CD-ROM Example on the CD-ROM

Related Items: None.

```
hash
host
hostname
href
pathname
port
protocol
search
target
```

See corresponding properties of the link object (Chapter 21).

shape

See `coords`.

MAP Element Object

For HTML element properties, methods, and event handlers, see Chapter 15.

Properties	Methods	Event Handlers
areas		onScroll
name		

Syntax

Accessing MAP element object properties:

```
(IE4+)      [window.]document.all.elemID.property | method([parameters])
(IE5+/NN6)  [window.]document.getElementById("elemID").property |
            method([parameters])
```

	NN2	NN3	NN4	NN6	IE3/J1	IE3/J2	IE4	IE5	IE5.5
Compatibility				✓			✓	✓	✓

About this object

The MAP element object is an invisible HTML container for all AREA elements, each of which defines a "hot" region for an image. Client-side image maps associate links (and targets) to rectangular, circular, or polygonal regions of the image.

By far, the most important properties of a MAP element object are the `areas` array and, to a lesser extent, its `name`. It is unlikely that you will change the name of a MAP. (It is better to define multiple MAP elements with different names, and then assign the desired name to an IMG element object's `useMap` property.) But you can use the `areas` array to change the makeup of the AREA objects inside a given client-side map.

Properties

`areas`

Value: Array of AREA element objects   Read/Write

	NN2	NN3	NN4	NN6	IE3/J1	IE3/J2	IE4	IE5	IE5.5
Compatibility				✓			✓	✓	✓

Use the `areas` array to iterate through all AREA element objects within a MAP element. While NN6 adheres closely to the document node structure of the W3C DOM, IE4+ provides more direct access to the AREA element objects nested inside a MAP. If you want to rewrite the AREA elements inside a MAP, you can clear out the old ones by setting the `length` property of the `areas` array to zero. Then assign AREA element objects to slots in the array to build that array.

On the CD-ROM

Example (with Listing 22-7) on the CD-ROM

Related Items: AREA element object.

✦   ✦   ✦

The Form and Related Objects

✦ ✦ ✦ ✦

In This Chapter

The FORM object as
a container of form
controls

How to submit forms
via e-mail

Processing form
validations

LABEL, FIELDSET, and
LEGEND element
objects

✦ ✦ ✦ ✦

Prior to the advent of dynamic object models and automatic page reflow, the majority of scripting in an HTML document took place in and around forms. Even with all the new DHTML powers, forms remain the primary user interface elements of HTML documents because they enable users to input information and make choices in very familiar user interface elements, such as buttons, option lists, and so on. The challenge of scripting forms and form elements often involves getting object references just right. The references can get pretty long by the time you start pointing to the property of a form element (which is part of a form, which is part of a document, which is part of a window or frame).

Expanded object models of IE4+ and NN6+ include scriptable access to form-related elements that are part of the HTML 4.0 specification. One pair of elements, FIELDSET and LEGEND, provides both contextual and visual containment of form controls in a document. Another element, LABEL, provides context for text labels that usually appear adjacent to form controls. While there is generally little need to script these objects, the browsers give you access to them just as they do for virtually every HTML element supported by the browser.

The Form in the Object Hierarchy

Take another look at the JavaScript object hierarchy in the lowest common denominator object model (refer back to Figure 14-1). The FORM element object can contain a wide variety of form element objects (sometimes called *form controls*), which I cover in Chapters 24 through 26. In this chapter, however, I focus primarily on the container.

The good news on the compatibility front is that much of the client-side scripting works on all scriptable browsers. While you are free to use newer ways of addressing forms and their nested elements when your audience exclusively uses the newer browsers, it can serve you well to be comfortable with the "old-fashioned" reference syntax. Therefore, almost all example code in this and the next three chapters uses syntax that is compatible with the earliest scriptable browsers. Besides, the only significant additions to the defining points of the form object in newer browsers are those characteristics that all other HTML elements share. The true scriptable heart of the form object has been within the scripter's reach since NN2.

FORM Object

For HTML element properties, methods, and event handlers, see Chapter 15.

Properties	Methods	Event Handlers
acceptCharset	handleEvent()	onReset
action	reset()	onSubmit
autocomplete	submit()	
elements		
encoding		
enctype		
length		
method		
name		
target		

Syntax

Accessing FORM object properties or methods:

```
(All)      [window.]document.formName. property | method([parameters])
(All)      [window.]document.forms[index]. property | method([parameters])
(All)      [window.]document.forms["formName"]. property | method([parameters])
(IE4+)     [window.]document.all.elemID.property | method([parameters])
(IE5+/NN6) [window.]document.getElementById("elemID").property |
           method([parameters])
```

About this object

Forms and their elements are the most common two-way gateways between users and JavaScript scripts. A form control element provides the only way that users can enter textual information. Form controls also provide somewhat standardized and recognizable user interface elements for the user to make a selection from a predetermined set of choices. Sometimes those choices appear in the form of an on/off checkbox, in a set of mutually exclusive radio buttons, or as a selection from a list.

As you have seen in many Web sites, the form is the avenue for the user to enter information that is sent to the server housing the Web files. Just what the server does with this information depends on the CGI (Common Gateway Interface) programs running on the server. If your Web site runs on a server directly under your control (that is, it is *in-house* or *hosted* by a service), you have the freedom to set up all kinds of data-gathering or database search programs to interact with the user. But with some of the more consumer-oriented Internet Service Providers (ISPs), you may have no CGI support available — or, at best, a limited set of popular but inflexible CGI programs available to all customers of the service. Custom databases or transactional services are rarely provided for this kind of Internet service.

Regardless of your Internet server status, you can find plenty of uses for JavaScript scripts in forms. For instance, rather than using data exchanges (and Internet bandwidth) to gather raw user input and report any errors, a JavaScript-enhanced document can preprocess the information to make sure that it employs the format that your back-end database or other programs most easily process. All corrective interaction takes place in the browser, without one extra bit flowing across the Net. I devote all of Chapter 43 to these kinds of form data-validation techniques.

How you define a FORM element (independent of the user interface elements described in subsequent chapters) depends a great deal on how you plan to use the information from the form's controls. If you intend to use the form completely for JavaScript purposes (that is, no queries or postings going to the server), you do not need to use the ACTION, TARGET, and METHOD attributes. But if your Web page will be feeding information or queries back to a server, you need to specify at least the ACTION and METHOD attributes. You need to also specify the TARGET attribute if the resulting data from the server is to be displayed in a window other than the calling window and the ENCTYPE attribute if your form's scripts fashion the server-bound data in a MIME type other than in a plain ASCII stream.

References to form control elements

For most client-side scripting, user interaction comes from the elements within a form; the FORM element object is merely a container for the various control elements. If your scripts perform any data validation checks on user entries prior to submission or other calculations, many statements have the form object as part of the reference to the element.

A complex HTML document can have multiple FORM objects. Each `<FORM>...</FORM>` tag pair defines one form. You don't receive any penalties (except for potential confusion on the part of someone reading your script) if you reuse a name for an element in each of a document's forms. For example, if each of three forms has a grouping of radio buttons with the name "choice," the object reference to each button ensures that JavaScript doesn't confuse them. The reference to the first button of each of those button groups is as follows:

```
document.forms[0].choice[0]
document.forms[1].choice[0]
document.forms[2].choice[0]
```

Remember, too, that you can create forms (or any HTML object for that matter) on the fly when you assemble HTML strings for writing into other windows or frames. Therefore, you can determine various attributes of a form from settings in an existing document.

Passing forms and elements to functions

When a form or form element contains an event handler that calls a function defined elsewhere in the document, you can use a couple of shortcuts to simplify the task of addressing the objects while the function does its work. Failure to grasp this concept not only causes you to write more code than you have to, but it also hopelessly loses you when you try to trace somebody else's code in his or her JavaScripted document. The watchword in event handler parameters is

```
this
```

which represents a reference to the current object that contains the event handler attribute. For example, consider the function and form definition in Listing 23-1. The entire user interface for this listing consists of form elements, as shown in Figure 23-1.

Listing 23-1: **Passing the Form Object as a Parameter**

```
<HTML>
<HEAD>
<TITLE>Beatle Picker</TITLE>
<SCRIPT LANGUAGE="JavaScript">
function processData(form) {
    for (var i = 0; i < form.Beatles.length; i++) {
        if (form.Beatles[i].checked) {
            break
```

Continued

Listing 23-1: **Passing the Form Object as a Parameter** *(Continued)*

```
        }
    }
    var chosenBeatle = form.Beatles[i].value
    var chosenSong = form.song.value
    alert("Looking to see if " + chosenSong + " was written by " +
chosenBeatle + "...")
}

function checkSong(songTitle) {
    var enteredSong = songTitle.value
    alert("Making sure that " + enteredSong + " was recorded by the Beatles.")
}
</SCRIPT>
</HEAD>

<BODY>
<FORM NAME-"Abbey Road">
Choose your favorite Beatle:
<INPUT TYPE="radio" NAME="Beatles" VALUE="John Lennon" CHECKED="true">John
<INPUT TYPE="radio" NAME="Beatles" VALUE="Paul McCartney">Paul
<INPUT TYPE="radio" NAME="Beatles" VALUE="George Harrison">George
<INPUT TYPE="radio" NAME="Beatles" VALUE="Ringo Starr">Ringo<P>

Enter the name of your favorite Beatles song:<BR>
<INPUT TYPE="text" NAME="song" VALUE="Eleanor Rigby"
onChange="checkSong(this)"><P>
<INPUT TYPE="button" NAME="process" VALUE="Process Request..."
onClick="processData(this.form)">
</FORM>
</BODY>
</HTML>
```

The `processData()` function, which needs to read and write properties of multiple form control elements, can reference the controls in two ways. One way is to have the `onClick` event handler (in the button element at the bottom of the document) call the `processData()` function and not pass any parameters. Inside the function, all references to objects (such as the radio buttons or the song field) must be complete references, such as

```
document.forms[0].song.value
```

to retrieve the value entered into the `song` field.

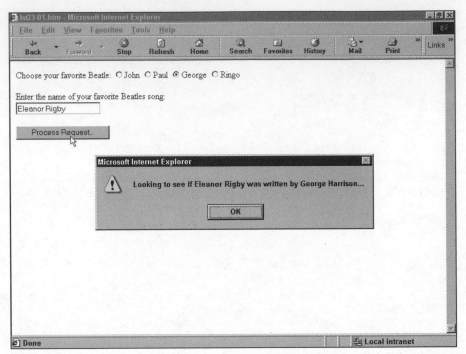

Figure 23-1: Controls pass different object references to functions in Listing 23-1.

A more efficient way is to send a reference to the FORM object as a parameter with the call to the function (as shown in Listing 23-1). By specifying `this.form` as the parameter, you tell JavaScript to send along everything it knows about the form from which the function is called. This works because `form` is a property of every form control element; the property is a reference to the form that contains the control. Therefore, `this.form` passes the value of the `form` property of the control.

At the function, the reference to the FORM object is assigned to a variable name (arbitrarily set to `form` here) that appears in parentheses after the function name. I use the parameter variable name `form` here because it represents an entire form. But you can use any valid variable name you like.

The reference to the form contains everything the browser needs to know to find that form within the document. Any statements in the function can therefore use the parameter value in place of the longer, more cumbersome reference to the form. Thus, here I can use `form` to take the place of `document.forms[0]` in any address. To get the value of the `song` field, the reference is:

```
form.song.value
```

Had I assigned the form object to a parameter variable called sylvester, the reference would have been:

```
sylvester.song.value
```

When a function parameter is a reference to an object, statements in the function can retrieve or set properties of that object as well as invoke the object's methods.

Another version of the this parameter passing style simply uses the word this as the parameter. Unlike this.form, which passes a reference to the entire form connected to a particular element, this passes a reference only to that one element. In Listing 23-1, you can add an event handler to the song field to do some validation of the entry (to make sure that the entry appears in a database array of Beatles' songs created elsewhere in the document). Therefore, you want to send only the field object to the function for analysis:

```
<INPUT TYPE="text" NAME="song" onChange="checkSong(this)"><P>
```

You then have to create a function to catch this call:

```
function checkSong(songTitle) {
    var enteredSong = songTitle.value
    alert("Making sure that " + enteredSong + " was recorded by the Beatles.")
}
```

Within this function, you can go straight to the heart — the value property of the field element without a long reference.

One further extension of this methodology passes only a single property of a form control element as a parameter. In the last example, the checkSong() function needs only the value property of the field, so the event handler can pass this.value as a parameter. Because this refers to the very object in which the event handler appears, the this.propertyName syntax enables you to extract and pass along a single property:

```
<INPUT TYPE="text" NAME="song" onChange="checkSong(this.value)"><P>
```

A benefit of this way of passing form element data is that the function doesn't have to do as much work:

```
function checkSong(songTitle) {
    alert("Making sure that " + songTitle + " was recorded by the Beatles.")
}
```

Unlike passing object references (like the form and text field objects above), when you pass a property value (for example, this.value), the property's value is passed with no reference to the object from which it came. This suffices when the function just needs the value to do its job. However, if part of that job is to modify the object's property (for example, converting all text from a field to uppercase and redisplaying the converted text), the value passed to the function does not maintain a "live" connection with its object. To modify a property of the object that invokes an event handler function, you need to pass some object reference so that the function knows where to go to work on the object.

Tip   Many programmers with experience in other languages expect parameters to be passed either by reference or by value, but not both ways. The rule of thumb in JavaScript, however, is fairly simple: object references are passed by reference; property values are passed by value.

Here are some guidelines to follow when deciding what kind of value to pass to an event handler function:

✦ Pass the entire form control object (this) when the function needs to make subsequent access to that same element (perhaps reading an object's value property, converting the value to all uppercase letters, and then writing the result back to the same object's value property).

✦ Pass only one property (this.propertyName) when the function needs read-only access to that property.

✦ Pass the entire FORM element object (this.form) for the function to access multiple elements inside a form (for example, a button click means that the function must retrieve a field's content).

Also be aware that you can submit multiple parameters (for example, onClick="someFunction (this.form, this.name)") or even an entirely different object from the same form (for example, onClick="someFunction(this.form. emailAddr.value)"). Simply adjust your function's incoming parameters accordingly. (See Chapter 41 for more details about custom functions.)

E-mailing forms

A common request among scripters is how to send a form via e-mail to the page's author. This includes the occasional desire to send "secret" e-mail to the author whenever someone visits the Web site. Let me address the privacy issue first.

A site visitor's e-mail address is valuable personal information that you should not retrieve without the visitor's permission or knowledge. That's one reason why Netscape plugged a privacy hole in Navigator 2 that allowed submitting a form to a mailto: URL without requesting permission from the user. You can use some workarounds for this in Navigator 3, but I do not condone surreptitiously lifting e-mail addresses and therefore choose not to publicize those workarounds here. Besides, as more users gravitate to newer browser versions, the workarounds fail anyway.

Microsoft, on the other hand, went too far in preventing forms e-mailing in the earliest browser versions. While Netscape's browsers reveal to the user in an alert that an e-mail message bearing the user's e-mail address (as stored in the browser's preferences) will be sent upon approval, Internet Explorer 3 does not send form content via e-mail at all. Internet Explorer 4 sends form content as an attachment through Microsoft Outlook, but only after displaying a mail composition window to the user. Starting with IE5, the process is much more fluid, but the action works best when Outlook is the default e-mail client on the computer.

Many ISPs that host Web sites provide standard CGIs for forwarding forms to an e-mail address of your choice. This manner of capturing form data, however, does not also capture the visitor's e-mail address unless your form has a field where the visitor voluntarily enters that information.

> Under no circumstances is a form submitted via the `mailto:` URL a secure document. The form data is embedded within a plain e-mail message that goes through the same Internet routes and servers as any e-mail message.

The remaining discussion about mailing forms focuses primarily on NN2+ and IE5+ browsers. You should be aware that mailing forms in the following ways is controversial in some Web standards circles. As of this writing, the W3C HTML specification does not endorse these techniques specifically. However, the latest browsers do support them nonetheless. Use these facilities judiciously and only after extensive testing on the client browsers you intend to support.

If you want to have forms submitted as e-mail messages, you must attend to three `<FORM>` tag attributes. The first is the `METHOD` attribute. You must set it to `POST`. Next comes `ENCTYPE`. If you omit this attribute, the e-mail client sends the form data as an attachment consisting of escaped name-value pairs, as in this example:

```
name=Danny+Goodman&rank=Scripter+First+Class&serialNumber=042
```

But if you set the `ENCTYPE` attribute to text/plain, the form name-value pairs are placed in the body of the mail message in a more human-readable format:

```
name=Danny Goodman
rank=Scripter First Class
serialNumber=042
```

The last attribute of note is the `ACTION` attribute, which is normally the spot to place a URL to another file or server CGI. Substitute the URL with the special `mailto:` URL followed by an optional parameter for the subject. Here is an example:

```
ACTION="mailto:prez@whitehouse.gov?subject=Opinion%20Poll"
```

To sum up, the following example shows the complete `<FORM>` tag for e-mailing the form in Navigator.

```
<FORM NAME="entry"
    METHOD=POST
    ENCTYPE="text/plain"
    ACTION="mailto:prez@whitehouse.gov?subject=Opinion Poll">
```

None of this requires any JavaScript at all. But seeing how you can use the attributes — and the fact that these attributes are exposed as properties of the FORM element object — you might see some extended possibilities for script control over forms.

Changing form attributes

With the exception of IE3 (whose FORM object properties are read-only), all scriptable browsers expose FORM element attributes as modifiable properties. Therefore, you can change, say, the action of a form via a script in response to user interaction on your page. For example, you can have two different CGI programs invoked on your server depending on whether a form's checkbox is checked.

Tip

The best opportunity to change the properties of a FORM element object is in a function invoked by the form's `onSubmit` event handler. The modifications are performed at the last instant prior to actual submission, leaving no room for user-induced glitches to get in the way.

Buttons in forms

A common mistake that newcomers to scripting make is defining all clickable buttons as the submit type of `input` object (`<INPUT TYPE="submit">`). The Submit button does exactly what it says — it submits the form. If you don't set any METHOD or ACTION attributes of the `<FORM>` tag, the browser inserts its default values for you: METHOD=GET and ACTION=pageURL. When you submit a form with these attributes, the page reloads itself and resets all field values to their initial values.

Use a Submit button only when you want the button to actually submit the form. If you want a button for other types of action, use the button style (`<INPUT TYPE="button">`). A regular button can invoke a function that performs some internal actions and then invokes the FORM element object's `submit()` method to submit the form under script control.

Redirection after submission

Undoubtedly, you have submitted a form to a site and seen a "Thank You" page come back from the server to verify that your submission was accepted. This is warm and fuzzy, if not logical, feedback for the submission action. It is not surprising that you would want to recreate that effect even if the submission is to a `mailto:` URL. Unfortunately, a problem gets in the way.

A common sense approach to the situation calls for a script to perform the submission (via the `form.submit()` method) and then navigate to another page that does the "Thank You." Here is such a scenario from inside a function triggered by a click of a link surrounding a nice, graphical Submit button:

```
function doSubmit() {
    document.forms[0].submit()
    location.href = "thanks.html"
}
```

The problem is that when another statement executes immediately after the `form.submit()` method, the submission is canceled. In other words, the script does not wait for the submission to complete itself and verify to the browser that all is well (even though the browser appears to know how to track that information given the statusbar feedback during submission). The point is, because JavaScript does not provide an event that is triggered by a successful submission, there is no sure-fire way to display your own "Thank You" page.

Don't be tempted by the `window.setTimeout()` method to change the location after some number of milliseconds following the `form.submit()` method. You cannot predict how fast the network and/or server is for every visitor. If the submission does not complete before the timeout ends, then the submission is still canceled — even if it is partially complete.

It's too bad we don't have this power at our disposal yet. Perhaps a future version of the document object model will provide an event that enables us to do something only after a successful submission.

Form element arrays

Starting with NN2 and IE4, document object models provide a feature that is beneficial to a lot of scripters. If you create a series of like-named objects, they automatically become an array of objects accessible via array syntax (see Chapter 7). This is particularly helpful when you create forms with columns and rows of fields, such as in an order form. By assigning the same name to all fields in a column, you can employ `for` loops to cycle through each row using the loop index as an array index.

As an example, the following code shows a typical function that calculates the total for an order form row (and calls another custom function to format the value):

```
function extendRows(form) {
    for (var i = 0; i < Qty.length; i++) {
        var rowSum = form.Qty[i].value * form.Price[i].value
        form.Total[i].value = formatNum(rowSum,2)
    }
}
```

All fields in the Qty column are named Qty. The item in the first row has an array index value of zero and is addressed as form.Qty[i].

Unfortunately, Internet Explorer 3 does not turn like-named fields into an array of references. But you can still script repetitive moves through an organized set of fields. The key is to assign names to the fields that include their index numbers: Qty0, Qty1, Qty2, and so on. You can even assign these names in a for loop that generates the table:

```
for (var i = 0; i <= rowcount; i++) {
    ...
    document.write("<INPUT TYPE='text' NAME='Qty" + i + "'>")
    ...
}
```

Later, when it comes time to work with the fields, you can use the indexing scheme to address the fields:

```
for (var i = 0; i < Qty.length; i++) {
    var rowSum = form.elements["Qty" + i].value * form.elements["Price" +
i].value
    form["Total" + i].value = formatNum(rowSum,2)
}
```

In other words, construct names for each item, and use those names as array index names. This solution is backward- and forward-compatible.

About <INPUT> element objects

While this chapter focuses strictly on the FORM element as a container of controls, the next three chapters discuss different types of controls that nest inside a form. Many of these controls share the same HTML tag: <INPUT>. Only the TYPE attribute of the <INPUT> tag determines whether the browser shows you a clickable button, a checkbox, a text field, or so on. The fact that one element has so many guises makes the system seem illogical at times to scripters.

An INPUT element has some attributes (and corresponding scriptable object properties) that simply don't apply to every type of form control. For example, while the maxLength property of a text box makes perfect sense in limiting the number of characters that a user can type into it, the property has no bearing whatsoever on form controls that act as clickable buttons. Similarly, you can switch a radio button or checkbox on or off by adjusting the checked property; however, that property simply doesn't apply to a text box.

As the document object models have evolved, they have done so in an increasingly object-oriented way. The result in this form-oriented corner of the model is that all elements created via the <INPUT> tag have a long list of characteristics that they all share by virtue of being types of INPUT elements — they inherit the properties and methods that are defined for any INPUT element. To try to limit the confusion, I divide the chapters in this book that deal with INPUT elements along functional lines (clickable buttons in one chapter, text fields in the other), and only list and discuss those INPUT element properties and methods that apply to the specific control type.

In the meantime, this chapter continues with details of the FORM element object.

Properties

acceptCharset

Value: String   Read/Write

	NN2	NN3	NN4	NN6	IE3/J1	IE3/J2	IE4	IE5	IE5.5
Compatibility				✓					

The acceptCharset property represents the ACCEPTCHARSET attribute of the FORM element in HTML 4.0. The value is a list of one or more recognized character sets that the server receiving the form must support. For a list of registered character set names, see ftp://ftp.isi.edu/in-notes/iana/assignments/character-sets.

Related Items: None.

action

Value: URL String   Read/Write (see text)

	NN2	NN3	NN4	NN6	IE3/J1	IE3/J2	IE4	IE5	IE5.5
Compatibility	✓	✓	✓	✓	✓	✓	✓	✓	✓

The action property (along with the method and target properties) primarily functions for HTML authors whose pages communicate with server-based CGI scripts. This property is the same as the value you assign to the ACTION attribute of a <FORM> tag. The value is typically a URL on the server where queries or postings are sent for submission.

User input may affect how you want your page to access a server. For example, a checked box in your document may set a form's action property so that a CGI script on one server handles all the input, whereas an unchecked box means the form data goes to a different CGI script or a CGI script on an entirely different server. Or, one setting may direct the action to one mailto: address, whereas another setting sets the action property to a different mailto: address.

Although the specifications for all three related properties indicate that they you can set them on the fly, such changes are ephemeral. A soft reload eradicates any settings you make to these properties, so you should make changes to these properties only in the same script function that submits the form (see form.submit() later in this chapter).

Note   The value of the action property is read-only in IE3.

On the CD-ROM   Example on the CD-ROM

Related Items: form.method, form.target, form.encoding properties.

autocomplete

Value: String   Read/Write

	NN2	NN3	NN4	NN6	IE3/J1	IE3/J2	IE4	IE5	IE5.5
Compatibility								✓	✓

Microsoft added a feature to forms with IE5 (but not IE5/Mac) that allows the browser to supply hints for filling out form controls if the controls' names map to a set of single-line text controls defined via some additional attributes linked to the vCard XML schema. For details on implementing this browser feature, see http://msdn.microsoft.com/workshop/author/forms/autocomplete_ovr. asp. Values for the autoComplete property are your choice of two strings: on or off. In either case, the FORM element object does not report knowing about this property unless you set the AUTOCOMPLETE attribute in the form's tag.

Related Items: None.

elements

Value: Array of form control elements   Read-Only

	NN2	NN3	NN4	NN6	IE3/J1	IE3/J2	IE4	IE5	IE5.5
Compatibility	✓	✓	✓	✓	✓	✓	✓	✓	✓

Elements include all the user interface elements defined for a form: text fields, buttons, radio buttons, checkboxes, selection lists, and more. The elements property is an array of all form control items defined within the current form. For example, if a form defines three <INPUT> items, the elements property for that form is an array consisting of three entries (one for each item in source code order). Each entry is a valid reference to that element; so, to extract properties or call methods for those elements, your script must dig deeper in the reference. Therefore, if the first element of a form is a text field and you want to extract the string currently showing in the field (a text element's value property), the reference looks like this:

```
document.forms[0].elements[0].value
```

Notice that this reference summons two array-oriented properties along the way: one for the document's forms property and one for the form's elements property.

In practice, I suggest you refer to form controls (and forms) by their names. This allows you the flexibility to move controls around the page as you fine-tune the design, and you don't have to worry about the source code order of the controls. The elements array comes in handy when you need to iterate through all of the controls within a form. If your script needs to loop through all elements of a form in search of particular kinds of elements, use the type property of every form object (NN3+ and IE4+) to identify which kind of object it is. The type property consists of the same string used in the TYPE attribute of an <INPUT> tag.

Overall, I prefer to generate meaningful names for each form control element and use those names in references throughout my scripts. The elements array helps with form control names, as well. Instead of a numeric index to the elements array, you can use the string name of the control element as the index. Thus, you can create a generic function that processes any number of form control elements, and simply pass the string name of the control as a parameter to the function. Then use that parameter as the elements array index value. For example:

```
function putVal(controlName, val) {
    document.forms[0].elements[controlName].value = val
}
```

If you want to modify the number of controls within a form, you should use the element and/or node management facilities of the browser(s) of your choice. For example, in IE4+ and NN6+, you can assemble the HTML string for an entirely new set of form controls and then assign that string to the innerHTML property of the FORM element object.

Example (with Listing 23-2 and Figure 23-2) on the CD-ROM

Related Items: text, textarea, button, radio, checkbox, and select objects.

encoding
enctype

Value: MIME Type String   Read/Write (see text)

	NN2	NN3	NN4	NN6	IE3/J1	IE3/J2	IE4	IE5	IE5.5
Compatibility	✓	✓	✓	✓	✓	✓	✓	✓	✓

You can define a form to alert a server when the data you submit is in a MIME type. The encoding property reflects the setting of the ENCTYPE attribute in the form definition. The enctype property name is defined for FORM element objects in the W3C DOM (with encoding removed), but NN6 provides both properties for backward and forward compatibility.

For mailto: URLs, I recommend setting this value (in the tag or via script) to "text/plain" to have the form contents placed in the mail message body. If the definition does not have an ENCTYPE attribute, this property is an empty string.

The value of the encoding property is read-only in IE3.

Example on the CD-ROM

Related Items: form.action, form.method properties.

length

Value: Integer   Read-Only

	NN2	NN3	NN4	NN6	IE3/J1	IE3/J2	IE4	IE5	IE5.5
Compatibility	✓	✓	✓	✓	✓	✓	✓	✓	✓

The `length` property of a FORM element object provides the same information as the `length` property of the form's `elements` array. The property provides a convenient, if not entirely logical, shortcut to retrieving the number of controls in a form.

On the CD-ROM Example on the CD-ROM

Related Items: `form.elements` property.

method

Value: String (GET or POST)   Read/Write (see text)

	NN2	NN3	NN4	NN6	IE3/J1	IE3/J2	IE4	IE5	IE5.5
Compatibility	✓	✓	✓	✓	✓	✓	✓	✓	✓

A form's `method` property is either the GET or POST value (not case-sensitive) assigned to the METHOD attribute in a `<FORM>` definition. Terminology overlaps here a bit, so be careful to distinguish a form's method of transferring its data to a server from the object-oriented method (action or function) that all JavaScript forms have.

The `method` property is of primary importance to HTML documents that submit a form's data to a server-based CGI script because it determines the format used to convey this information. For example, to submit a form to a `mailto:` URL, the `method` property must be POST. Details of forms posting and CGI processing are beyond the scope of this book. Consult HTML or CGI documentation to determine which is the appropriate setting for this attribute in your Web server environment. If a form does not have a METHOD attribute explicitly defined for it, the default value is GET.

Note   The method property is read-only in IE3.

Example on the CD-ROM

Related Items: form.action, form.target, form.encoding properties.

name

Value: Identifier String   Read/Write

	NN2	NN3	NN4	NN6	IE3/J1	IE3/J2	IE4	IE5	IE5.5
Compatibility	✓	✓	✓	✓	✓	✓	✓	✓	✓

Assigning a name to a form via the NAME attribute is optional but highly recommended when your scripts need to reference a form or its elements. This attribute's value is retrievable as the name property of a form. You don't have much need to read this property unless you inspect another source's document for its form construction, as in:

```
var formName = parent.frameName.document.forms[0].name
```

Moreover, because CGI programs frequently rely on the name of the form for validation purposes, it is unlikely you will need to change this property.

target

Value: Identifier String   Read/Write (see text)

	NN2	NN3	NN4	NN6	IE3/J1	IE3/J2	IE4	IE5	IE5.5
Compatibility	✓	✓	✓	✓	✓	✓	✓	✓	✓

Whenever an HTML document submits a query to a server for processing, the server typically sends back an HTML page — whether it is a canned response or, more likely, a customized page based on the input provided by the user. You see this situation all the time when you perform a search at Web sites. In a multiframe or multiwindow environment, you may want to keep the form part of this transaction in view for the user but leave the responding page in a separate frame or window for viewing. The purpose of the TARGET attribute of a <FORM> definition is to enable you to specify where the output from the server's query should be displayed.

The value of the target property is the name of the window or frame. For instance, if you define a frameset with three frames and assign the names Frame1, Frame2, and Frame3 to them, you need to supply one of these names (as a quoted string) as the parameter of the TARGET attribute of the <FORM> definition. Browsers also observe four special window names that you can use in the <FORM> definition: _top, _parent, _self, and _blank. To set the target as a separate subwindow opened via a script, use the window name from the window.open() method's second parameter and not the window object reference that the method returns.

The value of the target property is read-only in IE3.

Example on the CD-ROM

Related Items: form.action, form.method, form.encoding properties.

Methods

handleEvent(*event*)

Returns: Nothing.

	NN2	NN3	NN4	NN6	IE3/J1	IE3/J2	IE4	IE5	IE5.5
Compatibility			✓						

See the discussion of the window.handleEvent() method in Chapter 16 for a description of this NN4-specific method.

reset()

Returns: Nothing.

	NN2	NN3	NN4	NN6	IE3/J1	IE3/J2	IE4	IE5	IE5.5
Compatibility		✓	✓	✓			✓	✓	✓

A common practice, especially with a long form, is to provide a button that enables the user to return all the form elements to their default settings. The standard Reset button (a separate object type described in Chapter 24) does that task just fine. But if you want to clear the form using script control, you must do so by invoking the reset() method for the form. More than likely, such a call is initiated from outside the form, perhaps from a function or graphical button. In such cases, make sure that the reference to the reset() method includes the complete reference to the form you want to reset — even if the page only has one form defined for it.

On the CD-ROM   Example (with Listing 23-3) on the CD-ROM

Related Items: onReset event handler; reset object.

submit()

Returns: Nothing.

	NN2	NN3	NN4	NN6	IE3/J1	IE3/J2	IE4	IE5	IE5.5
Compatibility	✓	✓	✓	✓	✓	✓	✓	✓	✓

The most common way to send a form's data to a server's CGI program for processing is to have a user click a Submit button. The standard HTML Submit button is designed to send data from all named elements of a form according to the specifications listed in the <FORM> definition's attributes. But if you want to submit a form's data to a server automatically for a user, or want to use a graphical button for submission, you can accomplish the submission with the form.submit() method.

Invoking this method is almost the same as a user clicking a form's Submit button (except that the onSubmit event handler is not triggered). Therefore, you may have an image on your page that is a graphical submission button. If that image is surrounded by a link object, you can capture a mouse click on that image and trigger a function whose content includes a call to a form's submit() method (see Listing 23-3).

In a multiple-form HTML document, however, you must reference the proper form either by name or according to its position in a document.forms array. Always make sure that the reference you specify in your script points to the desired form before you submit any data to a server.

As a security and privacy precaution for people visiting your site, JavaScript ignores all submit() methods whose associated form actions are set to a mailto: URL. Many Web page designers would love to have secret e-mail addresses captured from visitors. Because such a capture can be considered an invasion of privacy, the power has been disabled since Navigator 2.02. You can, however, still use an explicit Submit button object to mail a form to you from browsers. (See the section, "E-mailing forms" earlier in this chapter.)

Because the form.submit() method does not trigger the form's onSubmit event handler, you must perform any presubmission processing and forms validation in the same script that ends with the form.submit() statement. You also do not want to interrupt the submission process after the script invokes the form.submit() method. Script statements inserted after one that invokes form.submit() — especially those that navigate to other pages or attempt a second submission — cause the first submission to cancel itself.

Example on the CD-ROM

Related Item: onSubmit event handler.

Event handlers
onReset

	NN2	NN3	NN4	NN6	IE3/J1	IE3/J2	IE4	IE5	IE5.5
Compatibility		✓	✓	✓			✓	✓	✓

Immediately before a Reset button returns a form to its default settings, JavaScript sends a reset event to the form. By including an onReset event handler in the form definition, you can trap that event before the reset takes place.

A friendly way of using this feature is to provide a safety net for a user who accidentally clicks the Reset button after filling out a form. The event handler can run a function that asks the user to confirm the action.

The onReset event handler employs a technique that surfaced with Navigator 3: The event handler must evaluate to return true for the event to continue to the browser. This may remind you of the way onMouseOver and onMouseOut event handlers work

for links and image areas. This requirement is far more useful here because your function can control whether the reset operation ultimately proceeds to conclusion.

Example (with Listing 23-4) on the CD-ROM

onSubmit

	NN2	NN3	NN4	NN6	IE3/J1	IE3/J2	IE4	IE5	IE5.5
Compatibility	✓	✓	✓	✓	✓	✓	✓	✓	✓

No matter how a form's data is actually submitted (by a user clicking a Submit
button or by a script invoking the `form.submit()` method), you may want your
JavaScript-enabled HTML document to perform some data validation on the user
input, especially with text fields, before the submission heads for the server. You
have the option of doing such validation while the user enters data (see Chapter
43) or in batch mode before sending the data to the server (or both). The place to
trigger this last-ditch data validation is the form's `onSubmit` event handler. Note,
however, that this event fires only from a genuine Submit type `<INPUT>` element
and not from the form's `submit()` method.

When you define an `onSubmit` handler as an attribute of a `<FORM>` definition,
JavaScript sends the `submit` event to the form just before it dashes off the data to
the server. Therefore, any script or function that is the parameter of the `onSubmit`
attribute executes before the data is actually submitted. Note that this event
handler fires only in response to a genuine Submit-style button and not from a
`form.submit()` method.

Any code executed for the `onSubmit` event handler must evaluate to an expression
consisting of the word `return` plus a Boolean value. If the Boolean value is `true`,
the submission executes as usual; if the value is `false`, no submission is made.
Therefore, if your script performs some validation prior to submitting data, make
sure that the event handler calls that validation function as part of a return statement (as shown in Listing 23-4).

Even after your `onSubmit` event handler traps a submission, JavaScript's security
mechanism can present additional alerts to the user depending on the server location of the HTML document and the destination of the submission.

Example on the CD-ROM

FIELDSET and LEGEND Element Objects

For HTML element properties, methods, and event handlers, see Chapter 15.

Properties	Methods	Event Handlers
align		
form		

Syntax

Accessing FIELDSET or LEGEND element object properties or methods:

```
(IF4+)      [window.]document.all.elemID.property | method([parameters])
(IE5+/NN6)  [window.]document.getElementById("elemID").property |
            method([parameters])
```

	NN2	NN3	NN4	NN6	IE3/J1	IE3/J2	IE4	IE5	IE5.5
Compatibility				✓				✓	✓

About these objects

The FIELDSET and LEGEND elements go hand in hand to provide some visual context to a series of form controls within a form. Browsers that implement the FIELDSET element draw a rectangle around the document space occupied by the form controls nested inside the FIELDSET element (although IE5/Mac drops the space into a debossed area on the page — a nice effect). The rectangle renders the full width of the body, unless its width is controlled by appropriate style sheet properties (for example, width). To that rectangle is added a text label that is assigned via the LEGEND element nested inside the FIELDSET element. (For IE5/Mac, the legend text is rendered just inside the debossed space.) None of this HTML-controlled grouping is necessary if you design a page layout that already provides graphical elements to group the form controls together.

Nesting the elements properly is essential to obtaining the desired browser rendering. A typical HTML sequence looks like the following:

```
<FORM>
<FIELDSET>
<LEGEND>Legend Text</LEGEND>
All your form controls and their labels go here.
</FIELDSET>
</FORM>
```

You can have more than one FIELDSET element inside a form. Each set has a rectangle drawn around it. This can help organize a long form into more easily digestible blocks of controls for users — yet the single form retains its integrity for submission to the server.

A FIELDSET element acts like any HTML container with respect to style sheets and the inheritance thereof. For example, if you set the `color` style property of a FIELDSET element, the color affects the text of elements nested within; however, the color of the border drawn by the browser is unaffected. Assigning a color to the FIELDSET style's `border-color` property colors just the border and not the textual content of nested elements.

Note that the content of the LEGEND element can be any HTML. Alternatively, you can assign a distinctive style sheet rule to the LEGEND element. If your scripts need to modify the text of the legend, you can accomplish this with the `innerText` (IE4+), `innerHTML` (IE4+, NN6+), or `nodeValue` (IE5+, NN6+) properties of HTML element objects.

Only two element-specific properties are assigned to this object pair. The first is the `align` property of the LEGEND object. This property matches the capabilities of the `ALIGN` attribute for the element as specified in the HTML 4.0 recommendation (albeit the property is deprecated in favor of style sheet rules). IE5+ for the Mac and IE5.5+ for Windows enable you to adjust this property on the fly (generally between your choices of "right" and "left") to alter the location of the legend at the top of the fieldset rectangle.

Because these elements are children of a FORM element, it makes sense that the DOM Level 2 specification supplies the read-only `form` property to both of these objects. That property returns a reference to the FORM element object that encloses either element. The `form` property for the FIELDSET and LEGEND objects is implemented only in IE5/Mac and NN6.

LABEL Element Object

For HTML element properties, methods, and event handlers, see Chapter 15.

Properties	Methods	Event Handlers
form		
htmlFor		

Syntax

Accessing LABEL element object properties or methods:

```
(IE4+)      [window.]document.all.elemID.property | method([parameters])
(IE5+/NN6)  [window.]document.getElementById("elemID").property |
            method([parameters])
```

	NN2	NN3	NN4	NN6	IE3/J1	IE3/J2	IE4	IE5	IE5.5
Compatibility				✓				✓	✓

About this object

With the push in the HTML 4.0 specification to provide context-oriented tags for just about every bit of content on the page, the W3C HTML working group filled a gap with respect to text that usually hangs in front of or immediately after INPUT, SELECT, and TEXTAREA form control elements. You use these text chunks as labels for the items to describe the purpose of the control. The only INPUT element that had an attribute for its label was the button input type. But even the newer BUTTON element did away with that.

A LABEL element enables you to surround a control's label text with a contextual tag. In addition, one of the element's attributes — FOR — enables you to associate the label with a particular form control element. In the HTML, the FOR attribute is assigned the ID of the control with which the label is associated. A LABEL element can be associated with a form control if the form control's tag is contained between the LABEL element's start and end tags.

At first glance, browsers do nothing special (from a rendering point of view) for a LABEL element. But for some kinds of elements, especially checkbox and radio input type elements, browsers help restore to users a vital user-interface convention: clicking the label is the same as clicking the control. For text elements, focus events are passed to the text input element associated with the label. In fact, all events that are directed at a label bubble upward to the form control associated with it. The following page fragment demonstrates how FIELDSET, LEGEND, and LABEL elements look in a form consisting of two radio buttons:

```
<FORM ...>
<FIELDSET ID="form1set1">
<LEGEND ID="form1set1legend">Choose the Desired Performance</LEGEND>
<INPUT TYPE="radio" NAME="speed" ID="speed1">
    <LABEL FOR="speed1">Fastest (lower quality)</LABEL><BR>
<INPUT TYPE="radio" NAME="speed" ID="speed2">
    <LABEL FOR="speed2">Slower (best quality)</LABEL>
</FIELDSET>
</FORM>
```

Even so, a LABEL and its associated form control element do not have to be adjacent to each other in the source code. For example, you can have a label in one cell of a table row with the form control in another cell (in the same or different row).

Properties

`htmlFor`

Value: Element Object Reference   Read/Write

	NN2	NN3	NN4	NN6	IE3/J1	IE3/J2	IE4	IE5	IE5.5
Compatibility				✓			✓	✓	✓

The `htmlFor` property is the scripted equivalent of the FOR attribute of the LABEL element. An acceptable value is a full reference to a form control element (INPUT, TEXTAREA, or SELECT element objects). It is highly unlikely that you would modify this property for an existing LABEL element. However, if your script is creating a new LABEL element (perhaps a replacement form), use this property to associate the label with a form control.

 On the CD-ROM   Example on the CD-ROM

✦   ✦   ✦

Button Objects

CHAPTER

24

♦ ♦ ♦ ♦

In This Chapter

Triggering action
from a user's click of
a button

Assigning hidden
values to radio and
checkbox buttons

Distinguishing
between radio button
families and their
individual buttons

♦ ♦ ♦ ♦

This chapter is devoted to those lovable buttons that
invite users to initiate action and make choices with a
single click of the mouse button. In this category fall the standard system-looking buttons with labels on them, as well as
radio buttons and checkboxes. For such workhorses of the
HTML form, these objects have a limited vocabulary of object-
specific properties, methods, and event handlers.

I group together the button, submit, and reset objects for an
important reason: They look alike yet they are intended for very
different purposes. Knowing when to use which button is important — especially when to differentiate between the button and
submit objects. Many a newcomer get the two confused and
wind up with scripting error headaches. That confusion won't
happen to you by the time you finish this chapter.

The BUTTON Element Object, and the Button, Submit, and Reset Input Objects

For HTML element properties, methods, and event handlers,
see Chapter 15.

Properties	Methods	Event Handlers
form	click()	onClick
name		onMouseDown
type		onMouseUp
value		

Syntax

Accessing button object properties or methods:

```
(All)      [window.]document.formName.buttonName.property |
           method([parameters])
(All)      [window.]document.formName.elements[index].property |
           method([parameters])
(All)      [window.]document.forms[index].buttonName.property |
           method([parameters])
(All)      [window.]document.forms["formName"].buttonName.property |
           method([parameters])
(All)      [window.]document.forms["formName"].elements[index].property |
           method([parameters])
(IE4+)     [window.]document.all.elemID.property | method([parameters])
(IE5+/NN6) [window.]document.getElementById("elemID").property |
           method([parameters])
```

About these objects

Button objects generate standard, pushbutton-style user interface elements on the page, depending on the operating system on which the particular browser runs. In the early days, the browsers called upon the operating systems to generate these standard interface elements. In more recent versions, the browsers define their own look, albeit frequently still different for each operating system. More recently, the appearance of a button may also be influenced by browser-specific customizations that browser makers put into their products. Even so, any computer user will recognize a button when the browser produces it on the page.

Starting with IE4 and NN6, you have two ways to put standard buttons into a page. The first, and completely backward-compatible way, is to use INPUT elements nested inside a FORM container. But a new HTML element, the BUTTON element, provides a slightly different way of specifying a button in a page, including the option of putting a button outside of a FORM (presumably for some client-side script execution, independent of form submission). From an HTML point of view, the difference between the two concerns itself with the way the label of the button is specified. With an INPUT element, the string assigned to the VALUE attribute becomes the label of the button; but a BUTTON element is a container (meaning with an end tag), whose content becomes the button's label. You can still assign a value to the VALUE attribute, which, if a form contains the button, gets submitted to the server, independent of the label text.

Always give careful thought to the label that you assign to a button. Because a button initiates some action, make sure that the verb in the label clearly defines what happens after you click it. Also, take cues from experienced user interface designers who craft operating system and commercial software buttons: Be concise. If you find your button labels going longer than two or three words, reconsider the design of your page so that the user can clearly understand the purpose of any button from a shorter label.

Browsers automatically display a button sized to accommodate the label text. But only browsers that support style sheets (IE4+ and NN6+) allow you to control more visual aspects of the button, such as size, label font, and coloration. And, as for the position of the button on the page, buttons, as in all in-line elements, appear where they occur in the source code. You can, of course, use element positioning of recent browsers (Chapter 31) to make a button appear wherever you want it. But if your pages run on multiple operating systems and generations of browsers, be aware that the appearance (and size) of a button will not be identical on all screens. Check out the results on as many platforms as possible.

Buttons in the Windows environment follow their normal behavior in that they indicate the focus with highlighted button-label text (usually with a dotted rectangle). Some newer browsers running on other operating systems offer this kind of highlighting and selection as a user option. IE5 provides additional INPUT element features that prevent buttons from receiving this kind of visible focus.

The lone button object event handler that works on all browser versions is one that responds to a user clicking the pointer atop the mouse: the onClick event handler. Virtually all action surrounding a button object comes from this event handler. You rarely need to extract property values or invoke the click() method (the method does not work correctly in Navigator 3). NN4 and IE4 add events for the components of a click: mouseDown and mouseUp; and IE4+ and NN6+ provide a plethora of user-initiated events for buttons.

Two special variants of the button object are the *submit* and *reset* button objects. With their heritages going back to early incarnations of HTML, these two button types perform special operations on their own. The submit-style button automatically sends the data within the same form object to the URL listed in the ACTION attribute of the <FORM> definition. The METHOD attribute dictates the format in which the button sends the data. Therefore, you don't have to script this action if your HTML page is communicating with a CGI program on the server.

If the form's ACTION attribute is set to a mailto: URL, you must provide the page visitor with a Submit button to carry out the action. Setting the form's ENCTYPE attribute to text/plain is also helpful so that the form data arrives in a more readable form than the normal encoded name-value pairs. See "E-Mailing forms" in Chapter 23 for details about submitting form content via e-mail.

The partner of the Submit button is the Reset button. This button, too, has special powers. A click of this button type restores all elements within the form to their default values. That goes for text objects, radio button groups, checkboxes, and selection lists. The most common application of the button is to clear entry fields of the last data entered by the user.

All that distinguishes these three types of buttons from each other in the `<INPUT>` tag or `<BUTTON>` tag is the parameter of the `TYPE` attribute. For buttons not intended to send data to a server, use the "button" style (this is the default value for the BUTTON element). Reserve "submit" and "reset" for their special powers.

If you want an image to behave like a button in all scriptable browsers, consider either associating a link with an image (see the discussion on the link object in Chapter 21) or creating a client-side image map (see the area object discussion in Chapter 22). But for IE4+ and NN6+, you can use the INPUT element with a `TYPE` attribute set to `image` (discussed later in this chapter).

Probably the biggest mistake scripters make with these buttons is using a Submit button to do the work of a plain button. Because these two buttons look alike, and the submit type of input element has a longer tradition than the button, confusing the two is easy. But if all you want is to display a button that initiates client-side script execution, use a plain button. The Submit button attempts to submit the form. If no `ACTION` attribute is set, then the page reloads, and all previous processing and field entries are erased. The plain button does its job quietly without reloading the page (unless the script intentionally does so).

Properties

`form`

Value: FORM object reference   Read-Only

	NN2	NN3	NN4	NN6	IE3/J1	IE3/J2	IE4	IE5	IE5.5
Compatibility	✓	✓	✓	✓	✓	✓	✓	✓	✓

A property of every INPUT element object is a reference to the FORM element that contains the control. This property can be very convenient in a script when you are dealing with one form control that is passed as a parameter to the function and you want to either access another control in the same form or invoke a method of the form. An event handler of any INPUT element can pass `this` as the parameter, and the function can still get access to the form without having to hard-wire the script to a particular form name or document layout.

On the CD-ROM Example on the CD-ROM

Related Items: FORM object.

name

Value: Identifier String   Read/Write (see text)

	NN2	NN3	NN4	NN6	IE3/J1	IE3/J2	IE4	IE5	IE5.5
Compatibility	✓	✓	✓	✓	✓	✓	✓	✓	✓

A button's name is fixed in the INPUT or BUTTON element's NAME attribute and cannot be adjusted via scripting except in newer browsers. You may need to retrieve this property in a general-purpose function handler called by multiple buttons in a document. The function can test for a button name and perform the necessary statements for that button. If you change the name of the object, even a soft reload or window resize restores its original name.

On the CD-ROM   Example on the CD-ROM

Related Items: name property of all form elements.

type

Value: String   Read-Only

	NN2	NN3	NN4	NN6	IE3/J1	IE3/J2	IE4	IE5	IE5.5
Compatibility		✓	✓	✓			✓	✓	✓

The precise value of the type property echoes the setting of the TYPE attribute of the <INPUT> or <BUTTON> tag that defines the object: button; submit; or reset.

value

Value: String   Read/Write (see text)

	NN2	NN3	NN4	NN6	IE3/J1	IE3/J2	IE4	IE5	IE5.5
Compatibility	✓	✓	✓	✓	✓	✓	✓	✓	✓

Both INPUT and BUTTON elements have the VALUE attribute, which is represented by the value property in the object model. But the purpose of the attribute/property in the two elements differs. For the INPUT element, the value property represents the label displayed on the button. For a BUTTON element, however, the label text is created by the HTML text between the start and end tags for the BUTTON element. In both cases, when the element has a NAME value associated with it, the name/value pair is submitted along with the form (assuming the BUTTON element is inside a form).

If you do not assign a VALUE attribute to a reset or submit style button, the browsers automatically assign the labels Reset and Submit without assigning a value. A value property can be any string, including multiple words.

You can modify this text on the fly in a script, but some cautions apply. Browsers prior to IE4 and NN6 do not resize the width of the button to accommodate a new name that is longer or shorter than the original. Moreover, any soft reload or resize of the window restores the original label. IE4+ and NN6, however, resize the button and reflow the page to meet the new space needs; the new label survives a window resizing, but not a soft reload of the page. Finally, IE4 for the Mac allows you to set this property, but it doesn't really stick.

Example on the CD-ROM

Related Items: value property of text object.

Methods

click()

Returns: Nothing.

	NN2	NN3	NN4	NN6	IE3/J1	IE3/J2	IE4	IE5	IE5.5
Compatibility	✓	✓	✓	✓	✓	✓	✓	✓	✓

A button's click() method should simulate, via scripting, the human action of clicking that button. Unfortunately, the method is highly unreliable in browsers prior to IE4 and NN4.

Example on the CD-ROM

Related Items: onClick event handler.

Event handlers
onClick

	NN2	NN3	NN4	NN6	IE3/J1	IE3/J2	IE4	IE5	IE5.5
Compatibility	✓	✓	✓	✓	✓	✓	✓	✓	✓

Virtually all button action takes place in response to the onClick event handler. A *click* is defined as a press and release of the mouse button while the screen pointer rests atop the button. The event goes to the button only after the user releases the mouse button.

For a Submit button, you should probably omit the onClick event handler and allow the form's onSubmit event handler to take care of lastminute data entry validation before sending the form. By triggering validation with the onSubmit event handler, your scripts can cancel the submission if something is not right (see the FORM object discussion in Chapter 23).

 On the CD-ROM Example (with Listing 24-1) on the CD-ROM

Related Items: button.onMouseDown, button.onMouseUp, form.onSubmit event handlers.

onMouseDown
onMouseUp

	NN2	NN3	NN4	NN6	IE3/J1	IE3/J2	IE4	IE5	IE5.5
Compatibility			✓	✓			✓	✓	✓

More recent browsers have event handlers for the components of a click event: the onMouseDown and onMouseUp event handlers. These events fire in addition to the onClick event handler.

The system-level buttons provided by the operating system perform their change of appearance while a button is being pressed. Therefore, trapping for the components of a click action won't help you in changing the button's appearance via scripting. Remember that a user can roll the cursor off the button while the button is still down. When the cursor leaves the region of the button, the button's appearance returns to its unpressed look, but any setting you make with the onMouseDown event handler won't undo itself with an onMouseUp counterpart, even after the user releases the mouse button elsewhere. On the other hand, if you can precache a click-on and click-off sound, you can use these events to fire the respective sounds in response to the mouse button action.

Related Items: button.onClick event handler.

Checkbox Input Object

For HTML element properties, methods, and event handlers, see Chapter 15.

Properties	Methods	Event Handlers
checked	click()†	onClick†
form†		
name†		
type		
value		

† See Button object.

Syntax

Accessing checkbox properties or methods:

```
(All)       [window.]document.formName.boxName.property | method([parameters])
(All)       [window.]document.formName.elements[index].property |
            method([parameters])
(All)       [window.]document.forms[index].boxName.property |
            method([parameters])
(All)       [window.]document.forms["formName"].boxName.property |
            method([parameters])
(All)       [window.]document.forms["formName"].elements[index].property |
            method([parameters])
(IE4+)      [window.]document.all.elemID.property | method([parameters])
(IE5+/NN6)  [window.]document.getElementById("elemID").property |
            method([parameters])
```

About this object

Checkboxes have a very specific purpose in modern graphical user interfaces: to toggle between "on" and "off" settings. As with a checkbox on a printed form, a mark in the box indicates that the label text is true or should be included for the individual who made that mark. When the box is unchecked or empty, the text is false or should not be included. If two or more checkboxes are physically grouped together, they should have no interaction: Each is an independent setting (see the discussion on the radio object for interrelated buttons).

I make these user interface points at the outset because, in order to present a user interface in your HTML pages consistent with the user's expectations based on exposure to other programs, you must use checkbox objects only for on/off choices that the user makes. Using a checkbox as an action button that, for example, navigates to another URL, is not good form. Just as they do in a Windows or Mac dialog box, users make settings with checkboxes and radio buttons and initiate action by clicking a standard button or image map.

That's not to say that a checkbox object cannot perform some limited action in response to a user's click, but such actions are typically related to the context of the checkbox button's label text. For example, in some Windows and Macintosh dialog boxes, turning on a checkbox may activate a bunch of otherwise inactive settings elsewhere in the same dialog box. IE4+ and NN6+ allow disabling (dimming) or hiding form elements, so a checkbox may control those visible attributes of related controls. Or, in a two-frame window, a checkbox in one frame may control whether the viewer is an advanced user. If so, the content in the other frame may be more detailed. Toggling the checkbox changes the complexity level of a document showing in the other frame (using different URLs for each level). The bottom line, then, is that you should use checkboxes for toggling between on/off settings. Provide regular buttons for users to initiate processing.

In the <INPUT> tag for a checkbox, you can preset the checkbox to be checked when the page appears. Add the constant CHECKED attribute to the definition. If you omit this attribute, the default, unchecked appearance rules. As for the checkbox label text, its definition lies outside the <INPUT> tag. If you look at the way checkboxes behave in HTML browsers, this location makes sense: The label is not an active part of the checkbox (as it typically is in Windows and Macintosh user interfaces, where clicking the label is the same as clicking the box).

Naming a checkbox can be an important part of the object definition, depending on how you plan to use the information in your script or document. For forms whose content goes to a CGI program on the server, you must word the box name as needed for use by the CGI program, so that the program can parse the form data and extract the setting of the checkbox. For JavaScript client-side use, you can assign not only a name that describes the button, but also a value useful to your script for making if...else decisions or for assembling strings that are eventually displayed in a window or frame.

document._formObject._**checkboxObject**

Properties

checked

Value: Boolean   Read/Write

	NN2	NN3	NN4	NN6	IE3/J1	IE3/J2	IE4	IE5	IE5.5
Compatibility	✓	✓	✓	✓	✓	✓	✓	✓	✓

The simplest property of a checkbox reveals (or lets you set) whether or not a checkbox is checked. The value is true for a checked box and false for an unchecked box. To check a box via a script, simply assign true to the checkbox's checked property:

```
document.forms[0].boxName.checked = true
```

Setting the checked property from a script does not trigger a click event for the checkbox object.

You may need an instance in which one checkbox automatically checks another checkbox elsewhere in the same or other form of the document. To accomplish this task, create an onClick event handler for the one checkbox and build a statement similar to the preceding one to set the other related checkbox to true. Don't get too carried away with this feature, however: For a group of interrelated, mutually exclusive choices, use a group of radio buttons instead.

If your page design requires that a checkbox be checked after the page loads, don't bother trying to script this checking action. Simply add the one-word CHECKED attribute to the <INPUT> tag. Because the checked property is a Boolean value, you can use its results as an argument for an if clause, as shown in the next example.

On the CD-ROM   Example (with Listing 24-2) on the CD-ROM

Related Items: defaultChecked, value properties.

defaultChecked

Value: Boolean   Read-Only

	NN2	NN3	NN4	NN6	IE3/J1	IE3/J2	IE4	IE5	IE5.5
Compatibility	✓	✓	✓	✓	✓	✓	✓	✓	✓

If you add the CHECKED attribute to the <INPUT> definition for a checkbox, the defaultChecked property for that object is true; otherwise, the property is false. Having access to this property enables your scripts to examine checkboxes to see if they have been adjusted (presumably by the user, if your script does not set properties).

On the CD-ROM   Example (with Listing 24-3) on the CD-ROM

Related Items: checked, value properties.

type

Value: String (checkbox)   Read-Only

	NN2	NN3	NN4	NN6	IE3/J1	IE3/J2	IE4	IE5	IE5.5
Compatibility		✓	✓	✓			✓	✓	✓

Use the type property to help you identify a checkbox object from an unknown group of form elements.

Related Items: form.elements property.

value

Value: String   Read/Write

	NN2	NN3	NN4	NN6	IE3/J1	IE3/J2	IE4	IE5	IE5.5
Compatibility	✓	✓	✓	✓	✓	✓	✓	✓	✓

document.*formObject.checkboxObject*.value

A checkbox object's `value` property is a string of any text that you want to associate with the box. Note that the checkbox's `value` property is not the label, as it is for a regular button, but hidden text associated with the checkbox. For instance, the label that you attach to a checkbox may not be worded in a way that is useful to your script. But if you place that useful wording in the `VALUE` attribute of the checkbox tag, you can extract that string via the `value` property.

When a checkbox object's data is submitted to a CGI program, the `value` property is sent as part of the name/value pair if the box is checked (nothing about the checkbox is sent if the box is unchecked). If you omit the `VALUE` attribute in your definition, the property always yields the string "on," which is submitted to a CGI program when the box is checked. From the JavaScript side, don't confuse this string with the on and off settings of the checkbox: Use the `checked` property to determine a checkbox's status.

Example (with Listing 24-4) on the CD-ROM

Related Items: `checked` property.

Methods

click()

Returns: Nothing.

	NN2	NN3	NN4	NN6	IE3/J1	IE3/J2	IE4	IE5	IE5.5
Compatibility	✓	✓	✓	✓	✓	✓	✓	✓	✓

The intention of the `click()` method is to enact, via script, the physical act of clicking a checkbox (but without triggering the `onClick` event handler). Unfortunately, this method does not work in Navigator 2 or 3 as expected. Even if this method worked flawlessly, your scripts are better served by setting the `checked` property so that you know exactly what the setting of the box is at any time.

Related Items: `checked` property; `onClick` event handler.

document.*formObject*.*checkboxObject*.click()

Event handlers

`onClick`

	NN2	NN3	NN4	NN6	IE3/J1	IE3/J2	IE4	IE5	IE5.5
Compatibility	✓	✓	✓	✓	✓	✓	✓	✓	✓

Because users regularly click checkboxes, the objects have an event handler for the `click` event. Use this event handler only if you want your page (or variable values hidden from view) to respond in some way to the action of clicking a checkbox. Most user actions, as mentioned earlier, are initiated by clicking standard buttons rather than checkboxes, so be careful not to overuse event handlers in checkboxes.

On the CD-ROM

Example (with Listing 24-5) on the CD-ROM

Related Items: checkbox mouse-related event handler.

Radio Input Object

Properties	*Methods*	*Event Handlers*
	See checkbox object.	

Syntax

Accessing radio object properties or methods:

```
(All)       [window.]document.formName.buttonGroupName[index].property |
            method([parameters])
(All)       [window.]document.formName.elements[index] [index].property |
            method([parameters])
(All)       [window.]document.forms[index]. buttonGroupName[index].property |
            method([parameters])
(All)       [window.]document.forms["formName"]. buttonGroupName[index].property |
            method([parameters])
(All)       [window.]document.forms["formName"].elements[index].property |
            method([parameters])
(IE4+)      [window.]document.all.elemID[index].property | method([parameters])
(IE5+/NN6)  [window.]document.getElementById("elemID")[index].property |
            method([parameters])
```

document.*formObject.radioObject*

About this object

A radio button object is an unusual one within the body of JavaScript applications. In every other case of form control elements, one object equals one visual element on the screen. But a radio object actually consists of a group of radio buttons. Because of the nature of radio buttons — a mutually exclusive choice among two or more selections — a group always has multiple visual elements. All buttons in the group share the same name — which is how the browser knows to group buttons together and to let the clicking of a button deselect any other selected button within the group. Beyond that, however, each button can have unique properties, such as its value or checked property.

Use JavaScript array syntax to access information about an individual button within the button group. Look at the following example of defining a button group and see how to reference each button. This button group lets the user select a favorite member of the Three Stooges:

```
<FORM>
<B>Select your favorite Stooge:</B><P>
<INPUT TYPE="radio" NAME="stooges" VALUE="Moe Howard" CHECKED>Moe
<INPUT TYPE="radio" NAME="stooges" VALUE="Larry Fine" >Larry
<INPUT TYPE="radio" NAME="stooges" VALUE="Curly Howard" >Curly
<INPUT TYPE="radio" NAME="stooges" VALUE="Shemp Howard" >Shemp
</FORM>
```

After this group displays on the page, the first radio button is preselected for the user. Only one property of a radio button object (length) applies to all members of the group. However, the other properties apply to individual buttons within the group. To access any button, use an array index value as part of the button group name. For example:

```
firstBtnValue = document.forms[0].stooges[0].value // "Moe Howard"
secondBtnValue = document.forms[0].stooges[1].value // "Larry Fine"
```

Any time you access the checked, defaultChecked, type, or value property, you must point to a specific button within the group according to its order in the array (or, in IE4+ and NN6, each button can also have a unique ID). The order of buttons in the group depends on the sequence in which the individual buttons are defined in the HTML document. In other words, to uncover the currently selected radio button, your script has to iterate through all radio buttons in the radio group. Examples of this come later in the discussion of this object.

Supplying a VALUE attribute to a radio button can be very important in your script. Although the text label for a button is defined outside the <INPUT> tag, the VALUE attribute lets you store any string in the button's hip pocket. In the earlier example, the radio button labels were just first names, whereas the value properties were set in the definition to the full names of the actors. The values could have been anything that the script needed, such as birth dates, shoe sizes, URLs, or the first names again (because a script has no way to retrieve the labels except through `innerHTML` or node property access in more modern browsers). The point is that the VALUE attribute should contain whatever string the script needs to derive from the selection made by the user. The VALUE attribute contents are also what is sent to a CGI program on a server in a submit action for the form.

How you decide to orient a group of buttons on the screen is entirely up to your design and the real estate available within your document. You can string them in a horizontal row (as shown earlier), place <BR> tags after each one to form a column, or do so after every other button to form a double column. Numeric order within the array is determined only by the order in which the buttons are defined in the source code, not by where they appear. To determine which radio button of a group is checked before doing processing based on that choice, you need to construct a repeat loop to cycle through the buttons in the group (shown in the next example). For each button, your script examines the checked property.

Tip

To be Navigator 2–friendly, be sure to always specify an `onClick` event handler to every radio button (even if `onClick=""`). This action overrides a bug that causes index values to be reversed among buttons in a group.

Properties

checked

Value: Boolean   Read/Write

	NN2	NN3	NN4	NN6	IE3/J1	IE3/J2	IE4	IE5	IE5.5
Compatibility	✓	✓	✓	✓	✓	✓	✓	✓	✓

Only one radio button in a group can be highlighted (checked) at a time (the browser takes care of highlighting and unhighlighting buttons in a group for you). That one button's checked property is set to `true`, whereas all others in the group are set to `false`.

Beginning with NN3 (and IE3), you can safely set the checked property of a radio button. By setting the checked property of one button in a group to `true`, all other buttons automatically uncheck themselves.

On the CD-ROM

Example (with Listing 24-6) on the CD-ROM

Related Items: `defaultChecked` property.

document.*formObject*.*radioObject*.checked

defaultChecked

Value: Boolean   Read-Only

	NN2	NN3	NN4	NN6	IE3/J1	IE3/J2	IE4	IE5	IE5.5
Compatibility	✓	✓	✓	✓	✓	✓	✓	✓	✓

If you add the CHECKED attribute to the <INPUT> definition for a radio button, the defaultChecked property for that object is true; otherwise, the property is false. Having access to this property enables your scripts to examine individual radio buttons to see if they have been adjusted (presumably by the user, if your script does not perform automatic clicking).

On the CD-ROM Example (with Listing 24-7) on the CD-ROM

Related Items: checked, value properties.

length

Value: Integer   Read-Only

	NN2	NN3	NN4	NN6	IE3/J1	IE3/J2	IE4	IE5	IE5.5
Compatibility	✓	✓	✓	✓	✓	✓	✓	✓	✓

A radio button group has *length* — the number of individual radio buttons defined for that group. Attempting to retrieve the length of an individual button yields a null value. The length property is valuable for establishing the maximum range of values in a repeat loop that must cycle through every button within that group. If you specify the length property to fill that value (rather than hard-wiring the value), the loop construction will be easier to maintain — as you make changes to the number of buttons in the group during page construction, the loop adjusts to the changes automatically.

On the CD-ROM Example on the CD-ROM

Related Items: None.

name

Value: Identifier String   Read-Only

	NN2	NN3	NN4	NN6	IE3/J1	IE3/J2	IE4	IE5	IE5.5
Compatibility	✓	✓	✓	✓	✓	✓	✓	✓	✓

The name property, while associated with an entire radio button group, can be read only from individual buttons in the group, such as

```
btnGroupName = document.forms[0].groupName[2].name
```

In that sense, each radio button element in a group inherits the name of the group. Your scripts have little need to extract the name property of a button or group. More often than not, you will hard-wire a button group's name into your script to extract other properties of individual buttons. Getting the name property of an object whose name you know is obviously redundant. But understanding the place of radio button group names in the scheme of JavaScript objects is important for all scripters.

Related Items: value property.

type

Value: String (radio)   Read-Only

	NN2	NN3	NN4	NN6	IE3/J1	IE3/J2	IE4	IE5	IE5.5
Compatibility		✓	✓	✓			✓	✓	✓

Use the type property to help identify a radio object from an unknown group of form elements.

Related Items: form.elements property.

value

Value: String   Read/Write

	NN2	NN3	NN4	NN6	IE3/J1	IE3/J2	IE4	IE5	IE5.5
Compatibility	✓	✓	✓	✓	✓	✓	✓	✓	✓

As described earlier in this chapter for the checkbox object, the value property contains arbitrary information that you assign when mapping out the <INPUT> definition for an individual radio button. Using this property is a handy shortcut to correlating a radio button label with detailed or related information of interest to your script or CGI program on a server. If you like, the value property can contain the same text as the label.

On the
CD-ROM   Example on the CD-ROM

Related Items: name property.

Methods

click()

Returns: Nothing.

	NN2	NN3	NN4	NN6	IE3/J1	IE3/J2	IE4	IE5	IE5.5
Compatibility	✓	✓	✓	✓	✓	✓	✓	✓	✓

The intention of the click() method is to enact, via a script, the physical act of clicking a radio button. Unfortunately, this method does not work in Navigator 2 or 3. Even if it worked flawlessly, you better serve your scripts by setting the checked properties of all buttons in a group so that you know exactly what the setting of the group is at any time.

Related Items: checked property; onClick event handler.

Event handlers

onClick

	NN2	NN3	NN4	NN6	IE3/J1	IE3/J2	IE4	IE5	IE5.5
Compatibility	✓	✓	✓	✓	✓	✓	✓	✓	✓

Radio buttons, more than any user interface element available in HTML, are intended for use in making choices that other objects, such as submit or standard buttons, act upon later. You may see cases in Windows or Mac programs in which highlighting a radio button — at most — activates or brings into view additional, related settings (see Listing 24-5).

I strongly advise you not to use scripting handlers that perform significant actions at the click of any radio button. At best, you may want to use knowledge about a user's clicking of a radio button to adjust a global variable or document.cookie setting that influences subsequent processing. Be aware, however, that if you script such a hidden action for one radio button in a group, you must also script similar actions for others in the same group. That way, if a user changes the setting back to a previous condition, the global variable is reset to the way it was. JavaScript, however, tends to run fast enough so that a batch operation can make such adjustments after the user clicks a more action-oriented button.

Example (with Listing 24-8) on the CD-ROM

Image Input Object

For HTML element properties, methods, and event handlers, see Chapter 15.

Properties	Methods	Event Handlers
complete		
form†		
name†		
src		
type		

† See Button object.

Syntax

Accessing image input object properties or methods:

```
(All)        [window.]document.formName.imageName.property |
             method([parameters])
(All)        [window.]document.formName.elements[index].property |
             method([parameters])
(All)        [window.]document.forms[index].imageName.property |
             method([parameters])
(All)        [window.]document.forms["formName"].imageName.property |
             method([parameters])
(All)        [window.]document.forms["formName"].elements[index].property |
             method([parameters])
(IE4+)       [window.]document.all.elemID.property | method([parameters])
(IE5+/NN6)   [window.]document.getElementById("elemID").property |
             method([parameters])
```

	NN2	NN3	NN4	NN6	IE3/J1	IE3/J2	IE4	IE5	IE5.5
Compatibility				✓			✓	✓	✓

About this object

Browsers with fuller document object models include the image input element among scriptable objects. The image input object most closely resembles the button input object but replaces the value property (which defines the label for the button) with the src property, which defines the URL for the image that is to be displayed in the form control. This is a much simpler way to define a clickable image icon, for example, than the way required for compatibility with older browsers: wrapping an IMG element inside an A element so that you can use the A element's event handlers.

Although this element loads a regular Web image in the document, you have virtually no control over the image, which the IMG element provides. Be sure the rendering is as you predict.

Properties

`complete`

Value: Boolean   Read-Only

	NN2	NN3	NN4	NN6	IE3/J1	IE3/J2	IE4	IE5	IE5.5
Compatibility							✓	✓	✓

The `complete` property works as it does for an IMG element, reporting `true` if the image has finished loading. Otherwise the property returns `false`. Interestingly, there is no `onLoad` event handler for this object.

Related Items: `Image.complete` property.

`src`

Value: URL String   Read/Write

	NN2	NN3	NN4	NN6	IE3/J1	IE3/J2	IE4	IE5	IE5.5
Compatibility				✓			✓	✓	✓

Like the IMG element object, the image input element's `src` property controls the URL of the image being displayed in the element. The property can be used for image swapping in a form control, just as it is for a regular IMG element. Because the image input element has all necessary mouse event handlers available (for example, `onMouseOver`, `onMouseOut`, `onMouseDown`) you can script rollovers, click-downs, or any other user interface technique that you feel is appropriate for your buttons and images. To adapt code written for link-wrapped images, move the event handlers from the A element to the image input element, and make sure the name of the image input element is the same as your old IMG element.

Older browsers load images into an image input element, but no event handlers are recognized.

Related Items: `Image.src` property.

type

Value: String (`image`) Read-Only

	NN2	NN3	NN4	NN6	IE3/J1	IE3/J2	IE4	IE5	IE5.5
Compatibility				✓			✓	✓	✓

Use the `type` property to help you identify an image input object from an unknown group of form elements.

Related Items: `form.elements` property.

✦　　✦　　✦

Text-Related Form Objects

The document object model for forms includes four text-related user interface objects — text, password, and hidden INPUT element objects, plus the TEXTAREA element object. All four of these objects are used for entry, display, or temporary storage of text data. While all of these objects can have text placed in them by default as the page loads, scripts can also modify the contents of these objects. Importantly, all but the hidden objects retain their user- or script-modified content during a soft reload (for example, clicking the Reload button), except in IE3. Hidden objects revert to their default values on all reloads in all browsers.

A more obvious difference between the hidden object and the rest is that its invisibility removes it from the realm of user events and actions. Therefore, the range of scripted possibilities is much smaller for the hidden object.

The persistence of text and TEXTAREA object data through reloads (and window resizes) makes these objects prime targets for off-screen storage of data that may otherwise be stored temporarily in a cookie. If you create a frame with no size (for example, you set the COLS or ROWS values of a <FRAMESET> tag to let all visible frames occupy 100 percent of the space and assign the rest — * — to the hidden frame), you can populate the frame with fields that act as shopping cart information or other data holders. Therefore, if users have cookies turned off or don't usually respond affirmatively to cookie requests, your application can still make use of temporary client storage. The field contents may survive unloading of the page, but whether this happens and for how many navigations away from the page the contents last depends on the visitor's cache settings (or if the browser is IE3, in which case no values preserve the unloading of a document). If the user quits the browser or closes the browser window, the field entry is lost.

Text Input Object

For HTML element properties, methods, and event handlers, see Chapter 15.

Properties	Methods	Event Handlers
defaultValue	select()	onAfterUpdate
form		onBeforeUpdate
maxLength		onChange
name		onErrorUpdate
readOnly		onSelect
size		
type		
value		

Syntax

Accessing text INPUT object properties or methods:

```
(All)      [window.]document.formName.fieldName.property | method([parameters])
(All)      [window.]document.formName.elements[index].property |
           method([parameters])
(All)      [window.]document.forms[index].fieldName.property |
           method([parameters])
(All)      [window.]document.forms["formName"].fieldName.property |
           method([parameters])
(All)      [window.]document.forms["formName"].elements[index].property |
           method([parameters])
(IE4+)     [window.]document.all.elemID.property | method([parameters])
(IE5+/NN6) [window.]document.getElementById("elemID").property |
           method([parameters])
```

About this object

The text INPUT object is the primary medium for capturing single-line, user-entered text. By default, browsers tend to display entered text in a monospaced font (usually Courier or a derivative), so that you can easily specify the width (SIZE) of a field based on the anticipated number of characters that a user may put into the field. Until you get to IE4+ and NN6+, the font is a fixed size and always is left-aligned in the field. In those later browsers, style sheets can control the font characteristics of a text field. If your design requires multiple lines of text, use the TEXTAREA object that comes later in this chapter.

Before document object models in IE4 and NN6 allowed dynamic modification of body content, a common practice was to use text objects to display results of a script calculation or other processing. Such fields may stand alone on a page or be part of a table.

Also prior to IE4 and NN6, these fields could not be made fully write-protected, so it was easy to understand how a novice user may become confused after he or she causes the text pointer or selection to activate a field used exclusively for output, simply by tabbing through a page.

Text object methods and event handlers use terminology that may be known to Windows users but not to Macintosh users. A field is said to have *focus* whenever the user clicks or tabs into the field. When a field has focus, either the text insertion pointer flashes, or any text in the field may be selected. Only one text object on a page can have focus at a time. The inverse user action — clicking or tabbing away from a text object — is called a *blur*. Clicking another object, whether it is another field or a button of any kind, causes a field that currently has focus to blur.

If you don't want the contents of a field to be changed by the user, you have three possibilities — depending on the vintage of browsers you need to support: forcing the field to lose focus; disabling the field; or setting the field's readOnly property.

The tactic that is completely backward compatible uses the following event handler in a field you want to protect:

```
onFocus="this.blur()"
```

Starting with IE4 and NN6, the object model provides a disabled property for form controls. Setting the property to true leaves the element visible on the page, but the user cannot access the control. The same browsers provide a readOnly property, which doesn't dim the field, but prevents typing in the field.

Text fields and events

Focus and blur also interact with other possible user actions to a text object: selecting and changing. *Selecting* occurs when the user clicks and drags across any text in the field; *changing* occurs when the user makes any alteration to the content of the field and then either tabs or clicks away from that field.

When you design event handlers for fields, be aware that a user's interaction with a field may trigger more than one event with a single action. For instance, clicking a field to select text may trigger both a focus and select event. If you have conflicting actions in the onFocus and onSelect event handlers, your scripts can do some weird things to the user's experience with your page. Displaying alert dialog boxes, for instance, also triggers blur events, so a field that has both an onSelect handler (which displays the alert) and an onBlur handler gets a nasty interaction from the two.

As a result, be very judicious with the number of event handlers you specify in any text object definition. If possible, pick one user action that you want to use to initiate some JavaScript code execution and deploy it consistently on the page. Not all fields require event handlers — only those you want to perform some action as the result of user activity in that field.

Many newcomers also become confused by the behavior of the change event. To prevent this event from being sent to the field for every character the user types, any change to a field is determined only *after* the field loses focus by the user's clicking or tabbing away from it. At that point, instead of a blur event being sent to the field, only a change event is sent, triggering an onChange event handler if one is defined for the field. This extra burden of having to click or tab away from a field may entice you to shift any onChange event handler tasks to a separate button that the user must click to initiate action on the field contents.

Starting with NN4 and IE4, text fields also have event handlers for keyboard actions, namely onKeyDown, onKeyPress, and onKeyUp. With these event handlers, you can intercept keystrokes before the characters reach the text field. Thus, you can use keyboard events to prevent anything but numbers from being entered into a text box while the user types the characters.

Text Boxes and the Enter/Return Key

Early browsers established a convention that continues to this day. When a form consists of only one text box, a press of the Enter/Return key acts the same as clicking a Submit button for the form. You have probably experienced this many times when entering a value into a single search field of a form. Press the Enter/Return key, and the search request goes off to the server.

The flip side is that if the form contains more than one text box, the Enter/Return key does no submission from any of the text boxes (IE4 for the Mac is an exception: it submits no matter how many text boxes there are). But with the advent of keyboard events, you can script this action (or the invocation of a client-side script) into any text boxes of the form you like. To make it work with all flavors of browsers capable of keyboard events requires a small conversion function that extracts the DOM-specific desired code from the keystroke. The following listing shows a sample page that demonstrates how to implement a function that inspects each keystroke from a text field and initiates processing if the key pressed is the Enter/Return key.

```
<HTML>
<HEAD>
<TITLE>Enter/Return Event Trigger</TITLE>
```

```
<SCRIPT LANGUAGE="JavaScript">
// Event object processor for NN4, IE4+, NN6
function isEnterKey(evt) {
    if (!evt) {
        // grab IE event object
        evt = window.event
    } else if (!evt.keyCode) {
        // grab NN4 event info
        evt.keyCode = evt.which
    }
    return (evt.keyCode == 13)
}

function processOnEnter(fld, evt) {
    if (isEnterKey(evt)) {
        alert("Ready to do some work with the form.")
        return false
    }
    return true
}
</SCRIPT>
</HEAD>

<BODY>
<H1>Enter/Return Event Trigger</H1>
<HR>
<FORM>
Field 1: <INPUT TYPE="text" NAME="field1"
onKeyDown="return processOnEnter(this,event)">
Field 2: <INPUT TYPE="text" NAME="field2"
onKeyDown="return processOnEnter(this,event)">
Field 3: <INPUT TYPE="text" NAME="field3"
onKeyDown="return processOnEnter(this,event)">
</FORM>
</BODY>
</HTML>
```

Notice that to accommodate the NN4+ event models, a reference to the event object must be passed as a parameter to the processing function. For more details on event handling, see Chapter 29.

Text field values and persistence

Text objects (including the related TEXTAREA object) have one unique behavior that can be very important to some document and script designs. Even if a default value is specified for the content of a field (in the VALUE attribute), any text entered into a field by a user or script persists in that field as long as the document is cached in the browser's memory cache (but Internet Explorer 3 has no such persistence). Therefore, if users of your page enter values into some fields, or your scripts display results in a field, all that data will be there later, even if the user performs a soft reload of the page or navigates to dozens of other Web pages or sites. Navigating back via the Go or Bookmarks menu entries causes the browser to retrieve the cached version (with its field entries). To force the page to appear with its default text object values, use the Open Location or Open File selections in the File menu, or script the location.reload() method. These actions cause the browser to load the desired page from scratch, regardless of the content of the cache. After you quit and relaunch the browser, the first time it goes to the desired page, the browser loads the page from scratch — with its default values.

This level of persistence is not as reliable as the document.cookie property because a user can reopen a URL at any time, thus erasing whatever was temporarily stored in a text or TEXTAREA object. Still, this method of temporary data storage may suffice for some designs. Unfortunately, you cannot completely hide a text object in case the data you want to store is for use only by your scripts. The TYPE="hidden" form element is not an alternative here because script-induced changes to its value do not persist across soft reloads.

If you prefer to use a text INPUT or TEXTAREA object as a storage medium but don't want users to see it, design the page to display in a non-resizable frame of height or width zero. Use proper frame references to store or retrieve values from the fields. Carrying out this task requires a great deal of work. The document.cookie may not seem so complicated after all that.

To extract the current content of a text object, summon the property document.*formName*.*fieldName*.value. After you have the string value, you can use JavaScript's string object methods to parse or otherwise massage that text as needed for your script. If the field entry is a number and you need to pass that value to methods requiring numbers, you have to convert the text to a number with the help of the parseInt() or parseFloat() global functions.

Properties

defaultValue

Value: String   Read-Only

	NN2	NN3	NN4	NN6	IE3/J1	IE3/J2	IE4	IE5	IE5.5
Compatibility	✓	✓	✓	✓	✓	✓	✓	✓	✓

document.*formObject*.*textObject*.defaultValue

Though your users and your scripts are free to muck with the contents of a `text` object by assigning strings to the value property, you can always extract (and thus restore, if necessary) the string assigned to the text object in its `<INPUT>` definition. The `defaultValue` property yields the string parameter of the `VALUE` attribute.

Example (with Listing 25-1) on the CD-ROM

Related Items: `value` property.

form

Value: FORM object reference   Read-Only

	NN2	NN3	NN4	NN6	IE3/J1	IE3/J2	IE4	IE5	IE5.5
Compatibility	✓	✓	✓	✓	✓	✓	✓	✓	✓

A property of every INPUT element object is a reference to the FORM element that contains the control. This property can be very convenient in a script when you are dealing with one form control that is passed as a parameter to the function and you want to either access another control in the same form or invoke a method of the form. An event handler of any INPUT element can pass `this` as the parameter, and the function can still get access to the form without having to hard-wire the script to a particular form name or document layout.

Example on the CD-ROM

Related Items: FORM object.

maxLength

Value: Integer   Read/Write

	NN2	NN3	NN4	NN6	IE3/J1	IE3/J2	IE4	IE5	IE5.5
Compatibility				✓			✓	✓	✓

The `maxLength` property controls the maximum number of characters allowed to be typed into the field. There is no interaction between the `maxLength` and `size` properties. This value is normally set initially via the MAXLENGTH attribute of the INPUT element.

Example on the CD-ROM

Related Items: size property.

name

Value: Identifier String   Read/Write

	NN2	NN3	NN4	NN6	IE3/J1	IE3/J2	IE4	IE5	IE5.5
Compatibility	✓	✓	✓	✓	✓	✓	✓	✓	✓

Text object names are important for two reasons. First, if your HTML page submits information to CGI scripts, the input device passes the name of the text object along with the data to help the server program identify the data being supplied by the form. Second, you can use a text object's name in its reference within JavaScript coding. If you assign distinctive, meaningful names to your fields, these names will help you read and debug your JavaScript listings (and will help others follow your scripting tactics).

Be as descriptive about your text object names as you can. Borrowing text from the field's on-page label may help you mentally map a scripted reference to a physical field on the page. Like all JavaScript object names, text object names must begin with a letter and be followed by any number of letters or numbers. Avoid punctuation symbols with the exception of the very safe underscore character.

Although I urge you to use distinctive names for all objects you define in a document, you can make a case for assigning the same name to a series of interrelated fields — and JavaScript is ready to help. Within a single form, any reused name for the same object type is placed in an indexed array for that name. For example, if you define three fields with the name entry, the following statements retrieve the value property for each field:

```
data = document.forms[0].entry[0].value
data = document.forms[0].entry[1].value
data = document.forms[0].entry[2].value
```

This construction may be useful if you want to cycle through all of a form's related fields to determine which ones are blank. Elsewhere, your script probably needs to know what kind of information each field is supposed to receive, so that it can process the data intelligently. I don't often recommend reusing object names, but you should be aware of how the object model handles them in case you need this construction. Unfortunately, IE3 does not turn like-named text input objects into arrays. See "Form Element Arrays" in Chapter 23 for more details.

 Example on the CD-ROM

Related Items: `form.elements` property; all other form element objects' `name` property.

readOnly

Value: Boolean   Read/Write

	NN2	NN3	NN4	NN6	IE3/J1	IE3/J2	IE4	IE5	IE5.5
Compatibility				✓			✓	✓	✓

To display text in a text field yet prevent users from modifying it, newer browsers offer the `readOnly` property (and tag attribute). When set to `true`, the property prevents users from changing or removing the content of the text field. Unlike a disabled text field, a read-only text field looks just like an editable one.

For older browsers, you can partially simulate this behavior by including the following event handler in the INPUT element:

```
onFocus="this.blur()"
```

The event handler approach is not foolproof, however, in that quick-fingered users may be able to change a field before the event handler completes its task. For NN4, you can also trap for any keyboard events and prevent them from putting characters in the field.

 Example on the CD-ROM

Related Items: `disabled` property.

size

Value: Integer   Read/Write

	NN2	NN3	NN4	NN6	IE3/J1	IE3/J2	IE4	IE5	IE5.5
Compatibility				✓			✓	✓	✓

Unless otherwise directed, a text box is rendered to accommodate approximately 20 characters of text for the font family and size assigned to the element's style sheet. You can adjust this under script control (in case the SIZE attribute of the tag wasn't enough) via the size property, whose value is measured in characters (not pixels). Be forewarned, however, that browsers don't always make completely accurate estimates of the space required to display a set number of characters. If you are setting the MAXLENGTH attribute of a text box, making the SIZE one or two characters larger is often a safe bet.

 On the CD-ROM Example on the CD-ROM

Related Items: maxLength property.

type

Value: String (text)   Read-Only

	NN2	NN3	NN4	NN6	IE3/J1	IE3/J2	IE4	IE5	IE5.5
Compatibility		✓	✓			✓	✓	✓	✓

Use the type property to help you identify a text input object from an unknown group of form elements.

Related Items: form.elements property.

value

Value: String   Read/Write

	NN2	NN3	NN4	NN6	IE3/J1	IE3/J2	IE4	IE5	IE5.5
Compatibility	✓	✓	✓	✓	✓	✓	✓	✓	✓

A text object's `value` property is the two-way gateway to the content of the field. A reference to an object's value property returns the string currently showing in the field. Note that all values coming from a text object are string values. If your field prompts a user to enter a number, your script may have to perform data conversion to the number-as-string value ("42" instead of plain, old 42) before a script can perform math operations on it. JavaScript tries to be as automatic about this data conversion as possible and follows some rules about it (see Chapter 34). If you see an error message that says a value is not a number (for a math operation), the value is still a string.

Your script places text of its own into a field for display to the user by assigning a string to the `value` property of a text object. Use the simple assignment operator. For example:

```
document.forms[0].ZIP.value = "90210"
```

JavaScript is more forgiving about data types when assigning values to a text object. JavaScript does its best to convert a value to a string on its way to a text object display. Even Boolean values get converted to their string equivalents `true` or `false`. Scripts can place numeric values into fields without a hitch. But remember that if a script later retrieves these values from the text object, they will come back as strings. About the only values that don't get converted are objects. They typically show up in text boxes as `[object]` or, in some browsers, a more descriptive label for the object.

Storing arrays in a field requires special processing. You need to use the `array.join()` method to convert an array into a string. Each array entry is delimited by a character you establish in the `array.join()` method. Later you can use the `string.split()` method to turn this delimited string into an array.

On the CD-ROM Example (with Listings 25-2 and 25-3) on the CD-ROM

Related Items: `defaultValue` property.

Methods

`blur()`

Returns: Nothing.

	NN2	NN3	NN4	NN6	IE3/J1	IE3/J2	IE4	IE5	IE5.5
Compatibility	✓	✓	✓	✓	✓	✓	✓	✓	✓

Just as a camera lens blurs when it goes out of focus, a text object blurs when it loses focus — when someone clicks or tabs out of the field. Under script control, `blur()` deselects whatever may be selected in the field, and the text insertion pointer leaves the field. The pointer does not proceed to the next field in tabbing order, as it does if you perform a blur by tabbing out of the field manually.

On the CD-ROM   Example on the CD-ROM

Related Items: `focus()` method; `onBlur` event handler.

`focus()`

Returns: Nothing.

	NN2	NN3	NN4	NN6	IE3/J1	IE3/J2	IE4	IE5	IE5.5
Compatibility	✓	✓	✓	✓	✓	✓	✓	✓	✓

For a text object, having focus means that the text insertion pointer is flashing in that text object's field (having focus means something different for buttons in a Windows environment). Giving a field focus is like opening it up for human editing.

Setting the focus of a field containing text does not let you place the cursor at any specified location in the field. The cursor usually appears at the beginning of the text (although in IE4+, you can use the `TextRange` object to position the cursor wherever you want in the field, as shown in Chapter 19). To prepare a field for entry to remove the existing text, use both the `focus()` and `select()` methods.

Note The focus() method does not work reliably in Navigator 3 for UNIX clients. While the select() method selects the text in the designated field, focus is not handed to the field.

On the CD-ROM Example on the CD-ROM

Related Items: select() method; onFocus event handler.

select()

Returns: Nothing.

	NN2	NN3	NN4	NN6	IE3/J1	IE3/J2	IE4	IE5	IE5.5
Compatibility	✓	✓	✓	✓	✓	✓	✓	✓	✓

Selecting a field under script control means selecting all text within the text object. A typical application is one in which an entry validation script detects a mistake on the part of the user. After alerting the user to the mistake (via a window.alert() dialog box), the script finishes its task by selecting the text of the field in question. Not only does this action draw the user's eye to the field needing attention (especially important if the validation code is checking multiple fields), but it also keeps the old text there for the user to examine for potential problems. With the text selected, the next key the user presses erases the former entry.

Trying to select a text object's contents with a click of a button is problematic. One problem is that a click of the button brings the document's focus to the button, which disrupts the selection process. For more ensured selection, the script should invoke both the focus() and the select() methods for the field, in that order. No penalty exists for issuing both methods, and the extra insurance of the second method provides a more consistent user experience with the page.

Internet Explorer for Windows is known to exhibit anomalous (meaning buggy) behavior when using the technique of focusing and selecting a text field after the appearance of an alert dialog box. The fix is not elegant, but it works: inserting an artificial delay via the setTimeout() method before invoking a separate function that focuses and selects the field. Better-behaved browsers accept the workaround with no penalty.

Selecting a text object via script does *not* trigger the same onSelect event handler for that object as the one that triggers if a user manually selects text in the field. Therefore, no event handler script is executed when a user invokes the select() method.

document.*formObject*.*textObject*.select()

On the CD-ROM

Example (with Listing 25-4) on the CD-ROM

Related Items: `focus()` method; `onSelect` event handler.

Event handlers

onAfterUpdate
onBeforeUpdate
onErrorUpdate

	NN2	NN3	NN4	NN6	IE3/J1	IE3/J2	IE4	IE5	IE5.5
Compatibility							✓	✓	✓

If you are using IE/Windows data binding on a text element, the element is subject to three possible events in the course of retrieving updated data. The `onBeforeUpdate` and `onAfterUpdate` events fire immediately before and after (respectively) the update takes place. If an error occurs in the retrieval of data from the database, the `onErrorUpdate` event fires.

All three events may be used for advisory purposes. For example, an `onAfterUpdate` event handler may temporarily change the font characteristics of the element to signify the arrival of fresh data. Or an `onErrorUpdate` event handler may fill the field with hyphens because no valid data exists for the field. These events apply only to INPUT elements of type text (meaning not password or hidden types).

Related Items: `dataFld`, `dataSrc` properties (Chapter 15).

onBlur
onFocus
onSelect

NN2	NN3	NN4	NN6	IE3/J1	IE3/J2	IE4	IE5	IE5.5
Compatibility	✓	✓	✓	✓	✓	✓	✓	✓

All three of these event handlers should be used only after you have a firm understanding of the interrelationships of the events that reach text objects. You must use extreme care and conduct lots of user testing before including more than one of these three event handlers in a text object. Because some events cannot occur without triggering others either immediately before or after (for example, an onFocus occurs immediately before an onSelect if the field did not have focus before), whatever actions you script for these events should be as distinct as possible to avoid interference or overlap.

> **Note**   The onSelect event handler does not work in Windows versions of NN at least through Version 4.

In particular, be careful about displaying modal dialog boxes (for example, window.alert() dialog boxes) in response to the onFocus event handler. Because the text field loses focus when the alert displays and then regains focus after the alert is closed, you can get yourself into a loop that is difficult to break out of. If you get trapped in this manner, try the keyboard shortcut for reloading the page (Ctrl+R or ⌘-R) repeatedly as you keep closing the dialog box window.

A question often arises about whether data-entry validation should be triggered by the onBlur or onChange event handler. An onBlur validation cannot be fooled, whereas an onChange one can be (the user simply doesn't change the bad entry as he or she tabs out of the field). What I don't like about the onBlur way is it can cause a frustrating experience for a user who wants to tab through a field now and come back to it later (assuming your validation requires data be entered into the field before submission). As in Chapter 43's discussion about form data validation, I recommend using onChange event handlers to trigger immediate data checking and then using another last-minute check in a function called by the form's onSubmit event handler.

Example (with Listing 25-5) on the CD-ROM

onChange

	NN2	NN3	NN4	NN6	IE3/J1	IE3/J2	IE4	IE5	IE5.5
Compatibility	✓	✓	✓	✓	✓	✓	✓	✓	✓

Of all the event handlers for a text object, you will probably use the onChange handler the most in your forms (see Listing 25-6). This event is the one I prefer for triggering the validation of whatever entry the user just typed in the field. The potential hazard of trying to do only a batch-mode data validation of all entries before submitting an entire form is that the user's mental focus is away from the entry of a given field as well. When you immediately validate an entry, the user is already thinking about the information category in question. See Chapter 43 for more about data-entry validation.

Note
In NN4 (only), if you have both `onChange` and any keyboard event handlers defined for the same text field tag, the `onChange` event handlers are ignored. This is not true for IE4, where all events fire.

On the CD-ROM
Example (with Listing 25-6) on the CD-ROM

Password Input Object

Properties	Methods	Event Handlers
See Text Input Object		

Syntax

See Text Input Object.

About this object

A password-style field looks like a text object, but when the user types something into the field, only asterisks or bullets (depending on your operating system) appear in the field. For the sake of security, any password exchanges should be handled by a server-side CGI program.

Many properties of the password object were blocked from scripted access in NN2. Scripts in later browsers can treat a password object exactly like a text INPUT object. This may lead a scripter to capture a user's Web site password for storage in the `document.cookie` of the client machine. A password object value property is returned in plain language, so that such a captured password would be stored in the cookie file the same way. Because a client machine's cookie file can be examined on the local computer (perhaps by a snoop during lunch hour), plain-language storage of passwords is a potential security risk. Instead, develop a scripted encryption algorithm for your page for reading and writing the password in the cookie. Most password-protected sites, however, usually have a CGI program on the server encrypt the password prior to sending it back to the cookie.

See the text object discussion for the behavior of password object's properties, methods, and event handlers. The `type` property for this object returns `password`.

Hidden Input Object

Properties	Methods	Event Handlers
See Text Input Object		

Syntax

See Text Input Object.

About this object

A hidden object is a simple string holder within a form object whose contents are not visible to the user of your Web page. Despite the long list of properties, methods, and event handlers that this input element type inherits by virtue of being an input element, you will be doing little with a hidden element beyond reading and writing its `value` property.

The hidden object plays a vital role in applications that rely on CGI programs on the server. Very often, the server has data that it needs to convey to itself the next time the client makes a submission (for example, a user ID captured at the application's login page). A CGI program can generate an HTML page with the necessary data hidden from the user but located in a field transmitted to the server at submit time.

Along the same lines, a page for a server application may present a user-friendly interface that makes data-entry easy for the user. But on the server end, the database or other application requires that the data be in a more esoteric format. A script located in the page generated for the user can use the `onSubmit` event handler to perform the last minute assembly of user-friendly data into database-friendly data in a hidden field. When the CGI program receives the request from the client, it passes along the hidden field value to the database.

I am not a fan of the hidden object for use on client-side-only JavaScript applications. If I want to deliver with my JavaScript-enabled pages some default data collections or values, I do so in JavaScript variables and arrays as part of the script.

Because scripted changes to the contents of a hidden field are fragile (for example, a soft reload erases the changes), the only place you should consider making such changes is in the same script that submits a form to a CGI program or in a function triggered by an `onSubmit` event handler. In effect, you're just using the hidden fields as holding pens for the scripted data to be submitted. For more persistent storage, use the `document.cookie` property or genuine text fields in hidden frames, even if just for the duration of the visit to the page.

For information about the properties of the hidden object, consult the earlier listing for the text input object. The `type` property for this object returns `hidden`.

TEXTAREA Element Object

For HTML element properties, methods, and event handlers, see Chapter 15.

Properties	Methods	Event Handlers
·cols	createTextRange()	onAfterUpdate†
form†	select()†	onBeforeUpdate†
name†		onChange
readOnly†		onErrorUpdate†
rows		
type†		
wrap		

† See text input object.

Syntax

Accessing TEXTAREA element object properties or methods:

(All)	`[window.]document.`*`formName.textareaName.property`* `|` *`method([parameters])`*
(All)	`[window.]document.`*`formName.`*`elements[`*`index`*`].`*`property`* `|` *`method([parameters])`*
(All)	`[window.]document.forms[`*`index`*`].`*`textareaName.property`* `|` *`method([parameters])`*
(All)	`[window.]document.forms["`*`formName`*`"].`*`textareaName.property`* `|` *`method([parameters])`*

```
(All)       [window.]document.forms["formName"].elements[index].property |
            method([parameters])
(IE4+)      [window.]document.all.elemID.property | method([parameters])
(IE5+/NN6)  [window.]document.getElementById("elemID").property |
            method([parameters])
```

About this object

Although not in the same HTML syntax family as other <INPUT> elements of a form, a TEXTAREA object is indeed a form input element, providing multiple-line text input facilities. Although some browsers let you put a TEXTAREA element anywhere in a document, it really should be contained by a FORM element.

A TEXTAREA object closely resembles a text object, except for attributes that define its physical appearance on the page. Because the intended use of a TEXTAREA object is for multiple-line text input, the attributes include specifications for height (number of rows) and width (number of columns in the monospaced font). No matter what size you specify, the browser displays a textarea with horizontal and vertical scrollbars in older browsers; more recent browsers tend to be smarter about displaying scrollbars only when needed (although there are exceptions). Text entered in the textarea wraps within the visible rectangle of the field if you set the WRAP attribute to virtual or physical in NN and soft or hard in IE; otherwise the text scrolls for a significant distance horizontally (the horizontal scrollbar appears when wrapping has the default off setting). This field is, indeed, a primitive text field by GUI computing standards in that font specifications made possible in newer browsers by way of style sheets apply to all text in the box.

All properties, methods, and event handlers of text objects apply to the TEXTAREA object. They all behave exactly the same way (except, of course, for the type property, which is textarea). Therefore, refer to the previous listings for the text object for scripting details for those items. Discussed next are a handful of additional properties that are unique to the TEXTAREA object.

Carriage returns inside textareas

The three classes of operating systems supported by Netscape Navigator — Windows, Macintosh, and UNIX — do not agree about what constitutes a carriage return character in a text string. This discrepancy carries over to the TEXTAREA object and its contents on these platforms.

After a user enters text and uses Enter/Return on the keyboard, one or more unseen characters are inserted into the string. In the parlance of JavaScript's literal string characters, the carriage return consists of some combination of the new line (\n) and return (\r) character. The following table shows the characters inserted into the string for each operating system category.

Operating System	Character String
Windows	\r\n
Macintosh	\r
Unix	\n

This tidbit is valuable if you need to remove carriage returns from a textarea for processing in a CGI or local script. The problem is that you obviously need to perform platform-specific operations on each. For the situation in which you must preserve the carriage return locations, but your server-side database cannot accept the carriage return values, I suggest you use the `string.escape()` method to URL-encode the string. The return character is converted to %0D and the newline character is converted to %0A. Of course these characters occupy extra character spaces in your database, so these additions must be accounted for in your database design.

As far as writing carriage returns into textareas, the situation is a bit easier. From NN3 and IE4 onward, if you specify any one of the combinations in the preceding table, all platforms know how to automatically convert the data to the form native to the operating system. Therefore, you can set the value of a TEXTAREA object to `1\r\n2\r\n3` in all platforms, and a columnar list of the numbers 1, 2, and 3 will appear in those fields. Or, if you URL-encoded the text for saving to a database, you can unescape that character string before setting the textarea value, and no matter what platform the visitor has, the carriage returns are rendered correctly. Upon reading those values again by script, you can see that the carriage returns are in the form of the platform (shown in the previous table).

Properties

```
cols
rows
```

Value: Integer   Read/Write

	NN2	NN3	NN4	NN6	IE3/J1	IE3/J2	IE4	IE5	IE5.5
Compatibility				✓			✓	✓	✓

The displayed size of a TEXTAREA element is defined by its COLS and ROWS attributes, which are represented in the object model by the `cols` and `rows` properties, respectively. Values for these properties are integers. For `cols`, the number represents the number of characters that can be displayed without horizontal scrolling of the textarea; for `rows`, the number is the number of lines of text that can be displayed without vertical scrolling.

Example on the CD-ROM

Related Items: `wrap` property.

wrap

Value: String   Read/Write

	NN2	NN3	NN4	NN6	IE3/J1	IE3/J2	IE4	IE5	IE5.5
Compatibility							✓	✓	✓

The `wrap` property represents the WRAP attribute, which, surprisingly, is not a W3C-sanctioned attribute as of HTML 4.0. In any case, IE4+ lets you adjust the property by scripting. Allowable string values are `soft`, `hard`, and `off`. The browser adds soft returns (the default in IE) to word-wrap the content, but no carriage return characters are actually inserted into the text. A setting for hard returns means that carriage return characters are added to the text (and would be submitted with the value to a server CGI). With wrap set to `off`, text continues to extend beyond the right edge of the textarea until the user manually types the Enter/Return key.

Related Items: `cols` property.

Methods
createTextRange()

Returns: `TextRange` object.

	NN2	NN3	NN4	NN6	IE3/J1	IE3/J2	IE4	IE5	IE5.5
Compatibility							✓	✓	✓

The `createTextRange()` method for a TEXTAREA operates just as the `document.createTextRange()` method, except that the range consists of text inside the TEXTAREA element, apart from the regular body content. This version of the `TextRange` object comes in handy when you want a script to control the location of the text insertion pointer inside a TEXTAREA element for the user.

Example on the CD-ROM

Related Items: `TextRange` object (Chapter 19).

✦   ✦   ✦

Select, Option, and FileUpload Objects

Selection lists — whether in the form of pop-up menus or scrolling lists — are space-saving form elements in HTML pages. They enable designers to present a lot of information in a comparatively small space. At the same time, users are familiar with the interface elements from working in their own operating systems' preference dialog boxes and application windows.

However, selection lists are more difficult to script, especially in older browsers, because the objects themselves are complicated entities. Scripts find all the real data associated with the form control in OPTION elements that are nested inside SELECT elements. As you can see throughout this chapter, backward-compatible references necessary to extract information from a SELECT element object and its OPTION objects can get pretty long. The results, however, are worth the effort.

The other object covered in this chapter, the fileUpload input object, is frequently misunderstood as being more powerful than it actually is. It is, alas, not the great file transfer elixir desired by many page authors.

SELECT Element Object

For HTML element properties, methods, and event handlers, see Chapter 15.

Properties	Methods	Event Handlers
form†	options[i].add()	onChange
length	item()	
multiple	namedItem()	
name†	options[i].remove()	
options		
selectedIndex		
size		
type		
value		

†See text input object (Chapter 25).

Syntax

Accessing SELECT element object properties:

```
(All)      [window.]document.formName.selectName.property |
           method([parameters])
(All)      [window.]document.formName.elements[index].property |
           method([parameters])
(All)      [window.]document.forms[index].selectName.property |
           method([parameters])
(All)      [window.]document.forms["formName"].selectName.property |
           method([parameters])
(All)      [window.]document.forms["formName"].elements[index].property |
           method([parameters])
(IE4+)     [window.]document.all.elemID.property | method([parameters])
(IE5+/NN6) [window.]document.getElementById("elemID").property |
           method([parameters])
```

About this object

SELECT element objects are perhaps the most visually interesting user interface elements among the standard built-in objects. In one format, they appear on the page as pop-up lists; in another format, they appear as scrolling list boxes. Pop-up lists, in particular, offer efficient use of page real estate for presenting a list of choices for the user. Moreover, only the choice selected by the user shows on the page, minimizing the clutter of unneeded verbiage.

Compared with other JavaScript objects, SELECT objects are difficult to script — mostly because of the complexity of data that goes into a list of items. What the user sees as a SELECT element on the page consists of both that element and OPTION elements that contain the actual choices from which the user makes a selection. Some properties that are of value to scripters belong to the SELECT object, while others belong to the nested OPTION objects. For example, you can extract the number (index) of the currently selected option in the list — a property of the entire SELECT object. To get the displayed text of the selected option, how-ever, you must zero in further to extract the `text` property of a single option among all options defined for the object.

When you define a SELECT object within a form, the construction of the `<SELECT>...</SELECT>` tag pair is easy to inadvertently mess up. First, most attributes that define the entire object — such as `NAME`, `SIZE`, and event handlers — are attributes of the opening `<SELECT>` tag. Between the end of the opening tag and the closing `</SELECT>` tag are additional tags for each option to be displayed in the list. The following object definition creates a selection pop-up list containing three color choices:

```
<FORM>
<SELECT NAME="RGBColors" onChange="changeColor(this)">
    <OPTION SELECTED>Red
    <OPTION>Green
    <OPTION>Blue
</SELECT>
</FORM>
```

The indented formatting of the tags in the HTML document is not critical. I indent the lines of options merely for the sake of readability.

By default, a SELECT element is rendered as a pop-up list. To make it appear as a scrolled list, assign an integer value greater than 1 to the `SIZE` attribute to specify how many options should be visible in the list without scrolling — how tall the list's box should be, measured in lines. Because scrollbars in GUI environments tend to require a fair amount of space to display a minimum set of clickable areas (includ-ing sliding "thumbs"), you should set list-box style sizes to no less than 4. If that makes the list box too tall for your page design, consider using a pop-up menu instead.

Significant differences exist in the way each GUI platform presents pop-up menus. Because each browser sometimes relies on the operating system to display its native pop-up menu style (and sometimes the browser designers go their own way), considerable differences exist among the OS and browser platforms in the size of a given pop-up menu. What fits nicely within a standard window width of one OS may not fit in the window of another OS in a different browser. In other words, you cannot rely on any SELECT object having a precise dimension on a page (in case you're trying to align a SELECT object with an image).

In list-box form, you can set a SELECT object to accept multiple, noncontiguous selections. Users typically accomplish such selections by holding down a modifier key (the Shift, Ctrl, or ⌘ key, depending on the operating system) while clicking additional options. To switch on this capability for a SELECT object, include the MULTIPLE attribute constant in the definition.

For each entry in a list, your <SELECT> tag definition must include an <OPTION> tag plus the text as you want it to appear in the list. If you want a pop-up list to show a default selection when the page loads, you must attach a SELECTED attribute to that item's <OPTION> tag. Without this attribute, the default item may be empty or the first item, depending on the browser. (I go more in depth about this in the OPTION object discussion later in this chapter.) You can also assign a string to each OPTION's VALUE attribute. As with radio buttons, this value can be text other than the wording displayed in the list. In essence, your script can act on that "hidden" value rather than on the displayed text, such as letting a plain-language select listing actually refer to a complex URL. This string value is also the value sent to a CGI program (as part of the name/value pair) when the user submits the SELECT object's form.

One behavioral aspect of the SELECT object may influence your page design. The onChange event handler triggers immediately when a user makes a new selection in a pop-up list (except in cases affected by a Navigator 2 bug on Windows versions). If you prefer to delay any action until the user makes other settings in the form, omit an onChange event handler in the SELECT object — but be sure to create a button that enables users to initiate an action governed by those user settings.

Modifying SELECT options (NN3+, IE4+)

Script control gives you considerable flexibility in modifying the contents and selection of a SELECT object. These powers are available only in NN3+ or IE4+. Some of this flexibility is rather straightforward, such as changing the *selectObj*.options[i].text property to alter the display of a single-option entry. The situation gets tricky, though, when the number of options in the SELECT object changes. Your choices include

✦ Removing an individual option (and thus collapsing the list)

✦ Reducing an existing list to a fewer number of options

✦ Removing all options

✦ Adding new options to a SELECT object

To remove an option from the list, set the specific option to `null`. For example, if a list contains five items and you want to eliminate the third item altogether (reducing the list to four items), the syntax (from the SELECT object reference) for doing that task is this:

```
selectObj.options[2] = null
```

After this statement, `selectObj.options.length` equals 4.

In another scenario, suppose that a SELECT object has five options in it and you want to replace it with one having only three options. You first must hard-code the `length` property to 3:

```
selectObj.options.length = 3
```

Then, set individual `text` and `value` properties for index values 0 through 2.

Perhaps you want to start building a new list of contents by completely deleting the original list (without harming the SELECT object). To accomplish this, set the `length` to 0:

```
selectObj.options.length = 0
```

From here, you have to create new options (as you do when you want to expand a list from, say, three to seven options). The mechanism for creating a new option involves an object constructor: `new Option()`. This constructor accepts up to four parameters, which enable you to specify the equivalent of an `<OPTION>` tag's attributes:

✦ Text to be displayed in the option

✦ Contents of the option's `value` property

✦ Whether the item is the `defaultSelected` option (Boolean)

✦ Whether the item is selected (Boolean)

You can set any (or none) of these items as part of the constructor and return to other statements to set their properties. I suggest setting the first two parameters (leave the others blank) and then setting the `selected` property separately. The following is an example of a statement that creates a new, fifth entry in a SELECT object and sets both its displayed `text` and `value` properties:

```
selectObj.options[4] = new Option("Yahoo","http://www.yahoo.com")
```

To demonstrate all of these techniques, Listing 26-1 enables you to change the text of a SELECT object — first by adjusting the text properties in the same number of options and then by creating an entirely new set of options. Radio button `onClick` event handlers trigger functions for making these changes — rare examples of when radio buttons can logically initiate visible action.

Listing 26-1: **Modifying SELECT Options**

```
<HTML>
<HEAD>
<TITLE>Changing Options On The Fly</TITLE>
<SCRIPT LANGUAGE="JavaScript">
// flag to reload page for older NNs
var isPreNN6 = (navigator.appName == "Netscape" &&
parseInt(navigator.appVersion) <= 4)

// initialize color list arrays
plainList = new Array(6)
hardList = new Array(6)
plainList[0] = "cyan"
hardList[0] = "#00FFFF"
plainList[1] = "magenta"
hardList[1] = "#FF00FF"
plainList[2] = "yellow"
hardList[2] = "#FFFF00"
plainList[3] = "lightgoldenrodyellow"
hardList[3] = "#FAFAD2"
plainList[4] = "salmon"
hardList[4] = "#FA8072"
plainList[5] = "dodgerblue"
hardList[5] = "#1E90FF"

// change color language set
function setLang(which) {
    var listObj = document.forms[0].colors
    // filter out old browsers
    if (listObj.type) {
        // find out if it's 3 or 6 entries
        var listLength = listObj.length
        // save selected index
        var currSelected = listObj.selectedIndex
        // replace individual existing entries
        for (var i = 0; i < listLength; i++) {
            if (which == "plain") {
                listObj.options[i].text = plainList[i]
            } else {
                listObj.options[i].text = hardList[i]
            }
        }
        if (isPreNN6) {
            history.go(0)
        } else {
            listObj.selectedIndex = currSelected
        }
    }
}
```

```
// create entirely new options list
function setCount(choice) {
    var listObj = document.forms[0].colors
    // filter out old browsers
    if (listObj.type) {
        // get language setting
        var lang = (document.forms[0].geekLevel[0].checked) ? "plain" : "hard"
        // empty options from list
        listObj.length = 0
        // create new option object for each entry
        for (var i = 0; i < choice.value; i++) {
            if (lang == "plain") {
                listObj.options[i] = new Option(plainList[i])
            } else {
                listObj.options[i] = new Option(hardList[i])
            }
        }
        listObj.options[0].selected = true
        if (isPreNN6) {
            history.go(0)
        }
    }
}
</SCRIPT>
</HEAD>

<BODY>
<H1>Flying Select Options</H1>
<FORM>
Choose a palette size:
<INPUT TYPE="radio" NAME="paletteSize" VALUE=3
onClick="setCount(this)" CHECKED>Three
<INPUT TYPE="radio" NAME="paletteSize" VALUE=6
onClick="setCount(this)">Six
<P>
Choose geek level:
<INPUT TYPE="radio" NAME="geekLevel" VALUE=""
onClick="setLang('plain')" CHECKED>Plain-language
<INPUT TYPE="radio" NAME="geekLevel" VALUE=""
onClick="setLang('hard')">Gimme hex-triplets!
<P>
Select a color:
<SELECT NAME="colors">
    <OPTION SELECTED>cyan
    <OPTION>magenta
    <OPTION>yellow
</SELECT>
</FORM>
</BODY>
</HTML>
```

In an effort to make this code easily maintainable, the color choice lists (one in plain language, the other in hexadecimal triplet color specifications) are established as two separate arrays. Repeat loops in both large functions can work with these arrays no matter how big they get.

The first two radio buttons (see Figure 26-1) trigger the `setLang()` function. This function's first task is to extract a reference to the SELECT object to make additional references shorter (just `listObj`). Then by way of the `length` property, you find out how many items are currently displayed in the list because you just want to replace as many items as are already there. In the repeat loop, you set the `text` property of the existing SELECT options to corresponding entries in either of the two array listings.

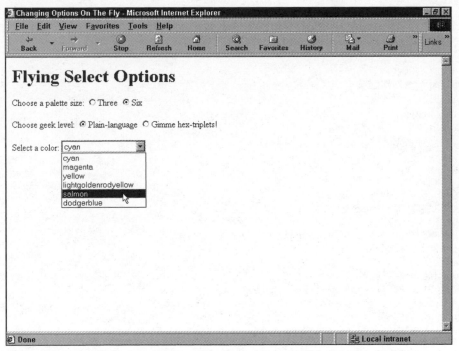

Figure 26-1: Radio button choices alter the contents of the SELECT object on the fly.

In the second pair of radio buttons, each button stores a value indicating how many items should be displayed when the user clicks the button. This number is picked up by the `setCount()` function and is used in the repeat loop as a maximum counting point. In the meantime, the function finds the selected language radio button and zeros out the SELECT object entirely. Options are rebuilt from scratch using the new Option() constructor for each option. The parameters are the corresponding display text entries from the arrays. Because none of these new options have other properties set (such as which one should be selected by default), the function sets that property of the first item in the list.

Notice that both functions call history.go(0) for NN3 and NN4 browsers after setting up their SELECT objects. The purpose of this call is to give these earlier Navigator versions an opportunity to resize the SELECT object to accommodate the contents of the list. The difference in size here is especially noticeable when you switch from the six-color, plain-language list to any other list. Without resizing, some long items are not readable. IE4+ and NN6, on the other hand, automatically redraw the page to the newly sized form element.

Modifying SELECT options (IE4+)

Microsoft offers another way to modify SELECT element options for IE4+, but the technique involves two proprietary methods of the options array property of the SELECT object. Because I cover all other ways of modifying the SELECT element in this section, I cover the IE way of doing things here as well.

The two options array methods are add() and remove(). The add() method takes one required parameter and one optional parameter. The required parameter is a reference to an OPTION element object that your script creates in another statement (using the document.createElement() method). If you omit the second parameter to add(), the new OPTION element is appended to the current collection of items. But you can also specify an index value as the second parameter. The index points to the position in the options array where the new item is to be inserted.

Listing 26-2 shows how to modify the two main functions from Listing 26-1 using the IE approach exclusively (changes and additions appear in bold). The script assumes that only IE browsers ever load the page (in other words, there is no filtering for browser brand here). When replacing one set of options with another, there are two approaches demonstrated. In the first (the setLang() function), the replacements have the same number of items, so the length of existing options provides a counter and index value for the remove() and add() methods. But when the number of items may change (as in the setCount() function), a tight loop removes all items before they are added back via the add() method without a second parameter (items are appended to the list). The approach shown in Listing 26-2 has no specific benefit over that of Listing 26-1.

Listing 26-2: **Modifying SELECT Options (IE4+)**

```
// change color language set
function setLang(which) {
    var listObj = document.forms[0].colors
    var newOpt
    // filter out old IE browsers
    if (listObj.type) {
        // find out if it's 3 or 6 entries
        var listLength = listObj.length
        // save selected index
        var currSelected = listObj.selectedIndex
        // replace individual existing entries
        for (var i = 0; i < listLength; i++) {
            newOpt = document.createElement("OPTION")
            newOpt.text = (which == "plain") ? plainList[i] : hardList[i]
            listObj.options.remove(i)
            listObj.options.add(newOpt, i)
        }
        listObj.selectedIndex = currSelected
    }
}

// create entirely new options list
function setCount(choice) {
    var listObj = document.forms[0].colors
    var newOpt
    // filter out old browsers
    if (listObj.type) {
        // get language setting
        var lang = (document.forms[0].geekLevel[0].checked) ? "plain" : "hard"
        // empty options from list
        while (listObj.options.length) {
            listObj.options.remove(0)
        }
        // create new option object for each entry
        for (var i = 0; i < choice.value; i++) {
            newOpt = document.createElement("OPTION")
            newOpt.text = (lang == "plain") ? plainList[i] : hardList[i]
            listObj.options.add(newOpt)
        }
        listObj.options[0].selected = true
    }
}
```

Modifying SELECT options (W3C DOM)

Yet another approach is possible in browsers that closely adhere to the W3C DOM Level 2 standard. In NN6, for example, you can use the add() and remove() methods of the SELECT element object. They work very much like the same-named methods for the options array in IE4+, but these are methods of the SELECT element object itself. The other main difference between the two syntaxes is that the NN6 add() method does not use the index value as the second parameter but rather a reference to the OPTION element object before which the new option is inserted. The second parameter is required, so to simply append the new item at the end of the current list, supply null as the parameter. Listing 26-3 shows the W3C-compatible version of the SELECT element modification scripts shown in Listings 26-1 and 26-2. I highlight source code lines in bold that exhibit differences between the IE4+ and W3C DOM versions.

Listing 26-3: **Modifying SELECT Options (NN6+)**

```
// change color language set
function setLang(which) {
    var listObj = document.forms[0].colors
    var newOpt
    // filter out old IE browsers
    if (listObj.type) {
        // find out if it's 3 or 6 entries
        var listLength = listObj.length
        // save selected index
        var currSelected = listObj.selectedIndex
        // replace individual existing entries
        for (var i = 0; i < listLength; i++) {
            newOpt = document.createElement("OPTION")
            newOpt.text = (which == "plain") ? plainList[i] : hardList[i]
            listObj.remove(i)
            listObj.add(newOpt, listObj.options[i])
        }
        listObj.selectedIndex = currSelected
    }
}

// create entirely new options list
function setCount(choice) {
    var listObj = document.forms[0].colors
    var newOpt
    // filter out old browsers
    if (listObj.type) {
        // get language setting
        var lang = (document.forms[0].geekLevel[0].checked) ? "plain" : "hard"
        // empty options from list
```

Continued

Listing 26-3 *(continued)*

```
    while (listObj.options.length) {
        listObj.remove(0)
    }
    // create new option object for each entry
    for (var i = 0; i < choice.value; i++) {
        newOpt = document.createElement("OPTION")
        newOpt.text = (lang == "plain") ? plainList[i] : hardList[i]
        listObj.add(newOpt, null)
    }
    listObj.options[0].selected = true
    }
}
```

As with the IE version, the W3C version offers no specific benefit over the original, backward-compatible approach. Choose the most modern one that fits the types of browsers you need to support with your page.

Properties

`length`

Value: Integer   Read/Write (see text)

	NN2	NN3	NN4	NN6	IE3/J1	IE3/J2	IE4	IE5	IE5.5
Compatibility	✓	✓	✓	✓	✓	✓	✓	✓	✓

Like all JavaScript arrays, the `options` array has a `length` property of its own. But rather than having to reference the `options` array to determine its length, the SELECT object has its own `length` property that you use to find out how many items are in the list. This value is the number of options in the object. A SELECT object with three choices in it has a `length` property value of 3.

In NN3+ and IE4+, you can adjust this value downward after the document loads. This is one way to decrease the number of options in a list. Setting the value to 0 causes the SELECT object to empty but not disappear.

Example on the CD-ROM

Related Item: options property.

multiple

Value: Boolean   Read/Write

	NN2	NN3	NN4	NN6	IE3/J1	IE3/J2	IE4	IE5	IE5.5
Compatibility				✓			✓	✓	✓

The multiple property represents the MULTIPLE attribute setting for a SELECT element object. If the value is true, the element accepts multiple selections by the user (for example, Ctrl+clicking in Windows). If you want to convert a pop-up list into a multiple SELECT pick list, you must also adjust the size property to direct the browser to render a set number of visible choices in the list.

Example on the CD-ROM

Related Item: size property.

options[*index*]

Value: Array of OPTION element objects   Read-Only

	NN2	NN3	NN4	NN6	IE3/J1	IE3/J2	IE4	IE5	IE5.5
Compatibility	✓	✓	✓	✓	✓	✓	✓	✓	✓

You typically don't summon this property by itself. Rather, it is part of a reference to a specific option's properties (or methods in later browsers) within the entire SELECT object. In other words, the options property is a kind of gateway to more specific properties, such as the value assigned to a single option within the list. In early versions of NN, displaying an alert that referenced the options array showed the HTML for the options. But more recent browsers simply return an indication that the value is an object.

In newer browsers (IE4+ and NN6+), you can reference individual options as separate HTML element objects. These references do not require the reference to the containing FORM or SELECT element objects. For backward compatibility, however, I recommend you stick with the long references through the SELECT objects.

I list the next several properties here in the SELECT object discussion because they are backward-compatible with all browsers, including browsers that don't treat the OPTION element as a distinct object. Be aware that all properties shown here that include options[*index*] as part of their references are also properties of the OPTION element object in IE4+ and NN6+.

Example on the CD-ROM

Related Items: All options[*index*].property items.

options[*index*].defaultSelected

Value: Boolean

Read-Only

	NN2	NN3	NN4	NN6	IE3/J1	IE3/J2	IE4	IE5	IE5.5
Compatibility	✓	✓	✓	✓	✓	✓	✓	✓	✓

If your SELECT object definition includes one option that features the SELECTED attribute, that option's defaultSelected property is set to true. The defaultSelected property for all other options is false. If you define a SELECT object that allows multiple selections (and whose SIZE attribute is greater than 1), however, you can define the SELECTED attribute for more than one option definition. When the page loads, all items with that attribute are preselected for the user (even in noncontiguous groups).

Example on the CD-ROM

Related Item: options[*index*].selected property.

options[*index*].index

Value: Integer

Read-Only

	NN2	NN3	NN4	NN6	IE3/J1	IE3/J2	IE4	IE5	IE5.5
Compatibility	✓	✓	✓	✓	✓	✓	✓	✓	✓

The index value of any single option in a SELECT object likely is a redundant value in your scripting. Because you cannot access the option without knowing the index anyway (in brackets as part of the options[*index*] array reference), you have little need to extract the index value. The value is a property of the item just the same.

On the CD-ROM Example on the CD-ROM

Related Item: options property.

options[*index*].selected

Value: Boolean   Read/Write

	NN2	NN3	NN4	NN6	IE3/J1	IE3/J2	IE4	IE5	IE5.5
Compatibility	✓	✓	✓	✓	✓	✓	✓	✓	✓

As mentioned earlier in the discussion of this object, better ways exist for determining which option a user selects from a list than looping through all options and examining the selected property. An exception to that "rule" occurs when you set up a list box to enable multiple selections. In this situation, the selectedIndex property returns an integer of only the topmost item selected. Therefore, your script needs to look at the true or false values of the selected property for each option in the list and determine what to do with the text or value data.

On the CD-ROM Example (with Listing 26-4) on the CD-ROM

Related Items: options[*index*].text, options[*index*].value, selectedIndex properties.

options[*index*].text

Value: String   Read/Write

	NN2	NN3	NN4	NN6	IE3/J1	IE3/J2	IE4	IE5	IE5.5
Compatibility	✓	✓	✓	✓	✓	✓	✓	✓	✓

The text property of an option is the text of the item as it appears in the list. If you can pass that wording along with your script to perform appropriate tasks, this property is the one you want to extract for further processing. But if your processing requires other strings associated with each option, assign a VALUE attribute in the definition and extract the options[*index*].value property (see Listing 26-6).

On the CD-ROM

Example (with Listing 26-5) on the CD-ROM

Related Item: options[*index*].value property.

options[*index*].value

Value: String   Read/Write

	NN2	NN3	NN4	NN6	IE3/J1	IE3/J2	IE4	IE5	IE5.5
Compatibility	✓	✓	✓	✓	✓	✓	✓	✓	✓

In many instances, the words in the options list appear in a form that is convenient for the document's users but inconvenient for the scripts behind the page. Rather than set up an elaborate lookup routine to match the selectedIndex or options[*index*].text values with the values your script needs, you can easily store those values in the VALUE attribute of each <OPTION> definition of the SELECT object. You can then extract those values as needed.

You can store any string expression in the VALUE attributes. That includes URLs, object properties, or even entire page descriptions that you want to send to a parent.frames[*index*].document.write() method.

Starting with IE4 and NN6, the SELECT element object itself has a value property that returns the value property of the selected option. But for backward compatibility, be sure to use the longer approach shown in the following example.

On the CD-ROM

Example (with Listing 26-6) on the CD-ROM

Related Item: options[*index*].text property.

selectedIndex

Value: Integer   Read/Write

	NN2	NN3	NN4	NN6	IE3/J1	IE3/J2	IE4	IE5	IE5.5
Compatibility	✓	✓	✓	✓	✓	✓	✓	✓	✓

When a user clicks a choice in a selection list, the selectedIndex property changes to a zero-based number corresponding to that item in the list. The first item has a value of 0. This information is valuable to a script that needs to extract the value or text of a selected item for further processing.

You can use this information as a shortcut to getting at a selected option's properties. To examine a SELECT object's selected property, rather than cycling through every option in a repeat loop, use the object's selectedIndex property to fill in the index value for the reference to the selected item. The wording gets kind of long; but from an execution standpoint, this methodology is much more efficient. Note, however, that when the SELECT object is a multiple-style, the selectedIndex property value reflects the index of only the topmost item selected in the list.

To script the selection of a particular item, assign an integer value to the SELECT element object's selectedIndex property, as shown in Listings 26-1 through 26-3.

Example (with Listing 26-7) on the CD-ROM

Related Item: options property.

size

Value: Integer   Read/Write

	NN2	NN3	NN4	NN6	IE3/J1	IE3/J2	IE4	IE5	IE5.5
Compatibility				✓			✓	✓	✓

The size property represents the SIZE attribute setting for a SELECT element object. You can modify the integer value of this property to change the number of options that are visible in a pick list without having to scroll.

Example on the CD-ROM

Related Item: multiple property.

type

Value: String   Read-Only

	NN2	NN3	NN4	NN6	IE3/J1	IE3/J2	IE4	IE5	IE5.5
Compatibility		✓	✓	✓			✓	✓	✓

Use the type property to help you identify a SELECT object from an unknown group of form elements. The precise string returned for this property depends on whether the SELECT object is defined as a single (select-one) or multiple (select-multiple) type.

Related Item: form.elements property.

value

Value: String   Read/Write (see text)

	NN2	NN3	NN4	NN6	IE3/J1	IE3/J2	IE4	IE5	IE5.5
Compatibility				✓			✓	✓	✓

The more recent browsers (and the W3C DOM) provide a value property for the SELECT element object. This property returns the string assigned to the VALUE attribute (or value property) of the currently selected OPTION element. If you do not assign a string to the attribute or property, the value property returns an empty string. For these browser generations, you can use this shortcut reference to the SELECT element object's value property instead of the longer version that requires a reference to the selectedIndex property and the options array of the element object.

If you assign a new string to this property (and that string does not match an existing option value), IE accepts the new `value` property and displays an empty item in the list. While this property is technically read/write also in NN6, assigning a string to this property does not override the string returned based on the user selection.

On the CD-ROM   Example on the CD-ROM

Related Item: `options[index].value` property.

Methods
`options[index].add(elementRef[, index])`
`options[index].remove()`

Returns: Nothing.

	NN2	NN3	NN4	NN6	IE3/J1	IE3/J2	IE4	IE5	IE5.5
Compatibility							✓	✓	✓

These two IE-specific methods belong to the `options` array property of a SELECT element object. See the discussion at the opening of the SELECT element object earlier in this chapter to see how to use these methods and their counterparts in other browser versions and object models.

`item(index)`
`namedItem("optionID")`

Returns: OPTION element reference.

	NN2	NN3	NN4	NN6	IE3/J1	IE3/J2	IE4	IE5	IE5.5
Compatibility				✓					

The `item()` and `namedItem()` methods are Netscape-specific convenience methods that access OPTION element objects nested inside a SELECT object. In a sense, they provide shortcuts to referencing nested options without having to use the `options` array property and the indexing within that array.

The parameter for the item() method is an index integer value. For example, the following two statements refer to the same OPTION element object:

```
document.forms[0].mySelect.options[2]
document.forms[0].mySelect.item(2)
```

If your script knows the ID of an OPTION element, then it can use the namedItem() method, supplying the string version of the ID as the parameter, to return a reference to that option element.

On the CD-ROM

Example on the CD-ROM

Related Item: options property.

Event handlers

onChange

	NN2	NN3	NN4	NN6	IE3/J1	IE3/J2	IE4	IE5	IE5.5
Compatibility	✓	✓	✓	✓	✓	✓	✓	✓	✓

As a user clicks a new choice in a SELECT object, the object receives a change event that the onChange event handler can capture. In examples earlier in this section (Listings 26-6 and 26-7, for example), the action is handed over to a separate button. This design may make sense in some circumstances, especially when you use multiple SELECT lists or any list box. (Typically, clicking a list box item does not trigger any action that the user sees.) But for most pop-up menus, triggering the action when the user makes a choice is desirable.

To bring a pop-up menu to life, add an onChange event handler to the <SELECT> definition. If the user makes the same choice as previously selected, the onChange event handler is not triggered. In this case, you can still trigger an action via the onClick event handler; but this event works for the SELECT object only in IE4+ and NN6+.

Note

A bug in the Windows versions of Navigator 2 (only) causes the onChange event handler in SELECT objects to fail unless the user clicks outside the SELECT object. If your audience includes users of these browsers, then consider adding a special routine that employs document.write() to include a "do nothing" button next to the SELECT object. This button should entice the user to click out of the SELECT object. The onChange event handler fires at a click of that button (or any other location on the page).

Example (with Listing 26-8) on the CD-ROM

OPTION Element Object

For HTML element properties, methods, and event handlers, see Chapter 15.

Properties	Methods	Event Handlers
defaultSelected		
form†		
label		
selected		
text		
value		

†See text input object (Chapter 25).

Syntax

Accessing OPTION object properties:

(All)	[window.]document.*formName*.*selectName*.options[*index*].*property* | *method*([*parameters*])
(All)	[window.]document.*formName*.elements[*index*].options[*index*].*property* | *method*([*parameters*])
(All)	[window.]document.forms[*index*].*selectName*.options[*index*].*property* | *method*([*parameters*])
(All)	[window.]document.forms["*formName*"].*selectName*.options[*index*].*property* | *method*([*parameters*])
(All)	[window.]document.forms["*formName*"].elements[*index*].options[*index*].*property* | *method*([*parameters*])
(IE4+)	[window.]document.all.*elemID*.*property* | *method*([*parameters*])
(IE5+/NN6+)	[window.]document.getElementById("*elemID*").*property* | *method*([*parameters*])
(NN6)	[window.]document.forms[*index*].*selectName*.item(*index*).*property* | *method*([*parameters*])
(NN6)	[window.]document.forms["*formName*"].*selectName*.namedItem(*elemID*).*property* | *method*([*parameters*])

About this object

OPTION elements are nested inside SELECT elements. Each option represents an item in the list of choices presented by the SELECT element. Properties of the OPTION element object let scripts inspect whether a particular option is currently selected or is the default selection. Other properties enable you to get or set the hidden value associated with the option as well as the visible text. For more details about the interaction between the SELECT and OPTION element objects, see the discussion about the SELECT object earlier in this chapter as well as the discussion of the properties and methods associated with the options array returned by the SELECT object's options property.

I discuss all backward-compatible OPTION object properties (defaultSelected, selected, text, and value) among the options property descriptions in the SELECT object section. The only items listed in this section are those that are unique to the OPTION element object defined in newer browsers.

In NN3+ and IE4+, there is a provision for creating a new option object via an Option object constructor function. The syntax is as follows:

```
var newOption = new Option("text","value")
```

Here, *text* is the string that is displayed for the item in the list, and *value* is the string assigned to the value property of the new option. This new option object is not added to a SELECT object until you assign it to a slot in the options array of the SELECT object. You can see an example of this approach to modifying options in Listing 26-1.

Properties

label

Value: String   Read/Write

	NN2	NN3	NN4	NN6	IE3/J1	IE3/J2	IE4	IE5	IE5.5
Compatibility				✓				✓	

The label property corresponds to the HTML 4.0 LABEL attribute of an OPTION element. This attribute (and property) enables you to assign alternate text for an option. The property is implemented in IE5/Mac and NN6.

In IE5/Mac, any string assigned to the LABEL attribute or corresponding property overrides the display of text found between the start and end tags of the OPTION element. Therefore, you can assign content to both the attribute and tag, but only browsers adhering to the HTML 4.0 standard for this element display the value assigned to the label. While the label property is implemented in NN6, the browser does not modify the option item's text to reflect the property's setting.

Example on the CD-ROM

Related Item: text property.

OPTGROUP Element Object

For HTML element properties, methods, and event handlers, see Chapter 15.

Properties	Methods	Event Handlers
form†		
label		

†See text input object (Chapter 25).

Syntax

Accessing OPTGROUP object properties:

```
(IE5/Mac)    [window.]document.all.elemID".property | method([parameters])
(NN6)        [window.]document.getElementById("elemID").property |
             method([parameters])
```

	NN2	NN3	NN4	NN6	IE3/J1	IE3/J2	IE4	IE5	IE5.5
Compatibility				(✓)				(✓)	

About this object

An OPTGROUP element in the HTML 4.0 specification enables authors to group options into subgroups within a SELECT list. The label assigned to the OPTGROUP element is rendered in the list as a non-selectable item, usually differentiated from the selectable items by some alternate display. In NN6, OPTGROUP items by default are shown in bold italic, while all OPTION elements nested within an OPTGROUP are indented but with normal font characteristics. The OPTGROUP element object has fewer properties, methods, and event handlers than most elements because (as of this writing) it is not part of the IE DOM in Windows versions — although it is implemented in IE5/Mac to provide nicely formatted hierarchical menus.

Browsers not recognizing this element ignore it. All options are presented as if the OPTGROUP elements are not there.

Properties

label

Value: String   Read/Write

	NN2	NN3	NN4	NN6	IE3/J1	IE3/J2	IE4	IE5	IE5.5
Compatibility				(✓)				(✓)	

The `label` property corresponds to the HTML 4.0 `LABEL` attribute of an OPTGROUP element. This attribute (and property) enables you to assign text to the label that encompasses a group of nested OPTION elements in the pop-up list display.

Note IE5/Mac exhibits a bug that prevents scripts from assigning values to the last OPT-GROUP element inside a SELECT element.

On the CD-ROM Example (with Listing 26-9) on the CD-ROM

Related Item: `OPTION.label` property.

File Input Element Object

For HTML element properties, methods, and event handlers, see Chapter 15.

Properties	Methods	Event Handlers
defaultValue†	select()†	onchange†
form†		
name†		
readOnly†		
size†		
type†		
value†		

†See text input object (Chapter 25).

Syntax

Accessing file INPUT element object properties:

```
(NN3+/IE4+)    [window.]document.formName.inputName.property |
               method([parameters])
(NN3+/IE4+)    [window.]document.formName.elements[index].property |
               method([parameters])
(NN3+/IE4+)    [window.]document.forms[index].inputName.property |
               method([parameters])
(NN3+/IE4+)    [window.]document.forms["formName"].inputName.property |
               method([parameters])
(NN3+/IE4+)    [window.]document.forms["formName"].elements[index].property |
               method([parameters])
(IE4+)         [window.]document.all.elemID.property | method([parameters])
(IE5+/NN6)     [window.]document.getElementById("elemID").property |
               method([parameters])
```

About this object

Some Web sites enable you to upload files from the client to the server, typically by using a form-style submission to a CGI program on the server. The INPUT element whose type is set to "file" (also known as a fileUpload object) is merely a user interface that enables users to specify which file on their PC they want to upload. Without a server process capable of receiving the file, the file input element does nothing. Moreover, you must also set two FORM element attributes as follows:

```
METHOD="POST"
ENCTYPE="multipart/form-data"
```

This element displays a field and a Browse button. The Browse button leads to an Open file dialog box (in the local operating system's interface vernacular) where a user can select a file. After you make a selection, the filename (or pathname, depending on the operating system) appears in the file input element's field. The value property of the object returns the filename.

You do not have to script much for this object on the client side. The value property, for example, is read-only in earlier browsers; in addition, a form cannot surreptitiously upload a file to the server without the user's knowledge or consent.

Listing 26-10 helps you see what the element looks like. The syntax is compatible in NN3+ and IE4+.

Listing 26-10: **File Input Element**

```
<HTML>
<HEAD>
<TITLE>FileUpload Object</TITLE>
</HEAD>
<BODY>
<FORM METHOD="POST" ACTION="yourCGIURL" ENCTYPE="multipart/form-data">
File to be uploaded:
<INPUT TYPE="file" SIZE=40 NAME="fileToGo"><P>
<INPUT TYPE="button" VALUE="View Value"
onClick="alert(this.form.fileToGo.value)">
</FORM>
</BODY>
</HTML>
```

In a true production environment, a Submit button and a URL to your CGI process are specified for the ACTION attribute of the <FORM> tag.

Table and List Objects– Summary

On the CD-ROM The full version of Chapter 27 is on the CD-ROM.

Tables are incredibly popular HTML constructions. When you consider that a lot of CGI programs search SQL databases and display data gathered from SQL tables, it's not unusual to find the table concept carried over from data storage to data display. Spreadsheet programs certainly put the notion of tabular display into the minds of most computer users.

One of the truly beneficial properties of tables in HTML is that they pack a lot of page organization and alignment punch in just a few tags and attributes. Even if you're not a graphics designer or a dedicated HTML jockey, you can get rows and columns of text and images to line up perfectly on the page. This behavior also lures many page designers to sculpt elaborately detailed pages out of what appear to be positioned elements. Earlier browsers didn't offer positioning facilities, so borderless tables were torqued into performing all kinds of placement tricks with the help of precisely sized, transparent images creating the illusion of white space between carefully placed elements. If you use some of the WYSIWYG authoring tools for HTML pages, you may not realize how much table-related HTML code is generated for you as you use the tool to drag an image to a particular location on the page.

The first part of this chapter focuses on the scriptable aspects of TABLE element objects and the shopping list of elements that support tables. All of these objects became scriptable objects in browsers starting with IE4 and NN6. Table-related elements in these later browsers offer a number of methods that simplify insertion and deletion of cells and rows. For many applications, truly dynamic tables provide the most exciting creative opportunities since the mouse rollover.

A chapter dedicated to tables seems like a logical place to also cover the special formatting elements for lists. Details of ordered and unordered lists, as well as definition elements, complete the chapter.

✦   ✦   ✦

The Navigator and Other Environment Objects— Summary

CHAPTER

28

◆ ◆ ◆ ◆

In This Chapter

Determining which browser the user has

Branching scripts according to the user's operating system

Detecting plug-in support

◆ ◆ ◆ ◆

On the CD-ROM   The full version of Chapter 28 is on the CD-ROM.

Client-side scripting primarily focuses on the document inside a browser window and the content of the document. As discussed in Chapter 16, the window, too, is an important part of how you apply JavaScript on the client. But stepping out even one more level is the browser application itself. Scripts sometimes need to know about the browser and the computing environment in which it runs so that they can tailor dynamic content for the current browser and operating system.

To that end, browsers provide objects that expose as much about the client computer and the browser as is feasible within accepted principles of preserving a user's privacy. In addition to providing some of the same information that CGI programs on the server receive as environment variables, these browser-level objects also include information about how well equipped the browser is with regard to plug-ins and Java. Another object defined for NN4+ and IE4+, the screen object, reveals information about the user's video monitor, which may influence the way your scripts calculate information displayed on the page.

The objects in this chapter don't show up on the document object hierarchy diagrams, except as freestanding groups (see Appendix A). The IE4+ object model, however, incorporates these environmental objects as properties of the `window` object. Because the `window` reference is optional, you can omit it for IE and wind up with a cross-browser, compatible script in many cases.

Where the IE (for Windows anyway) and NN environments diverge significantly is in the way scripts can find out whether a particular plug-in or support for a particular MIME type is available in the current browser. As you learn in this chapter, the IE for Windows methodology can be a bit roundabout. And yet the Macintosh version of IE5+ has adopted the more straightforward approach initiated by NN3, which employs the `plugins` and `mimeTypes` arrays. An extended discussion in this chapter about how browsers associate plug-ins with file types goes a long way to helping you understand the inner workings of the multi-plug-in sound API described in Chapter 44.

✦   ✦   ✦

Event Objects

Prior to NN4 and IE4, user and system actions — events — were captured predominantly by event handlers defined as attributes inside HTML tags. For instance, when a user clicked a button, the `click` event triggered the `onClick` event handler in the tag. That handler may invoke a separate function or perform some inline JavaScript script. Even so, the events themselves were rather dumb: Either an event occurred or it didn't. Where an event occurred (that is, the screen coordinates of the pointer at the moment the mouse button was clicked) and other pertinent event tidbits (for example, whether a keyboard modifier key was pressed at the same time) were not part of the equation. Until the Version 4 browsers, that is.

While remaining fully backward-compatible with the event handler mechanism of old, Version 4 browsers had the first event model that turned events into first-class objects whose properties automatically carry a lot of relevant information about the event when it occurs. These properties are fully exposed to scripts, allowing pages to respond more intelligently about what the user does with the page and its elements.

Another new aspect of Version 4 event models was the notion of "event propagation." It was possible to have an event processed by an object higher up the element containment hierarchy whenever it made sense to have multiple objects share one event handler. That the event being processed carried along with it information about the intended target, plus other golden information nuggets, made it possible for event handler functions to be smart about processing the event without requiring an event handler call to pass all kinds of target-specific information.

Unfortunately, the joy of this newly found power is tempered by the forces of object model incompatibility. No fewer than three event object models are in use today: The one initiated by NN4 (whose importance diminishes with each passing day as users migrate to other, newer browsers); the IE4+ model;

and the model adopted by the W3C DOM Level 2 as implemented in NN6+. Many of these distinctions are addressed in the overviews of the object models in Chapter 15. In this chapter, you find out more about the actual event objects that contain all the "goodies." Where possible, cross-browser concerns are addressed.

Why "Events"?

Graphical user interfaces are more difficult to program than the "old-fashioned" command-line interface. With a command-line or menu-driven system, users were intentionally restricted in the types of actions they could take at any given moment. The world was very modal, primarily as a convenience to programmers who led users through rigid program structures.

That all changed in a graphical user interface, such as Windows, MacOS, X Window System, and all others derived from the pioneering work of the Xerox Star system. The challenge for programmers is that a good user interface in this realm must make it possible for users to perform all kinds of actions at any given moment: roll the mouse, click a button, type a key, select text, choose a pull-down menu item, and so on. To accommodate this, a program (or, better yet, the operating system) must be on the lookout for any possible activity coming from all input ports, whether it be the mouse, keyboard, or network connection.

A common methodology to accomplish this at the operating system level is to look for any kind of event, whether it comes from user action or some machine-generated activity. The operating system or program then looks up how it should process each kind of event. Such events, however, must have some smarts about them so that the program knows what and where on the screen the event is.

What an event knows (and when it knows it)

Although the way to reference an event object varies a bit among the three event models, the one concept they all share is that an event object is created the instant the event action occurs. For instance, if you click a button, an event object is created in the browser's memory. As the object is created, the browser assigns values to its properties — properties that reflect numerous characteristics of that specific event. For a click event, that information includes the coordinates of the click and which mouse button was used to generate the event. To be even more helpful, the browser does some quick calculations to determine that the coordinates of the click event coincide with the rectangular space of a button element on the screen. Therefore, the event object has as one of its properties a reference to the "screen thing" that you clicked on.

Most event object properties (all of them in some event models) are read-only, because an event object is like a snapshot of an event action. If the event model were to allow modification of event properties, performing both potentially useful and potentially unfriendly actions would be possible. For example, how frustrating would it be to a user to attempt to type into a text box only to have a keystroke modified between the actual key press and then have a totally different character appear in the text box? On the other hand, perhaps it may be useful in some situations to make sure that anything typed into a text box is converted to uppercase characters, no matter what is typed. Each event model brings its own philosophy to the table in this regard. For example, the IE4+ event model allows keyboard character events to be modified by script; the NN4 and W3C DOM event models do not.

Perhaps the most important aspect of an event object to keep in mind is that it exists only as long as scripts process the event. An event can trigger an event handler — usually a function. That function, of course, can invoke other functions. As long as statements are still executing in response to the event handler, the event object and all its properties are still "alive" and available to your scripts. But after the last script statement runs, the event object reverts to an empty object.

The reason an event object has such a brief life is that there can be only one event object at a time. In other words, no matter how complex your event handler functions are, they are executed serially (for experienced programmers: there is one execution thread). The operating system buffers events that start to bunch up on each other. Except in rare cases in which the buffer gets full and events are not recorded, event handlers are executed in the order in which the events occur.

The static Event object

Up to this point, the discussion has been about the event object (with a lowercase "e"), which is one instance of an event, with all the properties associated with that specific event action. In the NN4 and W3C DOM event models, there is also a static Event object (with an uppercase "E"). In the W3C DOM event model are additional subcategories of the Event object. These subcategories are all covered later in this chapter, but they are introduced here to draw the contrast between the event and Event objects. The former, as you've seen, is a transient object with details about a specific event action; the latter serves primarily as a holder of event-related constant values that scripts can use. The static Event object is always available to scripts inside any window or frame. If you want to see a list of all Event object properties in NN4 and NN6+, use The Evaluator (Chapter 13): enter Event into the bottom text box (also check out the KeyEvent object in NN6+).

The static Event object also turns out to be the object from which event objects are cloned. Thus, the static Event object has a number of properties and methods that apply to (are inherited by) the event objects created by event actions. These relationships are more important in the W3C DOM event model, which builds upon the DOM's object-oriented tendencies to implement the event model.

Event Propagation

Prior to the Version 4 browsers, an event fired on an object. If an event handler was defined for that event and that object, the handler executed; if there was no event handler, the event just disappeared into the ether. Newer browsers, however, send events on a longer ride, causing them to propagate through the document object models. As you know by now, three propagation models exist, one for each of the event models in use today: NN4, IE4+, and W3C DOM as implemented in NN6+. Conceptually, the NN4 and IE4+ propagation models are diametrically opposite each other. But the W3C DOM model manages to implement both models simultaneously, albeit with all new syntax so as not to step on the older models.

At the root of all three models is the notion that every event has a target. For user-initiated actions, this is fairly obvious. If you click a button or type in a text box, that button is the target of your mouse-related event; the text box is the target of your keyboard event. System-generated events are not so obvious, such as the onLoad event after a page finishes loading. In all event models, this event fires on the window object. What distinguishes the event propagation models is how an event reaches its target, and what, if anything, happens to the event after it finishes executing the event handler associated with the target.

NN4 event propagation

Although the installed base of NN4 continues to diminish, its propagation model initiated some concepts that are found in the modern W3C DOM event propagation model. The name for the model is *event capture*.

In NN4, all events propagate from the top of the document object hierarchy (starting with the window object) downward to the target object. For example, if you click a button in a form, the click event passes through the window and document (and, if available, layer) objects before reaching the button (the form object is not part of the propagation path). This propagation happens instantaneously, so that there is no performance penalty by this extra journey.

The event that passes through the window, document, and layer objects is a fully formed event object, complete with all properties relevant to that event action. Therefore, if the event were processed at the window level, one of the event object's properties is a reference to the target object, so that the event handler scripts at the window level can find out information, such as the name of the button and even get a reference to its enclosing form.

By default, event capture is turned off. To instruct the window, document, or layer object levels to process that passing click object requires turning on event capture for the window, document, and/or layer object.

Enabling NN4 event capture

All three objects just mentioned—window, document, and layer—have a captureEvents() method. You use this method to enable event capture at any of those object levels. The method requires one or more parameters, which are the event types (as supplied by Event object constants) that the object should capture, while letting all others pass untouched. For example, if you want the window object to capture all keyPress events, you include the following statement in a script that executes as the page loads:

```
window.captureEvents(Event.KEYPRESS)
```

Defining event handlers in the intended targets is also a good idea, even if they are empty (for example, `onKeyPress=""`) to help NN4 generate the event in the first place. If you want the window to capture multiple event types, string the event type constants together, separated by the pipe character:

```
window.captureEvents(Event.KEYPRESS | Event.CLICK)
```

Now you must assign an action to the event at the window's level for each event type. More than likely, you have defined functions to execute for the event. Assign a function reference to the event handler by setting the handler property of the `window` object:

```
window.onKeyPress = processKeyEvent
window.onClick = processClickEvent
```

Hereafter, if a user clicks a button or types into a field inside that window, the events are processed by their respective window-level event handler functions.

Turning off event capture

As soon as you enable event capture for a particular event type in a document, that capture remains in effect until the page unloads or you specifically disable the capture. You can turn off event capture for each event via the `window`, `document`, or layer `releaseEvents()` method. The `releaseEvents()` method takes the same kind of parameters — Event object type constants — as the `captureEvents()` method.

The act of releasing an event type simply means that events go directly to their intended targets without stopping elsewhere for processing, even if an event handler for the higher-level object is still defined. And because you can release individual event types based on parameters set for the `releaseEvents()` method, other events being captured are not affected by the release of others.

To demonstrate not only the `captureEvents()` and `releaseEvents()` methods, but other event model techniques, I present a series of several versions of the same document. Each successive version implements an added feature to help you experience the numerous interactions among events and event handling methods. The document merely contains a few buttons, plus some switches to enable and disable various methods being demonstrated in the section. A layer object is also thrown into the mixture because a lot of impetus for capturing and modifying event handling comes from application of layers in a document.

Listing 29-1 is the first example, which shows the basic event capture and release from the outermost document level. A checkbox lets you enable or disable the document-level capture of `click` events (all checkboxes in these examples use `onMouseUp` event handlers to avoid getting in the way of tracing `click` events). Because all `click` events are being captured by the outermost document, even clicks to the layer's buttons get trapped by the outermost document when `captureEvents()` is set.

Listing 29-1: **NN4 Event Capture and Release**

```
<HTML>
<HEAD>
<SCRIPT LANGUAGE="JavaScript">
function setDocCapture(enable) {
    if (!enable) {
        document.captureEvents(Event.CLICK)
    } else {
        document.releaseEvents(Event.CLICK)
    }
}
function doMainClick(e) {
    if (e.target.type == "button") {
        alert("Captured in top document")
    }
}
document.captureEvents(Event.CLICK)
document.onclick=doMainClick
</SCRIPT>
</HEAD>
<BODY>
<B>Basic document-level capture of Event.CLICK</B>
<HR>
<FORM>
<INPUT TYPE="checkbox" onMouseDown="setDocCapture(this.checked)" CHECKED>Enable
Document Capture
<HR>
<INPUT TYPE="button" VALUE="Button 'main1'" NAME="main1"
    onClick="alert('Event finally reached Button:' + this.name)">
</FORM>

<LAYER ID="layer1" LEFT=200 TOP=150 BGCOLOR="coral">
<HEAD>
</HEAD>
<BODY>
<FORM>
<BR><P><INPUT TYPE="button" VALUE="Button 'layerButton1'"
    NAME="layerButton1"
    onClick="alert('Event finally reached Button:' + this.name)"></P>
<P><INPUT TYPE="button" VALUE="Button 'layerButton2'"
    NAME="layerButton2"
    onClick="alert('Event finally reached Button:' + this.name)"></P>
</FORM>
</BODY>
</LAYER>

</BODY>
</HTML>
```

With document-level event capture turned on (the default), all click events are trapped by the document's onclick event handler property, a function that alerts the user that the event was captured by the top document. Because all click events for buttons are trapped there, even click events of the layer's buttons are trapped at the top. But if you turn off event capture, the events reach their intended targets.

Caution

If the logic of the setDocCapture() function seems backwards to you, recall that when the onMouseDown event fires on the checkbox, its state is the opposite of what it is being changed to.

In Listing 29-2, I add some code (shown in boldface) that lets the layer object capture click events whenever the outer document event capture is turned off. Inside the <LAYER> tag, a script sets the layer to capture click events. Therefore, if you disable the outer document capture, the click event goes straight to the main1 button and to the layer event capture. Event capture in the layer object prevents the events from ever reaching the buttons in the layer, unless you disable event capture for both the document and the layer.

Listing 29-2: **Document and Layer Event Capture and Release**

```
<HTML>
<HEAD>
<SCRIPT LANGUAGE="JavaScript">
function setDocCapture(enable) {
    if (!enable) {
        document.captureEvents(Event.CLICK)
    } else {
        document.releaseEvents(Event.CLICK)
    }
}
function setLayerCapture(enable) {
    if (!enable) {
        document.layer1.captureEvents(Event.CLICK)
    } else {
        document.layer1.releaseEvents(Event.CLICK)
    }
}
function doMainClick(e) {
    if (e.target.type == "button") {
        alert("Captured in top document")
    }
}
document.captureEvents(Event.CLICK)
document.onclick=doMainClick
</SCRIPT>
</HEAD>
<BODY>
```

Continued

> ### Listing 29-2: *(continued)*

```
<B>Document-level and/or Layer-level capture of Event.CLICK</B>
<HR>
<FORM>
<INPUT TYPE="checkbox" onMouseDown="setDocCapture(this.checked)" CHECKED>Enable
Document Capture
<INPUT TYPE="checkbox" onMouseDown="setLayerCapture(this.checked)"
CHECKED>Enable Layer Capture
<HR>
<INPUT TYPE="button" VALUE="Button 'main1'" NAME="main1"
    onClick="alert('Event finally reached Button:' + this.name)">
</FORM>

<LAYER ID="layer1" LEFT=200 TOP=150 BGCOLOR="coral">
<HEAD>
<SCRIPT LANGUAGE="JavaScript">
function doLayerClick(e) {
    if (e.target.type == "button") {
        alert("Captured in layer1")
    }
}
layer1.captureEvents(Event.CLICK)
layer1.onclick=doLayerClick
</SCRIPT>
</HEAD>
<BODY>
<FORM>
 layer1<BR><P><INPUT TYPE="button" VALUE="Button 'layerButton1'"
    NAME="layerButton1"
    onClick="alert('Event finally reached Button:' + this.name)"></P>
<P><INPUT TYPE="button" VALUE="Button 'layerButton2'"
    NAME="layerButton2"
    onClick="alert('Event finally reached Button:' + this.name)"></P>
</FORM>
</BODY>
</LAYER>

</BODY>
</HTML>
```

Passing events toward their targets

If you capture a particular event type, your script may need to perform some limited processing on that event before letting it reach its intended target. For example, perhaps you want to do something special if a user clicks an element with the Shift metakey pressed. In that case, the function that handles the event at the document level inspects the event's modifiers property to determine if the Shift key was pressed at the time of the event. If the Shift key was not pressed, you want the event to continue on its way to the element that the user clicked.

To let an event pass through the object hierarchy to its target, you use the routeEvent() method, passing as a parameter the event object being handled in the current function. A routeEvent() method does not guarantee that the event will reach its intended destination, because another object in between may have event capturing for that event type turned on and will intercept the event. That object, too, can let the event pass through with its own routeEvent() method.

Listing 29-3 demonstrates event routing by adding onto the document being built in previous examples. While the clickable button objects are the same, additional powers are added to the document and layer function handlers that process events that come their way. For each of these event-capturing objects, you have additional checkbox settings to allow or disallow events from passing through after each level has processed them.

The default settings for the checkboxes are like the ones in Listing 29-2, where event capture (for the click event) is set for both the document and layer objects. Clicking any button causes the document object's event handler to process and none other. But if you then enable the checkbox that lets the event continue, you find that click events on the layer buttons cause alerts to display from both the document and layer object event handler functions. If you then also let events continue from the layer object, a click on the button displays a third alert, showing that the event has reached the buttons. Because the main1 button is not in the layer, none of the layer object event handling settings affect its behavior.

Listing 29-3: **NN4 Capture, Release, and Route Events**

```
<HTML>
<HFAD>
<SCRIPT LANGUAGE="JavaScript">
function setDocCapture(enable) {
    if (!enable) {
        document.captureEvents(Event.CLICK)
    } else {
        document.releaseEvents(Event.CLICK)
        document.forms[0].setDocRte.checked = false
        docRoute = false
    }

}
function setLayerCapture(enable) {
    if (!enable) {
        document.layer1.captureEvents(Event.CLICK)
    } else {
        document.layer1.releaseEvents(Event.CLICK)
        document.forms[0].setLyrRte.checked = false
        layerRoute = false
    }
}
```

Continued

Listing 29-3: *(continued)*

```
var docRoute = false
var layerRoute = false
function setDocRoute(enable) {
    docRoute = !enable
}
function setLayerRoute(enable) {
    layerRoute = !enable
}
function doMainClick(e) {
    if (e.target.type == "button") {
        alert("Captured in top document")
        if (docRoute) {
            routeEvent(e)
        }
    }
}
document.captureEvents(Event.CLICK)
document.onclick=doMainClick
</SCRIPT>
</HEAD>
<BODY>
<B>Capture, Release, and Routing of Event.CLICK</B>
<HR>
<FORM>
<INPUT TYPE="checkbox" NAME="setDocCap"
onMouseDown="setDocCapture(this.checked)" CHECKED>Enable Document Capture 
<INPUT TYPE="checkbox" NAME="setDocRte"
onMouseDown ="setDocRoute(this.checked)">And let event continue<P>
<INPUT TYPE="checkbox" NAME="setLyrCap"
onMouseDown ="setLayerCapture(this.checked)" CHECKED>Enable Layer Capture 
<INPUT TYPE="checkbox" NAME="setLyrRte"
onMouseDown ="setLayerRoute(this.checked)">And let event continue
<HR>
<INPUT TYPE="button" VALUE="Button 'main1'" NAME="main1"
    onClick="alert('Event finally reached Button:' + this.name)">
</FORM>

<LAYER ID="layer1" LEFT=200 TOP=150 BGCOLOR="coral">
<HEAD>
<SCRIPT LANGUAGE="JavaScript">
function doLayerClick(e) {
    if (e.target.type == "button") {
        alert("Captured in layer1")
        if (layerRoute) {
            routeEvent(e)
        }
    }
}
layer1.captureEvents(Event.CLICK)
layer1.onclick=doLayerClick
</SCRIPT>
```

```
</HEAD>
<BODY>
<FORM>
 layer1<BR><P><INPUT TYPE="button" VALUE="Button 'layerButton1'"
    NAME="layerButton1"
    onClick="alert('Event finally reached Button:' + this.name)"></P>
<P><INPUT TYPE="button" VALUE="Button 'layerButton2'"
    NAME="layerButton2"
    onClick="alert('Event finally reached Button:' + this.name)"></P>
</FORM>
</BODY>
</LAYER>

</BODY>
</HTML>
```

In some cases, your scripts need to know if an event that is passed onward by `routeEvent()` method activated a function that returns a value. This knowledge is especially valuable if your event must return a `true` or `false` value to let an object know if it should proceed with its default behavior (for example, whether a link should activate its `HREF` attribute URL or cancel after the event handler evaluates to `return true` or `return false`). When a function is invoked by the action of a `routeEvent()` method, the return value of the destination function is passed back to the `routeEvent()` method. That value, in turn, can be returned to the object that originally captured the event.

Event traffic cop

The last scenario is one in which a higher-level object captures an event and directs the event to a particular object elsewhere in the hierarchy. For example, you could have a document-level event handler function direct every click event whose `modifiers` property indicates that the Alt key was pressed to a Help button object whose own `onClick` event handler displays a help panel (perhaps shows an otherwise hidden layer).

You can redirect an event to any object via the `handleEvent()` method. This method works differently from the others described in this chapter, because the object reference of this method is the reference of the object to handle the event (with the event object being passed as a parameter, such as the other methods). As long as the target object has an event handler defined for that event, it will process the event as if it had received the event directly from the system (even though the event object's `target` property may be some other object entirely).

To demonstrate how this event redirection works, Listing 29-4 includes the final additions to the document being built so far in this chapter. The listing includes mechanisms that allow all `click` events to be sent directly to the second button in the layer (`layerButton2`). The previous interaction with document and layer event capture and routing is still intact, although you cannot have event routing and redirection on at the same time.

The best way to see event redirection at work is to enable both document and layer event capture (the default settings). When you click the `main1` button, the event reaches only as far as the document-level capture handler. But if you then turn on the "Send event to 'layerButton2'" checkbox associated with the document level, a click of the `main1` button reaches both the document-level event handler and `layerButton2`, even though the `main1` button is not anywhere near the layer button in the document object hierarchy. Click other checkboxes to work with the interaction of event capturing, routing, and redirection.

Listing 29-4: **NN4 Redirecting Events**

```
<HTML>
<HEAD>
<SCRIPT LANGUAGE="JavaScript">
function setDocCapture(enable) {
    if (!enable) {
        document.captureEvents(Event.CLICK)
    } else {
        document.releaseEvents(Event.CLICK)
        document.forms[0].setDocRte.checked = false
        docRoute = false
    }

}
function setLayerCapture(enable) {
    if (!enable) {
        document.layer1.captureEvents(Event.CLICK)
    } else {
        document.layer1.releaseEvents(Event.CLICK)
        document.forms[0].setLyrRte.checked = false
        layerRoute = false
    }
}
var docRoute = false
var layerRoute = false
function setDocRoute(enable) {
    docRoute = !enable
    document.forms[0].setDocShortCircuit.checked = false
    docShortCircuit = false
}
function setLayerRoute(enable) {
    layerRoute = !enable
    document.forms[0].setLyrShortCircuit.checked = false
    layerShortCircuit = false
}

var docShortCircuit = false
var layerShortCircuit = false
function setDocShortcut(enable) {
    docShortCircuit = !enable
    if (docShortCircuit) {
```

```
            document.forms[0].setDocRte.checked = false
            docRoute = false
        }
    }
    function setLayerShortcut(enable) {
        layerShortCircuit - !enable
        if (layerShortCircuit) {
            document.forms[0].setLyrRte.checked = false
            layerRoute = false
        }
    }

    function doMainClick(e) {
        if (e.target.type == "button") {
            alert("Captured in top document")
            if (docRoute) {
                routeEvent(e)
            } else if (docShortCircuit) {
                document.layer1.document.forms[0].layerButton2.handleEvent(e)
            }
        }
    }
    document.captureEvents(Event.CLICK)
    document.onclick=doMainClick
</SCRIPT>
</HEAD>
<BODY>
<B>Redirecting Event.CLICK</B>
<HR>
<FORM>
<INPUT TYPE="checkbox" NAME="setDocCap"
onMouseDown="setDocCapture(this.checked)" CHECKED>Enable Document Capture 
<INPUT TYPE="checkbox" NAME="setDocRte"
onMouseDown ="setDocRoute(this.checked)">And let event continue
<INPUT TYPE="checkbox" NAME="setDocShortCircuit"
onMouseDown ="setDocShortcut(this.checked)">Send event to 'layerButton2'<P>
<INPUT TYPE="checkbox" NAME="setLyrCap"
onMouseDown ="setLayerCapture(this.checked)" CHECKED>Enable Layer Capture 
<INPUT TYPE="checkbox" NAME="setLyrRte"
onMouseDown ="setLayerRoute(this.checked)">And let event continue
<INPUT TYPE="checkbox" NAME="setLyrShortCircuit"
onMouseDown ="setLayerShortcut(this.checked)">Send event to 'layerButton2'<P>
<HR>
<INPUT TYPE="button" VALUE="Button 'main1'" NAME="main1"
    onClick="alert('Event finally reached Button:' + this.name)">
</FORM>

<LAYER ID="layer1" LEFT=200 TOP=200 BGCOLOR="coral">
<HEAD>
<SCRIPT LANGUAGE="JavaScript">
function doLayerClick(e) {
    if (e.target.type == "button") {
```

Continued

Listing 29-4: *(continued)*

```
        alert("Captured in layer1")
        if (layerRoute) {
            routeEvent(e)
        } else if (layerShortCircuit) {
            document.forms[0].layerButton2.handleEvent(e)
        }
    }
}
layer1.captureEvents(Event.CLICK)
layer1.onclick=doLayerClick
</SCRIPT>
</HEAD>
<BODY>
<FORM>
 layer1<BR><P><INPUT TYPE="button" VALUE="Button 'layerButton1'"
    NAME="layerButton1"
    onClick="alert('Event finally reached Button:' + this.name)"></P>
<P><INPUT TYPE="button" VALUE="Button 'layerButton2'"
    NAME="layerButton2"
    onClick="alert('Event finally reached Button:' + this.name)"></P>
</FORM>
</BODY>
</LAYER>

</BODY>
</HTML>
```

IE4+ event propagation

Event propagation in IE4+ flows in the opposite direction of the NN4 event capture model. IE's model is called *event bubbling,* in which events "bubble" upward from the target object through the element containment hierarchy. It's important to distinguish between the old-fashioned document object hierarchy (followed in the NN4 event capture model) and the more modern notion of HTML element containment—a concept that carries to the W3C DOM as well.

A good way to demonstrate the effect of event bubbling—a behavior that is turned on by default—is to populate a simple document with lots of event handlers to see which ones fire and in what order. Listing 29-5 has onClick event handlers defined for a button inside a form, the form itself, and other elements and object all the way up the hierarchy out to the window.

Listing 29-5: **Event Bubbling Demonstration**

```
<HTML onClick="alert('Event is now at the HTML element.')">
<HEAD>
<TITLE>Event Bubbles</TITLE>
<SCRIPT LANGUAGE="JavaScript">
function init() {
    window.onclick = winEvent
    document.onclick = docEvent
    document.body.onclick = docBodEvent
}
function winEvent() {
    alert("Event is now at the window object level.")
}
function docEvent() {
    alert("Fvent is now at the document object level.")
}
function docBodEvent() {
    alert("Event is now at the BODY element.")
}

</SCRIPT>
</HEAD>
<BODY onLoad="init()">
<H1>Event Bubbles</H1>
<HR>
<FORM onClick="alert('Event is now at the FORM element.')">
<INPUT TYPE="button" VALUE="Button 'main1'" NAME="main1"
    onClick="alert('Event started at Button: ' + this.name)">
</FORM>
</BODY>
</HTML>
```

You can try this listing in IE4+ and even NN6, because the latter observes event bubbling. But you will notice differences in the precise propagation among IE4+/Windows, IE4+/Macintosh, and NN6. But first, notice that after you click the button in Listing 29-5, the event first fires at the target: the button. Then the event bubbles upward through the HTML containment to fire at the enclosing FORM element; next to the enclosing BODY element; and so on. Where the differences occur are after the BODY element. Table 29-1 shows the objects for which event handlers are defined in Listing 29-5 and which objects have the `click` event bubble to them in the three classes of browsers.

Table 29-1 **Event Bubbling Variations for Listing 29-5**			
Event Handler Location	*IE4+/Windows*	*IE4+/Macintosh*	*NN6*
BUTTON	yes	yes	yes
FORM	yes	yes	yes
BODY	yes	yes	yes
HTML	yes	no	yes
document	yes	yes	yes
window	no	no	yes

Despite the discrepancies in Table 29-1, events do bubble through the most likely HTML containers that come to mind. The object level with the most global scope and that works in all browser categories shown in the table is the document object.

Preventing IE event bubbling

Because bubbling occurs by default, there are times when you may prefer to prevent an event from bubbling up the hierarchy. For example, if you have one handler at the document level whose job is to deal with the click event from a related series of buttons, any other object that receives click events will allow those events to bubble upward to the document level unless the bubbling is cancelled. Having the event bubble up could conflict with the document-level event handler.

Each event object in IE has a property called cancelBubble. The default value of this property is false, which means that the event bubbles to the next outermost container that has an event handler for that event. But if, in the execution of an event handler, that property is set to true, the processing of that handler finishes its job, but the event does not bubble up any higher. Therefore, to stop an event from bubbling beyond the current event handler, include the following statement somewhere in the handler function:

```
event.cancelBubble = true
```

You can prove this to yourself by modifying the page in Listing 29-5 to cancel bubbling at any level. For example, if you change the event handler of the FORM element to include a statement that cancels bubbling, the event goes not further than the FORM in IE (the syntax is different for NN6, as discussed later):

```
<FORM
onClick="alert('Event is now at the FORM element.'); event.cancelBubble=true">
```

Redirecting events

Starting with IE5.5, you can redirect an event to another element, but with some limitations. The mechanism that makes this possible is the `fireEvent()` method of all HTML element objects (see Chapter 15). This method isn't so much redirecting an event as causing a brand-new event to be fired. But you can pass most of the properties of the original `event` object with the new event by specifying a reference to the old `event` object as the optional second parameter to the `fireEvent()` method.

The big limitation in this technique, however, is that the reference to the target element gets lost in this hand-off to the new event. The `srcElement` property of the old event gets overwritten with a reference to the object that is the target of the call to `fireEvent()`. For example, consider the following `onClick` event handler function for a button inside a FORM element:

```
function buttonEvent() {
    event.cancelBubble = true
    document.body.fireEvent("onclick", event)
}
```

By cancelling event bubbling, the event does not propagate upward to the enclosing FORM element. Instead, the event is explicitly redirected to the BODY element, passing the current `event` object as the second parameter. When the event handler function for the BODY element runs, its `event` object has information about the original event, such as the mouse button used for the click and the coordinates. But the `event.srcElement` property points to the `document.body` object. As the event bubbles upward from the BODY element, the `srcElement` property continues to point to the `document.body` object. You can see this at work in Listing 29-6 for IE5.5.

Listing 29-6: **Cancelling and Redirecting Events in IE5.5+**

```
<HTML onClick="revealEvent('HTML', event)">
<HEAD>
<TITLE>Event Cancelling & Redirecting</TITLE>
<SCRIPT LANGUAGE="JavaScript">
// display alert with event object info
function revealEvent(elem, evt) {
    var msg = "Event (from " + evt.srcElement.tagName + " at "
    msg += event.clientX + "," + event.clientY + ") is now at the "
    msg += elem + " element."
    alert(msg)
}
function init() {
    document.onclick = docEvent
    document.body.onclick = docBodEvent
}
```

Continued

Listing 29-6: *(continued)*

```
function docEvent() {
    revealEvent("document", event)
}
function docBodEvent() {
    revealEvent("BODY", event)
}
function buttonEvent(form) {
    revealEvent("BUTTON", event)
    // cancel if checked (IE4+)
    event.cancelBubble = form.bubbleCancelState.checked
    // redirect if checked (IE5.5+)
    if (form.redirect.checked) {
        document.body.fireEvent("onclick", event)
    }
}
</SCRIPT>
</HEAD>
<BODY onLoad="init()">
<H1>Event Cancelling & Redirecting</H1>
<HR>
<FORM onClick="revealEvent('FORM', event)">
<P><BUTTON NAME="main1" onClick="buttonEvent(this.form)">
Button 'main1'
</BUTTON></P>
<P><INPUT TYPE="checkbox" NAME="bubbleCancelState"
onClick="event.cancelBubble=true">Cancel Bubbling at BUTTON<BR>
<INPUT TYPE="checkbox" NAME="redirect" onClick="event.cancelBubble=true">
Redirect Event to BODY</P>
</FORM>
</BODY>
</HTML>
```

Listing 29-6 is a modified version of Listing 29-5. Major additions are enhanced event handlers at each level so that you can see the tag name of the event that is regarded as the srcElement of the event as well as the coordinates of the click event. With both checkboxes unchecked, events bubble upward from the button, and the BUTTON element is then shown to be the original target all the way up the bubble hierarchy. If you check the Cancel Bubbling checkbox, the event goes no further than the BUTTON element, because that's where event bubbling is turned off. If you then check the Redirect Event to BODY checkbox, the original event is cancelled at the BUTTON level, but a new event is fired at the BODY element. But notice that by passing the old event object as the second parameter, the click location properties of the old event are applied to the new event directed at the BODY. This event then continues to bubble upward from the BODY.

As a side note, if you uncheck the Cancel Bubbling checkbox but leave the Redirect Event box checked, you can see how the redirection is observed at the end of the BUTTON's event handler, and something special goes on. The original event is held aside by the browser while the redirected event bubbles upward. As soon as that event processing branch finishes, the original bubbling propagation carries on with the FORM. Notice, though that the event object still knows that it was targeted at the BUTTON element, and the other properties are intact. This means that for a time, two event objects were in the browser's memory, but only one is "active" at a time. While the redirected event is propagating, the window.event object refers to that event object only.

NN6+ event propagation

Yielding to arguments in favor of both event capture and event bubbling, the W3C DOM group managed to assemble an event model that employs both propagation systems. Although forced to use new syntax so as not to conflict with older browsers, the W3C DOM propagation model works like the NN4 one for capture and like IE4+ for bubbling. In other words, an event bubbles by default, but you can also turn on event capture if you want. Thus, an event first trickles down the element containment hierarchy to the target; then it bubbles up through the reverse path.

Event bubbling is on by default, just as in IE4+. To enable capture, you must apply a W3C DOM event listener to an object at some higher container. Use the addEventListener() method (see Chapter 15) for any visible HTML element or node. One of the parameters of the addEventListener() method determines whether the event listener function should be triggered while the event is bubbling or is captured.

Listing 29-7 is a simplified example that demonstrates how a click event aimed at a button can be both captured and allowed to bubble. Most event handling functions are assigned inside the init() function. Borrowing code from Listing 29-5, event handlers are assigned to the window, document, and BODY objects as property assignments. These are automatically treated as bubble-type event listeners. Next, two objects—the document and a form—are given capture-type event listeners for the click event. The document object event listener invokes the same function as the bubble-type event handler (the alert text includes some asterisks to remind you that it is the same alert being displayed in both the capture and bubble phases of the event). For the form object, however, the capture-type event listener is directed to one function, while a bubble-type listener for the same object is directed at a separate function. In other words, the form object invokes one function as the event trickles down to the target and another function when the event starts bubbling back up. Many of the event handler functions dynamically read the eventPhase property of the event object to reveal which phase of event propagation is in force at the instance the event handler is invoked.

Listing 29-7: **NN6 Event Capture and Bubble**

```
<HTML>
<HEAD>
<TITLE>W3C DOM Event Propagation</TITLE>
<SCRIPT LANGUAGE="JavaScript">
function init() {
    // using old syntax to assign bubble-type event handlers
    window.onclick = winEvent
    document.onclick = docEvent
    document.body.onclick = docBodEvent
    // turn on click event capture for two objects
    document.addEventListener("click", docEvent, true)
    document.forms[0].addEventListener("click", formCaptureEvent, true)
    // set event listener for bubble
    document.forms[0].addEventListener("click", formBubbleEvent, false)
}
function winEvent(evt) {
    alert("Event is now at the window object level (" + getPhase(evt) + ").")
}
function docEvent(evt) {
    alert("Event is now at the **document** object level (" + getPhase(evt) +
").")
}
function docBodEvent(evt) {
    alert("Event is now at the BODY level (" + getPhase(evt) + ").")
}
function formCaptureEvent(evt) {
    alert("This alert triggered by FORM only on CAPTURE.")
}
function formBubbleEvent(evt) {
    alert("This alert triggered by FORM only on BUBBLE.")
}
// reveal event phase of current event object
function getPhase(evt) {
    switch (evt.eventPhase) {
        case 1:
            return "CAPTURING"
            break
        case 2:
            return "AT TARGET"
            break
        case 3:
            return "BUBBLING"
            break
        default:
            return ""
    }
}
</SCRIPT>
```

```
</HEAD>
<BODY onLoad="init()">
<H1>W3C DOM Event Propagation</H1>
<HR>
<FORM>
<INPUT TYPE="button" VALUE="Button 'main1'" NAME="main1"  onClick=
    "alert('Event is now at the button object level (' + getPhase(event) +
').')">
</FORM>
</BODY>
</HTML>
```

If you want to remove event capture after it has been enabled, use the removeEventListener() method on the same object as the event listener that was originally added (see Chapter 15). And, because multiple event listeners can be attached to the same object, specify the exact same three parameters to the removeEventListener() method as applied to the addEventListener() method.

Preventing NN6 event bubbling or capture

Corresponding to the cancelBubble property of the IE4+ event object is an event object method in the W3C DOM. The method that prevents propagation in any event phase is the stopPropagation() method. Invoke this method anywhere within an event listener handler function. The current function executes to completion, but the event propagates no further.

Listing 29-8 extends the example of Listing 29-7 to include two checkboxes that let you stop propagation type at the FORM element in your choice of the capture or bubble phase.

Listing 29-8: **Preventing Bubble and Capture**

```
<HTML>
<HEAD>
<TITLE>W3C DOM Event Propagation</TITLE>
<SCRIPT LANGUAGE="JavaScript">
function init() {
    // using old syntax to assign bubble-type event handlers
    window.onclick = winEvent
    document.onclick = docEvent
    document.body.onclick = docBodEvent
    // turn on click event capture for two objects
    document.addEventListener("click", docEvent, true)
    document.forms[0].addEventListener("click", formCaptureEvent, true)
    // set event listener for bubble
```

Continued

Listing 29-8: *(continued)*

```
    document.forms[0].addEventListener("click", formBubbleEvent, false)
}
function winEvent(evt) {
    if (evt.target.type == "button") {
        alert("Event is now at the window object level (" + getPhase(evt) +
").")
    }
}
function docEvent(evt) {
    if (evt.target.type == "button") {
        alert("Event is now at the **document** object level (" +
getPhase(evt) + ").")
    }
}
function docBodEvent(evt) {
    if (evt.target.type == "button") {
        alert("Event is now at the BODY level (" +
getPhase(evt) + ").")
    }
}
function formCaptureEvent(evt) {
    if (evt.target.type == "button") {
        alert("This alert triggered by FORM only on CAPTURE.")
        if (document.forms[0].stopAllProp.checked) {
            evt.stopPropagation()
        }
    }
}
function formBubbleEvent(evt) {
    if (evt.target.type == "button") {
        alert("This alert triggered by FORM only on BUBBLE.")
        if (document.forms[0].stopDuringBubble.checked) {
            evt.preventBubble()
            }
    }
}
// reveal event phase of current event object
function getPhase(evt) {
    switch (evt.eventPhase) {
        case 1:
            return "CAPTURING"
            break
        case 2:
            return "AT TARGET"
            break
        case 3:
            return "BUBBLING"
            break
        default:
```

```
            return ""
        }
}
</SCRIPT>
</HEAD>
<BODY onLoad="init()">
<H1>W3C DOM Event Propagation</H1>
<HR>
<FORM>
<INPUT TYPE="checkbox" NAME="stopAllProp">Stop all propagation at FORM<BR>
<INPUT TYPE="checkbox" NAME="stopDuringBubble">Prevent bubbling past FORM
<HR>
<INPUT TYPE="button" VALUE="Button 'main1'" NAME="main1"  onClick=
    "alert('Event is now at the button object level (' + getPhase(event) +
').')">
</FORM>
</BODY>
</HTML>
```

Redirecting NN6 events

The mechanism for sending an event to an object outside the normal propagation pattern in NN6 is similar to that of IE4+, although with different syntax. In place of the IE4+ fireEvent() method, NN6 uses the W3C DOM dispatchEvent() method. The sole parameter of the method is an event object, such as the current event object. Listing 29-9 is the same as the IE4+ Listing 29-6, but with just a few modifications to run in the NN6 event model. Notice that the dispatchEvent() method passes the current event object as its sole parameter.

Listing 29-9: **Cancelling and Redirecting Events in NN6+**

```
<HTML onClick="revealEvent('HTML', event)">
<HEAD>
<TITLE>Event Cancelling & Redirecting</TITLE>
<SCRIPT LANGUAGE="JavaScript">
// display alert with event object info
function revealEvent(elem, evt) {
    var msg = "Event (from " + evt.target.tagName + " at "
    msg += evt.clientX + "," + evt.clientY + ") is now at the "
    msg += elem + " element."
    alert(msg)
}
function init() {
    document.onclick = docEvent
    document.body.onclick = docBodEvent
```

Continued

Listing 29-9: *(continued)*

```
}
function docEvent(evt) {
    revealEvent("document", evt)
}
function docBodEvent(evt) {
    revealEvent("BODY", evt)
}
function buttonEvent(form, evt) {
    revealEvent("BUTTON", evt)
    // redirect if checked
    if (form.redirect.checked) {
        document.body.dispatchEvent(evt)
    }
    // cancel if checked
    if (form.bubbleCancelState.checked) {
        evt.stopPropagation()
    }
}
</SCRIPT>
</HEAD>
<BODY onLoad="init()">
<H1>Event Cancelling & Redirecting</H1>
<HR>
<FORM onClick="revealEvent('FORM', event)">
<P><BUTTON NAME="main1" onClick="buttonEvent(this.form, event)">
Button 'main1'
</BUTTON></P>
<P><INPUT TYPE="checkbox" NAME="bubbleCancelState"
onClick="event.stopPropagation()">Cancel Bubbling at BUTTON<BR>
<INPUT TYPE="checkbox" NAME="redirect" onClick="event.stopPropagation()">
Redirect Event to BODY</P>
</FORM>
</BODY>
</HTML>
```

Referencing the event object

While there may be essentially three different event object models in today's browsers, the way your scripts access those objects is divided into two camps: the IE way; and the NN (and W3C) way. I start with the simpler, IE way.

IE4+ event object references

In IE4+, the `event` object is accessible as a property of the `window` object:

`window.event`

But, as you are well aware, the `window` part of references is optional, so your scripts can treat the `event` object as if it were a global reference:

`event.propertyName`

Thus, any statement in an event handler function can access the `event` object without any special preparation or initializations.

NN4+ (W3C) event object references

The situation is a bit more complicated in the NN4+ event model. In some cases you must explicitly pass the event object as a parameter to an event handler function, while in other cases, the event object is delivered as a parameter automatically. The difference depends on how the event handler function is bound to the object.

Using the original way of binding event handlers to objects — via an attribute in the element's tag — you must specify the event object as a parameter by passing `event` as a parameter, as in

`onClick="doSomething(event)"`

This is the only time in the NN4+ model that you see an explicit reference to the `event` (lowercase "e") object as if it were a global reference. This reference does not work in any other context — only as a parameter to an event handler function. If you have multiple parameters, the `event` reference can go in any order, but I tend to put it last:

`onClick="doSomething(this, event)"`

The function definition that is bound to the element should therefore have a parameter variable in place to "catch" the event object parameter:

`function doSomething(widget, evt) {...}`

You have no restrictions on how you name this parameter variable. In some examples of this book, you may see the variable assigned as `event` or, more commonly, `evt`. When working with cross-browser scripts, avoid using `event` as a parameter variable name so as not to interfere with IE's `event` property.

Other ways of binding event handler functions to objects — via property assignments and the addEventListener() method in NN6+ — assign references of those handlers to the desired objects in the document, as in either of the following:

```
document.forms[0].someButton.onclick = doSomething
document.getElementById("myButton").addEventListener("click", doSomething, false)
```

Event binding through these approaches prevents explicit passage of your own parameters to the invoked functions. But the NN4+ browsers automatically pass as the sole parameter a reference to the event object created in response to the user or system action that triggered the event. This means that your functions should "receive" the passed event object in a parameter variable:

```
function doSomething(evt) {...}
```

Recall that the event object contains a reference to the object that was the target of the event. From that, you can access any properties of that object, such as the form object that contains a form control object.

You can see the way the event object is passed as a parameter in Listing 29-9. For all event handlers that are assigned by reference (both to an event handler property of an object and to an addEventListener() method call), the functions have a parameter variable in place to act as a reference to the event object for statements within the function. If you need to invoke other functions from there, you can pass the event object reference further along as needed. The event object retains its properties as long as the chain of execution triggered by the event action continues.

event Object Compatibility

Despite the incompatible ways that NN and IE event objects arrive at an event handler function, you can easily stuff the object into one variable that both browser types can use. For example, the following function fragment receives an event object from NN but also accommodates the IE event object:

```
function doSomething(evt) {
    evt = (evt) ? evt : (window.event) ? window.event : ""
    if (evt) {
        // browser has an event to process
        ...
    }
}
```

If an event object arrives as a parameter, it continues to be available as evt; but if not, the function makes sure that a window.event object is available and assigns it to the evt variable; finally, if the browser doesn't know about an event object, the evt variable is made an empty string. Processing continues only if evt contains an event object.

That's the easy part. The madness comes in the details: reading properties of the event object when the property names can vary widely across the three event object models. Sections later in this chapter provide details of each property and method of all three event object models, but seeing an overview of the property terminology on a comparative basis is helpful. Table 29-2 lists the common information bits and actions you are likely to want from an event object and the property or method names used in the three event object models.

Table 29-2 Common event Object Properties and Methods

Property/Action	NN4	IE4+	NN6
Target element	target	srcElement	target
Event type	type	type	type
X coordinate in element	n/a†	offsetX	n/a†
Y coordinate in element	n/a†	offsetY	n/a†
X coordinate in positioned element	layerX	x	layerX
Y coordinate in positioned element	layerY	y	layerY
X coordinate on page	pageX	n/a†	pageX
Y coordinate on page	pageY	n/a†	pageY
X coordinate in window	n/a	clientX	client
X coordinate in window	n/a	clientY	clientY
X coordinate on screen	screenX	screenX	screenX
Y coordinate on screen	screenY	screenY	screenY
Mouse button	which	button	button
Keyboard key	which	keyCode	keyCode
Shift key pressed	modifiers	shiftKey	shiftKey
Alt key pressed	modifiers	altKey	altKey
Ctrl key pressed	modifiers	ctrlKey	ctrlKey
Previous Element	n/a	fromElement	relatedTarget
Next Element	n/a	toElement	relatedTarget
Cancel bubbling	n/a	cancelBubble	preventBubble()
Prevent default action	return false	returnValue	preventDefault()

†Value can be derived through calculations with other properties.

As you can see in Table 29-2, properties for the IE4+ and NN6 event objects have a lot in common. This is good news, especially as the installed base of NN4 users diminishes over time. The primary incompatibility is how to reference the element that is the intended target of the event. This, too, can be branched in your code to achieve a common variable that references the element. For example, embedded within the previous function fragment can be a statement, such as the following:

```
var elem = (evt.target) ? evt.target : evt.srcElement
```

Each event model has additional properties that are not shared by the other. Details about these are covered in the rest of this chapter.

Dueling Event Models

Despite the sometimes widely divergent ways event object models treat their properties, accommodating a wide range of browsers for event manipulation is not difficult. In this section, you see two scripts that examine important event properties. The first script reveals which, if any, modifier keys are held down during an event; the second script extracts the codes for both mouse buttons and keyboard keys. Both scripts work with all browsers that have event objects, including NN4. If your audience no longer uses NN4, you can eliminate the code branches that support it.

Cross-platform modifier key check

Listing 29-10 demonstrates branching techniques for examining the modifier key(s) being held down while an event fires. Details of the event object properties, such as `modifiers` and `altKey`, can be found later in this chapter. To see the page in action, click a link, type into a text box, and click a button while holding down any combination of modifier keys. A series of four checkboxes representing the four modifier keys is at the bottom. As you click or type, the checkbox(es) of the pressed modifier key(s) become checked.

Listing 29-10: **Checking Events for Modifier Keys**

```
<HTML>
<HEAD>
<TITLE>Event Modifiers</TITLE>
<SCRIPT LANGUAGE="JavaScript">
function checkMods(evt) {
    evt = (evt) ? evt : (window.event) ? window.event : ""
    if (evt) {
        var elem = (evt.target) ? evt.target : evt.srcElement
```

```
        var form = document.output
        if (evt.modifiers) {
            form.modifier[0].checked = evt.modifiers & Event.ALT_MASK
            form.modifier[1].checked = evt.modifiers & Event.CONTROL_MASK
            form.modifier[2].checked = evt.modifiers & Event.SHIFT_MASK
            form.modifier[3].checked = evt.modifiers & Event.META_MASK
        } else {
            form.modifier[0].checked = evt.altKey
            form.modifier[1].checked = evt.ctrlKey
            form.modifier[2].checked = evt.shiftKey
            form.modifier[3].checked = false
        }
    }
    return false
}
</SCRIPT>
</HEAD>
<BODY>
<H1>Event Modifiers</H1>
<HR>
<P>Hold one or more modifier keys and click on
<A HREF="javascript:void(0)" onMouseDown="return checkMods(event)">
this link</A> to see which keys you are holding.</P>
<FORM NAME="output">
<P>Enter some text with uppercase and lowercase letters:
<INPUT TYPE="text" SIZE=40 onKeyUp="checkMods(event)"></P>
<P><INPUT TYPE="button" VALUE="Click Here With Modifier Keys"
onClick="checkMods(event)"></P>
<P>
<INPUT TYPE="checkbox" NAME="modifier">Alt
<INPUT TYPE="checkbox" NAME="modifier">Control
<INPUT TYPE="checkbox" NAME="modifier">Shift
<INPUT TYPE="checkbox" NAME="modifier">Meta
</P>
</FORM>
</BODY>
</HTML>
```

Because all three event handlers call the same `checkMods()` function, branching is needed only in this function. Notice, though, that branching is done by object detection, rather than `navigator.userAgent` detection. This method makes the most sense for this example, because the scripts rely on the existence of particular objects and properties for their proper execution. For NN4, the event object is passed as a parameter (`evt`) whose `modifiers` property is Bitwise ANDed with an `Event` object constant for each modifier key. For IE4+ and NN6, the script checks the event object property for each of three modifiers.

Cross-platform key capture

To demonstrate keyboard events in both browsers, Listing 29-11 captures the key character being typed into a text box, as well as the mouse button used to click a button. As with Listing 29-10, NN4 has a very different way of getting this information compared to IE4+ and NN6. In this arena, however, NN6 continues to support the NN4 syntax as well, so you can use the old or new syntax as you like. Whereas NN4 combines the features of key character code and mouse button into one event object property (depending upon the event type), newer browsers have entirely separate properties for these values. Listing 29-11 is written such that NN6 follows the NN4 syntax path, but even if the NN4 syntax should disappear in a future NN version, the browser would follow the new syntax path without blinking an eye.

Listing 29-11: Checking Events for Key and Mouse Button Pressed

```
<HTML>
<HEAD>
<TITLE>Button and Key Properties</TITLE>
<SCRIPT LANGUAGE="JavaScript">
function checkWhich(evt) {
    evt = (evt) ? evt : (window.event) ? window.event : ""
    if (evt) {
        var thingPressed = ""
        var elem = (evt.target) ? evt.target : evt.srcElement
        if (evt.which) {
            thingPressed = evt.which
        } else {
            if (elem.type == "textarea") {
                thingPressed = evt.keyCode
            } else if (elem.type == "button") {
                thingPressed = evt.button
            }
        }
        status = thingPressed
    }
    return false
}
</SCRIPT>
</HEAD>
<BODY>
<H1>Button and Key Properties</H1> (results in the status bar)
<HR>
<FORM>
<P>Mouse down atop this
```

```
<INPUT TYPE="button" VALUE="Button" onMouseDown="checkWhich(event)">
this link</A> or this
<INPUT TYPE="button" VALUE="Button" onMouseDown="checkWhich(event)">
with either mouse button (if you have more than one).</P>
<P>Enter some text with uppercase and lowercase letters:
<TEXTAREA COLS=40 ROWS=4 onKeyPress="checkWhich(event)" WRAP="virtual">
</TEXTAREA></P>
</FORM>
</BODY>
</HTML>
```

The codes displayed for the keyboard event are equivalent to the ASCII values of character keys. If you need the codes of other keys, the onKeyDown and onKeyUp event handlers provide Unicode values for any key that you press on the keyboard. See the keyCode property listings for event objects later in this chapter for more details.

Event Types

Although browsers prior to Version 4 did not have an accessible event object, this is a good time to summarize the evolution of what in today's browsers is known as the type property. The type property reveals the kind of event that generates an event object (the event handler name minus the "on"). Object models in IE4+ and NN6+ provide event handlers for virtually every HTML element, so that it's possible, for example, to define an onClick event handler for not only a clickable button, but also a P or even an arbitrary SPAN element. We'll come back to the current crop of browsers in a moment. But first, in case you must write scripts that work on older browsers, you need to know which elements in those browsers support which event handlers. This knowledge will help you determine a common denominator of event handlers to implement in your pages, based on the browsers you anticipate will be accessing the pages.

Older browsers

Earlier browsers tended to limit the number of event handlers for any particular element to just those that made sense for the kind of element it was. Even so, many scripters wanted more event handlers on more objects. But until that became a reality in IE4+ and NN6+, authors had to know the limits of the object models. Table 29-3 shows the event handlers available for objects within three generations of early browsers. Each column represents the version in which the event type was introduced. For example, the `window` object started out with four event types and gained three more when NN4 was released. In contrast, the area object was exposed as an object for the first time in NN3, which is where the first event types for that object are listed.

	Table 29-3	**Event Types through the Early Ages**	
Object	*NN2/IE3*	*NN3*	*NN4*
window	blur		dragdrop
	focus		move
	load		resize
	unload		
layer			blur
			focus
			load
			mouseout
			mouseover
			mouseup
link	click	mouseout	dblclick
	mouseover		mousedown
			onmouseup
area		mouseout	click
		mouseover	
image		abort	
		error	
		load	
form	submit	reset	
text, textarea, password	blur		keydown
	change		keypress
	focus		keyup
	select		
all buttons	click		mousedown
			mouseup

Object	NN2/IE3	NN3	NN4
select	blur		
	change		
	focus		
fileUpload		blur	
		focus	
		select	

With the exception of the NN4 layer object, all objects shown in Table 29-3 have survived into the newer browsers, so that you can use these event handlers with confidence. Again, keep in mind that of the browsers listed in Table 29-3, only NN4 has an event object of any kind exposed to scripts.

Event types in IE4+ and NN6

By now you should have at least scanned the list of event handlers defined for elements in common, as shown in Chapter 15. This list of event types is enormous. A sizable number of the event types are unique to IE4, IE5, and IE5.5, and in some cases, just the Windows version at that.

If you compose pages for both IE4+ and NN6+, however, you need to know which event types these browser families and generations have in common. Event types for NN6 are based primarily on the W3C DOM Level 2 specification, although they also include keyboard events, which are not formally part of the Level 2 specification. Table 29-4 lists a common denominator of event types for modern browsers and the objects that support them. As you can see, many of these event types and corresponding objects go way back to the beginning. The biggest change is that mouse events are available for any visible element. While not as long as the IE event list, the event types in Table 29-4 are the basic set you should get to know for all browsers.

Table 29-4   IE4+ and NN6+ Event Types in Common

Event type	Applicable Elements
abort	OBJECT
blur	window, BUTTON, text, password, LABEL, SELECT, TEXTAREA
change	text, password, TEXTAREA, SELECT
click	All elements

Continued

	Table 29-4 *(continued)*
Event type	**Applicable Elements**
error	window, FRAMESET, OBJECT
focus	window, BUTTON, text, password, LABEL, SELECT, TEXTAREA
keydown	text, password, TEXTAREA
keypress	text, password, TEXTAREA
keyup	text, password, TEXTAREA
load	window, FRAMESET, OBJECT
mousedown	All elements
mousemove	All elements
mouseout	All elements
mouseover	All elements
mouseup	All elements
reset	FORM
resize	window
scroll	window
select	text, password, TEXTAREA
submit	FORM
unload	window, FRAMESET

NN4 event Object

Properties	**Methods**	**Event Handlers**
data		
layerX		
layerY		
modifiers		
pageX		
pageY		

Properties	Methods	Event Handlers
screenX		
screenY		
target		
type		
which		

Syntax

Accessing NN4 event object properties:

eventObject.property

	NN2	NN3	NN4	NN6	IE3/J1	IE3/J2	IE4	IE5	IE5.5
Compatibility			✓						

About this object

Most of the details about this object were covered in the comparative event object discussions earlier in this chapter. As the NN4 browser dissipates from the user-installed base, this object and its details will become less important.

Properties

data

Value: Array of Strings   Read-Only

	NN2	NN3	NN4	NN6	IE3/J1	IE3/J2	IE4	IE5	IE5.5
Compatibility			✓						

A DragDrop event contains information about the URL string being dragged to the browser window. Because dragging multiple items to a window is possible (for example, many icons representing URLs on some operating systems), the value of the property is an array of strings, with each string containing a single URL (including `file://` URLs for computer files).

URL information such as this is deemed to be private data, so it is exposed only to signed scripts after the user has granted permission to read browser data. If you want your signed script to capture this information without loading the URL into the window, the event handler must evaluate to return `false`.

Example (with Listing 29-12) on the CD-ROM

`layerX`
`layerY`
`pageX`
`pageY`
`screenX`
`screenY`

Value: Integer   Read-Only

	NN2	NN3	NN4	NN6	IE3/J1	IE3/J2	IE4	IE5	IE5.5
Compatibility			✓						

For many (but not all) mouse-related events, the NN4 event object contains a lot of information about the coordinates of the pointer when the event occurred. In the most complex case, a click in a layer object has three distinct pairs of horizontal and vertical (x and y) coordinate values relative to the layer, the page, and the entire screen. If no layers are specified for a document, the layer and page coordinate systems are identical. Note that these values are merely geographical in nature and do not, by themselves, contain any information about the object being clicked (information held by the *eventObject*.target property).

These mouse coordinate properties are set only with specific events. In the case of a link object, the `click` and all four mouse events pack these values into the event object. For buttons, however, only the mouse events (`mouseDown` and `mouseUp`) receive these coordinates.

Each of the two window event types (move and resize) uses one of these property pairs to convey the results of the user action involved. For example, when the user resizes a window, the resize event stuffs the *eventObject*.layerX and *eventObject*.layerY properties with the inner width and height (that is, the content area) of the browser window (you can also use the optional *eventObject*.width and *eventObject*.height property names if you prefer). When the user moves the window, the *eventObject*.screenX and *eventObject*.screenY properties contain the screen coordinates of the top-left corner of the entire browser application window.

Example (with Listing 29-13) on the CD-ROM

Related Items: window and layer object move and resize methods.

modifiers

Value: Constant   Read-Only

	NN2	NN3	NN4	NN6	IE3/J1	IE3/J2	IE4	IE5	IE5.5
Compatibility			✓						

The modifiers property of the NN4 event object refers to the modifier keys that can be pressed while clicking or typing. Modifier keys are Alt (also the Option key on the Macintosh keyboard), Ctrl, Shift, and what is known as a meta key (for example, the Command key, ⌘, on the Macintosh keyboard). You can use this property to find out if one or more modifier keys were pressed at the time the event occurred.

Values for these keys are integer values designed in such a way that any combination of keys generates a unique value. Fortunately, you don't have to know anything about these values, because the event model supplies some plain-language constants (properties of a global Event object always available behind the scenes) that a script can apply to the property value passed with the object. The constant names consist of the key name (all uppercase), followed by an underscore and the uppercase word MASK. For example, if the Alt key is pressed by itself or in concert with other modifier keys, you can use the bitwise AND operator (&) and the Event.ALT_MASK constant to test for the presence of the Alt key in the property value:

```
function handleMyEvent(evt) {
```

```
function handleMyEvent(evt) {
    if (evt.modifiers & Event.ALT_MASK) {
        //statements for Alt key handling
    }
}
```

Modifiers are not available with every event. You can capture them with `mouseDown` and `mouseUp` events in buttons and links. The only `click` event offering modifiers is with button objects. Keyboard events in text objects also include these modifiers. But be aware that accelerated keyboard combinations (for example, Ctrl+Q/⌘-Q for Quit) are not trappable by JavaScript event mechanisms because they are reserved for the browser's own menu shortcuts.

Example

See Listing 29-10 earlier in this chapter to see (in a cross-browser way) how the modifier keys are read for NN4.

target

Value: Object Reference   Read-Only

	NN2	NN3	NN4	NN6	IE3/J1	IE3/J2	IE4	IE5	IE5.5
Compatibility			✓						

Every event has a property containing a reference to the object that was clicked, typed into, or otherwise acted upon. Most commonly, this property is examined when you set up a page to trap for events at the window, document, or layer level, as described earlier in this chapter. The `target` property lets you better identify the intended destination of the event while handling all processing for that type of event in one place. With a reference to the target object at hand in this property, your scripts can extract and/or set properties of the object directly.

type

Value: String   Read-Only

	NN2	NN3	NN4	NN6	IE3/J1	IE3/J2	IE4	IE5	IE5.5
Compatibility			✓						

An event object's type is the name of the event that generated the event object. An event name is the same as the event handler's name, less the "on" prefix. Therefore, if a button's `onClick` event handler is triggered by a user's click, then the event type is `click` (all lowercase). If you create a multipurpose function for handling events, you can extract the *eventObject*.`type` property to help the function decide how to handle the current event. This sounds like a good job for the `switch` control structure (see Chapter 39).

which

Value: Integer   Read-Only

	NN2	NN3	NN4	NN6	IE3/J1	IE3/J2	IE4	IE5	IE5.5
Compatibility			✓						

The value of the `which` property depends on the event type: a mouse button indicator for mouse events and a character key code for keyboard events.

For a mouse-related event, the *eventObject*.`which` property contains either a 1 for the left (primary) mouse button or a 3 for the right (secondary) mouse button. Most Macintosh computers have only a one-button mouse, so exercise care in designing pages that rely on the second mouse button. Even on Windows and other platforms, you must program an object's `onMouseDown` event handler to `return false` for the secondary button to be registered instead of a browser pop-up menu appearing on-screen.

Keyboard events generate the ISO-Latin character code for the key that has been pressed. This value is an integer between 0 and 255. If your script needs to look at the actual character being typed, rather than the key code, use the `String.fromCharCode()` method (see Chapter 34) to make the conversion. If you have difficulty obtaining character codes from keyboard events, try using the `onKeyDown` and `onKeyUp` events rather than `onKeyPress`. In either case, the function keys do not present character codes.

Example
See Listing 29-10 for an example of using the *eventObject*.`which` property.

IE4+ event Object

Properties	Methods	Event Handlers
altKey		
altLeft		
behaviorCookie		
behaviorPart		
bookmarks		
boundElements		
button		
cancelBubble		
clientX		
clientY		
contentOverflow		
ctrlKey		
ctrlLeft		
dataFld		
dataTransfer		
fromElement		
keyCode		
nextPage		
offsetX		
offsetY		
propertyName		
qualifier		
reason		
recordset		
repeat		
returnValue		
saveType		
screenX		

Properties	Methods	Event Handlers
screenY		
shiftKey		
shiftLeft		
srcElement		
srcFilter		
srcUrn		
toElement		
type		
x		
y		

Syntax

Accessing IE4+ event object properties:

[window.]event.*property*

	NN2	NN3	NN4	NN6	IE3/J1	IE3/J2	IE4	IE5	IE5.5
Compatibility							✓	✓	✓

About this object

The IE4+ event object is a property of the window object. Its basic operation is covered earlier in this chapter.

You can see a little of what the event object is about with the help of The Evaluator (see Chapter 13). If you type event into the bottom text box, you can examine the properties of the event object for the event that triggers the function that displays the event object properties. If you press the Enter key in the text box, you see properties of the keypress event that caused the internal script to run; click the List Properties button to see the properties of the click event fired at the button. Hold down some of the modifier keys while clicking to see how this affects some of the properties.

As you review the properties for the event object, make special note of the compatibility table for each property. The list of properties for this object has grown over the evolution of the IE4+ event object model. Also, most properties are listed here as being read-only, which they were in IE4. But for IE5+, these properties are also Read/Write if the event is created artificially via methods, such as IE5.5's document.createEventObject() method. Event objects that are created by user or system action have very few properties that can be modified on the fly (to prevent your scripts from altering user actions).

Properties

altKey
ctrlKey
shiftKey

Value: Boolean   Read-Only

	NN2	NN3	NN4	NN6	IE3/J1	IE3/J2	IE4	IE5	IE5.5
Compatibility							✓	✓	✓

When an event object is created in response to a user or system action, these three properties are set based on whether their corresponding keys were being held down at the time — a Shift-click, for example. If the key was held down, the property is assigned a value of true; otherwise the value is false.

Most commonly, you use expressions consisting of this property as if construction condition statements. Because these are Boolean values, you can combine multiple properties in a single condition. For example, if you have a branch of a function that is to execute only if the event occurred with both the Shift and Control keys held down, the condition looks as the following:

```
if (event.shiftKey && event.ctrlKey) {
    // statements to execute
}
```

Conversely, you can take a more user-friendly approach to provide special processing if the user holds down any one of the three modifier keys:

```
if (event.shiftKey || event.ctrlKey || event.altKey) {
    // statements to execute
}
```

The rationale behind this approach is to offer perhaps some shortcut operation for users, but not force them to memorize a specific modifier key combination.

Example

See Listing 29-10, where the values of these three properties are used to set the checked properties of corresponding checkboxes for a variety of event types.

Related Items: altLeft, ctrlLeft, shiftLeft properties.

altLeft
ctrlLeft
shiftLeft

Value: Boolean   Read-Only

	NN2	NN3	NN4	NN6	IE3/J1	IE3/J2	IE4	IE5	IE5.5
Compatibility									✓

Some versions of Windows (notably Windows NT and Windows 2000) allow events to be modified by only the left-hand Alt, Ctrl, and Shift keys when using IE5.5+. For these modifiers to be recorded by the event object, focus must be on the document (body), and not in any form control. If the left-key version is false and the regular version is true, then your script knows that the right-hand key had been held down during the event.

Related Items: altKey, ctrlKey, shiftKey properties.

behaviorCookie
behaviorPart

Value: Integer   Read-Only

	NN2	NN3	NN4	NN6	IE3/J1	IE3/J2	IE4	IE5	IE5.5
Compatibility									✓

These two properties are related to a Windows technology that Microsoft calls *rendering behaviors*. Unlike the behaviors discussed under the `addBehavior()` method in Chapter 15, rendering behaviors are written in C++ and provide services for custom drawing on your Web page. For more details, consult the document "Implementing Rendering Behaviors" at `http://msdn.microsoft.com/workshop/browser/editing/imprendbehav.asp`.

bookmarks
boundElements
dataFld
qualifier
reason
recordset

Value: See Text   Read-Only

	NN2	NN3	NN4	NN6	IE3/J1	IE3/J2	IE4	IE5	IE5.5
Compatibility							✓	✓	✓

This group of `event` object properties is tied to using Data Binding in Windows versions of IE4+. Extensive details of Data Binding lie outside the scope of this book, but Table 29-5 provides a summary of these `event` object properties within that context (much of the terminology is used in Data Binding, but doesn't affect other scripting). For more details, search for ActiveX Data Objects (ADO) at `http://msdn.microsoft.com/workshop/`.

Table 29-5 **ADO-Related event Object Properties**

Property	Value	First Implemented	Description
bookmarks	Array	IE4	Array of ADO bookmarks (saved positions) for records within a recordset associated with the object that received the event.
boundElements	Array	IE5	Array of element references for all elements bound to the same data set that was touched by the current event.
dataFld	String	IE5	Name of the data source column that is bound to a table cell that receives a cellchange event.
qualifier	String	IE5	Name of the data member associated with a data source that receives a data-related event. Available only if the data source object (DSO) allows multiple-named data members or a qualifier has been explicitly set via the DATASRC attribute of the bound element. Read-write in IE5+.
reason	Integer	IE4	Set only from onDataSetComplete event, provides the result code of the data set loading (0=successful; 1=transfer aborted; 2=other error).
recordset	Object	IE4	Reference to the current recordset in a data source object.

button

Value: Integer   Read-Only

	NN2	NN3	NN4	NN6	IE3/J1	IE3/J2	IE4	IE5	IE5.5
Compatibility							✓	✓	✓

The button property reveals which button or buttons were pressed to activate a mouse event. If no mouse button is pressed to generate an event, this property is zero. But integers 1 through 7 reveal single and multiple button presses, including three-button mice when they are recognized by the operating system. Integer values correspond to buttons according to the following scheme:

Value	Description
0	No button
1	Left (primary) button
2	Right button
3	Left and right buttons together
4	Middle button
5	Left and middle buttons together
6	Right and middle buttons together
7	Left, middle, and right buttons together

Mouse buttons other than the primary one are easier to look for in mousedown or mouseup events, rather than onclick events. Be aware that as the user works toward pressing multiple buttons, each press fires a mousedown event. Therefore, if the user presses the left button first, the mousedown event fires, with the event.button property bearing the 1 value; as soon as the right button is pressed, the mousedown event fires again, but this time with an event.button value of 3. If your script intends to perform special action with both buttons pressed, it should ignore and not perform any action for a single mouse button, because that one-button event will very likely fire in the process, disturbing the intended action.

Exercise caution when scripting the event.button property for both IE4+ and NN6+. The W3C DOM event model defines different button values for mouse buttons (0, 1, and 2 for left, middle, and right) and no values for multiple buttons.

Example

See Listing 29-11, where the `event.button` property is revealed in the statusbar. Try pressing individual mouse buttons on, for example, the screen button. Then try combinations, watching the results very closely in the statusbar.

Related Items: None.

cancelBubble

Value: Boolean   Read/Write

	NN2	NN3	NN4	NN6	IE3/J1	IE3/J2	IE4	IE5	IE5.5
Compatibility							✓	✓	✓

The `cancelBubble` property (which sounds more as if it should be a method name) determines whether the current `event` object bubbles up any higher in the element containment hierarchy of the document. By default, this property is `false`, meaning that if the event is supposed to bubble, then it will do so automatically.

To prevent event bubbling for the current event, set the property to `true` anywhere within the event handler function. As an alternative, you can cancel bubbling directly in an element's event handler attribute, as in the following:

```
onClick="doButtonClick(this); event.cancelBubble = true"
```

Cancelling event bubbling works only for the current event. The very next event to fire will have bubbling enabled (provided the event bubbles).

Example

See Listing 29-6 to see the `cancelBubble` property in action. Even though that listing has some features that apply to IE5.5+, the bubble cancelling demonstration works all the way back to IE4.

Related Items: `returnValue` property.

```
clientX
clientY
offsetX
offsetY
screenX
screenY
x
y
```

Value: Integer   Read/Write

	NN2	NN3	NN4	NN6	IE3/J1	IE3/J2	IE4	IE5	IE5.5
Compatibility							✓	✓	✓

An IE `event` object provides coordinates for an event in as many as four coordinate spaces: the element itself, the parent element of the event's target, the viewable area of the browser window, and the entire video screen. Unfortunately, misleading values can be returned by some of the properties that correspond to these coordinate spaces, as discussed in this section. Note that no properties provide the explicit position of an event relative to the entire page, in case the user has scrolled the window.

Starting with the innermost space—that of the element that is the target of the event—the `offsetX` and `offsetY` properties should provide pixel coordinates within the target element. This is how, for example, you could determine the click point on an image, regardless of whether the image is embedded in the BODY or floating around in a positioned DIV. Windows versions through (at least) IE5.5 produce the correct values in most cases. But for some elements that are child elements of the BODY element, the vertical (y) value may be relative to the viewable window, rather than just the element itself. You can see an example of this when you work with Listing 29-14 and click the H1 or P elements near the top of the page. This problem does not affect IE for the Mac, but there is another problem on Mac versions: If the page is scrolled away from its normal original position, the scrolled values are subtracted from the `clientX` and `clientY` values. This is an incompatibility bug, and you must take this error into account if you need click coordinates inside an element for a potentially scrolled page. This error correction must be done only for the Mac, because Windows works OK.

Extending scope to the offset parent element of the event's target, the x and y properties in IE5+ for Windows should return the coordinates for the event relative to the target's offset parent element (the element that can be found via the offsetParent property). For most non-positioned elements, these values are the same as the clientX and clientY properties because, as discussed in a moment, the offset parent element has a zero offset with *its* parent, the BODY. Observe an important caution about the x and y properties: In IE4/Windows and through IE5/Macintosh, the properties do not take into account any offset parent locations other than the BODY. Even in IE5+ for Windows, this property can give false readings in some circumstances. By and large, these two properties should not be used.

The next set of coordinates, clientX and clientY, are relative to the visible document area of the browser window. When the document is scrolled all the way to the top (or the document doesn't scroll at all), these coordinates are the same as the coordinates on the entire page. But because the page can scroll "underneath" the viewable window, the coordinates on the page can change if the page scrolls. Also, in the Windows versions of IE, you can actually register mouse events that are up to two pixels outside of the BODY element, which seems weird, but true. Therefore, in IE/Windows, if you click the background of the BODY, the event fires on the BODY element, but the clientX/clientY values will be two pixels greater then offsetX/offsetY (they're equal in IE/Mac). Despite this slight discrepancy, you should rely on the clientX and clientY properties if you are trying to get the coordinates of an event that may be in a positioned element, but have those coordinates relative to the entire viewable window, rather than just the positioning context.

Taking the page's scrolling into account for an event coordinate is often important. After all, unless you generate a fixed-size window for a user, you don't know how the browser window will be oriented. If you're looking for a click within a specific region of the page, you must take page scrolling into account. The scrolling factor can be retrieved from the document.body.scrollLeft and document.body.scrollTop properties. When reading the clientX and clientY properties, be sure to add the corresponding scroll properties to get the position on the page:

```
var coordX = event.clientX + document.body.scrollLeft
var coordY = event.clientY + document.body.scrollTop
```

Do this in your production work without fail.

Finally, the screenX and screenY properties return the pixel coordinates of the event on the entire video screen. These properties may be more useful if IE provided more window dimension properties. In any case, because mouse events fire only when the cursor is somewhere in the content region of the browser window, don't expect to get screen values of anywhere outside this region.

If these descriptions seem confusing to you, you are not alone. Throw in a few bugs, and it may seem like quite a mess. But think how you may use event coordinates in scripts. By and large, you want to know one of two types of mouse event coordinates: within the element itself and within the page. Use the offsetX/offsetY properties for the former; use clientX/clientY (plus the scroll property values) for the latter.

While the coordinate properties are used primarily for mouse events, there is a little quirk that may let you determine if the user has resized the window via the maximize icon in the title bar (on the Mac, this is called the zoom box) or the resize handle at the bottom-right corner of the screen. Mouse event coordinates are recorded in the event object for a resize event. In the case of the maximize icon, the clientY coordinate is a negative value (above the client space) and the clientX coordinate is within about 45 pixels of the previous width of the window (document.body.clientWidth). This, of course, happens after the window has resized, so it is not a way to prevent window resizing.

Example (with Listing 29-14) on the CD-ROM

Related Items: fromElement, toElement properties.

dataTransfer

Value: Object   Read-Only

	NN2	NN3	NN4	NN6	IE3/J1	IE3/J2	IE4	IE5	IE5.5
Compatibility								✓	✓

The dataTransfer property is a reference to an IE/Windows-only object called the dataTransfer object. Use this object in drag-and-drop operations (that is, with drag-and-drop-related events) to control not only the data that gets transferred from the source to the target but also to control the look of the cursor along the way.

Table 29-6 lists the properties and methods of the dataTransfer object.

Table 29-6 dataTransfer object Properties and Methods

Property/Method	Returns	Description
dropEffect	String	An element that is a potential recipient of a drop action can use the onDragEnter, onDragOver, or onDrop event handler to set the cursor style to be displayed when the cursor is atop the element. Before this can work, the source element's onDragStart event handler must assign a value to the event.effectAllowed property. Possible string values for both properties are copy, link, move, or none. These properties correspond to the Windows system cursors for the operations users typically do with files and in other documents. You must also cancel the default action (meaning set event.returnValue to false) for all of these drop element event handlers: onDragEnter, onDragOver, and onDrop.
effectAllowed	String	Set in response to an onDragStart event of the source element, this property determines which kind of drag-and-drop action will be taking place. Possible string values are copy, link, move, or none. This property value must match the dropEffect property value for the target element's event object. Also, cancel the default action (meaning, set event.returnValue to false) in the onDragStart event handler.
clearData([format])	Nothing	Removes data in the clipboard. If no format parameters are supplied, all data are cleared. Data formats can be one or more of the following strings: Text, URL, File, HTML, Image.
getData(format)	String	Retrieves data of the specified format from the clipboard. The format is one of the following strings: Text, URL, File, HTML, Image. The clipboard is not emptied after you get the data, so that it can be retrieved in several sequential operations.
setData(format, data)	Boolean	Stores string data in the clipboard. The format is one of the following strings: Text, URL, File, HTML, Image. For non-text data formats, the data must be a string that specifies the path or URL to the content. Returns true if the transfer to the clipboard is successful.

(IE) event.dataTransfer

The `dataTransfer` object acts as a conduit and controller of data that your scripts need to transfer from one element to another in response to a user's drag-and-drop action. You need to adhere to a well-defined sequence of actions triggered by a handful of event handlers. This means that the object is invoked on different instances of the `event` object as different events fire in the process of dragging and dropping.

The sequence begins at the source element, where an `onDragStart` event handler typically assigns a value to the `dropEffect` property and uses the `getData()` method to explicitly capture whatever data it is about the source object that gets transferred to the eventual target. For example, if you drag an image, the information being transferred may simply be the URL of the image — data that is extractable from the `event.srcElement.src` property of that event (the `src` property of the image, that is).

At the target element(s), three event handlers must be defined: `onDragEnter`, `onDragOver`, and `onDrop`. Most commonly, the first two event handlers do nothing more than mark the element for a particular `dropEffect` (which must match the `effectAllowed` set at the source during the drag's start) and set `event.returnValue` to false so that the cursor displays the desired cursor. These actions are also carried out in the `onDrop` event handler, but that is also the handler that does the processing of the destination action at the target element. This is when the `dataTransfer` object's `getData()` method is invoked to pick up the data that has been "stored" away by `getData()` at the start of the drag. If you also want to make sure that the data is not picked up accidentally by another event, invoke the `clearData()` method to remove that data from memory.

Note that the style of dragging being discussed here is not the kind in which you see the source element actually moving on the screen (although you could script it that way). The intention is to treat drag-and-drop operations just as Windows does in, say, the Windows Explorer window or on the Desktop. To the user, the draggable component becomes encapsulated in the cursor. That's why the properties of the `dataTransfer` object control the appearance of the cursor at the drop point as a way of conveying to the user the type of action that will occur with the impending drop.

Example

An extensive example of the `dataTransfer` property in action can be found in Listing 15-37 in the section for the `onDrag` event handler.

Related Items: `onDragEnd`, `onDragEnter`, `onDragLeave`, `onDragOver`, `onDragStart`, `onDrop` event handlers.

fromElement
toElement

Value: Element Object   Read-Only

	NN2	NN3	NN4	NN6	IE3/J1	IE3/J2	IE4	IE5	IE5.5
Compatibility							✓	✓	✓

The fromElement and toElement properties allow an element to uncover where the cursor rolled in from or has rolled out to. These properties extend the power of the onMouseOver and onMouseOut event handlers by expanding their scope to outside the current element (usually to an adjacent element).

When the onMouseOver event fires on an element, the cursor had to be over some other element just beforehand. The fromElement property holds a reference to that element. Conversely, when the onMouseOut event fires, the cursor is already over some other element. The toElement property holds a reference to that element.

On the CD-ROM

Example (with Listing 29-15) on the CD-ROM

Related Items: srcElement property.

keyCode

Value: Integer   Read-Only

	NN2	NN3	NN4	NN6	IE3/J1	IE3/J2	IE4	IE5	IE5.5
Compatibility							✓	✓	✓

For keyboard events, the keyCode property returns an integer corresponding to the Unicode value of the character (for onKeyPress events) or the keyboard character key (for onKeyDown and onKeyUp events). There is a significant distinction between these numbering code systems.

If you want the Unicode values (the same as ASCII values for the Latin character set) for the key that a user pressed, get the keyCode property from the onKeyPress event handler. For example, a lowercase "a" returns 97, while an uppercase "A" returns 65. Non-character keys, such as arrows, page navigation, and function keys, return a null value for the keyCode property during onKeyPress events. In other words, the keyCode property for onKeyPress events is more like a character code than a key code.

To capture the exact keyboard key that the user presses, use either the onKeyDown or onKeyUp event handler. For these events, the event object captures a numeric code associated with a particular key on the keyboard. For the character keys, this varies with the language assigned as the system language. Importantly, there is no distinction between uppercase or lowercase: The "A" key on the Latin keyboard returns a value of 65, regardless of the state of the Shift key. At the same time, however, the press of the Shift key fired its own onKeyDown and onKeyUp events, setting the keyCode value to 16. Other non-character keys — arrows, page navigation, function, and similar — have their own codes as well. This gets very detailed, including special key codes for the numeric keyboard keys that are different from their corresponding numbers along the top row of the alphanumeric keyboard.

Be sure to see the extensive section on keyboard events in Chapter 15 for examples of how to apply the keyCode property in applications.

On the CD-ROM Example (with Listing 29-16) on the CD-ROM

Related Items: onKeyDown, onKeyPress, onKeyUp event handlers.

nextPage

Value: String   Read-Only

	NN2	NN3	NN4	NN6	IE3/J1	IE3/J2	IE4	IE5	IE5.5
Compatibility									✓

The nextPage property is applicable only if your IE5.5/Windows page uses a TemplatePrinter behavior. Values of this property are one of the following strings: left, right, or an empty string. For more information about the TemplatePrinter behavior for Windows-only versions of IE5.5+, see

```
http://msdn.microsoft.com/workshop/browser/hosting/printpreview/reference/
behaviors/TemplatePrinter.asp
```

propertyName

Value: String   Read-Only

	NN2	NN3	NN4	NN6	IE3/J1	IE3/J2	IE4	IE5	IE5.5
Compatibility								✓	✓

(IE) event.propertyName

The `propertyName` property is filled only after an `onPropertyChange` event fires. This property is not available through Version 5 of IE/Macintosh.

If a script modifies a property, the `onPropertyChange` event handler fires, and the string name of the property is stuffed into the `event.propertyName` property. If the property happens to be a property of the `style` object associated with the element, the `propertyName` is the full property reference, as in `style.backgroundColor`.

Example
See Listing 15-46 in the section about the `onPropertyChange` event handler for an example of the values returned by this property.

Related Items: `onPropertyChange` event handler (Chapter 15).

repeat

Value: Boolean   Read-Only

	NN2	NN3	NN4	NN6	IE3/J1	IE3/J2	IE4	IE5	IE5.5
Compatibility								✓	✓

The `repeat` property reveals for `onKeyDown` events only whether the key is in repeat mode (as determined by the Keyboard control panel settings in the system). With this information, you can prevent the automatic triggering of repeat mode from causing multiple characters from being recognized by the browser. This property can come in handy if users may be physically challenged and may occasionally and accidentally hold down a key too long. The following script fragment in an `onKeyDown` event handler for a text box or TEXTAREA prevents multiple characters from appearing even if the system goes into repeat mode:

```
if (event.repeat) {
    event.returnValue = false
}
```

By disabling the default action while in repeat mode, no further characters reach the text box until repeat mode goes away (meaning, with the press of another key). This property is not available in IE/Mac through Version 5.

Related Items: `onKeyDown` event handler.

returnValue

Value: Boolean   Read-Only

	NN2	NN3	NN4	NN6	IE3/J1	IE3/J2	IE4	IE5	IE5.5
Compatibility							✓	✓	✓

While IE4+ continues to honor the original way of preventing default action for an event handler (that is, having the last statement of the event handler evaluate to `return false`), the IE4+ event model provides a property that lets the cancellation of default action take place entirely within a function invoked by an event handler. By default, the `returnValue` property of the `event` object is `true`, meaning that the element processes the event after the scripted handler completes its job, just as if the script weren't there. Normal processing, for example, is displaying a typed character, navigating to a link's HREF URL upon being clicked, or submitting a form after the Submit button is clicked.

But you don't always want the default action to occur. For example, consider a text box that is supposed to allow only numbers be typed in it. The `onKeyPress` event handler can invoke a function that inspects each typed character. If the character is not a numeric character, then it should not reach the text box for display. The following validation function may be invoked from the `onKeyPress` event handler of just such a text box:

```
function checkIt() {
    var charCode = event.keyCode
    if (charCode < 48 || charCode > 57) {
        alert("Please make sure entries are numerals only.")
        event.returnValue = false
    }
}
```

By using this event handler, the errant character won't appear in the text box.

Note that this property is not a substitute for the `return` statement of a function. If you need a value to be returned to the invoking statement, you can use a `return` statement in addition to setting the `event.returnValue` property.

On the CD-ROM   Example on the CD-ROM

Related Items: `return` statement (Chapter 41).

saveType

Value: String   Read-Only

	NN2	NN3	NN4	NN6	IE3/J1	IE3/J2	IE4	IE5	IE5.5
Compatibility									✓

The saveType property is assigned a value only when an oncontentsave event is bound to an IE/Windows DHTML behavior (.htc). For more information about behaviors, see

http://msdn.microsoft.com/workshop/author/behaviors/overview.asp

Related Items: addBehavior() method.

srcElement

Value: Element Object Reference   Read-Only

	NN2	NN3	NN4	NN6	IE3/J1	IE3/J2	IE4	IE5	IE5.5
Compatibility							✓	✓	✓

The srcElement property is a reference to the HTML element object that is the original target of the event. Because an event may bubble up through the element containment hierarchy and be processed at any level along the way, having a property that points back to the element from which the event originated is comforting. After you have a reference to that element, you can read or write any properties that belong to that element or invoke any of its methods.

On the CD-ROM

Example (with Listing 29-17) on the CD-ROM

Related Items: fromElement, toElement properties.

srcFilter

Value: String   Read-Only

	NN2	NN3	NN4	NN6	IE3/J1	IE3/J2	IE4	IE5	IE5.5
Compatibility							✓	✓	✓

According to Microsoft, the srcFilter property should return a string of the name of the filter that was applied to trigger an onFilterChange event handler. While the property exists in the event object, its value is always null, at least through IE5.5. This property, because it is filter related, is a Windows-only property.

Related Items: onFilterChange event handler; style.filter object.

srcUrn

Value: String   Read-Only

	NN2	NN3	NN4	NN6	IE3/J1	IE3/J2	IE4	IE5	IE5.5
Compatibility								✓	✓

If an event is fired in an IE/Windows behavior attached to an element, and the behavior has a URN identifier defined for it, the srcUrn property returns the string from the URN identifier. For more information about behaviors, see

http://msdn.microsoft.com/workshop/author/behaviors/overview.asp

Related Items: addBehavior() method.

toElement

See fromElement

type

Value: String   Read-Only

	NN2	NN3	NN4	NN6	IE3/J1	IE3/J2	IE4	IE5	IE5.5
Compatibility							✓	✓	✓

You can find out what kind of event fired to create the current event object by way of the type property. The value is a string version of the event name — just the name of the event without the "on" prefix that is normally associated with event names in IE. This property can be helpful when you designate one event handler function to process different kinds of events. For example, both the onMouseDown and onClick event handlers for an object can invoke one function. Inside the function, a branch is written for whether the type comes in as mousedown or click, with different processing for each event type. That is not to endorse such event handler function sharing, but for you to be aware of this power should your script constructions find the property helpful.

This property and its values are fully compatible with the NN4 and NN6 event models.

Example on the CD-ROM

Related Items: All event handlers (Chapter 15).

NN6+ event Object

Properties	Methods	Event Handlers
altKey	preventDefault()	
bubbles	stopPropagation()	
button		
cancelBubble		
cancelable		
charCode		
clientX		
clientY		
ctrlKey		
currentTarget		
detail		
eventPhase		
isChar		

Continued

Properties	Methods	Event Handlers
keyCode		
layerX		
layerY		
metaKey		
pageX		
pageY		
relatedTarget		
screenX		
screenY		
shiftKey		
target		
timeStamp		
type		
view		

Syntax

Accessing NN6+ event object properties and methods:

eventObject.property | *method([parameters])*

	NN2	NN3	NN4	NN6	IE3/J1	IE3/J2	IE4	IE5	IE5.5
Compatibility				✓					

About this object

Although it is based largely on the event object as defined by the W3C DOM Level 2, the NN6+ event object also carries forward several characteristics from the NN4 event object. A few properties are continued primarily for backward compatibility. But because development for NN6 will likely forego the peculiarities of the NN4 DOM and event models, you should ignore these items (as highlighted below). Wherever possible, look forward and embrace the W3C DOM aspects of the event model.

While the NN6 event model provides a bubbling event propagation model just as IE4+, the incompatibility of referencing event objects between the event models is still there. In NN6 (as in NN4), an event object is explicitly passed as a parameter to event handler (or, rather, event listener) functions. But after you have a browser-specific event object assigned to a variable inside a function, a few important properties have the same names between the IE4+ and NN6+ event models. If Microsoft adopts more of the W3C DOM event model in future versions of IE, the compatibility situation should improve.

The event object discussed in this section is the instance of an event that is created as the result of a user or system event action. The NN6 DOM includes an additional static Event object. Many of the properties of the static Event object are inherited by the event instances, so the detailed coverage of those shared properties is in this section because it is the event object you'll be scripting for the most part.

In many code fragments in the following detail sections, you will see references that begin with the evt reference. This assumes that the statement(s) resides inside a function that has assigned the incoming event object to the evt parameter variable:

```
function myFunction(evt) {...}
```

As shown earlier in this chapter, you can equalize NN6 and IE4+ event object references when it is practical to do so because the scripts work on identical (or similar) event object properties.

Properties

altKey
ctrlKey
metaKey
shiftKey

Value: Boolean   Read-Only

	NN2	NN3	NN4	NN6	IE3/J1	IE3/J2	IE4	IE5	IE5.5
Compatibility				✓					

When an event object is created in response to a user or system action, these four properties are set based on whether their corresponding keys were being held down at the time—a Shift-click, for example. If the key was held down, the property is assigned a value of true; otherwise the value is false. The metaKey property corresponds to the Command key on the Macintosh keyboard but does not register for the Windows key on Wintel computers.

Most commonly, you use expressions consisting of this property as `if` construction condition statements. Because these are Boolean values, you can combine multiple properties in a single condition. For example, if you have a branch of a function that is to execute only if the event occurred with both the Shift and Control keys held down, the condition looks as the following:

```
if (evt.shiftKey && evt.ctrlKey) {
    // statements to execute
}
```

Conversely, you can take a more user-friendly approach to provide special processing if the user holds down any one of the four modifier keys:

```
if (evt.shiftKey || evt.ctrlKey || evt.metaKey || evt.altKey) {
    // statements to execute
}
```

The rationale behind this approach is to offer perhaps some shortcut operation for users, but not force them to memorize a specific modifier key combination.

Example

See Listing 29-10, where the values of these properties are used to set the `checked` properties of corresponding checkboxes for a variety of event types.

Related Items: None.

bubbles

Value: Boolean   Read-Only

	NN2	NN3	NN4	NN6	IE3/J1	IE3/J2	IE4	IE5	IE5.5
Compatibility				✓					

Not every event bubbles. For example, an `onsubmit` event propagates no further than the form object with which the event is associated. Events that do not bubble have their event object's `bubbles` property set to `false`; all others have the property set to `true`. You use this property in the rare circumstances of a single event handler function processing a wide variety of events. You may want to perform special operations only on events that can bubble and handle the others without special treatment. For this branch, you can use the property in an `if` condition statement:

```
if (evt.bubbles) {
    // special processing for bubble-able events
}
```

You do not have to branch, however, just to cancel bubbling. A non-propagating event doesn't mind if you tell it not to propagate.

Related Items: `cancelBubble` property.

button

Value: Integer   Read-Only

	NN2	NN3	NN4	NN6	IE3/J1	IE3/J2	IE4	IE5	IE5.5
Compatibility				✓					

The `button` property reveals the button that was pressed to activate the mouse event. The left (primary) button returns a value of 1. If the mouse is a three-button mouse, the middle button returns 2. The right button (on any multi-button mouse) returns a value of 3. Note that these values differ from those stated in the W3C DOM (0, 1, and 2, respectively), but these values are backward-compatible with the NN4 `which` property.

Mouse buttons other than the primary one are easier to look for in `mousedown` or `mouseup` events, rather than `onclick` events. In the case of a user pressing multiple buttons, only the most recent button is registered.

Exercise caution when scripting the `button` property for both IE4+ and NN6+. The respective event models define different button values for mouse buttons.

Example
See Listing 29-11, where the `button` property is revealed in the statusbar. Try pressing individual mouse buttons on, say, the screen button.

Related Items: None.

cancelBubble

Value: Boolean   Read/Write

	NN2	NN3	NN4	NN6	IE3/J1	IE3/J2	IE4	IE5	IE5.5
Compatibility				✓					

(NN6) *eventObject*.**cancelBubble**

The `cancelBubble` property is a rare instance of an IE4+ event property being implemented in NN6 even though the property is not defined in the W3C DOM. The property operates the same as in IE4+ in that it determines whether the current event object bubbles up any higher in the element containment hierarchy of the document. By default, this property is `false`, meaning that if the event is supposed to bubble, then it will do so automatically.

To prevent event bubbling for the current event, set the property to `true` anywhere within the event handler function. As an alternative, you can cancel bubbling directly in an element's event handler attribute, as in the following:

```
onClick="doButtonClick(this); event.cancelBubble = true"
```

Cancelling event bubbling works only for the current event. The very next event to fire will have bubbling enabled (provided the event bubbles).

If you are trying to migrate your code as much as possible to the W3C DOM, then use the `stopPropagation()` method instead of `cancelBubble`. For cross-browser compatibility, however, `cancelBubble` is a safe bet.

Example

See Listing 29-6 to see the `cancelBubble` property in action in an IE environment. Even though that listing has some features that apply to IE5.5+, the bubble cancelling demonstration works all the way back to IE4.

Related Items: `stopPropagation()` method.

cancelable

Value: Boolean   Read-Only

	NN2	NN3	NN4	NN6	IE3/J1	IE3/J2	IE4	IE5	IE5.5
Compatibility				✓					

If an event is cancelable, then its default action can be prevented from occurring with the help of a script. While most events are cancelable, some are not. The cancelable property lets you inquire about a particular event object to see if its event type is `cancelable`. Values for the property are Booleans. You may want to perform special operations only on events that are cancelable, and handle the others without special treatment. For this branch, you can use the property in an `if` condition statement:

```
if (evt.cancelable) {
    // special processing for cancelable events
}
```

You do not have to branch, however, just to prevent an event's default action. A non-cancelable event doesn't mind if you tell it to prevent the default action.

Related Items: preventDefault() method.

charCode
keyCode

Value: Integer   Read-Only

	NN2	NN3	NN4	NN6	IE3/J1	IE3/J2	IE4	IE5	IE5.5
Compatibility				✓					

The NN6 event object model clearly distinguishes between the Unicode character attached to the alphanumeric keys of the keyboard and the code attached to each of the keyboard (regardless of its character). To inspect the character of a key, use the onKeyPress event to create the event object, and then look at the event object's charCode property. This is the property that returns 97 for "a" and 65 for "A" because it's concerned with the character associated with the key action. This property's value is zero for onKeyDown and onKeyUp events.

In contrast, the keyCode property is filled with a non-zero value only from onKeyDown and onKeyUp events (onKeyPress sets the property to zero) when alphanumeric keys are pressed; for most other non-character keys, all three events fill the keyCode property. Through this property you can look for non-character keys, such as arrows, page navigation, and function keys. For the character keys, there is no distinction between uppercase or lowercase: The "A" key on the Latin keyboard returns a value of 65, regardless of the state of the Shift key. At the same time, however, the press of the Shift key fires its own onKeyDown and onKeyUp events, setting the keyCode value to 16. Other non-character keys — arrows, page navigation, function, and similar — have their own codes as well. This gets very detailed, including special key codes for the numeric keyboard keys that are different from their corresponding numbers along the top row of the alphanumeric keyboard.

Be sure to see the extensive section on keyboard events in Chapter 15 for examples of how to apply the keyCode property in applications.

(NN6) *eventObject*.charCode

On the CD-ROM Example (with Listing 29-18) on the CD-ROM

Related Items: onKeyDown, onKeyPress, onKeyUp event handlers.

clientX
clientY
layerX
layerY
pageX
pageY
screenX
screenY

Value: Integer   Read-Only

	NN2	NN3	NN4	NN6	IE3/J1	IE3/J2	IE4	IE5	IE5.5
Compatibility				✓					

The NN6 event object borrows mouse coordinate properties from both the NN4 and IE4+ event models. If you have worked with event coordinates in these other browsers, then you have nothing new to learn for NN6.

Like the IE4+ event object, the NN6 event object's clientX and clientY properties are the coordinates within the viewable content region of the window. These values are relative to the window space, not the document. But unlike IE4+, you don't have to calculate the position of the coordinates within the document because another pair of properties, pageX and pageY, provide that information automatically. If the page has not scrolled, then the values of the client and page coordinates are the same. Because it is usually more important to know an event's coordinates with respect to the document than the window, the pageX and pageY properties are used most often.

Another property pair, layerX and layerY, borrow terminology from the now defunct layer schemes of NN4, but the properties can still be quite valuable nonetheless. These coordinates are measured relative to the positioning context of the element that received the event. For regular, unpositioned elements in the BODY part of a document, that positioning context is the BODY element. Thus, for those elements, the values of the page and layer coordinates will be the same. But if you create a positioned element, the coordinate space is measured from the top-left corner of that space. Thus, if you are using the coordinates to assist in scripted dragging of positioned elements, you can confine your scope to just the positioned element.

One coordinate system missing from the NN6 repertoire is that of the target element itself (comparable to the `offsetX` and `offsetY` properties of IE4+). These values, however, can be calculated by subtracting from the page coordinate properties the `offsetLeft` and `offsetTop` properties of both the target element and its positioning context. For example, if you want to get the coordinates of a mouse event inside an image, the event handler can calculate those values as follows:

```
var clickOffsetX = evt.pageX - evt.target.offsetLeft - document.body.offsetLeft
var clickOffsetY = evt.pageY - evt.target.offsetTop - document.body.offsetTop
```

The last set of coordinate properties, `screenX` and `screenY`, provide values relative to the entire video display. Of all these properties, only the client and screen coordinates are defined in the W3C DOM Level 2 standard.

Keep in mind that in NN6, event targets include text nodes inside elements. Because nodes do not have all the properties of elements (for example, they have no offset properties signifying their location in the document), you may sometimes have to go to the target node's parent node to get an element object whose offset properties provide the necessary page geography. This matters, of course, only if your scripts need concern themselves with mouse events on text.

Example (with Listing 29-19) on the CD-ROM

Related Items: `target` property.

`currentTarget`

Value: Element Object Reference   Read-Only

	NN2	NN3	NN4	NN6	IE3/J1	IE3/J2	IE4	IE5	IE5.5
Compatibility				✓					

As an event courses its way through its propagation paths, an event listener may process that event along the way. While the event knows what the target is, it can also be helpful for the event listener function to know which element's event listener is now processing the event. The `currentTarget` property provides a reference to the element object whose event listener is processing the event. This allows one listener function to potentially process the event from different levels, branching the code to accommodate different element levels that process the event.

A valuable companion piece of information about the event is the `eventPhase` property, which helps your event listener function determine if the event is in capture mode, bubble mode, or is at the target. This property is demonstrated in the next section.

Example (with Listing 29-20) on the CD-ROM

Related Items: `eventPhase` property.

detail

Value: Integer   Read-Only

	NN2	NN3	NN4	NN6	IE3/J1	IE3/J2	IE4	IE5	IE5.5
Compatibility				✓					

The `detail` property is included in the W3C DOM specification as an extra property whose purpose can be determined by the browser maker. In theory, this integer property value can convey additional information about the event. While the property is present in the NN6 event object (and returns values for some events), it contains no additional data about events, but may in the future.

Related Items: None.

eventPhase

Value: Integer   Read-Only

	NN2	NN3	NN4	NN6	IE3/J1	IE3/J2	IE4	IE5	IE5.5
Compatibility				✓					

An event fires in one of three possible event phases: event capture, at the target, or bubbling. Because the same event listener function may be processing an event in multiple phases, it can inspect the value of the `eventPhase` property of the event object to see in which phase the event was when the function was invoked. Values for this property are integers 1 (capture), 2 (at target), or 3 (bubbling).

Example on the CD-ROM

Related Items: `currentTarget` property.

isChar

Value: Boolean   Read-Only

	NN2	NN3	NN4	NN6	IE3/J1	IE3/J2	IE4	IE5	IE5.5
Compatibility				✓					

You can find out from each keyboard event whether the key being pressed is a character key by examining the `isChar` property. Most typically, however, you are already filtering for character or non-character keys by virtue of the event handlers used to capture keyboard actions: `onKeyPress` for character keys; `onKeyDown` or `onKeyUp` for non-character keys. Be aware that the `isChar` property returns inconsistent values (even for the same key) in the first release of NN6.

Related Items: `charCode`, `keyCode` properties.

relatedTarget

Value: Element Object   Read-Only

	NN2	NN3	NN4	NN6	IE3/J1	IE3/J2	IE4	IE5	IE5.5
Compatibility				✓					

The `relatedTarget` property allows an element to uncover where the cursor rolled in from or has rolled out to. This property extends the power of the `onMouseOver` and `onMouseOut` event handlers by expanding their scope to outside the current element (usually to an adjacent element). This one property in NN6 does the same duty as the `fromElement` and `toElement` properties of the IE4+ `event` object.

When the onMouseOver event fires on an element, the cursor had to be over some other element just beforehand. The relatedTarget property holds a reference to that element. Conversely, when the onMouseOut event fires, the cursor is already over some other element. The relatedTarget property holds a reference to that element.

Example (with Listing 29-21) on the CD-ROM

Related Items: target property.

target

Value: Element Object Reference   Read-Only

	NN2	NN3	NN4	NN6	IE3/J1	IE3/J2	IE4	IE5	IE5.5
Compatibility				✓					

The target property is a reference to the HTML element object that is the original target of the event. Because an event may trickle down and bubble up through the element containment hierarchy and be processed at any level along the way, having a property that points back to the element from which the event originated is comforting. As soon as you have a reference to that element, you can read or write any properties that belong to that element or invoke any of its methods.

Example (with Listing 29-22) on the CD-ROM

Related Items: relatedTarget property.

timeStamp

Value: Integer   Read-Only

	NN2	NN3	NN4	NN6	IE3/J1	IE3/J2	IE4	IE5	IE5.5
Compatibility				✓					

Each event receives a time stamp in milliseconds, based on the same date epoch as the Date object (1 January 1970). Just as with the Date object, accuracy is wholly dependent on the accuracy of the system clock of the client computer.

While the precise time of an event may be of value in only some situations, the time between events can be useful for applications, such as timed exercises or action games. You can preserve the time of the most recent event in a global variable, and compare the time of the current time stamp against the stored value to determine the elapsed time between events.

Example (with Listing 29-23) on the CD-ROM

Related Items: Date object.

type

Value: String   Read-Only

	NN2	NN3	NN4	NN6	IE3/J1	IE3/J2	IE4	IE5	IE5.5
Compatibility				✓					

You can find out what kind of event fired to create the current event object by way of the type property. The value is a string version of the event name — just the name of the event without the "on" prefix that is normally associated with event listener names in NN6. This property can be helpful when you designate one event handler function to process different kinds of events. For example, both the onMouseDown and onClick event listeners for an object can invoke one function. Inside the function, a branch is written for whether the type comes in as mousedown or click, with different processing for each event type. That is not to endorse such event handler function sharing, but be aware of this power should your script constructions find the property helpful.

This property and its values are fully compatible with the NN4 and IE4+ event models.

Related Items: All event handlers (Chapter 15).

view

Value: Window Object Reference   Read-Only

	NN2	NN3	NN4	NN6	IE3/J1	IE3/J2	IE4	IE5	IE5.5
Compatibility				✓					

The closest that the W3C DOM Level 2 specification comes to acknowledging the browser window is an abstract object called an *abstract view* (AbstractView class). The object's only property is a reference to the document that it contains — the root document node that you've come to know and love. User events always occur within the confines of one of these views, and this is reflected in the event object's view property. NN6 returns a reference to the window object (which can be a frame) in which the event occurs. This reference allows an event object to be passed to scripts in other frames and those scripts can then gain access to the document object of the target element's window.

Related Items: window object.

Methods

preventDefault()

Returns: Nothing.

	NN2	NN3	NN4	NN6	IE3/J1	IE3/J2	IE4	IE5	IE5.5
Compatibility				✓					

While NN6+ continues to honor the original way of preventing default action for an event handler (that is, having the last statement of the event handler evaluate to return false), the NN6+ event model provides a method that lets the cancellation of default action take place entirely within a function invoked by an event handler. For example, consider a text box that is supposed to allow only numbers be typed in it. The onKeyPress event handler can invoke a function that inspects each typed character. If the character is not a numeric character, then it does not reach the text box for display. The following validation function may be invoked from the onKeyPress event handler of just such a text box:

```
function checkIt(evt) {
    var charCode = evt.charCode
    if (charCode < 48 || charCode > 57) {
        alert("Please make sure entries are numbers only.")
        evt.preventDefault()
    }
}
```

This way, the errant character won't appear in the text box.

Invoking the `preventDefault()` method in NN6 is the equivalent of assigning `true` to `event.returnValue` in IE5+.

Related Items: `cancelable` property.

stopPropagation()

Returns: Nothing.

	NN2	NN3	NN4	NN6	IE3/J1	IE3/J2	IE4	IE5	IE5.5
Compatibility				✓					

Use the `stopPropagation()` method to stop events from trickling down or bubbling up further through the element containment hierarchy. A statement in the event listener function that invokes

```
evt.stopPropagation()
```

is all that is needed. As an alternative, you can cancel bubbling directly in an element's event handler attribute, as in the following:

```
onClick="doButtonClick(this); event.stopPropagation()"
```

If you are writing cross-browser scripts, you also have the option of using the `cancelBubble` property, which is compatible with IE4+.

Related Items: `bubbles`, `cancelBubble` properties.

✦   ✦   ✦

Style Sheet and Style Objects

Version 4 browsers were the first to offer full-scale support for the concept of style sheets (although IE3 offered limited style sheet support). Style sheets promote a concept that makes excellent sense in the fast-paced, high-volume content creation environment that is today's World Wide Web: separating content from the rendering details of the content. Textual content may come from any number of electronic sources, but it may need to be dropped into different contexts — just like an online news feed that becomes amalgamated into dozens of Web portal sites, each with its own look and feel. All the content cares about is the text and its meaning; the Web page designer then decides how that content should be rendered on the page.

The concept has other advantages. Consider the large corporate Web site that wants to promote its identity through a distinct style. A family of style sheets can dictate the font face, font size, the look of emphasized text, and the margin width of all body text. To apply these styles on an element-by-element basis would not only be a tedious page authoring task, it is fraught with peril. If the style is omitted from the tags of one page, the uniformity of the look is destroyed. Worse yet, if the corporate design changes to use a different font face, the task of changing every style in every tag — even with a highly powered search-and-replace operation — is risky. But if a single external style sheet file dictates the styles, then the designer need make only one change in that one file to cause the new look to ripple ("cascade") through the entire Web site.

Learning how to create and apply style sheets is beyond the scope of this book, and this chapter assumes you already are familiar with style sheet terminology, such as a style sheet rule and a selector. If these terms are not in your vocabulary, you can find numerous tutorials on the subject both online and in books. Although IE and NN browsers adhere fairly closely to W3C standards for style sheets (called Cascading Style Sheets, or CSS for short), you should learn from an independent source. Microsoft, in particular, includes some extras in the style sheet vocabulary that work only on IE4+ for Windows. Unless that is your single target browser brand and client operating system, learning the common denominator of style sheet features is the right way to go. Details in this chapter cover all versions, so pay close attention to compatibility listings for each item.

One last compatibility note: While NN4 implements a fair amount of CSS, it does not expose style sheets or style rules to the object model. Part of this is linked to the static nature of an NN4 page. Because modifying a style may alter the physical layout of body elements, and because that browser does not reflow the page in response to such changes, altering styles of content that is already loaded is simply not possible. In NN6, however, the page reflows, and everything relating to styles is exposed to the scriptable object model.

Making Sense of the Object Names

The first task in this chapter is to clarify the seemingly overlapping terminology for the style sheet-related objects that you will be scripting. Some objects are more abstract than others, but they are all important. The objects in question are

> ✦ STYLE element object
>
> ✦ styleSheet object (a member of the styleSheets array)
>
> ✦ rule or cssRule object (a member of the rules or cssRules array)
>
> ✦ style object

A STYLE element object is the object that represents the <STYLE> tag in your document. Most of its properties are inherited from the basic HTML element objects you see detailed in Chapter 15. While the STYLE element object has a disabled property, by and large, you won't be accessing style sheets via the STYLE element object.

A style sheet can be embedded in a document via the <STYLE> tag or it may be linked in via a <LINK> tag. One property of the document object, the styleSheets property, returns an array (collection) of all styleSheet objects that are currently "visible" to the document, whether or not they are disabled. Even though the <STYLE> tag, for example, contains lines of code that make up the rules for a style sheet, the STYLE element object is not the path to reach the individual rules. The styleSheet object is. It is through the styleSheet object that you can enable or disable an entire sheet, access individual rules (via the rules or cssRules property array), and add or delete rules for that style sheet.

The meat of any style sheet is the rules that define how elements are to be rendered. At this object level, the terminology forks for IE4+ and NN6. The IE4+ object model calls each style sheet rule a rule object; NN6, adhering to the W3C DOM

Level 2 standard, calls each rule a cssRule object. IE5 for the Macintosh supports both references to the same object. Despite the incompatible object names, the two objects share key property names. Assembling a reference to a rule requires array references. For example, the reference to the first rule of the first styleSheet object in the document is as follows for the two browsers:

```
var oneRule = document.styleSheets[0].rules[0]        // IE4+
var oneRule = document.styleSheets[0].cssRules[0]      // IE5/Mac, NN6+
```

The style object is the last object of this quartet of style-related objects is the style object. This object is the motherlode, where actual style definitions take place. In earlier chapters, you have seen countless examples of modifying one or more style properties of an element. Most typically, this modification is accomplished through the style property of the HTML element. For example, you would set the font color of a SPAN element whose ID is "hot" as follows:

```
document.all.hot.style.color = "red"                  // IE4+
document.getElementById("hot").style.color = "red"    // IE5+, NN6+
```

The style object is also a property of a rule/cssRule object. Thus, if you need to modify the style of elements affected by an existing style sheet rule, you approach the style object through a different reference path, but the style object is treated just as it is for elements:

```
document.styleSheets[0].rules[0].style.color = "red"      // IE4+
document.styleSheets[0].cssRules[0].style.color = "red"   // IE5/Mac, NN6+
```

Many scripters concern themselves solely with the style object, and at that, a style object associated with a particular element object. Rare are instances that require manipulation of styleSheet objects beyond perhaps enabling and disabling them under script control. Therefore, if you are learning about these objects for the first time, pay closest attention to the style object details rather than to the other related objects.

Imported Style Sheets

Style sheets embedded in a document via the STYLE element can import additional style sheets via the @import selector:

```
<STYLE TYPE="text/css">
@import url(externalStyle.css);
P {font-size:16pt}
</STYLE>
```

In this example scenario, the document sees just one styleSheet object. But that object has a style sheet nested inside—the style sheet defined by the external file. IE4+ calls one of these imported styles sheets an import object. An import object has all the properties of any styleSheet object, but its parentStyle property is a reference to the styleSheet that "owns" the @import rule. In fact, the @import statement does not even appear among the rules collection of the IE styleSheet object. Therefore, to access the first rule of the imported style sheet, the reference is as the following:

```
document.styleSheets[0].imports[0].rules[0]
```

The W3C DOM and NN6 treat import rule objects differently from the IE model. To the W3C DOM, even an at-rule is considered one of the cssRules collection of a styleSheet object. One of the properties of a cssRule object is type, which conveys an integer code value revealing whether the rule is a plain CSS rule or one of several other types, including an import rule. Of course, an imported rule object then has as one of its properties the styleSheet object that, in turn, contains the rules defined in the external style sheet file. The parent-child relationship exists here, as well, whereby the styleSheet that contains the @import rule is referenced by the imported styleSheet object's parentStyle property (just as in IE4+).

Reading Style Properties

Both the IE4+ and NN6 (W3C) object models exhibit a behavior that at first glance may seem disconcerting. On the one hand, the W3C and good HTML practice encourage defining styles remotely (that is, embedded via <STYLE> or <LINK> tags) rather than as values assigned to the STYLE attribute of individual element tags throughout the document. This more closely adheres to the notion of separating style from content.

On the other hand, object models can be very literal beasts. Strictly speaking, if an element object presents a scriptable property that reflects an attribute for that element's tag, the first time a script tries to read that property, a value will be associated with that property *only* if the attribute is explicitly assigned in the HTML code. But if you assign style sheet settings via remote style sheets, the values are not explicitly set in the tag. Therefore, the style property of such an element comes up empty, even though the element is under the stylistic control of the remote style sheet. If all you want to do is assign a new value to a style property, that's not a problem, because your assignment to the element object's style property overrides whatever style is assigned to that property in the remote style sheet (and then that new value is subsequently readable from the style property). But if you want to see what the current setting is, the initial value won't be in the element's style object.

To the rescue, in IE5+ anyway, comes an extra, read-only property—
currentStyle—that reveals the style sheet values that are currently being
applied to the element, regardless of where the style sheet definitions are. The
currentStyle property returns an object that is in the same format and has the
same properties as the regular style property. If your audience runs browsers no
earlier than IE5, then you should make a habit of reading styles for an element via
its currentStyle property. If you want a change to a style object's property to
apply to only one element, then use the element's style property to set that value;
but if the change is to apply to all elements covered by the same remote style sheet
rule, then modify the style property of the rule object.

STYLE Element Object

See Chapter 15 for items shared by all HTML elements.

Properties	Methods	Event Handlers
media		
type		

Syntax

Accessing STYLE element object properties and methods:

```
(IE4+)       document.all.objectID.property | method([parameters])
(IE5+/NN6)   document.getElementById(objectID).property | method([parameters])
```

	NN2	NN3	NN4	NN6	IE3/J1	IE3/J2	IE4	IE5	IE5.5
Compatibility				✓			✓	✓	✓

About this object

The STYLE element is among the classification of HTML directive elements (see
Chapter 20) in that it goes in the HEAD portion of a document and does not have
any of its own content rendered in the page. But the contents obviously have a

great amount of control over the rendering of other elements. Most of the properties, methods, and event handlers that the STYLE element inherits from all HTML elements are irrelevant.

One exception is the Boolean disabled property. Although there are additional ways to disable a style sheet (the disabled property of the styleSheet object), it may be easier to disable or enable a style sheet by way of the STYLE element object. Because you can assign an ID to this element and reference it explicitly, doing so may be more convenient than trying to identify which styleSheet object among the document's styleSheets collection you intend to enable or disable.

Properties

media

Value: String   Read/Write

	NN2	NN3	NN4	NN6	IE3/J1	IE3/J2	IE4	IE5	IE5.5
Compatibility				✓			✓	✓	✓

The media property represents the MEDIA attribute of a STYLE element. This attribute can define what kind of output device is governed by the style sheet. The HTML 4.0 specification has lofty goals for this attribute, but at best, computer browsers are limited to the following values: screen, print, and all. Thus, you can design one set of styles to apply when the page is viewed on the computer screen and a different set for when it's printed.

type

Value: String   Read/Write

	NN2	NN3	NN4	NN6	IE3/J1	IE3/J2	IE4	IE5	IE5.5
Compatibility				✓			✓	✓	✓

The type property represents the TYPE attribute of the STYLE element. For CSS style sheets, this property is always set to text/css. If your scripts assign some other value to this property and the browser does not support that style sheet type, the style sheet no longer functions as a CSS style sheet, and any styles it controls revert to their default styles.

styleSheet Object

Properties	Methods	Event Handlers
cssRules	addImport()	
cssText	addRule()	
disabled	deleteRule()	
href	insertRule()	
id	removeRule()	
imports		
media		
ownerNode		
ownerRule		
owningElement		
pages		
parentStyleSheet		
readOnly		
rules		
title		
type		

Syntax

Accessing styleSheet object properties and methods:

(IE4+/NN6)   document.styleSheets[*index*].*property* | *method*([*parameters*])

	NN2	NN3	NN4	NN6	IE3/J1	IE3/J2	IE4	IE5	IE5.5
Compatibility				✓			✓	✓	✓

About this object

If the STYLE element object is the concrete incarnation of a style sheet, then the styleSheet object is its abstract equivalent. A styleSheet object exists by virtue of a style sheet definition being embedded in the current document either by way of the <STYLE> tag or linked in from an external file via the <LINK> tag. Each element that introduces a style sheet into a document creates a separate styleSheet object. Access to a styleSheet object is via the document.styleSheets array. If the document contains no style sheet definitions, then the array has a length of zero. Styles that are introduced into a document by way of an element's STYLE attribute are not considered styleSheet objects.

Although both IE4+ and NN6+ present styleSheet objects — and the object represents the same "thing" in both browser families — the set of properties and methods diverges widely between browsers. In many cases, the object provides the same information but through differently named properties in the two families. Interestingly, on some important properties, such as the ones that return the array of style rules and a reference to the HTML element that is responsible for the style sheet's being in the document, IE5+/Mac provides both the Microsoft and W3C terminology. Methods for this object focus on adding rules to and deleting rules from the style sheet. For the most part, however, your use of the styleSheet object will be as a reference gateway to individual rules (via the rules or cssRules array).

Properties

cssRules

Value: Array of rule objects   Read-Only

	NN2	NN3	NN4	NN6	IE3/J1	IE3/J2	IE4	IE5	IE5.5
Compatibility				✓				(✓)	(✓)

The cssRules property returns an array of style sheet rule objects. Strictly speaking, the objects are called cssRule objects in the W3C DOM terminology. This property is implemented in the Mac version of IE5+, but not in the Windows version as of IE5.5. The list of rule objects is in source code order. The corresponding IE4+/Windows property is rules.

Example on the CD-ROM

Related Items: `rules` property; `cssRule`, `rule` objects.

cssText

Value: String   Read/Write

	NN2	NN3	NN4	NN6	IE3/J1	IE3/J2	IE4	IE5	IE5.5
Compatibility								✓	✓

The `cssText` property contains a string of the style sheet rules contained by the styleSheet object. Parsing this text in search of particular strings is not wise because the text returned by this property can have carriage returns and other formatting that is not obvious from the text that is assigned to the rules in the style sheet. But you can use this property as a way to completely rewrite the rules of a style sheet in a rather brute-force manner: Assemble a string consisting of all the new rules and assign that string to the `cssText` property. The more formal way of modifying rules (adding and removing them) is perhaps better form, but there is no penalty for using the `cssText` property if your audience is strictly IE5+.

 On the CD-ROM   Example on the CD-ROM

Related Items: `addRule()`, `deleteRule()`, `insertRule()`, `removeRule()` methods.

disabled

Value: Boolean   Read/Write

	NN2	NN3	NN4	NN6	IE3/J1	IE3/J2	IE4	IE5	IE5.5
Compatibility				✓			✓	✓	✓

While the `disabled` property of the STYLE element object works with that element only, the styleSheet object's `disabled` property works with a styleSheet object that comes into the document by a LINK element as well.

Enabling and disabling style sheets is one way to swap different appearance styles for a page, allowing the user to select the preferred style. The page can contain multiple style sheets that control the same selectors, but your script can enable one and disable another to change the overall style. You can even perform this action via the onLoad event handler. For example, if you have separate style sheets for Windows and Mac browsers, you can put both of them in the document, initially both disabled. An onLoad event handler determines the operating system and enables the style sheet tailored for that OS. Unless your style sheets are very extensive, there is little download performance penalty for having both style sheets in the document.

Example on the CD-ROM

Related Items: disabled property of the STYLE element object.

href

Value: String   Read/Write (See Text)

	NN2	NN3	NN4	NN6	IE3/J1	IE3/J2	IE4	IE5	IE5.5
Compatibility				✓			✓	✓	✓

When a style sheet is linked into a document via a LINK element, the href property of the styleSheet object contains a string with the URL to that file. Essentially, the href property of the LINK element is passed along to the styleSheet object that loads as a result. In IE4+ for Windows only, this property is read/write, allowing you to dynamically link in an external style sheet file after the page has loaded. In IE/Mac and NN6, this property is read-only.

Related Items: LINK element object.

id

Value: String   Read-Only

	NN2	NN3	NN4	NN6	IE3/J1	IE3/J2	IE4	IE5	IE5.5
Compatibility							✓	✓	✓

The id property of a styleSheet object inherits the id property of its containing element (STYLE or LINK element). This can get confusing, because it may appear as though two objects in the document have the same ID. The id string, however, can be used as an index to the `document.styleSheets` array in IE4+ (for example, `document.styleSheets["winLINK"]`). NN6 does not provide a comparable identifier associated with a styleSheet object.

Related Items: `id` property of all element objects.

imports

Value: Array of styleSheet Objects   Read-Only

	NN2	NN3	NN4	NN6	IE3/J1	IE3/J2	IE4	IE5	IE5.5
Compatibility							✓	✓	✓

A style sheet can contain one or more `@import` rules to import an external style sheet file into the document. Each imported styleSheet object is treated as an `import` object. The `imports` property is a collection of all imported styleSheet objects that belong to the current styleSheet object. Imported style sheets are not added to the `document.styleSheets` collection, so that references to an imported styleSheet object must be through the `document.styleSheets[i].imports[i]` array.

An `import` object is, itself, a styleSheet object. All properties and methods applicable to a styleSheet object also apply to an `import` object. Therefore, if you want to load a different external style sheet into the page, you can assign the new URL to the imported styleSheet object's `href` property:

```
document.styleSheets[0].imports[0].href = "alternate.css"
```

Modifications of this nature work in IE for Windows, but not in IE/Mac as of Version 5.

Related Items: styleSheet object.

media

Value: See Text   Read/Write

	NN2	NN3	NN4	NN6	IE3/J1	IE3/J2	IE4	IE5	IE5.5
Compatibility				✓			✓	✓	✓

CSS style sheets can be defined to apply to specific output media, such as the video display screen, printer, and, in the future, devices such as speech synthesizers or Braille generators. A style sheet gets this direction from the MEDIA attribute of a STYLE or LINK element. That value is represented in the media property of the styleSheet object.

In IE4+, the media property value is a string with one of three possible values: screen, printer, all. The W3C DOM and NN6 take this one step further by allowing for potentially multiple values being assigned to the MEDIA attribute. The NN6 value is an array of string media names.

Related Items: None.

ownerNode

Value: Node Reference   Read-Only

	NN2	NN3	NN4	NN6	IE3/J1	IE3/J2	IE4	IE5	IE5.5
Compatibility				✓					

The ownerNode property is a reference to the document node in which the styleSheet object is defined. For styleSheet objects defined inside STYLE and LINK elements, the ownerNode property is a reference to that element. The corresponding property in IE4+ is owningElement. Oddly, IE5/Mac has an additional, misnamed property called owningNode, whose value equals that of the owningElement property.

Example on the CD-ROM

Related Items: ownerRule, owningElement property.

ownerRule

Value: cssRule Object   Read-Only

	NN2	NN3	NN4	NN6	IE3/J1	IE3/J2	IE4	IE5	IE5.5
Compatibility				✓					

The `ownerRule` property applies to a styleSheet object that has been imported into a document via the `@import` rule. The property returns a reference to the `@import` rule responsible for loading the external style sheet. There is an interaction between the `ownerRule` and `ownerNode` properties in that an imported rule has an `ownerRule` but its `ownerNode` property is `null`; conversely, a regular styleSheet has an `ownerNode`, but its `ownerRule` property is `null`. Note that NN6 does not expose imported style sheets as objects, so this property is not yet applicable to NN.

Related Items: `ownerNode` property.

owningElement

Value: Element Reference　　　　　　　　　　　　　　　　　　Read-Only

	NN2	NN3	NN4	NN6	IE3/J1	IE3/J2	IE4	IE5	IE5.5
Compatibility							✓	✓	✓

The `owningElement` property is a reference to the element object in which the styleSheet object is defined. For styleSheet objects defined inside STYLE and LINK elements, the `owningElement` property is a reference to that element. The corresponding property in NN6+ is `ownerNode`. Oddly, IE5/Mac has an additional, misnamed property called `owningNode`, whose value equals that of the `owningElement` property.

 Example on the CD-ROM

Related Items: `ownerNode` property.

pages

Value: Array of @page Rules　　　　　　　　　　　　　　　　　Read-Only

	NN2	NN3	NN4	NN6	IE3/J1	IE3/J2	IE4	IE5	IE5.5
Compatibility									✓

An @page style rule defines the dimensions and margins for printed versions of a Web page. The `pages` property returns a collection of @page rules contained by the current styleSheet object. If no @page rules are defined in the style sheet, the array has a length of zero.

While an @page rule has the same properties as any rule object, it has one more read-only property, the pseudoClass property, which returns any pseudo-class definitions in the rule. For example, the following @page rules define different rectangle specifications for the left and right printed pages:

```
@page :left {margin-left:4cm; margin-right:3cm;}
@page :right {margin-left:3cm; margin-right:4cm;}
```

Values for the pseudoClass property of these two page rules are :left and :right, respectively.

To the W3C DOM, an @page rule is just another rule object, but one whose type property returns page.

For more information about the paged media specification, see http://www.w3.org/TR/REC-CSS2/page.html.

Related Items: None.

parentStyleSheet

Value: styleSheet Object   Read-Only

	NN2	NN3	NN4	NN6	IE3/J1	IE3/J2	IE4	IE5	IE5.5
Compatibility				✓			✓	✓	✓

An imported style sheet is present thanks to the hosting of a styleSheet object created by a STYLE or LINK element. That host styleSheet object is referenced by the parentStyleSheet property. For most styleSheet objects (that is, those not imported via the @import rule), the parentStyleSheet property is null. Take note of the distinction between the parentStyleSheet property, which points to a styleSheet object, and the various properties that refer to the HTML element that "owns" the styleSheet object.

Related Items: None.

readOnly

Value: Boolean   Read-Only

	NN2	NN3	NN4	NN6	IE3/J1	IE3/J2	IE4	IE5	IE5.5
Compatibility							✓	✓	✓

The readOnly property's name is a bit misleading. Its Boolean value lets your script know whether the current style sheet was embedded in the document by way of the STYLE element or brought in from an external file via the LINK element or @import rule. When embedded by a STYLE element, the readOnly property is false; for style sheets defined outside the page, the property is true. But a value of true doesn't mean that your scripts cannot modify the style properties. Style properties can still be modified on the fly, but of course the changes will not be reflected in the external file from which the initial settings came.

Related Items: owningElement property.

rules

Value: Array of rule Objects   Read-Only

	NN2	NN3	NN4	NN6	IE3/J1	IE3/J2	IE4	IE5	IE5.5
Compatibility							✓	✓	✓

The rules property returns an array of all rule objects (other than @ rules) defined in the current style sheet. The order of rule objects in the array is based on source code order of the rules defined in the STYLE element or in the external file.

Use the rules array as the primary way to reference an individual rule inside a style sheet. If you use a for loop to iterate through all rules in search of a particular rule, you will most likely be looking for a match of the rule object's selectorText property. This assumes, of course, that each selector is unique within the style sheet. Using unique selectors is good practice, but no restrictions prevent you from reusing a selector name in a style sheet for additional style information applied to the same selector elements.

The corresponding property name for NN6 is cssRules. IE5/Mac responds to both the rules and cssRules properties.

 On the CD-ROM   Example on the CD-ROM

Related Items: rule object; cssRules property.

title

Value: String   Read/Write

	NN2	NN3	NN4	NN6	IE3/J1	IE3/J2	IE4	IE5	IE5.5
Compatibility				✓			✓	✓	✓

If you assign a value to the TITLE attribute of a STYLE element or a LINK element
that loads a style sheet, that string value filters down to the title property of the
styleSheet object. You can use the string value as a kind of identifier, but it is not
usable as a true identifier that you can use as an index to the styleSheets array. In
visible HTML elements, the TITLE attribute usually sets the text that displays with
the tooltip over the element. But for the unseen STYLE and LINK elements, the
attribute has no impact on the rendered display of the page. Therefore, you can use
this attribute and corresponding property to convey any string value you want.

Related Items: title property of all HTML elements.

type

Value: String   Read/Write

	NN2	NN3	NN4	NN6	IE3/J1	IE3/J2	IE4	IE5	IE5.5
Compatibility				✓			✓	✓	✓

The type property of a styleSheet object picks up the TYPE attribute of the STYLE
or LINK element that embeds a style sheet into the page. Unless you are experimenting with some new types of style sheet language (assuming it is even supported in the browser), the value of the type property is text/css.

Related Items: None.

Methods
addImport("*URL*"[, *index*])

Returns: Integer.

	NN2	NN3	NN4	NN6	IE3/J1	IE3/J2	IE4	IE5	IE5.5
Compatibility							✓	✓	✓

The addImport() method lets you add an @import rule to a styleSheet object. A required first parameter is the URL of the external .css file that contains one or more style sheet rules. If you omit the second parameter, the @import rule is appended to the end of rules in the styleSheet object. Or you can specify an integer as the index of the position within the rules collection where the rule should be inserted. The order of rules in a styleSheet object can influence the cascading order of overlapping style sheet rules (that is, multiple rules that apply to the same elements).

The value returned by the method is an integer representing the index position of the new rule within the rules collection of the styleSheet. If you need subsequent access to the new rule, you can preserve the value returned by the addImport() method and use it as the index to the rules collection.

Related Items: addRule() method.

addRule("*selector*", "*styleSpec*"[, *index*]) removeRule(*index*)

Returns: Integer (for addRule()).

	NN2	NN3	NN4	NN6	IE3/J1	IE3/J2	IE4	IE5	IE5.5
Compatibility							✓	✓	✓

The addRule() method appends or inserts a style sheet rule into the current styleSheet object. The first two parameters are strings for the two components of every rule: the selector and the style specification. Any valid selector, including multiple, space-delimited selectors, is permitted. For the style specification, the string should contain the semicolon-delimited list of style *attribute:value* pairs, but without the curly braces that surround the specification in a regular style sheet rule.

If you omit the last parameter, the rule is appended to the end of the rules collection for the style sheet. Or, you can specify an integer index value signifying the position within the rules collection where the new rule should go. The order of rules in a styleSheet object can influence the cascading order of overlapping style sheet rules (meaning multiple rules that apply to the same elements).

The return value conveys no meaningful information.

To remove a rule from a styleSheet object's rules collection, invoke the removeRule() method. Exercise some care here, because you must have the correct index value for the rule that you want to remove. Your script can use a for loop to iterate through the rules collection, looking for a match of the selectorText property (assuming that you have unique selectors). The index for the matching rule can then be used as the parameter to removeRule(). This method returns no value.

For NN6, the corresponding methods are called insertRule() and deleteRule().

On the CD-ROM   Example on the CD-ROM

Related Items: deleteRule(), insertRule() methods.

deleteRule(*index*)
insertRule("*rule*", *index*)

Returns: Integer (for insertRule()).

	NN2	NN3	NN4	NN6	IE3/J1	IE3/J2	IE4	IE5	IE5.5
Compatibility				✓					

The insertRule() method appends or inserts a style sheet rule into the current styleSheet object. The first parameter is a string containing the style rule as it would normally appear in a style sheet, including the selector and curly braces surrounding the semicolon-delimited list of style *attribute:value* pairs.

You must supply an index location within the cssRules array where the new rule is to be inserted. If you want to append the rule to the end of the list, use the length property of the cssRules collection for the parameter. The order of rules in a styleSheet object can influence the cascading order of overlapping style sheet rules (meaning multiple rules that apply to the same elements).

The return value is an index for the position of the inserted rule.

To remove a rule from a styleSheet object's cssRules collection, invoke the deleteRule() method. Exercise some care here, because you must have the correct index value for the rule that you want to remove. Your script could use a for loop to iterate through the `cssRules` collection, looking for a match of the `selectorText` property (assuming that you have unique selectors). The index for the matching rule can then be used as the parameter to `deleteRule()`. This method returns no value.

For IE4+, the corresponding methods are called `addRule()` and `removeRule()`.

 Example on the CD-ROM

Related Items: `addRule()`, `removeRule()` methods.

cssRule and rule Objects

Properties	Methods	Event Handlers
cssText		
parentStyleSheet		
readOnly		
selectorText		
style		
type		

Syntax

Accessing rule or cssRule object properties:

```
(IE4+)          document.styleSheets[index].rules[index].property
(IE5-Mac/NN6+)  document.styleSheets[index].cssRules[index].property
```

About these objects

The rule and cssRule objects are different object model names for the same objects. For IE4+, the object is known as a *rule* (and a collection of them the `rules` collection); for NN6 (and IE5/Mac), the object follows the W3C DOM recommendation, calling the object a *cssRule* (and a collection of them the `cssRules` collection). For the remainder of this section, they will be referred to generically as the rule object.

A rule object has two major components. The first is the selector text, which governs which element(s) are to be influenced by the style rule. The second component is the style definition, with its set of semicolon-delimited *attribute:value* pairs. In both the IE4+ and NN6 object models, the style definition is treated as an object: the `style` object, which has tons of properties representing the style attributes available in the browser. The `style` object that belongs to a rule object is precisely the same `style` object that is associated with every HTML element object. Accessing `style` properties of a style sheet rule requires a fairly long reference, as in

```
document.styleSheets[0].rules[0].style.color = "red"
```

but the format follows the logic of JavaScript's dot-syntax to the letter.

Properties

cssText

Value: String   Read/Write

	NN2	NN3	NN4	NN6	IE3/J1	IE3/J2	IE4	IE5	IE5.5
Compatibility				✓				(✓)	

The `cssText` property returns the full text of the current cssRule object. This property is available in NN6 and IE5/Macintosh. While the text returned from this property can be parsed to locate particular strings, it is easier and more reliable to access individual style properties and their values via the `style` property of a cssRule object.

Related Items: `style` property.

parentStyleSheet

Value: styleSheet Object   Read-Only

	NN2	NN3	NN4	NN6	IE3/J1	IE3/J2	IE4	IE5	IE5.5
Compatibility				✓				(✓)	

The parentStyleSheet property is a reference to the styleSheet object that contains the current cssRule object. This property is available in NN6 and IE5/Macintosh. The return value is a reference to a styleSheet object, from which scripts can read and write properties related to the entire style sheet.

Related Items: parentRule property.

readOnly

Value: Boolean

Read-Only

	NN2	NN3	NN4	NN6	IE3/J1	IE3/J2	IE4	IE5	IE5.5
Compatibility							✓	✓	✓

The readOnly property's name is a bit misleading. Its Boolean value lets your script know whether the current rule's styleSheet was embedded in the document by way of the STYLE element or brought in from an external file via the LINK element or @import rule. When embedded by a STYLE element, the readOnly property is false; for style sheets defined outside the page, the property is true. But a value of true doesn't mean that your scripts cannot modify the style properties. Style properties can still be modified on the fly, but of course the changes are not reflected in the external file from which the initial settings came.

Related Items: styleSheet.readOnly property.

selectorText

Value: String

Read-Only

	NN2	NN3	NN4	NN6	IE3/J1	IE3/J2	IE4	IE5	IE5.5
Compatibility				✓			✓	✓	✓

The selectorText property returns only the selector portion of a style sheet rule. The value is a string, and if the selector contains multiple, space-delimited items, the selectorText value returns the same space-delimited string. For selectors that are applied to classes (preceded by a period) or ids (preceded by a crosshatch), those leading characters are returned as part of the string as well.

If you want to change the selector for a rule, removing the original rule and adding a new one in its place is better. You can always preserve the `style` property of the original rule and assign the style to the new rule.

Example on the CD-ROM

Related Items: `style` property.

style

Value: `style` Object   Read/Write

	NN2	NN3	NN4	NN6	IE3/J1	IE3/J2	IE4	IE5	IE5.5
Compatibility				✓			✓	✓	✓

The `style` property of a rule (or cssRule) is, itself, an object whose properties consist of the CSS style attributes supported by the browser. Modifying a property of the `style` object requires a fairly long reference, as in

```
document.styleSheets[0].rules[0].style.color = "red"
```

Any change you make to the rule's `style` properties is reflected in the rendered style of whatever elements are denoted by the rule's selector. If you want to change the style of just one element, then access the `style` property of just that element. Style values applied directly to an element override whatever style sheet style values are associated with the element.

Example on the CD-ROM

Related Items: `style` object.

type

Value: Integer   Read-Only

	NN2	NN3	NN4	NN6	IE3/J1	IE3/J2	IE4	IE5	IE5.5
Compatibility				✓					

The W3C DOM defines several classes of style sheet rules. To make it easier for a script to identify the kind of cssRule it is working with, the `type` property returns an integer whose value is associated with one of the known cssRule types. While not all of these rule types may be implemented in NN6, the complete W3C DOM list is as follows:

Type	Description
0	Unknown type
1	Regular style rule
2	@charset rule
3	@import rule
4	@media rule
5	@font-face rule
6	@page rule

Most of the style sheet rules you work with are type 1. To learn more about these rule types, consult the W3C specification for CSS at `http://www.w3.org/TR/REC-CSS2`.

Related Items: None.

currentStyle , runtimeStyle , and style Objects

Properties	Methods	Event Handlers
(See below)		

Syntax

Accessing `currentStyle`, `runtimeStyle`, or `style` object properties:

```
(IE4+/NN6)     elementReference.style.property
(IE4+/NN6)     document.styleSheets[index].style.property
(IE5+)         elementReference.currentStyle.property
(IE5.5)        elementReference.runtimeStyle.property
```

About these objects

All three of these objects — `currentStyle`, `runtimeStyle`, and `style` — return an object that contains dozens of properties related to style sheet specifications associated either with a styleSheet object (for the `style` object only) or any rendered HTML element object. With the browser page reflow facilities of IE4+ and NN6+, changes made to the properties of the `style` and IE-specific `runtimeStyle` objects are reflected immediately by the rendered content on the page.

The primary object, the `style` object, is accessed as a property of either a styleSheet object or an HTML element object. It is vital to remember that style properties of an HTML element are reflected by the `style` object only if the specifications are made via the STYLE attribute inside the element's tag. If your coding style requires that style sheets be applied via STYLE or LINK tags, and if your scripts need to access the `style` property values as set by those style sheets, then you must read the properties through the read-only `currentStyle` property (available in IE5+). The `currentStyle` object returns the effective style sheet being applied to an HTML element object.

IE's `currentStyle` object does not have precisely the same properties as its `style` object. Missing from the `currentStyle` object are the properties that contain combination values, such as `border` or `borderBottom`. On the other hand, `currentStyle` provides separate properties for each of the sides of a clipping rectangle (`clipTop`, `clipRight`, `clipBottom`, and `clipLeft`), which the `clip` property does not provide.

Microsoft introduced one more flavor of style object — the `runtimeStyle` object — in IE5.5. This object lets scripts override any style property that is set in a style sheet or via the STYLE attribute. In other words, the `runtimeStyle` object is like a read/write version of `currentStyle` except that assigning a new value to one of its properties does not modify the style sheet definition or the value assigned in a STYLE attribute. By and large, however, your scripts will modify the `style` property of an element to make changes, unless you modify styles by enabling and disabling style sheets (or changing the `className` property of an element so that it is under the control of a different selector).

Style properties

If you add up all the `style` object properties available in browsers starting with IE4 and NN6, you have a list approximately 180 properties long. A sizable percentage are in common among all browsers and are scriptable versions of W3C CSS style sheet attributes. The actual CSS attribute names are frequently script-unfriendly in that multiple-worded attributes have hyphens in them, such as `font-size`. JavaScript identifiers do not allow hyphens, so multiple-worded attributes are converted to interCap versions, such as `fontSize`.

Not all style properties are supported by all browsers that have the `style` object in their object models. Microsoft, in particular, has added many properties that are sometimes unique to IE and sometimes unique to just IE for Windows (or even just to Windows 2000). On the Netscape side, you find some properties that appear to be supported by the `style` object, but the browser doesn't genuinely support the attributes. For example, the CSS specification defines several attributes that enhance the delivery of content that is rendered through a speech synthesizer. While NN6 does not qualify, the Gecko browser engine at the core of NN6 could be adapted to such a browser. Therefore, if you see a property in the following listings that doesn't make sense to you, test it out in the compatible browsers to verify that it works as you need it.

Some browsers also expose advanced `style` object properties to scripters, when, in fact, they are not genuinely supported in the browser. For example, an inspection of the `style` object for IE5/Mac and NN6 shows a `quotes` property, which matches the `quotes` style attribute in the W3C CSS2 specification. But in truth, the `quotes` style property cannot be set by script in these browsers. When you see that a property is supported by IE5/Mac and NN6 but none others, testing out the `style` property (and the style sheet attribute as well) in The Evaluator is a good idea before attempting to employ the property in your application.

With so many properties associated with an object, it may be difficult to locate the specific property you need for a particular style effect. To help you locate properties, the listings that follow are divided into functional categories, ordered by popularity:

Category	*Description*
Text & Fonts	Font specifications, text rendering, text alignment
Inline Display & Layout	Element flow, alignment, and display
Positioning	Explicit positioning of "layers"
Background	Background images and colors
Borders & Edges	Borders, padding, and margins around elements
Lists	Details for UL and OL elements
Scrollbars	Scrollbar colors (IE5.5/Windows only)
Tables	Details for TABLE elements and components
Printing	Page breaks and alignment for printed pages
Miscellaneous	Odds and ends
Aural	For rendering via speech-synthesis

Property values

All `style` object property values are strings. Moreover, many groups of style properties share the same format for their values. Knowing the formats for the frequently used values is helpful. The purpose of this chapter is not to teach you about style sheets but to show you how to script them. Therefore, if you see unfamiliar terminology here, consult online or print instructional material about CSS style sheets.

Length

Values for length cover a wide range, but they all define an amount of physical space in the document. Because content can be displayed on a video monitor or printed on a sheet of paper, any kind of length value should include a unit of measure as well as the quantity. One group of units (px, em, ex) are considered *relative* units, because the precise size depends on factors beyond the control of the style sheet (for example, the pixel density of the display) or units set by elements with more global scope (for example, a P element's margin em length dependent upon the BODY element's font-size setting). *Absolute* units (in, cm, mm, pi, pt) are more appropriate for printed output. Length units are referred in script according to the following table:

Unit	Script Version	Example
pixel	px	14px
em	em	1.5em
ex	ex	1.5ex
inch	in	3.0in
centimeter	cm	4.0cm
millimeter	mm	40mm
pica	pi	72pi
point	pt	14pt

A length value can also be represented by a percentage as a string. For example, the `lineHeight` style for a paragraph would be set to 120% of the font size established for the paragraph by the following statement:

```
document.getElementById("myP").style.lineHeight = "120%"
```

Style inheritance — an important CSS concept — often has significant impact on style properties whose values are lengths.

Color

Values for colors can be one of three types:

- ✦ RGB values (in a few different formats)
- ✦ plain-language versions of the color names
- ✦ plain-language names of system user interface items

RGB values can be expressed as hexadecimal values. The most common way is with a crosshatch character followed by six hex numbers, as in #ff00ff (letters can be uppercase or lowercase). A special shortcut is also available to let you specify three numbers with the assumption that they will be expanded to pairs of numbers. For example, a color of #f0f is expanded internally to be #ff00ff.

An alternative RGB expression is with the rgb() prefix and three numbers (from 0 to 255) or percentages corresponding to the red, green, and blue components of the color. Here are a couple of examples:

```
document.styleSheets[0].rules[0].style.color = "rgb(0, 255, 0)"
document.styleSheets[0].rules[0].style.color = "rgb(0%, 100%, 0%)"
```

Browsers also respond to a long list of plain-language color names originally devised by Netscape. You can see the list with sample colors at http://developer.netscape.com/docs/manuals/htmlguid/colortab.htm. Not all of those colors are necessarily part of what are known as "Web safe" colors. For a demonstration of Web safe colors, visit http://www.lynda.com/hexh.html.

activeborder	graytext	menutext
activecaption	highlight	scrollbar
appworkspace	highlighttext	threeddarkshadow
background	inactiveborder	threedface
buttonface	inactivecaption	threedhighlight
buttonhighlight	inactivecaptiontext	threedlightshadow
buttonshadow	infobackground	threedshadow
buttontext	infotext	window
captiontext	menu	windowframe
windowtext		

The last category of color values references user interface pieces, many of which are determined by the user's control panel for video display. The string values correspond to recognizable UI components (also called system colors), as follows:

Using these color settings may be risky for public sites, because you are at the mercy of the color settings the user has chosen. For a corporate environment where system installations and preferences are strictly controlled, these values could help define a safe color scheme for your pages.

Rectangle sides

Many style properties control the look of sides of rectangles (for example, thickness of a border around a block element). In most cases, the style values can be applied to individual sides or combinations of sides, depending on the number of values supplied to the property. The number of values affects the four sides of the rectangle according to the following matrix:

Number of Values	Impact
1	All four sides set to the one value
2	Top and bottom sides set to first value; left and right sides set to second value
3	Top side set to first value; left and right sides set to second value; bottom side set to third value
4	Top, right, bottom, and left sides set to individual values in that order

For example, to set the border color of an element so that all sides are red, the syntax is

```
elementRef.style.borderColor = "red"
```

To set the top and bottom to red but the left and right to green, the syntax is

```
elementRef.style.borderColor = "red green"
```

Properties that accept these multiple values cover a wide range of styles. Values may be colors, lengths, or selections from a fixed list of possible values.

Combination values

Another category of style values includes properties that act as shortcuts for several related properties. For example, the border property encompasses the borderWidth, borderStyle, and borderColor properties. This is possible because very different classes of values represent the three component properties: `borderWidth` is a length; `borderStyle` is based on a fixed list of values; and `borderColor` is a color value. Therefore, you can specify one or more of these property values (in any order), and the browser knows how to apply the values to the detailed sub-property. Only one value is permitted for any one of these sub-properties, which means that if the property is one of the four-sided styles described in the previous section, the value is applied to all four sides equally.

For example, setting the `border` property to a single value, as in

```
elementRef.style.border = "blue"
```

is the same as setting

```
elementRef.style.borderColor = "blue"
```

But if you set multiple items, as in

```
elementRef.style.border = "groove blue 3px"
```

then you have set the equivalent of the following three statements:

```
elementRef.style.borderStyle = "groove"
elementRef.style.borderColor = "blue"
elementRef.style.borderWidth = "3px"
```

In the property descriptions that follow, these combination values are denoted by their scripted property names and the OR (| |) operator, as in

```
border = "borderStyle || borderColor || borderWidth"
```

URLs

Unlike other property values containing URLs, a `style` property requires a slightly different format. This format includes the `url()` prefix, with the actual URL (relative or absolute) located inside the parentheses. The URL itself is not quoted, but the entire property value is, as in

```
elementRef.style.backgroundImage = "url(chainlink.jpg)"
```

URLs should not have any spaces in them, but if they do, then use the URL-encoded version for the file specification: convert spaces to %20. This format distinguishes a URL value from some other string value for shortcut properties.

Text and font properties

color

	IE/Windows	IE/Mac	NN	W3C CSS2
Compatibility	4	4	6	Yes

Controls: Foreground color of an element, primarily used to assign color to text. May also affect edges and highlights of other elements in some browsers.

Value: Color specification.

Example: *elementRef*.style.color = "rgb(#22FF00)"

font

	IE/Windows	IE/Mac	NN	W3C CSS2
Compatibility	4	4	6	Yes

Controls: Up to six font-related style properties.

Value: Combination values: *fontStyle* || *fontVariant* || *fontWeight* || *fontSize* || *lineHeight* || *fontFamily*. See individual properties for their value formats.

Example: *elementRef*.style.font = "bold sans-serif 16px"

fontFamily

	IE/Windows	IE/Mac	NN	W3C CSS2
Compatibility	4	4	6	Yes

Controls: Font family to be applied to an element in order of priority.

Value: Comma-delimited list of font families to be applied to element, starting with the most preferred font family name. You can also use one of several generic family names that rely on the browser to choose the optimal font to match the class: `serif | sans-serif | cursive | fantasy | monospace`. Not all browsers support all constants, but `serif`, `sans-serif`, and `monospace` are commonly implemented.

Example: `elementRef.style.fontFamily = "Bauhaus 93, Arial, monospace"`

fontSize

	IE/Windows	IE/Mac	NN	W3C CSS2
Compatibility	4	4	6	Yes

Controls: Size of the characters of the current font family.

Value: Lengths (generally px or pt values); relative size constants: `larger | smaller`; absolute size constants: `xx-small | x-small | small | medium | large | x-large | xx-large`

Examples: `elementRef.style.fontSize = "16px"`

`elementRef.style.fontSize = "small"`

fontSizeAdjust

	IE/Windows	IE/Mac	NN	W3C CSS2
Compatibility	—	5	6	Yes

Controls: Aspect value of a secondary font family so that it maintains a similar character height as the primary font family.

Value: Number (including floating-point value) or `none`.

Example: `elementRef.style.fontSizeAdjust = "1.05"`

fontStretch

	IE/Windows	IE/Mac	NN	W3C CSS2
Compatibility	—	5	6	Yes

Controls: Rendered width of a font's characters.

Value: Constant `ultra-condensed` | `extra-condensed` | `condensed` | `semi-condensed` | `semi-expanded` | `expanded` | `extra-expanded` | `ultra-expanded` or `wider` | `narrower` | `inherit` | `normal`

Example: `elementRef.style.fontStretch = "expanded"`

fontStyle

	IE/Windows	IE/Mac	NN	W3C CSS2
Compatibility	4	4	6	Yes

Controls: Italic style of characters.

Value: Constant `normal` | `italic` | `oblique` | `inherit`

Example: `elementRef.style.fontStyle = "italic"`

fontVariant

	IE/Windows	IE/Mac	NN	W3C CSS2
Compatibility	4	4	6	Yes

Controls: Rendering characters as small caps.

Value: Constant `normal` | `small-caps` | `inherit`

Example: `elementRef.style.fontVariant = "small-caps"`

fontWeight

	IE/Windows	IE/Mac	NN	W3C CSS2
Compatibility	4	4	6	Yes

Controls: Rendering characters in bold or light weights. Fonts that support numbered gradations can be controlled by those numbers. Normal = 400; Bold = 700.

Value: Constant bold | bolder | lighter | normal | 100 | 200 | 300 | 400 | 500 | 600 | 700 | 800 | inherit

Example: *elementRef*.style.fontWeight = "bold"

letterSpacing

	IE/Windows	IE/Mac	NN	W3C CSS2
Compatibility	4	4	6	Yes

Controls: Spacing between characters. Used to override a font family's own characteristics.

Value: Length (usually em units, relative to current font size); Constant normal | inherit

Example: *elementRef*.style.letterSpacing = "1.2em"

lineBreak

	IE/Windows	IE/Mac	NN	W3C CSS2
Compatibility	5	—	—	No

Controls: Line break rules for Japanese text content.

Value: Constant normal | strict

Example: *elementRef*.style.lineBreak = "strict"

lineHeight

	IE/Windows	IE/Mac	NN	W3C CSS2
Compatibility	4	4	6	Yes

Controls: Height of the rectangular space that holds a line of text characters.

Value: Length (usually em units, relative to current font size); number (a multiplier on the inherited line height); percentage (relative to inherited line height); constant normal l inherit

Example: *elementRef*.style.lineHeight = "1.1"

quotes

	IE/Windows	IE/Mac	NN	W3C CSS2
Compatibility	—	5	6	Yes

Controls: Characters to be used for quotation marks.

Value: Space-delimited pairs of open and close quotation symbols; Constant none l inherit

Example: *elementRef*.style.quotes = "« »"

rubyAlign

	IE/Windows	IE/Mac	NN	W3C CSS2
Compatibility	5	5	—	No

Controls: Alignment of ruby text within a RUBY element.

Value: Constant `auto | left | center | right | distribute-letter | distribute-space | line-edge`

Example: *RUBYelementRef*`.style.rubyAlign = "distribute=letter"`

rubyOverhang

	IE/Windows	IE/Mac	NN	W3C CSS2
Compatibility	5	5	—	No

Controls: Overhang of ruby text within a RUBY element.

Value: Constant `auto | whitespace | none`

Example: *RUBYelementRef*`.style.rubyOverhang - "whitespace"`

rubyPosition

	IE/Windows	IE/Mac	NN	W3C CSS2
Compatibility	5	5	—	No

Controls: Placement of ruby text with respect to the RUBY element's base text.

Value: Constant `above | inline`

Example: *RUBYelementRef*`.style.rubyPosition = "inline"`

textAlign

	IE/Windows	IE/Mac	NN	W3C CSS2
Compatibility	4	4	6	Yes

Controls: Horizontal alignment of text with respect to its containing element.

Value: Constant center I justify I left I right

Example: *elementRef*.style.textAlign = "center"

textAlignLast

	IE/Windows	IE/Mac	NN	W3C CSS2
Compatibility	5.5	—	—	No

Controls: Horizontal alignment of last line of text in a paragraph.

Value: Constant auto I center I justify I left I right

Example: *elementRef*.style.textAlignLast = "justify"

textAutospace

	IE/Windows	IE/Mac	NN	W3C CSS2
Compatibility	5	—	—	No

Controls: Extra spacing between ideographic and non-ideographic text.

Value: Constant none I ideograph-alpha I ideograph-numeric I ideograph-parenthesis I ideograph-space

Example: *elementRef*.style.textAutospace = "ideograph-alpha"

textDecoration

	IE/Windows	IE/Mac	NN	W3C CSS2
Compatibility	4	4	6	Yes

Controls: Display of underline, overline, or line-through with text.

Value: Constant none I blink I line-through I overline I underline

Example: *elementRef*.style.textDecoration = "underline"

textDecorationBlink
textDecorationLineThrough
textDecorationNone
textDecorationOverline
textDecorationUnderline

	IE/Windows	IE/Mac	NN	W3C CSS2
Compatibility	4	4	—	No

Controls: Individual text decoration characteristics for text, allowing for multiple decorations to be applied to the same text.

Value: Boolean (not strings) true | false

Example: *elementRef*.style.textDecorationUnderline = true

textIndent

	IE/Windows	IE/Mac	NN	W3C CSS2
Compatibility	4	4	6	Yes

Controls: Amount of indentation for the first line of a block text element (e.g., P).

Value: Length (negative values for outdenting); percentage (relative to inherited value)

Example: *elementRef*.style.textIndent = "2.5em"

textJustify

	IE/Windows	IE/Mac	NN	W3C CSS2
Compatibility	5	5	—	No

Controls: Additional detailed specifications for an element whose `textAlign` property is set to `justify`.

Value: Constant `auto` | `distribute` | `distribute-all-lines` | `distribute-center-last` | `inter-cluster` | `inter-ideograph` | `inter-word` | `kashida` | `newspaper`

Example: `elementRef`.`style`.`textJustify` = `"distribute"`

textJustifyTrim

	IE/Windows	IE/Mac	NN	W3C CSS2
Compatibility	5	5	—	No

Reserved for future use.

textKashidaSpace

	IE/Windows	IE/Mac	NN	W3C CSS2
Compatibility	5.5	—	—	No

Controls: Ratio of kashida expansion to white space expansion for Arabic writing systems.

Value: Percentage

Example: `elementRef`.`style`.`textKashidaSpace` = `"90%"`

textShadow

	IE/Windows	IE/Mac	NN	W3C CSS2
Compatibility	—	5	6	Yes

Controls: Shadow rendering around text characters. *Note:* The style attribute for this property is not implemented in IE5/Mac or NN6, but the property is listed as valid for a `style` object.

Value: Each shadow specification consists of an optional color and three space-delimited length values (horizontal shadow offset, vertical shadow offset, blur radius length). Multiple shadow specifications are comma-delimited.

textTransform

	IE/Windows	IE/Mac	NN	W3C CSS2
Compatibility	4	4	6	Yes

Controls: Case rendering of the text (meaning without altering the case of the original text).

Value: Constant none | capitalize | lowercase | uppercase

Example: *elementRef*.style.textTransform = "uppercase"

textUnderlinePosition

	IE/Windows	IE/Mac	NN	W3C CSS2
Compatibility	5.5	—	—	No

Controls: Whether an underline text decoration is displayed above or below the text. Seems redundant with textDecorationUnderline and textDecorationOverline.

Value: Constant above | below

Example: *elementRef*.style.textUnderlinePosition = "above"

unicodeBidi

	IE/Windows	IE/Mac	NN	W3C CSS2
Compatibility	5	5	6	Yes

Controls: Within bi-directional text (for example, English and Arabic), to what extent an alternate direction text block is embedded within the outer element.

Value: Constant `normal | embed | bidi-override`

Example: `elementRef`.`style.unicodeBidi = "embed"`

whiteSpace

	IE/Windows	IE/Mac	NN	W3C CSS2
Compatibility	4	4	6	Yes

Controls: Treatment of white space characters within an element's source code.

Value: Constant `normal | nowrap | pre`

Example: `elementRef`.`style.whiteSpace = "nowrap"`

wordBreak

	IE/Windows	IE/Mac	NN	W3C CSS2
Compatibility	5	—	—	No

Controls: Word breaking characteristics, primarily for Asian-language text or text containing a mixture of Asian and Latin characters.

Value: Constant `normal | break-all | keep-all`

Example: `elementRef`.`style.wordBreak = "break-all"`

wordSpacing

	IE/Windows	IE/Mac	NN	W3C CSS2
Compatibility	4	4	6	Yes

Controls: Spacing between words.

Value: Length (usually in em units); Constant `normal`

Example: *elementRef*.style.wordSpacing = "1em"

wordWrap

	IE/Windows	IE/Mac	NN	W3C CSS2
Compatibility	5.5	—	—	No

Controls: Word wrapping characteristics of text in a block element, explicitly sized inline element, or positioned element.

Value: Constant normal | break-word

Example: *elementRef*.style.wordWrap = "break-word"

writingMode

	IE/Windows	IE/Mac	NN	W3C CSS2
Compatibility	5.5	—	—	No

Controls: Direction of content flow (left-to-right/top-to-bottom or top-to-bottom/ right-to-left, as in some Asian languages).

Value: Constant lr-tb | tb-rl

Example: *elementRef*.style.writingMode = "tb-rl"

Inline display and layout properties

clear

	IE/Windows	IE/Mac	NN	W3C CSS2
Compatibility	4	4	6	Yes

Controls: Layout orientation of an element with respect to a neighboring floating element.

Value: Constant both | left | none | right

Example: *elementRef*.style.clear = "right"

clip

	IE/Windows	IE/Mac	NN	W3C CSS2
Compatibility	4	4	6	Yes

Controls: The clipping rectangle of an element (that is, the position of the rectangle through which the user sees an element's content).

Value: rect(*topLength*, *rightLength*, *bottomLength*, *leftLength*) | auto

Example: *elementRef*.style.clip = "rect(10px, 300px, 200px, 0px)"

clipBottom
clipLeft
clipRight
clipTop

	IE/Windows	IE/Mac	NN	W3C CSS2
Compatibility	5	—	—	No

Controls: Individual edges of the clipping rectangle of an element. These properties are Read-Only properties of the currentStyle object.

Value: Length | auto

Example: var leftEdge = *elementRef*.currentStyle.clipLeft

content

	IE/Windows	IE/Mac	NN	W3C CSS2
Compatibility	—	5	6	Yes

Controls: The content rendered by an element. *Note:* The style attribute for this property is not implemented in IE5/Mac or NN6, but the property is listed as valid for a `style` object.

Value: See `http://www.w3.org/TR/REC-CSS2/generate.html#propdef-content`.

counterIncrement

	IE/Windows	IE/Mac	NN	W3C CSS2
Compatibility	—	5	6	Yes

Controls: The jumps in counter values to be displayed via the `content` style property. *Note:* The style attribute for this property is not implemented in IE5/Mac or NN6, but the property is listed as valid for a `style` object.

Value: One or more pairs of counter identifier and integers.

counterReset

	IE/Windows	IE/Mac	NN	W3C CSS2
Compatibility	—	5	6	Yes

Controls: Resets a named counter for content to be displayed via the `content` style property. *Note:* The style attribute for this property is not implemented in IE5/Mac or NN6, but the property is listed as valid for a `style` object.

Value: One or more pairs of counter identifier and integers.

cssFloat

	IE/Windows	IE/Mac	NN	W3C CSS2
Compatibility	—	5	6	Yes

Controls: Horizontal alignment of an element that allows other content to wrap around the element (usually text wrapping around an image). Corresponds to the CSS `float` style attribute. See also the `floatStyle` property, below. Floating (non-positioned) elements follow a long sequence of rules for their behavior, detailed at `http://www.w3.org/TR/REC-CSS2/visuren.html#propdef-float`.

Value: Constant `left | right | none`

Example: `elementRef.style.cssFloat = "right"`

cursor

	IE/Windows	IE/Mac	NN	W3C CSS2
Compatibility	4	4	6	Yes

Controls: The icon used for the cursor on the screen from a library of system-generated cursors. The CSS2 specification defines syntax for downloadable cursors, but this feature is not implemented as of IE5.5 or NN6.

Value: Constant `auto | crosshair | default | e-resize | help | move | n-resize | ne-resize | nw-resize | pointer | s-resize | se-resize | sw-resize | text | w-resize | wait`

Example: `elementRef.style.cursor = "hand"`

direction

	IE/Windows	IE/Mac	NN	W3C CSS2
Compatibility	5	5	6	Yes

Controls: Layout direction (left-to-right or right-to-left) of inline text (same as `DIR` attribute of an element).

Value: Constant `ltr | rtl`

Example: `elementRef.style.direction = "rtl"`

display

	IE/Windows	IE/Mac	NN	W3C CSS2
Compatibility	4	4	6	Yes

Controls: Whether an element is displayed on the page. Content surrounding an undisplayed element cinches up to occupy the undisplayed element's space—as if the element didn't exist for rendering purposes (see the `visibility` property for a different approach). Commonly used to hide or show segments of a graphical tree structure. Also used to direct the browser to display an element as inline or block-level element. Some special-purpose values are associated with specific element types (for example, lists, table cells, and so on).

Value: Constant `block` | `compact` | `inline` | `inline-table` | `list-item` | `none` | `run-in` | `table` | `table-caption` | `table-cell` | `table-column-group` | `table-footer-group` | `table-header group` | `table-row` | `table-row-group`

Example: `elementRef.style.display = "none"`
`    // removes element from page`

filter

	IE/Windows	IE/Mac	NN	W3C CSS2
Compatibility	4	4	—	No

Controls: Rendering effects on static content and on transitions between hiding and showing elements. Microsoft made a massive overhaul of the `filter` style sheet syntax for IE5.5/Windows (using the DXImageTransform ActiveX control). A handy online utility lets you preview the filter results and provides copy-and-paste code you can use to start adding filters and scripted control of filters to your pages. See `http://msdn.microsoft.com/workshop/samples/author/dhtml/DXTidemo/DXTidemo.htm`. Scripting transitions require several steps to load the transition and actions before playing the transition. Use `style.filter` to read or write the entire filter specification string; use the `elem.styles[i]` object to access individual filter properties. See discussion of the `filter` object later in this chapter.

Value: Filter specification as string.

Example: `var filterSpec = elementRef.style.filter = "alpha (opacity=50) flipH()"`

floatStyle

	IE/Windows	IE/Mac	NN	W3C CSS2
Compatibility	—	4	—	Yes

Controls: Horizontal alignment of an element that allows other content to wrap around the element (usually text wrapping around an image). Corresponds to the CSS `float` style attribute. See also the `cssFloat` property, above. Floating (non-positioned) elements follow a long sequence of rules for their behavior, detailed at `http://www.w3.org/TR/REC-CSS2/visuren.html#propdef-float`.

Value: Constant `left` | `right` | `none`

Example: `elementRef`.`style.floatStyle = "right"`

layoutGrid

	IE/Windows	IE/Mac	NN	W3C CSS2
Compatibility	5	—	—	No

Controls: Page grid properties (primarily for Asian-language pages).

Value: Combination values: `layoutGridMode` || `layoutGridType` || `layoutGridLine` || `layoutGridChar`. See individual properties for their value formats.

Example: `elementRef`.`style.layoutGrid = "2em strict"`

layoutGridChar

	IE/Windows	IE/Mac	NN	W3C CSS2
Compatibility	5	—	—	No

Controls: Size of the character grid (Asian languages).

Value: Length; Percentage; Constant `none` | `auto`

Example: *elementRef*.style.layoutGridChar = "2em"

layoutGridLine

	IE/Windows	IE/Mac	NN	W3C CSS2
Compatibility	5	—	—	No

Controls: Line height of the grid (Asian languages).

Value: Value: Length; Percentage; Constant none | auto

Example: *elementRef*.style.layoutGridLine = "110%"

layoutGridMode

	IE/Windows	IE/Mac	NN	W3C CSS2
Compatibility	5	—	—	No

Controls: One- or two-dimensional grid (Asian languages).

Value: Constant both | none | line | char

Example: *elementRef*.style.layoutGridMode = "both"

layoutGridType

	IE/Windows	IE/Mac	NN	W3C CSS2
Compatibility	5	—	—	No

Controls: Type of grid for text content (Asian languages).

Value: Constant loose | strict | fixed

Example: *elementRef*.style.layoutGridType = "strict"

markerOffset

	IE/Windows	IE/Mac	NN	W3C CSS2
Compatibility	—	5	6	Yes

Controls: Distance between the edges of a marker box (content whose display is of a marker type) and a block-level element's box. *Note:* The style attribute for this property is not implemented in IE5/Mac or NN6, but the property is listed as valid for a `style` object.

Value: Length; Constant `auto`

Example: *elementRef*`.style.markerOffset = "2em"`

marks

	IE/Windows	IE/Mac	NN	W3C CSS2
Compatibility	—	5	6	Yes

Controls: Rendering of crop marks and the like on the printed page. *Note:* The style attribute for this property is not implemented in IE5/Mac or NN6, but the property is listed as valid for a `style` object.

Value: Constant `crop || cross | none`

Example: *elementRef*`.style.marks = "crop"`

maxHeight
maxWidth
minHeight
minWidth

	IE/Windows	IE/Mac	NN	W3C CSS2
Compatibility	—	5	6	Yes

Controls: Maximum or minimum height or width of an element. The corresponding style attribute is implemented in NN6.

Value: Length; Percentage; Constant (for max properties only) `none`

Example: `elementRef`.style.maxWidth = "300px"

overflow

	IE/Windows	IE/Mac	NN	W3C CSS2
Compatibility	4	4	6	Yes

Controls: The rendering of a block-level element's content when its native rectangle exceeds that of its next outermost rectangular space. A `hidden` overflow clips the block-level content; a `scrolled` overflow forces the outermost rectangle to display scrollbars so that users can scroll around the block-level element's content; a `visible` overflow causes the block-level element to extend beyond the outermost container's rectangle (indeed, "overflowing" the container).

Value: Constant `auto | hidden | scroll | visible`

Example: `elementRef`.style.overflow = "scroll"

overflowX
overflowY

	IE/Windows	IE/Mac	NN	W3C CSS2
Compatibility	5	—	—	No

Controls: The rendering of a block-level element's content when its native rectangle exceeds the width (`overflowX`) or height (`overflowY`) of its next outermost rectangular space. A hidden overflow clips the block-level content; a scrolled overflow forces the outermost rectangle to display scrollbars so that users can scroll around the block-level element's content; a visible overflow causes the block-level element to extend beyond the outermost container's rectangle (indeed, "overflowing" the container).

Value: Constant `auto` | `hidden` | `scroll` | `visible`

Example: `elementRef`.`style.overflowX = "scroll"`

styleFloat

	IE/Windows	IE/Mac	NN	W3C CSS2
Compatibility	4	4	—	Yes

Controls: Horizontal alignment of an element that allows other content to wrap around the element (usually text wrapping around an image). Corresponds to the CSS `float` style attribute. See also the `cssFloat` property, above. Floating (non-positioned) elements follow a long sequence of rules for their behavior, detailed at `http://www.w3.org/TR/REC-CSS2/visuren.html#propdef-float`.

Value: Constant `left` | `right` | `none`

Example: `elementRef`.`style.styleFloat = "right"`

verticalAlign

	IE/Windows	IE/Mac	NN	W3C CSS2
Compatibility	4	4	6	Yes

Controls: How inline and table cell content aligns vertically with surrounding content. Not all constant values are supported by all browsers.

Value: Constant `baseline` | `bottom` | `middle` | `sub` | `super` | `text-bottom` | `text-top` | `top`; Length; Percentage.

Example: `elementRef`.`style.verticalAlign = "baseline"`

visibility

	IE/Windows	IE/Mac	NN	W3C CSS2
Compatibility	4	4	6	Yes

Controls: Whether an element is displayed on the page. The element's space is preserved as empty space when the element is hidden. To cinch up surrounding content, see the `display` property. This property is used frequently for hiding and showing positioned element under script control.

Value: Constant `collapse | hidden | visible`

Example: `elementRef.style.visibility = "hidden"`

width

	IE/Windows	IE/Mac	NN	W3C CSS2
Compatibility	4	4	6	Yes

Controls: Horizontal dimension of a block-level element. Earlier browsers exhibit unexpected behavior when nesting elements that have their `width` style properties set.

Value: Length; Percentage; Constant `auto`

Example: `elementRef.style.width = "200px"`

zoom

	IE/Windows	IE/Mac	NN	W3C CSS2
Compatibility	5.5	—	—	No

Controls: Magnification factor of a rendered element.

Value: Constant `normal`; Percentage (where `100%` is normal); floating-point number (scale multiplier, where 1.0 is normal)

Example: `elementRef.style.zoom = ".9"`

Positioning properties

(See Chapter 31 for coding examples of positioned elements and their `style` properties.)

bottom
right

	IE/Windows	IE/Mac	NN	W3C CSS2
Compatibility	5	5	6	Yes

Controls: The offset measure of a positioned element from its containing rectangle's bottom and right edges, respectively. In practice, you should adjust the size of a positioned element via the style's `height` and `width` properties.

Value: Length; Percentage; Constant `auto`

Example: `elementRef.style.bottom = "20px"`

left
top

	IE/Windows	IE/Mac	NN	W3C CSS2
Compatibility	4	4	6	Yes

Controls: The offset measure of a positioned element from its containing rectangle's left and top edges, respectively. In practice, use these properties to position an element under script control. To position an absolute-positioned element atop an inline element, calculate the position of the inline element via the `offsetTop` and `offsetLeft` properties with some browser-specific adjustments, as shown in Chapter 31.

Value: Length; Percentage; Constant `auto`

Example: `elementRef.style.top = "250px"`

height
width

	IE/Windows	IE/Mac	NN	W3C CSS2
Compatibility	4	4	6	Yes

Controls: Height and width of a block-level element's box. Used most commonly to adjust the dimensions of a positioned element (Chapter 31).

Value: Length; Percentage; Constant `auto`

Example: `elementRef.style.height = "300px"`

pixelBottom
pixelHeight
pixelLeft
pixelRight
pixelTop
pixelWidth

	IE/Windows	IE/Mac	NN	W3C CSS2
Compatibility	4	(4)	—	No

Controls: Integer pixel values for (primarily positioned) elements. Because the non-pixel versions of these properties return strings that also contain the unit measure (for example, `30px`), these properties let you work exclusively in integers for pixel units. The same can be done cross-platform by using `parseInt()` on the non-pixel versions of these properties. The `pixelBottom` and `pixelRight` properties are not in IE4/Mac.

Value: Integer

Example: `elementRef.style.pixelTop = elementRef.style.pixelTop + 20`

```
posBottom
posHeight
posLeft
posRight
posTop
posWidth
```

	IE/Windows	IE/Mac	NN	W3C CSS2
Compatibility	4	(4)	—	No

Controls: Numeric values for (primarily positioned) elements in whatever unit was specified by the corresponding style attribute. Because the non-pos versions of these properties return strings that also contain the unit measure (for example, `1.2em`), these properties let you work exclusively in numbers in the same units as the style was originally defined. The same can be done cross-platform by using `parseFloat()` on the non-pixel versions of these properties.

Value: Integer

Example: `elementRef.style.posTop = elementRef.style.posTop + 0.5`

position

	IE/Windows	IE/Mac	NN	W3C CSS2
Compatibility	4	4	6	Yes

Controls: The type of positioning to be applied to the element. An element that is not explicitly positioned is said to be *static*. A relative-positioned element appears in its normal page flow location but can be explicitly positioned relative to that location. An absolute-positioned element must have its `top` and `left` style attributes set to give the element a set of coordinates for its location. IE5/Mac and NN6 also allow for a fixed positioned element, which remains at its designated position in the browser window, even if the page scrolls (for example, for a watermark effect). See Chapter 31 for more information on positioned elements.

Value: Constant `absolute | fixed | relative | static`

Example: *elementRef*.style.position = "absolute"

zIndex

	IE/Windows	IE/Mac	NN	W3C CSS2
Compatibility	4	4	6	Yes

Controls: Front-to-back layering of positioned elements. Multiple items with the same zIndex value are layered in source code order (earliest item at the bottom). The higher the value, the closer to the user's eye the element is.

Value: Integer number; Constant auto

Example: *elementRef*.style.zIndex = "3"

Background properties

background

	IE/Windows	IE/Mac	NN	W3C CSS2
Compatibility	4	4	6	Yes

Controls: Up to five background style properties for an element.

Value: Combination values: *backgroundAttachment* || *backgroundColor* || *backgroundImage* || *backgroundPosition* || *backgroundRepeat*

Example: *elementRef*.style.background = "scroll url(bricks.jpg) repeat-x"

backgroundAttachment

	IE/Windows	IE/Mac	NN	W3C CSS2
Compatibility	4	4	6	Yes

Controls: Whether the background image remains fixed or scrolls with the content. Default is `scroll`.

Value: Constant `fixed | scroll`

Example: `elementRef.style.backgroundAttachment = "fixed"`

backgroundColor

	IE/Windows	IE/Mac	NN	W3C CSS2
Compatibility	4	4	6	Yes

Controls: Solid, opaque color for the background, or completely transparent. If you assign a background image, the color is layered behind the image so that any transparent spots of the image show the background color.

Value: Color value; Constant `transparent`

Example: `elementRef.style.backgroundColor = "salmon"`

backgroundImage

	IE/Windows	IE/Mac	NN	W3C CSS2
Compatibility	4	4	6	Yes

Controls: The URL (if any) of an image to be used for the background for the element.

Value: URL value; Constant `none`

Example: `elementRef.style.backgroundImage = "url(bricks.jpg)"`

backgroundPosition

	IE/Windows	IE/Mac	NN	W3C CSS2
Compatibility	4	4	6	Yes

Controls: The left-top location of the background image. Any offset from the left-top corner (default value "0% 0%") allows background color to show through along left and top edges of the element.

Value: Length values; Percentages; Constant `left | center | right || top | center | bottom`. While single values are accepted, their behavior may not be as expected. Providing space-delimited pairs of values is more reliable.

Example: `elementRef.style.backgroundPosition = "left top"`

backgroundPositionX
backgroundPositionY

	IE/Windows	IE/Mac	NN	W3C CSS2
Compatibility	4	4	–	No

Controls: The left (`backgroundPositionX`) and top (`backgroundPositionY`) locations of the background image. Any offset from the left-top corner (default value "0%") allows background color to show through along left and top edges of the element.

Value: Length value; Percentage; Constant `left | center | right` (for `backgroundPositionX`); Constant `top | center | bottom` (for `backgroundPositionY`).

Example: `elementRef.style.backgroundPositionX = "5px"`

backgroundRepeat

	IE/Windows	IE/Mac	NN	W3C CSS2
Compatibility	4	4	6	Yes

Controls: Image repetition characteristics of a background image. You can force the image to repeat along a single axis, if you want.

Value: Constant `repeat | repeat-x | repeat-y | no-repeat`

Example: `elementRef.style.backgroundRepeat = "repeat-y"`

Border and edge properties

`border`

	IE/Windows	IE/Mac	NN	W3C CSS2
Compatibility	4	4	6	Yes

Controls: Up to three border characteristics (color, style, and width) for all four edges of an element.

Value: Combination values *borderColor* || *borderStyle* || *borderWidth*

Example: *elementRef*.style.border = "green groove 2px"

borderBottom
borderLeft
borderRight
borderTop

	IE/Windows	IE/Mac	NN	W3C CSS2
Compatibility	4	4	6	Yes

Controls: Up to three border characteristics (color, style, and width) for a single edge of an element.

Value: Combination values

(**for** borderBottom)
borderBottomColor || *borderBottomStyle* || *borderBottomWidth*

(**for** borderLeft)
borderLeftColor || *borderLeftStyle* || *borderLeftWidth*

(**for** borderRight)
borderRightColor || *borderRightStyle* || *borderRightWidth*

(**for** borderTop) *borderTopColor* ||
borderTopStyle || *borderTopWidth*

elementRef.style.borderBottom

Example: *elementRef*.style.borderLeft = "#3300ff solid 2px"

borderBottomColor
borderLeftColor
borderRightColor
borderTopColor

	IE/Windows	IE/Mac	NN	W3C CSS2
Compatibility	4	4	6	Yes

Controls: Color for a single border edge of an element.

Value: Color values; Constant transparent.

Example: *elementRef*.style.borderTopColor = "rgb(30%, 50%, 0%)"

borderBottomStyle
borderLeftStyle
borderRightStyle
borderTopStyle

	IE/Windows	IE/Mac	NN	W3C CSS2
Compatibility	4	4	6	Yes

Controls: Rendered style for a border edge of an element.

Value: Constant none | hidden | dotted | dashed | solid | double | groove | ridge | inset | outset. IE versions for Windows prior to IE5.5 do not respond to the dotted or dashed types; IE/Mac does not respond to the hidden type.

Example: *elementRef*.style.borderRightStyle = "double"

borderBottomWidth
borderLeftWidth
borderRightWidth
borderTopWidth

	IE/Windows	IE/Mac	NN	W3C CSS2
Compatibility	4	4	6	Yes

Controls: Thickness of a border edge of an element.

Value: Length value; Constant thin | medium | thick (precise measure is at browser's discretion).

Example: *elementRef*.style.borderBottomWidth = "5px"

borderColor

	IE/Windows	IE/Mac	NN	W3C CSS2
Compatibility	4	4	6	Yes

Controls: Rendered color for one to four sides of an element.

Value: Color values for one to four rectangle sides.

Example: *elementRef*.style.borderColor = "green black"

borderStyle

	IE/Windows	IE/Mac	NN	W3C CSS2
Compatibility	4	4	6	Yes

Controls: Rendered style for one to four sides of an element.

Value: One to four rectangle side constants none I hidden I dotted I dashed I solid I double I groove I ridge I inset I outset. IE versions for Windows prior to IE5.5 do not respond to the dotted or dashed types; IE/Mac does not respond to the hidden type.

Example: `elementRef.style.borderStyle = "ridge"`

borderWidth

	IE/Windows	IE/Mac	NN	W3C CSS2
Compatibility	4	4	6	Yes

Controls: Thickness of border for one to four sides of an element.

Value: One to four rectangle side length value or constants thin I medium I thick (precise dimension is at browser's discretion).

Example: `elementRef.style.borderWidth = "5px 4px 5px 3px"`

margin

	IE/Windows	IE/Mac	NN	W3C CSS2
Compatibility	4	4	6	Yes

Controls: Thickness of transparent margin space outside the element's borders for one to four edges.

Value: One to four rectangle side length values.

Example: `elementRef.style.margin = "10px 5px"`

```
marginBottom
marginLeft
marginRight
marginTop
```

	IE/Windows	IE/Mac	NN	W3C CSS2
Compatibility	4	4	6	Yes

Controls: Thickness of transparent margin space outside the element's borders for a single border edge.

Value: Length value

Example: *elementRef*.style.marginBottom = "50px"

outline

	IE/Windows	IE/Mac	NN	W3C CSS2
Compatibility	–	5	6	Yes

Controls: Up to three characteristics of an outline surrounding an element (such as a border, but not shifting the location of internal content). This style is not fully supported in the above browsers, even though the properties are reflected in the style object.

Value: Combination values: *outlineColor* || *outlineStyle* || *outlineWidth*

Example: *elementRef*.style.outline = "red groove 2px"

outlineColor

	IE/Windows	IE/Mac	NN	W3C CSS2
Compatibility	–	5	6	Yes

Controls: Color of all four edges of an outline. This style is not fully supported in the above browsers, even though the properties are reflected in the `style` object.

Value: Color values; Constant `invert`

Example: `elementRef.style.outlineColor = "cornflowerblue"`

outlineStyle

	IE/Windows	IE/Mac	NN	W3C CSS2
Compatibility	—	5	6	Yes

Controls: Rendered style for all four sides of an element outline. This style is not fully supported in the above browsers, even though the properties are reflected in the `style` object.

Value: Constant `none | hidden | dotted | dashed | solid | double | groove | ridge | inset | outset`

Example: `elementRef.style.outlineStyle = "ridge"`

outlineWidth

	IE/Windows	IE/Mac	NN	W3C CSS2
Compatibility	—	5	6	Yes

Controls: Thickness of all four sides of an element outline. This style is not fully supported in the above browsers, even though the properties are reflected in the `style` object.

Value: Length value or constant `thin | medium | thick` (precise dimension is at browser's discretion)

Example: `elementRef.style.outlineWidth = "4px"`

padding

	IE/Windows	IE/Mac	NN	W3C CSS2
Compatibility	4	4	6	Yes

Controls: Thickness of space between an element's content and its borders for one to four edges.

Value: One to four rectangle side length values.

Example: *elementRef*.style.padding = "5px"

paddingBottom
paddingLeft
paddingRight
paddingTop

	IE/Windows	IE/Mac	NN	W3C CSS2
Compatibility	4	4	6	Yes

Controls: Thickness of space between an element's content and its borders for a single edge.

Value: Length value

Example: *elementRef*.style.paddingBottom = "20px"

List Properties

listStyle

	IE/Windows	IE/Mac	NN	W3C CSS2
Compatibility	4	4	6	Yes

Controls: Up to three characteristics of a list (OL or UL) presentation. Also applies to DD, DT, and LI elements.

Value: Combination values *listStyleImage* || *listStylePosition* || *listStyleType*

Example: *elementRef*.style.listStyle = "none inside lower-alpha"

listStyleImage

	IE/Windows	IE/Mac	NN	W3C CSS2
Compatibility	4	4	6	Yes

Controls: URL of the image to be used as a marker for a list item.

Value: URL value; Constant none

Example: *elementRef*.style.listStyleImage = "url(custombullet.jpg)"

listStylePosition

	IE/Windows	IE/Mac	NN	W3C CSS2
Compatibility	4	4	6	Yes

Controls: Whether the marker should be formatted inside the wrapped text of its content or dangle outside the wrapped text (default).

Value: Constant inside | outside

Example: *elementRef*.style.listStylePosition = "inside"

listStyleType

	IE/Windows	IE/Mac	NN	W3C CSS2
Compatibility	4	4	6	Yes

Controls: Which of the standard marker sets should be used for items in the list. A change to this property for a single LI element causes succeeding items to be in the same style.

Value: For UL elements, constant `circle` | `disc` | `square`

For OL elements, constant `decimal` | `lower-alpha` | `lower-roman` | `upper-alpha` | `upper-roman`

Example: `elementRef`.style.listStyleType = "upper-roman"

Scrollbar properties

```
scrollbar3dLightColor
scrollbarArrowColor
scrollbarBaseColor
scrollbarDarkShadowColor
scrollbarFaceColor
scrollbarHighlightColor
scrollbarShadowColor
scrollbarTrackColor
```

	IE/Windows	IE/Mac	NN	W3C CSS2
Compatibility	5.5	—	—	No

Controls: Colors of individual components of scrollbars when they are displayed for APPLET, BODY, DIV, EMBED, OBJECT, or TEXTAREA elements. To experiment with how different colors can affect the individual components, visit `http://msdn.microsoft.com/workshop/samples/author/dhtml/refs/scrollbarColor.htm`.

Value: Color values; Constant `none`

Example: `elementRef`.style.scrollbarTrackColor = "hotpink"

Table properties

borderCollapse

	IE/Windows	IE/Mac	NN	W3C CSS2
Compatibility	—	5	6	Yes

Controls: Whether a TABLE element adheres to the CSS2 separated borders model or the collapsed borders model. Style is not fully supported in IE5/Mac.

Value: Constant `collapse | separate`

Example: *elementRef*`.style.borderCollapse = "separate"`

borderSpacing

	IE/Windows	IE/Mac	NN	W3C CSS2
Compatibility	—	5	6	Yes

Controls: For a table following the separated borders model, the thickness of the spacing between cell rectangles (akin to the `CELLSPACING` attribute of TABLE elements). Style is not fully supported in IE5/Mac.

Value: One length value (for horizontal and vertical spacing) or comma-delimited list of two length values (the first for horizontal; the second for vertical).

Example: *elementRef*`.style.borderSpacing = "10px"`

captionSide

	IE/Windows	IE/Mac	NN	W3C CSS2
Compatibility	—	5	6	Yes

Controls: Position of the CAPTION element inside a TABLE element. Style is not implemented in IE5/Mac and is only partially implemented in NN6.

Value: Constant top | right | bottom | left

Example: *elementRef*.style.captionSide = "bottom"

emptyCells

	IE/Windows	IE/Mac	NN	W3C CSS2
Compatibility	—	5	6	Yes

Controls: Rendering of cells and their borders when the cells have no content. Default behavior is to not render borders around empty cells. Style is not implemented in IE5/Mac and is only partially implemented in NN6.

Value: Constant show | hide

Example: *elementRef*.style.emptyCells = "show"

tableLayout

	IE/Windows	IE/Mac	NN	W3C CSS2
Compatibility	5	5	6	Yes

Controls: Whether table is rendered progressively based on fixed width settings of the first row of cells or is rendered after the widths of all row content can be determined. Modifying this property after a table loads has no effect on the table.

Value: Constant auto | fixed

Example: *elementRef*.style.tableLayout = "auto"

Page and printing properties

orphans
widows

	IE/Windows	IE/Mac	NN	W3C CSS2
Compatibility	—	5	6	Yes

Controls: The minimum number of lines of a paragraph to be displayed at the bottom of a page (orphans) or top of a page (widows) when a page break occurs.

Value: Integer

Example: *elementRef*.style.orphans = "4"

page

	IE/Windows	IE/Mac	NN	W3C CSS2
Compatibility	—	5	6	Yes

Controls: The page (defined in an @page rule) with which the current element should be associated for printing.

Value: Identifier assigned to an existing @page rule

Example: *elementRef*.style.page = "landscape"

pageBreakAfter
pageBreakBefore

	IE/Windows	IE/Mac	NN	W3C CSS2
Compatibility	4	4	6	Yes

Controls: Whether a printed page break should be before or after the current element and the page break type. Style is not fully implemented in the IE4 browsers.

Value: Constant auto | always | avoid | left | right

Example: *elementRef*.style.pageBreakBefore = "always"

pageBreakInside

	IE/Windows	IE/Mac	NN	W3C CSS2
Compatibility	—	5	6	Yes

Controls: Whether a printed page break is allowed inside an element.

Value: Constant auto | avoid

Example: *elementRef*.style.pageBreakInside = "avoid"

size

	IE/Windows	IE/Mac	NN	W3C CSS2
Compatibility	—	—	6	Yes

Controls: The size or orientation of the page box (linked to the style rule via the page property) used to determine printed pages.

Value: One (same value for width and height) or two space-delimited (width and height) length values; constant auto | portrait | landscape

Example: *elementRef*.style.size = "portrait"

Miscellaneous properties

accelerator

	IE/Windows	IE/Mac	NN	W3C CSS2
Compatibility	5	—	—	No

Controls: Whether an accelerator key is defined for an element.

Value: Boolean

Example: *elementRef*`.style.accelerator = "true"`

behavior

	IE/Windows	IE/Mac	NN	W3C CSS2
Compatibility	5	—	—	No

Controls: The external behavior to be applied to the current element.

Value: Space-delimited list of URL values. URLs can be a file location, an OBJECT element id, or one of the built-in (default) behaviors.

Example: *elementRef*`.style.behavior = "url(#default#anchorClick)"`

cssText

	IE/Windows	IE/Mac	NN	W3C CSS2
Compatibility	4	4	6	No

Controls: Actual CSS rule text (Read-Only). This property exists by virtue of the browser's object model and is not part of the CSS specification. There is no corresponding CSS attribute.

Value: String

Example: var cssRuleText = *elementRef*`.style.cssText`

imeMode

	IE/Windows	IE/Mac	NN	W3C CSS2
Compatibility	5	—	—	No

Controls: Whether text is entered into a text INPUT or TEXTAREA element through the Input Method Editor (for languages, such as Chinese, Japanese, or Korean).

Value: Constant auto | active | inactive | disabled

Example: *elementRef*.style.imeMode = "active"

Aural properties

Although these properties are defined in the CSS2 specification and placeholders exist for them in NN6, the styles are not implemented in NN6. The script equivalent properties are listed here for the sake of completeness only.

```
azimuth
cue
cueAfter
cueBefore
elevation
pause
pauseAfter
pauseBefore
pitch
pitchRange
playDuring
richness
speak
speakHeader
speakNumeral
speakPunctuation
speechRate
stress
voiceFamily
volume
```

	IE/Windows	IE/Mac	NN	W3C CSS2
Compatibility	–	–	6	Yes

Controls: A variety of styles primarily for browsers that support speech synthesis output.

Value: Consult `http://www.w3.org/TR/REC-CSS2/aural.html` for details on aural style sheets.

filter Object

Properties	Methods	Event Handlers
See text		

Syntax

Accessing `filter` object properties and methods:

```
(IE4+)    document.all.objectID.stylefilters[i].property |
          method([parameters])
(IE5.5+)  document.all.objectID.stylefilters[filterName].
          property | method([parameters])
```

	NN2	NN3	NN4	NN6	IE3/J1	IE3/J2	IE4	IE5	IE5.5
Compatibility							✓	✓	✓

About this object

Earlier in this chapter, the `style.filter` property was shown to allow reading and writing of the string value that is assigned to an element's `style.filter` property. Filters are available in IE for Windows only, and not for the Mac as of IE5/Mac, even though IE5/Mac returns the `style.filter` property value. The purpose of this section is to teach you not how to use filters but rather, how to script them.

Multiple filters are merely part of the space-delimited list of filters. Some filter types have additional specifications. For example, the glow() filter has three properties that more clearly define how the element should be rendered with a glow effect. The style sheet rule for an element whose ID is glower looks like the following:

```
#glower {filter:glow(color=yellow, strength=5, enabled=true)}
```

Accessing the currentStyle.filter property for that element yields the string value:

```
glow(color=yellow, strength=5, enabled=true)
```

Attempting to modify a single sub-property of the glow() filter by way of string parsing would be cumbersome and hazardous at best. For example, imagine trying to increment the glow filter's strength property by 5.

Reading and writing sub-properties

A cleaner way to work with individual properties of a filter is to access the filter as an object belonging to the element affected by the filter. Each type of filter object has as its properties the individual sub-properties that you set in the style sheet. Continuing with the glow() filter example, you could access just the color property of the filter as follows:

```
var currColor = document.all.glower.currentStyle.filters["glow"].color
```

The reference is through the currentStyle property for reading the value, because in this case, the filter is applied in a style sheet definition, and only the currentStyle property reveals the effective style properties acting on an element. To modify the color, assign a new value to the filter object's property, but do so through the element's style property:

```
document.all.glower.style.filters["glow"].color = "green"
```

To increment a numeric value, such as increasing the glow() filter's strength property by 5, use a construction such as the following (long-winded though it may be):

```
document.all.glower.style.filters["glow"].strength =
document.all.glower.currentStyle.filters["glow"].strength + 5
```

Table 30-1 lists the filter object names that work all the way back to IE4 and the properties associated with each filter type.

Table 30-1   IE4-Compatible Static Filter Types

Filter Name	Description and Properties		
alpha()	Transparency level		
	Properties:	opacity	(0 to 100)
		finishopacity	(0 to 100)
		style	(gradient shape 0 to 3)
		startX	(coordinate integer)
		startY	(coordinate integer)
		finishX	(coordinate integer)
		finishY	(coordinate integer)
blur()	Simulating blurred motion		
	Properties:	add	(1 or 0)
		direction	(0, 45, 90, 135, 180, 225, 270, 315)
		strength	(pixel count)
chroma()	Color transparency		
	Properties:	color	(color value)
dropShadow()	Shadow effect		
	Properties:	color	(color value)
		offx	(horizontal offset pixels)
		offy	(vertical offset pixels)
		positive	(1 or 0)
flipH()	Horizontally mirrored image		
	Properties:	None	
flipV()	Vertically mirrored image		
	Properties:	None	
glow()	Outer edge radiance		
	Properties:	color	(color value)
		strength	(intensity 1 to 255)
gray()	Eliminate color		
	Properties:	None	

Continued

	Table 30-1 *(continued)*		
invert()	**Opposite hue, saturation, brightness levels**		
	Properties:	**None**	
light()	**Add light source (controlled by methods)**		
	Properties:	**None**	
mask()	**Overlay transparent mask**		
	Properties:	color	**(color value)**
shadow()	**Render as silhouette**		
	Properties:	color	**(color value)**
		direction	**(0, 45, 90, 135, 180, 225, 270, 315)**
wave()	**Add sine-wave distortion**		
	Properties:	add	**(1 or 0)**
		freq	**(integer number of waves)**
		light	**(strength 0 to 100)**
		phase	**(percentage offset 0 to 100)**
		strength	**(intensity 0 to 255)**
xRay()	**Render edges only**		
	Properties:	**None**	

In addition to the static filter types, which are applied to content and sit there unless modified by script, the IE4+ filter object also provides types for blends and reveals for transitions between visible and invisible elements. Scripting transitions to act when a script hides or shows an element requires a few lines of code, including calls to some of the filter object's methods. First, Table 30-2 shows the IE4+ syntax for transition filters.

Table 30-2 **IE4+ Transition Filters**

FilterName	*Description and Properties*			
blendTrans()	**Fades out old element, fades in new element**			
	Properties:	duration	(floating point number of seconds)	
	Methods:	apply()	(freezes current display)	
		play()	(plays the transition)	
		stop()	(stops transition mid-stream)	
revealTrans()	**Reveals element to be Shown through an effect**			
	Properties:	duration	(floating-point number of seconds)	
		transition	(code number for effect)	
			0	Box in
			1	Box out
			2	Circle in
			3	Circle out
			4	Wipe up
			5	Wipe down
			6	Wipe right
			7	Wipe left
			8	Vertical blinds
			9	Horizontal blinds
			10	Checker-board across
			11	Checker board down

Continued

Table 30-2 *(continued)*			
FilterName	*Description and Properties*		
		12	Random dissolve
		13	Split vertical in
		14	Split vertical out
		15	Split horizontal in
		16	Split horizontal out
		17	Strips left down
		18	Strips left up
		19	Strips right down
		20	Strips right up
		21	Random bars horizontally
		22	Random bars vertically
		23	Random effect
	Methods:	apply()	(freezes current display)
		play()	(plays the transition)
		stop()	(stops transition mid-stream)

To make a transition work under script control, a filter must be applied to the element that you want the transition to work on. That can be done by script or by assigning a filter style to the element. As for the scripting, you begin by invoking the apply() method of the desired filter object. Next, script the change, such as assigning a new URL to the src property of an IMG element. While you do this, the apply() method freezes the image until you invoke the play() method on the filter. Listing 30-1 effects a checkerboard transition between two images after you click the image.

Listing 30-1: **A Reveal Transition Between Images**

```
<HTML>
<HEAD>
<TITLE>IE4+ Transition</TITLE>
<STYLE TYPE="text/css">
IMG {filter:revealTrans(transition=10)}
</STYLE>
<SCRIPT LANGUAGE="JavaScript">
function doReveal() {
    document.all.myIMG.filters["revealTrans"].apply()
    if (document.all.myIMG.src.indexOf("desk1") != -1) {
        document.all.myIMG.src = "desk3.gif"
    } else {
        document.all.myIMG.src = "desk1.gif"
    }
    document.all.myIMG.filters["revealTrans"].play()
}
</SCRIPT>
</HEAD>
<BODY>
<H1>IE4+ Transition</H1>
<HR>
<P>Click on the image to cause a reveal transition.</P>
<IMG ID="myIMG" SRC="desk1.gif" HEIGHT=90 WIDTH=120 onClick="doReveal()">
</BODY>
</HTML>
```

Building on the example in Listing 30-1, the next example in Listing 30-2 demonstrates how a script can also modify a `filter` object's property, including a transition filter. Before the transition filter has its `apply()` method invoked, the script sets the transition type based on a user choice in a SELECT list.

Listing 30-2: **Choosing Reveal Transitions Between Images**

```
<HTML>
<HEAD>
<TITLE>IE4+ Transition and Choices</TITLE>
<STYLE TYPE="text/css">
IMG {filter:revealTrans(transition=10)}
</STYLE>
<SCRIPT LANGUAGE="JavaScript">
function doReveal() {
    document.all.myIMG.filters["revealTrans"].transition =
document.forms[0].transChoice.value
```

```
            document.all.myIMG.filters["revealTrans"].apply()
            if (document.all.myIMG.src.indexOf("desk1") != -1) {
                document.all.myIMG.src = "desk3.gif"
            } else {
                document.all.myIMG.src = "desk1.gif"
            }
            document.all.myIMG.filters["revealTrans"].play()
}
</SCRIPT>
</HEAD>
<BODY>
<H1>IE4+ Transition and Choices</H1>
<HR>
<FORM>
<P>Choose the desired transition type:
<SELECT NAME="transChoice">
    <OPTION VALUE=0>Box in
    <OPTION VALUE=1>Box out
    <OPTION VALUE=2>Circle in
    <OPTION VALUE=3>Circle out
    <OPTION VALUE=4>Wipe up
    <OPTION VALUE=5>Wipe down
    <OPTION VALUE=6>Wipe right
    <OPTION VALUE=7>Wipe left
    <OPTION VALUE=8>Vertical blinds
    <OPTION VALUE=9>Horizontal blinds
    <OPTION VALUE=10>Checkerboard across
    <OPTION VALUE=11>Checkerboard down
    <OPTION VALUE=12>Random dissolve
    <OPTION VALUE=13>Split vertical in
    <OPTION VALUE=14>Split vertical out
    <OPTION VALUE=15>Split horizontal in
    <OPTION VALUE=16>Split horizontal out
    <OPTION VALUE=17>Strips left down
    <OPTION VALUE=18>Strips left up
    <OPTION VALUE=19>Strips right down
    <OPTION VALUE=20>Strips right up
    <OPTION VALUE=21>Random bars horizontally
    <OPTION VALUE=22>Random bars vertically
    <OPTION VALUE=23>Random effect
</SELECT>
</FORM>
<P>Click on the image to cause a reveal transition.</P>
<IMG ID="myIMG" SRC="desk1.gif" HEIGHT=90 WIDTH=120 onClick="doReveal()">
</BODY>
</HTML>
```

IE5.5 filter syntax changes

While IE5.5/Windows still supports the original IE4 way of controlling filters, the browser also implements a new filter component, which Microsoft strongly encourages authors to use (as evidenced by the difficulty in finding documentation for the IE4 syntax at its developer Web site). In the process of implementing this new filter component, the names of many filters change, as do their individual properties. Moreover, the way the filter component is invoked in the style sheet is also quite different from the original component.

The style sheet syntax requires a reference to the new component as well as the filter name. Here is the old way:

```
#glower {filter:glow(color=yellow, strength=5, enabled=true)}
```

And here is the new way:

```
#glower {filter:progid:DXImageTransform.Microsoft.Glow(color=yellow, strength=5, enabled=true)}
```

Don't overlook the extra `progid:` pointer in the reference. This program identifier becomes part of the filter name that your scripts use to reference the filter:

```
document.all.glower.style.filters["DXImageTransform.Microsoft.Glow"].color = "green"
```

While some of the filter names and properties stay the same (except for the huge prefix), several older properties are subsumed by new filters whose properties help identify the specific effect. The former `revealTrans()` filter is now divided among several new filters dedicated to transition effects. Table 30-3 shows the IE5.5 syntax.

Note   Using the new syntax in IE5.5 can cause frequent crashes of the browser (at least early released versions), especially transition filters. If you implement the new syntax, be sure to torture-test your pages extensively.

Table 30-3   IE5.5 DXImageTransform.Microsoft Filter Names

FilterName	Description and Properties		
Alpha()	Transparency level		
	Properties:	opacity	(0 to 100)
		finishopacity	(0 to 100)
		style	(gradient shape 0 to 3)

Continued

elementRef.style.*filterObject*

	Table 30-3 (continued)		
FilterName	**Description and Properties**		
		startX	(coordinate integer)
		startY	(coordinate integer)
		finishX	(coordinate integer)
		finishY	(coordinate integer)
Barn()	**Barn-door style transition**		
	Properties:	duration	(floating-point number of seconds)
		motion	(in **or** out)
		orientation	(horizontal **or** vertical)
		percent	(0 to 100)
		status	0 (stopped), 1 (applied), 2 (playing)
	Methods:	apply()	(freezes current display)
		play()	(plays the transition)
		stop()	(stops transition mid-stream)
BasicImage()	**Element rotation, flip, color effects, and opacity**		
	Properties:	grayScale	(1 or 0)
		invert	(1 or 0)
		mask	(1 or 0)
		maskColor	(color value)
		mirror	(1 or 0)
		opacity	(0.0 to 1.0)
		rotation	0 (no rotation), 1 (90°), 2 (180°), 3 (270°)
		xRay	(1 or 0)
Blinds()	**Action transition with Venetian blind effect**		
	Properties:	**direction**	(up, down, right, left)
		squaresX	(integer column count)
		squaresY	(integer row count)
		status	0 (stopped), 1 (applied), 2 (playing)
	Methods:	apply()	(freezes current display)
		play()	(plays the transition)

FilterName	*Description and Properties*		
		stop()	(stops transition mid-stream)
Checkerboard()	**Action transition with checkerboard effect**		
	Properties:	bands	**(1 to 100)**
		direction	(up, down, right, left)
		duration	**(floating-point number of seconds)**
		percent	**(0 to 100)**
		slideStyle	(HIDE, PUSH, SWAP)
		status	**0 (stopped), 1 (applied), 2 (playing)**
	Methods:	apply()	**(freezes current display)**
		play()	**(plays the transition)**
		stop()	**(stops transition mid-stream)**
Chroma()	**Color transparency**		
	Properties:	color	**(color value)**
DropShadow()	**Shadow effect**		
	Properties:	color	**(color value)**
		offx	**(horizontal offset pixels)**
		offy	**(vertical offset pixels)**
		positive	**(1 or 0)**
Fade()	**Blend transition**		
	Properties:	duration	**(floating-point number of seconds)**
		overlap	**(0.0 to 1.0 seconds)**
		percent	**(0 to 100)**
		status	**0 (stopped), 1 (applied), 2 (playing)**
	Methods:	apply()	**(freezes current display)**
		play()	**(plays the transition)**
		stop()	**(stops transition mid-stream)**
Glow()	**Outer edge radiance**		
	Properties:	color	**(color value)**
		strength	**(intensity 1 to 255)**

Continued

	Table 30-3 *(continued)*		
FilterName	*Description and Properties*		
Iris()	Action transition with zoom effect		
	Properties:	duration	(floating-point number of seconds)
		irisStyle	(CIRCLE, CROSS, DIAMOND, PLUS, SQUARE, STAR)
		motion	(in **or** out)
		percent	(0 to 100)
		status	0 (stopped), 1 (applied), 2 (playing)
	Methods:	apply()	(freezes current display)
		play()	(plays the transition)
		stop()	(stops transition mid-stream)
Light()	Add light source (controlled by methods)		
	Properties:	None	
	Methods:	addAmbient (*red, green, blue, strength*)	
		addCone (*sourceLeft, sourceTop, sourceZAxis, targetLeft, targetTop, red, green, blue, strength, spreadAngle*)	
		addPoint (*sourceLeft, sourceTop, sourceZAxis, red, green, blue, strength*)	
		changeColor (*lightID, red, green, blue, absoluteColorFlag*)	
		changeStrength (*lightID, strength, absoluteIntensityFlag*)	
		clear()	
		moveLight (*lightID, sourceLeft, sourceTop, sourceZAxis, absoluteMovementFlag*)	
MaskFilter()	Overlay transparent mask		
	Properties:	color	(color value)
MotionBlur()	Simulating blurred motion		
	Properties:	add	(1 or 0)

FilterName	Description and Properties		
		direction	(0, 45, 90, 135, 180, 225, 270, 315)
		strength	(pixel count)
RandomDissolve()	**Pixelated dissolve transition**		
	Properties:	duration	(floating-point number of seconds)
		percent	(0 to 100)
		status	0 (stopped), 1 (applied), 2 (playing)
	Methods:	apply()	(freezes current display)
		play()	(plays the transition)
		stop()	(stops transition mid-stream)
RandomBars()	**Bar style transition**		
	Properties:	duration	(floating-point number of seconds)
		orientation	(horizontal or vertical)
		percent	(0 to 100)
		status	0 (stopped), 1 (applied), 2 (playing)
	Methods:	apply()	(freezes current display)
		play()	(plays the transition)
		stop()	(stops transition mid-stream)
Shadow()	**Render as silhouette**		
	Properties:	color	(color value)
		direction	(0, 45, 90, 135, 180, 225, 270, 315)
Strips()	**Striped style transition**		
	Properties:	duration	(floating-point number of seconds)
		motion	(in or out)
		percent	(0 to 100)
		status	0 (stopped), 1 (applied), 2 (playing)
	Methods:	apply()	(freezes current display)
		play()	(plays the transition)
		stop()	(stops transition mid-stream)
Wave()	**Add sine-wave distortion**		
	Properties:	add	(1 or 0)

Continued

elementRef*.style.*filterObject

FilterName	Description and Properties		
		freq	(integer number of waves)
		light	(strength 0 to 100)
		phase	(percentage offset 0 to 100)
		strength	(intensity 0 to 255)
xRay()	Render edges only		
	Properties:	None	

For more details on deploying filters in IE for Windows, visit `http://msdn.microsoft.com/workshop/author/filter/filters.asp`. Because most of the live examples require IE5.5+/Windows, be sure to use that version for the best experience at that page.

✦   ✦   ✦

Positioned Objects— Summary

♦ ♦ ♦ ♦

In This Chapter

Layer concepts

How to move, hide, and show content

The end of the LAYER element

♦ ♦ ♦ ♦

 On the CD-ROM   The full version of Chapter 31 is on the CD-ROM.

This is an oddball chapter within the scheme of Part III. Thus far, I have devoted each chapter to a distinct set of object model objects. This chapter breaks away from that mold for just a moment. The main reason that this chapter even exists has to do more with the history of Dynamic HTML — the capability to alter content on the fly in response to user interaction — particularly with respect to Netscape Navigator 4. The impetus for this separate discussion is the NN4 LAYER element and its associated object. What makes this discussion awkward is that the LAYER element and object became dead-end entities that never made it into the W3C standards process. NN6 instead has adopted the W3C standards for dynamic content, which more closely mimic the way Microsoft implemented its DHTML features starting with IE4. NN6 explicitly does not provide backward compatibility with scripted LAYER element objects, which also means that you must rewrite legacy applications to work in NN6.

That leaves an ungainly task in this chapter to create a bridge between the LAYER element and the more modern way of working with elements that can be positioned on the page, flown across the page, stacked in front of other elements, or hidden from view. The IE4+ and NN6 way to accomplish all of this is through CSS style sheets and the scripting thereof. In years to come, the NN4 LAYER element will be only a distant memory. Until then, we must acknowledge it and understand how to work the same magic with style sheets. To that end, this chapter provides details on both the NN4 layer object and the comparable syntax for using IE4+ and NN6 style sheets to get and set properties or invoke methods. Chapter 48 applies these techniques in some DHTML applications.

What Is a Layer?

Terminology in the area of positioned elements has become a bit confusing over time. Because NN4 was the earliest browser to be released with positioned elements (the LAYER element), the term *layer* became synonymous with any positioned element. When IE4 came on the scene, it was convenient to call a style sheet-positioned element (in other words, an element governed by a style sheet rule with the `position` attribute) a *layer* as a generic term for any positioned element. In fact, NN4 even treated an element that was positioned through style sheets as if it were a genuine layer object (although with some minor differences).

In the end, the layer term made good sense because no matter how it was achieved, a positioned element acted like a layer in front of the body content of a page. Perhaps you have seen how animated cartoons were created before computer animation changed the art. Layers of clear acetate sheets were assembled atop a static background. Each sheet contained one character or portion of a character. When all the sheets were carefully positioned atop each other, the view (as captured by a still camera) formed a composite frame of the cartoon. To create the next frame of the cartoon, the artist moved one of the layers a fraction of an inch along its intended path and then took another picture.

If you can visualize how that operation works, you have a good starting point for understanding how layers work. Each layer contains some kind of HTML content that exists in its own plane above the main document that loads in a window. You can change or replace the content of an individual layer on the fly without affecting the other layers; you can also reposition, resize, or hide the entire layer under script control.

The rest of this chapter has two distinct sections. The first is the same level of in-depth treatment of the NN4 layer object that other objects in this book receive. Along the way, the descriptions of various properties and methods demonstrate dynamic manipulation of layers and their content. The second section replicates the dynamic tasks in syntax that are compatible with the IE4+ and W3C DOMs. If you are making the transition away from the NN4 layer object, you can easily compare dynamic HTML actions for NN4 layers with the same actions in the other DOMs, especially as your NN4 scripting migrates to the W3C DOM world of NN6.

✦   ✦   ✦

Embedded Objects— Summary

On the CD-ROM

The full version of Chapter 32 is on the CD-ROM.

In addition to the typical content that you see in Web pages — primarily text and images — you can embed other kinds of content into the page. Such embedded content usually requires the powers of additional software, such as plug-in players or other external code processors, to load and display the content. All of this external content is added to a page by one of three HTML elements: APPLET, EMBED, or OBJECT. In the HTML 4.0 standard, the APPLET element, which was intended originally for loading Java applets, is deprecated in favor of the newer OBJECT element. An OBJECT element is intended to be more extensible, meaning that it has enough attributes and power to summon the Java virtual machine if the incoming code is a Java applet, or run an ActiveX program (in IE for Windows, that is). The EMBED element is commonly used to display a plug-in control panel directly in the document, rather than having the panel appear in a separate window.

In all cases, when a visual element is embedded via any of these elements, the control panel or applet occupies a segregated rectangular space on the page, and generally confines its activities to that rectangle. But in many cases, JavaScript can also interact with the content or the player, allowing your scripts to extend themselves with powers for actions, such as controlling audio playback or the operation of a Java applet.

This chapter's primary focus is not on the content and players that you can control as it is on the HTML element objects that load the content or players into the page in the first place. Most of the properties represent nothing more than scriptable access to the element HTML attributes. The property descriptions in this chapter are therefore not extensive. Online HTML references (including the W3C HTML 4.0 specification and the Microsoft Developer Network documentation) should fill in the attribute value information quite well.

In practice, scripts have very little interaction with these element objects, because once a plug-in or embedded controller loads into a page, scripts don't modify the behavior of the plug-in or controller through element properties. But if you ever need to know what parts of the HTML elements are scriptable, you'll find that information in this chapter. As for controlling applets and plug-ins, you can find information about that in Chapter 44, where you also see code for a JavaScript library that acts an intermediary for controlling sound playback through Windows Media Player, QuickTime, and LiveAudio plug-ins.

✦   ✦   ✦

XML Objects— Summary

33

CHAPTER

◆ ◆ ◆ ◆

In This Chapter

Treating XML
elements as objects

Creating IE XML data
islands

Accessing XML
element attributes

◆ ◆ ◆ ◆

 On the CD-ROM   The full version of Chapter 33 is on the CD-ROM.

XML (eXtensible Markup Language) is an undeniably hot topic in the Internet world. Not only has the W3C organization formed multiple working groups and recommendations for XML and its offshoots, but the W3C DOM recommendation also has XML in mind when it comes to defining how elements, attributes, and data of any kind — not just the HTML vocabulary — are exposed to browsers as an object model. Most of the arcana of the W3C DOM Core specification — especially the structure based on the node — are in direct response to the XML possibilities of documents that are beginning to travel the Internet.

While XML documents can stand alone as containers of structured data in both IE5+ and NN6, the Windows version of IE5+ permits XML data to be embedded as "islands" in an HTML document. Such islands are encased in an XML element — an IE-specific extension of HTML.

It's important to distinguish between "the" XML element — the element generated in a document by the IE-specific <XML> tag set — and a generic XML element that is a part of the XML data island. Generic XML elements have tag names that are meaningful to a data application, and they are usually defined by a separate Document Type Declaration (DTD) that contains a formal specification of the element names, their attributes (if any), and the nature of the data they can contain. Out of necessity, this book assumes that you are already familiar with XML such that your server-based applications serve up XML data exclusively, embed XML islands into HTML documents, or convert database data into XML. The focus of this chapter, and an extended application example of Chapter 57, is how to access custom elements that reside inside an IE XML element.

The rest of the chapter on the CD-ROM continues by exploring the relationship between application-specific XML elements and the core portion of the W3C DOM. The W3C DOM standard defines a sizable set of properties and methods that apply to nodes, elements, and attributes. You will recognize the properties and methods from their association with generic HTML elements described in Chapter 15, because in the W3C DOM world, HTML elements inherit the core object characteristics. You then meet the IE5+/Windows XML element object (the one generated by the ⟨XML⟩ tag) to understand how it turns XML data into JavaScript-accessible objects.

✦　　✦　　✦

JavaScript Core Language Reference

The String
Object

C hapter 6's tutorial introduced you to the concepts of
values and the types of values that JavaScript works
with — features, such as strings, numbers, and Boolean values. In this chapter, you look more closely at the very important String data type, as well as its relationship to the Number
data type. Along the way, you encounter the many ways in
which JavaScript enables scripters to manipulate strings.

Note   Much of the syntax that you see in this chapter is identical
to that of the Java programming language. Because the
scope of JavaScript activity is narrower than that of Java,
you don't have nearly as much to learn for JavaScript as for
Java. At the same time, certain string object language features apply to scripting but not to Java programming.
Improvements to the string object's methods in Navigator
4 greatly simplify a number of string manipulation tasks. If
you must script for a lower common denominator of
browser, however, you may need some of the same kind of
string micro-management skills that a C programmer
needs. I soften the blow by providing some general purpose functions that you can plug into your scripts to make
those jobs easier.

String and Number Data Types

Although JavaScript is not what is known as a "strongly
typed" language, you still need to be aware of several data
types because of their impact on the way you work with the
information in those forms. In this section, I focus on strings
and two types of numbers.

Simple strings

A *string* consists of one or more standard text characters between matching quote marks. JavaScript is forgiving in one regard: You can use single or double quotes, as long as you match two single quotes or two double quotes around a string. Another benefit to this scheme becomes apparent when you try to include a quoted string inside a string. For example, say that you're assembling a line of HTML code in a variable that you will eventually write to a new window completely controlled by JavaScript. The line of text that you want to assign to a variable is the following:

```
<INPUT TYPE="checkbox" NAME="candy">Chocolate
```

To assign this entire line of text to a variable, you have to surround the line in quotes. But because quotes appear inside the string, JavaScript (or any language) has problems deciphering where the string begins or ends. By carefully placing the other kind of quote pairs, however, you can make the assignment work. Here are two equally valid ways:

```
result = '<INPUT TYPE="checkbox" NAME="candy">Chocolate'
result = "<INPUT TYPE='checkbox' NAME='candy'>Chocolate"
```

Notice that in both cases, the same unique pair of quotes surrounds the entire string. Inside the string, two quoted strings appear that are treated as such by JavaScript. I recommend that you settle on one form or the other, and then use that form consistently throughout your scripts.

Building long string variables

The act of joining strings together — concatenation — enables you to assemble long strings out of several little pieces. This feature is very important for some of your scripting — for example, when you need to build an HTML page's specifications entirely within a variable before writing the page to another frame with one `document.write()` statement.

One tactic that I use keeps the length of each statement in this building process short enough so that it's easily readable in your text editor. This method uses the add-by-value assignment operator (+=) that appends the right-hand side of the equation to the left-hand side. Here is a simple example, which begins by initializing a variable as an empty string:

```
var newDocument = ""
newDocument += "<HTML><HEAD><TITLE>Life and Times</TITLE></HEAD>"
newDocument += "<BODY><H1>My Life and Welcome to It</H1>"
newDocument += "by Sidney Finortny<HR>"
```

Starting with the second line, each statement adds more data to the string being stored in newDocument. You can continue appending string data until the entire page's specification is contained in the newDocument variable.

Joining string literals and variables

In some cases, you need to create a string out of literal strings (characters with quote marks around them) and string variable values. The methodology for concatenating these types of strings is no different from that of multiple string literals. The plus-sign operator does the job. Therefore, in the following example, a variable contains a name. That variable value is made a part of a larger string whose other parts are string literals:

```
yourName = prompt("Please enter your name:","")
var msg = "Good afternoon, " + yourName + "."
alert(msg)
```

Some common problems that you may encounter while attempting this kind of concatenation include the following:

✦ Accidentally omitting one of the quotes around a literal string

✦ Failing to insert blank spaces in the string literals to accommodate word spaces

✦ Forgetting to concatenate punctuation after a variable value

Also, don't forget that what I show here as variable values can be any expression that evaluates to a string, including property references and the results of some methods. For example

```
var msg = "The name of this document is " + document.title + "."
alert(msg)
```

Special inline characters

The way string literals are created in JavaScript makes adding certain characters to strings difficult. I'm talking primarily about adding quotes, carriage returns, apostrophes, and tab characters to strings. Fortunately, JavaScript provides a mechanism for entering such characters into string literals. A backslash symbol, followed by the character that you want to appear as inline, makes that task happen. For the "invisible" characters, a special set of letters following the backslash tells JavaScript what to do.

The most common backslash pairs are as follows:

✦ \"   Double quote

✦ \'   Single quote (apostrophe)

✦ \\   Backslash

✦ \b   Backspace

✦ \t   Tab

✦ \n   New line

✦ \r   Carriage return

✦ \f   Form feed

Use these "inline characters" (also known as "escaped characters," but this terminology has a different connotation for Internet strings) inside quoted string literals to make JavaScript recognize them. When assembling a block of text that needs a new paragraph, insert the \n character pair. Here are some examples of syntax using these special characters:

```
msg = "You\'re doing fine."
msg = "This is the first line.\nThis is the second line."
msg = document.title + "\n" + document.links.length + " links present."
```

Technically speaking, a complete carriage return, as known from typewriting days, is both a line feed (advance the line by one) and a carriage return (move the carriage all the way to the left margin). Although JavaScript strings treat a line feed (\n new line) as a full carriage return, you may have to construct \r\n breaks when assembling strings that go back to a CGI script on a server. The format that you use all depends on the string-parsing capabilities of the CGI program. (Also see the special requirements for the TEXTAREA object in Chapter 22.)

Confusing the strings assembled for display in TEXTAREA objects or alert boxes with strings to be written as HTML is easy. For HTML strings, make sure that you use the standard HTML tags for line breaks (<BR>) and paragraph breaks (<P>) rather than the inline return or line feed symbols.

String Object

Properties	Methods
constructor	anchor()
length	big()

Properties	Methods
prototype†	blink()
	bold()
	charAt()
	charCodeAt()
	concat()
	fixed()
	fontcolor()
	fontsize()
	fromCharCode()†
	indexOf()
	italics()
	lastIndexOf()
	link()
	localeCompare()
	match()
	replace()
	search()
	slice()
	small()
	split()
	strike()
	sub()
	substr()
	substring()
	sup()
	toLocaleLowerCase()
	toLocaleUpperCase()
	toLowerCase()
	toString()
	toUpperCase()
	valueOf()

†Member of the static String object

Syntax

Creating a string object:

```
var myString = new String("characters")
```

Accessing static `String` object properties and methods:

```
String.property | method([parameters])
```

Accessing string object properties and methods:

```
string.property | method([parameters])
```

About this object

JavaScript draws a fine line between a string value and a string object. Both let you use the same methods on their contents, so that by and large, you do not have to create a string object (with the `new String()` constructor) every time you want to assign a string value to a variable. A simple assignment operation (`var myString = "fred"`) is all you need to create a string value that behaves on the surface very much like a full-fledged string object.

Where the difference comes into play is when you want to exploit the "object-ness" of a genuine string object, which I explain further in the discussion of the `string.prototype` property later in this chapter. You may also encounter the need to use a full-fledged string object when passing string data to Java applets. If you find that your applet doesn't receive a string value as a Java String data type, then create a new string object via the JavaScript constructor function before passing the value onto the applet.

With string data often comes the need to massage that text in scripts. In addition to concatenating strings, you at times need to extract segments of strings, delete parts of strings, and replace one part of a string with some other text. Unlike many plain-language scripting languages, JavaScript is fairly low-level in its built-in facilities for string manipulation. This characteristic means that unless you can take advantage of the regular expression powers of NN4+ and IE4+, you must fashion your own string handling routines out of very elemental powers built into JavaScript. Later in this chapter, I provide several functions that you can use in your own scripts for common string handling in a manner fully compatible with older browsers.

As you work with string values, visualize every string value as an object with properties and methods like other JavaScript objects. The latest versions of JavaScript define a few properties and a slew of methods for any string value (and one extra property for the static `String` object that is always present in the context of the browser window). The syntax is the same for string methods as it is for any other object method:

```
stringObject.method()
```

What may seem odd at first is that the `stringObject` part of this reference can be any expression that evaluates to a string, including string literals, variables containing strings, methods or functions that return strings, or other object properties. Therefore, the following examples of calling the `toUpperCase()` method are all valid:

```
"george burns".toUpperCase()
yourName.toUpperCase() // yourName is a variable containing a string
window.prompt("Enter your name","").toUpperCase()
document.forms[0].entry.value.toUpperCase() // entry is a text field object
```

An important concept to remember is that invoking a string method does not change the string object that is part of the reference. Rather, the method returns a value, which can be used as a parameter to another method or function call, or assigned to a variable value.

Therefore, to change the contents of a string variable to the results of a method, you must use an assignment operator, as in

```
yourName = yourName.toUpperCase() // variable is now all uppercase
```

Note

In Navigator 2, avoid nesting method calls for the same string object when the methods modify the string. The evaluation does not work as you may expect. Instead, break out each call as a separate JavaScript statement.

Properties

constructor

Value: Function Reference   Read/Write

	NN2	NN3	NN4	NN6	IE3/J1	IE3/J2	IE4	IE5	IE5.5
Compatibility			✓	✓			✓	✓	✓

The `constructor` property is a reference to the function that was invoked to create the current string. For a native JavaScript string object, the constructor function is the built-in `String()` constructor.

When you use the `new String()` constructor to create a string object, the type of the value returned by the constructor is `object` (meaning the `typeof` operator returns `object`). Therefore, you can use the `constructor` property on an object value to see if it is a string object:

```
if (typeof someValue == "object" ) {
    if (someValue.constructor == String) {
        // statements to deal with string object
    }
}
```

Although the property is read/write, and you can assign a different constructor to the `String.prototype`, the native behavior of a `String` object persists through the new constructor.

 Example on the CD-ROM

Related Items: `prototype` property.

length

Value: Integer   Read-Only

	NN2	NN3	NN4	NN6	IE3/J1	IE3/J2	IE4	IE5	IE5.5
Compatibility	✓	✓	✓	✓	✓	✓	✓	✓	✓

The most frequently used property of a string is `length`. To derive the length of a string, read its property as you would read the `length` property of any object:

```
string.length
```

The length value represents an integer count of the number of characters within the string. Spaces and punctuation symbols count as characters. Any backslash special characters embedded in a string count as one character, including such characters as newline and tab. Here are some examples:

```
"Lincoln".length // result = 7
"Four score".length // result = 10
"One\ntwo".length // result = 7
"".length // result = 0
```

The `length` property is commonly summoned when dealing with detailed string manipulation in repeat loops.

prototype

Value: Object   Read/Write

	NN2	NN3	NN4	NN6	IE3/J1	IE3/J2	IE4	IE5	IE5.5
Compatibility		✓	✓	✓			✓	✓	✓

String objects defined with the `new String("stringValue")` constructor are robust objects compared with plain, old variables that are assigned string values. You certainly don't have to create this kind of string object for every string in your scripts, but these objects do come in handy if you find that strings in variables go awry. This happens occasionally while trying to preserve string information as script variables in other frames or windows. By using the string object constructor, you can be relatively assured that the string value will be available in the distant frame when needed.

Another byproduct of true string objects is that you can assign prototype properties and methods to all string objects in the document. A *prototype* is a property or method that becomes a part of every new object created after the prototype items are added. For strings, as an example, you may want to define a new method for converting a string into a new type of HTML font tag not already defined by the JavaScript string object. Listing 34-1 shows how to create and use such a prototype.

Listing 34-1: **A String Object Prototype**

```
<HTML>
<HEAD>
<TITLE>String Object Prototype</TITLE>
<SCRIPT LANGUAGE="JavaScript1.1">
function makeItHot() {
    return "<FONT COLOR='red'>" + this.toString() + "</FONT>"
}
String.prototype.hot = makeItHot
</SCRIPT>
<BODY>
<SCRIPT LANGUAGE="JavaScript1.1">
document.write("<H1>This site is on " + "FIRE".hot() + "!!</H1>")
</SCRIPT>
</BODY>
</HTML>
```

A function definition (`makeItHot()`) accumulates string data to be returned to the object when the function is invoked as the object's method. The `this` keyword refers to the object making the call, which you convert to a string for concatenation with the rest of the strings to be returned. In the page's Body, that prototype method is invoked in the same way one invokes existing `String` methods that turn strings into HTML tags (discussed later in this chapter).

In the next sections, I divide string object methods into two distinct categories. The first, parsing methods, focuses on string analysis and character manipulation within strings. The second group, formatting methods, is devoted entirely to assembling strings in HTML syntax for those scripts that assemble the text to be written into new documents or other frames.

Parsing methods

string`.charAt(`*index*`)`

Returns: One-Character String

	NN2	NN3	NN4	NN6	IE3/J1	IE3/J2	IE4	IE5	IE5.5
Compatibility	✓	✓	✓	✓	✓	✓	✓	✓	✓

Use the *string*`.charAt()` method to read a single character from a string when you know the position of that character. For this method, you specify an index value in the string as a parameter to the method. The index value of the first character of the string is 0. To grab the last character of a string, mix string methods:

```
myString.charAt(myString.length - 1)
```

If your script needs to get a range of characters, use the *string*`.substring()` method. Using *string*`.substring()` to extract a character from inside a string is a common mistake, when the *string*`.charAt()` method is more efficient.

On the CD-ROM   Example on the CD-ROM

Related Items: `string.lastIndexOf()`, `string.indexOf()`, `string.substring()` methods.

string.charCodeAt([*index*])
String.fromCharCode(*num1* [, *num2* [, ...
numn]])

Returns: Integer code number for a character; concatenated string value of code numbers supplied as parameters.

	NN2	NN3	NN4	NN6	IE3/J1	IE3/J2	IE4	IE5	IE5.5
Compatibility			✓	✓			✓	✓	✓

Conversions from plain language characters to their numeric equivalents have a long tradition in computer programming. For a long time, the most common numbering scheme was the ASCII standard, which covers the basic English, alphanumeric characters and punctuation within 128 values (numbered 0 through 127). An extended version with a total of 256 characters, with some variations depending on the operating system, accounts for other roman characters in other languages, particularly vowels with umlauts and other pronunciation marks. To bring all languages, including pictographic languages and other nonroman alphabets, into the computer age, a world standard called Unicode provides space for thousands of characters.

In JavaScript, the character conversions are string methods. Acceptable values depend on the browser that you are using. NN4 works only with the 256 ISO-Latin-I values; NN6 and IE4+ work with the Unicode system.

The two methods that perform these conversions work in very different ways syntactically. The first, *string*.charCodeAt(), converts a single string character to its numerical equivalent. The string being converted is the one to the left of the method name — and the string may be a literal string or any other expression that evaluates to a string value. If no parameter is passed, the character being converted is by default the first character of the string. However, you can also specify a different character as an index value into the string (first character is 0), as demonstrated here:

```
"abc".charCodeAt()  // result = 97
"abc".charCodeAt(0) // result = 97
"abc".charCodeAt(1) // result = 98
```

If the string value is an empty string or the index value is beyond the last character, the result is NaN.

To convert numeric values to their characters, use the `String.fromCharCode()` method. Notice that the object beginning the method call is the static `String` object, not a string value. Then, as parameters, you can include one or more integers separated by commas. In the conversion process, the method combines the characters for all of the parameters into one string, an example of which is shown here:

```
String.fromCharCode(97, 98, 99)  // result "abc"
```

Note The `string.charCodeAt()` method is broken on the first release of the Macintosh version of Navigator 4, and always returns `NaN`. This error is fixed in subsequent releases.

On the CD-ROM Example (with Listing 34-2) on the CD-ROM

Related Items: None.

string.concat(*string2*)

Returns: Combined string.

	NN2	NN3	NN4	NN6	IE3/J1	IE3/J2	IE4	IE5	IE5.5
Compatibility			✓	✓			✓	✓	✓

JavaScript's add-by-value operator (+=) provides a convenient way to concatenate strings. Recent browsers, however, include a string object method that performs the same task. The base string to which more text is appended is the object or value to the left of the period. The string to be appended is the parameter of the method, as the following example demonstrates:

```
"abc".concat("def")  // result: "abcdef"
```

As with the add-by-value operator, the `concat()` method doesn't know about word endings. You are responsible for including the necessary space between words if the two strings require a space between them in the result.

Related Items: Add-by-value (+=) operator.

string.indexOf(*searchString* [, *startIndex*])

Returns: Index value of the character within *string* where *searchString* begins.

	NN2	NN3	NN4	NN6	IE3/J1	IE3/J2	IE4	IE5	IE5.5
Compatibility	✓	✓	✓	✓	✓	✓	✓	✓	✓

Like some languages' offset string function, JavaScript's indexOf() method enables your script to obtain the number of the character in the main string where a search string begins. Optionally, you can specify where in the main string the search should begin—but the returned value is always relative to the very first character of the main string. Such as all string object methods, index values start their count with 0. If no match occurs within the main string, the returned value is -1. Thus, this method is a convenient way to determine whether one string contains another, regardless of position.

A bug exists in some versions of Navigator 2 and 3 that can trip up your scripts if you don't guard against it. If the string being searched is empty, the indexOf() method returns an empty string rather than the expected -1 value. Therefore, you may want to test to make sure the string is not empty before applying this method. A look at the following examples tells you more about this method than a long description. In all examples, you assign the result of the method to a variable named offset.

On the CD-ROM Example on the CD-ROM

Related Items: string.lastIndexOf(), string.charAt(), string.substring() methods.

string.lastIndexOf(*searchString*[, *startIndex*])

Returns: Index value of the last character within string where *searchString* begins.

	NN2	NN3	NN4	NN6	IE3/J1	IE3/J2	IE4	IE5	IE5.5
Compatibility	✓	✓	✓	✓	✓	✓	✓	✓	✓

The *string*.lastIndexOf() method is closely related to the method *string*.indexOf(). The only difference is that this method starts its search for a match from the end of the string (*string*.length - 1) and works its way backward through the string. All index values are still counted, starting with 0, from the front of the string. The examples that follow use the same values as in the examples for *string*.indexOf() so that you can compare the results. In cases where only one instance of the search string is found, the results are the same; but when multiple instances of the search string exist, the results can vary widely—hence the need for this method.

 This string method has experienced numerous bugs, particularly in Navigator 2, and in later versions for UNIX. Scripts using this method should be tested exhaustively.

 Example on the CD-ROM

Related Items: string.lastIndexOf(), string.charAt(), string.substring() methods.

string.localeCompare(*string2*)

Returns: Integer.

	NN2	NN3	NN4	NN6	IE3/J1	IE3/J2	IE4	IE5	IE5.5
Compatibility				✓					✓

The localeCompare() method lets a script compare the cumulative Unicode values of two strings, taking into account the language system for the browser. The need for this method affects only some language systems (Turkish is said to be one). If the two strings, adjusted for the language system, are equal, the value returned is zero. If the string value on which the method is invoked (meaning the string to the left of the period) sorts ahead of the parameter string, the value returned is a negative integer; otherwise the returned value is a positive integer.

The ECMA standard for this method leaves the precise positive or negative values up to the browser designer. NN6 calculates the cumulative Unicode values for both strings and subtracts the string parameter's sum from the string value's sum. IE5.5, on the other hand, returns -1 or 1 if the strings are not colloquially equal.

Related Items: string.toLocaleLowerCase(), string.toLocaleUpperCase() methods.

string.match(*regExpression*)

Returns: Array of matching strings.

	NN2	NN3	NN4	NN6	IE3/J1	IE3/J2	IE4	IE5	IE5.5
Compatibility			✓	✓			✓	✓	✓

The *string*.match() method relies on the RegExp (regular expression) object introduced to JavaScript in NN4 and IE4. The string value under scrutiny is to the left of the dot, while the regular expression to be used by the method is passed as a parameter. The parameter must be a regular expression object, created according to the two ways these objects can be generated.

This method returns an array value when at least one match turns up; otherwise the returned value is null. Each entry in the array is a copy of the string segment that matches the specifications of the regular expression. You can use this method to uncover how many times a substring or sequence of characters appears in a larger string. Finding the offset locations of the matches requires other string parsing.

On the CD-ROM   Example (with Listing 34-3) on the CD-ROM

Related Items: RegExp object (Chapter 38).

string.replace(*regExpression, replaceString*)

Returns: Changed string.

	NN2	NN3	NN4	NN6	IE3/J1	IE3/J2	IE4	IE5	IE5.5
Compatibility			✓	✓			✓	✓	✓

Regular expressions are commonly used to perform search-and-replace operations. JavaScript's *string*.replace() method provides a simple framework in which to perform this kind of operation on any string.

Searching and replacing requires three components. The first is the main string that is the target of the operation. Second is the regular expression to search for. And third is the string to replace each instance of the text found by the operation. For the `string.replace()` method, the main string is the string value or object referenced to the left of the period. This string can also be a literal string (that is, text surrounded by quotes). The regular expression to search for is the first parameter, while the replacement string is the second parameter.

The regular expression definition determines whether the replacement is of just the first match encountered in the main string or all matches in the string. If you add the g parameter to the end of the regular expression, then one invocation of the `replace()` method performs global search-and-replace through the entire main string.

As long as you know how to generate a regular expression, you don't have to be a whiz to use the `string.replace()` method to perform simple replacement operations. But using regular expressions can make the operation more powerful. Consider these soliloquy lines by Hamlet:

```
To be, or not to be: that is the question:
Whether 'tis nobler in the mind to suffer
```

If you wanted to replace both instances of "be" with "exist," you can do it in this case by specifying

```
var regexp = /be/g
soliloquy.replace(regexp, "exist")
```

But you can't always be assured that the letters "b" and "e" will be standing alone as a word. What happens if the main string contains the word "being" or "saber"? The above example replaces the "be" letters in them as well.

The regular expression help comes from the special characters to better define what to search for. In the example here, the search is for the word "be." Therefore, the regular expression surrounds the search text with word boundaries (the \b special character), as in

```
var regexp = /\bbe\b/g
soliloquy.replace(regexp, "exist")
```

This syntax also takes care of the fact that the first two "be" words are followed by punctuation, rather than a space, as you may expect for a freestanding word. For more about regular expression syntax, see Chapter 38.

On the CD-ROM   Example (with Listing 34-4) on the CD-ROM

Related Items: `string.match()` method; `RegExp` object.

string.search(*regExpression*)

Returns: Offset Integer.

	NN2	NN3	NN4	NN6	IE3/J1	IE3/J2	IE4	IE5	IE5.5
Compatibility			✓	✓			✓	✓	✓

The results of the *string*.search() method may remind you of the *string*.indexOf() method. In both cases, the returned value is the character number where the matching string first appears in the main string, or -1 if no match occurs. The big difference, of course, is that the matching string for *string*.search() is a regular expression.

On the CD-ROM

Example on the CD-ROM

Related Items: string.match() method; RegExp object.

string.slice(*startIndex* [, *endIndex*])

Returns: String.

	NN2	NN3	NN4	NN6	IE3/J1	IE3/J2	IE4	IE5	IE5.5
Compatibility			✓	✓			✓	✓	✓

The *string*.slice() method resembles the method *string*.substring() in that both let you extract a portion of one string and create a new string as a result (without modifying the original string). A helpful improvement in *string*.slice(), however, is that specifying an ending index value relative to the end of the main string is easier.

Using *string*.substring() to extract a substring that ends before the end of the string requires machinations, such as the following:

```
string.substring(4, (string.length-2))
```

Instead, you can assign a negative number to the second parameter of *string*.slice() to indicate an offset from the end of the string:

```
string.slice(4, -2)
```

The second parameter is optional. If you omit the second parameter, the returned value is a string from the starting offset to the end of the main string.

On the CD-ROM Example (with Listing 34-5) on the CD-ROM

Related Items: `string.substr()`, `string.substring()` methods.

string.split("*delimiterCharacter*" [, *limitInteger*])

Returns: Array of delimited items.

	NN2	NN3	NN4	NN6	IE3/J1	IE3/J2	IE4	IE5	IE5.5
Compatibility		✓	✓	✓			✓	✓	✓

The `split()` method is the functional opposite of the *array*.`join()` method (see Chapter 37). From the string object point of view, JavaScript splits a long string into pieces delimited by a specific character and then creates a dense array with those pieces. You do not need to initialize the array via the `new Array()` constructor. Given the powers of array object methods, such as *array*.`sort()`, you may want to convert a series of string items to an array to take advantage of those powers. Also, if your goal is to divide a string into an array of single characters, you can still use the `split()` method, but specify an empty string as a parameter. For NN3 and IE4, only the first parameter is observed.

In NN4+ and IE4+, you can use a regular expression object for the first parameter, enhancing the powers of finding delimiters in strings. For example, consider the following string:

```
var nameList = "1.Fred,2.Jane,3.Steve"
```

To convert that string into a three-element array of only the names takes a lot of parsing without regular expressions before you can even use *string*.`split()`. However, with a regular expression as a parameter,

```
var regexp = /,*\d.\b/
var newArray = nameList.split(regexp)
    // result = an array "Fred", "Jane", "Steve"
```

the new array entries hold only the names and not the leading numbers or periods. A second addition is an optional second parameter. This integer value allows you to specify a limit to the number of array elements generated by the method.

And finally, NN4+ provides some extra (but non-ECMA-standard) functionality if you use the *string*.split() method inside a <SCRIPT> tag that specifies JavaScript1.2 (only). A space character as a single parameter, such as *string*.split(" "), is interpreted to mean any white space (spaces, tabs, carriage returns, line feeds) between runs of characters. Even if the number of spaces between elements is not uniform, they are treated all the same. This special feature may not be adopted by ECMA and is omitted from later JavaScript versions in NN.

On the CD-ROM　Example on the CD-ROM

Related Items: array.join() method.

string.substr(*start* [, *length*])

Returns: String.

	NN2	NN3	NN4	NN6	IE3/J1	IE3/J2	IE4	IE5	IE5.5
Compatibility			✓	✓			✓	✓	✓

The *string*.substr() method offers a variation of the *string*.substring() method that has been in the language since the beginning. The distinction is that the *string*.substr() method's parameters specify the starting index and a number of characters to be included from that start point. In contrast, the *string*.substring() method parameters specify index points for the start and end characters within the main string.

As with all string methods requiring an index value, the *string*.substr() first parameter is zero-based. If you do not specify a second parameter, the returned substring starts at the indexed point and extends to the end of the string. A second parameter value that exceeds the end point of the string means that the method returns a substring to the end of the string.

Even though this method is newer than its partner, it is not part of the ECMA standard as of Edition 3 of the language spec. But because the method is so widely used, the standard does acknowledge it so that other scripting contexts can implement the method consistent with browser practice.

Caution

NN4/Mac users should avoid setting the second parameter to a negative number to prevent a crash.

On the CD-ROM

Example (with Listing 34-6) on the CD-ROM

Related Items: `string.substring()` method.

string.substring(*indexA, indexB*)

Returns: String of characters between index values *indexA* and *indexB*.

	NN2	NN3	NN4	NN6	IE3/J1	IE3/J2	IE4	IE5	IE5.5
Compatibility	✓	✓	✓	✓	✓	✓	✓	✓	✓

The *string*.substring() method enables your scripts to extract a copy of a contiguous range of characters from any string. The parameters to this method are the starting and ending index values (first character of the string object is index value 0) of the main string from which the excerpt should be taken. An important item to note is that the excerpt goes up to, but does not include, the character pointed to by the higher index value.

It makes no difference which index value in the parameters is larger than the other: The method starts the excerpt from the lowest value and continues to (but does not include) the highest value. If both index values are the same, the method returns an empty string; and if you omit the second parameter, the end of the string is assumed to be the endpoint.

Note

NN4 experimented with a slight variation of this method. If you use this method in a `<SCRIPT LANGUAGE="JavaScript1.2">` tag, the first index value is always the start of the excerpt, and the end is at the second index value, even if it means that the string value comes out in reverse. This variation has not been carried forward in later versions of JavaScript in NN.

On the CD-ROM

Example (with Listing 34-7) on the CD-ROM

Related Items: `string.substr()`, `string.slice()` methods.

string.toLocaleLowerCase()
string.toLocaleUpperCase()

Returns: String.

	NN2	NN3	NN4	NN6	IE3/J1	IE3/J2	IE4	IE5	IE5.5
Compatibility				✓					✓

These two methods are variations on the standard methods for changing the case of a string. They take into account some language systems whose cases for a particular character don't necessarily map to the Latin alphabet character mappings.

Related Items: `string.toLowerCase()`, `string.toUpperCase()` methods.

string.toLowerCase()
string.toUpperCase()

Returns: The string in all lower- or uppercase, depending on which method you invoke.

	NN2	NN3	NN4	NN6	IE3/J1	IE3/J2	IE4	IE5	IE5.5
Compatibility	✓	✓	✓	✓	✓	✓	✓	✓	✓

A great deal of what takes place on the Internet (and in JavaScript) is case-sensitive. URLs on some servers, for instance, are case-sensitive for directory names and filenames. These two methods, the simplest of the string methods, return a copy of a string converted to either all lowercase or all uppercase. Any mixed-case strings get converted to a uniform case. If you want to compare user input from a field against some coded string without worrying about matching case, you can convert both strings to the same case for the comparison.

On the CD-ROM
Example on the CD-ROM

Related Items: `string.toLocaleLowerCase()`, `string.toLocaleUpperCase()` methods.

string.toString()
string.valueOf()

Returns: String value.

	NN2	NN3	NN4	NN6	IE3/J1	IE3/J2	IE4	IE5	IE5.5
Compatibility			✓	✓			✓	✓	✓

Both of these methods return string values (as opposed to full-fledged string objects). If you have created a string object via the new String() constructor, the type of that item is object. Therefore, if you want to examine more precisely what kind of value is held by the object, you can use the valueOf() method to get the value and then examine it via the typeof operator. The toString() method is present for this object primarily because a string object inherits the method from the root object of JavaScript.

On the CD-ROM　Example on the CD-ROM

Related Items: typeof operator (Chapter 40).

String Utility Functions

Figuring out how to apply the various string object methods to a string manipulation challenge is not always an easy task, especially if you need backward compatibility with older scriptable browsers. I also find it difficult to anticipate every possible way you may need to massage strings in your scripts. But to help you get started, Listing 34-8 contains a library of string functions for inserting, deleting, and replacing chunks of text in a string. If your audience uses browsers capable of including external .js library files, that would be an excellent way to make these functions available to your scripts.

Listing 34-8: **Utility String Handlers**

```
// extract front part of string prior to searchString
function getFront(mainStr,searchStr){
    foundOffset = mainStr.indexOf(searchStr)
    if (foundOffset == -1) {
        return null
```

```
    }
    return mainStr.substring(0,foundOffset)
}

// extract back end of string after searchString
function getEnd(mainStr,searchStr) {
    foundOffset = mainStr.indexOf(searchStr)
    if (foundOffset == -1) {
        return null
    }
    return mainStr.substring(foundOffset+searchStr.length,mainStr.length)
}

// insert insertString immediately before searchString
function insertString(mainStr,searchStr,insertStr) {
    var front = getFront(mainStr,searchStr)
    var end = getEnd(mainStr,searchStr)
    if (front != null && end != null) {
        return front + insertStr + searchStr + end
    }
    return null
}

// remove deleteString
function deleteString(mainStr,deleteStr) {
    return replaceString(mainStr,deleteStr,"")
}

// replace searchString with replaceString
function replaceString(mainStr,searchStr,replaceStr) {
    var front = getFront(mainStr,searchStr)
    var end = getEnd(mainStr,searchStr)
    if (front != null && end != null) {
        return front + replaceStr + end
    }
    return null
}
```

The first two functions extract the front or end components of strings as needed for some of the other functions in this suite. The final three functions are the core of these string-handling functions. If you plan to use these functions in your scripts, be sure to notice the dependence that some functions have on others. Including all five functions as a group ensures that they work as designed.

Formatting methods

Now we come to the other group of string object methods, which ease the process of creating the numerous string display characteristics when you use JavaScript to assemble HTML code. The following is a list of these methods:

```
string.anchor("anchorName")      string.link(locationOrURL)
string.blink()                   string.big()
string.bold()                    string.small()
string.fixed()                   string.strike()
string.fontcolor(colorValue)     string.sub()
string.fontsize(integer1to7)     string.sup()
string.italics()
```

First examine the methods that don't require any parameters. You probably see a pattern: All of these methods are font-style attributes that have settings of on or off. To turn on these attributes in an HTML document, you surround the text in the appropriate tag pairs, such as <B>...</B> for boldface text. These methods take the string object, attach those tags, and return the resulting text, which is ready to be put into any HTML that your scripts are building. Therefore, the expression

```
"Good morning!".bold()
```

evaluates to

```
<B>Good morning!</B>
```

Of course, nothing is preventing you from building your HTML by embedding real tags instead of by calling the string methods. The choice is up to you. One advantage to the string methods is that they never forget the ending tag of a tag pair. Listing 34-9 shows an example of incorporating a few simple string methods in a string variable that is eventually written to the page as it loads. Internet Explorer does not support the <BLINK> tag and therefore ignores the *string*.blink() method.

Listing 34-9: **Using Simple String Methods**

```
<HTML>
<HEAD>
<TITLE>HTML by JavaScript</TITLE>
</HEAD>
```

```
<BODY>
<SCRIPT LANGUAGE="JavaScript">
var page = ""
page += "JavaScript can create HTML on the fly.<P>Numerous string object methods
facilitate creating text that is " + "boldfaced".bold() + ", " +
"italicized".italics() + ", or even the terribly annoying " + "blinking
text".blink() + "."
document.write(page)
</SCRIPT>
</BODY>
</HTML>
```

Of the remaining string methods, two more ($string$.fontsize() and $string$.fontcolor()) also affect the font characteristics of strings displayed in the HTML page. The parameters for these items are pretty straightforward — an integer between 1 and 7 corresponding to the seven browser font sizes and a color value (as either a hexadecimal triplet or color constant name) for the designated text. Listing 34-10 adds a line of text to the string of Listing 34-9. This line of text not only adjusts the font size of some parts of the string but also nests multiple attributes inside one another to set the color of one word in a large-font-size string. Because these string methods do not change the content of the string, you can safely nest methods here.

Listing 34-10: **Nested String Methods**

```
<HTML>
<HEAD>
<TITLE>HTML by JavaScript</TITLE>
</HEAD>

<BODY>
<SCRIPT LANGUAGE="JavaScript">
var page = ""
page += "JavaScript can create HTML on the fly.<P>Numerous string object methods
facilitate creating text that is " + "boldfaced".bold() + ", " +
"italicized".italics() + ", or even the terribly annoying " + "blinking
text".blink() + ".<P>"
page += "We can make " + "some words big".fontsize(5) + " and some words both "
+ ("big and " + "colorful".fontcolor('coral')).fontsize(5) + " at the same
time."
document.write(page)
</SCRIPT>
</BODY>
</HTML>
```

The final two string methods let you create an anchor and a link out of a string. The *string*.anchor() method uses its parameter to create a name for the anchor. Thus, the following expression

```
"Table of Contents".anchor("toc")
```

evaluates to

```
<A NAME="toc">Table of Contents</A>
```

In a similar fashion, the *string*.link() method expects a valid location or URL as its parameter, creating a genuine HTML link out of the string:

```
"Back to Home".link("index.html")
```

This evaluates to the following:

```
<A HREF="index.html">Back to Home</A>
```

Again, the choice of whether you use string methods to build HTML anchors and links over assembling the actual HTML is up to you. The methods may be a bit easier to work with if the values for the string and the parameters are variables whose content may change based on user input elsewhere in your Web site.

URL String Encoding and Decoding

When browsers and servers communicate, some non-alphanumeric characters that we take for granted (such as a space) cannot make the journey in their native form. Only a narrower set of letters, numbers, and punctuation is allowed. To accommodate the rest, the characters must be encoded with a special symbol (%) and their hexadecimal ASCII values. For example, the space character is hex 20 (ASCII decimal 32). When encoded, it looks like %20. You may have seen this symbol in browser history lists or URLs.

JavaScript includes two functions, escape() and unescape(), that offer instant conversion of whole strings. To convert a plain string to one with these escape codes, use the escape function, as in

```
escape("Howdy Pardner") // result = "Howdy%20Pardner"
```

The unescape() function converts the escape codes into human-readable form. Both of these functions and some newer, more robust versions for recent browsers are covered in Chapter 42.

✦   ✦   ✦

The Math, Number, and Boolean Objects

The introduction to data types and values in Chapter 6's tutorial scratched the surface of JavaScript's numeric and Boolean powers. In this chapter, you look more closely at JavaScript's way of working with numbers and Boolean data.

Math often frightens away budding programmers; but as you've seen so far in this book, you don't really have to be a math genius to program in JavaScript. The powers described in this chapter are here when you need them — if you need them. So if math is not your strong suit, don't freak out over the terminology here.

An important point to remember about the objects described in this chapter is that (like string values and string objects) numbers and Booleans are both values and objects. Fortunately for script writers, the differentiation is rarely, if ever, a factor unless you get into some very sophisticated programming. To those who actually write the JavaScript interpreters inside the browsers we use, the distinctions are vital.

For most scripters, the information about numeric data types and conversions as well as the Math object are important to know. I present other details in this chapter about the number and Boolean objects primarily for completeness because their direct powers are almost never used in day-to-day scripting of Web applications.

Numbers in JavaScript

More powerful programming languages have many different kinds of numbers, each related to the amount of memory it occupies in the computer. Managing all these different types may be fun for some, but it gets in the way of quick scripting. A JavaScript number has only two possibilities. It can be an integer or a floating-point value. An *integer* is any whole number within a humongous range that does not have any fractional part. Integers never contain a decimal point in their representation. *Floating-point numbers* in JavaScript spread across the same range, but they are represented with a decimal point and some fractional value. If you are an experienced programmer, refer to the discussion about the Number object later in this chapter to see how the JavaScript number type lines up with numeric data types you use in other programming environments.

Integers and floating-point numbers

Deep inside a computer, the microprocessor has an easier time performing math on integer values as compared to any number with a decimal value tacked on it, which requires the microprocessor to go through extra work to add even two such floating-point numbers. We, as scripters, are unfortunately saddled with this historical baggage and must be conscious of the type of number used in certain calculations.

Most internal values generated by JavaScript, such as index values and length properties, consist of integers. Floating-point numbers usually come into play as the result of the division of numeric values, special values such as pi, and human-entered values such as dollars and cents. Fortunately, JavaScript is forgiving if you try to perform math operations on mixed numeric data types. Notice how the following examples resolve to the appropriate data type:

```
3 + 4 = 7 // integer result
3 + 4.1 = 7.1 // floating-point result
3.9 + 4.1 = 8 // integer result
```

Of the three examples, perhaps only the last result is unexpected. When two floating-point numbers yield a whole number, the result is rendered as an integer.

When dealing with floating-point numbers, be aware that not all browser versions return the precise same value down to the last digit to the right of the decimal. For example, the following table shows the result of 8/9 as calculated by numerous scriptable browsers (all Windows 95) and converted for string display:

Navigator 2	0.88888888888888884
Navigator 3	.8888888888888888
Navigator 4	.8888888888888888

Navigator 6	0.8888888888888888
Internet Explorer 3	0.888888888888889
Internet Explorer 4+	0.8888888888888888

Clearly, from this display, you don't want to use floating-point math in JavaScript browsers to plan space flight trajectories. For everyday math, however, you need to be cognizant of floating-point errors that accrue in PC arithmetic.

In Navigator, JavaScript relies on the operating system's floating-point math for its own math. Operating systems that offer accuracy to as many places to the right of the decimal as JavaScript displays are exceedingly rare. As you can detect from the preceding table, the modern versions of browsers from Netscape and Microsoft agree about how many digits to display and how to perform internal rounding for this display. That's good for the math, but not particularly helpful when you need to display numbers in a specific format.

Until you get to IE5.5 and NN6, JavaScript does not offer built-in facilities for formatting the results of floating-point arithmetic. (For the newer browsers, see the Number object later in this chapter for formatting methods.) Listing 35-1 demonstrates a generic formatting routine for positive values, plus a specific call that turns a value into a dollar value. Remove the comments and the routine is fairly compact.

Listing 35-1: **A Generic Number-Formatting Routine**

```
<HTML>
<HEAD>
<TITLE>Number Formatting</TITLE>
<SCRIPT LANGUAGE="JavaScript">
// generic positive number decimal formatting function
function format (expr, decplaces) {
    // raise incoming value by power of 10 times the
    // number of decimal places; round to an integer; convert to string
    var str = "" + Math.round (eval(expr) * Math.pow(10,decplaces))
    // pad small value strings with zeros to the left of rounded number
    while (str.length <= decplaces) {
        str = "0" + str
    }
    // establish location of decimal point
    var decpoint = str.length - decplaces
    // assemble final result from: (a) the string up to the position of
    // the decimal point; (b) the decimal point; and (c) the balance
    // of the string. Return finished product.
    return str.substring(0,decpoint) + "." + str.substring(decpoint,str.length);
}
```

Continued

Listing 35-1 *(continued)*

```
// turn incoming expression into a dollar value
function dollarize (expr) {
    return "$" + format(expr,2)
}
</SCRIPT>
</HEAD>
<BODY>
<H1>How to Make Money</H1>
<FORM>
Enter a positive floating-point value or arithmetic expression to be converted
to a currency format:<P>
<INPUT TYPE="text" NAME="entry" VALUE="1/3">
<INPUT TYPE="button" VALUE=">Dollars and Cents>"
onClick="this.form.result.value=dollarize(this.form.entry.value)">
<INPUT TYPE="text" NAME="result">
</FORM>
</BODY>
</HTML>
```

This routine may seem like a great deal of work, but it's essential if your application relies on floating-point values and specific formatting for all browsers.

You can also enter floating-point numbers with exponents. An exponent is signified by the letter "e" (upper- or lowercase), followed by a sign (+ or -) and the exponent value. Here are examples of floating-point values expressed as exponents:

```
1e6 // 1,000,000 (the "+" symbol is optional on positive exponents)
1e-4 // 0.0001 (plus some error further to the right of the decimal)
-4e-3 // -0.004
```

For values between 1e-5 and 1e15, JavaScript renders numbers without exponents (although you can force a number to display in exponential notation in IE5.5 and NN6). All other values outside these boundaries return with exponential notation in all browsers.

Hexadecimal and octal integers

JavaScript enables you to work with values in decimal (base-10), hexadecimal (base-16), and octal (base-8) formats. You have only a few rules to follow when dealing with any of these values.

Decimal values cannot begin with a leading 0. Therefore, if your page asks users to enter decimal values that begin with a 0, your script must strip those zeroes from the input string or use the number parsing global functions (described in the next section) before performing any math on the values.

Hexadecimal integer values are expressed with a leading 0x or 0X. (That's a zero, not the letter "o.") The A through F values can appear in upper- or lowercase, as you prefer. Here are some hex values:

```
0X2B
0X1a
0xcc
```

Don't confuse the hex values used in arithmetic with the hexadecimal values used in color property specifications for Web documents. Those values are expressed in a special *hexadecimal triplet* format, which begins with a crosshatch symbol followed by the three hex values bunched together (such as #c0c0c0).

Octal values are represented by a leading 0 followed by any digits between 0 and 7. Octal values consist only of integers.

You are free to mix and match base values in arithmetic expressions, but JavaScript renders all results in decimal form. For conversions to other number bases, you have to employ a user-defined function in your script. Listing 35-2, for example, is a function that converts any decimal value from 0 to 255 into a JavaScript hexadecimal value.

Listing 35-2: **Decimal-to-Hexadecimal Converter Function**

```
function toHex(dec) {
    hexChars = "0123456789ABCDEF"
    if (dec > 255) {
        return null
    }
    var i = dec % 16
    var j = (dec - i) / 16
    result = "0X"
    result += hexChars.charAt(j)
    result += hexChars.charAt(i)
    return result
}
```

The toHex() conversion function assumes that the value passed to the function is a decimal integer. If you simply need a hexadecimal representation of a number in string format, see the toString() method in Chapter 42.

Converting strings to numbers

What is missing so far from this discussion is a way to convert a number represented as a string to a number with which the JavaScript arithmetic operators can work. Before you get too concerned about this, be aware that most JavaScript operators and math methods gladly accept string representations of numbers and handle them without complaint. You will run into data type incompatibilities most frequently when trying to accomplish addition with the + operator (which is also the string concatenation operator). Also know that if you perform math operations on values retrieved from form text boxes, those object value properties are strings. Therefore, in many cases, you need to convert those values to values of the number type for math operations.

Conversion to numbers requires one of two JavaScript functions:

```
parseInt(string [,radix])
parseFloat(string  [,radix])
```

These functions, inspired by the Java language. The term *parsing* has many implied meanings in programming. One meaning is the same as *extracting*. The parseInt() function returns whatever integer value it can extract from the string passed to it; the parseFloat() function returns the floating-point number that can be extracted from the string. Here are some examples and their resulting values:

```
parseInt("42")          // result = 42
parseInt("42.33")       // result = 42
parseFloat("42.33")     // result = 42.33
parseFloat("42")        // result = 42
parseFloat("fred")      // result = NaN
```

Because the parseFloat() function can also work with an integer and return an integer value, you may prefer using this function in scripts that have to deal with either kind of number, depending on the string entered into a text field by a user.

An optional second parameter to both functions enables you to specify the base of the number represented by the string. This comes in handy particularly when you need a decimal number from a string that starts with one or more zeros. Normally, the leading zero indicates an octal value. But if you force the conversion to recognize the string value as a decimal, it is converted the way you expect:

```
parseInt("010")         // result = 8
parseInt("010",10)      // result = 10
parseInt("F2")          // result = NaN
parseInt("F2", 16)      // result = 242
```

Use these functions wherever you need the integer or floating-point value. For example:

```
var result = 3 + parseInt("3")    // result = 6
var ageVal = parseInt(document.forms[0].age.value)
```

The latter technique ensures that the string value of this property is converted to a number (although you should do more data validation—see Chapter 43—before trying any math on a user-entered value).

Both the `parseInt()` and `parseFloat()` methods start working on the first character of a string and continue until there are no more numbers or decimal characters. That's why you can use them on strings—such as the one returned by the `navigator.appVersion` property (for example, `4.0 (compatible; MSIE 5.5; Windows95)`)—to obtain just the leading, numeric part of the string. If the string does not begin with an acceptable character, the methods return `NaN` (not a number).

Converting numbers to strings

If you attempt to pass a numeric data type value to many of the string methods discussed in Chapter 34, JavaScript complains. Therefore, you should convert any number to a string before you, for example, find out how many digits make up a number.

There are several ways to force conversion from any numeric value to a string. The old-fashioned way is to precede the number with an empty string and the concatenation operator. For example, assume that a variable named `dollars` contains the integer value of `2500`. To use the string object's `length` property (discussed later in this chapter) to find out how many digits the number has, use this construction:

```
("" + dollars).length    // result = 4
```

The parentheses force JavaScript to evaluate the concatenation before attempting to extract the `length` property.

A more elegant way is to use the `toString()` method. Construct such statements as you do to invoke any object's method. For example, to convert the `dollars` variable value to a string, use this statement:

```
dollars.toString()    // result = "2500"
```

This method has one added power in NN3+ and IE4+: You can specify a number base for the string representation of the number. Called the *radix,* the base number is added as a parameter to the method name. Here is an example of creating a numeric value for conversion to its hexadecimal equivalent as a string:

```
var x = 30
var y = x.toString(16)    // result = "1e"
```

Use a parameter of 2 for binary results and 8 for octal. The default is base 10. Be careful not to confuse these conversions with true numeric conversions. You cannot use results from the `toString()` method as numeric operands in other statements.

Finally, in IE5.5 and NN6, three additional methods of the `Number` object—`toExponential()`, `toFixed()`, and `toPrecision()`—return string versions of numbers formatted according to the rules and parameters passed to the methods. I describe these in detail later in this chapter.

When a number isn't a number

In a couple of examples in the previous section, you probably noticed that the result of some operations was a value named `NaN`. That value is not a string but rather a special value that stands for Not a Number. For example, if you try to convert the string `"joe"` to an integer with `parseFloat()`, the function cannot possibly complete the operation. It reports back that the source string, when converted, is not a number.

When you design an application that requests user input or retrieves data from a server-side database, you cannot be guaranteed that a value you need to be numeric is, or can be converted to, a number. If that's the case, you need to see if the value is a number before performing some math operation on it. JavaScript provides a special global function, `isNaN()`, that enables you to test the "numberness" of a value. The function returns `true` if the value is not a number and `false` if it is a number. For example, you can examine a form field that should be a number:

```
var ageEntry = parseInt(document.forms[0].age.value)
if (isNaN(ageEntry)) {
    alert("Try entering your age again.")
}
```

Note   `NaN` and `isNaN()` are implemented in Navigator 2 only on UNIX versions. You can find these terms on all OS platforms of NN3+ and IE4+.

Math Object

Whenever you need to perform math that is more demanding than simple arithmetic, look through the list of `Math` object methods for the solution.

Syntax

Accessing `Math` object properties and methods:

```
Math.property
Math.method(value [, value])
```

About this object

In addition to the typical arithmetic operations (covered in detail in Chapter 40), JavaScript includes more advanced mathematical powers that you can access in a way that may seem odd to you if you have not programmed in true object-oriented environments before. Although most arithmetic takes place on the fly (such as var result = 2 + 2), the rest requires use of the JavaScript internal Math object (with a capital "M"). The Math object brings with it several properties (which behave like some other languages' constants) and many methods (which behave like some other languages' math functions).

The way you use the Math object in statements is the same way you use any JavaScript object: You create a reference beginning with the Math object's name, a period, and the name of the property or method you need:

```
Math.property | method([parameter]. . . [,parameter])
```

Property references return the built-in values (things such as pi). Method references require one or more values to be sent as parameters of the method. Every method returns a result.

Properties

JavaScript Math object properties represent a number of valuable constant values in math. Table 35-1 shows you those methods and their values as displayed to 16 decimal places.

Table 35-1 JavaScript Math Properties

Property	Value	Description
Math.E	2.718281828459045091	Euler's constant
Math.LN2	0.6931471805599452862	Natural log of 2
Math.LN10	2.302585092994045901	Natural log of 10
Math.LOG2E	1.442695040888963387	Log base-2 of E
Math.LOG10E	0.4342944819032518167	Log base-10 of E
Math.PI	3.141592653589793116	π
Math.SQRT1_2	0.7071067811865475727	Square root of 0.5
Math.SQRT2	1.414213562373095145	Square root of 2

Because these property expressions return their constant values, you use them in your regular arithmetic expressions. For example, to obtain the circumference of a circle whose diameter is in variable d, employ this statement:

```
circumference = d * Math.PI
```

Perhaps the most common mistakes scripters make with these properties are failing to capitalize the Math object name and observing the case-sensitivity of property names.

Methods

Methods make up the balance of JavaScript Math object powers. With the exception of the Math.random() method, all Math object methods take one or more values as parameters. Typical trigonometric methods operate on the single values passed as parameters; others determine which of the numbers passed along are the highest or lowest of the group. The Math.random() method takes no parameters but returns a randomized, floating-point value between 0 and 1 (note that the method does not work on Windows or Macintosh versions of Navigator 2). Table 35-2 lists all the Math object methods with their syntax and descriptions of the values they return.

Table 35-2	**Math Object Methods**
Method Syntax	**Returns**
Math.abs(*val*)	Absolute value of *val*
Math.acos(*val*)	Arc cosine (in radians) of *val*
Math.asin(*val*)	Arc sine (in radians) of *val*
Math.atan(*val*)	Arc tangent (in radians) of *val*
Math.atan2(*val1, val2*)	Angle of polar coordinates *x* and *y*
Math.ceil(*val*)	Next integer greater than or equal to *val*
Math.cos(*val*)	Cosine of *val*
Math.exp(*val*)	Euler's constant to the power of *val*
Math.floor(*val*)	Next integer less than or equal to *val*
Math.log(*val*)	Natural logarithm (base e) of *val*
Math.max(*val1, val2*)	The greater of *val1* or *val2*
Math.min(*val1, val2*)	The lesser of *val1* or *val2*

Method Syntax	Returns
Math.pow(*val1*, *val2*)	*Val1* to the *val2* power
Math.random()	Random number between 0 and 1
Math.round(*val*)	N+1 when *val* >= N.5; otherwise N
Math.sin(*val*)	Sine (in radians) of *val*
Math.sqrt(*val*)	Square root of *val*
Math.tan(*val*)	Tangent (in radians) of *val*

HTML is not exactly a graphic artist's dream environment, so using trig functions to obtain a series of values for HTML-generated charting is not a hot JavaScript prospect. Only with the advent of positionable elements have scripters been able to apply their knowledge of using these functions to define fancy trajectories for flying elements. For scripters who are not trained in programming, math is often a major stumbling block. But as you've seen so far, you can accomplish a great deal with JavaScript by using simple arithmetic and a little bit of logic — leaving the heavy-duty math for those who love it.

Creating random numbers

The Math.random() method returns a floating-point value between 0 and 1. If you design a script to act like a card game, you need random integers between 1 and 52; for dice, the range is 1 to 6 per die. To generate a random integer between zero and any top value, use the following formula:

```
Math.floor(Math.random() * n)
```

Here, *n* is the top number. To generate random numbers between a different range, use this formula:

```
Math.floor(Math.random() * n) + m
```

Here, *m* is the lowest possible integer value of the range and *n* equals the top number of the range. For the dice game, the formula for each die is

```
newDieValue = Math.floor(Math.random() * 6) + 1
```

Math object shortcut

In Chapter 39, you see details about a JavaScript construction that enables you to simplify the way you address multiple Math object properties and methods in statements. The trick is to use the with statement.

In a nutshell, the `with` statement tells JavaScript that the next group of statements (inside the braces) refers to a particular object. In the case of the `Math` object, the basic construction looks like this:

```
with (Math) {
    //statements
}
```

For all intervening statements, you can omit the specific references to the `Math` object. Compare the long reference way of calculating the area of a circle (with a radius of six units)

```
result = Math.pow(6,2) * Math.PI
```

to the shortcut reference way:

```
with (Math) {
    result = pow(6,2) * PI
}
```

Though the latter occupies more lines of code, the object references are shorter and more natural when reading the code. For a longer series of calculations involving `Math` object properties and methods, the `with` construction saves keystrokes and reduces the likelihood of a case-sensitive mistake with the object name in a reference. You can also include other full-object references within the `with` construction; JavaScript attempts to attach the object name only to those references lacking an object name. On the downside, the `with` construction is not particularly efficient in JavaScript because it must perform a lot of internal tracking in order to work.

Number Object

Properties	Methods
constructor	toExponential()
MAX_VALUE	toFixed()
MIN_VALUE	toLocaleString()
NaN	toString()
NEGATIVE_INFINITY	toPrecision()
POSITIVE_INFINITY	valueOf()
prototype	

Syntax

Creating a number object:

```
var val = new Number(number)
```

Accessing number and Number object properties and methods:

```
number.property | method([parameters])
Number.property | method([parameters])
```

	NN2	NN3	NN4	NN6	IE3/J1	IE3/J2	IE4	IE5	IE5.5
Compatibility		✓	✓	✓		✓	✓	✓	✓

About this object

The Number object is rarely used because (for the most part) JavaScript satisfies day-to-day numeric needs with a plain number value. But the Number object contains some information and power of value to serious programmers.

First on the docket are properties that define the ranges for numbers in the language. The largest number (in both Navigator and Internet Explorer) is 1.79E+308; the smallest number is 2.22E-308. Any number larger than the maximum is POSITIVE_INFINITY; any number smaller than the minimum is NEGATIVE_INFINITY. Rarely will you accidentally encounter these values.

More to the point of a JavaScript object, however, is the prototype property. In Chapter 34, you see how to add a method to a string object's prototype such that every newly created object contains that method. The same goes for the Number.prototype property. If you have a need to add common functionality to every number object, this is where to do it. This prototype facility is unique to full-fledged number objects and does not apply to plain number values. For experienced programmers who care about such matters, JavaScript number objects and values are defined internally as IEEE double-precision 64-bit values.

Properties

constructor

See string.constructor (Chapter 34).

```
MAX_VALUE
MIN_VALUE
NEGATIVE_INFINITY
POSITIVE_INFINITY
```

Value: Number   Read-Only

	NN2	NN3	NN4	NN6	IE3/J1	IE3/J2	IE4	IE5	IE5.5
Compatibility		✓	✓	✓		✓	✓	✓	✓

The `Number.MAX_VALUE` and `Number.MIN_VALUE` properties belong to the static `Number` object. They represent constants for the largest and smallest possible positive numbers that JavaScript (and ECMAScript) can work with. Their actual values are $1.7976931348623157 * 10^{308}$, and $5 * 10^{-324}$, respectively.

A number that falls outside the range of allowable numbers is equal to the constant `Number.POSITIVE_INFINITY` or `Number.NEGATIVE_INFINITY`.

On the CD-ROM   Example on the CD-ROM

Related Items: `NaN` property; `isNaN()` global function.

```
NaN
```

Value: NaN   Read-Only

	NN2	NN3	NN4	NN6	IE3/J1	IE3/J2	IE4	IE5	IE5.5
Compatibility		✓	✓	✓		✓	✓	✓	✓

The `NaN` property is a constant that JavaScript uses to report when a number-related function or method attempts to work on a value other than a number or the result is something other than a number. You encounter the `NaN` value most commonly as the result of the `parseInt()` and `parseFloat()` functions whenever a string undergoing conversion to a number lacks a numeral as the first character. Use the `isNaN()` global function to see if a value is an `NaN` value.

Example

See the discussion of the isNaN() function in Chapter 42.

Related Item: isNaN() global function.

prototype

See String.prototype (Chapter 34).

Methods

number.toExponential(*fractionDigits*)
number.toFixed(*fractionDigits*)
number.toPrecision(*precisionDigits*)

Returns: String.

	NN2	NN3	NN4	NN6	IE3/J1	IE3/J2	IE4	IE5	IE5.5
Compatibility				✓					✓

A recent addition to the ECMA language — and thus to the JavaScript-enabled browsers — are three Number object methods that let scripts control the formatting of numbers for display as string text. Each method has a unique purpose, but they all return strings. You should perform all math operations as unformatted number objects because the values have the most precision. Only after you are ready to display the results should you use one of these methods to convert the number to a string for display as body text or assignment to a text field.

The toExponential() method forces a number to display in exponential notation, even if the number is in the range in which JavaScript normally uses standard notation. The parameter is an integer specifying how many digits to the right of the decimal should be returned. All digits to the right of the decimal are returned, even if they are zero. For example, if a variable contains the numeric value 345, applying toExponential(3) to that value yields 3.450e+2, which is JavaScript's exponential notation for 3.45×10^2.

Use the toFixed() method when you want to format a number with a specific number of digits to the right of the decimal. This is the method you use, for instance, to display the results of a financial calculation in units and hundredths of units (for example, dollars and cents). The parameter to the method is an integer indicating the number of digits to be displayed to the right of the decimal. If the number being formatted has more numbers to the right of the decimal than the number of digits specified by the parameter, the method rounds the rightmost visible digit — but only with respect to the unrounded value of the next digit. For example, the value 123.455 fixed to two digits to the right of the decimal is rounded up to 123.46. But if the starting value is 123.4549, the method ignores the 9 and sees that the 4 to the right of the 5 should be rounded down; therefore, the result is 123.45. Do not consider the toFixed() method to be an accurate rounder of numbers; however, it does a satisfactory job in most cases.

The final method is toPrecision(), which enables you to define how many total digits (including digits to the left and right of the decimal) to display of a number. In other words, you define the precision of a number. The following list demonstrates the results of several parameter values signifying a variety of precisions:

```
var num = 123.45
num.toPrecision(1)    // result = 1e+2
num.toPrecision(2)    // result = 1.2e+2
num.toPrecision(3)    // result = 123
num.toPrecision(4)    // result = 123.5
num.toPrecision(5)    // result = 123.45
num.toPrecision(6)    // result = 123.450
```

Notice that the same kind of rounding can occur with toPrecision() as it does for toFixed().

On the CD-ROM   Example on the CD-ROM

Related Item: Math object.

number.toLocaleString()

Returns: String.

	NN2	NN3	NN4	NN6	IE3/J1	IE3/J2	IE4	IE5	IE5.5
Compatibility				✓					✓

According to the ECMA Edition 3 standard, browsers have some leeway in determining exactly how the toLocaleString() method should return a string value that conforms with the language standard of the client system or browser. IE5.5 appears to return the same value as the toFixed(2) method.

Related Items: number.toFixed(), number.toString() methods.

number.toString([*radix*])

Returns: String.

	NN2	NN3	NN4	NN6	IE3/J1	IE3/J2	IE4	IE5	IE5.5
Compatibility	✓	✓	✓			✓	✓	✓	✓

The number.toString() method returns a string value version of the current number. The default radix parameter (10) converts the value to base-10 notation if the original number isn't already of that type. Or you can specify other number bases (for example, 2 for binary, 16 for hexadecimal) to convert the original number to the other base—as a string, not a number, for further calculation.

Example on the CD-ROM

Related Item: toLocaleString() method.

number.valueOf()

See string.valueOf( ) (Chapter 34).

Boolean Object

Properties	Methods
constructor	toString()
prototype	valueOf()

Syntax

Creating a Boolean object:

```
var val = new Boolean(BooleanValue)
```

Accessing `Boolean` object properties:

BooleanObject.property | method

	NN2	NN3	NN4	NN6	IE3/J1	IE3/J2	IE4	IE5	IE5.5
Compatibility		✓	✓	✓		✓	✓	✓	✓

About this object

You work with Boolean values a lot in JavaScript—especially as the result of conditional tests. Just as string values benefit from association with string objects and their properties and methods, so, too, do Boolean values receive aid from the `Boolean` object. For example, when you display a Boolean value in a text box, the `"true"` or `"false"` string is provided by the `Boolean` object's `toString()` method so you don't have to invoke it directly.

The only time you need to even think about a `Boolean` object is if you wish to attach some property or method to `Boolean` objects that you create with the new `Boolean()` constructor. Parameter values for the constructor include the string versions of the values, numbers (0 for `false`; any other integer for `true`), and expressions that evaluate to a Boolean value. Any such new `Boolean` object is imbued with the new properties or methods you add to the `prototype` property of the core `Boolean` object.

For details about the properties and methods of the `Boolean` object, see the corresponding listings for the `String` object in Chapter 34.

✦   ✦   ✦

The Date Object

Perhaps the most untapped power of JavaScript is its
date and time handling. Scripters passed over the Date
object with good cause in the early days of JavaScript,
because in earlier versions of scriptable browsers, significant
bugs and platform-specific anomalies made date and time programming hazardous without significant testing. Even with the
improved bug situation, working with dates requires a working knowledge of the world's time zones and their relationships with the standard reference point, known as Greenwich
Mean Time (GMT) or Coordinated Universal Time (abbreviated UTC).

Now that date- and time-handling has improved in the latest
browsers, I hope more scripters look into incorporating these
kinds of calculations into their pages. In Chapter 54, for example, I show you an application that lets your Web site highlight
the areas that have been updated since each visitor's last surf
ride through your pages — an application that relies heavily
on date arithmetic and time zone conversion.

Before getting to the JavaScript part of date discussions, however, the chapter summarizes key facts about time zones and
their impact on scripting date and time on a browser. If you're
not sure what GMT and UTC mean, the following section is
for you.

Time Zones and GMT

By international agreement, the world is divided into distinct
time zones that allow the inhabitants of each zone to say with
confidence that when the Sun appears directly overhead, it is
roughly noon, squarely in the middle of the day. The current
time in the zone is what we set our clocks to — the local time.

That's fine when your entire existence and scope of life go no
further than the width of your own time zone. But with instant
communication among all parts of the world, your scope

reaches well beyond local time. Periodically you must be aware of the local time in other zones. After all, if you live in New York, you don't want to wake up someone in Los Angeles before dawn with a phone call from your office.

> **Note**   For the rest of this section, I speak of the Sun "moving" as if Earth were the center of the solar system. I do so for the convenience of our daily perception of the Sun arcing across what appears to us as a stationary sky. In point of fact, I believe Copernicus's theories, so delete that e-mail you were about to send me.

From the point of view of the time zone over which the Sun is positioned at any given instant, all time zones to the east have already had their noon, so it is later in the day for them—one hour later per time zone (except for those few time zones offset by fractions of an hour). That's why when U.S. television networks broadcast simultaneously to the eastern and central time zones, the announced schedule for a program is "10 eastern, 9 central."

Many international businesses must coordinate time schedules of far-flung events. Doing so and taking into account the numerous time zone differences (not to mention seasonal national variations, such as daylight saving time) would be a nightmare. To help everyone out, a standard reference point was devised: the time zone running through the celestial observatory at Greenwich (pronounced GREN-itch), England. This time zone is called Greenwich Mean Time, or GMT for short. The "mean" part comes from the fact that on the exact opposite side of the globe (through the Pacific Ocean) is the international date line, another world standard that decrees where the first instance of the next calendar day appears on the planet. Thus, GMT is located at the middle, or mean, of the full circuit of the day. Not that many years ago, GMT was given another abbreviation that is not based on any one language of the planet. The abbreviation is UTC (pronounced as its letters: yu-tee-see), and the English version is Coordinated Universal Time. Whenever you see UTC, it is for all practical purposes the same as GMT.

If your personal computer's system clock is set correctly, the machine ticks away in GMT time. But because you set your local time zone in the appropriate control panel, all file time stamps and clock displays are in your local time. The machine knows what the offset time is between your local time and GMT. For daylight saving time, you may have to check a preference setting so that the offset is adjusted accordingly; in Windows 95 and later, the operating system knows when the changeover occurs and prompts you if changing the offset is okay. In any case, if you travel across time zones with a laptop, you should change the computer's time zone setting, not its clock.

JavaScript's inner handling of date and time works a lot like the PC clock (on which your programs rely). Date values that you generate in a script are stored internally in GMT time; however, almost all the displays and extracted values are in the local time of the visitor (not the Web site server). And remember that the date values are created on the visitor's machine by virtue of your script's generating that value— you don't send "living" date objects to the client from the server. This concept is perhaps the most difficult to grasp as you work with JavaScript date and time.

Whenever you program time and date in JavaScript for a public Web page, you must take the worldview. This view requires knowing that the visitor's computer settings determine the accuracy of the conversion between GMT and local time. You'll also have to do some testing by changing your PC's clock to times in other parts of the world and making believe you are temporarily in those remote locations, which isn't always easy to do. It reminds me of the time I was visiting Sydney, Australia. I was turning in for the night and switched on the television in the hotel. This hotel received a live satellite relay of a long-running U.S. television program, *Today*. The program broadcast from New York was for the morning of the same day I was just finishing in Sydney. Yes, this time zone stuff can make your head hurt.

The Date Object

Like a handful of other objects in JavaScript and the document object models, there is a distinction between the single, static Date object that exists in every window (or frame) and a date object that contains a specific date and time. The static Date object (uppercase "D") is used in only a few cases: Primarily to create a new instance of a date and to invoke a couple of methods that the Date object offers for the sake of some generic conversions.

Most of your date and time work, however, is with instances of the Date object. These instances are referred to generically as date objects (lowercase "d"). Each date object is a snapshot of an exact millisecond in time, whether it be for the instant at which you generate the object or for a specific time in the past or future you need for calculations. If you need to have a live clock ticking away, your scripts will repeatedly create new date objects to grab up-to-the-millisecond snapshots of your computer's clock. To show the time on the page, extract the hours, minutes, and seconds from the snapshot date object, and then display the values as you like (for example, a digital readout, a graphical bar chart, and so on). By and large, it is the methods of a date object instance that your scripts invoke to read or modify individual components of a date object (for example, the month or hour).

Despite its name, every date object contains information about date and time. Therefore, even if you're concerned only about the date part of an object's data, time data is standing by as well. As you learn in a bit, the time element can catch you off-guard for some operations.

Creating a date object

The statement that asks JavaScript to make an object for your script uses the special object construction keyword new. The basic syntax for generating a new date object is as follows:

```
var dateObjectName = new Date([parameters])
```

The date object evaluates to an object data type rather than to some string or numeric value.

With the date object's reference safely tucked away in the variable name, you access all date-oriented methods in the dot-syntax fashion with which you're already familiar:

```
var result = dateObjectName.method()
```

With variables, such as result, your scripts perform calculations or displays of the date object's data (some methods extract pieces of the date and time data from the object). If you then want to put some new value into the date object (such as adding a year to the date object), you assign the new value to the object by way of the method that lets you set the value:

```
dateObjectName.method(newValue)
```

This example doesn't look like the typical JavaScript assignment statement, which has an equals sign operator. But this statement is the way in which methods that set date object data work.

You cannot get very far into scripting dates without digging into time zone arithmetic. Although JavaScript may render the string equivalent of a date object in your local time zone, the internal storage is strictly GMT.

Even though you haven't yet seen details of a date object's methods, here is how you use two of them to add one year to today's date.

```
var oneDate = new Date()          // creates object with current GMT date
var theYear = oneDate.getYear()   // theYear is now storing the value 98
theYear = theYear + 1             // theYear now is 99
oneDate.setYear(theYear)          // new year value now in the object
```

At the end of this sequence, the oneDate object automatically adjusts all the other date components for the next year's date. The day of the week, for example, will be different, and JavaScript takes care of that for you, should you need to extract that data. With next year's data in the oneDate object, you may now want to extract that new date as a string value for display in a field on the page or submit it quietly to a CGI program on the server.

The issue of parameters for creating a new date object is a bit complex, mostly because of the flexibility that JavaScript offers the scripter. Recall that the job of the new Date() statement is to create a place in memory for all data that a date needs to store. What is missing from that task is the data — what date and time to enter into that memory spot. That's where the parameters come in.

If you leave the parameters empty, JavaScript takes that to mean you want today's date and the current time to be assigned to that new date object. JavaScript isn't any smarter, of course, than the setting of the internal clock of your page visitor's personal computer. If the clock isn't correct, JavaScript won't do any better of a job identifying the date and time.

Note Remember that when you create a new date object, it contains the current time as well. The fact that the current date may include a time of 16:03:19 (in 24-hour time) may throw off things, such as days-between-dates calculations. Be careful.

To create a date object for a specific date or time, you have five ways to send values as a parameter to the new Date() constructor function:

```
new Date("Month dd, yyyy hh:mm:ss")
new Date("Month dd, yyyy")
new Date(yy,mm,dd,hh,mm,ss)
new Date(yy,mm,dd)
new Date(milliseconds)
```

The first four variations break down into two styles — a long string versus a comma-delimited list of data — each with optional time settings. If you omit time settings, they are set to 0 (midnight) in the date object for whatever date you entered. You cannot omit date values from the parameters — every date object must have a real date attached to it, whether you need it or not.

In the long string versions, the month is spelled out in full in English. No abbreviations are allowed. The rest of the data is filled with numbers representing the date, year, hours, minutes, and seconds, even if the order is different from your local way of indicating dates. For single-digit values, you can use either a one- or two-digit version (such as 4:05:00). Colons separate hours, minutes, and seconds.

The short versions contain a non-quoted list of integer values in the order indicated. JavaScript cannot know that a 30 means the date if you accidentally place it in the month slot.

You use the last version only when you have the millisecond value of a date and time available. This generally occurs after some math arithmetic (described later in this chapter), leaving you with a date and time in millisecond format. To convert that numeric value to a date object, use the new Date() constructor. From the new date object created, you can retrieve more convenient values about the date and time.

Native object properties and methods

Like the String and Array objects, the Date object features a small handful of properties and methods that all native JavaScript objects have in common. On the property side, the Date object in NN3+ and IE3/J2+ has a prototype property, which enables you to apply new properties and methods to every date object created in the current page. You can see examples of how this works in discussions of the prototype property for String and Array objects (Chapters 34 and 37, respectively). At the same time, every instance of a date object in IE4+ and NN6 has a constructor property that references the constructor function that generated the object.

Methods in common are `toString()` and `valueOf()` (both NN4+ and IE3/J2+). A date object has numerous methods that convert date object types to strings, most of which are more specific than the generic `toString()` one. The `valueOf()` method returns the millisecond integer that is stored for a particular date—the same value that you get with the more object-specific `getUTCMilliseconds()` method (see the following section).

Date methods

The bulk of a date object's methods are for reading parts of the date and time information and for changing the date and time stored in the object. These two categories of methods are easily identifiable because they all begin with the word "get" or "set." Table 36-1 lists all of the methods of both the static `Date` object and, by inheritance, date object instances. The list is impressive—some would say frightening—but there are patterns you should readily observe. Most methods deal with a single component of a date and time value: year, month, date, and so forth. Each block of "get" and "set" methods also has two sets of methods: one for the local date and time conversion of the date stored in the object; one for the actual UTC date stored in the object. After you see the patterns, the list should be more manageable. Unless otherwise noted, a method has been part of the `Date` object since the first generation of scriptable browsers.

Table 36-1	**Date Object Methods**	
Method	*Value Range*	*Description*
dateObj.getFullYear()	1970-...	Specified year (NN4+, IE3/J2+)
dateObj.getYear()	70-...	(See Text)
dateObj.getMonth()	0-11	Month within the year (January = 0)
dateObj.getDate()	1-31	Date within the month
dateObj.getDay()	0-6	Day of week (Sunday = 0)
dateObj.getHours()	0-23	Hour of the day in 24-hour time
dateObj.getMinutes()	0-59	Minute of the specified hour
dateObj.getSeconds()	0-59	Second within the specified minute
dateObj.getTime()	0-...	Milliseconds since 1/1/70 00:00:00 GMT
dateObj.getMilliseconds()	0-...	Milliseconds since 1/1/70 00:00:00 GMT (NN4+, IE3/J2+)
dateObj.getUTCFullYear()	1970-...	Specified UTC year (NN4+, IE3/J2+)

Method	Value Range	Description
dateObj.getUTCMonth()	0-11	UTC month within the year (January = 0) (NN4+, IE3/J2+)
dateObj.getUTCDate()	1-31	UTC date within the month (NN4+, IE3/J2+)
dateObj.getUTCDay()	0-6	UTC day of week (Sunday = 0) (NN4+, IE3/J2+)
dateObj.getUTCHours()	0-23	UTC hour of the day in 24-hour time (NN4+, IE3/J2+)
dateObj.getUTCMinutes()	0-59	UTC minute of the specified hour (NN4+, IE3/J2+)
dateObj.getUTCSeconds()	0-59	UTC second within the specified minute (NN4+, IE3/J2+)
dateObj.getUTCMilliseconds()	0-...	UTC milliseconds since 1/1/70 00:00:00 GMT (NN4+, IE3/J2+)
dateObj.setYear(*val*)	1970-...	Be safe: always specify a four-digit year
dateObj.setFullYear(*val*)	1970-...	Specified year (NN4+, IE3/J2+)
dateObj.setMonth(*val*)	0-11	Month within the year (January = 0)
dateObj.setDate(*val*)	1-31	Date within the month
dateObj.setDay(*val*)	0-6	Day of week (Sunday = 0)
dateObj.setHours(*val*)	0-23	Hour of the day in 24-hour time
dateObj.setMinutes(*val*)	0-59	Minute of the specified hour
dateObj.setSeconds(*val*)	0-59	Second within the specified minute
dateObj.setMilliseconds(*val*)	0-...	Milliseconds since 1/1/70 00:00:00 GMT (NN4+, IE3/J2+)
dateObj.setTime(*val*)	0-...	Milliseconds since 1/1/70 00:00:00 GMT
dateObj.setUTCFullYear(*val*)	1970-...	Specified UTC year (NN4+, IE3/J2+)
dateObj.setUTCMonth(*val*)	0-11	UTC month within the year (January = 0) (NN4+, IE3/J2+)
dateObj.setUTCDate(*val*)	1-31	UTC date within the month (NN4+, IE3/J2+)

Continued

Method	Value Range	Description
dateObj.setUTCDay(*val*)	0-6	UTC day of week (Sunday = 0) (NN4+, IE3/J2+)
dateObj.setUTCHours(*val*)	0-23	UTC hour of the day in 24-hour time (NN4+, IE3/J2+)
dateObj.setUTCMinutes(*val*)	0-59	UTC minute of the specified hour (NN4+, IE3/J2+)
dateObj.setUTCSeconds(*val*)	0-59	UTC second within the specified minute (NN4+, IE3/J2+)
dateObj.setUTCMilliseconds(*val*)	0–...	UTC milliseconds since 1/1/70 00:00:00 GMT (NN4+, IE3/J2+)
dateObj.getTimezoneOffset()	0–...	Minutes offset from GMT/UTC
dateObj.toDateString()		Date-only string in a format determined by browser (IE5.5)
dateObj.toGMTString()		Date/time string in universal format
dateObj.toLocaleDateString()		Date-only string in your system's localized format (NN6, IE5.5)
dateObj.toLocaleString()		Date/time string in your system's localized format
dateObj.toLocaleTimeString()		Time-only string in your system's localized format (NN6, IE5.5)
dateObj.toString()		Date/time string in a format determined by browser
dateObj.toTimeString()		Time-only string in a format determined by browser (IE5.5)
dateObj.toUTCString()		Date/time string in universal format (NN4+, IE3/J2+)
Date.parse("*dateString*")		Converts string date to milliseconds integer
Date.UTC(*date values*)		Converts GMT string date to milliseconds integer

Deciding between using the UTC or local versions of the methods depends on several factors. If the browsers you must support go back to the beginning, you will be stuck with the local versions in any case. But even for newer browsers, activities, such as calculating the number of days between dates or creating a countdown timer for a quiz, won't care which set you use, but you must use the same set for all calculations. If you start mixing local and UTC versions of date methods, you'll be destined to get wrong answers. Where the UTC versions come in most handy is when your date calculations must take into account the time zone of the client machine compared to some absolute in another time zone — calculating the time remaining to the chiming of Big Ben signifying the start of the New Year in London.

JavaScript maintains its date information in the form of a count of milliseconds (thousandths of a second) starting from January 1, 1970, in the GMT (UTC) time zone. Dates before that starting point are stored as negative values (but see the section on bugs and gremlins later in this chapter). Regardless of the country you are in or the date and time formats specified for your computer, the millisecond is the JavaScript universal measure of time. Any calculations that involve adding or subtracting times and dates should be performed in the millisecond values to ensure accuracy. Therefore, though you may never display the milliseconds value in a field or dialog box, your scripts will probably work with them from time to time in variables. To derive the millisecond equivalent for any date and time stored in a date object, use the *dateObj*.getTime() method, as in

```
var startDate = new Date()
var started = startDate.getTime()
```

Although the method has the word "time" in its name, the fact that the value is the total number of milliseconds from January 1, 1970, means the value also conveys a date.

Other date object get methods read a specific component of the date or time. You have to exercise some care here, because some values begin counting with 0 when you may not expect it. For example, January is month 0 in JavaScript's scheme; December is month 11. Hours, minutes, and seconds all begin with 0, which, in the end, is logical. Calendar dates, however, use the actual number that would show up on the wall calendar: The first day of the month is date value 1. For the twentieth century years, the year value is whatever the actual year number is, minus 1900. For 1996, that means the year value is 96. But for years before 1900 and after 1999, JavaScript uses a different formula, showing the full year value. This means you have to check whether a year value is less than 100 and add 1900 to it before displaying that year.

```
var today = new Date()
var thisYear = today.getYear()
if (thisYear < 100) {
    thisYear += 1900
}
```

This assumes, of course, you won't be working with years before A.D. 100. If your audience is strictly IE3/J2+ and NN4+, then use only the getFullYear() method, which returns the complete set of year digits from all ranges.

To adjust any one of the elements of a date value, use the corresponding set method in an assignment statement. If the new value forces the adjustment of other elements, JavaScript takes care of that. For example, consider the following sequence and how some values are changed for us:

```
myBirthday = new Date("September 11, 2001")
result = myBirthday.getDay() // result = 2, a Tuesday
myBirthday.setYear(2002) // bump up to next year
result = myBirthday.getDay() // result = 3, a Wednesday
```

Because the same date in the following year is on a different day, JavaScript tracks that for you.

Accommodating time zones

Understanding the *dateObj*.getTimezoneOffset() method involves both your operating system's time control panel setting and an internationally recognized (in computerdom, anyway) format for representing dates and times. If you have ignored the control panel stuff about setting your local time zone, the values you get for this property may be off for most dates and times. In the eastern part of North America, for instance, the eastern standard time zone is five hours earlier than Greenwich Mean Time. With the getTimezoneOffset() method producing a value of minutes' difference between GMT and the PC's time zone, the five hours difference of eastern standard time is rendered as a value of 300 minutes. On the Windows platform, the value automatically changes to reflect changes in daylight saving time in the user's area (if applicable). Offsets to the east of GMT (to the date line) are expressed as negative values.

Dates as strings

When you generate a date object, JavaScript automatically applies the toString() method to the object if you attempt to display that date either in a page or alert box. The format of this string varies with browser and operating system platform. For example, in Navigator 4 for Windows 98, the string is in the following format:

```
Wed Oct 31 11:43:34 GMT-0800 (Pacific Standard Time) 2001
```

But in the same version for Macintosh, the string is

```
Wed Oct 31 11:43:34 GMT-0800 2001
```

Internet Explorer returns its own variations on the string. The point is not to rely on a specific format and character location of this string for the components of dates. Use the date object methods to read date object components.

JavaScript does, however, provide two methods that return the date object in more constant string formats. One, *dateObj*.toGMTString(), converts the date and time to the GMT equivalent on the way to the variable that you use to store the extracted data. Here is what such data looks like:

```
Wed, 1 Nov 2000 04:25:28 GMT
```

If you're not familiar with the workings of GMT and how such conversions can present unexpected dates, exercise great care in testing your application. Eight o'clock on a Friday evening in California in the winter is four o'clock on Saturday morning GMT.

If time zone conversions make your head hurt, you can use the second string method, *dateObj*.toLocaleString(). In Navigator 3 for North American Windows users, the returned value looks like this:

```
10/31/2000 20:25:28
```

Starting with IE5.5 and NN6, you can also have JavaScript convert a date object to just the date or time portions in a nicely formatted version. The best pair of methods for this are toLocaleDateString() and toLocaleTimeString(), because these methods return values that make the most sense to the user, based on the localization settings of the user's operating system and browser.

Friendly date formats for older browsers

If you don't have the luxury of writing only for IE5.5+ or NN6+, you can create your own formatting function to do the job for a wide range of browsers. Listing 36-1 demonstrates one way of creating this kind of string from a date object (in a form compatible with Navigator 2 and Internet Explorer 3 pseudo-arrays).

Listing 36-1: **Creating a Friendly Date String**

```
<HTML>
<HEAD>
<TITLE>Date String Maker</TITLE>
<SCRIPT LANGUAGE="JavaScript">
function MakeArray(n) {
    this.length = n
    return this
}
monthNames = new MakeArray(12)
monthNames[1] = "January"
monthNames[2] = "February"
monthNames[3] = "March"
```

Continued

Listing 36-1: *(continued)*

```
monthNames[4] = "April"
monthNames[5] = "May"
monthNames[6] = "June"
monthNames[7] = "July"
monthNames[8] = "August"
monthNames[9] = "September"
monthNames[10] = "October"
monthNames[11] = "November"
monthNames[12] = "December"

dayNames = new MakeArray(7)
dayNames[1] = "Sunday"
dayNames[2] = "Monday"
dayNames[3] = "Tuesday"
dayNames[4] = "Wednesday"
dayNames[5] = "Thursday"
dayNames[6] = "Friday"
dayNames[7] = "Saturday"

function customDateString(oneDate) {
    var theDay = dayNames[oneDate.getDay() + 1]
    var theMonth = monthNames[oneDate.getMonth() + 1]
    var theYear = oneDate.getYear()
    theYear += (theYear < 100) ? 1900 : 0
    return theDay + ", " + theMonth + " " + oneDate.getDate() + ", " + theYear
}
</SCRIPT>
</HEAD>

<BODY>
<H1> Welcome!</H1>
<SCRIPT LANGUAGE="JavaScript">
document.write(customDateString(new Date()))
</SCRIPT>

<HR>
</BODY>
</HTML>
```

Assuming the user has the PC's clock set correctly (a big assumption), the date appearing just below the opening headline is the current date — making it appear as though the document had been updated today. The downside to this approach (as opposed to the newer `toLocaleDateString()` method) is that international users are forced to view dates in the format you design, which may be different from their local custom.

More conversions

The last two methods shown in Listing 36-1 are methods of the static Date object. These utility methods convert dates from string or numeric forms into millisecond values of those dates. The primary beneficiary of these actions is the *dateObj*.setTime() method, which requires a millisecond measure of a date as a parameter. You use this method to throw an entirely different date into an existing date object.

Date.parse() accepts as a parameter date strings similar to the ones you've seen in this section, including the internationally approved version. Date.UTC(), on the other hand, requires the comma-delimited list of values (in proper order: *yy,mm,dd, hh,mm,ss*) in the GMT zone. The Date.UTC() method gives you a backward-compatible way to hard-code a GMT time (you can do the same in NN4+ and IE4+ via the UTC methods). The following is an example that creates a new date object for 6 p.m. on March 4, 2002, GMT in IE5/Windows:

```
var newObj = new Date(Date.UTC(2002,2,4,18,0,0))
result = newObj.toString()    // result = "Mon, Mar 04 10:00:00 PST 2002"
```

The second statement returns a value in a local time zone, because all non-UTC methods automatically convert the GMT time stored in the object to the client's local time.

Date and time arithmetic

You may need to perform some math with dates for any number of reasons. Perhaps you need to calculate a date at some fixed number of days or weeks in the future or figure out the number of days between two dates. When calculations of these types are required, remember the *lingua franca* of JavaScript date values: milliseconds.

What you may need to do in your date-intensive scripts is establish some variable values representing the number of milliseconds for minutes, hours, days, or weeks, and then use those variables in your calculations. Here is an example that establishes some practical variable values, building on each other:

```
var oneMinute = 60 * 1000
var oneHour = oneMinute * 60
var oneDay = oneHour * 24
var oneWeek = oneDay * 7
```

With these values established in a script, I can use one to calculate the date one week from today:

```
var targetDate = new Date()
var dateInMs = targetDate.getTime()
dateInMs += oneWeek
targetDate.setTime(dateInMs)
```

Another example uses components of a date object to assist in deciding what kind of greeting message to place in a document, based on the local time of the user's PC clock. Listing 36-2 adds to the scripting from Listing 36-1, bringing some quasi-intelligence to the proceedings. Again, this script uses the older array creation mechanism to be compatible with Navigator 2 and Internet Explorer 3.

Listing 36-2: **A Dynamic Welcome Message**

```
<HTML>
<HEAD>
<TITLE>Date String Maker</TITLE>
<SCRIPT LANGUAGE="JavaScript">
function MakeArray(n) {
    this.length = n
    return this
}
monthNames = new MakeArray(12)
monthNames[1] = "January"
monthNames[2] = "February"
monthNames[3] = "March"
monthNames[4] = "April"
monthNames[5] = "May"
monthNames[6] = "June"
monthNames[7] = "July"
monthNames[8] = "August"
monthNames[9] = "September"
monthNames[10] = "October"
monthNames[11] = "November"
monthNames[12] = "December"
dayNames = new MakeArray(7)
dayNames[1] = "Sunday"
dayNames[2] = "Monday"
dayNames[3] = "Tuesday"
dayNames[4] = "Wednesday"
dayNames[5] = "Thursday"
dayNames[6] = "Friday"
dayNames[7] = "Saturday"

function customDateString(oneDate) {
    var theDay = dayNames[oneDate.getDay() + 1]
    var theMonth = monthNames[oneDate.getMonth() + 1]
    var theYear = oneDate.getYear()
    theYear += (theYear < 100) ? 1900 : 0
    return theDay + ", " + theMonth + " " + oneDate.getDate() + ", " + theYear
}
function dayPart(oneDate) {
    var theHour = oneDate.getHours()
    if (theHour <6 )
```

```
            return "wee hours"
    if (theHour < 12)
            return "morning"
    if (theHour < 18)
            return "afternoon"
    return "evening"
}
</SCRIPT>
</HEAD>

<BODY>
<H1> Welcome!</H1>
<SCRIPT LANGUAGE="JavaScript">
today = new Date()
var header = (customDateString(today)).italics()
header += "<BR>We hope you are enjoying the "
header += dayPart(today) + "."
document.write(header)
</SCRIPT>
<HR>
</BODY>
</HTML>
```

The script divides the day into four parts and presents a different greeting for each part of the day. The greeting that plays is based, simply enough, on the hour element of a date object representing the time the page is loaded into the browser. Because this greeting is embedded in the page, the greeting does not change no matter how long the user stays logged on to the page.

Counting the days. . .

You may find one or two more date arithmetic applications useful. One displays the number of shopping days left until Christmas (in the user's time zone); the other is a countdown timer to the start of the year 2100.

Listing 36-3 demonstrates how to calculate the number of days between the current day and some fixed date in the future. The assumption in this application is that all calculations take place in the user's time zone. The example shows the display of the number of shopping days before the next Christmas day (December 25). The basic operation entails converting the current date and the next December 25 to milliseconds, calculating the number of days represented by the difference in milliseconds. If you let the millisecond values represent the dates, JavaScript automatically takes care of leap years.

The only somewhat tricky part is setting the year of the next Christmas day correctly. You can't just slap the fixed date with the current year, because if the program is run on December 26, the year of the next Christmas must be incremented by one. That's why the constructor for the Christmas date object doesn't supply a fixed date as its parameters but, rather, sets individual components of the object.

Listing 36-3: **How Many Days Until Christmas**

```
<HTML>
<HEAD>
<TITLE>Christmas Countdown</TITLE>
<SCRIPT LANGUAGE="JavaScript">
function getDaysUntilXmas() {
    var oneMinute = 60 * 1000
    var oneHour = oneMinute * 60
    var oneDay = oneHour * 24
    var today = new Date()
    var nextXmas = new Date()
    nextXmas.setMonth(11)
    nextXmas.setDate(25)
    if (today.getMonth() == 11 && today.getDate() > 25) {
        nextXmas.setFullYear(nextXmas.getFullYear() + 1)
    }
    var diff = nextXmas.getTime() - today.getTime()
    diff = Math.floor(diff/oneDay)
    return diff
}
</SCRIPT>
</HEAD>

<BODY>
<H1>
<SCRIPT LANGUAGE="JavaScript">
var header = "You have <I>" + getDaysUntilXmas()  + "</I> "
header += "shopping days until Christmas."
document.write(header)
</SCRIPT>
</H1><HR>
</BODY>
</HTML>
```

The second variation on calculating the amount of time before a certain event takes time zones into account. For this demonstration, the page is supposed to display a countdown timer to the precise moment when the flame for the 2004 Summer Games in Athens is to be lit. That event takes place in a time zone that may be different from that of the page's viewer, so the countdown timer must calculate the time difference accordingly.

Listing 36-4 shows a simplified version that simply displays the ticking timer in a text field. The output, of course, could be customized in any number of ways, depending on the amount of dynamic HTML you want to employ on a page. The time of the lighting for this demo is set at 17:00 GMT on August 13, 2004 (the date is certainly accurate, but the officials may set a different time closer to the actual event).

Because this application is implemented as a live ticking clock, the code starts by setting some global variables that should be calculated only once so that the function that gets invoked repeatedly has a minimum of calculating to do (to be more efficient). The Date.UTC() method provides the target time and date in standard time. The getTimeUntil() function accepts a millisecond value (as provided by the targetDate variable) and calculates the difference between the target date and the actual internal millisecond value of the client's PC clock.

The core of the getCountDown() function peels off the number of whole days, hours, minutes, and seconds from the total number of milliseconds difference between now and the target date. Notice that each chunk is subtracted from the total so that the next smaller chunk can be calculated from the leftover milliseconds.

One extra touch on this page is that users of Windows operating systems have a display of the local date and time of the actual event. The Mac is excluded because it does not provide accurate daylight saving time adjustments for local dates. Some UNIX flavors may do the right thing, but they were not tested for this example.

Listing 36-4: **Summer Games Countdown**

```
<HTML>
<HEAD>
<TITLE>Summer Games Countdown</TITLE>
<SCRIPT LANGUAGE="JavaScript">
// globals -- calculate only once
// set target date to 1700GMT on August 13, 2004
var targetDate = Date.UTC(2004, 7, 13, 17, 0, 0, 0)
var oneMinute = 60 * 1000
var oneHour = oneMinute * 60
var oneDay = oneHour * 24

function getTimeUntil(targetMS) {
    var today = new Date()
    var diff = targetMS - today.valueOf()
    return Math.floor(diff)
}
```

Continued

Listing 36-4: *(continued)*

```
function getCountDown() {
    var ms = getTimeUntil(targetDate)
    var output = ""
    var days, hrs, mins, secs
    if (ms >= 0) {
        days = Math.floor(ms/oneDay)
        ms -= oneDay * days
        hrs = Math.floor(ms/oneHour)
        ms -= oneHour * hrs
        mins = Math.floor(ms/oneMinute)
        ms -= oneMinute * mins
        secs = Math.floor(ms/1000)
        output += days + " Days, " +
                  hrs + " Hours, " +
                  mins + " Minutes, " +
                  secs + " Seconds"
    } else {
        output += "The time has passed."
    }
    return output
}
function updateCountDown() {
    document.forms[0].timer.value = getCountDown()
    setTimeout("updateCountDown()", 1000)
}
</SCRIPT>
</HEAD>

<BODY onLoad="updateCountDown()">
<H1>Athens Games Torch Lighting Countdown</H1>
<P>
<SCRIPT LANGUAGE="JavaScript">
if (navigator.userAgent.indexOf("Win") >= 0) {
    document.write("(" + (new Date(targetDate)).toLocaleString())
    document.write(" in your time zone.)")
}
</SCRIPT>
</P>
<FORM>
<INPUT TYPE="text" NAME="timer" SIZE=60>
</FORM>
<HR>
</BODY>
</HTML>
```

Date bugs and gremlins

Each new browser generation improves the stability and reliability of scripted date objects. Unfortunately, Navigator 2 has enough bugs and crash problems across many platforms to make scripting complex world-time applications for this browser impossible. The Macintosh version also has bugs that throw off dates by as much as a full day. I recommend avoiding NN2 on all platforms for serious date and time scripting.

The situation is much improved for NN3. Still, some bugs persist. One bug in particular affects Macintosh versions of NN3. Whenever you create a new date object with daylight saving time engaged in the Date and Time control panel, the browser automatically adds one hour to the object. See the time-based application in Chapter 54 for an example of how to counteract the effects of typical time bugs. Also afflicting the Macintosh in NN3 is a faulty calculation of the time zone offset for all time zones east of GMT. Instead of generating these values as negative numbers (getting lower and lower as you head east), the offset values increase continuously as you head west from Greenwich. While the Western Hemisphere is fine, the values continue to increase past the international date line, rather than switch over to the negative values.

Internet Explorer 3 isn't free of problems. It cannot handle dates before January 1, 1970 (GMT). Attempts to generate a date before that one result in that base date as the value. IE3 also completely miscalculates the time zone offset, following the erroneous pattern of Navigator 2. Even Navigators 3 and 4 have problems with historic dates. You are asking for trouble if the date extends earlier than January 1, A.D. 1. Internet Explorer 4, on the other hand, appears to sail very well into ancient history.

You should be aware of one more discrepancy between Mac and Windows versions of Navigator through Version 4. In Windows, if you generate a date object for a date in another part of the year, the browser sets the time zone offset for that object according to the time zone setting for that time of year. On the Mac, the current setting of the control panel governs whether the normal or daylight saving time offset is applied to the date, regardless of the actual date within the year. This discrepancy affects Navigator 3 and 4 and can throw off calculations from other parts of the year by one hour.

It may sound as though the road to Date object scripting is filled with land mines. While date and time scripting is far from hassle free, you can put it to good use with careful planning and a lot of testing.

Validating Date Entries in Forms

Given the bug horror stories in the previous section, you may wonder how you can ever perform data entry validation for dates in forms. The problem is not so much in the calculations as it is in the wide variety of acceptable date formats around the world. No matter how well you instruct users to enter dates in a particular format, many will follow their own habits and conventions. Moreover, how can you know whether an entry of 03/04/2002 is the North American March 4, 2002, or the European April 3, 2002? The answer: You can't.

My recommendation is to divide a date field into three components: month, day, and year. Let the user enter values into each field and validate each field individually for its valid range. Listing 36-5 shows an example of how this is done. The page includes a form that is to be validated before it is submitted. Each component field does its own range checking on the fly as the user enters values. But because this kind of validation can be defeated, the page includes one further check triggered by the form's onSubmit event handler. If any field is out of whack, the form submission is canceled.

Listing 36-5: **Date Validation in a Form**

```
<HTML>
<HEAD>
<TITLE>Date Entry Validation</TITLE>
<SCRIPT LANGUAGE="JavaScript">
<!--
// **BEGIN GENERIC VALIDATION FUNCTIONS**
// general purpose function to see if an input value has been entered at all
function isEmpty(inputStr) {
    if (inputStr == "" || inputStr == null) {
        return true
    }
    return false
}


// function to determine if value is in acceptable range for this application
function inRange(inputStr, lo, hi) {
    var num = parseInt(inputStr, 10)
    if (num < lo || num > hi) {
        return false
    }
    return true
}
// **END GENERIC VALIDATION FUNCTIONS**

function validateMonth(field, bypassUpdate) {
    var input = field.value
    if (isEmpty(input)) {
```

```
            alert("Be sure to enter a month value.")
            select(field)
            return false
        } else {
            input = parseInt(field.value, 10)
            if (isNaN(input)) {
                alert("Entries must be numbers only.")
                select(field)
                return false
            } else {
                if (!inRange(input,1,12)) {
                    alert("Enter a number between 1 (January) and 12 (December).")
                    select(field)
                    return false
                }
            }
        }
        if (!bypassUpdate) {
            calcDate()
        }
        return true
}

function validateDate(field) {
    var input = field.value
    if (isEmpty(input)) {
        alert("Be sure to enter a date value.")
        select(field)
        return false
    } else {
        input = parseInt(field.value, 10)
        if (isNaN(input)) {
            alert("Entries must be numbers only.")
            select(field)
            return false
        } else {
            var monthField = document.birthdate.month
            if (!validateMonth(monthField, true)) return false
            var monthVal = parseInt(monthField.value, 10)
            var monthMax = new Array(31,31,29,31,30,31,30,31,31,30,31,30,31)
            var top = monthMax[monthVal]
            if (!inRange(input,1,top)) {
                alert("Enter a number between 1 and " + top + ".")
                select(field)
                return false
            }
        }
    }
    calcDate()
    return true
```

Continued

Listing 36-5: *(continued)*

```
}

function validateYear(field) {
    var input = field.value
    if (isEmpty(input)) {
        alert("Be sure to enter a year value.")
        select(field)
        return false
    } else {
        input = parseInt(field.value, 10)
        if (isNaN(input)) {
            alert("Entries must be numbers only.")
            select(field)
            return false
        } else {
            if (!inRange(input,1900,2005)) {
                alert("Enter a number between 1900 and 2005.")
                select(field)
                return false
            }
        }
    }
    calcDate()
    return true
}

function select(field) {
    field.focus()
    field.select()
}

function calcDate() {
    var mm = parseInt(document.birthdate.month.value, 10)
    var dd = parseInt(document.birthdate.date.value, 10)
    var yy = parseInt(document.birthdate.year.value, 10)
    document.birthdate.fullDate.value = mm + "/" + dd + "/" + yy
}

function checkForm(form) {
    if (validateMonth(form.month)) {
        if (validateDate(form.date)) {
            if (validateYear(form.year)) {
                return true
            }
        }
    }
    return false
}
```

```
//-->
</SCRIPT>
</HEAD>
<BODY>
<FORM NAME="birthdate" ACTION="mailto:fun@dannyg.com" METHOD=POST
onSubmit="return checkForm(this)">
Please enter your birthdate...<BR>
Month:<INPUT TYPE="text" NAME="month" VALUE=1 SIZE=2
onChange="validateMonth(this)">
Date:<INPUT TYPE="text" NAME="date" VALUE=1 SIZE=2
onChange="validateDate(this)">
Year:<INPUT TYPE="text" NAME="year" VALUE=1900 SIZE=4
onChange="validateYear(this)">
<P>
Thank you for entering:<INPUT TYPE="text" NAME="fullDate" SIZE=10><P>
<INPUT TYPE="submit"> <INPUT TYPE="Reset">
</FORM>
</BODY>
</HTML>
```

The page shows the three entry fields as well as a field that is normally hidden on a form to be submitted to a CGI program. On the server end, the CGI program responds only to the hidden field with the complete date, which is in a format for entry into, for example, an Informix database.

Not every date entry validation must be divided in this way. For example, an intranet application can be more demanding in the way users are to enter data. Therefore, you can have a single field for date entry, but the parsing required for such a validation is quite different from that shown in Listing 36-5. See Chapter 43 for an example of such a one-field date validation routine.

✦   ✦   ✦

The Array Object

An array is the sole JavaScript data structure provided for storing and manipulating ordered collections of data. But unlike some other programming languages, JavaScript's arrays are very forgiving as to the kind of data you store in each cell or entry of the array. This allows, for example, an array of arrays, providing the equivalent of multi-dimensional arrays customized to the kind of data your application needs.

If you have not done a lot of programming in the past, the notion of arrays may seem like an advanced topic. But if you ignore their capabilities, you set yourself up for a harder job when implementing many kinds of tasks. Whenever I approach a script, one of my first thoughts is about the data being controlled by the application and whether handling it as an array will offer some shortcuts for creating the document and handling interactivity with the user.

I hope that by the end of this chapter, you will not only be familiar with the properties and methods of JavaScript arrays, but you will begin to look for ways to make arrays work for you.

Structured Data

In programming, an *array* is defined as an ordered collection of data. You can best visualize an array as a table, not much different from a spreadsheet. In JavaScript, arrays are limited to a table holding one column of data, with as many rows as needed to hold your data. As you have seen in many chapters in Part III, a JavaScript-enabled browser creates a number of internal arrays for the objects in your HTML documents and browser properties. For example, if your document contains five links, the browser maintains a table of those links. You access them by number (with 0 being the first link) in the array syntax: the array name is followed by the index number in square brackets, as in `document.links[0]`, which represents the first link in the document.

For many JavaScript applications, you will want to use an array as an organized warehouse for data that users of your page access, depending on their interaction with form elements. In the application shown in Chapter 50, for example, I demonstrate an extended version of this usage in a page that lets users search a small table of data for a match between the first three digits of their U.S. Social Security numbers and the state in which they registered with the agency. Arrays are the way JavaScript-enhanced pages can recreate the behavior of more sophisticated CGI programs on servers. When the collection of data you embed in the script is no larger than a typical .gif image file, the user won't experience significant delays in loading your page; yet he or she has the full power of your small database collection for instant searching without any calls back to the server. Such database-oriented arrays are important applications of JavaScript for what I call *serverless CGIs*.

As you design an application, look for clues as to potential application of arrays. If you have a number of objects or data points that interact with scripts the same way, you have a good candidate for array structures. For example, in every browser, with the exception of Internet Explorer 3, you can assign like names to every text field in a column of an order form. In that sequence, like-named objects are treated as elements of an array. To perform repetitive row calculations down an order form, your scripts can use array syntax to perform all the extensions within a handful of JavaScript statements, rather than perhaps dozens of statements hard-coded to each field name. Chapter 51 shows an example of this application.

You can also create arrays that behave like the Java hash table: a lookup table that gets you to the desired data point instantaneously if you know the name associated with the entry. If you can conceive your data in a table format, an array is in your future.

Creating an Empty Array

Arrays are treated in JavaScript like objects, but the extent to which your scripts can treat them as objects depends on whether you're using the first version of JavaScript (in Navigator 2 and Internet Explorer 3 with the Version 1 JScript DLL) or more recent versions (in Navigator 3 or later and Internet Explorer with JScript DLL Version 2 or later). For the sake of compatibility, I begin by showing you how to create arrays that work in all scriptable browsers.

You begin by defining an object *constructor* function that assigns a passed parameter integer value to the length property of the object:

```
function makeArray(n) {
    this.length = n
    return this
}
```

Then, to actually initialize an array for your script, use the new keyword to construct the object for you while assigning the array object to a variable of your choice:

```
var myArray = new makeArray(n)
```

where *n* is the number of entries you anticipate for the array. This initialization does not make any array entries or create any placeholders. Such preconditioning of arrays is not necessary in JavaScript.

In one important aspect, an array created in this "old" manner does not exhibit an important characteristic of standard arrays. The length property here is artificial in that it does not change with the size of the array (true JavaScript arrays are completely dynamic, letting you add items at any time). The length value here is hard-wired by assignment. You can always change the value manually, but it takes a great deal of scripted bookkeeping to manage that task.

Another point to remember about this property scheme is that the value assigned to this.length in the constructor actually occupies the first entry (index 0) of the array. Any data you want to add to an array should not overwrite that position in the array if you expect to use the length to help a repeat loop look through an array's contents.

What a full-fledged array object gains you is behavior more like that of the arrays you work with elsewhere in JavaScript. You don't need to define a constructor function, because it's built into the JavaScript object mechanism. Instead, you create a new array object, such as this:

```
var myArray = new Array()
```

An array object automatically has a length property (0 for an empty array). Most importantly, this length value does not occupy one of the array entries; the array is entirely for data.

Should you want to presize the array (for example, preload entries with null values), you can specify an initial size as a parameter to the constructor. For example, here is how to create a new array to hold information about a 500-item compact disc collection:

```
var myCDCollection = new Array(500)
```

Presizing an array does not give you any particular advantage, because you can assign a value to any slot in an array at any time: The length property adjusts itself accordingly. For instance, if you assign a value to myCDCollection[700], the array object adjusts its length upward to meet that slot (with the count starting at 0):

```
myCDCollection [700] = "Gloria Estefan/Destiny"
collectionSize = myCDCollection.length    // result = 701
```

A true array object also features a number of methods and the capability to add prototype properties, described later in this chapter.

Populating an Array

Entering data into an array is as simple as creating a series of assignment statements, one for each element of the array. Listing 37-1 (not on the CD-ROM) assumes that you're using the newer style array object and that your goal is to generate an array containing a list of the nine planets of the solar system.

Listing 37-1: **Generating and Populating a New Array**

```
solarSys = new Array(9)
solarSys[0] = "Mercury"
solarSys[1] = "Venus"
solarSys[2] = "Earth"
solarSys[3] = "Mars"
solarSys[4] = "Jupiter"
solarSys[5] = "Saturn"
solarSys[6] = "Uranus"
solarSys[7] = "Neptune"
solarSys[8] = "Pluto"
```

This way of populating a single array is a bit tedious when you're writing the code, but after the array is set, it makes accessing information collections as easy as any array reference:

```
onePlanet = solarSys[4]      // result = "Jupiter"
```

A more compact way to create an array is available if you know that the data will be in the desired order (as the preceding solarSys array). Instead of writing a series of assignment statements (as in Listing 37-1), you can create what is called a *dense array* by supplying the data as parameters to the Array() constructor:

```
solarSys = new Array("Mercury","Venus","Earth","Mars","Jupiter","Saturn",
"Uranus","Neptune","Pluto")
```

The term "dense array" means that data is packed into the array, without gaps, starting at index position 0.

The example in Listing 37-1 shows what you may call a vertical collection of data. Each data point contains the same type of data as the other data points — the name of a planet — and the data points appear in the relative order of the planets from the Sun.

But not all data collections are vertical. You may, for instance, just want to create an array that holds various pieces of information about one planet. Earth is handy, so use some of its astronomical data to build a completely separate array of earthly info in Listing 37-2 (not on the CD-ROM).

Listing 37-2: **Creating a "Horizontal" Array**

```
earth = new Array()
earth.diameter = "7920 miles"
earth.distance = "93 million miles"
earth.year = "365.25 days"
earth.day = "24 hours"
earth.length      // result = 4
```

What you see in Listing 37-2 is an alternative way to populate an array. In a sense, you saw a preview of this approach for the creation of an array in the old style, where the `length` property name was assigned to its first entry. If you assign a value to a property name that has not yet been assigned for the array, JavaScript is smart enough to append a new property entry for that value.

In an important change from the old style of array construction, the way you define an array entry affects how you access that information later. For example, when you populate an array based on numeric index values (Listing 37-1), you can retrieve those array entries only via references that include the index values. Conversely, if you define array entries by property name (as in Listing 37-2), you cannot access those values via the numeric index way. In Navigator 2, for instance, the array assignments of Listing 37-2 can be retrieved by their corresponding index values:

```
earth.diameter        // result = "7920 miles"
earth["diameter"]     // result = "7920 miles"
earth[0]              // result = "7920 miles"
```

In Navigator 3 or 4, however, because these entries are defined as named properties, they must be retrieved as properties, not as numeric index values:

```
earth.diameter        // result = "7920 miles"
earth["diameter"]     // result = "7920 miles"
earth[0]              // result = null
```

The impact here on your scripts is that you need to anticipate how you expect to retrieve data from your array. If an indexed repeat loop is in the forecast, populate the array with index values (as in Listing 37-1); if the property names are more important to you, then populate the array that way (as in Listing 37-2). Your choice of index value type for a single-column array is driven by the application, but you will want to focus on the named array entry style for creating what appear to be two-dimensional arrays.

JavaScript 1.2 Array Creation Enhancements

The JavaScript version in NN4+ and IE4+ provides one more way to create a dense array and also clears up a bug in the old way. A new, simpler way to create a dense array does not require the `Array` object constructor. Instead, JavaScript 1.2 (and later) accepts what is called *literal notation* to generate an array. To demonstrate the difference, the following statement is the regular dense array constructor that works with Navigator 3:

```
solarSys = new Array("Mercury","Venus","Earth","Mars","Jupiter","Saturn",
"Uranus","Neptune","Pluto")
```

While JavaScript 1.2+ fully accepts the preceding syntax, it also accepts the new literal notation:

```
solarSys = ["Mercury","Venus","Earth","Mars","Jupiter","Saturn",
"Uranus","Neptune","Pluto"]
```

The square brackets stand in for the call to the `Array` constructor. You have to judge which browser types your audience will be using before deploying this streamlined approach to array creation.

The bug fix has to do with how to treat the earlier dense array constructor if the scripter enters only the numeric value 1 as the parameter — `new Array(1)`. In NN3 and IE4, JavaScript erroneously creates an array of length 1, but that element is `undefined`. For NN4 (and inside a `<SCRIPT LANGUAGE="JavaScript1.2">` tag) and all later browsers (IE5+, NN6), the same statement creates that one-element array and places the value in that element.

Deleting Array Entries

You can always set the value of an array entry to `null` or an empty string to wipe out any data that used to occupy that space. But until the `delete` operator in NN4 and IE4, you could not completely remove the element.

Deleting an array element eliminates the index from the list of accessible index values but does not reduce the array's length, as in the following sequence of statements:

```
myArray.length    // result: 5
delete myArray[2]
myArray.length    // result: 5
myArray[2]        // result: undefined
```

The process of deleting an array entry does not necessarily release memory occupied by that data. The JavaScript interpreter's internal garbage collection mechanism (beyond the reach of scripters) is supposed to take care of such activity. See the delete operator in Chapter 40 for further details.

Parallel Arrays

Using an array to hold data is frequently desirable so that a script can do a lookup to see if a particular value is in the array (perhaps verifying that a value typed into a text box by the user is permissible); however, even more valuable is if, upon finding a match, a script can look up some related information in another array. One way to accomplish this is with two or more parallel arrays: the same indexed slot of each array contains related information.

Consider the following three arrays:

```
var regionalOffices = new Array("New York", "Chicago", "Houston", "Portland")
var regionalManagers = new Array("Shirley Smith", "Todd Gaston", "Leslie Jones",
"Harold Zoot")
var regOfficeQuotas = new Array(300000, 250000, 350000, 225000)
```

The assumption for these statements is that Shirley Smith is the regional manager out of the New York office, and her office's quota is 300,000. This represents the data that is included with the document, perhaps retrieved by a CGI program on the server that gets the latest data from a SQL database and embeds the data in the form of array constructors. Listing 37-3 shows how this data appears in a simple page that looks up the manager name and quota values for whichever office is chosen in the SELECT element. The order of the items in the list of SELECT is not accidental: The order is identical to the order of the array for the convenience of the lookup script.

Lookup action in Listing 37-3 is performed by the getData() function. Because the index values of the options inside the SELECT element match those of the parallel arrays index values, the selectedIndex property of the SELECT element makes a convenient way to get directly at the corresponding data in other arrays.

Listing 37-3: **A Simple Parallel Array Lookup**

```
<HTML>
<HEAD>
<TITLE>Parallel Array Lookup</TITLE>
<SCRIPT LANGUAGE="JavaScript">
// the data
var regionalOffices = new Array("New York", "Chicago", "Houston", "Portland")
var regionalManagers = new Array("Shirley Smith", "Todd Gaston", "Leslie Jones",
"Harold Zoot")
var regOfficeQuotas = new Array(300000, 250000, 350000, 225000)
// do the lookup into parallel arrays
function getData(form) {
    var i = form.offices.selectedIndex
    form.manager.value = regionalManagers[i]
    form.quota.value = regOfficeQuotas[i]
}
</SCRIPT>
</HEAD>

<BODY onLoad="getData(document.officeData)">
<H1>Parallel Array Lookup</H1>
<HR>
<FORM NAME="officeData">
<P>
Select a regional office:
<SELECT NAME="offices" onChange="getData(this.form)">
    <OPTION>New York
    <OPTION>Chicago
    <OPTION>Houston
    <OPTION>Portland
</SELECT>
</P><P>
The manager is:
<INPUT TYPE="text" NAME="manager" SIZE=35>
<BR>
The office quota is:
<INPUT TYPE="text" NAME="quota" SIZE=8>
</P>
</FORM>
</BODY>
</HTML>
```

On the other hand, if the content to be looked up is typed into a text box by the user, you have to loop through one of the arrays to get the matching index. Listing 37-4 is a variation of Listing 37-3, but instead of the SELECT element, a text field asks users to type in the name of the region. Assuming that users will always spell the input correctly (an outrageous assumption), the version of getData() in

Listing 37-4 performs actions that more closely resemble what you may think a "lookup" should be doing: looking for a match in one array, and displaying corresponding results from the parallel arrays. The `for` loop iterates through items in the `regionalOffices` array. An `if` condition compares all uppercase versions of both the input and each array entry. If there is a match, the `for` loop breaks, with the value of `i` still pointing to the matching index value. Outside the `for` loop, another `if` condition makes sure that the index value has not reached the length of the array, which means that no match is found. Only when the value of `i` points to one of the array entries does the script retrieve corresponding entries from the other two arrays.

Listing 37-4: A Looping Array Lookup

```
<HTML>
<HEAD>
<TITLE>Parallel Array Lookup II</TITLE>
<SCRIPT LANGUAGE="JavaScript">
// the data
var regionalOffices = new Array("New York", "Chicago", "Houston", "Portland")
var regionalManagers = new Array("Shirley Smith", "Todd Gaston", "Leslie Jones",
"Harold Zoot")
var regOfficeQuotas = new Array(300000, 250000, 350000, 225000)
// do the lookup into parallel arrays
function getData(form) {
    // make a copy of the text box contents
    var inputText = form.officeInp.value
    // loop through all entries of regionalOffices array
    for (var i = 0; i < regionalOffices.length; i++) {
        // compare uppercase versions of entered text against one entry
        // of regionalOffices
        if (inputText.toUpperCase() == regionalOffices[i].toUpperCase()) {
            // if they're the same, then break out of the for loop
            break
        }
    }
    // make sure the i counter hasn't exceeded the max index value
    if (i < regionalOffices.length) {
        // display corresponding entries from parallel arrays
        form.manager.value = regionalManagers[i]
        form.quota.value = regOfficeQuotas[i]
    } else {  // loop went all the way with no matches
        // empty any previous values
        form.manager.value = ""
        form.quota.value = ""
        // advise user
        alert("No match found for " + inputText + ".")
    }
}
```

Continued

Listing 37-4: *(continued)*

```
</SCRIPT>
</HEAD>

<BODY>
<H1>Parallel Array Lookup II</H1>
<HR>
<FORM NAME="officeData">
<P>
Enter a regional office:
<INPUT TYPE="text" NAME="officeInp" SIZE=35>
<INPUT TYPE="button" VALUE="Search" onClick="getData(this.form)">
</P><P>
The manager is:
<INPUT TYPE="text" NAME="manager" SIZE=35>
<BR>
The office quota is:
<INPUT TYPE="text" NAME="quota" SIZE=8>
</P>
</FORM>
</BODY>
</HTML>
```

Multidimensional Arrays

An alternate to parallel arrays is the simulation of a multidimensional array. While it's true that JavaScript arrays are one-dimensional, you can create a one-dimensional array of other arrays or objects. A logical approach is to make an array of custom objects, because the objects easily allow for naming of object properties, making references to multidimensional array data more readable (custom objects are discussed at length in Chapter 41).

Using the same data from the examples of parallel arrays, the following statements define an object constructor for each "data record." A new object is then assigned to each of four entries in the main array.

```
// custom object constructor
function officeRecord(city, manager, quota) {
    this.city = city
    this.manager = manager
    this.quota = quota
}

// create new main array
var regionalOffices = new Array()
```

```
// stuff main array entries with objects
regionalOffices[0] = new officeRecord("New York", "Shirley Smith", 300000)
regionalOffices[1] = new officeRecord("Chicago", "Todd Gaston", 250000)
regionalOffices[2] = new officeRecord("Houston", "Leslie Jones", 350000)
regionalOffices[3] = new officeRecord("Portland", "Harold Zoot", 225000)
```

The object constructor function (officeRecord()) assigns incoming parameter values to properties of the object. Therefore, to access one of the data points in the array, you use both array notations to get to the desired entry in the array and the name of the property for that entry's object:

```
var eastOfficeManager = regionalOffices[0].manager
```

You can also assign string index values for this kind of array, as in

```
regionalOffices["east"] = new officeRecord("New York", "Shirley Smith", 300000)
```

and access the data via the same index:

```
var eastOfficeManager = regionalOffices["east"].manager
```

But if you're more comfortable with the traditional multidimensional array (from your experience in other programming languages), you can also implement the above as an array of arrays with less code:

```
// create new main array
var regionalOffices = new Array()
// stuff main array entries with arrays
regionalOffices[0] = new Array("New York", "Shirley Smith", 300000)
regionalOffices[1] = new Array("Chicago", "Todd Gaston", 250000)
regionalOffices[2] = new Array("Houston", "Leslie Jones", 350000)
regionalOffices[3] = new Array("Portland", "Harold Zoot", 225000)
```

or, for the extreme of unreadable brevity with literal notation:

```
// create new main array
var regionalOffices = [ ["New York", "Shirley Smith", 300000],
                        ["Chicago", "Todd Gaston", 250000],
                        ["Houston", "Leslie Jones", 350000],
                        ["Portland", "Harold Zoot", 225000] ]
```

Accessing a single data point of an array of arrays requires a double array reference. For example, retrieving the manager's name for the Houston office requires the following syntax:

```
var HoustonMgr = regionalOffices[2][1]
```

The first index in brackets is for the outermost array (regionalOffices); the second index in brackets points to the item of the array returned by regionalOffices[2].

Array Object Properties

constructor

See `string.constructor` (Chapter 34).

length

Value: Integer   Read/Write

	NN2	NN3	NN4	NN6	IE3/J1	IE3/J2	IE4	IE5	IE5.5
Compatibility		✓	✓	✓		✓	✓	✓	✓

A true array object's `length` property reflects the number of entries in the array. An entry can be any kind of JavaScript value, including `null`. If an entry is in the 10th cell and the rest are `null`, the length of that array is `10`. Note that because array index values are zero-based, the index of the last cell of an array is one less than the length. This characteristic makes it convenient to use the property as an automatic counter to append a new item to an array:

```
myArray[myArray.length] = valueOfAppendedItem
```

Thus, a generic function does not have to know which specific index value to apply to an additional item in the array.

prototype

Value: Variable or Function   Read/Write

	NN2	NN3	NN4	NN6	IE3/J1	IE3/J2	IE4	IE5	IE5.5
Compatibility		✓	✓	✓		✓	✓	✓	✓

Inside JavaScript, an array object has its dictionary definition of methods and `length` property—items that all array objects have in common. The `prototype` property enables your scripts to ascribe additional properties or methods that apply to all the arrays you create in the currently loaded documents. You can override this prototype, however, for any individual objects as you want.

To demonstrate how the prototype property works, Listing 37-5 creates a proto-type property for all array objects generated from the static Array object. As the script generates new arrays (instances of the Array object, just as a date object is an instance of the Date object), the property automatically becomes a part of those arrays. In one array, c, you override the value of the prototype sponsor property. By changing the value for that one object, you don't alter the value of the prototype for the Array object. Therefore, another array created afterward, d, still gets the original sponsor property value.

Listing 37-5: **Adding a prototype Property**

```
<HTML>
<HEAD>
<TITLE>Array prototypes</TITLE>
<SCRIPT LANGUAGE="JavaScript1.1">
// add prototype to all Array objects
Array.prototype.sponsor = "DG"
a = new Array(5)
b = new Array(5)
c = new Array(5)
// override prototype property for one 'instance'
c.sponsor = "JS"
// this one picks up the original prototype
d = new Array(5)
</SCRIPT>
<BODY><H2>
<SCRIPT LANGUAGE="JavaScript">
document.write("Array a is brought to you by: " + a.sponsor + "<P>")
document.write("Array b is brought to you by: " + b.sponsor + "<P>")
document.write("Array c is brought to you by: " + c.sponsor + "<P>")
document.write("Array d is brought to you by: " + d.sponsor + "<P>")
</SCRIPT>
</H2>
</BODY>
</HTML>
```

You can assign properties and functions to a prototype. To assign a function, define the function as you normally would in JavaScript. Then assign the function to the prototype by name:

```
function newFunc(param1) {
    // statements
}
Array.prototype.newMethod = newFunc  // omit parentheses in this reference
```

When you need to call upon that function (which has essentially become a new temporary method for the `Array` object), invoke it as you would any object method. Therefore, if an array named `CDCollection` has been created and a proto-type method `showCoverImage()` has been attached to the array, the call to invoke the method for a tenth listing in the array is

```
CDCollection.showCoverImage(9)
```

where the parameter of the function uses the index value to perhaps retrieve an image whose URL is a property of an object assigned to the 10th item of the array.

Array Object Methods

After you have information stored in an array, JavaScript provides several methods to help you manage that data. These methods, all of which belong to array objects you create, have evolved over time, so observe carefully which browser versions a desired method works with.

array.concat(*array2*)

Returns: array Object.

	NN2	NN3	NN4	NN6	IE3/J1	IE3/J2	IE4	IE5	IE5.5
Compatibility			✓	✓			✓	✓	✓

The *array*.concat() method allows you to join two array objects into a new, third array object. The action of concatenating the arrays does not alter the contents or behavior of the two original arrays. To join the arrays, you refer to the first array object to the left of the period before the method; a reference to the second array is the parameter to the method. For example:

```
var array1 = new Array(1,2,3)
var array2 = new Array("a","b","c")
var array3 = array1.concat(array2)
    // result: array with values 1,2,3,"a","b","c"
```

If an array element is a string or number value (not a string or number object), the values are copied from the original arrays into the new one. All connection with the original arrays ceases for those items. But if an original array element is a reference to an object of any kind, JavaScript copies a reference from the original array's entry into the new array. So if you make a change to either array's entry, the change occurs to the object, and both array entries reflect the change to the object.

Example (with Listing 37-6) on the CD-ROM

Related Items: `array.join()` method.

array.join(*separatorString*)

Returns: String of entries from the array delimited by the *separatorString* value.

	NN2	NN3	NN4	NN6	IE3/J1	IE3/J2	IE4	IE5	IE5.5
Compatibility	✓	✓	✓		✓	✓	✓	✓

You cannot view data in an array when it's in that form. Nor can you put an array into a form element for transmittal to a server CGI program. To make the transition from discrete array elements to string, the `array.join()` method handles what would otherwise be a nasty string manipulation exercise.

The sole parameter for this method is a string of one or more characters that you want to act as a delimiter between entries. For example, if you want commas between array items in their text version, the statement is

```
var arrayText = myArray.join(",")
```

Invoking this method does not change the original array in any way. Therefore, you need to assign the results of this method to another variable or a value property of a form element.

Example (with Figure 37-1 and Listing 37-7) on the CD-ROM

Related Items: `string.split()` method.

array.pop()
array.push(*valueOrObject*)
array.shift()
array.unshift(*valueOrObject*)

Returns: One array entry value.

	NN2	NN3	NN4	NN6	IE3/J1	IE3/J2	IE4	IE5	IE5.5
Compatibility			✓	✓					✓

The notion of a *stack* is well known to experienced programmers, especially those who know about the inner workings of assembly language at the CPU level. Even if you've never programmed a stack before, you have encountered the concept in real life many times. The classic analogy is the spring-loaded pile of cafeteria trays. If the pile were created one tray at a time, each tray would be pushed into the stack of trays. When a customer comes along, the topmost tray (the last one to be pushed onto the stack) gets popped off. The last one to be put on the stack is the first one to be taken off.

JavaScript in NN4+ and IE5.5 lets you turn an array into one of these spring-loaded stacks. But instead of placing trays on the pile, you can place any kind of data at either end of the stack, depending on which method you use to do the stacking. Similarly, you can extract an item from either end.

Perhaps the most familiar terminology for this is *push* and *pop*. When you push() a value onto an array, the value is appended as the last entry in the array. When you issue the *array*.pop() method, the last item in the array is removed from the stack and is returned, and the array shrinks in length by one. In the following sequence of statements, watch what happens to the value of the array used as a stack:

```
var source = new Array("Homer","Marge","Bart","Lisa","Maggie")
var stack = new Array()
    // stack = <empty>
stack.push(source[0])
    // stack = "Homer"
stack.push(source[2])
    // stack = "Homer","Bart"
var Simpson1 = stack.pop()
    // stack = "Homer" ; Simpson1 = "Bart"
var Simpson2 = stack.pop()
    // stack = <empty> ; Simpson2 = "Homer"
```

While push() and pop() work at the end of an array, another pair of methods works at the front. Their names are not as picturesque as push() and pop(). To insert a value at the front of an array, use the *array*.unshift() method; to grab the first element and remove it from the array, use *array*.shift(). Of course, you are not required to use these methods in matching pairs. If you push() a series of values onto the back end of an array, you can shift() them off from the front end without complaint. It all depends on how you need to process the data.

Related Items: array.concat(), array.slice() method.

array.reverse()

Returns: Array of entries in the opposite order of the original.

	NN2	NN3	NN4	NN6	IE3/J1	IE3/J2	IE4	IE5	IE5.5
Compatibility		✓	✓	✓		✓	✓	✓	✓

Occasionally, you may find it more convenient to work with an array of data in reverse order. Although you can concoct repeat loops to count backward through index values, a CGI program on the server may prefer the data in a sequence opposite to the way it was most convenient for you to script it.

You can have JavaScript switch the contents of an array for you: Whatever element was last in the array becomes the 0 index item in the array. Bear in mind that if you do this, you're restructuring the original array, not copying it, even though the method also returns a copy of the reversed version. A reload of the document restores the order as written in the HTML document.

On the CD-ROM   Example (with Listing 37-8) on the CD-ROM

Related Items: array.sort() method.

array.slice(*startIndex* [, *endIndex*])

Returns: Array.

	NN2	NN3	NN4	NN6	IE3/J1	IE3/J2	IE4	IE5	IE5.5
Compatibility			✓	✓			✓	✓	✓

Behaving as its like-named string method, *array*.slice() lets you extract a contiguous series of items from an array. The extracted segment becomes an entirely new array object. Values and objects from the original array have the same kind of behavior as arrays created with the *array*.concat() method.

One parameter is required—the starting index point for the extraction. If you don't specify a second parameter, the extraction goes all the way to the end of the array; otherwise the extraction goes to, *but does not include,* the index value supplied as the second parameter. For example, extracting Earth's neighbors from an array of planet names looks as the following.

```
var solarSys = new Array("Mercury","Venus","Earth","Mars","Jupiter","Saturn",
"Uranus","Neptune","Pluto")
var nearby = solarSys.slice(1,4)
    // result: new array of "Venus", "Earth", "Mars"
```

Related Items: array.splice(), string.slice() methods.

array.sort([*compareFunction*])

Returns: Array of entries in the order as determined by the *compareFunction* algorithm.

	NN2	NN3	NN4	NN6	IE3/J1	IE3/J2	IE4	IE5	IE5.5
Compatibility		✓	✓	✓		✓	✓	✓	✓

JavaScript array sorting is both powerful and a bit complex to script if you haven't had experience with this kind of sorting methodology. The purpose, obviously, is to let your scripts sort entries of an array by almost any kind of criterion that you can associate with an entry. For entries consisting of strings, the criterion may be their alphabetical order or their length; for numeric entries, the criterion may be their numerical order.

Look first at the kind of sorting you can do with the *array*.sort() method by itself (for example, without calling a comparison function). When no parameter is specified, JavaScript takes a snapshot of the contents of the array and converts items to strings. From there, it performs a string sort of the values. ASCII values of characters govern the sort, which means that numbers are sorted by their string values, not their numeric values. This fact has strong implications if your array consists of numeric data: The value 201 sorts before 88, because the sorting mechanism compares the first characters of the strings ("2" versus "8") to determine the sort order. For simple alphabetical sorting of string values in arrays, the plain `array`.sort() method does the trick.

Fortunately, additional intelligence is available that you can add to array sorting. The key tactic is to define a function that helps the sort() method compare items in the array. A comparison function is passed two values from the array (what you don't see is that the `array`.sort() method rapidly sends numerous pairs of values from the array to help it sort through all entries). The comparison function lets the sort() method know which of the two items comes before the other, based on the value the function returns. Assuming that the function compares two values, a and b, the returned value reveals information to the sort() method, as shown in Table 37-1.

Table 37-1   Comparison Function Return Values

Return Value Range	Meaning
< 0	Value b should sort later than a
0	The order of a and b should not change
> 0	Value a should sort later than b

Consider the following example:

```
myArray = new Array(12, 5, 200, 80)
function compare(a,b) {
    return a - b
}
myArray.sort(compare)
```

The array has four numeric values in it. To sort the items in numerical order, you define a comparison function (arbitrarily named compare()), which is called from the sort() method. Note that unlike invoking other functions, the parameter of the sort() method uses a reference to the function, which lacks parentheses.

When the compare() function is called, JavaScript automatically sends two parameters to the function in rapid succession until each element has been compared with the others. Every time compare() is called, JavaScript assigns two of the array's values to the parameter variables (a and b). In the preceding example, the returned value is the difference between a and b. If a is larger than b, then a positive value goes back to the sort() method, telling it to sort a later than b (that is, position a at a higher value index position than b). Therefore, b may end up at myArray[0], whereas a ends up at a higher index-valued location. On the other hand, if a is smaller than b, then the returned negative value tells sort() to put a in a lower index value spot than b.

Evaluations within the comparison function can go to great lengths, as long as some data connected with array values can be compared. For example, instead of numerical comparisons, as just shown, you can perform string comparisons. The following function sorts alphabetically by the last character of each array string entry:

```
function compare(a,b) {
    // last character of array strings
    var aComp = a.charAt(a.length - 1)
    var bComp = b.charAt(b.length - 1)
    if (aComp < bComp) {return -1}
    if (aComp > bComp) {return 1}
    return 0
}
```

First, this function extracts the final character from each of the two values passed to it. Then, because strings cannot be added or subtracted like numbers, you compare the ASCII values of the two characters, returning the corresponding values to the sort() method to let it know how to treat the two values being checked at that instant.

When an array's entries happen to be objects, you can even sort by properties of those objects. If you bear in mind that the a and b parameters of the sort function are references to two array entries, then by extension you can refer to properties of those objects. For example, if an array contains objects whose properties define information about employees, one of the properties of those objects can be the employee's age as a string. You can then sort the array based on the numeric equivalent of age property of the objects by way of the following comparison function:

```
function compare(a,b) {
    return parseInt(a.age) - parseInt(b.age)
}
```

Array sorting, unlike sorting routines you may find in other scripting languages, is not a stable sort. Not being stable means that succeeding sort routines on the same array are not cumulative. Also, remember that sorting changes the sort order of the original array. If you don't want the original array harmed, make a copy of it before sorting or reload the document to restore an array to its original order.

Should an array element be null, the method sorts such elements at the end of the sorted array starting with Navigator 4 (instead of leaving them in their original places as in Navigator 3).

Note Unfortunately, this powerful method does not work in the Macintosh version of Navigator 3. Starting with Navigator 4, all platforms have the feature.

JavaScript array sorting is extremely powerful stuff. Array sorting is one reason why it's not uncommon to take the time during the loading of a page containing an IE XML data island to make a JavaScript copy of the data as an array of objects (see

Chapter 57). Converting the XML to JavaScript arrays makes the job of sorting the data much easier and faster than cobbling together your own sorting routines on the XML elements.

Example (with Listing 37-9) on the CD-ROM

Related Items: `array.reverse()` method.

Note

As I show you in Chapter 38, many regular expression object methods generate arrays as their result (for example, an array of matching values in a string). These special arrays have a custom set of named properties that assist your script in analyzing the findings of the method. Beyond that, these regular expression result arrays behave like all others.

array.splice(*startIndex* , *deleteCount*[, *item1*[, *item2*[,...*itemN*]]])

Returns: Array.

	NN2	NN3	NN4	NN6	IE3/J1	IE3/J2	IE4	IE5	IE5.5
Compatibility			✓	✓					✓

If you need to remove items from the middle of an array, the *array*.splice() method (not implemented in IE5/Mac) simplifies a task that would otherwise require assembling a new array from selected items of the original array. The first of two required parameters is a zero-based index integer that points to the first item to be removed from the current array. The second parameter is another integer that indicates how many sequential items are to be removed from the array. Removing array items affects the length of the array, and those items that are removed are returned by the splice() method as their own array.

You can also use the splice() method to replace array items. Optional parameters beginning with the third let you provide data elements that are to be inserted into the array in place of the items being removed. Each added item can be any JavaScript data type, and the number of new items does not have to be equal to the number of items removed. In fact, by specifying a second parameter of zero, you can use splice() to insert one or more items into any position of the array.

Example on the CD-ROM

Related Items: `array.slice()` method.

array.toLocaleString()

Returns: String.

	NN2	NN3	NN4	NN6	IE3/J1	IE3/J2	IE4	IE5	IE5.5
Compatibility				✓					✓

array.toString()

Returns: String.

	NN2	NN3	NN4	NN6	IE3/J1	IE3/J2	IE4	IE5	IE5.5
Compatibility		✓	✓	✓		✓	✓	✓	✓

The `array.toLocaleString()` and the older, more compatible `array.toString()` are methods to retrieve the contents of an array in string form. Browsers use the `toString()` method on their own whenever you attempt to display an array in text boxes, in which case the array items are comma-delimited.

The precise string conversion of the `toLocaleString()` is left up to the specific browser implementation. That IE5.5 and NN6 differ in some details is not surprising, even in the U.S. English versions of operating systems and browsers. For example, if the array contains integer values, IE5.5's `toLocaleString()` method returns the numbers comma-and-space-delimited, formatted with two digits to the right of the decimal (as if dollars and cents). NN6, on the other hand, returns just the integers, but these are also comma-and-space-delimited.

If you need to convert an array to a string for purposes of passing array data to other venues (for example, as data in a hidden text box submitted to a server or as search string data conveyed to another page), use the `array.join()` method instead. `Array.join()` gives you more reliable and flexible control over the item delimiters, and you are assured of the same results regardless of locale.

Related Items: `array.join()` method.

✦   ✦   ✦

The Regular Expression and RegExp Objects— Summary

On the CD-ROM

The full version of Chapter 38 is on the CD-ROM.

Web programmers who have worked in Perl (and other Web application programming languages) know the power of regular expressions for processing incoming data and formatting data for readability in an HTML page or for accurate storage in a server database. Any task that requires extensive search and replacement of text can greatly benefit from the flexibility and conciseness of regular expressions. Navigator 4 and Internet Explorer 4 (more fully fleshed out in IE5.5) bring that power to JavaScript.

Most of the benefit of JavaScript regular expressions accrues to those who script their CGI programs on servers that support a JavaScript version that contains regular expressions. But that's not to exclude the client-side from application of this "language within a language." If your scripts perform client-side data validations or any other extensive text entry parsing, then consider using regular expressions, rather than cobbling together comparatively complex JavaScript functions to perform the same tasks.

In several chapters earlier in this book, I describe an expression as any sequence of identifiers, keywords, and/or operators that evaluates to some value. A regular expression follows that description, but has much more power behind it. In essence, a regular expression uses a sequence of characters and symbols to define a pattern of text. Such a pattern is used to locate a chunk of text in a string by matching up the pattern against the characters in the string.

As you learn in this chapter, regular expression syntax is almost a language unto itself, replete with shortcut symbols and other characters that are far from the plain-language of JavaScript. If you are new to regular expressions, the obscurity of the syntax may be daunting; but if you have used regular expressions in the past, you will be right at home with the implementation in the JavaScript core language.

✦   ✦   ✦

Control Structures and Exception Handling

◆ ◆ ◆ ◆

CHAPTER 39

In This Chapter

Branching script
execution down
multiple paths

Looping through
ordered collections of
data

Applying exception
handling techniques

◆ ◆ ◆ ◆

Y ou get up in the morning, go about your day's business, and then turn out the lights at night. That's not much different from what a program does from the time it starts to the time it ends. But along the way, both you and a program take lots of tiny steps, not all of which advance the "processing" in a straight line. At times, you have to control what's going on by making a decision or repeating tasks until the whole job is finished. Control structures are the facilities that make these tasks possible in JavaScript.

JavaScript control structures follow along the same lines of many programming languages, particularly with additions made in Navigator 4 and Internet Explorer 4. Basic decision-making and looping constructions satisfy the needs of just about all programming tasks.

Another vital program control mechanism — error (or exception) handling — is formally addressed in Edition 3 of the ECMA-262 language standard. The concept of exception handling is new to the JavaScript version that comes in IE5.5 and NN6, but it is well known to programmers in many other environments. Adopting exception handling techniques in your code can greatly enhance recovery from processing errors caused by errant user input or network glitches.

If and If. . .Else Decisions

	NN2	NN3	NN4	NN6	IE3/J1	IE3/J2	IE4	IE5	IE5.5
Compatibility	✓	✓	✓	✓	✓	✓	✓	✓	✓

JavaScript programs frequently have to make decisions based on the current values of variables or object properties. Such decisions can have only two possible outcomes at a time. The factor that determines the path that the program takes at these decision points is the truth of some statement. For example, when you enter a room of your home at night, the statement under test is something such as "It is too dark to see without a light." If that statement is true, you switch on the light; if that statement is false, you carry on with your primary task.

Simple decisions

JavaScript syntax for this kind of simple decision always begins with the keyword if, followed by the condition to test, and then the statements that execute if the condition yields a true result. JavaScript uses no "then" keyword (as some other languages do); the keyword is implied by the way parentheses and braces surround the various components of this construction. The formal syntax is

```
if (condition) {
    statementsIfTrue
}
```

This construction means that if the condition is true, program execution takes a detour to execute statements inside the braces. No matter what happens, the program continues executing statements beyond the closing brace (}). If household navigation were part of the scripting language, the code would look as this:

```
if (tooDark == true) {
    feel for light switch
    turn on light switch
}
```

If you're not used to C/C++, the double equals sign may have caught your eye. You learn more about this type of operator in the next chapter, but for now, know that this operator compares the equality of items on either side of it. In other words, the condition statement of an if construction must always yield a Boolean (true or false) value. Some object properties, you may recall, are Booleans, so you can stick a reference to that property into the condition statement by itself. Otherwise, the condition statement consists of two values separated by a comparison operator, such as == (equals) or != (does not equal).

Next, look at some real JavaScript. The following function receives a form object containing a text object called entry:

```
function notTooHigh(form) {
    if (parseInt(form.entry.value) > 100) {
        alert("Sorry, the value you entered is too high. Try again.")
        return false
    }
    return true
}
```

The condition (in parentheses) tests the contents of the field against a hard-wired value of 100. If the entered value is larger than that, the function alerts you and returns a false value to the calling statement elsewhere in the script. But if the value is less than 100, all intervening code is skipped and the function returns true.

About (*condition*) expressions

A lot of condition testing for control structures compares a value against some very specific condition, such as a string's being empty or a value's being null. You can use a couple of shortcuts to take care of many circumstances. Table 39-1 details the values that evaluate to a true or false (or equivalent) to satisfy a control structure's *condition* expression.

Table 39-1	Condition Value Equivalents
True	*False*
Nonempty string	Empty string
Nonzero number	0
Nonnull value	Null
Object exists	Object doesn't exist
Property is defined	Undefined property

Instead of having to spell out an equivalency expression for a condition involving these kinds of values, you can simply supply the value to be tested. For example, if a variable named myVal may reach an if construction with a value of null, an empty string, or a string value for further processing, you can use the following shortcut:

```
if (myVal) {
    // do processing on myVal
}
```

All null or empty string conditions evaluate to `false`, so that only the cases of `myVal`'s being a processable value get inside the `if` construction. This mechanism is the same that you have seen elsewhere in this book to employ object detection for browser branching. For example, the code nested inside the following code segment executes only if the `document` object has an `images` array property:

```
if (document.images) {
    // do processing on image objects
}
```

Complex decisions

The simple type of `if` construction described earlier is fine when the decision is to take a small detour before returning to the main path. But not all decisions — in programming or in life — are like that. To present two alternate paths in a JavaScript decision, you can add a component to the construction. The syntax is

```
if (condition) {
    statementsIfTrue
} else {
    statementsIfFalse
}
```

By appending the `else` keyword, you give the `if` construction a path to follow in case the condition evaluates to false. The *statementsIfTrue* and *statementsIfFalse* do not have to be balanced in any way: One statement can be one line of code, the other one hundred lines. But when either one of those branches completes, execution continues after the last closing brace. To demonstrate how this construction can come in handy, the following example is a script fragment that assigns the number of days in February based on whether or not the year is a leap year (using modulo arithmetic, explained in Chapter 40, to determine if the year is evenly divisible by four, and setting aside all other leap year calculation details for the moment):

```
var howMany = 0
var theYear = 2002
if (theYear % 4 == 0) {
    howMany = 29
} else {
    howMany = 28
}
```

Here is a case where execution has to follow only one of two possible paths to assign the number of days to the `howMany` variable. Had I not used the `else` portion, as in

```
var howMany = 0
var theYear = 2002
if (theYear % 4 == 0) {
    howMany = 29
}
howMany = 28
```

then the variable would always be set to 28, occasionally after momentarily being set to 29. The `else` construction is essential in this case.

Nesting if. . .else statements

Designing a complex decision process requires painstaking attention to the logic of the decisions your script must process and the statements that must execute for any given set of conditions. The need for many complex constructions disappears with the advent of `switch` construction in NN4+ and IE4+ (described later in this chapter), but there may still be times when you must fashion complex decision behavior out of a series of nested `if. . .else` constructions. Without a JavaScript-aware text editor to help keep everything properly indented and properly terminated (with closing braces), you have to monitor the authoring process very carefully. Moreover, the error messages that JavaScript provides when a mistake occurs (see Chapter 45) may not point directly to the problem line but only to the region of difficulty.

Note Another important point to remember about nesting `if. . .else` statements in JavaScript before Version 1.2 is that the language does not provide a mechanism for script execution to break out of a nested part of the construction. For that reason, you have to construct complex assemblies with extreme care to make sure only the desired statement executes for each set of conditions. Extensive testing, of course, is also required (see Chapter 45).

To demonstrate a deeply nested set of `if. . .else` constructions, Listing 39-1 presents a simple user interface to a complex problem. A single text object asks the user to enter one of three letters—A, B, or C. The script behind that field processes a different message for each of the following conditions:

✦ The user enters no value.

✦ The user enters A.

✦ The user enters B.

✦ The user enters C.

✦ The user enters something entirely different.

Listing 39-1: **Deeply Nested if. . .else Constructions**

```
<HTML>
<HEAD>
<SCRIPT LANGUAGE="JavaScript">
function testLetter(form){
    inpVal = form.entry.value  // assign to shorter variable name
    if (inpVal != "") {  // if entry is not empty then dive in...
        if (inpVal == "A") {  // Is it an "A"?
            alert("Thanks for the A.")
        } else if (inpVal == "B") {  // No.  Is it a "B"?
            alert("Thanks for the B.")
        } else if (inpVal == "C") {  // No.  Is it a "C"?
            alert("Thanks for the C.")
        } else {          // Nope.  None of the above
            alert("Sorry, wrong letter or case.")
        }
    } else {   // value was empty, so skipped all other stuff above
        alert("You did not enter anything.")
    }
}
</SCRIPT>
</HEAD>
<BODY>
<FORM>
Please enter A, B, or C:
<INPUT TYPE="text" NAME="entry" onChange="testLetter(this.form)">
</FORM>
</BODY>
</HTML>
```

Each condition executes only the statements that apply to that particular condition, even if it takes several queries to find out what the entry is. You do not need to break out of the nested construction because when a true response is found, the relevant statement executes, and no other statements occur in the execution path to run.

Even if you understand how to construct a hair-raising nested construction, such as the one in Listing 39-1, the trickiest part is making sure that each left brace has a corresponding right brace. My technique for ensuring this pairing is to enter the right brace immediately after I type the left brace. I typically type the left brace, press Enter twice (once to open a free line for the next statement, once for the line that is to receive the right brace); tab, if necessary, to the same indentation as the line containing the left brace; and then type the right brace. Later, if I have to insert something indented, I just push down the right braces that I entered earlier. If I keep up this methodology throughout the process, the right braces appear at the desired indentation after I'm finished, even if the braces end up being dozens of lines below their original spot.

What's with the Formatting?

Indentation of the `if` construction and the further indentation of the statements executed on a true condition are not required by JavaScript. What you see here, however, is a convention that most JavaScript scripters follow. As you write the code in your text editor, you can use the Tab key to make each indentation level. The browser ignores these tab characters when loading the HTML documents containing your scripts.

Conditional Expressions

	NN2	NN3	NN4	NN6	IE3/J1	IE3/J2	IE4	IE5	IE5.5
Compatibility	✓	✓	✓	✓	✓	✓	✓	✓	✓

While I'm showing you decision-making constructions in JavaScript, now is a good time to introduce a special type of expression that you can use in place of an `if. . .else` control structure for a common type of decision—the instance where you want to assign one of two values to a variable, depending on the outcome of some condition. The formal definition for the conditional expression is as follows:

```
variable = (condition) ? val1 : val2
```

This expression means that if the Boolean result of the `condition` statement is true, JavaScript assigns `val1` to the variable; otherwise, it assigns `val2` to the variable. Like other instances of condition expressions, this one must also be written inside parentheses. The question mark is key here, as is the colon separating the two possible values.

A conditional expression, though not particularly intuitive or easy to read inside code, is very compact. Compare an `if. . .else` version of an assignment decision that follows

```
var collectorStatus
if (CDCount > 500) {
    collectorStatus = "fanatic"
} else {
    collectorStatus = "normal"
}
```

with the conditional expression version:

```
var collectorStatus = (CDCount > 500) ? "fanatic" : "normal"
```

The latter saves a lot of code lines (although the internal processing is the same as that of an if. . .else construction). Of course, if your decision path contains more statements than just one setting the value of a variable, the if. . .else or switch construction is preferable. This shortcut, however, is a handy one to remember if you need to perform very binary actions, such as setting a true-or-false flag in a script.

Repeat (for) Loops

	NN2	NN3	NN4	NN6	IE3/J1	IE3/J2	IE4	IE5	IE5.5
Compatibility	✓	✓	✓	✓	✓	✓	✓	✓	✓

As you have seen in numerous examples throughout other chapters, the capability to cycle through every entry in an array or through every item of a form element is vital to many JavaScript scripts. Perhaps the most typical operation is inspecting a property of many similar items in search of a specific value, such as to determine which radio button in a group is selected. One JavaScript structure that allows for these repetitious excursions is the for loop, so named after the keyword that begins the structure. Two other structures, called the while loop and do-while loop, are covered in following sections.

The JavaScript for loop lets a script repeat a series of statements any number of times and includes an optional loop counter that can be used in the execution of the statements. The following is the formal syntax definition:

```
for ( [initial expression]; [condition]; [update expression]) {
    statements
}
```

The three statements inside the parentheses (parameters to the for statement) play a key role in the way a for loop executes.

An initial expression in a for loop is executed one time, the first time the for loop begins to run. The most common application of the initial expression is to assign a name and starting value to a loop counter variable. Thus, seeing a var statement that both declares a variable name and assigns an initial value (generally 0 or 1) to it is not uncommon. An example is

```
var i = 0
```

You can use any variable name, but conventional usage calls for the letter i, which is short for *index*. If you prefer the word counter or another word that reminds you of what the variable represents, that's fine, too. In any case, the important point to remember about this statement is that it executes once at the outset of the for loop.

The second statement is a *condition*, precisely like the condition statement you saw in if constructions earlier in this chapter. When a loop-counting variable is established in the initial expression, the condition statement usually defines how high the loop counter should go before the looping stops. Therefore, the most common statement here is one that compares the loop counter variable against some fixed value — is the loop counter less than the maximum allowed value? If the condition is false at the start, the body of the loop is not executed. But if the loop does execute, then every time execution comes back around to the top of the loop, JavaScript reevaluates the condition to determine the current result of the expression. If the loop counter increases with each loop, eventually the counter value goes beyond the value in the condition statement, causing the condition statement to yield a Boolean value of false. The instant that happens, execution drops out of the for loop entirely.

The final statement, the *update expression*, is executed at the end of each loop execution — after all statements nested inside the for construction have run. Again, the loop counter variable can be a factor here. If you want the counter value to increase by one the next time through the loop (called incrementing the value), you can use the JavaScript operator that makes that happen: the ++ operator appended to the variable name. That task is the reason for the appearance of all those i++ symbols in the for loops that you've seen already in this book. You're not limited to incrementing by one. You can increment by any multiplier you want or even drive a loop counter backward by decrementing the value (i).

Now, take this knowledge and beef up the formal syntax definition with one that takes into account a typical loop-counting variable, i, and the common ways to use it:

```
// incrementing loop counter
for (var i = minValue; i <= maxValue; i++) {
    statements
}
// decrementing loop counter
for (var i = maxValue; i >= minValue; i--) {
    statements
}
```

In the top format, the variable, i, is initialized at the outset to a value equal to that of minValue. Variable i is immediately compared against maxValue. If i is less than or equal to maxValue, processing continues into the body of the loop. At the end of the loop, the update expression executes. In the top example, the value of i is incremented by 1. Therefore, if i is initialized as 0, then the first time through the loop, the i variable maintains that 0 value during the first execution of statements in the loop. The next time around, the variable has the value of 1.

As you may have noticed in the formal syntax definition, each of the parameters to the for statement is optional. For example, the statements that execute inside the loop may control the value of the loop counter based on data that gets manipulated in the process. Therefore, the update statement would probably interfere with the intended running of the loop. But I suggest that you use all three parameters until such time as you feel absolutely comfortable with their roles in the for loop. If you omit the condition statement, for instance, and you don't program a way for the loop to exit on its own, your script may end up in an infinite loop—which does your users no good.

Putting the loop counter to work

Despite its diminutive appearance, the i loop counter (or whatever name you want to give it) can be a powerful tool for working with data inside a repeat loop. For example, examine a version of the classic JavaScript function that creates a Navigator 2-compatible array while initializing entries to a value of 0:

```
// initialize array with n entries
function MakeArray(n) {
    this.length = n
    for (var i = 1; i <= n; i++) {
        this[i] = 0
    }
    return this
}
```

The loop counter, i, is initialized to a value of 1, because you want to create an array of empty entries (with value 0) starting with the one whose index value is 1 (the zeroth entry is assigned to the length property) in the previous line. In the condition statement, the loop continues to execute as long as the value of the counter is less than or equal to the number of entries being created (n). After each loop, the counter increments by 1. In the nested statement that executes within the loop, you use the value of the i variable to substitute for the index value of the assignment statement:

```
this[i] = 0
```

The first time the loop executes, the value expression evaluates to

```
this[1] = 0
```

The next time, the expression evaluates to

```
this[2] = 0
```

and so on, until all entries are created and stuffed with 0.

Recall the HTML page in Listing 37-3, where a user chooses a regional office from a SELECT list (triggering a script to look up the manager's name and sales quota for that region). Because the regional office names are stored in an array, the page could be altered so that a script populates the SELECT element's options from the array. That way, if there is ever a change to the alignment of regional offices, there need be only one change to the array of offices, and the HTML doesn't have to be modified. As a reminder, here is the definition of the regional offices array, created while the page loads:

```
var regionalOffices = new Array("New York", "Chicago", "Houston", "Portland")
```

A script inside the HTML form can be used to dynamically generate the SELECT list as follows:

```
<SCRIPT LANGUAGE="JavaScript">
var elem = "" // start assembling next part of page and form
elem += "<P>Select a regional office: "
elem += "<SELECT NAME='offices' onChange='getData(this.form)'>"
// build options list from array office names
for (var i = 0; i < regionalOffices.length; i++) {
    elem += "<OPTION"    // OPTION tags
    if (i == 0) {        // pre-select first item in list
        elem += " SELECTED"
    }
    elem += ">" + regionalOffices[i]
}
elem += "</SELECT></P>" // close SELECT item tag
document.write(elem)     // write element to the page
</SCRIPT>
```

Notice one important point about the `condition` statement of the `for` loop: JavaScript extracts the `length` property from the array to be used as the loop counter boundary. From a code maintenance and stylistic point of view, this method is preferable to hard-wiring a value there. If the company added a new regional office, you would make the addition to the array "database," whereas everything else in the code would adjust automatically to those changes, including creating a longer pop-up menu in this case.

Notice, too, that the operator for the `condition` statement is less-than (<): The zero-based index values of arrays mean that the maximum index value we can use is one less than the actual count of items in the array. This is vital information, because the index counter variable (`i`) is used as the index to the `regionalOffices` array each time through the loop to read the string for each item's entry. You also use the counter to determine which is the first option, so that you can take a short detour (via the `if` construction) to add the `SELECTED` attribute to the first option's definition.

The utility of the loop counter in `for` loops often influences the way you design data structures, such as two-dimensional arrays (see Chapter 37) for use as databases. Always keep the loop-counter mechanism in the back of your mind when you begin writing JavaScript script that relies on collections of data that you embed in your documents.

Breaking out of a loop

Some loop constructions perform their job as soon as a certain condition is met, at which point they have no further need to continue looping through the rest of the values in the loop counter's range. A common scenario for this is the cycling of a loop through an entire array in search of a single entry that matches some criterion. That criterion test is set up as an `if` construction inside the loop. If that criterion is met, you break out of the loop and let the script continue with the more meaningful processing of succeeding statements in the main flow. To accomplish that exit from the loop, use the `break` statement. The following schematic shows how the `break` statement may appear in a `for` loop:

```
for (var i = 0; i < array.length; i++) {
    if (array[i].property == magicValue) {
        statements that act on entry array[i]
        break
    }
}
```

The `break` statement tells JavaScript to bail out of the nearest `for` loop (in case you have nested `for` loops). Script execution then picks up immediately after the closing brace of the `for` statement. The variable value of `i` remains whatever it was at the time of the break, so that you can use that variable later in the same script to access, say, that same array entry.

I use a construction similar to this in Chapter 24. There, the discussion of radio buttons demonstrates this construction, where, in Listing 24-8, you see a set of radio buttons whose `VALUE` attributes contain the full names of four members of the Three Stooges. A function uses a `for` loop to find out which button was selected and then uses that item's index value — after the for loop breaks out of the loop — to alert the user. Listing 39-2 (not on the CD-ROM) shows the relevant function.

Listing 39-2: **Breaking Out of a for Loop**

```
function fullName(form) {
    for (var i = 0; i < form.stooges.length; i++) {
        if (form.stooges[i].checked) {
            break
        }
    }
    alert("You chose " + form.stooges[i].value + ".")
}
```

In this case, breaking out of the for loop was for more than mere efficiency; the value of the loop counter (frozen at the break point) is used to summon a different property outside of the for loop. In NN4+ and IE4+, the break statement assumes additional powers in cooperation with the new label feature of control structures. This subject is covered later in this chapter.

Directing loop traffic with continue

One other possibility in a for loop is that you may want to skip execution of the nested statements for just one condition. In other words, as the loop goes merrily on its way round and round, executing statements for each value of the loop counter, one value of that loop counter may exist for which you don't want those statements to execute. To accomplish this task, the nested statements need to include an if construction to test for the presence of the value to skip. When that value is reached, the continue command tells JavaScript to immediately skip the rest of the body, execute the update statement, and loop back around to the top of the loop (also skipping the condition statement part of the for loop's parameters).

To illustrate this construction, you create an artificial example that skips over execution when the counter variable is the superstitious person's unlucky 13:

```
for (var i = 0; i <= 20; i++) {
    if (i == 13) {
        continue
    }
    statements
}
```

In this example, the *statements* part of the loop executes for all values of i except 13. The continue statement forces execution to jump to the i++ part of the loop structure, incrementing the value of i for the next time through the loop. In the case of nested for loops, a continue statement affects the for loop in whose immediate scope the if construction falls. The continue statement is enhanced in NN4+ and IE4+ in cooperation with the new label feature of control structures. This subject is covered later in this chapter.

The while Loop

	NN2	NN3	NN4	NN6	IE3/J1	IE3/J2	IE4	IE5	IE5.5
Compatibility	✓	✓	✓	✓	✓	✓	✓	✓	✓

The `for` loop is not the only kind of repeat loop you can construct in JavaScript. Another statement, called a `while` statement, sets up a loop in a slightly different format. Rather than providing a mechanism for modifying a loop counter, a `while` repeat loop assumes that your script statements will reach a condition that forcibly exits the repeat loop.

The basic syntax for a `while` loop is

```
while (condition) {
    statements
}
```

The *condition* expression is the same kind that you saw in `if` constructions and in the middle parameter of the `for` loop. You introduce this kind of loop if some condition exists in your code (evaluates to `true`) before reaching this loop. The loop then performs some action, which affects that condition repeatedly until that condition becomes `false`. At that point, the loop exits, and script execution continues with statements after the closing brace. If the statements inside the `while` loop do not affect the values being tested in *condition*, your script never exits, and it becomes stuck in an infinite loop.

Many loops can be rendered with either the `for` or `while` loops. In fact, Listing 39-3 (not on the CD-ROM) shows a `while` loop version of the `for` loop from Listing 39-2.

Listing 39-3: A while Loop Version of Listing 39-2

```
function fullName(form) {
    var i = 0
    while (!form.stooges[i].checked) {
        i++
    }
    alert("You chose " + form.stooges[i].value + ".")
}
```

One point you may notice is that if the condition of a `while` loop depends on the value of a loop counter, the scripter is responsible for initializing the counter prior to the `while` loop construction and managing its value within the `while` loop.

Should you need their powers, the `break` and `continue` control statements work inside `while` loops as they do in `for` loops. But because the two loop styles treat their loop counters and conditions differently, be extra careful (do lots of testing) when applying `break` and `continue` statements to both kinds of loops.

No hard-and-fast rules exist for which type of loop construction to use in a script. I generally use `while` loops only when the data or object I want to loop through is already a part of my script before the loop. In other words, by virtue of previous statements in the script, the values for any condition or loop counting (if needed) are already initialized. But if I need to cycle through an object's properties or an array's entries to extract some piece of data for use later in the script, I favor the `for` loop.

Another point of style, particularly with the `for` loop, is where a scripter should declare the `i` variable. Some programmers prefer to declare (or initialize if initial values are known) all variables in the opening statements of a script or function. That is why you tend to see a lot of `var` statements in those positions in scripts. If you have only one `for` loop in a function, for example, nothing is wrong with declaring and initializing the `i` loop counter in the initial expression part of the `for` loop (as demonstrated frequently in the previous sections). But if your function utilizes multiple `for` loops that reuse the `i` counter variable (that is, the loops run completely independently of one another), then you can declare the `i` variable once at the start of the function and simply assign a new initial value to `i` in each `for` construction.

The do-while Loop

	NN2	NN3	NN4	NN6	IE3/J1	IE3/J2	IE4	IE5	IE5.5
Compatibility			✓	✓			✓	✓	✓

JavaScript in NN4+ and IE4+ brings you one more looping construction, called the `do-while` loop. The formal syntax for this construction is as follows:

```
do {
    statements
} while (condition)
```

An important difference distinguishes the `do-while` loop from the `while` loop. In the `do-while` loop, the statements in the construction always execute at least one time before the condition can be tested; in a `while` loop, the statements may never execute if the condition tested at the outset evaluates to `false`.

Use a `do-while` loop when you know for certain that the looped statements are free to run at least one time. If the condition may not be met the first time, use the `while` loop. For many instances, the two constructions are interchangeable, although only the `while` loop is compatible with all scriptable browsers.

Looping through Properties (for-in)

	NN2	NN3	NN4	NN6	IE3/J1	IE3/J2	IE4	IE5	IE5.5
Compatibility	✓	✓	✓	✓	✓	✓	✓	✓	✓

JavaScript includes a variation of the for loop, called a for-in loop, which has special powers of extracting the names and values of any object property currently in the browser's memory. The syntax looks like this:

```
for (var in object) {
    statements
}
```

The object parameter is not the string name of an object but a reference to the object itself. JavaScript delivers an object reference if you provide the name of the object as an unquoted string, such as window or document. Using the var variable, you can create a script that extracts and displays the range of properties for any given object.

Listing 39-4 shows a page containing a utility function that you can insert into your HTML documents during the authoring and debugging stages of designing a JavaScript-enhanced page. In the example, the current window object is examined and its properties are presented in the page.

Listing 39-4: **Property Inspector Function**

```
<HTML>
<HEAD>
<SCRIPT LANGUAGE="JavaScript">
function showProps(obj,objName) {
    var result = ""
    for (var i in obj) {
        result += objName + "." + i + " = " + obj[i] + "<BR>"
    }
    return result
}
</SCRIPT>
</HEAD>
<BODY>
<B>Here are the properties of the current window:</B><P>
<SCRIPT LANGUAGE="JavaScript">
document.write(showProps(window, "window"))
</SCRIPT>
</BODY>
</HTML>
```

For debugging purposes, you can revise the function slightly to display the results in an alert dialog box. Replace the
 HTML tag with the \n carriage return character for a nicely formatted display in the alert dialog box. You can call this function from anywhere in your script, passing both the object reference and a string to it to help you identify the object after the results appear in an alert dialog box. If the showProps() function looks familiar to you, it is because it closely resembles the property inspector routines of The Evaluator (see Chapter 13). In Chapter 45, you can see how to embed functionality of The Evaluator into a page under construction so that you can view property values while debugging your scripts.

The with Statement

	NN2	NN3	NN4	NN6	IE3/J1	IE3/J2	IE4	IE5	IE5.5
Compatibility	✓	✓	✓	✓	✓	✓	✓	✓	✓

A with statement enables you to preface any number of statements by advising JavaScript on precisely which object your scripts will be talking about, so that you don't have to use full, formal addresses to access properties or invoke methods of the same object. The formal syntax definition of the with statement is as follows:

```
with (object) {
    statements
}
```

The object reference is a reference to any valid object currently in the browser's memory. An example of this appears in Chapter 35's discussion of the Math object. By embracing several Math-encrusted statements inside a with construction, your scripts can call the properties and methods without having to make the object part of every reference to those properties and methods.

An advantage of the with structure is that it can make heavily object-dependent statements easier to read and understand. Consider this long version of a function that requires multiple calls to the same object (but different properties):

```
function seeColor(form) {
    newColor = (form.colorsList.options[form.colorsList.selectedIndex].text)
    return newColor
}
```

Using the with structure, you can shorten the long statement:

```
function seeColor(form) {
    with (form.colorsList) {
        newColor = (options[selectedIndex].text)
    }
    return newColor
}
```

When JavaScript encounters an otherwise unknown identifier inside a with statement, it tries to build a reference out of the object specified as its parameter and that unknown identifier. You cannot, however, nest with statements that build on one another. For instance, in the preceding example, you cannot have a with (colorsList) nested inside a with (form) statement and expect JavaScript to create a reference to options out of the two object names.

As clever as the with statement may seem, be aware that it introduces some inherent performance penalties in your script (because of the way the JavaScript interpreter must artificially generate references). You probably won't notice degradation with occasional use of this construction, but if it's used inside a loop that must iterate many times, processing speed will almost certainly be affected negatively.

Labeled Statements

	NN2	NN3	NN4	NN6	IE3/J1	IE3/J2	IE4	IE5	IE5.5
Compatibility			✓	✓			✓	✓	✓

Crafting multiple nested loops can sometimes be difficult when the final condition your script is looking for is met deep inside the nests. The problem is that the break or continue statement by itself has scope only to the nearest loop level. Therefore, even if you break out of the inner loop, the outer loop(s) continue to execute. If all you want to do is exit the function after the condition is met, a simple return statement performs the same job as some other languages' exit command. But if you also need some further processing within that function after the condition is met, you need the NN4+ and IE4+ facility that lets you assign labels to blocks of JavaScript statements. Your break and continue statements can then alter their scope to apply to a labeled block other than the one containing the statement.

A *label* is any identifier (that is, name starting with a letter and containing no spaces or odd punctuation other than an underscore) followed by a colon preceding a logical block of executing statements, such as an if. . .then or loop construction. The formal syntax looks like the following:

```
labelID:
    statements
```

For a break or continue statement to apply itself to a labeled group, the label is added as a kind of parameter to each statement, as in

```
break labelID
continue labelID
```

To demonstrate how valuable this can be in the right situation, Listing 39-5 contains two versions of the same nested loop construction. The goal of each version is to loop through two different index variables until both values equal the target values set outside the loop. When those targets are met, the entire nested loop construction should break off and continue processing afterward. To help you visualize the processing that goes on during the execution of the loops, the scripts output intermediate and final results to a textarea.

In the version without labels, when the targets are met, only the simple break statement is issued. This breaks the inner loop at that point, but the outer loop picks up on the next iteration. By the time the entire construction has ended, a lot of wasted processing has gone on. Moreover, the values of the counting variables max themselves out, because the loops execute in their entirety several times after the targets are met.

But in the labeled version, the inner loop breaks out of the labeled outer loop as soon as the targets are met. Far fewer lines of code are executed, and the loop counting variables are equal to the targets, as desired. Experiment with Listing 39-5 by changing the break statements to continue statements. Then closely analyze the two results in the Results textarea to see how the two versions behave.

Listing 39-5: **Labeled Statements**

```
<HTML>
<HEAD>
<TITLE>Breaking Out of Nested Labeled Loops</TITLE>
<SCRIPT LANGUAGE="JavaScript">
var targetA = 2
var targetB = 2
var range = 5
function run1() {
    var out = document.forms[0].output
    out.value = "Running WITHOUT labeled break\n"
    for (var i = 0; i <= range; i++) {
        out.value += "Outer loop #" + i + "\n"
        for (var j = 0; j <= range; j++) {
            out.value += "  Inner loop #" + j + "\n"
            if (i == targetA && j == targetB) {
                out.value += "**BREAKING OUT OF INNER LOOP**\n"
                break
            }
```

Continued

label

Listing 39-5 *(continued)*

```
        }
    }
    out.value += "After looping, i = " + i + ", j = " + j + "\n"
}
function run2() {
    var out = document.forms[0].output
    out.value = "Running WITH labeled break\n"
    outerLoop:
    for (var i = 0; i <= range; i++) {
        out.value += "Outer loop #" + i + "\n"
        innerLoop:
        for (var j = 0; j <= range; j++) {
            out.value += "  Inner loop #" + j + "\n"
            if (i == targetA && j == targetB) {
                out.value += "**BREAKING OUT OF OUTER LOOP**\n"
                break outerLoop
            }
        }
    }
    out.value += "After looping, i = " + i + ", j = " + j + "\n"
}
</SCRIPT>
</HEAD>
<BODY>
<H1>Breaking Out of Nested Labeled Loops</H1>
<HR>
<P>Look in the Results field for traces of these button scripts:</P>
<FORM>
<P><INPUT TYPE="button" VALUE="Execute WITHOUT Label" onClick="run1()"></P>
<P><INPUT TYPE="button" VALUE="Execute WITH Label" onClick="run2()"></P>
<P>Results:</P>
<TEXTAREA NAME="output" ROWS=43 COLS=60> </TEXTAREA>
</FORM>
</BODY>
</HTML>
```

The switch Statement

	NN2	NN3	NN4	NN6	IE3/J1	IE3/J2	IE4	IE5	IE5.5
Compatibility			✓	✓			✓	✓	✓

In some circumstances, a binary — true or false — decision path is not enough to handle the processing in your script. An `object` property or `variable` value may contain any one of several values, and a separate execution path is required for each one. In the past, the way to accommodate this was with a series of `if. . .else` constructions. The more conditions you must test, the less efficient the processing is, because each condition must be tested. Moreover, the sequence of clauses and braces can get very confusing.

In NN4+ and IE4+, a control structure in use by many languages comes to JavaScript. The implementation is similar to that of Java and C, using the switch and case keywords. The basic premise is that you can create any number of execution paths based on the value of some expression. At the beginning of the structure, you identify what that expression is and then, for each execution path, assign a label matching a particular value.

The formal syntax for the `switch` statement is

```
switch (expression) {
    case label1:
        statements
        [break]
    case label2:
        statements
        [break]
    ...
    [default:
        statements]
}
```

The *expression* parameter of the `switch` statement can evaluate to any string or number value. Labels are not surrounded by quotes, even if the labels represent string values of the expression. Notice that the `break` statements are optional. A `break` statement forces the switch expression to bypass all other checks of succeeding labels against the expression value. Another option is the `default` statement, which provides a catchall execution path when the expression value does not match any of the `case` statement labels. If you'd rather not have any execution take place with a non-matching expression value, omit the default part of the construction.

To demonstrate the syntax of a working `switch` statement, Listing 39-6 provides the skeleton of a larger application of this control structure. The page contains two separate arrays of different product categories. Each product has its name and price stored in its respective array. A SELECT list displays the product names. After a user chooses a product, the script looks up the product name in the appropriate array and displays the price.

The trick behind this application is the values assigned to each product in the select list. While the displayed text is the product name, the VALUE attribute of each <OPTION> tag is the array category for the product. That value is the expression used to decide which branch to follow. Notice, too, that I assign a label to the entire switch construction. The purpose of that is to let the deeply nested repeat loops for each case completely bail out of the switch construction (via a labeled break statement) whenever a match is made. You can extend this example to any number of product category arrays with additional case statements to match.

Listing 39-6: The switch Construction in Action

```
<HTML>
<HEAD>
<TITLE>Switch Statement and Labeled Break</TITLE>
<SCRIPT LANGUAGE="JavaScript1.2">
// build two product arrays, simulating two database tables
function product(name, price) {
    this.name = name
    this.price = price
}
var ICs = new Array()
ICs[0] = new product("Septium 900MHz","$149")
ICs[1] = new product("Septium Pro 1.0GHz","$249")
ICs[2] = new product("Octium BFD 750MHz","$329")
var snacks = new Array
snacks[0] = new product("Rays Potato Chips","$1.79")
snacks[1] = new product("Cheezey-ettes","$1.59")
snacks[2] = new product("Tortilla Flats","$2.29")

// lookup in the 'table' associated with the product
function getPrice(selector) {
    var chipName = selector.options[selector.selectedIndex].text
    var outField = document.forms[0].cost
    master:
        switch(selector.options[selector.selectedIndex].value) {
            case "ICs":
                for (var i = 0; i < ICs.length; i++) {
                    if (ICs[i].name == chipName) {
                        outField.value = ICs[i].price
                        break master
                    }
                }
                break
            case "snacks":
                for (var i = 0; i < snacks.length; i++) {
                    if (snacks[i].name == chipName) {
                        outField.value = snacks[i].price
                        break master
```

```
                      }
                  }
              break
          default:
              outField.value = "Not Found"
          }
      }
</SCRIPT>
</HEAD>
<BODY>
<B>Branching with the switch Statement</B>
<HR>
Select a chip for lookup in the chip price tables:<P>
<FORM>
Chip:<SELECT NAME-"chips" onChange="getPrice(this)">
    <OPTION>
    <OPTION VALUE="ICs">Septium 900MHz
    <OPTION VALUE="ICs">Septium Pro 1.0GHz
    <OPTION VALUE="ICs">Octium BFD 750MHz
    <OPTION VALUE-"snacks">Rays Potato Chips
    <OPTION VALUE="snacks">Cheezey-ettes
    <OPTION VALUE="snacks">Tortilla Flats
    <OPTION>Poker Chipset
</SELECT> 
Price:<INPUT TYPE="text" NAME="cost" SIZE=10>
</FORM>
</BODY>
</HTML>
```

If you need this kind of functionality in your script but your audience is not all running level 4 or later browsers, see Listing 39-1 for ways to simulate the `switch` statement with `if. . .else` constructions.

Exception Handling

The subject of exception handling is relatively new to JavaScript. Formalized in Edition 3 of ECMA-262, parts of the official mechanism are implemented in IE5, with a more complete implementation in NN6. As you see in the rest of this chapter, both IE5+ and NN6 follow many of the same rules with respect to controlling execution paths (the primary subject of this chapter). But IE's departure from the ECMA-262 specification on some of the details can force scripters to take some extra steps to make exception handling work smoothly across browsers. More on that later. First, an overview of exception handling.

Exceptions and errors

If you've done any scripting, you are certainly aware of JavaScript errors, whether they be from syntax errors in your code, or what are known as *runtime* errors — errors that occur while scripts are processing information. Ideally, a program should be aware of when an error occurs and handle it as gracefully as possible. This self-healing can prevent lost data (usually not a big problem in Web applications) and prevent users from seeing the ugliness of error messages. In Chapter 16, you learn about the `onError` event handler (and `window.onerror` property), which were early attempts at letting scripts gain a level of control over runtime errors. This event-driven mechanism works on a global level (that is, in the `window` object) and processes every error that occurs throughout the page. This event handler ends up being used primarily as a last-ditch defense against displaying any error message to the user and is a long way from what programmers consider to be exception handling.

In the English language, the term "exception" can mean the same as something out of the ordinary, or something abnormal. This definition seems quite distant from the word "error," which usually means a mistake. In the realm of programming languages, however, the two words tend to be used interchangeably, and the difference between the two depends primarily on one's point of view.

Consider, for example, a simple script whose job is to multiply numbers that the user enters into two text fields on the page. The script is supposed to display the results in a third text box. If the script contains no data entry validation, JavaScript will attempt to multiply whatever values are entered into the text boxes. If the user enters two numbers, JavaScript is smart enough to recognize that even though the `value` properties of the two input text fields are strings, the strings contain numbers that can be converted to number types for the proper multiplication. Without complaint, the product of the two numbers gets calculated and displayed into the results.

But what if the user types a letter into one of the text boxes? Again, without any entry validation in the script, JavaScript has a fixed way of responding to such a request: The result of the multiplication operation is the `NaN` (not a number) constant. If you are an untrained user, you have no idea what `NaN` means, but your experience with computers tells you that some kind of error has occurred. You may blame the computer or you may blame yourself.

To shift the point of view to the programmer, however, the script was designed to be run by a user who never makes a typing mistake, intentional or not. That, of course, is not very good programming practice. Users make mistakes. Therefore, anticipating user input that is not what would be expected is the programmer's job — input that is an exception to the rules your program wants to operate by. You must include some additional code that handles the exceptions gracefully so as to not confuse the user with unintelligible output and perhaps even help the user repair the input to get a result. This extra programming code handles the undesirable and erroneous input.

As it turns out, JavaScript and the W3C Document Object Model liberally mix terms of exception and error within the vocabulary used to handle exceptions. As you see shortly, an exception creates an *error object*, which contains information about the exception. It is safe to say that you can think of exceptions and errors as the same things.

The exception mechanism

Newcomers to JavaScript (or any programming environment, for that matter) may have a difficult time at first creating a mental model of how all this stuff runs within the context of the browser. It may be easy enough to understand how pages load and create object models, and how event handlers (or listeners in the W3C DOM terminology) cause script functions to run. But a lot of action also seems to be going on in the background. For example, the event object that is generated automatically with each event action (see Chapter 29) seems to sit "somewhere" while event handler functions run so that they can retrieve details about the event. After the functions finish their processing, the event object disappears, without even leaving behind a Cheshire Cat smile. Mysterious.

Browsers equipped for exception handling have more of this "stuff" running in the background, ready for your scripts when you need it. Because you have certainly viewed the details of at least one scripting error, you have already seen some of the exception handling mechanism that is built into browsers. If a script error occurs, the browser creates in its memory an error object, whose properties contain details about the error. The precise details (described later in this chapter) vary from one browser brand to the next, but what you see in the error details readout is the default way the browser handles exceptions/errors. As browsers have matured, their makers have gone to great lengths to tone down the intrusion of script errors. For example in NN4+, errors appear in a separate JavaScript Console window (which must be invoked in NN4 by typing javascript: into the Location field; or opened directly via the Tools menu in NN6), while users see only a message about the existence of an error in the statusbar. In IE4+ for Windows, the statusbar comes into play again, as the icon at the bottom-left corner turns into an alert icon: Double-clicking the icon displays more information about the error. IE/Mac users can turn off scripting error alerts altogether.

True exception handling, however, goes further than just displaying error messages. It also provides a uniform way to let scripts guard against unusual occurrences. Ideally, the mechanism makes sure that *all* runtime errors get funneled through the same mechanism to help simplify the scripting of exception handling. The mechanism is also designed to be used intentionally as a way for your own code to generate errors in a uniform way so that other parts of your scripts can handle them quietly and intelligently. In other words, you can use the exception handling mechanism as a kind of "back channel" to communicate from one part of your scripts to another.

The JavaScript exception handling mechanism is built around two groups of program execution statements. The first group consists of the `try-catch-finally` statement triumvirate; the second group is the single `throw` statement.

Using try-catch-finally constructions

The purpose of the `try-catch-finally` group of related statements is to provide a controlled environment in which script statements that may encounter runtime errors can run, such that if an exception occurs, your scripts can act upon the exception without alarming the rest of the browser's error mechanisms. Each of the three statements precedes a block of code in the following syntax:

```
try {
    statements to run
}
catch (errorInfo) {
    statements to run if exception occurs in try block
}
finally {
    statements to run whether or not an exception occurred [optional]
}
```

Each `try` block must be mated with a `catch` and/or `finally` block at the same nesting level, with no intervening statements. For example, a function can have a one-level `try-catch` construction inside it as follows:

```
function myFunc() {
    try {
        statements
    }
    catch (e) {
        statements
    }
}
```

But if there were another `try` block nested one level deeper, a balancing `catch` or `finally` block would also have to be present at that deeper level:

```
function myFunc() {
    try {
        statements
        try {
```

```
            statements
      }
    catch (e) {
        statements
      }
  }
  catch (e) {
      statements
    }
}
```

The statements inside the `try` block include statements that you believe are capable of generating a runtime error because of user input errors, the failure of some page component to load, or a similar error. The presence of the `catch` block prevents errors from appearing in the browser's regular script error reporting system (for example, the JavaScript Console of NN6).

An important term to know about exception handling of this type is *throw*. The convention is that when an operation or method call triggers an exception, it is said to "throw an exception." For example, if a script statement attempts to invoke a method of a string object, but that method does not exist for the object (perhaps you mistyped the method name), JavaScript throws an exception. Exceptions have names associated with them — a name that sometimes, but not always, reveals important information about the exception. In the mistyped method example just cited, the name of that exception is a `TypeError` (yet more evidence of how "exception" and "error" become intertwined).

The JavaScript language (in IE5+ and NN6+) is not the only entity that can throw exceptions. The W3C DOM also defines categories of exceptions for DOM objects. For example, according to the Level 2 specification, the `appendChild()` method (see Chapter 15) can throw (or *raise*, in the W3C terminology) one of three exceptions:

Exception Name	When Thrown
HIERARCHY_REQUEST_ERR	If the current node is of a type that does not allow children of the type of the *newChild* node, or if the node to append is one of this node's ancestors
WRONG_DOCUMENT_ERR	If *newChild* was created from a different document than the one that created the current node
NO_MODIFICATION_ALLOWED_ERR	If the current node is read-only

Because the `appendChild()` method is capable of throwing exceptions, a JavaScript statement that invokes this method should ideally be inside a `try` block.

try-catch-finally

If an exception is thrown, then script execution immediately jumps to the `catch` or `finally` block associated with the `try` block. Execution does not come back to the `try` block.

A `catch` block has special behavior. Its format looks similar to a function in a way, because the `catch` keyword is followed by a pair of parentheses and an arbitrary variable that is assigned a reference to the error object whose properties are filled by the browser when the exception occurs. One of the properties of that error object is the name of the error. Therefore, the code inside the `catch` block can examine the name of the error and perhaps include some branching code to take care of a variety of different errors that are caught.

To see how this construction may look in code, look at a hypothetical generic function whose job is to create a new element and append it to some other node. Both the type of element to be created and a reference to the parent node are passed as parameters. To take care of potential misuses of this function through the passage of improper parameter values, it includes extra error handling to treat all possible exceptions from the two DOM methods: `createElement()` and `appendChild()`. Such a function looks like Listing 39-7.

Listing 39-7: **A Hypothetical try-catch Routine**

```
// generic appender
function attachToEnd(theNode, newTag) {
    try {
        var newElem = document.createElement(newTag)
        theNode.appendChild(newElem)
    }
    catch (e) {
        switch (e.name) {
            case "INVALID_CHARACTER_ERR" :
                statements to handle this createElement() error
                break
            case "HIERARCHY_REQUEST_ERR" :
                statements to handle this appendChild() error
                break
            case "WRONG_DOCUMENT_ERR" :
                statements to handle this appendChild() error
                break
            case "NO_MODIFICATION_ALLOWED_ERR" :
                statements to handle this appendChild() error
                break
            default:
                statements to handle any other error
        }
        return false
    }
```

```
    return true
}
```

The single `catch` block in Listing 39-7 executes only if one of the statements in the `try` block throws an exception. The exceptions may be not only one of the four specific ones named in the `catch` block but also syntax or other errors that could occur inside the `try` block. That's why you have a last-ditch case to handle truly unexpected errors. Your job as scripter is to not only anticipate errors but also to provide clean ways for the exceptions to be handled, whether they be through judiciously worded alert dialog boxes or perhaps even some self-repair. For example, in the case of the invalid character error for `createElement()`, your script may attempt to salvage the data passed to the `attachToEnd()` function and reinvoke the method passing `theNode` value as-is and the repaired value originally passed to `newTag`. If your repairs were successful, the `try` block would execute without error and carry on with the user's being completely unaware that a nasty problem had been averted.

A `finally` block contains code that always executes after a `try` block, whether or not the `try` block succeeds without throwing an error. Unlike the `catch` block, a `finally` block does not receive an error object as a parameter, so it operates very much in the dark about what transpires inside the `try` block. If you include both `catch` and `finally` blocks after a `try` block, the execution path depends on whether an exception is thrown. If no exception is thrown, the `finally` block executes after the last statement of the `try` block runs. But if the `try` block throws an exception, program execution runs first to the `catch` block. After all processing within the `catch` block finishes, the `finally` block executes. In development environments that give programmers complete control over resources, such as memory allocation, a `finally` block may be used to delete some temporary items generated in the `try` block, whether or not an exception occurs in the `try` block. Currently, JavaScript has less need for that kind of maintenance, but you should be aware of the program execution possibilities of the `finally` block in the `try-catch-finally` context.

Real-life exceptions

The example shown in Listing 39-6 is a bit idealized. The listing assumes that the browser dutifully reports every W3C DOM exception precisely as defined in the formal specification. Unfortunately, that's not how it is (yet) in browsers through IE5.5 and NN6. Both browsers implement additional error naming conventions and layers between actual DOM exceptions and what gets reported with the error object at the time of the exception.

If you think these discrepancies make cross-browser exception handling difficult, you're right. Even simple errors are reported differently among the two major browser brands and the W3C DOM specification. Until the browsers exhibit a greater unanimity in exception reporting, the smoothest development road will be for those scripters who have the luxury of writing for one of the browser platforms, such as IE5 for Windows or NN6.

That said, however, one aspect of exception handling can still be used in both IE5+ and NN6. You can take advantage of `try-catch` constructions to throw your own exceptions — a practice that is quite common in advanced programming environments.

Throwing Exceptions

The last exception handling keyword not covered yet — `throw` — makes it possible to utilize exception handling facilities for your own management of processes, such as data entry validation. At any point inside a `try` block, you can manually throw an exception that gets picked up by the associated `catch` block. The details of the specific exception are up to you.

Syntax for the `throw` statement is as follows:

```
throw value
```

The value you throw can be of any type, but good practice suggests that the value be an error object (described more fully later in this chapter). Whatever value you throw is assigned to the parameter of the `catch` block. Look at the following two examples. In the first, the value is a string message; in the second, the value is an error object.

Listing 39-8 presents one input text box for a number between 1 and 5. Clicking a button looks up a corresponding letter in an array and displays the letter in a second text box. The lookup script has two simple data validation routines to make sure the entry is a number and is in the desired range. Error checking here is done manually by script. If either of the error conditions occurs, `throw` statements force execution to jump to the `catch` block. The `catch` block assigns the incoming `string` parameter to the variable e. The design here assumes that the message being passed is text for an alert dialog box. Not only does a single `catch` block take care of both error conditions (and conceivably any others to be added later), but the `catch` block runs within the same variable scope as the function, so that it can use the reference to the input text box to focus and select the input text if there is an error.

Listing 39-8: **Throwing String Exceptions**

```
<HTML>
<HEAD>
<TITLE>Throwing a String Exception</TITLE>
<SCRIPT LANGUAGE="JavaScript">
var letters = new Array("A","B","C","D","E")
function getLetter(fld) {
    try {
        var inp = parseInt(fld.value, 10)
        if (isNaN(inp)) {
            throw "Entry was not a number."
        }
        if (inp < 1 || inp > 5) {
            throw "Enter only 1 through 5."
        }
        fld.form.output.value = letters[inp]
    }
    catch (e) {
        alert(e)
        fld.form.output.value = ""
        fld.focus()
        fld.select()
    }
}
</SCRIPT>
</HEAD>
<BODY>
<H1>Throwing a String Exception</H1>
<HR>
<FORM>
Enter a number from 1 to 5:
<INPUT TYPE="text" NAME="input" SIZE=5>
<INPUT TYPE="button" VALUE="Get Letter" onClick=getLetter(this.form.input)>
Matching Letter is:<INPUT TYPE="text" NAME="output" SIZE=5>
</FORM>
</BODY>
</HTML>
```

The flaw with Listing 39-8 is that if some other kind of exception were thrown inside the `try` block, the value passed to the `catch` block would be an error object, not a string. The alert dialog box displayed to the user would be meaningless. Therefore, it is better to be uniform in your `throw-catch` constructions and pass an error object.

Listing 39-9 is an updated version of Listing 39-8, demonstrating how to create an error object that gets sent to the catch block via throw statements. The one glitch in generating an error object comes in IE5 and IE5.5. The ECMA-262 standard allows a script statement to set the message property of an error object to directly by passing a string as the parameter to the new Error() constructor. This is how NN6 works. But the error object in IE5 does not have the message property at all, and in IE5.5, the parameter is not assigned to the message property. Therefore, Listing 39-9 contains a separate utility function (getErrorObj()) that fills the gap when an error object does not have the message property to begin with or doesn't have the property set automatically. If a future version of IE adopts the ECMA standard way, then the extra branch is avoided, just as it is for NN6.

Listing 39-9: **Throwing an Error Object Exception**

```
<HTML>
<HEAD>
<TITLE>Throwing an Error Object Exception</TITLE>
<SCRIPT LANGUAGE="JavaScript">
var letters = new Array("A","B","C","D","E")
function getErrorObj(msg) {
    var err = new Error(msg)
    // take care of IE5/5.5
    if (!err.message) {
        err.message = msg
    }
    return err
}
function getLetter(fld) {
    try {
        var inp = parseInt(fld.value, 10)
        if (isNaN(inp)) {
            throw getErrorObj("Entry was not a number.")
        }
        if (inp < 1 || inp > 5) {
            throw getErrorObj("Enter only 1 through 5.")
        }
        fld.form.output.value = letters[inp]
    }
    catch (e) {
        alert(e.message)
        fld.form.output.value = ""
        fld.focus()
        fld.select()
    }
}
</SCRIPT>
</HEAD>
<BODY>
```

```
<H1>Throwing an Error Object Exception</H1>
<HR>
<FORM>
Enter a number from 1 to 5:
<INPUT TYPE="text" NAME="input" SIZE=5>
<INPUT TYPE="button" VALUE="Get Letter" onClick=getLetter(this.form.input)>
Matching Letter is:<INPUT TYPE="text" NAME="output" SIZE=5>
</FORM>
</BODY>
</HTML>
```

The only difference to the catch block is that it now reads the message property of the incoming error object. This means that if some other exception is thrown inside the try block, the browser-generated message will be displayed in the alert dialog box.

In truth, however, the job really isn't complete. In all likelihood, if a browser-generated exception is thrown, the message in the alert dialog box won't mean much to the user. The error message will probably be some kind of syntax or type error — the kind of meaningless error message you often get from your favorite operating system. A better design is to branch the catch block so that "intentional" exceptions thrown by your code are handled through the alert dialog box messages you've put there, but other types are treated differently. To accomplish this, you can take over one of the other properties of the error object — name — so that your catch block treats your custom messages separately.

In Listing 39-10, the getErrorObj() function adds a custom value to the name property of the newly created error object. The name you assign can be any name, but you want to avoid exception names used by JavaScript or the DOM. Even if you don't know what all of those are, you can probably conjure up a suitably unique name for your error. Down in the catch block, a switch construction branches to treat the two classes of errors differently. Notice that because IE5's error object does not have a name property, the switch expression (e.name) evaluates to –undefined, which forces the default case to execute whenever a native exception is thrown (and you have to be careful about which error object properties you use in the default case statements). In this simplified example, about the only possible problem other than the ones being trapped for explicitly in the try block would be some corruption to the page during downloading. Therefore, for this example, the branch for all other errors simply asks that the user reload the page and try again. The point is, however, that you can have as many classifications of custom and system errors as you want and handle them in a single catch block accordingly.

Listing 39-10: **A Custom Object Exception**

```
<HTML>
<HEAD>
<TITLE>Throwing a Custom Error Object Exception</TITLE>
<SCRIPT LANGUAGE="JavaScript">
var letters = new Array("A","B","C","D","E")
function getErrorObj(msg) {
    var err = new Error(msg)
    // take care of IE5/5.5
    if (!err.message) {
        err.message = msg
    }
    err.name = "MY_ERROR"
    return err
}
function getLetter(fld) {
    try {
    var inp = parseInt(fld.value, 10)
        if (isNaN(inp)) {
            throw getErrorObj("Entry was not a number.")
        }
        if (inp < 1 || inp > 5) {
            throw getErrorObj("Enter only 1 through 5.")
        }
        fld.form.output.value = letters[inp]
    }
    catch (e) {
        switch (e.name) {
            case "MY_ERROR" :
                alert(e.message)
                fld.form.output.value = ""
                fld.focus()
                fld.select()
                break
            default :
                alert("Reload the page and try again.")
        }
    }
}
</SCRIPT>
</HEAD>
<BODY>
<H1>Throwing a Custom Error Object Exception</H1>
<HR>
<FORM>
Enter a number from 1 to 5:
<INPUT TYPE="text" NAME="input" SIZE=5>
```

```
<INPUT TYPE="button" VALUE="Get Letter" onClick=getLetter(this.form.input)>
Matching Letter is:<INPUT TYPE="text" NAME="output" SIZE=5>
</FORM>
</BODY>
</HTML>
```

If you want to see how the alternative branch of Listing 39-10 looks, copy the listing file from the CD-ROM to your hard disk and modify the last line of the `try` block so that one of the letters is dropped from the name of the array:

```
fld.form.output.value = letter[inp]
```

This may simulate the faulty loading of the page. If you enter one of the allowable values, the reload alert appears, rather than the actual message of the error object: letter is undefined. Your users will thank you.

All that's left now on this subject are the details on the error object.

Error Object

Properties	Methods
Error.prototype	
errorObject.toString()	
errorObject.constructor	
errorObject.description	
errorObject.filename	
errorObject.lineNumber	
errorObject.message	
errorObject.name	
errorObject.number	

Syntax

Creating an error object:

```
var myError = new Error("message")
var myError = Error("message")
```

Accessing static `Error` object property:

```
Error.property
```

Accessing error object properties and methods:

```
errorObject.property | method([parameters])
```

	NN2	NN3	NN4	NN6	IE3/J1	IE3/J2	IE4	IE5	IE5.5
Compatibility				✓				✓	✓

About this object

An error object instance is created whenever an exception is thrown or when you invoke either of the constructor formats for creating an error object. Properties of the error object instance contain information about the nature of the error so that `catch` blocks can inspect the error and process error handling accordingly.

IE5 implemented an error object in advance of the ECMA-262 formal error object, and the IE5 version ends up having its own set of properties that are not part of the ECMA standard. Those proprietary properties are still part of IE5.5, which includes the ECMA properties as well. NN6, on the other hand, starts with the ECMA properties and adds two proprietary properties of its own. The browser uses these additional properties in its own script error reporting. The unfortunate bottom line for cross-browser developers is that no properties in common among all browsers support the error object. However, two common denominators (`name` and `message`) are between IE5.5 and NN6.

As described earlier in this chapter, you are encouraged to create an error object whenever you use the `throw` statement for your own error control. See the discussion surrounding Listing 39-9 about handling missing properties in IE.

Properties

`constructor`

See `string.constructor` (Chapter 34)

`description`

Value: String   Read/Write

	NN2	NN3	NN4	NN6	IE3/J1	IE3/J2	IE4	IE5	IE5.5
Compatibility								✓	✓

The `description` property contains a descriptive string that provides some level of detail about the error. For errors thrown by the browser, the description is the same text that appears in the script error dialog box in IE. Although this property continues to be supported, the `message` property in IE5.5 and NN6 is preferred.

Related Items: `message` property.

`fileName`
`lineNumber`

Value: String   Read/Write

	NN2	NN3	NN4	NN6	IE3/J1	IE3/J2	IE4	IE5	IE5.5
Compatibility				✓					

The NN6 browser uses the `fileName` and `lineNumber` properties of an error object for its own internal script error processing — these values appear as part of the error messages that are listed in the JavaScript Console. The `fileName` is the URL of the document causing the error; the `lineNumber` is the source code line number of the statement that threw the exception. These properties are exposed to JavaScript, as well, so that your error processing may use this information if it is meaningful to your application.

Both of these properties (along with the message property) have been in the Navigator vernacular since NN3. See the discussion of the window.error property in Chapter 16 for further ideas on how to use this information for bug reporting from users.

Related Items: window.error property.

message

Value: String   Read/Write

	NN2	NN3	NN4	NN6	IE3/J1	IE3/J2	IE4	IE5	IE5.5
Compatibility				✓					✓

The message property contains a descriptive string that provides some level of detail about the error. For errors thrown by the browser, the message is the same text that appears in the script error dialog box in IE and the JavaScript Console in NN6. By and large, these messages are more meaningful to scripters than to users. Unfortunately, there are no standards for the wording of a message for a given error. Therefore, it is hazardous at best to use the message content in a catch block as a means of branching to handle particular kinds of errors. You may get by with this approach if you are developing for a single browser platform, but you have no assurances that the text of a message for a particular exception may not change in future browser versions.

Custom messages for errors that your code explicitly throws can be in user-friendly language if you intend to display such messages to users. See Listings 39-8 through 39-10 for examples of this usage.

Related Items: description property.

name

Value: String   Read/Write

	NN2	NN3	NN4	NN6	IE3/J1	IE3/J2	IE4	IE5	IE5.5
Compatibility				✓					✓

The `name` property generally contains a word that identifies the type of error that has been thrown. The most general kind of error (and the one that is created via the `new Error()` constructor) has a name `Error`. But JavaScript errors can be of several varieties: `EvalError`, `RangeError`, `ReferenceError`, `SyntaxError`, `TypeError`, and `URIError`. Some of these error types are not necessarily intended for exposure to scripters (they're used primarily in the inner workings of the JavaScript engine), but some browsers do expose them. Unfortunately, there are some discrepancies as to the specific name supplied to this property for script errors.

When JavaScript is being used in a browser environment that employs the W3C DOM, some DOM exception types are returned via the `name` property. But browsers frequently insert their own error types for this property, and, as is common in this department, little uniformity exists among browser brands.

For custom exceptions that your code explicitly throws, you can assign names as you want. As shown in Listings 39-9 and 39-10, this information can assist a `catch` block in handling multiple categories of errors.

Related Items: message property.

number

Value: Number   Read/Write

	NN2	NN3	NN4	NN6	IE3/J1	IE3/J2	IE4	IE5	IE5.5
Compatibility								✓	✓

IE5+ assigns unique numbers to each error description or message. The `number` property, however, is problematical. While Microsoft documents a sequence of syntax and runtime errors and their numbers, in practice, IE browsers do not report the numbers shown in Microsoft's own documentation. This is unfortunate, because the number can be a language-independent way of branching `catch` block code based on the error number, rather than the description or message. And, because the `number` property was born at the same time as the `description` property (now superseded by the `message` property), it is unknown how reliable the number values (if you can figure them out) will be going forward.

Related Items: description property.

Methods

`toString()`

Returns: String (see text).

	NN2	NN3	NN4	NN6	IE3/J1	IE3/J2	IE4	IE5	IE5.5
Compatibility				✓				✓	✓

The `toString()` method for an error object should return a string description of the error. In IE5 and 5.5, however, the method returns a reference to the very same error object. In NN6, the method returns the `message` property string, preceded by the string `Error:` (with a space after the colon). Most typically, if you want to retrieve a human-readable expression of an error object, read its `message` (or, in IE5, `description`) property.

Related Items: message property.

✦   ✦   ✦

JavaScript Operators

✦ ✦ ✦ ✦

In This Chapter

Understanding operator categories

Exploring the role of operators in script statements

Recognizing operator precedence

✦ ✦ ✦ ✦

JavaScript is rich in *operators*: words and symbols in expressions that perform operations on one or two values to arrive at another value. Any value on which an operator performs some action is called an *operand*. An expression may contain one operand and one operator (called a *unary operator*) or two operands separated by one operator (called a *binary operator*). Many of the same symbols are used in a variety of operators. The combination and order of those symbols are what distinguish their powers.

> **Note** The vast majority of JavaScript operators have been in the language since the very beginning. But, as you may expect from an evolving language, some new entries have been added to the lexicon. In the rest of this chapter, compatibility charts typically govern an entire category of operator. If there are version anomalies for a particular operator within a category, they are covered in the text.

Operator Categories

To help you grasp the range of JavaScript operators, I group them into seven categories. I assign a wholly untraditional name to the second group — but a name that I believe better identifies its purpose in the language. Table 40-1 shows the operator types.

Table 40-1	JavaScript Operator Categories
Type	**What It Does**
Comparison	Compares the values of two operands, deriving a result of either true or false (used extensively in condition statements for `if...else` and `for` loop constructions)
Connubial	Joins together two operands to produce a single value that is a result of an arithmetical or other operation on the two
Assignment	Stuffs the value of the expression of the right-hand operand into a variable name on the left-hand side, sometimes with minor modification, as determined by the operator symbol
Boolean	Performs Boolean arithmetic on one or two Boolean operands
Bitwise	Performs arithmetic or column-shifting actions on the binary (base-2) representations of two operands
Object	Helps scripts examine the heritage and capabilities of a particular object before they need to invoke the object and its properties or methods
Miscellaneous	A handful of operators that have special behaviors

Any expression that contains an operator evaluates to a value of some kind. Sometimes the operator changes the value of one of the operands; other times the result is a new value. Even this simple expression

```
5 + 5
```

shows two integer operands joined by the addition operator. This expression evaluates to 10. The operator is what provides the instruction for JavaScript to follow in its never-ending drive to evaluate every expression in a script.

Doing an equality comparison on two operands that, on the surface, look very different is not at all uncommon. JavaScript doesn't care what the operands look like — only how they evaluate. Two very dissimilar-looking values can, in fact, be identical when they are evaluated. Thus, an expression that compares the equality of two values, such as

```
fred == 25
```

does, in fact, evaluate to true if the variable fred has the number 25 stored in it from an earlier statement.

Comparison Operators

	NN2	NN3	NN4	NN6	IE3/J1	IE3/J2	IE4	IE5	IE5.5
Compatibility	✓	✓	✓	✓	✓	✓	✓	✓	✓

Any time you compare two values in JavaScript, the result is a Boolean `true` or `false` value. You have a wide selection of comparison operators to choose from, depending on the kind of test you want to apply to the two operands. Table 40-2 lists all comparison operators.

Table 40-2   JavaScript Comparison Operators

Syntax	Name	Operand Types	Results
==	Equals	All	Boolean
!=	Does not equal	All	Boolean
===	Strictly equals	All	Boolean (IE4+, NN4+)
!==	Strictly does not equal	All	Boolean (IE4+, NN4+)
>	Is greater than	All	Boolean
>=	Is greater than or equal to	All	Boolean
<	Is less than	All	Boolean
<=	Is less than or equal to	All	Boolean

For numeric values, the results are the same as those you'd expect from your high school algebra class. Some examples follow, including some that may not be obvious.

```
10 == 10        // true
10 == 10.0      // true
9 != 10         // true
9 > 10          // false
9.99 <= 9.98    // false
```

Strings can also be compared on all of these levels:

```
"Fred" == "Fred"    // true
```

```
"Fred" == "fred"    // false
"Fred" > "fred"     // false
"Fran" < "Fred"     // true
```

To calculate string comparisons, JavaScript converts each character of a string to its ASCII value. Each letter, beginning with the first of the left-hand operator, is compared to the corresponding letter in the right-hand operator. With ASCII values for uppercase letters being less than those of their lowercase counterparts, an uppercase letter evaluates to being less than its lowercase equivalent. JavaScript takes case-sensitivity very seriously.

Values for comparison can also come from object properties or values passed to functions from event handlers or other functions. A common string comparison used in data-entry validation is the one that sees if the string has anything in it:

```
form.entry.value != ""    // true if something is in the field
```

Equality of Disparate Data Types

For all versions of JavaScript before 1.2, when your script tries to compare string values consisting of numerals and real numbers (for example, "123" == 123 or "123" != 123), JavaScript anticipates that you want to compare apples to apples. Internally it does some data type conversion that does not affect the data type of the original values (for example, if the values are in variables). But the entire situation is more complex, because other data types, such as objects, need to be dealt with. Therefore, prior to JavaScript 1.2, the rules of comparison are as shown in Table 40-3.

Table 40-3	**Equality Comparisons for JavaScript 1.0 and 1.1**	
Operand A	*Operand B*	*Internal Comparison Treatment*
Object reference	Object reference	Compare object reference evaluations
Any data type	Null	Convert nonnull to its object type and compare against null
Object reference	String	Convert object to string and compare strings
String	Number	Convert string to number and compare numbers

The logic to what goes on in equality comparisons from Table 40-3 requires a lot of forethought on the scripter's part, because you have to be very conscious of the particular way data types may or may not be converted for equality evaluation (even though the values themselves are not converted). In this situation, supplying the proper conversion where necessary in the comparison statement is best. This ensures that what you want to compare — for example, the string versions of two values or the number versions of two values — is compared, rather than leaving the conversion up to JavaScript.

Backward compatible conversion from a number to string entails concatenating an empty string to a number:

```
var a = "09"
var b = 9
a == "" + b  // result: false, because "09" does not equal "9"
```

For converting strings to numbers, you have numerous possibilities. The simplest is subtracting zero from a numeric string:

```
var a = "09"
var b = 9
a-0 == b  // result: true because number 9 equals number 9
```

You can also use the parseInt() and parseFloat() functions to convert strings to numbers:

```
var a = "09"
var b = 9
parseInt(a, 10) == b  // result: true because number 9 equals number 9
```

To clear up the ambiguity of JavaScript's equality internal conversions, JavaScript 1.2 in NN4 and IE4 adds two more operators to force the equality comparison to be extremely literal in its comparison. The strictly equals (===) and strictly does not equal (!==) operators compare both the data type and value. The only time the === operator returns true is if the two operands are of the same data type (for example, both are numbers) and the same value. Therefore, no number is ever automatically equal to a string version of that same number. Data and object types must match before their values are compared.

JavaScript 1.2 also provides some convenient global functions for converting strings to numbers and vice versa: String() and Number(). To demonstrate these methods, the following examples use the typeof operator to show the data type of expressions using these functions:

```
typeof 9           // result: number
typeof String(9)   // result: string
typeof "9"         // result: string
typeof Number("9") // result: number
```

None of these functions alters the data type of the value being converted. But the value of the function is what gets compared in an equality comparison:

```
var a = "09"
var b = 9
a == String(b)    // result: false, because "09" does not equal "9"
typeof b          // result: still a number
Number(a) == b    // result: true, because 9 equals 9
typeof a          // result: still a string
```

This discussion should impress upon you the importance of considering data types when testing the equality of two values.

Connubial Operators

	NN2	NN3	NN4	NN6	IE3/J1	IE3/J2	IE4	IE5	IE5.5
Compatibility	✓	✓	✓	✓	✓	✓	✓	✓	✓

Connubial operators is my terminology for those operators that join two operands to yield a value related to the operands. Table 40-4 lists the connubial operators in JavaScript.

Table 40-4   JavaScript Connubial Operators

Syntax	Name	Operand Types	Results
+	Plus	Integer, float, string	Integer, float, string
-	Minus	Integer, float	Integer, float
*	Multiply	Integer, float	Integer, float
/	Divide	Integer, float	Integer, float
%	Modulo	Integer, float	Integer, float
++	Increment	Integer, float	Integer, float
--	Decrement	Integer, float	Integer, float
+val	Positive	Integer, float, string	Integer, float
-val	Negation	Integer, float, string	Integer, float

The four basic arithmetic operators for numbers are straightforward. The plus operator also works on strings to join them together, as in

```
"Howdy " + "Doody" // result = "Howdy Doody"
```

In object-oriented programming terminology, the plus sign is considered *overloaded*, meaning that it performs a different action depending on its context. Remember, too, that string concatenation does not do anything on its own to monitor or insert spaces between words. In the preceding example, the space between the names is part of the first string.

Modulo arithmetic is helpful for those times when you want to know if one number divides evenly into another. You used it in an example in Chapter 39 to figure out if a particular year was a leap year. Although some other leap year considerations exist for the turn of each century, the math in the example simply checked whether the year was evenly divisible by four. The result of the modulo math is the remainder of division of the two values: When the remainder is 0, one divides evenly into the other. Here are some samples of years evenly divisible by four:

```
2002 % 4     // result = 2
2003 % 4     // result = 3
2004 % 4     // result = 0 (Bingo! Leap year!)
```

Thus, I used this modulo operator in a condition statement of an `if. . .else` structure:

```
var howMany - 0
today = new Date()
var theYear = today.getYear()
if (theYear % 4 == 0) {
    howMany = 29
} else {
    howMany = 28
}
```

Some other languages offer an operator that results in the integer part of a division problem solution: integral division, or `div`. Although JavaScript does not have an explicit operator for this behavior, you can recreate it reliably if you know that your operands are always positive numbers. Use the `Math.floor()` or `Math.ceil()` methods with the division operator, as in

```
Math.floor(4/3)     // result = 1
```

In this example, `Math.floor()` works only with values greater than or equal to 0; `Math.ceil()` works with values less than 0.

The increment operator (++) is a *unary* operator (only one operand) and displays two different behaviors, depending on the side of the operand on which the symbols lie. Both the increment and decrement (--) operators can be used in conjunction with assignment operators, which I cover next.

As its name implies, the increment operator increases the value of its operand by one. But in an assignment statement, you have to pay close attention to precisely when that increase takes place. An assignment statement stuffs the value of the right operand into a variable on the left. If the ++ operator is located in front of the right operand (prefix), the right operand is incremented before the value is assigned to the variable; if the ++ operator is located after the right operand (postfix), the previous value of the operand is sent to the variable before the value is incremented. Follow this sequence to get a feel for these two behaviors:

```
var a = 10     // initialize a to 10
var z = 0      // initialize z to zero
z = a          // a = 10, so z = 10
z = ++a        // a becomes 11 before assignment, so a = 11 and z becomes 11
z = a++        // a is still 11 before assignment, so z = 11; then a becomes 12
z = a++        // a is still 12 before assignment, so z = 12; then a becomes 13
```

The decrement operator behaves the same way, except that the value of the operand decreases by one. Increment and decrement operators are used most often with loop counters in for and while loops. The simpler ++ or -- symbology is more compact than reassigning a value by adding 1 to it (such as, z = z + 1 or z += 1). Because these are unary operators, you can use the increment and decrement operators without an assignment statement to adjust the value of a counting variable within a loop:

```
function doNothing() {
    var i = 1
    while (i < 20) {
        ++i
    }
    alert(i) // breaks out at i = 20
}
```

The last pair of connubial operators are also unary operators (operating on one operand). Both the positive and negation operators can be used as shortcuts to the Number() global function, converting a string operand consisting of number characters to a number data type. The string operand is not changed, but the operation returns a value of the number type, as shown in the following sequence:

```
var a = "123"
var b = +a     // b is now 123
typeof a       // result: string
typeof b       // result: number
```

The negation operator (-val) has additional power. By placing a minus sign in front of any numeric value (no space between the symbol and the value), you instruct JavaScript to evaluate a positive value as its corresponding negative value, and vice versa. The operator does not change the operand's value, but the expression returns the modified value. The following example provides a sequence of statements to demonstrate:

```
var x = 2
var y = 8
var z = -x          // z equals -2, but x still equals 2
z = -(x + y)        // z equals -10, but x still equals 2 and y equals 8
z = -x + y          // z equals 6, but x still equals 2 and y equals 8
```

To negate a Boolean value, see the Not (!) operator in the discussion of Boolean operators.

Assignment Operators

	NN2	NN3	NN4	NN6	IE3/J1	IE3/J2	IE4	IE5	IE5.5
Compatibility	✓	✓	✓	✓	✓	✓	✓	✓	✓

Assignment statements are among the most common statements you write in your JavaScript scripts. These statements appear everywhere you copy a value or the results of an expression into a variable for further manipulation of that value.

You assign values to variables for many reasons, even though you could probably use the original values or expressions several times throughout a script. Here is a sampling of reasons why you should assign values to variables:

✦ Variable names are usually shorter

✦ Variable names can be more descriptive

✦ You may need to preserve the original value for later in the script

✦ The original value is a property that cannot be changed

✦ Invoking the same method several times in a script is not efficient

Newcomers to scripting often overlook the last reason. For instance, if a script is writing HTML to a new document, it's more efficient to assemble the string of large chunks of the page into one variable before invoking the document.write()

method to send that text to the document. This approach is more efficient than literally sending out one line of HTML at a time with multiple `document.writeln()` method statements. Table 40-5 shows the range of assignment operators in JavaScript.

Table 40-5	JavaScript Assignment Operators		
Syntax	**Name**	**Example**	**Means**
=	Equals	x = y	x = y
+=	Add by value	x += y	x = x + y
-=	Subtract by value	x -= y	x = x - y
*=	Multiply by value	x *= y	x = x * y
/=	Divide by value	x /= y	x = x / y
%=	Modulo by value	x %= y	x = x % y
<<=	Left shift by value	x <<= y	x = x << y
>=	Right shift by value	x >= y	x = x > y
>>=	Zero fill by value	x >>= y	x = x >> y
>>>=	Right shift by value	x >>>= y	x = x >>> y
&=	Bitwise AND by value	x &= y	x = x & y
|=	Bitwise OR by value	x |= y	x = x | y
^=	Bitwise XOR by value	x ^= y	x = x ^ y

As clearly demonstrated in the top group (see "Bitwise Operators" later in the chapter for information on the bottom group), assignment operators beyond the simple equals sign can save some characters in your typing, especially when you have a series of values that you're trying to bring together in subsequent statements. You've seen plenty of examples in previous chapters, where you used the add-by-value operator (+=) to work wonders with strings as you assemble a long string variable that you eventually send to a `document.write()` method. Look at this variation of a segment of Listing 37-3, where you could use JavaScript to create the HTML content of a SELECT element on the fly:

```
var elem = "" // start assembling next part of page and form
elem += "<P>Select a regional office: "
elem += "<SELECT NAME='offices' onChange='getData(this.form)'>"
// build options list from array office names
for (var i = 0; i < regionalOffices.length; i++) {
```

```
    elem += "<OPTION"          // OPTION tags
    if (i == 0) {              // pre-select first item in list
        elem += " SELECTED"
    }
    elem += ">" + regionalOffices[i]
}
elem += "</SELECT></P>"        // close SELECT item tag
document.write(elem)           // write element to the page
```

The script segment starts with a plain equals assignment operator to initialize the
elem variable as an empty string. In many of the succeeding lines, you use the add-
by-value operator to tack additional string values onto whatever is in the elem variable at the time. Without the add-by-value operator, you are forced to use the plain
equals assignment operator for each line of code to concatenate new string data to
the existing string data. In that case, the first few lines of code look as shown:

```
var elem = "" // start assembling next part of page and form
elem = elem + "<P>Select a regional office: "
elem = elem + "<SELECT NAME='offices' onChange='gctData(this.form)'>"
```

Within the for loop, the repetition of elem + makes the code very difficult to read,
trace, and maintain. These enhanced assignment operators are excellent shortcuts
that you should use at every turn.

Boolean Operators

	NN2	NN3	NN4	NN6	IE3/J1	IE3/J2	IE4	IE5	IE5.5
Compatibility	✓	✓	✓	✓	✓	✓	✓	✓	✓

Because a great deal of programming involves logic, it is no accident that the arithmetic of the logic world plays an important role. You've already seen dozens of
instances where programs make all kinds of decisions based on whether a statement or expression is the Boolean value true or false. What you haven't seen
much of yet is how to combine multiple Boolean values and expressions — a quality
that scripts with slightly above average complexity may need to have in them.

In the various condition expressions required throughout JavaScript (such as in an
if construction), the condition that the program must test for may be more complicated than, say, whether a variable value is greater than a certain fixed value or
whether a field is not empty. Look at the case of validating a text field entry for
whether the entry contains all the numbers that your script may want. Without
some magical JavaScript function to tell you whether or not a string consists of all

numbers, you have to break apart the entry character by character and examine whether each character falls within the range of 0 through 9. But that examination actually comprises two tests: You can test for any character whose ASCII value is less than 0 or greater than 9. Alternatively, you can test whether the character is greater than or equal to 0 and is less than or equal to 9. What you need is the bottom-line evaluation of both tests.

Boolean math

That's where the wonder of Boolean math comes into play. With just two values — true and false — you can assemble a string of expressions that yield Boolean results and then let Boolean arithmetic figure out whether the bottom line is true or false.

But you don't add or subtract Boolean values the same way you add or subtract numbers. Instead, you use one of three JavaScript Boolean operators at your disposal. Table 40-6 shows the three operator symbols. In case you're unfamiliar with the characters in the table, the symbols for the Or operator are created by typing Shift-backslash.

Table 40-6   JavaScript Boolean Operators

Syntax	Name	Operands	Results
&&	And	Boolean	Boolean
||	Or	Boolean	Boolean
!	Not	One Boolean	Boolean

Using Boolean operators with Boolean operands gets tricky if you're not used to it, so I have you start with the simplest Boolean operator: Not. This operator requires only one operand. The Not operator precedes any Boolean value to switch it back to the opposite value (from true to false, or from false to true). For instance:

```
!true          // result = false
!(10 > 5)      // result = false
!(10 < 5)      // result = true
!(document.title == "Flintstones")    // result = true
```

As shown here, enclosing the operand of a Not expression inside parentheses is always a good idea. This forces JavaScript to evaluate the expression inside the parentheses before flipping it around with the Not operator.

The And (&&) operator joins two Boolean values to reach a true or false value based on the results of both values. This brings up something called a *truth table,* which helps you visualize all the possible outcomes for each value of an operand. Table 40-7 is a truth table for the And operator.

Table 40-7	**Truth Table for the And Operator**		
Left Operand	*And Operator*	*Right Operand*	*Result*
True	&&	True	True
True	&&	False	False
False	&&	True	False
False	&&	False	False

Only one condition yields a true result: Both operands must evaluate to true. Which side of the operator a true or false value lives doesn't matter. Here are examples of each possibility:

```
5 > 1 && 50 > 10    // result = true
5 > 1 && 50 < 10    // result = false
5 < 1 && 50 > 10    // result = false
5 < 1 && 50 < 10    // result = false
```

In contrast, the Or (||) operator is more lenient about what it evaluates to true. The reason is that if one or the other (or both) operands is true, the operation returns true. The Or operator's truth table is shown in Table 40-8.

Table 40-8	**Truth Table for the Or Operator**		
Left Operand	*Or Operator*	*Right Operand*	*Result*
True	||	True	True
True	||	False	True
False	||	True	True
False	||	False	False

Boolean Operators

Therefore, if a `true` value exists on either side of the operator, a `true` value is the result. Take the previous examples and swap the And operators with Or operators so that you can see the Or operator's impact on the results:

```
5 > 1 || 50 > 10    // result = true
5 > 1 || 50 < 10    // result = true
5 < 1 || 50 > 10    // result = true
5 < 1 || 50 < 10    // result = false
```

Only when both operands are `false` does the Or operator return `false`.

Boolean operators at work

Applying Boolean operators to JavaScript the first time just takes a little time and some sketches on a pad of paper to help you figure out the logic of the expressions. Earlier I talked about using a Boolean operator to see whether a character fell within a range of ASCII values for data-entry validation. Listing 40-1 (not on the CD-ROM) is a function discussed in more depth in Chapter 43. This function accepts any string and sees whether each character of the string has an ASCII value less than 0 or greater than 9 — meaning that the input string is not a number.

Listing 40-1: **Is the Input String a Number?**

```
function isNumber(inputStr) {
    for (var i = 0; i < inputStr.length; i++) {
        var oneChar = inputStr.substring(i, i + 1)
        if (oneChar < "0" || oneChar > "9") {
            alert("Please make sure entries are numerals only.")
            return false
        }
    }
    return true
}
```

Combining a number of JavaScript powers to read individual characters (substrings) from a `string` object within a `for` loop, the statement that you're interested in is the condition of the `if` construction:

```
(oneChar < "0" || oneChar > "9")
```

In one condition statement, you use the Or operator to test for both possibilities. If you check the Or truth table (Table 40-8), you see that this expression returns `true` if either one or both tests returns `true`. If that happens, the rest of the function alerts the user about the problem and returns a `false` value to the calling statement. Only if both tests within this condition evaluate to `false` for all characters of the string does the function return a `true` value.

From the simple Or operator, I go to the extreme, where the function checks — in one `condition` statement — whether a number falls within several numeric ranges. The script in Listing 40-2 comes from the array lookup application in Chapter 50, in which a user enters the first three digits of a U.S. Social Security number.

Listing 40-2: **Is a Number within Discontiguous Ranges?**

```
// function to determine if value is in acceptable range for this application
function inRange(inputStr) {
    num = parseInt(inputStr)
    if (num < 1 || (num > 586 && num < 596) || (num > 599 && num < 700) ||num >
728) {
        alert("Sorry, the number you entered is not part of our database.  Try
another three-digit number.")
        return false
    }
    return true
}
```

By the time this function is called, the user's data entry has been validated enough for JavaScript to know that the entry is a number. Now the function must check whether the number falls outside of the various ranges for which the application contains matching data. The conditions that the function tests here are whether the number is

✦ Less than 1

✦ Greater than 586 and less than 596 (using the And operator)

✦ Greater than 599 and less than 700 (using the And operator)

✦ Greater than 728

Each of these tests is joined by an Or operator. Therefore, if any one of these conditions proves `true`, the whole `if` condition is `true`, and the user is alerted accordingly.

The alternative to combining so many Boolean expressions in one `condition` statement would be to nest a series of `if` constructions. But such a construction requires not only a great deal more code but also much repetition of the alert dialog box message for each condition that could possibly fail. The combined Boolean condition is, by far, the best way to go.

Bitwise Operators

	NN2	NN3	NN4	NN6	IE3/J1	IE3/J2	IE4	IE5	IE5.5
Compatibility	✓	✓	✓	✓	✓	✓	✓	✓	✓

For scripters, bitwise operations are an advanced subject. Unless you're dealing with external processes on CGIs or the connection to Java applets, it's unlikely that you will use bitwise operators. Experienced programmers who concern themselves with more specific data types (such as long integers) are quite comfortable in this arena, so I simply provide an explanation of JavaScript capabilities. Table 40-9 lists JavaScript bitwise operators.

Table 40-9   JavaScript's Bitwise Operators

Operator	Name	Left Operand	Right Operand
&	Bitwise And	Integer value	Integer value
|	Bitwise Or	Integer value	Integer value
^	Bitwise XOR	Integer value	Integer value
~	Bitwise Not	(None)	Integer value
<<	Left shift	Integer value	Shift amount
>>	Right shift	Integer value	Shift amount
>>>	Zero fill right shift	Integer value	Shift amount

The numeric value operands can appear in any of the JavaScript language's three numeric literal bases (decimal, octal, or hexadecimal). As soon as the operator has an operand, the value is converted to binary representation (32 bits long). For the first three bitwise operations, the individual bits of one operand are compared with their counterparts in the other operand. The resulting value for each bit depends on the operator:

✦ **Bitwise And:** 1 if both digits are 1

✦ **Bitwise Or:** 1 if either digit is 1

✦ **Bitwise Exclusive Or:** 1 if only one digit is a 1

Bitwise Not, a unary operator, inverts the value of every bit in the single operand. The bitwise shift operators operate on a single operand. The second operand specifies the number of positions to shift the value's binary digits in the direction of the arrows of the operator symbols. For example, the left shift (<<) operator has the following effect:

```
4 << 2 // result = 16
```

The reason for this shifting is that the binary representation for decimal 4 is 00000100 (to eight digits, anyway). The left shift operator instructs JavaScript to shift all digits two places to the left, giving the binary result 00010000, which converts to 16 in decimal format. If you're interested in experimenting with these operators, use The Evaluator (Chapter 13) to evaluate sample expressions for yourself. More advanced books on C and C++ programming are also of help.

Object Operators

The next group of operators concern themselves with objects (including native JavaScript, DOM, and custom objects) and data types. Most of these have been implemented after the earliest JavaScript browsers, so each one has its own compatibility rating.

delete

	NN2	NN3	NN4	NN6	IE3/J1	IE3/J2	IE4	IE5	IE5.5
Compatibility			✓	✓			✓	✓	✓

Array objects do not contain a method to remove an element from the collection, nor do custom objects offer a method to remove a property. You can always empty the data in an array item or property by setting its value to an empty string or null, but the array element or property remains in the object. With the delete operator, you can completely remove the element or property.

There is special behavior about deleting an array item that you should bear in mind. If your array uses numeric indices, a deletion of a given index removes that index value from the total array but without collapsing the array (which would alter index values of items higher than the deleted item). For example, consider the following simple dense array:

```
var oceans = new Array("Atlantic", "Pacific", "Indian","Arctic")
```

This kind of array automatically assigns numeric indices to its entries for addressing later in constructions, such as `for` loops:

```
for (var i = 0; i < oceans.length; i++) {
    if (oceans[i] == form.destination.value) {
        statements
    }
}
```

If you then issue the statement

```
delete oceans[2]
```

the array undergoes significant changes. First, the third element is removed from the array. Note that the length of the array does not change. Even so, the index value (2) is removed from the array, such that schematically the array looks as the following:

```
oceans[0] = "Atlantic"
oceans[1] = "Pacific"
oceans[3] = "Arctic"
```

If you try to reference `oceans[2]` in this collection, the result is `undefined`.

The `delete` operator works best on arrays that have named indices. Your scripts will have more control over the remaining entries and their values, because they don't rely on what could be a missing entry of a numeric index sequence.

One aspect of this deletion action that JavaScript doesn't provide is absolute control over memory utilization. All garbage collection is managed by the JavaScript interpreter engine, which tries to recognize when items occupying memory are no longer needed, at which time the unused browser's application memory may be recovered. But you cannot force the browser to perform its garbage collection task.

in

	NN2	NN3	NN4	NN6	IE3/J1	IE3/J2	IE4	IE5	IE5.5
Compatibility				✓					✓

The `in` operator lets a script statement inspect an object to see if it has a named property or method. The operand to the left of the operator is a string reference to the property or method (just the method name, without parentheses); the operand to the right of the operator is the object being inspected. If the object knows the property or method, the expression returns `true`. Thus, you can use the `in` operator in expressions used for conditional expressions.

You can experiment with this operator in The Evaluator. For example, to prove that the `write()` method is implemented for the `document` object, the expression you type into the top text box of The Evaluator is:

```
"write" in document
```

But compare the implementation of the W3C DOM `document.createAttribute()` method in IE5.5 and NN6:

```
"createAttribute" in document
```

In NN6, the result is `true`, while in IE5.5, the result is `false`.

Having this operator around for conditional expressions lets you go much beyond simple object detection for branching code. For example, if you intend to use `document.createAttribute()` in your script, you can make sure that the method is supported before invoking it (assuming your users all have browsers that know the in operator).

instanceof

	NN2	NN3	NN4	NN6	IE3/J1	IE3/J2	IE4	IE5	IE5.5
Compatibility				✓				✓	✓

The `instanceof` operator (not implemented in IE5/Mac) lets a script test whether an object is an instance of a particular JavaScript native object or DOM object (in NN6). The operand to the left side of the operator is the value under test; the value to the right of the operand is a reference to the root class from which the value is suspected of being constructed.

For native JavaScript classes, the kinds of object references to the right of the operator include such static objects as `Date`, `String`, `Number`, `Boolean`, `Object`, `Array`, and `RegExp`. You sometimes need to be mindful of how native JavaScript classes can sometimes be children of other native classes, which means that a value may be an instance of two different static objects. For example, consider the following sequence (which you can follow along in The Evaluator):

```
a = new Array(1,2,3)
a instanceof Array
```

The second statement yields a result of `true`, because the `Array` constructor was used to generate the object. But the JavaScript `Array` is, itself, an instance of the root `Object` object. Therefore both of the following statements evaluate to `true`:

```
a instanceof Object
Array instanceof Object
```

NN6 also supports this functionality for W3C DOM objects to some degree. For instance, you can see that the `document` node is an instance of the root `Node` object:

```
document instanceof Node
```

But NN6 also erroneously reports instances of a variety of nodes and elements outside the strict inheritance hierarchy of the W3C DOM (for instance, NN6 also reports that `document` is an instance of `HTMLElement`, which it clearly is not).

new

	NN2	NN3	NN4	NN6	IE3/J1	IE3/J2	IE4	IE5	IE5.5
Compatibility	✓	✓	✓	✓	✓	✓	✓	✓	✓

Most JavaScript core objects have constructor functions built into the language. To access those functions, you use the `new` operator along with the name of the constructor. The function returns a reference to the object instance, which your scripts can then use to get and set properties or invoke object methods. For example, creating a `new` date object requires invoking the `Date` object's constructor, as follows:

```
var today = new Date()
```

Some object constructor functions require parameters to help define the object. Others, as in the case of the `Date` object, can accept a number of different parameter formats, depending on the format of date information you have to set the initial object. The `new` operator can be used with the following core language objects:

JavaScript 1.0	JavaScript 1.1	JavaScript 1.2	JavaScript 1.5
Date	Array	RegExp	Error
Object	Boolean		
(Custom object)	Function		

JavaScript 1.0	JavaScript 1.1	JavaScript 1.2	JavaScript 1.5
	Number		
	String		

this

	NN2	NN3	NN4	NN6	IE3/J1	IE3/J2	IE4	IE5	IE5.5
Compatibility	✓	✓	✓	✓	✓	✓	✓	✓	✓

JavaScript includes an operator that allows script statements to refer to the very object in which they are located. The self-referential operator is this.

The most common application of the this operator is in event handlers that pass references of themselves to functions for further processing, as in

```
<INPUT TYPE="text" NAME="entry" onChange="process(this)">
```

A function receiving the value assigns it to a variable that can be used to reference the sender, its properties, and its methods.

Because the this operator references an object, that object's properties can be exposed with the aid of the operator. For example, to send the value property of a text input object to a function, the this operator stands in for the current object reference and appends the proper syntax to reference the value property:

```
<INPUT TYPE="text" NAME="entry" onChange="process(this.value)">
```

The this operator also works inside other objects, such as custom objects. When you define a constructor function for a custom object, using the this operator to define properties of the object and assign values to those properties is common practice. Consider the following example of an object creation sequence:

```
function bottledWater(brand, ozSize, flavor) {
    this.brand = brand
    this.ozSize = ozSize
    this.flavor = flavor
}
var myWater = new bottledWater("Crystal Springs", 16, "original")
```

When the new object is created via the constructor function, the this operators define each property of the object and then assign the corresponding incoming value to that property. Using the same names for the properties and parameter variables is perfectly fine and makes the constructor easy to maintain.

By extension, if you assign a function as an object's property (to behave as a method for the object), the this operator inside that function refers to the object invoking the function, offering an avenue to the object's properties. For example, if I add the following function definition and statement to the myWater object created just above, the function can directly access the brand property of the object:

```
function adSlogan() {
    return "Drink " + this.brand + ", it's wet and wild!"
}
myWater.getSlogan = adSlogan
```

When a statement invokes the myWater.getSlogan() method, the object invokes the adSlogan() function, but all within the context of the myWater object. Thus, the this operator applies to the surrounding object, making the brand property available via the this operator (this.brand).

Miscellaneous Operators

The final group of operators doesn't fit into any of the previous categories, but they are no less important.

	NN2	NN3	NN4	NN6	IE3/J1	IE3/J2	IE4	IE5	IE5.5
Compatibility	✓	✓	✓	✓	✓	✓	✓	✓	✓

The comma operator indicates a series of expressions that are to be evaluated in left-to-right sequence. Most typically, this operator is used to permit multiple variable initializations. For example, you can combine the declaration of several variables in a single var statement, as follows:

```
var name, address, serialNumber
```

Another situation where you could use this operator is within the expressions of a for loop construction. In the following example, two different counting variables are initialized and incremented at different rates. When the loop begins, both variables are initialized at zero (they don't have to be, but this example starts that way); for each subsequent trip through the loop, one variable is incremented by one, while the other is incremented by 10:

```
for (var i=0, j=0; i < someLength; i++, j+10) {
    ...
}
```

Don't confuse the comma operator with the semi-colon delimiter between statements.

? :

	NN2	NN3	NN4	NN6	IE3/J1	IE3/J2	IE4	IE5	IE5.5
Compatibility	✓	✓	✓	✓	✓	✓	✓	✓	✓

The conditional operator is a shortcut way of expressing an `if. . .else` conditional construction covered in Chapter 39. This operator is typically used in concert with an assignment operator to assign one of two values to a variable based on the result of a condition expression. The formal syntax for the conditional operator is:

```
condition ? expressionIfTrue : expressionIfFalse
```

If used with an assignment operator, the syntax is:

```
var = condition ? expressionIfTrue : expressionIfFalse
```

No matter how you use the operator, the important point to remember is that an expression that contains this operator evaluates to one of the two expressions following the question mark symbol. In truth, either expression could invoke any JavaScript, including calling other functions or even nesting further conditional operators within one of the expressions to achieve the equivalent of nested `if. . .else` constructions. To assure proper resolution of nested conditionals, surround inner expressions with parentheses to make sure that they evaluate before the outer expression evaluates. As an example, the following statement assigns one of three strings to a variable depending on the date within a month:

```
var monthPart = (dateNum <= 10) ? "early" : ((dateNum <= 20) ? "middle" : "late")
```

When the statement is evaluated, the inner conditional expression at the right of the first colon is evaluated, returning either `middle` or `late`; then the outer conditional expression is evaluated, returning either `early` or the result of the inner conditional expression.

typeof

	NN2	NN3	NN4	NN6	IE3/J1	IE3/J2	IE4	IE5	IE5.5
Compatibility		✓	✓	✓	✓	✓	✓	✓	✓

Unlike most other operators, which are predominantly concerned with arithmetic and logic, the unary typeof operator defines the kind of value to which a variable or expression evaluates. Typically, this operator is used to identify whether a variable value is one of the following types: number, string, boolean, object, function, or undefined.

Having this investigative capability in JavaScript is helpful because variables cannot only contain any one of those data types but can change their data type on the fly. Your scripts may need to handle a value differently based on the value's type. The most common use of the typeof property is as part of a condition. For example:

```
if (typeof myVal == "number") {
    myVal = parseInt(myVal)
}
```

The evaluated value of the typeof operation is, itself, a string.

void

	NN2	NN3	NN4	NN6	IE3/J1	IE3/J2	IE4	IE5	IE5.5
Compatibility		✓	✓	✓		✓	✓	✓	✓

In all scriptable browsers you can use the javascript: pseudo-protocol to supply the parameter for HREF and SRC attributes in HTML tags, such as links. In the process, you have to be careful that the function or statement being invoked by the URL does not return or evaluate to any values. If a value comes back from such an expression, then that value or sometimes the directory of the client's hard disk often replaces the page content. To avoid this possibility use the void operator in front of the function or expression being invoked by the javascript: URL.

The best way to use this construction is to place the operator before the expression or function and separate them by a space, as in

```
javascript: void doSomething()
```

On occasion, you may have to wrap the expression inside parentheses after the void operator. Using paranthenses is necessary only when the expression contains operators of a lower precedence than the void operator (see the following section, "Operator Precedence"). But don't automatically wrap all expressions in parentheses, because some browsers can experience problems with these. Even so, it is common practice to assign the following URL to the HREF attribute of an A link whose onClick event handler does all of the work:

```
HREF="javascript: void (0)"
```

The void operator makes sure the function or expression returns no value that the HTML attribute can use. Such a link's onClick event handler should also inhibit the natural behavior of a clicked link (for example, by evaluating to return false).

Operator Precedence

When you start working with complex expressions that hold a number of operators (for example, Listing 40-2), knowing the order in which JavaScript evaluates those expressions is vital. JavaScript assigns different priorities or weights to types of operators in an effort to achieve uniformity in the way it evaluates complex expressions.

In the following expression

```
10 + 4 * 5 // result = 30
```

JavaScript uses its precedence scheme to perform the multiplication before the addition — regardless of where the operators appear in the statement. In other words, JavaScript first multiplies 4 by 5, and then adds that result to 10 to get a result of 30. That may not be the way you want this expression to evaluate. Perhaps your intention was to add the 10 and 4 first and then to multiply that sum by 5. To make that happen, you have to override JavaScript's natural operator precedence. To do that, you must use parentheses to enclose an operator with lower precedence. The following statement shows how you adjust the previous expression to make it behave differently:

```
(10 + 4) * 5 // result = 70
```

That one set of parentheses has a great impact on the outcome. Parentheses have the highest precedence in JavaScript, and if you nest parentheses in an expression, the innermost set evaluates first.

For help in constructing complex expressions, refer to Table 40-10 for JavaScript's operator precedence. My general practice: When in doubt about complex precedence issues, I build the expression with lots of parentheses according to the way I want the internal expressions to evaluate.

	Table 40-10 **JavaScript Operator Precedence**	
Precedence Level	*Operator*	*Notes*
1	`()`	From innermost to outermost
	`[]`	Array index value
	`function()`	Any remote function call
2	`!`	Boolean Not
	`~`	Bitwise Not
	`-`	Negation
	`++`	Increment
	`--`	Decrement
	`new`	
	`typeof`	
	`void`	
	`delete`	Delete array or object entry
3	`*`	Multiplication
	`/`	Division
	`%`	Modulo
4	`+`	Addition
	`-`	Subtraction
5	`<<`	Bitwise shifts
	`>`	
	`>>`	
6	`<`	Comparison operators
	`<=`	
	`>`	
	`>=`	
7	`==`	Equality
	`!=`	
8	`&`	Bitwise And
9	`^`	Bitwise XOR
10	`|`	Bitwise Or

Precedence Level	Operator	Notes
11	&&	Boolean And
12	||	Boolean Or
13	?	Conditional expression
14	=	Assignment operators
	+=	
	-=	
	*=	
	/=	
	%=	
	<<=	
	>=	
	>>=	
	&=	
	^=	
	|=	
15	,	Comma (parameter delimiter)

This precedence scheme is devised to help you avoid being faced with two operators from the same precedence level that often appear in the same expression. When it happens (such as with addition and subtraction), JavaScript begins evaluating the expression from left to right.

One related fact involves a string of Boolean expressions strung together for a `condition` statement (Listing 40-2). JavaScript follows what is called *short-circuit evaluation*. As the nested expressions are evaluated left to right, the fate of the entire condition can sometimes be determined before all expressions are evaluated. Any time JavaScript encounters an And operator, if the left operand evaluates to `false`, the entire expression evaluates to `false` without JavaScript's even bothering to evaluate the right operand. For an Or operator, if the left operand is `true`, JavaScript short-circuits that expression to `true`. This feature can trip you up if you don't perform enough testing on your scripts: If a syntax error or other error exists in a right operand, and you fail to test the expression in a way that forces that right operand to evaluate, you may not know that a bug exists in your code. Users of your page, of course, will find the bug quickly. Do your testing to head bugs off at the pass.

Note   Notice, too, that all math and string concatenation is performed prior to any comparison operators. This enables all expressions that act as operands for comparisons to evaluate fully before they are compared.

The key to working with complex expressions is to isolate individual expressions and to try them out by themselves, if you can. See additional debugging tips in Chapter 45.

✦   ✦   ✦

Functions and Custom Objects

By now, you've seen dozens of JavaScript functions in action and probably have a pretty good feel for the way they work. This chapter provides the `function` object specification and delves into the fun prospect of creating objects in your JavaScript code. (That includes objects that have properties and methods, just like the big boys.)

Function Object

Properties	Methods
arguments	apply()
arity	call()
caller	toString()
constructor	valueOf()
length	
prototype	

Syntax

Creating a function object:

```
function functionName([arg1,...[,argN]]) {
    statement(s)
}
var funcName = new Function(["argName1",...[,"argNameN"],
"statement1;...[;statementN]"])
object.eventHandlerName = function([arg1,...[,argN]])
{statement(s)}
```

Accessing function object properties and methods:

```
functionObject.property | method([parameters])
```

	NN2	NN3	NN4	NN6	IE3/J1	IE3/J2	IE4	IE5	IE5.5
Compatibility	(✓)	✓	✓	✓	(✓)	✓	✓	✓	✓

About this object

JavaScript accommodates what other languages might call procedures, subroutines, and functions all in one type of structure: the *custom function*. A function may return a value (if programmed to do so with the `return` keyword), but it does not have to return any value. Except for JavaScript code that executes as the document loads, all deferred processing takes place in functions.

While you can create functions that are hundreds of lines long, I recommend you break up longer processes into shorter functions. Among the reasons for doing so: smaller chunks are easier to write and debug; building blocks make it easier to visualize the entire script; you can make functions generalizable and reusable for other scripts; and other parts of the script or other open frames can use the functions.

Learning how to write good, reusable functions takes time and experience. But the earlier you understand the importance of this concept, the more you will be on the lookout for good examples in other people's scripts on the Web.

Creating functions

The standard way of defining a function in your script means following a simple pattern and then filling in the details. The formal syntax definition for a function is:

```
function functionName( [arg1] ... [, argN]) {
    statement(s)
}
```

The task of assigning a function name helps you determine the precise scope of activity of the function. If you find that you can't reduce the planned task for the function to a simple one- to three-word name (which is then condensed into one contiguous sequence of characters for the *functionName*), perhaps you're asking the function to do too much. A better idea may be to break the job into two or more functions. As you start to design a function, be on the lookout for functions that you can call from the one you're writing. If you find yourself copying and pasting lines of code from one part of a function to another because you're performing the same operation in different spots within the function, it may be time to break that segment out into its own function.

Starting with Navigator 3 (and Internet Explorer 3 with JScript.dll version2), you can also create what is called an *anonymous function* using the `new Function()` constructor. In reality, you assign a name to this "anonymous" function as follows:

```
var funcName = new Function(["argName1",...[,"argNameN"],
"statement1;...[;statementN]"])
```

This other way of building a function is particularly helpful when your scripts need to create a function after a document loads. All the components of a function are present in this definition. Each function parameter name is supplied as a string value, separated from each other by commas. The final parameter string consists of the statements that execute whenever the function is called. Separate each JavaScript statement with a semicolon, and enclose the entire sequence of statements inside quotes, as in the following:

```
var willItFit = new Function("width","height",
"var sx = screen.availWidth; var sy = screen.availHeight; return (sx >= width &&
sy >= height)")
```

The `willItFit()` function takes two parameters; the body of the function defines two local variables (`sx` and `sy`) and then returns a Boolean value of `true` if the incoming parameters are smaller than the local variables. In traditional form, this function is defined as follows:

```
function willItFit(width, height) {
    var sx = screen.availWidth
    var sy = screen.availHeight
    return (sx >= width && sy >= height)
}
```

Once this function exists in the browser's memory, you can invoke it like any other function:

```
if (willItFit(400,500)) {
    statements to load image
}
```

One last function creation format is available in NN4+. This advanced technique, called a *lambda expression,* provides a shortcut for creating a reference to an anonymous function (truly anonymous because the function has no name that you can reference later). The common application of this technique is to assign function references to event handlers when the NN event object also must be passed. The following is an example of how to assign an anonymous function to an `onChange` event handler for a form control:

```
document.forms[0].age.onchange = function(event)
{isNumber(document.forms[0].age)}
```

Nesting functions

NN4+ and IE4+ also provide for nesting functions inside one another. In all prior scripting, each function definition is defined at the global level whereby every function is exposed and available to all other scripting. With nested functions, you can encapsulate the exposure of a function inside another and make that nested function private to the enclosing function. Of course I don't recommend reusing names in this fashion, but you can create nested functions with the same name inside multiple global level functions, as the following skeletal structure shows:

```
function outerA() {
    statements
    function innerA() {
        statements
    }
    statements
}
function outerB() {
    statements
    function innerA() {
        statements
    }
    function innerB() {
        statements
    }
    statements
}
```

A good time to apply a nested function is when a sequence of statements need to be invoked in multiple places within a large function but those statements have meaning only within the context of the larger function. In other words, rather than break out the repeated sequence as a separate global function, you keep it all within the scope of the larger function.

You can access a nested function only from statements in its containing function (and in any order). Moreover, all variables defined in the outer function (including parameter variables) are accessible to the inner function; but variables defined in an inner function are not accessible to the outer function. See the section, "Variable Scope: Globals and Locals" later in this chapter for details on how variables are visible to various components of a script.

Function parameters

The function definition requires a set of parentheses after the *functionName*. If the function does not rely on any information arriving with it when invoked, the parentheses can be empty. But when some kind of data is arriving with a call to the function, you need to assign names to each parameter. Virtually any kind of value can be a parameter: strings, numbers, Booleans, and even complete object references such as a form or form element. Choose names for these variables that help you remember the content of those values; also, avoid reusing existing object names as variable names because it's easy to get confused when objects and variables with the same name appear in the same statements. You must avoid using JavaScript keywords (including the reserved words listed in Appendix B) and any global variable name defined elsewhere in your script. (See more about global variables in the following sections.)

JavaScript is forgiving about matching the number of parameters in the function definition with the number of parameters passed along from the calling statement. If you define a function with three parameters and the calling statement specifies only two, the third parameter variable value in that function is assigned a null value. For example:

```
function oneFunction(a, b, c) {
    statements
}
oneFunction("George","Gracie")
```

In the preceding example, the values of a and b inside the function are "George" and "Gracie", respectively; the value of c is null.

At the opposite end of the spectrum, JavaScript also doesn't balk if you send more parameters from the calling statement than the number of parameter variables specified in the function definition. In fact, the language includes a mechanism — the arguments property — that you can add to your function to gather any extraneous parameters that should read your function.

Properties

arguments

Value: Array of arguments   Read-Only

	NN2	NN3	NN4	NN6	IE3/J1	IE3/J2	IE4	IE5	IE5.5
Compatibility	✓	✓	✓			✓	✓	✓	✓

When a function receives parameter values from the statement that invokes the function, those parameter values are silently assigned to the arguments property of the function object. This property is an array of the values, with each parameter value assigned to a zero-based index entry in the array — whether or not parameters are defined for it. You can find out how many parameters are sent by extracting *functionName*.arguments.length. For example, if four parameters are passed, *functionName*.arguments.length returns 4. Then, you can use array notation (*functionName*.arguments[*i*]) to extract the values of any parameter(s) you want.

Theoretically, you never have to define parameter variables for your functions by extracting the desired arguments array entry instead. Well-chosen parameter variable names, however, are much more readable, so I recommend them over the arguments property in most cases. But you may run into situations in which a single function definition needs to handle multiple calls to the function when each call may have a different number of parameters. The function knows how to handle any arguments over and above the ones given names as parameter variables.

See Listings 41-1 and 41-2 for a demonstration of both the arguments and caller properties.

arity

Value: Integer   Read-Only

	NN2	NN3	NN4	NN6	IE3/J1	IE3/J2	IE4	IE5	IE5.5
Compatibility			✓	✓					

See the discussion of the length property later in this chapter.

caller

Value: Function Object Reference   Read-Only

	NN2	NN3	NN4	NN6	IE3/J1	IE3/J2	IE4	IE5	IE5.5
Compatibility		✓	✓			✓	✓	✓	✓

Note The caller property, not part of the ECMA-262 standard, was removed from NN for version 6.

When one function invokes another, a chain is established between the two primarily so that a returned value knows where to go. Therefore, a function invoked by another maintains a reference to the function that called it. Such information is automatically stored in a function object as the `caller` property. This relationship reminds me a bit of a subwindow's `opener` property, which points to the window or frame responsible for the subwindow's creation. The value is valid only while the called function is running at the request of another function; when a function isn't running, its `caller` property is `null`.

The value of the `caller` property is a reference to a function object, so you can inspect its `arguments` and `caller` properties (in case it was called by yet another function). Thus, a function can look back at a calling function to see what values it was passed.

The *functionName*.`caller` property reveals the contents of an entire function definition if the current function was called from another function (including an event handler). If the call for a function comes from a regular JavaScript statement not originating from inside a function, the *functionName*.`caller` property is `null`.

To help you grasp all that these two properties yield, study Listing 41-1.

Listing 41-1: **A Function's arguments and caller Properties**

```
<HTML>
<HEAD>
<SCRIPT LANGUAGE="JavaScript">
function hansel(x,y) {
    var args = hansel.arguments
    document.write("<P>hansel.caller is " + hansel.caller + "<BR>")
    document.write("hansel.arguments.length is " + hansel.arguments.length +
"<BR>")
    for (var i = 0; i < args.length; i++) {
        document.write("argument " + i + " is " + args[i] + "<BR>")
    }
    document.write("</P>")
}

function gretel(x,y,z) {
    today = new Date()
    thisYear = today.getFullYear()
    hansel(x,y,z,thisYear)
}
</SCRIPT>
</HEAD>
<BODY>
<SCRIPT LANGUAGE="JavaScript">
hansel(1, "two", 3);
gretel(4, "five", 6, "seven");
</SCRIPT>
</BODY>
</HTML>
```

When you load this page, the following results appear in the browser window (although the `caller` property values show `undefined` for NN6):

```
hansel.caller is null
hansel.arguments.length is 3
argument 0 is 1
argument 1 is two
argument 2 is 3

hansel.caller is function gretel(x, y, z) { today = new Date(); thisYear =
today.getFullYear(); hansel(x, y, z, thisYear); }

hansel.arguments.length is 4
argument 0 is 4
argument 1 is five
argument 2 is 6
argument 3 is 2001 (or whatever the current year is)
```

As the document loads, the `hansel()` function is called directly in the body script. It passes three arguments, even though the `hansel()` function defines only two. The `hansel.arguments` property picks up all three arguments just the same. The main body script then invokes the `gretel()` function, which, in turn, calls `hansel()` again. But when `gretel()` makes the call, it passes four parameters. The `gretel()` function picks up only three of the four arguments sent by the calling statement. It also inserts another value from its own calculations as an extra parameter to be sent to `hansel()`. The `hansel.caller` property reveals the entire content of the `gretel()` function, whereas `hansel.arguments` picks up all four parameters, including the year value introduced by the `gretel()` function.

Neither the `caller` nor `arguments` properties of a `function` object appear in the ECMA-262 Edition 3 specification. While NN6 dropped the `caller` property, it continues to support the `arguments` property probably because a lot of scripters use it.

constructor

See `string.constructor` (Chapter 34).

length

Value: Integer   Read-Only

	NN2	NN3	NN4	NN6	IE3/J1	IE3/J2	IE4	IE5	IE5.5
Compatibility			✓	✓		✓	✓	✓	✓

As the `arguments` property of a function proves, JavaScript is very forgiving about matching the number of parameters passed to a function with the number of parameter variables defined for the function. But a script can examine the `length` property of a function object to see precisely how many parameter variables are defined for a function. A reference to the property starts with the function name representing the object. For example, consider the following function definition shell:

```
function identify(name, rank, serialNum) {
    ...
}
```

A script statement anywhere outside of the function can read the number of parameters with the reference:

```
identify.length
```

The value of the property in the preceding example is 3. The `length` property supercedes the NN-only `arity` property.

prototype

See `Array.prototype` (Chapter 37).

Methods

```
apply([thisObj[, argumentsArray]])
call([thisObj[, arg1[, arg2[,...argN]]]])
```

Returns: Nothing.

	NN2	NN3	NN4	NN6	IE3/J1	IE3/J2	IE4	IE5	IE5.5
Compatibility				✓					✓

The `apply()` and `call()` methods of a function object invoke the function. This may seem redundant to the normal way in which script statements invoke functions by simply naming the function, following it with parentheses, passing parameters, and so on. The difference with these methods is that you can invoke the function if your script has only a reference to the function. For example, if your script defines a function via the `new Function()` constructor (or other anonymous shortcut supported by the browser), you receive a reference to the function as a result of the constructor. To invoke the function later using only that reference (presumably preserved in a global variable), use either the `apply()` or `call()` method. Both of these methods achieve the same result, but choosing one method over the other depends on the form in which the function's parameters are conveyed (more about that in a moment).

The first parameter of both methods is a reference to the object that the function treats as the current object. For garden-variety functions defined in your script, use the keyword `this`, which means that the function's context becomes the current object (just like a regular function). In fact, if there are no parameters to be sent to the function, you can omit parameters to both methods altogether.

The object reference comes into play when the function being invoked is one that is normally defined as a method to a custom object. (I cover some of these concepts later in this chapter, so you may need to return here after you are familiar with custom objects.) Consider the following code that generates a custom object and assigns a method to the object to display an alert about properties of the object:

```
// function to be invoked as a method from a 'car' object
function showCar() {
    alert(this.make + " : " + this.color)
}
// 'car' object constructor function
function car(make, color) {
    this.make = make
    this.color = color
    this.show = showCar
}
// create instance of a 'car' object
var myCar = new car("Ford", "blue")
```

The normal way of getting the `myCar` object to display an alert about its properties is:

```
myCar.show()
```

At that point, the `showCar()` function runs, picking up the current `car` object as the context for the `this` references in the function. In other words, when the `showCar()` function runs as a method of the object, the function treats the object as the "current object."

With the `call()` or `apply()` methods, however, you don't have to bind the `showCar()` function to the `myCar` object. You can omit the statement in the `car()` constructor that assigns the `showCar` function to a method name for the object. Instead, a script can invoke the `showCar()` method and instruct it to treat `myCar` as the current object:

```
showCar.call(myCar)
```

The `showCar()` function operates just as before, and the object reference in the `call()` method's first parameter slot is treated as the current object for the `showCar()` function.

As for succeeding parameters, the `apply()` method's second parameter is an array of values to be passed as parameters to the current function. The order of the values must match the order of parameter variables defined for the function. The `call()` method, on the other hand, enables you to pass individual parameters in a comma-delimited list. Your choice depends on how the parameters are carried along in your script. If they're already in array form, then use the `apply()` method; otherwise, use the `call()` method. The (ECMA) recommended way to invoke a function through this mechanism when no parameters need to be passed is via the `call()` method.

toString()
valueOf()

Returns: String.

	NN2	NN3	NN4	NN6	IE3/J1	IE3/J2	IE4	IE5	IE5.5
Compatibility			✓	✓			✓	✓	✓

Scripts rarely, if ever, summon the `toString()` and `valueOf()` methods of a function object. They work internally to allow debugging scripts to display a string version of the function definition. For example, when you enter the name of a function defined in The Evaluator into the top text box, JavaScript automatically converts the function to a string so that its "value" can be displayed in the Results box. Using these methods or parsing the text they return has little, if any, practical application.

Function Application Notes

Understanding the ins and outs of JavaScript functions is the key to successful scripting, especially for complex applications. Additional topics covered in this chapter include the ways to invoke functions, variable scope in and around functions, recursion, and the design of reusable functions.

Invoking Functions

A function doesn't perform any work until a script calls it by name or reference. Scripts invoke functions (that is, get functions to do something) via four routes: document object event handlers; JavaScript statements; HREF attributes pointing to a javascript: URL; and the more recent call() and apply() methods of function objects. The one approach not discussed at length yet in this book is the javascript: URL (some say pseudo-URL).

Several HTML tags have HREF attributes that normally point to Internet URLs for navigating to another page or loading a MIME file that requires a helper application or plug-in. These HTML tags are usually tags for clickable objects, such as links and client-side image map areas.

A JavaScript-enabled browser has a special, built-in URL pseudo-protocol — javascript: — that lets the HREF attribute point to a JavaScript function or method rather than to a URL out on the Net. For example, it is common practice to use the javascript: URL to change the contents of two frames from a single link. Because the HREF attribute is designed to point to only a single URL, you'd be out of luck without a convenient way to put multiframe navigation into your hands. Implement multiframe navigation by writing a function that sets the location.href properties of the two frames; then invoke that function from the HREF attribute. The following example shows what the script may look like:

```
function loadPages() {
    parent.frames[1].location.href = "page2.html"
    parent.frames[2].location.href = "instrux2.html"
}
...
<A HREF="javascript:loadPages()">Next</A>
```

Note   These kinds of function invocations can include parameters, and the functions can do anything you want. One potential side effect to watch out for occurs when the function returns a value (perhaps the function is also invoked from other script locations where a returned value is expected). Because the HREF attribute sets the TARGET window to whatever the attribute evaluates to, the returned value is assigned to the TARGET window — probably not what you want.

To prevent the assignment of a returned value to the HREF attribute, prefix the function call with the void operator:

```
<A HREF="javascript:void loadPages()">
```

If you don't want the HREF attribute to do anything (that is, let the onClick event handler do all the work), then assign a blank function after the operator:

```
<A HREF="javascript:void (0)">
```

Experienced programmers of many other languages recognize this operator as a way of indicating that no values are returned from a function or procedure. The operator has that precise functionality here, but in a nontraditional location.

Variable Scope: Globals and Locals

A variable can have two scopes in JavaScript. As you might expect, any variable initialized within the main flow of a script (not inside a function) is a *global variable* in that any statement in the same document's script can access it by name. You can, however, also initialize variables inside a function (in a var statement) so the variable name applies only to statements inside that function. By limiting the scope of the variable to a single function, you can reuse the same variable name in multiple functions thereby enabling the variables to carry very different information in each function. Listing 41-2 demonstrates the various possibilities.

Listing 41-2: **Variable Scope Workbench Page**

```
<HTML>
<HEAD>
<TITLE>Variable Scope Trials</TITLE>
<SCRIPT LANGUAGE="JavaScript">
var headGlobal = "Gumby"
function doNothing() {
    var headLocal = "Pokey"
    return headLocal
}
</SCRIPT>
</HEAD>

<BODY>
<SCRIPT LANGUAGE="JavaScript">
// two global variables
var aBoy = "Charlie Brown"
var hisDog = "Snoopy"
function testValues() {
    var hisDog = "Gromit"  // initializes local version of "hisDog"
    var page = ""
    page += "headGlobal is: " + headGlobal + "<BR>"
    // page += "headLocal is: " + headLocal + "<BR>" // : headLocal not defined
    page += "headLocal value returned from head function is: " + doNothing() +
"<P>"
    page += " aBoy is: " + aBoy + "<BR>" // picks up global
    page += "local version of hisDog is: " + hisDog + "<P>" // "sees" only local
    document.write(page)
}
```

Continued

Listing 41-2: *(continued)*

```
testValues()
document.write("global version of hisDog is intact: " + hisDog)
</SCRIPT>
</BODY>
</HTML>
```

In this page, you define a number of variables — some global, others local — that are spread out in the document's Head and Body sections. When you load this page, it runs the `testValues()` function, which accounts for the current values of all the variable names. The script then follows up with one more value extraction that was masked in the function. The results of the page look like this:

```
headGlobal is: Gumby
headLocal value returned from head function is: Pokey

aBoy is: Charlie Brown
local version of hisDog is: Gromit

global version of hisDog is intact: Snoopy
```

Examine the variable initialization throughout this script. In the Head, you define the first variable (`headGlobal`) as a global style outside of any function definition. The `var` keyword for the global variable is optional but often helpful for enabling you to see at a glance where you initialize your variables. You then create a short function, which defines a variable (`headLocal`) that only statements in the function can use.

In the Body, you define two more global variables: `aBoy` and `hisDog`. Inside the Body's function (for purposes of demonstration), you reuse the `hisDog` variable name. By initializing `hisDog` with the `var` statement inside the function, you tell JavaScript to create a separate variable whose scope is only within the function. This initialization does not disturb the global variable of the same name. It can, however, make things confusing for you as the script author.

Statements in this script attempt to collect the values of variables scattered around the script. Even from within this script, JavaScript has no problem extracting global variables directly — including the one defined in the Head. But JavaScript cannot get the local variable defined in the other function — that `headLocal` variable is private to its own function. Trying to run a script that references that variable value will result in an error message saying that the variable name is not defined. In the eyes of everyone else outside of the `doNothing()` function, that's true. If you really need that value, you can have the function return the value to a calling statement as you do in the `testValues()` function.

Near the end of the function, the script reads the aBoy global value without a hitch. But because you initialized a separate version of hisDog inside that function, only the localized version is available to the function. If you reassign a global variable name inside a function, you cannot access the global version from inside that function.

As proof that the global variable — whose name was reused inside the testValues() function — remains untouched, the script writes that value to the end of the page for all to see. Charlie Brown and his dog are reunited.

A benefit of this variable-scoping scheme is that you can reuse "throw-away" variable names in any function you like. For instance, you can use the i loop counting variable in every function that employs loops. (In fact, you can reuse it in multiple for loops of the same function because the for loop reinitializes the value at the start of the loop.) If you pass parameters to a function, you can assign to those parameter variables the same names to aid in consistency. For example, a common practice is to pass an entire form object reference as a parameter to a function (using a this.form parameter in the event handler). For every function that catches one of these objects, you can use the variable name form in the parameter:

```
function doSomething(form) {
    statements
}
...
<INPUT TYPE="button" VALUE="Do Something" onClick="doSomething(this.form)">
```

If five buttons on your page pass their form objects as parameters to five different functions, each function can assign form (or whatever you want to use) to that parameter value.

I recommend reusing variable names only for these "throwaway" variables. In this case, the variables are all local to functions, so the possibility of a mix-up with global variables does not exist. But the thought of reusing a global variable name as, say, a special case inside a function sends shivers up my spine. Such a tactic is doomed to cause confusion and error.

Some programmers devise naming conventions to avoid reusing global variables as local variables. A popular scheme puts a lowercase "g" in front of any global variable name. In the example from Listing 41-2, you can name the global variables

```
gHeadGlobal
gABoy
gHisDog
```

Then, if you define local variables, don't use the leading "g." Any scheme you employ to prevent the reuse of variable names in different scopes is fine as long as it does the job.

In a multiframe or multiwindow environment, your scripts can also access global variables from any other document currently loaded into the browser. For details about this level of access, see Chapter 16.

Variable scoping rules apply equally to nested functions in NN4+ and IE4+. Any variables defined in an outer function (including parameter variables) are exposed to all functions nested inside. But if you define a new local variable inside a nested function, that variable is not available to the outer function. Instead, you can return a value from the nested function to the statement in the outer function that invokes the nested function.

Parameter variables

When a function receives data in the form of parameters, remember that the values may be copies of the data (in the case of run-of-the-mill data values) or references to real objects (such as a form object). In the latter case, you can change the object's modifiable properties in the function when the function receives the object as a parameter, as shown in the following example:

```
function validateCountry (form) {
    if (form.country.value == "") {
        form.country.value = "USA"
    }
}
```

Therefore, whenever you pass an object reference as a function parameter, be aware that the changes you make to that object in its "passed" form affect the real object.

As a matter of style, if my function needs to extract properties or results of methods from passed data (such as object properties or string substrings), I like to do that at the start of the function. I initialize as many variables as needed for each piece of data used later in the function. This task enables me to assign meaningful names to the data chunks, rather than rely on potentially long references within the working part of the function (such as using a variable like inputStr instead of form.entry.value).

Recursion in functions

Functions can call themselves — a process known as *recursion*. The classic example of programmed recursion is the calculation of the factorial (the factorial for a value of 4 is 4 * 3 * 2 * 1), shown in Listing 41-3 (not on the CD-ROM).

In the third line of this function, the statement calls itself, passing along a parameter of the next lower value of n. As this function executes, diving ever deeper into itself, JavaScript watches intermediate values and performs the final evaluations of the nested expressions. Be sure to test any recursive function carefully. In particular, make sure that the recursion is finite: that a limit exists for the number of times it can recurse. In the case of Listing 41-3, that limit is the initial value of n. Failure to watch out for this limit may cause the recursion to overpower the limits of the browser's memory and even lead to a crash.

Listing 41-3: A JavaScript Function Utilizing Recursion

```
function factorial(n) {
    if (n > 0) {
        return n * (factorial(n-1))
    } else {
        return 1
    }
}
```

Turning functions into libraries

As you start writing functions for your scripts, be on the lookout for ways to make functions generalizable (written so that you can reuse the function in other instances, regardless of the object structure of the page). The likeliest candidates for this kind of treatment are functions that perform specific kinds of validation checks (see examples in Chapter 43), data conversions, or iterative math problems.

To make a function generalizable, don't let it make any references to specific objects by name. Object names generally change from document to document. Instead, write the function so that it accepts a named object as a parameter. For example, if you write a function that accepts a text object as its parameter, the function can extract the object's data or invoke its methods without knowing anything about its enclosing form or name. Look again, for example, at the factorial() function in Listing 41-4 — but now as part of an entire document.

Listing 41-4: Calling a Generalizable Function

```
<HTML>
<HEAD>
<TITLE>Variable Scope Trials</TITLE>
<SCRIPT LANGUAGE="JavaScript">
function factorial(n) {
    if (n > 0) {
        return n * (factorial(n - 1))
    } else {
```

Continued

Listing 41-4: *(continued)*

```
        return 1
    }
}
</SCRIPT>
</HEAD>

<BODY>
<FORM>
Enter an input value: <INPUT TYPE="text" NAME="input" VALUE=0>
<P><INPUT TYPE="button" VALUE="Calc Factorial"
    onClick="this.form.output.value = factorial(this.form.input.value)">
<P>Results: <INPUT TYPE="text" NAME="output">
</FORM>
</BODY>
</HTML>
```

This function is designed to be generalizable, accepting only the input value (n) as a parameter. In the form, the onClick event handler of the button sends only the input value from one of the form's fields to the factorial() function. The returned value is assigned to the output field of the form. The factorial() function is totally ignorant about forms, fields, or buttons in this document. If I need this function in another script, I can copy and paste it into that script knowing that it has been pretested. Any generalizable function is part of my personal library of scripts — from which I can borrow — and saves me time in future scripting tasks.

You cannot always generalize a function. Somewhere along the line in your scripts, you must have references to JavaScript or custom objects. But if you find that you're frequently writing functions that perform the same kind of actions, see how you can generalize the code and put the results in your library of ready-made functions. And if your audience uses browsers from Navigator 3 onward (and later versions of Internet Explorer 3 onward), consider placing these library functions in an external .js library file. See Chapter 13 for details on this convenient way to share utility functions among many documents.

Custom Objects

In all the previous chapters of this book, you've seen how conveniently the browser document object models organize all the information about the browser window and its document. What may not be obvious from the scripting you've done so far is that JavaScript enables you to create your own objects in memory — objects with properties and methods. These objects are not user-interface elements on the page but rather the kinds of objects that may contain data and script functions (behaving as methods) whose results the user can see displayed in the browser window.

You actually had a preview of this power in Chapter 37's discussion about arrays. An array, you recall, is an ordered collection of data. You can create a JavaScript array in which entries are labeled just like properties that you access via the now-familiar dot syntax (`arrayName[index].propertyName`). An object typically contains different kinds of data. It doesn't have to be an ordered collection of data — although your scripts can use objects in constructions that strongly resemble arrays. Moreover, you can attach any number of custom functions as methods for that object. You are in total control of the object's structure, data, and behavior.

An example — planetary objects

Building on your familiarity with the planetary data array created in Chapter 37, this chapter shows you how convenient it is to use the data when it is constructed in the form of custom objects. The application goal for the extended example in this section is to present a pop-up list of the nine planets of the solar system and display data about the selected planet. From a user-interface perspective (and for more exposure to multiframe environments), the resulting data displays in a separate frame of a two-frame window. This means your object method builds HTML on the fly and plugs it into the display frame. If you implement this application strictly for IE4+ and NN6, you can apply the same data to reconstruct the displayed table data for each user selection. The example as shown, however, is fully backward-compatible for all scriptable browsers.

In this chapter, instead of building arrays to hold the data, you build objects — one object for each planet. The design of your object has five properties and one method. The properties of each planet are: name, diameter, distance from the sun, year length, and day length. To assign more intelligence to these objects, you give each of them the capability to display their data in the lower frame of the window. You can conveniently define one function that knows how to behave with any of these planet objects, rather than having to define nine separate functions.

Listing 41-5 shows the source code for the document that creates the frameset for your planetary explorations; Listing 41-6 shows the entire HTML page for the object-oriented planet document, which appears in the top frame.

Listing 41-5: **Framesetting Document for a Two-Frame Window**

```
<HTML>
<HEAD>
<TITLE>Solar System Viewer</TITLE>
<SCRIPT LANGUAGE="JavaScript">
function blank() {
    return "<HTML><BODY></BODY></HTML>"
}
```

Continued

Listing 41-5: *(continued)*

```
</SCRIPT>
</HEAD>
<FRAMESET ROWS="50%,50%"
onLoad="Frame1.doDisplay(Frame1.document.forms[0].planetsList)">
    <FRAME NAME="Frame1" SRC="lst41-06.htm">
    <FRAME NAME="Frame2" SRC="javascript:parent.blank()">
</FRAMESET>
</HTML>
```

One item to point out in Listing 41-5 is that because the lower frame isn't filled until the upper frame's document loads, you need to assign some kind of URL for the SRC attribute of the second frame. Rather than add the extra transaction and file burden of a blank HTML document, here you use the javascript: URL to invoke a function. In this instance, I want the value returned from the function (a blank HTML page) to be reflected into the target frame (no void operator here). This method provides the most efficient way of creating a blank frame in a frameset.

Listing 41-6: **Object-Oriented Planetary Data Presentation**

```
<HTML>
<HEAD>
<TITLE>Our Solar System</TITLE>
<SCRIPT LANGUAGE="JavaScript">
<!-- start script
// method definition
function showPlanet() {
    var result = "<HTML><BODY><CENTER><TABLE BORDER=2>"
    result += "<CAPTION ALIGN=TOP>Planetary data for: <B>" + this.name +
"</B></CAPTION>"
    result += "<TR><TD ALIGN=RIGHT>Diameter:</TD><TD>" + this.diameter +
"</TD></TR>"
    result += "<TR><TD ALIGN=RIGHT>Distance from Sun:</TD><TD>" + this.distance +
"</TD></TR>"
    result += "<TR><TD ALIGN=RIGHT>One Orbit Around Sun:</TD><TD>" + this.year +
"</TD></TR>"
    result += "<TR><TD ALIGN=RIGHT>One Revolution (Earth Time):</TD><TD>" +
this.day + "</TD></TR>"
    result += "</TABLE></CENTER></BODY></HTML>"
    // display results in a second frame of the window
    parent.Frame2.document.write(result)
    parent.Frame2.document.close()
```

```
}

// definition of planet object type;
// 'new' will create a new instance and stuff parameter data into object
function planet(name, diameter, distance, year, day) {
    this.name = name
    this.diameter = diameter
    this.distance = distance
    this.year = year
    this.day = day
    this.showPlanet = showPlanet  // make showPlanet() function a planet method
}

// create new planet objects, and store in a series of variables
var Mercury = new planet("Mercury","3100 miles", "36 million miles", "88 days",
"59 days")
var Venus = new planet("Venus", "7700 miles", "67 million miles", "225 days",
"244 days")
var Earth = new planet("Earth", "7920 miles", "93 million miles", "365.25
days","24 hours")
var Mars = new planet("Mars", "4200 miles", "141 million miles", "687 days",
"24 hours, 24 minutes")
var Jupiter = new planet("Jupiter","88,640 miles","483 million miles",
"11.9 years", "9 hours, 50 minutes")
var Saturn = new planet("Saturn", "74,500 miles","886 million miles",
"29.5 years", "10 hours, 39 minutes")
var Uranus = new planet("Uranus", "32,000 miles","1.782 billion miles",
"84 years", "23 hours")
var Neptune = new planet("Neptune","31,000 miles","2.793 billion miles",
"165 years", "15 hours, 48 minutes")
var Pluto = new planet("Pluto", "1500 miles", "3.67 billion miles", "248 years",
"6 days, 7 hours")

// called from push button to invoke planet object method
function doDisplay(popup) {
    i = popup.selectedIndex
    eval(popup.options[i].text + ".showPlanet()")
}
// end script -->
</SCRIPT>
<BODY>
<H1>The Daily Planet</H1>
<HR>
<FORM>
<P>Select a planet to view its planetary data:
```

Continued

Listing 41-6: *(continued)*

```
<SELECT NAME='planetsList' onChange='doDisplay(this)'>
    <OPTION>Mercury
    <OPTION>Venus
    <OPTION SELECTED>Earth
    <OPTION>Mars
    <OPTION>Jupiter
    <OPTION>Saturn
    <OPTION>Uranus
    <OPTION>Neptune
    <OPTION>Pluto
</SELECT></P>
</FORM>
</BODY>
</HTML>
```

The first task in the Head is to define the function that becomes a method in each of the objects. You must do this task before scripting any other code that adopts the function as its method. Failure to define the function ahead of time results in an error — the function name is not defined. If you compare the data extraction methodology with the function in the array version, notice that the parameter for the index value is gone and the reference to each property begins with this. Later, I return to the custom method after giving you a look at the rest of the Head code.

Next comes the object constructor function, which performs several important tasks. For one, everything in this function establishes the structure of your custom object: the properties available for data storage and retrieval and any methods that the object can invoke. The name of the function is the name you use later to create new instances of the object. Therefore, choosing a name that truly reflects the nature of the object is important. And, because you probably want to stuff some data into the function's properties to get one or more instances of the object loaded and ready for the page's user, the function definition includes parameters for each of the properties defined in this object definition.

Inside the function, you use the this keyword to assign data that comes in as parameters to labeled properties. For this example, I use the same names for both the incoming parameter variables and the properties. That's primarily for convenience (and is very common practice), but you can assign any variable and property names you want and connect them any way you like. In the planet() constructor function, five property slots are reserved for every instance of the object whether or not any data actually is placed in every property (any unassigned slot has a value of null).

The last entry in the planet() constructor function is a reference to the showPlanet() function defined earlier. Notice that the assignment statement doesn't refer to the function with its parentheses — just to the function name. When JavaScript sees this assignment statement, it looks back through existing definitions (those functions defined ahead of the current location in the script) for a match. If it finds a function (as it does here), JavaScript knows to assign the function to the identifier on the left side of the assignment statement. In doing this task with a function, JavaScript automatically sets up the identifier as a method name for this object. As you do in every JavaScript method you encounter, you must invoke a method by using a reference to the object, a period, and the method name followed by a set of parentheses. You see that syntax in a minute.

The next long block of statements creates the individual objects according to the definition established in the planet() constructor. Similar to an array, an assignment statement and the keyword new create an object. I assign names that are not only the real names of planets (the Mercury object name is the Mercury planet object) but that also can come in handy later when the doDisplay() function extracts names from the pop-up list in search of a particular object's data.

The act of creating a new object sets aside space in memory (associated with the current document) for this object and its properties. In this script, you create nine object spaces, each with a different set of properties. Notice that no parameter is sent (or expected at the function) that corresponds to the showPlanet() method. Omitting that parameter here is fine because the specification of that method in the object definition means that the script automatically attaches the method to every version (instance) of the planet object that it creates.

The last function definition, doDisplay(), is invoked whenever the user makes a choice from the list of planets in the upper frame. This function is also invoked via the frameset's onLoad event handler so that an initial table is displayed from the default selected item (see Figure 41-1). Invoking the function from the upper frame's onLoad event handler can cause problems (such as the failure of the other frame) if the frameset is not completely loaded.

The onChange event handler in the SELECT list passes that SELECT element's reference to the doDisplay() function. In that function, the SELECT object is assigned to a variable called popup to help you visualize that the object is the pop-up list. The first statement extracts the index value of the selected item. Using that index value, the script extracts the text. But things get a little tricky because you need to use that text string as a variable name — the name of the planet — and append it to the call to the showPlanet() method. To make the disparate data types come together, use the eval() function. Inside the parentheses, extract the string for the planet name and concatenate a string that completes the reference to the object's showPlanet() method. The eval() function evaluates that string, which turns it into a valid method call. Therefore, if the user selects Jupiter from the pop-up list, the method call becomes Jupiter.showPlanet().

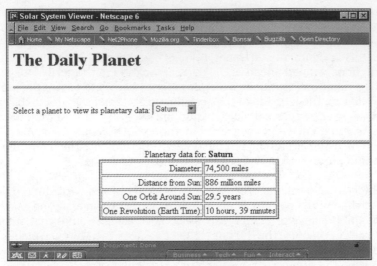

Figure 41-1: An external and internal face-lift for an earlier application

Now it's time to look back to the showPlanet() function/method definition at the top of the script. When that method runs in response to a user selection of the planet Jupiter, the method's only scope is of the Jupiter object. Therefore, all references to this.propertyName in showPlanet() refer to Jupiter only. The only possibility for this.name in the Jupiter object is the value assigned to the name property for Jupiter. The same goes for the rest of the properties extracted in the function/method.

Creating an array of objects

In Listing 41-6, each of the planet objects is assigned to a global variable whose name is that of the planet. If the idea of custom objects is new to you, this idea probably doesn't sound so bad because it's easy to visualize each variable representing an object. But, as shown in the doDisplay() function, accessing an object by name requires use of the eval() function to convert a string representation to a valid object reference. While it's not too important in this simple example, the eval() function is not particularly efficient in JavaScript. If you find yourself using an eval() function, look for ways to improve efficiency such that you can reference an object by string. The way to accomplish that streamlining for this application is to place the objects in an array whose index values are the planet names.

To assign the custom objects in Listing 41-6 to an array, first create an empty array and then assign the result of each object constructor call to an entry in the array. The modified code section looks like the following (formatted to fit this printed page):

```
// create array
var planets = new Array()
// populate array with new planet objects
planets["Mercury"] =
    new planet("Mercury","3100 miles", "36 million miles",
    "88 days", "59 days")
planets["Venus"] =
    new planet("Venus", "7700 miles", "67 million miles",
    "225 days", "244 days")
planets["Earth"] =
    new planet("Earth", "7920 miles", "93 million miles",
    "365.25 days","24 hours")
planets["Mars"] =
    new planet("Mars", "4200 miles", "141 million miles",
    "687 days", "24 hours, 24 minutes")
planets["Jupiter"] =
    new planet("Jupiter","88,640 miles","483 million miles",
    "11.9 years", "9 hours, 50 minutes")
planets["Saturn"] =
    new planet("Saturn", "74,500 miles","886 million miles",
    "29.5 years", "10 hours, 39 minutes")
planets["Uranus"] =
    new planet("Uranus", "32,000 miles","1.782 billion miles",
    "84 years", "23 hours")
planets["Neptune"] =
    new planet("Neptune","31,000 miles","2.793 billion miles",
    "165 years", "15 hours, 48 minutes")
planets["Pluto"] =
    new planet("Pluto", "1500 miles", "3.67 billion miles",
    "248 years", "6 days, 7 hours")
```

The supreme advantage to this approach comes in a modified `doDisplay()` function, which can use the string value from the SELECT element directly without any conversion to an object reference:

```
// called from push button to invoke planet object method
function doDisplay(popup) {
    i = popup.selectedIndex
    planets[popup.options[i].text].showPlanet()
}
```

The presence of so many similar objects cries out for their storage as an array. Because the names play a key role in their choice for this application, the named index values work best; in other situations, you may prefer to use numeric indexes to facilitate looping through the array.

Adding a custom method

You're approaching advanced subject matter at this point, so I merely mention and briefly demonstrate an additional power of defining and using custom objects. A custom object can have a reference to another custom object as a property. Let's extend the planet example to help you understand the implications.

Say that you want to beef up the planet page with a photo of each planet. Each photo has a URL for the photo file; each photo also contains other information, such as the copyright notice and a reference number, which displays on the page for the user. One way to handle this additional information is to create a separate object definition for a photo database. Such a definition may look like this:

```
function photo(name, URL, copyright, refNum) {
    this.name = name
    this.URL = URL
    this.copyright = copyright
    this.refNum = refNum
}
```

You then need to create individual photo objects for each picture. One such definition may look like this:

```
mercuryPhoto = new photo("Planet Mercury", "/images/merc44.gif", "(c)1990 NASA",
28372)
```

Attaching a photo object to a planet object requires modifying the planet constructor function to accommodate one more property. The new planet constructor looks like this:

```
function planet(name, diameter, distance, year, day, photo) {
    this.name = name
    this.diameter = diameter
    this.distance = distance
    this.year = year
    this.day = day
    this.showPlanet = showPlanet
    this.photo = photo // add photo property
}
```

Once the photo objects are created, you can then create each planet object by passing one more parameter — a photo object you want associated with that object:

```
// create new planet objects, and store in a series of variables
Mercury = new planet("Mercury","3100 miles",  "36 million miles",   "88 days",
"59 days",  mercuryPhoto)
```

To access a property of an `photo` object, your scripts then have to assemble a reference that works its way through the connection with the `planet` object:

```
copyrightData = Mercury.photo.copyright
```

The potential of custom objects of this type is enormous. For example, you can embed all the copy elements and image URLs for an online catalog in a single document. As the user selects items to view (or cycles through them in sequence), a new JavaScript-written page displays the information in an instant. This requires only the image to be downloaded — unless the image was precached, as described in the image object discussion in Chapter 18. In this case, everything works instantaneously — no waiting for page after page of catalog.

If, by now, you think you see a resemblance between this object-within-an-object construction and a relational database, give yourself a gold star. Nothing prevents multiple objects from having the same subobject as their properties — like multiple business contacts having the same company object property.

More ways to create objects

The examples in Listings 41-5 and 41-6 show a way of creating objects that works with all scriptable browsers. If your audience is limited to users with more modern browsers, additional ways of creating custom objects exist.

From NN3+ and IE4+, you can use the `new Object()` constructor to generate a blank object. From that point on, you can define property and method names by simple assignment, as in the following:

```
var Earth = new Object()
Earth.diameter = "7920 miles"
Earth.distance = "93 million miles"
Earth.year = "365.25"
Earth.day = "24 hours"
Earth.showPlanet = showPlanet  // function reference
```

When you create a lot of like-structured objects, the custom object constructor shown in Listing 41-6 is more efficient. But for single objects, the `new Object()` constructor is more efficient.

NN4+ and IE4+ scripters can also benefit from a shortcut literal syntax for creating a new object. You can set pairs of property names and their values inside a set of curly braces, and you can assign the whole construction to a variable that becomes the object name. The following script shows how to organize this kind of object constructor:

```
var Earth = {diameter:"7920 miles", distance:"93 million miles", year:"365.25",
        day:"24 hours", showPlanet:showPlanet}
```

Colons link name/value pairs, and commas separate multiple name/value pairs. The value portion of a name/value pair can even be an array (using the [...] constructor shortcut) or a nested object (using another pair of curly braces). In fact, you can nest arrays and objects to your heart's content to create exceedingly complex objects. All in all, this is a very compact way to embed data in a page for script manipulation. If your CGI, XML, and database skills are up to the task, consider using a server program to convert XML data into this compact JavaScript version with each XML record being its own JavaScript object. For multiple records, assign the curly-braced object definitions to an array entry. Then your scripts on the client can iterate through the data and generate the HTML to display the data in a variety of forms and sorted according to different criteria (thanks to the JavaScript array-sorting powers).

Object watcher methods

NN4+ includes two special functions for objects that were designed primarily for use with external debugging tools: watch() and unwatch(). The watch() method instructs JavaScript to keep an eye on a particular property in an object (any JavaScript-accessible object) and execute a function when the value of the property changes by assignment (that is, not by user interaction).

You can see how this works in the simplified example of Listing 41-7. Three buttons set the value property of a text box. You can turn on the watch() method, which calls a handler and passes the name of the property, the old value, and the new value. An alert in the listing's function demonstrates what those values contain.

Listing 41-7: **Object Watching in NN4+**

```
<HTML>
<HEAD>
<TITLE>Object Watching</TITLE>
<SCRIPT LANGUAGE="JavaScript1.2">
function setIt(msg) {
    document.forms[0].entry.value = msg
}
function watchIt(on) {
    var obj = document.forms[0].entry
    if (on) {
        obj.watch("value",report)
    } else {
        obj.unwatch("value")
    }
}
function report(id, oldval, newval) {alert("The field's " + id +
" property on its way from \n'" + oldval + "'\n to \n'" + newval + "'.")
    return newval
}
</SCRIPT>
```

```
<BODY>
<B>Watching Over You</B>
<HR>
<FORM>
Enter text here:
<INPUT TYPE="text" NAME="entry" SIZE=50 VALUE="Default Value"><P>
<INPUT TYPE="button" VALUE="Set to Phrase I" onClick="setIt('Four score and
seven years ago...')"><BR>
<INPUT TYPE="button" VALUE="Set to Phrase 2" onClick="setIt('When in the course
of human events...')"><BR>
<INPUT TYPE="reset" onClick="setIt('Default Value')"><P>
<INPUT TYPE="button" VALUE="Watch It" onClick="watchIt(true)">
<INPUT TYPE="button" VALUE="Don't Watch It" onClick="watchIt(false)">
</FORM>
</BODY>
</HTML>
```

Better ways exist to intercept and preprocess user input, but the `watch()` function can be a helpful debugging tool when you want to monitor the hidden workings of scripts.

Defining object property getters and setters

A future version of the ECMA-262 language specification will likely include a pair of facilities called *getter* and *setter*. Until such time as the formal syntax is finalized, you can begin to experiment with this technique in NN6 using temporary syntax that adheres to the likely format (but intentionally uses different keywords until the standard is adopted). When the standard is adopted, a subsequent version of NN will include the standard keywords.

I introduced the idea of creating a getter and setter for an object briefly in Chapter 14, where the NN6 syntax style extended properties of some W3C DOM objects to include some of the Microsoft-specific (and very convenient) DOM syntax. Most notably, you can define a getter for any container to return an array of nested elements just like the IE-only `document.all` collection.

The purpose of a getter is to assign a new property to the prototype of an object and to define how the value returned by the property should be evaluated. A setter does the same, but it also defines how a new value assigned to the property should apply the value to the object. Both definitions are written in the form of anonymous functions, such that reading or writing an object's property value can include sophisticated processing for either operation.

Getters and setters are assigned to the `prototype` property of an object, thus enabling you to customize native and DOM objects. The NN6 syntax fashions getters, setters, and methods of an object's prototype with the following syntax:

```
object.prototype.__defineGetter__("propName", function)
object.prototype.__defineSetter__("propName", function)
```

Note that the underscores before and after the method names are actually pairs of underscore characters (that is, _, _, defineGetter, _, _). This double underscore was chosen as a syntax that the ECMA standard will not use, so it will not conflict with the eventual syntax for this facility.

The first parameter of the method is the name of the property for which the getter or setter is defined. This can be an existing property name that you want to override. The second parameter can be a function reference; but more likely it will be an anonymous function defined in place. By using an anonymous function, you can take advantage of the context of the object for which the property is defined. For each property, define both a getter and setter — even if the property is meant to be read-only or write-only.

To see how this mechanism works, let's use the getter and setter shown in Chapter 14 to add an `innerText` property to HTML elements in NN6. This property is read/write, so functions are defined for both the getter and setter. The getter definition is as follows:

```
HTMLElement.prototype.__defineGetter__("innerText", function () {
    var rng = document.createRange()
    rng.selectNode(this)
    return rng.toString()
})
```

The modified object is the basic `HTMLElement` object — the object that NN6 uses to create instances of every HTML element for the page. After the statement above executes, every HTML element on the page inherits the new `innerText` property. Each time the `innerText` property is read for an element, the anonymous function in this getter executes. Thus, after a text range object is created, the range is set to the node that is the current element. This is an excellent example of how the context of the current object allows the use of the `this` keyword to refer to the very same object. Finally, the string version of the selected range is returned. It is essential that a getter function include a `return` statement and that the returned value is of the desired data type. Also take notice of the closing of the function's curly brace and the getter method's parenthesis.

By executing this function each time the property is read, the getter always returns the current state of the object. If content of the element has changed since the page loaded, you are still assured of getting the current text inside the element. This is far superior to simply running the statements inside this function once as the page loads to capture a static view of the element's text.

The corresponding setter definition is as follows:

```
HTMLElement.prototype.__defineSetter__("innerText", function (txt) {
    var rng = document.createRange()
    rng.selectNodeContents(this)
    rng.deleteContents()
    var newText = document.createTextNode(txt)
    this.appendChild(newText)
    return txt
})
```

To assign a value to an object's property, the setter function requires that a parameter variable receive the assigned value. That parameter variable plays a role somewhere within the function definition. For this particular setter, the current object (`this`) also manipulates the text range object. The contents of the current element are deleted, and a text node comprising the text passed as a parameter is inserted into the element. To completely simulate the IE behavior of setting the `innerText` property, the text is returned. While setters don't always return values, this one does so that the expression that assigns a value to the `innerText` property evaluates to the new text.

If you want to create a read-only property, you still define a setter for the property but you also assign an empty function, as in:

```
Node.prototype.__defineSetter__("all", function() {})
```

This prevents assignment statements to a read-only property from generating errors. A write-only property should also have a getter that returns `null` or an empty string, as in:

```
HTMLElement.prototype.__defineGetter__("outerHTML", function() {return ""})
```

Because the getter and setter syntax shown here is unique to NN6, you must obviously wrap such statements inside object detection or browser version detection statements. And, to reiterate, this syntax will change in future browser versions once ECMA adopts the formal syntax.

Using custom objects

There is no magic to knowing when to use a custom object instead of an array in your application. The more you work with and understand the way custom objects work, the more likely you will think about your data-carrying scripts in these terms — especially if an object can benefit from having one or more methods associated with it. This avenue is certainly not one for beginners, but I recommend that you give custom objects more than a casual perusal once you gain some JavaScripting experience.

Object-Oriented Concepts

As stated several times throughout this book, JavaScript is object-based rather than object-oriented. Instead of adhering to the class, subclass, and inheritance schemes of object-oriented languages such as Java, JavaScript uses what is called *prototype inheritance*. This scheme works not only for native and DOM objects but also for custom objects.

Adding a prototype

A custom object is frequently defined by a constructor function, which typically parcels out initial values to properties of the object, as in the following example:

```
function car(plate, model, color) {
    this.plate = plate
    this.model = model
    this.color = color
}
var car1 = new car("AB 123", "Ford", "blue")
```

NN4+ and IE4+ offer a handy shortcut, as well, to stuff default values into properties if none are provided (the supplied value is null, 0, or an empty string). The OR operator (||) can let the property assignment statement apply the passed value, if present, or a default value you hard-wire into the constructor. Therefore, you can modify the preceding function to offer default values for the properties:

```
function car(plate, model, color) {
    this.plate = plate || "missing"
    this.model = model || "unknown"
    this.color = color || "unknown"
}
var car1 = new car("AB 123", "Ford", "")
```

After the preceding statements run, the car1 object has the following properties:

```
car1.plate    // value = "AB 123"
car1.model    // value = "Ford"
car1.color    // value = "unknown"
```

If you then add a new property to the constructor's prototype property, as in

```
car.prototype.companyOwned = true
```

any car object you already created or are about to create automatically inherits the new companyOwned property and its value. You can still override the value of the companyOwned property for any individual car object. But if you don't override the property for instances of the car object, the car objects whose companyOwned property is not overridden automatically inherit any change to the `prototype.companyOwned` value. This has to do with the way JavaScript looks for `prototype` property values.

Prototype inheritance

Each time your script attempts to read or write a property of an object, JavaScript follows a specific sequence in search of a match for the property name. The sequence is as follows:

1. If the property has a value assigned to the current (local) object, this is the value to use.

2. If there is no local value, check the value of the property's prototype of the object's constructor.

3. Continue up the prototype chain until either a match of the property is found (with a value assigned to it) or the search reaches the native `Object` object.

Therefore, if you change the value of a constructor's `prototype` property and you do not override the property value in an instance of that constructor, JavaScript returns the current value of the constructor's `prototype` property.

Nested objects and prototype inheritance

When you begin nesting objects, especially when one object invokes the constructor of another, there is an added wrinkle to the prototype inheritance chain. Let's continue with the `car` object defined earlier. In this scenario, consider the `car` object to be akin to a root object that has properties shared among two other types of objects. One of the object types is a company fleet vehicle, which needs the properties of the root `car` object (`plate`, `model`, `color`) but also adds some properties of its own. The other object that shares the `car` object is an object representing a car parked in the company garage — an object that has additional properties regarding the parking of the vehicle. This explains why the `car` object is defined on its own.

Now look at the constructor function for the parking record, along with the constructor for the basic `car` object:

```
function car(plate, model, color) {
    this.plate = plate || "missing"
    this.model = model || "unknown"
    this.color = color || "unknown"
}
function carInLot(plate, model, color, timeIn, spaceNum) {
    this.timeIn = timeIn
    this.spaceNum = spaceNum
    this.carInfo = car
    this.carInfo(plate, model, color)
}
```

The carInLot constructor not only assigns values to its unique properties (timeIn and spaceNum), but it also includes a reference to the car constructor arbitrarily assigned to a property called carInfo. This property assignment is merely a conduit that allows property values intended for the car constructor to be passed within the carInLot constructor function. To create a carInLot object, use a statement like the following:

```
var car1 = new carInLot("AA 123", "Ford", "blue", "10:02AM", "31")
```

After this statement, the car1 object has the following properties and values:

```
car1.timeIn      // value = "10:02AM"
car1.spaceNum    // value = "31"
car1.carInfo     // value = reference to car object constructor function
car1.plate       // value = "AA 123"
car1.model       // value = "Ford"
car1.color       // value = "blue"
```

Let's say that five carInLot objects are created in the script (car1 through car5). The prototype wrinkle comes into play if, for example, you assign a new property to the car constructor prototype:

```
car.prototype.companyOwned = true
```

Even though the carInLot objects use the car constructor, the instances of carInLot objects do not have a prototype chain back to the car object. As the preceding code stands, even though you've added a companyOwned property to the car constructor, no carInLot object inherits that property (even if you were to create a new carInLot object after defining the new prototype property for car). To get the carInLot instances to inherit the prototype.companyOwned property, you must explicitly connect the prototype of the carInLot constructor to the car constructor prior to creating instances of carInLot objects:

```
carInLot.prototype = new car()
```

The complete sequence, then, is as follows:

```
function car(plate, model, color) {
    this.plate = plate || "missing"
    this.model = model || "unknown"
    this.color = color || "unknown"
}
function carsInLot(plate, model, color, timeIn, spaceNum) {
    this.timeIn = timeIn
    this.spaceNum = spaceNum
    this.carInfo = car
    this.carInfo(plate, model, color)
}
```

```
carsInLot.prototype = new car()
var car1 = new carsInLot("123ABC", "Ford","blue","10:02AM", "32")
car.prototype.companyOwned = true
```

After this stretch of code runs, the `car1` object has the following properties and values:

```
car1.timeIn          // value = "10:02AM"
car1.spaceNum        // value = "31"
car1.carInfo         // value = reference to car object constructor function
car1.plate           // value = "AA 123"
car1.model           // value = "Ford"
car1.color           // value = "blue"
car1.companyOwned    // value = true
```

NN4+ provides one extra, proprietary bit of syntax in this prototype world. The `__proto__` property (that's with double underscores before and after the word "proto") returns a reference to the object that is next up the prototype chain. For example, if you inspect the properties of `car1.__proto__` after the preceding code runs, you see that the properties of the object next up the prototype chain are as follows:

```
car1.__proto__.plate          // value = "AA 123"
car1.__proto__.model          // value = "Ford"
car1.__proto__.color          // value = "blue"
car1.__proto__.companyOwned   // value = true
```

This property can be helpful in debugging custom objects and prototype inheritance chain challenges, but the property is not part of the ECMA standard. Therefore, I discourage you from using the property in your production scripts.

Object Object

Properties	Methods
constructor	hasOwnProperty()
prototype	isPrototypeOf()
	propertyIsEnumerable()
	toLocaleString()
	toString()
	valueOf()

Syntax

Creating an object object:

```
function constructorName([arg1,...[,argN]]) {
    statement(s)
}
var objName = new constructorName(["argName1",...[,"argNameN"])
var objName = new Object()
var objName = {propName1:propVal1[, propName2:propVal2[,...N]]}
```

Accessing an object object properties and methods:

```
objectReference.property | method([parameters])
```

	NN2	NN3	NN4	NN6	IE3/J1	IE3/J2	IE4	IE5	IE5.5
Compatibility	(✓)	✓	✓	✓	(✓)	✓	✓	✓	✓

About this object

While it might sound like doubletalk, the Object object is a vital native object in the JavaScript environment. It is the root object on which all other native objects — such as Date, Array, String, and the like — are based. This object also provides the foundation for creating custom objects, as described earlier in this chapter.

By and large, your scripts do not access the properties of the native Object object. The same is true for many of its methods, such as toString() and valueOf(), which internally allow debugging alert dialog boxes (and The Evaluator) to display something when referring to an object or its constructor.

You can use a trio of methods, described next, in IE5.5 and NN6 to perform some inspection of the prototype environment of an object instance. They are of interest primarily to advanced scripters who are building extensive, simulated object-oriented applications.

Methods

hasOwnProperty("*propName*")

Returns: Boolean.

	NN2	NN3	NN4	NN6	IE3/J1	IE3/J2	IE4	IE5	IE5.5
Compatibility				✓					✓

The hasOwnProperty() method returns true if the current object instance has the property defined in its constructor or in a related constructor function. But if this property is defined externally, as via assignment to the object's prototype property, the method returns false.

Using the example of the car and carInLot objects from earlier in this chapter, the following expressions evaluate to true:

```
car1.hasOwnProperty("spaceNum")
car1.hasOwnProperty("model")
```

Even though the model property is defined in a constructor that is invoked by another constructor, the property belongs to the car1 object. The following statement, however, evaluates to false:

```
car1.hasOwnProperty("companyOwned")
```

This property is defined by way of the prototype of one of the constructor functions and is not a built-in property for the object instance.

isPrototypeOf(*objRef*)

Returns: Boolean.

	NN2	NN3	NN4	NN6	IE3/J1	IE3/J2	IE4	IE5	IE5.5
Compatibility				✓					✓

The isPrototypeOf() method is intended to reveal whether or not the current object has a prototype relation with an object passed as a parameter. In practice, the IE5.5 and NN6 versions of this method not only operate differently, but they also do not appear in either browser to report prototype relationships correctly between objects. If any updated information is available for this method within these browsers, I will post it to the *JavaScript™ Bible,* 4th Edition Support Center at http://www.dannyg.com/update.html.

propertyIsEnumerable("*propName*")

Returns: Boolean.

	NN2	NN3	NN4	NN6	IE3/J1	IE3/J2	IE4	IE5	IE5.5
Compatibility				✓					✓

In the terminology of the ECMA-262 language specification, a value is enumerable if constructions such as the `for-in` property inspection loop (Chapter 39) can inspect it. Enumerable properties include values such as arrays, strings, and virtually every kind of object. According to the ECMA specification, this method is not supposed to work its way up the prototype chain. IE5.5 appears to adhere to this, whereas NN6 treats a property inherited from an object's prototype as a valid parameter value.

✦ ✦ ✦

Global Functions and Statements

In addition to all the objects and other language constructs described in the preceding chapters of this reference part of the book, several language items need to be treated on a global scale. These items apply to no particular objects (or any object), and you can use them anywhere in a script. If you read earlier chapters, you were introduced to many of these functions and statements. This chapter serves as a convenient place to highlight these all-important items that are otherwise easily forgotten. At the end of the chapter, note the brief introduction to several objects that are built into the Windows-only versions of Internet Explorer. Some of these objects have pointers to more details at Microsoft's Web site.

This chapter begins with coverage of the following global functions and statements that are part of the core JavaScript language:

Functions	Statements
decodeURI()	// and /*...*/ (comment)
decodeURIComponent()	const
encodeURI()	var
encodeURIComponent()	
escape()	
eval()	
isFinite()	
isNaN()	
Number()	
parseFloat()	

Functions	Statements
parseInt()	
toString()	
unescape()	
unwatch()	
watch()	

Global functions are not tied to the document object model. Instead, they typically enable you to convert data from one type to another type. The list of global statements is short, but a couple of them appear extensively in your scripting.

Functions

```
decodeURI("encodedURI")
decodeURIComponent("encodedURIComponent")
encodeURI("URIString")
encodeURIComponent("URIComponentString")
```

Returns: String.

	NN2	NN3	NN4	NN6	IE3/J1	IE3/J2	IE4	IE5	IE5.5
Compatibility				✓					✓

The ECMA-262 Edition 3 standard, as implemented in IE5.5 and NN6, provides utility functions that perform a more rigorous conversion of strings to valid URI strings and vice versa than was achieved earlier via the escape() and unescape() functions (described later in this chapter). The purpose of the encoding functions is to convert any string to a version that you can use as a Uniform Resource Identifier, such as a Web page address or an invocation of a server CGI script. While Latin alphanumeric characters pass through the encoding process untouched, you must use the encoding functions to convert some symbols and other Unicode characters to a form (hexadecimal representations of the character numbers) that the Internet can pass from place to place. The space character, for example, must be encoded to its hex version: %20.

Perhaps the biggest difference between the encodeURI() and escape() functions (and their decodeURI() and unescape() counterparts) is that the more modern versions do not encode a wide range of symbols that are perfectly acceptable as URI characters according to the syntax recommended in RFC2396 (http://www.ietf.org/rfc/rfc2396.txt). Thus, the following characters are not encoded via the encodeURI() function:

```
; / ? : @ & = + $ , - _ . ! ~ * ' ( ) #
```

Use the encodeURI() and decodeURI() functions only on complete URIs. Applicable URIs can be relative or absolute, but these two functions are wired especially so symbols that are part of the protocol (://), search string (? and =, for instance), and directory level delimiters (/) are not encoded. The decodeURI() function should work with URIs that arrive from servers as page locations, but be aware that some server CGIs encode spaces into plus symbols (+) that are not decoded back to spaces by the JavaScript function. If the URIs your script needs to decode contain plus symbols in place of spaces, you need to run your decoded URI through a string replacement method to finish the job (regular expressions come in handy here). If you are decoding URI strings that your scripts encoded, use the decode functions only on URIs that were encoded via the corresponding encode function. Do not attempt to decode a URI that was created via the old escape() function because the conversion processes work according to different rules.

The difference between a URI and a URI component is that a *component* is a single piece of a URI, generally not containing delimiter characters. For example, if you use the encodeURIComponent() function on a complete URI, almost all of the symbols (other than things such as periods) are encoded into hexadecimal versions — including directory delimiters. Therefore, you should use the component-level conversion functions only on quite granular pieces of a URI. For example, if you assemble a search string that has a name/value pair, you can use the encodeURIComponent() function separately on the name and on the value. But if you use that function on the pair that is already in the form *name=value*, the function encodes the equal symbol to a hexadecimal equivalent.

Use The Evaluator (Chapter 13) to experiment with the differences between encoding a full URI and a component and encoding and escaping a URI string. For example, compare the results of the following three statements:

```
escape("http://www.giantco.com/index.html?code=42")
encodeURI("http://www.giantco.com/index.html?code=42")
encodeURIComponent("http://www.giantco.com/index.html?code=42")
```

Because the sample URI string is valid as is, the encodeURI() version makes no changes. Experiment further by making the search string value into a string with a space, and see how each function treats that character.

```
escape("URIString" [,1])
unescape("escapedURIString")
```

Returns: String.

	NN2	NN3	NN4	NN6	IE3/J1	IE3/J2	IE4	IE5	IE5.5
Compatibility	✓	✓	✓	✓	✓	✓	✓	✓	✓

If you watch the content of the Location field in your browser, you may occasionally
see URLs that include a lot of % symbols plus some numbers. The format you see is
URL encoding (more accurately called *URI encoding*—Uniform Resource Identifier
rather than Uniform Resource Locator). This format allows even multiple word
strings and nonalphanumeric characters to be sent as one contiguous string of a
very low, common-denominator character set. This encoding turns a character,
such as a space, into its hexadecimal equivalent value preceded by a percent symbol. For example, the space character (ASCII value 32) is hexadecimal 20, so the
encoded version of a space is %20.

All characters, including tabs and carriage returns, can be encoded in this way and
sent as a simple string that can be decoded on the receiving end for reconstruction.
You can also use this encoding to preprocess multiple lines of text that must be
stored as a character string in databases. To convert a plain-language string to its
encoded version, use the escape() method. This function returns a string consisting of the encoded version. For example:

```
var theCode = escape("Hello there")
    // result: "Hello%20there"
```

Most, but not all, nonalphanumeric characters are converted to escaped versions
with the escape() function. One exception is the plus sign, which URLs use to separate components of search strings. If you must encode the plus symbol, too, then
add the optional second parameter to the function to make the plus symbol convert to its hexadecimal equivalent (2B):

```
var a = escape("Adding 2+2")
    // result: "Adding%202+2
var a = escape("Adding 2+2",1)
    // result: "Adding%202%2B2
```

To convert an escaped string back into plain language, use the unescape() function. This function returns a string and converts all URL-encoded strings—
including those encoded with the optional parameter.

The escape() function operates in a way that is approximately midway between the newer functions encodeURI() and encodeComponentURI(). The escape() function is best used on portions of URIs, such as the search string. If your scripts bounce back and forth between escaped and unescaped strings, be sure to balance the functions of the same type; use unescape() only on URI strings that are encoded via the escape() function.

Finally, be aware of slightly different behavior with regard to the @ symbol in various browsers. This character is not encoded in IE, but it is encoded (to %40) in NN.

eval("*string*")

Returns: Object reference.

	NN2	NN3	NN4	NN6	IE3/J1	IE3/J2	IE4	IE5	IE5.5
Compatibility	✓	✓	✓	✓	✓	✓	✓	✓	✓

Expression evaluation, as you probably are well aware by now, is an important concept to grasp in scripting with JavaScript (and programming in general). An expression evaluates to some value. But occasionally you need to force an additional evaluation on an expression to receive the desired results. The eval() function acts on a string value to force an evaluation of that string expression.

Perhaps the most common application of the eval() function is to convert a string version of an object reference to a genuine object reference. For example, one technique for creating a Dynamic HTML script that accommodates the different ways that IE and NN4 reference positionable objects is to assemble references out of the comparable pieces of references. In the following function, the name of a positionable object is passed as a parameter. This example assumes that global variable flags are set elsewhere for isNav4 and isIE4. The function must create a valid reference to the object depending on which browser the user runs:

```
function getReference(objName) {
    if (navigator.appVersion.charAt(0) == "4") {
        if (navigator.appName == "Netscape") {
            var range = ""
            var styleObj = ""
        } else {
            var range = ".all"
            var styleObj = ".style"
        }
        var theObj = eval("document" + range + "." + objName + styleObj)
```

```
        return theObj
    }
    return null
}
```

In the NN4 branch of the preceding example, the variables `range` and `styleObj` are assigned empty strings; for the Microsoft branch, each variable assumes the components that must be inserted into an object reference for the Microsoft syntax. If the components are concatenated without the `eval()` function, the result simply is a concatenated string (which is not the same as the object reference). By forcing an additional evaluation with the `eval()` function, the script invokes JavaScript to see if one more level of evaluation is needed. If JavaScript finds that the evaluation of that string is a valid object reference, it returns the reference as the result; otherwise, the function returns `undefined`.

The `eval()` function can evaluate any JavaScript statement or expression stored as a string. This includes string equivalents of arithmetic expressions, object value assignments, and object method invocation.

I do not recommend that you rely on the `eval()` function, however, because this function is inherently inefficient (from the standpoint of performance). Fortunately, you may not need the `eval()` function to get from a string version of an object's name to a valid object reference. For example, if your script loops through a series of objects whose names include serial numbers, you can use the object names as array indices rather than use `eval()` to assemble the object references. The inefficient way to set the value of a series of fields named `data0`, `data1`, and so on, is as follows:

```
function fillFields() {
    var theObj
    for (var i = 0; i < 10; i++) {
        theObj = eval("document.forms[0].data" + i)
        theObj.value = i
    }
}
```

A more efficient way is to perform the concatenation within the index brackets for the object reference:

```
function fillFields() {
    for (var i = 0; i < 10; i++) {
        document.forms[0].elements["data" + i].value = i
    }
}
```

Tip   Whenever you are about to use an `eval()` function, look for ways to use string index values of arrays of objects instead. The W3C DOM (in IE5+ and NN6) makes it even easier with the help of the `document.getElementById()` method, which takes a string as a parameter and returns a reference to the named object.

isFinite(*number*)

Returns: Boolean.

	NN2	NN3	NN4	NN6	IE3/J1	IE3/J2	IE4	IE5	IE5.5
Compatibility			✓	✓			✓	✓	✓

It is unlikely that you will ever need the isFinite() function, but its purpose is to advise whether a number is beyond the absolute minimum or maximum values that JavaScript can handle. If a number is outside of that range, the function returns false. The parameter to the function must be a number data type.

isNaN(*expression*)

Returns: Boolean.

	NN2	NN3	NN4	NN6	IE3/J1	IE3/J2	IE4	IE5	IE5.5
Compatibility	(✓)	✓	✓	✓	✓	✓	✓	✓	✓

For those instances in which a calculation relies on data coming from a text field or other string-oriented source, you frequently need to check whether the value is a number. If the value is not a number, the calculation may result in a script error.

Use the isNaN() function to test whether a value is a number prior to passing the value onto the operation. The most common use of this function is to test the result of a parseInt() or parseFloat() function. If the strings submitted for conversion to those functions cannot be converted to a number, the resulting value is NaN (a special symbol indicating "not a number"). The isNaN() function returns true if the value is not a number.

A convenient way to use this function is to intercept improper data before it can do damage, as follows:

```
function calc(form) {
    var inputValue = parseInt(form.entry.value)
    if (isNaN(inputValue)) {
        alert("You must enter a number to continue.")
    } else {
        statements for calculation
    }
}
```

Probably the biggest mistake scripters make with this function is failing to observe the case of all the letters in the function name. The trailing uppercase "N" is easy to miss.

Note   The `isNaN()` function works in Navigator 2 only on UNIX platforms. It is available on all platforms in Navigator 3+ and Internet Explorer 3+.

```
Number("string")
parseFloat("string")
parseInt("string" [,radix])
```

Returns: Number.

	NN2	NN3	NN4	NN6	IE3/J1	IE3/J2	IE4	IE5	IE5.5
Compatibility	(✓)	(✓)	✓	✓	(✓)	(✓)	✓	✓	✓

All three of these functions convert a string value into a numeric value. The `parseInt()` and `parseFloat()` functions are compatible across all versions of all browsers; the `Number()` function is new with NN4 and IE4.

Use the `Number()` function when your script is not concerned with the precision of the value and prefers to let the source string govern whether the returned value is a floating-point number or an integer. The function takes a single parameter — a string to convert to a number value.

The `parseFloat()` function also lets the string source value determine whether the returned value is a floating-point number or an integer. If the source string includes any non-zero value to the right of the decimal, the result is a floating-point number. But if the string value were, say, `"3.00"`, the returned value would be an integer value.

An extra, optional parameter for `parseInt()` enables you to define the number base for use in the conversion. If you don't specify a radix parameter, JavaScript tries to look out for you; but in doing so, JavaScript may cause some difficulty for you. The primary problem arises when the string parameter for `parseInt()` starts with a zero, which a text box entry or database field might do. In JavaScript, numbers starting with zero are treated as octal (base-8) numbers. Therefore, `parseInt("010")` yields the decimal value 8.

When you apply the `parseInt()` function, always specify the radix of 10 if you are working in base-10 numbers. You can, however, specify any radix value from 2 through 36. For example, to convert a binary number string to its decimal equivalent, assign a radix of 2 as follows:

```
var n = parseInt("011",2)
    // result: 3
```

Similarly, you can convert a hexadecimal string to its decimal equivalent by specifying a radix of 16:

```
var n = parseInt("4F",16)
    // result: 79
```

Both `parseInt()` and `parseFloat()` exhibit a very useful behavior: If the string passed as a parameter starts with at least one number followed by, say, letters, the functions do their jobs on the numeric part of the string and ignore the rest. This is why you can use `parseFloat()` on the `navigator.appVersion` string to extract just the reported version number without having to parse the rest of the string. For example, NN6 for Windows reports a `navigator.appVersion` value as

```
5.0 (Windows; en-US)
```

But you can get just the numeric part of the string via `parseFloat()`:

```
var ver = parseFloat(navigator.appVersion)
```

Because the result is a number, you can perform numeric comparisons to see, for instance, whether the version is greater than or equal to 4.

toString([*radix*])

Returns: String.

	NN2	NN3	NN4	NN6	IE3/J1	IE3/J2	IE4	IE5	IE5.5
Compatibility	(✓)	✓	✓	✓	(✓)	✓	✓	✓	✓

Every JavaScript core language object and every DOM `document` object has a `toString()` method associated with it. This method is designed to render the contents of the object in as meaningful a way as possible. Table 42-1 shows the result of applying the `toString()` method on each of the convertible core `language` object types.

Table 42-1 toString() Method Results for Object Types	
Object Type	**Result**
String	The same string
Number	String equivalent (but numeric literals cannot be converted)
Boolean	"true" or "false"
Array	Comma-delimited list of array contents (with no spaces after commas)
Function	Decompiled string version of the function definition

Many DOM objects can be converted to a string. For example, a `location` object returns its URL. But when an object has nothing suitable to return for its content as a string, it usually returns a string in the following format:

```
[object objectType]
```

The `toString()` method is available on all versions of all browsers. However, a convenient improvement to `toString()` for NN3 and IE3/J2 is the optional `radix` parameter. By setting this parameter between 2 and 16, you can convert numbers to string equivalents in different number bases. Listing 42-1 calculates and draws a conversion table for decimal, hexadecimal, and binary numbers between 0 and 20. In this case, the source of each value is the value of the index counter variable each time the `for` loop's statements execute.

Listing 42-1: **Using toString() with Radix Values**

```
<HTML>
<HEAD>
<TITLE>Number Conversion Table</TITLE>
</HEAD>
<BODY>
<B>Using toString() to convert to other number bases:</B>
<HR>
<TABLE BORDER=1>
<TR>
<TH>Decimal</TH><TH>Hexadecimal</TH><TH>Binary</TH></TR>
<SCRIPT LANGUAGE="JavaScript">
var content = ""
for (var i = 0; i <= 20; i++) {
    content += "<TR>"
    content += "<TD>" + i.toString(10) + "</TD>"
    content += "<TD>" + i.toString(16) + "</TD>"
```

```
        content += "<TD>" + i.toString(2) + "</TD></TR>"
    }
    document.write(content)
</SCRIPT>
</TABLE>
</BODY>
</HTML>
```

The toString() method of user-defined objects does not convert the object into a meaningful string, but you can create your own method to do just that. For example, if you want to make your custom object's toString() method behave like an array's method, then define the action of the method and assign that function to a property of the object (as shown in Listing 42-2).

Listing 42-2: **Creating a Custom toString() Method**

```
<HTML>
<HEAD>
<TITLE>Custom toString()</TITLE>
<SCRIPT LANGUAGE="JavaScript">
function customToString() {
    var dataArray - new Array()
    var count = 0
    for (var i in this) {
        dataArray[count.++] = this[i]
        if (count > 2) {
            break
        }
    }
    return dataArray.join(",")
}
var book = {title:"The Aeneid", author:"Virgil", pageCount:543}
book.toString = customToString
</SCRIPT>
</HEAD>
<BODY>
<B>A user-defined toString() result:</B>
<HR>
<SCRIPT LANGUAGE="JavaScript">
document.write(book.toString())
</SCRIPT>
</BODY>
</HTML>
```

When you run Listing 42-2, you can see how the `custom` object's `toString()` handler extracts the values of all elements of the object except for the last one, which is the function handler reference. You can customize how the data should be labeled and/or formatted.

```
unwatch(property)
watch(property, handler)
```

Returns: Nothing.

	NN2	NN3	NN4	NN6	IE3/J1	IE3/J2	IE4	IE5	IE5.5
Compatibility			✓	✓					

To supply the right kind of information to external debuggers, JavaScript in NN4+ implements two global functions that belong to every object — including user-defined objects. The `watch()` function keeps an eye on a desired object and property. If that property is set by assignment, the function invokes another user-defined function that receives information about the property name, its old value, and its new value. The `unwatch()` function turns off the watch functionality for a particular property. See Listing 41-7 in Chapter 41 for an example of how to use these functions that you can assign to any object.

Statements

```
//
/*...*/
```

	NN2	NN3	NN4	NN6	IE3/J1	IE3/J2	IE4	IE5	IE5.5
Compatibility	✓	✓	✓	✓	✓	✓	✓	✓	✓

Comments are statements that the JavaScript interpreter (or server-side compiler) ignores. However, these statements enable authors to leave notes about how things work in their scripts. While lavish comments are useful to authors during a script's creation and maintenance, the full content of a client-side comment is downloaded with the document. Every byte of non-operational content of the page takes a bit more time to download. Still, I recommend lots of comments — particularly as you create a script.

JavaScript offers two styles of comments. One style consists of two forward slashes (no spaces between them). JavaScript ignores any characters to the right of those slashes on the same line, even if they appear in the middle of a line. You can stack as many lines of these single-line comments as is necessary to convey your thoughts. I typically place a space between the second slash and the beginning of my comment. The following are examples of valid, one-line comment formats:

```
// this is a comment line usually about what's to come
var a = "Fred"  // a comment about this line
// You may want to capitalize the first word of a comment
// sentence if it runs across multiple lines.
//
// And you can leave a completely blank line, like the one above.
```

For longer comments, it is usually more convenient to enclose the section in the other style of comment. The following comment opens with a forward slash and asterisk (/*) and ends with an asterisk and forward slash (*/). JavaScript ignores all statements in between — including multiple lines. If you want to comment out briefly a large segment of your script for debugging purposes, it is easiest to bracket the segment with these comment symbols. To make these comment blocks easier to find, I generally place these symbols on their own lines as follows:

```
/*
some
  commented-out
    statements
*/
```

If you are developing rather complex documents, you might find using comments a convenient way to help you organize segments of your scripts and make each segment easier to find. For example, you can define a comment block above each function and describe what the function is about, as in the following example.

```
/*------------------------------------------------
  calculate()
  Performs a mortgage calculation based on
  parameters blah, blah, blah.  Called by blah
  blah blah.
------------------------------------------------*/
function calculate(form) {
    statements
}
```

const

	NN2	NN3	NN4	NN6	IE3/J1	IE3/J2	IE4	IE5	IE5.5
Compatibility				✓					

The const keyword initializes a constant. Unlike a variable, whose data is subject to change while a page loads, a constant's value cannot be modified once it is assigned. It is common practice in many programming languages to define constant identifiers with all uppercase letters, usually with underscore characters to delimit multiple words. This style makes it easier to see a constant's application later in the program.

Listing 42-3 shows how you can use a constant. The page conveys temperature data for several cities. (Presumably, this data is updated on the server and fashioned into an array of data when the user requests the page.) For temperatures below freezing, the temperature is shown in a distinctive text style. Because the freezing temperature is a constant reference point, it is assigned as a constant.

Listing 42-3: **Using the const Keyword**

```
<HTML>
<HEAD>
<TITLE>const(ant)</TITLE>
<STYLE TYPE="text/css">
.cold {font-weight:bold; color:blue}
TD {text-align:center}
</STYLE>
<SCRIPT LANGUAGE="JavaScript">
const FREEZING_F = 32
var cities = ["London", "Moscow", "New York", "Tokyo", "Sydney"]
var tempsF = [33, 12, 20, 40, 75]
function showData() {
    var tableData = ""
    for (var i = 0; i < cities.length; i++) {
        tableData += "<TR><TD>" + cities[i] + "</TD><TD "
        tableData += (tempsF[i] < FREEZING_F) ? "CLASS='cold'" : ""
        tableData += ">" + tempsF[i] + "</TR>"
    }
    document.getElementById("display").innerHTML = tableData
}
</SCRIPT>
</HEAD>
<BODY onLoad="showData()">
<H1>The const keyword</H1>
```

```
<HR>
<TABLE ID="temps">
<TR><TH>City<TH>Temperature</TR>
<TBODY ID="display">
</TBODY>
</TABLE>
</BODY>
</HTML>
```

The `const` keyword likely will be adopted in the next version of the ECMA-262 standard and will become part of the JavaScript vernacular in future browsers.

var

	NN2	NN3	NN4	NN6	IE3/J1	IE3/J2	IE4	IE5	IE5.5
Compatibility	✓	✓	✓	✓	✓	✓	✓	✓	✓

Before using any variable, you should declare it (and optionally initialize it with a value) via the `var` statement. If you omit the `var` keyword, the variable is automatically assigned as a global variable within the current document. To keep a variable local to a function, you must declare or initialize the variable with the `var` keyword inside the function's braces.

If you assign no value to a variable, it evaluates to `null`. Because a JavaScript variable is not limited to one variable type during its lifetime, you don't need to initialize a variable to an empty string or zero unless that initial value helps your scripting. For example, if you initialize a variable as an empty string, you can then use the add-by-value operator (+=) to append string values to that variable in a future statement in the document.

To save statement lines, you can declare and/or initialize multiple variables with a single `var` statement. Separate each *varName=value* pair with a comma, as in

```
var name, age, height  // declare as null
var color="green", temperature=85.6 // initialize
```

Variable names (also known as identifiers) must be one contiguous string of characters, and the first character must be a letter. Many punctuation symbols are also banned, but the underscore character is valid and often is used to separate multiple words in a long variable name. All variable names (like most identifiers in JavaScript) are case-sensitive, so you must name a particular variable identically throughout the variable's scope.

IE/Windows Objects

	NN2	NN3	NN4	NN6	IE3/J1	IE3/J2	IE4	IE5	IE5.5
Compatibility							✓	✓	✓

Microsoft prides itself on the integration between Web browser functionality and the Windows operating system. The linkage between browser and OS is most apparent in IE's facilities for accessing ActiveX objects. Microsoft has fashioned several such objects for access to scripters — again, provided the deployment is intended only for Windows versions of Internet Explorer. Some objects also exist as a way to expose some Visual Basic Script (VBScript) functionality to JavaScript. Because these objects are more within the realm of Windows and ActiveX programming, the details and quirks of working with them from IE/Windows is best left to other venues. But in case you are not familiar with these facilities, the following discussions introduce the basic set of IE/Windows objects. You can find more details at the Microsoft Developer Network (MSDN) Web site; in addition, I provide appropriate URLs for your further exploration.

The objects mentioned here are the `ActiveXObject`, `Dictionary`, `Enumerator`, `FileSystemObject`, and `VBArray` objects. Microsoft documents these objects as if they are part of the native JScript language. However, you can be sure that they will remain proprietary certainly to Internet Explorer, if not exclusively for Windows-only versions.

ActiveXObject

`ActiveXObject` is a generic object that allows your script to open and access what Microsoft sometimes calls *automation objects*. An automation object is an executable program that might run on the client or be served from a server. This can include local applications, such as applications from the Microsoft Office suite, executable DLLs (dynamic-link libraries), and so on.

Use the constructor for the `ActiveXObject` to obtain a reference to the object according to the following syntax:

```
var objRef = new ActiveXObject(appName.className[, remoteServerName])
```

This JScript syntax is the equivalent of the VBScript `CreateObject()` method. You need to know a bit about Windows programming to determine the application name and the classes or types available for that application. For example, to obtain a reference to an Excel worksheet, use this constructor:

```
var mySheet = new ActiveXObject("Excel.Sheet")
```

Once you have a reference to the desired object, you must also know the names of the properties and methods of the object you'll be addressing. You can access much of this information via Microsoft's developer tools, such as Visual InterDev or the tools that come with Visual Basic. These tools enable you to query an object to discover its properties and methods. Unfortunately, an `ActiveXObject`'s properties are not enumerable through a typical JavaScript `for-in` property inspector.

Accessing an `ActiveXObject`, especially one on the client, involves some serious security considerations. The typical security setup for an IE client prevents scripts from accessing client applications, at least not without asking the user if it's okay to do so. While it's foolhardy to state categorically that you cannot perform surreptitious inspection or damage to a client without the user's knowledge (hackers find holes from time to time), it is highly unlikely. In a corporate environment, where some level of access to all clients is desirable, the client may be set up to accept instructions to work with ActiveX objects when they come from trusted sources. The bottom line is that unless you are well versed in Windows programming, don't expect the `ActiveXObject` to become some kind of magic portal that enables you to invade the privacy or security of unsuspecting users.

For more details, visit `http://msdn.microsoft.com/scripting/jscript/doc/jsobjActiveXObject.htm`.

Dictionary

While the `Dictionary` object is very helpful to VBScript authors, JavaScript already provides the equivalent functionality natively. A `Dictionary` object behaves very much like a JavaScript array that has string index values (similar to a Java hash table), although numeric index values are also acceptable in the `Dictionary`. Indexes are called *keys* in this environment. VBScript arrays do not have this facility natively, so the `Dictionary` object supplements the language for the sake of convenience. Unlike a JavaScript array, however, you must use the various properties and methods of the `Dictionary` object to add, access, or remove items from it.

You create a `Dictionary` object via `ActiveXObject` as follows:

```
var dict = new ActiveXObject("Scripting.Dictionary")
```

You must create a separate `Dictionary` object for each array. Table 42-2 lists the properties and methods of the `Dictionary` object. After you create a blank `Dictionary` object, populate it via the `Add()` method for each entry. For example, the following statements create a `Dictionary` object to store U.S. state capitals:

```
var stateCaps = new ActiveXObject("Scripting.Dictionary")
stateCaps.Add("Illinois", "Springfield")
```

You can then access an individual item via the Key property (which, thanks to its VBScript heritage, looks more like a JavaScript method). One convenience of the Dictionary object is the Keys() method, which returns an array of all the keys in the dictionary — something that a string-indexed JavaScript array could use.

Table 42-2	**Dictionary Object Properties and Methods**
Property	**Description**
Count	Integer number of entries in the dictionary (read-only)
Item("*key*")	Reads or writes a value for an entry whose name is *key*
Key("*key*")	Assigns a new key name to an entry
Method	**Description**
Add("*key*", *value*)	Adds a value associated with a unique key name
Exists("*key*")	Returns Boolean *true* if *key* exists in dictionary
Items()	Returns VBArray of values in dictionary
Keys()	Returns VBArray of keys in dictionary
Remove("*key*")	Removes *key* and its value
RemoveAll()	Removes all entries

For more details, visit http://msdn.microsoft.com/scripting/jscript/doc/jsobjDictionary.htm.

Enumerator

An Enumerator object provides JavaScript with access to collections that otherwise do not allow direct access to their items via index number or name. This object isn't necessary when working with DOM collections, such as document.all, because you can use the item() method to obtain a reference to any member of the collection. But if you are scripting ActiveX objects, some of these objects' methods or properties may return collections that cannot be accessed through this mechanism or the JavaScript for-in property inspection technique. Instead, you must wrap the collection inside an Enumerator object.

To wrap a collection in an Enumerator, invoke the constructor for the object, passing the collection as the parameter:

```
var myEnum = new Enumerator(someCollection)
```

This enumerator instance must be accessed via one of its four methods to position a "pointer" to a particular item and then extract a copy of that item. In other words, you don't access a member directly (that is, by diving into the collection with an item number to retrieve). Instead, you move the pointer to the desired position and then read the item value. As you can see from the list of methods in Table 42-3, this object is truly intended for looping through the collection. Pointer control is limited to positioning it at the start of the collection and incrementing its position along the collection by one:

```
myEnum.moveFirst()
for (; !myEnum.atEnd(); myEnum.moveNext()) {
    val = myEnum.item()
    // more statements that work on value
}
```

Table 42-3	**Enumerator Object Methods**
Method	**Description**
atEnd()	Returns true if pointer is at end of collection
item()	Returns value at current pointer position
moveFirst()	Moves pointer to first position in collection
moveNext()	Moves pointer to next position in collection

For more details, visit http://msdn.microsoft.com/scripting/jscript/doc/ jsobjEnumerator.htm.

FileSystemObject

Of all the IE/Windows objects, the one whose capabilities most scripters want to have as a cross-browser native object is FileSystemObject. A common wish among scripters is to be able to save some user-entered data on the client in file form rather than as a cookie. Of course, there can't be wide-open access to the file system because unscrupulous scripters could wreak havoc with a user's system and privacy — especially in such a well-documented and constant OS file structure as Windows. Netscape Navigator can accomplish many of these same operations via direct access to Java classes and signed scripts (which obtain the user's permission before accessing the file system).

`FileSystemObject` has a large library of methods (and one property) that scripts with the proper security clearance and permission can use to read and write files, create and delete files and directories, and, essentially, have its way with the contents of the client's hard disk. Table 42-4 shows a summary of these methods.

Table 42-4   FileSystemObject Property and Methods

Property	Description
`Drives`	Returns a collection of (disk) `Drive` objects (a `Drive` object has 15 properties)

Method	Description
`BuildPath(path, name)`	Appends name to existing *path*
`CopyFile(src, dest[, overwrite])`	Copies file at *src* path to *dest* path, optionally to automatically overwrite existing *dest* file of same name
`CopyFolder(src, dest[, overwrite])`	Copies directory at *src* path to *dest* path, optionally to automatically overwrite existing *dest* directory of same name
`CreateFolder(path)`	Creates folder with name specified in *path*
`CreateTextFile(path[, overwrite[, unicode]])`	Returns `TextStream` object after opening an empty file at *path*, optionally to overwrite existing file at *path* and optionally to save characters in Unicode (instead of ASCII)
`DeleteFile(path[, force])`	Deletes file at *path*, optionally to force deletion of read-only file
`DeleteFolder(path[, force])`	Deletes directory at *path*, optionally to force deletion of read-only directory
`DriveExists(drivespec)`	Returns `true` if specified drive exists on client
`FileExists(filespec)`	Returns `true` if specified file exists
`FolderExists(folderspec)`	Returns `true` if specified directory exists
`GetAbsolutePathName(pathspec)`	Returns full path based on parameters supplied in *pathspec*
`GetBaseName(filespec)`	Returns base name of rightmost item in *filespec* but without file extension
`GetDrive(drivespec)`	Returns `Drive` object referenced by *drivespec* (for example, `c:\`)

Method	Description
GetDriveName(*path*)	Returns name of the drive for a given *path*
GetExtensionName(*path*)	Returns file extension for rightmost item in the *path*
GetFile(*filespec*)	Returns File object (a File object has 12 properties and 4 methods of its own)
GetFileName(*filespec*)	Returns the full filename of rightmost item in *pathspec*
GetFileVersion(*filespec*)	Returns version number associated with a file
GetFolder(*folderspec*)	Returns Folder object (a Folder object has 15 properties and 4 methods of its own)
GetParentFolderName(*path*)	Returns name of parent directory of *path*
GetSpecialFolder(*type*)	Returns Folder object of type 0 (Windows), 1 (Windows\System), or 2 (Windows\Temp)
GetTempName()	Returns a nonsense name for use as a temp filename
MoveFile(*src*, *dest*)	Moves *src* file(s) to *dest*
MoveFolder(*src*, *dest*)	Moves *src* folder(s) to *dest*
OpenTextFile(*path*[, *iomode*[, *create*[, *format*]]])	Returns a TextStream object after opening a file at *path* for mode (ForReading, ForWriting, ForAppending); optionally to create file if not existing; optionally to treat characters as Unicode (TristateTrue), ASCII (TristateFalse), or system default (TristateUseDefault)

As for the basic task of writing some data to a hard disk, the sequence involves creating an instance of FileSystemObject, opening an output stream for text, writing content to the file, and closing the file. Such a sequence might look like the following:

```
function saveLocalData(theData) {
    var fsObj = new ActiveXObject("Scripting.FileSystemObject")
    var theFile = fsObj.CreateTextFile("c:\\giantco.txt", true)
    theFile.WriteLine(theData)
    theFile.Close()
}
```

The `WriteLine()` method belongs to the `TextStream` object, which is returned by `FileSystemObject`'s `CreateTextFile()` method. You can read more about the `TextStream` object and the details of the `FileSystemObject` at http://msdn.microsoft.com/scripting/jscript/doc/jsobjtextstream.htm and http://msdn.microsoft.com/scripting/jscript/doc/jsobjFileSystem.htm.

VBArray

The `VBArray` object provides JavaScript access to Visual Basic *safe arrays*. Such an array is read-only and is commonly returned by ActiveX objects. Such arrays can be composed in VBScript sections of client-side scripts. Visual Basic arrays by their very nature can have multiple dimensions. For example, the following code creates a three-by-two VB array:

```
<SCRIPT LANGUAGE="VBScript">
Dim myArray(2, 1)
myArray(0, 0) = "A"
myArray(0, 1) = "a"
myArray(1, 0) = "B"
myArray(1, 1) = "b"
myArray(2, 1) = "C"
myArray(2, 2) = "c"
</SCRIPT>
```

Once you have a valid VB array, you can convert it to an object that the JScript interpreter can't choke on:

```
<SCRIPT LANGUAGE="JavaScript">
var theVBArray = new VBArray(myArray)
</SCRIPT>
```

Global variables from one script language block can be accessed by another block, even in a different language. But at this point, the array is not in the form of a JavaScript array yet. You can either convert it to such via the `VBArray.toArray()` method or access information about the `VBArray` object through its other methods (described briefly in Table 42-5). Once you convert a `VBArray` to a JavaScript array, you can then iterate through the values just like any JavaScript array.

Table 42-5 **VBArray Object Methods**

Method	Description
dimensions()	Returns number of dimensions of the original array
getItem(*dim1*[, *dim2*[,...*dimN*]])	Returns value at array location defined by dimension addresses
ibound(*dim*)	Returns lowest index value for a given dimension
toArray()	Returns JavaScript array version of VBArray
ubound(*dim*)	Returns highest index value for a given dimension

When you use the toArray() method and the source array has multiple dimensions, values from dimensions after the first "row" are simply appended to the JavaScript array with no nesting structure. IE through version 5.5 provides no backward conversion from a JavaScript array to a VB array.

For more details, visit http://msdn.microsoft.com/scripting/jscript/doc/jsobjVBArray.htm.

✦   ✦   ✦

JavaScript™ Bible, Gold Edition Preview

P A R T

V

◆ ◆ ◆ ◆

In This Part

Fifteen Extra
Chapters

Development Tips

Debugging Tools and
Techniques

Sample Applications

◆ ◆ ◆ ◆

There is much more to developing and deploying applications with JavaScript than has been described in the tutorial and reference sections of the book you are now reading. The JavaScript™ Bible, Gold Edition is not only published in a durable hardcover, but it also contains fifteen additional chapters of particular value to serious scripters and Web application developers. This section describes each of the chapters.

The first six chapters of the Gold Edition extension (Part V in that title) focus on "nuts and bolts" development issues and techniques. Chapters on client-side data-entry validation, cross-browser Dynamic HTML, and (perhaps most important of all) debugging get down to the practical side of developing applications with JavaScript enhancements. Among the nine full-blown applications documented in the remaining chapters is an all-new application for transforming XML data in a document.

The following is a rundown of each of the Gold Edition's extra chapters.

Chapter 43. Data-Entry Validation

One of the most practical applications of JavaScript on the client—the usage that prompted the development of the language to start with—is validating user input to forms before submitting the forms to the server. In this chapter, you will see how to apply both real-time and batch validation for a variety of data-entry types. The key to efficient data validation is building a library of interlocking validation functions. Individual data validation routines are invoked both by user action within a form and by the act of submitting the form—one last check to make sure the user hasn't tried to trick the server into processing incorrect or missing data. You will see lots of code samples from an "industrial-strength" data validation library derived from a real-world high-volume data-entry application that demanded not only perfect accuracy, but also helpful advice and suggestions to weary entry operators who needed reminders about acceptable date ranges, ID number formats, and the like. You may just get some hot ideas about how to design form fields for your next application.

Chapter 44. Scripting Java Applets and Plug-ins

Most browsers that support Java applets also provide a communications pathway between JavaScript scripts on the page and the applets loaded into the page. Netscape calls this technology LiveConnect, but Microsoft (not using the LiveConnect trademark) provides the same powers in IE4+ for Windows.

Java applets don't always have to be visible on the page. One of my favorite applications of applets is to create "faceless" applets that open powers to scripts that JavaScript on its own cannot provide. One of the faceless applets described in Chapter 44 is one that reads a text file on the server, storing the content in a variable within the applet. Then the communications between JavaScript and the applet let the script gain access to that file content. Other developers have used this faceless applet technique to provide a gateway between client-side scripts and Java servlets on the server. In this case, the applet and servlet maintain their own live connection over the network, even after the page has loaded. Applets can also talk to JavaScript, but you must build your applet according to instructions contained in this chapter.

Scripts can also communicate with other kinds of embedded objects, such as plug-ins and (in IE/Windows) ActiveX objects. Plug-ins designed to be scripted provide a set of properties and/or methods that scripts can use to manipulate the activity of the plug-in. One of the examples in Chapter 44 is a client-side music jukebox player that knows how to control the Windows Media Player, QuickTime, and the Netscape LiveAudio sound players (see Figure V-1). Use scripts to change the tunes, play or stop playback, and control the volume level. In other words, you can design your own user interface to very sophisticated playback technologies. To accomplish this, of course, the example in this chapter applies the plug-in detection techniques described in Chapter 32.

Chapter 45. Debugging Scripts

Assuming you've had your hand in scripting by the time you are reading this, you have certainly come across JavaScript error messages. Sometimes error messages are helpful; more often than not, however, they fail to provide enough information to help you hunt down the true source of the problem. Internet Explorer for Windows can be especially obtuse in reporting what the specific problem is and where in the source code it occurs. The first job of Chapter 45, therefore, is to decipher the most common error messages you encounter. You finally uncover what it means when an IE/Windows error alert says "Object expected" at a line number that contains an event handler that invokes what appears to be a perfectly valid function.

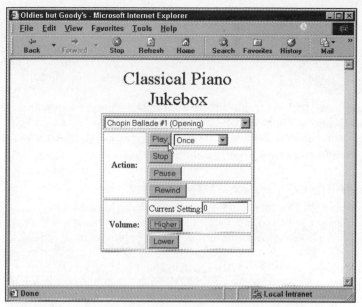

Figure V-1: Design your own interfaces for plug-in controls.

Next, I give you the benefit of my years of experience in debugging scripts. If the error messages fail to help you, you can find where a problem is really occurring with the help of my time-tested debugging techniques.

Part of those years of experience was spent designing my own debugging tools (using JavaScript, of course!). For a popular and accessible technology, JavaScript implementations in browsers have abominable debugging support. Both Microsoft and Netscape have devised debuggers, which are pretty cranky themselves, so I built my own tools. The first of two debugging utilities that you will find helpful lets you signal points in your code to dump traces of values to a listing you can view. This tracing is especially useful when you want to observe the values of variables inside for loops or the values being passed as parameters to frequently invoked functions. While a previous version of this trace utility worked only in NN, the new version supports IE, too. The second tool is an embeddable version of The Evaluator (see Chapter 13). With this tool embedded temporarily in a document that you're constructing, you can view global variable values and inspect values of properties of both browser objects and objects created in your code. The embeddable Evaluator gives you a microscope into the innards of your errant scripts.

Everyone dreams of writing totally bug-free code the first time. To point you toward that goal, this chapter ends with a discussion about how best to prevent bugs in the first place. Good design principles — saving the user from himself or herself — come into play, as well.

Chapter 46. Security and Netscape Signed Scripts

Due to the potential for severe abuse of privacy and security, JavaScript scripts tend to be tucked away pretty securely in their own corner of your browser. This chapter begins with a discussion about the JavaScript security model — notably the same-origin security policy — and how it can affect your application designs.

Netscape developers can then learn about the concept of signed scripts and how, with the user's permission, otherwise off-limits areas of the browsers can be examined and modified. You get an overview of how the Netscape Signing Tool lets you turn script libraries into JAR (Java Archive) files.

Chapter 47. Cross-Browser Dynamic HTML Issues

Chapter 47 provides a cohesive introduction to Dynamic HTML concepts. More importantly, you discover how implementations of various standards and proprietary technologies have both helped and hindered the deployment of DHTML applications in the past. If you have developed cross-browser DHTML applications for NN4 and IE4, you are well aware of the situation. In this chapter, you receive guidance about how to move forward to the W3C DOM, with the goal of reducing the amount of code branching necessary to make one page work in as many DHTML-capable browsers as possible. Until the installed base of NN4 browsers withers to a tiny fraction of the world, you may still have to acknowledge the NN4 proprietary — and dead-end — layer object. Making the transition to the W3C DOM standard in NN6 will be painful for some developers, but this chapter attempts to soften the blow.

Chapter 48. Internet Explorer Behaviors

In a few places throughout the Part III reference section of this book, you have seen mention of IE behaviors. Behaviors are external components that combine XML and JavaScript (or VBScript, if that's your cup of tea) to create specifications about how objects should behave in response to user or system events. This chapter describes the structure of a behavior file and how to go about developing behaviors for your IE5+/Windows applications.

Chapter 49. Application: Tables and Calendars

In Chapter 49, you begin seeing JavaScript used for real-world applications. This chapter demonstrates three ways to use JavaScript on the client to compose and modify a table — in this case, a table that displays a calendar (see Figure V-2). The first version is a static table, which is fully backward compatible with all scriptable browsers. The same goes for the second version, which uses text boxes within a table to allow immediate updating of a calendar to display different months and years without having to reload the page. All new for this edition is a third version, which takes advantage of the table manipulation and page reflowing features of IE4+ and NN6. You see tables and calendars in nicely formatted HTML change right before your very eyes and with a minimum of code.

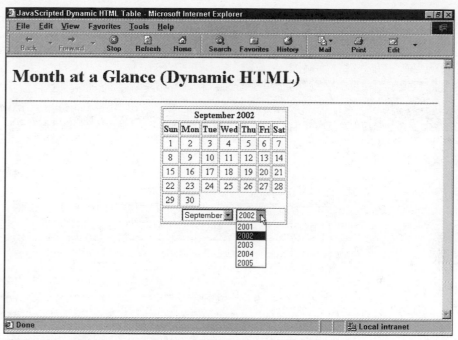

Figure V-2: With IE4+ and NN6, calendar tables can be dynamic.

Chapter 50. Application: A Lookup Table

A convenient way to offload simple data lookup or calculation operations from your server to the client is to embed small chunks of data (up to about 15KB) into the document in the form of arrays or objects. Then let the client-side scripts respond to user input to perform lookups of the data. The response is instantaneous for the user. The application in Chapter 50 provides demonstrations of a few techniques along this line. The subject of the lookup is the U.S. state associated with the first three digits of a Social Security number. This is more than a simple one-for-one lookup, because there are ranges of values that apply to a given state. Therefore, the part of the lookup mechanism has to include a streamlined way of defining each numeric range and linking a state to that range.

User interface elements for this application are simple enough: one text box for entry and one for readout (to be backward compatible). But even with this seemingly simple data-entry field, validation is necessary to make sure only three-digit numbers are entered before the lookup task starts up. Therefore, techniques from Chapter 43 are put to use for real here.

Chapter 51. Application: A "Poor Man's" Order Form

Calling the application in this chapter an "order form" is a ruse to demonstrate some significant scripting techniques affecting rows and columns of form text fields inside a table (see Figure V-3). The purpose of wrapping this example in the guise of an order form is to also demonstrate efficient ways of calculating totals across rows and down columns. The table and form are generated by script. Some additional suggestions are provided for applying the table manipulation and page reflow of IE4+ and NN6.

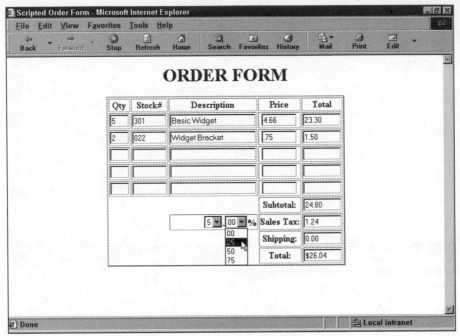

Figure V-3: Scripts can write tables and calculate totals efficiently.

Chapter 52. Application: Outline-Style Table of Contents

Perhaps one of the most popular applications from the JavaScript(tm) Bible is the collapsible hierarchical list. To be backward compatible with older browsers, the code rewrites the outline each time the user expands or collapses a segment. This chapter includes a second version that takes advantage of IE4+ and NN6 style sheets to operate even more quickly and cleanly. The latest version of the collapsible list is designed for IE5+/Windows. This version takes advantage of XML data islands and the Outline Processor Markup Language (OPML) format for outline data. Scripts convert the XML data into flexible JavaScript data structures. Scripts then render the outline in a very professional-looking form (see Figure V-4).

Chapter 53. Application: Calculations and Graphics

Another popular application (among electronics geeks, anyway) is the graphical resistor value calculator described in this chapter (see Figure V-5). This application demonstrates techniques of pre-caching images, image swapping, and calculating values based on chosen options of a SELECT form element. The application also suggests that what may otherwise be a boring electronics calculator can be turned into an inviting and engaging application.

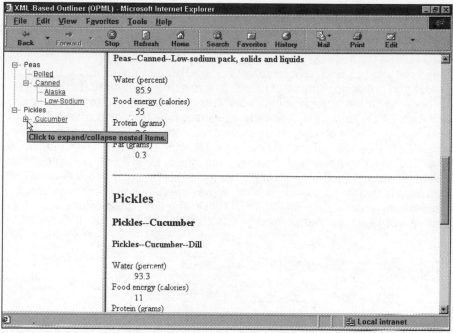

Figure V-4: Expandable/collapsible lists are fast under script control.

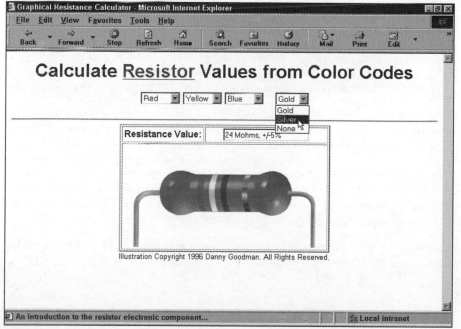

Figure V-5: Calculators don't have to be boring or server-slow.

Chapter 54. Application: Intelligent "Updated" Flags

Whenever you visit a Web site that has an icon next to an item indicating that the item is new or updated, can you be sure that it is new since your last visit? Or is it new as of the last time the page author updated that item? And what if you haven't visited the site in a couple of months? The goal of the application in this chapter is to let you attribute some intelligence to items on a page so that any item that has been updated since the visitor's last trip to the site is flagged as being new (see Figure V-6). Thus, this application gets into how to date-stamp a visit, storing that value in a client cookie. Date calculations compare the date stamp of each item updated on the page and the cookie value, allowing the page to dynamically add "New" icon flags to items that the user hasn't seen, even if you've made a dozen updates to the site in the meantime. This feature is one of those "added value" applications that lets JavaScript enhance the experience of those with script-enabled browsers, while not penalizing those who have JavaScript turned off or are running a browser without scripting capabilities.

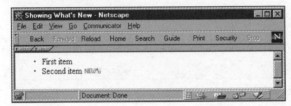

Figure V-6: Let your scripts show the user what's new.

Chapter 55. Application: Decision Helper

The Decision Helper is a Web version of an application that performs weighting analysis on factors affecting a choice among several possibilities (for example, which of five computer models to buy). This application is the most complex in the book, and it demonstrates several advanced JavaScript techniques (see Figure V-7).

With the application laid out in a frameset, navigation buttons affect the navigation of two other frames in the frameset: One loading different pages and the other navigating to different anchors within a single page. This application must also preserve locally (and temporarily) many individual pieces of data that the user enters (for example, computer model numbers, factors being compared, how important each factor is to the user, and so on). Two versions of the application show how to use cookies to preserve this data (including the fact that you have more data points than cookie spaces) or variables in the frameset.

Results of the user's input entry are calculated and presented graphically. Thus, you can see how to generate colorful bar charts based on real data. All of this takes place without one line of CGI code on the server.

Chapter 56. Application: Cross-Browser DHTML Map Puzzle

In this chapter, you see practical application of the information discussed in Chapters 31 (on positioned objects) and 48. In this application, the user is asked to drag U.S. state maps (only a handful are provided in the example) onto a blank outline of the lower 48 states (see Figure V-8). If the user successfully releases the state within five pixels of its true position, the dragged item snaps into position, and the state is rated as being complete. After all of the supplied states are successfully placed, the user sees a congratulatory message. One more technique displayed here shows a help "window" flying in from one side of the browser window and centering itself.

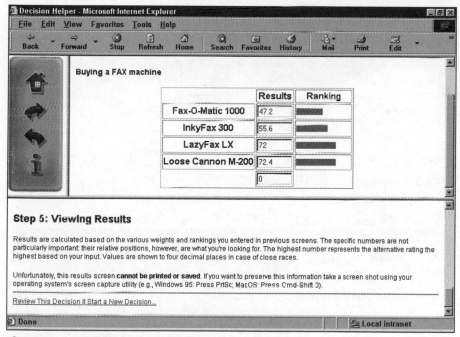

Figure V-7: A full-fledged application on the client

Chapter 57. Application: Transforming XML Data Islands

With the XML data island facilities in IE5+, the application in this chapter has some XML data embedded within the document. Scripts turn the XML data into JavaScript objects, which makes it easy to sort and render the data in multiple ways without having to request alternate views from the server (see Figure V-9). You can see that for many XML data custom rendering jobs, JavaScript (along with CSS and HTML in browsers) offers several benefits over the less robust XML Style Sheet Transform (XSLT) technology.

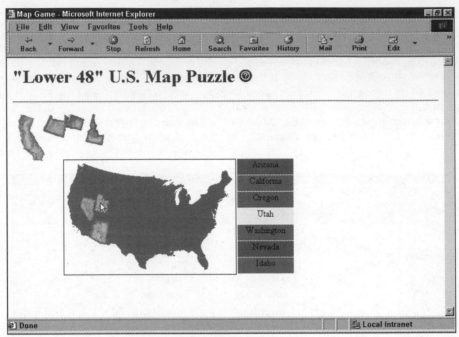

Figure V-8: A fun application of Dynamic HTML

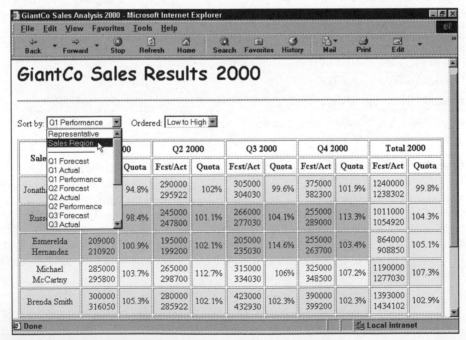

Figure V-9: Use JavaScript to sort and render XML data in IE.

Appendixes

◆ ◆ ◆ ◆

◆ ◆ ◆ ◆

JavaScript and Browser Object Quick Reference

The following pages contain reduced printouts of a handy pamphlet whose Adobe Acrobat (.pdf) file you can find on the companion CD-ROM. I modified the arrangement of the following material for printing in this appendix. The .pdf file on the CD-ROM, which you can print for quick reference, contains all of the pages you see in this appendix.

This compact guide enables you to see at a glance the breadth of each object's properties, methods, and event handlers. The core JavaScript language section applies to all scriptable browsers. The document object model, however, is divided into the three basic model types that developers must support:

- ❖ Fully compatible with all browsers
- ❖ Internet Explorer proprietary object model
- ❖ W3C DOM-compatible browsers

As a measure of how much the language — and especially the object models — have grown in recent times, the same quick reference for the previous edition of this book amounted to four printable sides. This edition requires no fewer than 12 sides.

The large vocabularies and divisive nature of the existing object models (complicated ever further in the IE browser due to operating system incompatibilities) create a major challenge in designing a portable, quick reference like the one shown on the following pages. Object model groupings in the

Quick Reference are designed to be as consistent as possible across the three models; so if you attempt to build applications for multiple object models, you can find, say, the `document` object's property listings in similar positions in each of the three model references. Development for the IE4+ and W3C DOM environments still requires knowledge about the original object model because that legacy model persists in current practice.

To conserve space in the IE4+ and W3C DOM sections, I do not list all HTML element objects (even though I cover them in chapters of this book). A large percentage of HTML elements share the same properties, methods, and event handlers — all of which are listed in each object model's section (in a box labeled "All HTML Elements"). For example, the DIV element has a specific role and behavior from the point of view of the HTML rendering engine; however, as a scriptable object, it has no properties, methods, or event handlers beyond the ones it shares with all HTML elements. Therefore, the only HTML elements that I list within the IE4+ and W3C DOM sections are those that have one or more properties, methods, and event handlers that are either unique to that object or are shared by only a few related elements. Once you are acquainted with the items in common with all elements, it is easier to find the items that are special to a listed object.

If you choose to print the Acrobat files, first read the CD-ROM file `Choose a Version.txt` to determine the format you'd like to print. Then read the `howtoprt.txt` file in the folder dedicated to your chosen format. This file contains printing and assembly directions for optimum convenience with respect to the format you choose.

Core JavaScript/JScript/ECMAScript (NN2+, IE3+) Quick Reference

Array N3,J2 — 37

constructor N4, IE4
length
prototype

concat(array2)N4, IE4
join("char")
push()N4, IE5.5
pop()N4, IE5.5
reverse()
shift()N4, IE4
slice(i,[j]) N4, IE4
sort(compareFunc)
splice(i,j, items)N4, IE5.5
toLocaleString() N6, IE5.E
toString()
unshift()N4, IE5.5

Date — 36

constructor N4, IE4
prototype N3, IE4

getFullYear()N4, J2
getYear()
getMonth()
getDate()
getDay()
getHours()
getMinutes()
getSeconds()
getTime()
getMilliseconds() N4, J2
getUTCFullYear()N4, J2
getUTCMonth()N4, J2
getUTCDate()N4, J2
getUTCDay()N4, J2
getUTCHours()N4, J2
getUTCMinutes()N4, J2
getUTCSeconds()N4, J2
getUTCMilliseconds() N4, J2
setYear(val)
setFullYear(val)N4, J2
setMonth(val)
setDate(val)
setDay(val)
setHours(val)
setMinutes(val)
setSeconds(val)
setMilliseconds(val)N4, J2
setTime(val)
setUTCFullYear(val)N4, J2
setUTCMonth(val)N4, J2
setUTCDate(val)N4, J2
setUTCHours(val)N4, J2
setUTCMinutes(val)N4, J2
setUTCSeconds(val)N4, J2
setUTCMilliseconds(val)N4, J2
getTimezoneOffset()
toLocaleDateString() IE5.5, N6
toLocaleString()
toLocaleTimeString() IE5.5, N6
toString()
toUTCString()N4, J2
Date.parse("dateString")
Date.UTC(date values)

String — 34

constructor N4, IE4
length
prototype N4, J2

anchor("anchorName")
big()
blink()
bold()
charAt(index)
charCodeAt(i)N4, IE4
concat(string2)N4, IE4
fixed()
fontcolor(# rgbhb)
fontsize(1to7)
fromCharCode(n1...)(1),N4, IE5.5
indexOf(str [,i])
italics()
lastIndexOf(str [,i])
link(URL)
localeCompare() N6, IE5.5
match(regexp)N4, IE4
replace(regexp, str)N4, IE4
search(regexp)N4, IE4
slice(i [,j])N4, IE4
small()
split(i [,j])N3, (2), IE4
substr(start, length)N4, IE4
substring(intA, intB)
sup()
toLocaleLowerCase() N6, IE5.5
toLocaleUpperCase() N6, IE5.5
toLowerCase()
toString()N4, IE4
toUpperCase()
valueOf()N4, IE4

(1) Method of the static String object.
(2) Added behavior in N4 indicates: ability to accept a regexp parameter; second parameter (limit integer) to limit the number of splits to be included; a space string parameter signifying any white space character.

Math(1) — 35

E
LN2
LN10
LOG2E
LOG10E
PI
SQRT1_2
SQRT2

abs(val)
acos(val)
asin(val)
atan(va)
atan2(val1, val2)
ceil(val)
cos(val)
exp(val)
floor(val)
log(val)
max(val1, val2)
min(val1, val2)
pow(val1, power)
random(va)
round(va)
sin(val)
sqrt(val)
tan(val)

(1)All properties & methods are of the static Math object.

Number N3,J2 — 35

constructor N4, IE4
MAX_VALUE
MIN_VALUE
NaN
NEGATIVE_INFINITY
POSITIVE_INFINITY
prototype

toExponential(n)N6, IE5.5
toFixed(n)N6, IE5.5
toLocaleString() N6, IE5.5
toString(radix)N4, IE4
toPrecision(n)N6, IE5.5
valueOf()N4, IE4

Function N3,J2 — 41

arguments
arity(1)
caller(1)
constructor N4, IE4
length
prototype

apply(this, argsArray)N6, IE5.5
call(this [,arg1[...argN]])N6, IE5.5
toString()
valueOf()

(1) Discontinued for N6.

Regular Expressions N4,IE4 — 38

global
ignoreCase
input(1), IE5.5
lastIndex
multiline (1), IE5.5
lastMatch (1), IE5.5
lastParen (1), IE5.5
leftContext (1), IE5.5
prototype
rightContext (1)
source
$1...$9

compile(regexp)
exec(" string")(2)
test("string")
str.match(regexp)
str.replace(regexp, str)
str.search(regexp)
str.split(regexp, limit1)

(1) Property of the static RegExp object.
(2) Returns an array with properties: index, input, [0], [1]...[n]

Globals — 42

Functions

decodeURI(" encodedURI")N6, IE5.5
decodeURIComponent(" encComp")N6, IE5.5
encodeURI("URI/String")N6, IE5.5
encodeURIComponent("compString")N6, IE5.5
escape(" string" [,1])
eval("string")
isFinite(number)N4, IE4
isNaN(expression)
Number(sizing)N4, IE4
parseFloat("string")
parseInt("s,img" [,radix])
toString(radix)
unescape("string")
unwatch(prop)N4
watch(prop, handler)N4

Statements

// ..." ;
const N6
var

Boolean N3,J2 — 35

constructor N4, IE4
prototype3

toString()N4, IE4
valueOf()N4, IE4

Control Statements — 39

```
if (condition) {
    statements/fTrue
}

If (condition) {
    statements/fTrue
} else {
    statements/fFalse
}

result = condition ? expr1 : expr2

for ([init expr]; [condition]; [update]   ]) {
    statements

for (var in object) {          with (object) {
    statements                      statements
}                              }

while (condition) {            do {
    statements                      statements
}                              } while (condition )N4, IE4

switch ( expression) {
    case labelN :
        [break]
    ...
    [default :
        statements ]
}N4, IE4

label : N4, IE4
continue [ label]N4, IE4
break [label]N4, IE4

try {
    statements to test
} catch (errorInfo) {
    statements to run, exception or not
}[finally {
    statements if exception occurs in try block
}]

throw value N4, W5
```

Error N6,W5 — 39

prototype   toString()
constructor W5
description W5
fileName N6
lineNumber N6
message N6, IE5.5
name N6, IE5.5
number W5

JavaScript and Browser Objects Quick Reference

Appendix A

JavaScript Bible, 4th Edition by Danny Goodman

How to Use This Quick Reference

This guide contains quick reference info for the core JavaScript language, the original document object model (2 pp), the IE4+DHTML object model (4 pp), and the W3C DOM object model (4 pp) as implemented in IE5+ and NN6. All-uppercase object names refer to HTML elements (IE4+ and W3C DOMs). The three columns in each box list the object's properties, methods, and event handlers in that order. Read the compatibility guides for each section.

Numbers in the upper left corners of object squares are chapter numbers in which the object is covered in detail.

Basic browser and operating system notation codes are as follows:

N — Netscape Navigator	IE — MS Internet Explorer
W — Win32 OS	M — Macintosh OS

See the accompanying file for printing and collating instructions in booklet or broadside configurations.

Operators | 40

Comparison

==	Equals	N4, IE4
===	Strictly equals	
!=	Does not equal	
!==	Strictly does not equal	N4, IE4
>	Is greater than	
>=	Is greater than or equal to	
<	Is less than	
<=	Is less than or equal to	

Arithmetic

+	Plus (and string concat.)
-	Minus
*	Multiply
/	Divide
%	Modulo
++	Increment
--	Decrement
-val	Negation

Assignment

=	Equals
+=	Add by value
-=	Subtract by value
*=	Multiply by value
/=	Divide by value
%=	Modulo by value
<<=	Left shift by value
>>=	Right shift by value
>>>=	Zero fill by value
&=	Bitwise AND by value
|=	Bitwise OR by value
^=	Bitwise XOR by value

Boolean

&&	AND
||	OR
!	NOT

Bitwise

&	Bitwise AND
		Bitwise OR
^	Bitwise XOR
~	Bitwise NOT
<<	Left shift
>>	Right shift
>>>	Zero fill right shift

Miscellaneous

delete	N4, IE4	Series delimiter
in	N6, IE5.5	Property destroyer
instanceof	N6,W5	Item in object
new		Instance of
this		Object creator
typeof	N3, IE3	Object self-reference
void	N3, IE3	Value type
		Return no value

IE4+, NN6+ style Object Properties

style IE4,N6 | 30

Text & Fonts

color IE4, N6
font IE4, N6
fontFamily IE4, N6
fontSize IE4, N6
fontSizeAdjust M5, N6
fontStretch M5, N6
fontStyle IE4, N6
fontVariant IE4, N6
fontWeight IE4, N6
letterSpacing IE4, N6
lineBreak IE5
lineHeight IE4, N6
quotes M5, N6
rubyAlign IE5
rubyOverhang IE5
rubyPosition IE5
textAlign IE4, N6
textAlignLast IE5.5
textAutospace W5
textDecoration IE4, N6
textDecorationBlink IE-Only
textDecorationLineThrough IE-Only
textDecorationNone IE-Only
textDecorationOverline IE-Only
textDecorationUnderline IE-Only
textIndent IE5
textJustify IE5
textJustifyTrim IE5.5
textKashidaSpace IE5.5
textShadow M5, N6
textTransform IE4, N6
textUnderlinePosition IE5.5
unicodeBidi IE5, N6
whiteSpace IE4, N6
wordBreak W5
wordSpacing IE4, N6
wordWrap W5
writingMode IE5.5

Positioning

bottom IE5, N6
height IE4, N6
left IE4, N6
right IE5, N6
top IE4, N6
width IE4, N6
pixelBottom IE/W-Only
pixelHeight IE/W-Only
pixelLeft IE/W-Only
pixelRight IE/W-Only
pixelTop IE/W-Only
pixelWidth IE/W-Only
posBottom IE/W-Only
posHeight IE/W-Only
posLeft IE/W-Only
posRight IE/W-Only
posTop IE/W-Only
posWidth IE/W-Only
position IE4, N6
zIndex IE4, N6

Borders & Edges

border IE4, N6
borderBottom IE4, N6
borderLeft IE4, N6
borderRight IE4, N6
borderTop IE4, N6
borderBottomColor IE4, N6
borderLeftColor IE4, N6
borderRightColor IE4, N6
borderTopColor IE4, N6
borderBottomStyle IE4, N6
borderLeftStyle IE4, N6
borderRightStyle IE4, N6
borderTopStyle IE4, N6
borderBottomWidth IE4, N6
borderLeftWidth IE4, N6
borderRightWidth IE4, N6
borderTopWidth IE4, N6
borderColor IE4, N6
borderStyle IE4, N6
borderWidth IE4, N6
margin IE4, N6
marginBottom IE4, N6
marginLeft IE4, N6
marginRight IE4, N6
marginTop IE4, N6
outline M5, N6
outlineColor M5, N6
outlineStyle M5, N6
outlineWidth M5, N6
padding IE4, N6
paddingBottom IE4, N6
paddingLeft IE4, N6
paddingRight IE4, N6
paddingTop IE4, N6

Lists

listStyle IE4, N6
listStyleImage IE4, N6
listStylePosition IE4, N6
listStyleType IE4, N6

Tables

borderCollapse M5, N6
borderSpacing IE5.5
captionSide M5, N6
emptyCells M5, N6
tableLayout IE5, N6

Background

background IE4, N6
backgroundAttachment IE4, N6
backgroundColor IE4, N6
backgroundImage IE4, N6
backgroundPosition IE4, N6
backgroundPositionX IE/W-Only
backgroundPositionY IE/W-Only
backgroundRepeat IE4, N6

Inline Display & Layout

clear IE4, N6
clip IE4, N6
clipBottom W5
clipLeft W5
clipRight W5
clipTop W5
content M5, N6
counterIncrement M5, N6
counterReset M5, N6
cssFloat M5, N6
cursor IE4, N6
direction IE5, N6
display IE4, N6
filter W4
floatStyle M4
layoutGrid W5
layoutGridChar W5
layoutGridLine W5
layoutGridMode W5
layoutGridType W5
marks M5, N6
markerOffset M5, N6
maxHeight M5, N6
maxWidth M5, N6
minHeight M5, N6
minWidth M5, N6
overflow IE4, N6
overflowX W5
overflowY W5
styleFloat IE-Only
verticalAlign IE4, N6
visibility IE4, N6
width IE5.5
zoom IE5.5

Printing

orphans M5, N6
widows M5, N6
page M6, N6
pageBreakAfter IE4, N6
pageBreakBefore IE4, N6
pageBreakInside W5
size N6

Miscellaneous

accelerator W5
behavior W5
cssText IE4, N6
imeMode W5

Scrollbars

scrollbar3dLightColor IE5.5
scrollbarArrowColor IE5.5
scrollbarBaseColor IE5.5
scrollbarDarkShadowColor IE5.5
scrollbarFaceColor IE5.5
scrollbarHighlightColor IE5.5
scrollbarShadowColor IE5.5
scrollbarTrackColor IE5.5

Original DOM (NN2+, IE3+) Quick Reference — Page 1 of 2

JS84

window (16)

Properties	Methods	Event Handlers
content N6	alert("msg")	onAbort N6
appCore N6	attachEvent(" evt", func) IE5	onAfterPrint W5
clientInformation IE4	back() N4	onBeforePrint W5
clipboardData W5	blur() N3, IE4	onBeforeUnload IE4
closed N3, IE4	captureEvents(type) N4-Only	onBlur N3, IE4
Components[] N6	clearInterval(ID) N4, IE4	onChange N6
controllers[] N6	clearTimeout(ID)	onClick N6
crypto N6	close()	onClose N6
defaultStatus	confirm("msg") IE5.5	onDragDrop N4,(S)
dialogArguments W4	createPopup() IE5.5	onError N3, IE4
dialogHeight W4	detachEvent(" evt", func) IE5	onFocus N3, IE4
dialogLeft W4	disableExternalCapture() N4-Only	onHelp IE4
dialogTop W4	enableExternalCapture() N4-Only	onKeyDown N6
dialogWidth W4	execScript(" expr"[,lang]) IE4	onKeyPress N6
directories N4,(S)	find([" str"[,case, bkwd]])N4-Only	onKeyUp N6
document	fireEvent(" evt"[,evtObj])IE5.5	onLoad
event IE4	focus() N3, IE4	onMouseDown N6
external W4	forward() N4	onMouseMove N6
frameElement IE5.5	handleEvent(event)N4-Only	onMouseOut N6
frames[]	home() N4	onMouseOver N4-Only
history	moveBy(Δx,Δy) N4, IE4	onMouseUp N6
innerHeight N4	moveTo(x,y)N4, IE4	onMove N4-Only
innerWidth N4	navigate() IE3	onReset N6
length N4, IE4	open("URL","name", "specs")[1],(S)	onResize N4, IE4
loading N4-Only	print() N4, IE5	onScroll IE4
location	prompt("msg", "reply")	onSelect N6
locationbar N4,(S)	releaseEvents(type)N4-Only	onSubmit N6
menubar N4,(S)	resizeBy(Δx,Δy) N4, IE4	onUnload
name	resizeTo(width,height)N4, IE4	
navigator N5, IE4	routeEvent(event)N4-Only	
offscreenBuffering W4	scroll(x,y)N3, IE4	
opener IE3, N3	scrollBy(Δx,Δy)N4, IE4	
outerHeight N4	scrollTo(x,y)N4, IE4	
outerWidth N4	setActive() IE5.5	
pageXOffset N4	setInterval(func, msec [,args])N4,IE4,(2)	
pageYOffset N4	setTimeout(func, msec [,args])(2)	
parent	showHelp() N4	
personalbar N4,(S)	showModalDialog() W4	
pkcs11 N6	showModelessDialog() W5	
prompter N6	stop()N4	
returnValue W4		
screen N6, IE4		
screenLeft W5		
screenTop W5		
screenX N6		
scrollbars N4,(S)		
scrollX N6		
scrollY N6		
self		
sidebar N4,(S)		
status		
statusbar N4,(S)		
toolbar N4,(S)		
top		
window		

(1) New window specs for all browsers: height, width, toolbar, location, directories, status, menubar, scrollbars, resizable, copyHistory. For N4+: alwaysLowered, alwaysRaised, dependent, hotkeys, innerHeight, innerWidth, outerHeight, outerWidth, screenX, screenY, titlebar(S), z-lock(S). Add'l specs for IE4+: channelmode, fullscreen, left, top. Add'l spec for IE5+: title.
(2) Optional args parameter added to N4; 3rd parameter in IE4 is for scripting language.

document (18)

Properties	Methods	Event Handlers
alinkColor N3, IE4	captureEvents(type)N4-Only	(None)
anchors[]	clear()	
applets[] N3, IE4	close()	
bgColor	getSelection() N4,(2)	
cookie	handleEvent(event)N4-Only	
domain N3, IE4	open("mimetype" [,"replace"])N4-Only(3)	
embeds[] N3, IE4	releaseEvents(event)N4-Only	
fgColor	routeEvent(event)N4-Only	
forms[]	write("string")	
height N4	writeln("string")	
images[] N3, IE4		
lastModified		
layers[]N4-Only		
linkColor		
links[]		
location (1)		
referrer		
title		
URL N3, IE4		
vlinkColor		
width N4		

(1) Replaced by the URL property in Navigator 3.
(2) N4 has a document.selection property to retrieve the currently selected text.
(3) mimetype parameter new in N4, but only "text/html" type supported.

layer N4-Only (31)

Properties	Methods	Event Handlers
above	load("filename", y)	onBlur
background	moveAbove(layerObj)	onFocus
below	moveBelow(layerObj)	onLoad
bgColor	moveBy(Δ x, Δy)	onMouseOut
clip.bottom	moveTo(x, y)	onMouseOver
clip.height	moveToAbsolute(x, y)	onMouseUp
clip.left	resizeBy(Δ x, Δy)	
clip.right	resizeTo(width, height)	
clip.top		
clip.width		
document		
left		
name		
pageX		
pageY		
parentLayer		
siblingAbove		
siblingBelow		
src		
top		
visibility		
zIndex		

location (17)

Properties	Methods	Event Handlers
hash	assign(" URL")	(None)
host	reload([unconditional])N3, E4	
hostname	replace(" URL")N3,IE4	
href		
pathname		
port		
protocol		

link (<A HREF=...></A>) (21)

Properties	Methods	Event Handlers
hash	(None)	onClick
host		onDblClick N4,(1), IE4
hostname		onMouseDown N4, IE4
href		onMouseOut N4, IE4
pathname		onMouseOver
port		onMouseUp N4, IE4
protocol		
search		
target		
text N4		
x N4		
y N4		

(1) Not implemented in NN4/Mac.

anchor (<A NAME=...></A>) (21)

Properties	Methods	Event Handlers
name N4, IE4	(None)	(None)
text N4		
x N4		
y N4		

image N3,(1),IE4 (22)

Properties	Methods	Event Handlers
border	(None)	onAbort
complete		onError
height		onLoad
hspace		
lowsrc		
name		
src		
vspace		
width		
x N4		
y N4		

(1) Implemented in IE3.01/Macintosh but not Windows until IE4.

area N3,IE4 (22)

Properties	Methods	Event Handlers
hash	(None)	onClick N4
host		onMouseOut
hostname		onMouseOver
href		
pathname		
port		
protocol		
search		
target		

history (17)

Properties	Methods	Event Handlers
length	back()	(None)
	forward()	
	go(int | "URL")	
	current (S),(1)	
	next (S),(1)	
	previous (S),(1)	

(1) Accessible in NN2 via a security technique no longer in use. Available in NN4+ with signed scripts.

Page 2 of 2 — Original DOM (NN2+, IE3+) Quick Reference

JSB4

form 23

```
action            handleEvent( evt)N4   onResetN3, IE4
elements[]        reset()N3, IE4        onSubmit
encoding          submit()
length
method
name
target
```

button, reset, submit 24

```
checked           click()              onClick
form              handleEvent( evt)N3   onMouseDown N4, IE4
name                                   onMouseUp N4, IE4
typeN3, IE4
value
```

checkbox 24

```
checked           click()              onClick
defaultChecked    handleEvent( evt)N3   onMouseDown N4, IE4
form                                   onMouseUp N4, IE4
nameN3, M4
typeN3, IE4
value
```

radio 24

```
checked           click()              onClick
defaultChecked    handleEvent( evt)N3   onMouseDown N4, IE4
form                                   onMouseUp N4, IE4
length
name
typeN3, IE4
value
```

text, textarea, password, hidden 25

```
defaultValue (1)  blur()               onBlur
form              focus()              onChange
name              handleEvent( evt)N4   onFocus
typeN3, IE4       select()             onKeyDown N4, IE4
value (2)                              onKeyPress N4, IE4
                                       onKeyUp N4, IE4
                                       onSelect
```
(1) Not available for textarea object.
(2) Password value property returns empty string in NN2.

file input controlN3, (1), IE4 26

```
form              blur()               onBlur
name              focus()              onFocus
type              handleEvent( evt)N4   onSelect
value             select()
```
(1) Netscape also calls this the fileUpload object.

select 26

```
length            blurN3, IE4          onBlur
name              focus()N3, IE4       onChange
options[]         handleEvent( evt)N4   onFocus
options[].defaultSelected
options[].index
options[].selected
options[].text
options[].value
selectedIndex
typeN3, IE4
```

navigator 28

```
appCodeName               javaEnabled()N3, M4
appMinorVersion IE4       preference(name[, val])N4, (S)
appName                   taitEnabled()N3, M4
appVersion
browserLanguage IE4
cookieEnabled N6, IE4
cpuClass IE4
language N4
mimeTypes[] N3, M4
onLine IE4
platform N4, IE4
plugins[] N3, M4
productN6
productSub N6
securityPolicy N6
systemLanguage IE4
userAgent
userLanguage IE4
userProfile IE4
vendorN6
vendorSub N6
```

mimeTypeN3, M4 28

```
description       (None)
enabledPlugin
type
suffixes
```

pluginN3, M4 28

```
name              refresh()
filename
description
length
```

screenN4, IE4 28

```
availHeight       (None)
availLeft (1)
availTop (1)
availWidth
bufferDepth(2)
colorDepth
fontSmoothingEnabled (2)
height
pixelDepth
updateInterval (2)
width
```
(1) NN4+ only.
(2) IE4+ only.

Original DOM Compatibility Guide

Baseline browsers for this section are NN2, IE3&/1, and IE 3.01/Mac. An item with no notation is compatible back to that level. Notations indicate the browser and version in which the property, method, or event handler was introduced. An item showing to be introduced only in IE, for example, does not exist for any NN version.

Except for the window and navigator objects (whose listings cover all browsers and versions), new features listed in this section cover only through NN4 (and IE4 when they matched a new NN4 feature). Notations are as follows:

```
N3  —  New in NN3
N4  —  New in NN4
J2  —  New in IE3, JScript.dll ver.2
IE4 —  New in IE4, all OSes
(S) —  Requires signed scripts (NN)
```

Additional window and navigator object notations are:

```
W4   —  IE4+Windows only
W5   —  IE5+Windows only
IE5  —  IE5+ all OSes
IE5.5 — IE5.5+ only Win tested)
M4   —  IE4+/Mac only
M5   —  IE5+/Mac only
N6   —  New in NN6
```

Except for items marked N4-Only (which are not carried over into NN6), an item listed for an early browser is also available in the IE4+ and/or W3C DOM object models. "(None)" means that no methods or events exist for the current object through IE3 and NN4.

IE4+ DHTML DOM Quick Reference — Page 1 of 4

All HTML Elements 15

accessKey
all[]
behaviorUrns[] W5
canHaveChildren W5
canHaveHTML IE5.5
className
clientHeight
clientLeft
clientTop
clientWidth
contentEditable IE5
currentStyle IE5
dataFld W4
dataFormatAs W4
dataSrc W4
disabled
document
filters[] W4
hideFocus IE5.5
id
innerHTML
innerText
isContentEditable IE5.5
isDisabled IE5.5
isMultiLine IE5.5
isTextEdit W4
lang
language
length W5
offsetHeight
offsetLeft
offsetParent
offsetTop
offsetWidth
outerHTML
outerText
parentElement W4
parentTextEdit
readyState
recordNumber W4
runtimeStyle W5
scopeName W5
scrollHeight
scrollLeft
scrollTop
scrollWidth
sourceIndex
style
tabIndex
tagName
tagUrn W5
title
uniqueID W5

addBehavior(" URL") W5
applyElement(elem[, type]) W5
attachEvent(" evt", func) W5
blur()
clearAttributes() W5
click()
componentFromPoint(x,y) W5
contains(elem)
detachEvent(" evt", func) W5
fireEvent(" evt"[, evt]) IE5.5
focus()
getAdjacentText(" case")
getAttribute(" attr"[, case])
getBoundingClientRect() W5
getClientRects() W5
getExpression() W5
insertAdjacentElement() W5
insertAdjacentHTML()
insertAdjacentText()
item(index[, subindex])(1)
mergeAttributes() W5
releaseCapture() W5
removeAttribute(" attr"[, case])
removeBehavior(" ID) W5
removeExpression(" prog") W5
removeNode(children) W5
replaceAdjacentText(" loc", "txt") W5
replaceNode(new) W5
scrollIntoView(top)
setActive() IE5.5
setAttribute(" attr", val[, case])
setCapture(container) W5
setExpression(" prog", "expr", "lang") W5
swapNode(node) W5
tags(" tag")(1)
urns(" URN") W5, (1)

(1) Property or method of all object collections.

onActivate IE5.5
onBeforeCopy W5
onBeforeCut W5
onBeforeDeactivate IE5.5
onBeforeEditFocus W5
onBeforePaste W5
onBlur
onClick
onContextMenu W5
onControlSelect IE5.5
onCopy W5
onCut W5
onDblClick
onDeactivate IE5.5
onDrag W5
onDragEnd W5
onDragEnter W5
onDragLeave W5
onDragOver W5
onDragStart W5
onDrop W5
onFilterChange W4
onFocus
onHelp W4,M5
onKeyDown
onKeyPress
onKeyUp
onLoseCapture W5
onMouseDown
onMouseEnter IE5.5
onMouseLeave IE5.5
onMouseMove
onMouseOut
onMouseOver
onMouseUp
onPaste W5
onPropertyChange W5
onReadyStateChange
onResize
onResizeEnd IE5.5
onResizeStart IE5.5
onSelectStart

popup W5.5 15

document
isOpen

hide()
show()

(None)

FRAMESET 16

border
borderColor
cols
frameBorder
frameSpacing
rows

FRAME 16

borderColor
Document
frameBorder
height
marginHeight
marginWidth
noResize
scrolling
src
width

IFRAME 16

align
Document
frameBorder
frameSpacing
hspace
marginHeight
marginWidth
scrolling
src
vspace

BASE 20

href
target

BASEFONT 20

color
face
size

META 20

charset
content
http-Equiv
name
url

TITLE 20

text

document 18

activeElement
alinkColor
all
anchors[]
applets[]
bgColor
body
charset
cookie
defaultCharset
designMode W5
doctype
domain
embeds[]
expando
fgColor
fileCreatedDate
fileModifiedDate
fileSize
forms[]
frames[]
images[]
lastModified
linkColor
links[]
location
media IE5.5
mimeType W5
namespaces[] IE5.5
parentWindow
plugins[]
protocol
readyState
referrer
scripts[]
security IE5.5
selection
styleSheets[]
title
uniqueID
URL
URLUnencoded IE5.5
vlinkColor

attachEvent(" evt", func) IE5
clear()
clearAttributes() IE5
close()
createElement(" tag")
createEventObject([evt]) IE5.5
createStyleSheet([" URL"[, index]])
detachEvent(" evt", func) IE5
elementFromPoint(x,y)
execCommand(" cmd"[, UI][, arg])
focus()
mergeAttributes(obj) W5
open([" mimeType"[, replace])
queryCommandEnabled(" cmd")
queryCommandIndterm(" cmd")
queryCommandState(" cmd")
queryCommandSupported(" cmd")
queryCommandValue(" cmd")
recalc(allFlag) W5
releaseCapture() IE5.5
setActive() IE5.5
write(" str")
writeln(" str")

onActivate IE5.5
onBeforeCut IE5.5
onBeforeDeactivate IE5.5
onBeforeEditFocus W5
onBeforePaste W5
onClick
onContextMenu W5
onControlSelect IE5.5
onCut
onDblClick
onDeactivate IE5.5
onDragEnd W5
onDragEnter W5
onDragLeave W5
onDragOver W5
onDragStart W5
onDrop W5
onHelp W4,M5
onKeyPress
onKeyUp
onMouseDown
onMouseMove
onMouseOut
onMouseOver
onMouseUp
onPaste
onPropertyChange W5
onReadyStateChange
onResize
onSelectionChange
onStop IE5

BODY 18

aLink
background
bgColor
bgProperties
bottomMargin
leftMargin
link
noWrap
rightMargin
scroll
scrollLeft
scrollTop
text
topMargin
vLink

createControlRange() W5
createTextRange()
doScroll([" scrollAction "]) W5

onAfterPrint W5
onBeforePrint W5
onScroll

Page 2 of 4 — IE4+ DHTML DOM Quick Reference

IMG [22]

```
align
alt
border
complete
dynsrc
fileCreatedDate
fileModifiedDate
fileSize
fileUpdatedDate
height
href
hspace
isMap
loop
lowsrc
name
nameProp  W5
protocol
src
start
useMap
vspace
width
```

(None)

onAbort
onError
onLoad

A (anchor/link) [21]

```
hash
host
hostname
href
Methods
mimeType
name
nameProp
pathname
port
protocol
protocolLong
rel
rev
search
target
urn
```

AREA [22]

```
alt
coords
hash
host
hostname
href
noHref
pathname
port
protocol
search
shape
target
```

(None)

MAP [22]

```
areas[]
name
```

(None)

onScroll

MARQUEE [19]

```
behavior
bgColor
direction
height
hspace
loop
scrollAmount
scrollDelay
trueSpeed
vspace
width
```

start()
stop()

onBounce
onFinish
onStart

FORM [23]

```
action
autocomplete  W5
elements[]
encoding
enctype
length
method
name
target
```

reset()
submit()

onReset
onSubmit

LABEL [23]

```
htmlFor
```

(None)

BUTTON [24]
INPUT (button, reset, submit, radio, checkbox)

(See original object model button, reset, submit, radio, and checkbox object listings.)

INPUT (image) [24]

```
complete
form
name
src
type
```

(None)

INPUT (text, password, hidden) [25]

(See original object model text, password, and hidden object listings.)

```
maxLength
readOnly
size
```

(None)

onAfterUpdate W4
onBeforeUpdate W4
onErrorUpdate W4

TEXTAREA [25]

```
cols
readOnly
rows
wrap
```

(See original object model textarea object listing.)
createTextRange()

onAfterUpdate W4
onBeforeUpdate W4
onErrorUpdate W4

SELECT [26]

```
length
multiple
size
value
```

(See original object model select object listing.)
options[i].add(elem[,index])
options[i].remove()

(None)

OPTION [26]

```
defaultSelected
form
selected
text
value
```

(None)

IE44+ DHTML DOM Compatibility Guide

The baseline browser for this section is MSIE 4. An item with no notation is compatible back to that level for all OS versions. Notations as follows:

W4 — IE4+/Windows only
W5 — IE5+/Windows only
IE5 — IE5+ all OSes
IE5.5 — IE5.5+ (only Win tested)
M5 — IE5+/Mac

All HTML element objects share items from "All HTML" box on Page 1. "(None)" means no special methods or events for the current object.

OL [27]

```
compact
start
type
```

UL [27]

```
compact
type
```

LI [27]

```
type
value
```

DL, DT, DD, DIR, MENU

```
compact
```

IE4+ DHTML DOM Quick Reference — Page 3 of 4

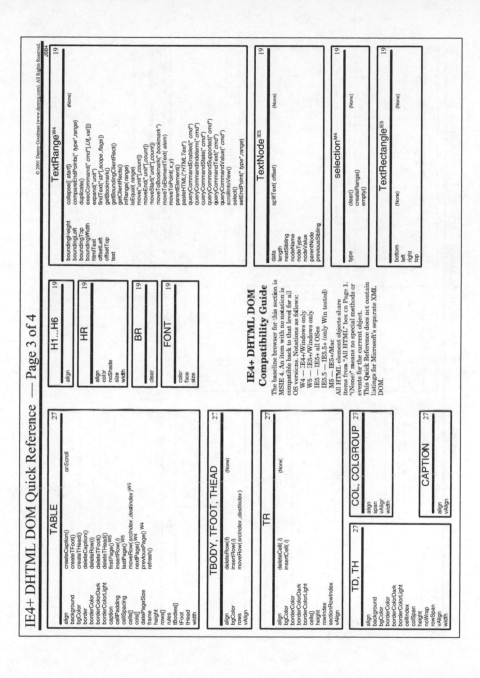

TABLE [27]

align
background
bgColor
border
borderColor
borderColorDark
borderColorLight
caption
cellPadding
cellSpacing
cells[]
cols[]
datePageSize
frame
height
rows[]
rules
tBodies[]
tFoot
tHead
width

onScroll

createCaption()
createTFoot()
createThead()
deleteCaption()
deleteRow()
deleteTFoot()
deleteThead()
firstPage() W5
insertRow()
lastPage() W5
moveRow(*srcindex*, *destindex*) W5
nextPage() W4
previousPage() W4
refresh()

TBODY, TFOOT, THEAD [27]

align
bgColor
rows
vAlign

(None)

deleteRow()
insertRow()
moveRow(*srcindex*, *destindex*)

TR [27]

align
bgColor
borderColor
borderColorDark
borderColorLight
cells[]
height
rowIndex
sectionRowIndex
vAlign

(None)

deleteCell()
insertCell()

TD, TH [27]

align
background
bgColor
borderColor
borderColorDark
borderColorLight
cellIndex
colSpan
height
noWrap
rowSpan
vAlign
width

COL, COLGROUP [27]

align
span
vAlign
width

CAPTION [27]

align
vAlign

H1...H6 [19]

align

HR [19]

align
color
noShade
size
width

BR [19]

clear

FONT [19]

color
face
size

IE4+ DHTML DOM Compatibility Guide

The baseline browser for this section is MSIE 4. An item with no notation is compatible back to that level for all OS versions. Notations as follows:

W4 — IE4+/Windows only
W5 — IE5+/Windows only
IE5 — IE5+ all OSes
IE5.5 — IE5.5+ (only Win tested)
M5 — IE5+/Mac

All HTML element objects share items from "All HTML" box on Page 1. "(None)" means no special methods or events for the current object. This Quick Reference does not contain listings for Microsoft's separate XML DOM.

TextRange W4 [19]

boundingHeight
boundingLeft
boundingTop
boundingWidth
htmlText
offsetLeft
offsetTop
text

collapse([*start*])
compareEndPoints(" *type* ",*range*)
duplicate()
execCommand(" *cmd* "[,*UI*[,*val*]])
expand(" *unit* ")
findText(" *str* "[,*scope*,*flags*])
getBookmark()
getBoundingClientRect()
getClientRects()
inRange(*range*)
isEqual(*range*)
move(" *unit* "[,*count*])
moveEnd(" *unit* "[,*count*])
moveStart(" *unit* "[,*count*])
moveToBookmark(" *bookmark* ")
moveToElementText(*elem*)
moveToPoint(*x*,*y*)
parentElement()
pasteHTML(" *HTMLText* ")
queryCommandEnabled(" *cmd* ")
queryCommandIndeterm(" *cmd* ")
queryCommandState(" *cmd* ")
queryCommandSupported(" *cmd* ")
queryCommandText(" *cmd* ")
queryCommandValue(" *cmd* ")
scrollIntoView()
select()
setEndPoint(" *type* ",*range*)

(None)

TextNode IE5 [19]

data
length
nextSibling
nodeName
nodeType
nodeValue
parentNode
previousSibling

splitText(*offset*)

(None)

selection M4 [19]

type

clear()
createRange()
empty()

(None)

TextRectangle IE5 [19]

bottom
left
right
top

(None)

Page 4 of 4 — IE4+ DHTML DOM Quick Reference

STYLE 30

(None)

media
type

---

styleSheet 30

addImport("URL"[,index])
addRule("selector","styleSpec"[,index])
removeRule(index)

cssText IE5
disabled
href
id
imports[]
media
owningElement
pages[] IE5.5
parentStyleSheet
readOnly
rules[]
title
type

---

currentStyle IE5 , **runtimeStyle** IE5.5 30

(See **style** object)

---

rule 30

(None)

readOnly
selectorText
style

LINK 20

(None)   onLoad

disabled
href
hreflang
media
rel
rev
styleSheet
target
type

SCRIPT 20

(None)

defer
event
htmlFor
language
src
text
type

---

event 29

altKey
altLeft IE5.5
behaviorCookie W5.5
behaviorPart W5.5
bookmarks W4
boundElements
button
cancelBubble
clientX
clientY
contentOverflow
ctrlKey
ctrlLeft IE5.5
dataFld W4
dataTransfer W5
fromElement
keyCode
nextPage W5.5
offsetX
offsetY
propertyName W5
qualifier W4
reason W4
recordset W4
repeat W5
returnValue
saveType W5.5
screenX
screenY
shiftKey
shiftLeft IE5.5
srcElement
srcFilter W4
srcUrn W5
toElement
type
x
y

APPLET 32

(None)

onCellChange W5
onDataAvailable W5
onDatasetChanged W5
onDatasetComplete W5
onLoad
onRowEnter W5
onRowExit W5
onRowsDelete W5
onRowsInserted W5
onScroll

align
altHTML
code
codeBase
height
hspace
name
vspace
width

OBJECT 32

(None)

onCellChange W5
onDataAvailable W5
onDatasetChanged W5
onDatasetComplete W5
onLoad
onRowEnter W5
onRowExit W5
onRowsDelete W5
onRowsInserted W5
onScroll

align
altHTML
BaseHref
classid
code
codeBase
codeType
height
hspace
name
object
type
vspace
width

EMBED 32

(None)   onLoad
            onScroll

align
height
hidden
name
pluginspage
src
units
width

XML W5 32

(None)

src
XMLDocument

W3C DOM (IE5+, NN6+) Quick Reference — Page 1 of 4

JSB4

All HTML Elements (15)

Properties	Methods	Event Handlers
attributes[]	addEventListener(" evt" func, capt)(2)	onBlur
childNodes[]	appendChild(elem)	onClick
className	blur()	onDblClick
dir	click()	onFocus
firstChild	cloneNode(deep)	onKeyDown
id	dispatchEvent(evt)(2)	onKeyPress
innerHTML(1)	focus()	onKeyUp
lang	getAttribute(" attr")	onMouseDown
lastChild	getAttributeNode(" attr")(3)	onMouseMove
length (3)	getElementsByTagName(" tag")	onMouseOut
localName	hasChildNodes()	onMouseOver
namespaceURI	insertBefore(new, ref)	onMouseUp
nextSibling	item(index)(3)	onResize
nodeName	normalize()(2)	
nodeType	removeAttribute(" attr")	
nodeValue	removeAttributeNode(noda)(2)	
offsetHeight (1)	removeChild(node)	
offsetLeft (1)	removeEventListener(" evt" func, capt)(2)	
offsetParent (1)	replaceChild(new, old)	
offsetTop (1)	setAttribute(" attr", val)	
offsetWidth (1)	setAttributeNode(node)(2)	
ownerDocument	supports(" feature")(2)	
parentNode		
prefix		
previousSibling		
style		
tabIndex		
tagName		
title		

(1) Originating from the IE4 Object Model, this non-W3C item is implemented in N6 for convenience.
(2) Not implemented in IE through 5.5.
(3) Property or method of all object collections.

HTML (20)

Properties	Methods	Event Handlers
version (1)	(None)	(None)

(1) Not implemented in IE through 5.5.

FRAMESET (16)

Properties	Methods	Event Handlers
cols	(None)	(None)
rows		

FRAME (16)

Properties	Methods	Event Handlers
contentDocument (1)	(None)	(None)
frameBorder		
longDesc (1)		
marginHeight		
marginWidth		
noResize		
scrolling		
src		

(1) Not implemented in IE through 5.5.

HEAD (20)

Properties	Methods	Event Handlers
profile (1)		

(1) Not implemented in IE through 5.5.

BASE (20)

Properties	Methods	Event Handlers
href		
target		

BASEFONT (20)

Properties	Methods	Event Handlers
color		
face		
size		

META (20)

Properties	Methods	Event Handlers
charset		
content		
httpEquiv		
name		
url		

TITLE (20)

Properties	Methods	Event Handlers
text		

W3C DOM Compatibility Guide

Baseline browsers for this section are IE5 and NN6. An item with no notation is compatible with these browsers for all OS versions. Observe footnotes for items missing from IE.

All HTML element objects share items from "All HTML" box on Page 1. "(None)" means no special methods or events for the current object.

document (18)

Properties	Methods	Event Handlers
alinkColor	clear()	onBlur
anchors[]	close()	onClick
applets[]	createAttribute(" name")	onDblClick
attributes[]	createDocumentFragment()	onFocus
bgColor	createElement(" tag")	onKeyDown
body	createTextNode(" txt")	onKeyPress
characterSet (1)	focus()	onKeyUp
childNodes[]	getElementById(" ID")	onMouseDown
cookie	getElementsByName(" name")	onMouseMove
doctype (1)	getElementsByTagName(" tag")	onMouseOut
documentElement	open(" mimeType" [," replace"])	onMouseOver
domain	write(" str")	onMouseUp
embeds[]	writeln(" str")	onResize
fgColor		
firstChild		
forms[]		
height (1)		
images[]		
implementation (1)		
lastChild		
lastModified		
linkColor		
links[]		
location		
namespaceURI		
nextSibling		
nodeName		
nodeType		
ownerDocument (1)		
parentNode		
plugins		
previousSibling		
referrer		
styleSheets[]		
title		
URL		
vlinkColor		
width(1)		

(1) Not implemented in IE through 5.5.

IFRAME (16)

Properties	Methods	Event Handlers
align		
contentDocument (1)		
frameBorder		
longDesc (1)		
marginHeight		
marginWidth		
scrolling		
src		

(1) Not implemented in IE through 5.5.

BODY (18)

Properties	Methods	Event Handlers
alink	(None)	
background		
bgColor		
link		
text		
vLink		

(1) Not implemented in IE through 5.5.

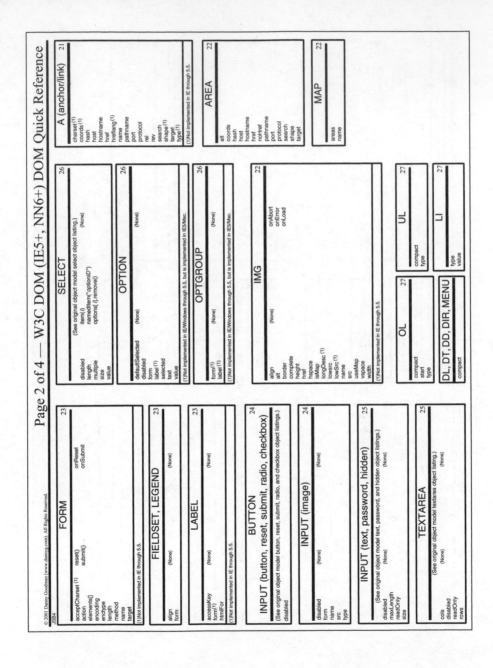

Page 2 of 4 — W3C DOM (IE5+, NN6+) DOM Quick Reference

FORM [23]
```
acceptCharset (1)    reset()      onReset
action               submit()     onSubmit
elements[]
encoding
enctype
length
method
name
target
```
(1)Not implemented in IE through 5.5.

FIELDSET, LEGEND [23]
```
(None)               (None)
```

LABEL [23]
```
accessKey            (None)
form(1)
htmlFor
```
(1)Not implemented in IE through 5.5.

BUTTON [24]
INPUT (button, reset, submit, radio, checkbox)
(See original object model button, reset, submit, radio, and checkbox object listings.)
disabled

INPUT (image) [24]
```
disabled             (None)
form
name
src
type
```

INPUT (text, password, hidden) [25]
(See original object model text, password, and hidden object listings.)
```
disabled             (None)
maxLength
readOnly
size
```

TEXTAREA [25]
(See original object model textarea object listing.)
```
cols                 (None)
disabled
readOnly
rows
```

SELECT [26]
(See original object model select object listing.)
```
disabled     item()                      (None)
length       namedItem("optionID")
multiple     options[.j.remove()
size
value
```

OPTION [26]
```
defaultSelected      (None)
disabled
form
label (1)
selected
text
value
```
(1)Not implemented in IE/Windows through 5.5, but is implemented in IE5/Mac.

OPTGROUP [26]
```
form(1)              (None)
label(1)
```
(1)Not implemented in IE/Windows through 5.5, but is implemented in IE5/Mac.

IMG [22]
```
align        (None)       onAbort
alt                       onError
border                    onLoad
complete
height
href
hspace
isMap
longDesc (1)
lowsrc
lowSrc (1)
name
src
useMap
vspace
width
```
(1)Not implemented in IE through 5.5.

OL [27]
```
compact
start
type
```

UL [27]
```
compact
type
```

DL, DT, DD, DIR, MENU
```
compact
```

LI [27]
```
type
value
```

A (anchor/link) [21]
```
charset(1)           (None)
coords(1)
hash
host
hostname
href
hreflang(1)
name
pathname
port
protocol
rel
rev
search
shape(1)
target
type(1)
```
(1)Not implemented in IE through 5.5.

AREA [22]
```
alt
coords
hash
host
hostname
href
noHref
pathname
port
protocol
search
shape
target
```

MAP [22]
```
areas
name
```

W3C DOM (IE5+, NN6+) Quick Reference — Page 3 of 4

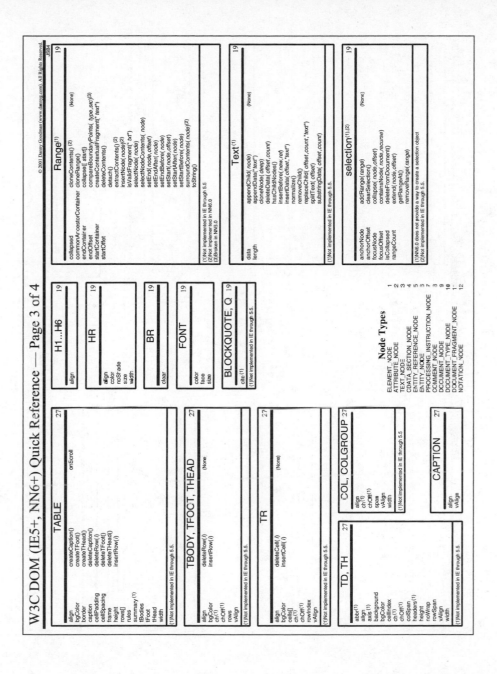

TABLE (27)

align
bgColor
border
caption
cellPadding
cellSpacing
frame
height
rows[]
rules
summary(1)
tBodies
tFoot
tHead
width

createCaption()
createTFoot()
createTHead()
deleteCaption()
deleteRow()
deleteTFoot()
deleteTHead()
insertRow()

onScroll

(1)Not implemented in IE through 5.5.

TBODY, TFOOT, THEAD (27)

align
bgColor
ch(1)
chOff(1)
rows
vAlign

deleteRow(/)
insertRow(/)

(None)

(1)Not implemented in IE through 5.5.

TR (27)

align
bgColor
cells[]
ch(1)
chOff(1)
rowIndex
vAlign

deleteCell(/)
insertCell(/)

(None)

(1)Not implemented in IE through 5.5.

TD, TH (27)

abbr(1)
align
axis (1)
background
bgColor
cellIndex
ch(1)
chOff(1)
colSpan
headers(1)
height
noWrap
rowSpan
vAlign
width

(1)Not implemented in IE through 5.5.

COL, COLGROUP (27)

align
ch(1)
chOff(1)
span
vAlign
width

(1)Not implemented in IE through 5.5.

CAPTION (27)

align
vAlign

H1...H6 (19)

align

HR (19)

align
color
noShade
size
width

BR (19)

clear

FONT (19)

color
face
size

BLOCKQUOTE, Q (19)

cite (1)

(1)Not implemented in IE through 5.5.

Range(1) (19)

collapsed
commonAncestorContainer
endContainer
endOffset
startContainer
startOffset

cloneContents() (2)
cloneRange()
collapse(start)
compareBoundaryPoints(type, src)(3)
createContextualFragment(" text")(3)
deleteContents()
detach()
extractContents() (2)
insertNode(node)(2)
isValidFragment(node)
selectNode(node)
selectNodeContents(node)
setEnd(node, offset)
setEndAfter(node)
setEndBefore(node)
setStart(node, offset)
setStartAfter(node)
setStartBefore(node)
surroundContents(node)(2)
toString()

(1)Not implemented in IE through 5.5.
(2)Not implemented in NN6.0
(3)Broken in NN6.0

Text(1) (19)

data
length

appendChild(node)
appendData("text")
cloneNode(deep)
deleteData(offset, count)
hasChildNodes()
insertBefore(new, ref)
insertData(offset, "text")
normalize()
removeChild()
replaceChild(offset, count, "text")
splitText(offset)
substringData(offset, count)

(None)

(1)Not implemented in IE through 5.5.

selection(1),(2) (19)

anchorNode
anchorOffset
focusNode
focusOffset
isCollapsed
rangeCount

addRange(range)
clearSelection()
collapse(node, offset)
containsNode(node, recurse)
deleteFromDocument()
extend(node, offset)
getRangeAt()
removeRange(range)

(None)

(1)NN6.0 does not provide a way to create a selection object
(2)Not implemented in IE through 5.5.

Node Types

ELEMENT_NODE	1
ATTRIBUTE_NODE	2
TEXT_NODE	3
CDATA_SECTION_NODE	4
ENTITY_REFERENCE_NODE	5
ENTITY_NODE	6
PROCESSING_INSTRUCTION_NODE	7
COMMENT_NODE	8
DOCUMENT_NODE	9
DOCUMENT_TYPE_NODE	10
DOCUMENT_FRAGMENT_NODE	11
NOTATION_NODE	12

JSB4

Page 4 of 4 — W3C DOM (IE5+, NN6+) DOM Quick Reference

JSB4

STYLE 30
(None)

media
type

styleSheet 30

deleteRule(*index*)(1)
insertRule(*rule*, *index*)(1)

disabled
href
media
ownerNode(1)
ownerRule(1)
parentStyleSheet
title
type

(1)Not implemented in IE through 5.5.

cssRule 30
(None)

cssText (2)
parentStyleSheet (2)
selectorText
style
type(1)

(1)Not implemented in IE through 5.5.
(2)Not implemented in IE through 5.5, but implemented in IE5/Mac.

LINK 20
(None)

charset(1)
disabled
href
hreflang
media
rel
rev
target
type

(1)Not implemented in IE through 5.5.

SCRIPT 20
(None)

defer
event
htmlFor
language
src
text
type

event(1) 29

initEvent(" *type*",*bubble* ,*cancelable*)   (None)
initKeyEvent(" *type*", *evtArgs*)
initMouseEvent(" *type*", *evtArgs*)
initUIEvent(" *type*", *evtArgs*)
preventDefault()
stopPropagation()

altKey
bubbles
button
cancelBubble
cancelable
charCode
clientX
clientY
ctrlKey
currentTarget
detail
eventPhase
isChar
keyCode
layerX
layerY
metaKey
pageX
pageY
relatedTarget
screenX
screenY
shiftKey
target
timeStamp
type
view

(1)Not implemented in IE through 5.5.

EMBED 32
(None)

align
height
name
src
width

APPLET 32
(None)

align
alt(1)
archive (1)
code
codeBase
height
hspace
name
object(1)
vspace
width

(1)Not implemented in IE through 5.5.

OBJECT 32

onLoad
onScroll

align
alt(1)
code
codeBase
codeType
contentDocument
height
hspace
name
object
type
vspace
width

(1)Not implemented in IE through 5.5.

W3C DOM Compatibility Guide

Baseline browsers for this section are IE5 and NN6. An item with no notation is compatible with these browsers for all OS versions. Observe footnotes for items missing from IE.
All HTML element objects share items from "All HTML" box on Page 1. "(None)" means no special methods or events for the current object.

JavaScript Reserved Words

Every programming language has a built-in vocabulary of keywords that you cannot use for the names of variables and the like. Because a JavaScript function is an object that uses the function name as an identifier for the object, you cannot employ reserved words for function names either. Netscape's list of reserved words closely echoes that of the Java language; thus, many of the keywords in the list do not — at least yet — apply to JavaScript. Remember that JavaScript keywords are case-sensitive. While you may get away with using these words in other cases, it may lead to unnecessary confusion for someone reading your scripts.

abstract	boolean	break	byte
case	catch	char	class
const	continue	debugger	default
delete	do	double	else
enum	export	extends	false
final	finally	float	for
function	goto	if	implements
import	in	instanceof	int
interface	long	native	new
null	package	private	protected
public	return	short	static
super	switch	synchronized	this
throw	throws	transient	true
try	typeof	var	void
while	with		

Answers to Tutorial Exercises

This appendix provides answers to the tutorial exercises that appear in Part II of this book (Chapters 4 through 12).

Chapter 4 Answers

1. The music jukebox (a) and temperature calculator (d) are good client-side JavaScript applications. Even though the jukebox relies on server storage of the music files, you can create a more engaging and responsive user interface of buttons, swappable images, and information from a plug-in, such as LiveAudio, Windows Media Player, or QuickTime. The temperature calculator is a natural, because all processing is done instantaneously on the client, rather than having to access the server for each conversion.

The Web site visit counter (b) that accumulates the number of different visitors to a Web site is a server-side CGI application, because the count must be updated and maintained on the server. At best, a client-side counter could keep track of the number of visits the user has made to a site and report to the user how many times he or she has been to the site. The storage requires scripting the cookie (Chapter 16). A chat room application (c) done properly requires server facilities to open up communication channels among all users connected simultaneously. Client-side scripting by itself cannot create a live chat environment.

2. The first task is to determine a valid identifier for the General Motors location in the hierarchy. Then "connect the dots":

   a. General_Motors.Chevrolet.Malibu

   b. General_Motors.Pontiac.Firebird

   c. General_Motors.Pontiac.Bonneville

3. **a.** Valid, because it is one contiguous word. InterCap spelling is fine.

   b. Valid, because an underscore character is acceptable between words.

   c. Not valid, because an identifier cannot begin with a numeral.

   d. Not valid, because no spaces are allowed.

   e. Not valid, because apostrophes and most other punctuation are not allowed.

4. The names that I assign here are arbitrary, but the paths are not.

```
document.myLink
document.entryForm
document.entryForm.nameField
document.entryForm.addressField
document.entryForm.phoneField
document.entryForm.noArchiveBox
```

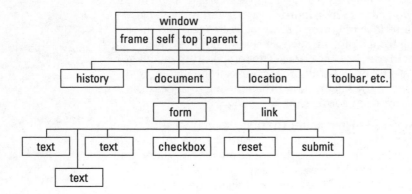

5.
```
<INPUT TYPE="button" NAME="Hi" VALUE="Howdy"
onClick="alert('Hello to you, too!')">
```

Chapter 5 Answers

1.
```
<SCRIPT LANGUAGE="JavaScript">

<!--
document.write("Hello, world.")
// -->
</SCRIPT>
```

2.
```
<HTML>
<BODY>
<SCRIPT LANGUAGE="JavaScript">
<!--
document.write("Hello, world.")
// -->
</SCRIPT>
</BODY>
</HTML>
```

3.
```
<HTML>
<BODY>
<SCRIPT LANGUAGE="JavaScript">
<!--
// write a welcome message to the world
document.write("Hello, world.")
// -->
</SCRIPT>
</BODY>
</HTML>
```

4. My answer is written so that both event handlers call separate functions. You can also have each event handler invoke the `alert()` method inline.

```
<HTML>
<HEAD>
<TITLE>An onLoad= script</TITLE>
<SCRIPT LANGUAGE="JavaScript">
<!--
function done() {
    alert("The page has finished loading.")
}
function alertUser() {
    alert("Ouch!")
}
// -->
</SCRIPT>
</HEAD>
<BODY onLoad="done()">
Here is some body text.
```

```
<FORM>
    <INPUT TYPE="button" NAME="oneButton" VALUE="Press Me!"
onClick="alertUser()">
</FORM>
</BODY>
</HTML>
```

5.   **a.** The page displays two text fields.

      b. The user enters text into the first field and either clicks or tabs out of the field to trigger the onChange event handler.

      c. The function displays an all-uppercase version of one field into the other.

Chapter 6 Answers

1.   **a.** Valid.

      b. Not valid. The variable needs to be a single word, such as howMany or how_many.

      c. Valid.

      d. Not valid. The variable name cannot begin with a numeral. If the variable needs a number to help distinguish it from other similar variables, then put the numeral at the end: address1.

2.   **a.** 4

      b. 40

      c. "4020"

      d. "Robert"

3. The functions are parseInt() and parseFloat(). Strings to be converted are passed as parameters to the functions: parseInt(document.forms[0].entry.value).

4. Both text field values are strings that must be converted to numbers before they can be arithmetically added together. You can use the parseFloat() functions either on the variable assignment expressions (for example, var value1 = parseFloat(document.adder.inputA.value)) or in the addition expression (document.adder.output.value = parseFloat(value1) + parseFloat(value2)).

5. Concatenate means to join together two strings to become one string.

Chapter 7 Answers

1. Because the references in the function point to a text field named `entry` inside a form named `entryForm`, be sure to assign those names to the `NAME` attributes in the respective HTML tags.

```
<HTML>
<HEAD>
<SCRIPT LANGUAGE="JavaScript">
var USStates = new Array(51)
USStates[0] = "Alabama"
USStates[1] = "Alaska"
USStates[2] = "Arizona"
USStates[3] = "Arkansas"
USStates[4] = "California"
USStates[5] = "Colorado"
USStates[6] = "Connecticut"
USStates[7] = "Delaware"
USStates[8] = "District of Columbia"
USStates[9] = "Florida"
USStates[10] = "Georgia"
USStates[11] = "Hawaii"
USStates[12] = "Idaho"
USStates[13] = "Illinois"
USStates[14] = "Indiana"
USStates[15] = "Iowa"
USStates[16] = "Kansas"
USStates[17] = "Kentucky"
USStates[18] = "Louisiana"
USStates[19] = "Maine"
USStates[20] = "Maryland"
USStates[21] = "Massachusetts"
USStates[22] = "Michigan"
USStates[23] = "Minnesota"
USStates[24] = "Mississippi"
USStates[25] = "Missouri"
USStates[26] = "Montana"
USStates[27] = "Nebraska"
USStates[28] = "Nevada"
USStates[29] = "New Hampshire"
USStates[30] = "New Jersey"
USStates[31] = "New Mexico"
USStates[32] = "New York"
USStates[33] = "North Carolina"
USStates[34] = "North Dakota"
USStates[35] = "Ohio"
USStates[36] = "Oklahoma"
USStates[37] = "Oregon"
USStates[38] = "Pennsylvania"
USStates[39] = "Rhode Island"
```

```
USStates[40] = "South Carolina"
USStates[41] = "South Dakota"
USStates[42] = "Tennessee"
USStates[43] = "Texas"
USStates[44] = "Utah"
USStates[45] = "Vermont"
USStates[46] = "Virginia"
USStates[47] = "Washington"
USStates[48] = "West Virginia"
USStates[49] = "Wisconsin"
USStates[50] = "Wyoming"

var stateEntered = new Array(51)
stateEntered[0] = 1819
stateEntered[1] = 1959
stateEntered[2] = 1912
stateEntered[3] = 1836
stateEntered[4] = 1850
stateEntered[5] = 1876
stateEntered[6] = 1788
stateEntered[7] = 1787
stateEntered[8] = 0000
stateEntered[9] = 1845
stateEntered[10] = 1788
stateEntered[11] = 1959
stateEntered[12] = 1890
stateEntered[13] = 1818
stateEntered[14] = 1816
stateEntered[15] = 1846
stateEntered[16] = 1861
stateEntered[17] = 1792
stateEntered[18] = 1812
stateEntered[19] = 1820
stateEntered[20] = 1788
stateEntered[21] = 1788
stateEntered[22] = 1837
stateEntered[23] = 1858
stateEntered[24] = 1817
stateEntered[25] = 1821
stateEntered[26] = 1889
stateEntered[27] = 1867
stateEntered[28] = 1864
stateEntered[29] = 1788
stateEntered[30] = 1787
stateEntered[31] = 1912
stateEntered[32] = 1788
stateEntered[33] = 1789
stateEntered[34] = 1889
stateEntered[35] = 1803
stateEntered[36] = 1907
stateEntered[37] = 1859
stateEntered[38] = 1787
stateEntered[39] = 1790
stateEntered[40] = 1788
```

```
stateEntered[41] = 1889
stateEntered[42] = 1796
stateEntered[43] = 1845
stateEntered[44] = 1896
stateEntered[45] = 1791
stateEntered[46] = 1788
stateEntered[47] = 1889
stateEntered[48] = 1863
stateEntered[49] = 1848
stateEntered[50] = 1890

function getStateDate() {
    var selectedState = document.entryForm.entry.value
    for (var i = 0; i < USStates.length; i++) {
        if (USStates[i] == selectedState) {
            break
        }
    }
    alert("That state entered the Union in " +
stateEntered[i] + ".")
}
</SCRIPT>
</HEAD>
<BODY>
<FORM NAME="entryForm">
Enter the name of a state:
<INPUT TYPE="text" NAME="entry">
<INPUT TYPE="button" VALUE="Look Up Entry Date"
onClick="getStateDate()">
</FORM>
</BODY>
</HTML>
```

2. Several problems plague this function definition. Parentheses are missing from the first `if` construction's condition statement. Curly braces are missing from the second nested `if...else` construction. A mismatch of curly braces also exists for the entire function. The following is the correct form (changes and additions in boldface):

```
function format(ohmage) {
    var result
    if (ohmage >= 10e6) {
        ohmage = ohmage / 10e5
        result = ohmage + " Mohms"
    } else {
        if (ohmage >= 10e3) {
            ohmage = ohmage / 10e2
            result = ohmage + " Kohms"
        } else {
            result = ohmage + " ohms"
        }
    }
    alert(result)
}
```

Part VI ✦ Appendixes

3. Here is one possibility:

```
for (var i = 1; i < tomatoes.length; i++) {
    if (tomatoes[i].looks == "mighty tasty") {
        break
    }
}
var myTomato = tomatoes[i]
```

4. The new version defines a different local variable name for the dog.

```
<HTML>
<HEAD>
<SCRIPT LANGUAGE="JavaScript">
var aBoy = "Charlie Brown"   // global
var hisDog = "Snoopy"        // global
function sampleFunction() {
    // using improper design to demonstrate a point
    var WallacesDog = "Gromit" // local version of hisDog
    var output = WallacesDog + " does not belong to " +
        aBoy + ".<BR>"
    document.write(output)
}
</SCRIPT>
<BODY>
<SCRIPT LANGUAGE="JavaScript">
sampleFunction()    // runs as document loads
document.write(hisDog + " belongs to " + aBoy + ".")
</SCRIPT>
</BODY>
</HTML>
```

5. The application uses three parallel arrays and is structured very much like the solution to question 1. Learn to reuse code whenever you can.

```
<HTML>
<HEAD>
<SCRIPT LANGUAGE="JavaScript">
var planets = new Array(4)
planets[0] = "Mercury"
planets[1] = "Venus"
planets[2] = "Earth"
planets[3] = "Mars"

var distance = new Array(4)
distance[0] = "36 million miles"
distance[1] = "67 million miles"
distance[2] = "93 million miles"
distance[3] = "141 million miles"

var diameter = new Array(4)
diameter[0] = "3100 miles"
diameter[1] = "7700 miles"
diameter[2] = "7920 miles"
diameter[3] = "4200 miles"
```

```
function getPlanetData() {
    var selectedPlanet = document.entryForm.entry.value
    for ( var i = 0; i < planets.length; i++) {
        if (planets[i] == selectedPlanet) {
            break
        }
    }
    var msg = planets[i] + " is " + distance[i]
    msg += " from the Sun and "
    msg += diameter[i] + " in diameter."
    document.entryForm.output.value = msg
}
</SCRIPT>
</HEAD>
<BODY>
<FORM NAME="entryForm">
Enter the name of a planet:
<INPUT TYPE="text" NAME="entry">
<INPUT TYPE="button" VALUE="Look Up a Planet"
onClick="getPlanetData()">
<BR>
<INPUT TYPE="text" SIZE=70 NAME="output">
</BODY>
</HTML>
```

Chapter 8 Answers

1.   **a.** Close, but no cigar. Array references are always plural:

        `window.document.forms[0]`.

    b. @NL2:Not valid: `self` refers to a window and `entryForm` must refer to a form. Where's the document? It should be `self.document.entryForm.entryField.value`.

    c. Valid.

    d. Not valid. The `document` reference is missing from this one.

    e. Valid, assuming that `newWindow` is a variable holding a reference to a subwindow.

2. `window.status = "Welcome to my Web page."`

3. `document.write("<H1>Welcome to my Web page.</H1>")`

4. A script in the Body portion invokes a function that returns the text entered in a `prompt()` dialog box.

```
<HTML>
<HEAD>
<SCRIPT LANGUAGE="JavaScript">
function askName() {
    var name = prompt("What is your name, please?","")
```

```
        return name
}
</SCRIPT>
</HEAD>
<BODY>
<SCRIPT LANGUAGE="JavaScript">
document.write("Welcome to my web page, " + askName() + ".")
</SCRIPT>
</BODY>
</HTML>
```

5. The URL can be derived from the `href` property of the `location` object.

```
<HTML>
<HEAD>
<SCRIPT LANGUAGE="JavaScript">
function showLocation() {
    alert("This page is at: " + location.href)
}
</SCRIPT>
</HEAD>
<BODY onLoad="showLocation()">
Blah, blah, blah.
</BODY>
</HTML>
```

Chapter 9 Answers

1. For Listing 9-1, pass the text object because that's the only object involved in the entire transaction.

```
<HTML>
<HEAD>
<TITLE>Text Object value Property</TITLE>
<SCRIPT LANGUAGE="JavaScript">
function upperMe(field) {
    field.value = field.value.toUpperCase()
}
</SCRIPT>
</HEAD>
<BODY>
<FORM onSubmit="return false">
<INPUT TYPE="text" NAME="convertor" VALUE="sample"
onChange="upperMe(this)">
</FORM>
</BODY>
</HTML>
```

For Listing 9-2, the button invokes a function that communicates with a different element in the form. Pass the form object.

```
<HTML>
<HEAD>
```

```
<TITLE>Checkbox Inspector</TITLE>
<SCRIPT LANGUAGE="JavaScript">
function inspectBox(form) {
    if (form.checkThis.checked) {
        alert("The box is checked.")
    } else {
        alert("The box is not checked at the moment.")
    }
}
</SCRIPT>
</HEAD>
<BODY>
<FORM>
<INPUT TYPE="checkbox" NAME="checkThis">Check here<BR>
<INPUT TYPE="button" VALUE="Inspect Box"
onClick="inspectBox(this.form)">
</FORM>
</BODY>
</HTML>
```

For Listing 9-3, again the button invokes a function that looks at other elements in the form. Pass the form object.

```
<HTML>
<HEAD>
<TITLE>Extracting Highlighted Radio Button</TITLE>
<SCRIPT LANGUAGE="JavaScript">
function fullName(form) {
    for (var i = 0; i < form.stooges.length; i++) {
        if (form.stooges[i].checked) {
            break
        }
    }
    alert("You chose " + form.stooges[i].value + ".")
}
</SCRIPT>
</HEAD>

<BODY>
<FORM>
<B>Select your favorite Stooge:</B>
<INPUT TYPE="radio" NAME="stooges" VALUE="Moe Howard"
CHECKED>Moe
<INPUT TYPE="radio" NAME="stooges" VALUE="Larry Fine"> Larry
<INPUT TYPE="radio" NAME="stooges" VALUE="Curly Howard">
Curly<BR>
<INPUT TYPE="button" NAME="Viewer" VALUE="View Full Name..."
onClick="fullName(this.form)">
</FORM>
</BODY>
</HTML>
```

For Listing 9-4, all action is triggered by and confined to the SELECT object. Pass only that object to the function.

```html
<HTML>
<HEAD>
<TITLE>Select Navigation</TITLE>
<SCRIPT LANGUAGE="JavaScript">
function goThere(list) {
    location = list.options[list.selectedIndex].value
}
</SCRIPT>
</HEAD>

<BODY>
<FORM>
Choose a place to go:
<SELECT NAME="urlList" onChange="goThere(this)">
    <OPTION SELECTED VALUE="index.html">Home Page
    <OPTION VALUE="store.html">Shop Our Store
    <OPTION VALUE="policies.html">Shipping Policies
    <OPTION VALUE="http://www.yahoo.com">Search the Web
</SELECT>
</FORM>
</BODY>
</HTML>
```

2. This requires a bit of surgery. The Submit button is replaced with a standard button whose VALUE attribute is set to "Submit." The button's onClick event handler calls the checkForm() function, which performs the validation. If an empty field exists, the function must return to bail out of the loop. Because the event handler is not expecting any returned value, you can simply issue the return statement to stop the function altogether. If all the tests pass, then the form is submitted with the submit() method. Functions that have a return statement inside an if construction must also have a return statement outside the construction so that it always returns a value (including the null value used here). The other change is that the onSubmit event handler has been removed from the <FORM> tag, because it is no longer needed (the submit() method does not trigger an onSubmit event handler).

```html
<HTML>
<HEAD>
<TITLE>Validator</TITLE>
<SCRIPT LANGUAGE="JavaScript">
function checkForm(form) {
    for (var i = 0; i < form.elements.length; i++) {
        if (form.elements[i].value == "") {
            alert("Fill out ALL fields.")
            return
        }
    }
    form.submit()
```

```
      return
   }
</SCRIPT>
</HEAD>

<BODY>
<FORM>
Please enter all requested information:<BR>
First Name:<INPUT TYPE="text" NAME="firstName"><BR>
Last Name:<INPUT TYPE="text" NAME="lastName"><BR>
Rank:<INPUT TYPE="text" NAME="rank"><BR>
Serial Number:<INPUT TYPE="text" NAME="serialNumber"><BR>

<A HREF="javascript:void checkForm(document.forms[0])">
Submit Form</A>
</FORM>
</BODY>
</HTML>
```

3. The `this` keyword refers to the text field object, so that `this.value` refers to the `value` property of that object.

```
function showText(txt) {
    alert(txt)
}
```

4. `document.accessories.acc1.value = "Leather Carrying Case"`

   `document.forms[1].acc1.value = "Leather Carrying Case"`

5. The SELECT object invokes a function that does the job.

```
<HTML>
<HEAD>
<TITLE>Color Changer</TITLE>
<SCRIPT LANGUAGE="JavaScript">
function setColor(list) {
    var newColor = list.options[list.selectedIndex].value
    document.bgColor = newColor
}
</SCRIPT>
</HEAD>

<BODY>
<FORM>
Select a background color:
<SELECT onChange="setColor(this)">
<OPTION VALUE="red">Stop
<OPTION VALUE="yellow">Caution
<OPTION VALUE="green">Go
</SELECT>
</FORM>
</BODY>
```

```
</HTML>
```

Chapter 10 Answers

1. Use *string*.indexOf() to see if the field contains the "@" symbol.

```
<HTML>
<HEAD>
<TITLE>E-mail Validator</TITLE>
<SCRIPT LANGUAGE="JavaScript">
function checkAddress(form) {
    if (form.email.value.indexOf("@") == -1) {
        alert("Check the e-mail address for accuracy.")
        return false
    }
    return true
}
</SCRIPT>
</HEAD>

<BODY>
<FORM onSubmit="return checkAddress(this)">
Enter your e-mail address:
<INPUT TYPE="text" NAME="email" SIZE=30><BR>
<INPUT TYPE="submit">
</FORM>
</BODY>
</HTML>
```

2. Remember that the substring goes up to, but does not include, the index of the second parameter. Spaces count as characters.

```
myString.substring(0,3)     // result = "Net"
myString.substring(13,18)   // result = "gator"
myString.substring(4,12)    // result = "cape Nav"
```

3. The missing for loop is in boldface. You could also use the increment operator on the count variable (++count) to add 1 to it for each letter "e."

```
function countE(form) {
    var count = 0
    var inputString = form.mainstring.value.toLowerCase()
    for (var i = 0; i < inputString.length; i++) {
        if (inputString.charAt(i) == "e") {
            count += 1
        }
    }
    var msg = "The string has " + count
```

```
        msg += " instances of the letter e."
        alert(msg)
    }
```

4. The formula for the random throw of one die is in the chapter.

```
<HTML>
<HEAD>
<TITLE>E-mail Validator</TITLE>
<SCRIPT LANGUAGE="JavaScript">
function roll(form) {
    form.die1.value = Math.floor(Math.random() * 6) + 1
    form.die2.value = Math.floor(Math.random() * 6) + 1
}
</SCRIPT>
</HEAD>

<BODY>
<FORM>
<INPUT TYPE="text" NAME="die1" SIZE=2>
<INPUT TYPE="text" NAME="die2" SIZE=2><BR>
<INPUT TYPE="button" VALUE="Roll the Dice"
onClick="roll(this.form)">
</FORM>
</BODY>
</HTML>
```

5. If you used the `Math.round()` method in your calculations, that is fine for your current exposure to the `Math` object. Another method, `Math.ceil()`, may be more valuable because it rounds up any fractional value.

```
<HTML>
<HEAD>
<TITLE>Waiting for Santa</TITLE>
<SCRIPT LANGUAGE="JavaScript">
function daysToXMAS() {
    var oneDay = 1000 * 60 * 60 * 24
    var today = new Date()
    var XMAS = new Date("December 25, 2001")
    var diff = XMAS.getTime() - today.getTime()
    return Math.ceil(diff/oneDay)
}
</SCRIPT>
</HEAD>

<BODY>
<SCRIPT LANGUAGE="JavaScript">
document.write(daysToXMAS() + " days until Christmas.")
</SCRIPT>
</BODY>
</HTML>
```

Chapter 11 Answers

1. `onLoad="parent.currCourse = 'history101'"`

2.

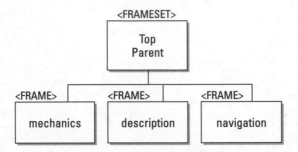

3. All three frames are siblings, so references include the parent.

```
parent.mechanics.location.href = "french201M.html"
parent.description.location.href = "french201D.html"
```

4. A script in one of the documents is attempting to reference the `selector` object in one of the frames but the document has not fully loaded, causing the object to not yet be in the browser's object model. Rearrange the script so that it fires in response to the `onLoad` event handler of the framesetting document.

5. From the subwindow, the `opener` property refers back to the frame containing the `window.open()` method. To extend the reference to the frame's parent, the reference includes both pieces: `opener.parent.ObjVarFuncName`.

Chapter 12 Answers

1. As the document loads, the `<IMG>` tag creates a document image object. A memory image object is created with the new `Image()` constructor. Both objects have the same properties, and assigning a URL to the `src` property of a memory object loads the image into the browser's image cache.

2. `var janeImg = new Image(100,120)`

   `janeImg.src = "jane.jpg"`

3. `document.images["people"].src = janeImg.src`

4. Surround `<IMG>` tags with link (A element) tags, and use the link's `onClick`, `onMouseOver`, and `onMouseOut` event handlers. Set the image's `BORDER` attribute to zero if you don't want the link highlight to appear around the image.

✦   ✦   ✦

JavaScript and DOM Internet Resources

As an online technology, JavaScript has plenty of support online for scripters. Items recommended here were taken as a snapshot of Internet offerings in early 2001. But beware! Sites change. URLs change. Be prepared to hunt around for these items if the information provided here becomes out-of-date by the time you read this.

Support and Updates for this Book

The most up-to-date list of errata and other notes of interest pertaining to this edition of the *JavaScript Bible* can be found at the official Support Center, located at:

```
http://www.dannyg.com/update.html
```

If you are experiencing difficulty with the example listings in this book, first check with the Support Center to see if your question has been answered. As mentioned earlier, you are encouraged to enter the tutorial listings yourself to get used to typing JavaScript (and HTML) code. If, after copying the examples from Part II, you can't make something work (and a fix hasn't already been posted to the Support Center), send the file you've typed to me via e-mail, along with a description of what's not working for you. Also tell me the browser version and operating system that you're using. My e-mail address is `dannyg@dannyg.com`. Regretfully, I am unable to answer general questions about JavaScript or how to apply examples from the book to your own projects.

Newsgroups

The best places to get quick answers to your pressing questions are online newsgroups. Here are the top JavaScript-related newsgroups:

On most news servers:

```
comp.lang.javascript
```

On news://msnews.microsoft.com

```
microsoft.public.scripting.jscript
microsoft.public.windows.inetexplorer.ie5.programming.dhtml
microsoft.public.windows.inetexplorer.ie5.programming.dhtml.scripting
microsoft.public.inetsdk.programming.scripting.jscript
```

On news://secnews.netscape.com

```
netscape.public.mozilla.dom
netscape.public.mozilla.jseng
```

Before you post a question to a newsgroup, however, read about FAQs in the following section and also use the extremely valuable Deja.com newsgroup archive, which is now owned by Google. Look for links to "Usenet Advanced Search" at:

```
http://groups.google.com
```

Enter the keyword or phrase into the top text box, but then also try to narrow your search by limiting the newsgroup(s) to search. For example, if you have a question about weird behavior you are experiencing with the borderCollapse style property in IE, enter borderCollapse into the keyword field, and then first try narrowing the search to the newsgroup comp.lang.javascript. If you don't find the answer there, try again with all the Microsoft newsgroups by specifying microsoft.public.* in the Newsgroups field.

If you post a question to a newsgroup, you will most likely get a quick and intelligent response if you also provide either some sample code that's giving you a problem, or a link to a temporary file on your server that others can check out. Visualizing a problem you've spent days on is very hard for others. Be as specific as possible, including the browser(s) on which the code must run and the nature of the problem.

FAQs

One situation that arises with a popular and accessible technology, such as JavaScript and DHTML authoring, is that the same questions get asked over and over, as newcomers arrive on the scene daily. Rather than invoke the ire of newsgroup users, look through existing FAQ files to see if your concern has already been raised and answered. Here are some of the best JavaScript FAQ sites:

```
javascript.faqts.com
developer.irt.org/script/script.htm
```

For less-frequently asked questions — but previously asked and answered in a public form — use the dejanews.com archive search, described earlier in this appendix.

Online Documentation

Locations of Web sites that dispense official documentation for one browser or another are extremely fluid. Therefore, the following information contains links only to top-level areas of appropriate Web sites, along with tips on what to look for after you are at the site.

For Netscape browser technologies, start at:

```
http://developer.netscape.com/library/
```

You can also find some interesting future-oriented developer documentation at:

```
http://www.mozilla.org/docs
```

Microsoft has condensed its developer documentation into a massive site called MSDN (Microsoft Developer Network). The place to begin is:

```
http://msdn.microsoft.com/workshop/
```

This page is the portal to many technologies, but the one most applicable to JavaScript and client-side scripting is one labeled "DHTML, HTML & CSS". Look for subject headers covering Document Object Model and DHTML References. The core JScript language is detailed in a separate section:

```
http://msdn.microsoft.com/scripting/jscript/techinfo/jsdocs.htm
```

Finally, you can read the industry standards for HTML, CSS, and ECMAScript technologies online. Be aware that these documents are primarily intended for developers of tools that we use — browsers, WYSIWYG editors,and so forth — to direct them on how their products should respond to tags, style sheets, scripts, and so on. Reading these documents has frequently been cited as a cure for insomnia.

```
http://www.ecma.ch/ecma1/STAND/ECMA-262.HTM
http://www.w3.org/TR/html4
http://www.w3.org/TR/REC-CSS2
```

Please note that just because a particular item is described in an industry standard doesn't mean that it is implemented in any or all browsers. In the real world, we must develop for the way the technologies are actually implemented in browsers.

World Wide Web

The number of Web sites devoted to JavaScript tips and tricks is mind-boggling. Many sites come and go in the middle of the night, leaving no trace of their former existence. If you are looking for more example code for applications not covered in this book, perhaps the best place to begin your journey is through the traditional search engines. Narrowing your search through careful keyword choice is vital. In addition to the Netscape and (heavily Windows-oriented) Microsoft developer Web sites (plus numerous online articles of mine listed at `http://www.dannyg.com/recentwriting.html`), a couple other venerable sites are:

```
http://builder.com
http://www.webreference.com
```

These sites are by no means the only worthwhile JavaScript and DHTML destinations on the Web. Sometimes having too many sources is as terrifying as having not enough. The links and newsgroups described in this appendix should take you a long way.

✦   ✦   ✦

What's on the CD-ROM

The accompanying Windows–Macintosh CD-ROM contains nearly 300 HTML document listings from the book, substantial supplemental book material, electronic versions of the Quick Reference shown in Appendix A, a complete, searchable version of the book, trial software, and the Adobe Acrobat Reader.

System Requirements

To derive the most benefit from the example listings, you should have both Netscape Navigator 6 (or later) and Internet Explorer 5 (or later) installed on your computer. While many scripts run in both browsers, several scripts demonstrate features that are available on only one browser or the other. To write scripts, you can use a simple text editor, word processor, or dedicated HTML editor.

To use the Adobe Acrobat Reader, you need the following:

✦ For Windows 95, Windows 98, or Windows NT4.0 (with SP3 or later), you should be using a 486 or Pentium computer with 16MB of RAM and 10MB of hard disk space.

✦ Macintosh users require a PowerPC, System 7.1,2 or later, at least 8MB of RAM, and 8MB of disk space.

Disc Contents

Platform-specific software is located in the appropriate Windows and Macintosh directories on the CD-ROM. The contents include the following items.

JavaScript listings for Windows and Macintosh text editors

Starting with Part III of the book, almost all example listings are on the CD-ROM in the form of complete HTML files, which you can load into a browser to see the language item in operation. A directory called Listings contains the HTML and related files, with nested folders named for each chapter. Each HTML file's name is keyed to the Listing number in the book. For example, the file for Listing 15-1 is named `lst15-01.htm`. Note that no listings are provided for the tutorial chapters of Part II, because you are encouraged to enter HTML and scripting code manually.

For your convenience, an `index.html` file in the Listings folder provides a front-end table of contents to the HTML files for the book's program listings. Open that file from your browser whenever you want to access the program listing files. If you intend to access that index page frequently, you can bookmark it in your browser(s). Using the index file to access the listing files can be very important in some cases, because several individual files must be opened within their associated framesets to work properly. Accessing the files through the `index.html` file assures that you open the frameset. The `index.html` file also shows browser compatibility ratings for all the listings. This saves you time from opening listings that are not intended to run on your browser. To examine and modify the HTML source files, open them from your favorite text editor program (for Windows editors, be sure to specify the `.htm` file extension in the Open File dialog box).

You can open all listing files directly from the CD-ROM, but if you copy them to your hard drive, access is faster and you will be able to experiment with modifying the files more readily. Copy the folder named Listings from the CD-ROM to any location on your hard drive.

JavaScript and Browser Object Quick Reference from Appendix A (Adobe Acrobat format)

If you like the quick reference in Appendix A, you can print it out in your choice of format with the help of the Adobe Acrobat Reader, included with the CD-ROM. The files are located on the CD-ROM in the `:Author-Files: JS Object Reference:` folder in PDF format. To decide on the format that is best for you, read the file named `Choose a Version.txt`. The `.pdf` file for each version is contained in its own subdirectory, where you also find full assembly and collating instructions in a companion text file. Start Acrobat Reader on your computer and open the desired file from either the CD-ROM or from a copy made to your hard drive. Before printing out the document, be sure to choose Landscape orientation in the Page Setup dialog box of Acrobat Reader.

Adobe Acrobat Reader

The Adobe Acrobat Reader is a helpful program that enables you to view the reference example sections for Parts III and IV of the book, the Quick Reference from Appendix A, and the searchable version of this book, all of which are in .pdf format on the CD-ROM. To install and run Adobe Acrobat Reader, follow these steps:

For Windows

1. Start Windows Explorer or Windows NT Explorer and then open the Acrobat folder on the CD-ROM.

2. In the Acrobat folder, double-click rs405eng.exe and follow the instructions presented on-screen for installing Adobe Acrobat Reader.

For Macintosh

1. Open the Acrobat folder on the CD-ROM.

2. In the Acrobat folder, double-click the Adobe Acrobat Installer icon and follow the instructions presented on-screen for installing Adobe Acrobat Reader.

Reference examples from Parts III and IV

In many places throughout the reference chapters of Parts III and IV, you see an icon that directs you to the CD-ROM for an example of the language term being discussed. All of these examples are located in Adobe Acrobat files on the CD-ROM in a directory named Examples. For the fastest access to these example sections, copy the Examples directory and its contents to your hard disk.

An example may consist of a detailed description of a listing or directions on how to experiment with the term through a handy learning utility on the CD-ROM, called The Evaluator. While many of these example sections contain listings, the Acrobat files are distinct from the HTML listing files that you run in your browser and edit with your text editor.

Searchable version of the book

This is a complete, searchable version of the book, provided in Adobe Acrobat .pdf format. Access it from the JSB4 folder after installing Adobe Acrobat Reader. To take advantage of the full-text search, you must add the book's index file (.pdx file) to the list of indexes available to your copy of Acrobat Reader. Here are the steps to add the index:

1. Choose Search from the Edit menu.

2. Choose Select Indexes from the submenu.

3. Click the Add button.

4. Locate the `.pdx` file on the CD-ROM in the directory containing the book's `.pdf` files and open the `.pdx` file. The *JavaScript Bible* index should be listed in the Index Selection window. If the checkbox next to the name is not yet checked, check it now.

5. Click OK.

To begin an actual search, click the Search icon (binoculars in front of a sheet of paper). Enter the text for which you're searching. The search also covers the text of example listings. To access the index and search facilities in future sessions, the CD-ROM must be in your CD-ROM drive.

Commercial software products

Included on the CD-ROM is a licensed version of Microsoft Internet Explorer for Windows. Also included is a link through which you can download Netscape Navigator 6.0. Prior to installing either product, be sure that you read and understand the installation instructions.

Commercial, trial, and shareware software

We also include the following software for your review:

Index Stock Imagery WebSpice Objects

The CD-ROM contains the full version of WebSpice Objects. The product contains 3,000 high-quality buttons, labels, borders, and other art to give the professional look to your Web pages.

Helios Software Solutions TextPad (Windows only)

TextPad is a favorite Windows text editor for programmers. TextPad is a significant improvement over the Notepad and WordPad editors that come with Windows, but doesn't have all the overhead that you find in word processors. TextPad is shareware. Registration information is included with the product.

Bare Bones Software BBEdit (Macintosh only)

BBEdit is the most popular text editor for the Macintosh. The version on the CD-ROM is a demo version.

✦   ✦   ✦

Index

Symbols & Numbers

, (comma) operator, 1046–1047
?: (conditional) operator, 1047
</ /> comment tag, 172
<!—comment—> tag, 28
=+ (add-by-value operator), 133
<> delimiter characters, 5
!= (does not equal comparison operator), 80
= (equals assignment operator), location object and, 488
== (equals comparison operator), 80, 96
> (greater than comparison operator), 80
>= (greater than/equal to comparison operator), 80
< (less than comparison operator), 80
<= (less than/equal to comparison operator), 80
@ symbol, 33–34

A

A element object, 588–592
abbr property, CD-140–CD-141
above property, CD-211–CD-212
acceptCharset property, 637
accessKey property, 247–248
action property, 637–638
activeElement property, 510–511
ActiveX controls, 7
ActiveXObject object, 1106–1107
add( ) method, 713
add-by-value operators, 133
addBehavior( ) method, 292–293
AddDesktopComponent( ) method, 390
addEventListener( ) method, 229, 293–296
AddFavorite( ) method, 390
addImport( ) method, 814–815
addReadRequest( ) method, CD-201–CD-202
addRule( ) method, 815–816
Adobe Acrobat Reader, 7
alert( ) method, 55, 132, 410–411
alertUser( ) function, 65
align property
    APPLET element object, CD-257–CD-258
    EMBED element object, CD-271
    heading elements, CD-7–CD-8
    HR element object, CD-9
    IFRAME element object, 475–476
    Image element object, 605–606
    IMG element object, 605–606
    OBJECT element object, CD-264
    TABLE element object, CD-113

alignment
    IFRAME element object, 475–476
    images, 605–606
    rules, CD-9
aLink property, 574–575
alinkColor property, 511–512
all property, 248–250
    simulator, 239–240
alt property
    APPLET element object, CD-258
    AREA element object, 620–621
    Image element object, 606
    IMG element object, 606
    OBJECT element object, CD-264
altHTML property
    APPLET element object, CD-258
    OBJECT element object, CD-265
altKey property
    event object (IE4), 766–767
    event object (NN6+), 785–786
altLeft property, 767
Anchor element object, 588–592
anchors, location object and, 489
anchors property
    document object, 512–513
    links property and, 541
animation, 7
    applets and, 7
appCodeName property, CD-156
appCore property, 380–381
appendChild( ) method, 223, 295–296
appendData( ) method, CD-44–CD-45
APPLET element object, CD-256–CD-257
    properties, CD-257–CD-261
applets array, 513
applets (Java), 7–8
    animation, 7
    playing, 8
applets property, 513–514
application level, CD-155
apply( ) method, 1061–1063
applyElement( ) method, 297
appMinorVersion property, CD-161–CD-162
appName property, CD-156
appVersion property, CD-156–CD-159
archive property, CD-259
AREA element object, 619–620
    properties, 620–622, CD-662
areas property, 623

O

Hungry Minds, Inc.
End-User License Agreement

READ THIS. You should carefully read these terms and conditions before opening the software packet(s) included with this book ("Book"). This is a license agreement ("Agreement") between you and Hungry Minds, Inc. ("HMI"). By opening the accompanying software packet(s), you acknowledge that you have read and accept the following terms and conditions. If you do not agree and do not want to be bound by such terms and conditions, promptly return the Book and the unopened software packet(s) to the place you obtained them for a full refund.

1. **License Grant.** HMI grants to you (either an individual or entity) a nonexclusive license to use one copy of the enclosed software program(s) (collectively, the "Software") solely for your own personal or business purposes on a single computer (whether a standard computer or a workstation component of a multi-user network). The Software is in use on a computer when it is loaded into temporary memory (RAM) or installed into permanent memory (hard disk, CD-ROM, or other storage device). HMI reserves all rights not expressly granted herein.

2. **Ownership.** HMI is the owner of all right, title, and interest, including copyright, in and to the compilation of the Software recorded on the disk(s) or CD-ROM ("Software Media"). Copyright to the individual programs recorded on the Software Media is owned by the author or other authorized copyright owner of each program. Ownership of the Software and all proprietary rights relating thereto remain with HMI and its licensers.

3. **Restrictions On Use and Transfer.**

   (a) You may only (i) make one copy of the Software for backup or archival purposes, or (ii) transfer the Software to a single hard disk, provided that you keep the original for backup or archival purposes. You may not (i) rent or lease the Software, (ii) copy or reproduce the Software through a LAN or other network system or through any computer subscriber system or bulletin-board system, or (iii) modify, adapt, or create derivative works based on the Software.

   (b) You may not reverse engineer, decompile, or disassemble the Software. You may transfer the Software and user documentation on a permanent basis, provided that the transferee agrees to accept the terms and conditions of this Agreement and you retain no copies. If the Software is an update or has been updated, any transfer must include the most recent update and all prior versions.

(b) In no event shall HMI or the author be liable for any damages whatsoever (including without limitation damages for loss of business profits, business interruption, loss of business information, or any other pecuniary loss) arising from the use of or inability to use the Book or the Software, even if HMI has been advised of the possibility of such damages.

(c) Because some jurisdictions do not allow the exclusion or limitation of liability for consequential or incidental damages, the above limitation or exclusion may not apply to you.

7. **U.S. Government Restricted Rights.** Use, duplication, or disclosure of the Software for or on behalf of the United States of America, its agencies and/or instrumentalities (the "U.S. Government") is subject to restrictions as stated in paragraph (c)(1)(ii) of the Rights in Technical Data and Computer Software clause of DFARS 252.227-7013, or subparagraphs (c) (1) and (2) of the Commercial Computer Software - Restricted Rights clause at FAR 52.227-19, and in similar clauses in the NASA FAR supplement, as applicable.

8. **General.** This Agreement constitutes the entire understanding of the parties and revokes and supersedes all prior agreements, oral or written, between them and may not be modified or amended except in a writing signed by both parties hereto that specifically refers to this Agreement. This Agreement shall take precedence over any other documents that may be in conflict herewith. If any one or more provisions contained in this Agreement are held by any court or tribunal to be invalid, illegal, or otherwise unenforceable, each and every other provision shall remain in full force and effect.

CD-ROM Installation Instructions

The files on this CD-ROM can be accessed and used from both Windows 95 (or later) and Macintosh environments. Some Macintosh program files require MacOS 8.6 or later, but program listing text files can be opened with any MacOS version. For Windows, access the software with My Computer or Windows Explorer. Macintosh users can access files by using the Finder.

You can open all of the example file listings directly from the CD-ROM, but access will be faster — and you will be able to experiment with modifying the files more readily — if you copy the listings to your hard drive. Copy the folder named Listings from the CD-ROM to any location on your hard drive.

To open the listing scripts on this CD-ROM, you should have a copy of Microsoft Internet Explorer 5 (or later), Netscape Navigator 6 (or later), or both browsers installed on your computer. You will find installers for recommended minimum versions of the two browsers on this CD-ROM.

To run the listing scripts from your browser, open the file named index.html in the Listings folder. This page provides a table of contents consisting of direct links to the listings, showing which browsers are compatible with each listing.

Access the Adobe Acrobat (PDF) files for the book's contents from the CD-ROM. Be sure to install the index files into your copy of Acrobat to take advantage of full-text search.

For more details on installing and running the CD-ROM contents, see Appendix E.